Gandhi

Gandhi

The Years That Changed the World

1914 – 1948

Ramachandra Guha

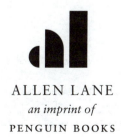

ALLEN LANE
an imprint of
PENGUIN BOOKS

ALLEN LANE

UK | USA | Canada | Ireland | Australia
India | New Zealand | South Africa

Penguin Books is part of the Penguin Random House group of companies
whose addresses can be found at global.penguinrandomhouse.com.

First published in India by Penguin Random House India 2018
First published in Great Britain by Allen Lane 2018
001

Printed and bound in Great Britain by Clays Ltd, Elcograf S.p.A.

A CIP catalogue record for this book is available from the British Library

ISBN: 978–1–846–14267–3

For Suja

Albert Einstein, writing about Gandhi in 1944:

> *A leader of his People, unsupported by any outward authority, a politician whose success rests not upon craft nor the mastery of technical devices, but simply on the convincing power of his personality; a victorious fighter who has always scorned the use of force; a man of wisdom and humility, armed with resolve and inflexible consistency, who has devoted all his strength to the uplifting of his people and the betterment of their lot; a man who has confronted the brutality of Europe with the dignity of the simple human being, and thus at all times rises superior.*
>
> *Generations to come, it may be, will scarce believe that such a one as this ever in flesh and blood walked upon this earth.*

Lord Willingdon, Viceroy of India, writing about Gandhi in 1933:

> *It's a beautiful world if it wasn't for Gandhi who is really a perfect nuisance . . . At the bottom of every move he makes which he always says is inspired by God, one discovers the political manoeuvre. . . . I see the American Press is saying what a wonderful man he is in that if he threatens to starve there is a terrible hullaballoo over here. It's true, but the fact is that we live in the midst of very unpractical, mystical, and superstitious folk who look upon Gandhi as something holy, whereas I look upon him as the biggest humbug alive.*

Gandhi, writing about himself in 1934:

> *I make no hobgoblin of consistency. If I am true to myself from moment to moment, I do not mind all the inconsistencies that may be flung in my face.*

Contents

Preface

I

When Mohandas K. Gandhi landed in Bombay in January 1915, he was already forty-five, and had been away a long time from his homeland. Gandhi grew up in two small chiefdoms in Gujarat, insulated from the social and political changes taking place in British India. He studied law in London, and then, after failing to establish himself at the Bar in Bombay and Rajkot, moved to South Africa, where he developed a flourishing legal practice before turning to activism and social work.

The two decades that Gandhi spent in the diaspora were crucial to his intellectual and moral development. Living outside India, he came to appreciate the enormous linguistic and religious diversity of his homeland. It was in South Africa that he forged a regimen of extreme personal austerity, experimenting with different foods and methods of healing. It was here that he first thought of, and applied, the technique of non-violent resistance known as satyagraha.

Gandhi's years in South Africa were important to him, personally, yet his years in India were of far greater historic import. In South Africa, he sought to represent the Indian diaspora, roughly 1,50,000 people in all. In his homeland, he strove to become the leader of its 300 million people. In South Africa, he worked only in towns and districts where Indians were present; in India, he made his ideas known in every corner of the subcontinent. In one place, he led a relatively small community of migrants; in the other, he became the central figure in the largest colony of the world's greatest Empire.

The India that Gandhi returned to in 1915 was by no means politically quiescent. The Indian National Congress, set up in 1885, had a 'Moderate' faction, which politely and respectfully petitioned the British to grant Indians greater rights; and an 'Extremist' faction, which resorted to street protest and the burning of British cloth to demand political and economic independence for India. Whereas the Congress professed to represent all Indians regardless of caste or creed, the Muslim League was established in 1906 specifically to protect the interests of the subcontinent's largest religious minority. There were also some revolutionary groups, small but very active, who sought through bombings and assassinations to scare the British out of India.

These political groups and tendencies were resolutely urban as well as middle class. They had no roots in the villages. After his return to India in 1915, Gandhi took this city-based and elite-dominated opposition to British rule and made it into a mass movement, reaching deep into the countryside, bringing in millions of peasants, workers, artisans and women. The techniques Gandhi used, the travels he undertook, and the friendships he forged to accomplish this transformation, form a major part of the narrative. This biography of India's most famous patriot is inevitably also a history of the most important political party of the time, the Indian National Congress, and of the freedom movement itself.

To deliver India from British rule was by no means Gandhi's only preoccupation. The forging of harmonious relations between India's often disputatious religious communities was a second. The desire to end the pernicious practice of untouchability in his own Hindu faith was a third. And the impulse to develop economic self-reliance for India and moral self-reliance for Indians was a fourth.

These campaigns were conducted by Gandhi in parallel. All were to him of equal importance. In 1933, he wrote to a close friend that 'my life is one indivisible whole. . . . I can't devote myself entirely to untouchability and say: "Neglect Hindu–Muslim unity or swaraj". All these things run into one another and are inter-dependent. You will find at one time in my life an emphasis on one thing, at another time on another. But that is just like a pianist, now emphasizing one note and now another. But they are all related to [one] another.'[1]

For Gandhi, political independence meant nothing at all unless it was accompanied by religious harmony, caste and gender equality, and the development of self-respect in every Indian. Other patriots had used the Hindi word *swaraj* to signify national independence; Gandhi made Indians aware of its true or original meaning, swa-raj, or *self*-rule.

II

Gandhi's life in India was, among other things, a series of often intense and long-running arguments. In each of his four callings, Gandhi adopted innovative methods, which to some appeared daringly revolutionary, to others timid and reformist. A friend from his London days, who had followed his subsequent career closely, remarked in 1934 that Gandhi 'is a problem. To Rulers and Governors he is a thorn in their side. To logicians he is a fool. To economists he is a hopeless ignoramus. To materialists he is a dreamer. To communists he is a drag on the wheel. To constitutionalists he represents rank revolution.'[2] To this list we might add: 'To Muslim leaders he was a communal Hindu. To Hindu extremists he was a notorious appeaser of Muslims. To the "untouchables" he appeared a defender of high-caste orthodoxy. To the Brahmin he was a reformer in too much of a hurry.'

This book tracks Gandhi's arguments in the fields of politics, social reform, religious relations and self-improvement. These arguments were sometimes private, conducted through letters written and received; but more often public, conducted in widely circulated newspapers and books and pamphlets. Gandhi's critics were often considerable figures, who possessed a commitment that sometimes equalled his own, and an intelligence that sometimes surpassed his. I have sought to reconstruct these arguments as they unfolded at the time, regardless of how they have subsequently been interpreted, projected, or (as is sadly often the case) distorted.

Gandhi actively engaged with every important aspect of social and public life in India: the impact of colonialism, the caste system, religious conflict, the emancipation of women, the role of the State in social life, the role of technology in economic reconstruction, the role of language in social and national renewal. These engagements were important to Gandhi, and for the history of his country. Through what he said and did, and whom he battled with or argued against, Gandhi helped enable India's transition from empire to nation, from autocracy to democracy, from a society whose laws sanctioned the most extreme forms of discrimination to a country whose Constitution mandated equality of all citizens regardless of caste, gender, language or religion.

While living and working in India, Gandhi was inevitably drawn into profoundly important political developments that originated outside his homeland, such as the two World Wars, and the rise of Bolshevism and Nazism. Between his return to India in 1915 and his death in 1948, Gandhi made but one single trip outside South Asia. However, his work was keenly followed in many continents. British politicians and statesmen wrote of him, and he had an extraordinary impact on ordinary British people too. Gandhi never visited the United States, yet his ideas and movements were discussed in American newspapers, magazines, books and radio shows. They even made their way into popular advertisements.

• Gandhi's public role looms large, but this is not a book about Gandhi the public man alone. I examine here his own continuing examinations into himself, pre-eminently on the question of celibacy. I study his complex and often tortured relations with his wife and his four children. And I pay tribute to the men and women who, by joining in the struggle for freedom, helped make Gandhi the best-known person in India, perhaps the best-known person in the world. More details of these 'secondary' characters in Gandhi's life and struggles will emerge in the pages that follow. But of the fact that they were absolutely central to his career and fame, there should be no doubt. Of the most remarkable of these characters, whose role previous biographers have (perhaps unwittingly) tended to underplay, Gandhi himself wrote that this man's 'greatest characteristic' was 'his ability to reduce himself to zero, whenever occasion demanded it'.[3]

III

This book is a free-standing sequel to *Gandhi Before India*, my account of Mohandas K. Gandhi's years as a schoolboy in Rajkot and a law student in London, and, above all, of his decades as a lawyer-activist in Natal and the Transvaal. That book ended with Gandhi's departure from South Africa in 1914; this book takes the story up to Gandhi's death in 1948. A reading of its prequel is not mandatory to a fuller understanding of *Gandhi: The Years That Changed the World*, whose events are played out against a very different historical and geographical landscape. However, I have, wherever necessary, referred the interested reader to the relevant pages in *Gandhi Before India*, particularly with regard to individuals who feature fleetingly in this book but more substantially in the other.

The playwright Michael Frayn once remarked that 'ideas adopt you, like a lost dog on a walk'. Historians are adopted by characters, rather than ideas. I have myself been stalked by the shadow (and the substance) of Mohandas K. Gandhi all my working life. I spent the first fifteen years of my career working on the history of Indian environmentalism, whose main actors were influenced by Gandhian methods of analysis, critique, struggle and reconstruction. I spent the next ten years studying the history of India since Independence, where the main actors were often inspired, sometimes challenged, and occasionally disgusted by Gandhi.

That Gandhi should loom large in these areas of research was perhaps not entirely a surprise. But he followed me even in the most unexpected places. When I wrote a social history of cricket, I found the name of Gandhi popping up everywhere. This was odd, because Gandhi had a profound distaste for popular passions such as cinema and sport. He is known to have watched only one film in his life. He occasionally attended a football match in South Africa, but then only because the players were his fellow resisters against racial discrimination. He knew nothing of cricket, football, hockey or any other sport. But while Gandhi did not watch, play or talk about cricket, he influenced how cricket was watched, played and talked about in the decades between the wars. In fighting their own battles on and off the field, cricket-mad Indians invoked the name of the cricket-ignorant Gandhi all the time. And so a book on a sport in which Gandhi had absolutely no interest ended with forty index entries against his name.

Since I had been shadowed by Gandhi for so long, it was time I properly and formally settled my accounts with him. A second reason for writing a new biography of Gandhi was that existing biographies were written by scholars much older than myself.[4] Every generation of Indians needed, I thought, its own assessment or reassessment of Gandhi; just as every generation of Britons would revisit Churchill afresh; every generation of the French, De Gaulle; every generation of Americans, Franklin Roosevelt, and so on.

But there was a third reason, and this the most compelling. All previous biographies had relied largely on the ninety-seven volumes of Gandhi's *Collected Works*. As a biographer, I knew that one must go beyond the works or writings of one's subject. As a historian, in the course of my wanderings through the archives, I had come across hundreds of fascinating references to Gandhi in sources other than the *Collected Works*.

The years up to Gandhi's departure from South Africa cover a mere twelve volumes of the *Collected Works*. The Indian period, by contrast, extends over more than eighty volumes. Gandhi's own writings—whether letters, articles, editorials, speeches or interviews—were more substantial, and far better documented, in the years he spent in India. Since the campaigns he undertook in his homeland were more important than those in South Africa, they provoked greater reflection, analysis and reanalysis.

A close, chronological reading of the *Collected Works* was therefore mandatory. The exercise was immensely interesting. Gandhi, who had adopted the British taste for self-deprecation, once said that 'I have no university education worth the name. My high school career was never above the average. I was thankful if I could pass my examinations. Distinction in the school was beyond my aspiration.'[5] This was true so far as it went. Yet no twentieth-century politician or reformer so intensely immersed himself in the thoughts and actions of ordinary people. He may not have gone to Oxford or Cambridge, nor even to Calcutta or Bombay University, but Gandhi had a near-continuous education in the University of Life.

Reading the *Collected Works* was instructive in terms of both content and style. Gandhi was a wonderfully clear writer, who (as one contemporary remarked) had developed a prose style 'all his own, composed of short sentences shot-out like shrapnel in a *feu de joie* at a new-year parade, dynamic in force and devastating in effect'.[6] The Trinidadian writer Seepersad Naipaul told his son (the future Nobel laureate V.S. Naipaul) that good literature boiled down to 'writing from the belly rather than from the cheek'. While most people wrote from the cheek, added Naipaul père, 'Gandhi's writing is great' because he wrote from the belly.[7]

I studied Gandhi's own writings, but I had to go beyond them, to juxtapose what Gandhi himself said with what others wrote to him or said about him, whether in public or in private. This involved research on the vast collection of letters to Gandhi housed in the Sabarmati Ashram in Ahmedabad; in the private papers of his friends, contemporaries, colleagues and rivals; in the institutional collections of organizations that impinged on his work; in the archival records of the British Raj, these located in London and New Delhi, as well as in provincial archives in Bombay, Lucknow and Nagpur; and in runs of contemporary newspapers, in English and in Hindi. I also consulted printed secondary sources such as memoirs and biographies, but used them sparingly, since retrospective accounts are often less credible, and always less vivid, than those written at the time the events they describe actually occurred.

In reconstructing Gandhi's life and struggles, this book draws upon more than sixty different archival collections, located in repositories around the world. These include a colossal hoard of papers belonging to Mohandas K. Gandhi himself, which have only recently been placed in the public domain, and whose significance is explained below.

In or about the year 1920, a young man from the Punjab named Pyarelal Nayar joined Gandhi. He served him devotedly for the next three decades, first as the assistant to Gandhi's secretary Mahadev Desai, and then, after Mahadev's death in 1942, as his main and often only secretary. In the 1930s, Pyarelal's younger sister, Sushila Nayar, a medical doctor, also joined Gandhi's entourage.

Shortly after Gandhi's death in New Delhi in January 1948, Pyarelal visited Sevagram, the rural settlement Gandhi had founded in central India. He collected the papers kept there, and took them back to Delhi. Over the next thirty years, Pyarelal sought to write a multivolume life of Gandhi. By the time he died, in 1982, several volumes had appeared, albeit not in a chronological order. The task now devolved on his sister, Sushila Nayar. Dr Nayar sought to complete the project, unsuccessfully. She herself died in 2000.

Despite their closeness to Gandhi, neither Pyarelal nor Dr Nayar were scholars (or indeed writers). The volumes they published have some interesting details, but the narrative is often disconnected and rambling. When, during the 1960s and 1970s, the project to compile Gandhi's *Collected Works* was under way, its legendary chief editor, Professor K. Swaminathan, sought unavailingly to have Pyarelal allow full access to the collection under his control. This he would not do, instead offering the editors of the *Collected Works* letters by Gandhi himself in dribs and drabs, while withholding other relevant material which would have placed these letters in context. ('When it came to his material on Gandhi', remarked K. Swaminathan once, Pyarelal was 'like Othello guarding Desdemona'.[8])

Why Pyarelal was so possessive about these papers must remain a matter of speculation. Perhaps he had resolved, as someone who had been with Gandhi for the better part of three decades, to be to him what Boswell had been to Dr Johnson. Perhaps he was jealous of D.G. Tendulkar, the independent-minded Bombay scholar who—before the *Collected Works* had got off the ground—produced an eight-volume chronological account of Gandhi's life, based on newspaper reports, Gandhi's own printed statements and writings, and books. Pyarelal may have felt even more determined to publish a more authoritative account, which meant keeping other Gandhi scholars away from the materials he had.

After Pyarelal died in 1982, a far-sighted archivist, Dr Hari Dev Sharma, persuaded Sushila Nayar to transfer the papers to the Nehru Memorial Museum and Library (NMML), of which he was then deputy director. Until Dr Nayar's own death, she had the right to withhold permission to use them, which she usually did, since she still hoped—despite her own infirmity and advanced age—to complete her brother's task. Although the NMML knew that these were in effect the personal papers of the greatest modern Indian, given the closeness of the brother-and-sister duo to Gandhi himself, they did not broach the matter of making them available to the larger scholarly community while they were alive. But then Dr Nayar herself died. Neither she nor her brother had any children. So, the NMML made the wise and undeniably public-spirited decision to have these papers made open to researchers.

However, this could not be done overnight. For, Pyarelal was not a trained historian, still less a trained archivist. The papers he had collected from Sevagram were kept in hundreds of boxes, these very loosely categorized according to subject, year or correspondent. The size of the collection and the haphazard state it was in meant that its sorting, classification, preservation and indexing took several years. One massive chunk of the collection was made available for consultation in 2007; a second and almost as substantial a chunk, five years later.

Containing thousands of files, many of which are several hundred pages in extent, this recently opened collection covers all the major themes in Gandhi's wide-ranging and often controversial career from the 1920s till his death. The files include numerous petitions and pamphlets sent to Gandhi, a great deal of correspondence concerning Gandhi, thousands of fascinating and often important letters to Gandhi, and even some key letters written *by* Gandhi which were accidentally or deliberately kept out of the *Collected Works*. The newly opened Gandhi Papers at the NMML have been an absolutely indispensable source for this book (as the references to them scattered through the endnotes reveal), and I feel deeply privileged to be the first Gandhi biographer to have used them.

Apart from Pyarelal, of course. Possessiveness is not an unusual trait among historians, and it is very nearly ubiquitous among biographers. For all his quirkiness when alive, I think one must be extremely grateful to Pyarelal for having preserved the papers of his master for so long. We Indians have an appalling record when it comes to preserving or maintaining historical records. Family papers are sold as *raddi*, government papers are incinerated. And what man cannot destroy, nature—in the form of dust, fungus and the monsoon—takes care of. Scholars much younger than myself, and of many nationalities, shall have reason to be grateful for Pyarelal's possessive devotion and devoted possessiveness.

PART I

CLAIMING A NATION (1914–1922)

CHAPTER ONE

The Returning Hero

I

On 18 July 1914, Mohandas Gandhi sailed from Cape Town for London. With him were his wife, Kasturba, and his closest friend, a Jewish architect named Hermann Kallenbach. Gandhi was leaving South Africa for good, after two decades spent there in various roles: lawyer, editor, food faddist, activist and prisoner. He had been the unquestioned leader of the small Indian community in South Africa. Now he wished to work with, and for, the several hundred million people of his homeland.

One of the Gandhis' four children was already in India; the others were on their way, part of a larger group of students from Phoenix, the settlement that Gandhi had established in rural Natal. The patriarch wished to go to London first, because his mentor, the great Poona* educationist and politician Gopal Krishna Gokhale, was there. Ever since they first met in 1896, Gokhale had been the Indian whom Gandhi most admired. In his years in the diaspora he wrote to him regularly, consulting him on matters of politics and social reform. Gokhale, in turn, visited Gandhi in South Africa in

---

* Poona is now Puné, just as Bombay is now Mumbai. However, in this book I use the place names current at the time Gandhi lived.

1912, and raised money from wealthy Indians for the causes that Gandhi was fighting for.

Gandhi had first gone to South Africa in May 1893, as a legal adviser to a Gujarati merchant fighting a court case. After the dispute was resolved, he stayed on to build a successful law practice. Over time, he moved from lawyering to activism, leading campaigns in Natal and the Transvaal against racial laws that bore down heavily on Indians. He went to jail several times; his wife Kasturba too courted arrest. In between campaigns he read and thought deeply on religious matters, practised and advocated the simple life, and ran a weekly newspaper, *Indian Opinion* (much of which he wrote himself).

Gandhi's desire to consult Gokhale was born as much out of respect (for the older man) as ignorance (about his own country). At this stage he probably knew South Africa better than he knew India. He was intimately familiar with the peninsula of Kathiawar, where he was born and raised. He had lived briefly in Bombay, and visited Madras, Calcutta and Banaras. But vast areas of the subcontinent were unknown to him. Peasants constituted the majority of Indians; Gandhi had no knowledge of how they lived and laboured.

Gokhale was a leader of the Moderate wing of the Congress party. He believed in debate and dialogue, and in appealing to reason and justice. By these methods he hoped to persuade the colonial government to grant self-rule to his people. At the other end of the spectrum was a group of young Indian revolutionaries, some of whom Gandhi had met (and argued with) in London in 1909. These radicals believed that armed struggle was the only way to win freedom for India.

In South Africa, Gandhi had evolved a method of protest distinct and different both from the polite pleading of the Moderates and the bomb-throwing of the revolutionaries. He called this satyagraha, or truth-force. This involved the deliberate violation of laws deemed to be unjust. Protesting individually or in batches, satyagrahis courted arrest, and courted it again, until the offending law was repealed. In 1909, Gandhi asked the Congress to apply his method to India too. Satyagraha, he said, 'is the only weapon suited to the genius of our people and our land'. For 'the many ills we suffer from in India it is an infallible panacea'.[1]

There were other ideas about India that Gandhi developed in South Africa. Himself a Hindu, he worked closely with Muslims. Himself a native Gujarati speaker, in South Africa he came into contact with Indians speaking Tamil, Telugu, Hindi, Urdu and Bengali. He saw that the sustenance of religious and linguistic pluralism was central to the nurturing of nationhood. Living in London and Johannesburg, he became disenchanted with industrialism; he hoped that India would base its economic future on its peasant and craft traditions rather than mindlessly emulate the West.

Though largely unfamiliar with life in India, Gandhi had a reasonably clear idea of what he could contribute to his country. What he was not clear about was where he would base himself, what organizational affiliation he would seek, and what activities he would undertake. That is why he thought it prudent to first visit Gokhale in London. He needed to consult his guru and seek his guidance before embarking on a career in a land where he was, in political and social terms, an outsider.

II

Gandhi had first gone to England in 1888, to qualify as a lawyer. He went again in 1906 and 1909, representing to the Imperial Government the case for humane treatment of Indians in South Africa. This was his fourth visit, but the first time he was travelling in third class. On board, the Gandhis and Kallenbach lived mostly on fruits, nuts and milk. Every day, Gandhi spent an hour reading the Gita or the Ramayana to his wife, and another hour teaching Gujarati to his companion.[2]

Gandhi and Kallenbach had first met in Johannesburg in 1904. The lawyer and the architect shared a common hero in Leo Tolstoy, under whose influence they abandoned their professions in favour of social work. Kallenbach was devoted to Gandhi, so devoted that the Indians in South Africa called him 'Hanuman' (after the monkey god who had served Lord Rama). When the Gandhis decided to return to India, he said he would also come with them.[3]

The simplicity that Tolstoy prescribed was harder for Kallenbach than for Gandhi. In Johannesburg he had liked going to the best barbers. He owned one of the first automobiles in the city. Gandhi was able to wean him off these luxuries, but the enchantment with modern technology remained. Now, on board the *S.S. Kinfaus*, the two argued about a pair of expensive binoculars that the architect owned—and cherished. Kallenbach (out of a mixture of genuine respect and blind reverence) gave way, and the field glasses were flung into the sea.[4]

These private arguments were soon overshadowed by the onset of war in Europe. On 28 June—when the Gandhis were still in South Africa—Archduke Franz Ferdinand, heir to the Austro-Hungarian throne, was assassinated by a Bosnian Serb. The *S.S. Kinfaus* sailed on 18 July towards a Europe still at peace. Ten days into the journey, Austria declared war on Serbia. Russia started mobilizing in defence of the Serbs, prompting the Germans to do the same on behalf of the Austrians. On 1 August, Germany and Russia were officially at war. Two days later, Germany invaded Belgium. Now France also stood threatened; on 4 August, Britain declared war on Germany. Underwater mines had been laid in the English Channel; negotiating them carefully, the ship Gandhi was on docked in Southampton on 6 August.

III

When Gandhi arrived in London, Gokhale himself was stranded in France. He had gone to Vichy to rest; with the war, ships had temporarily been suspended between Paris and London. So Gokhale asked a friend, the poet Sarojini Naidu—then holidaying in London—to welcome the visitors on his behalf.

The Gandhis were staying with a Gujarati friend in Bayswater. It was raining when Mrs Naidu called on them, climbing (as she later wrote) 'the staircase of an ordinary London dwelling home to find myself confronted with a true Hindu idyll of radiant and domestic simplicity'. Gandhi, the 'great South African leader', was 'reclining, a little ill and weary, on the floor eating his frugal meals of nuts and fruits (which I shared) and his wife was busy and content as though she were a mere modest housewife absorbed in a hundred details of household service, and not the world-famed heroine of a hundred noble sufferings in a nation's cause'.

From their first meeting, Mrs Naidu got the sense that 'Mrs. Gandhi was like a bird with eager outstretched wings longing to annihilate the time and distance that lay before her and her far-off India, and impatient of the brief and necessary interruption in her homeward flight. The woman's heart within her was full of yearning for the accustomed sounds and scenes of her own land and the mother's heart within her full of passionate hunger for the beloved faces of her children.'[5]

Kasturba's yearning could not yet be realized, for her husband had decided that he must stay on in England to help with the War effort. In 1914, Gandhi was still an Empire loyalist. He believed that the racial laws in South Africa were an aberration, a departure from the equality of all subjects that Queen Victoria had promised. In his struggles against discrimination he had sometimes found support among English officials and politicians. Now that Britain was at war, the Empire's subjects must—regardless of their race—rally round to defend it.[6]

In 1899, Gandhi had raised an ambulance corps during the Anglo-Boer war, and done so again in 1906, when the Natal government suppressed a Zulu rebellion.[7] On both occasions, Gandhi had taken the side of the ruler, without bearing arms himself. Now, for the third time in fifteen years, he would lead his fellow Indians in nursing the wounded.

IV

Ten days after landing in London, Gandhi and Kasturba were guests of honour at a reception in Hotel Cecil. Sarojini Naidu was present, as were the nationalist politicians Lala Lajpat Rai and Muhammad Ali Jinnah. Gandhi gave a speech, mostly on the South African satyagraha of 1913–14, in which his wife and he, as well as several thousand others, had gone to jail. Praising the courage and sacrifice of the Tamil satyagrahis in Natal, he said: 'These men and women are the salt of India; on them will be built the Indian nation that is to be.'[8]

The long sea journey had exhausted Gandhi. He was suffering from pain in his legs. A doctor he saw suspected pleurisy. But he carried on with his work; by the end of August, close to a hundred Indians had signed up for a training class in nursing.

Gandhi's decision to help in the war effort attracted criticism. Henry Polak, a radical Jew who had been his political lieutenant in South Africa, told him it was a departure from his professions of ahimsa, or non-violence. So did Gandhi's nephew Maganlal. The novelist Olive Schreiner—a white South African passionately opposed to racism and imperialism—wrote to Gandhi an anguished letter of protest. War, she said, 'was against my religion—whether it is Englishmen travelling thousands of miles to kill Indians in India, or Indians travelling thousands of miles to kill white men whom they have never seen in Europe'. She was 'struck to the heart with sorrow' to read that Gandhi and the 'beautiful and beloved Indian poetess' (Sarojini Naidu) had offered to serve the British Government '*in any way* they might demand of you'. She continued: 'Surely you, who would not take up arms even in the cause of your own oppressed people cannot be willing to shed blood in this wicked cause.'[9]

Gandhi's reply to Olive Schreiner is unrecorded. To his nephew Maganlal, he said that since London owed its food and supplies to the protection of the navy, merely by living there he was participating in the conflict. Attending to the war wounded was his way of repayment for this protection. Otherwise, he wrote, 'there was only one right course left, which was to go away to live in some mountain or cave in England itself and subsist on whatever food or shelter Nature might provide . . . I do not yet possess the spiritual strength necessary for this.'[10]

When another Gujarati friend complained that Gandhi's war work was an abdication of ahimsa, he answered that he was not shooting, merely nursing. He hoped to get a chance to attend to wounded Germans so that he 'could nurse them without any partisan spirit'.[11]

V

Gokhale had now returned to London and had long conversations with Gandhi. Each was anxious about the other person's health. Gandhi worried that his mentor was overweight and did not exercise enough. Gokhale, on his part, thought Gandhi's pleurisy a consequence of his fruit-and-nut diet.

Gokhale was keen that Gandhi join his Servants of India Society, which focused on education and social reform. Perhaps he could start a chapter of the society in his home province of Gujarat. However, he advised Gandhi to refrain from public work for a year after his return. He should use this period of 'probation' to travel around a country he scarcely knew.[12]

Gokhale sailed for Bombay on 24 October 1914. The Gandhis would have followed him immediately, except that the British government had refused to grant permission to Kallenbach to accompany them to India, for he was technically a German citizen, and now an 'enemy alien'. Gandhi made several representations, saying that since he had lived for many years in South Africa, Kallenbach considered himself a naturalized Briton. Influential Englishmen whom Gandhi knew were asked to plead on behalf of Kallenbach. The Colonial Office was unmoved; Gandhi's 'German' friend could not go to India; he was shipped off to an internment camp on the Isle of Man instead.[13] The Gandhis had to return home without Kallenbach.

What would Gandhi do on his return to India after two decades in exile? An interesting prediction was offered by C.F. Andrews, an English priest and friend of Gokhale's who had taught for many years at St Stephen's College in Delhi. In January 1914, Andrews had worked closely with Gandhi in mediating a settlement with the South African authorities, which abolished a poll tax levied on Indians and also lifted some other restrictions on them. In December of that year, Andrews wrote to Gokhale that

> I have been thinking a great deal about what Mr. Gandhi will do on his return. Perhaps it is no use thinking as he is bound to take his own course, whatever it may be. *He is not one who can be bound*. I do feel positive about one thing, that he could not for long [fit] in with the *general* work of the Servants of India [Society]. He might take up some special sphere, such as work among the depressed classes [i.e. the 'untouchables'], but *he would need to be quite independent*.[14]

VI

The ship carrying Gandhi and Kasturba back home, the *S.S. Arabia*, landed in Bombay at 9 a.m. on Saturday, 9 January 1915. A large crowd had gathered at the port. When the Gandhis stepped ashore, they were 'cheered again and again, and the press of people was so great that it was with difficulty that they reached their motor car, and by the time they did so they were almost hidden by garlands'. Eventually, they got into the car, which drove off, with 'many of the crowd pursuing it for some distance'.[15]

Bombay in 1915 had a thriving textile industry, an energetic press (operating in many languages), and many prosperous (and some very philanthropic) merchants. Whereas Calcutta was to a large extent a Bengali city, and Madras a Tamil town, Bombay was a microcosm of the subcontinent, home to migrants from all over India and of all religions and ethnicities.

Bombay was an active centre of politics and of social reform. Gandhi's work in South Africa had been widely discussed among its intelligentsia. Gokhale had done much to make his protégé better known; as had Henry Polak, who in 1909–10 had spent time in the city, writing and speaking about Gandhi's struggles.[16] Bombay was also home to a large Gujarati community, whose pride in their man was provincial and very intense.

Gandhi and Kasturba stayed at the home of a friend in the northern suburb of Santa Cruz. On 9 January itself, Gandhi met up with Gokhale, and gave an interview to the *Times of India*. The next day was spent visiting relatives, some of whom had, many years before, opposed his decision to cross the oceans to study law in London. That was in 1888, when he was young and obscure; now, having won fame in a foreign land, he was proudly owned by his caste and community. When Gandhi entered the Gujarati locality of Bazar Gate, he was given a rousing welcome. 'The windows of *chawls* were full with people and they were showering flowers. Everyone was equally enthusiastic. The shops of the Parsis were also decorated with flowers.'[17]

On the morning of 12 January, Gandhi paid his respects to Dadabhai Naoroji, the Parsi veteran whose role in Gandhi's early career was second only to Gokhale's. The same evening, a grand party was thrown for the Gandhis at the mansion of the fabulously wealthy Petit family. As a reporter on the spot wrote: 'Every single sect and community in this cosmopolitan city was represented, and few more influential gatherings have been witnessed in Bombay.' Among those present were high court judges, European civil servants and the city's most prominent Parsis, Hindus and Muslims. The main speech was delivered by Sir Pherozeshah Mehta, who praised the returning hero's courage, selflessness and patriotism. While they were proud of Mr Gandhi, said Sir Pherozeshah, they were prouder of Mrs Gandhi, for 'standing shoulder-to-shoulder with him in the fight and in the sufferings and privations he was prepared to undergo' in South Africa.[18]

On 13 January, Gandhi attended a gathering hosted by the Bombay National Union, a less westernized group of activists and professionals. Here, Bal Gangadhar Tilak praised Gandhi for having 'fought for the honour of India in a distant land'.[19] Tilak was the foremost 'Extremist' leader of the Congress much as Gokhale was its foremost 'Moderate'. Both factions had now temporarily united to praise the leader of the struggle in South Africa.

There were more meetings in Bombay, of which two were especially significant. The first was hosted by the Gurjar Sabha, the representative body of the city's Gujaratis. The proceedings were opened by the young lawyer-novelist K.M. Munshi, who called the gathering 'a public expression of the feelings of reverence to and admiration for the greatest son of modern Gujarat'.[20]

The main speech here was made by Muhammad Ali Jinnah. Some aspects of Jinnah's career resembled Gandhi's. Born in 1876, like Gandhi he was from Kathiawar; he had likewise studied law in London and sought to build a career at the Bombay Bar. In 1897 he was in correspondence with Gandhi in South Africa. The letters they exchanged are lost—they may have been about a legal partnership the two were hoping to build in Durban.[21]

Jinnah eventually stayed on in Bombay, and built a successful practice. He became active in the Congress and simultaneously in the Muslim League (Jinnah was a Shia). An eloquent speaker in English, he was much in demand at public meetings. In 1909, still in his thirties, he was elected to the Imperial Legislative Council, an elite body of policymakers which had only sixty members from across India.[22]

Jinnah had spoken several times in support of Gandhi's struggle in the Transvaal. They were acquaintances rather than friends. Each knew of the other's reputation. Even so, Jinnah must have had mixed feelings on hearing Gandhi being described as 'the greatest son of modern Gujarat'. As a member of the Imperial Legislature, he enjoyed an exceptionally high status himself. In terms of proximity to power and authority, Jinnah would, in 1915, probably have counted as the most influential Gujarati alive.

Jinnah's speech to the Gurjar Sabha was carefully crafted. He praised Gandhi's 'strenuous and hard labour' on behalf of the Indians in the diaspora, and 'the trials, the sufferings [and] the sacrifices' he had to undergo on their behalf. But he wondered if Gandhi's return to India was not 'a terrible loss to South Africa'. The condition of the community was still precarious, and with Gandhi's departure, 'there was nobody who could take his place and fight their battle'.

The caveat stated, Jinnah welcomed the hero home, calling him a 'worthy ornament' to the nation-in-the-making. He then drew Gandhi's attention to the relationship between their respective communities. Hindus and Muslims had been 'absolutely one, on the South African question'—the 'first occasion' on which they had stood so solidly together. The challenge now was to bring 'that frame of mind' to Hindu–Muslim relations within India itself. Jinnah asked Gandhi to pay special attention to this central problem: 'namely, how to bring about unanimity and co-operation between the two communities so that the demands of India may be made absolutely unanimously'.[23]

Jinnah had spoken in English. Gandhi made a brief reply, in Gujarati. That a Muslim had been the main speaker in a meeting dominated by Hindus was for Gandhi a happy augury. Now that he was back, he would first 'study all the Indian questions and then enter upon the service of the country'.[24]

The last meeting for the returnees was composed exclusively of women. Its guest of honour was Kasturba Gandhi. A 1000-

strong crowd heard speeches in praise of Kasturba by two wives of Parsi knight-millionaires, the widow of the reformer M.G. Ranade, and a representative of the famous Tyabji family. A printed tribute, presented in a silver casket, spoke of Kasturba's 'rare qualities of courage, devotion and self-sacrifice [which] had so signally justified and fulfilled the high traditions of Indian womanhood'.

Unlike her husband, Kasturba was unused to public speaking. Her speech was brief but graceful. She thanked 'the women of this great and historic city' for their generosity. She said the honour being accorded to her was really due to the Indian women of South Africa, 'some of whom had even died in jail'.[25]

VII

After a week in Bombay, the Gandhis proceeded to their native Kathiawar. On 17 January they reached Rajkot, where Gandhi had gone to high school and where the couple had spent their early married years. The reception at Rajkot, wrote one observer, 'crossed all limits. A pandal was erected at the station. The coaches and engine were decorated with flowers.' After the Gandhis disembarked from the train, they were taken in a horse-driven carriage through the town, cheered by the large crowd that lined the streets.[26]

The Gandhis then proceeded to Porbandar, where both of them were born. Gandhi's father and grandfather had served as diwans of the state. The residents of Porbandar had closely followed his struggle in South Africa, and raised money for it. Now, streets were decorated with arches, and homes with colourful banners. Schools and colleges were closed for the day. The car carrying the returning couple was preceded by horsemen of the state's cavalry, and followed by a contingent of the infantry and the military band. Even the ruler came out of his palace to watch the show.

The next day, a crowd in excess of 5000 (including many women) heard a local merchant speak of the simplicity of their home-town hero. The shawl Gandhi was wearing perhaps cost two rupees, he said, but due to wear and tear it was now worth less than two annas. However, since it had been worn by Mohandas Gandhi, he would pay 100 rupees for it. Gandhi handed over the shawl and asked the merchant to donate the money to charity.

After depositing Kasturba in Rajkot, Gandhi proceeded to Ahmedabad, the largest city in the region, and under direct British rule. At a well-attended public meeting, Gandhi thanked Ahmedabad for having provided some of the best satyagrahis for his struggle in South Africa. He wished, if the citizens would accommodate him, to make the city his base in India.[27]

In the first week of February, Gandhi travelled to Poona to meet Gokhale. His mentor was welcoming, but the other members of the Servants of India Society were discomfited by his presence. As Gandhi recalled: 'There was a difference between my ideals and methods of work, and theirs.' He was unhappy with the dependence of the Servants on servants for their cooking, cleaning and washing; Gandhi, by contrast, preferred to perform these tasks himself.

Gandhi told Gokhale he hoped to settle down in Gujarat, where he would start an ashram on the model of Phoenix, the settlement he had established in South Africa. The older man promised to raise money to support the initiative. As for the Servants of India Society, said Gokhale, 'whether you are formally admitted as a member or not, I am going to look upon you as one'.[28]

Gandhi and Kasturba now travelled across the subcontinent to Bengal. C.F. Andrews had asked him to visit Santiniketan, the rural settlement established by the poet Rabindranath Tagore, who, two years previously, had become the first Asian to win a Nobel Prize. Tagore was not at home when the Gandhis arrived. Gandhi had hoped to stay several weeks in Santiniketan, but news reached him that Gokhale had died in Poona. At a spontaneous memorial meeting in Santiniketan, Gandhi spoke movingly of his mentor. He praised Gokhale's contributions to politics and social reform, his 'fearlessness', 'zest', 'truthfulness', 'thoroughness', and his 'love and reverence' for the motherland. 'I was in quest of a really truthful hero in India,' said Gandhi, 'and I found him in Gokhale.'[29]

Gandhi retraced his steps westward, reaching his mentor's home town on 22 February. Arriving in Poona on the same train as Gandhi was the Madras scholar V.S. Srinivasa Sastri, an active member of the Servants of India Society. Sastri and Gandhi were born in the same year, 1869, and both were devoted to Gokhale. There the similarities ended. Sastri was Brahminical in both the good and bad senses of the term: deeply learned in the scriptures, but entirely dependent on the labour of others for his sustenance. As a constitutionalist, he abhorred Gandhi's use—in South Africa—of strikes, fasts and boycotts to make his case.[30]

An entry in Sastri's diary for 27 February reads:

> At night there was a meeting with Gandhi and a scene.
>
> Spoke up for Society but rather warmly.
>
> Hariji figured well, remarkably so and struck out the phrase 'moral intoxication'.
>
> H.N. Apte too did well. Poor Gandhi—he sat like a man rebuked.[31]

There are no recorded minutes of the meeting. A police report claimed that Gandhi and the society had fallen out because of their 'different' and 'irreconcilable' ideals. Gandhi, inspired by Tolstoy, wanted to found a rural community 'where the youth of India will be taught the dignity of manual labour'. The society, on the other hand, wished its members to 'take part in every movement of modern life, educational, political and economic'. Noting the lack of support for his views, Gandhi withdrew his membership application.[32]

C.F. Andrews had warned Gokhale that Gandhi might find the methods of the Servants of India Society confining. So it turned out. Later in 1915, V.S. Srinivasa Sastri succeeded Gokhale as the society's president.

VIII

Gandhi now returned to Santiniketan, to spend a few days with Tagore and Andrews. The residents of Santiniketan had been told beforehand about Gandhi's capacity for hard physical work. He lived up to this image, telling the students of Tagore's school that they should dispense with paid cooks and do all the cooking and cleaning themselves.[33]

Gandhi's next stop was Rangoon, where his close friend and patron Pranjivan Mehta was based. A prosperous jeweller, Mehta had been a fellow student with Gandhi in London, had financially supported his work in South Africa, and was the first person to call him 'Mahatma'.

Pranjivan Mehta had long wanted Gandhi to leave South Africa for India. Mehta believed Gandhi needed a larger theatre for his work; and the motherland needed *him*. Now, having turned his back on the Servants of India Society, Gandhi wished to consult Mehta about what direction his work might take.[34]

From Rangoon, Gandhi took a boat to Calcutta before journeying northward to the holy town of Haridwar, on the banks of the Ganga. He arrived at the time of the Kumbh Mela, ostensibly a great show of faith, yet with 'very little goodness on display'. The *akhada*s of the sadhus—crowded, unkempt, reeking of marijuana—disappointed him. He was more impressed by the Gurukul Kangri, a school set up by a visionary preacher and friend of C.F. Andrews named Swami Shraddhananda.[35]

After a week in Haridwar, Gandhi proceeded to Delhi, where he spoke at an institution where Andrews had taught, St Stephen's College. He refused to offer the students advice on Indian problems, since Gokhale had told him to first spend a year acquainting himself with a country that he, at this time, scarcely knew. Addressing an audience of Hindu and Muslim students in a Christian college, he focused on his mentor's ecumenism. Gokhale, said Gandhi,

> was a Hindu, but of the right type. A Hindu Sannyasi once came
> to him and made a proposal to push the Hindu political cause in
> a way which would suppress the Mahommedan and he pressed his
> proposal with many specious religious reasons. Mr. Gokhale replied
> to this person in the following words: 'If to be a Hindu I must do as
> you wish me to do, please publish it abroad that I am not a Hindu.'[36]

From Delhi, Gandhi travelled across the subcontinent to Madras, continuing his education into the habits and mores of his countrymen. In this city he was even more of a hero than in Bombay. A majority of those who went to prison in the South African satyagrahas had been

Tamils. Some were women, which is why Kasturba accompanied him on this trip.

When the train carrying the Gandhis reached Madras Central Station, a large crowd was waiting to receive them. They made for the first-class compartment, only to be directed by the guard to the back of the train, where they found their hero, 'thin and emaciated' after four days of continuous travel. The Gandhis 'stepped out of a crowded third class [coach] with no posh travel trunks but bundles of old clothes, like a family of peasants'. With shouts of 'Long Live Mr and Mrs Gandhi', the admirers conducted the visitors to a waiting carriage, from which the horses had been unyoked. The coach was pulled through the streets, 'being cheered all the way'.[37]

Gandhi's host in Madras was G.A. Natesan, editor of *Indian Review*. Natesan was an early admirer, raising money for Gandhi in South Africa, publishing pamphlets by and about him. Gandhi attended several receptions in his honour, variously organized by Gujarati, Christian and Muslim groups, with one all-embracing ecumenical party hosted by Natesan himself. At a meeting of the local Social Service League, Gandhi gently criticized the orthodoxy of the Madrasi Hindu. He himself approved of Panchama (Untouchable) and high-caste students studying together, insisting that 'neither the Panchama boys nor the caste boys would be prejudicially affected in any way'.

In late April and early May, Gandhi travelled through the Madras Presidency, visiting the towns and villages from which the indentured labourers in Natal had come. In a speech in Mayavaram, he said it was 'no part of real Hinduism to have in its hold a mass of people whom I would call "untouchables". If it was proved to me that this is an essential part of Hinduism, I for one would declare myself an open rebel against Hinduism itself.'[38]

From the town of Nellore, Gandhi wrote to his friend Albert West, who had helped found the Phoenix settlement, and was now running it more or less on his own. 'I am going through very varied experiences,' wrote Gandhi to West. 'India continues to satisfy my aspirations. I see much to dishearten me and I see much to encourage me.'[39]

For part of the tour in South India, Gandhi was accompanied by V.S. Srinivasa Sastri. Although they had argued about Gokhale's legacy, their personal relations remained civil. In Mayavaram, Sastri translated Gandhi's speeches from English into Tamil. This was noble of him, since his diary entry after the event read: 'Procession: tedious and annoying.'[40] The refined scholar recoiled from the spontaneous (but to him somewhat vulgar) show of affection for Gandhi by the ordinary Tamil.

IX

In his first few months in India, Gandhi was continuously on the move. He had no office or secretariat—not even a permanent address. Only a few letters written to him in this period survive. They suggest that he was becoming known across the country. In April he was invited to the third Andhra conference, to be held in Vizagapatnam in the middle of May. The conference was part of a wider movement to create a cohesive state of Telugu speakers, then spread across different provinces and chiefdoms. Its organizers hoped that Gandhi, by blessing the Andhra movement, would endorse the 'spread of knowledge and culture through the medium of the mother-tongue and the speedy realisation of Indian nationhood by the division of the country into autonomous units on linguistic basis'.[41]

In the same week, a letter in Hindi was posted to Gandhi from the Himalayan foothills. 'Since you are touring India now and have decided to serve the country,' it said, 'please improve the conditions of the people in the Himalaya.' The writer enumerated the problems of hill peasants: the extraction of forced labour by officials, restrictions on access to forests (a vital source of fuel and fodder), no proper schools for their children. 'Since you are an experienced man,' the correspondent told Gandhi, 'I have related our problems to you. Please come to Naini Tal and Almora, so that I can acquaint you with our difficulties. . . . Do begin the good work from here and carry on till Cape Comorin.'[42]

Some letters asked for advice, others offered it. A Bombay editor wrote to complain about Gandhi's strident criticisms of modern life, since despite its many faults, 'Western civilization, taken as a whole, tends more strongly to justice for all than any older civilization.' 'Your career and character is such a vast public asset,' the editor told Gandhi, 'that one feels that it is a pity it should be rendered less useful than it might and should be by this prejudice, as I must hold it to be, against modernity as such.'[43]

Among the letters Gandhi received in the early months of 1915 was one from his son, Harilal. Unlike previous letters between the two, this was not handwritten, but printed. Harilal had originally intended to release it to the public, but in the end sent it only to family and close friends.

Gandhi and his eldest son had a deeply troubled relationship. Shortly after Harilal was born, in July 1888, his father left to study law in London. Between 1893 and 1896 Gandhi again lived alone, in Durban. The family were reunited for a few years, but then separated again, as Harilal studied in high school in India while his parents and brothers lived in South Africa.

In 1906, Harilal journeyed to South Africa to join the family. He stayed there for four years, in which time he went to jail in the satyagrahas led by Gandhi. He wished to become a barrister like his father. But Gandhi insisted that his eldest son abandon personal ambition and work selflessly for the community. Harilal resisted, and in 1910, now in his early twenties, returned to India to continue his studies.[44]

After Gandhi himself returned to India, father and son met, only to fight once more. On 14 March 1915, Gandhi wrote to a nephew: '[T]here has been a misunderstanding between Harilal and me. He has parted from me completely. He will receive no monetary help from me.'[45]

After this quarrel, Harilal composed the long letter that he then had printed. The letter rehearsed their decade of disagreement, the son saying that the father had 'oppressed' him, and paid him 'no attention at all'. 'Whenever we tried to put across our views on any subject to you,' said Harilal, 'you have lost your temper quickly and told us, "You are stupid, you are in a fallen state, you lack comprehension."' Harilal also accused Gandhi of bullying Kasturba, writing: 'It is beyond my capacity to describe the hardships that my mother had to undergo.'

Gandhi had disapproved of Harilal's marriage, since he fell in love and chose his bride, rather than, as was the custom, have his parents choose a wife for him. Harilal's relationship with his wife, Chanchi, was intensely romantic; this wasn't to Gandhi's liking either, since he believed sex was strictly for procreation and a true satyagrahi should be celibate. Harilal emphatically disagreed. 'No one can be made an ascetic,' he told his father. 'A person becomes an ascetic on his own volition . . . I cannot believe a salt-free diet, or abstinence from ghee or milk [all of which Gandhi preached and practised] indicates strength of character and morality.'

Harilal claimed he spoke on behalf of his younger brothers as well. Gandhi had imposed his will on his four sons, without ever giving them a hearing. 'My entire letter stresses one point,' remarked Harilal. 'You have never considered our rights and capabilities, you have never seen the person in us.' The argument stated, at length and with force, Harilal ended on a note of contrition:

> You know I have not disobeyed you on purpose. It is possible that my views are wrong. I hope that they prove to be wrong—if I realise that they are wrong I shall not hesitate to reform myself. In the deep recesses of my conscience, my only desire is that I be your son—that is, if I am good enough to be your son.[46]

Harilal's criticisms were, on the whole, fair. For, Gandhi was the traditional overbearing Hindu patriarch: insensitive to the wishes and desires of his wife; demanding that his children obey his instructions even when they had reached adulthood. Even now, Gandhi failed to reflect on where he might have gone wrong. 'One will not easily find a parallel to what Harilal has done,' wrote Gandhi to his nephew Narandas: 'When a son writes in that manner, there is bound to be bitterness between father and son . . . Harilal has written to say that he has recovered his calm and that he is sorry he wrote that letter. The letter was all error, and I know that, with experience, he will understand things better.'[47]

X

In the second week of May, Gandhi returned to Gujarat, his travels temporarily on hold. He wished to start a community of social workers that would be a model of its kind. He had chosen the city of Ahmedabad as his base. There were several reasons for this. Ahmedabad had prosperous Hindu and Jain merchants who could fund his projects. The language of the city was his mother tongue, Gujarati. Ahmedabad was located in British India, but—unlike Bombay, Calcutta or Madras—was not greatly influenced by British culture. It had a large Muslim population, allowing him to test his ideas of religious pluralism. And it did not yet have a political leader with an all-India reputation.

Sited on the banks of the Sabarmati River, Ahmedabad was a thriving commercial centre, a major market for gold, cloth and grain. Its Hindu and Jain businessmen were legendary for their acumen. Some fifty textile mills were established here in the decades before Gandhi arrived, earning the city the moniker, 'the Manchester of India'.

The population of Ahmedabad in 1915 was about 2,40,000. The bulk of the population still lived within the medieval city walls; slowly, families were shifting out, building residential colonies on the open land across the river.[48]

An Ahmedabad businessman who had come forward to back Gandhi was the mill owner Mangaldas Girdhardas.[49] On 11 May, Gandhi submitted to Mangaldas a meticulously detailed description of all that the proposed ashram in Ahmedabad would need. The items listed included the number and size of cooking pots, cups, plates, frying pans, kettles, carpenter's and cobbler's tools, agricultural implements, inkstands, blackboards, chamber pots, and maps (of Gujarat, the Bombay Presidency, India and the world). The ashram would have about fifty inmates. Its annual expenditure (excluding land and buildings) would be in the region of Rs 6000.[50]

Gandhi had hoped to acquire at least ten acres for the ashram. That was not immediately forthcoming, so he rented a building from a local barrister named Jivanlal Desai. This was located in Kochrab, across the river from the main city. Desai's bungalow was spacious;

with a dozen rooms spread across two floors, a lovely tiled roof and a large garden. It would do until a larger plot was identified and purchased.[51]

On 20 July 1915, Gandhi and a few followers formally took over the building in Kochrab. On the same day, he drafted a constitution for the ashram. Inmates had 'to learn how to serve the motherland one's whole life'. They would take personal vows of truth, non-violence, celibacy, non-stealing, non-possession and 'control of the palate'. They would also commit themselves to the wearing and promotion of hand-spun cloth and the abolition of untouchability. A school for children would also be established, with instruction in the mother tongue.

Gandhi had founded two such settlements in South Africa. One, Phoenix, took the name of a nearby railway station. The second was called Tolstoy Farm, since the land originally belonged to his fellow Tolstoyan, Hermann Kallenbach. Among the names suggested for Gandhi's first Indian settlement were 'Sevashram' (the home of service) and 'Tapovan' (the home of austerities). Gandhi eventually decided to call it 'Satyagraha Ashram', which, as he noted, conveyed 'both our goal and our method of service'.

The daily routine of the ashram was similar to that of Phoenix. The inmates woke up at 4 a.m., and bathed. Community prayers (with hymns and texts drawn from Hindu, Christian, Parsi and Muslim traditions) were followed by breakfast. The adults spent the bulk of the day doing manual labour, the children alternating between classes and work. The evening meal was followed by a second round of prayers. The children were to go to bed by 9 p.m., and adults by 10 p.m.[52]

Gandhi had circulated the ashram's constitution to a few friends. One, the Moderate politician Satyananda Bose, wrote a searing critique of the emphasis on *brahmacharya*, or celibacy. While self-control and self-discipline were important attributes, did one have to enforce them in such a rigorous way? 'It is not desirable that the country should be peopled by monks and nuns,' remarked Bose acidly. If the 'best men' were 'called away as celibate Sannyasis', wrote Bose, 'the society will consist of mediocres'.[53]

Gandhi's reply is unavailable. For him, abstinence from sex was absolutely an article of faith. An early teacher, the Jain preacher

Raychandbhai, had termed celibacy 'that state supreme', whereby an individual surrendered his desires to 'tread the path trodden by the wise and the great'. Another major influence, Leo Tolstoy, also embraced celibacy in later life, celebrating it as 'a man's liberation from the lusts'.[54]

Gandhi's obsession with celibacy was akin to that of early Christian ascetics in North Africa and the Middle East. For them, writes one historian of the subject, 'sex typified the kingdom of evil'. They believed that 'the supremely dangerous desires inside us are sexual'. In later life, the most famous of these celibates, St Augustine, looked back on the sexual encounters of his youth with 'horror and disdain'.[55]

Like St Augustine, Gandhi gave up sex in his thirties, when fully capable of enjoying its pleasures. Having once experienced it vigorously, and even fathered four children, he came to view sex with disgust. Gandhi was not a young virgin when he embraced celibacy (as was and often still is the case with many Buddhist, Christian, Jain as well as Hindu monks). Neither was he an old man. Yet Gandhi felt that he had arrived at brahmacharya too late. Now, those who came under his own influence were asked—or mandated—to take the vow as early as possible.[56]

XI

By early September, the ashram had about thirty members. They included Gandhi's own family, some Indians from South Africa, and a handful of brave young men who had abandoned their careers in pursuit of an ideal. Recruits were welcome, so long as they were willing to take the vows. The social worker A.V. Thakkar now wrote to Gandhi that 'a humble and honest untouchable family is desirous of joining your Ashram. Will you accept them?'

This letter, recalled Gandhi in his autobiography, 'perturbed' him.[57] He had taken a public stance against the practice of untouchability. However, in matters of caste the Hindus of Ahmedabad were cautious and conservative. So soon after he had moved to their city, should he challenge their prejudices in so open a manner?

Varnashramadharma, the rules of caste, strictly forbade members of different castes from living under the same roof or eating at the same table. In July 1915, there were no 'untouchables' in the ashram, but there were members from the four main orders: Brahmin, Kshatriya, Vaishya and Sudra. To justify their cohabitation, the ashram manifesto as drafted by Gandhi said: 'The Ashram does not follow the *varnashram dharma*.' This, he argued, was because the inmates were in the stage of *sannyas* (renunciation) where such rules did not apply. Then, in a bow to orthodox opinion, Gandhi added: 'Apart from this, the Ashram has a firm belief in the *varnashram* dharma. The discipline of caste seems to have done no harm to the country . . . There is no reason to believe that eating in company promotes brotherhood ever so slightly.'[58]

Shortly after Gandhi reached India, he had received a long letter on the problem of untouchability from a friend in South Africa. The writer, a Tamil Christian named J.M. Lazarus, told Gandhi that in the Madras Presidency, 'even today, a Pariah dare not walk into a Street inhabited by Brahmins, nor will he even wear his Dhotis below his knees before his Brahmin Lord, nor will he even draw his drinking water from a well used by the Brahmins'.

Comprising some 15 per cent of the Indian population, the 'untouchables' were confined to professions such as scavenging and leatherwork, which caste Hindus regarded as 'unclean'. Though technically Hindus, they were not considered part of the varna system, and not allowed to worship in temples, nor allowed to draw water from the same wells as upper-caste Hindus. In some parts of India even the sight of an 'untouchable' was said to 'pollute' the Brahmins. The economic degradation and social humiliation that 'untouchables' in India experienced had no parallel elsewhere in the world.*

---

* The erstwhile 'untouchables' are now known as Dalits, a term which has come into common use only in recent decades. In this book, I use the terms current at the time Gandhi lived and worked, such as 'Depressed Classes', used widely in the official literature at the time, and also often used by Gandhi's great contemporary B.R. Ambedkar; and 'untouchables', the inverted commas conveying the inhuman treatment that these people had to suffer at the hands of the Hindu caste order. In the early 1930s, Gandhi coined the term 'Harijan' (Children of God) as a substitute for 'untouchables'; I use that term when specifically referring to his own activities and those of his followers.

Under British rule the situation of the 'untouchables' had marginally improved. They could convert to Christianity (as Lazarus had himself done), or abandon their traditional, stigmatized professions to take up jobs in factories and government offices. The growing movement for self-government was no doubt welcome, argued Lazarus, but where did it place the 'untouchables'? Gandhi's Tamil friend argued that the Congress was dominated by high-caste men who had 'not done anything to elevate the oppressed classes'. He worried that if India got political independence, 'the Brahmins could again pursue their old Steam Roller Policy upon this much neglected and wretched community'.

Lazarus asked Gandhi to pay this 'great question' his fullest attention. He understood that 'by bringing this question forward it may hamper Congress's aims in some respects and so it behooves us to find some solution of the difficulty'. For, if a solution was not found, 'the realisation of the ideal of a National India is an utter impossibility'.[59]

Gandhi himself believed that the practice of untouchability was immoral and unjust. Friends like Lazarus pushed him to make its abolition an active part of his programme. On the other side, he was sensible of the strong feelings of the orthodox Hindu. Gandhi was himself not a Brahmin; born in the Bania, or merchant caste, and without a deep knowledge of Sanskrit, he did not have a formal mandate to prescribe what Hindus should or should not do.

A.V. Thakkar's letter to him had now placed Gandhi in a quandary. Should he accept the 'untouchable' family recommended by Thakkar, or would that imperil the future of the ashram?

Gandhi decided to accept Thakkar's suggestion. The family consisted of Dudhabhai, his wife, Danibehn, and their baby daughter, Lakshmi. When they arrived at the Satyagraha Ashram on 11 September, there was much grumbling, not least from Gandhi's own family members. Kasturba was not happy with this decision to defy the orthodox. Danibehn was prevented from drawing water from the common well until Gandhi said in that case he would not use the well either.[60]

On 23 September, Gandhi wrote to Srinivasa Sastri about the turmoil caused by the admission of the 'untouchable' family. 'There was quite a flutter in the Ashram,' he remarked. 'There is a flutter even in Ahmedabad. I have told Mrs. Gandhi she could leave me and we should part good friends. The step is momentous because it so links me with the suppressed classes mission that I might have at no distant time to carry out the idea of shifting to some *Dhed* quarters and sharing their life with the *Dheds*.'[61]

The argument raged within the ashram, and without. Gandhi was able to persuade Kasturba that the step was necessary. However, their principal patron, Mangaldas Girdhardas, decided to withdraw his funding. He was an orthodox Hindu who, after visiting his factory and meeting workers of different castes, would have a purificatory bath before his meal. Gandhi's decision to admit an 'untouchable' family was not something he could abide.

Mangaldas was funding the ashram on a monthly basis. If the next cheque did not come, Gandhi's experiment, barely three months old, faced extinction. Fortunately, another Ahmedabad industrialist stepped in. In his autobiography, Gandhi does not identify the man, referring to him simply as the 'Sheth' (merchant). But we know him to be Ambalal Sarabhai. Twenty-eight years younger than Mangaldas, he was of a more progressive cast of mind, and had travelled widely overseas.[62]

Sarabhai and Gandhi had only met once. The businessman had not stepped inside the ashram. But on hearing that the experiment was in trouble, Sarabhai drove to Kochrab and sent word (through one of the schoolchildren) that he wanted to see the founder. Gandhi went outside, where the 'Sheth' was waiting in his car. He asked whether Gandhi needed any help. Gandhi replied: 'Most certainly. And I confess I am at the present moment at the end of my resources.'

Sarabhai told Gandhi that he would come again the following day. Twenty-four hours later, a car horn was heard outside the ashram. Once more, a child was sent to summon Gandhi. From within the car, the 'Sheth' handed over a large bundle of currency notes, and drove away.

The notes were worth Rs 13,000, or two years' expenses. The ashram had been saved, by a benefactor who had not so much as entered the premises.[63] But the grumblings continued. Visiting the ashram in October 1915, the district magistrate of Ahmedabad found that 'the Institution evidently still excites interest. I saw half a dozen students from Bombay, waiting to be shown round, or perhaps to see the great man. But it has come to grief on the matter of caste, and Mr. Gandhi prefers to have things as they are to giving in over what is to him a vital Principle.'[64]

In the last week of December, Gandhi attended the annual session of the Indian National Congress in Bombay. He moved a resolution deploring the treatment of Indians in South Africa. Later, he heard G.A. Natesan praise him from the podium. 'The problem of Indian nationality for the solution of which this Congress has been started,' remarked Natesan, 'seems to be very satisfactorily solved in South Africa with such brave leaders as Mr. Gandhi.' Gandhi, said his Tamil admirer, had 'returned to his motherland after winning a brave feat of arms with weapons unique and almost unparalleled in the history of the world'.[65]

Gandhi's travels in 1915 had exponentially expanded his knowledge of his homeland. He could now apply his mind and his methods to all problems of Indian nationality, whether social, political or religious.

CHAPTER TWO

Coming out in Banaras

I

The year's probation mandated by Gokhale had ended. Gandhi was now free to speak out on political matters. Although he perhaps did not realize it, he was also freed by Gokhale's premature death. Had his mentor been alive, Gandhi would have framed his utterances in the light of what Gokhale would make of them. Gokhale may also have tried to keep him within the Servants of India Society, a body that focused on social work and stayed out of political controversies.

Gandhi spent the first month of 1916 in Gujarat. On 1 February, he travelled to Banaras. He had been invited to the founding ceremonies of the Banaras Hindu University, whose prime movers were the theosophist Annie Besant and the Allahabad scholar Madan Mohan Malaviya. A centre of learning and of pilgrimage, Banaras was probably the oldest and certainly the most storied of Indian cities. The creation of a modern university in an ancient town was originally Mrs Besant's idea. Malaviya was instrumental in raising the money and in acquiring land for the campus. Among the patrons were some influential (and very rich) maharajas. They would be in attendance at the inaugural ceremony where the chief guest was the viceroy, Lord Hardinge.[1]

A massive amphitheatre had been constructed for the opening. The spectators were seated in fifteen different stands, their cards of admission issued in five colours to help them find their place. The band in attendance struck up 'God Save the King' as the viceroy came and took his seat. Around him sat sundry maharajas, high officials of the Raj and Indians with knighthoods.

The ceremony began at noon on 4 February, with a speech welcoming the viceroy by a major patron of the university, the maharaja of Darbhanga. The maharaja said they hoped to produce men of intellect and character 'who love their Motherland, are loyal to the King and are in every way fit to be useful members of the community and worthy citizens of a great Empire'.[2]

The viceroy then made a speech of his own, before laying the foundation stone amidst the chanting of Sanskrit hymns. After lunch he was driven off to the railway station on a shining metalled road specially built for the occasion. In his memoirs, the chief guest wrote of how it had been 'a very big function and a very successful one. . . . The Durbar at Benares was extraordinarily picturesque with the Ruling Chiefs and all the Indians in their smartest clothes, in bright colours and parti-coloured turbans . . . There were 6,000 people present and all very enthusiastic.'[3]

The viceroy had stayed only for the first day, 4 February. From the 5th to the 8th, the ceremonies carried on, featuring dances, plays, cricket matches and lectures.

Apart from scholars and scientists, some public figures had also been asked to deliver lectures. On the evening of 6 February, Annie Besant spoke on 'The University as a Builder of Character'. Immediately after her, Gandhi was due to speak. The title of his talk was not listed on the programme; but it was assumed that he would speak about his experiences in South Africa.

Gandhi's autobiography does not mention this visit to Banaras. Whether the omission was deliberate one cannot say. (The book was written as a series of newspaper articles, and in any case, memoirists have the freedom to include or exclude memories as they please.) Nonetheless the omission is striking. For, Gandhi's speech in Banaras was the first properly *public* statement he made after his return to the homeland. What he said created a stir; how the audience responded to what he said created a stir too.

The text of Gandhi's Banaras speech in the *Collected Works* is taken from an anthology of his writings published by G.A. Natesan in 1918. In sending his text to Natesan, Gandhi said he had 'merely removed some of the verbiage which in cold print would make the speech bad reading'. The provincial archives in Lucknow contain the unexpurgated version, this based on the notes in shorthand of a reporter from the *Leader* newspaper.[4]

Among the sections excised by Gandhi was a broadside against Lord Macaulay. In making English the language of instruction in India, Macaulay had hoped 'to form a class who may be interpreters between us and the millions whom we govern . . . a class of persons Indian in blood and colour, but English in tastes, in opinions, in morals and in intellect'.[5] Gandhi commented acidly that 'Lord Macaulay made many blunders in his life, all unconsciously, but so far as India is concerned there was never a greater blunder made than when he penned that minute on education'.

Also excised by Gandhi was a paragraph suggesting that the new university was in danger of isolating itself from the masses. The salvation of the country, he had remarked, 'is only going to come when the agriculturist, when the artisan of India is educated up to his sense of responsibility, when he finds that he has at least enough to feed himself on, to clothe himself. And you are not going to learn all these things in the university . . .'

For all that it left out, the text that Gandhi sent to the printer was powerful and provocative enough. One section directly attacked the princes who were the new university's main patrons. Was it necessary, asked Gandhi, 'that in order to show the truest loyalty to our King-Emperor, it is necessary for us to ransack our jewellery-boxes and to appear bedecked from head to toe'? Gandhi told the invitees that 'there is no salvation for India unless you strip yourself of this jewellery and hold it in trust for your countrymen in India ("Hear, hear" and applause)'. 'There can be no spirit of self-government about us,' he went on, 'if we take away or allow others to take away from the peasants almost the whole of the results of their labour.'

The previous day, Gandhi had visited the city's most famous shrine, the Kashi Vishwanath temple. He found it filthy, the state of the temple symptomatic of the state of Indian society. As he told his audience in the university, 'If a stranger dropped from above on to this great temple and he had to consider what we as Hindus were, would he not be justified in condemning us? Is not this great temple a reflection of our own character? . . . Is it right that the lanes of our sacred temple should be as dirty as they are? . . . If even our temples are not models of roominess and cleanliness, what can our self-government be?'

Hearing Gandhi's strictures against princely excess and Hindu custom were the princes themselves. One, the maharaja of Alwar, left the podium in protest. As he walked out, he passed the commissioner of Banaras, and said, 'I am simply disgusted, the man must be mad.' The commissioner replied, 'Well Maharaja Sahib, this is no place for us.'[6]

Gandhi carried on, asking why, when the viceroy came to Banaras, there were so many detectives on the streets and on rooftops. Was this a sign of fear? He then spoke of the anarchists of Bengal, who sought to throw bombs at high officials in the hope that they would be terrorized into fleeing India. Gandhi termed their zeal 'misdirected, and wondered why they were so afraid to come into the open'. At this stage, Annie Besant, sitting behind Gandhi, intervened, saying: 'Stop! Please Stop!' More princes began leaving the stage. The students in the audience, on the other hand, shouted: 'Go On! Go On!' Gandhi asked the chairman (the maharaja of Darbhanga) what he should do. The chairman answered: 'Please explain your object.' Gandhi then said that 'there is no room for anarchism in India'. He himself wished 'to purge India of the atmosphere of suspicion on either side' so as to create an empire 'based on mutual love and mutual trust'.

The caveat entered, Gandhi returned to the polemical mode. He deplored 'the atmosphere of sycophancy and falsity' that surrounded the high officials of the Raj. He characterized their behaviour as 'overbearing' and 'tyrannical'. He then said that Indians would never be granted self-government; they had to take it for themselves, as the Boers had done in South Africa. The suggestion of a rebellion against the Raj led to more agitation on the stage. Mrs Besant asked Gandhi once more to stop; the chairman, an arch-loyalist like the rest of his ilk, declared the meeting closed.

As the princes left the podium, Madan Mohan Malaviya walked over and addressed the crowd. He was sorry that Gandhi's speech had 'given offence in high quarters'. The references to anarchists had alarmed the chiefs; had they waited, they would have come to know that Gandhi was in fact deploring their methods. What Gandhi wanted to do, said Malaviya, was 'to wean from all time our students from the evil influences of those who themselves hiding behind the screen, turn young men into the wrong part'.[7]

A member of the audience later recalled that 'everybody was offended' by Gandhi's speech: 'the Ruling Princes because of his ungenerous attack on their jewellery, the University authorities because of the slight cast on them by his riling at their princely patrons, the C.I.D. officers because of his appreciation of sedition mongers, and lastly Mr. Gandhi himself, because the meeting terminated abruptly without even a "by your leave" to the speaker.'[8]

II

The day after his speech, Gandhi wrote a letter to the maharaja of Darbhanga, clarifying that he held 'very strong views against all acts of violence and anarchy'. His mission was 'securing the utmost freedom for my country but never by violence'. The maharaja was unpersuaded. On 7 February, when presiding over another public lecture, the maharaja of Darbhanga said that 'they had heard with grief and pain the remarks of Mr. Gandhi [the previous day] and he was sure they all disapproved the attitude Mr. Gandhi had taken up'.[9]

Gandhi had, meanwhile, left Banaras for Bombay. On 9 February, a correspondent from the Associated Press asked why his speech had become so controversial. Gandhi clarified that while he thought the anarchists had 'patriotic motives', their methods did great damage in the long run. He had never endorsed violence; indeed, it was his 'firm belief that, but for Mrs. Besant's hasty and ill-conceived interruption, nothing would have happened and my speech in its completed state would have left no room for any doubt as to its meaning'.[10]

When a report of this interview reached Mrs Besant, she hastened to defend herself. She had, she said, heard a police officer sitting behind her say, 'Everything he says is being taken down, and will be sent to the Commissioner.' Since Gandhi's remarks were 'capable of a construction' contrary to what he intended, she had told the chairman that 'politics is out of place in that meeting'. 'If the meeting had been called by Mr. Gandhi,' said Mrs Besant, 'it would have been no one's business but his own what he chose to say.' But as a member of the university committee, she was responsible to the invitees, to whom Gandhi's remarks did seem a provocation.[11]

Mrs Besant was correct on one count; the government was keenly following what Gandhi had to say. The superintendent of police in Banaras wired his bosses in Lucknow about the visitor's 'objectionable speech'. The copy of the speech prepared by the *Leader* was obtained; and the newspaper was prohibited from publishing it. In a long report on the incident, the commissioner of Banaras grimly noted that 'the reception by the students of Gandhi's address indicated the spirit which permeates them. The remarks which they cheered were those which referred to the giving up of English, and the turning of the English—bag and baggage—out of the country.'[12]

The authorities were confused as to how to deal with the provocation. The police and the legal remembrancer to the United Provinces (UP) government both held Gandhi's remarks to be 'seditious and disloyal', and recommended that he be arrested and prosecuted under the Indian Penal Code. The chief secretary disagreed; Gandhi, he noted, 'is already a popular hero, and prosecution will only madden him still further and increase his influence with the students. Cold water seems better than the martyr's stake.'[13]

These notes and opinions went back and forth between the different departments of the UP government. On 17 March—a full five weeks after the speech—the lieutenant governor, James Meston, summed up the debate in magisterial terms:

> My own impression is that Gandhi started with the intention of talking against the use of violence in the nationalist campaign and the importance of cultivating higher qualities than brute force. . . . But however well designed the outlines of his address might have been, Gandhi clearly got carried away by his own rhetoric and by the applause with which the students received some unguarded expressions which he used. In his growing excitement, he lost control of himself, and let out his real sentiments. Part of his speech was admirable; part was in thoroughly bad taste; the rest, though

not a deliberate or intentional incitement to sedition, was in effect
seditious and open to grave objection.

The lieutenant governor also advised against prosecution, since
'influential men in his own community' had distanced themselves from
Gandhi's views, and since action against him would spoil the success of
the university's inauguration as a whole. The 'wisest course' therefore,
would be for the government to let the matter drop, and allow the
incident caused by Gandhi's speech to 'slip into obscurity and oblivion'.[14]

III

Although Gandhi disassociated himself from the methods of the
anarchists, his suggestion that their motives were patriotic caused
disquiet. No group of Indians was more loyal to the Empire than
the maharajas. And Madan Mohan Malaviya himself belonged to
the 'Moderate' wing of the Congress party, which believed in slow,
incremental gains for Indians granted by Britons from above.

The princes and the Moderates both had a horror of violent
protest. That the viceroy had inaugurated the university was further
evidence that this was an establishment affair. Gandhi's mere mention
of terror and assassination muddied the waters. Lord Hardinge had
himself narrowly escaped an attempt on his life in December 1912,
when a bomb had been thrown at him while he was on an elephant
in a grand public procession in Delhi.[15] The detectives who shadowed
the viceroy as he drove through the streets of Banaras were there to
forestall a second attack.

The official commentary on Gandhi's speech focused on whether
the references to anarchism were 'seditious'. But in fact, the speech
was—and is—notable for far more than its treatment of violence and
non-violence. In Banaras, Gandhi made four fundamental claims
about how Indians should conduct their affairs.

First, Gandhi argued in favour of instruction in the mother
tongue. English, the foreign language imposed on India, should have
no place in education or public affairs;

Second, Gandhi pointed to the sharp inequalities between different groups in India. He contrasted the luxuriant lifestyles of the maharajas with the desperate poverty of the majority of Indians. That is why he asked the princes to cast off their jewels, and told the students that they must acquaint themselves with the living conditions of peasants, artisans and labourers;

Third, he asked that officials of the state identify more closely with those they governed over. He deplored the arrogance of the elite Indian Civil Service (ICS), whose officers saw themselves as members of a ruling caste rather than as servants of the people;

Finally, Gandhi asked for a more critical attitude towards religious orthodoxy. The Kashi Vishwanath was the most famous temple in all of Banaras. Why then was it so filthy? If Indians were incapable of maintaining even their places of worship, how then could they justify their claims for self-rule?

Gandhi's speech was an act of courage. In February 1916, he was altogether without any influence or power in British India. And yet, he made direct and telling criticisms of wealthy princes, important officials and the guardians of religious orthodoxy. In India's holiest city, at a function inaugurated by the viceroy and patronized by his leading collaborators, a lawyer lately returned from many years abroad had served notice of his intention to transform his faith and his country.

IV

In the third week of February 1916, Gandhi travelled to Poona to mark the first anniversary of Gokhale's death. Addressing a 2000-strong audience at the Kirloskar Theatre, Gandhi spoke of how he had found 'that the country was vibrating with a passionate spirit of patriotism, but the bugbear of "fear" loomed large on the horizon. . . . The spiritual liberty of the people was usurped by the priests; in politics they were afraid to give expression to their views.'[16]

From Poona, Gandhi travelled north-west to Sindh. He spent several days in the port city of Karachi, where there was a large community of Gujarati traders. In a speech in the inland town of Hyderabad, he said 'swaraj and swadeshi must go together'. Political freedom, or swaraj, was being coupled with economic self-reliance, or swadeshi.[17]

In July, Gandhi published a pamphlet in Gujarati on the problems of railway passengers. This was based on his own extensive travels over the past year and a half. He told stationmasters that by 'using courtesy in your dealings with poor passengers you can set an example to your subordinates'. Booking clerks were asked to issue tickets promptly, and policemen not to accept bribes. As for his fellow passengers, Gandhi urged them not to rush to board the train or carry excessive luggage, not to smoke if others in the coach objected, and to use lavatories with care. Finally, they were asked to disregard differences of caste and language while they travelled: 'If you think of all [passengers] as children of India who have for the nonce assembled under one roof, and cherish a brotherly feeling for all, you will be happy this very moment and bring glory to India.'[18]

Some months later, Gandhi published, in both Gujarati and Marathi, a long essay on the caste system. This fourfold division of Hindu society had, he argued, 'struck such deep roots in India that I think it will be far more advisable to try to improve it, rather than uproot it'. He thought that prohibitions on different castes intermarrying and eating together were conducive to self-control. 'With an arrangement of this kind, there is a good chance that loose conduct will be kept down.' At the same time, he said, the system should allow exceptions so that 'if I eat in the company of a *Bhangi* [from the "untouchable" sweeper caste] there being, from my point of view, greater self-control in doing so, the community should have nothing to do with the matter'.[19]

While condemning untouchability outright, Gandhi was not prepared to criticize the caste system itself. He thought that by restricting oneself to a bride of one's own caste, the predatory instincts of young men would be checked. But, for those who had already achieved a greater degree of 'self-control' (such as himself), mixing and mingling with other castes was permissible. The system, he seemed to be saying, would not be brought down; but heretics should not be persecuted either.

V

From June to November 1916, Gandhi was mostly in Ahmedabad, where he was building a cadre of devoted co-workers. A young lecturer of English named Valji Govind Desai resigned his job and joined Gandhi. So did a precocious scholar named Vinoba Bhave, who had studied Sanskrit in Banaras, where he had attended and been moved by Gandhi's famous/notorious talk at the university's inauguration. This new recruit practised an extreme physical austerity. 'Your son,' wrote Gandhi admiringly to Bhave's father, 'has acquired at so tender an age such high-spiritedness and asceticism as took me years of patient labour to do.'[20]

Gandhi was also garnering devotees elsewhere in India. An idealistic merchant named Jamnalal Bajaj—based in Wardha in the Central Provinces—visited the ashram several times and started funding it. Also keenly following Gandhi's work was C. Rajagopalachari, a young lawyer based in Salem. In February 1916, Rajagopalachari wrote a long essay outlining, for a southern audience, Gandhi's 'Message to India', namely an emphasis on Hindu–Muslim harmony, non-violence, and the promotion of handicrafts to foster self-reliance.[21]

In late October, a conference of political workers in the Bombay Presidency was held in Ahmedabad. M.A. Jinnah was elected president of the conference, his name proposed by Gandhi, who described him as a 'learned Muslim gentleman', 'a person who holds [a] respected position in the eyes of both parties'. Gandhi went on to say that 'the feeling we should outwardly show, that moderates or extremists, Surtis or Kathiawaris or Ahmedabadis, Hindus or Muslims, all are our brethren, should be there in our hearts'.[22]

In November, his South African comrade Henry Polak came visiting. To their mutual friend Hermann Kallenbach, Polak wrote that 'G. looks better than I have seen him looking in years. Evidently India, with its many disappointments, has offered him a more

congenial atmosphere. Mrs G., too, looks much better and fuller than
I have seen her for a long time.'[23]

VI

In 1916, as Gandhi was clearing a space for himself, two more
famous names in Indian politics founded 'Home Rule Leagues'. Bal
Gangadhar Tilak and Annie Besant were both enormously charismatic
individuals. Tilak was a fiery orator who had recently served a long
jail term on charges of 'sedition'. He was popular in western India,
especially in his native Maharashtra, where he had promoted a cult
of the medieval warrior-king Shivaji. Besant's appeal was more to the
English-speaking middle classes, who were flattered by this Western
woman's romance with Hinduism, and genuinely admired her work
on education.

Tilak started his Home Rule League in April 1916; Besant started
hers in September of the same year. Both experiments were inspired
by the struggle for independence in Ireland. They aimed at nudging—
or pushing—the British rulers towards granting self-government to
Indians.[24]

Tilak and Besant both had their eye on the annual meeting of
the Congress, held that year at the same time, and in the same town,
Lucknow, as the annual meeting of the Muslim League. This was by
choice; through 1916, the two organizations had tried to establish a
working relationship. In recent times, Muslims had stayed away from
the Congress, weakening its credibility. Now an attempt was being
made to heal the breach. The prime movers were Tilak, from the
side of the Congress, and Jinnah, on behalf of the League. The two
men were friends; Jinnah had even served as Tilak's lawyer in a case
brought against him by the government.

The last time Tilak had attended a Congress meeting was at Surat
in 1907, when the party split into Extremist and Moderate factions.
Now the factions had come together on the same platform once more.
For his journey to the Lucknow Congress in December, Tilak had
arranged for a special train to carry his supporters. As the 'Home
Rule Special' pulled into Lucknow station, it was met by a large

crowd, 'showering roses on [Tilak] and offering countless bouquets and garlands'. Tilak was conveyed through the city's streets in an open carriage drawn by young men shouting the slogan he had made famous: 'Swaraj is my birthright and I shall have it.'[25]

If Tilak was the star of the Congress, the leading light of the Muslim League was Jinnah. He had been elected president for the session. The League was dominated by large landlords and nawabs who were abjectly loyal to the British. Jinnah, however, recognized the growing force of nationalist sentiment, and his election signalled a shift in the League's orientation.

Leading up to the meeting, Jinnah had appealed to his 'Hindu friends to be generous and liberal and welcome and encourage other activities of Muslims even if it involves some sacrifice in the matter of separate electorates'. Back in 1909, the British had granted separate electorates to Muslims on the grounds that otherwise they would be swamped by the Hindus. The move was bitterly opposed by the Congress. Jinnah now offered a quid pro quo: in exchange for the retention of this special provision, the Muslim League would join hands with the Congress in demanding self-government for India.[26]

In Lucknow, the Congress and the Muslim League committed themselves to a common programme. Through this 'Lucknow Pact', they jointly demanded that 'India should be lifted from the position of a dependency to that of an equal partner in the Empire'. The Congress and the League asked for four-fifths of the central and provincial legislatures to be composed of elected (rather than nominated) members, and for provinces to have autonomy in designing their laws and running their administrations; for, in sum, India to be placed on par with self-governing dominions such as Australia and Canada.[27]

Attending the Congress and League meetings in Lucknow was a brilliant and beautiful girl named Ruttie Petit. Her father, a massively wealthy Bombay Parsi, was a long-time client of Jinnah's. In the summer of 1916, Jinnah had taken a holiday at the Petits' bungalow in the hill station of Darjeeling. He and Ruttie had taken walks and rides together; and had fallen in love. It was, for the times, an unorthodox, controversial romance, for the courting couple were of different religions, and also many years apart in age.[28]

Ruttie came to Lucknow with her parents, attending the Congress sessions with keen interest. Later, she wrote to a friend about how Lucknow, 'the City of Mosques', had

> welcomed the worshippers of the Lords Krishna and Buddha. It has heard the carefully measured words of the Moderates and also the reckless indictments of the Extremists against an alien Government. It has thrilled to the passionate appeal of the Nationalists who have sacrificed all at the feet of the Motherland.[29]

Like Ruttie Petit, Mohandas Gandhi was in attendance in Lucknow during that week of political meetings. He played a modest part in the proceedings; chairing a session of the Congress devoted to a common language policy, and addressing the Muslim League about the conditions of Indians in South Africa. In between, he loaned his blanket to Srinivasa Sastri—late December was icily cold in North India, and the scholarly Madrasi needed protection more—much more—than the ascetic Gujarati.[30]

CHAPTER THREE

Three Experiments in Satyagraha

I

One of the resolutions passed at the Lucknow Congress related to the conditions of peasants in Bihar's indigo plantations. Speaking on the resolution, a peasant from Champaran named Raj Kumar Shukla said the European planters 'have become so powerful that they decide civil and criminal cases themselves and punish the poor ryots [peasants] as they choose'. Shukla continued: 'I do not know what I shall have to suffer when I go back to Champaran for my coming here and relating the story to you all.'[1]

Shukla had spent much of the past decade mobilizing the peasants of Champaran against the forcible exaction of indigo. He and another peasant activist named Shaikh Gulab sent petitions to the collector, and organized peaceful marches, and even a strike, which ended with the striking peasants being beaten up by the planters and the police.

Shukla was at the 1916 Congress, where he spoke to Bal Gangadhar Tilak about the indigo question; but Tilak was not inclined to take it up, seeing it as a diversion from the larger struggle for independence from British rule. Then Shukla approached Gandhi, and seizing Gandhi's legs, said (in Hindi): 'Please come to Champaran and save us peasants from the exactions of the indigo planters!'[2]

Gandhi refused, politely, and proceeded from Lucknow to his next stop, Kanpur. Shukla followed him there: 'Champaran is very near here. Please give a day,' he pleaded. Gandhi now said—perhaps out of courtesy rather than intention—that he would come when he was free.

Gandhi returned to his ashram at Ahmedabad, to find 'the ubiquitous Rajkumar was there too'. He demanded that a date be fixed for the promised visit. Gandhi, forced to commit himself, said he would be in Calcutta in April, and could come to Bihar then.[3]

Why did Shukla seek out Gandhi? Tilak and Malaviya had rebuffed him; perhaps, as a second-rung Congress leader, Gandhi was more likely to find the time to visit a remote rural district. Shukla also knew that there were plantation workers from Bihar in South Africa, some of whom had been Gandhi's clients.

Once Shukla had settled on Gandhi as the leader he wanted, he was remarkably persistent. After he returned to Champaran, he wrote to Gandhi that 'nineteen lakh oppressed subjects of Champaran are awaiting eagerly to have a "darsan" of your lotus feet and they have not hope but full belief that they shall be emancipated as soon as your honour will set foot in Champaran . . .'[4]

Notably, Raj Kumar Shukla was not the only person from Champaran seeking Gandhi's intervention. Equally active in this regard was Pir Muhammad Munis, a correspondent with *Pratap*, the Hindi daily edited from Kanpur by the nationalist Ganesh Shankar Vidyarthi. Munis wrote often of the travails of the indigo farmers, and hoped that Gandhi, with his experience in South Africa, would come and fight for them.[5]

II

Indigo had been cultivated in the subcontinent since ancient times. In the late eighteenth century, the East India Company seized on indigo as likely to command a market in Europe. Settlers came to Bengal and Bihar, establishing plantations to make the highly prized dye that the crop produced.

The British planters in eastern India were sons of lawyers, clergymen and army officers. While distinctly lower in status than men of the Indian Civil Service, they often enjoyed a higher standard of living. In addition to his salary, the manager of an indigo plantation got a share of the factory's profits. He was provided oil and other fuel free, and sometimes grain and vegetables too. The countryside teemed with wildlife, with leopards and tigers to be had for trophies, and deer and partridges for the pot.

In the second half of the nineteenth century, close to 1,00,000 acres of indigo were cultivated in Champaran alone. In 1897, synthetic indigo was invented in Germany. This led to a steep fall in the price of natural indigo, and soon, a fall in production as well. In 1896, there were 112 plantations in Bihar producing an average of 2.6 million kilograms each. By 1914, there were only fifty-nine plantations producing a mere 3,00,000 kilograms apiece.

The First World War, and the stoppage of trade with Germany, renewed the demand for indigo from Bihar. Its price tripled; and production began to expand once more. Keen to take advantage of the shortfall, the planters began to press hard on the peasantry. The acreage under indigo, which had reduced to 8100 acres in 1914, had expanded to 21,900 acres two years later.

Indigo was cultivated both on land owned by factories and by peasants on their own plots. Under a harsh colonial law (known as *tinkathia*), peasants were obliged to put a proportion of their land (once 3/20, then 1/10) under indigo, or else pay an enhanced rent (known as *sharabeshi*) to the factory. Those who refused to meet this obligation had their land confiscated. Peasants had long been unhappy with the demand to grow indigo. They wanted the freedom to grow the crops they wished. The European planters were resented for their brash, often brutal, manner. Using their influence with the state, the planters appropriated communal pastures and cultivated indigo on them.[6]

From the early twentieth century the peasants protested their condition, sending petitions to the government and holding meetings. In 1907–08, some villages took a collective vow not to grow indigo. Raj Kumar Shukla joined the movement. In 1914, Shukla was briefly sent to jail for quarrelling with a European manager. Two years later, he took the issue to the Lucknow Congress, after which he persuaded Gandhi to visit Champaran.[7]

III

Gandhi reached Muzaffarpur, north Bihar's largest town, on 11 April
1917. The next morning he wrote to the commissioner saying he had
come to study the indigo plantations, with, he hoped, 'the cognizance
and even co-operation . . . of the local administration'.

In Muzaffarpur, Gandhi's host was a lanky scholar from Sindh
named J.B. Kripalani. The two had first met in Santiniketan in
1915. Now Kripalani was teaching history at a local college. He
received Gandhi at Muzaffarpur station and brought him home
in a carriage hauled by enthusiastic students. The boys wanted
the visitor to be honoured in the traditional manner, with an
aarti. This ritual required a couple of coconuts, which the agile
Kripalani, rather than the students, obtained from a tree in the
college compound.[8]

On 13 April, Gandhi called on the commissioner, L.F. Morshead.
After their meeting, Morshead wrote to the district magistrate (DM)
of Champaran warning him that Gandhi was coming his way. Since
(in the commissioner's view) 'his object is probably agitation rather
than a genuine search for knowledge', and 'there is a danger of
disturbance to the public tranquility should he visit your district', the
DM was advised to deport Gandhi from Champaran under Section
144 of the Criminal Procedure Code.[9]

The same day, Gandhi wrote to his nephew Maganlal that 'the
situation here is more serious than I had imagined. It [the treatment
of indentured labourers] seems to be worse than in Fiji and Natal.'
Then he added: 'I have seen the authorities. They may be thinking of
apprehending me.'[10]

Gandhi arrived in the district town of Motihari on 15 April. The
next morning he set out for a village named Jasaulipatti, where tenants
complained about oppression by the planters. The most convenient
mode of transport was an elephant. It was a hot day, and Gandhi
had never sat on an elephant before. Swaying from side to side, he
engaged his companions on the purdah system then widely prevalent
in North India. When they defended the purdah, Gandhi called it
'pernicious', for it damaged the wife's health and did not allow her to
work alongside her husband.

The conversation was interrupted by a man on a bicycle, who shouted out to Gandhi that the district magistrate wished to meet him. The messenger identified himself as a police subinspector. Gandhi dismounted, and said he was expecting this. Asking his companions to proceed to Jasaulipatti, he made his way back to Motihari (using a bullock cart procured by the policeman).[11]

In the town, Gandhi was served a notice by the DM, telling him to leave the district 'by the next available train'. Gandhi replied that he would stay, since he had come 'purely and simply for a genuine search for knowledge'.[12] Meanwhile, he wrote to the viceroy that 'the ryots are living under a reign of terror and their property, their persons, and their minds are all under the planters' heels'.[13]

While this was Gandhi's first encounter with the sufferings of peasants in India, in South Africa he had fought for the rights of plantation workers. His knowledge of the British legal system and his prior experience with agrarian oppression made the situation in Champaran a perfect test case for him.

Since Gandhi had declined to leave the district, he was served with a notice to appear before a magistrate on the afternoon of 18 April. His mood was buoyant. To his old comrade Henry Polak (who was then touring India), he wrote: 'I am recalling the best days of South Africa. . . . The people are rendering all assistance. We shall soon find out Naidoos and Sorabjis and Imams. I don't know that we shall stumble upon a Cachalia' (these being his closest associates in South Africa).[14]

Gandhi spent the morning of 18 April taking testimonies from indigo cultivators. Shortly after noon he went to the court, where a large and excited crowd had collected. Gandhi was asked to sit in the court's library while the police secured the building from intrusion.

At the hearing, Gandhi said he had come to Champaran to render 'humanitarian and national service'. The ryots had invited him to see how they were 'not being fairly treated by the planters'. While he had no intention of disturbing the peace, as 'a self-respecting man' he was bound to disobey the DM's order and stay on in the district.[15]

Gandhi agreed to the DM's request to stay in Motihari town and not venture further into the villages. On 20 April, the chief secretary tersely informed the commissioner that he 'did not go about the matter in the right way'. Gandhi had said he would work with the local authorities; why wasn't he taken at his word? The lieutenant governor, advised of the situation, advised that the legal proceedings against Gandhi be abandoned.[16]

Gandhi was now free to make his inquiries. He based himself alternately in Champaran's two main towns, Motihari and Bettiah. Some days he ventured into the villages himself. He met many peasants, and also spoke to European planters and factory managers. Everywhere, he was followed by policemen in civilian clothing, who took notes of what he said at his meetings.

A group of lawyers had arrived from Patna to assist Gandhi. They included Brajkishore Prasad, whose interest in Champaran was of long standing, and Rajendra Prasad, a scholar educated in Calcutta and a rising star at the Bar. They travelled from Patna on 18 April, with Henry Polak, who filled the hours on the train by recounting tales of Gandhi's 'doings in South Africa'. The next day, Gandhi's other great English friend, C.F. Andrews, also arrived in Motihari to check on his new campaign.[17]

The Patna lawyers had brought their own servants to cook their meals. These men ate well and they ate late, with *nashta* (snacks, frequently fried) at dusk, and a full dinner at 11 p.m. Gandhi persuaded the lawyers to dispense with their servants and help with the cooking, and to eat earlier and more frugally too. Seeing Gandhi wash his own clothes, they were forced to follow suit.[18]

The coming of these educated Indians enraged the Europeans of the district. The secretary of the Bihar Planters Association wrote angrily to the commissioner that 'whatever Mr. Gandhi's real aims may be, there is unfortunately no question as to the objects of the band of disloyal and seditious agitators who are in his train'.[19] The local branch of the European Defence Association passed a resolution stating that the presence of Gandhi in the district 'has been accompanied by unrest and crime', and that 'his continued presence is likely to be disastrous to the welfare of the Europeans in Champaran and the welfare of the district'.[20]

Two weeks after Gandhi's arrival, the subdivisional magistrate of Bettiah, W.H. Lewis, observed that 'by the planters Mr. Gandhi is very naturally regarded as their natural enemy'. But while Europeans may 'look upon Mr. Gandhi as an idealist, a fanatic or a revolutionary according to our particular opinions', to 'the *raiyats* he is their liberator, and they credit him with extraordinary powers. He moves about in the villages, asking them to lay their grievances before him, and he is daily transfiguring the imagination of masses of ignorant men with visions of an early millennium.'[21]

IV

By the end of May, Gandhi had collected almost 7000 testimonies. In early June he travelled to Bihar's summer capital, Ranchi, to place them before the lieutenant governor of the state. The evidence was overwhelming. On 10 June, a Champaran Agrarian Enquiry Committee was appointed by the Bihar government. Gandhi was a member, as were four British officers of the Indian Civil Service. The chairman was an official from the Central Provinces.

Gandhi had now decided to open some schools in Champaran. A range of volunteers came to assist him. Kasturba Gandhi also arrived to join her husband. Her presence attracted the attention of a planter named W.S. Irwin, whose dislike for Gandhi was intense even by the standards of his class. Irwin wrote an angry letter to the *Statesman*, saying that while Gandhi had promised the commissioner that he would not indulge in public activities, he had been giving contentious speeches on cow slaughter and Hindu–Muslim relations. Meanwhile, claimed Irwin,

> During the absences of her lord and master at Home Rule and such-like functions Mrs. Gandhi . . . scatters similar advice broadcast, and has recently, under the shallow pretence of opening a school, started a bazaar in the *dehat* . . . This is obviously and palpably done to shut down and ruin two neighbouring bazaars belonging to the factory. Can all this above be palpably construed into an honest fulfilment of Mr. Gandhi's undertaking to Government?[22]

Gandhi at once wrote to the *Statesman* in reply. His speeches, he said, were aimed at stemming strife between religious communities.

He invited the planters to assist him in this 'onerous mission'. He turned then to his 'innocent wife who will never even know the wrong your correspondent has done her'. If Irwin were to be introduced to her, 'he will soon find that Mrs. Gandhi is a simple woman, almost unlettered, who knows nothing about the two bazaars mentioned by him'. Her husband added, with an uncharacteristic touch of sarcasm, that 'Mrs. Gandhi has not yet learnt the art of making speeches or addressing letters to the Press'.[23]

V

The Champaran Enquiry Committee discussed whether sharabeshi (the rent paid in case the peasant grew something other than indigo) was illegal, and whether tinkathia—the mandatory requirement to devote a portion of one's holdings to indigo—should be abolished. It studied the peasant testimonies supplied by Gandhi, and invited planters to state their case.

Among the planters who appeared before the committee was W.S. Irwin. 'If Mr. Gandhi were to remain in this part of the country for the length of time I have (and it is 35 years),' said Irwin, 'he would be convinced what a consummate liar the Champaran ryot is.'[24] The committee took a different view. The evidence placed before it by Gandhi and his colleagues had demonstrated how the peasants had been exploited and abused for decades. In partial compensation, the committee decided that on existing agreements, sharabeshi would be reduced by roughly 20 per cent. On tinkathia, the demand of the raiyats (and Gandhi) was accepted in toto, and the committee recommended 'the voluntary system', in which 'the tenant must be absolutely free to enter into the contract [with the planters] or to refrain from making it.'[25]

The Champaran Enquiry Committee submitted its report—largely favourable to the tenants—on 3 October 1917. Gandhi then proceeded to Motihari to consult with the peasants and their leaders. On 11 October he left Motihari for Bettiah, where he was to spend two days before returning home to Ahmedabad. When his train reached Bettiah station, some 4000 people were waiting to receive him. A police intelligence report takes up the story:

No sooner the train stopped than people began to shout 'Gandhiji ki jai', 'Gandhi Maharajki jai'. There were *bajas* [bands] and flags at the station and all men from neighbouring and distant villages including schoolboys and *mukhtiars* [lawyers] were present. They showered flowers on Mr. Gandhi and garlanded him. There was a red cloth spread at the platform for Mr. Gandhi. Surajmal Marwari of Bettiah had brought his phaeton and a horse of Puran Babu Raj, an engineer, was harnessed. It is not understood how Puran Babu lent his horse and why the railway servants allowed so much rush and show at the station.[26]

Gandhi's first satyagraha in India had been a success. So great had been his impact that, four years after he had left the area, an official touring Muzaffarpur and Champaran found that 'the name of Mr. Gandhi is still one to conjure with . . .'[27]

VI

Since his return to India, Gandhi had travelled extensively through the subcontinent, but interacted mostly with townspeople. His stay in Champaran was his first direct experience of peasant life in his homeland. Notably, Gandhi's campaign improved his standing in the city where he lived, Ahmedabad. The city's westernized professionals had previously treated him with disdain. Ahmedabad's doctors, lawyers and professors were attached to two institutions: a discussion group named the Gujarat Sabha and a recreational space called the Gujarat Club. Neither the club nor the sabha had much time for Gandhi; nor, it must be said, he for them.

The historian David Hardiman writes that 'before 1917, Gujarat had a reputation in nationalist circles for being a torpid backwater of ideological conservatism'. The Gujarat Sabha was dominated by loyalist lawyers, some of whom took Gandhi to be a 'misguided religious crank'. Their attitude to him changed dramatically when Gandhi refused to obey the order to leave Champaran in April 1917. When the news reached Ahmedabad, 'the legal fraternity at the Gujarat Club leapt to their feet', and decided to have this 'brave man' as the next president of their sabha.[28]

A leading light of the Gujarat Club was Vallabhbhai Patel. Born in 1875, Patel was the son of a farmer who owned a modest ten acres of land. Because of family and farming duties his attendance at school was erratic, and he only matriculated at the age of twenty-two. He then passed the local bar exam, and became a lawyer in the district towns of Gujarat.

Patel was keen to qualify as a barrister in England. He finally travelled to London when he was thirty-five; returning with his qualification two years later, he now started practising in Ahmedabad. He prospered professionally as well as socially, spending his evenings at the Gujarat Club. He was playing bridge at the club when he came to hear of Gandhi's challenge in Champaran.[29]

Patel's career trajectory was rather different from Gandhi's. Gandhi came from a comfortable and completely urban background; his father and grandfather were chief ministers in princely states. Gandhi was only nineteen when he went to England to qualify as a lawyer, his expenses met by an elder brother. Patel, on the other hand, had to pull himself out of the village, and himself fund his legal education.

We do not know precisely when Patel and Gandhi first met. It was most likely in August–September 1917. Patel had already served a term as a municipal councillor. Meeting Gandhi took him further away from his work at the bar towards full-time public service.

Two other Gujarati lawyers also joined Gandhi in the second half of 1917. Their names were Mahadev Desai and Narhari Parikh. They had studied law together in Bombay, and then moved to Ahmedabad to practise. Sometime towards the end of 1915, they came across Gandhi's ashram manifesto, and sent him a letter criticizing the emphasis on celibacy and on handicrafts. Gandhi invited them for a discussion, after which Narhari Parikh decided to join the ashram school as a teacher.

Gandhi was happy to have Parikh work with him. But he was keener on Mahadev Desai. Desai was a scholar who had just translated John Morley's classic work, *On Compromise*, into Gujarati. He also had a practical side, with a keen interest in cooperative societies. Gandhi asked Desai to come visit him every day. Finally, on 31 August, he told Desai that 'I have found in you just the type of young man for whom I have been searching for the last two years'. He had discovered 'three outstanding qualities' in him, these being 'regularity, fidelity and intelligence'. 'I have got in you the man I wanted,' Gandhi told Desai: 'The man to whom I can entrust all my work some day and be at ease, and to whom I can rely with confidence.'

Mahadev Desai was charmed—and persuaded. In November 1917, he joined Gandhi as his secretary, and more. He was constantly at hand, to take notes, to translate Gandhi's articles from Gujarati to English (and vice versa), to receive guests, and to make travel arrangements.[30]

VII

With more people joining, the bungalow at Kochrab was proving inadequate for the ashram. In the summer of 1917, an Ahmedabad merchant named Punjabhai Hirachand offered a plot three miles north of Kochrab. It was bare and treeless, but large, extending along the banks of the Sabarmati River. Gandhi saw its potential immediately. He was attracted by the proximity to the site of a prison. 'As jail-going was understood to be the normal lot of Satyagrahis,' he wrote later, 'I liked this position.'[31]

On one side of the new site was a prison; on the other, a cremation ground, also a place every satyagrahi was bound to visit. The buildings were put in place in the second half of 1917, supervised by Gandhi's nephew Maganlal. Unlike in Kochrab, the inmates had the space to experiment with farming, weaving and animal husbandry. Their activities were supervised by Gandhi, whom everybody in the settlement called 'Bapu', father.[32]

In the first week of November 1917, Gandhi organized the first-ever Gujarat Political Conference. Jinnah and Tilak both attended. Asked by Gandhi to speak in their shared mother tongue, Jinnah 'made a brave show of stammering out his speech in Gujarati'.[33] Gandhi thanked him, while (somewhat patronizingly) adding that he should practise speaking in the mother tongue. Jinnah was a member of the Imperial Legislative Council, but if reforms came and a wider franchise was granted, he might, said Gandhi, soon 'have to approach

Hindus and Muslims, Ghanchis, Golas and others not knowing English for votes. He should, therefore, learn Gujarati if he doesn't know it.'[34]

Gandhi began his own speech with a joking reference to the late arrival of Tilak. He invoked the defaulter's own famous slogan about swaraj (freedom) being his birthright. 'If one does not mind arriving late by three-quarters of an hour at a conference summoned for the purpose,' remarked Gandhi, 'one should not mind if swaraj comes correspondingly late.'

Gandhi then referred to a petition being prepared for submission to the secretary of state for India, Edwin Montagu. This articulated the demand of the Congress and the Muslim League for self-government. Thousands of signatures had already been collected. Gandhi insisted that literacy by itself was not crucial for achieving swaraj: what 'is essential is the idea itself, the desire itself'. The signatories to the resolution were all city based, and middle class. But, as Gandhi noted, 'When the peasantry of India understands what swaraj is, the demand will become irresistible.'

In Gandhi's view, the movement for swaraj was weak because two major constituencies had been kept away. Since the movement had only men, and no women, 'the nation walks with one leg only'. Besides, the educated classes had not freely mixed with the peasantry. Gandhi argued that 'we dare not turn away from a single section of the community or disown any. We shall make progress only if we carry all with us.'[35]

Gandhi's talk drew on his recent experiences in Champaran, where he had discovered the political promise of the peasantry, and witnessed how well-fed and well-dressed lawyers from the cities could be made to mingle with the masses. His convening of the conference, his treatment of Jinnah and Tilak, the contents of his own speech— all reflected a remarkable self-assurance, a growing awareness of his present and future role in the public life of India.

VIII

At the conference in Godhra, Gandhi asked the Gujaratis present to tour the countryside and study peasant grievances. The monsoon in 1917 had been late and severe: seventy inches of rain instead of the usual thirty. In the otherwise prosperous district of Kheda, crops had been badly damaged. A local leader named Mohanlal Pandya got villagers to write to the authorities, asking for the postponement of land revenue in view of the failure of their crops. Some 18,000 peasants signed these letters, which were posted on 15 November, the Gujarati New Year's Day.[36]

Gandhi now wrote to the commissioner asking him to suspend land revenue for the year. When the commissioner refused, the peasants started a no-tax campaign. They were encouraged by, among others, Vallabhbhai Patel and the fiery young socialist Indulal Yagnik. The government responded by stiffening its stance, and replaced an officer sympathetic to the peasants with one known to enforce the law more strictly.[37]

The peasants remained defiant. They stopped supplies of milk to dairies which produced butter and cheese for troops stationed in Bombay. One station in Kheda, which usually supplied 12,000 gallons of milk to the city daily, had to be closed due to this 'organized agitation'.[38]

The unpaid dues of the peasants in Kheda were mounting. Two friends from the Servants of India Society suggested to Gandhi that a public subscription of one lakh rupees be raised to pay off the debts. This would save the peasants from going to jail or having their lands confiscated. Gandhi refused the offer, since 'the object behind the idea of satyagraha is to make the people fearless and free, and not to maintain our own reputation anyhow'.[39]

As the peasant satyagraha in Kheda was developing, a conflict was emerging in Ahmedabad as well. The rains that had destroyed crops in the countryside had led to the onset of plague in the city. By November 1917, some 550 deaths had been reported. Schools, colleges and offices had shut down.

The onset of plague led to a panic migration out of the city. This worried the textile mill owners. If the workers fled to their villages, who was to produce the fabrics? To persuade their staff to stay, the mill owners offered a 'plague bonus' of 75 per cent. This was to be paid to all categories of workers, except the relatively well-off warpers. These incentives permitted the mills in Ahmedabad to function while everything else came to a halt. There were now some 1,06,000 spindles at work in the city's mills, supplying 22,000 looms. To meet the growing demand, factories worked two shifts instead of one.[40]

By January 1918, the plague had subsided. The owners decided to dispense with the plague bonus. When the workers complained, citing rising prices, they were offered—uniformly across all categories—a flat 20 per cent pay increase. This was not accepted, with the weavers in particular finding the offer hopelessly inadequate.

On 2 January, Gandhi was in Bombay. Also in the city was the Ahmedabad mill owner Ambalal Sarabhai, who had saved Gandhi's ashram by his gift of Rs 13,000 back in 1915. When Ambalal met Gandhi in Bombay, he conveyed his concern that the workers in the mills might strike on the question of the bonus.

On returning to Ahmedabad, Gandhi asked his associates to give him data on the workers' living conditions, and on wages in Ahmedabad's mills as compared to other cities. The evidence suggested that the workers deserved a better deal. They wanted a flat 50 per cent increase in wages; Gandhi persuaded them to settle for 35 per cent.

However, the mill owners refused to improve on their original offer of a 20 per cent increase. Now, as Mahadev Desai recalled, 'an element of doggedness . . . characterized both the sides'.[41]

Leading the mill owners in their obstinacy was Ambalal Sarabhai. Leading the workers in their intransigence was his sister Anasuya. This class conflict was also a family dispute, surely an unprecedented situation in the history of worker–capitalist relations in India—or anywhere else perhaps.

Heirs to a prosperous family business, the Sarabhais were orphaned early. Anasuya, who was several years older, helped bring Ambalal up. However, she was married off at thirteen to a man who would not let her attend school. Eventually, she left her husband, and went back to live with her brother.

Ambalal ran the family business while his sister ran the household. After her brother got married, Anasuya decided to go to England to fulfil her long-suppressed desire to educate herself. She attended classes at the newly founded London School of Economics and Political

Science, met trade unionists, and was impressed by the commitment of the suffragettes, although their methods (stone throwing and window breaking) did not appeal to her Jain sentiments. She was admitted to St Hilda's, a women's college in Oxford, but before she could join, news came that her younger sister had died. Anasuya abandoned her studies and returned home. Since Ambalal was now happily married and with children of his own, she sought fulfilment outside the home. She started a day school for the children of mill-hands, and a night school for workers who were illiterate. She also helped with access to healthcare and housing.[42]

Anasuya and her brother had first come into conflict in December 1917. This was when the warpers, denied the plague bonus, asked for a 25 per cent 'dearness allowance' instead. The demand was taken by Anasuya to her brother. When he refused, she wrote to Gandhi (then in Champaran) to intervene. He did. 'Why should not the mill-owners feel happy paying a little more to the workers?' wrote Gandhi to Ambalal. He added: 'How could a brother be the cause of suffering to a sister?—and that, too, a sister like Anasuyabehn?'[43]

Now, two months later, the mill owners and workers were once more in disagreement. Ambalal stood with his class; Anasuya for her cause. Once more, Gandhi was asked to settle the dispute.

IX

When the mill owners refused to enhance the wages by 35 per cent, Gandhi and Anasuya Sarabhai advised the workers to stop going to the factories. A millworkers' strike began on 22 February 1918. Every afternoon, a meeting was held outside a large babul tree on the banks of the Sabarmati. Gandhi would drive to the meeting in Anasuya's Overland roadster, while workers would walk several miles from their chawls. At the meeting, Gandhi spoke, while a leaflet of instructions and reflections on the dispute was distributed. Afterwards, Gandhi and Anasuya drove back to her brother's house for tea. Gandhi had told the magnate that it was best if they discussed the dispute every day in a spirit of understanding and trust.[44]

The civility between brother and sister notwithstanding, the middle class of Ahmedabad was consumed by anxiety. 'Every one was afraid that the angry workers would cause trouble on thoroughfares, commit thefts, and provoke scuffles, and riots.' Nothing of the sort happened. The workers remained non-violent, meeting with Gandhi every evening under the babul tree. After Gandhi had spoken, the workers began to sing, the songs freshly composed for the occasion.[45]

The Gujarati leaflets distributed at these daily meetings were composed by Gandhi, Anasuya and an energetic trade unionist named Shankarlal Banker. One leaflet asked workers not to gamble, to spend their time—now that they were not at the mill—reading or repairing their homes. They were advised to work part-time as tailors or carpenters. Another leaflet recalled the satyagrahas in South Africa and the sacrifices made by the mining and plantation workers there. A third urged the strikers not to make 'distinctions of Hindu, Muslim, Gujarati, Madrasi, Punjabi, etc.', for 'in public work we are all one or wish to be one'. A fourth deplored the callous attitude of the mill owners, saying, 'we had confidently hoped that the Jain and Vaishnava employers in the capital city of this worthy land of Gujarat would never consider it a victory to beat down the workers or deliberately to give them less than their due.'[46]

On 1 March 1918, Gandhi wrote Ambalal Sarabhai a remarkable letter, telling him that if his class of mill owners succeeded in their aims,

> the poor, already suppressed, will be suppressed still more, will be more abject than ever and the impression will have been confirmed that money can subdue everyone. If, despite your efforts, the workers succeed in getting the increase, you, and others with you, will regard the result as your failure. Can I possibly wish you success in so far as the first result is concerned? Is it your desire that the arrogance of money should increase? Or that the workers be reduced to utter submission? . . . Do you not see that in your failure lies your success, that your success is fraught with danger for you? . . . Kindly look deep into your heart, listen to the still small voice within and obey it, I pray you. Will you dine with me?[47]

Ambalal came over to dine with Gandhi at the ashram. What they spoke about is not recorded. At any rate, they did not reach a settlement on the question of workers' wages.

The strike was now into its third week. The workers had begun to lose heart. The attendance at the daily meetings held by Gandhi dwindled. In the beginning, several thousand workers came. By 10 March, the figure was down to a few hundreds. Some millhands had gone back to work, accepting the magnates' offer of a 20 per cent increase.[48]

One day, Gandhi's nephew Chhaganlal went to the Jugaldas chawl to ask the workers why they had not attended the daily meeting. A worker responded: 'What is it to Anasuyabehn and Gandhiji? They come and go in their car; they eat sumptuous food, but we are suffering death-agonies; attending meetings does not prevent starvation.'[49]

When these words reached Gandhi, he recognized the truths they contained. He decided to go on a fast to force the issue. Gandhi had fasted before, but for reasons internal to the family and his ashram (such as departures from celibacy). This was the first occasion on which he chose to fast for a larger social or political purpose. The criticisms of the workers had stung him, forcing him to put his body on the line for their rights.

On 15 March, Gandhi told the workers that he would not eat, and not sit in a motorcar either. On 17 March, he invoked the example of Tilak, who had gone to jail for the national cause, and thus 'undergone the sufferings of internment with a spiritual motive'. His own decision to fast was taken to 'keep' the 10,000 striking workers from 'falling'.[50]

Gandhi's fast put pressure on the mill owners. Ambalal and his colleagues could not allow the situation to deteriorate. By the fourth day of the fast, they had been coerced into a settlement. On 18 March, the mill owners agreed to arbitration by a third party, a respected Ahmedabad academic named Anandshankar Dhruva. In the spirit of compromise the workers would be paid 35 per cent extra wages on the first day, but 20 per cent (what the employers had agreed on) on the next day, and so on till the award came.[51]

Professor Dhruva gave his award only in August 1918, and it was in favour of the workers, giving them a 35 per cent increase in wages, to be paid retrospectively. In this battle of siblings, the sister had triumphed in the end.

X

Gandhi now returned to the agrarian conflict in Kheda. Six months into the struggle, thousands of peasants had refused to pay the land revenue due to the government. In some talukas, the percentage of defaulters was close to 30 per cent.

On 30 March 1918, the collector ordered the confiscation of the crops of those who had not paid taxes. On 5 April, Gandhi met the collector to try and effect a compromise. The official was unyielding. Police parties raided villages, breaking locks and taking away grain, vessels, furniture and buffaloes.[52]

Gandhi sent Vallabhbhai Patel to canvass support in Bombay for the peasants of Kheda. Vallabhbhai tried to meet Jinnah but failed. When he returned to Ahmedabad, he angrily told Gandhi: 'For two long hours we waited, but Jinnah Saheb couldn't find time to grant us an audience. And this is whom they call our Mazzini of India!' (Gandhi's reply is unrecorded.)[53]

Jinnah was a 'Mazzini' to the educated classes alone. Others were comparing Gandhi himself to the great Italian patriot, on the grounds that he appealed to far more than city-based lawyers and editors. A Gujarati newspaper said that while some intellectuals dismissed villagers as 'ignorant and illiterate', 'the salvation of India will be achieved only by the agriculturists. If there be a leader in India the people are ready to follow him, but the question is who should be regarded as the leader. Italy produced only one Mazzini who brought about her regeneration. Gujarat has also produced only one Mazzini in Mr. Gandhi. May God make him infuse new life into Gujarat! It is prayed that this spiritual fight put up by the Kheda agriculturists may be closely watched by the entire agricultural class in India.'[54]

On 23 April, Gandhi was in Bombay, speaking at a public meeting held in solidarity with the peasants of Kheda. The struggle, he said, 'did not originate with the Home Rulers or with any barristers or lawyers as some people allege'. Rather, it was 'started by the tillers themselves'. Men and women had both participated equally. Gandhi had himself witnessed 'wonderful scenes . . . at the village meetings. The women declare that even if the Government seize their buffaloes, attach their jewellery or confiscate their lands, the men must honour their pledge. This is a grand struggle . . . Its fragrance is spreading everywhere.'

Gandhi was addressing an audience many of whose members had never been to a village. His own experience in Kheda and Champaran, on the other hand, had taught him 'this one lesson, that, if the leaders move among the people, live with them, eat and drink with them, a momentous change will come about in two years'.[55]

From Bombay, Gandhi proceeded to Delhi for a conference called by the viceroy, Lord Chelmsford, aimed at soliciting support for the War. (A former governor of the Australian state of Queensland and New South Wales, Chelmsford had replaced Hardinge as viceroy in March 1916.) The conflict between Britain and Germany had entered a crucial stage. Close to a million Indians had already volunteered to fight in the War. Now, with the Germans pressing hard, a fresh round of recruits was required.

Gandhi still thought the British Empire could or would redeem itself. He still believed that if unfair laws and unjust practices were brought to the attention of the highest officials, they would be revoked or corrected. It was in this spirit, or expectation, that he responded to the viceroy's appeal to help with the War. However, he was disappointed that Tilak had not been called for the conference, and that important Muslim leaders like Shaukat Ali and Mohammad Ali were under house arrest (on suspicion of being supporters of the Turkish state, against whom the British were at war). Gandhi boycotted the first day of the conference, but was persuaded by Charlie Andrews to show up for the second. The viceroy also met Gandhi privately, and urged him to support the recruitment drive.

Before he left Delhi, Gandhi wrote the viceroy a long and intensely felt letter. Not calling Tilak and the Ali Brothers was, he said, a 'grave blunder'. For, they were 'among the most powerful leaders of powerful opinion'. The protest registered, Gandhi acknowledged that in this hour of danger, it was necessary to provide 'ungrudging and unequivocal support to the Empire, of which we aspire, in the near future, to be partners in the same sense as the Dominions overseas'.

In cooperating with the British war effort, Gandhi was acting similarly to other subjects of the Empire who hoped one day to see their nation free. The great Israeli nationalist David Ben-Gurion was even more energetic in his support for the rulers; raising, and himself volunteering for, a Jewish battalion to fight alongside the British in the Great War. As with Gandhi, the hope here was that a good turn done in the Empire's time of crisis would be rewarded with self-rule after the crisis had passed.

Loyalty to the Empire was, in Gandhi's mind, directly linked to the securing of Home Rule. Support for the War involved 'the consecration of our lives to the common cause'. But since India, unlike Canada or South Africa, was not yet a partner in the Empire, this was 'a consecration based on the hope of a better future'.

After returning to Gujarat, Gandhi wrote again to the viceroy, asking for 'relief regarding the Kheda trouble'. If revenue was suspended for the year, he cannily argued, he and his co-workers would be free to devote their energies to getting recruits for the War.[56]

Through much of May and June, Gandhi toured Kheda, asking peasants to enlist to save the Empire. A Gujarati leaflet issued by him claimed 'the easiest and the straightest way to win swaraj is to participate in the defence of the Empire'. Gandhi even offered to lead one unit, but without carrying arms himself. That way he would (admittedly uneasily) balance his desire to help the British with his own commitment to non-violence. The peasants were unpersuaded. On 9 July, Gandhi wrote to his son Devadas: 'I have not had a single recruit so far, so deplorable is the plight of the country.' Two weeks later, about 100 men—still a meagre number—had come forward.[57]

Gandhi was counting on his own appeal and that of Vallabhbhai Patel. He failed, because the peasants were reluctant soldiers, and because some now saw him as a hypocrite. They were appalled that he, who had recently been counselling non-violent protest against the Raj, was now advocating that they enlist as soldiers to fight in the Empire's cause. The attendance at his meetings was thin; on occasion, he was denied transport and food, and at one gathering, peasants shouted at him: 'We made you great! We helped you make Satyagraha work! And see what you ask of us now.'[58]

That Gandhi tried so hard to get recruits did, however, make an impression on the authorities. In June, following a meeting between Gandhi and the collector of Kheda, an order was issued suspending the collection of revenue from those who could not afford it, while asking well-to-do cultivators to voluntarily pay up.[59]

In Champaran and in Ahmedabad, the struggles led and conceived by Gandhi had met with a substantial degree of success. On the other hand, this third experiment with satyagraha resulted in what can (at best) be termed a face-saving compromise.

XI

In the first week of March 1918, Gandhi wrote to Henry Polak's wife, Millie: 'I am here attending to the Kheda trouble as also a big strike. My passive resistance is therefore beginning to have full play in all the departments of life.' The excitement was palpable. Three months later, the intensity of the struggle had begun to take its toll. In late June, he wrote to another woman friend, the secretary of his South African years, Sonja Schlesin: 'My work has involved constant railway travelling. I am longing for solitude and rest. They may never be my lot.'[60]

In the first half of 1918, Gandhi was continually on the move. In his absence, the ashram in Ahmedabad limped along. Among those desolated by the patriarch's absence was his wife Kasturba. Her letters are lost, but from Gandhi's replies we can tell she missed him terribly. One letter, addressed to 'Beloved Kastur', begins: 'I know you are pining to stay with me. I feel, though, that we must go on with our tasks. At present, it is right that you remain where you are [in the Ashram] . . . As you come to love others and serve them, you will have a joy welling up from within.' Working alone in the ashram was evidently little consolation for Kasturba. For, two days later, Gandhi wrote again: 'Your being unhappy makes me unhappy. If it had been possible to bring ladies, I would have brought you. Why should you lose your head because I may have to go out? We have learnt to find our happiness in separation. If God has so willed, we shall meet again and live together. There are many useful things one can do in the Ashram and you are bound to keep happy if you occupy yourself with them.'[61]

Once the Kheda settlement was secured, Gandhi came back home to Kasturba and the ashram. The construction was proceeding smoothly, supervised by his nephew Maganlal. Gandhi hoped to provide accommodation for 100 people and install sixteen looms. This would cost 1,00,000 rupees, of which 40,000 had been collected. For the balance he approached his friend Pranjivan Mehta. 'I have to tax you for a large amount,' wrote Gandhi to Mehta. 'Please give, if you can, what I have asked for, so that my anxieties can end.'[62]

From August through November, Gandhi was almost continually in Ahmedabad. His stay was not entirely voluntary. In the second week of August, he came down with a bad bout of dysentery. He was flat on his back, 'passing through the severest illness of my life', and could hardly write because of the pain.[63]

Gandhi had vowed to abstain from milk for life. He had lived without it for the past few years. But his recent sickness had weakened him. The doctors asked him to resume drinking milk to build up his body. So did Kasturba. Gandhi was reluctant to break his vow. He wrote to the Bengali chemist P.C. Ray to ask whether the protein provided by milk could be found in vegetables instead.

In October, Gandhi's health turned bad again. His heartbeats became irregular. He was being administered arsenic, iron and strychnine injections to bring back his appetite. Kasturba pointed out that his vow had been taken with regard to cow's milk only. Why could he not take goat's milk instead? That would not be a lapse of conscience. The lawyer had been outwitted by his unlettered wife, on technical grounds. He agreed to take the substitute.[64]

Gandhi's young colleagues Narhari Parikh and Mahadev Desai found their mentor's attitude puzzling. Either he should not have taken the vow, they said, or he should have kept to it. When Mahadev conveyed their disquiet to Henry Polak, he wrote back that at least Gandhi's health was on the mend. 'I only hope the improvement continues,' wrote Polak to Mahadev. 'I entirely share your feelings as regards his [Gandhi's] attitude. It seems to be wholly illogical; but I prefer his lack of logic and his life to his logic and his death. In any case, his vow was illogical, and as two negatives make an affirmative, I am perfectly satisfied with the result'.[65]

XII

In April 1918, Gandhi's eldest son, Harilal, was accused of embezzling funds from his employer. He wrote in panic to his father for advice. Gandhi replied: 'What shall I write to you? Man behaves according to the impulses of his nature. But it is the *dharma* of every one of us to gain mastery over them. Make that effort, and all your faults will be forgotten and forgiven. Since you are emphatic that you did not commit the theft, I will believe you, but the world will not.'

Gandhi advised Harilal not to engage a pleader, but to 'tell everything to the advocate on the other side'. The letter ended by saying that Mahadev Desai

> satisfies my need for you. He has taken your place, but the wish that it had been you refuses still to die. If others had not become my sons and soothed my feelings, I would simply have died of the pain of separation from you. Even now, if you wish to be an understanding son without displacing anyone who has made himself [dear] to me, your place is assured.[66]

In the first week of July, Gandhi was in Nadiad, a town some forty miles from Ahmedabad. He heard (perhaps from Kasturba) that Harilal was to pass through on his way from Bombay. 'I must go and see him,' said Gandhi to Mahadev, and went to Nadiad station at night. One train stopped, but Harilal was not on it. Another came a little later, and Gandhi found his son 'sound asleep in a second class compartment'. Harilal was surprised to see his father. They spoke for a while, 'but there was no warmth in it'. Gandhi came back to where Mahadev and he were staying, 'sorely disappointed and grieved', remarking to his secretary that 'the very face of the boy has undergone a change and lost its colour'.[67]

Gandhi's second son, Manilal, had been sent away to South Africa. With Albert West, he was running the Phoenix settlement and publishing the magazine Gandhi had founded in 1903, *Indian Opinion*. Manilal was lonely, and desperately keen to get married (he was now in his mid-twenties, well past the age at which Indian males then found their brides).

Gandhi insisted that Manilal continue to be celibate. In January 1918, Gandhi wrote to him that 'You may consider marriage only when you can leave *Indian Opinion* in good order. . . . We have a thousand desires; all of them cannot be satisfied.' To West's sister, Gandhi wrote that if Manilal 'can stand a few more years of bachelor life, he will get hardened'.[68]

Writing to Manilal, Gandhi fretted that he 'could not attract Harilal to my path of a truth-seeker and he dropped away from it'. He thought he might yet succeed with his second son. Gandhi told Manilal that

> You have stayed on in my life, but are discontented. You can't bring yourself to go out of it, and yet do not altogether like being in it. This is why you are not at peace with yourself. . . . I have not harmed you intentionally. All I have done I did in the belief that it was for your good. Is not this enough to bring down your anger against me?[69]

This is the letter of a purist and perfectionist, of one who had radically simplified his life, abandoned his career, devoted himself to the service of society. At the same time, it is dogmatic and unfeeling. Gandhi greatly admired the medieval poet Narasinha Mehta, whose hymn '*Vaishnava Jana To*' was now sung daily at his ashram.[70] Mehta's hymn emphasized that only those who understood the pain of others could come close to God. As an upper-caste Hindu, Gandhi himself understood, and responded to, the pain of peasants, workers, Muslims and 'untouchables'. His views on women—asking for the abolition of purdah, seeking their support in social movements—were moderately progressive for the time. And yet, for all his empathy and concern for those outside his family, Gandhi was curiously blind to the pain of his own sons.

Harilal and Manilal were both independent and strong-willed. The third son, Ramdas, was timid and shy. Gandhi did not think him capable of public work. But when Ramdas found it difficult to get stable employment, he did disappoint the father. So Gandhi pinned his hopes on his youngest son, Devadas, who was intelligent, hard-working, and less inclined to disagree with his father than the two eldest boys.

Mahadev Desai records a conversation in the spring of 1918, where Gandhi told him:

> Harilal threw away his whole life in a moment by one false step. I see in him all my faults magnified and my merits minimised, as we see in some special mirrors' reflections of objects larger and smaller than their size. . . . Dev[a]das had been born to compensate me for the dissatisfaction I feel from my other three sons.[71]

In June 1918, Gandhi sent Devadas, then aged eighteen, to Madras to teach Hindi to South Indians, since they were unfamiliar with what would one day become an independent nation's lingua franca. After six months away from home, Devadas wished to return. Gandhi told him that his 'interest' and 'duty' required him to stay on. 'When your task in Madras is over,' he wrote, 'I shall satisfy your desire for studies. But believe me, the experience you have gained very few must have.' The tone here is different from his letters to Harilal. The father would still direct and exhort, but in a gentler and kinder way.[72]

XIII

Gandhi had decidedly mixed success in winning his sons over to his cause. He was luckier elsewhere. As he conducted his first experiments with satyagraha, young men and, more occasionally, women flocked to his call.

In Champaran, those who came to work with Gandhi included 'barristers, Pleaders, dismissed school masters, Politicians, local agitators . . .'[73] When he started his schools in Champaran, volunteers came from across the country. They included S.L. Soman, a Marathi-speaking Brahmin from Belgaum, who was a lawyer and Sanskrit scholar; Pranlal Prabhu, a yogi from Bhavnagar in Kathiawad, who 'lives on fruits only, does not take rice, bread, etc.' and who distributed medicines free to the villagers; Avanti and Baban Gopal Gokhale, a couple from Bombay, he an engineer, she a teacher; and Hari D. Deo, a member of the Servants of India Society from Poona.[74]

In Kheda and Ahmedabad too, idealistic young Indians came to assist Gandhi, abandoning their legal or teaching careers to do so. And he also found sustenance among the subaltern classes. In Champaran, the indigo tenants were looking to Gandhi to lead them. In his native Gujarat, peasants in the countryside and workers in the city were mobilized by Gandhi's associates, taking their cues from what their leader asked or expected from them.

Of the educated followers whom Gandhi attracted to himself in 1917–18, three stood out. These were J.B. Kripalani, Vallabhbhai Patel and Mahadev Desai. What they had in common was independence of mind. Their admiration for Gandhi did not shade into blind reverence. They often argued with him, and sometimes even made him change his views.

Patel and Kripalani were men of action. Neither kept a diary. What we know of their early encounters with Gandhi is partial and incomplete. Mahadev Desai, on the other hand, kept a record of all that Gandhi said to him. Sometimes he also noted what he said in return. We thus know that the disciple did not always concur with what his master had to say.

In late May 1918, travelling by train in Bihar, Mahadev and Gandhi had an argument about reincarnation. Gandhi insisted that if one was a Hindu (as Mahadev certainly was) one must accept the cycle of births and rebirths. His secretary spiritedly answered: 'Call me a non-Hindu or a Christian or whatever you like, but why should I hide what I honestly feel?' How could a horse become a man in his next life, he asked, or a man a horse?

A month later, back in Ahmedabad, Mahadev disagreed with Gandhi once more. This time they were discussing the position of women. Gandhi said it was 'in the very nature of womankind' to be dependent on others. Mahadev answered that her 'dependence is not as natural as all that'. He cited Annie Besant as an example of a woman who was truly independent.[75]

In South Africa, Gandhi had a devoted secretary, Sonja Schlesin, and an outstanding second in command, Henry Polak. In March 1918, six months after Mahadev joined him, Gandhi described him to Polak as 'a capable helper', whose 'ambition is to replace you. It is a mighty feat. He is making the attempt.'[76]

Mahadev had one great advantage over his predecessor; he was a native Gujarati speaker. Polak perhaps understood Gandhi's political philosophy better than anyone else in South Africa. As one who had shared a home with Gandhi, he knew his personal eccentricities rather well too. However, as an Englishman, he was denied access to the mental and moral world of Gujarat and Gujarati. Mahadev was as well read in history and politics as Polak. He had a deep love for English literature. And he was a Gujarati, shaped by the same stock of songs, stories and sayings as Gandhi himself.

In April, Gandhi wrote to his secretary's father: 'Mahadev has relieved me of many of my worries. I was in search of a loving helpmate of his character and learning. Having got Mahadev, I have succeeded in the search.'[77]

In May, Gandhi wrote to Mahadev himself: 'You have made yourself indispensable to me. I meant what I wrote to Polak. . . . It is for your efficiency and character that I have chosen you to help me in my political work and you have not disappointed me. Add to this the fact that you can cook *khichdi* for me, with so much love.'[78]

Gandhi had written to his eldest son, Harilal, that Mahadev had taken his place. But Mahadev was more than a surrogate son. He also served as Gandhi's secretary, interpreter, travel manager, interlocutor and (when necessary) cook. A year after he joined the ashram, Gandhi told his nephew Maganlal that Mahadev 'has come to be my hands and feet, and my brain as well, so that without him I feel like one who has lost the use of legs and speech. The more I know him, the more I see his virtues. And he is as learned as [he is] virtuous.'[79]

Like Henry Polak—to whom Gandhi compared him—Mahadev Desai had a ready wit and great personal charm, qualities altogether rare in activists who seek to transform the world. Like Polak again, his role in the making of the Mahatma deserves to be far better known than it is.

CHAPTER FOUR

Going National

I

In his recruitment drive in the district of Kaira, Gandhi had meagre pickings. Gujaratis were not naturally oriented towards military service. But men from other parts of India were. Punjabis, Pathans, Tamils, Malayalis, Garhwalis, Kumaunis and Purbiyas all enlisted in large numbers to serve in the World War. Some 10,00,000 Indians took up arms on behalf of the king-emperor, playing a major role in both the European and the Middle Eastern fronts.

This massive contribution to the war brought forth calls for greater rights for Indians. A leading proponent of self-government was the secretary of state for India, Edwin S. Montagu. Montagu had served as undersecretary of state for India from 1910 to 1914. He had toured India in the winter of 1912–13, and had been keen to succeed Lord Hardinge as viceroy in 1916.

The prize post of viceroy was denied Montagu, with Lord Chelmsford being appointed instead. As consolation, he was appointed secretary of state in July 1917. His Majesty's Government had talked about giving 'responsible government' for India; Montagu thought this a mealy-mouthed term, preferring the more emphatic 'self-government' instead. He told his Cabinet colleagues that 'if we do not use the word "Self-government", I do not believe any announcement will fulfil its purpose, and the fact that we have avoided using it will be pounced upon by the Home Rulers.'[1]

In the second week of November 1917, Montagu arrived in India to expedite the process of political reform. He spent six months in the country, consulting with the viceroy and his advisers, and with governors and officials in the provinces. In between his talks he indulged himself in shikar expeditions.

Montagu kept a diary of his conversations, which offers fascinating insights into the men who ruled India. He was shocked by the racism of Europeans in the cities, whose clubs were closed to Indians. In his view, 'the social question, the fact that the civil servants are willing to work with the Indians but not to play with them, the fact that the Boxwallah will have nothing to do with them, has really brought the present political situation upon us.'[2]

Montagu spoke with a representative section of Indian opinion. Among those summoned to Delhi to meet the visitor were Jinnah and Gandhi. The secretary of state found Jinnah to be 'young, perfectly mannered, impressive-looking, armed to the teeth with dialectics, and insistent upon the whole of his scheme'. Jinnah was 'a very clever man', concluded Montagu, 'and it is, of course, an outrage that such a man should have no chance of running the affairs of his own country'.

Montagu was told that 'at the root of Jinnah's activities is ambition. He believes that when Mrs Besant and Tilak have disappeared he will be the leader, and he is collecting around him a group of young men, whom he says he is keeping from revolutionary movements, and professes a great influence over them.'

Also of the generation following Tilak and Besant was Mohandas K. Gandhi. Montagu had been briefed about the conflict in Champaran and the Gujarati's role in it. Meeting Gandhi immediately after Jinnah, Montagu jotted down his impressions of the man: 'He is a social reformer; he has a real desire to find grievances and to cure them, not for any reason of self-advertisement, but to improve the conditions of his fellow men. . . . He dresses like a coolie, forswears all personal advancement, lives practically on the air, and is a pure visionary. He does not understand details of schemes; all he wants is that we should get India on our side.'[3]

On 13 December, when in the bath in Calcutta's Government House, Montagu had an idea that 'seems to me the most brilliant that has ever entered my head'. This was to ask the prime minister to appoint Sir S.P. Sinha, the eminent lawyer who had been the first Indian member of the viceroy's executive council, secretary of state for India. Montagu would voluntarily take a demotion and become his undersecretary. This would be an object lesson for arrogant ICS officers, that 'a British statesman who, however undeservedly, has reached Cabinet rank, finds nothing derogatory in assisting rather than controlling an Indian'.

Montagu believed that 'the dead hand of the Government of India is over everything, blighting it'. His scheme of reform rested on three pillars: wider representation, provincial autonomy and absolute racial equality.[4] His conservative Cabinet colleagues thought he was giving Indians too much, too quickly. Within India, the governors of provinces damned his scheme 'all the way up hill and down dale'.[5]

The viceroy, Lord Chelmsford, was also lukewarm. In July 1918, a 'Montagu–Chelmsford' scheme was announced, a compromise decidedly weighted in favour of the latter party. Montagu had asked for 'complete provincial decentralization'. Instead, the Government of India retained a tight leash, by dividing administrative categories into 'reserved' and 'transferred'. The former remained under the control of the unelected governor (always an Englishman) and his unelected officials, while the latter were to be dealt with by elected ministers under the overall supervision of the governor.

'Reserved' categories included finance, law and order, justice, development of mineral resources, factories, and the control/ censorship of books, films and newspapers. Thus, in practice, every major economic and political subject was under the direct control of the governor and his advisers. 'Transferred' categories included health and education, agriculture and fisheries, and such fields as 'weights and measures; libraries, museums, and zoological gardens'.[6]

The franchise on which the members of provincial legislatures would be elected was based on a property and income qualification, which excluded the vast majority of the population. For example, of the 42 million residents of the Madras Presidency, only half a million would be voters; of the 20 million in the Punjab, a mere 2,37,000.

Prosperous Bombay was slightly better served—with about 6,50,000 voters in a population of 21 million (this still less than 4 per cent). Women were excluded altogether, since the government felt that 'the social conditions of India' made it 'premature' to extend the franchise to them. (Women in Britain had only just been permitted to vote.)

Montagu's scheme for self-government was massively watered down by the viceroy and his council. His daring, even revolutionary, proposal to elevate Sir S.P. Sinha to his own post was not accepted by the prime minister. Instead, Sinha was appointed undersecretary of state for India, serving as Montagu's deputy so that it remained clear to all concerned (not least Montagu) that Indians needed guidance and direction from above.

II

In October 1917, the Bolsheviks had taken power in Russia. This increased the already intense paranoia of the Government of India. In December, it appointed a committee to inquire into 'the nature and extent of the criminal conspiracies connected with the revolutionary movement in India', and to advise on the legislation needed to deal effectively with the (real or imaginary) threat this movement posed.

These revolutionaries were most active in Bengal, where young Hindus, devoted to Goddess Kali and to a cult of sacrifice, had formed secret societies where they manufactured bombs and plotted murders of colonial officials. Their activities achieved mixed success: although many acts were planned, few were successfully carried out.[7]

The new committee was to be chaired by Justice Sidney Rowlatt, a high court justice in England. It had four other members, two British, two Indian. Edwin Montagu was in Bombay when Justice Rowlatt's ship landed. When they met, the liberal politician explained to the judge that 'government by means of internment and police was naturally a delightful method which built up only trouble for our successors, and that I hoped he would remember what was parliamentarily defensible in listening to the plan which had been prepared for him by the Government'.[8]

The advice was disregarded. In April 1918, Justice Rowlatt submitted his report to the Government of India. The first part, replete with charts and tables, documented acts of violence such as assassinations, murders, dacoities and bomb attacks. There was one chapter apiece on revolutionary activities in Bombay, Madras, the United Provinces and the Punjab, but five chapters on Bengal alone.

The evidence assembled by his committee, said Justice Rowlatt, showed 'that the intentions of the revolutionaries were eventually to subvert by violent means British rule in India, and meanwhile to assassinate Government officials, to obtain such help as might be obtainable from the Indian army, and to finance their enterprises by plundering their fellow-countrymen'.

Until the outbreak of the World War, the troublemakers had all been Hindus. However, when the War found Turkey and Britain on opposite sides, some Muslims also became disaffected with the Raj. Now, 'Muhammadan fanatics' were working 'to provoke first sedition and then rebellion in India'.

The second part of the Rowlatt report outlined ways to tame and defeat revolutionary terrorism. Noting 'the remarkable length of trials in India', Justice Rowlatt recommended that seditious crimes be tried by a three-judge bench without juries. 'It is of the utmost importance,' he argued, 'that punishment or acquittal should be speedy, both in order to secure the moral effect which punishment should produce and also to prevent the prolongation of the excitement which the proceedings may set up.' His committee suggested that all trials be held in camera; that the press and the public be excluded; and that no part of the proceedings be disclosed.[9]

When a copy of the report reached Edwin Montagu in London, he was dismayed. 'There is much in its recommendations which is most repugnant to my mind,' he wrote to the viceroy. During the War, the government had promulgated a Defence of India Act which mandated restricted liberties and strict censorship; why, asked Montagu, had Rowlatt retained these harsh provisions even though the War was coming to an end? Invoking by name two of the more reactionary governors in India (of Madras and Punjab), Montagu said he would 'hate to give the Pentlands of this world and the O'Dwyers the chance of locking a man up without trial'.

The viceroy wrote back defending the report. In 'the face of the Bengal anarchic movement', he said, 'it would be impossible for my Government to do otherwise than come forward with legislation carrying out the [Rowlatt] Committee's recommendations'. He hoped the secretary of state would assent to the proposed legislation, which was required (in his view) 'to defend our friends in India from the criminal few'.[10]

III

In the first months of 1918, Gandhi was active in the Kheda and Ahmedabad satyagrahas. At the time, he was apparently not aware of the Rowlatt Committee. The committee's report was for restricted circulation; while Montagu got a copy, Gandhi and other Indian leaders would not have been sent one.

Gandhi spent the second half of 1918 mostly in his ashram in Ahmedabad. He had a bad bout of dysentery, and did not recover in time to attend the 1918 Congress, held in December in Calcutta. The following month, Gandhi went to Bombay to be operated on for piles. He was sedated, and slept fitfully. Mahadev Desai, by his hospital bedside, heard him speaking in his sleep. Mahadev, characteristically, began to take notes. We thus know that 'the last outburst during [Gandhi's] delirium was very significant: "These two things are a 'must' for the Government. It has to annul the Salt Tax and nationalize the milk industry. It passes my understanding how such a cruel tax as this on salt was meekly accepted by the people. The whole country could have been inflamed to revolt against the Government at the time the law was passed. How could there be a tax on salt so indispensable to human life?"'[11]

From Bombay, Gandhi proceeded to Ahmedabad for a month of rest and recuperation. While he was there, the government published two bills based on the recommendations of the Rowlatt Committee. Now that the bills were public, Gandhi immediately recognized the opportunity for popular mobilization that they represented. His dream in Bombay seemed to convey a desire to take up a cause that would affect all of India. The Salt Act could wait: why not inflame the country to revolt against this new bill instead?

In South Africa, Gandhi had often challenged particular laws: a law which mandated that Indians carried passes, a law that disallowed Hindu and Muslim marriages, a law that made every Indian labourer pay a tax. In India itself, he had conducted three localized satyagrahas: with indigo farmers in Champaran; peasants in Kaira; and workers in Ahmedabad. However, like the Salt Tax, the Rowlatt Act affected not one particular district but the whole of British India. A movement against it would allow Gandhi to define—or redefine—himself as a national leader.

On 8 February 1919, Gandhi wrote to Madan Mohan Malaviya proposing a countrywide agitation against the 'obnoxious' Rowlatt Bills if they were not withdrawn. The next day he told Srinivasa Sastri that Malaviya and he should resign from the Imperial Legislative Council in protest. The Rowlatt Bills, said Gandhi, were 'evidence of a determined policy of repression'; therefore, 'civil disobedience seems to be a duty imposed upon every lover of personal and public liberty'. The same day he wrote to a South African friend: 'The Rowlatt Bills have agitated me very much. It seems I shall have to fight the greatest battle of my life.'[12]

In the last week of February, Gandhi convened a meeting in his ashram in Ahmedabad. Those in attendance included Vallabhbhai Patel, Sarojini Naidu, the Bombay merchant Umar Sobani and B.G. Horniman, the British-born, India-loving editor of the nationalist newspaper, the *Bombay Chronicle*. At this meeting a 'Satyagraha Pledge' was drawn up, whose signatories would court arrest unless the Rowlatt Bills were withdrawn.

Also at this meeting was Jamnadas Dwarkadas, a young protégé of Annie Besant's who was gradually being drawn towards Gandhi. Mrs Besant herself was sceptical of the uses of satyagraha, resting her faith instead in meetings, speeches, books, newspaper articles and petitions. Her protégé now tried to explain the merits of Gandhi's method to her. In satyagraha, wrote Dwarkadas,

> There is no hatred, no bitterness of any kind. The government's action [in bringing about the Rowlatt Bills] shows that their

conscience is sleeping, so the satyagrahi tries to awaken the conscience of the government . . . by civilly disobeying some laws and inviting punishment on himself. A number of people doing that will make the rulers realize that they have done a grievous wrong, and ultimately will have to give in. Gandhi thinks that this is a weapon patent to India, and will teach a lesson not to our rulers only, but to the world, and will enable us to proclaim ourselves as supreme teachers of spirituality.[13]

IV

From his South African days, Gandhi had followed a standard procedure: threaten a movement against an unfair or unjust law, but not begin the protests before giving the authorities the chance to withdraw it. Here, too, he wrote to the viceroy after the 24 February meeting, asking him to withdraw the bills, since even the 'most autocratic' government 'finally owes its power to the will of the governed'.

Lord Chelmsford did not respond, so Gandhi travelled to Delhi to seek an interview in person. They met on 5 March, with Gandhi writing later to his son Devadas that 'the talk was extremely cordial and friendly. I got the impression that both of us understand each other, but neither succeeded in convincing the other. An Englishman will not be argued into yielding; he yields only under compulsion of events.'[14]

From Delhi, Gandhi visited Lucknow and Allahabad, taking soundings and having meetings on the Rowlatt Bills. In Allahabad he stayed with Motilal Nehru, a prominent local lawyer active in Congress circles, who had supported Gandhi's movement in South Africa. Motilal's son, Jawaharlal, had studied science at Cambridge and later qualified as a lawyer too. Practice at the Allahabad Bar bored him; now, with Gandhi staying at their home, the younger Nehru began contemplating a career in nationalist politics. Motilal was lukewarm about Gandhi's plans for civil disobedience, whereas his son Jawaharlal was 'afire with enthusiasm and wanted to join the Satyagraha Sabha immediately'.[15]

From the United Provinces Gandhi returned to Bombay, giving more speeches on the Rowlatt Bills. By mid-March, there were 600 signatories to the Satyagraha Pledge in the Bombay Presidency. 'The younger generation appears to be catching on very enthusiastically,' said an intelligence report, 'and the cloth merchants have determined to follow Gandhi through thick and thin.'[16]

Meanwhile, the government had passed one of the Rowlatt Bills into law. This prompted several Indian members to resign from the Imperial Legislative Council. They included Jinnah who, in a powerful speech, called the Acts 'admittedly obnoxious and decidedly coercive'. In his opinion, 'the Government that passes or sanctions such a law in times of peace, forfeits its claim to be called a civilized Government . . .'[17]

The government remained intransigent. On the other side, funds were pouring in for Gandhi's movement, mostly from cotton merchants and wealthy lawyers. The money was used for the printing of posters, and the travel and board of leaders.[18]

In early March, Gandhi received an invitation to visit Madras. The invitation came from C. Rajagopalachari, a brilliant, self-made lawyer who had for some time admired Gandhi. Rajagopalachari had sent money to support Gandhi's work in South Africa, translated his writings into Tamil, and written articles about him in the Madras press.

Gandhi had a deep fondness for the people of the Tamil country. They had sustained his struggle in Natal and the Transvaal; perhaps they would do the same now? He left Bombay on 16 March, reaching Madras two days later. Shortly after his arrival, he learnt that the Imperial Legislative Council in Delhi had passed the second Rowlatt Bill.

Gandhi spent five days in Madras. He gave several public talks, these translated into Tamil by Rajagopalachari. In the evenings the two had long conversations about the meanings of satyagraha. Gandhi was impressed by the lawyer's intelligence, and by his willingness to abandon his career to court arrest.[19]

Gandhi proceeded next to the temple towns of Tanjore and Madurai, carrying on to Tuticorin, Trichy and Nagapattinam. To bring the audiences to his side, he spoke of the Tamils who had sacrificed their livelihood, their properties and even their lives in the struggles led by him in South Africa.

Speaking in Tuticorin on 28 March, Gandhi announced that Sunday, 6 April, would witness a nationwide statement of protest against the Rowlatt Bills. People were asked to observe a day-long fast, and hold public meetings demanding that the secretary of state for India repeal the legislation.[20]

It was in early February that Gandhi first thought of launching an agitation against the Rowlatt Act. Within a month, he had garnered support from across the country. He was helped by one enormous stroke of luck: Bal Gangadhar Tilak was away in England, fighting a court case. Tilak was a militant who had in the past taken to the streets. He also had a much longer record of public service than Gandhi, and was much better known (and more widely admired) across India. Had Tilak been around, Gandhi might not have acted so swiftly and autonomously. Tilak's absence allowed Gandhi to set himself up as *the* leader of a mass movement against a law that in theory threatened every Indian.

V

Gandhi had called for an all-India hartal to be observed on Sunday, 6 April 1919. But some eager nationalists in Delhi decided to observe it on the previous Sunday itself. On 30 March, young men moved around the streets of the capital of British India, shouting slogans in praise of Gandhi and in condemnation of the Rowlatt Act. In the narrow, densely crowded streets of the Old City, the protesters clashed with the police. The conflict escalated, and a detachment of infantrymen was sent to restore order. Tear gas and rubber bullets were answered by sticks and stones. Finally, the troops fired live bullets, killing at least eight people and injuring many others.[21]

On 3 April, the prominent Bengali Moderate Surendranath Banerjee wrote to the 'home member' of the viceroy's council, suggesting that a commission be appointed to inquire into the incident in Delhi, and Gandhi be made a member. 'Such a committee would help to soothe public feeling and the appointment of Mr. Gandhi would serve to deepen the favourable impression,' he wrote. Besides, putting Gandhi to committee work would 'take him away from the work of agitation in which he is over engaged'.[22]

The home member rejected Banerjee's suggestion, leaving Gandhi free to go ahead with his planned day of protest on 6 April.

Gandhi had decided to lead the hartal in Bombay. He arrived at the Chowpatty beach by 6.30 a.m. People bathed in the sea and then came and sat around him. By 8 a.m. a 'huge mass of people' had assembled. One reporter estimated that 1,50,000 were present— 'Mahomedans, Hindus, Parsis, etc., and one Englishman'. In his speech, Gandhi referred to the recent police firing on the satyagrahis in Delhi, and then asked the crowd to endorse the resolutions asking the viceroy to withdraw the Rowlatt Act. Reminding the crowd of the sacrifice 'of the innocents of Delhi', he asked them to 'promise that we shall continue to suffer by civil disobedience till the hearts of the rulers are softened'.[23]

An Urdu weekly published in Bombay termed the hartal against the Rowlatt Act a 'splendid success'. The government's passing of the bills had 'united the Hindus and the Musalmans like sugar and water, although these two communities once stood apart from one another owing to the long-standing differences between them'. This was a genuine mass upsurge, wrote the weekly, and 'it is wrong to suppose that Mahatma Gandhi or any other person is the originator of the movement. Hundreds of Gandhis will be produced from the soil of India.'[24]

Other cities and towns also observed the hartal called by Gandhi on 6 April, and likewise in the spirit of inter-religious solidarity. Karachi, one local newspaper reported, 'closed its shops and centres of business: when did such a stupendous thing happen before in the history of the city? . . . One was impressed at yesterday's function with one soul-stirring fact—the disappearance of communal, parochial and sectarian impulses. They were "Hindus", "Muhammadans", "Parsis", "Khojas", "Jains", yesterday; but they all felt they belonged to one community—the Indian; they all felt there was the One Religion in various religions, the Religion of Self-respect, the Religion of guarding India's rights for the service of Humanity.'[25]

In Patna, capital of Bihar, 'nearly all shops closed' on 6 April, and a mass meeting in the evening was attended by more than 10,000 people. Orissa was largely quiet, but Bengal was not—with shops closing in the towns of Dacca, Murshidabad and Midnapore, as well as the great city of Calcutta. Madras observed a complete hartal, with close to 1,00,000 people congregating on the beach in the evening. Other towns in the Presidency—Tanjore, Madurai, Kumbakonam, Chittoor—also responded to Gandhi's call.[26]

In the days after 6 April, Gandhi had printed a series of leaflets for satyagrahis. One listed a series of books/booklets prohibited by the censor—such as a life of the Egyptian patriot Mustafa Kemal Pasha and Gandhi's own *Hind Swaraj*. By printing and distributing these banned works, the satyagrahis could court arrest. (Under a provision of the new bill, anyone carrying a 'prohibited' publication could be sent to jail for two years.) A second leaflet asked the satyagrahis to take a 'swadeshi' vow committing themselves to wearing clothes of cotton, grown, spun and woven in India. A third asked nationalists to take this pledge:

> With God as witness we Hindus and Mahomedans declare that we shall behave towards one another as children of the same parents, that we shall have no differences, that the sorrows of each will be the sorrows of the other and that each shall help the other in removing them. We shall respect each other's religion and religious feelings and shall not stand in the way of our respective religious practices. We shall always refrain from violence to each other in the name of religion.[27]

VI

Gandhi was now very keen to travel to the Punjab. He had not previously visited that politically conscious province, which had taken an active part in the swadeshi movement of 1905–07. More recently, it was the centre of the Ghadar movement, where Sikhs who had migrated to North America returned to the Punjab to mobilize the peasantry. Many Punjabis had also served in the World War, often forcibly recruited by the British.

Gandhi was quite well known in the Punjab. As the chief secretary of the province later recalled, in one speech 'the coming of Mr. Gandhi was compared to the coming of Christ, to the coming of Muhammad and the coming of Krishna. Now that was the man who, if I should use the words of a speaker at Amritsar, was to break the power of the bureaucracy, that was the man around whom the whole of the agitation centred; that was the man who by his new device of passive resistance was to relieve the people of the burden with which they were threatened.'[28]

On 8 April, Gandhi boarded a train to Delhi, from where he hoped to proceed to the Punjab. When the Government of India heard of his plans, they consulted the chief commissioner of Delhi and the lieutenant governor of Punjab, both of whom said 'it would be most dangerous to allow Mr. Gandhi to enter their jurisdictions'. If he came he would have to be arrested, since 'his avowed intention was to break the law of the land'.[29]

The government now decided to stop Gandhi. At the station of Kosi Kalan (about sixty miles short of his immediate destination), the police served Gandhi an order prohibiting him from entering Delhi and the Punjab, and restricting his movements to the Bombay Presidency.[30]

The detention of Gandhi provoked protests all across India. Shops and offices shut down in Bombay. In Calcutta, a large crowd gathered at the Nakhoda mosque, with Hindus mixing with Muslims.[31] On the morning of 10 April, when the news of Gandhi's arrest reached Ahmedabad, workers in mills downed tools, and shops shut down. The next day, a rumour gathered ground that Anasuya Sarabhai had also been arrested. This led to a riot, with an excited crowd, composed largely of millhands, attacking Europeans, torching government buildings and looting the homes of officials. The trouble continued the next day, and subsided only when troops were called in to fire at the rioters and the city placed under martial law. At least twenty-three people were killed and more than 100 injured in the shooting.[32]

Gandhi returned to Ahmedabad on 13 April. When he heard of the violence caused in his name, he broke down. He was 'exceedingly ashamed' to hear of the disturbances in his city. He wrote to the viceroy that he had 'over-calculated the measure of permeation of satyagraha among the people'. But, he added, externing him from the Punjab was itself a 'grievous blunder', since 'the mad incendiarism that has taken place in Ahmedabad would never have occurred, if the orders had not been served upon me. . . . Rightly or wrongly, I seem to command, at the present moment, in an excessive degree the respect and affection of the people all over India.'[33]

On 14 April, Gandhi addressed a large meeting in his ashram. The recent happenings in the city were, he said, 'most disgraceful'. He had said 'times without number that satyagraha admits of no violence, no pillage, no incendiarism; and still in the name of satyagraha, we burnt down buildings, forcibly captured weapons, extorted money, stopped trains, cut off telegraph wires, killed innocent people and plundered shops and private houses'. These events in Ahmedabad had 'most seriously damaged the satyagraha movement'. Had 'an entirely peaceful agitation followed my arrest', added Gandhi, 'the Rowlatt Act would have been out or on the point of being out of the Statute-book today. It should not be a matter of surprise if the withdrawal of the Act is now delayed.'

Gandhi had now decided to 'offer satyagraha against ourselves for the violence that has occurred'. This would take the form of a seventy-two-hour fast. Gandhi asked those assembled to also 'observe a twenty-four-hour fast in slight expiation of these sins'.[34]

Gandhi's address, reported the Bombay government, 'had a very beneficial effect and the disturbances at Ahmedabad practically came to an end on . . . 14th April' itself.[35]

VII

Against this backdrop of the hartal on the 6th, Gandhi's detention on the 8th, and the violent protests on the 10th, there occurred a fascinating exchange of letters between Gandhi and Rabindranath Tagore. Apart from being India's most famous writer, Tagore was also a social reformer, who preached against caste and religious discrimination, and was establishing a 'University of the World' in his native Bengal.

When he planned his satyagraha against the Rowlatt Act, Gandhi was very keen to get Tagore's blessing. On 5 April, he wrote to the poet that he was anxious to gather for the satyagraha campaign 'the ennobling assistance of those who approve it. I will not be happy until I have your considered opinion on this endeavour to purify the political life of the country.'

Gandhi was hoping for an endorsement; what he got instead were words of caution. Tagore acknowledged that Gandhi returned to the 'motherland in the time of her need to remind her of her mission . . . to purge her present-day politics of its feebleness . . .' But he warned that

> passive resistance is a force which is not necessarily moral in itself; it can be used against truth as well as for it. The danger inherent in all force grows stronger when it is likely to gain success, for then it becomes temptation.

Tagore knew that Gandhi's own desire was to 'fight against evil by the help of the good'. But 'such a fight', he warned, 'is for heroes and not for men led by impulses of the moment'.[36]

The words were prescient. As the violence that followed Gandhi's arrest demonstrated, not all those who joined his movement had his own calm resolution and steady commitment to non-violence. On 18 April, Gandhi announced the suspension of civil disobedience. He hoped satyagraha could be resumed in a few months, by which time his associates would have spread and cultivated a spirit of disciplined non-violence.[37]

VIII

As Gandhi started and stopped his movement in the Bombay Presidency, events were moving swiftly in the Punjab. Three days after the hartal of 6 April was Ram Navami, the festival celebrating the birth of Lord Ram. This was normally observed by Hindus alone. But on this day in Amritsar, 'contrary to previous practice, the festival was very largely participated in by Muhammadans, and along with the usual shouts political cries were freely raised, "Mahatma Gandhi ki Jai", "Hindu–Mussalman ki jai"'.

On the evening of 9 April, orders were issued for the deportation of two prominent local Congressmen, Satyapal and Dr Saifuddin Kitchlew. One was Hindu, the other Muslim. When news of Gandhi's arrest reached Amritsar on 10 April, a large and angry crowd collected on the streets. British banks were set on fire and three bank managers murdered. A female missionary was beaten up and left for dead.

The violence continued through the 10th and the 11th. With the police unable to control the crowds, the city was placed under de facto martial law. The collector handed over charge to Brigadier General Reginald Dyer, who had come with a contingent of Gurkha and Pathan troops.

The martial law regime in the Punjab was extremely harsh. Mail was censored. Temples and mosques were closed to worshippers. Water and electricity was cut off from the homes of those whose political affiliations were suspect. Worse still were public floggings of select rebels; and most incredible was an order making it mandatory for all Indians to crawl along the street that had witnessed the attack on the woman missionary.[38]

The protesters remained defiant. They called for a meeting to be held at one of the town's public parks, Jallianwala Bagh, on the afternoon of 13 April. General Dyer issued a proclamation banning the meeting, sending soldiers with megaphones into the streets to warn people against attending. A crowd of several thousand gathered nonetheless. Enraged that his proclamation was disregarded, Dyer proceeded to the meeting place with some fifty soldiers and two armoured cars.

The 13th of April was Baisakhi, Sikh New Year's Day. From the morning, pilgrims had filed into the Golden Temple. After visiting the shrine, many worshippers walked over to the nearby Jallianwala Bagh, to rest and chat in the park before returning home. By the time Dyer reached the park, this mixed crowd of protesters and worshippers was several thousand strong.

The armoured cars could not negotiate the narrow lanes of the old town, so Dyer and his men disembarked and proceeded on foot. Having deployed his troops, the general at once gave orders to open fire on the crowd facing him in the enclosure. In panic the crowd dispersed, towards the park's single entrance, now blocked by the troops. Dyer shouted to his men to continue shooting. Asking them to reload their magazines, he personally directed fire at the densest parts of the crowd. Some 1650 rounds were fired. Almost 400 people died in the carnage.[39]

The drama, intensity and brutality of the week's events are all captured in the diary of J.P. Thompson, the chief secretary of the Punjab at the time. On 6 April, Thompson noted down the popular rumours about the Rowlatt Bills. 'Few understand what it is. One story is that police permission will be required for weddings and funerals. Another that anyone who does not *salaam* a policeman will be arrested.' The hartal called by Gandhi for 6 April was 'complete' in Amritsar and in 'most towns of importance'.

On 8 April, the chief secretary confided to his diary that 'the situation is serious. Gandhi and company have started hawking prescribed pamphlets in the streets of Bombay.' On the 9th, he noted Gandhi's departure for Delhi: 'We have sent an order directing him not to enter the Punjab.' The next day was described as 'memorable'; with a crowd of 5000 rushing the civil station in Amritsar, and burning the town hall. 'Troops fired—30 casualties.'

Thompson seems to have ignored his diary on 14 April. The entry for the 12th deals with Lahore where troops marched through the city, closing the magnificent Badshahi mosque to worshippers. 'Temper of mob very bad,' noted the chief secretary grimly. Portraits of the king and queen were smashed, and at least two railway stations looted.

The entry for 13 April reads: 'Late at night mutilated wire came through from Amritsar. . . . Meeting held in spite of prohibition—200 killed!' On the 14th, at a party at the Governor's House, Thompson met Watkins, the principal of Amritsar's Khalsa College, who told him that in Jallianwala Bagh the troops 'shot men down like rabbits as they ran', adding, 'in an excited state' that the 'only thing that can save the situation was that LG [the lieutenant governor] should disown action taken'. Thompson's own view was that while it 'seems to have been a bloody business—200–300 killed in a garden', 'probably it will be justified by [the] result'.[40]

IX

Under martial law, there was strict press and postal censorship in the Punjab. The facts of the Jallianwala Bagh incident were largely unknown to the outside world. But rumours and counter-rumours were rife.

A month after the massacre in Amritsar, Gandhi wrote to the viceroy's private secretary: 'I have not said a word about the events in the Punjab, not because I have up to now not thought or felt over them, but because I have not known what to believe and what not to believe.'[41]

In early June, the first reports on the Amritsar massacre began appearing in the Indian press. Gandhi now broke his public silence on the Punjab, with an article criticizing the imprisonment of Kalinath Roy, the editor of the province's leading English paper, the *Tribune*. Roy had been tried and jailed for sedition, when in fact, his writings were marked by 'sobriety' and 'self-restraint'. Gandhi next took up the case of Radha Krishna, the editor of *Pratap*, likewise sent to jail by the Punjab government for allegedly inflammatory articles. He urged that he be released too.[42]

Gandhi's writings were now appearing regularly in a weekly called *Young India*. This journal was started by Shankarlal Banker and Umar Sobani in Bombay. In May, the government suspended the widely read *Bombay Chronicle* newspaper and deported its editor, B.G. Horniman, for taking the side of the anti-Rowlatt agitators. To fill the gap, *Young India* now became a biweekly. Gandhi and Mahadev Desai also began the process of shifting it to Ahmedabad.[43]

While it was being published in Bombay, *Young India* carried advertisements. Those paying for space included soap and almirah merchants, jewellers, booksellers, an orphanage that was an 'ideal institution for Homeless Hindus of all ages and both sexes', and a certain A. Ratna and Co., Madras, who for Re 1 plus postage would supply a 'fine photo of Mr. M.K. Gandhi'.

After the magazine shifted to Ahmedabad in early October 1919, it reverted to being a weekly, and stopped carrying advertisements. *Young India* now reprinted, in full, statements and speeches by Gandhi. Each issue also carried one and frequently several articles especially written by him for the journal. In the autumn of 1919, for example, Gandhi published more than a dozen articles about the Punjab—these dealing with the plight of the families whose members had been killed in the Amritsar firing, miscarriages of justice and the apathy of officials.

X

The satyagraha had been suspended. Gandhi now turned his attention away from politics and to the promotion of spinning and weaving. He had long believed that the decline of handicrafts was one of the causes of India's poverty. In the past, weaving had been an important subsidiary occupation in villages, taking up the slack in the lean season. Machine-made goods had destroyed India's hand-spun textile industry. Its rejuvenation was key to Gandhi's plans for national renewal. In his ashram, he had set up looms, and made it mandatory for members to spin every day.

For Gandhi, swaraj and swadeshi, freedom and self-reliance, went hand in hand. In the summer and autumn of 1919, he gave many talks on the importance of economic self-reliance. Speaking in Bombay, he said that 'because of its neglect of swadeshi, the nation has been ruined'. Speaking in the town of Godhra, he said that if the free hours of men and women in rural homes were occupied in spinning and weaving, crores of rupees of foreign exchange would be saved.[44]

A journalist from Madras, coming to meet him in Bombay, found Gandhi sitting cross-legged on a couch, wearing handwoven clothes, writing a letter to a friend in Gujarati, using materials 'of the more common swadeshi type'. The 'paper was none too fine, the pencil had to be pressed hard to make an impression, and the envelope would not easily open in the prevailing [monsoon] weather'. The reporter (a westernized Tamil Brahmin) also noticed 'that one of the curls of [Gandhi's] spectacles had broken midway and was being held in position by a piece of thread knotted round his head. I was wondering why a fresh curl had not been put in, but soon found a broken curl was not without its uses, as it serves well enough for a toothpick on occasions.'

The journalist asked what Gandhi's message was for the people of South India. He replied: 'I want every man, woman and child to learn hand-spinning and weaving.'[45]

The theme of swadeshi also figured heavily in Gandhi's personal correspondence. Writing to Jinnah in the last week of June, he said, 'Pray tell Mrs. Jinnah [the erstwhile Ruttie Petit] that I shall expect her on her return to join the hand-spinning class that Mrs. Banker Senior and Mrs. Ramabai, a Punjabi lady, are conducting [in Bombay].' Then he gratuitously added, 'And, of course, I have your promise that you would take up Gujarati and Hindi as quickly as possible. May I then suggest that like Macaulay you learn at least one of these languages on your return voyage [from England]?'[46]

Jinnah was a political colleague. Their relations were civil, though by no means warm. But even to perfect strangers, Gandhi was prone to offer similar advice. The Bombay Presidency now had a new governor, George Lloyd. Gandhi had been unsuccessfully seeking an interview with him for some time. While the request was being processed, he sent the governor's private secretary a note explaining his programme of swadeshi, and its importance for the economic survival of the peasantry, for whom spinning and weaving could become 'an automatic famine insurance'. He then made four requests of the governor. The first three were straightforward—viz., that the governor issue a statement approving of hand-spinning and hand-weaving, that the registrar of cooperative societies be instructed to encourage these activities, and that district officers be instructed likewise.

The last request was more unusual. Thus Gandhi wrote:

And, if it is not a presumption, I would respectfully ask H.E. on my behalf to secure Lady George Lloyd's patronage for my spinning classes. Several titled ladies are, with a view to encouraging the industry among the poor classes, taking spinning lessons. I would consider it an honour to be allowed to present a spinning-wheel to Her Excellency and to send her a lady teacher or to give her the lessons myself. I may mention that the art of spinning is incredibly easy to learn.[47]

This was cheeky, even insolent, reflecting Gandhi's extraordinary sense of self-belief. That his proposal could ever be accepted beggars

the imagination—a titled and grandly dressed English lady, meant
to grace ballrooms, racecourses, and guards of honour, squatting on
the floor of her palace while working on a wooden spinning wheel,
instructed by a little brown man in a loincloth.

XI

Swadeshi and hand-spinning were interests of long-standing.
Meanwhile, Gandhi had discovered a new cause, the protection
of the Ottoman Caliphate. The sultan of Turkey had himself been
the *khalifa* of Islam, the protector of the holy shrines in Mecca and
Medina. Now, with the defeat of the Ottomans in the War, Indian
Muslims feared that Turkey would not get justice from the Allies
(since it had sided with Germany). They worried that the Ottoman
Empire would be dismembered, the sultanate itself abolished, and the
status of Islam's holiest shrines called into question.

In theory, the caliph was both the spiritual and temporal head of
the Sunni Muslims. After Mughal rule was finally extinguished in India
in 1857, the Ottoman sultan was the only major Sunni potentate, and
he began to be acknowledged as the true caliph in India. His name
was read out in Friday prayers across the subcontinent. When the
Ottomans fought against the Russians in 1877 and against the Greeks
twenty years later, Indian Muslims raised funds for them.[48]

Gandhi had long been aware of the respect the Muslims of India
had for the caliph in Istanbul. In August 1900, when he was a lawyer
in Durban, he was commissioned to draft an address on behalf of
the Indian Muslims of Natal to 'His Imperial Majesty Ghazi Abdul
Hamid Khan, Sultan of Turkey, Ameer-ul-Momeneen, Lord of the
Two Seas, Protector of the Holy Cities, and Defender of the Islamic
Faith'. The caliph, bearer of even more titles than Queen Victoria, had
just entered the twenty-fifth year of his reign. The Muslims of Natal
wished to publicly 'rejoice with the whole Mahomedan world in the
advent of the auspicious and unique occasion'. They asked Gandhi
to draft a letter conveying their congratulations and their hope that
'Your Majesty [would] continue for many years to administer the
sacred office of the Commander of the Faithful in health and peace,

and may the faith of our Prophet (on whom be peace) thrive and be the solace of the millions of true believers is our earnest prayer to Allah-ul-malik.'[49]

The war of 1914–18 had placed Indian Muslims in an uncomfortable position. They were traditionally loyal to the British Raj, but they also venerated the caliph. Some Muslim leaders sided with the Turks. They included the brothers Shaukat and Mohammad Ali, both educated in Aligarh, both powerful orators and writers. The Ali Brothers were detained in 1915 and interned in the remote town of Chhindwara lest they sway Indian Muslims away from loyalty to the British Empire and in favour of the Ottoman Empire instead.

Gandhi had corresponded with the Ali Brothers, and was keen to meet them. He wrote several letters to the viceroy asking for permission to visit them in their internment home in Chhindwara, deep in the Central Provinces, but was denied each time.

Gandhi did, however, meet with another influential Muslim leader. This was Maulana Abdul Bari, the senior cleric of Firangi Mahal, a famous Lucknow seminary established in the seventeenth century. Performing the hajj in 1910–11, Bari returned via Turkey, 'entranced [by] the last vestige of Turkish greatness'. After the World War ended, he canvassed for the restoration of the Khilafat.[50]

Gandhi and Abdul Bari first met in March 1918, at the home of a respected leader of the Congress, Dr M.A. Ansari. A year later, Gandhi visited Bari in Lucknow. They had long conversations, discussing Hindu–Muslim cooperation. Bari told Gandhi that a commission should be formed of 'a few well-wishers of the motherland, Mussalmans and Hindu'. The commission would tour India and find out the reasons—economic, political, theological— which 'initiate the disruption in the relation between the Mussalmans and the Hindus and should then think over the means of removing these reasons altogether. Means should be adopted which may place the Hindu–Moslem Unity on a stable foundation.'[51]

Gandhi was moved by Bari's patriotism and concern for religious harmony. The maulana from Lucknow had told him that 'Islam will fall to pieces if it ever takes and never gives'; he had even asked his followers to refrain from killing cows since the animal was sacred to their Hindu neighbours. In September 1919, Bari sent Gandhi a telegraph saying, 'In celebration of Hindu–Muslim unity no cow sacrifices in Firangi Mahal this Bakrid', to which Gandhi wired back, 'Delighted with your great act of renunciation. Pray, accept Id Mubarak.'[52]

That same month, a conference of Muslim leaders was held in Lucknow on the Khilafat question. Gandhi now decided to lend his name to this movement. On 18 September, Gandhi told a predominantly Muslim meeting in Bombay that 'you have the whole of the Hindus with you in this your just struggle' (for the Turkish sultan to continue having control over Mecca and Medina).[53]

Gandhi's statement was a conceit. Why would the ordinary Hindu concern himself with an institution external to India, such as the Caliphate? Gandhi was acting here largely on his own, hoping it would lead to a wider unity between Hindus and Muslims.

Gandhi asked Muslims to make their case peacefully but firmly, and urged Hindus to support the demand of 'their respected neighbours and brethren'. As he put it, 'All those born in India have to live and die together. No community can rise at the cost of another, or preserve its rights if it permits those of others to be sacrificed.'[54]

On 17 October an All India Khilafat Day was observed, with prayers, fasting and hartals. Gandhi asked Hindus to participate out of solidarity, and 'thus put a sacred seal on the Hindu–Mohammedan bond'.[55]

Back in April, some Muslims had observed a hartal against the Rowlatt Act in response to Gandhi, a Hindu; now, some Hindus were showing sympathy with what was essentially a Muslim question. The possibility of an entente between India's two largest religious groupings alarmed the authorities. Shortly after the successful observance of the Khilafat Day, the governor of Bombay wrote to a colleague that

> It is maddening to see all the Moslems gradually leaving us to make common cause with the Brahmans whom they despise and hate because they can get no sympathy from us: it is more than alarming to see the measured skill with which the Brahmans are exploiting the Moslem unrest in order to tear from us our hitherto never failing prop of Moslem loyalty and military support.[56]

XII

Through the first nine months of 1919, Gandhi maintained a ferocious pace: travelling, speaking, planning campaigns, supervising the ashram, mentoring his disciples. He had now acquired two new platforms—*Young India* and a Gujarati magazine called *Navajivan*. This was started by the socialist activist Indulal Yagnik, as a monthly. After Gandhi took over, it began to appear every week.

The two journals played different roles. *Young India* acted as a bridge between different parts of the country. *Navajivan* was specifically targeted at Gandhi's own linguistic group. In his English newspaper, Gandhi wrote in measured tones, conveying news and providing context and analysis. In his own language he was more intimate: 'In simple, easy Gujarati, he addressed the people directly, argued with them, coaxed and rebuked them as one of themselves.'[57]

By the end of September 1919, *Navajivan* had as many as 12,000 subscribers, each copy read by four or five people. Gandhi was 'proud to think that I have numerous readers among farmers and workers'. *Young India*, however, had only 1200 subscribers and, now without advertisements, needed to double its subscription base to pay its way. Gandhi appealed to his 'Tamil friends' in particular to come forward and meet the shortfall.[58]

Along with eager subscribers, Gandhi's Gujarati newspaper was also attracting a large volume of unsolicited submissions. In an essay entitled 'Request to Contributors', Gandhi offered some suggestions to those who wished to have their work published in *Navajivan*. They were advised to write on one side of each sheet only (out of 'pity for the editor and poor compositors'), to write 'in a clear and beautiful hand' (since 'some are under the impression that any kind of handwriting is good enough in Gujarati'), and to revise, rewrite and shorten their drafts before submitting an essay for publication (although 'even after all this, you will find the editor so merciless that he will have to cut out something else').[59]

An excess of contributors and contributions—this was a pleasant dilemma for an editor to have, and so soon after beginning publication.

XIII

In October, the government finally allowed Gandhi to visit the Punjab. He left Ahmedabad on 22 October, reaching Lahore two days later. The crowd at the station to receive him was so large that it took Gandhi forty minutes to get from the platform to the car.

In Lahore, Gandhi was staying at the home of Saraladevi Chaudhurani. Born in 1872, the daughter of one of Rabindranath Tagore's sisters, Saraladevi was a gifted singer and writer herself. She was also striking-looking, with a lush head of hair that hung down to her shoulders. She liked dressing up; pearls were among her favourite jewels. She was what Bengalis call a *bhadramahila*: a well-born, well-dressed, well-spoken lady.

The Tagore family held extremely progressive views on women, but even by their standards, Saraladevi was liberated and self-willed. Unlike other women of her class she was not content to make a good marriage and run a home. She took her first degree at the age of seventeen, in English literature. Then she studied physics, a subject in those days meant only for boys—she was the only girl in the class. Meanwhile, she pursued her interests in the creative arts. She was the first to set the great patriotic poem '*Vande Mataram*' to music. She also wrote stories and poems of her own in Bengali. Sarala was particularly close to her uncle Rabindranath; the two discussing, among other things, the respective merits of Browning, Keats and Shelley, and of South Indian and North Indian classical music. A composition of hers in praise of the motherland, '*Namo Hindustan*', was sung at the Calcutta Congress in December 1901.

Among those greatly impressed by Saraladevi was the charismatic and influential spiritual leader, Swami Vivekananda. He wanted her to join his movement, and make it better known in India and abroad. 'If bold and talented women like yourself,' wrote Vivekananda to Sarala, 'go to England to preach, I am sure that every year hundreds of men and women will be blessed by adopting the religion of the land of Bharata.'[60]

Sarala did not join Vivekananda, instead moving south to Mysore to teach in a school, since (as she wrote) 'to know oneself one must be away from the cloying atmosphere of one's home'. After a spell in the south, she retraced her steps northwards, well beyond her native Bengal to the Kumaun hills. She was planning a pilgrimage to Mansarovar in Tibet when she got a telegram saying her mother was at death's door, and her last wish was to get Sarala married.

This was in 1905, when Sarala was already thirty-three. The groom chosen for her was a widower named Rambhuj Dutt Chaudhuri, who was a successful lawyer in Lahore. On moving to the Punjab, Saraladevi continued to write, sing and speak. In 1910 she founded a Bharat Stree Mahamandal (literally, the Great Circle of Indian Women), which aimed (in her words) to free them from 'the shade of [the patriarchal lawmaker] Manu' that had thus far kept Hindu women 'under thraldom at every stage of their growth'.[61]

Sarala's husband, Rambhuj, had been active in the anti-Rowlatt Act protests of 1919, and made many fiery speeches. These landed him in jail, so when Gandhi reached their home he was received by the wife alone.

Gandhi had briefly met Saraladevi in 1901, when she sang the opening song at the Calcutta Congress which he had attended. One does not know what impression she made then. But staying under her roof, with both their spouses absent, meant that they spoke long and often. In a 'Punjab Letter' for his Gujarati readers, Gandhi observed:

> In Lahore I am the guest of Smt. Sar[a]ladevi Choudhrani and have been bathing in her deep affection. I first met Sar[a]ladevi in 1901. She comes from the famous Tagore family. Of her learning and sincerity, too, I get evidence in ever so many ways.[62]

The India of 1919 was conservative and deeply patriarchal. The women's place was in the home, as Gandhi's own wife Kasturba knew only too well. There were few women in India as variously gifted as Saraladevi, so active in so many public causes. And perhaps none so widely travelled. Those long conversations, possible only because the husband was away, left a profound impression on Gandhi. He would be back for more.

After a week in Lahore, Gandhi left for Amritsar. With him was C.F. Andrews. The Englishman knew Amritsar well, but this was his friend's first visit to the holy city of the Sikhs, the city where the massacre took place in April. To his Gujarati readers, Gandhi described his arrival thus:

> The entire area outside the station was packed with the citizens of Amritsar. Their cheers and shouts almost overwhelmed me. This huge procession proceeded towards the city. The people filled the car with flowers. I was taken to the mosque, which was thronged with Hindus and Muslims. With great difficulty I made my way from the mosque back to the car, and it was a long time before it reached the Golden Temple of the Sikhs.[63]

Gandhi's account of the spectacular reception he got is confirmed by a reporter on the spot. 'Monday was a veritable Gandhi day for the whole of Amritsar,' wrote the *Bombay Chronicle*, adding:

> Business houses and shops were decked with rich clothes and tapestries and every street and shop had laid its store of rose petals and garlands to shower on the distinguished guest of the city. Hours before the time, streams of humanity were moving to the railway station. Hindus, Mahommaddans and Sikhs had suspended business in honour of the event. In their determination to honour Mahatma Gandhi, women lined the roadsides, crowded windows and balconies and thousands of rupees worth [of] flowers were purchased and carried in cartfuls to the station and stocked en route.[64]

It was, of course, not merely, in the Punjab that Gandhi now had admirers. The satyagraha against the Rowlatt Act made him an all-India figure, known in the major towns and cities of the subcontinent. Yet, this might never have been the case had the acknowledged leader of Congress's radical wing, Bal Gangadhar Tilak, been around when the movement started. Tilak was in London for almost all of 1919. When he returned to India in the last week of November, he told a public meeting that 'he wished he had been in Bombay when Mr. Gandhi began satyagraha. He would have borne the difficulties with him and undergone the hardships.'[65] This was both gracious and generous; for, Gandhi was Tilak's junior in age as well as length of service to the national cause. Indeed, had Tilak been in India in early 1919 it might have been he, and not Gandhi, who would have led and directed the protests against the Rowlatt Act.

XIV

The government had set up a committee to inquire into the Punjab disturbances. Chaired by Lord Hunter, a former solicitor general of Scotland, it had seven other members—four British and three Indian. Meanwhile, the Congress set up an inquiry committee of its own, with five members, among them Gandhi and the Allahabad lawyer Motilal Nehru.

Through most of November and December, Gandhi travelled through the Punjab countryside, taking statements from people about martial law, the Jallianwala firing and other instances of state repression. He stayed on in the Punjab until the end of 1919, so as to attend the annual Congress meeting. This year it was being held, for both symbolic and political reasons, in Amritsar. The stars of the show were the Ali Brothers, who had recently been released as part of a general amnesty. They arrived in Amritsar 'amid cheers, tears, embraces, and a veritable mountain of garlands'. The highlight of the Congress session was 'an impromptu oration by Mohammad Ali, during which he proclaimed that he and all the other released leaders would rather return to prison indefinitely than see India in chains'.[66]

Gandhi, for his part, struck a more conciliatory note. After Tilak and the Bengal leader C.R. Das had characterized the Montagu–Chelmsford Reforms as 'disappointing', Gandhi argued that 'these reforms can be used as a stepping-stone to full responsible government'. Besides, 'Indian culture demands that we shall trust the man who extends the hand of fellowship. The King-Emperor has extended the hand of fellowship.' Therefore, the Congress should offer cooperation under such conditions as it may see fit to lay down. Gandhi went on to say:

> If I get a sour loaf, I reject it; I do not take it. But if I get a loaf which is not enough or which does not contain sufficient condiments in it,

> I shall see to it that I get condiments too at a later stage, but I take a
> bite; then it is not disappointing.[67]

The metaphor that Gandhi used was much favoured by his one-time
mentor, the English vegetarian Henry Salt, who likewise believed that
'improvements never come in the mass, but always by instalment;
and it is only reactionaries who deny that half a loaf is better than no
bread'.[68]

Gandhi was at this stage both an incrementalist and an Empire
loyalist. His faith in British justice was shaken but not broken. Perhaps
the Hunter Committee would properly punish those responsible for
the Punjab atrocities; perhaps the Rowlatt Act would be withdrawn;
perhaps the Caliphate, so important to Indian Muslims, would be
safeguarded. So long as these possibilities existed, the Congress
could, he felt, work with the government in a spirit of constructive
cooperation.

CHAPTER FIVE

The Personal and the Political

I

In South Africa, Gandhi's first struggles against racial discrimination had largely been funded and staffed by Muslims. In the diaspora such trans-religious solidarity was easier, since Hindus, Muslims, Christians and Parsis from India all faced the same disabilities. In the homeland, however, the different communities were established in their particular ways of life. To build a joint Hindu–Muslim union against colonial rule was more difficult, not least because the British were adept at playing off one community against another. But, for a movement to count as truly 'national', it could not be restricted to Hindus alone. Hence, Gandhi's efforts to reach out to Muslims, first by supporting the restoration of the Caliphate, and now by canvassing the support of the Ali Brothers. Since they were 'the eyes of the Muslims', Gandhi hoped that by befriending them he could cement Hindu–Muslim unity.[1]

Gandhi believed that personal relationships were a reliable route to intercommunity cooperation. His closest friends in the diaspora included a Parsi merchant and a Muslim merchant, both Gujarati-speaking like himself, both willing to repeatedly court arrest under his leadership; two Jews—an architect and a journalist-turned-lawyer; and a Christian priest who was also his first biographer. Now, in

India, men such as the Ali Brothers and Maulana Abdul Bari were to be both his personal friends as well as his political comrades. Gandhi thought that if individuals of different religions could inspire trust and affection among one another, surely the wider communities of which they were part of could do likewise.

In January 1920, Gandhi proceeded to Lahore, continuing his investigations into the Punjab atrocities, and incidentally also furthering his friendship with Saraladevi Chaudhurani. The day he reached Lahore, Gandhi wrote to his nephew Maganlal that 'Saraladevi has been showering her love on me in every possible way'. In return, Gandhi hoped to convert her to his ways. He asked Maganlal to send a good spinning instructor for Saraladevi.[2]

In the last week of January, Sarala's husband was released from prison. The day he came home, Gandhi 'saw a new glow on Smt. Saraladevi's face. The face which had been lined with care was today bright with joy. Or perhaps I am doing her an injustice. Even during separation Saraladevi had not lost the light on her face.'[3]

In his first two weeks in the Punjab, Gandhi visited Gujrat, Sargodha and other districts in the interior. 'Saraladevi Chowdhrani accompanied me on this journey,' wrote Gandhi, but it is not clear whether her husband did. The peasants of Punjab were much taken with the lady, for, as her companion noted, 'many men and women address Saraladevi as *Mataji* or Mother'.[4]

Gandhi and his associates had now recorded the testimonies of some 1700 witnesses to the happenings of March–April 1919. With this mountain of material, he proceeded, alone, to Banaras, where he stayed in Madan Mohan Malaviya's house and hammered out a first draft of the Congress report on the Punjab. Taking a walk at sunrise, he saw a 'golden sheen appear on the Ganga', and as the sun came into view over the horizon, 'there seemed to stand in the water of the river a great pillar of gold'. This beautiful sight was soon spoilt by another, that of people defecating on the banks of the river. One could not walk along the Ganga barefoot, one dare not drink its water, and one could not visit with pleasure the still dirt-and-garbage-filled Kashi Vishwanath Temple either. When he started his morning walk Gandhi was moved to sing the gayatri hymn (an invocation to the sun); by the time he ended, he was reflecting gloomily on 'the cause of [the] degradation of the Hindus'.[5]

The report drafted, Gandhi took the night train from Banaras to Delhi, where he was once again joined by Saraladevi (coming from Lahore), the two travelling together to Ahmedabad. One does not know what Kasturba made of the new arrival. On 27 February, Sarala was the main speaker at a public meeting held in the dry riverbed of the Sabarmati River. A crowd of 3000 heard her speak on the Punjab troubles, her words translated from Hindi into Gujarati by her companion. Speaking after her, Gandhi said that 'unless our sisters in the country give their blessings to the brothers, India's progress is impossible'. In Ahmedabad he had found a sister in Anasuya Sarabhai, and now, in the Punjab, he had found Saraladevi. When he stayed with her, said Gandhi, 'I had from her as much service as from one's own sister and thus became her debtor.'[6]

Gandhi was enchanted with, and by, Saraladevi Chaudhurani. A sign of this was the regularity with which her name appeared in the columns of his newspaper. In February 1920, *Young India* reprinted several letters connected with Saraladevi's membership of the 'Lahore Purdah Club', a society which brought together high-born Indian women and wives of senior British officials. In April 1919, the president of the club was Una O'Dwyer, wife of the province's lieutenant governor. After Sarala's husband had been arrested for his part in the Rowlatt satyagraha, the president wrote to the Purdah Club's managing committee, demanding that they ask 'the Chaudhurani' to resign her membership, failing which she would be removed from the list of members. 'It is obvious,' said Lady O'Dwyer, 'that the wife of the Lieutenant Governor cannot belong to the same club as the wife of Chaudhari Ram Bhuj.'

Young India printed Mrs O'Dwyer's letter, along with a letter from the secretary of the Purdah Club, asking Saraladevi to resign. This had the signatures of all the committee members, several of whom were Indian. In reproducing this correspondence, Gandhi's newspaper remarked: 'It is painful to find cultured Indian ladies being so terror-struck as to easily expose themselves to ridicule and insult. For in sending the notice they did to Saraladevi Chaudhurani they insulted not Mrs Chaudhari but themselves. Shrimati Saraladevi is a member of the Bengali aristocracy, wife of a noted leader of the Punjab and what is more, one of the few highly educated and gifted ladies India possesses. It was the Club that was honoured by her being its member.'[7]

The treatment by the Lahore Purdah Club of Saraladevi was unquestionably petty. But did it merit extended commentary in the main organ of Gandhi's political struggle? That an individual's club membership was treated alongside serious articles on education and the condition of workers must be reckoned an example of the editor's extreme partiality to this subject.

The next month, *Young India* printed an article by Saraladevi on how the Punjab was awoken from its slumber by an unnamed man from Gujarat. 'He had never seen the Punjab but he had a message for her as for the rest of India. Many read it, some only understood it. . . . The people of the Punjab did not sign his pledge. They did not grasp the inwardness of Satyagraha, nevertheless its freedom-giving spirit permeated the Punjab air and the Punjab was vitalised. A new power came into being—the power of suffering—and so the citizens of Lahore received bullets in their breasts without retaliating . . .'[8]

A second article by Saraladevi praised Gandhi by name, for having, in his ashram school, 'reproduce[d] all the best of our ancient Gurukuls'. A third referred to him as 'the national visionary who is blessed with prevision through the lens of a lofty mission'.[9]

This was a mutual admiration society, and a very public one too.

II

Gandhi was becoming increasingly engaged with the Khilafat question. The 19th of March 1920 was to be observed as 'Khilafat Day', with fasting and cessation of business. In a letter to the press, Gandhi summarized the Muslim claim as follows: the Turkish Empire should be fully restored in the European parts it once controlled, subject to protection of the rights of non-Muslim subjects; and the sultan should be assured control over the holy places of Islam in Arabia, although the Arabs could be granted self-governing rights.

'To deprive the Khalif [Caliph] of the suzerainty of Arabia,' wrote Gandhi, 'is to reduce the Khilafat to a nullity.'[10]

Muslim leaders had made several unsuccessful representations to the viceroy. The victorious Allies had not forgiven Turkey for siding with Germany. They also claimed that the Ottomans had grossly oppressed the Arabs. To free the Arabs from Turkish control, and to bring them under their own influence, the British and the French were in the process of elevating tribal chiefs into full-fledged monarchs, by creating kingdoms in Jordan, Syria, Iraq and Saudi Arabia. If this happened, Turkey would shrink to a fraction of the size it enjoyed under the Ottomans; crucially, it would lose control of the holy sites of Mecca and Medina.

The attitude of the Allies put a great strain on Gandhi's Empire loyalty. Back in December, at the Congress session in Amritsar, Gandhi had suggested that the party work with the government in making the Montagu–Chelmsford Reforms effective. But he was now arguing that, with the refusal of the Allies to grant the Turkish claim, 'non-co-operation is therefore the only remedy left open for us'. A fresh satyagraha might make the government reconsider. Gandhi thus asked: 'If every Hindu and every Muslim resigns from the service of the Government, what will be the result?'[11]

In pursuit of their case, a 'Khilafat Delegation' was sent to England in March 1920. It was led by the respected Delhi doctor M.A. Ansari, a friend of Gandhi's. Its most prominent member was Mohammad Ali, who addressed a series of public meetings in London. Islam, he told the British public, 'does not recognise geographical and racial barriers such as the nationalism of modern Europe has set up in the way of the freest human intercourse and the widest human sympathies'. Thus, 'to the Muslim of India the Turk is not only a man, but a brother' with whom he shared 'a common outlook on life and common institutions and laws'. And Islam was 'a complete scheme of life', which had two centres, 'the personal centre' of the caliph and 'the local centre' of Mecca and Medina. The two centres were connected, which was why it was vital that the holy places of Arabia be under the control of the caliph. Mohammad Ali hoped for a loose federation of Turk and Arab that would keep the caliphate intact and which 'will give the Arab all the freedom he desires or demands'.[12]

The Khilafat Delegation made speeches, and met with MPs, Cabinet ministers and the prime minister, Lloyd George. Their efforts were unsuccessful. In the first week of May, the Allies formally announced the peace terms that Turkey was compelled to accept. Turkey was granted the Constantinople sector and the Turkish areas of Asia Minor. However, Syria, Mesopotamia and Palestine were to become quasi-independent states, the first under a French Mandate, the latter two under a British Mandate. Hejaz (part of present-day Saudi Arabia) was to be recognized as 'a free and independent State', with its ruler to control access to Mecca and Medina for pilgrims from other countries.[13]

The Khilafat Delegation was devastated. So was their friend Gandhi, who claimed that this offer broke a 'solemn promise' made to the Turks by Prime Minister Lloyd George. He called for direct action in response. 'If India—both Hindu and Mohammedan—can act as one man and can withdraw her partnership in this crime against humanity which the peace terms represent, she will soon secure a revision of the treaty and give herself and the Empire at least, if not the world, a lasting peace. There is no doubt that the struggle would be bitter, sharp and possibly prolonged, but it is worth all the sacrifice that it is likely to call forth.'[14]

From its inception in 1885, the Indian National Congress had a mixed record in attracting Muslims to its ranks. The formation of the Muslim League in 1906 and the creation of separate electorates had further muddied the waters. The League and the Congress were initially suspicious of one another, until Jinnah and Tilak brought them together in Lucknow in 1916.

The Rowlatt satyagraha of April 1919 had seen Hindus and Muslims come together on a common platform. In taking up the Khilafat question, Gandhi was hoping to consolidate this unity. He had already befriended the Ali Brothers and Maulana Abdul Bari. More recently, he had got to know Maulana Abul Kalam Azad, a respected scholar and journalist who was now increasingly active in the Khilafat movement.

Not all prominent Muslims were in favour of the restoration of the Khalifa, however. Muhammad Ali Jinnah, for one, had mixed feelings. As a Shia, he did not share the Sunni reverence for the Caliphate. As a constitutionalist, he was not in favour of street protests demanding its restoration.[15]

And was Khilafat the best way to promote inter-religious solidarity? C.F. Andrews was unsure. The Khilafatists in India, wrote Andrews to Gandhi, were too 'pro-Turkish' and 'have lamentably failed to understand the awakening of the Arab speaking people'. They were asking for the Turkish caliphate to once more have dominion over non-Turkish territories such as Syria, Palestine, Arabia, Armenia and Mesopotamia. But, as Andrews pointed out, 'these lands have been won by the sword and lost by the sword. They have *never* been populated by Turks.'[16]

Many Hindus also did not agree with Gandhi on the Khilafat question. The historian Jadunath Sarkar argued that the idea that the ruler of Turkey was the spiritual head of all Muslims did not have the antiquity Gandhi accorded it. Rather, it was a creation of the late nineteenth century; a response to the absorption of other sovereign Muslim states into Western empires. The liberal editor K. Natarajan accepted that the Turks had been treated harshly by the Allies; but, as he pointed out, with the dismemberment of the Ottoman Empire, 'the Indian Mussulman's freedom to follow his religious tenets has not suffered a bit'.[17]

Hindu intellectuals worried about Gandhi's enchantment with Khilafat; so did the Hindu orthodoxy. If they made common cause with the Muslims, would they have to eat together (breaking the rules of caste) and perhaps even sanction inter-religious marriages? Gandhi assuaged their fears, saying that 'in order that we may help them on the Khilafat issue, there is absolutely no need to drink water from the same glass, sit together at meals or give sons and daughters in marriage'. He offered his own personal experience as proof. When he stayed with Maulana Abdul Bari in Lucknow, the maulana 'sent for a Brahmin cook for me and even had his milk warmed by him. He is a non-vegetarian but he did not let me catch even a glimpse of meat in his house. Because of his observing such decorum, our friendship was strengthened, not weakened.'[18]

Finally, to modernist and orthodox Hindu alike, Gandhi offered an instrumental argument: 'If twenty-two crores of Hindus intelligently plead for the Muslims on the Khilafat issue, I believe that they would for ever win the vote of the eight crores of Muslims.'

Meanwhile, the Congress and the government had released their respective reports on the Punjab troubles. The Congress report, drafted by Gandhi, recommended that both General Dyer, the butcher of Amritsar, and the lieutenant governor at the time, Sir Michael O'Dwyer, be relieved from 'any responsible office under the Crown'. It also called for the recall of the viceroy, the refund of fines collected from the people, and an end to the corrupt practices of local officials.[19]

The official report acknowledged the excesses under martial law, and chastised General Dyer for not thinking before he acted. However, it shied away from punishing errant officials. The viceroy, forwarding the report to London, euphemized Dyer's action, saying, 'in the face of a great crisis an officer may be thrown temporarily off the balance of his judgement'. He also gave the much-hated Michael O'Dwyer a resounding certificate of character, praising his 'experience and courage' as well as his 'decision and vigour', which, in the viceroy's view, 'was largely responsible for quelling a dangerous rising which might have had widespread and disastrous effects on the rest of India'.[20]

To the rejection of the Khilafat demand was now added the whitewashing of the egregious behaviour of the Punjab government. This was a double betrayal, putting enormous strain on Gandhi's once fervent faith in British justice. He now decided that the only way to make the rulers see reason was to launch a fresh movement of protest. He outlined in print a programme of 'non-co-operation', to unfold in four stages. The first entailed the giving up of titles; the second the resignation from government service of select officials; the third stage—a 'distant goal'—the resignation of policemen and soldiers; the fourth stage, 'still more remote', the non-payment of taxes. He added that 'non-co-operation as a voluntary movement can only succeed if the feeling is genuine and strong enough to make people suffer to the utmost'.[21]

III

Even as he thought and wrote about political matters, Gandhi's relationship with Saraladevi steadily grew more intimate. He persuaded her to write an article for *Navajivan*; introducing it in print, he asked readers to read it several times over since 'its sweetness is inexhaustible'.[22] In April, Sarala travelled with him to Bombay, where he had to attend a Khilafat meeting—6 to 13 April was observed as 'National Week', since, exactly a year ago, the Rowlatt Act hartal had occurred on the 6th and the Jallianwala Bagh shooting on the 13th. Gandhi spoke at several meetings, Sarala each time accompanying him to the venue. Afterwards, he penned this endearing (and extended) tribute to his companion:

> The swadeshi movement received the finest impetus from Shrimati Saraladevi Chowdhrani. During the National Week, she expressed a desire to wear a sari and blouse of khadi [homespun cloth]. I have not so far succeeded in inducing any woman to wear a sari made of khadi and so at first I thought Saraladevi was joking. But she was perfectly sincere in what she said and, what is more, she meant khadi as rough as what I wear. I got a sari and blouse made for her and she celebrated the National Week in these. When her maternal uncle [Tagore, also in Bombay at the time] saw her in this dress, he also remarked: 'If you don't feel embarrassed yourself, there is nothing wrong with this dress. You can go anywhere in it.' There was a big party on the 11th at Mrs. Petit's in honour of the poet [Tagore] and she had to decide whether she could attend it in khadi. She then remembered the poet's remark and honoured that party by attending it in this same khadi dress. She received no less respect than she used to in her costly silk saris. After this she went to all meetings and functions in khadi and at every one of them which I attended I could see that people's respect for her had increased because of this dress.[23]

However, Gandhi's other 'sister', Anasuya Sarabhai, had steadfastly refused to wear khadi. As she later recalled: 'The first person to wear khadi was Saraladevi Chaudharani. She chose the thickest cloth with an enormous border—the one used for curtains.' Gandhi kept trying to get Anasuya herself to wear khadi, but she always refused, saying, 'you keep sending me khadi, but I find it so thick'.[24]

From Bombay, Saraladevi proceeded to Lahore to arrange the marriage of her stepson, Jagdish (the child of her husband by his first wife), while Gandhi returned to Kasturba and the ashram in Ahmedabad. Then he proceeded, via Bombay, for a five-day retreat in the fort of Sinhagad, close to Poona. His pleurisy had recurred, with pain in his chest and legs, and his doctor had advised a period of rest in the hills.

From Sinhagad, Gandhi wrote to Saraladevi every day. A letter posted on 30 April began:

> I have just got up with two dreams, one about you and [the] other about Khilafat. To my great joy, you returned within two days. I asked, 'How so quickly?' You replied, 'Oh it was Panditji's [her husband] trick to have me by him. Jagdish's marriage is as far off as ever. I have therefore returned.' I discovered that it was a dream. I fell off again to sleep in disgust . . .[25]

The next day, Gandhi wrote again. He had 'a most torturing headache' the previous night, and his leg still ached. Then he continued: 'I ask you however not to worry about me. I thought you should know my condition, if only to keep you to the fortnight's limit if Jagdish's marriage is then over or if it is postponed. If you would persuade Panditji too to come so much the better. He must see and live the Ashram life.'

Despite the prefatory 'I ask you not to worry about me . . .' the letter is redolent of emotional blackmail. He seems to have extracted a promise from Sarala that she would return from Lahore in a fortnight; he would hold her to it, even if it meant parading his physical (and mental) pain.

This second letter from Sinhagad ended with a very telling paragraph:

> And now for a boon. I know you have granted many. The appetite has grown with the receiving. You said you were shy over working at the Ashram. Will you not get rid of your shyness by commencing household work there? . . . Great and good though you are, you are not a complete woman without achieving the ability to do

household work. You have preached it to others. Your preaching
will be more effective when people know that even at your time of
life and in your station you do not mind doing it.[26]

Gandhi wanted Sarala near him, for her charm and her conversation.
But he also wanted to mould her in his image. In her own home,
Sarala would have left housework to the servants, leaving her free
to paint, write, sing and converse. Gandhi wanted her words and
her songs, but he also wished to make her a model ashramite who
cooked, cleaned and span too.

On 2 May, Gandhi wrote his third letter to Sarala in as many
days. He was missing her terribly. He wrote:

> You still continue to haunt me even in my sleep. No wonder Panditji
> calls you the greatest *shakti* of India. You may have cast that spell
> over him. You are performing the trick over me now.

Gandhi continued:

> I was certain of a letter from you yesterday. But none came. Today
> too there is a blank. I wonder, however. I know you have not failed
> me. It is the wretched post.[27]

We owe the existence of these letters to Mahadev Desai, who noted
them in his diary, from where they finally found their way to the
Collected Works. Almost all of Sarala's own letters to Gandhi
were destroyed by Gandhi's family. But even from one side of the
correspondence we can see how intimate the friendship was.

Gandhi was besotted by his new friend, and she, most certainly,
by him. Sarala was loyal to her husband—but he was no Mahatma,
merely a minor provincial leader rather than a major national leader.
Gandhi was loyal to Kasturba—but she was merely a homemaker, no
poet, singer or political activist.

The relationship was intense, but not equal. Gandhi had taken
to signing his letters 'Law Giver', a self-regarding appellation that
reveals his desire to have Sarala conform to his ways, to modify or
change her lifestyle so that it might more closely approximate his

own. The aristocratic bhadramahila would, under his close and direct supervision, become a simple servant of the nation.

IV

In the India in which Gandhi was born and raised, friendship between boys and girls, men and women, was impermissible. Education was strictly segregated. Working-class and peasant women ventured out alone into factory, field or street; but middle-class women did not. Apart from his wife, the only women an Indian man of Gandhi's generation and class would have had any intimacy with were his mother, sisters, daughters, grandmothers, aunts, nieces and (at a stretch) servants.

By living outside India, Gandhi had been able to free himself from custom and convention, and forge friendships across the gender divide. In his years in the diaspora he was close to three women in particular: his long-time secretary in South Africa, Sonja Schlesin; Henry Polak's wife, Millie, since the Polaks and the Gandhis shared a home in Johannesburg; and Polak's sister, Maud, whom he had met in London.

Maud Polak was in love with Gandhi—this was not reciprocated. With Millie and Sonja the friendship was entirely platonic. He liked and respected them—indeed, they were among the few colleagues who dared challenge or criticize him.

Saraladevi was Gandhi's first woman friend in India, and also his first *Indian* woman friend. Their relationship was shot through with passion and romance. He found her stimulating, interesting, even glamorous. He was possessive about her, he wished to be with her as much as possible.

The relationship between Gandhi and Saraladevi was never consummated sexually. But it seems it came very close to doing so. Years later, in an exchange with a Gujarati colleague about the merits of brahmacharya, Gandhi remarked: 'I myself am a proof before you that sex does not discriminate between the young and the old. Even today I have to erect all sorts of walls around me for the sake of safety.' Then he continued: 'Despite this, I was in danger of succumbing a few years ago.'[28]

Notably, Gandhi wished to share the intensity of his feelings for Saraladevi with his closest male friends. Some months after he first met Saraladevi, Gandhi was finally able to discover the whereabouts of his old Johannesburg companion Hermann Kallenbach. He had, he told Kallenbach, got his address 'after the greatest search'. He had feared that Kallenbach was dead. 'How I wish I could go over to see you and hug you,' he wrote.

The friends had not been in contact for five years—since Kallenbach had been denied permission to come to India. Gandhi filled him in on the news. 'Dev[a]das is with me, ever growing in every way and in every direction. Mrs. Gandhi is at [the] Ashram. She has aged considerably but is as brave as ever. She is the same woman you know with her faults and virtues. Manilal and Ramdas are at Phoenix looking after *Indian Opinion*. Harilal is at Calcutta doing his business.'

Gandhi mentioned that he was 'engaged in a fierce struggle with the Government'. He told Kallenbach that 'my life is simpler than ever. My food is not now fruit and nuts. I am living on goat's milk and bread and raisins.'

Amidst the news, familial and dietary, Gandhi did not fail to tell Kallenbach about his newest friend: 'I have come in close touch with a lady who often travels with me. Our relationship is indefinable. I call her my spiritual wife. A friend has called it an intellectual wedding. I want you to see her. It was under her roof that I passed several months at Lahore in the Punjab.'[29]

The friend who had called it 'an intellectual wedding' was almost certainly Mahadev Desai, who had transcribed Gandhi's letters, opened Saraladevi's letters, and been somewhere in the background in Ahmedabad, Bombay, Lahore, Sinhagad and all the other places Gandhi went with or without his new companion.

Apart from Kallenbach, Gandhi had also written about his new friend to his Tamil protégé C. Rajagopalachari (popularly known as Rajaji). Gandhi's letter has been lost, but we do have fragments of Rajaji's reply. Where Mahadev was approving of, or at least acquiescent in, the development of the relationship, Rajaji was dismayed. In his letter, Gandhi seems to have suggested that Sarala and he were thinking of taking the friendship a step further. What this was is not clear—perhaps a public proclamation of their 'spiritual marriage'? Rajaji wrote back that this would bring 'unutterable shame and ruin' to Gandhi, and destroy 'all saintliness, all purity, all asceticism, all India's hope'.

That Gandhi had even contemplated such a step filled his protégé with horror. 'How could you venture out,' wrote Rajaji agitatedly, 'when in your boat was the faith and fate of millions of simple souls who if the boat had capsized would have seen neither beauty nor love nor grandeur, but unspeakable shame and death.'

Rajaji had met Saraladevi briefly, and been unimpressed. 'I fail to see any "greatness" in the lady,' he wrote to Gandhi. 'She is like a hundred other women, whom a little education makes very attractive. I have seen scores of bigger-minded [and] better-souled women.' Rajaji thought Saraladevi was 'not worthy to unloose the latchet of Miss Faring [a Danish missionary who admired Gandhi and joined the ashram] and as to Mrs Gandhi, it would be like comparing a kerosene oil Ditmar lamp to the morning sun . . .'

Rajaji chastised Gandhi, but blamed Saraladevi too. 'It is difficult to forgive her reckless indifference to consequences,' he remarked. He advised Gandhi to 'pray disengage yourself at once completely: No delay is allowable when you hold such great trusts' (namely, the fate of the nation itself).[30]

This was a brave and necessary letter: brave because few of Gandhi's Indian admirers ever criticized him directly; necessary because Gandhi does not seem to have recognized the enormous risks of the step he was contemplating. Gandhi's asceticism was a vital part of his mass appeal. Although polygamy was allowed under Hindu law, Hindu myths and Hindu social custom were both strongly in favour of monogamous marriages. Had Gandhi publicly taken another wife, albeit even a 'spiritual' one, it might have massively eroded his standing among his fellow Hindus, endangering the wider movement for political and social change that he was leading.

Gandhi was taken aback by Rajaji's forthrightness, and he did heed his advice—in part. He would not publicly take Saraladevi as his spiritual wife, but he would not—or not yet—disengage from her completely.

V

In the first week of June 1920, the Khilafat Committee met with major Congress leaders in Allahabad. The meeting began with Motilal Nehru and Madan Mohan Malaviya saying that they would wait and watch for some time before committing themselves to a policy of non-cooperation with the government. At this Shaukat Ali said angrily that 'they had already enough time to make up their minds'. Maulana Abdul Bari was equally upset; the Khilafat, he said, was 'a matter in which the very life of the Mussalmans was at stake and still the Hindus thought it proper to play with it'.

Gandhi now stepped in to calm tempers. He had, he reminded Bari and Shaukat Ali, pledged his own support to the Khilafat movement, but they must, in return, commit themselves to non-violence. He then outlined his four-stage approach to non-cooperation. It was decided that a decision as to whether to implement these stages would be taken at a special session of the Congress, to be held in Calcutta in September.

Saraladevi Chaudhurani attended this meeting in Allahabad, although she does not appear to have spoken. Another silent participant was a mole of the intelligence department. He later reported that the striking feature of the meeting was 'Gandhi's astounding assumption of dictatorship', and the Muslim leaders' acquiescence in it. Shaukat Ali said 'the Mahomedans were quite prepared to leave themselves under the guidance of Gandhi'.[31]

In the third week of June, Gandhi wrote a long letter to the viceroy on Khilafat. 'The whole of Mussalman India', he said, had 'behaved in a singularly restrained manner during the past five years'. The reward for their loyalty and restraint was a 'cruel' settlement imposed on Turkey by the Allies. Indian Muslims now had three alternatives: violence, emigration and non-cooperation, with the last being the 'only dignified and constitutional' option. 'But there is yet an escape from non-co-operation,' said Gandhi—the viceroy could identify with the Indian Muslims and pressure London to revise the settlement.[32]

In July, Gandhi toured the Punjab and Sindh, speaking on the importance of non-cooperation. If the programme was implemented, it would consist of the renouncing of titles, the boycotting of legislatures, the withdrawal of children from government schools, the giving up of practice by lawyers, and the refusal of invitations to all government functions. Gandhi expressed his 'firm belief' that the British could be made to yield under the pressure of a non-violent struggle. For, 'no European nation is more amenable to the pressure of moral force than the British'.[33]

The 1st of August was to be observed as Khilafat Day. Gandhi wished to be in Bombay to lead the hartal there. He returned to Ahmedabad from Sindh on 26 July, spent two days in the ashram, and on the 28th, took the night train to Bombay. He spent the morning in preparatory meetings. In the afternoon he heard that Bal Gangadhar Tilak was seriously ill, having just suffered two heart attacks. When Gandhi reached the home where Tilak was staying, a massive crowd had collected. Gandhi made his way into the house to see the patient. Tilak was delirious, so no words were exchanged.[34]

Tilak died in the early hours of 1 August. The news spread through the city, bringing thousands to the home where he lay. People of all ages and from all communities came to pay their respects. A dense 'mass of humanity' accompanied the body to the cremation grounds.[35]

In the vanguard of this crowd of worshippers was Gandhi. He acted as one of the pall-bearers. Later, at the Khilafat meeting scheduled for that day, rich tributes were paid to Tilak by Hindu and Muslim leaders. The main speech was made by Gandhi, who stressed the renouncing of posts and titles, non-violence in word and deed, and 'a vigorous prosecution of swadeshi'.[36]

On the same day, Gandhi wrote to the viceroy returning the three medals the king-emperor had awarded him, for services rendered in the Boer, Zulu and World Wars. 'Valuable as these honours have been to me,' said Gandhi, 'I cannot wear them with an easy conscience so long as my Mussulman countrymen have to labour under a wrong done to their religious sentiments.'[37]

That Gandhi returned the medals on the day Tilak died was a striking coincidence. For, of all the Congress leaders of the previous generation, Tilak was the most uncompromising in his opposition to colonial rule. Swaraj was his birthright and he would have it. By being in Bombay on the day Tilak died, and helping carry his body to the bier, Gandhi had further signalled that he would inherit the mantle of the departed leader. If Gokhale's death in 1915 freed Gandhi from the confines of social service, Tilak's death in 1920 allowed Gandhi to emerge as the leader of the militant tendency in the Congress-led national movement.

CHAPTER SIX

Capturing the Congress

I

Gandhi's growing militancy through the first half of 1920 alarmed the British authorities. There had been questions in Parliament about his threatened programme of non-cooperation. Conservative MPs, as well as the Conservative press, were pressing the secretary of state and the viceroy to arrest him.

In July 1920, Montagu had hinted in the House of Commons that if non-cooperation was carried out, Gandhi would be arrested. Gandhi immediately wrote an article in response to Montagu's threat. He listed three aims the government might have in arresting him:

1. 'To frighten me into changing my views.
2. To separate me from the people and thus weaken public opinion.
3. By removing me from their midst, to test the people and see whether they are really agitated over the subject.'

If he was indeed arrested, Gandhi hoped that 'the people will go ahead with non-co-operation with still greater vigour'.[1]

On 4 August, Chelmsford wrote to Montagu that they did not intend to arrest the chief troublemaker, since 'once you have made a martyr you do not know where his martyrdom may land you'. Besides, the viceroy was confident that the programme of non-cooperation would be 'a fiasco, since it runs counter to the common sense of the community at large'. If the leader's campaign was going to fizzle out anyway, why bother to arrest him?[2]

II

Gandhi spent most of August in the Madras Presidency, speaking on non-cooperation. He started his tour in Madras city, with a speech to a massive crowd assembled on the beach opposite Presidency College.

Gandhi began by speaking of his 'boundless faith' in the Tamil people, whom he had known since 1893. He then answered the question on people's minds: 'What is this non-co-operation about which you have heard much, and why do we want to offer this non-co-operation?' The two key issues were Khilafat and the Punjab. On the first, Gandhi believed the Hindus must 'perform a neighbourly duty', since 'they have an opportunity of a lifetime which will not occur for another hundred years, to show their goodwill, fellowship and friendship and to prove what they have been saying for all these long years that the Mussulman is the brother of the Hindu'. On the second, he insisted that 'the Punjab has wounded the heart of India as no other question has for the past century. I do not exclude from my calculation the Mutiny of 1857.'[3]

During his tour, Gandhi was joined by Shaukat Ali. The two addressed meetings in Kumbakonam, Nagore, Madurai, Trichy, Calicut, Kasargod and Mangalore, speaking to mixed audiences of Hindus and Muslims, often with women also present. For most of their journey, they were accompanied by C. Rajagopalachari, who translated their speeches into Tamil.

Gandhi and Shaukat Ali presented a striking contrast. The Muslim dressed stylishly, in a great green cloak and a cap with a crescent on it. And he had a booming voice. Gandhi was clothed more modestly, in a homespun dhoti, and shirt, and spoke softly.[4] Yet the travelling companions got on famously. Their joint tour in the Madras Presidency, Gandhi told C.F. Andrews, 'has confirmed . . . my belief in the greatness and goodness of Shaukat Ali. He is really one of the most sincere of men I have met. He is generous, frank, brave and gentle.'⁵

Admittedly, they had differing views on violence. Unlike Gandhi, Shaukat Ali 'believes one can kill an enemy and, for doing so, even deceit can be employed'. But for the present, Ali had accepted Gandhi's methods: 'He tells the people frankly that, at the present time, my way is the best for them.'⁶

During his tour of Madras, Saraladevi wrote several letters to Gandhi. A bare but most intriguing summary of their contents is provided by Mahadev Desai. Here is his diary entry for 23 August 1920:

> Bezwada. Seven or eight letters were received from Saraladevi during the Madras tour. They indicate her suspicion about . . . her charge that Bapu is dazzled by him and her complaint that Bapu's letters betray 'mental exhaustion'. She says that for Bapu's sake she made such an inordinate sacrifice. She put in one pan all the joys of life and pleasures of the world and in the other 'Bapu and his laws' and committed the folly of choosing the latter!⁷

The person denoted by those ellipses was almost certainly Shaukat Ali. Sarala was unhappy with Gandhi's enchantment with him; whether out of possessiveness or reservations regarding Khilafat we cannot say. And Sarala was clearly tired of being told what to wear, what to eat, how to cook and clean. She was not an ashramite who had voluntarily taken a series of vows—asked by Gandhi to live like one, she was resisting.

Like many lawgivers, Gandhi failed to see the signs of rebellion. In one of her letters, Sarala had said she wished to visit her family in Calcutta. Gandhi, writing from Bezwada on 23 August (the same day as Mahadev's diary entry above) told her to do so only 'after you have perfected your spinning-wheel and Hindi and put our Lahore work on a sound footing'. The next day, he wrote again: 'Your letters have caused me distress. You do not like my sermons. . . . I do not at all like your doubting the necessity of the life adopted by you or the life you are trying to adopt. . . . If I am your Law-giver and if I do not always lay down the law, surely I must at least reason with you on things of eternity or supreme importance for the country for which we live and which we love so well.'[8]

III

Gandhi had taken his message of non-cooperation to the Punjab, Sindh and the United Provinces; to Bombay and Ahmedabad; to the large and small towns of the Madras Presidency. The north, the west and the south of the country had been reasonably well covered. Only the east remained.

Gandhi now proceeded to Calcutta, the venue for the special session of the Congress, held in the first week of September. Calcutta in 1920 was the greatest city in India, the former capital of the British Raj, and—not least—an epicentre of the national movement. Many early leaders of the Congress had been Bengalis from Calcutta. The revolutionary terrorists had also been most active in this city and province.

One suspects Gandhi might have approached his journey east with some trepidation. His earlier visits to Calcutta had not always been happy or productive. He first went there in 1896, seeking support for his campaign for Indian rights in South Africa. Every newspaper editor he met showed him the door. In the twenty-four years since that first visit, Gandhi had become much better known in Bengal. No editor in Calcutta—or anywhere else in India—could afford to ignore him. But he was keenly aware of the Bengali bhadralok's sense of superiority. They had been the first to take to English education, the first to ask for rights for women, the first to articulate the demand for political freedom.

Gokhale had once said that what Bengal thinks today, India thinks tomorrow. This was extremely generous, for Gokhale's native Maharashtra had produced its precocious social reformers too. Bengal and Bengalis might allow that Maharashtrians were also politically sophisticated and culturally emancipated. But they were less willing to acknowledge a mere Gujarati as an equal. Gandhi's asceticism also grated on the epicurean Bengalis, themselves fond of good food and wine, and of music and art, tastes which Gandhi had conspicuously failed to cultivate.[9]

Gandhi arrived at Calcutta's Howrah station on the night of 3 September. He was received by his son Harilal, to whose home in Pollock Street he then proceeded. The next morning he visited the venue of the Congress. The pandal was adorned with flags and slogans saying 'Nations by Themselves are Made', 'Remember Jallianwala Bagh', 'Home Rule is our Birthright' and 'Hindu–Mussalman ki jai'.[10]

At a session on the first day, Annie Besant was shouted down by the delegates, because of her opposition to the policy of non-cooperation. Gandhi stood up on a chair and with folded hands asked the hecklers to quieten down. Every speaker, he said, must be given a patient hearing. This was a handsome gesture, since, back in 1916, Mrs Besant had demanded that he stop speaking in Banaras when his words offended her.[11]

On 5 September, Gandhi circulated a note he had freshly drafted on non-cooperation. This asked for seven forms of action: surrender of titles and honorary posts; refusal to attend government functions; 'gradual withdrawal' of children from government schools and colleges, and establishment of national schools and colleges in their place; 'gradual boycott' of British courts by lawyers and litigants, and establishment of private arbitration courts in their place; refusal by Indians to serve as soldiers, labourers or clerks in the new British government in Mesopotamia; boycott of legislative councils; and boycott of foreign goods.[12]

On 8 September, Gandhi formally moved his resolution on non-cooperation. Speeches and the 'mere expression of angry feeling', he said, had proved inadequate 'to bend the Government to our will'. Carried away by the moment, Gandhi now made what (even at the time) must have seemed an extremely reckless promise. 'If there is a sufficient response to my scheme,' he proclaimed, 'I make bold to reiterate my statement that you can gain swarajya in the course of a year.'

Gandhi's resolution was seconded by Motilal Nehru, who, pressed by his radical son Jawaharlal, had come around to the virtues of non-cooperation. On the other side, Jinnah, Malaviya and Mrs Besant spoke vigorously against the motion. After the speeches, the votes were cast and counted—1855 delegates voted for Gandhi's resolution, 873 against. The provincial break-up was revealing:

Bombay (243 yes, 93 no), UP (259 vs 28) and Punjab (254 vs 92) most strongly supported Gandhi, while Madras (161 to 135) and Bengal (551 to 395) were more divided. In the Central Provinces, Gandhi's supporters were actually in a minority (30 to 33).[13]

In terms of numbers, Gandhi had won the day. But the debates had been prolonged, and many long-serving Congressmen had opposed the motion. The Bengal leaders B.C. Pal and C.R. Das now worked to effect a compromise. The annual session of the Congress was due to meet in Nagpur in December. Why not wait until then to have the decision ratified? The meeting ended with the acceptance of non-cooperation in principle, but a deferral of the decision to put it into practice.[14]

IV

From Calcutta, Gandhi returned to Ahmedabad for a week's rest, and then resumed his travels. In October, he spent two weeks in the United Provinces, speaking in ten different towns. By far the most important of these was Aligarh. The town was home to the great Muslim University, alma mater of both Shaukat and Mohammad Ali, but also a bastion of Empire loyalism. Gandhi and the Ali Brothers arrived in Aligarh on 11 October, hoping to win its students over to the cause of non-cooperation.[15] They gave a series of speeches in Aligarh that had mixed results; the students finding it difficult to follow Gandhi's still imperfect Hindustani.[16]

Even less impressed were the trustees of the university. They refused outright the request of Gandhi and the Ali Brothers that they return their government grant and become a 'National University'. Writing to Gandhi, the trustees said they would 'firmly adhere to our old established policy' of staying away from politics, which, in effect, meant taking the side of the authorities.[17]

Accompanying Gandhi on this trip was Mahadev Desai. He did not entirely share his master's enchantment with the Ali Brothers. 'This Shaukat Ali is becoming intolerable now,' wrote Mahadev to Devadas Gandhi, 'he is fond of pomp [and] there was nothing but tamasha in Mathura yesterday.' At Aligarh, Mahadev wanted Gandhi to meet with groups of students, but they were overruled by Shaukat and his programme of 'endless hustle and processions and public meetings'.[18]

Gandhi and the Ali Brothers now decided to start their own 'National University' in Aligarh. Their hope was that the poet-philosopher Muhammad Iqbal, a man comparable in stature to Tagore, would agree to be its vice chancellor. Gandhi wrote to Iqbal in Lahore urging him to accept the post. 'I am sure it [the National University] will prosper under your cultured leadership,' he said, adding, 'Hakimji Ajmal Khan and Dr. Ansari and of course the Ali Brothers desire it. I wish you could see your way to respond. Your expenses on a scale suited to the new awakening can be easily guaranteed.'[19]

Iqbal wrote back declining the offer. The poet, understandably, did not want to be diverted by academic politics and the raising of funds. But he did have an important suggestion to make. Iqbal observed that 'the Muslims of India are far behind the other communities of this country. Their principal need is not Literature and Philosophy but technical Education which would make them Economically independent.' Therefore, he said, those who were behind the new university 'will be well advised if they make it an institution devoted mainly to the technical side of Natural Sciences supplemented by such religious Education as may be considered necessary'.[20]

Having failed with Iqbal, Gandhi then persuaded the educationist Zakir Husain to take up the assignment. The university itself was shifted from Aligarh to Delhi. Named the Jamia Millia Islamia, it would function as a 'Nationalist Muslim' alternative to the solidly pro-British university at Aligarh.

V

In the last week of October, Gandhi published a letter addressed 'To Every Englishman in India', signed by 'Your faithful friend, M.K. Gandhi'. The letter began by recalling his 'free and voluntary co-operation' with the British government for three decades, and the services he had rendered them during their wars with the Zulus, Boers and Germans. However, said Gandhi, the unwillingness to restore the Khilafat and the 'atrocities in the Punjab' had 'completely shattered my faith in the good intentions of the Government and the nation which is supporting it'.

Gandhi listed other grievances: such as the exploitation of India's economic resources for the benefit of England; the high salaries, high military expenditure and other official extravagances 'in utter disregard of India's poverty'; the 'repressive legislation' to silence the voices 'seeking to give expression to a nation's agony'; and the 'degrading treatment' of Indians in British dominions.

Gandhi urged the English to 'repent of the wrong done to Indians', and to abandon repression in favour of an 'honourable solution'. He ended by asking the rulers to 'make common cause with the people of India whose salt you are eating. To seek to thwart their aspirations is disloyalty to the country.'[21]

Gandhi's letter evoked some interesting responses from Englishmen in India. Two schoolteachers in Bangalore praised the 'generous tone' of the letter. Acknowledging the 'arrogant attitude to Indians' among many Englishmen, they themselves believed the Empire should be 'a commonwealth of free peoples voluntarily linked together by the ties of common experience in the past and common aspirations for the future, a commonwealth which may hope to spread liberty and progress through the whole earth'.[22]

Another letter, by a certain Edward Foy of Ambala Cantonment, was less measured. This called Gandhi 'the ungratefulest of men'. 'After all that the British Government has done,' wrote this man angrily, 'you have no good word for it! Where would you have been today but for the British Government which saved India from the iron grip of Germany?' Gandhi claimed to be a 'peace-maker', but in the eyes of Mr Foy he was in fact a 'peace-breaker', 'manufacturing worse and worse forms of agitation which threaten the lives and property of all others and of your own countrymen also'.[23]

Even more intemperate was a letter sent under the pseudonym 'Pro Bono Publico'. The letter began by calling Gandhi a 'Prince of Liars, Son of Seven Prostitutes and Father of a thousand criminal bastards'. How can 'an idolatrous farting Hindu', it asked, 'side with a pharaisical Mahomeddan'? 'What sympathy or thought,' the letter continued, 'you miserable swine, can pretend to have for the lecherous, murdering Turk, he would not piss on you or the Muslims of this country.' Had Gandhi lived 'under the German Govt. the first time you acted the "nimakharam" and uttered a crooked word against them, you would have been hung like the dog you are'. Yet the 'benign and benevolent [British] government has most stupidly given you no end of rope . . .'[24]

Amidst this barrage of criticism and abuse, Gandhi received a letter from an Irishman who wrote 'to wish you success in trying to obtain Swaraj. India belongs to your people and not to the English . . .' The writer spoke of how the 'English have oppressed Ireland, my own dear country, for hundreds of years but we Irish never gave in and always strived for freedom and although we are not yet a Republic we shall go on doing our very best to obtain it'. With the Irish example before him, Gandhi was urged to 'fight on for liberty' himself.[25]

VI

As he travelled through India, Gandhi continued to be reminded that what all parts of the country had in common was the treatment of certain castes as 'untouchable'. He was appalled by this stigmatization by his fellow Hindus of their co-religionists. In May 1920, he emphatically declared that

> We cannot compare the sufferings of the untouchables with those of any other section in India. It passes my understanding how we consider it dharma to treat the depressed classes as untouchables; I shudder at the very thought of this. My conscience tells me that untouchability can never be a part of Hinduism. I do not think it too much to dedicate my whole life to removing the thick crust of sin with which Hindu society has covered itself for so long by stupidly regarding these people as untouchables. I am only sorry that I am unable to devote myself wholly to that work.[26]

Gandhi had now started a college in Ahmedabad to go with the school he had already founded. Called the Gujarat Vidyapith, this would be autonomous of the government and avail of no state funds. It was run as a 'national' college, supported by voluntary donations, and with a curriculum more suited to Indian needs than the state-run colleges that sought to train clerks for the civil service.

In October 1920, the Gujarat Vidyapith passed a resolution that no school which refused to admit 'Antyaja', or untouchable children, would be given approval by it. This provoked uproar among upper-caste Gujaratis, with articles and statements attacking Gandhi for undermining Hindu dharma. To these criticisms, Gandhi pointedly asked: 'Do we hope to win swaraj while reviving the practice of untouchability at the same time?'[27]

In his own ashram, of course, no caste distinctions were observed at all. Visiting Sabarmati, the Moderate politician M.R. Jayakar saw Gandhi 'ready to eat a boiled potato with a Harijan [untouchable] girl although it had been half bitten by her'. Jayakar himself lived in Bombay, professedly a cosmopolitan city, albeit one where his fellow lawyers would not break bread with people of other castes. 'I have,' he wrote later, 'never found a man so free from caste aversion as Gandhi.' Jayakar was impressed that Gandhi, 'the foremost leader of India', had 'practically rooted out caste sense from his daily concerns'.[28]

In early December, Gandhi wrote a long essay in *Young India* outlining his understanding of caste. He said that while he accepted the traditional fourfold division known as varnashramadharma, he condemned the practice of untouchability. 'I believe that caste has saved Hinduism from disintegration,' he remarked. 'But like every other institution it has suffered from excrescences.'

It was customary to rank the four varnas as follows: the Brahmins, or priests, at the top; the Kshatriyas, or warriors, next; the Vaishyas, or merchants (Gandhi's own caste), third; the Sudras, or peasants and labourers, fourth, with a fifth class, that of the 'untouchables', literally beyond the pale. However, in Gandhi's (rather revisionist) view, 'the caste system is not based on inequality, there is no question of inferiority, and so far as there is any such question arising . . . the tendency should undoubtedly be checked. But there appears to be no valid reason for ending the system because of its abuse. It lends itself easily to reformation. The spirit of democracy, which is fast spreading through India and the rest of the world will, without a shadow of doubt, purge the institution of the idea of predominance and subordination.'

Each of these four varnas had hundreds of jatis, or sub-castes. Traditionally, a member of a particular jati would not mix, marry or eat with the member of a jati other than his own. These prohibitions Gandhi did not as yet challenge, claiming that 'interdrinking, interdining, intermarrying, I hold, are not essential for the promotion of the spirit of democracy'. He did not 'contemplate under a most democratic constitution a universality of manners and customs about eating, drinking and marrying. We shall ever have to seek unity in diversity, and I decline to consider it a sin for a man not to drink or eat with anybody and everybody.'

Gandhi now added a crucial caveat:

> Thus whilst I am prepared to defend, as I have always done, the division of Hindus into four castes . . . I consider untouchability to be a heinous crime against humanity. It is not a sign of self-restraint but an arrogant assumption of superiority. It has served no useful purpose and it has suppressed, as nothing else in Hinduism has, vast numbers of the human race who are not only every bit as good as ourselves, but are rendering in many walks of life an essential service to the country.[29]

Gandhi's attitude towards caste, ca 1920, can be summed up in four propositions:

1. While the orthodox or literal-minded saw caste as a vertical system based on hierarchy, he would reconfigure it as a horizontal system in which no group was superior or inferior;
2. Eating, mixing and marrying were personal or communal choices—while in his own ashram he promoted inter-dining and intermingling, he would not presume to impose this on all Indians;
3. In dealing with his fellows, man must not follow the scriptures, but his own conscience.

4. Untouchability was not just a social question, but also a moral one. The practice was wrong, unjust, cruel. Therefore, it had to be eradicated.

By 1920, Gandhi saw the abolition of untouchability as being as significant as the consolidation of Hindu–Muslim unity. For the movement for swaraj to be politically strong, it had to transcend religious differences; for it to be morally credible, it had to put an end to the treatment of a large section of Indians as less-than-human.

VII

After the special session of the Congress in Calcutta, Gandhi resumed his travels. In October, he toured the Punjab and the United Provinces; in November, the Bombay Presidency and his native Gujarat. The magnificently detailed chronology of his life by Chandubhai Dalal[30] tells us that he visited nineteen towns and cities in the first month, and as many as twenty-nine in the second. Everywhere, he spoke at public meetings and, before or after these meetings, talked to delegates likely to attend the Congress session in Nagpur in December.

Gandhi's travels were mostly by train, on tracks built by British firms after the Great Rebellion of 1857. At the time of the rebellion there were merely a few hundred miles of railway track in the subcontinent; by the end of the century, this had jumped to more than 30,000. The railways criss-crossed the country, connecting east and west, south and north.[31]

Gandhi usually spent a day (or less) in the places he visited. His longest stay was at Allahabad, where he spent as many as four days. He was welcomed at the station by Motilal and Jawaharlal Nehru, and with 'blowing conches and ringing bells'.[32] Talks to students at Allahabad University and a large public meeting had been arranged. In between, he had long conversations with the Nehrus. Jawaharlal had recently visited the district of Pratapgarh, where discontented peasants, led by a sadhu called Baba Ram Chandra, had started a no-tax campaign. This direct exposure to rural poverty had further radicalized the younger Nehru. He was now urging his father to put his weight more fully behind Gandhi's movement.[33]

VIII

As Gandhi combed the country, canvassing support for non-cooperation, his relationship with Saraladevi Chaudhurani once more came under strain. This is visibly manifest in a series of letters written by Sarala to Gandhi in October 1920, these among the very few by her to have survived.[34]

In the second week of October, Sarala journeyed to Ahmedabad in the hope of spending some time with Gandhi. However, he was out, on the road. From the ashram, she wrote to him about what she was doing while he was away—wearing saris made of khaddar, and persuading society women in Ahmedabad to do likewise. But she wished he was there. 'The bathroom is the only place to receive my sobs,' she wrote. 'But I am hoping they will come to an end very soon.'[35]

Eventually, tired of waiting, Sarala travelled back to her home in Lahore. From there she wrote to Gandhi about the 'misconceptions' between them, and of her 'anger' at his not giving her 'a free hand' in how she wished to live her life. When, in a recent conversation, she had accused him of harbouring 'harsh thoughts' and of having an 'adamantine' pride, Gandhi had answered that he was 'activated by love' in his 'punishment' of her. Now, Sarala challenged him to directly declare his feelings for her. 'If it be love,' she told Gandhi, 'tell me . . . in simple touching language you are missing me daily, suffering the pangs of separation yourself [as she was], longing for the dawn of the day when we shall meet again. If it be love, let pride be prostrate once and for all and love use its language in a free flow once more.'

On the other hand, said Sarala to Gandhi, if it was the case that 'love is killed and cannot be revived any more', then he should 'confess that freely and do not bear a "White man's burden" for the uplift of the Black'.[36]

Two days later, Sarala wrote again. She was hurt that Gandhi had charged her 'with a new sin to [add to] my many older ones—that of jealousy'. Sarala admitted that like other human beings, she was not entirely free of that emotion. 'But what of that in our relationship?' she remarked. 'Do you mean to say that I am jealous of you? I can only laugh at the charge & wonder at your biased reading of me.' Sarala concluded that Gandhi and she were 'at cross purposes, it seems'. 'The misunderstandings can't be cleared up by the post,' she added.[37] It seems that Gandhi thought so too, for after his United Provinces tour, he decided to carry on to the Punjab to meet her.

Gandhi reached Lahore on 19 October. He stayed two days with the Chaudhuris. However, Sarala and he could not get much time to themselves, since an unending stream of students came to pay their respects to the visitor. In a letter written to Gandhi the day after he left, Sarala suggested a temporary truce. As she somewhat poetically put it: 'Let us not tread on delicate grounds for some time and agree to differ in our respective views on certain topics. Shall we? Let God's light be thrown on the actions & motives & thoughts of both of us & not our individual lights.'[38]

In Gandhi's life, politics was now rapidly taking precedence over friendship. On 11 December, Gandhi wrote Sarala an answer to 'a longish letter which shows that you do not understand my language or my thoughts. I have certainly not betrayed any annoyance over your complex nature, but I have remarked upon it.' He continued: 'In you I have an enigma to solve. I shall not be impatient. Only bear with me whenever I try to point [out] what to me appear to be your obvious limitations. We all have them. It is the privilege of friendship to lay the gentle finger on the weak spots.'[39]

Sarala was tired of being asked to live the simple life. And she seemed to have reservations about Gandhi's political programme too. Mahadev Desai's diary for 17 December 1920 has this entry: 'Saraladevi had written: Non-co-operation was based on hatred [of the British] and she loved Bapu the less therefore. She would love Bapu more if he was free of hatred; an activity, moreover, like non-co-operation could be taken up by others also.'[40]

Sarala's reservations may have been stoked by her famous uncle. Gandhi's campaign of non-co-operation provoked ambivalent feelings in Tagore; as he wrote to their mutual friend C.F. Andrews, he wished the emotion would flow along constructive channels. If that happened, said Tagore, 'I shall be willing to sit at his [Gandhi's] feet and do his bidding, if he commands me to co-operate with my countrymen in service of love. I refuse to waste my manhood in lighting the fire of anger and spreading it from house to house.'[41]

On receiving Saraladevi's letter of 17 December, Gandhi wrote back immediately. He first answered her reservations about his political method. 'You would be right in your regret over my being engaged in N[on]-C[o-]O[peration] if it was a matter of politics with me,' remarked Gandhi. 'As it is, with me it is my religion. I am gathering together all the forces of hate and directing them in a proper channel. . . . If I could but show our countrymen that we need not fear the English, we will cease to hate them.'

The second, and more significant, paragraph of the letter turned to their relationship. I have reproduced it more or less in extenso, deleting only the odd repetitive thought/sentence:

I have been analysing my love for you. I have reached a definite meaning of spiritual wife. It is a partnership between two persons of the opposite sex where the physical is wholly absent. . . . It is possible only between two *brahmacharis* in thought, word and deed. I have felt drawn to you, because I have recognized in you an identity of ideals and aspirations and a complete self-surrender. You have been 'wife' because you have recognized in me a fuller fruition of the common ideal than in yourself. . . . It follows from what I have stated that spiritual partners can never be physically wedded either in this life or a future, for it is possible only when there is no carnality, latent or patent. Are you spiritual wife to me of that description? Have we that exquisite purity, that perfect coincidence, that perfect merging, that identity of ideals, that self-forgetfulness, that fixity of purpose, that trustfulness? For me I can answer plainly that it is only an aspiration. I am unworthy to have that companionship with you. I require in me an infinitely higher purity than I possess in thought. I am too physically attached to you to be worthy of enjoying that sacred association with you. By physical attachment I here mean I am too much affected by your weaknesses. I must not be teacher to you, if I am your spiritual husband, if coincidence or merging is felt. On the contrary there are sharp differences between you and me so often. So far as I can see our relationship, it is one of brother and sister. I must lay down the law for you, and thus ruffle you. I must plead gently like a brother ever taking care to use the right word even as I do to my oldest sister. I must not be father, husband, friend, teacher all rolled into one. This is the big letter I promised. With dearest love I still subscribe myself,

Yours
LAW-GIVER[42]

This letter lacks the clarity and precision that marks Gandhi's writings. Amidst the confusion and complexity, one can, however, discern a few distinct strands. The first is the strongly patriarchal tone—the husband is the Law-Giver, to whose superior will the wife must bend. A second and allied note is the presumption that Gandhi's way of life is also superior—he has achieved a 'fuller fruition' of the nationalist ideal. A third is the visible tension between Gandhi's commitment to celibacy and his attraction to Saraladevi. He does not, he confesses here, have that 'infinitely higher purity [in practice] that I possess in thought'.

This letter does seem to have taken their relationship almost to breaking point. After this missive of 17 December, Saraladevi Chaudhurani's name appears very infrequently in the *Collected Works*. That it was Gandhi who took the decision to end their friendship/spiritual marriage is manifest from a letter he wrote to C. Rajagopalachari three years later. 'Yes, your guess is correct,' writes Gandhi. 'The fair friend is Sar[a]ladevi. She wants to bombard me with more stuff but I have refused to give further accommodation.'[43]

As the colleague who had cautioned Gandhi against deepening the relationship, Rajaji must have read these words with a sense of relief and also, one supposes, vindication.

IX

Gandhi arrived in Nagpur for the Congress on 20 December 1920, accompanied by Shaukat Ali. They were received by a large crowd, which took them in an open carriage through the streets. Gandhi was staying in a lodge run by his fellow vegetarians, the Marwari community.[44]

On Christmas Day—the day before the Congress began—Gandhi gave two talks, one to a group of weavers, the other to a meeting of 'untouchables'. He told the former that 'I regard myself a farmer-weaver', urged them to revive their profession, and expressed dismay that the cloth they wore was not produced by themselves.

The speech to the 'untouchables' was longer and more personal. Here Gandhi spoke of how 'I have to suffer much in trying to carry my wife with me in what I have been doing' (to end untouchability). He noted that 'at present I am engaged in a great dispute with the Hindus in Gujarat' on the same question. Calling the practice of untouchability 'a great Satanism in Hinduism', he observed: 'I have said to the Hindus, and say it again today, that till Hindu society is purged of this sin, swaraj is an impossibility.'

Even so, Gandhi advocated a cautious, incrementalist approach to the activists who had gathered to hear him. They wanted to have a resolution passed at the Congress demanding that 'untouchables' should be allowed to enter all temples. Gandhi responded: 'How is this possible? So long as *Varnashram dharma* occupies the central place in Hinduism, it is vain that you ask that every Hindu should be free to enter a temple right now. It is impossible to get society to accept this. It is not prepared for this yet.'

Gandhi noted that some temples in South India were closed even to him (because he had refused to wear a thread signifying his upper-caste status). Others were open only to members of certain sects. 'I don't feel unhappy about this,' he remarked. 'I am not even prepared to say that this betrays the Hindus' narrow outlook or that it is a wrong they are committing. Maybe it is, but we should consider the line of thinking behind it. If their action is inspired by considerations of discipline, I would not say that everyone should be free to go to any temple.'

Gandhi added: 'I myself eat and drink in the company of Antyajas. I have adopted the daughter of an Antyaj ["untouchable"] family and she is dearer to me than my own life.' The girl was Lakshmi, daughter of Dudhabhai and Danibehn, admitted to the ashram in 1915. While himself extremely heterodox, Gandhi felt that he could not yet 'tell Hindu society that it might abandon its self-control'.[45]

From social reform, Gandhi plunged straight into politics.[46] On 30 December, he spoke to the Congress on the crucial non-cooperation resolution. This asked for 'the establishment of an Indian Republic' through the programme already outlined by Gandhi in Calcutta, namely, the boycotting by students of government schools and colleges, by lawyers of courts, by merchants of foreign goods, by voters and representatives of councils. Policemen and soldiers were requested to 'refuse to subordinate their creed and country to the fulfilment of orders of their [British] officers'. The resolution also appealed to all government servants, 'pending the call of the nation for resignation of their service, to help the national cause by importing greater kindness and stricter honesty in their dealings with the people'.

The resolution was in eleven paragraphs, the last of which called for individuals and organizations to 'advance Hindu–Muslim unity', for 'the leading Hindus to settle the disputes between Brahmin and non-Brahmin' (these particularly acute in the Madras Presidency), and for a 'special effort to rid Hinduism of the reproach of untouchability'.[47]

Gandhi asked the delegates to carry the resolution 'with a prayer to God from the deepest recesses of your heart', and to 'show no violence in thought, deed or word whether in connection with the Government or whether in connection with ourselves'. His exhortations were met with loud cries and cheers of 'Mahatma Gandhi ki jai'.[48]

Gandhi was the star of what was the biggest Congress yet. As many as 14,582 delegates came. There were also more Muslims (1050) and more women (169) than ever before. The Congress was presided over by the veteran C. Vijayaraghavachariar, who was completely in thrall to Gandhi. In a long, rambling presidential address, he quoted Burke, Lincoln and the 'Hindu idea of polity', before speaking of the 'process of national unification' that had 'greatly expanded and intensified under the auspices of Mahatmaji Gandhi and the stalwart patriots who are co-operating with him'.[49]

The vast majority of the delegates at Nagpur were with Gandhi, and so were the leaders. As the official history of the Congress was to later put it, the support that Gandhi obtained at Nagpur was undoubtedly greater than what he had in Calcutta. In Calcutta, the only top-notch politician [who] had lent a helping hand to Gandhi, and that rather late in the day, was Pandit Motilal Nehru . . . Else the stool of [non-co-operation] was resting on but one leg. At Nagpur, it stood on all its four legs with perfect equipoise. Gandhi and Nehru, Das and Lalaji [Lajpat Rai] were all for it.[50]

Although the party historian would not mention it, there was in fact a 'top-notch politician' who did not go along with Gandhi in Nagpur. This was Muhammad Ali Jinnah. Jinnah had stayed away from the Khilafat movement, uncomfortable with the strident militancy of the Ali Brothers; now he would stay away from Gandhi's struggle too. In a speech of controlled passion, Jinnah opposed the non-cooperation resolution for two reasons: because so long as the British were in control of the government machinery, a unilateral declaration of swaraj, or independence, was 'mere sentimental feeling and expression of anger and desperation', a 'declaration which you have not the means to carry out'; and because he did not want to make a fetish of non-cooperation, a method which in his view would 'not succeed in destroying the British Empire'. The Congress under Gandhi's direction was, said Jinnah, adopting a course that was 'neither logical nor politically sound'.

Jinnah was booed and barracked at regular intervals. When he referred to 'Mr. Muhammad Ali' there were angry cries of 'Maulana', 'Maulana', the honorific usually used before Mohammad Ali's name. When Jinnah ended his speech, by appealing to Gandhi 'to pause, to cry halt before it is too late', he was answered by shouts of 'Shame! Shame!' and 'Mahatma Gandhi ki jai'.[51]

Jinnah's dissent apart, this was from first to last a Gandhi show. The Congress organization was now effectively his to control and direct. A week after the meeting, the viceroy, Lord Chelmsford, wrote to the secretary of state in London that 'Gandhi has had undoubtedly a great personal triumph, and I gather . . . that he really dominated the whole situation'. Then he hopefully added: 'Yet I fancy that a feeling of soreness has been left behind with those who do not see eye to eye with Gandhi . . .'[52]

CHAPTER SEVEN

The Rise and Fall of Non-cooperation

I

Gandhi wanted to make the Congress more *Indian*, and he wanted it to have a properly representative character. So it was resolved to have party units at different levels: that of the province, the district and the taluk (sub-district). Taluk, district and provincial committees were constituted, their members chosen by election. The provinces would in turn send members for the All India Congress Committee (AICC). The most select and powerful body was the Congress Working Committee (CWC), which had about fifteen members and was where all major party decisions were taken.

In its own workings, the Congress had now replaced the administrative divisions of British India with one which explicitly recognized the linguistic diversity of the subcontinent. Outside the Hindi-speaking heartland, every major language group had its own provincial unit. There was no longer a Madras Presidency Congress, but there were now a Karnataka Provincial Congress Committee (KPCC), an Andhra PCC, a Maharashtra PCC, etc. The party's apex body, the CWC, took care to reflect this diversity. In 1921, for example, it had a member apiece from Gujarat (represented by Gandhi), Maharashtra, Bengal and Assam, Bihar and Orissa, and Andhra. Of the three general secretaries, Motilal Nehru was from the United Provinces, C. Rajagopalachari from Tamilnadu, and Dr M.A. Ansari from Delhi. The treasurer, Jamnalal Bajaj, was from the Central Provinces. Meanwhile, the AICC, second only to the CWC in importance, was also becoming more representative. In 1919, it had a mere eighteen Muslim members; three years later it had as many as eighty-four (out of a total of 350). This was part of Gandhi's attempt to ensure that the Congress could not be dismissed as a 'Hindu party'.

The Nagpur constitution introduced the idea of paid membership. For the modest sum of four annas (one-fourth of a rupee), anyone over eighteen years of age could become a member of the Congress, and participate in its discussions at the taluk or district level, or join a trade union, peasant organization or women's group working under the Congress umbrella.[1]

Gandhi's attempts to make the Congress a mass organization were successful. In the months after the Nagpur Congress, tens of thousands of primary members enrolled in each of the provinces. By the end of the year, the party had close to 2 million members. Before Gandhi took charge, the Congress was dominated by lawyers, editors and scholars, who brought the high status of their professional position to their work in the party. But with the non-cooperation movement, the ability or desire to abandon one's profession became a critical attribute. As one historian of the party puts it: 'The significant difference between the pre-1920 and the post-1920 Congress leadership lay in the fact that before 1920 it was social position which automatically conferred a leading role in the movement; after 1920 it was the renunciation of social position and the demonstration of willingness to accept sacrifice that was demanded of those who aspired to lead.'[2] Men such as C.R. Das, Motilal Nehru and C. Rajagopalachari gained in prestige and public acclaim because they had abandoned their lucrative legal practices to serve the nation.

II

Gandhi spent the second half of January 1921 in Bengal, raising money for the non-cooperation movement. His wife, Kasturba, was with him. While he was in Calcutta, Gandhi received a letter from C.F. Andrews, complaining that he was spending too much time on his campaign against untouchability. Gandhi replied that while, as an Englishman and Christian, Andrews was merely an observer, as an Indian and Hindu, Gandhi was 'an affected and afflicted party. You *can* be patient, and I *cannot*. . . . I have to deal with the Hindu Dyers.'

By comparing upper-caste Hindus to General Dyer, Gandhi was underlining his disgust with the practice of untouchability. He was, he told Andrews, 'engaged *as a Hindu* in showing that it is not a sin and that it is sin to consider that touch a sin'. It was 'a bigger problem than that of gaining Indian independence', said Gandhi, continuing prophetically: 'It is not impossible that India may free herself from English domination before India has become free of the curse of untouchability.'[3]

From Calcutta, Gandhi proceeded to the mineral-rich areas of Bihar. In the coalfield town of Jharia, where there was a large community of Gujaratis, he held a public meeting, and collected 60,000 rupees in cash and jewellery. A lady in the crowd put her gold necklace around Kasturba's neck and was about to adorn her wrists with gold bracelets. Kasturba protested—taking off the necklace, she said the collection was for the nation's swaraj, not for her personally. The lady then gave Gandhi the necklace, but begged Kasturba to at least wear the bracelets. As Mahadev Desai wryly noted in his diary: 'Kasturba refused—with the result that the Swaraj fund was robbed of the bracelets.'[4]

The incident showed the long distance Kasturba had travelled in her own political journey. Back in 1901, when the grateful Indians of Natal presented the Gandhis with jewellery, husband and wife had a terrific row. He wanted to return the gifts, but she, thinking of her future daughters-in-law, thought that since they were given in good faith the jewels could be retained.[5] Now, twenty years later, Kasturba would accept gifts of necklaces and bracelets to aid Gandhi's campaigns, while denying them for herself.

From Bihar, Kasturba went back to Ahmedabad, while her husband continued his non-cooperation tour. He visited several towns in the United Provinces, before moving on to the Punjab.

Then he moved south, where, in the first week of April, the AICC
met at Vijayawada. In attendance was an Andhra Congressman
named P. Venkayya, who for several years had been pressing
Gandhi to adopt a 'national' flag for the nation-in-the-making.
This time too Venkayya made the same proposal, but in the design
he offered, Gandhi 'saw nothing to stir the nation to its depths'.
Then Lala Hansraj of Jullundur suggested that the spinning wheel
should find a place on the Swaraj Flag. Gandhi was struck by the
suggestion, and asked Venkayya to give him a design containing a
spinning wheel on a background of saffron (denoting Hindu) and
green (denoting Muslim).

The enthusiastic Venkayya produced a design in three hours.
Gandhi looked at it, and realized that a colour was also needed for the
other religions of India. He suggested white be added to the saffron
and the green. For, 'Hindu–Muslim unity is not an exclusive term; it
is an inclusive term, symbolic of the unity of all faiths domiciled in
India. If Hindus and Muslims can tolerate each other, they are bound
to tolerate all other faiths.'

Gandhi further suggested the order in which the colours should
be placed: white first, next green, finally saffron, in progressive order
of numerical importance, 'the idea being that the strongest should act
as a shield to the weakest'. Eventually, the white was placed in the
middle, between the saffron and the green, the two major religions
symbolically surrounding and protecting the others.[6]

III

In his travels through India, Gandhi was often accompanied
by one or both the Ali Brothers. At public meetings they would
appear jointly, and speak in turn. This double act signified both
the growing Hindu–Muslim unity and the coupling of Khilafat and
non-cooperation.

The Ali Brothers do seem to have genuinely admired Gandhi.
Speaking to a mixed audience of Hindus and Muslims in a town in
the United Provinces, Mohammad Ali called Gandhi 'a brave man,
a true man', who would 'sacrifice his life and property for the cause

of India'.[7] Speaking in another United Provinces town, Shaukat Ali proclaimed that 'today Mahatmaji is the leader of all of us, Hindus and Muslims, and if you Hindus and Muslims obey Mahatmaji and act on his advice and sacrifice your life and property for country and religion you will be gifted with all the blessings of this world and the next'. Then he continued:

> The fact is though [his] bones are small and Mahatma Gandhi is a lean and thin man and I have repeatedly said I could if I liked place him in my pocket with my left hand, yet his heart is so large that this Government has no power save that of fear . . . Brethren, the work of Mahatma Gandhi is now the work of the whole country . . . Each one of the 33 crores [of Indians] is now a Gandhi.[8]

These joint tours of Hindu and Muslim leaders caused some discomfort among the authorities. There can 'be no doubt', wrote a senior official of the Madras Presidency, 'that both Gandhi and the Ali Brothers create tremendous temporary enthusiasm and attract enormous crowds wherever they go'. Some came out of mere curiosity, 'but a large number, and especially women, seem to be inspired with feelings of real adoration for the Mahatma and many thousand rupees worth of jewels were collected at his meetings'.[9]

For all their mutual affection, the Ali Brothers did not share Gandhi's principled commitment to ahimsa, or non-violence. This extract from a speech made by Mohammad Ali in the town of Fyzabad in February 1921 is illustrative:

> The Mussalmans wanted to seek the alliance of Gandhiji in the work of the Khilafat but I told them that we could not make him our ally as he wanted to banish from our hearts all thought of using the sword. I declared that God has given me the right to use the sword against any adversary when I had the power to do so and that no one could then stop me. This is our creed. But now we know and we see that our country does not possess that power and so long as we do not have that power we will be his (Gandhiji's) associates . . . [W]e are, therefore, standing today on the same platform—he for reasons of principle and we for those of policy.[10]

The adherence of the Ali Brothers to non-violence was purely tactical. In a speech in the Gujarati town of Broach, Mohammad Ali said that while for the present they would keep the sword in its sheath, 'we must reserve the right to take up arms against the enemies of Islam'.[11]

In response to the British refusal to restore the Khilafat, some Muslims had migrated to Afghanistan. They were following an ancient practice known as *hijrat*, sanctioned by the Prophet himself, whereby one left a state that refused to honour Islam for a state that upheld the principles of the faith.[12] Afghanistan was an independent Islamic state, whose amir did not have the best relations with the Raj. Speaking in Madras in April 1921, Mohammad Ali said if the amir of Afghanistan invaded India to overthrow the British, it was the duty of Indian Muslims to support him.[13]

This was an extremely provocative statement, for only two years previously, the British and the Afghans had fought a bloody war, with thousands of casualties on both sides. Gandhi was unhappy with Mohammad Ali seeming to favour the amir. The British were absolutely livid. In May, Gandhi was in Simla, the summer capital of the Raj, when Madan Mohan Malaviya suggested that he meet the new viceroy, Lord Reading. Gandhi, with his long-standing belief in dialogue, agreed. Reading was new to India; this was the time to press upon him the demands of the Indians.

In the third week of May, Gandhi had several meetings with the viceroy. Afterwards, Lord Reading wrote to his son: 'There is no hesitation about him, there is a ring of sincerity in all he utters, save when discussing some political questions. . . . [H]e is convinced to a point almost bordering on fanaticism, that non-violence and love will give India its independence . . .'[14]

One of the subjects Gandhi and Reading discussed was the language of the Ali Brothers. The viceroy's advisers told him that in their speeches the brothers had offered incitements to violence, and were thus liable to prosecution and arrest. When this was put to Gandhi, he said he would get the brothers to commit themselves to his own creed of non-violence. He hoped that would persuade the viceroy to stay their arrest.

On Gandhi's suggestion, the Ali Brothers issued a statement clarifying that they did not intend prescribing violence as a means of bringing about political change. This led to a certain amount of gloating in government circles, and on the other side, anger against Gandhi among some Muslims. His friend Abdul Bari wrote him a letter saying that by making the Ali Brothers 'apologize for fictitious violence', he had humiliated them in the eyes of the community and lowered the prestige of the movement itself.[15]

IV

While mobilizing popular support, Gandhi also set about collecting money for his movement. The Congress had started a 'Tilak Swaraj Fund', for which Gandhi had set a target of Rs 1 crore (equivalent to 10 million, or 100 lakh). Each province had been assigned a target of its own.

Gandhi first focused on Kathiawar, the part of Gujarat where he had himself been born and raised. 'Kathiawaris claim me as one of themselves,' he wrote. 'Their love for me will now be tested. If, despite their love for me, I fail in convincing them, how can I ever hope to win over other Indians?'[16]

The Kathiawaris contributed Rs 2 lakh to the Tilak Fund, four times the target specified for them. The British-ruled areas of Gujarat responded even more energetically to Gandhi's call. The state contributed more than Rs 13 lakh, almost half coming from Ahmedabad alone.[17]

Gandhi next trained his eye on the city of Bombay, whose Gujarati merchants belonged to three distinct religions: Hinduism, Islam and Zoroastrianism. While Gujarati Hindus and Gujarati Muslims had long supported Gandhi, the Parsis were mostly Empire loyalists. In an open letter 'To the Parsis', Gandhi recalled the 'sacred ties' that bound him to them, such as the mentorship of Dadabhai Naoroji and the support given to his movement in South Africa by the Parsis.[18] Some Parsis were persuaded by his appeal. One, from the famous Godrej family that manufactured safes and almirahs, donated Rs 3 lakh to the Tilak fund, by far the largest single contribution. 'Mr. Godrej's generosity,' remarked Gandhi, 'puts the Parsis easily first in India.' Meanwhile, his friend Parsi Rustomji had sent Rs 52,000 from South Africa.[19]

Gandhi appealed for funds through print, and in person. He spent almost a month in Bombay, going from one locality to the next, gathering notes, coins, cheques and jewels. On 26 June 1921, some 20,000 people gathered in a merchant's godown in central Bombay, to present a purse to Gandhi. As one eyewitness reported, 'The heat was oppressive and owing to the over-crowding the audience endured much discomfort. Many of them unable to bear it any longer left the place before Gandhi arrived, but dropped their contributions into the collecting boxes as they left. Gandhi, however, stuck it out to the end, intent only on the collection of as large a sum as possible.'

Gandhi collected nearly Rs 5 lakh in this one meeting. These included small donations by individuals as well as larger contributions by guilds or trade bodies.

Other days in Bombay were even more successful. In C.B. Dalal's chronology of Gandhi's Indian years, the entry for 30 June 1921 reads: 'Bombay: Visited, accepted purses from, and addressed various institutions and organizations'.

From the intelligence reports of the Bombay government, we can flesh out the day in greater and richer detail. Gandhi's first meeting was at the northern suburb of Borivili. Collecting Rs 45,000 from its residents, he then traced his way back to the city. At 1 p.m. he visited the Mangaldas Cloth Market in the company of the Ali Brothers and Sarojini Naidu, collecting upward of Rs 35,000. He then attended a meeting of Lohanas at Mandvi, around three thousand-strong, some eight hundred women among them. This Gujarati merchant caste had raised Rs 1,10,000 for their compatriot. The Lohanas were advised by Gandhi 'to use *Swadeshi* clothes, to give national education to their children and to take up national work'.

Gandhi's next stop was Grant Road, where, at 3.30 p.m., he met the jewellers of Bombay. A group collection of Rs 10,000 was offered to him, after which a jeweller named Gulab Devchand handed over the impressive sum of Rs 2,32,000, 'together with an address which was written out on a khadi handkerchief and contained a prayer that God would help Gandhi in reaching the goal of *Swaraj* to which they all aspired'. Gandhi's merchant friend Revashankar Jagjivan gave him Rs 25,000, while a further Rs 60,000 'were collected from small associations and bodies, including the Grass Merchants, Plumbers, etc. . . .'

At 5 p.m., the indefatigable Gandhi was in the posh locality of Colaba. Here, after the Colaba cotton merchants had presented him a purse of Rs 1,54,000, 'two bales of cotton were also put up for auction; the one on which Gandhi was sitting went for Rs 6,100; the other, not so pleasantly favoured, only fetched Rs 2,500'.

Gandhi's next meeting was with the Parsis, at a place well suited for a community which pioneered modern Indian drama—the Excelsior Theatre. 'The leaders of Parsi Society were conspicuous by their absence'; but sections of the Parsi middle class were present, among them the prominent lawyer K.F. Nariman. A purse of Rs 30,000 was handed over, after which 'Gandhi and the various Parsi speakers flattered each other on their many noble qualities and achievements, and Gandhi suggested that the Parsi ladies should come out and assist the volunteers on picketing duty'.

Gandhi then seems to have been taken by his minders for supper. The next meeting, the last for the day, started at 9.30 p.m. It was organized by the Mandvi District Congress Committee. Admission was by tickets priced at Re 1 and Rs 2. Some 10,000 people were present, and 'the usual speeches advising the use of *Swadeshi* cloth instead of foreign and the adoption of the *Charkha* were made by Gandhi, the Ali Brothers and Mrs. Naidu'. About a lakh of rupees was collected along with a few items of jewellery.

It had been an exhausting day for Gandhi, but also a productive one. The police mole following him around from meeting to meeting surely shared his weariness, but perhaps not his satisfaction.[20]

V

All through 1921, members of the Congress acted on the principles of non-cooperation. Some returned medals or honours bestowed upon them by the colonial government. Teachers in government schools stayed away from work. So did many students in government colleges. Members of provincial legislative councils resigned. So did those who served on university senates or town municipalities.

A file in the papers of the AICC contains a register, ninety-five pages long, with names of individuals in different provinces who, in various ways, sought not to cooperate with the government. Thus 'the three Desai brothers of Hubli resigned [from] the membership of the Taluka Local Board'. The chief imam of Madras, Maulvi Shah Zahid Hussain Khadri, returned the title of Shamsul Ulama that the viceroy had accorded him. The students of the Sanatana Dharma Sabha High School in Amritsar went on strike until it stopped receiving government funds and became a certifiably 'national' school. So did the students of the Islamia High School, Etawah.[21]

Withdrawing association with the government was one canon of the non-cooperation creed. The boycott of foreign cloth was another. Back in 1919, Gandhi had urged that patriots wear Indian clothes. At the same time, he had explicitly ruled out the burning of foreign cloth on the grounds that it would promote ill will against Europeans. But now, pressed by the militants in his ranks, he sanctioned a practice he had previously opposed. The precedent that was invoked was the swadeshi movement of 1905–07, where foreign goods had often been burnt in public meetings.

On 31 July, Gandhi himself inaugurated a nationwide campaign, lighting a bonfire of foreign cloth in Bombay, his act accompanied by shouts and cheers. The crowd was huge: 'overflowing with men and women dressing handsomely in white khadi caps and khadi clothes, [it] gave one the impression that the entire population of Bombay had assembled there'.

Gandhi told the gathering that 'we are purifying ourselves by discarding foreign cloth which is the badge of our slavery'. After the meeting, the crowd—men, women and children—went to Chowpatti to pay homage to Bal Gangadhar Tilak, who had been cremated on that spot a year previously.[22]

In Bombay and elsewhere, women were particularly active in picketing liquor shops. The temperance campaign, in which Gandhi took a special interest, led to a dramatic fall in the consumption of alcohol and in state revenue from its sale. As a government report mournfully noted, in the financial year 1921–22 the excise revenue of Punjab fell by 33 lakh rupees, of Bihar and Orissa by 10 lakh rupees and of Bombay by 6 lakh rupees.[23]

These activities were all, so to say, 'authorized' by the Congress and in conformity with its creed. But the name and appeal of Gandhi also inspired acts that he and his party would have regarded as transgressive or even wrong. Peasants in the Indo-Gangetic plains refused to pay taxes, saying 'Gandhi Maharaj' had told them not to do so. They also travelled ticketless on trains, invoking the same authority. Peasants in the Himalaya broke forest laws and refused to carry the luggage of officials, again using Gandhi's name. Disenchanted workers in factories were emboldened by the non-cooperation campaign to go on strike.[24]

VI

Two among Gandhi's close friends were not entirely sympathetic with his movement. C.F. Andrews wrote that he was 'supremely happy' when Gandhi took on evils like drink, drugs and race arrogance. 'But lighting bonfires of foreign cloth and telling people it is a religious *sin* to wear it, destroying in the fire the noble handiwork of one's fellow-men and women, one's brothers and sisters abroad, saying it would be "defiling" to wear it, I cannot tell you how different all this appears to me.'

Gandhi defended his position. 'If the emphasis were on all foreign things,' he told Andrews, 'it would be racial, parochial and wicked. The emphasis is on all foreign cloth. The restriction makes all the difference in the world.' Gandhi did not want to shut out such exquisite handcrafted items as European watches or Japanese lacquerwork. But 'love of foreign cloth has brought foreign domination, pauperism and what is worst, shame to many a home'. Gandhi believed that importing foreign cloth had not only put many weavers out of work, but forced the women in their families into prostitution.[25]

Joining Andrews in his disenchantment with Gandhi's methods was their mutual friend Rabindranath Tagore. Tagore was travelling in North America in 1921, raising funds for his university, when a recent article by Gandhi was brought to his attention. Entitled 'Evil Wrought by the English Medium', it claimed that 'Rammohun Roy would have been a greater reformer, and Lokmanya Tilak would have been a greater scholar, if they had not to start with the handicap of having to think in English and transmit their thoughts chiefly in English'. Gandhi argued that 'of all the superstitions that affect India, none is so great as that a knowledge of the English language is necessary for imbibing ideas of liberty, and developing accuracy of thought'. As a result of the system of education introduced by the English, 'the tendency has been to dwarf the Indian body, mind and soul'.[26]

Tagore was dismayed by the article, and wrote to C.F. Andrews that 'I strongly protest against Mahatma Gandhi's trying to cut down such great personalities of Modern India as Rammohan Roy in his blind zeal for crying down our modern education'. These criticisms, added Tagore tellingly, showed that Gandhi 'is growing enamoured of his own doctrines—a dangerous form of egotism, that even great people suffer from at times'.

The Mahatma believed that the nineteenth-century reformer Rammohan Roy was limited by his familiarity with English. To the contrary, Tagore argued that through his engagement with other languages, Roy 'could be perfectly natural in his acceptance of the West, not only because his education had been perfectly Eastern,—he had the full inheritance of the Indian wisdom. He was never a school boy of the West, and therefore he had the dignity to be the friend of the West.'[27]

Andrews shared the letter with the press. The criticisms stung Gandhi, who immediately published a clarification in his journal, *Young India*. He pointed to his own friendship with white men (Andrews among them), and the hospitality granted to Englishmen by many non-cooperators. Neither he nor his flock were guilty of chauvinism or xenophobia. His defence was then summed up in these words: 'I hope I am as great a believer in free air as the great Poet. I do not want my house to be walled in on all sides and my windows to be stuffed. I want the cultures of all the lands to be blown about my house as freely as possible. But I refuse to be blown off my feet by any.'[28]

In July 1921, Tagore returned home from his travels. To his dismay, many members of the staff at Santiniketan had enthusiastically embraced the non-cooperation movement, thus giving themselves up to 'narrow nationalist ideas that were already out of date'.

In the first week of September, Gandhi met Tagore at his family home in Calcutta. They had a long and argumentative conversation. Tagore told Gandhi that 'the whole world is suffering today from the cult of a selfish and short-sighted nationalism. India has all down her history offered hospitality to the invader of whatever nation, creed or colour. I have come to believe that, as Indians, we not only have much to learn from the West but that we also have something to contribute. We dare not therefore shut the West out.'[29]

Gandhi's answer is not recorded. But apparently, Tagore was not satisfied, since he chose to make his criticisms public in the influential Calcutta journal *Modern Review*. In his recent travels in the West, said Tagore, he had met many people who sought 'to achieve the unity of man, by destroying the bondage of nationalism'. Then he returned home, to be confronted with a political movement suffused with negativity. Are 'we alone to be content with telling the beads of negation', asked Tagore, 'harping on other's faults and proceeding with the erection of Swaraj on a foundation of quarrelsomeness'?[30]

Gandhi responded immediately, defending the non-cooperation movement as 'a refusal to co-operate with the English administrators on their own terms'. Indian nationalism, he insisted, 'is not exclusive, nor aggressive, nor destructive. It is health-giving, religious and therefore humanitarian. India must learn to live before she can aspire to die for humanity. The mice which helplessly find themselves between the cat's teeth acquire no merit from their enforced sacrifice.'[31]

Tagore's own elder brother was on Gandhi's side in this debate. Himself a poet and composer of distinction, Dwijendranath Tagore was a much-loved figure in Bengal, universally known as 'Bordada' (elder brother). In September 1920, he had sent *Young India* an article on the 'inner meaning' of non-cooperation. This argued that 'in this extreme crisis of our country, it is incumbent upon the wisest in the land to stand apart from the blood-sucking influence of the authorities, and with their own exertions and in their own ways to give a full expression to their own ideal'.[32]

A year later, when his brother was publicly rebuking the Mahatma, Dwijendranath sent Gandhi a short but telling private note:

Dearest and most revered Mahatma,

Robi[ndranath] is taking a wrong course. He is creating an atmosphere of mirth & music around him while India is travailing to give birth to her new child 'Swaraj'.

He is unnecessarily pouring water on the widespread branches of Universal brotherhood leaving its root to wither for want of water. Poor kindhearted Mr Andrews is in danger of being perverted from his course.

To tell you the truth I am sick at heart. You are my only pole star of hope. May God shower blessing on your head day and night.

Your unworthy Bordada
Dwijendranath Tagore[33]

Another celebrated Bengali who favoured Gandhi over Tagore was the scientist-entrepreneur Prafulla Chandra Ray. Ray called Gandhi 'a veritable miracle worker—the saviour of modern and builder of future India'. Then he added: 'There are occasions when silence is golden and speech is but silver. I think Rabindranath would have best consulted the interests of the country if he had followed this precept.'[34]

Dwijendranath Tagore was a full twenty years older than his brother. At the age of eighty, he surely hoped to see swaraj come before he was gone. P.C. Ray had faced much opposition from British entrepreneurs and British officials in starting his own factories. That the two supported Gandhi so wholeheartedly was proof of their nationalism, and of the Mahatma's own power to move and to inspire. Their consent, however, perhaps makes Tagore's dissent all the more noteworthy.

A hundred years on, the Tagore–Gandhi debate still makes for compelling reading. The Mahatma insisted that a colonized nation had first to discover itself before discovering the world. The poet answered that there was a thin line between nationalism and xenophobia—besides, hatred of the foreigner could easily turn into a hatred of Indians of other castes, classes or communities. He was particularly sceptical of the claim that non-cooperation had or would dissolve Hindu–Muslim differences.

VII

In a bid to curb the non-cooperation movement, the government sought to control the press. The first step was to disallow nationalist periodicals from carrying government advertisements. A list of 'newspapers unsuitable to receive official advertisements and for perusal by Indian troops' was prepared. More than 300 periodicals were included in this list, including Gandhi's own *Young India* and *Navajivan*, the *Bombay Chronicle*, as well as journals in Urdu, Hindi, Tamil, Telugu, Marathi, Bengali and other Indian languages.[35]

Despite the ban, these newspapers survived. And the nationalist message was conveyed as much by word of mouth as through print. So the government decided to arrest the non-cooperators. From July 1921, thousands of protesters were booked under various sections of the Indian Penal Code. These included Section 121 (waging, or attempting to wage war, or abetting waging of war, against the Government of India), Section 124 (assaulting government officials or otherwise seeking to restrain the exercise of any lawful power), Section 124A (the preaching or practice of sedition), Section 131 (abetting mutiny, or attempting to seduce a soldier, sailor or airman from his duty), Section 150 (hiring, or conniving at hiring, of persons to join an unlawful assembly), Section 151 (knowingly joining or continuing in an assembly of five or more persons after it had been commanded to disperse), Sections 153 and 153A (promoting enmity between different groups on grounds of religion, race, place of birth, residence, language, etc.), and Section 447 (criminal trespass).

In late August, seeking to spread the message of swadeshi and non-cooperation, Gandhi visited Assam for the first time, and then went from there by train to Chittagong and eastern Bengal. With him was Mohammad Ali. They spoke together at many public meetings, some held in parks, others in mosques.

The eastern tour ended in Calcutta in the second week of September. Here, shops that still stocked goods from abroad were picketed daily by energetic nationalists led by Maulana Abul Kalam Azad. Gandhi, with Azad next to him, participated in several bonfires of foreign cloth.

While he was in Calcutta, Gandhi got a letter from Shaukat Ali saying he had heard from friends that he and his brother would soon he arrested. On 21 October, the Central Khilafat Committee planned to meet in Delhi. 'I doubt we will be allowed to attend . . .' wrote Shaukat. Yet he was 'sure our arrest would advance our sacred cause and we have no fear for the future'. Sending 'his love and devoted affection', the elder of the Ali Brothers placed his total trust in his Hindu friend. 'You need no certificate from any of us,' he remarked, 'but I must press my honest conviction that there could be no more considerate, insightful and patient chief to lead us than you whom India loves and respects.'[36]

From Calcutta, Gandhi and Mohammad Ali took a train down the Coromandel coast. On 14 September, they halted at Waltair for a public meeting. Here (as they had anticipated), Mohammad Ali was arrested and taken away by the police. Shaukat Ali, then in North India, was arrested shortly afterwards.

While incarcerating the Ali Brothers, the government stayed their hand as regards Gandhi. In this they were following the advice of the Allahabad Moderate Tej Bahadur Sapru, then law member of the viceroy's executive council. Sapru argued that the arrest could wait till 'Mr. Gandhi by some overt act will place himself so much in the wrong that we should be doing the right thing in prosecuting him, or we may reach a stage when a considerable body of opinion will have detached itself from Mr. Gandhi and the situation will then have become easier'.[37]

After his companion was detained, Gandhi addressed a meeting in Waltair, before carrying on to Madras and further south. In the town of Madurai he took a decision to simplify his dress even further. He would now discard the shirt, and wear a loincloth only.

The idea had been in Gandhi's mind for some time. He first thought of it in Barisal in Bengal. He finally took the step only in Madurai, when people told him that they had not enough khadi or where khadi was available, not enough money. When he communicated his decision to his co-workers, Maulana Azad understood immediately, but the others, including C. Rajagopalachari, were unhappy. 'They felt such radical change might make people uneasy, some might not understand it; some might take me to be a lunatic . . .' Typically, the opposition made Gandhi even more resolute in his decision.[38]

VIII

Gandhi had hoped to go on to Malabar, the Malayalam-speaking district of the Madras Presidency. He was stopped from doing so, because a major rebellion had broken out in the district, and martial law had been declared. In the agrarian system of Malabar, the tenants were predominantly Muslim (belonging to a community known as the Moplahs), and the landlords largely Hindu. The Moplahs were a militant lot, who had rebelled several times in the nineteenth century. The present uprising was partly a class war of tenants versus landlords, and partly a religious war, of Muslims versus Hindus.

From September 1921, armed bands of Moplahs began attacking the homes of landlords, torching government offices and police stations, tearing up railway tracks and telegraph lines, and, occasionally, abducting women. Hindus captured by the rebels were offered the choice of Islam or death.

The ranks of the rebels were populated by coolies, cultivators, keepers of tea shops, petty merchants, Koran readers and mosque attendants. At its height, there were nearly 10,000 armed Moplahs on the move. Two brigades of infantry and 700 special police were needed to suppress the rebellion. More than 2000 Moplahs were killed in the exchanges, as well as some fifty soldiers and policemen.[39]

The Moplah rebellion raised a large question mark over the future of Gandhi's movement. The uprising was not non-violent, and it had ruptured rather than furthered Hindu–Muslim unity. As the district magistrate of Malabar noted, among the rebels 'the talk of Hindu–Muslim unity was nonsense and the main idea was the vision of *swaraj* and Malabar for the Mapilla and the Mapilla alone'.[40]

Gandhi accepted that the Moplah rebellion was a setback to his struggle. But he did not despair, 'for the simple reason that no sane Muslim approves of what a few Moplahs have done'. Later, at a public meeting on the Marina beach, Gandhi said the Moplahs 'have committed a sin against the Khilafat and against their own country'. Yet he hoped 'that my Hindu countrymen will keep their senses', since he did 'not know a single sensible Mussulman who approves either secretly or openly of these forcible conversions . . .'[41]

In an article for *Navajivan*, Gandhi admitted that his recent tour of Madras 'was something of a disappointment'. The province lagged behind in the production of khadi, the 'untouchables' suffered 'more indignities than they do in almost any other part of the country', and the Moplah rebellion had undermined his cherished dream of Hindu–Muslim unity. Gandhi was consoled by his growing friendship with C. Rajagopalachari, who accompanied him for much of his tour. Praising Rajaji's 'wisdom, integrity and ability', Gandhi noted that his Tamil colleague had 'fully understood the meaning of our struggle and, in a moment of crisis, he can be resolute and patient'.[42]

IX

Gandhi spent October shuttling between Ahmedabad and Bombay, attending to his ashram in the one place and pursuing the non-cooperation agenda in the other. He had taken a vow to spin half an hour every day before lunch, and forgo the meal if he failed to do so. The vow was not binding when he was on a train.[43]

For most of 1921, Mahadev Desai was away in Allahabad, where he was assisting Motilal Nehru in running a new nationalist paper called *The Independent*. In his absence, a new recruit named Pyarelal was acting as Gandhi's secretary. From the Punjab, he had freshly graduated with a degree in English literature. One of Pyarelal's assets was an excellent memory; he had made it his business to learn entire passages from Gandhi's writings and speeches.

The Prince of Wales was due to tour India that winter. Gandhi asked the public to boycott the visit, since it was a 'crime' to bring the prince over 'for personal pleasure and sport when India is seething with discontent'. The ship carrying the prince landed in Bombay on 17 November; on Gandhi's instructions, at the very hour the heir to the English throne was disembarking, a massive bonfire of foreign cloth was lit in central Bombay.[44]

While Gandhi called for a boycott, Indians loyal to the Raj enthusiastically welcomed the visitor. This led to clashes in the streets, between the non-cooperators burning cloth and the Empire loyalists chanting slogans in praise of the prince. The conflict revealed and built upon cleavages of religion, class and political affiliation. Parsis and Christians (identified by their headgear or clothing) were singled out for attack by Hindus and Muslims, presumably because they were seen as pro-British (and were also relatively prosperous). Millworkers were prominent among the rioters, who from time to time raised the cry of 'Mahatma Gandhi ki jai'.

Gandhi was appalled by the violence. The day after the riot, he composed a long essay for *Young India*. He heard of the trouble at 1 p.m., and at once motored to the Two Tanks area, where he

> found a liquor shop smashed, two policemen badly wounded and lying unconscious on cots without anybody caring for them. I alighted. Immediately the crowd surrounded me and yelled *Mahatma Gandhi ki jai*. That sound usually grates on my ears, but it has grated never so much as it did yesterday when the crowd unmindful of the two sick brethren choked me with the shout at the top of their voices. I rebuked them and they were silent. Water was brought for the two wounded men. I requested two of my companions and some from the crowd to take the dying policemen to the hospital. I proceeded then to the scene a little further up where I saw a fire rising. They were two tram-cars which were burnt by the crowd. On returning I witnessed a burning motor car. I appealed to the crowd to disperse, told them that they had damaged the cause of the Khilafat, the Punjab and swaraj. I returned sick at heart and in a chastened mood.

After the events in Bombay, wrote Gandhi, 'the hope of reviving mass civil disobedience has once more in my opinion been dashed to pieces. . . . If I can have nothing to do with the organized violence of the Government, I can have less to do with the unorganized violence of the people.'

Gandhi went on a fast from 19 November, breaking it four days later when the violence had subsided. As he wrote in *Young India*, 'for me fast was a necessity. I was the guilty party. I was the bankrupt.'[45]

The violence in Bombay provoked a series of sombre articles by Gandhi in *Young India*. Non-cooperators, he said, must now 'retrace our steps and scrupulously insure minorities against the least molestation'. For, if they could not tolerate Parsis and Christians, what was the guarantee that 'Hindus . . . would not impose their will upon the Mussulman minority, or the Mussulmans, if they believed themselves to be capable of wielding superior brute strength, would not crush the weak Hindu in spite of his numerical superiority?'[46]

X

From November 1921, the government renewed its crackdown on the non-cooperators. Arrests were made of people picketing liquor shops, holding meetings, selling prohibited literature, etc. By the middle of December, 1500 protesters had been arrested in Bengal alone, and several hundred apiece in Madras, UP, Bombay and Sindh. Among those in jail was Harilal Gandhi, arrested in Calcutta.

The police now began to target the senior leadership. In early December, C.R. Das, president-elect of the Congress to be held in Ahmedabad later that month, was arrested in Calcutta. A group of women, who included C.R. Das's wife and sister, were also detained for selling khadi on the road (they were charged with blocking traffic, and thus became the first women arrested in the movement).

On 6 December, Abul Kalam Azad wrote to Gandhi that 'the repression in Calcutta is much more severe than what we heard while at Bombay. The Government is determined to strike at the very root and crush the movement.' Azad himself was planning 'to organise a successful "HARTAL" on the 24th and to maintain Peace and Order which the Government wishes otherwise'.[47] A week in advance of the hartal he hoped to organize, Azad was taken into custody by the police. J.B. Kripalani was arrested in Banaras; Motilal Nehru and Mahadev Desai in Allahabad; and C. Rajagopalachari in Madras.

Many Congress leaders were now in jail. It was now more than twelve months since Gandhi had promised 'swaraj in one year'. Despite the struggle and the sacrifice, political freedom seemed as distant as ever. Gandhi wrote that he was 'being implored, on the one hand, not to carry out my threat to retire to the Himalayas if we do not get swaraj by the end of this year. On the other hand, I am asked what face I shall show to the people if we fail to get swaraj.'

Gandhi now provided himself with an escape route, writing that 'swaraj means self-reliance. To hope that I shall get swaraj for them is the opposite of self-reliance.' The Hindu/Muslim vs Parsi/Christian riots had 'put an obstacle in our path. We ourselves had planned to start a fight and invite suffering upon ourselves; Bombay made this impossible.'[48]

The next Congress was to be held in Ahmedabad in December 1921. On the eve of the Congress, Gandhi reminded the readers of *Young India* of the four key elements of the nationalist credo: unity between Hindus and Muslims and all other faiths; manufacture and use of handmade cloth; abolition of untouchability; and a strict adherence to non-violence. 'These are like the four posts of a bedstead,' he wrote. 'Remove one of them and it cannot stand.'[49]

Some 4700 delegates attended the Congress, coming from all the provinces of British India. There were vigorous debates, the most important of which was between the prominent cleric Maulana Hasrat Mohani and Gandhi. Mohani claimed that the Muslims had contributed disproportionately to the struggle—according to one (probably embroidered) report, he said that while Hindus outnumbered Muslims four to one among the general population, 95 per cent of those who went to jail were Muslim. Gandhi disputed these figures, saying the Hindus had courted arrest in large numbers too.[50]

Maulana Mohani asked for the removal, in the Congress's main resolution, of all clauses making non-violence mandatory. He also wanted a complete severance of the British connection. Gandhi, speaking for the resolution (which eventually passed with a large majority), said that while within the Congress there could be differences on whether swaraj should come within the British Empire or outside it, 'there could be no room for those who wanted to resort to violence'.

In his home town, Gandhi was in command. As a news report on the Congress commented, when he reached 'the rostrum in his usual loin-cloth, there was an enthusiastically devotional and deafening applause'.[51]

XI

A year had come and gone, and the swaraj that Gandhi had promised in this time was as distant as ever. So he now began preparing for a fresh round of civil disobedience. This would begin in the taluks of Bardoli and Anand, in his native Gujarat, and where his lieutenant of peasant background, Vallabhbhai Patel, had great influence. Peasants were to be asked to stop paying taxes and refuse all cooperation with the government. Gandhi hoped that if the experiment in Gujarat succeeded, it could be replicated elsewhere in India.[52]

The Bombay government was now very keen to arrest Gandhi. The governor wrote to the viceroy that since Gandhi was preparing to 'completely throw off [his] disguise' and launch 'a general attack on Government', it was dangerous to wait any longer. He submitted a list of articles written by Gandhi in *Young India* which clearly counted as 'seditious'. The viceroy consulted his senior officials, who counselled caution. Action against Gandhi would alienate even the Moderates. As the home secretary of the Government of India put it,

> In the fight for position the tactical advantage has already to a very undesirable extent passed to Gandhi and his arrest and prosecution at the present juncture would seriously increase that advantage . . . [T]he arrest of Gandhi at the present moment so far from lessening our difficulties, would add to them considerably.[53]

On 26 January Gandhi left his ashram at Ahmedabad, telling the inmates that he was going to Bardoli for the preparation of civil disobedience and the non-payment of taxes. He added: 'I shall be back here in a week, maybe a month, or a year, or perhaps I may not return here at all.'[54]

Gandhi was then called away to Bombay, where the Moderates, led by Jinnah, urged him to abandon his planned satyagraha in Bardoli and wait for the government to convene a round table conference. Gandhi was unpersuaded, and carried on to Bardoli, reaching there on 29 January. He toured the villages, giving speeches urging Hindu–Muslim unity and the abolition of untouchability, and asking peasants to stop paying land revenue and other government taxes.[55]

On 1 February, Gandhi wrote to the viceroy, informing him that Bardoli, a taluk in the Surat district with a population of 87,000, had been made 'the first unit for mass civil disobedience in order to mark the national revolt against the Government for its consistently criminal refusal to appreciate India's resolve regarding the [restoration of the] Khilafat, [justice for the victims of] the Punjab [atrocities] and [the attainment of] swaraj'. Characteristically, he left a window open, 'respectfully' asking the viceroy to set free all political prisoners, declare 'a policy of absolute non-interference with all non-violent activities in the country' with regard to Khilafat, swaraj, etc., and 'free the Press from all administrative control'. If the viceroy could make a declaration assuring this within the next week, said Gandhi, then the 'aggressive civil disobedience' planned for Bardoli and elsewhere would be suspended.[56]

On 6 February, the government issued a 'communiqué' in response to Gandhi's letter. As a consequence of the non-cooperation movement, said the government, 'the issue is no longer between this or that programme of political advance but between lawlessness with all its dangerous consequences on the one hand, and on the other, the maintenance of those principles which lie at the root of all civilized governments. Mass civil disobedience is fraught with such dangers to the State that it must be met with sternness and severity.'[57]

The next day Gandhi replied to the communiqué, accusing the government of 'official lawlessness and barbarism', through the repression of peaceful protests and the victimization of innocent individuals. The letter ended with this sharp sentence: 'I hold that it is impossible for any body of self-respecting men, for fear of unknown dangers, to sit still and do nothing effective while looting of property and assaulting of innocent men are going on all over the country in the name of law and order.'[58]

Two days earlier, a police station in an obscure hamlet in the Gorakhpur district of the United Provinces had been burnt by nationalist protesters. The hamlet was named Chauri Chaura. On 4 February, a large crowd of volunteers marched through the streets, shouting slogans in praise of Gandhi and the Khilafat. They clashed with the police—sticks and stones versus bullets. The constables had the advantage of modern arms, but were massively outnumbered.

When the crowd grew larger and the hail of rocks grew fiercer, they retreated into the police station. The protesters doused the building with kerosene and set it on fire. Twenty-three policemen perished in the conflagration.[59]

News of the arson at Chauri Chaura took two days to travel from rural North India to rural Gujarat. Gandhi got the news after he had sent his second letter to the viceroy on the 7th. On the next day, the 8th, he wrote to the members of the CWC. This was the third time he had 'received a rude shock' on the eve of embarking on mass civil disobedience. The first occasion was in April 1919, when his fellow Ahmedabadis rioted after he had been stopped from entering the Punjab. The second was in November 1921, the violence in Bombay ensuing from the boycott of the Prince of Wales's visit. Now again, he had been 'violently agitated' by the events in Chauri Chaura. He had convened a CWC meeting at Bardoli on the 11th, to discuss whether mass civil disobedience should be suspended for the time being.[60]

On 10 February—the day before the CWC met—Gandhi spoke with a group of Congress workers in Bardoli. He asked whether civil disobedience should be suspended in view of 'the terrible happening at Chauri Chaura'. All but three said the movement should go on, for after Gandhi's challenge to the viceroy if he (and they) now retreated, 'the whole country would be disgraced before the world'. Gandhi was dismayed by the response, which showed that even the 'best workers' of the Congress had 'failed to understand the message of non-violence'. He was now resolved to 'immediately stop the movement for civil disobedience'.[61]

The CWC, meeting the next day, passed a series of resolutions drafted by Gandhi. In view of 'the tragic and terrible events at Chauri Chaura', the Congress had decided to suspend civil disobedience, advise cultivators to pay land revenue, and not hold processions or public meetings. The working committee outlined a new programme for the Congress, focusing on the promotion of spinning and of temperance, the abolition of untouchability, and the organization of village and town panchayats to settle disputes peaceably.[62]

To atone for the violence at Chauri Chaura, Gandhi went on a five-day fast. 'Surely I could not have done less, could I?' he wrote to his son Devadas. For, 'to start civil disobedience in an atmosphere of incivility is like putting one's hand in a snake-pit'.[63]

Gandhi's decision to call off the struggle divided the Congress leadership. While older Congressmen such as M.A. Ansari supported him, younger radicals like Jawaharlal Nehru were 'terribly cut up'.[64] Why should the leader allow one isolated episode to derail a vigorous mass upsurge that had otherwise eschewed violence? Tens of thousands had already courted arrest. Tens of thousands more were ready to follow them. The whole country was afire with the spirit of swaraj. The British Raj was nervous—as its policies of repression showed. Why, when energy and enthusiasm ran so high, did the leader abandon the movement?

Gandhi was unmoved. He had been told that the policemen at Chauri Chaura had 'given much provocation'. But 'no provocation can possibly justify the brutal murder of men who had been rendered defenceless and who had virtually thrown themselves on the mercy of the mob'. After what had happened in Chauri Chaura, Gandhi 'would think 50 times before embarking upon mass civil disobedience'.[65]

XII

By early February 1922, the viceroy could hold out no longer. On the 8th of the month, he passed an order asking 'that action should be taken at once for the immediate arrest and prosecution of Gandhi'. But before the order could be acted upon, the CWC had called off civil disobedience. The home secretary now advised the viceroy to stay the arrest. On 15 February, Lord Reading issued a fresh order asking that 'the prosecution of Gandhi be postponed for the moment'. Ten days later, the AICC met in Delhi and endorsed the CWC's resolutions in Bardoli, adding a caveat that civil disobedience had been postponed temporarily, not indefinitely. This persuaded the government that there had been 'no fundamental change in the policy of the non-co-operation party'. Fresh orders were now issued for Gandhi's arrest.[66]

The Bombay government had decided to arrest Gandhi on 9 March. The previous day, Gandhi left Ahmedabad for a meeting of nationalist ulemas in Ajmer. The authorities waited until he had returned. On the evening of 10 March, the deputy superintendent of police (DSP) of Ahmedabad drove in his car to the Sabarmati Ashram. On his way he saw Shankarlal Banker and Anasuya Sarabhai out on a postprandial walk. The DSP told Banker he had a warrant for his arrest and for Gandhi's.

Banker's crime was that he was the publisher of *Young India*, and thus complicit in Gandhi's 'seditious' articles. The DSP reported that on hearing the news, Banker 'seemed very pleased and said he was expecting it'. Anasuya was told to ask Gandhi to get his things ready. When the police officer arrived, Gandhi congratulated him on coming without an escort. He asked the ashramites to sing his favourite Narasinha Mehta hymn, '*Vaishnava Jana To*'. His parting words were that they should 'strain every nerve to propagate peace and goodwill all over India, among all communities'.[67]

The DSP took Gandhi, Kasturba, Shankarlal and Anasuya to the jail in his car. He woke up the prison superintendent (it was now past 11 p.m.), and handed over the two men to him, before dropping the two ladies back at the ashram. He then went to the Navajivan Press to obtain documentary proof of Gandhi's and Shankarlal's connection with *Young India*.[68]

The ashram at Sabarmati had been chosen in part because of its proximity to the Sabarmati jail. Gandhi and Shankarlal were lodged in a section of the prison which had a row of eight rooms facing a courtyard. Both were allotted single rooms, each furnished with an iron cot, a mattress, two sheets, a pillow and a blanket.

The next morning the accused were presented to the court, held in the commissioner's office. Gandhi, asked about his profession, said he was 'a farmer and weaver'. The magistrate was startled, pausing before noting it down, to check whether Gandhi was being serious.

Both Banker and Gandhi pleaded guilty, and the trial was set for 18 March. It was held at the Circuit House, and many leading Congressmen attended, sometimes travelling long distances. They included Jawaharlal Nehru, Sarojini Naidu and Madan Mohan Malaviya. Saraladevi Chaudhurani was also there, having come all the way from Lahore. She sat two seats away from Kasturba—the sources do not tell us whether they exchanged any words.

After Gandhi and Banker had pleaded guilty, the advocate general, Sir J.T. Strangman, made his presentation. The articles published by Gandhi in *Young India*, he said, were part of an 'organized campaign ... to preach disaffection towards the existing Government'. Since the accused 'was a man of high educational qualifications' and 'a recognised leader', the 'harm that was likely to be caused was considerable'. As for the second accused, Shankarlal Banker, 'his offence was lesser. He did the publication and he did not write.'

Gandhi then read out a statement he had prepared. He spoke of his work in South Africa, his belief that the treatment of Indians there was an aberration and that British rule was 'intrinsically and mainly good'. He mentioned his work raising ambulance corps in 1899, 1906 and 1914, these 'actuated by the belief that it was possible by such services to gain a status of full equality in the Empire for my countrymen'.

The 'first shock' to Gandhi's faith in the British Empire was the Rowlatt Act, 'a law designed to rob the people of all freedom'. Then 'followed the Punjab horrors', and finally, the going back on the promise regarding the Khilafat. His 'hope shattered', Gandhi 'came reluctantly to the conclusion that the British connection had made India more helpless than she ever was before, politically and economically'. Hence the movement which he had started, based on the belief that 'non-co-operation with evil is as much a duty as is co-operation with the good'.

It was time now for the judge, C.N. Broomfield, to deliver his judgment. The son of a London barrister, he had spent almost two decades in the Indian Civil Service. After saying that Gandhi had made it easy for him by pleading guilty, Broomfield remarked that it was

> impossible to ignore the fact that you are in a different category from any person I have ever tried or am likely to have to try. It would be impossible to ignore the fact that in the eyes of millions of your countrymen, you are a great patriot and a great leader. Even those who differ from you in politics look upon you as a man of high ideals and of noble and even saintly life.

The law, however, was 'no respector of persons'. Gandhi had by his own admission broken the law. The judge had agonized as to what

would be a just sentence, and—addressing the accused directly—said
he had finally decided on a jail term of six years, which he hoped
Gandhi would not consider 'unreasonable', since Bal Gangadhar
Tilak had once got the same sentence under the same section of the
law. Then, in what must surely be among the most unusual wishes
offered by a judge anywhere at any time, Justice Broomfield remarked
that 'if the course of events in India should make it possible for the
Government to reduce the period and release you, no one will be
better pleased than I'.

Since Shankarlal Banker's offence was less serious, he was
sentenced to a year and a half in jail.[69]

When I first read Judge Broomfield's words some three decades
ago, I was moved almost to tears. In rereading them now, my response
is only slightly less emotional. The judge himself saw the matter in
more detached terms. In his diary for 18 March, he had pencilled the
following entries:

> Golf before breakfast
> Try Gandhi[70]

In the evening, the judgment delivered, Broomfield most likely went
for a drink in the club. A day later, the men he had sentenced were
taken in a special train bound for Poona, where they would be lodged
in the Yerwada Jail.

CHAPTER EIGHT

The Mahatma from Above and Below

I

After Gandhi had called off the non-cooperation movement and himself gone to jail, the Government of India commissioned a history of the struggles that he had led. Khilafat and non-cooperation together constituted the most widespread resistance to British authority since the great rebellion of 1857. They had also displayed a comparable level of Hindu–Muslim solidarity. The Government wished therefore to understand their origins and causes, to be better able to handle such movements when they next occurred.

This official history was written by a senior officer of the Intelligence Bureau. The book starts with these prefatory words:

> The success which attended the Non-co-operation and Khilafat Movements in India is undoubtedly attributable to the Great War, for neither agitation could have attained the dimensions which it did but for the economic pressure to which the people were subjected in consequence of the prolonged and wide-spread hostilities. The pressure aggravated and magnified local grievances and spread the spirit of unrest, thus making, for a time, the work of agitators easy.[1]

The analysis was not incorrect. The War led to high inflation, caused by the printing of currency to finance it. There was a scarcity of essential commodities across India. The million-plus Indians who went to serve under the British flag were often heads of households; in their absence, the family profession (most often farming) seriously suffered.

While economics played a role, so did individuals, and one individual in particular. The official history underestimated the personal charisma of Mohandas K. Gandhi. His name, and his methods, fired the popular imagination. It was he who conceived of and led the campaign against the Rowlatt Act, he who conceived and led non-cooperation, he, who, by making common cause with the Muslims on the Khilafat, brought India's two major communities together against the Raj.

This chapter steps back from the chronological narrative to consider how Gandhi was perceived at home and abroad in these years, as he so adeptly moved from a position of relative marginality to the very centre of public life. Why did so many Indians respond so positively to him, his leadership and his movement? Why did some Indians criticize him? And how did Gandhi and his ideas become known in Europe and America?

II

The merchants of Bombay were among Gandhi's earliest and most consistent supporters. Their support was based in part on the camaraderie of caste; Gandhi too was a Bania by birth, indeed the first major political leader from that background. (Tilak and Gokhale were both Brahmins, as were many other Congressmen). Then there was the linguistic affinity; for, successful traders in Bombay tended to be Gujarati speakers. Gandhi's asceticism and personal integrity also appealed to the merchants. Finally, even among this traditionally cautious and risk-averse community, who put family, faith and finances above all else, there was a residual patriotism. Here was a direct challenge to foreign rule, and it was led by one of their own.

In July 1921, when the non-cooperation movement was at its height, the finance secretary of the Government of Bombay met with the president of the Bombay Piece-goods Dealers Association. Reporting the conversation to the Government of India, the official reproduced what were 'more or less' the merchant's 'actual words', namely:

> Here at last is a National leader, who, whatever may be the merits and demerits of his practical policy, has devoted his life to uplifting us as a country, and who, unlike other leaders, is not out for any personal gain. It is up to us, therefore, not to let him down, or at any rate to do what we can to save his face.[2]

Bombay was a city where Gandhi had once practised as a lawyer, and which he visited often. It was also a hub of nationalist activity. Yet Gandhi was known and admired in towns in many other parts of India too.

In the last months of 1919, Gandhi made his first-ever visit to the Punjab. With Gandhi on this trip was C.F. Andrews. Andrews had already spent a decade in the subcontinent, based at St Stephen's College in Delhi. He knew the Punjab particularly well, and wrote often for its leading English newspaper, the *Tribune*.

Gandhi and Andrews reached Amritsar on 4 November. In an article written soon afterwards, the Englishman described it as

> one of the most remarkable days that I have ever spent in India. It revealed in a light I had not seen before, the psychology of the Indian crowd during a time of intense devotional fervour and excitement. The procession through the city, which occupied altogether nearly five hours, was altogether transformed by the multitude into a religious ceremony. No one had instructed them. From first to last it was spontaneous, to the fullest sense of the word.

Andrews had been to the Punjab shortly after the tragedies of April 1919. Then, when he passed down those same streets, 'the fear caused by martial law and punitive police was still fresh in people's minds'. On some faces he had noticed a 'sullen gloom', on others, a 'cowed submission'. But now, wrote Andrews, 'the coming of Mahatma Gandhi has effectively broken this evil spell . . . Indeed his victory has been so great that it has extended over the police themselves. Joyful news was spread from street to street, that the police were joining with the multitude on that day of universal rejoicing.'[3]

Andrews was a close friend of Gandhi's, and missionaries (even lapsed missionaries) are prone to hyperbole anyway. Even so, it seems clear that Gandhi received a rapturous reception on this, his first trip to Amritsar. His activities elsewhere in India had been published in the local press, and conveyed by word of mouth. Like the Bombay merchant, the citizen of Amritsar understood that here was a leader who worked not for himself but for the nation-in-the-making.

From the far north let us move to the deep south. We have noted, in Chapter 4, the countrywide observance of 6 April 1919 as Satyagraha Day. In the temple town of Kumbakonam there was a total hartal, with all shops, schools and colleges being closed. In the evening there was a public meeting attended by more than 10,000 people. Among the resolutions passed by the gathering was this one:

> This Meeting offers its humble prayer to the All Wise Providence for sending Mahathma Gandhi to advise and organise this and other meetings and to infuse into them the spirit of Love and Charity.[4]

One sign of this veneration of Gandhi was the title 'Mahatma', used unselfconsciously by both his friend Charlie Andrews and by the public of Kumbakonam (a town Gandhi had not yet visited). Loosely translated as 'Great Soul', it is an honorific rarely granted. It denotes great spiritual power as well as moral purity.

It is conventionally believed that it was the poet Rabindranath Tagore who first called Gandhi 'Mahatma'. But the ascription is incorrect. As early as 1910, Gandhi's friend Pranjivan Mehta referred to him as a 'Mahatma' in a letter he wrote to Gopal Krishna Gokhale.[5]

Mehta's was a private declaration. The first public occasion on which the title may have been used was in the Kathiawari town of Gondal, which Gandhi and Kasturba visited shortly after their return to India. On 27 January 1915, the citizens of Gondal organized a reception for the Gandhis, to mark their return to the homeland and to honour their work in South Africa. At this reception, a locally respected priest named Jivram Kalidas Shastri presented Gandhi with a scroll which referred to him as a 'Mahatma'.[6]

By the time of the Rowlatt satyagraha of 1919, the honorific 'Mahatma' was being widely used by Gandhi's admirers across India. And sometimes misused. In January 1921, the bearer of the title was told that a brand of 'Mahatma Gandhi Cigarettes' was being marketed and sold. Gandhi was appalled, for in his view smoking was an 'expensive vice' which 'fouls the breath, discolours the teeth and sometimes even causes cancer'. Through the columns of *Young India*, he urged the errant firm to withdraw the labels bearing his name from the market.[7]

III

In 1919, Gandhi turned fifty. His birthday by the Western calendar fell on 2 October. However, going by the traditional Indian calendar, his fiftieth birthday was marked on 21 September 1919.

The occasion was widely celebrated. In Bombay, a women's group named the Bhagini Samaj held a public meeting, where 'the proceedings began with music. The soul stirring song of "Bharat Hamara Desh Hai" was sung by Mrs. Avantibai Gokhale', a follower of Gandhi who had worked with him in Champaran.

Meanwhile, in the inland town of Satara, a photo of the Mahatma was carried in a procession through the streets, ending in a public meeting where 'speeches were made about the life and doings of Gandhi'. Further south, in a meeting in Belgaum, one speaker said that 'since the Mutiny [of 1857], Mr. Gandhi was the first man to prove that Government could be made to yield to Satyagraha. The audience, he hoped, would be infected by [a] hundredth part of Gandhi's brilliant character.' Another speaker claimed that 'whatever Tilak and others did in words, Gandhi had done in deeds'.

A most remarkable tribute to Gandhi on his fiftieth birthday came in the form of an epic poem, almost 400 lines long. Entitled 'The Ascetic of Gujarat', it was written in Gujarati by one Nanalal D. Kavi. The Bombay government's hard-working police department had it translated in its entirety. A few select verses follow:

A Brahmin seer in investigating rules of life
A valiant Kshatriya hero in battleplay,

A wise great Vaishya in determining policy
A thorough-going Shudra in service of man,
All the Varnas are well concentrated in him . . .
Newest of the new,
He is the oldest of the old.
Truth is his motto.
Asceticism is his armour,
His banner is of Brahmacharya, his saint's bowl,
Inexhaustible waters of forgiveness are in,
His skin is of forbearance,
An heir to the Yoga of the eternal Yogi family,
Above storm-winds of passions,
The great living teacher of Bharata,
He is the ascetic of Gujarat,
The great-souled Mahatma Gandhi.[8]

To this Hindu male's very public profession of admiration, let me juxtapose a private declaration by a Muslim woman. This was Raihana Tyabji, whose father, Abbas Tyabji, was a former chief justice of Baroda state who had abandoned power and position to join the non-cooperation movement. Gandhi and Abbas Tyabji were extremely fond of one another, addressing each other in their correspondence with the peculiar greeting 'BHRR', apparently an abbreviation of 'Brother'.

Tyabji's daughter, Raihana, was a gifted singer, specializing in the devotional songs of Mirabai, the medieval poet-mystic, born of royal blood, who had worshipped Krishna, an avatar of Vishnu. Gandhi liked conversing with Abbas, and liked hearing Raihana sing Mira bhajans even more. From 1919, she began visiting the Sabarmati Ashram regularly, often staying for long periods of time.

When Gandhi was arrested in March 1922, Raihana Tyabji was at her father's home in Baroda. She wrote Gandhi an impassioned letter of love and loyalty. 'What you have done for us, words may not express,' she began. Then she continued in words none the less:

We were slaves, and you have freed us. Our hearts were empty, you have filled them with love of country and firm resolve. Our minds were empty, you have filled them with the one great idea—service of the motherland. We were bound hand and foot with a desolating sense of our own inferiority and worthlessness. I remember the time when I envied English girls—for they were free—and they had white skins. You have made us see that we are in no way inferior to any people, you have made us men and women again. Our bodies may be in thrall, but our souls are the souls of free Indians.

Raihana ended her letter by declaring Gandhi to be 'today the freest man in the world'. The British might have put him in jail, 'but from your new Ashram your soul will guide us and keep us to the straight path'. For, Gandhi had given all Indians 'a new ideal. You have given us new life. You have given us freedom. You have given us truth and love.'[9]

IV

In February 1921, Gandhi had toured the district of Gorakhpur in the United Provinces, bordering Nepal. From there he took a train to Banaras. Mahadev Desai's diary contains an arresting description of how the villagers en route showed their affection for Gandhi. He writes that 'at every station peasants with long lathis and torches in their hands would come to us and raise cries loud enough to split the very drums of our ears'. They would go from compartment to compartment, asking, 'Who is Mahatma Gandhi?' At one station an exasperated Desai, seeking to protect his master, identified his bald and bespectacled self as Gandhi. Then he felt guilty at having told a lie.

The train proceeded, haltingly, till

We reached Bhatni and the craze for Gandhiji's darshan reached its climax. As it was, owing to the previous invasions, the train reached there at 12 midnight instead of the scheduled 11 p.m. As the people could not have the darshan [Gandhi was trying to sleep, and Mahadev did not want to disturb him], they got furious and stood, in spite of all our earnest pleading, between the railway lines in front

of the engine. Cries of, 'We won't allow the train to start till we have
the darshan' came out from many lips. I got down again and fell at
their feet—all to no purpose. I grew wild . . . I warned them that, as
a result of this tumult, Gandhiji might stop travelling altogether . . .
But they were stone-deaf to all my frantic appeals. On the contrary,
they tried to put us to shame by repeatedly asserting, 'We have come
for darshan of the Lord. How ever can we feel ashamed of it.'[10]

After Gandhi left Gorakhpur, all kinds of rumours circulated about
the Mahatma and his magic touch. These were published in a local
Hindi newspaper, *Sandesh*. There were tales of a lawyer who went
back on his promise to give up his practice and had his house filled
with faeces; of a sadhu who abused Gandhi and whose body then
began to stink awfully; of a milkman whose entire stock of ghee went
bad after he had made sarcastic remarks about the Mahatma; of a
mango tree bent badly in a storm that straightened itself because, it
was said, it had the grace of Gandhi; of a follower of Gandhi who
went around telling his fellow villagers to stop gambling—all obeyed
him except one, whose goats were then bitten by his own dogs.

One of the most vivid of these stories concerned an Anglo-Indian
engine driver, who had a nightmare and ran towards the railway
colony

shouting 'Man, run, man! Gandhi is marching at the head of several
strong Indians decimating the English'. This caused a panic and all
the local white population emerged from their bedrooms in a state
of undress and ran towards the station. The key to the armoury at
the station was asked for, but could not be found as the officer-
in-charge was away. English women were locked up in boxes and
almirahs, and some Englishmen were heard saying, 'Man! The cries
of "jai jai" are still reaching our ears. We shall not go back to our
bungalows.'[11]

Gorakhpur lay in the northernmost part of the United Provinces.
Meanwhile in the central UP districts of Rae Bareilly and Faizabad,
a preacher named Baba Ram Chandra had catalysed a vigorous
movement of peasants demanding lower rents and an end to arbitrary

eviction. In a massive gathering of peasants in the temple town of Ayodhya, 'Mr. Gandhi's name was freely used.' The peasants, 'while taking no interest in the schemes of the non-co-operators were moved by the agitators to advance the more forcible expression of their own grievances'.[12]

To show their discontent, peasants burnt the crops of their landlords, and let loose the landlords' cattle in the sugar cane fields. In January 1921, the chief secretary described the situation in these districts as 'extremely serious'. The peasants, he wrote,

> had been persuaded by perambulating agitators that not only the Taluqdars [landlords] but the British Raj would shortly cease to exist and that under the beneficent rule of Mr. Gandhi they would enter on a golden age of prosperity in which they would be able to buy good cloth at 0-4-0 [four annas] and other necessaries of life at similar cheap rates.[13]

The situation in the Indo-Gangetic plains was reproduced in the Eastern Himalaya. In January 1922, the Government of Assam sent the Government of India a 'note on the meanings assigned to swaraj by various sections of the population'. Thus the peasants of the Kamrup District believed that when swaraj came,

> the revenue will be largely reduced, and that most of the forest taxes, including the grazing tax will be abolished, the royalty on timber will remain, but like the land revenue will only be a fraction of what it is now. . . . [N]o tolls would be levied either on *hats* [local markets] or on people who fish. Those who wish to do so will be allowed to grow the poppy and to manufacture opium and ganja for their own use.

Such was the peasant understanding of, or expectations for, the dawn of political freedom. The note continued: 'In a vague sort of way, it is thought that Gandhi will be raja; but the real point of the movement is the reduction and abolition of taxation and the cheapening of commodities which in some mysterious ways is to accompany swaraj.'

It was further noted that 'a European passing along the Trunk Road to Polasbari is assailed with cries of Mahatma Gandhi ki jai by all the cowherds'.[14]

In Assam, Gandhi's appeal was not restricted to the peasants alone. In May 1921, there was a series of strikes in the tea gardens of the province. Some 6000 coolies left work, telling the managers that Gandhi had ordered them to do so. A local newspaper reported that 'Mahatma's name is in their mouths. Mahatma's image is in their hearts.'[15]

V

Gandhi had visited some of the sites of the protests narrated earlier. But his visits were always fleeting, a speech on the stump before moving on to the next town. Even those who attended his talks didn't always hear or understand his words. He spoke softly, and microphones were not yet in common use.

Yet he had a presence. This was communicated by his dress, the ordinary loincloth that denoted a life of simplicity and sacrifice. His words—when they were heard—were clear and direct, addressing the everyday life of Indians, in an idiom derived from their own myths and traditions.

The Congress leaders of the past had an elitist air about them. They dressed formally, whether in a Western suit and tie or in an Indian tunic and turban. They were most comfortable speaking in university senate houses and city clubs. Some were more daring—Bal Gangadhar Tilak had reached out to the workers of Bombay, Lajpat Rai to the peasants of the Punjab. But none had the audacity to make theirs a genuinely all-India and all-class campaign.

Gandhi's clothes were homespun. His manner of speaking was homespun as well. Both helped him reach out to a far wider public than his predecessors. Yet, even more critical was the scale of his political ambition. Tilak was a mass leader in western Maharashtra alone. If he ventured outside his province, it was to address city audiences in English. But Gandhi travelled *everywhere*. UP, Bihar, Bengal, Assam, the Tamil and Telugu country, Maharashtra, Punjab—Gandhi went to all these places, visiting cities and towns small and even smaller. He spoke not in English but in Hindustani, the lingua franca of much of northern and eastern India, with interpreters at hand to render his words into Tamil or Bengali or Marathi or Telugu or whatever the local language would have been.

Those who attended Gandhi's meetings conveyed their wonder to their fellows, and the word passed on, and on. The restructuring of the Congress had made it a decentralized and truly democratic party. The flourishing of nationalist newspapers, printed in all the languages of the subcontinent, their contents often read aloud to groups in villages and small towns, took the Gandhian message to all corners of the land.

In every district, sometimes in every taluk, there were now young men who had taken aboard Gandhi's four pillars of swaraj—non-violence, Hindu–Muslim harmony, swadeshi and the abolition of untouchability—and preached their necessity to the people of their own taluk or district. Although these activists were mostly or exclusively men, their audiences, like Gandhi's own, often included women as well. The sage-like nature of his personality, the simplicity and directness of his message, his relentless and near-continuous travels, the commitment of his followers—these all help explain the extent of Gandhi's reach and influence during the days of the non-cooperation movement. That he was so widely known and revered was truly astonishing, when we consider that in 1920–21 the radio had not yet arrived in India, and television and the Internet had not been invented. Compared to the technologies of communication available to the political leaders of today, those that Gandhi had to make use of seem very primitive indeed.

By 1921, Gandhi was admired by men and women; doctors, lawyers, teachers; workers, peasants, pastoralists; Hindus, Muslims, Sikhs; high castes and low castes. And even by convicts. My personal favourite among all the stories from the years of non-cooperation relates to an incident that took place in the late summer of 1921 in the southern town of Trichy. Here, a group of prisoners escaped from the local jail. An official inquiry into the jailbreak revealed 'that there are some grounds for believing it to be political and based upon the belief that the British rule was on the point of yielding to Gandhi's swaraj'.[16]

VI

Gandhi had his Indian admirers, and he had his Indian critics, among them the Moderate politicians whom he had relegated to the sidelines. The Moderates were constitutionalists, who abhorred street protest, preferring earnest petitions to the government. They were extremely trusting of the British. As they saw it, the Raj had brought order and stability to a divided and desperately poor land; it would bring progress and welfare; and, in time, freedom and liberty as well. On the other hand, Gandhi's movement of militant non-cooperation was a direct challenge to the Raj, and through methods radically opposed to those favoured by the Moderates.

The most famous Moderate attack on Gandhi was C. Sankaran Nair's *Gandhi and Anarchy*, published in 1922. Nair was a considerable public figure in India. Born in Malabar in 1857, he moved to Madras and established a successful law practice. Visiting England in 1893, he was confirmed in his belief that the country 'was the home of freedom'.

Nair served as president of the (then extremely loyalist) Congress party in 1897. He later became advocate general of Madras, and, in 1915, a member of the viceroy's executive council, the highest post to which an Indian could aspire (he was only the third Indian to be elevated in this manner). He resigned from the council in protest after the Amritsar massacre in 1919.[17]

Sankaran Nair vehemently disliked Gandhi. This may have been in part a product of jealousy, for when Nair was already Congress president, Gandhi was a relatively unknown lawyer in Durban. His book reeks of personal bitterness, at being put in the shadows by a man much younger than himself. But beyond the animosity, there was also a larger political argument that Nair was making and that we must not lose sight of.

After years of trying, wrote Nair in *Gandhi and Anarchy*, the Moderates at last 'obtained a Reform scheme which brought India directly on to the path leading to Home Rule'. But 'Mr. Gandhi is standing right athwart their path, thus preventing or at least retarding and dangerously imperilling the indispensable reforms'.

As Nair saw it, 'the violent section led by Mr. Gandhi' sought 'the expulsion of the British Government from India'. 'What is

Mr. Gandhi doing?' he asked, before providing this answer: 'He is doing everything possible to increase racial and class hatred.'

As a Hindu from Malabar, Nair was horrified by the Moplah revolt. 'For sheer brutality on women, I cannot remember anything in history to match the Moplah rebellion,' he remarked. The uprising was at least in part a product of the Khilafat movement. And yet, 'Gandhi and his dupes have led Khilafatists to understand that the Hindus will stand by them in any contingency'. Nair then offered this dire prediction: 'Gandhi and his followers have greatly encouraged the growth of Indian Pan Islamism which will in future always be opposed to other Religions and civilizations.'[18]

Nair's attack on Gandhi attracted much attention at the time, largely because of his reputation and the high posts he had occupied. However, a more wide-ranging Moderate critique came from a Tamil named M. Ruthnaswamy. His book, also published in 1922, was (so far as I know) the first careful and considered, if in the end critical, analysis of Gandhi's political philosophy.

Born in 1885, Ruthnaswamy studied in India before taking a history tripos at Cambridge and qualifying as a barrister in London. After his return home he became principal of Pachaiyappa's College and a nominated member of the Madras legislative council. He does not seem to have ever been a member of the Congress, although he briefly joined the Justice Party, which sought to represent the non-Brahmins of the presidency.

Ruthnaswamy began by acknowledging the distinctiveness of Gandhi's method. 'We may not accept Mr. Gandhi as the pre-destined guide to the Promised Land of political emancipation,' he remarked, 'but we cannot deny that he has brought politics from the clouds to the earth of rural India.' Gandhi had 'knocked out of popular esteem' both the timid Moderates as well as the bomb-throwing revolutionaries. His philosophy was 'popular not because it ministers to the prejudices or tickles the palate of the people, but because it appeals to something in their soul'.

Ruthnaswamy praised Gandhi for drawing attention to the problem of 'over-government', for making the people 'themselves responsible for their political and social government', for insisting that social reform must go hand in hand with political reform (in contrast to other nationalists who claimed that 'once political reform was secured in India, social reform would follow immediately and certainly').

Finally, and most significantly, Gandhi had

> brought politics from the Congress platforms to the beach and the maidan. He has interested the common people, the masses, in politics, that is in matters concerning national well-being. This in itself is a great achievement. For, the misfortune in India has been not that people have taken up the wrong brand of politics but that they have not taken to politics at all.

Gandhi had taken politics to the masses, but in ways that did not resonate with modern needs and values. Gandhi's criticisms of modern civilization, wrote Ruthnaswamy, were 'not the product of an occasion, the passing phase of an irritated mind, or an argument *ad hoc*. It was the conviction of his soul and revealed itself long before he began to think ill of British rule.'

Despite taking politics to the people, argued Ruthnaswamy, Gandhi's ideas were out of date, and perhaps also his methods. Collective boycotts, practised in the past by a caste or a village, required unanimity among the members of a small, well-defined community. They were unfeasible 'in the divided society of modern India'. Gandhi had attempted to make satyagraha 'a general movement when, to succeed, it has to be local. A village expedient, he has tried to apply it to urban areas. Non-Co-operation in the form of social boycott was a caste device; he has tried to convert it into a national process.'

For the Madras critic, Gandhi was a 'protagonist of the past' who 'wants to bring back the village civilisation of ancient India'. Ironically, while he disliked modern civilization, Gandhi sought to introduce two modern, Western ideas into India—those of liberty and equality. Yet these modern ideas required modern institutions to make them a reality. For, 'you cannot fight an institution with an idea, however great and sublime it may be. The idea of untouchability is embodied in an institution which is Caste. If you want to destroy untouchability you must attack the institution of Caste. If you want to establish the ideas of liberty and equality you must introduce institutions embodying those ideas.'

Ruthnaswamy came to 'the melancholy conclusion' that Gandhi had 'put his character, the tremendous influence he wields over his people and the political truths which he has seized hold of to the service of reaction'. The last paragraph of his unjustly forgotten book suggests that while

> Mr. Gandhi might have been the saviour of India, he is content to be the saviour of Hinduism. He might have been a second Buddha, leading his people to social freedom, as that other led them to religious freedom. But he is content to be a second Tilak. . . . He might have saved his country, but he is anxious only to save his theories. With regret and with despondency—for this seems to be the fate of almost all the great men that have been given to India— we must set Mr. Gandhi down as one of the great Might-Have-Beens of Indian history.[19]

This last judgement was premature. With Gandhi in jail, Ruthnaswamy may have thought that his political career was declining, or even at an end. That said, his was a courageous and often perceptive critique of a man so widely hailed as the nation's redeemer.

VII

Moderates thought Gandhi too radical. Marxists thought him not radical enough. The success of the Bolshevik Revolution had attracted some intelligent and idealistic young Indians to communism. One was Sripad Amrit Dange, a trade union activist based in Bombay. In 1920, when he was still in his early twenties, Dange published a slim book called *Gandhi vs. Lenin*. This acknowledged some parallels between the two thinkers and their systems. Like Leninism, Gandhism accepted that 'all the vices from which society' was suffering emanated from 'the rule of capitalism'. Notwithstanding his sincerity, argued Dange, Gandhi was a reactionary thinker obsessed with religion and the individual conscience. On the other hand, Lenin had identified the structural roots of economic oppression and sought to end it though collective mass action. While Gandhi looked to recreate the past, Lenin would preserve the 'existing achievements' of modern civilization, further building upon them by organizing the proletariat in a revolutionary transformation of society.[20]

Dange was based in Bombay. The most famous Indian Marxist of the day was in exile. This was M.N. Roy, a widely travelled polymath who had helped set up the Mexican Communist Party as well as the Communist International. Dange knew Lenin only through his writings, but Roy knew Lenin in person.

Roy had been out of India since 1915. However, he keenly followed developments in his homeland. He published a Marxist journal from Zurich, copies of which were smuggled into the subcontinent. In an essay in his journal, Roy declared that 'the cult of non-violence is inseparable from an anti-revolutionary spirit. Those who do not want a revolution in India, can pin their hope on non-violent methods. Strictly non-violent methods are hardly distinguishable from constitutional agitation, and no people on the face of the earth has ever made a revolution by constitutional methods.'

Having spoken of (and dismissed) the principle, Roy then came to the person. 'The greatness of Mahatma Gandhi,' he remarked,

> is to be found in his ability to discover before any other [Indian] the potentiality of mass agitation. But a vast social upheaval is greater than the greatest of men. The Mahatmaji did not fail to take 'fullest advantage' of the situation, but he was not capable, he was not bold enough to identify himself with the mass movement as soon as it began to assume proportions of revolutionary violence. His failure proved the non-revolutionary nature of his ideal, which was the cult of non-violence.[21]

VIII

Dange and Roy, Nair and Ruthnaswamy, may all be largely forgotten now, but at the time they were all public figures. The last Indian critic of Gandhi I shall consider was unknown even while he lived.

His name was Kantilal Amratlal, and his criticisms are contained in a Gujarati letter he wrote Gandhi on the last day of 1920, a copy of which is in the archives of the Sabarmati Ashram.

The critic began by challenging Gandhi's claim to the title 'Mahatma'. He conceded that 'it is well known that your mental strength is very strong'. But, he added, Gandhi would 'not claim to be free of human weaknesses—all types of weaknesses. Christ was a Mahatma. Buddha was a Mahatma. Lord Krishna was a Mahatma. Ramchandra was a Mahatma. Can you be placed among them? Surely not. Then why do you introduce yourself as a Mahatma?'

Gandhi had not coined the term for himself, but surely he should not encourage its use, said the critic. Yet, even the magazines edited by him, such as *Navajivan*, referred to Gandhi as 'Mahatma'. 'Is it fine for a cultured man like you to allow such things?' asked Amratlal.

The correspondent then argued that morality and politics were incompatible. 'The burden of sin is increasing in Hindustan and in the world,' he remarked. 'People don't hesitate in lying. Thousands of evil deeds are done.' Rather than engage in politics, he asked Gandhi, 'Why don't you take up the best of all missions to stop people and lead them on the path of morality?'

The third charge the critic laid at Gandhi's door was hypocrisy. Gandhi had called for the boycott of government grants, schools and offices. Yet, he accepted the 'money of those Mill owners who exploit their labourers mercilessly and the traders who do lots of malpractices'.

The fourth charge Gandhi was accused of was chauvinism. 'How it can be a sin not to use *swadeshi* goods?' asked the critic. 'Pride in one's nation [*swadeshabhiman*] is not the ultimate sentiment.' Gandhi's was a 'narrow vision', since 'country and life are transient', not eternal.[22]

His letter tells us that the critic lived in Ahmedabad—in the locality of Shahpur—and that he had written several times to Gandhi in the past. Perhaps he belonged to the segment of Ahmedabad's merchant class that was resolutely hostile to the Sabarmati Ashram and its founder. This may be why the letter elicited no reply. Motivated though it may have been, this letter echoed criticisms made by people Gandhi knew and respected, such as Rabindranath Tagore. Notably, it was written, and received, at the moment of Gandhi's greatest political triumph, the Nagpur Congress.

IX

Gandhi also attracted a range of responses from British officials who had to deal with him and his movement. Some were irritated by Gandhi—one member of the viceroy's executive council, W.S. Marris, describing him as a 'self-constituted redresser of wrongs'.[23] Others were simply confused, such as the home secretary who wrote that 'Gandhi is a follower of Tolstoi and Thoreau; and I am under the impression that there is a good deal in common—not in practice but in theory—between their doctrines and Bolshevism'.[24]

Non-official Englishmen in India were also hostile to Gandhi. An early critic was the planter W.S. Irwin, whom we met in Chapter 3. In a series of articles in pro-Raj papers, he argued that the European planters had converted dangerous jungle into prosperous farmland. The peasants of Champaran, he claimed, were quite contented until the agitator Gandhi came along. In a splendid piece of vituperation, Irwin said that

> the genuineness of Mr. Gandhi's 'mission' would have been much in doubt if his methods had been less theatrical. Notwithstanding [his] familiarity in England and elsewhere with the minor amenities of Western civilization, he (in Champaran at least) discards the use of head covering or shoes, sits on the floor, cooks his own food, and affects to follow the footsteps of the much greater philanthropist of 2,000 years ago [i.e. the Buddha] . . . Firmly dealt with, this agitation would have died a natural death, the sole purpose of it being to get the non-official portion of the European Community out of the district and to hand over to the tender mercies of the lawyer and mahajan the ryot for whose welfare so much solicitude is being advertised.[25]

In 1917, Gandhi was making trouble merely in one district. Four years later, when the non-cooperation movement had made him a national leader, the Anglican bishops of India issued a pamphlet whose language was more elevated than W.S. Irwin's, but whose intent was the same—the delegitimizing of Gandhi and his methods. The Indian leader had long claimed that he admired Jesus. In their response, the bishops noted that in Jesus's time there 'was a violent Nationalist party among the Jews and also a moderate party which was content with the Roman sway'. A malignant group of Jews, wrote the bishops, 'tried to carry Him off to head a Nationalist revolt. But He would have none of it. His ideal was both broader and deeper, and His method of winning acceptance for His ideal was very different from that of political rebellion.'

The Anglican bishops were convinced that the British had 'conferred great benefits on India. They have protected her against foreign foes. They have protected her people against themselves.' However, with the emergence of Gandhi's movement, 'it is race hatred which now in India threatens to submerge all that has been laboriously built of social order, economic prosperity, political progress and even religion'.

The bishops professed admiration for Gandhi's campaign against untouchability. Yet, they claimed that the practice 'will never be removed till the clear light of the knowledge of God as universal King and impartially loving Father has penetrated the hearts of the people of this land'—that is, till all Hindus in India—and perhaps all Muslims and Sikhs too—had converted to Christianity.[26]

Confusion, anger, paranoia, racial and theological arrogance—these were the ways in which the British in India met Gandhi's challenge. Yet, there were exceptions, of Englishmen who provided more subtle understandings of the man and his movement. One such Englishman was W.B. Heycock, the district magistrate of Champaran at the time of Gandhi's campaign there in the summer of 1917. In the weeks and months that Gandhi had been in his district, Heycock had become increasingly fascinated by the man. He spoke with him, he spoke to others about him. He even procured pamphlets about and by Gandhi, dating from his South African period. This was how the magistrate summed up his adversary:

> Gandhi seems a curious mixture of the East and West. He owes
> a large part of his belief to Ruskin and Tolstoi, particularly the
> latter; and couples these to the asceticism of a Jogi. Were his ideas

only those of the East, he would have been content to have applied
them to his personal existence in a life of meditative seclusion. It is
only the teachings of the West that have made him an active social
reformer.[27]

This was written in June 1917. Exactly four years later, another
insightful assessment was provided by the home secretary of the
Government of India, H.D. Craik. No one else in India—not even
Gandhi—knew as much about the political situation in the country
as he did. For, it was to the home secretary that came the fortnightly
reports, province by province and district by district, of the progress
and impact of the political campaigns of 1920 and 1921.

In Gandhi's mind, Khilafat and non-cooperation were
complementary and conjoined. The home secretary, on the other hand,
argued that 'the two movements are in origin and character distinct'.
Non-cooperation was 'in its essence political and social in character';
and its leaders had urged that 'it must disassociate itself from violence
of any kind'. On the other hand, Khilafat was essentially a religious
question, and its leaders, far from being always wedded to non-violence,
'have openly preached the doctrine that it may become necessary at any
moment to declare *jehad*, or, in their phrase, to draw the sword'.

Gandhi felt that by supporting Khilafat, he would cement the
unity between Hindus and Muslims. The home secretary, on the
other hand, believed that there was 'no guarantee' that the unity was
'anything but temporary'. For,

> those who make much of it do so largely to promote political aims.
> They deliberately overlook the lessons of history, the ignorance of
> the masses and the essential differences which divide the two great
> religions—differences due to conflicting ethical standards as much
> as to political jealousy.[28]

X

How was Gandhi received in Britain itself? The first assessment of
Gandhi in the British press after his return to India was an article

published in January 1918 by the Oxford classicist Gilbert Murray. At this time, Gandhi's reputation still rested largely on his work in South Africa. Murray thus provided a summary of Gandhi's early life, his abandonment of a lucrative legal career for activism, and his leadership of the struggles of Indians against racially exclusive laws, this a 'battle of the unaided human soul against overwhelming material force'. Noting how the South African satyagrahas of 1913–14 had compelled the government to amend its laws, Murray remarked:

> Persons in power should be very careful how they deal with a man who cares nothing for sensual pleasure, nothing for riches, nothing for comfort or praise or promotion, but is simply determined to do what he believes to be right. He is a dangerous and uncomfortable enemy—because his body, which you can always conquer, gives you so little purchase upon his soul.[29]

Murray was not unsympathetic to pacifism, and came from a colonial background (he was born and raised in Australia). The empathy he showed with Gandhi and his methods was not reproduced by other British writers. They were largely sceptical of a man whose leadership of the Rowlatt satyagraha and the non-cooperation movement had thrown a direct challenge to British rule in India.

One British journalist who had made many visits to India was Valentine Chirol, foreign editor of *The Times*. In a book published in 1910, he had characterized Bal Gangadhar Tilak as 'the father of Indian unrest', claiming he was a man 'impatient of all restraint' who held reactionary social and religious views.[30] A decade later, when Chirol wrote a second book on the subcontinent, the title of 'father of Indian unrest' had passed on to Gandhi. *The Times* man saw him as a 'strange and incalculable figure . . . who, favoured by an extraordinary combination of untoward circumstances, was to rally around him some of the most and many of the least reputable forces' in India. For all 'his visionary idealism', wrote Chirol, Gandhi was 'letting loose dangerous forces which reeked naught of *ahimsa* [non-violence]'.[31]

Chirol's strictures were relatively mild compared to British journalists who knew India (and Gandhi) only at second-hand. In early 1922, a popular London monthly published a blistering attack on Gandhi, calling him an 'arch-agitator', the 'leader of sedition, incessantly fomenting unrest, and though deprecating violence and preaching peace, really inciting to riot and bloodshed'. The writer, a high Tory imperialist, claimed that in Gandhi 'all the distillation of the East against the West is incarnate'. He spoke disparagingly of 'the illiterate mobs, stuck in ignorance, whose racial passions [Gandhi] stirred to frenzy'.

The article ended with this unequivocal denunciation: 'It would be difficult to discover a more perfect example of fanaticism and utter self-deception, for the evil [Gandhi] has wrought, the wicked unrest and misery he [brought] across India like a black shadow.'[32]

Meanwhile, an influential London magazine had opened its columns to Michael O'Dwyer, the recently retired lieutenant governor of the Punjab. O'Dwyer was unrepentant of his martial law administration, arguing that Indians responded only to tough rules and tough-minded rulers. The spread of Gandhi's movement, he believed, had been enabled and encouraged by the feebleness of the viceroy and (especially) the secretary of state. He accused Montagu of a policy of 'placating your enemies at all costs', and of displaying 'an almost Oriental obsequiousness' towards Gandhi and company.

As for Gandhi himself, O'Dwyer called him an 'unctuous hypocrite' who, through a mixture of 'threats or money', had mobilized a traditionally loyalist population to support his 'seditious' activities. Gandhi was, in fact, 'a most dangerous criminal [who] has set himself up, while an impotent Government was looking on, to disrupt society and subvert authority under the hypocritical guise of a religious and social reformer'.[33]

Amidst the abuse and scepticism there were a few dissonant notes. The *Glasgow Herald*, run by a liberal editor named Robert Bruce, printed a long and thoughtful piece called 'Gandhi Sahib'. This began by asking 'Who is this "egregious Mr. Gandhi"' (the adjective favoured by some Tories and Tory papers), and then providing this answer: 'He is the soul of India in revolt, the spirit of Indian discontent, the assertion of the East's equality with the West, the most powerful and at the same time the most puzzling personality in India today.' Gandhi, said the Scottish journal, 'is not to be dismissed by the fine sarcasm of an editorial in an English newspaper nor rendered ridiculous by the foolish worship of admiring disciples'.

The unsigned piece was written by someone who had travelled widely in India and spoken to many Indians. He called Gandhi a 'patriot', who is 'human enough to break through the conventions of caste and custom to eat with pariahs'. While 'a partisan in politics, Gandhi is no bigot in religion. He calls himself a Hindu but that is a term exceedingly broad, and in many matters he shares common ground with Christians and Mahomedans.' The journalist further added that 'he is singularly free from race prejudice'.

This unusually sympathetic piece ended with a prediction: 'When in course of time the "United States of India" come into existence, I hazard the opinion that history will regard the spectacle as an outcome of the work and worth of the "egregious Mr. Gandhi", as well as the crowning triumph of British statesmanship in India.'[34]

XI

Gandhi was being noticed across the Atlantic too. The American President, Woodrow Wilson, was an internationalist, whose famous Fourteen Points had included a commitment to national self-determination. And although America had acquired its own colonial possessions, the self-image of Americans was that they were an anti-colonial people. Their origin myth had them wresting freedom from the British, which made them sympathetic to others who too wished the British to get off their backs.

In October 1920, the *New York Tribune* published an article by its London correspondent on Gandhi and the non-cooperation movement. The writer, an American, had not been to India himself. Basing his piece on conversations with Indians in London and with British officials, he wrote that the non-violent movement led by Gandhi 'appears a greater menace to the British Empire than all the revolutionists, Bolshevik agitators, Indian fanatics and other troublemakers of the last fifty years'. To his countrymen, Gandhi apparently combined 'the wisdom of a statesman, the cleverness of a politician, [and] the simplicity of a peasant'.[35]

Six months later, the *Tribune*'s main competitor, the *New York Times*, printed a five-column, full-page laudatory article on Gandhi. It was not clear whether the author (Clare Price) had met the man or visited his country. The article rehearsed his career thus far, the influence on his thought of Tolstoy and Ruskin, his work in South Africa and his struggles in India. 'Not even the British are able to cast the slightest aspersion on the high sincerity of the man,' wrote Price. Although Gandhi was 'a dark little wisp of a man' who looked as if he could be cradled like a child, 'in point of personal following he is far and away the greatest man living in the world today'.[36]

This last sentence, or judgement, was not original. It seems to have been cribbed from a New York clergyman named John Haynes Holmes. Holmes had discovered Gandhi through reading Gilbert Murray's article in the *Hibbert Journal*. He looked for more material on Gandhi; the more he read, the more he was convinced that he was 'a great and wonderful man'. Finally, on Sunday, 10 April 1921, he chose as the topic for his sermon the question, 'Who is the Greatest Man in the World?' The answer was Gandhi, who, of all those then living, reminded the clergyman most of Jesus. Like Jesus, 'he lives his life; he speaks his word, he suffers, strives, and will some day nobly die, for his kingdom upon earth'.[37]

British Anglicans thought Gandhi's methods to be opposed to Jesus's methods. Radical American priests saw them as akin and even identical. After that first sermon, Holmes returned to the subject at regular intervals. When Gandhi was arrested in February 1922, he preached on his 'world significance'. Comparing him to Garibaldi and George Washington, Holmes added that unlike those other patriots and makers of nations, 'Gandhi is far more, infinitely greater, than a nationalistic leader. At bottom, he is a great religious leader . . . His movement in this respect is a movement for world redemption. Gandhi is thus undertaking to do exactly what Jesus did when he proclaimed the kingdom of God on earth.'[38]

Some well-known African Americans were also impressed by the Indian freedom struggle and its leader. 'White Christianity stood before Gandhi,' wrote W.E.B. Du Bois in 1922, 'and, let us face it, it cut a sorry figure.' A year previously, the socialist bishop Reverdy C. Ransom called Gandhi 'a messiah and saint', 'the new "Light of

Asia", [who] would deliver his countrymen from the rule of British imperialism, not by violent resistance, but through the peaceful method of non-co-operation'.

Some black intellectuals were more sceptical. The sociologist E. Franklin Frazier thought non-violence would not work in the barbarous conditions of the American South. 'Suppose there should arise a Gandhi to lead Negroes without hate in their hearts,' he wrote, 'I fear we would witness an unprecedented massacre of defenseless black men and women in the name of Law and Order . . .'

In fact, Frazier's own intervention showed how actively Gandhi was being discussed in the black press. It was because black newspapers from Chicago to New York and down into the Deep South were writing so appreciatively about Gandhi's relevance to America that the sociologist sought to temper their enthusiasm.[39]

These African-American commentators had not met or seen Gandhi. Nor, as yet, had John Haynes Holmes. Those Americans who had, wrote about him in only slightly less fulsome tones. A couple who had spent two years teaching in India praised Gandhi's 'mental alertness', his 'charm' and his 'wonderful courage', his work in forging Hindu–Muslim unity, but worried that his message of non-violence was too complex for the 'average Indian peasant to understand'.[40] A young Quaker who visited Gandhi found him a 'wonderful little man', with compassion towards people of other faiths and towards animals too.[41] A journalist who travelled with Gandhi marvelled at the manifest love of the people for him, while deploring the British colonialist's lack of understanding of what he really stood for.[42]

These gushing tributes attracted the hostile attentions of a former member of the Indian Civil Service named Maurice Joachin, who put forward the British point of view in a series of articles in the American press. 'Americans, beware!' he wrote. 'Do not lend an atom of support to Gandhism, which is nothing more nor less than the most formidable menace to Western culture and a cleverly devised conspiracy against the progress of civilization.'

Joachim went on to suggest that Gandhi's movement was aimed not merely at the West, but at America in particular. The party of 'Nationalists led by Mohandas K. Gandhi', he claimed, was

slowly but surely paving the way to make his brother American
a pariah in the East; is unconsciously helping to drive out every
American from India; is aiding and abetting the abolishment of
American enterprise in the East; is contributing [its] time and money
to uproot and disrupt all the good work that American missionaries,
the American Salvation Army and the American YMCA have
performed after years and years of self-sacrifice; in short, is
cooperating in a movement to turn back the clock of civilization.[43]

The first mention of Gandhi in the American press actually dates to
as far back as 1897, when the *Nation* carried an article on racial
discrimination in Natal, and the young lawyer's attempts to combat
it.[44] Twenty-four years later, this still radical, anti-imperialist paper
carried a glowing assessment of Gandhi's struggle in India, published
under the tell-all title, 'The New Light of Asia'. In a 'cynical,
materialistic, and disillusioned' age, wrote the *Nation*, there had
emerged a man 'whose singular devotion, unselfishness and spiritual
power have won him the almost superstitious reverence of his own
people and the respect of the sceptical critics'. At a time when the
Western world had just concluded an extended and very bloody war,
Gandhi had committed himself and his people to a credo of non-
violence. Thus, through all the strikes and boycotts, 'Gandhi has kept
his own soul free from hate. The literature of revolution contains no
documents so uncompromising, yet so reasonable and sweet-spirited,
as his "Letter to Every Englishman". . .'

The *Nation*'s editorial was admittedly written on the basis of
'meagre and often contradictory despatches from British sources'. Yet,
it was insightful, and perhaps the first serious American appreciation
of Gandhi and his movement. It ended with this remarkable passage:

> The complete verdict on the course of Indian nationalism can only
> be written by time. But even now it is possible to say that British,
> or rather Western imperialism is doomed. We are witnessing one of
> the great historic movements of our time in the awakening of Asia.
> However that awakening manifests within India, whether in the
> slow or constitutional progress of the Moderates, the spontaneous
> revolt, half blind and often violent, of exploited workers and hungry

peasants; or the ordered resistance, spiritual and economic, of the non-co-operators, the struggle of the long-oppressed deserves the sympathetic understanding of every man who waits for a new birth of freedom in every land. But if the triumph of India should mean the triumph of the spirit and method of Gandhi, then, indeed, would a new day dawn for all mankind. For war would be shown to be as unnecessary for the outer semblance of freedom, as it is destructive to the realisation of its inner spirit.[45]

XII

Gandhi's movement was also being noticed in Europe. In April 1922, a French literary journal published an extended analysis which began with this vivid description of the man:

> A shy flame burning from deep eye sockets; a hooked nose between emaciated cheeks; a colour which overshadows the black mass of the moustache and hair; under a puny appearance an intense impression of nervous force and concentrated power: thus appears to us the agitator, the prophet, the apostle, the Messiah of contemporary India, an India which depends on him from day to day for its salvation and liberty—Mohandas Karamchand Gandhi.

The rest of the article was written in a more detached tone. It summarized Gandhi's education in London, his political apprenticeship in South Africa, and the course of the movements he led in India. While appreciative of his ability to move and mobilize people, the writer wished Gandhi had unleashed that power more fully instead of restraining it after the first episodes of violence. 'Ascetic and saint which he was in the eyes of the masses and perhaps in reality,' wrote the critic, 'in condemning the violence does he not try to turn away from himself the power of lightning?'[46]

The interest in France was perhaps unexpected. Not so the interest in Africa, a continent Gandhi had spent close to two decades in. His son Manilal was now based in Natal, running *Indian Opinion*, the journal his father had founded in 1903. That journal, as well as other periodicals published by the community, dutifully reported the protests against the Rowlatt Act and the progress of the non-cooperation movement.

In Kenya too, expatriate Indians were reading Gandhi and, in their own way, seeking to apply his techniques. A Gujarati immigrant named Manibhai Desai was a close colleague of a Kenyan labour leader named Harry Thuku. When Thuku was arrested and deported following a strike, Desai pressed C.F. Andrews to intervene. The priest did his 'very best at the time to make his voice heard in England, but without effect'. He then wrote to Gandhi about Thuku's troubles. Gandhi publicized the matter through his newspaper, *Young India*. Contemporary accounts suggest that Thuku saw himself as a Kenyan analogue of the Mahatma. A British settler wrote in disgust that 'this lad Harry Thuku . . . likens himself to [Gandhi] in India'. When, after a successful strike, some Indians in Kenya threw a party for Thuku, he is reported to have said; 'Gandhi is going to be King in India and I'm going to be King here.'[47]

XIII

Although formally based in Ahmedabad, Gandhi's real home was not so much the ashram on the banks of the Sabarmati as a third-class railway compartment. In and through his journeys by train, Gandhi saw a great deal of India and Indians, and they saw a great deal of him in return.

The folklore and rumours about Gandhi's personality among peasants and tribals were a product of these travels. So were the printed appreciations and denunciations by middle-class Indians, although these additionally drew on his own writings.

The non-cooperation movement was the first real challenge to British rule since the great uprising of 1857. In 1857, the Indian press was primitive and undeveloped. The message of the rebels was largely transmitted by word of mouth. By Gandhi's day, however, there was a flourishing newspaper industry, with hundreds of titles published in many languages. The spread of the railway network facilitated the distribution of these papers between and within provinces. Each issue of every paper was usually read by more than one person, and also often read out to those who were illiterate.

The Indian press of 1919–22 did not speak with one voice. There were newspapers that saw British rule as beneficent, and were resolutely opposed to self-government. There were papers that were run by Moderates, which advocated political reform, to be achieved in slow, incremental stages. There were papers run by various religious sects. And there were papers that presented the Congress, or more particularly, the Gandhian point of view.

We do not have firm data on the relative reach and influence of these different kinds of periodicals. But we do know that there were enough in the last category, that these were present in all provinces and published in all languages, and that they conveyed the zest and vigour of the political movement they had linked themselves with.[48]

That Gandhi and his ideas were so actively debated within India was not therefore surprising. What was more noteworthy was the interest in the man across the globe. At this time, Gandhi had little interest in world affairs. He did not even comment on such vital matters as the Treaty of Versailles or the Paris Peace Conference.

Gandhi was not interested in the politics and social life in Europe, North America or even Africa. But writers and thinkers in those countries were interested in him. No political leader before Gandhi had so radically simplified his life. The clothes he wore, the food he ate, the homes he lived in, all brought Gandhi far closer to the masses than professedly socialist leaders like Lenin. While 'passive resistance' had been practised by particular groups (such as suffragettes and Non-Conformists in England, and by the Doukhobors in Russia), it had never before been made part of a wider national struggle. That both man and movement had set themselves up against the great British Empire was a further marvel.

Between 1919 and 1922, Gandhi and Gandhism were actively discussed within India. And they did not pass unnoticed outside India. The debates of these years foreshadowed the greater and more intense debates of later years, when the world came to know Gandhi better, and when Gandhi himself, reluctantly but inevitably, came to know more about the world.

PART II

REACHING OUT TO THE WORLD (1922–1931)

CHAPTER NINE

Prisoner Number 827

I

Gandhi had been arrested, tried and sentenced in Ahmedabad itself. But the state thought it prudent not to imprison him in the same city where his family and close disciples resided. Escorted by a posse of police, he was taken by train to Poona, where, on the evening of 21 March 1922, he was placed in the custody of the superintendent of the Yerwada jail.[1]

Shortly after Gandhi reached Yerwada, his name was entered into the prison roll. He was given the serial number 827, his health described as 'fair', his crime defined as violation of Section 124(A) of the Indian Penal Code (uttering or writing words exciting disaffection towards the government established by law). Under the column 'Previous Convictions' was entered 'Nil', an entry that was not strictly accurate, if one included countries other than India.

As a satyagrahi in South Africa, Gandhi had been to jail on four separate occasions. The terms ranged from three weeks to three months. He was thus a fairly experienced prisoner, who knew how to occupy himself when separated from his family, how to deal with whimsical or bullying jail authorities, how to spend his time reading and writing.

In Yerwada, Gandhi was allowed one group of visitors every three months, their names vetted beforehand by the jail authorities. He first availed himself of this privilege a mere ten days after he was jailed. On 1 April, his son Devadas, his protégé C. Rajagopalachari, and his friend A.V. Thakkar came to see Gandhi. In an article published in *Young India*, Rajagopalachari shared with a wider audience the life their leader was now obliged to lead. Gandhi was kept in solitary confinement and his cell locked up at night. The cell had two small ventilators to let in light and air. During the day, Gandhi was allowed to walk on the veranda.

The chamber pot was in the cell. At the visitors' request, the superintendent had it replaced with a commode. Gandhi had been given two blankets but no pillow. He was allowed writing paper which he was using to learn Urdu.[2]

Gandhi spent his first weeks in Yerwada writing a Gujarati primer for the students of the ashram school in Ahmedabad. Presented in the form of a dialogue between a mother and child, this stressed the significance of cleanliness, regular exercises, the importance of spinning, and the knowledge of the seasons and of crops grown in the region. A son was told to 'help with the housework, just as your sister Shanta does'.[3]

Gandhi was permitted to write one letter every three months. He wrote the first on 14 April, to Hakim Ajmal Khan, latterly the president of the Ahmedabad Congress and one of the few important nationalists still at large. The letter described his prison routine in some detail. Gandhi was allowed to retain the seven books he brought with him, among them the Gita, the Koran, the Ramayana, a presentation copy of the Sermon on the Mount (sent him 'by schoolboys of a high school in California with the hope that [he] would always carry it with [him]'), and an Urdu guide gifted by Maulana Abul Kalam Azad. He was also allowed to borrow books from the jail library. He asked to be supplied with a newspaper; knowing that the nationalist *Bombay Chronicle* would be verboten, he requested the establishment-oriented *Times of India* instead. The request was refused.

Another request was granted—permission to sleep in the open. Gandhi rose at 4 a.m., said his prayers, and when light dawned, commenced his studies. There was no electric light in his cell. He read the whole day, the reading interrupted by walks in the veranda outside his cell (beyond which he could not go). Here he often met a prisoner from the Gulf, who spoke only Arabic, so they merely exchanged greetings.

Gandhi's spinning wheel was confiscated when he first arrived, but after persistent pleas, it was returned. Now the routine became slightly more varied: reading and walking, interspersed with spinning.

The superintendent of the prison had 'pleasant manners', noted Gandhi, but otherwise 'the human element is largely, if not entirely, absent in the jail system'.

Gandhi ended the letter by asking his friend to 'please persuade Mrs. Gandhi not to think of visiting me. Dev[a]das created a scene when he visited me. He could not brook the idea of my standing in the Superintendent's office while he was brought in. This proud and sensitive boy burst out weeping aloud and it was with difficulty that I could restrain him. He should have realized that I was a prisoner and as such I had no right to sit in the presence of the Superintendent.'[4]

The letter to Hakim Ajmal Khan was deemed by the censor to be insufficiently non-political. It was retained in Yerwada, to be returned to the prisoner on the completion of his term. Then, a week later, the superintendent yielded to Gandhi's request to be given more space for exercise. The veranda he was presently given access to measured a mere seventy feet. The official, noting that Gandhi was 'not a man who would assault another prisoner in the same yard', recommended that he be allowed to walk in the prison yard escorted by a constable.[5]

In July 1922, on Kasturba's request, Gandhi sent some ten pounds of yarn he had spun in the jail via the prison authorities to Sabarmati. Hearing of this, the *Kesari* newspaper (founded by Bal Gangadhar Tilak) ran a story suggesting that the yarn, which 'ought to fetch more than its weight in gold', be auctioned in public. The material spun by Gandhi, said the newspaper, 'will occupy an honoured position in any swadeshi exhibition and the person who purchases it and his descendant will be highly respected by the public'.

This report alarmed the authorities. As the inspector general of prisons commented: 'We cannot permit Mr. Gandhi's followers to go wild over Mr. Gandhi's yarn.' Kasturba was told that it was a keepsake for her only, while further supplies were to be stopped.[6]

II

In jail, with time on his hands, Gandhi kept a diary, which mostly contained a list of books he read, borrowed from the prison library. In his first months in Yerwada, Gandhi read *A History of Scotland*, *Stories from the History of Rome*, *Tom Brown's Schooldays* (he found 'some portions of it beautiful'), the Gujarati translation of Valmiki's Ramayana, Edward Bellamy's utopian novel *Equality*, R.L. Stevenson's *The Strange Case of Dr. Jekyll and Mr. Hyde*, Kipling's *The Jungle Book*, Macaulay's *Lays of Ancient Rome*, Tilak's book on the Gita, Govardhanram Tripathi's great multivolume Gujarati novel *Saraswatichandra* (which he had read several times before), some volumes of Gibbon's *Decline and Fall*, and a translation of Goethe's *Faust*.[7]

Gandhi set aside several hours a day for reading Urdu, the lingua franca of much of northern India, and a language identified with Muslim aspirations. Once he had become reasonably fluent, he read a life of the Prophet and of his companions. From this he reached two conclusions. The first was that Urdu and Hindi, once closely allied under the composite rubric of 'Hindustani', were becoming separate and distinct languages, with the former relying more on Arabic and Persian grammar, and the Hindi writers turning to classical Sanskrit. Gandhi now saw that 'if we are to have a common national language being a mixture of Hindi and Urdu, special and prolonged effort will have to be made to effect a juncture between the two streams which seem at present to be diverging more and more one from the other'.

The second conclusion was more cheering. Reading about the early history of the faith, he became convinced 'that it was not the sword that won a place for Islam in those days in the scheme of life. It was the rigid simplicity, the utter self-effacement of the Prophet, the scrupulous regard for pledges, his intense devotion to his friends and followers, his intrepidity, his fearlessness, his absolute trust in God and his own mission.'[8]

While he read, spun, walked or wrote, Gandhi was under the watch of 'convict warders', the prisoners who had been in Yerwada for a long time and whose good behaviour allowed them to supervise new entrants. The first warder assigned to look after Gandhi was a

Punjabi Hindu called Harkaran, who had been convicted of murder, and already served nine years of a fourteen-year sentence. Harkaran was a master of stealing and hiding trifles, as indeed were many other prisoners in Yerwada. As Gandhi was to wryly write later: 'If the whole of the jail yard were to be dug up twelve inches deep, it would yield up many a secret in the shape of spoons, knives, pots, cigarettes, soaps, and such like.' Harkaran, 'being one of the oldest inmates of Yerwada, was a sort of purveyor-general to the prisoners'. If an inmate wanted a knife, spoon, pot or pan, he knew where and how to get one.

Harkaran watched over Gandhi during the day. At night, he was replaced by a powerful Baloch named Shabaskhan, also convicted of murder. Gandhi thought the authorities had deliberately chosen a Muslim to balance the Hindu. Not that he minded, for Shabaskhan's build reminded him of his friend Shaukat Ali, while he told Gandhi on the very first day: 'I am not going to watch you at all. Treat me as your friend and do exactly as you like.'[9]

III

Gandhi was sentenced on 18 March 1922. In early April, the Congress decided that so long as their leader was behind bars, they would observe the 18th of every month as 'Gandhi Day', where prayers would be 'offered in all the temples, mosques and churches for Mahatmaji's health in prison, and for the speedy success of the Cause'.[10] On 2 October, Gandhi's birthday, a group of about a hundred women from Bombay took the train to Poona and then hired a bus to ferry them to Yerwada jail. The superintendent refused the ladies permission to meet their hero, but promised to take him the flowers and garlands they had brought with them.[11]

On the same day, an American journalist named Drew Pearson interviewed the governor of Bombay, Sir George Lloyd, in Poona. The governor spoke animatedly of the man he had put in jail. 'Just a thin, spindly shrimp of a fellow he was,' said His Excellency,

but he swayed 319,000,000 people and held them at his beck and call. He didn't care for material things, and preached nothing but

the ideas and morals of India. You can't govern a country with
ideals. Still that was where he got his grip upon the people. He was
their god. India must always have its god. First it was Tilak, then
Gandhi now, then someone else tomorrow. He gave us a scare! His
programme filled the jails, you can't go arresting people forever,
you know, not when there are 319,000,000 of them. And if they
had taken the next step and refused to pay the taxes, God knows
where we should have been! . . . Gandhi's was the most colossal
experiment in history, and he came within an inch of succeeding . . .

Pearson then asked whether he could meet Gandhi in prison.
'Absolutely impossible,' answered the governor, adding: 'If we
allowed people to come here and make a fuss over him, he would
become a martyr, and the gaol would be a Mecca for the world.' The
journalist next asked if there was any chance of Gandhi being released
before his sentence of six years was over. 'Not while I'm here,' replied
the governor. 'Of course, my term expires in December. They can do
whatever they like with him after I go back to England.'[12]

Another American travelling in India in the cold season of
1922–23 was the Chicago social worker Jane Addams. She spent
two months in the country, meeting women's groups and sundry
nationalists, but 'found it impossible to see Gandhi, he is allowed
but two visitors in . . . three months, naturally his wife is one and his
followers [bargain] for the other chance'.[13]

On 10 November 1922, in London, a 'Bench Table' meeting of the
Inner Temple's management ordered that 'Mohandas Karamchand
Gandhi, having been convicted by a competent tribunal of an offence
which, in the opinion of the Bench, disqualifies him from continuing as
a member of the Inn, should have his name removed from the books'.
The decision was to be communicated 'to the judges of the Supreme
Court of Judicature, to the other Inns of Court, to the General Council
of the Bar and by registered letter to the said Mohandas Karamchand
Gandhi, and be screened in the Hall'.[14]

The news of Gandhi's disbarment was reported in the Indian
press. We do not know whether the letter sent to him by the Inner
Temple was passed on to him by the authorities. Not that the news
would have disturbed him. It had been more than a decade since he

had functioned as a practising lawyer. His more recent appearances in court had been as someone charged with having broken the law.

IV

In their leader's absence, the inmates of the Sabarmati Ashram doggedly went about their work. There were a series of stand-in editors who ran *Young India*: first, Shuaib Qureshi, and then, after his arrest, C. Rajagopalachari. The journal's pages were filled with reports of khadi work from across the country, and with reprints of articles by the founder. A series Gandhi had written in 1908 on his jail experiences in South Africa was republished for the Indian reader; so also extracts from his 1910 book, *Hind Swaraj*.

A new contributor to the pages of *Young India* was Kasturba Gandhi. Her husband and their eldest son, Harilal, were already in prison. In May 1922, when Devadas was also arrested, Kasturba issued a message asking students 'to go on with the Khadi propaganda with all your youthful vigour and intensity and either release your brothers from the jails or fill up the jails to overflowing, thus showing to the world that India is determined to prove her self-respect to the last'.[15]

Later that month, Kasturba gave the presidential address to a political conference in Ahmedabad. She urged the delegates to promote spinning and weaving, since 'no Empire can detain Gandhiji in jail a minute more as soon as India has fully realized the significance of khadi'.[16] In June, when *Navajivan* printed a special number on women, Kasturba told them to show the same 'passionate love for the Motherland' as the young men were doing. Recalling how, in South Africa, many Indian women came forward to court arrest, she asked, 'Will the women here come out if a similar occasion arose? I have my doubts.'[17]

In July, *Navajivan* printed a special number on the suppressed castes. Kasturba now called upon the upper castes to 'purge yourselves of all your sins—and what sin is greater than your refusing to touch your brothers?'[18] Then, on the occasion of Gandhi's birthday, Kasturba sent a message via *Young India* suggesting that the best way to celebrate the day would be to 'redouble our efforts for Swadeshi and recognise the claim of our untouchable brethren to our kinship in a practical manner'.[19]

Ever since her return to India in 1915, Kasturba had stayed away from politics and public affairs. Now, with her husband in jail, she came forward to commend his programme to those still at large. Kasturba was a poor writer and indifferent speaker. The messages she put out were most likely drafted on her behalf by her nephew Maganlal Gandhi. Yet, the sentiments they conveyed were indisputably her own.

V

The annual December session of the Congress met in 1922 in the town of Gaya, in Bihar, near where the Buddha had achieved enlightenment under the Bodhi tree. Presiding over the session was C.R. Das, who had recently been released from jail. Das praised Gandhi as 'one of the greatest men that the world has ever seen'. The tribute paid, Das now sought to move the Congress away from the great Gandhi's policies. He wanted the party to end its boycott of the legislative councils set up under the Montagu–Chelmsford scheme. The mass movement having exhausted itself, entering the councils seemed the pragmatic thing to do.

Das's resolution asking for the ending of the boycott of councils was defeated. The Calcutta barrister now resigned from the presidency of the Congress, and founded a new Swaraj Party, whose members included Motilal Nehru, Hakim Ajmal Khan and Vithalbhai Patel (elder brother of Vallabhbhai). This party would, however, still remain within the Congress. The other faction, which stood by the boycott and came to be known as the 'No-Changers' had as its prominent members Dr Ansari, Mrs Naidu, Maulana Azad and Rajagopalachari.[20]

The AICC met in Bombay in the last week of May 1923. It had been five months since the Gaya Congress, and in this period, Das swayed more people to his side, among them his fellow Bengali, the dynamic young Congressman Subhas Chandra Bose. Hardcore devotees of the Mahatma such as Mahadev Desai and

Rajagopalachari still held out, but in this meeting, Das was able to get majority support for his policy of council entry (with ninety-six AICC members voting for, seventy-one against).[21]

With Gandhi in prison, the Congress had abandoned the boycott of the councils. The campaign against untouchability was also visibly slowing down. In a note to the AICC, the radical priest Swami Shraddhananda bitterly complained that 'the question of raising the depressed classes has been relegated to an obscure corner'. Travelling through the Punjab and the United Provinces, the swami 'found the question of removing the disability of the untouchables everywhere ignored or shelved'. What, he asked, had happened to all the pious resolutions committing the Congress and Congressmen to ending this pernicious practice?[22]

Shraddhananda made his criticisms public. 'People who oppress a section of their own community,' he wrote in a widely circulated booklet, 'do not have any right to complain about the oppressive measures of foreign rulers.' So long as 'the iniquities of untouchability' persist, continued the swami, 'so long is it impossible for the National Congress to be successful in any kind of programme of criticism or development'.[23]

With Gandhi in prison, the question of inter-religious relations was also not getting the attention it deserved. Ten months after Gandhi had been sentenced, the viceroy wrote to the secretary of state for India: 'The Hindu–Muslim entente, which has been fostered by Hindu politicians for their own reasons, is now visibly cracking.'[24] The note of smug satisfaction, of schadenfreude, was palpable.

VI

Gandhi maintained his diary in 1923, again mostly a record of his reading. The books he read this year included Max Müller's translation of the Upanishads, some works by Rabindranath Tagore, Patrick Geddes's The Evolution of Cities, books on Sikh history, a biography of the medieval saint Ramanujacharya, George Bernard Shaw's Man and Superman, and William James's The Varieties of Religious Experience.

There was the odd entry on his health—thus on Saturday, 7 July, Gandhi 'suffered great pains'. The 'fault was entirely mine,' the entry continued, 'I ate more than I should have of the figs sent by Anasuyabehn.'[25]

More important (from the public point of view) was the diary entry for Monday, 26 November, which noted that Gandhi had now 'commenced writing the history of Satyagraha in South Africa'. During those extended periods of solitude, away from his Indian comrades and co-workers, Gandhi had been thinking a great deal about how and where the idea of satyagraha was born and first applied. These recollections were now finding their way on to paper.

Every three months, Gandhi continued to be allowed one group of visitors, their names vetted by the authorities. His political associates—Jawaharlal Nehru and Mahadev Desai—were denied permission, but his wife Kasturba and their son Ramdas were allowed in. They found he had lost a couple of pounds in weight, but was (in his own words) 'quite happy and feels free as a bird'.[26]

Books, magazines and letters sent to Gandhi were also carefully screened. In December 1922, one E.H. James, a resident of Concord, Massachusetts, wrote to Gandhi. He had 'with a certain thrill of pleasure' read of the Indian's admiration for Henry David Thoreau. He enclosed a copy of the essays of Emerson, Thoreau's friend and fellow Concordian. The letter (re)told the story of Thoreau's going to jail for not paying taxes when America was at war; and of Emerson going to visit him and saying, 'Henry, why are you here?', to be answered by the return query: 'Ralph, why are you not here?'

Neither the letter nor the book was passed on to the prisoner.

In January 1923, Gandhi had asked for two Gujarati magazines, *Vasant* and *Samalochak*, to be supplied to him. When his request was refused, Gandhi asked for a reconsideration. Even prisoners had rights, he argued, among them the right to water and food, and 'the right to have such mental nourishment given to me as I am used to'.[27]

The matter was sent up to the inspector general of prisons, who ruled in favour of the jail authorities, since 'any magazine allowed to Mr. Gandhi should be like Caesar's wife' (that is, above suspicion).

In March, a friend sent Gandhi a Gujarati translation of Aurobindo Ghose's *Essays on the Gita*. The jail authorities got a report prepared on the book by the Bombay government's oriental translator. When he confirmed that it confined itself to spiritual matters, the book was passed on to the prisoner.

Anything with a whiff of politics or social reform was withheld, but purely religious works were allowed to be read. A certain J. Lambert Disney of Philadelphia, who described himself as a 'Healer-by-Faith and Drugless Physician', sent Gandhi pamphlets on the Bible and faith healing; these were duly delivered to Prisoner Number 827. So were several works on the Buddha and Buddhism sent by one Dr A.L. Nair of Bombay. So also a study of the Chandogya Upanishad posted by Gandhi's friend and follower Jamnalal Bajaj.[28]

One of the more intriguing letters in the prison records was written by Gandhi in December 1922. For some reason, it escaped the editors of the *Collected Works*, although it appeared in print in an anthology of documents published as far back as 1968. Here is the letter in full:

The Superintendent   21st December 1922
Yerwada Central Jail

Sir,
Shrimati Sarala Devi Chaudhrani (Mazang Road, Lahore) in her letter handed to me says that she sent about six months ago [a] certain manuscript and wishes it to be returned to her. I have not been given any manuscript from her. If it has been received from her at the Gaol, will you kindly return it to her. If it has not, will you kindly write to her to the effect that it was never received.

I am
Yours obediently
M.K. Gandhi
[Prisoner] No. 827[29]

What was the nature of the manuscript sent by Saraladevi to Gandhi? Was it a memoir, a poetry collection, a novel? And what had she said in the letter recently handed over to Gandhi? Was it merely a polite or anxious inquiry about his health, or a larger meditation on Indian politics, or even a personal reflection on their relationship? We shall never know. But the fact that three years after their spiritual wedding had been aborted, Saraladevi still wrote to and thought of Gandhi is not without significance.

VII

During the Rowlatt satyagraha and the non-cooperation movement, Gandhi had lived his life in the public eye. From March 1919 to March 1922, there were daily reports in the press about his words and actions. But now, in prison, he was denied access to the newspapers. And they were denied access to him. There was little reliable public information about Gandhi and how he coped in prison. With no hard news available, speculation was rife.

In the first week of April 1922, a rumour was abroad that Gandhi had been flogged in Yerwada jail. The home department issued a statement that 'there is not a germ of truth in this rumour which is a sheer invention'. The origins of this rumour were traced to a clerk in Yerwada, who had overheard Gandhi asking the prison superintendent what the penalty for disobeying jail regulations was. The superintendent answered that they included flogging, which the clerk somehow assumed had been the fate of Gandhi himself.

In September 1923, a nationalist periodical named the *Voice of India* said it was strongly rumoured that Gandhi would be awarded the Nobel Peace Prize that year. Surely, the British authorities would release him so that he could accept the prize in person? The paper commented that 'as it stands, the news is too good to be true, and yet there is every indication to show it may be true. For of the fifteen hundred million living men of the earth, if it can be said of any one that he lives and suffers for the peace of the world and for the brotherhood of men, it can be said of one man alone, and that man is Mahatma Gandhi.'

Voice of India contrasted Gandhi with the warmongering Europeans; for, if the news was indeed correct, it would mean that 'in spite of the false lead given to humanity by the Lloyd Georges and the Clemenceaus of Europe, and in spite of the stupendous efforts made by the Curzons and Poincarés of today to keep [alive] the poisonous weeds of national hatred and domination, mankind has kept the kernel of its heart sound and known to look for true worth and true guidance . . .'[30]

The story was without any foundation. No Nobel Peace Prize was awarded in 1923, a year that came and went with Gandhi still confined in prison.

VIII

The 1923 Congress was held in Kakinada, in the Andhra country. The president that year was Mohammad Ali. His presidential address dealt with a wide range of political subjects, while returning repeatedly to Gandhi, for whom 'all eyes search in vain in this Pandal today'. Ever since he first attended a Congress in 1919, said Mohammad Ali, Gandhi had 'been the one dominating personality'. 'More than ever,' he continued, 'we need our great chief Mahatma Gandhi today.'

Calling himself one of Gandhi's 'humblest followers', the Congress president told the party's members that 'the only one who can lead you is the one who had led you at Amritsar, at Calcutta, at Nagpur and at Ahmedabad, though each session of the Congress has its own elected President. Our generalissimo is today a prisoner of war in the hands of the enemy, and none can fill the void that his absence from our midst has caused.' In a strange and bitter irony, said Mohammad Ali feelingly, 'it was reserved for a Christian government to treat as a felon the most Christ-like man of our times'.[31]

In the first week of January 1924, Gandhi came down with high fever. This was followed by acute pain in the stomach. The jail doctor, unable to cope, sent for Colonel Maddox, the civil surgeon of Poona. After examining Gandhi, Maddox asked for his stools and blood to be tested. The doctor examined Gandhi again on Thursday, 10 January, when he seemed a little better.

The next day, however, Gandhi developed acute pain. When he saw him again on the morning of Saturday, 12 January, Maddox had no doubt that Gandhi had appendicitis. With the jail superintendent's permission, the civil surgeon conveyed the prisoner in his own car to

Poona's Sassoon Hospital. Gandhi said he did not want to be operated upon until he had seen Dr Dalal, who had operated on him for piles in 1919. Maddox tried calling Dalal in Bombay but could not get through. Gandhi was told that if the operation was delayed, he could develop peritonitis. He agreed to have the operation performed that night.

Before taking him to the operating theatre, Maddox asked Gandhi whom he would like to see. The patient asked for his fellow Gokhale protégé V.S. Srinivasa Sastri, and a Poona doctor named V.D. Phatak. Both were called to meet Gandhi, with Dr Phatak being present during the operation as well. The lights failed during the procedure, so the doctors had to continue their work with the help of kerosene lamps.[32]

By the morning of the 13th, word of Gandhi being moved out of jail had reached Bombay. A reporter was sent down to Poona, where he met Dr Phatak, who conveyed the reassuring news that Gandhi 'had no fever and his pulse was all right. He was looking cheerful. He is taking sips of hot water now and then and some lemon juice. He is kept in a private special surgical ward under the care of a special European nurse. All the medical staff is looking after him with respectful attention.'[33]

Kasturba and Devadas had rushed from Ahmedabad to be with him, as had Mahadev Desai and Anasuya Sarabhai. A steady stream of Congress workers and leaders were demanding admission. This placed some strain on Colonel Maddox, who found Gandhi 'a bit upset about the restriction of visitors and . . . a terribly difficult bird to handle'.[34] The doctor would, however, have been comforted by praise from the nationalist *Bombay Chronicle*, which remarked that his 'bold and unconventional step of removing the Mahatma to the Hospital in his own car, and his scrupulous care and treatment—all have preserved a life that is held in the highest esteem by millions of Indians'.[35]

On 15 January—three days after Gandhi's operation—the home secretary of Bombay noted that his illness 'has redoubled popular interest and concern in him and we may expect strong, if not intensive, feeling to be aroused if he is sent back to prison when he is well again. The question is: is it worth keeping him in prison any longer; is Gandhi in prison, in the circumstance and in view of the general

situation, a greater force than when at large?' The official thought
that 'Gandhi at large will be a restraining force against the adoption
of violent methods which the more extreme sections are beginning to
coquette with'. There would, he argued, be 'much political advantage'
in the government releasing him now as an act of clemency.[36]

On 18 January, there was a mass meeting of all communities at
Bombay's Chowpatty beach, held to pray for the good health of Gandhi
and ask for his immediate release. Meanwhile, prominent public
figures in the Bombay Presidency, including the lawyers M.A. Jinnah
and M.R. Jayakar, and the industrial magnates Sir Purushottamdas
Thakurdas and Sir Dinshaw Petit, urged the government not to
send Gandhi back to jail after he had recovered from his operation,
but set him free instead. Jinnah spoke for many when he hoped the
government would remit the remaining period of Gandhi's sentence,
and have him 'restored to his family, friends and countrymen'.[37]

The Government of India was reluctant to release Gandhi.
However, there was now a new governor of Bombay, Leslie Wilson,
who was more sympathetic to the popular sentiment. His officials
told him that, if he was set free, Gandhi would exercise a 'restraining
influence' on the Ali Brothers. Besides, sending Gandhi back to
prison 'might easily lead to outbreaks of violence, which, in view
of the present industrial situation in Bombay, would very probably
lead to a more serious position'. This was a reference to the growing
communist influence among the textile millworkers in Bombay,
whose philosophy of violent revolution Gandhi was known to oppose
and abhor.[38]

Pressing their case, the Bombay government added that Colonel
Maddox could get an undertaking from Gandhi not to take part in
politics till he had fully recovered, which the doctor had estimated
would take at least six months. Maddox and Gandhi had talked about
where he might best recoup his strength. The doctor thought that
what he needed most of all was some months of continuous exposure
to cool and fresh winds from the sea. A couple of possible locations
in Surat district were discussed.[39]

Meanwhile, visitors continued to pour into the hospital ward.
Mohammad Ali came on 28 January; the next day his brother,
Shaukat, joined him. They spent a long time chatting with Gandhi.

As they were leaving, Shaukat told Gandhi: 'Take plenty of food now. Don't you starve yourself!' Gandhi replied: 'But if I grow fat, how will you find it possible to thrust me into the pocket' (this a reference to their joint tours of 1920–21, when the elder Ali had said he always kept his little Hindu friend with him, in his pocket).

Later, speaking to C. Rajagopalachari, Gandhi expressed his worries about the growing rift between Hindus and Muslims. The Arya Samaj and the Mahasabha-ites were urging Hindus to 'get as strong as the Muslims', and enrol in gymnasia and *akhara*s. Gandhi found this talk 'absurd'. As he told Rajagopalachari, 'admit the use of armed force and you will make the country an armed camp in no time'. Gandhi also deprecated the Muslim belief that the Word of God as passed on to Muhammad was eternal and infallible. He admired the Prophet's simplicity and spirit of sacrifice, but did not think that his 'message was final and for all time'.

There were political colleagues who came to see Gandhi, and also some trophy hunters. Two American journalists turned up with cameras, begging the nurses to allow them to take photographs of the great man in his hospital bed. 'This is a hospital,' said one nurse angrily. 'Gandhi is a patient here. It is not a museum, nor is Gandhi a specimen. Get away!'[40]

On 4 February 1924, the government chose to release Gandhi unconditionally. Two Englishmen were at his bedside when the release order reached Gandhi. These were his old friend Charlie Andrews, and the doctor who had recently operated on him, Colonel Maddox. It fell to the doctor to read the text out loud; he was, an eyewitness wrote, 'most enthusiastic in congratulating' his patient. As the news spread, a crowd of people from all over Poona came to offer their congratulations in person; which they could not do, since the doctor did not want to take any chances with a still weak and recovering patient. Telegrams from all over India also came pouring in; these were selectively read to Gandhi by his son Devadas.[41]

Three days after he was officially set free, but while he was still convalescing in the Sassoon Hospital, Gandhi wrote a long letter to Mohammad Ali, the serving president of the Congress. This assessed the changes in the Indian political scene in the time he had been incarcerated. 'It is clear,' wrote Gandhi to the younger of the Ali Brothers,

> that without unity between Hindus, Mahomedans, Sikhs, Parsis and Christians and other Indians, all talk of swaraj is idle. The unity which I fondly believed, in 1922, had been nearly achieved has, so far as Hindus and Mussalmans are concerned, I observe, suffered a severe check. Mutual trust has given place to distrust. . . . When I heard in the jail of the tensions between Hindus and Mussalmans in certain places, my heart sank within me.

Gandhi then moved on to the promotion of spinning and the abolition of untouchability, two other projects in urgent need of renewal. Finally, he raised the 'vexed question' of whether Congressmen should resume entering legislative councils, a growing demand within the party, for which he had 'no data for coming to a judgment' just yet.[42]

In early March, Gandhi read in the newspapers of the abolition of the Khilafat. This act had been undertaken not by the conquering Europeans, but by the Turks themselves, directed by their new and aggressively secularizing leader Kemal Atatürk. Gandhi wrote at once to Mohammad Ali to console him. While 'the decision must cause deep grief and distress to you', he remarked, his friend should remember that 'the future of Islam lies in the hand of the Mussalmans of India'.[43]

On 11 March, Gandhi was finally discharged from the Sassoon Hospital. He caught a train to Bombay, where—on the advice of his doctors—he would stay at a seaside cottage in Juhu owned by the Gujarati industrialist Narottam Morarjee. This was on the outskirts of Bombay, so Gandhi would have access to good medical care, and could also easily consult Colonel Maddox in Poona if need be.

The cottage in Juhu faced the sea, and at high tide, the waves came right up to its boundary wall. Here, a man born on the coast and who had spent so much of his early life in ports and ships, would recover his health while planning his, and his country's, future.

CHAPTER TEN

Picking Up the Pieces

I

Once he was out of jail, Gandhi's daily schedule was modified. He still woke up at 4.30 a.m. and said his prayers. At six he had a light breakfast, then took a short walk within the compound of the cottage. From then until midday he attended to his correspondence in English and in Gujarati, dictating letters and articles to a shorthand typist. He rested in the afternoon, saw visitors, and then took a forty-minute walk on the seashore. On his doctor's advice, he had not yet resumed spinning.

Juhu, the suburb where Gandhi was recovering, was easily accessible from the city by rail and road. A stream of visitors, mostly uninvited and unannounced, descended daily from Bombay. Gandhi was finally forced to issue a public appeal, asking people to come see him between five and six in the evening only. 'The capital of energy at my disposal is very small,' he wrote, 'and I want to utilize it only in service. I wish to resume editorship of *Navajivan* and *Young India* from next week. And I need absolute quiet for that work. If all my time and energy are taken up in seeing and entertaining you, it will not be possible for me to edit the weeklies in the way I desire.'[1]

Among those keen to see Gandhi was M.A. Jinnah's young wife, Ruttie. She sent a basket of strawberries, with a note saying she wanted to come too, but was nervous lest it interfere with his health. 'I should hate to think,' wrote Ruttie Jinnah, 'that what to me is a source of pleasure must to you inevitably prolong the struggle for recovery.' Then she hopefully added: 'But you must know, that like the rest of the world, I too am dying to see you, so when I can legitimately do so, I shall expect a line or a word of permission.'[2]

It is not clear whether Mrs Jinnah in fact visited Gandhi. But plenty of other admirers descended on the cottage in Juhu. 'I understand that Juhu has become another general hospital,' sarcastically wrote C. Rajagopalachari to Mahadev Desai, adding: 'At Poona it was a special ward; but it is now a general ward of all consumptives and melancholics—and a ward without divisions for sexes.'[3]

In the last week of March, Gandhi's old comrade in South Africa, Henry Polak, now based in London, cabled him with a request: the prestigious *Spectator* magazine wanted an exclusive article 'giving summarily your present programme'.[4] Gandhi was not up to writing the piece. However, he gave an interview to a visiting British journalist. Here he said, among other things, that 'if Britain is unwilling to give us complete independence, I would welcome and accept Home Rule'. When asked how India could rule itself amidst 'the irreconcilable differences of her castes, religions and tribes', Gandhi answered:

> Of course there are differences. No nation is without them. The United Kingdom was born amidst the Wars of the Roses. Probably we, too, shall fight. But, when we are tired of breaking each other's heads, we shall discover that, despite the disparities of our races and religions, we can live together, just as the Scotch and Welsh manage to live together.[5]

Even as Gandhi spoke these words, a bitter conflict was brewing between different castes in the southern princely state of Travancore. In the forefront of this struggle was T.K. Madhavan, a journalist and follower of the social reformer Narayana Guru. Born in a lowly caste of toddy tappers known as Ezhavas, Narayana Guru had started a social movement to remove caste distinctions altogether. He believed that all humans were the same, hence his slogan, 'One Caste, One Religion, One God'.[6]

T.K. Madhavan had first met Gandhi in Tirunelveli in September 1921. The follower of Narayana Guru told the reformer from Gujarat that he was keen on promoting inter-caste marriages, and temple entry for 'untouchables'. Gandhi, however, urged Madhavan to begin with opening wells and schools to 'untouchables' rather than roads or temples.[7]

Clearly, the Ezhava reformers were several steps ahead of Gandhi in their critique of caste. By the end of 1923, Madhavan had identified, as the first target of their movement, roads in the town of Vaikom that were barred to lower castes and 'untouchables'. These roads ringed a famous shrine to Siva, administered and patronized by Nairs and Namboodiris, the two dominant castes in this part of South India.

Like Narayana Guru, Madhavan was an Ezhava, from the caste of toddy tappers that were ritually considered to be on the border that divided the 'touchables' from the 'untouchables'. His strongest local ally was K.P. Kesava Menon, an upper-caste Nair who served as secretary of the Kottayam District Congress Committee. In the last week of January 1924—when Gandhi was at the Sassoon Hospital and still officially a prisoner—Madhavan and Kesava Menon formed an 'Anti-Untouchability Committee'. A month later, this committee held a large public meeting in Vaikom, where it was decided that the rule barring the temple roads to low castes would be defied by a group of satyagrahis. The 30th of March was fixed as the date when this defiance would take place.[8]

On 12 March, Kesava Menon wrote to Gandhi of the satyagraha, saying: 'A message from you would instil fresh courage in us.' Three years previously, Gandhi had been lukewarm about temple entry. However, now that a movement was actually under way, he supported it, asking only that it be non-violent. Writing to Kesava Menon, Gandhi said that 'there should be no show of force if any of our people oppose their progress. You should meekly submit and take all the beating, if any.'[9]

On 30 March, volunteers arrived in Vaikom from different parts of Travancore. Some came from Malabar, the Malayalam-speaking district of the Madras Presidency. The atmosphere in the satyagrahis' camp 'was charged with the austere serenity of Gandhian idealism and the burning odour of nationalist sentiment'. After the Mahatma's message was read out to them, three men—a Pulaya (a caste considered not just 'untouchable', but also 'unapproachable'), an Ezhava and a Nair—were garlanded, before marching hand in hand towards the prohibited road. When they were stopped by the police, the satyagrahis refused to turn back, but squatted on the road. A further batch of three men from different castes then came forward to break the law. The six protesters were arrested and taken off to court—one apologized, but the others stayed firm, and were sentenced to six months in prison.

A week later, both Madhavan and Kesava Menon courted arrest. More volunteers came forward to take their place. The authorities now changed their tactics, in part because the jails of Travancore were not capacious enough to house many more protesters. They had a large barricade erected across the road and placed a police guard next to it.

As the satyagraha proceeded, songs were composed in Malayalam juxtaposing admiration for Gandhi with denunciations of the caste system. Gandhi was praised as 'the fountain of humaneness and sympathy', who had invented the art of satyagraha 'with a view to rescu[ing] his mother country'.[10]

The roads to the temple remained barred to the lower castes. The satyagrahis responded by sitting outside the barricade and refusing to eat or drink. This part of India is always hot and humid—and the men were unaccustomed to fasting anyway. Several fainted, and were rushed to hospital.[11]

When Gandhi heard of these new developments, he sent a wire to the satyagrahis asking them to 'QUIT FASTING BUT STAND OR SQUAT IN RELAYS WITH QUIET SUBMISSION TILL ARRESTED'. The next day, a letter followed, where Gandhi elaborated on his advice. 'You cannot fast against a tyrant,' said Gandhi. 'Fasting can only be resorted to against a lover [by which Gandhi meant 'one you love'], not to extort rights but to reform him, as when a son fasts for a parent who drinks. My fast at Bombay, and then at Bardoli, was of that character. I fasted to reform those who loved me. But I will not fast to reform, say, General Dyer, who not only does not love me, but who regards himself as my enemy.'[12]

After Madhavan and Kesava Menon were arrested, the leadership
of the satyagraha was assumed by George Joseph, a London-educated
barrister and devoted Congressman. Joseph had edited *Young India* in
1923–24, stepping in for Rajagopalachari who, in turn, was stepping
in for Gandhi.

Gandhi admired Joseph, but thought a Christian should not play
a prominent role in a struggle within and for the soul of Hinduism.
'You should let the Hindus do the work,' he wrote to Joseph. 'It is
they who have to purify themselves. You can help by your sympathy
and your pen, but not by organizing the movement and certainly
not by offering satyagraha.' As a Christian, Joseph had 'nothing to
expiate'. Untouchability, insisted Gandhi, was 'the sin of the Hindus',
and it is they who must 'suffer for it', and 'pay the debt they owe their
suppressed brothers and sisters'.[13]

In a long, reflective article in *Young India*, Gandhi took
up the larger meaning of the Vaikom satyagraha. He had been
criticized for suggesting that while the satyagraha continued, the
organizers should simultaneously send petitions and deputations
to the authorities. His critics claimed Gandhi was 'partial to the
[Travancore] State authorities because they represent[ed] Indian
rule', whereas he was 'hostile to the British authorities because they
represent an alien rule'. In reply, Gandhi noted that even in South
Africa, he had carried on negotiations with the authorities while the
satyagraha proceeded.

In advocating an approach of determined incrementalism, Gandhi
remarked that 'in Travancore, the satyagrahis are not attacking a whole
system. . . . They are fighting sacerdotal prejudice. . . . Satyagrahis
would, therefore, be deviating from their path if they did not try to
court junction with the authorities and cultivate public support by
means of deputations, meetings, etc. Direct action does not always
preclude other consistent methods. Nor is petitioning, etc., in every
case a sign of weakness on the part of a satyagrahi. Indeed, he is no
satyagrahi who is not humble.'[14]

In the third week of May, a group of volunteers from Vaikom
arrived to meet Gandhi in Juhu. When asked what their future
course of struggle might be, Gandhi suggested that caste Hindus
who supported reform should march peacefully from Vaikom to the

state capital, Trivandrum. They should ask the ruler for an audience, and urge him to have removed the disabilities of the 'untouchables'. Gandhi told the deputation that 'the caste Hindus comprising the procession must be prepared to suffer the inconveniences incidental to a slow march on foot. They must camp in places away from villages and towns and make their own arrangements for food.'[15]

Here too, Gandhi must certainly had his South African experience in mind. In November 1913, he had led a slow, peaceful and yet spectacular march of several thousand Indians in Natal, who defied racial laws by crossing provincial boundaries into the Transvaal and courting arrest.[16] By marching and sleeping in the open, and cooking their own food, and thus voluntarily inflicting suffering on themselves, the satyagrahis could draw attention to, and garner support for, their cause.

II

With the collapse of the non-cooperation movement, demoralization had set in within the Congress. Gandhi's own misjudgements had contributed to this; notably, his hasty promise that if Indians followed his call, the country would be free within one year of the beginning of the struggle. Young men who had joined the Congress in the hope that swaraj was around the corner had now abandoned it to make their peace with the workaday world. The leadership remained divided, between those who wished to take part in council elections and those who stuck doggedly to the old policy of boycott.

In the last week of March 1924, Motilal Nehru travelled down to Juhu to meet Gandhi. The two had long discussions, each failing to convince the other of their point of view. The firmness of the elder Nehru's belief, acknowledged Gandhi, was a manifestation of genuine commitment. If the swarajists were so passionate in their convictions, he concluded, 'their place is undoubtedly in the Councils. . . . If their work prospers and the country benefits, such an ocular demonstration cannot but convince sceptics like me of our error and I know the Swarajists to be patriotic enough to retrace their steps when experience disillusioned them.'[17]

Motilal Nehru was back in Juhu a month later, this time with C.R. Das in tow. These two formidable barristers were the leaders of the swarajists. For a long, hot week in May, Gandhi and his visitors talked and argued. Afterwards, the two parties issued separate press statements. Gandhi's was shorter, saying that since he had failed to convince his swarajist friends, 'their place is undoubtedly in the Councils'. The 'No-changers' (who still upheld the 1920 non-cooperation credo) would adopt an attitude of 'perfect neutrality' towards council entry.

In their statement, Motilal Nehru and C.R. Das expressed regret that they had failed to convince Gandhi of the soundness of council entry. Their plan within the councils was to vote against proposals which consolidated the bureaucracy's power and led to the drain of wealth from India, and, on the other side, to 'introduce all resolutions, measures and bills which are necessary for the healthy growth of our national life and the consequent displacement of the bureaucracy'. Outside the legislatures, they planned to give 'whole-hearted support to the constructive programme of Mahatma Gandhi'.[18]

III

In his first months as a free man, Gandhi became increasingly preoccupied with the deteriorating relations between Hindus and Muslims. This had the potential of being even more damaging to the nationalist cause than the persistence of untouchability or a rift within the Congress.

In the summer of 1924, there was a series of religious riots across northern India. 'Daily the gulf was widening', commented one journal of record: 'Vernacular papers cropped up like mushrooms simply to indulge into the most unbridled license in ridiculing the religion and social customs of the opposite community, and they sold like hot cakes.'[19]

Several factors contributed to the rising tension. The Hindu missionary organization, the Arya Samaj, had launched an aggressive programme of 're-converting' Hindus whose forefathers had, long ago, converted to Islam. Muslims were demoralized after the abolition of the Khilafat, an outcome which also led them to suspect the (mostly Hindu) Congress leaders who had promised to help restore it.

In the last week of April, the Delhi Congress leader Asaf Ali wrote to Gandhi deploring 'the disgraceful outburst of distrust and passion which has engulfed us in the North'. He laid a large share of the blame on partisan newspaper accounts, where 'every street brawl is a communal fight, and every worthless delinquent who bears a Hindu or Muslim name is held up as a type of the civilization which each name is supposed to represent'.[20]

Gandhi was reading the newspapers, and also speaking to Congressmen from the districts most seriously affected. In the last week of May, he published a long essay in *Young India* entitled 'Hindu–Muslim Tension: Its Cause and Cure'. He began by narrating some of the complaints he had been receiving. A Hindu had written to say that Gandhi was responsible for the recent riots in Multan, because he had asked them to make common cause with Muslims, and now 'the awakened Mussalmans have proclaimed a kind of jehad against us Hindus'. A Muslim wrote to say that through Gandhi's advocacy of the boycott of colleges the great university in Aligarh had been 'utterly spoilt'. The Muslim boys left their colleges, but the Hindus stayed on to study. This embittered reader further claimed that Mohammad Ali, who was 'doing solid work for the Muslim community, was won over to your side, and he is now a loss to the community'.

Replying to both kinds of critics, Gandhi said he was 'totally unrepentant' about his role in the Khilafat agitation. He believed that 'in spite of the present strained relations between the two communities, both have gained. The awakening of the masses was a necessary part of the training. I would do nothing to put the people to sleep again. Our wisdom consists now in directing the awakening in the proper channel.'

Gandhi then examined what he saw as 'two constant causes of friction' between Hindus and Muslims: the persistence of cow slaughter and the playing of music before mosques. First addressing the Hindus, Gandhi remarked that they said nothing about the daily killings of animals by Englishmen, yet 'our anger becomes red-hot when a Mussalman slaughters a cow'. Besides, 'living as they do in glass houses, [Hindus] have no right to throw stones at their Mussalman neighbours. . . . In the history of the world religions, there is perhaps nothing like our treatment of the suppressed classes.' Then, addressing the Muslims, Gandhi pointed out that 'just as Hindus cannot compel Mussalmans to refrain from killing cows, so can Mussalmans not compel Hindus to stop music or *arati* at the point of a sword'. If there was to be a durable peace, this could come only through voluntary restraint on both sides.[21]

The simmering rift within the Congress, and the open breach between Hindus and Muslims, delighted the *Times of India*, a newspaper then solidly behind the British Raj. 'The Gandhi Raj has broken up,' it chortled in delight, 'and on all sides we see fighting swamis, truculent maulvis, Bengali admirers of assassins and uncertain quantities like Mr. [Motilal] Nehru vigorously getting back to realities.' Gandhi, said the newspaper, 'should realize that he can no longer carry the country with him'. Since 'huge sections of his followers have already deserted him', it advised Gandhi to retire from politics altogether.[22]

IV

After eight weeks by the sea in Juhu, his doctors permitted Gandhi to return to Ahmedabad. He reached the Sabarmati Ashram on 29 May 1924, two years and two months after his arrest. He had now also been allowed to resume spinning, an act that for him was not merely an individual practice, but part of a larger programme for social and national renewal.

Amidst the clash of factions, castes and religions, Gandhi took a quiet satisfaction in the spread of khadi. In *Young India*, he reproduced a report on the steady promotion of khadi in Bengal, led by the chemist P.C. Ray and the social worker Satis Chandra Dasgupta. 'If the whole nation, irrespective of parties, co-operates in the spinning programme,' remarked Gandhi, 'it will be found that we can banish foreign cloth and with it pauperism from our midst in an incredibly short space of time.'[23]

Gandhi was also pleased with the progress of the Gujarat Vidyapith, the autonomous body he had established to provide schooling outside the sphere of the state. By 1924, the vidyapith had 140 institutions affiliated to it, of which three were colleges and the rest high schools. There were 800 teachers in these national schools, instructing 30,000 children, of which as many as 500 were girls.[24]

In the last week of June, the AICC met in Ahmedabad. Here, Gandhi moved a resolution making it mandatory for all Congress representatives/office-bearers to spin for at least half an hour a day except when travelling, and to send to the All India Khadi Board at least ten *tola*s (about 1.8 kg) of 'even and well-twisted' yarn every month. The resolution passed, by seventy-eight votes to seventy. Among those resolute in their opposition were Motilal Nehru and C.R. Das. The narrowness of Gandhi's victory suggested that he no longer had complete control over the Congress.[25]

Friends continued to be anxious about Gandhi's health. Motilal Nehru, whose affection for the Mahatma had survived political differences, thought that he should stop all work, even writing, editing and answering letters till he had completely recovered. 'I should cut you off from all communication with India for a time,' wrote Motilal, 'and send you out in the open sea for a fairly long cruise without any land being in sight for six weeks.'[26]

Other Congressmen were, however, asking Gandhi to play a more active role in party affairs. Leaders from several provinces had asked him to be the president of the next Congress, to be held in the southern town of Belgaum in December. Writing in *Young India*, Gandhi said that since he was a sort of partisan, 'an out-and-out advocate of the old programme of non-co-operation', the president should be someone more neutral. He himself thought that the best candidate would be Sarojini Naidu, since she was identified with neither camp, and stood 'for solid Hindu–Muslim unity'. Besides, the Congress had not yet had an Indian woman as its president (Gandhi was here counting Annie Besant as foreign-born), making this 'the fittest opportunity for paying our Indian sisters the compliment that is long overdue'.[27]

V

In the third week of August Gandhi travelled to Delhi, his first long trip since his release from jail. He was now travelling second, and not third, class on trains, on his doctor's advice. In Delhi, Gandhi addressed a public meeting and met with Hindu and Muslim leaders. He returned to Ahmedabad on 23 August, spent a week in the ashram, and then was off again, to Bombay and Poona. Meanwhile, more reports of riots were coming in.

The climax of the rising Hindu–Muslim tension was reached in the town of Kohat, in the North-West Frontier Province (NWFP). In the second week of September, a Hindu preacher in Kohat published a pamphlet with hostile references to Islam and the Koran, whereupon angry Muslims torched the homes and shops of Hindus and Sikhs. The latter fought back, but as they were less than 10 per cent of the population, it was an unequal battle. More than a hundred people perished, with the entire Hindu (and Sikh) population of the town fleeing to Rawalpindi, 100 miles from Kohat, and in the province of the Punjab.

Gandhi wanted to visit Kohat, but the government denied him permission. On 17 September, Gandhi started a twenty-one-day fast in the house of Mohammad Ali in Delhi. Mahadev Desai communicated to the press a short statement dictated by his master, which said the fast was a 'prayer both to Hindus and Mussalmans, who have hitherto worked in unison, not to commit suicide'.

Mahadev had himself pleaded with Gandhi not to fast. He had understood the decision to fast after Bombay in 1919 and Chauri Chaura in 1922, when the violence that broke out was in some ways a (degenerate) byproduct of the movements Gandhi had initiated. With Kohat, however, Mahadev could not see what Gandhi's own fault was that he had to undergo this penance. Gandhi replied that he had 'committed a breach of faith with the Hindus. I asked them to befriend Muslims. . . . Even today I am asking them to practice ahimsa, to settle quarrels by dying but not by killing. And what do I find to be the result? How many temples have been desecrated? How many sisters have come to me with complaints?' So this fast was addressed in the first instance to Muslims, the main perpetrators of the violence in Kohat.[28]

After the fast began, there was no deviation in Gandhi's daily routine. He slept at 10 p.m., and awoke six hours later for his prayers. He met visitors, gave interviews, spun for at least half an hour a day, and wrote articles for *Young India* and *Navajivan*. He also sometimes took a drive in the afternoon through the streets of Delhi.[29]

The day after the fast began, Maulana Shaukat Ali met Gandhi and tried to persuade him to give up his fast. Gandhi was unmoved, saying 'it is a matter between me and my Maker'.[30]

On 20 September, his wife Kasturba and his son Ramdas arrived from Ahmedabad. So did Gandhi's trusty lieutenants Anasuya Sarabhai and Shankarlal Banker. He was comforted by their presence; the chatter around his bedside was now mostly in Gujarati, while the ashramites also helped Mahadev regulate the unceasing flow of visitors.

On 22 September—four days after the fast began—Gandhi issued a statement explaining why he had chosen to fast in the home of a Muslim friend. 'I know instinctively what is necessary for Hinduism,' he remarked. 'But I must labour to discover the Mussalman mind. The closer I come to the best of Mussalmans, the juster I am likely to be in my estimate of the Mussalman and their doings.'[31]

Gandhi's fast was closely covered in the press. One Hindi paper, *Aaj*, ran a daily health bulletin and op-ed column devoted to Gandhi, commending his call to the conscience of the ordinary Indian. '*Ishvar Se Toh daro*', ran the title of one column—'At Least Fear the Lord', before continuing: '*Aaj Mahatmaji ke upvaas ka chautha din hai. Aap aur hum khaate hain, sote hain, haste hain, khelte hain. Mahatmaji faanke kar rahe hain, rote hain aur param karunik parmatma se raat-din lagaatar prarthna kar rahe hain.*' ('Today is the fourth day of the Mahatma's fast. The rest of us eat, sleep, laugh and play, while the Mahatma grieves [for our sins] and prays to the Lord day and night.')[32]

In response to Gandhi's fast, a 'Unity Conference' was held in Delhi on 26 and 27 September. Mohammad Ali was the first speaker, while Motilal Nehru was in the chair. The meeting unanimously passed a resolution condemning 'any desecration of places of worship to whatsoever faith they may belong, and any persecution or punishment of any person for adopting or reverting to any faith'. It further condemned 'any attempt by compulsion to convert people to one's faith or to secure or to enforce one's own religious observances at the cost of the rights of others'.

At the end of the conference, its participants trooped to Gandhi's bedside and begged him to give up his fast. Gandhi calmly answered that the matter was between him and his God. The fast would continue. The doctors, meanwhile, reported that Gandhi was physically weak, but his face looked brighter and happier.[33]

Among those attending the Unity Conference was C. Rajagopalachari. He stayed on afterwards to be with Gandhi. Writing to Devadas Gandhi as a disciple to a son, he reported that the Mahatma was having a daily oil massage, and drinking plenty of water. Now well into the second week of his fast, Gandhi's 'facial symptoms are most satisfactory as far as an anxious layman can judge'. Having given these personal details, Rajaji continued:

> I am a changed man now as regards the Mussulman leaders. I don't like them at all. I see no change of heart in them. They have not realized the least bit the psychology of the fast—that Bapu is in deepest grief over the ingratitude of the Mussulmans and the sufferings of the Hindus and the indifference and heartlessness of the Mussulman leaders, and gropes with unvarnished faith still towards God crying for light and help in his great anguish. I see no change whatever in the hardened hearts of the Mussulman leaders.

Rajagopalachari ended his letter on a despairing note: 'One thing is clear, that a long period of suspension of all Swaraj activities is before us.'[34]

While Rajaji placed the burden of the blame on the Muslims, many Muslims, on their part, thought the Hindus were more guilty. A clerk in Simla wrote Gandhi a long letter charging that across northern India, Hindu mobs were attacking 'unarmed peaceful Muslims'. He blamed the Arya Samaj in particular for their aggressive campaigns of 'Shuddhi', or reconversion.[35]

As Gandhi's fast entered its third week, there was increasing anxiety about his health. The doctors urged him to at least stop spinning; he refused. On 1 October, Gandhi's urine was analysed, and large amounts of poisonous acids detected. The doctors pleaded with Gandhi to at least take a spoon of glucose every day. He declined. Now, Dr Ansari stayed by his bedside the whole night.

A second urine analysis a day later showed the poisons had now largely disappeared. Gandhi, his body—or will—having trumped the doctors, went out into the veranda to enjoy the sunlight. A ladies' deputation from Bombay came to see him. They inevitably asked him to give up the fast, and he, just as inevitably, refused.[36]

Gandhi broke his fast at 12.30 p.m. on 9 October, after completing the three-week period he had set himself. Among those present when Dr Ansari handed him a glass of orange juice were Anasuya Sarabhai, Sarojini Naidu, Swami Shraddhananda, Hakim Ajmal Khan, Motilal Nehru, C.R. Das, the Ali Brothers, Charlie Andrews, and his old friend from South Africa, Imam Abdul Kadir Bawazir. Gandhi asked Imam Kadir to read a prayer from the Koran, this followed by a Christian hymn from Andrews, and a Hindu hymn from Anasuya Sarabhai. Afterwards, Mohammad Ali presented Gandhi a cow that he had purchased from a butcher so that the Mahatma could present it to a *pinjrapole*, a shelter for cows.[37]

VI

After the fast was broken, Gandhi did not resume his normal diet at once. Instead, he sought to replenish his energy with orange juice, honey and glucose. Later, he graduated to goat's milk and bread. The doctors had asked him to have a prolonged period of 'mental rest'. Gandhi refused, attending to his work, meeting colleagues, and telling Mahadev (more pliant in this respect than the doctors) to brief him daily about the news and to place all important correspondence before him.[38]

On 15 October, Gandhi again asked the viceroy for permission to visit the riot-torn town of Kohat in the company of Shaukat Ali. The viceroy answered that the 'time was not propitious'.[39] So Gandhi turned his attention to the still simmering dispute within the Congress itself. He travelled to Calcutta to meet C.R. Das, and also had long conversations with Motilal Nehru. On 6 November, the three of them issued a joint statement asking the Congress to suspend the non-cooperation programme, except insofar as it related to the wearing of foreign cloth.

In December 1924, Shaukat Ali and Gandhi chose to go together to Rawalpindi, where the refugees from Kohat were currently located. After the two men had visited the refugee camps, Gandhi told the *Tribune* newspaper that he hoped 'the Mussalmans of Kohat will see their way to meet the refugees and invite them to return to Kohat under a promise of friendship and full security'.[40]

Gandhi now moved back south, towards the town of Belgaum, in the Deccan, the venue for that year's Congress of which he had been chosen president. In his presidential address, Gandhi spoke with feeling about the prevailing 'disunity and ill feeling' among Hindus and Muslims. He then discussed the growing opposition within the Congress to the mandatory spinning that went with party membership. It remained his conviction that 'every revolution of the charkha was bringing swaraj nearer and nearer to us'.[41]

And so ended the year 1924. In the ten months after Gandhi's release, he had to retreat, regroup, reconsider. The enthusiasm of the non-cooperation movement had now visibly fizzled out. His leadership of the Congress was no longer unquestioned. And Hindu–Muslim riots were breaking out everywhere.

VII

While Gandhi had been pursuing Hindu–Muslim harmony in the North, the movement for the emancipation of 'untouchables' carried on in the South. The focal point remained Vaikom, the temple town whose roads were closed to lower castes. Among the new volunteers was E.V. Ramasamy, a radical Congressman with a deep antipathy to the caste system. Ramasamy threw himself into the struggle, being arrested twice. His commitment earned him the appellation *Vaikom Virar*, the valiant hero of Vaikom.[42]

In the second week of February 1925, the Travancore Legislative Council voted by the narrowest of margins (twenty-two to twenty-one) against the entry of 'untouchables' to the temple road. A satyagrahi from Vaikom now urged Gandhi to visit the town. If they did not have his sustenance and support, he said, the movement would wane, and perhaps die out altogether.[43]

In March, Gandhi visited Vaikom. He found the volunteers squatting in front of the barricades put up to guard the temple's four entrances. Each batch was stationed for six hours, its members spinning or singing.

Gandhi asked the satyagrahis 'to forget the political aspect of the programme'. We 'are endeavouring to rid Hinduism of its greatest blot', he remarked. The aim was to get all roads in Travancore to be opened up to the 'untouchables', as a prelude to an end to caste discrimination itself.[44]

Gandhi urged the protesters to cultivate a 'detached state of mind', adding that 'three fourths of the miseries and misunderstandings in the world will disappear, if we step into the shoes of our adversaries and understand their standpoint'. Gandhi himself sought an audience with the high-caste Namboodiri Brahmins who were most bitterly opposed to granting the Ezhavas and Pulayas the right to walk on the roads outside the temple.

The conversation between Gandhi and the Namboodiri orthodoxy in Vaikom was recorded by Mahadev Desai. When asked why they treated the low castes so harshly, the leader of the Namboodiris—named Indanturuttil—said placidly that the Ezhavas and Pulayas were merely 'reaping the reward of their karma'. It was for their (bad) behaviour in their past life that they had been relegated to the bottom of the pile in this one.

Gandhi told Indanturuttil Namboodiri that their conduct was as shocking, and as brutal, as the actions of General Dyer in Jallianwala Bagh. The Brahmin said, in justification, that the practice he and his caste men followed had been started by Adi Sankara, the eighth-century preacher from Kerala who had helped create a sense of unity among Hindus. Gandhi asked that if indeed this was an ancient custom, why was it not practised elsewhere in India? To this the Namboodiri answered: 'Surely untouchability is there in every part of India. We carry untouchability a little further. That's all.'

What, asked Gandhi, if the courts ruled in favour of granting access to the road to all regardless of caste? If that happened, said the

Namboodiri, then 'we should use the roads no longer, and we should leave the temples'.[45]

While in Travancore, Gandhi also visited Narayana Guru, the great Ezhava reformer among whose protégés was the originator of the Vaikom satyagraha, T.K. Madhavan. In Gandhi's version of the meeting, when the Guru told him 'religion was one', he respectfully disagreed; in his view, 'so long as there are different human heads, so long will there be different religions, but the secret of a true religious life is to tolerate one another's religion'.

The two men were sitting in an open courtyard under a mango tree. As recorded in the *Collected Works*, Gandhi told Narayana Guru that 'no two leaves of this very tree, under whose shadow we are sitting, are alike, though they spring from the same root, but, even as the leaves live together in perfect harmony and present to us a beautiful whole, so must we, divided humanity present to the outsider looking upon us as a beautiful whole'.[46]

The version told by the Guru's biographers uses the same metaphor, but with a crucial twist. Here, Gandhi plucked two leaves from the tree, and, pointing to their different textures, sizes and shapes, said they illustrated the variety of humanity, and hence of their religious affiliations. In response, the Guru bit into the stem of one leaf, and then the other, and asked Gandhi to do so as well. He would find that the juice of the two stems tasted exactly the same. Likewise, men may appear to differ in size or skin colour or caste or religious identity, but in essence they were the same. Hence, Narayan Guru's slogan, 'One Caste, One God, One Humanity'.[47]

A poem attributed to Narayana Guru beautifully conveys his egalitarian and universalist philosophy. It reads well enough in English, and must surely be even more evocative in its native Malayalam. Here are a few lines:

> One of kind, one of faith, and one of God is man
> Of one womb, of one form, difference herein none
> Within a species, is it not, that offspring truly bred?
> The community of man thus viewed to a single caste belongs
> Of the human species is even a Brahmin born,
> And the Pariah too.[48]

Despite their different theological positions, Gandhi was greatly impressed by Narayana Guru, and by the manifest influence he had on the self-esteem of the Ezhavas. In a public meeting held in the state capital, Trivandrum, he said it 'hurt his sense of religion, humanity and nationalism', that someone like Narayana Guru could not enter the prohibited roads in Vaikom. He thought the issue should be settled by a popular referendum, or by an impartial arbitrator. Gandhi believed that 'blind orthodoxy could not stand the fierce light of local public criticism provided it was sympathetic, non-violent and humble. There were only sixty thousand Brahmins, compared to eight lakh non-Brahmins and 17 lakh untouchables in [the State], and . . . they should not be refused the rights of common humanity.'[49]

On this trip, Gandhi also met the ruling maharani of Travancore, and urged her to have the obnoxious restrictions in Vaikom removed. Later in the year, some concessions were granted, with three sides of the road outside the temple being thrown open to all regardless of caste. But one side remained closed, while the temple itself remained out of bounds for all except caste Hindus.[50]

VIII

Gandhi had been prevented from visiting the riot-torn town of Kohat. He did, however, make several trips to Rawalpindi, where he had extensive conversations with the refugees. In the last week of March, six months after the riots themselves, Gandhi published a statement in *Young India*. He argued here that while there was provocation from both sides, the Muslim response was excessive, their 'fury [knowing] no bounds', with attacks on people and property (including temples and gurdwaras). Gandhi also blamed the local government, which had 'betrayed callous indifference, incompetence and weakness'.

Gandhi advised the Hindus of Kohat, now in Rawalpindi, not to return to their home town 'till there is complete reconciliation between them and the Mussalmans, and until they feel that they are able to live at peace with the latter without the protection of the British bayonet'.

Young India also printed Shaukat Ali's article on the Kohat riots. Their statements show subtle differences of emphasis. Gandhi pointed out that the Muslims were the aggressors, and that the government was criminally negligent. Shaukat Ali accepted that since the Muslims were in a majority they must take a greater share of the blame, but felt the Hindus had been unnecessarily provocative by publishing a pamphlet insulting the Prophet. He also said the old Muslim elite in the NWFP had been made insecure by the growing wealth of Hindu merchants who 'aggressively' flaunted their prosperity.[51]

Back in the days of Khilafat and non-cooperation, Gandhi and Shaukat Ali acted and felt like brothers. That now they could not even agree on a joint statement was reflective of a growing rift between the two men, and the two communities they represented.

The deteriorating relations between Hindus and Muslims depressed Gandhi, but cheered British imperialists. Lord Birkenhead, the secretary of state for India, wrote in glee to the viceroy, Lord Reading, that 'I have always placed my highest and most permanent hopes [for the continuance of the British Raj] upon the eternity of the communal situation'.[52]

In the winter of 1924–25, the American scholar E.A. Ross was touring India. Ross, a professor of sociology at Wisconsin, met with a wide cross section of people, including Gandhi. He sympathized with Indian hopes and aspirations, but wondered if a free and united India would be feasible. He had observed the recent religious riots, and noticed the sentiment among educated Muslims that once they had been 'the masters' (of Hindus and of India). And so Ross presciently remarked: 'The Punjab and Bengal have a majority of Mohammodans and, unless their feeling undergoes a wonderful change, it is possible that these great provinces would elect to remain outside an Indian Union just as North Ireland remains outside the Irish Free State.'[53]

IX

As, after his release from jail, Gandhi made his way back into the centre of Indian politics, he continued to be noticed and written about overseas. A sociologist at the State University of Iowa analysed how, through Gandhi and his movement, 'new social values emerge through the actions of individual attitudes upon pre-existing social attitudes'.[54]

A Methodist minister and founding member of the American Civil Liberties Union wrote of how Lenin and Gandhi had become 'the two most influential men of this period'. Both were born middle class, both identified themselves with the masses, both commanded enormous prestige in their respective countries. Yet, they differed radically in their political programme—Lenin seeking to conquer the oppressor by force, Gandhi by a form of 'spiritual resistance'.[55]

The most important foreigner to write about Gandhi was undoubtedly the French novelist Romain Rolland. Born in 1866, Rolland had never been to India, but had met and corresponded with his fellow Nobel laureate in literature, Rabindranath Tagore.

Rolland first heard of Gandhi in 1920, from the Bengali musician and mystic Dilip Kumar Roy, and from Tagore. They told him of Gandhi's 'extraordinary influence' in India, and of his 'ideal pacifism which the rest of the world pursues in vain'. Gandhi, Rolland learnt, was 'a nationalist, but of the greatest, the loftiest kind, a kind which should be a model for all the petty, base, or even criminal nationalisms of Europe'.[56]

After Gandhi was jailed in March 1922, Rolland began work on a book about him. His sources were Gandhi's own writings, reports in the Indian and European press, and pamphlets and books issued by the Madras publishers G.A. Natesan and S. Ganesan. His book was published in 1924 in French, and, in the same year, in an English translation in London and New York. It was called *Mahatma Gandhi: The Man Who Became One with the Universal Being*.

Romain Rolland was a man of faith, albeit one attracted more to individual mystics than to religious ceremonies or institutions. Gandhi appealed to him as a fellow ecumenist, and for his philosophy of non-violence, which spoke directly to a Frenchman who had just lived through the bloodiest war in European history. Praising Gandhi's 'childlike simplicity' and 'gentle and courteous' manner, Rolland said the Indian leader had 'introduced into human politics the strongest religious impetus of the last two thousand years'.[57]

Rolland's book presented a factual overview of Gandhi's life, interspersed with the author's own comments and reflections. Rolland laid particular emphasis on the catholicity of Gandhi's beliefs, his deep interest in religions other than his own, and his admiration for Western thinkers such as Tolstoy and Ruskin. He also provided an extended, and even-handed, discussion of the debates between Gandhi and Tagore.

The chronological narrative of Rolland's book ended with Gandhi's trial and arrest in 1922. 'Ever since the great apostle's voice has been silent,' he wrote. 'His body is walled in as in a tomb. But never did a tomb act as a barrier to thought, and Gandhi's invisible soul still animates India's vast body.'[58]

Rolland ended his book with some powerful passages on Gandhi's message. 'The world is swept by the wind of violence,' he remarked. 'All—be they nationalists, Fascists, Bolshevists, members of the oppressed classes, members of the oppressing classes—claim that they have the right to use force, while refusing this right to others.' Meanwhile, 'the church gives innocuous advice, virtuous and dosed, carefully worded, so as not to antagonize the mighty'.

In this 'old, crumbling world', there was 'no refuge, no hope, no great light'—except Gandhi. Rolland ended with the mystical hope that

> either Gandhi's spirit will triumph, or it will manifest itself again, as were manifested, centuries before, the Messiah and Buddha, till there is finally manifested, in a mortal half-god, the perfect incarnation of the principle of life which will lead a new humanity on to a new path.[59]

Rolland sent a copy of his book to his fellow Gandhi worshipper, the American clergyman John Haynes Holmes. The two had not yet met, but had been in correspondence. 'To see your name on the title page as the author of a book on Gandhi,' wrote Holmes to Rolland, 'has brought to me one of the most profound sensations of my life and I must thank you again not merely for sending me a copy of your book, but for having undertaken the task of writing it. You have done what nobody else could have done so efficiently and well.'

Holmes excitedly told Rolland of how, 'in a strange and decidedly impressive sort of way, Gandhi is leaping into great prominence here in America, after a period of obscurity which began with his imprisonment'. A short biography of Gandhi had been published in

Chicago, as well as an edition of *Hind Swaraj*, with an introduction by Holmes. And now, to round it off, came this 'extraordinarily fine piece of work' by Rolland.[60]

Gandhi himself read Rolland's book when it appeared, and began to correspond with the author. But he does not seem to have read another assessment of his work, written by a writer as admired in his continent as the Frenchman was in his. This was José Carlos Mariátegui, a Peruvian by nationality, but known and read all across Latin America.[61]

Born in 1894, Mariátegui left Peru in 1920 to spend several years in Europe. On his travels he read about Gandhi in French and Spanish newspapers. He returned to his homeland in 1923, and two years later, published his first book, *La Escena Contemporánea*, collecting articles he had published in the press during his European sojourn. One section dealt with the 'Orient'—this contained essays on the Turks, Tagore and Gandhi.

Mariátegui had closely read Rolland's book, but as a secular socialist, agreed only with parts of it. While accepting that Gandhi was 'one of the greatest figures of contemporary history', he was not convinced of the merits of non-violence. Mariátegui saw Gandhi's calling off of non-cooperation after Chauri Chaura as a mistake; as he put it, 'this retreat, ordered at the moment of the greatest tension and a time of burning passions, debilitated the revolutionary wave'.

Mariátegui also had problems with Gandhi's economic ideas. 'Having acquired the machine,' he remarked, 'it is difficult for humanity to renounce it.' He also charged Gandhi with having exaggerated the defects of Western civilization. Western man was 'not so prosaic and small-minded as many contemplative spirits and ecstatics imagine. Socialism and unionism, despite their materialist conception of history, are less materialistic than they appear. They support the interest of the majority, but they are inclined to ennoble and dignify life.'

While disagreeing with his politics, Mariátegui yet admired Gandhi's personality. After Gandhi had come out of jail, he wrote, 'the number of his supporters had declined. But if his authority as leader had eroded, his fame as ascetic and saint had spread. One journalist tells of how people from different races and all parts of Asia flocked to Gandhi's dwelling. Without ceremony or protocol, Gandhi received everyone who came to him.'

That said, if one had to choose between the 'moralism' of Gandhi and the 'realism' of Lenin, the Peruvian had no doubt that he would choose the latter. Revolutions, argued Mariátegui, do 'not come by fasting. The revolutionaries of all parts of the world have to choose between suffering violence and using it. If spirit and intelligence are not to be commanded by force, then it must be resolved to put force at the command of intelligence and spirit.'[62]

Rolland and Mariátegui present two verdicts on Gandhi, each fascinating and intriguing, but ultimately one set against the other—faith versus reason, spirit versus matter, morality versus instrumentalism, non-violence versus violence. Both, however, demonstrate the ever-wider interest in Gandhi, with the Indian in his ashram being scrutinized with fascinated awe by some of the world's leading minds.

X

In the first week of May 1925, Gandhi commenced a long tour of Bengal, a province crucial in many respects: for its delicate demographic balance between Hindus and Muslims; for its (largely merited) self-perception as a leading centre of the national movement; for historically being less hospitable to Gandhi himself than Bombay, Madras or the Punjab.

The pre-eminent Congress leader in Bengal was the barrister C.R. Das, popularly known as 'Deshbandhu'. In June, Gandhi spent five days with Das at his summer home in Darjeeling. His host had thoughtfully arranged for five goats to be sent up from the plains to supply milk to the eccentric and demanding guest. The two spent much of the time discussing the affairs of the province, with Gandhi concluding from Das's account that 'Bengal political life is one of mutual jealousy and back-biting'.[63]

In between these conversations, Gandhi gave Das spinning lessons, with the Bengal stalwart promising 'that he would try to learn spinning and spin so long as his body allowed'. Watching him at the wheel, Gandhi concluded that Das found 'spinning harder than giving defeats to the Government or winning cases for his clients'.

After he had left Darjeeling for the plains, Gandhi wrote mischievously to Das reminding him of his promise to improve his spinning: 'If the Governor [of Bengal] said "Spin and take what you want", you will work at the wheel for twenty-four hours and master it. Well, it is not the Governor who is saying it; but one who loves you and loves India does say: "Spin and take swaraj."'[64]

Alas, C.R. Das had little time to put this advice into practice. On 16 June 1925, he died in Darjeeling, at the relatively young age of fifty-five. Gandhi was in Khulna, in the eastern part of the province; on hearing the news, he proceeded immediately to Calcutta, where Das's body would be received and cremated. On reaching the city, Gandhi issued a public statement, asking citizens not to rush the train carrying Das's remains when it arrived at Sealdah station, not to shout, and to clear the way for the coffin-bearers to pass, and likewise to be orderly at the cremation ground itself. As he pointed out, 'respect for the memory of the deceased patriot demands not any outward temporary show of affection, but an inward determination to deserve the heritage the Deshbandhu has left us'.[65]

Gandhi now decided to stay on for an extra month in Bengal. He consoled Das's widow, Basanti Devi, protecting her from the rush of wailing mourners. He also started a public fund in memory of the deceased nationalist, for a 'hospital for women irrespective of caste or creed' as well as a school for training nurses.[66]

Back in 1920, Gandhi was in Bombay when Tilak died in that city. Now, five years later, he was near Calcutta when C.R. Das passed away. On both occasions, Gandhi played a prominent role in the obsequies. His actions and words were no doubt sincere. Nonetheless, by being able to lead the mourning for these two leaders, Gandhi consolidated his own standing in two very important provinces of British India.

XI

In June 1925, Annie Besant wrote to a friend: 'I hear that a strenuous attempt is being made to rescue the Congress from being strangled by Gandhi's yarn.'[67] The sarcasm owed itself perhaps to Mrs Besant's feeling of being sidelined by Gandhi. But the Mahatma's own loyal followers were despairing of their party's future. In July 1925, C. Rajagopalachari wrote to a friend of how the Congress was beset with confusion and faction-fighting, its members squabbling over mandatory spinning, council entry, etc. 'What a hopeless muddle we are in,' wrote Rajagopalachari, adding, 'and I am in a greater muddle than anyone else. I wish I had been a private gentleman pure and simple—and I should then have been less of a fool than I am now.'[68]

Gandhi was having trouble holding together his party. In his private life, he was having trouble keeping control of his sons. In Calcutta, Gandhi had met his eldest son, Harilal. They talked for three hours, the young man telling his father of a fresh set of difficulties. He had lent his name to a Calcutta firm called 'All India Stores', which, by virtue of having the Mahatma's son on its masthead, was garnering investors and investments from, as it were, 'All India'.

Among those who had sent money to the new enterprise was a Muslim from Lyallpur, in the Punjab. Receiving no replies from the firm, the investor feared that this was 'a bogus affair'. He asked his lawyer to send a notice to *Young India*, whose editor was the father of one of the directors of the All India Stores. Gandhi answered the lawyer and his client in the columns of the journal, for the 'important principles' that were involved called for a public reply. Harilal was indeed his son, wrote Gandhi, but 'his ideals and mine having been discovered fifteen years ago to be different, he has been living separately from me and since 1915 has not been supported by or through me'. Harilal, said the father, 'chose, as he had every right to do, a different and independent path. He was and still is ambitious. He wants to become rich and that too, easily.'

Gandhi then came to the matter raised by the Lyallpur lawyer. He pointed out that Harilal had 'started the Stores in question without the least assistance of any kind whatsoever from me. I did not lend my name to them. I never recommended his enterprise to anybody either privately or openly. Those who helped him did so on the merits of the enterprise.'

Having made clear his personal and professional distance from his son, Gandhi said those who have invested in Harilal's firm 'have my sympathy, but beyond that, nothing more. . . . If he [Harilal] is honest . . . he will not rest till he has paid all the creditors in full.'[69]

XII

As a biological son was going out of Gandhi's life, an adoptive daughter was coming in. Her name was Madeleine Slade. She was born in 1892, the daughter of a British admiral who had served in India. While her father was away on foreign postings, Madeleine grew up in the English countryside, riding, hunting and playing the piano. Her first real interest was in music, particularly German music and still more particularly, the music of Beethoven. After reading Romain Rolland's little book on the composer and his big novel, *Jean-Christophe*, she went to Villeneuve to meet him in the autumn of 1924. She found the writer scanning proofs of his latest work, the short but entirely appreciative study of Mahatma Gandhi. Miss Slade had not, at this time, heard of Gandhi. She bought the book when it appeared, and knew at once that the 'call was absolute'. She decided to prepare by practising spinning and weaving, and giving up eating meat and 'the drinking of all wines, beers or spirits'.

In May 1925, Miss Slade wrote to Gandhi of her 'fervent' desire to join him, to 'learn to live' his 'ideals and principles', to become a 'fit servant' of his cause. She sent Gandhi samples of wool she had spun. Gandhi replied that it was 'excellent', and asked her to come 'whenever you choose'. Sailing from Marseille on 25 October, she landed in Bombay on 6 November, and took the night train to Ahmedabad.[70]

Gandhi gave the new entrant an Indian name, Mira. The name was short and simple, and easy to pronounce. Mira was the name of a medieval poetess of royal blood, who had refused to get married, turned her back on a life of privilege, and instead spent her time composing songs in praise of Lord Krishna. This upper-class Englishwoman would be Mira to Gandhi's Krishna, although her devotion was fulfilled in more prosaic terms, by preparing her master's meals, screening his visitors, and spinning alongside him. The ashramites called her 'Mira Behn', Sister Mira.

Among the first to befriend Mira was Mahadev Desai. Always keen to expand his knowledge, Mahadev began to take lessons in French from the well-bred Englishwoman. When Gandhi learnt of this, he asked Mahadev to discontinue the classes, because in his view much of the best French literature was available in English translation, and because when he toured with Gandhi the lessons would be interrupted anyway. When 'we are engaged in a life and death struggle', asked Gandhi of his secretary, 'how could you think of learning French? You may read as much French as you like after swaraj.'

Gandhi suggested that Mahadev instead teach Mira Hindustani to ease her transition into life in India.[71]

In early December, with both Mahadev and Mira in tow, Gandhi left for a vacation in Wardha. The home town of his merchant-disciple Jamnalal Bajaj, Wardha was in the very centre of India. It was boiling in summer but crisp and dry in the cold season. For some years now, Gandhi had been spending a week in December with Bajaj. It was from there that he made another annual pilgrimage, to the Congress session, convened as always in the last week of December.

The 1925 Congress was held in the northern industrial city of Kanpur. The president this year was Sarojini Naidu who, in her address, termed the Hindu–Muslim question 'the most baffling and most tragic of all the problems before us'.[72] Also present at the Kanpur Congress was the British writer Aldous Huxley. Huxley had heard much about Gandhi, and expected to see someone whose appearance matched the legend. In his mind's eye he had visualized the saint of popular imagination to have 'a large intellectual forehead, expressive and luminous eyes, and a good deal of waved hair, preferably of a snowy whiteness'.

But the Gandhi whom Huxley saw in Kanpur did not look like this at all. Anyone who saw Mrs Naidu in her gorgeous silk sari, or Motilal Nehru with his erect bearing, would know at once that these people were 'somehow intrinsically important; their faces proclaimed it'. But, wrote Huxley, the casual observer who came to the Congress looking for its leaders

> would never even have noticed the little man in the dhoti, with the
> shawl over his naked shoulders; the emaciated little man with the

shaved head, the large ears, the rather foxy appearance; the quiet little man, whose appearance is only remarkable when he laughs— for he laughs with the whole-hearted laughter of the child, and his smile has an unexpected and boyish charm. No, the casual observer would probably never have even noticed Mahatma Gandhi.[73]

Not the casual foreign observer perhaps. But all the Indians present in Kanpur knew exactly who Gandhi was and why—his unprepossessing appearance notwithstanding—he was the most important man or woman among the several thousand Congress workers in the pandal. The rush to meet Gandhi and have his darshan was terrific. As Mira Behn wrote to Devadas Gandhi from Kanpur, 'the crowds of people have worn poor Bapu to a shadow . . . He is right down to the bottom of his strength.'

At Kanpur, Dr M.A. Ansari checked Gandhi, and concluded that his body and nervous system needed an extended period of rest. He asked Gandhi to take a break from editorial work, get others to attend to his correspondence, and add bread to his mostly fruitarian diet. 'How glad we shall all be to get back to Sabarmati!' wrote the adopted daughter (Mira) to the favourite son (Devadas), adding: 'And you have heard, no doubt, that Bapu has decided to stay at the Ashram for a *whole year*! Is that not the best of news!'[74]

It was, for Mira at any rate. She looked forward to an uninterrupted stretch of devoted service, where—with no meetings or travels or other distractions—she could focus on peeling her master's oranges, mixing his milk, filing his correspondence, taking out and putting away his spinning wheel.

CHAPTER ELEVEN

Spinning in Sabarmati

I

In *Young India*'s first issue for 1926, Gandhi made public his sabbatical from travelling as mandated by his doctors. He would stay put in Sabarmati, he wrote, for three reasons: to rest his 'tired limbs', to give 'personal attention to the Ashram', and to put the affairs of the All India Spinners Association in order.[1]

The Satyagraha Ashram in Ahmedabad was built on both sides of a public road. Gandhi's cottage was one of seven on the eastern, or river-facing, side. The cottage had several rooms, but the occupant himself favoured the veranda. Unless it rained, he slept there at night. During the day he did his writing there too.

In front of Gandhi's cottage was a large open space with a clear view of the river. It was here that the prayer meetings were held, once just before sunrise and a second time just after sunset. Verses from various religious texts were read, and hymns sung.

Spinning was Gandhi's main preoccupation during this sabbatical year. In an article for his Gujarati weekly *Navajivan*, he presented a succinct description of all that the activity involved:

Spinning does not mean drawing out bits of yarn of any sort as if we were merely playing at spinning. Spinning, in fact, means learning all the preliminary processes—sitting down properly, with a mind completely at rest, and spinning daily for a fixed number of hours good, uniform and well-twisted yarn, spraying it, measuring its length and taking its weight, rolling it neatly, and if it is to be sent out to some other place, packing it carefully and sticking a label to it with details of the variety of cotton used, the count, the length and weight of the yarn, and tying a tag on it with particulars of the contributor's name and address in clear handwriting; when all this is done, one will have completed the spinning-*yajna* for the day.[2]

In his book, *Hind Swaraj*, written in 1909 on the boat from London to Cape Town, Gandhi had asked middle-class Indian men to take to spinning and to promote handmade cloth. After his return to India he led by example. Spinning was for him many things: a breaking down of the barriers (so integral to the caste system) between mental and manual labour; a demonstration of self-reliance at the most basic, or individual, level; a renewal of indigenous skills and techniques that had atrophied or been destroyed under colonialism. Social reform, personal uplift, economic self-sufficiency, national pride: the making of khadi symbolized, and contributed, to all these.[3]

II

By taking a year's break from travel, Gandhi sought to shut out the world, yet the world came looking for him. In the first weeks of 1926, he was visited by, among others, Swami Shraddhananda, Jamnalal Bajaj and Motilal Nehru. A little later came two American women representing the 'Fellowship of Faith, League of Neighbours, and Union of East and West', and then another American woman with an agenda more focused than merely fostering fellowship and unity. This was Katherine Mayo, a journalist and writer who wished to write a book presenting a more favourable picture of the British Raj than was appearing in her country's press. To that end, she had got His Majesty's Government in London to smooth her way, by introducing her to provincial governments in India who could assist her with travel, translation, and the like.[4]

Katherine Mayo visited the Sabarmati Ashram on 17 March. She asked Gandhi a series of questions about his work, and then asked him for a message for her compatriots. Gandhi answered: 'My message to America is simply the hum of this wheel', adding that 'untouchability for me is more insufferable than British rule'.[5]

Although Gandhi had never visited America, the interest in him in that country was growing by the minute. In April 1926, a cultural entrepreneur based in New York wrote to Gandhi suggesting he undertake a speaking tour of the United States. He was assured of 'large and genuinely interested audiences everywhere'. The terms were generous: with Gandhi to get 75 per cent of the income from ticketed events, in addition to travel and local hospitality. The visitor would be in safe hands; for, as the correspondent assured him, he had 'managed very successfully the tours of people who have been under political difficulties, without the slightest annoyance to them, and am expert in the management of the newspaper publicity'.[6]

Gandhi's doctors had prescribed an extended period of rest; but even if he had been allowed to travel, it is unlikely that he would have been interested in this audacious American proposal.

III

Based in Ahmedabad, having temporarily quit travelling, and with the momentum of the political movement noticeably waning, Gandhi had time to answer letters from friends and strangers on Hindu–Muslim relations, celibacy, untouchability, and spinning. And on more mundane matters too, as in this reply to a query from a certain S. Mehtah of Grey Street in Durban:

> Dear Sir,
> You have enquired of me whether your brother Sheikh Amir Khan was a fellow passenger with me in 1896 on board S.S. *Courland* when I returned from India to Natal during that year. I have to state in reply that your said brother was a fellow passenger with me during that year.
>
> Yours truly
> M.K. Gandhi[7]

Among the more important letters written by Gandhi in the first half of 1926 was one to his son Manilal. Still based in Natal, running the Phoenix Ashram, Manilal had fallen in love with a girl named Fatima Gool, whose parents, based in Cape Town, were also of Gujarati descent, but Muslim rather than Hindu. Fatima loved Manilal too, and was even amenable to the idea of converting to Hinduism. When Manilal wrote to his father about the relationship, Gandhi conveyed his strong disagreement, writing to his son that

> what you desire is contrary to dharma. If you stick to Hinduism and Fatima follows Islam it will be like putting two swords in one sheath; or you both may lose your faith. And then what should be your children's faith? . . . It is not *dharma*, only *adharma* if Fatima agrees to conversion just for marrying you. Faith is not a thing like a garment which can be changed to suit our convenience. For the sake of dharma a person shall forgo matrimony, forsake his home, why, even lay down his life; but for nothing may faith be given up. May not Fatima have meat at her father's? If she does not, she has as good as changed her religion.

Gandhi continued: 'Nor is it in the interests of our society to form this relationship. Your marriage will have a powerful impact on the Hindu–Muslim question. Intercommunal marriages are no solution to this problem. You cannot forget nor will society forget that you are my son.'

Manilal seems to have asked his father to speak to his mother on his behalf. 'I cannot ask for Ba's permission,' said Gandhi. 'She will not give it. Her life will be embittered for ever.'

Looking at this correspondence through the lens of the twenty-first century, it may seem that the father was a bullying busybody, interfering with choices freely and voluntarily made by two adults. One might conclude that this was, as it were, an example of Hindu patriarchy at its most oppressive. Looked at from the perspective of its own time, one might view Gandhi's intervention less harshly. For, he was trying desperately to build a modus vivendi between India's two largest religious communities. There could be no united front against colonialism unless Hindus and Muslims came together. There would be no end to riots and clashes about cow slaughter and music before mosques unless Hindus and Muslims came together. In this delicate, fraught social and political environment, the Mahatma's son marrying a Muslim girl—and, even worse, allowing her to convert to Hinduism—would at a stroke ruin Gandhi's attempts to bring about unity and harmony. Had Manilal married Fatima, and had she then changed her name to Lakshmi or Parvati, there would be sermons in a thousand mosques across India about how Gandhi's call for Hindus and Muslims to work together was merely a devious camouflage to kill Islam by capturing its women.

Gandhi's principal reason for opposing the marriage was political. But there was also a personal element, the sense that his son had let him down by abandoning brahmacharya. He insinuated that in contemplating marriage, Manilal's 'main urge [was] carnal pleasure'; an unfair and unfeeling charge whether read in his time or ours. He urged his son to 'get out of your infatuation', added that his brothers Ramdas and Devadas 'also have arrived independently at the same conclusion, as mine', and ended by reiterating that 'I could not embolden myself to discuss this with Ba.'[8]

IV

In September 1926, a group of nationalists—Hindu, Muslim and Christian—signed a public appeal to Gandhi, urging him, 'the unquestioned leader of the Indian people', to come out of his 'self-imposed seclusion' and 'resume the reins' of the national movement.[9] Gandhi was unmoved, writing to his friend, the Calcutta entrepreneur G.D. Birla, that 'I know that I have served the country through my silence; however, I am not confident that I can unite the various parties. My heart shrinks from the idea of going to Gauhati [for the annual Congress].'[10]

In 1915, his mentor Gokhale had made him take a vow not to speak on public matters for a year. This new vow, applicable through the year 1926, was, however, self-imposed. By now, Gandhi had also decided to observe a weekly day of silence. Every Monday, he would not speak at all, communicating through signs or, if necessary, through writing notes on chits of paper.

Although Gandhi had not appeared in public for almost a year, his name and fame still resonated across India. In December 1926, a new nationalist newspaper in Bombay organized a readers' poll to choose the 'Ten Greatest Living Indians'. Such contests had come into vogue in the United States, but this may well have been the first such exercise in India. When the votes were counted, the list of people selected was as follows:

Person	Votes Polled
Gandhi	9308
Tagore	7391
Bose, Jagdish Chandra	5954
Nehru, Motilal	4035
Ghose, Aurobindo	3907
Ray, P.C.	3524
Naidu, Sarojini	3519
Malaviya, M.M.	2618
Lajpat Rai	2568
Srinivasa Sastri, V.S.	1516

The chart was accompanied by an essay interpreting these choices. This noted that 'every sphere of life has received its meed', with poets, philosophers and scientists all represented, as also politicians of different ideological tendencies.[11] The commentary however missed the biases: there was one woman (perhaps par for the times), but as many as five Bengalis, this a reflection not merely of that province's leading contribution to public life but also of the intense patriotism of its middle class, which may have prompted them to vote in larger numbers than their compatriots elsewhere in India. Even more remarkably, all ten of these 'Greatest Living Indians' were Hindu. The readers, and the newspaper, did not see fit to choose or nominate a single Muslim or Sikh or Christian or Parsi.

V

In the second week of December, Gandhi went for his usual week's retreat in Wardha. The annual meeting of the All India Spinners

Association (AISA) was held to coincide with his visit. The AISA now had on its rolls 110 carders, 42,959 spinners and 3407 weavers, working in some 150 production centres across the country.[12]

Despite his reluctance, Gandhi could not really afford to absent himself from that year's Congress, held in the Assamese town of Gauhati. While he was on the train to Gauhati, a telegram was delivered to Gandhi at a wayside station. It was from Lala Lajpat Rai, and it contained the news of the murder in Delhi of the Arya Samaj leader Swami Shraddhananda.

The swami had been ill and was resting at home, when a young man named Abdul Rashid came to visit him. The servant told the visitor that his master was too sick to receive guests, but the man insisted. Hearing the argument, the swami told the servant to allow the visitor into his room. The guest asked for a glass of water, and while the servant went to get it, pulled out a revolver and shot and killed the swami.[13]

Despite his reservations about the proselytizing methods of the Arya Samaj, Gandhi admired Swami Shraddhananda for his fearlessness and his commitment to the extirpation of untouchability. On the evening of the 24 December, he spoke movingly of his late colleague at a meeting of the AICC in Gauhati. With the murder of a famous Hindu swami at the hands of a Muslim, this was, said Gandhi, 'a testing time for [both] Hindus and Muslims. Let the Hindus remain peaceful and refrain from seeking revenge for this murder. Let them not think that the two communities are now enemies of each other and that unity is not possible. . . . And, in my opinion, if a Mussalman thinks that Abdul Rashid did well he will be disgracing his religion. . . . May God give us faith and wisdom to survive this test and to behave towards each other, after this deed, in such a way that God can say that the two communities did what they ought to have done.'[14]

In Gauhati, Gandhi was staying in a hut on the banks of the great river Brahmaputra. His dwelling, specially erected for the Congress, was made of bamboo and thatch. The mattress was on a bed of straw, and the bed sheet made in khadi—all from materials locally available in Assam. Gandhi was impressed by his temporary home, since 'it costs very little, takes only a day or two to put up, and requires no great skill. This is so with all true art. It is always simple and natural.'[15]

VI

His sabbatical over, Gandhi now resumed his typically hectic pace of travel. From Gauhati, he journeyed to Calcutta, and from there to the eastern districts of Bengal. A brief visit to Banaras followed—to allow him to attend a meeting of homage to Swami Shraddhananda—before he carried on to the mining districts of Bihar, and from there to the north of the province, to the towns of Bettiah and Motihari which had been his base during his first satyagraha on Indian soil a decade previously.[16]

Travelling through eastern and central India, Gandhi found the purdah system far more prevalent than in other parts of the country. In western and southern India, women were attending schools and colleges and even participating in public life. The Tamil women he knew in South Africa had raised money for his struggle and even courted arrest. But in Bihar and the United Provinces the situation was altogether different. The women who attended his meetings were dressed in purdah, and sat behind a screen segregating them from the rest of the crowd.

In an article for *Young India*, Gandhi wrote of how the treatment of women had 'pained and humiliated' him. 'Why do not our women enjoy the same freedom we do?' he asked. 'Why should they not be able to walk out and have fresh air?' Purdah was a 'barbarous custom which, whatever use it might have had when it was first introduced, had now become totally useless and [was] doing incalculable harm to the country'.[17]

The rights of women also figured in a letter Gandhi wrote to his son Manilal. Gandhi had not allowed Manilal to marry the girl of his choice (Fatima Gool, of Cape Town), but he had finally reconciled himself to the boy not remaining a lifelong brahmachari. Manilal had consented to an arranged marriage; once it was finalized, he would sail from South Africa to claim his wife.

The girl chosen for Manilal by his father was Sushila Mashruwala, a relative of Kishore Mashruwala, a member of the Ahmedabad Ashram. Sushila was an accomplished artist and musician, and spoke Gujarati, Marathi and Hindi fluently, and English adequately. The wedding was scheduled for the first week of March 1927, in Sushila's home town, Akola.

Writing to Manilal, Gandhi asked for a 'solemn assurance that you shall honour Sushila's freedom; that you shall treat her as your companion, never as a slave; that you shall take as much care of her person as your own; that you shall not force her to surrender to your passion . . .' The father continued: 'You know my attitude towards women. Men have not been treating them well. I have proposed this alliance assuming you to be capable of coming up to my ideals.'

To Sushila, Gandhi wrote that 'God alone would know how fortunate you are but Manilal, I think, has certainly been lucky in getting you'.[18]

The wedding was held on 6 March. Gandhi gifted his new daughter-in-law a copy of the Gita and a spinning wheel. At his request, it was a simple ceremony, with only close relatives present. The next day was Gandhi's day of silence. The newly wedded couple, who had only set sight on one another the previous day, were too shy to talk amidst the family gathered around them. Noticing this, Gandhi wrote a note for his son which read:

> Now that I have got you married and introduced you [to your wife] it is for you to take the initiative and run your own house. Go and sit near Sushila. See what clothes she has got, find out her wishes and then make a note of what she needs. This will break the ice and things will get moving. Or you may try another approach. Or shall I ask her to come near you and tell the others to move away?[19]

This is a sweet note, displaying a tenderness absent in Gandhi's letters to Harilal, and in many of his previous letters to Manilal as well. The father was growing softer, and about time, too.

VII

In the years after he had left Yerwada prison, Gandhi's most important political disagreements had been with the swarajists. He had urged a continuation of the boycott of the councils; whereas C.R. Das, Motilal Nehru and others wanted an active engagement with the institutions set up by the colonial state. Interestingly, whereas the swarajists considered Gandhi too radical, a group of militants on the Left thought him too reformist. Their own preferred path was to use bombs and bullets to throw the British out of India.

In February 1925, Gandhi had reproduced in *Young India* an exchange he had with one of these young revolutionaries. Gandhi's programme, argued this critic, 'was not in keeping with Indian culture and traditions'. He claimed that 'India will not hesitate to shed blood just in the same way as a surgical operation necessitates the shedding of blood. To an ideal Indian, violence or non-violence has the same significance provided they ultimately do good to humanity.'

Gandhi, in response, characterized his own philosophy as a 'mixture of Tolstoy and Buddha'. 'I hold that the world is sick of armed revolutions,' he remarked. He was, he said, 'not ashamed to stand erect before the heroic and self-sacrificing revolutionary because I am able to pit an equal measure of non-violent men's heroism and sacrifice untarnished by the blood of the innocent'.[20]

Two years later, Gandhi was once more engaged in a public defence of ahimsa against the votaries of revolutionary struggle. His critic this time was Shapurji Saklatvala, a former director of the House of Tatas who had embraced communism while living in England. Known as 'Comrade Sak', in 1922 Saklatvala became one of the first two communists to be elected a member of the British Parliament.[21]

Saklatvala visited India in the spring of 1927. He met Gandhi, later publishing an 'Open Letter' in the Indian newspapers accusing Gandhi of 'misguided sentimentality', and—through his charkha movement—of launching 'an attack upon machinery, upon physical sciences, upon material progress'. Saklatvala compared Gandhi unfavourably to Kemal Atatürk, Sun Yat-sen and, above all, Lenin. Whereas those other leaders had 'express[ed] boldly and fearlessly the unexpressed voice of the people', Gandhi, claimed the communist, had prepared Indians 'for servile obedience and for a belief that there are superior persons on earth'.[22]

Gandhi replied to his critic in the columns of *Young India*. The 'impatient communist', he pointed out, focused only on the cities and ignored altogether the real India that lived in the villages. Here, the charkha that Saklatvala so deplored could become 'the centre' of rural renewal.

Unlike the communist, Gandhi did not think that the interests of capital and labour were always antagonistic. As he put it, 'bloody revolutions just do not appeal to me. I never wish to kill even a venomous snake, not to speak of a venomous man.'

Beyond these political differences, there was a fundamental philosophical difference, this relating to the ends of human life. Thus, Gandhi wrote that

> unlike 'Comrade' Saklatvala, I do not believe that multiplication of wants and machinery contrived to supply them is taking the world a single step nearer its goal. 'Comrade' Saklatvala swears by the modern rush. I whole-heartedly detest this mad desire to destroy distance and time, to increase animal appetites and go to the ends of the earth in search of their satisfaction.[23]

VIII

In the first week of April 1927, Gandhi fell ill. He was then touring the princely state of Savantvadi, adjoining Goa. A doctor friend, Jivraj Mehta, came down from Bombay to examine him. They had first met in London in 1915, when Mehta had treated Gandhi for pleurisy. Now, twelve years later, the patient was diagnosed as having high blood pressure and apoplexy, brought on by excessive travel and overwork. 'The strain you were putting yourself to,' said Dr Mehta to Gandhi, 'was abnormal.' He was advised to stop seeing visitors, but allowed to do 'light reading' and continue writing his autobiography, instalments of which had begun appearing in both *Young India* and *Navajivan*.

Dr Mehta thought Gandhi needed several months of continuous rest to recoup his strength. Summer was approaching; in Ahmedabad, temperatures would soon approach forty degrees Centigrade. So the doctor suggested that Gandhi go to Nandidurg, a hill station close to the city of Bangalore, and at an elevation of 4800 feet.[24]

Gandhi spent six weeks in Nandidurg, from 20 April to 5 June. He worked on his autobiography, attended to his correspondence, and (disregarding his doctor's advice) continued to write for his periodicals. His devoted disciple Rajagopalachari had arranged for goat's milk to be sent every day on the Madras–Bangalore train; it was collected at Tumkur station, and ferried up the hill to Nandi.[25]

While Gandhi was in Nandi, he received a letter from a friend in the western Indian town of Mahad, where a clash had broken out between upper castes and 'untouchables', over the latter's drinking of water from a public tank. The 'untouchables' were led by a brilliant young scholar named B.R. Ambedkar, who had taken doctoral degrees from Columbia and the London School of Economics and also qualified as a barrister.[26]

Gandhi wrote an essay on the controversy in Mahar, under the telling title 'Untouchability and Unreason'. The Bombay Legislative Council and the Mahad municipality had both passed resolutions permitting 'untouchables' access to public water sources. Gandhi felt that Dr Ambedkar was therefore 'fully justified' in 'advising the so-called untouchables to go to the tank to quench their thirst'. For, continued Gandhi, 'untouchability has no reason behind it. It is an inhuman institution. It is tottering and it is . . . supported by the so-called orthodox party by sheer force.'[27]

In Nandi, Gandhi received a letter from Motilal Nehru suggesting that his son Jawaharlal be made the next Congress president. The father had always had large ambitions for his only son. When Jawaharlal was at Harrow, Motilal wrote to him:

I think I can without vanity say that I am the founder of the Nehru family. I look upon you, my dear son, as the man who will build upon the foundations I have laid and have the satisfaction of seeing a noble structure of renown rearing up its head to the skies.

Then, when Jawaharlal had finished school and gained admission into Trinity College, Cambridge, Motilal assured him:

It would be something for any man to speak about his connections with these great institutions, but in your case it will be the institutions who will own you with pride as one of their brightest jewels.[28]

In 1927, Jawaharlal Nehru had been active in the Congress for a little less than a decade. He had a wide interest in international affairs,

and strongly socialist inclinations. Despite Jawaharlal's intelligence
and energy, and his own personal feelings of affection for him,
Gandhi considered the younger Nehru too inexperienced to be made
president. So he wrote delicately to the pushy father:

> The idea of Jawaharlal presiding has an irresistible appeal for me.
> But I wonder whether it would be proper in the present atmosphere
> to saddle the responsibility on him. It seems to me to be a thankless
> task. All discipline has vanished. Communalism is at its height.
> Intrigue is triumphant everywhere. Good and true men are finding
> it difficult to hold on to their position in the Congress. Jawahar's
> time will be simply taken away in keeping the Congress tolerably
> pure and he will simply sicken.[29]

To Jawaharlal himself, Gandhi wrote that 'I do not myself see the
way so clear as to make me force the crown on you and plead with
you to work it'. He also pointed out that were he to become Congress
president, with all the attendant committee work, Jawaharlal would
not be able to continue the mass contact programme he had so far
energetically pursued, taking the Congress message to students,
peasants and workers.[30]

Despite Gandhi's hesitation, Motilal Nehru continued to press
his son's case. To be fair to Jawaharlal, he was less keen to become
president than was his father on his behalf. In fact, when the idea
was first mooted in April, he had written to Gandhi that 'I do not
feel inclined to welcome the proposal about the presidentship'.
He believed that the respected Delhi doctor M.A. Ansari, and
not himself, would be 'the best choice' to lead the Congress come
December.[31]

Gandhi too wanted Dr Ansari to become president, since as a
Muslim he could help 'solve the almost insoluble problem' of inter-
communal relations.[32] But Ansari himself was hesitant to assume the
presidency. The Congress was ridden with factions; and as a man
of science, he had no talent for political intrigue. Gandhi assured
him that he could keep his distance from debates on council entry
and constitution-making, and focus on the Hindu–Muslim question.
'You owe it to the country,' wrote the Mahatma to the doctor, 'as a

Mussalman and a staunch nationalist to vindicate the religion of the Prophet and the honour of the country by giving all the talents you have for securing a domestic peace honourable to all parties.'[33]

IX

In the summer of 1927, the American writer Katherine Mayo— who had visited Gandhi in Sabarmati the previous year—published a searing critique of Hindu society in a book titled *Mother India*. Miss Mayo said she was writing this book since all that the average American knew about India was 'that Mr. Gandhi lives there; also tigers'.[34]

Mother India began with a description of the Kalighat temple in Calcutta, whose goddess was 'black of face' with 'a monstrous lolling tongue, dripping blood', and whose worshippers sacrificed hundreds of goats daily to placate the deity.[35] This set the tone for a consistently disparaging account of Indian and, more particularly, Hindu customs. Miss Mayo wrote at length about the ubiquity of child marriage, of the shocking conditions under which girls were made to have sex and bear children at the ages of twelve and thirteen, of the lack of medical care for pregnant women, of the prohibitions against widow remarriage, of the pernicious practice of purdah, of the oppressions of the caste system, and much else.

The practices described by Miss Mayo undoubtedly existed in India. What was tendentious was her presentation: she minimized the efforts of Indian reformers to end these evils (there were several sneering remarks about Gandhi himself), and she completely exonerated the British colonial authorities from any responsibility. As she squarely stated:

> The British administration of India, be it good, bad, or indifferent, has nothing whatever to do with the conditions above indicated. Inertia, helplessness, lack of initiative and originality, lack of staying power and of sustained loyalties, sterility of enthusiasm, weakness of life-vigor itself—all are traits that truly characterize the Indian not only of today, but of long-past history.[36]

Or, as she continued, now substituting 'Hindu' for 'Indian':

> The whole pyramid of the Hindu's woes, material and spiritual—
> poverty, sickness, ignorance . . . melancholy, ineffectiveness,
> not forgetting that subconscious conviction of inferiority which
> he forever bares and advertises by his gnawing and imaginative
> alertness for social affronts—rests upon a rock-bottom physical
> base. The base is, simply, his manner of getting into the world and
> his sex-life thereafter.[37]

Katherine Mayo contrasted the 'honesty, sincerity and devotion' of
British colonial officials with the 'utter apathy of the Indian peoples,
based on their fatalistic creed'.[38] The India Office was delighted with
the book—according to one report, it bought 5000 copies of *Mother
India* to distribute to the British public. A free copy was presented to
every member of Parliament, and the book was widely and generously
reviewed in the British press.[39]

The reception in India was very different. The veteran nationalist
Lala Lajpat Rai wrote a book-length rejoinder entitled *Unhappy
India*, where he called the book 'a jumble of truths, half-truths and
lies', describing the author as an 'apologist for British rule'.[40] Annie
Besant called Miss Mayo's book 'most mischievous' and worthy of
being prosecuted 'for stirring up bad feeling and for being obscene'.[41]
Rabindranath Tagore charged Miss Mayo of having grossly
misrepresented him—as allegedly being in favour of sex before
puberty, among other calumnies. Yet, Tagore urged Indians not to
reply in kind, for that would play into 'the malignant contagion of race-
hatred' and lead to an 'endless vicious cycle of mutual recrimination
and ever-accumulating misunderstanding that are perilous for the
peace of the world'.[42]

Tagore's advice went unheeded—more than fifty books and
pamphlets were published by Indians in response to *Mother India*.[43]
Gandhi himself wrote a long assessment of the book in his journal
Young India, describing it as 'the report of a drain inspector sent
out with the one purpose of opening the drains of the country to be
reported upon, or to give a graphic description of the stench exuded
by the open drains'.

Gandhi charged Miss Mayo with a selective representation of the facts, the selection done with a view to praising British rule and criticizing Indian culture. The author of *Mother India* had claimed 'for the British Government merits which cannot be sustained and which many an honest British officer would blush to see the Government credited with'.

Katherine Mayo's book presented the case to 'perpetuate white domination in India on the plea of India's unfitness to rule herself'. Yet, Gandhi would not dismiss it out of hand, characteristically arguing that the 'indignation which we are bound to express against the slanderous book must not blind us to *our obvious imperfections and our great limitations*'. Indians, he insisted, must 'not resent being made aware of the dark side of the picture wherever it exists. Overdrawn her pictures of our insanitation, child marriages, etc., undoubtedly are. But let them serve as a spur to much greater effort than we have hitherto put forth in order to rid [Indian] society of all cause of reproach.'[44]

X

In the last week of August 1927, his health fully restored, Gandhi began a tour of the Tamil country, his itinerary chosen by C. Rajagopalachari. He visited and spoke at, among other places, Vellore, Madras, Chidambaram, Tanjore, Kumbakonam, Coimbatore, Madurai and Trichy. Everywhere, the meetings ended with a box passed from hand to hand in the audience, gathering donations for a fund to promote spinning.

From the Tamil country, Gandhi moved on to Travancore, where he spent two weeks touring and speaking. Gandhi pressed home the importance of ending untouchability regardless of whether or not it had scriptural sanction. At one town, Nagercoil, he told his audience that not everything written in Sanskrit had a binding effect on social behaviour. 'That which is opposed to the fundamental maxims of morality,' he remarked, 'that which is opposed to trained reason, cannot be claimed as Shastras no matter how ancient it may be.' At another town, Quilon, he said that 'untouchability poisons Hinduism as a drop of arsenic poisons milk'. He himself had 'not a shadow of doubt that in the great turmoil now taking place either untouchability has to die or Hinduism has to disappear'.[45]

While touring in the south, Gandhi had received an invitation from the new viceroy, Lord Irwin, to come see him in New Delhi. A former Cabinet minister and Fellow of All Souls, Irwin was a devout Anglo-Catholic. Gandhi met the viceroy alone, on 31 October, and again the next day, this time with a larger group of Indian leaders. Afterwards, Gandhi wrote to a Gujarati friend that 'the Viceroy did not wish to know others' views; he wished only to express his own'. To Charlie Andrews, Gandhi described Irwin as 'a good man with no power' (presumably to overrule the officials who ran the Raj). He had particularly wanted to discuss khaddar, but the viceroy was more keen to talk about politics and the Hindu–Muslim question.[46]

The viceroy himself wrote to his father that he found Gandhi 'an interesting personality', albeit one 'singularly remote from practical politics'. Gandhi had suggested that India should be accorded Dominion Status, without (in Irwin's view) recognizing the institutional constraints and parliamentary procedures which stood in the way of such a declaration. Irwin remarked to his father that 'it was rather like talking to someone who had stepped off another planet on to this for a short visit of a fortnight and whose mental outlook was quite other to that which was regulating most of the affairs on the planet to which he had descended'.[47]

From Delhi, Gandhi proceeded to Ahmedabad, his first visit home since March. He stayed merely two days, before returning south, travelling by rail to Tuticorin, on the tip of the peninsula, and then by boat to Colombo.

Gandhi had been invited to Ceylon by three young students from Jaffna, who had met him in Bangalore back in June. A month later, they renewed their invitation, adding as an inducement that they were 'quite hopeful that we can raise in Ceylon a large purse for khadi work'.[48]

Gandhi arrived in Colombo by boat on the evening of Saturday, 12 November. Several thousand people had gathered to receive him, with the jetty festooned with flags and pot palms. On 15 November, Gandhi was given a public reception in Colombo's town hall, the first coloured man ever to be so honoured by the municipality. Also notable was a reception thrown for him by the Buddhist priests of Vidyodaya College, with 500 monks in yellow robes chanting their benediction on the visitor.

In Colombo, Gandhi was besieged by autograph hunters. He signed his name for them, asking in return that they take a promise to wear khadi. A well-born lady was taken aback at the condition, presenting to Gandhi 'her various difficulties—parties, official invitations, this thing and that thing. How could she wear Khadi on all occasions?' Eventually, she withdrew her request for an autograph, murmuring that she would not hastily make a promise she could not keep.[49]

In the southern part of the island, dominated by Sinhala Buddhists, Gandhi suggested a kinship between his faith and their own. As he put it in a speech in Colombo, 'Buddha never rejected Hinduism, but he broadened its base. He gave it a new life and a new interpretation.' The same day, Gandhi spoke to the Young Men's Christian Association of Colombo, offering them a revisionist view of *their* faith. Had 'I to face only the Sermon on the Mount and my own interpretation of it,' he observed, 'I should not hesitate to say, "Oh yes, I am a Christian."' Then he continued: 'But negatively I have to say that in my humble opinion, much of what passes as Christianity is a negation of the Sermon on the Mount.'

Gandhi now made his way towards the north of the island, where Tamil-speaking Hindus were in the majority. On the day Gandhi arrived in the main Tamil town, Jaffna, 'the avenues to the [train] station were impassable'. A large police contingent was in place to manage the crowd, which yet resorted to 'promiscuous charging' when the train carrying their hero arrived. With much difficulty, the police cleared a passage for Gandhi to walk to the car that was waiting to receive him.[50]

Gandhi's programme in Jaffna was crowded even by his standards. For Sunday, 27 November 1927, it went like this:

9 to 10 a.m.: Visits Jaffna Hindu, Parameshwara and Manipay Hindu colleges

3 to 5 p.m.: Visits [the localities of] Puttur, Achveli, Velvettiturai, Tondaimannar, Point Pedro, Chavakachcheri and Chiviateru

6 to 6.15 p.m.: Ladies' meeting at Ridgeway Hall
6.15 to 6.30 p.m.: Cigar Factory Workers' Meeting
6.30 to 7 p.m.: General Public meeting[51]

Gandhi was dismayed to find that among Ceylon's Tamils, caste distinctions were as rigid as in India. 'Living in a country over which the spirit of Buddha is brooding,' he told his audience, 'I had felt you would be free from this taint of untouchability.' Here, as in India, 'ancient traditions and ancient laws have been dragged almost out of the tomb to justify the hideous doctrine of untouchability'.[52]

Gandhi spent two and a half weeks in Ceylon, speaking to an impressively wide range of audiences. He also collected a great deal of money for his khaddar work. The students of Jaffna were most active in raising funds, while among the largest donors were the Chettiar merchants of the island. But others chipped in too. Even the barbers of Colombo contributed a purse of Rs 400. The total collections amounted to Rs 1,05,000 and 2 annas, the name of each contributor and the amount he/she contributed detailed in a chart extending over five pages of Mahadev Desai's book on his master's travels in Ceylon.[53]

XI

While travelling within India, Gandhi usually had Mahadev Desai as his main companion. But, for this trip to Ceylon he also took his wife Kasturba along. In one speech, at Matale, he referred to their relationship in part-serious, part-jocular terms. After his own parents died, he remarked, Kasturba had 'been my mother, friend, nurse, cook, bottle-washer and all these things'. And they had 'come to a reasonable understanding that I should have all the honours and she should have all the drudgery'.[54]

Gandhi and Kasturba had now been married forty-five years. In the first decade of their marriage, they were often separated, with Gandhi in London and Durban and his wife in Rajkot. In 1897, Kasturba joined him in South Africa. They had some sharp disagreements, these largely dealing with the patriarch's desire to put the demands of his public work above the claims of his family. Over time, Kasturba came to see the strength of Gandhi's convictions, and even joined the struggle herself.

By 1927, Gandhi and Kasturba had been back in India for more than a decade. Once more, Kasturba was often left alone while Gandhi was on the road. However, in the ashram at Ahmedabad, with her sons and nephews around her, and with the language of the home as well as of the street being her mother tongue, Gujarati, she was far less lonely than in South Africa. To be sure, she'd rather her husband stayed more at home. Their relationship had also been tested by the coming into Gandhi's life of Saraladevi. But now that Sarala had been kept at arm's length, the marriage was more or less on an even keel. Gandhi and Kasturba, as he told the audience in Matale, had come to a 'reasonable understanding'.

What, however, of Gandhi and his sons? The eldest, Harilal, was still estranged. The second, Manilal, had at times felt suppressed and suffocated by the father. Now they were reconciled, with Gandhi agreeing to the son not being a brahmachari, and Manilal accepting the father's choice of bride. The third son, Ramdas, always the most docile, had meanwhile been betrothed to a Gujarati Bania girl named Nirmala, chosen for him by Gandhi. The marriage had been fixed for January 1928.

The son still single and still a brahmachari was Devadas. He was greatly beloved of the mother, and of the father too—indeed, it was only with his youngest son that Gandhi had something like a normal relationship. Now, however, Devadas had fallen in love with Lakshmi, the daughter of C. Rajagopalachari (Rajaji). While his parents were in Ceylon, they had received a letter from a family friend about how Devadas was pining for Lakshmi, and was determined to marry her. Gandhi wrote back that

> Dev[a]das's state is extremely pitiable. Rajaji is not likely at all to let him marry Lakshmi, and rightly so. Lakshmi will not take one step without his consent. She is happy and cheerful, whereas Dev[a]das has gone mad after her and is pining for her and suffering. If he had such love for God, he would have been revered as a saintly man and become a great dedicated worker.

But how can even Dev[a]das act against his very nature? He wishes to obey me, but his soul rebels against him. He seems to believe that I stand in the way of his marriage with Lakshmi and so feels angry with me. I do not know at present [how] he can be brought out of this condition. Try and see if you can help him recover peace of mind and explain to him his dharma. It is possible that I have not understood him and am, therefore, doing him injustice.[55]

In the India of the 1920s, 'love' marriages were almost unknown. Whether one was Hindu, Muslim, Sikh or Jain, whether working class or middle class or aristocratic, one's spouse was chosen by one's parents or guardians. To be sure, with growing urbanization and the growth of university education, young men and women were occasionally falling in love, and, still more occasionally, persuading their parents to let them marry the person of their choice. But perhaps 99 per cent (if not 99.99 per cent) of all marriages in India in 1927 were arranged by the respective families of the bride and bridegroom.

Gandhi's eldest son, Harilal, was one of the rare transgressors. When his parents were away in South Africa, he had fallen in love. He chose the girl; even so, her father was a friend of Gandhi's, and likewise a Gujarati-speaking Bania. Because of these extenuating factors, Gandhi had acquiesced. But he had forbidden Manilal from marrying Fatima Gool, in part because the boy had chosen the girl himself, and in larger part because his own son marrying a Muslim would have serious and perhaps unmanageable repercussions on his public career.

Now Devadas too had fallen in love, with the daughter of one of Gandhi's closest friends. But Rajagopalachari was a Brahmin, not a Bania, and a Tamil, not a Gujarati. An inter-caste and inter-regional marriage had its own complications. Would the orthodoxy seize on this Brahmin–Bania union to represent Gandhi as a dangerous radical, thus undermining his still unfolding campaign against untouchability?

The patriarch had however got one salient fact wrong. The boy's love *was* reciprocated. Lakshmi too was pining for Devadas. The two had first met in June 1924, when Gandhi was visiting Bangalore, and Rajagopalachari had come with his daughter to meet him. Family lore has it that it was on a park bench in Bangalore that Devadas first declared his love for Lakshmi. Later, he formally approached her father to grant permission to marry her.

Rajaji himself was extremely fond of Devadas. He had known the boy from 1918, when Gandhi sent his youngest son to Madras to promote Hindi in South India. Despite his affection for Devadas, Rajaji was not sure he wanted his own daughter to marry him. He conferred with Gandhi, and they decided to put the couple on probation. They would have no meetings, no letters, so as to test their love for one another. If, after some years had passed, they still wanted to get married, their fathers would not stand in the way.[56]

XIII

Through the 1920s, relations between Hindus and Muslims continued to deteriorate. In the Punjab, a major controversy broke out over the publication of a pamphlet called 'Rangila Rasool', which may be loosely translated as 'Colourful Prophet'. This anonymous pamphlet, which focused on the polygamous tendencies of the Prophet Muhammad, was published in Lahore by a Hindu named Rajpal. Aggrieved Muslims filed a case under Section 153A of the Indian Penal Code ('Promoting enmity between different groups on grounds of religion, race, place of birth, residence, language, etc., and doing acts prejudicial to maintenance of harmony'). Rajpal was at first found guilty, and sentenced to ten months in prison. He went on appeal, and succeeded in getting the conviction overturned by the Lahore High Court, which judged that the defendant had not wantonly set out to cause offence.

The acquittal of the publisher of 'Rangila Rasool' sparked outrage among the Muslims of northern India. The judgment was announced on 4 May 1927; two days later, speaking at Delhi's Jama Masjid, Mohammad Ali said the verdict 'had opened the floodgates of mischief, much greater than Hindu–Muslim quarrels over cow-slaughter and music before mosques'. The younger of the Ali Brothers asked for a change in the law to make such public insults of the Prophet impermissible.[57]

Meanwhile, the older Ali brother, Shaukat, wrote Gandhi a series of sorrowful letters on the deepening religious divide. He complained about the 'rabid if not wicked' outpourings of Arya Samajist newspapers, expressing a 'mad desire for revenge' for the killing of Swami Shraddhananda. This 'wild talk' had 'wiped out all the good effect which swamiji's unfortunate murder had brought about in sobering down the Moslems'. With Hindus and Muslims 'being led astray by mischievous [and] greedy wire-pullers', Shaukat Ali could 'see nothing but grief for both' communities.[58]

As Hindu–Muslim relations deteriorated, several 'Unity Conferences' were held. The first, in Simla in the third week of September 1927, was attended by Jinnah, Azad and the Hindu Mahasabha leaders Madan Mohan Malaviya and B.S. Moonje. It discussed the cow slaughter and music before mosque questions, without arriving at any agreement.[59]

A second 'Unity Conference' was held in Calcutta in the last week of October. Among those attending were Ansari, Azad, Motilal Nehru, Sarojini Naidu and Subhas Chandra Bose. Once more, the questions of cow slaughter and the playing of music before mosques were discussed. Militant Hindus were angry at the two issues being placed on a par, saying it showed 'a regrettable disregard of the deep seated Hindu sentiment regarding the cow and is not likely to lead to unity and peace, but on the contrary, is calculated to lead to greater discord and strife'.[60]

Gandhi did not attend either conference. But he was briefed on their discussions. In the first week of December 1927, he published a long essay on the subject. He said here that while his 'interest and faith in Hindu–Muslim unity' was as 'strong as ever', his approach had changed. While previously he pursued the path of meetings and joint resolutions, now, 'in an atmosphere which is surcharged with distrust, fear and hopelessness', those older methods 'rather hinder than help heart-unity. I therefore rely upon prayer and such individual acts of friendship as are possible.'[61]

Later in December, the annual Congress met in Madras. The day before the Congress began, Gandhi wrote to the president-elect, M.A. Ansari, that he hoped a pact would be put in place, whereby Muslims eschewed cow slaughter and Hindus stopped playing music before mosques. In the event, though there was no formal pact, a resolution was passed asking Muslims to 'spare Hindu feelings as much as possible in the matter of the cow', and Hindus, in return, 'to spare Mussalman feelings as much as possible in the matter of music before mosques'.[62]

The Congress also resolved to boycott a statutory commission appointed by the British government to report 'into the working of the system of government, the growth of education, and the development of representative institutions, in British India'. In both character and composition, the commission was a noticeable regress from the Indianization that Edwin Montagu had once hoped for. The commission had seven members: all were MPs (four Tory, two Labour, one Liberal) and, more crucially, all were white. It was to be chaired by Sir John Simon, a Liberal politician and former attorney general of Great Britain.

The absence of Indian representation on a body discussing *Indian* reforms outraged both Moderate and Radical opinion. So did the absence of any reference in the commission's terms of reference to the granting of 'Dominion Status', which would place India on par with other self-governing units of the Empire such as Canada and Australia. Jinnah and the Muslim League, Tej Bahadur Sapru and the Indian Liberal Federation, Sir Purushottamdas Thakurdas and the Mill-owners' Association, all signed a joint petition of protest. The weighty Congress party now chipped in, resolving in Madras that 'the only self-respecting course for India is to boycott the Commission in every form'.[63]

At the Madras Congress, Jawaharlal Nehru was appointed working secretary of the party, an important post, if not quite the presidency his father desired for him. Earlier that year, Jawaharlal had toured Soviet Russia, a trip that reinforced his leftward turn.[64] Gandhi was unhappy with his protégé's growing radicalism. When the younger Nehru had an 'Independence Resolution' passed at the Madras Congress, Gandhi wrote to him that 'you are going too fast. . . . Most of the resolutions you framed and got carried could have been delayed for one year. . . . But I do not mind these acts of yours so much as I mind your encouraging mischief-makers and hooligans. I do not know whether you still believe in unadulterated non-violence.'[65]

Nehru, in reply, defended the Independence Resolution, saying it was drafted 'after prolonged and careful thought'. He then outlined his growing disenchantment with Gandhi's leadership. During the non-cooperation movement, wrote Jawaharlal to Gandhi,

> you were supreme; you were in your element and automatically you took the right step. But since you came out of prison something seems to have gone wrong and you have been very obviously ill at ease. . . . All you have said is that within a year or eighteen months you expected the khadi movement to spread rapidly and in a geometric ratio and then some direct action in the political field might be indulged in. Several years and eighteen months have passed since then and the miracle has not happened. It was difficult to believe it would happen but faith in your amazing capacity to bring off the impossible kept us in an expectant mood. But such faith for an irreligious person like me is a poor reed to rely on and I am beginning to think if we are to wait for freedom till khadi becomes universal in India we shall have to wait till the Greek Kalends.[66]

Gandhi wrote back in hurt tones. 'The differences between you and me appear to be so vast,' he remarked, 'that there seems to be no meeting-ground between us. I can't conceal from you my grief that I should lose a comrade so valiant, so faithful, so able and so honest as you always have been . . .'[67]

Jawaharlal's letter worried Gandhi, for he knew the younger Nehru spoke not merely for himself. His views were representative of the younger generation of Congressmen as a whole. How long would Gandhi persist with spinning and his call to end untouchability? When would he call once more for a direct confrontation with colonial rule? The patriarch was being pressured from below, and he sensed it.

CHAPTER TWELVE

The Moralist

I

This book thus far has focused on the *public* Gandhi, the social reformer who preached and struggled against untouchability; the bridge-builder who sought to reconcile India's two largest communities, Hindus and Muslims; the constructive worker who energetically promoted hand-spinning across India as a means of combating rural poverty and unemployment; the partyman who, despite the long stretches he spent in his ashram in Sabarmati, always found time to attend the annual meetings of the Congress while playing a key role in choosing who, each year, would be the party's president; the anti-colonial activist who mobilized his compatriots across caste, class and religious lines to seek to win political freedom for India.

This chapter by contrast, turns the gaze inwards, examining key aspects of Gandhi's personal faith, his personal morality, as expressed in his words and actions in this decade of the 1920s. The next chapter examines the intent of Gandhi's two memoirs, also written in the 1920s, which are his enduring literary legacy. From Chapter 14, we pick up the story of Gandhi the public man once more.

Gandhi was born and raised a Hindu, albeit a heterodox one. His mother was a follower of a sect called the Pranamis, whose temples had verses of the Gita as well as the Koran on their walls. An early mentor was the Jain sage Raychandbhai, who Gandhi met in 1891 on his return from his law studies in London, and with whom he maintained a regular correspondence until Raychand's death a decade later.[1]

As a boy, growing up in Rajkot, Gandhi's understanding of religion was experiential. He went with his mother to the temple, and observed her during her fasts at home. His textual understanding of Hinduism, however, really began in London, when he read the Bhagavad Gita with some English friends. Ever since, the Gita remained his favourite text, to which he regularly returned.

Gandhi's considered views on the Gita found expression through a series of discourses that he delivered to inmates of the Sabarmati Ashram in the spring and summer of 1926. In his sabbatical year from public life, he chose to distil the essence of those readings for a close and select audience.

Gandhi argued that the Gita should be read metaphorically, not as a work of history. In the text, 'the physical body is only an occasion for describing the battle-field of the human body. In this view the names mentioned are not of persons but the qualities they represent. What is described is the conflict within the human body between opposing moral tendencies imagined as distinct figures.'[2]

In the Gita, Krishna asked Arjuna to 'give up all thought of acquiring, holding and defending possessions', and to 'cultivate detachment in that respect'. Likewise, argued Gandhi, the ashramites should give up possessiveness: 'We should think that the things we keep in the Ashram belong to others as much as to us, and so remain indifferent towards them.' That was how one could become what the Gita calls a *sthitaprajna*, 'a person who has become completely free from attachments and aversions'.[3]

In his lectures at the ashram, Gandhi spoke repeatedly of the Gita's emphasis on work without expectation of reward. Thus, 'karma means work which circumstances make it necessary for us to undertake, not that which we do of our own choice'. Again: 'The Gita's karma is not karma done under compulsion; it must be prompted by some little measure at any rate of knowledge' (as well as self-knowledge).[4]

In these talks, delivered daily during morning prayers, Gandhi ranged widely beyond the Gita itself. Among the people he referred to were Buddha, Jesus, Prophet Muhammad, Tolstoy, the Bengali saint Chaitanya, the Gujarati poet Narasinha Mehta and the British antivivisectionist Anna Kingsford. He told his audience of how a lump of sugar placed on the tongue of Chaitanya stayed undissolved, like a piece of stone, since for the saint 'pleasure . . . had completely died away'; that to Prophet Muhammad, 'fasting brought happiness, for it was an occasion when he could live constantly in the presence of God'; that Jesus fasted for forty days in solitude, after which 'he felt that he heard a mysterious voice, that God was talking to him and that the veil which hid God from him had lifted'.[5]

One discourse glossed the term yajna, or ritual sacrifice, which in the period the Gita was composed, often involved the sacrifice of animals, a practice which still prevailed in parts of India. In the past, it was thought that sacrificing a buffalo would bring rainfall and help the crops, but now 'we serve the good of the world by refraining from causing suffering to other creatures'. Gandhi argued that the term was metaphorical, and that 'we can perform a *yajna* with the mind as much as with the body. Of these two meanings of *yajna*, we should accept that which suits the context every time'. 'There is no harm,' continued Gandhi, 'in our enlarging the meaning of the word *yajna*, even if the new meaning we attach to the term was never in Vyasa's mind. We shall do no injustice to Vyasa by expanding the meaning of his words. Sons should enrich the legacy of their fathers.'

In Gandhi's view, 'the original intention behind the idea of *yajna* was that people should do physical work'. At the time the Gita was written, cutting trees to clear the land for agriculture was a form of yajna. Gandhi claimed that 'at the present time, spinning has become a *yajna*'. Likewise, 'if water was scarce and we had to fetch it from a distance of two miles, fetching water would be a *yajna*'.[6]

On 6 April 1926, Gandhi started his morning discourse by recalling that on that day in 1919, Hindus 'had kept a fast, bathed in a river and gone to temples; Muslims had offered prayers in mosques and Parsis in their fire-temples'. That was a day both of 'religious awakening' and of 'political significance'. At the time, recalled Gandhi nostalgically, 'everyone seemed to be sincere'.

Returning to the (politically quiescent) present, Gandhi argued that Indians could still get 'swaraj through the spinning-wheel'. Since 'the Bhagavad Gita says that women, Vaisyas and Sudras, all classes of people, can win freedom', Gandhi remarked that 'in the same way, all of us can do this [spin to win swaraj]'.[7]

In his last discourse, Gandhi described the Gita as 'a valuable provision for the mind in one's life-journey, as the spinning-wheel is for the body'. The Gita, he continued, 'is a big knowledge feast, as it is the very *amrita* [nectar] of knowledge'.[8]

In his own commentary on Gandhi's commentary on the Bhagavad Gita, Mahadev Desai remarked that 'there is nothing exclusive about the Gita which should make it a gospel only for the Brahmana or the Hindu. Having all the light and colour of the Indian atmosphere, it naturally must have the greatest fascination for the Hindu, but the central teaching should not have any the less appeal for a non-Hindu as the central teaching of the Bible or the Koran should not have any the less appeal for a non-Christian or a non-Muslim.' This was, theologically speaking, perhaps a stretch; but it did represent Mahadev's own ecumenism, his moral conviction (akin to, indeed derived from, Gandhi's own) that 'in the deepest things of life, the Hindu and the Mussalman and the Christian, the Indian and the European, in fact all who have cared and endeavoured to read the truth of things, are so spiritually akin'.[9]

II

The Gita was Gandhi's favourite text. A close second was the Bible. This eclecticism drew hostility from the orthodoxy. In August 1926, a controversy broke out regarding Gandhi's attempts to interpret the Bible to the students of the Gujarat Vidyapith. 'Is there nothing useful in our literature?' wrote one angry correspondent. 'Is the *Gita* less to you than the Bible? You are never tired of saying that you are a staunch sanatani Hindu. Have you not now been found out as a Christian in secret?'

In an extended reply, Gandhi explained why he chose the text he did. When he decided to spend an hour a week with the students, he offered them three alternatives: sessions based on the Gita, Tulsidas's Ramayana, or the New Testament. The students, thinking that they could read the Ramayana and the Gita with other teachers, themselves decided by 'a majority of votes' to read the New Testament with Gandhi as they knew he had 'made a fair study of it'.

Gandhi told his critics that 'it is the duty of every cultured man or woman to read sympathetically the scriptures of the world'. Then he continued: 'For myself, I regard my study of and reverence for the Bible, the Koran, and the other scriptures to be wholly consistent with my claim to be a staunch *sanatani* Hindu. He is no *sanatani* Hindu who is narrow, bigoted and considers evil to be good if it has the sanction of antiquity and is to be found supported in any Sanskrit book.'

Gandhi insisted that his study of other faiths had 'broadened my view of life. They have enabled me to understand more clearly many an obscure passage in the Hindu scriptures.' In 'the other world', he continued, 'there are neither Hindus, nor Christians, nor Mussalmans'. But in this world it was impossible to escape such labels. Gandhi therefore chose 'to retain the label of my forefathers so long as it does not cramp my growth and does not debar me from assimilating all that is good anywhere else'.

The unspoken corollary was that Muslims and Christians should likewise stick with the religion of their forefathers, but also broaden and deepen it by sympathetically studying the scriptures of other religions and, where necessary, 'assimilating all that is good' in them.[10]

In January 1928, a meeting of the International Fellowship of Religions was held in Sabarmati. In his address to the gathering, Gandhi succinctly expressed his own pluralist credo. 'All religions were true and also all had some error in them,' he remarked; therefore, 'we can only pray, if we are Hindus, not that a Christian should become a Hindu, or if we are Mussalmans, not that a Hindu or a Christian should become a Mussalman, nor should we even secretly pray that anyone should be converted, but our inmost prayer should be that a Hindu should be a better Hindu, a Muslim a better Muslim and a Christian a better Christian. That is the fundamental truth of fellowship.' He had, he told a mixed audience of padres, pandits and maulvis, 'broaden[ed] my Hinduism by loving other religions as my own'.[11]

Among those attending this meeting was a young English priest named Verrier Elwin, 'fresh from Oxford, come to India, as he said, to do some atonement for the sins of his countrymen in keeping India in chains'.[12] Elwin was deeply impressed by Gandhi's personality, less so by his ideas. Writing to a Christian friend, Elwin said that Gandhi had a 'saint's heroism, a saintly joy, and a saint's love'; all the same, he was 'intellectually singularly unsound', his religious doctrine neither 'genuinely Eastern' nor 'genuinely modern', an 'amalgam of Ruskin, Tolstoi, Emerson and that gang—a type which I have never understood or liked'. Elwin continued:

> But when I think of Bapu, as we call him, the light of his life, his courtesy, his joy, his charm, his prayerfulness, his self-control, his peace, his sway over his noble splendid followers, I can only bow in reverence. Cut off his head, and I would mark him Xt. But his mind is far behind his life . . .[13]

To someone formally trained in theology (as Elwin was), Gandhi's attitude to religion seemed puzzling. Gandhi believed that the sacred texts of all religions had contradictory trends and impulses; sometimes sanctioning one thing, at other times, its opposite. He himself wished to recover and reaffirm those trends that opposed violence and discrimination while promoting justice and non-violence. Orthodox Hindus claimed that untouchability was sanctioned by the Shastras; Gandhi answered that in that case the Shastras did not represent the true traditions (or real intentions) of Hinduism. Likewise, a Christian must place the pacifism of Jesus's life above passages in the Bible calling for retribution against people of other faiths.

For Gandhi, all faiths were fallible, not least his own. As he wrote in *Young India* not long after the Sabarmati meeting, at the root of all missionary effort—whether by Christians, Muslims or Arya Samajists—was 'the assumption that one's own belief is true not only for oneself but for all the world; whereas the truth is that God reaches us through millions of ways not understood by us'. He himself had 'no feeling that from a spiritual standpoint I am necessarily superior to the so-called savage. And spiritual superiority is a dangerous thing to feel.'[14]

III

Christians were a small minority in India. Thus, Gandhi's encounters with priests like Andrews and Elwin, while interesting for what they revealed of his own faith, did not provoke wider discussion. On the other hand, what he said—or sometimes did not say—about Islam did. For instance, when in December 1926 Gandhi wrote a tribute to Swami Shraddhananda in *Young India*, some readers felt that he should have more directly criticized Islam's cult of violence for the murder of the swami. An angry Hindu asked Gandhi why he had stopped short of 'condemning . . . those who are responsible for this act (those who describe Hindu leaders as Kafirs—the hot Muslim propagandists and the mad Muslim priests)'. The critic continued:

> I am sure if such a black act had been committed by a Hindu against a Muslim leader (which Heaven forbid!), you would have condemned the murderer and the community in unsparing terms. You would have asked Hindus to repent in sack-cloth and ashes, to offer fasts, hold [a] hartal, raise [a] memorial to the departed Muslim and many other things. Why do you accord preferential treatment to your 'blood brothers' the Muslims?

As was his wont, Gandhi printed the criticism and then patiently set out to refute it. He thought the swami's murderer was 'himself a victim of foul irreligious propaganda in the name of religion'—this conducted both by newspapers and by maulvis. But that Islam itself had to be painted in the darkest colours he would not accept. He continued:

> What is the meaning of the treatment of untouchables by us Hindus? Let not the pot call the kettle black. The fact is that we are all growing. I have given my opinion that the followers of Islam are too free with the sword. But that is not due to the teachings of the Koran. That is due in my opinion to the environment in which Islam was born. Christianity has a bloody record against it, not because Jesus was found wanting, but because the environment in which it spread was not responsive to his lofty teaching.

These two, Christianity and Islam, are after all religions of but
yesterday. They are yet in the course of being interpreted. I reject
the claim of maulvis to give a final interpretation to the message
of Mahomed as I reject that of the Christian clergy to give a final
interpretation of the message of Jesus. Both are being interpreted
in the lives of those who are living these messages in silence and in
perfect self-dedication.[15]

Here, directly and crisply stated, is the essence of Gandhi's philosophy
of religion. This consisted of five, interconnected, propositions. First,
the claim that no religion is perfect, with all religions being a mixture
of truth and error. Second, the assumption that all religions are in a
process of evolving, of ridding themselves of error and groping towards
the truth. Third, the argument that it was through interfaith dialogue,
by seeing one's faith in the mirror of another, that one could rid it of
imperfections. Fourth, the conviction that a person of faith must not
always trust priests or the so-called 'authorized' interpreters to give
the correct interpretation. Fifth, the belief that when interpreting or
judging a religion, one must trust its best practitioners rather than its
most powerful.

    Just as Gandhi rejected the Christian priest's or the Muslim imam's
claim to certitude and absolute religious authority, so too he would
reject the claim of the Sankaracharyas to give a 'final interpretation'
of Hinduism.

IV

Pluralism of faith was for Gandhi a political choice as well as a moral
obligation. Hindus and Muslims had to collaborate and cooperate if
they were to effectively challenge the British Raj. At the same time,
as a Hindu himself, Gandhi saw his faith as fallible and flawed. He
would not abandon it, but he would seek to deepen and enrich it
by sympathetically studying the faiths of others, and by befriending
Muslims, Christians, Sikhs, Jews and Parsis.

    Likewise, the practice of non-violence was for Gandhi both a
political as well as ethical choice. It was the best way to win freedom

from colonial rule, as well as the most honourable way to deal with one's fellow human beings.

When it came to non-violence in politics, Gandhi would brook no compromise. He had called off the non-cooperation movement in April 1922 after the killing of policemen in Chauri Chaura. Although the intensity and scale of the protests had severely shaken the Raj, Gandhi had no hesitation in aborting the movement, since that single act of violence had, in his mind, sullied the cause.

Gandhi knew that many Indian nationalists did not share his doctrinal commitment to non-violence. In fact, his book *Hind Swaraj*, published in 1910 while he was still in South Africa, explicitly set out to refute those Indians who had adopted forms of armed struggle against the Raj. These armed revolutionaries were sidelined by Gandhi after he returned to India, but they did not entirely disappear. Attacks on British officials and colonial targets took place occasionally, and when they did, their perpetrators were invariably chastised by Gandhi.

When it came to politics, Gandhi was uncompromising in his adherence to non-violence. However, when it came to everyday life, he was not so rigid. There were no circumstances in which a human being could kill another human being, but there might be circumstances when humans were permitted to kill animals.

In 1926, the compound of a textile mill in Ahmedabad was overrun by rabid dogs. The mill owner (Gandhi's friend Ambalal Sarabhai) got the dogs killed, leading to outraged protests by the Ahmedabad Humanitarian League and by many Jains. When the magnate asked Gandhi to intervene, he approved of the decision to kill the dogs, even though it appeared contrary to his professed belief in ahimsa.

In a series of articles published both in Gujarati and English, Gandhi defended his support of the apparently heartless actions of the mill owner. He pointed out that 'a principle is the expression of a perfection, and as imperfect beings like us cannot practice perfection, we devise every moment limits of its compromise in practice'. Thus, 'a recluse, who is living in a forest and is compassion incarnate, may not destroy a rabid dog. For in his compassion he has the virtue of making it whole. But a city dweller who is responsible for the protection of lives under his care and who does not possess the virtues of the recluse, but is capable of destroying a rabid dog, is faced with a conflict of duties. If he kills the dog, he commits a sin. If he does not kill it, he commits a graver sin.'

Gandhi told his readers about a group of Jains who came to the ashram at night, when he was about to go to sleep, and berated him in tones of 'anger, bitterness and arrogance' for his defence of the killing of rabid dogs. Gandhi stood his ground, saying that ideally, each dog would have an owner, and those without an owner could be kept together in a shelter for them. But if neither alternative was available, there was no option but to get rid of the rabid dogs. For, 'a dog without an owner is a danger to society and a swarm of them is a menace to its very existence'.

The complaints continued to pour in. So Gandhi defended his position with fresh examples and arguments. He noted that Ahmedabad's Civil Hospital had recorded 1117 cases of hydrophobia in 1925 and 995 in the first nine months of 1926. From this he concluded that 'stray dogs do not drop from heaven. They are a sign of the idleness, indifference and ignorance of society.' He recalled that when he was living in England as a student in the 1890s, and an epidemic of rabies broke out, orders were passed asking all owners to put collars with their names and addresses on their dogs, with dogs without collars being killed. 'The measure was taken purely in the public interest,' commented Gandhi. The conclusion he reached was that 'the ideal of humanity is perhaps lower [in England than in India], but the practice of it is very much [more] thorough than ours'.[16]

Two years later, the debate about whether one could ever kill animals broke out afresh in Ahmedabad. The object this time was not dogs, about whom Hindus were (so to say) neutral, but cows, whom Hindus worshipped. A badly injured calf was put to death in the Sabarmati Ashram; provoking outrage among Jain and Vaishnava circles in the city.

Gandhi defended the killing, comparing it to a surgical operation that removed a diseased part of the body. In both cases, he wrote, the object was 'to relieve the suffering soul within from pain. In the one case you do it by severing the diseased portion from the body, in the other you do it by severing from the soul the body that has become an instrument of torture to it.' Then, in a sharp attack on his critics, he remarked that

the trouble with our votaries of ahimsa is that they have made
of ahimsa blind fetish and put the greatest obstacle in the way of
the spread of true ahimsa in our midst. The current (and in my
opinion, mistaken) view of ahimsa has drugged our conscience
and rendered us insensible to a host of other and more insidious
forms of *himsa* [violence] like harsh words, harsh judgements,
ill-will, anger and spite and lust of cruelty; it has made us forget
that there may be far more *himsa* in the slow torture of men
and animals, the starvation and exploitation to which they
are subjected out of selfish greed, the wanton humiliation and
oppression of the weak and the killing of their self-respect that
we witness all around today than in mere benevolent taking
of life.[17]

Gandhi's defence of the killing of the maimed cow brought upon
him a further torrent of criticism. He received so many hostile letters
that, in a rare resort to sarcasm, he said his critics 'seem bent upon
improving the finances of the Postal Department'. Most letters were
'full of abuse'; they were 'practising himsa in the name of ahimsa'.
But one letter deserved a reply; this had suggested that Gandhi's
position might lend itself to an argument in favour of the selective
assassination of tyrants and dictators. For, if 'a man begins to oppress
a whole people and there is no other way to stop his oppression', then
it would be 'an act of ahimsa to rid society of his presence by putting
him to death'. The correspondent added: 'You say that there is no
himsa in killing off animal pests that destroy a farmer's crops; then
why should it not be ahimsa to kill human pests that threaten society
with destruction and worse?'

In response, Gandhi clarified that his definition of ahimsa did
not in any way endorse manslaughter. The killing of the calf was
undertaken for the sake of the animal itself. Recalling his earlier
defence of killing monkeys that destroy crops, Gandhi noted that
'society as yet knows of no means by which to effect a change of heart
in the monkeys and their killing may therefore be pardonable, but
there is no evil-doer or tyrant who can be considered beyond reform.
*That is why the killing of a human being out of self-interest can never
find a place in the scheme of ahimsa.*'[18]

Writing to Rajagopalachari, Gandhi hoped that 'the calf controversy [in *Young India*] provides some amusement for you, if it provides no instruction. If I took seriously all the correspondence that comes to me I should have to drown myself in the Sabarmati.'[19]

V

Pluralism and non-violence were two core aspects of Gandhi's faith. Celibacy, or brahmacharya, was a third. Gandhi had struggled hard but unavailingly to practise celibacy as a young man, finally taking a firm vow to give up sex in 1906.

Gandhi imposed his vow of celibacy on all who lived with him in the ashram. This was for him a mark of sacrifice, and also of moral purity. Among the worldly pleasures that social workers had to abandon when choosing to serve society were fine food, alcohol, tobacco, jewellery and sex.

Gandhi's relationship with Saraladevi Chaudhurani was not free of passion. But he managed to keep his vow of celibacy. Meanwhile, the ashram school had boys and girls studying together, in what Gandhi called a 'delicate' and 'novel' experiment. Gandhi knew Gujarati society to be deeply conservative; so, in an address to the students, he explained 'certain rules of conduct' they must follow. Thus, boys and girls must sit in separate rows in the class, and outside the classroom must not mix with one another. Boys could converse and joke with other boys, girls with other girls, but 'they should neither converse nor joke with one another'. Or touch one another, or carry on private correspondence with one another. For, as he emphatically noted, 'physical contact disturbs brahmacharya'.

In 1920, after the ashram school had been established, Gandhi outlined a long defence and explanation of brahmacharya, addressed, one supposes, chiefly to the boys. This took the form of a series of exhortations:

> As days pass I realize with increasing clearness that preservation of
> the vital fluid is imperative if one is to serve the country;
>   All of you must conserve this fluid and build up your bodies;

If I display so much vigour at this age of 51 it is only because I have conserved it. If I had done so from the beginning, I cannot imagine to what heights I should have soared by now;

A hot-tempered person can acquire knowledge, and so can a dishonest person, but one who does not observe *brahmacharya* can never acquire knowledge;

I appeal to all parents and guardians present here to help their boys in every way to conserve the vital fluid;

Whoever feels that it is not possible for him to restrain himself any longer, that his physical urge has grown so strong that it is impossible for him to curb it, should immediately quit this place rather than bring shame to the Ashram and break up this holy experiment.[20]

In both Jain and Hindu traditions, celibacy—or to use Gandhi's expression, 'the preservation of the vital fluid'—was crucial to acquiring spiritual power. Self-control and the suppression of the desires brought one closer to the Divine. Gandhi's innovation was to make celibacy central to social service.

Notably, Gandhi did not ask his political colleagues in the Congress Party to be celibate. Jawaharlal Nehru, Maulana Azad, Rajendra Prasad and Vallabhbhai Patel, as well as lesser-known Congressmen across India, were free if they so chose to have sex and raise a family. But those who were inmates of the ashram, who were his spiritual rather than his political disciples, had to take the pledge of brahmacharya.

In the last week of November 1925, Gandhi was dismayed to hear of 'irregularities on the part of many boys' in the ashram. Having discovered transgressions 'among the boys and somewhat among the girls', he decided to go on a week-long fast. It was the least he owed to the ashram's patrons, who had given him money 'in the hope that I am building up character'. Hence, the fast, undertaken 'to bring the youngsters to a sense of their error', and to make 'the Ashram free from errors which are sapping the manhood of the nation and undermining the character of the nation'.[21]

It was not just to his disciples in the ashram that Gandhi gave lessons on personal behaviour. Two letters written on the same day—19 August 1927—give a flavour of Gandhi's non-political concerns—or obsessions. Both were to young men who had written about the personal (including sexual) problems they faced. To T.W. Kalani of Sukkur in Sindh, Gandhi wrote instructing him to 'omit all novel-reading, and [to] repeat Ramanama [the name of Ram]. Learn *Bhagavad Gita* if possible in the original. Take a cold bath every day. Sleep out in the open air. . . . Do not brood over discharges when they occur. Find out each time the reason, and avoid the reason next time. Tell your father of the disease and tell him that it is perfectly useless to go to London [to study] till you have conquered these discharges and your thoughts.'

A certain 'R.B.T.' of Banaras had also written to Gandhi about similar anxieties. Gandhi offered his sympathies, while suggesting that he should stop 'excessive self-abuse. The vital fluid is evidently now passed even without stimulation. My advice to you is not to go to your wife at all for at least for one year and not till you have acquired mastery of yourself . . .'

The advice Gandhi offered went beyond the practice of sexual restraint. The young man in Banaras was told to wake up early, take regular walks, read the Gita and chant the name of Ram. Advice on diet was also forthcoming; fresh milk was recommended (without sugar), green rather than starchy vegetables, plenty of fruits and nuts and raisins if they weren't too expensive. Finally, the correspondent was told to 'keep your bowels in good order. And at the time of retiring at night take an earth bandage.'[22]

To contemporary eyes these exchanges might seem strange, even bizarre. The condemnation of masturbation was, of course, widespread at the time; here Gandhi was sharing in a more general prejudice. The other suggestions originated in his own personal experience. The Gita was always at his side; the name of Ram often on his lips. Since they had given him moral purpose and self-control, might they not do likewise to younger Indians? Early nights, long walks and a fruit-and-nut diet had kept him in good health; and they might do so for others too.

To my mind, what is truly remarkable is the fact that Gandhi engaged in such exchanges at all. One can more easily appreciate his interest in who would, each year, be best suited to be president of the

Congress, which, after all, was the premier political organization in British India. His concern for Hindu–Muslim harmony, his stress on the importance of spinning, his continuing attacks on the practice of untouchability—these too we can comprehend, for they represented the necessary preconditions for Indians to be capable of self-rule.

It is those other, idiosyncratic and deeply personal concerns, that mark Gandhi out from the major political leaders of his time. Gandhi differed from men such as Woodrow Wilson, Lloyd George, V.I. Lenin and Sun Yat-sen in substantive matters of political theory and practice. His belief in non-violence and his scepticism about industrial society was not shared by them. But in terms of his interest in matters outside politics, he differed even more radically. One can scarcely imagine Wilson or Lenin receiving unsolicited letters from unknown young men on dietary or sexual matters—and, even if they did, answering them at such length.

CHAPTER THIRTEEN

The Memoirist

I

In November 1923, during his first term in Yerwada prison, Gandhi had begun to write a history of the struggles he had led in South Africa. Time hung heavily on his hands; writing helped fill the hours (and days). The natural outlets for his literary ambitions, his own journals *Young India* and *Navajivan*, were temporarily unavailable to him. And he had now reached middle age, a time when one begins to reflect on the years left behind.

Gandhi wrote thirty chapters of his South African memoir in Yerwada, many of them dictated to his fellow prisoner Indulal Yagnik. After his release, he completed the book while recuperating in Juhu.

The serial publication of *Dakshina Africana Satyagrahano Itihas*, as it was called in Gujarati, began with *Navajivan*'s issue of 13 April 1924. Further instalments appeared, week by week, the last episode being printed in *Navajivan*'s issue of 22 November 1925. The English translation, undertaken by the long-time ashramite (and former English teacher) Valji Desai, was published in quarterly instalments in the Madras journal *Current Thought*, brought out by the nationalist publisher S. Ganesan and Co.

The serial publication of Gandhi's South African experiences was immediately followed by the serial publication of a more intimate memoir, carrying the Gujarati title *Satyana Prayogo Athava Atmakatha*. This appeared in weekly instalments in *Navajivan* from 29 November 1925 to 3 February 1929. The English version appeared more or less simultaneously, every week in *Young India*, from 3 December 1925 to 7 February 1929. The translator this time was the other and even more loyal ashramite Desai, namely, Mahadev, his English drafts improved and refined by Mira. A few chapters, written while Mahadev was away from the ashram, were translated by Pyarelal.

Dakshina Africana Satyagrahano Itihas was also published as a book in Gujarati, but in two parts, these appearing in 1924 and 1925 respectively. The English version, under the straightforward title *Satyagraha in South Africa*, was published by S. Ganesan in 1928. The book was dedicated to his lately deceased nephew, Maganlal Gandhi.

The second memoir was likewise published in Gujarati and English. Both versions appeared under the imprint of the newly started Navajivan Publishing House, based in the ashram. The autobiography originally appeared in two volumes, these published in 1926 and 1928 in Gujarati, and in 1927 and 1929 in English. The English edition was printed at the Karnatak Press, Bombay, and bound in khadi cloth. It was called *The Story of My Experiments with Truth*, although a more accurate rendition of the Gujarati might have been *Truth's Experiments, Or an Autobiography*, since the original suggests that the protagonist is 'truth', with the author, Gandhi, being merely an instrument used by it.[1]

There is inevitably some overlap between the memoirs. Yet, the tone of the second is markedly different from the first. Thus, while describing the early years of the struggle in South Africa in his autobiography, Gandhi writes: 'If I found myself entirely absorbed in the service of the community, the reason behind it was my desire for self-realization. I had made the religion of service my own, as I felt that God could only be realized through service.'

These were not Gandhi's first books. Back in 1909, while on a ship between London and Cape Town, he had written a spirited polemic against industrial civilization called *Hind Swaraj*.[2] In 1921, he had published a pamphlet called *A Guide to Health*. But *Satyagraha in*

South Africa and *My Experiments with Truth* were his first excursions
in autobiography, lending them a special poignancy, as well as
significance. Gandhi himself was not unaware of their importance.
In October 1926—shortly after finishing his South African memoir
and while he was writing *Experiments*—Gandhi executed a new
will. This stated that he owned no property, while bequeathing to
the Navajivan Trust that ran the ashram 'all my rights in whatever
books and whatever articles I have written or I may write thereafter',
the income from these to be used 'for carrying out the objects of the
Satyagraha Ashram according to their discretion'.[3]

Gandhi had no estate except a literary one, but this, as he sensed
in 1926, was likely to be invaluable. The books he wrote have been
continuously in print, with the autobiography in particular appearing
in many editions and many translations.[4] For ninety years now, the
Navajivan Trust has been almost entirely sustained by the royalties
from Gandhi's writings.

In the 1920s, in between one jail term and the next, while
campaigning against untouchability and for Hindu–Muslim harmony,
while seeking ways to launch a fresh political challenge to the Raj,
while monitoring the moral and sexual habits of his family and his
disciples, Gandhi yet found time to write two memoirs. What do
these two books tell us about the man, the writer, the thinker, the
propagandist?

II

The preface to the first book notes that the idea of satyagraha was
invented in South Africa. Gandhi remarks here that he had 'long
entertained a desire to write a history of that struggle myself. Some
things only I could write. Only the general who conducts a campaign
can know the objective of each particular move. And as this was the first
attempt to apply the principle of Satyagraha to politics on a large scale,
it is necessary . . . that the public should have an idea of its development.'

Satyagraha in South Africa starts with the geographical and
historical setting, the rivalry between the two main groups of
European colonists in South Africa, the Dutch and the British. Of

the boom town of Johannesburg, built on the extraction of gold, a city where he spent almost a decade, and where satyagraha itself was born, Gandhi writes: 'It would be no exaggeration to say that the citizens of Johannesburg do not walk but seem as if they ran. No one has the leisure to look at any one else, and every one is apparently engrossed in thinking how to amass the maximum wealth in the minimum of time!'[5]

When Gandhi first went to South Africa, in 1893, he was prone to think of Africans as backward and uncivilized. At the time, he believed in a hierarchy of civilizations, with Europeans at the top, Indians slightly below them, and Africans at the very bottom. He shed some of these prejudices in the two decades he lived in South Africa. Now, in this book written many years after he had left Africa, he revealed a further maturation. He praised the beauty of the Zulu language, and the Africans' moral sense (writing that they are more honest than Europeans or Indians), while condemning the economic and political exploitation they were subject to.

By the time he published *Satyagraha in South Africa*, Gandhi had moved decisively from parochialism to universalism. 'In my opinion,' he wrote here, 'there is no place on earth and no race, which is not capable of producing the finest types of humanity, given suitable opportunities and education.'[6]

The main subject of the book, however, was the condition of the Indians in South Africa. Gandhi distinguished between two sets of migrants: indentured labourers for sugar plantations and coal mines, these mostly from South India; and a smaller group of Gujarati traders, both Muslim and Hindu, who had set up shops in the towns of Natal and the Transvaal, initially catering to Indian workers but over time servicing Africans as well.

Successive chapters detailed the laws and practices that discriminated against Indians, province by province. Indians were restricted from owning property in the Transvaal. In Natal, labourers who wished to stay on after the expiry of their indenture had to pay a hefty annual tax. There were stringent curbs on Indians crossing provincial boundaries.

The narrative then moved on to the first protests against racial laws that bore down heavily on Indians. These took the form of petitions written to the government, and lobbying with legislators. Gandhi spoke of the founding, in 1894, of the Natal Indian Congress, as an organizational platform to campaign for Indian rights.

In 1899 the Anglo-Boer war broke out. Gandhi analysed the fallout of the war on the Indians, and why, after the warring sides signed a peace treaty, he based himself in Johannesburg. It was here, in September 1906, that a famous meeting was held where Indians vowed to court arrest unless a particularly noxious ordinance was withdrawn. Gandhi, imbuing the meeting with a retrospective glow of patriotism, claimed that 'the Ordinance [sought] to humiliate not only ourselves but also the motherland'. Discriminations against, and restrictions on, individual Indians were 'tantamount to insulting the [Indian] nation as a whole'.[7]

Later chapters marked the major milestones in the satyagraha: the bonfire of certificates in 1908; the march across provincial borders in 1913; the arrests and jail terms of the leaders and the rank and file; the deportation to India of many brave satyagrahis; and the eventual compromise forged between General Smuts and Gandhi in 1914.

In his account of these satyagrahas, Gandhi was at pains to stress that the participation cut across religious and linguistic boundaries. Hindus, Muslims, Parsis and Christians, as well as Tamil speakers, Telugu speakers, Hindi speakers, and Gujarati speakers, all came forward to court arrest. A separate chapter was devoted to Ahmad Muhammad Kachhalia, a Muslim merchant from Johannesburg who was one of the heroes of the campaign. 'I have never, whether in South Africa or in India,' writes Gandhi, 'come across a man who could surpass Mr Kachhalia in courage and steadfastness. He sacrificed all for the community's sake. . . . Perfectly fearless and impartial as he was, he never hesitated to point out their faults to Hindus as well as Musalmans whenever he found it necessary.'[8]

One chapter dealt with the role of *Indian Opinion*, the multilingual journal Gandhi founded in South Africa. He remarked that 'we could not perhaps have educated the local Indian community, nor kept Indians all over the world in touch with the course of events in South Africa in any other way, with the same ease and success as through *Indian Opinion*, which therefore was certainly a most useful and potent weapon in our struggle'.[9]

There was also a chapter on the (mostly Tamil) women who joined the satyagraha of 1913–14, whose 'bravery was beyond words'.[10] Another chapter detailed the contributions of sympathetic Europeans. Gandhi paid tribute to Albert West, who helped run *Indian Opinion* and the Phoenix settlement; Henry Polak, who often mediated between Gandhi and the authorities; and Hermann Kallenbach, who donated his farm to house satyagrahis and sustain the movement. 'One of my objects in enumerating the names of European helpers,' remarked Gandhi, 'is to mark the Satyagrahis' gratefulness to them.'[11]

A brief conclusion pointed to the larger implications of the struggles led by Gandhi in South Africa. The concessions wrought by the Indians in that colony, he argued, 'more or less served as a shield for Indian emigrants in other parts of the Empire, who, if they are suppressed, will be suppressed thanks to the absence of Satyagraha among themselves . . .' More broadly, Gandhi hoped that the book had 'demonstrated with some success that Satyagraha is a priceless and matchless weapon, and that those who wield it are strangers to disappointment or defeat'.[12]

At one level, the book can be read as a straightforward narrative of the satyagrahas in South Africa, as told by the man—or General— who both conceived and led them. At another level, the book can be read as a handbook of political techniques, instructing potential satyagrahis (whether in India or elsewhere) on what methods to use and which to eschew. At once descriptive and didactic, the book was written to educate, but also to instruct.

But there may be a third way to read the book: as an extended thank you note to the community he had left behind. Gandhi came to India fully formed, his social philosophy and his political repertoire in place, to be now applied to a much wider theatre of action. *Satyagraha in South Africa* is a grateful backward look at the men and women, Indian as well as European, who sustained and supported him in those formative years in the diaspora.

III

The tone of the narrative of *Satyagraha in South Africa* may be described as 'author-inflected'. The personal note is by no means absent, but it is not dominant either. On the other hand, the narrative of *The Story of My Experiments with Truth* is 'author-saturated', if not 'author-supersaturated'.[13] The difference in tone is deliberate, as indicated by Gandhi himself in the introduction to the latter book:

> My experiments in the political field are now known, not only in India, but to a certain extent to the 'civilized' world. For me, they have not much value; and the title of Mahatma that they have won for me has, therefore, even less. Often the title has pained me; and there is not a moment I can recall when it may be said to have tickled me. But I should certainly like to narrate my experiments in the spiritual field which are known only to myself, and from which I have derived such power as I possess for working in the political field.

Gandhi's autobiography begins with his birth and upbringing in a Bania family of Kathiawar that was steeped in piety and food restrictions. He was, he recalled, 'very shy and avoided all company'. He also remembered, some fifty years after the event, how he disgraced himself in the eyes of his teacher by failing to spell 'kettle' accurately.[14]

The narrative then moves on to his marriage at the age of thirteen, and his early possessiveness about his wife Kasturba, who became the object of his 'carnal appetite'. A friend he made in school subjected him to various temptations—eating meat and visiting a brothel, among them. A key chapter (still much cited and discussed) describes how, at the precise moment his father was dying, he was having sex with his wife and could not attend to his filial duties.

A dozen short chapters at the end of Part I deal with his years in London as a law student, where he took dancing lessons in a bid to play the English gentleman, before finding succour in the Vegetarian Society of London. It was in London that Gandhi made his first Christian friends, the beginning of a lifelong engagement with people of religious faiths other than his own. This outer quest was accompanied by the (continuing) search for inner perfection. Thus, he relates, not without pride, how he successfully adhered to the three vows he had made to his mother before leaving India—that he would not eat meat, drink alcohol, or have sex with a woman who was not his wife.

Part II begins with Gandhi's return to India, and his failure to establish himself at the Bombay Bar. In and from this failure he learnt a lesson, here conveyed to the 'briefless barristers' of the generations after his. Since he was short of money, he walked to the court and back from his house several miles away. This walk, remarked Gandhi, 'saved a fair amount of money, and when many of my friends in Bombay used to fall ill, I do not remember having once had an illness. Even when I began to earn money, I kept up the practice of walking to and from the office, and I am still reaping the benefits of that practice.'[15]

Gandhi was rescued from professional mediocrity by an invitation from South Africa. His arrival in that country, his first clients, and the racial slurs and insults he was victim to, are all narrated, but also, perhaps more notably, his discussions with Christians whose faith he sought to understand but who were uncomprehending, and even occasionally contemptuous, of his own faith. We learn how he first read the works of Tolstoy and Ruskin, two thinkers who were to profoundly influence him. Other chapters outline his personal and moral debts to his pre-eminent Indian mentors, the Jain mystic Raychandbhai and the Poona statesman Gopal Krishna Gokhale.[16]

Gandhi's path to self-realization had several hurdles. The most notable was the struggle with his sexuality. His early mentor Raychandbhai had urged him to practise brahmacharya. It took him more than a decade to put his teacher's precepts into practice. The path was arduous, for true brahmacharya 'means control of the senses in thought, word and deed'. Writing twenty years after he took the vow of celibacy, Gandhi was 'filled with pleasure and wonderment. The more or less successful practice of self-control had been going on since 1901. But the freedom and joy that came to me after taking the vow had never been experienced before 1906. Before the vow I had been open to being overcome by temptation at any moment. Now the vow was a sure shield against temptation.'[17]

In the late summer of 1896, Gandhi returned to India to take his wife and children back with him to South Africa. Part III of his autobiography begins with the return journey, the growing hysteria among the whites at Indian emigration resulting in a mob attack on Gandhi (as the alleged leader or facilitator of this emigration). He was saved by a white policeman and his wife, confirming his view that even among the Europeans he could make friends and allies.

Scattered throughout the book are episodes from his forty and more years of married life with Kasturba. Several misunderstandings are recalled, and retold from his point of view. Gandhi writes that his own experiences in three continents had led him to observe 'no distinctions between relatives and strangers, countrymen and foreigners, white and coloured, Hindus and Indians of other faiths, whether Musalmans, Parsis, Christians or Jews'.

Kasturba, however, remained bound within the conventions (and prejudices) of her religion and caste. When they were living in Durban in the late 1890s, a clerk of Gandhi's, a Tamil Christian, lived with them in their house. Kasturba refused to clean his chamber pot on the twin grounds that this now Christianized Hindu had been born in an untouchable caste. Gandhi, in a fit of rage, almost pushed her out of the house, but recovered his senses just in time.

Remembering the incident almost thirty years later, Gandhi remarked that he was then 'a cruelly kind husband. I regarded myself as [Kasturba's] teacher, and so harassed her out of my blind love for her.' The phrase 'cruelly kind' is intriguing—was he at once cruel and kind, or cruel in a cause that was itself kindly? Probably the latter, since through his actions Gandhi hoped that he would make his wife elevate her moral self by acknowledging kinship with all humans, regardless of caste or colour. Back in 1898, Gandhi regarded his wife as 'born to do her husband's behest', whereas now he saw her rather as 'a helpmate, a comrade and a partner in the husband's joys and sorrows'.[18]

Gandhi also recounts arguments with his friend and housemate Henry Polak. Gandhi believed that 'Indian parents who train their children to think and talk in English from their infancy betray their children and their country. They deprive them of the spiritual and social heritage of the nation, and render them to that extent unfit for the service of the country.' Holding these views, Gandhi always spoke to his children in Gujarati. Polak thought that he was thus closing a window to them. 'He contended,' wrote Gandhi, 'with all the love and vigour at his command, that, if children were to learn a universal language like English from their infancy, they would easily gain considerable advantage over others in the race of life. He failed to convince me.'[19]

Later in the narrative, Gandhi returns to the significance of the mother tongue, while remembering the reception thrown for him by Bombay's Gujarati community back in 1915. The principal speaker, M.A. Jinnah, 'made a short and sweet little speech in English'. Most of the other speeches were also in the language of the conqueror. But, recalls Gandhi with a touch of pride, 'when my turn came, I expressed my thanks in Gujarati explaining my partiality for Gujarati and Hindustani, and entering my humble protest against the use of English in a Gujarati gathering'.[20]

Gandhi's ever-changing diet is the subject of several chapters. An account of his giving up milk ends with this statement: 'Those who make light of dietetic restrictions and fasting are as much in error as those who stake their all on them.' The next chapter argues that 'fasting can help to curb animal passion, only if it is undertaken with a view to self-restraint'. Later in the book, he insists that 'my experiments in dietetics are dear to me as a part of my researches in Ahimsa. They give me recreation and joy.'[21]

Part V of the book runs from 1915 to 1920, from his return to India to the special session of the Congress in Calcutta where he authoritatively established his control over the Congress. Gandhi rehearses his travels by train around the subcontinent, and revisits the death of Gokhale and his own decision not to join the Servants of India Society. He speaks of the setting up of the Sabarmati Ashram, and the controversy over admitting an 'untouchable' family. There is a fairly long account of his first satyagraha in Champaran, and shorter accounts of the peasant movement in Kheda and the millworkers' strike in Ahmedabad.

In describing his travels around India in 1918–19, Gandhi said he was 'seeking the friendship of good Mussalmans, and was eager to understand the Mussalman mind through contact with their purest and most patriotic representatives'. His South African experiences had convinced him that 'it would be on the question of Hindu–Muslim unity that my Ahimsa would be put to its severest test, and that the question presented the widest field for my experiments in Ahimsa. The conviction is still there. Every moment of my life I realize that God is putting me on my trial.'[22]

The last chapter of the book, entitled 'Farewell', explains why the narrative ends in September 1920. For, his life since then 'has been so public that there is hardly anything about it that people do not know'.

IV

As the two memoirs were being serialized in *Young India* and *Navajivan*, friends wrote in offering opinions. To his Indian colleagues, who knew almost nothing about his South African days, the books came as a revelation.

The reactions of Gandhi's South African colleagues were more ambivalent. Henry Polak wondered how he had left out Gabriel Isaacs, a South African jeweller (of Jewish extraction) who had wholeheartedly supported the Indians.[23] Sonja Schlesin complained about the omission of Mrs Vogt, a Jewish lady who had formed an Indian women's club in Johannesburg.[24] Gandhi's former secretary had other, and more serious, complaints. Thus, Miss Schlesin noticed that 'again and again in your autobiography you mention conversations and incidents which one feels that the people concerned would not have liked mentioned'. She thought letters and private conversations should be regarded as confidential; to publish them without first taking permission from the writer or speaker was 'a distinct breach of confidence'.[25]

A month later, Miss Schlesin wrote Gandhi an eight-page, intensely felt letter on the serialization of the autobiography in *Young India* and the 'misrepresentations' about her and her work it contained, which she hoped Gandhi 'will not perpetuate in book-form'. She listed these mistakes: Gandhi had got her age when she joined him wrong, misstated some facts about an educational loan she had taken, called her the principal of a girls' school when she was merely one of the teachers, etc. She urged him to have these errors corrected, acidly commenting: 'A Mahatma cannot lie; therefore, people reading your misrepresentations would naturally come to the conclusion that the unfortunate victim of the misrepresentation had been responsible for them.'[26]

His son Manilal also asked his father about significant omissions in the two memoirs. Gandhi defensively answered that 'my aim in giving certain names is that they should be remembered as long as the "Autobiography" is recognized as an important work'.[27]

On the other hand, some correspondents in South Africa were impressed by the frankness with which Gandhi discussed his mistakes of judgement. One wrote in to compliment him on the revelations about his ill treatment of Kasturba. Gandhi wrote back: 'Of course you have not imagined that I am in any way proud of recalling the brutality or that I am today capable of any such brutality. But I thought that if people recognize me as a gentle peace-loving man, they should know that at one time I could be a positive beast even though at the same time I claimed to be a loving husband. It was not without good cause that a friend described me as a combination of sacred cow and fierce tiger.'[28]

Gandhi had been frank about his own marital problems. Yet, he had prudently left out another woman with whom he had a significant relationship. The omission of Saraladevi Chaudhurani both pleased and relieved his closest disciples. Thus, as Rajagopalachari wrote to Mahadev Desai, 'as the story is proceeding I am afraid a certain lady is trembling in agonised fear as to the future chapters though I know there is no need to fear. For the "simplicity" that the Manchester Guardian admires in Bapu is tempered with an enormous amount of caution and moderation.'[29]

Apart from these private letters, there were also some public responses to Gandhi's autobiography. The pro-British *Times of India* claimed that the book showed its author to be a 'supreme egotist' and served merely as 'a smug and self-complacent justification of his amazing experiments with human nature'. Of Gandhi's injunctions to ashram inmates to give up their belongings and embrace celibacy, the newspaper observed that the desires for property and sex 'are instinctive in the unregenerate but normal and natural human being'. The Bolsheviks in Russia had tried but failed to abolish private property, but apparently 'Mr. Gandhi hopes to do what the Soviets have given up as hopeless'.[30]

Gandhi almost certainly saw this attack in the *Times of India*, since the newspaper came into his ashram in Ahmedabad. And he almost certainly did not see a more nuanced assessment, published in an English journal out of Shanghai. This found the autobiography a book 'of extreme interest to everybody', for 'few saints have exposed their souls so unflinchingly to the ordeal of publicity'. The reviewer acknowledged Gandhi was far from being a 'profound and patient thinker'; rather, he was 'half a mere faddist', who inflicted on the reader 'page after page full of his experiments in diet, medicine, and hand spinning'. Even so, the reviewer concluded, the book 'is easy reading, and he keeps our sympathy partly because of his perfect courage, but still more because of the genuine spirit of candour and Christian charity which somehow manages to keep fresh and sweet the whole of this astonishing farrago'.[31]

V

As Gandhi's memoirs appeared in instalments in *Navajivan* and *Young India*, letters began pouring into the Sabarmati Ashram asking for translation rights. The interest was naturally more keen in the autobiography per se than in the book about South Africa. There were queries about Hindi, Punjabi, Urdu, Tamil and Bengali editions, and about French, German, Danish, Japanese and Norwegian editions too.

Gandhi was happy for *The Story of My Experiments with Truth* to appear in Indian languages, 'so long as nothing is omitted from the book'.[32] He was also happy to see an English edition appear in India itself. But about other foreign rights he wished to wait and see. In 1926, his admirer, the New York clergyman John Haynes Holmes, had asked for permission to negotiate with Macmillan of New York for an English edition to be sold around the world. Gandhi asked him to go ahead, without committing himself.[33]

The first instalment of the English version of *Experiments* appeared in India in 1927. A year later, a friend wrote about the possibility of a British edition. Gandhi told him the rights had been provisionally granted to Macmillan, adding: 'The second volume of the book is not to be published just now. It will take some time, because I do not know how the chapters of Indian experience will run. I have no definite plan mapped out. I am, therefore, unable to say how many more chapters I shall have to write, and it is for that reason that publication of the second volume has been suspended.'[34]

In the event, the narrative of the autobiography stopped in 1920. In explaining why this was so, Gandhi remarked that his 'principal experiments during the past seven years', had 'all been made through the Congress. A reference to my relations with the leaders would therefore be unavoidable, if I set about describing my experiments further. And this I may not do so, any rate for the present, if only from a sense of propriety.'[35]

In April 1928, the *Observer* of London printed excerpts from Gandhi's autobiography as they had appeared in *Young India*. Entitled 'Gandhi on Himself', these dealt with his experiments with diet and celibacy as he sought to 'subdue flesh to the spirit'. Reading this piece with interest across the Atlantic was an editor at the Baltimore *Sun*. As he commented in his column, even the brief excerpts offered by the newspaper 'make clear the vastness of the difference between East and West. We in the West may admire Gandhi but we could not follow him. . . . And that, I believe, is just as well.' The article was unsigned, but the phrasing bears the signature of Baltimore's most famous son, H.L. Mencken.[36]

The article in the *Observer* was, of course, read more widely in Britain itself. A prominent literary agent, David Higham of Curtis Brown Associates, wrote to the newspaper asking it to put him in touch with Gandhi. Higham said that Curtis Brown 'could be of real service to Mr. Gandhi for the publication arrangements for his autobiography. A very large number of separate rights in such a work ought to be valuable and I think we can reasonably claim to be in a better position than anyone else for securing the largest possible return from these.' He added that the authors the agency represented included David Lloyd George and Winston Churchill.[37]

The letter reached Ahmedabad, for it now rests in the Sabarmati Ashram's archives. Whether it was read by Gandhi himself is not clear. However, he seems to have trusted the work to his friends rather than a commercial agency. In January 1929, on the advice of John Haynes Holmes, Gandhi sold the American rights to his autobiography to Macmillan Company of New York, for about a lac of rupees (equivalent to about 7500 pounds sterling), the entire sum to be handed over by Gandhi for khadi work.[38]

Meanwhile, C.F. Andrews had opened negotiations with George Allen and Unwin for a British edition of Gandhi's autobiography. Andrews had been told that rather than a word-for-word reproduction, a thematic selection might be a better option. Indians were naturally interested in an exhaustive account of their Mahatma's experiments. British and American readers, on the other hand, might welcome a truncated version omitting themes and subjects foreign to them.[39]

VI

Like all self-testimonies of famous men, these two books were pre-emptive strikes against future chroniclers of Gandhi's life and influence. Gandhi wanted his version of the satyagraha in South Africa published before the events it described were subject to the dispassionate gaze of the academic historian; and he wanted his own account of his personal struggles with truth and morality out in the public domain before biographers set about critically scrutinizing his personality.

At the same time, Gandhi's memoirs are also meant to be instructional manuals. But whereas the pedagogic intent of *Satyagraha in South Africa* was political, with *The Story of My Experiments with Truth* it is personal. We learn of how the child Gandhi learnt not to tell lies or cheat in school examinations, how the young adult strove to simplify his diet and take control of his passions, how the husband learnt to respect his wife and school his children, how the upper-caste Hindu learnt to transcend the boundaries of identity and faith, how the successful lawyer chose to elevate community over career. Perhaps, by reading this frank self-testimony of their famous countryman, younger Indians battling their own personal, sexual, dietary, familial or professional problems would learn how to combat or overcome them.

At the time Gandhi wrote his memoirs, autobiographies written in the West were broadly of two types: those written when the author was young, and those written when the author was old. Prominent in the first category were books by poets such as Robert Graves and Edmund Blunden, who, having fought in the First World War, were encouraged to tell their life's story when still in their early thirties. At the other pole were men of science, who typically turned to autobiography when their real work was done. Among the great works of this kind that Gandhi may have known of were the autobiographies of Charles Darwin and Benjamin Franklin.

Gandhi's memoirs did not fit into either type (or stereotype). They were written in his fifties. Here, the autobiographer had a substantial reservoir of experience to draw upon, and more to look forward to. The tone was at once reflective and pedagogic. Gandhi's hope— particularly with regard to *Experiments*—was that the reader would be inspired and educated by the experiences, errors, judgements and actions of the autobiographer. Yet, the teachings were addressed also to himself. The autobiographer knew that he was not done with life yet. Might he not, in the years that remained, implement with more certainty the credo that he had so strenuously worked out?

CHAPTER FOURTEEN

Once More into the Fray

I

On 27 January 1928, Gandhi's third son, Ramdas Gandhi, was married in the Sabarmati Ashram. His bride, Nirmala, had been chosen for him by his father. Gandhi gifted the couple a copy of the Gita and two spinning wheels. In a speech to the gathering, he remarked that Ramdas and Devadas were the two sons 'brought up exclusively' by him and under his care, adding that neither had ever deceived him, nor hidden from him their faults or failings. The unspoken comparison was with the two elder sons, with whom Gandhi's relations had been far more contentious.[1]

One reason Gandhi was staying put in the ashram was his indifferent health. As he wrote to a Sindhi colleague, the 'doctors' instruments do give alarming readings, and therefore I have agreed to take full rest'.[2] Elsewhere in India, protests were gathering ground against the Simon Commission that arrived in India in the first week of February 1928. While its mandate was to prescribe constitutional reforms for India, the commission was vitiated from the start by the fact that not one of its members was an Indian.

A vivid account of these protests is contained in the travelogue of Edward Cadogan, a member of the Simon Commission. In Bombay, wrote Cadogan, they were met with 'the first of those hostile

294

demonstrations with which we were destined to become so familiar all over India'. Then, in Delhi, their convoy of cars was stalled by 'a concourse of more or less hostile riff-raff' waving 'banners with "Go back, Simon," inscribed thereon'. Next, in Kanpur, a group of students 'had blocked all the approaches in our neighbourhood and shouted themselves hoarse'. The pattern was repeated wherever they went—in Guntur, Lucknow, Lahore and Poona, where the commissioners could travel only under heavy police escort in the face of fervent opposition by crowds in which college students were prominent.

Edward Cadogan was struck by the depth of the protests, and by the hostility of one family in particular. 'Of all the bitter and irreconcilable opponents with whom the Government of India had been brought into contact during recent years,' remarked Cadogan, 'Motilal Nehru and his son stand out [as] the most conspicuous.' The visiting Englishman was puzzled by Motilal's volte-face; once a 'warm friend of the English community', he had 'suddenly and for some reason' become their 'inveterate foe'. And he was angered by Jawaharlal, who had organized 'the most spectacular of all the demonstrations' against the commission, and whose propaganda among students was 'doing infinite harm with complete impunity'.[3]

In the third week of February, the Central Legislative Assembly discussed a resolution, proposed by Lala Lajpat Rai, expressing 'the Assembly's entire lack of confidence' in the Simon Commission. Lajpat Rai remarked that even 'with the best of intentions and motives, the Commissioners could only be the gramophone of the [British] Indian bureaucracy, and eventually the gramophone of the Secretary of State for India'. His fellow Congressman Srinivasa Iyengar acidly remarked that 'the Britisher's [belief in] fair play never crossed the English Channel'. Then Motilal Nehru added that 'Sir John Simon is a big man but I for one will not advise my countrymen to surrender their right to the biggest man in the world. That right is the right of self-determination.'

The Congress leaders were buoyed by the support they received from Moderate politicians such as M.A. Jinnah. Addressing the British members of the assembly, Jinnah said they were making 'a great mistake by trying to represent that all the parties are determined on the boycott for some sinister motive'. If they persisted in this attitude, he warned, the British 'will lose the whole of India'.

With the bulk of the Indian members voting for it, and all official members against, Lajpat Rai's motion passed by a narrow majority: sixty-eight to sixty-two. The result was greeted with shouts of '*Vande Mataram*' (the invocation to the motherland composed by the Bengali writer Bankim Chandra Chatterjee).[4]

II

Gandhi watched these protests against the Simon Commission from afar. He was more closely involved, however, with a localized struggle, that of the peasants of Bardoli in southern Gujarat. The government had imposed an enhanced revenue on this taluk, which the villagers were refusing to pay. At a meeting of peasants on 4 February, Vallabhbhai Patel urged them to show the government 'as to what evil consequences result through awakening a sleeping lion'.[5] Patel himself resigned from his presidentship of the Ahmedabad Municipality, and moved back to the Gujarat countryside where he had been born and raised. He organized and spoke at many meetings, while writing to the authorities to suspend the enhanced assessment, and conduct an impartial inquiry into the condition of the peasantry. 'Vallabhbhai's name,' remarked a colleague, 'is now a synonym for honest cooperation with Government when possible and clean and honest fight where necessary.' Helping him in the campaign were Mohanlal Pandya and Abbas Tyabji, the latter urging Muslim cultivators not to stay aloof from the movement.[6]

The government responded by confiscating the properties of those who refused to pay the enhanced tax. In a further show of strength, police parties were sent to the defaulting villages. The peasants were undeterred. At a meeting in Varad on 28 April,

> enthusiastic scenes of devotion and worship showered upon
> Mr. Vallabhbhai Patel were witnessed. Women dressed in Khadi,
> with garlands of hand-spun yarn and offerings of flowers, cocoanut,

red powder and rice were paying their respects and making obeisance in unending chains. Songs composed by pious matrons among women-folk, in some places altered to suit the present occasion, invoking God to bless them in their holy struggle for truth were recited by about five hundred women, which gave a religious turn to the congregation consisting of about 2,500 souls.[7]

On 2 May, one of the satyagraha leaders, Ravishankar Vyas, was arrested and sentenced to five months in jail for telling peasants not to carry the luggage of the revenue officials. Other satyagrahis were also arrested and sentenced for intimidating public servants. Meanwhile, the government seized and auctioned lands and cattle owned by the protesting peasants.[8]

Writing in *Young India*, Gandhi said the people of Bardoli 'have lost their possessions' but 'kept their honour'. He urged them to stay firm. 'Imprisonments, forfeitures, deportations, death, must all be taken in the ordinary course by those who count honour before everything else.'

Gandhi compared the Bardoli struggle to a great 'yajna', or sacrifice. The government was using a fourfold method to crush the satyagraha: namely, *sama* (appeasement), *dama* (bribery), *danda* (punishment) and *bheda* (promotion of divisiveness). But the peasants of Bardoli, led by 'their beloved Sardar', had thus far resisted all attempts to appease, bribe, divide or punish them.[9]

This appears to have been the first reference in print by Gandhi to Vallabhbhai as 'Sardar', the term by which he was now commonly known to the peasants of Bardoli, a term variously connoting patriarch, community leader and commander, all definitions applying to this man of peasant stock who, after winning wealth and fame in the city, had returned to lead his people in their fight against a harsh and unfeeling government.

III

The ashram in Sabarmati now had a total of 277 residents: 133 men, 66 women and 78 children. Spread across 132 acres, it had homes, a school, a printing press, and sheds for carpentry and spinning. Among the latest reforms Gandhi had initiated were a common kitchen where everyone had to eat; private or family kitchens in individual cottages were no longer permitted. The thirty-odd ashram 'servants' were also now dispensed with; the inmates had do all the cleaning and clearing themselves, working in batches of six in the kitchen.[10] A Sindhi professor who joined the ashram thought its 'most striking social feature' was 'the utter absence of servants and so also of masters. It was a large family of equals in the sense that no work or occupation was considered too low or too high.' This was broadly true, except that there was one person more equal than others: Gandhi, 'Bapu' to all in the ashram, who drafted the community's rules, supervised its functioning, and resolved or adjudicated disputes among its members.[11]

Kasturba was happy to have her husband at home for a stretch. Three of their sons were now productively engaged: Manilal running *Indian Opinion* and the Phoenix settlement in Natal; Ramdas promoting khadi in rural Kathiawar; Devadas working in Jamia Millia Islamia, the new 'Nationalist Muslim' university in Delhi. But the eldest boy, Harilal, continued to be estranged from his parents. 'Harilal has practically forsaken me,' wrote Gandhi to a friend in South Africa. 'He drinks, eats and makes himself merry. But he is a brave boy in one sense that he makes no secret of his vice and his rebellion is an open rebellion. If he had not done his creditors down, I would not have minded his other lapses as I mind this betrayal of his creditors.'[12]

Harilal's absence hurt; but what hurt far more was the premature death, in late April 1928, of his nephew Maganlal Gandhi. Maganlal had died of typhoid, contracted while touring in rural Bihar. In an eloquent tribute, Gandhi spoke of his nephew's work in running the Phoenix settlement in South Africa and his vital role in nurturing the Sabarmati Ashram. Maganlal was, in Gandhi's eyes, a model celibate, a model constructive worker, and a model civil resister too. Terming Maganlal 'my best comrade', Gandhi feelingly wrote: 'He was my hands, my feet and my eyes. The world knows so little of how much my so-called greatness depends upon the incessant toil and drudgery of silent, devoted, able and pure workers, men as well as women.

And among them all Maganlal was to me the greatest, the best and the purest.'[13]

IV

From his ashram, Gandhi monitored the ongoing struggle in Bardoli. Thousands of rupees were being collected for the 'Bardoli Satyagraha Fund' from sympathizers in Gujarat's two largest towns, Surat and Ahmedabad, and from Bombay as well.[14]

In the third week of July 1928, the governor of Bombay, Sir Leslie Wilson, visited Surat, and had a three-hour-long discussion with Vallabhbhai Patel. The details were not shared with the press. However, rumours leaked out that while the governor had agreed to an inquiry into the terms of assessment, he insisted it would be carried out by a revenue officer. Patel wanted a judicial officer to be appointed, on the grounds that he was likely to be more impartial.

On 23 July, the governor spoke in the Bombay Legislative Council about his meeting with Vallabhbhai Patel. He was prepared to offer 'a full, open and independent enquiry' into the Bardoli dispute, to commence once the revenue now due to the government had been paid. The payment of arrears was non-negotiable, for the question was 'whether the writ of His Majesty the King-Emperor is to run in a portion of His Majesty's Dominions or whether the edict of some unofficial body of individuals is to be obeyed'. The peasants of Bardoli were told they had fourteen days to pay up.[15]

In a note prepared for the governor, a senior official wrote that 'Bardoli has been chosen with great care as the arena for this trial of strength. Gandhi's influence over this area is paramount and he has for some years sedulously trained the inhabitants to practise his principles of Satyagraha and civil disobedience. There are in this area a number of people who were in South Africa with Gandhi.'[16]

This note was dated 28 July. Another note, sent to the governor three days later, observed that 'in the Bardoli Taluka there is complete contempt for Government and except for the Police, civil authority exists only on sufferance'.[17]

On 2 August, as the deadline indicated by the governor of Bombay approached, Gandhi left for Bardoli. He stayed in the area, while Vallabhbhai Patel went to Poona to meet the governor. Writing to Vallabhbhai's daughter Manibehn on 4 August, Gandhi was hopeful that a settlement would be reached, for 'the Government is not in a sufficiently strong position now to prolong the fight. Public opinion is against it and it has made many mistakes.'

Gandhi's optimism was not misplaced. On 6 August, the government agreed to an inquiry 'by a Judicial Officer associated with a Revenue Officer, the opinion of the former prevailing in all disputed points'. The satyagrahis under arrest were all released, and the village headmen who had resigned, reinstated. More good news followed, when it was announced that the inquiry would be conducted by R.S. Broomfield, who had made that memorable speech praising Gandhi while sentencing him to prison back in March 1922.[18]

Vallabhbhai Patel now returned in triumph to Bardoli. At a mass meeting held on 12 August, he recalled the abandonment of the non-cooperation movement after the Chauri Chaura incident. 'After the year 1922,' remarked Vallabhbhai, 'people were doubtful whether the teachings of Mahatma Gandhi were practicable and whether people would hear them or not? God gave us this opportunity and we have been able to prove that it was practicable and people have now got faith in the message of Mahatma Gandhi.'[19]

In November, Judge Broomfield and his colleagues commenced their inquiry. Mahadev Desai and his fellow ashramite Narhari Parikh shadowed them, making sure the villagers' testimonies were properly translated and recorded. It was found that the settlement officers had grossly overestimated crop and cattle yields in the taluka. On these inflated estimates they had arrived at an enhanced assessment for the taluka of Rs 1,87,492—the figure that had provoked outrage and then protest. The inquiry commission now radically revised this downwards—to an increase of a mere Rs 48,648. The satyagrahis had been handsomely vindicated. As Mahadev Desai wrote at the time, the peasants of Bardoli had 'dealt a severe moral blow to the Government', and 'added to the moral stature of the peasant throughout the length and breadth of India'.[20] Mahadev's verdict was endorsed by the viceroy of India, who told the governor of Bombay that the peasant agitation in Bardoli was 'without doubt the most serious thing we have had to face since I came to India'.[21]

V

In answer to the all-white Simon Commission, a conference held in Bombay on 19 May 1928 tasked a group of Indians with drafting a preliminary constitution for a free India. Chaired by Motilal Nehru, the committee had ten members, among them two Muslims and one Sikh, as well as representatives of the Hindu Mahasabha and of the Indian Liberal Federation. The committee had twenty-five sittings, while also canvassing proposals and suggestions from the wider public.

On 10 August, Motilal Nehru submitted the committee's report to the Congress president, M.A. Ansari. This envisaged, once the British departed, a House of Parliament, with 500 members elected on the basis of universal adult franchise; and a Senate, whose 200 members would be sent by the legislatures of individual provinces (themselves based on adult franchise). In this federal system, the Union would have control of, among other things, defence, foreign affairs, monetary policy, and civil and criminal law; with subjects such as land, water, public health and education dealt with by the provinces.

The report also considered relations between what was currently British India and the 500-odd princely states which covered a little over one-third of the subcontinent. It said an Indian government would respect existing treaty rights between the Crown and individual rulers; but hoped that the princes would eventually join the federation, in view of the 'historical, religious, sociological and economic affinities', as well as the shared 'aspirations and ambitions', of the residents of princely and non-princely India.[22]

The most important—and contentious—sections of the Nehru Report dealt with the Hindu–Muslim question. For India as a whole, Hindus were then 65.9 per cent of the population; Muslims, 24.1 per cent. Yet, there were significant regional variations, with Muslims in a majority in Bengal, the Punjab and the NWFP. The Nehru Report recognized that the 'whole [Hindu–Muslim] problem resolves itself into the removal from the minds of each of a baseless fear of the other and of giving a feeling of security to all communities'. However, the 'clumsy and objectionable' system of separate electorates introduced by the British did 'not give this security. They only keep up an armed truce.'[23] The committee also considered, and rejected, a proposal that the Muslims of Bengal and the Punjab should have guaranteed reservation of seats in the legislature in order to protect their 'majority'.

Universal adult franchise would secure Muslims political security in the Punjab and Bengal. In other provinces, where their numbers might not translate into many seats, the Nehru Report advised minority reservation in proportion to population, but for a fixed period of ten years only. However, it rejected the suggestion of one of its members that the Central Legislature should have one-third of its seats reserved for Muslims.[24]

On receiving a copy of the report, Gandhi sent Motilal Nehru a note of congratulation. 'I was not prepared,' he remarked, 'for the endorsement of the franchise, for instance, or of your solution of the Native States. But I see that the Hindu–Muslim question is still to be a thorny question.'[25]

Gandhi admired Motilal Nehru, and appreciated his labours. But the work of constitution-making per se did not appeal to him. While urging the acceptance of the Nehru Report in public, in private he wrote to an English friend that while 'the way to constitutional swaraj may lie through Lucknow [where the Nehru Committee had met]', the 'way to organic swaraj which is synonymous with *Ramrajya* lies through Bardoli'.[26]

VI

The Nehru Report was envisaged as an Indian response to the Simon Commission. The latter explicitly ruled out self-government; the former took self-government as the basis for its deliberations. As Motilal Nehru and his colleagues met in Allahabad and Lucknow in the summer of 1928, Sir John Simon and his fellow Englishmen fled the heat of the Indian plains for the comparative cool of London.

While Simon was in London, C.P. Scott of the *Manchester Guardian* arranged for Charlie Andrews to meet him. Writing to Gandhi, Andrews said he made it 'quite clear' to Simon 'that India did not want any Commission to frame India's constitution. That must be left to India herself.'[27]

The Simon Commission returned to India in early October. Once more, they were met with a hostile reception on landing in Bombay. Hundreds of protesters, led by K.F. Nariman and Shaukat Ali, marched to Ballard Pier raising slogans such as 'Simon Go Back', and 'Down with British Imperialism'. These physical demonstrations of protest were accompanied by posters put up across the city. One poster urged the students of Bombay to follow the example of students in Egypt:

WHAT EGYPT DID

INDIA CAN DO

In Egypt the hated Milner Commission was avoided everywhere

Like the plague.

When some of the members entered the Law Court,

the Judge walked out to show his contempt.

If they went to a restaurant,

the waiter refused to serve them.

If they wanted a taxi,

the chauffeur refused to carry them.

Everywhere the mark of the people's

DISPLEASURE

pursued them

Baffled, humiliated, their machinations frustrated,

they beat an inglorious retreat to their

own country.

Youths of Bombay!

Who brought About

THIS WONDERFUL AWAKENING?

None but the

BRAVE EGYPTIAN YOUTHS

Therefore
Youths of Bombay
BE UP AND DOING
To Break the Simonites

Another poster listed 'Bombay's Blacklegs', the politicians who were cooperating with, rather than boycotting the Simon Commission. Among the 'Blacklegs' mentioned by name was 'B.R. Ambedkar, Professor of Political Mendicancy'.[28]

Ambedkar had once been professor of political economy at Sydenham College. By now, he had increasingly turned from scholarship to advocacy. He saw no future for himself in the Congress, where—like everyone else in that organization—he would have to subordinate himself to Gandhi. So he decided to work outside and even in opposition to it. During the Simon Commission's second stint, Ambedkar testified before its members in Poona. He told them that the 'untouchable' castes to whom he belonged were a 'distinct minority separate from the Hindu community'. He urged that they get reservation on the same basis as the Muslims. 'We claim reserved seats if accompanied by adult suffrage,' stated Ambedkar, 'but in the absence of adult suffrage we want separate electorates.'[29]

From Poona, the Simon Commission proceeded northwards, to the Punjab. In the provincial capital, Lahore, they were faced with one of the largest demonstrations yet. Hindus, Muslims and Sikhs marched together through the old city, shouting slogans against the visiting Englishmen. There were clashes with the police, in which the veteran Congressman Lala Lajpat Rai was injured on the chest and shoulder. Gandhi, while deploring the assault, said it added to Lajpat Rai's already considerable prestige as 'one of the most beloved and esteemed leaders in all [of] India'.[30]

Three weeks after this incident, Lajpat Rai died. He was sixty-three, and ailing. But it was widely believed that the injuries inflicted by the police had hastened his passing. Gandhi wrote in *Young India* that the best tribute to his memory would be to 'work for swaraj and all it implies with redoubled zeal'.[31] The viceroy, for his part, worried that Lajpat Rai's death had 'done great harm in stirring up feeling'. When the Congress was held in late December, Irwin wrote to a colleague: 'There will be a good deal of inflammable material about in Calcutta at that time—what with Congress, Independence Leagues, Youth Leagues and another four or five whose names I cannot remember.'[32]

VII

In 1928, as in previous years, it fell to Gandhi to play a critical role in choosing the Congress president. Back in July, Motilal Nehru had written suggesting that Vallabhbhai Patel or alternatively Jawaharlal Nehru be appointed. Gandhi had a long chat with Vallabhbhai, who said that because of his immersion in the Bardoli struggle he could not serve as Congress president that year. Gandhi, however, agreed with Motilal that it was time their generation gave way to younger men. So, he assured the thrusting father, he was going to recommend Jawaharlal's name for adoption by the provincial committees.[33]

Two days after Gandhi wrote to Motilal, he received a telegram from Subhas Chandra Bose, which read: 'Bengal unanimous in favour of Motilalji's Presidentship. Kindly recommend him otherwise pray remain neutral.' Gandhi replied that Motilal himself seemed 'disinclined to accept the honour'; even so, he assured Bose that 'I shall say nothing about the election in the pages of *Young India* or elsewhere unless Bengal friends would let me'.[34]

The Congress was being held that year in Calcutta. The Bengal Congress was naturally keen that the president be someone it approved of. Motilal Nehru was a close associate of the great, and lately deceased, Bengal Congressman C.R. Das. These two barristers had once kept the Swaraj Party going. More recently, Motilal had overseen the drafting of a putative constitution for free India.

Gandhi decided to honour Bengal's wishes. In an essay in *Young India*, he remarked that while Vallabhbhai Patel's name was 'naturally on everybody's lips', nominating him was 'out of the question just now' because of his commitments in Bardoli. So the choice was between the two Nehrus, father and son. Who should it be, asked Gandhi: 'Pandit Motilalji the weather-beaten warrior or Pandit Jawaharlal Nehru, the disciplined young soldier who by his sterling worth has captured the imagination of the youth of the country?'

Gandhi told the readers of *Young India* that 'Bengal wants Motilalji to guide the Congress barque through the perilous seas that threaten to overwhelm us during the coming year'. So the senior Nehru it would be, said Gandhi, advising 'the impatient youth of the country [to] wait a while. They will be all the stronger for the waiting.'[35]

Reading the article in *Young India*, Subhas Bose wired Gandhi saying 'we are grateful to you for your kind help in connection with the decision regarding the Congress Presidentship'.[36]

VIII

Far more serious than factions within the Congress were the still unresolved tensions between Hindus and Muslims. As Gandhi had feared, sections of the Muslim leadership were not happy with the Nehru Report and its desire to do away with communal electorates. When he called for a renewed emphasis on religious toleration, Gandhi received a charming letter from an Indian in England which must be reproduced in full:

> Dear Mr. Gandhi,
> I am very glad to learn from the press here that you have at last decided to take the platform again to bring about the union between Hindus and Mohammadans. Since I am also deeply interested in the problem I feel I must return to India and help you in the work. On my return I shall settle down in my old town of Delhi.
>
> I regret however that I am unable to collect money enough to pay my passage back. I am writing this to ask you if you could assist me in the matter.
>
> Kindly let me hear from you since if you cannot help, I shall seriously consider walking back. It will take some time but I feel I must do my duty by my country even at some inconvenience.
>
> Yours fraternally
> Saiyid Haider Raza[37]

Saiyid Haider Raza was an Indian patriot with an interesting past. Back in 1907–08, when Gandhi was still in South Africa, Raza had been a political militant in Delhi, urging Hindus and Muslims to unite and oppose colonial tax policies. As the police closed in on him he escaped to England.[38] The records of the Middle Temple list Raza as having been admitted to their rolls in 1910.[39] His letter to Gandhi, written eighteen years later, was posted from a seaside village in Sussex, so we may presume him to have now been a briefless barrister, nostalgic for his homeland and keen to contribute to its liberation. Gandhi did not, it seems, reply to Raza, perhaps because he was already engaged in conversations with a Muslim based in India and extremely active in its politics.

This was Shaukat Ali. Since the Kohat riots of 1924, Gandhi and his erstwhile 'blood brother' had been drifting apart. The Nehru Report now made the split wide open. Writing to Gandhi, Shaukat Ali claimed that Motilal Nehru was following the Hindu Mahasabha's lead in asking Muslims to give up reservation of seats, thus making 'the position of Moslem Congressmen . . . most unpleasant'. He then attacked Motilal personally, writing: 'In my opinion he ruined our non-co-operation movement, he has ruined the Swaraj Party and now he will bring disruption in the ranks of the Congress.' Shaukat Ali complained that 'we Moslems have given a fight all along the line to the reactionary element in our camp. I think we had a right to expect our Hindu co-workers to tackle their mischief-making militant groups.'[40]

Note the use of the pronoun 'our', denoting the joint ownership by the Ali Brothers and Gandhi of the now long dead non-cooperation movement. Gandhi disregarded the appeal to nostalgia, writing back that in his view Motilal Nehru was 'incapable of wilfully coming to a perverse decision. . . . He may be mistaken but he is sincere and frank.'[41]

In November, reports reached Gandhi of an inflammatory speech made by Shaukat Ali at Kanpur, where he fulminated against Hindus and challenged them to a fight to the finish. Gandhi wrote a letter of complaint, but his estranged comrade was unrepentant. His speech at Kanpur had two purposes, said Shaukat Ali: 'One to warn the Hindus and stop them from creating an atmosphere for civil war or family quarrel or any thing of that kind whatsoever we may call it. The second object was to drag out even the reactionary Mussalmans from playing into the hands of the English, and bring them more in line with ourselves. Frankly I wanted and do want Mussalmans not to depend for their future either on the English or on the Hindus. I want them to stand on their own legs and think and act for themselves, doing what was best in the interest of Islam and our Motherland.'[42]

In this twin declaration of loyalty, Islam preceded the motherland. Shaukat Ali had a deep love of country, but a prior and perhaps deeper love of faith. It is also notable that his letters to Gandhi were written on the letterhead of 'The Central Khilafat Committee (India), Khilafat House, Bombay'. Although it was now several years since the Caliphate had been abolished by Kemal Atatürk, in the minds of this Indian Muslim that idea/fantasy was still very alive.

Replying more in sorrow than anger, Gandhi told Shaukat Ali that this was 'not the Maulana with whom I have been so long familiar and with whom I have passed so many happy days as with a blood-brother and bosom friend'. Gandhi told the older of the Ali Brothers that he would go 'all the way with you in accusing the Hindu of his many misdeeds; but I am unable to hold with you that he has ever been the aggressor, ever the tyrant and his Mussalman brother always the injured victim'. In his Kanpur speech, Shaukat Ali had 'been terribly dogmatic and emphatic. The assumption of infallibility is unworthy of you.' Gandhi now played the nostalgia card in turn, urging him to 'recall those stirring days of our joint peregrinations from shop to shop where Hindus vied with one another to pay even to the Khilafat Fund as to the Tilak Swaraj Fund'.[43]

Shaukat Ali and Gandhi had once worked shoulder to shoulder in the non-cooperation and Khilafat movements. These quarrels between them presaged deeper and more pervasive problems between India's two major religious communities.

IX

Shortly before the Calcutta Congress, news reached Gandhi of the murder in Lahore of a British policeman named Saunders, apparently in revenge for the police assault on Lajpat Rai which had led to his death. Gandhi, while accepting that the provocation was 'great', hoped to 'convince the hot[-headed] youth of the utter futility of such revenge'. For, as he wrote in *Young India*, the 'freedom of a nation cannot be won by solitary acts of heroism'; rather, it 'requires the patient, intelligent, and constructive effort of tens of thousands of men and women, young and old'.[44]

At the Calcutta Congress, a resolution was passed urging the British government to accept the recommendations of the Nehru Report. A deadline of one year was specified; if, by 31 December 1929, the provisions of the Nehru Report were not enacted into law, the Congress would begin a countrywide campaign of non-violent non-cooperation. Addressing the delegates, Gandhi praised the Nehru Report 'as a great contribution towards the solution of India's political and communal problems'. Younger Congressmen such as Subhas Bose wanted to repudiate Dominion Status, which would place India on par with Canada and Australia, and push for complete independence, which would sunder the British connection completely. Gandhi, however, felt that it would be 'a grievous blunder to pit Independence against Dominion Status or compare the two and suggest that Dominion Status carries humiliation with it and that Independence is something that is triumphant'.[45]

As Gandhi once more engaged actively with politics, he came to encounter fresh problems: the disenchantment of many leading Muslims with the Congress, and of a few Depressed Classes leaders too. But he remained what he had been since 1919, the pre-eminent public figure in India. A Tamil chapbook issued in 1928, while speaking of the ubiquity of Gandhi's name and its veneration, noted that 'all kinds of stuff are being named for him. . . . Gandhi hotel, Gandhi umbrella, Gandhi soda, Gandhi beedi, Gandhi cigarette, Gandhi balm, Gandhi vest, Gandhi saree, Gandhi matches . . . Is Mahatma Gandhi manufacturing these? Does he smoke beedis and cigarettes? . . . Alas, some are even selling toddy wearing a Gandhi cap!'[46]

CHAPTER FIFTEEN

Father, Son, Holy Spirit

I

In April 1929, Gandhi commenced a tour of the Andhra country, the Telugu-speaking districts of the Madras Presidency, which had been active in the non-cooperation movement and in the promotion of khadi. He was in the town of Vijayawada when news reached him of a bomb thrown in the Central Assembly in Delhi on 8 April. As the assembly's president, Vithalbhai Patel (brother of Vallabhbhai), rose to speak, there was (an eyewitness wrote) 'suddenly a very loud "bang", the whole assembly filled with dust and falling plaster from the dome and I saw the bomb exploding on the Government benches below our ladies gallery'. Then a second bomb was thrown, followed by two revolver shots.[1]

After the bombs exploded, two young men rose from the visitors' gallery claiming responsibility. 'Inquilab Zindabad' (Long Live Revolution), they shouted, as they rained pamphlets of their 'Hindustan Socialist Republican Army' down on the members below. The police quickly moved towards the protesters, who offered no resistance, allowing themselves to be arrested and taken away from the building.[2]

No one was killed or seriously injured in the incident. But, from Gandhi's point of view, the use or threat of violence was itself abhorrent. Speaking at a public meeting in Vijayawada, he said that 'Swaraj has receded a step by this crime. The two youths involved in the bomb outrage have set back the progress of our national movement. The Congress members must cleanse themselves from the taint of violence.'

The bombs were thrown on 8 April; two days earlier, a young Muslim man had knifed and killed Rajpal, the publisher of the inflammatory pamphlet 'Rangila Rasul'. Writing in *Young India*, Gandhi remarked that both actions rested on a 'mad philosophy of mad revenge and impotent rage. The bomb-throwers have discredited the cause of freedom in whose name they threw the bombs; the user of the knife has discredited Islam in whose name the perpetrator did the mad deed.' He added that 'Rajpal's assassination has given him a martyrdom and a name which he did not deserve'.

Gandhi thought that both 'the bomb and the knife derive their lease of life from the world's belief in violence as a remedy for securing supposed justice'. 'We can,' he insisted, 'to a great extent checkmate the bomb-thrower, if we would have faith in our own programme [of non-violence] and work for it.'[3]

For their part, the two bomb throwers were unrepentant. In their statement in court, Bhagat Singh and Batukeshwar Dutt said they had sought by their actions to 'draw the world's attention to the condition in India'. The bombs were 'necessary to wake England from her dreams', to 'make the deaf hear and to give the heedless a timely warning'. The assembly itself was 'a symbol of India's humiliation and helplessness'; for, the 'labouring millions had nothing to expect' from an institution 'that stood as a menacing monument to the strangling powers of the exploiters and the serfdom of helpless labourers'.

Singh and Dutt attacked Gandhi by implication, although not by name. Their actions, they hoped, would mark 'the end of the era of utopian non-violence of whose futility the rising generation has been convinced beyond the shadow of a doubt'. They offered as alternative role models 'Guru Govind Singh and Shivaji, Kemal Pasha and Riza Khan, Washington and Garibaldi, Lafayette and Lenin', all leaders who had used arms against their adversaries. Their statement ended with an affirmation of faith in radical socialism. 'Revolution is the inalienable right of mankind,' they proclaimed. 'Freedom is the imprescriptible birthright of all.'[4]

II

Gandhi spent five weeks in the Andhra country, speaking at countless meetings, garnering contributions small and large for his khadi work. In his day by day chronology of Gandhi's life, Chandubhai Dalal names more than two hundred villages, towns and cities visited by Gandhi between 8 April, when he arrived in Andhra, and 21 May, when he finally left, taking a train from the town of Adoni to Bombay.

At these meetings, Gandhi spoke on the cultivation of Hindu–Muslim unity, the abolition of untouchability, the boycott of foreign cloth and the promotion of khadi. He ended his speeches by asking for contributions for khadi work. In successive issues of *Young India*, he itemized the takings, hamlet by hamlet. By 12 April he had collected Rs 21,570; by the 24th this had risen to Rs 1,11,653; by 16 May, to Rs 2,43,282.

Gandhi also kept meticulous accounts of the money spent by and on him in this tour. He was driven from village to village in locally hired vehicles; these included a Ford, a Chevrolet and a Dodge. Cars and fuel accounted for some 90 per cent of his expenses; with postage and printing of handbills taking care of the rest. (He usually stayed at the home of local Congress workers.) By his estimate, his personal expenses came to a mere 5 per cent of the total funds collected on the tour.[5]

By late April, the temperature in the shade was in excess of 100 degrees Fahrenheit. The weather was hot; the countryside poorly connected. And Gandhi himself was now pushing sixty. Yet, he took to the task with zest and vigour. Normally, when Gandhi was on the road, he wrote regular letters back to his disciples in the ashram; some addressed collectively, some to particular individuals. On this Andhra tour, these letters became less frequent. One who felt their lack was his devoted and dependent English 'daughter', Mira. When she complained of being neglected, Gandhi wrote back that it was not so much lack of love as lack of technology that explained his silence.

'This letter,' he remarked, 'will be sent by a cyclist who will have to ford two streams and cover a distance of twelve miles to reach a branch line station. Whether it will catch the correct mail train I do not know. Well you cannot expect Western conveniences in typically Eastern tracts.' Then he added: 'I see nothing wrong in people living miles apart not corresponding with one another daily through letters or wires. It used to be enough that they corresponded through their hearts.'[6]

In his last speech in Andhra, Gandhi said that of all his many tours after returning to India in 1915, this had been 'the longest and the most intensive . . . in any single province'. It had also been the most successful in terms of public subscriptions, excepting that frenzied year, 1921, when he collected as much money in a single day in Bombay as he now had in six weeks in Andhra.[7]

III

By 1929, the two Nehrus had emerged as perhaps the closest political allies of the Mahatma. Gandhi respected Motilal's legal acumen, and was charmed by Jawaharlal's spontaneity and zest. He looked to the elder Nehru for advice on constitutional matters, and to his son to build bridges with the younger generation, and with the world. They, in turn, treated Gandhi as a preceptor who provided them guidance on moral and even familial matters. When Motilal's daughter Sarup fell in love with a Muslim journalist, it was Gandhi who urged her not to marry him, on the same grounds as he had once urged his son Manilal not to marry a Muslim girl. Then, when Sarup agreed to marry a Hindu scholar from Maharashtra, it was Gandhi's wife Kasturba who wove the sari that she wore on her wedding day.[8]

Motilal Nehru was now the Congress president, and Jawaharlal, the Congress secretary. Guided by Gandhi, both had crucial roles to play in a rapidly developing political situation. The Congress had given a deadline of twelve months to the government to accept the Nehru Report. The annual meeting of the Congress was to be held in December in the historic city of Lahore, on the banks of the river Ravi. Once more, among the names put forward for the presidency was that of Jawaharlal Nehru. The younger Nehru was ambivalent about succeeding his father as president. He had been the working secretary of the party for the past three years. He now wanted a break from office work, to renew his engagement with the masses. As he wrote to Gandhi, he 'wanted to educate myself and try to get at the back of the mind of the villager'.

Jawaharlal told Gandhi that if (as was expected) the government did not implement his father's report, and a new round of civil disobedience was planned, the Mahatma should serve as the formal head of the party. 'Of course you could lead, as you have done in the past, without being Congress President,' wrote Jawaharlal. 'But it would help matters certainly if you are also the official head of the organization. I feel that it would be a great gain if you would preside. That would strike the imagination of the country and of other countries.'[9]

Gandhi had been Congress president once, in 1924. He had no wish to take up the post again, in part because he knew that he could shape and direct the party in any case. Meanwhile, he was being pushed by the younger generation of Congressmen to take a more militant stance vis-à-vis the government. Appointing Jawaharlal as president would send a positive signal to the youth; it would also be just reward for his work in making the case for Indian freedom more widely known abroad.

In recent years, Jawaharlal Nehru had travelled extensively in the West. In February 1927, he attended a 'Congress of Oppressed Nationalities' in Brussels, where he interacted with anti-colonial activists from Asia, Africa and Latin America. In November of that year, he visited Soviet Russia, impressed by the absence of the extreme inequalities that he had witnessed in Western Europe. Where other Congress leaders 'never rose above their limited national horizon', Jawaharlal Nehru was now advocating that the party adopt 'the most intense internationalism'.[10]

In nominating the younger Nehru as the next president of the Congress, Gandhi was surely mindful of the increasing attractions of left-wing ideas among younger Indians. The glow of the Russian Revolution had not yet dimmed. There was now an active Communist Party in India that was gaining ground among the textile workers of

Bombay in particular. Even further to the Left was the Hindustan Socialist Republican Army (HSRA), recently responsible for the murder of the police officer Saunders in Lahore and the spectacular bomb attack on the Central Assembly in Delhi.

For some years now, Gandhi was being pressed by younger Congressmen to abandon Dominion Status in favour of Purna Swaraj, or complete independence. If older Congressmen did not keep pace with the young radicals in their own party, the danger was that they might move over to the communists or even the HSRA. Hence the decision to make Jawaharlal Nehru the Congress president, in the hope that (as Gandhi put it) 'responsibility will mellow and sober the youth, and prepare them for the burden they must discharge'.

Jawaharlal was still hesitant to accept the responsibility. Ultimately, helped no doubt by a word and a nudge from Motilal, Gandhi 'wrung consent' out of him.[11] The presidentship of the Congress would pass from father to son for the first time in its history.

IV

In 1929, as in previous years, Gandhi was exercised about the place of India's largest minority, the Muslims. A colleague from the Khilafat days wrote to him complaining that 'nobody [in the Congress] has yet cared to give them [the Muslims] a patient hearing, but everyone dubs them as rank communalists'.[12] The Muslim League was split into several sections; one section had collaborated with the Simon Commission, a second section had backed the Nehru Report, a third—led by Jinnah—had not yet revealed its hand.[13]

The most prominent Muslim on the side of Gandhi was Dr M.A. Ansari. In July 1929, a meeting of pro-Congress Muslims was convened in Allahabad by Dr Ansari. In his speech to the gathering, Ansari criticized those Muslims 'bent upon opposing the Congress' and who had 'taken up the profession of flattering Government'. (The Muslim League was not mentioned by name, but clearly it was the target of this criticism.) The meeting resolved to form an 'All-India Nationalist Muslim Party' to inspire in Muslims 'a greater confidence in Indian national ideals', thus to 'take their proper share in the national struggle'.[14]

Motilal Nehru was convinced that the support of Ansari and company was all that mattered. He wrote to Gandhi that 'the only way to reach a compromise with the truly nationalist Musalmans is to ignore Mr. Jinnah and the Ali Brothers completely. All three of them are totally discredited and have no following worth the name.'[15]

Gandhi received contrary advice from Sarojini Naidu. Mrs Naidu was a close friend of Jinnah's, whom she had once hailed as the 'ambassador of Hindu–Muslim unity'. She now arranged for Gandhi to meet him in the second week of August. 'I go to Bombay on the 11th to meet Jinnah,' wrote Gandhi to Jawaharlal Nehru, adding: 'I admire Sarojini Devi's optimism. But I am going to Bombay without much hope.'[16]

When Gandhi reached Bombay, he found that the Ali Brothers were also in town. He met all three leaders, but the talks were inconclusive. In a brief public statement, Gandhi did not divulge what was (or was not) spoken about, while asking those 'who believe in prayer [to] pray with me that there may soon be peace between Hindus, Mussalmans and all the other communities'.[17]

V

In the autumn of 1929, Gandhi undertook a long tour of the United Provinces. Before he left Ahmedabad, he issued detailed instructions for the local organizers of his tour. He asked them to 'beware of multiplying functions or expecting long speeches from me'. He had 'a horror of touching-the-feet-devotion. . . . It interferes with free and easy movement, and I have been hurt by the nails of the devotees cutting into the flesh.' They were not to construct costly platforms for his speeches, but to take his car to the centre of the meeting and use it as a platform instead. 'This proved a most effective and expeditious method in Andhra.'[18]

Gandhi's United Provinces tour started in Agra on 11 September. He spent nearly two and a half months in the province, interspersed with brief visits to Delhi and the hill station of Mussoorie. He spent several days apiece in the province's major cities—Agra, Lucknow, Kanpur, Allahabad, Banaras—while also calling at smaller towns such as Ghazipur, Azamgarh, Gorakhpur, Moradabad and Aligarh. He spoke at many colleges, urging students to wear khadi and join the Congress to participate in the struggle for freedom.

With Gandhi on this trip was J.B. Kripalani, his old comrade from Champaran. Kripalani had since set up a series of khadi centres in the United Provinces, and was extremely familiar with the terrain and its people. As Gandhi gratefully noted, Kripalani had erected a 'wall of protection' between the visitor and his legion of fans; he was 'sometimes really angry and more often feigned anger when leaders of places visited wanted more time and more appointments or when people insisted on seeing me or crowding into my car'.[19]

While he was in the United Provinces, Gandhi received a letter from Raihana Tyabji, the poet and singer who lived in the Sabarmati Ashram. The Tyabjis were an extremely progressive family, the first Muslim women in western India to emerge out of purdah, to travel overseas, to go to school and college, and to write at length of their experiences.[20] Raihana now asked Gandhi to write a 'strong article' on the question of women's rights.

So he did. 'I am uncompromising in the matter of women's rights,' he began. 'In my opinion she should labour under no legal disability not suffered by man. I should treat the daughters and sons on a footing of perfect equality. As women begin to realize their strength, as they must in proportion to the education they receive, they will naturally resent the glaring inequalities to which they are subjected.'

Gandhi argued, however, that to remove or amend laws that discriminated against women would be 'a mere palliative. The root of the evil lies much deeper than most people realize. It lies in man's greed of power and fame and deeper still in mutual lust. Man has always desired power. Ownership of property gives this power.' While men were greedy and lustful, argued Gandhi, 'woman is the embodiment of sacrifice and suffering, and her advent to public life should therefore result in purifying it, in restraining unbridled ambition and accumulation of property'.

Gandhi ended by asking 'the enlightened daughters of Bharat Mata' to 'not ape the manner of the West which may be suited to its environment. They must apply methods suited to the Indian genius and Indian environment. Theirs must be the strong, controlling, purifying, steadying hand, conserving what is best in our culture and unhesitatingly rejecting what is base and degrading.'[21]

In the United Provinces, women were even more rigorously suppressed than in other parts of India. Purdah was de rigueur among Hindus as well as Muslims. After spending several weeks in the plains, Gandhi visited the hill station of Mussoorie, where women had gone over, it seemed to him, to the other extreme. In a letter to the women of the ashram, he described Mussoorie as 'one of those places where pleasure-seeking abounds. There is no *purdah* here. Wealthy ladies spend their time in dancing at parties, paint their lips, deck themselves in all sorts of ways and blindly imitate the West in a good many ways.'

The working women in the plains were severely exploited; the upper-class women in these hill resorts, excessively emancipated. 'Ours is a middle path,' Gandhi told the ashramites. 'We do not wish to keep alive superstition and *purdah* nor to encourage shamelessness and self-indulgence. The middle path is straight but difficult to follow. It is our aim to seek it and follow it steadily.'[22]

VI

While Gandhi was travelling in the United Provinces, the viceroy, Lord Irwin, was in London, consulting with His Majesty's Government. After his return, he issued a statement on 31 October, saying that a round table conference would be convened in London sometime in 1930 to discuss the 'Indian constitutional progress'. The government would invite 'representatives of different parties and interests in British India', as well as representatives of the princely states, to this conference. Lord Irwin hoped that the meeting would result in the submission of 'proposals to Parliament which may command a wide measure of general assent'.[23]

In early November, Sarojini Naidu met Jinnah who offered to arrange a meeting of Congress leaders with the viceroy, to prepare the way for their participation in the conference. Sarojini was herself very keen that this came about. 'I know that you have always the patience,' she wrote to Gandhi, 'to attempt till the last moment all proper and reasonable methods of preliminary discussion, argument, consultation & persuasion before you finally . . . close the door.'[24]

Also anxious that Gandhi attend the London conference was his old friend Henry Polak, who was now based in England. The Congress still hadn't got the guarantees from the British government with regard to Dominion Status (which the Nehru Report had asked for). However, Polak reminded Gandhi that, back in 1914, when fighting for the rights of Indians in South Africa, he had met General Smuts without any written assurances. Polak thus implored his friend 'not to take up a position of intransigence which may result in the losing of a great opportunity for mutual understanding'.[25]

There was now a Labour government in power in the United Kingdom. Polak thought this boded well for India and Indian aspirations. 'Whatever the Conservatives may, or may not, have meant,' he told Gandhi, 'there is no doubt that there is a complete and fundamental change in the attitude towards the Indian problem on the part of the Labour Party. They most earnestly want a settlement in India and a very friendly one.'[26]

Gandhi was prepared to keep the conversations going. On 30 November, Vithalbhai Patel (president of the Central Legislative Assembly, and very much a Moderate) and Jinnah met with Gandhi at the Sabarmati Ashram. 'The subject of their talk is not known,' ran a news report, 'but it is believed that it was about the Round Table Conference.'[27]

On 21 December, Gandhi took a train to Delhi, to attend the meeting with the viceroy fixed up as promised by Jinnah. Irwin was on tour, and was scheduled to return to Delhi on 23rd morning. At Nizamuddin, a few miles before the Delhi station, there was an attack on the viceroy's special train. Two bombs had been planted on the tracks, connected by a long wire to a battery placed several hundred yards away. With the press of a button, the bombs had been activated. Two bogies were detached from the train as a result of the explosion. The viceroy fortunately escaped unhurt. It was exactly seventeen years to the day since the attack on Lord Hardinge.[28]

Ironically, it was on the same day that the Irwins became the first occupants of the grand new Viceregal Palace, sited on Raisina Hill in central New Delhi. So, hours after the failed attempt on his life, Irwin convened the first formal meeting in his new home. On the afternoon of the 23rd, the viceroy conferred with Gandhi, Jinnah, Motilal Nehru and the Moderate politicians Tej Bahadur Sapru and Vithalbhai Patel. Gandhi began by expressing his 'horror' at the attempt on the viceroy's train that morning. The talk then turned to the proposed Round Table Conference. Sapru saw 'great value' in the conference, which, even if it did not guarantee Dominion Status for India, would help in framing a policy towards that end. The viceroy added that the conference 'would have the fullest opportunity to discuss any proposals put before it'. Canada, he pointed out, did not achieve Dominion Status 'in a [single] jump', but through several stages.

Gandhi, however, was firm that unless the granting of Dominion Status was the 'immediate objective' of the conference, he would not himself take part in it. However, he had no objection if others did. Motilal Nehru agreed with Gandhi; he thought 'the British people exaggerated the difficulties in the way of Dominion Status for India'.

The conversation now got somewhat testy. The viceroy asked whether Gandhi and his colleagues believed 'in British purpose'. Gandhi replied that he 'doubted the sincerity of British purpose broadly, though he recognised that of individuals'. He added that while India was 'weak and disunited', he did not see the point of travelling to London unless on the promise of Dominion Status. He blamed British rule for this lack of unity. The viceroy sarcastically asked Gandhi, as 'a matter of historical interest', whether India had ever been united as it now was under British rule. To this, Sapru added the thought that 'if India had really been united then the British would not be here at all'. Gandhi answered that in the time the British had been here, they had done little to bring about unity. Jinnah now asked Gandhi if he thought it 'logical' for Indians to ask for Dominion Status when they were 'thus divided'.

The meeting ended with the viceroy saying he had 'run no small political risk' in calling this meeting. He contrasted the 'stiffness of attitude' shown by Gandhi and Motilal with the 'generous' approach of His Majesty's Government.[29]

VIII

On the night of 23 December, Gandhi left Delhi for Lahore, where an impressive new township had been erected for the Congress. Travelling with Gandhi were his wife Kasturba, his son Devadas, and his English disciple Mira. To avoid a large crowd, they got off at Lahore Cantonment instead of the city's main station. Even so, Gandhi was recognized, with a group of people, including the station coolies, rushing to touch his feet. Seeing Gandhi emerge on to the platform, the crowd shouted, among other things, 'Mahatma Gandhi ki jai', 'Vande Mataram', and 'Bhagat Singh Zindabad', thus coupling the non-violent Mahatma, their national icon, with the young proponent of armed struggle who was a native of Lahore.[30]

Gandhi arrived in Lahore on Christmas Eve. The same day, there was a conference of ulemas in Kanpur, where the main speech was by his now estranged comrade, Maulana Mohammad Ali, 'who referred to the past glories of the Islamic world and deplored the present decline'. Later in his talk, the Maulana said that 'though he was an ex-colleague of Mahatma Gandhi he could not accept Hindu Raj as contemplated by the Nehru Report'.[31]

Jawaharlal Nehru arrived in Lahore on Christmas Day. As a journalist on the spot reported, 'the crowd on the platform became mad, and surged and swayed making it impossible for Panditji to alight'. It took the younger Nehru more than half an hour to emerge from his compartment and get out of the station. There,

> countless human heads were visible. And this sea of human heads was fed by streams of visitors from the mufassil. It is stated that in Amritsar [35 miles away] people closed their shops and pulled down the shutters just to take part in the Presidential Procession. People were perched on the tops of the trees and the roofs of the railway buildings.

Nehru was taken on horseback through the city, flanked by 100 Punjabi youths, shouting slogans in his praise.[32]

The Congress was formally inaugurated on the 29th, in a pandal decorated with banners proclaiming 'Country First, Religion Next',

'Only wear Khaddar and no Other', 'World Peace Depends on India's Freedom' and 'Remove Curse of Untouchability'. An estimated 50,000 people attended the opening ceremony. There was 'a whole host' of photographers 'seen cudgeling their brains to find out the best position. Lenses were adjusted, cameras clicked, and Pandit Jawaharlal's movements at the flag staff were faithfully recorded on plates after plates.'

In his presidential address, Jawaharlal Nehru announced that the 'day of European domination is already approaching its end'. The 'future is with America and Asia', he added. In its struggle for freedom, India placed itself on the side of China, Turkey, Persia and Egypt. Nehru highlighted three major problems that the Congress had to tackle—the place of minorities, the position of the princely states, and the rights of peasants and labourers. His socialist inclinations were manifest in his declaring the problems of peasants and workers 'the biggest of all', and in his ending with the slogan, 'Inquilab Zindabad'.[33]

On 31 December, Gandhi moved a resolution proposing 'Purna Swaraj', or complete independence, as the goal of the Congress. He had also drafted the resolution, which began: 'The Congress deplores the bomb outrage perpetrated on the Viceregal train, and reiterates its own conviction that such action is not only contrary to the creed of the Congress but results in harm being done to the national cause.'[34]

Since a year had passed since the Nehru Report was submitted, the Congress now declared its commitment to complete independence. Congress members were asked to boycott councils and legislatures, and engage in constructive work. Meanwhile, the AICC was authorized 'wherever it deems fit, to launch upon a programme of Civil Disobedience, including non-payment of taxes, whether in selected areas or otherwise and under such safeguards as it may consider necessary'.

The mention of the AICC was a mere formality. For the AICC would, in turn, 'authorize' Gandhi to choose where, when, and in what manner to launch a fresh campaign of civil disobedience. For the moment, the Mahatma held his cards close to his chest. He told no one in Lahore, not even the Nehrus, of what was brewing in his mind. They, and India itself, would have to wait until the New Year.[35]

In December 1929, Saraladevi Chaudhurani still lived in Lahore, although her husband had died some years previously. It is likely that Saraladevi attended the Congress, although the sources don't tell us whether she and Gandhi met and spoke. If a week is a long time in politics, a decade was clearly an eternity when it came to personal relationships. The 1920s began with the couple intensely involved with one another; it ended with them barely in touch, with Gandhi having resolutely channelled his passion and his energy into winning freedom for India.

CHAPTER SIXTEEN

The March to the Sea

I

Lahore, where the 1929 Congress was held, was where Lajpat Rai died as a result of police violence, where the British policeman Saunders was murdered in revenge, where Bhagat Singh, who carried out the bomb attack on the Central Assembly, was born and raised. Addressing a public meeting in Lahore just before the Congress began, Gandhi declared: 'Freedom can never be attained by exploding bombs on innocent men.'[1]

On the train back from Lahore, Gandhi drafted a major essay restating the case for non-violence. This was published in *Young India*'s first issue for 1930. The essay began: 'There is so much violence in the atmosphere immediately surrounding us, politically minded part of India, that a bomb thrown here and a bomb thrown there causes little perturbation and probably there is even joy over such an event in the hearts of some.' But, said Gandhi, in his travels around India he observed that the 'vast masses who have become conscious of the fact that they must have freedom are untouched by the spirit of violence'. He now proposed 'to reason with those who may not be so much saturated with violence as to be beyond the pale of reason'.

Gandhi put forward two practical arguments against the use of violence by freedom fighters. First, violence led to increased repression by the rulers. Thus, 'every time violence has occurred we have lost heavily, that is to say, military expenditure has risen'. Second, a culture or cult of violence ultimately turns on the society that breeds it. For, 'from violence done to the foreign ruler, violence to our own people whom we may consider to be obstructing the country's progress is an easy natural step'.

Seeking to drive out Englishmen through violence, would, in Gandhi's view, 'lead not to independence but to utter confusion. We can establish independence only by adjusting our differences through an appeal to the head and the heart, by evolving organic unity amongst ourselves, not by terrorizing or killing those who, we fancy, may impede our march, but by patient and gentle handling, by converting the opponent . . .'[2]

Gandhi's essay was read by the young radicals of the Punjab. They drafted a combative reply, printed it as a pamphlet, and posted a copy to the Sabarmati Ashram. The pamphlet began with a stirring evocation of the revolutionary credo. Armed struggle, said these members of the HSRA, 'instills fear in the hearts of the oppressors, it brings hopes of revenge and redemption to the oppressed masses, it gives courage and self confidence to the wavering, it shatters the spell of the superiority of the ruling class and raises the status of the subject race in the eyes of the world . . .'

The revolutionaries claimed that, unlike Gandhi, they knew how the masses lived and thought. And 'the average human being' understood 'little of the fine theological niceties of "Ahimsa" and "loving one's enemy"'. The pamphlet continued:

> The way of the world is like this. You have a friend; you love him, sometimes so much that you even die for him. You have an enemy, you shun him, you fight against him, and, if possible, kill him. It is what it has been since the days of Adam and Eve and no man has any difficulty about understanding it.[3]

II

The HSRA pamphlet was one of several critiques of Gandhi by political opponents in the first weeks of 1930. A student of Sanskrit, writing from the temple town of Rishikesh, asked Gandhi to reflect why the 'pandit samaj', the community of Hindu priests and scholars, were so angry with him. Was it not because he supported the Sarda Bill raising the age of consent and of marriage? The young scholar, writing in chaste Sanskritized Hindi, told Gandhi that by violating the ancient code of dharma, the Sarda Bill had cut at the root of national unity. He argued that whether India was to prosper or to decay depended on its adherence to the Hindu faith. If faith went, then nothing could save the land.[4]

Gandhi was attacked by left-wing revolutionaries and right-wing reactionaries, and by centrist liberals too. Back in 1915, a Bengali Moderate named Satyananda Bose had criticized Gandhi's emphasis on celibacy. Fifteen years later, Bose now urged him not to launch a fresh struggle against the British. 'Civil disobedience is possible,' wrote Bose, 'only in respect of a particular measure which has outraged popular sentiment. Civil disobedience for obtaining independence is psychologically impossible. It will not arouse public feeling.'[5]

Also critical of Gandhi's plans was his erstwhile 'blood-brother' Shaukat Ali. The elder Ali noted that 'we have certainly drifted apart', for which he blamed Gandhi's failure 'to check the militant reactionaries' in the Hindu fold. With regard to the Lahore Congress and its declaration of Purna Swaraj, Gandhi's former comrade-in-arms commented: 'Any declaration of war against the Government over the heads of the Moslem[s] and without consulting them would probably result in a civil war and bitter quarrels amongst ourselves, leading to the failure of all plans either made by you or us.'[6]

The Ali Brothers had stopped attending Congress meetings. They had publicly attacked the Nehru Report. However, Shaukat Ali's advice was independently endorsed by that patriotic Muslim and loyal Congressman M.A. Ansari. In a long, intensely felt letter, Dr Ansari told Gandhi that 'you are taking on a great responsibility on yourself by declaring war against the Government', since 'the situation today is quite the reverse of what it was in 1920, when you started the campaign of non-co-operation'.

The situation was different with regard to Hindu–Muslim relations in particular. In 1920, they were united; now they were estranged. As proof of this, Ansari provided a rather telling table, reproduced below:

1920	1930
1. Great dissatisfaction against the Government, owing to war-time promises not having been kept. Dissatisfaction against Rowlatt Act, Martial Law, and Khilafat Wrongs	1. Large number of people believe in the goodwill of Labour Government and sincerity of the Viceroy, rightly or wrongly
2. Highest water-mark reached in Hindu–Muslim unity	2. Lowest water-mark reached in Hindu–Muslim unity
3. Sikhs entirely with the Congress	3. Sikhs almost entirely against the Congress
4. Complete unity inside the Congress. Great enthusiasm amongst the workers and rank and file	4. Disunity in the Congress, diversity of purpose, complete lack of enthusiasm amongst the workers. Lukewarmness among the rank and file
5. Complete non-violent atmosphere and yet breaking [out] of violence in Chauri Chaura	5. Obvious existence of violence, even large number of Congressmen believing in it and the certainty of violence breaking out[7]

Rather than take on the Raj, Ansari thought the Congress should first work harder to 'wean the Muslims away from the influence of communalism and reactionary leaders and think and act in terms of "nationalism"'.[8]

Gandhi did not reply to the bomb thrower, the Hindu reactionary, the polite, pussyfooted Moderate, or the Islamic radical. He had answered them and their ilk many times in the past. They were irreconcilable. But he could not let his friend and fellow Congressman Dr Ansari go unanswered. He agreed 'that the Hindu–Muslim problem is the problem of problems'. But, he pointed out, 'meanwhile the third party—the evil British power—has got to be sterilized. . . . Hence must civil disobedience be forged from day to day by those who believe that there is no escape from non-violence and that violence will *never* bring freedom to India.'

Gandhi told his sceptical colleague that 'my personal line is cast. I fancy that I see my way clear now. . . . If all this be hallucination I must perish in the flames of my own lighting.'[9]

M.A. Ansari had sent a copy of his letter to Gandhi to Motilal Nehru, perhaps hoping that, as a constitutionalist, he would second his reservations about beginning a mass movement without the Muslims. However, the older Nehru, pressed by his son Jawaharlal, was completely on Gandhi's side. He thought that the time for petitions and representations had come and gone. Motilal was now almost seventy years old; he was in ill health too. But the passion of his son and of their common mentor had cast aside all his reservations. As he now told Ansari: 'Nothing but a deep conviction that the time for the greatest effort and the greatest sacrifice has come would have induced me to expose myself at my age and with my physical disabilities and with my family obligations to the tremendous risks I am incurring [in courting arrest]. I hear the clarion call of the country and I obey.'[10]

III

Gandhi was keenly aware of the enchantment among the young with revolutionary violence. In the Punjab, he had witnessed at first-hand the cult-like status of Bhagat Singh and his comrades. Meanwhile, within the Congress itself, radicals such as Jawaharlal Nehru and Subhas Bose wanted to get rid of the British connection entirely. They demanded Purna Swaraj, complete independence, not mere Dominion Status, which to them meant a continuing tutelage to the Raj.

Challenged by the revolutionary critics of the Congress, pressed by the younger members of his own party, Gandhi knew that he had to leave the ashram and enter, or re-enter, active politics once more. He had thus made up his mind to launch a fresh round of civil disobedience. But what form would it take? Writing to Jawaharlal Nehru on 10 January, he said that 'ever since we have separated at Lahore, I have been evolving schemes of civil disobedience. I have not seen my way clear as yet.'[11]

In Lahore, the Congress had decided to mark the last Sunday of January as 'Independence Day'. All over India, meetings were to be held where the national tricolour would be raised, patriotic songs sung, and vows to work for freedom made. Through the columns of his newspaper, Gandhi urged everyone to maintain 'complete discipline, restraint, reserve, dignity and real strength'. Volunteers could 'pass the day in doing some constructive work, whether it is spinning, or service of "untouchables", or reunion of Hindus and Mussalmans, or prohibition work, or even all these together . . .'[12]

In the event, the first 'Independence Day' was a spectacular success. As a government intelligence report admitted, in cities and towns across India the celebrations 'were attended by considerable crowds and their effect was serious and impressive'.[13]

The province of the Punjab, where the last Congress had been held, was representative of the popular mood. Amritsar, a colleague wired Gandhi, 'observed independence day flag hoisting procession meeting and illumination most successfully surpassing previous occasions thousands fixed and hoisted flags whole district giving proof of readiness to fight under national movement'. In Lahore, wrote another Congressman, 'thousands of men, women and children, students, businessmen, clerks, of all castes, communities and creeds were vying with each other to get the best possible accommodation in the meeting'—in a 'unique demonstration' of how 'the hearts of the people are throbbing with the impulse of becoming independent of all foreign yoke'.[14]

Gandhi received similar reports from across the country. They greatly encouraged him. To be sure, an overwhelming majority of those who had celebrated 'Independence Day' on 26 January were Hindus. Muslims and even Christians had largely stayed away. However, the reports that Congressmen were sending Gandhi from across the country only stressed the numbers who attended these ceremonies, not their social composition. This convinced Gandhi that the country was ready for a new round of civil disobedience.

IV

In *Young India*'s last issue for January 1930, Gandhi began revealing his hand. He outlined eleven demands for the government to meet; these included prohibition, the reduction of land revenue, abolition of the salt tax, the reduction of military expenditure and of official salaries, and the imposition of a protective tariff on foreign cloth. If the viceroy satisfied 'these very simple but vital needs of India', wrote Gandhi, 'he will then hear no talk of civil disobedience, and the Congress will heartily participate in any conference where there is perfect freedom of expression and demand'.[15]

Four weeks later, in another article for *Young India*, Gandhi focused on one of these demands: the state's monopoly over the production and sale of salt. The price of this essential commodity in the open market was greatly enhanced by a tax that the state levied on it, of about three rupees per maund. Gandhi termed this a 'nefarious monopoly', since next only to air and water, salt was 'perhaps the greatest necessity of life'. It was vital for the poor, and for cattle too.

A retired salt officer had told Gandhi that the whole west coast from Cambay to Ratnagiri was a 'huge natural salt-work', from which 'salt can be easily prepared in every creek'. The officer (who chose to be anonymous) continued: 'If a band of volunteers begin the work all along the coast, it will be impossible for the whole strength of the police and customs staff to prevent them from collecting natural salt and salt earth, turning them into salt . . . and retaining it.'

After quoting this telling letter, Gandhi remarked: 'When therefore the time comes, civil resisters will have an ample opportunity of their ability to conduct their campaign regarding the tax in a most effective manner. The illegality is in a Government that steals the people's salt and makes them pay heavily for the stolen article. The people, when they become conscious of their power, will have every right to take possession of what belongs to them.'[16]

In 1919, when Gandhi was operated on in Bombay, Mahadev Desai had heard Gandhi say that 'it passes my understanding how such a cruel tax as this on salt was meekly accepted by the people.

The whole country could have been inflamed to revolt against the Government at the time the law was passed. How could there be a tax on salt so indispensable to human life?'

A hundred years before Gandhi, the liberal reformer Rammohan Roy had alerted the British Parliament to the vital importance of salt in the daily lives of the poor. In Bengal, the salt trade was controlled by the East India Company, which used its monopoly to malevolent effect, such that the commodity was four times as expensive as in England. The 'dearth of salt', wrote Roy, is 'felt by the whole community', with 'poorer peasants' in particular 'ready to surrender everything else in order to procure a small proportion of this article'. Thus, 'if salt were rendered cheaper and better, it must greatly promote the common comforts of the people'.[17]

That the state monopoly on salt was unpopular was known to the more sensitive members of the ruling race. In 1902, the Liberal politician Charles Dilke said the salt tax of the Government of India was 'probably one of the worst ever levied in the civilized world'.[18] Four years later, a young district officer in the Punjab called the monopoly 'thoroughly iniquitous'. When peasants were caught by the police extracting salt from the saline soils of their own property, they were brought before this officer, who later wrote to his mother: 'I had to convict, but I hated it.'[19] In between these two statements, Gandhi, then in South Africa, had himself written that it was 'a great shame' that the British taxed salt in India, and demanded that 'the tax should be immediately abolished'.[20]

In 1919, Gandhi had shelved the issue of salt in favour of a movement against the Rowlatt Act. Now, eleven years later, he had chosen to make it the centrepiece of a new countrywide movement against the colonial government. On 2 March, he wrote to the viceroy again, sending the letter through a young English Quaker named Reginald Reynolds. Gandhi gave Irwin advance warning of civil disobedience. While he had 'the privilege of claiming many Englishmen as dearest friends', remarked Gandhi, he regarded British rule as 'a curse', for, among other reasons, the 'terrific pressure of land revenue', the destruction of hand-spinning and other artisanal industries, and the absurdly high official salaries, with the viceroy himself paid more than five thousand times the average Indian income (by contrast, the British prime minister was paid only ninety times the average income).

Having spelt out the complaint, Gandhi then outlined the means of redressal. 'If you cannot see your way to deal with these evils, and my letter makes no appeal to your heart,' wrote Gandhi to the viceroy, then he would 'proceed with such co-workers of the Ashram as I can take, to disregard the provisions of the salt laws. I regard this tax to be the most iniquitous of all from the poor man's standpoint.'[21]

Irwin did not reply to Gandhi's letter directly. He sent a two-sentence answer through his private secretary, conveying the viceroy's regret that 'you contemplate a course of action which is clearly bound to involve violation of the law and danger to the public peace'.[22]

The viceroy's curt response seems to have been based on a note prepared for him by one of his officials. This argued that 'salt does not appear, at first sight, to be a very promising field in which to inaugurate a campaign for the withholding of taxes. . . . The most that would happen would be that relatively small quantities of bad salt would be sporadically produced. . . . At the worst it is unlikely that the loss of revenue would be really serious.'

The note complacently recalled that 'the agitation, stirred up by and among the politically-minded in regard to the raising of the Salt Duty in Lord Reading's time, evoked singularly little response among the masses, who probably realize that there is a salt tax, and in normal circumstances neither feel nor resent its existence'.[23]

The viceroy's scepticism about a popular movement based on salt was shared by more than one Congress leader. On 15 February, when the CWC met at Ahmedabad, Motilal Nehru dismissed a campaign around salt as 'quixotic'. Jamnalal Bajaj suggested that instead of protesting against the salt tax, Gandhi should march—peacefully of course—towards the viceroy's house in New Delhi.[24]

The CWC meeting started at 9 a.m. on the 15th, and at 4 p.m. a statement was issued to the press announcing a campaign of non-violent civil disobedience 'for the purpose of achieving Purna Swaraj'. The statement did not mention the specific forms of protest, but this was indeed discussed and decided upon. After the meeting ended, Sarojini Naidu wrote to her daughter: 'So the final decision is taken and salt is to be the issue! But no one seems particularly enthusiastic and everyone is more than a little doubtful how things will pan out.'[25]

Elegant and well bred, Mrs Naidu was by no means a natural satyagrahi. One who was, Vallabhbhai Patel, was ready and willing to join the fight. After the CWC meeting he toured Gujarat, telling village audiences that a *dharmayudh*, a battle of righteousness, of good against evil, 'unprecedented in the history of the world will commence within a few days, and its beginning will be made in Gujarat. Those who are afraid of death should go on a pilgrimage and those who possess riches should go to foreign countries. Those who are true Gujaratis should not sit behind closed doors.'

In his speeches, Patel asked lawyers not to attend court, and students to stay away from government schools. Attacking the salt and land laws, he sarcastically commented that 'only the air remained to be taxed' by the government.[26]

V

On 7 March, Vallabhbhai Patel was arrested and sentenced to three months rigorous imprisonment for a speech in Borsad taluka in defiance of prohibitory orders. Reports of the arrest created a 'great sensation' in Ahmedabad. The textile mills in the city all closed down on the instructions of Anasuya Sarabhai, the president of the labour union.[27] On the evening of Saturday, 8 March, Gandhi addressed a massive meeting in the city, attended by about 60,000 people, including many women. He praised Vallabhbhai Patel, whose 'services to Gujarat, and more particularly to this city, exceed mine a thousand times'. If the government had 'arrested and removed one Vallabhbhai', he remarked, 'you, the men and women of Ahmedabad, should take his place and work as his representatives'. His own aim was 'to get the Salt Tax abolished. That is for me one step, the first step, towards full freedom.'[28]

Gandhi had now decided to break the salt laws. There were inland salt deposits near the town of Badalpur. But these were just a few days walk from Ahmedabad, whereas Gandhi wanted this to be a long march, or pilgrimage perhaps, where his leisurely progress would enthuse people along the way and attract wider publicity too. He finally decided to break the law at Dandi, a village by the sea where the retreating tide left drying pools of salt water.[29]

Gandhi's choice was very likely influenced by the last of his satyagrahas in South Africa. There, Indians were prohibited from crossing provincial boundaries without explicit permission. In November 1913, Gandhi had led several thousand marchers across the border between Natal and the Transvaal, to draw attention to this particular law and to other forms of discrimination against Indians.[30] Now, sixteen and a half years later, he would march to the sea to defy the salt law, thus bringing into sharp focus the more general hurt and injustice that Indians were subjected to under British rule.

Through his Gujarati paper, Gandhi issued instructions for the villages that would host them on the way. He asked them to provide the 'simplest possible' food, with 'no oil, spices and chillies', and, since the marchers were carrying their own bedding, merely 'a clean place to rest in'. He also asked them to compile information on the religious composition of their village, the number of 'untouchables', the number of spinning wheels, the number of cows and buffaloes, and its educational facilities.[31]

On 11 March, the night before the march was to begin, 'there was great excitement all over Ahmedabad city'. A crowd of people came to the ashram, many staying on the riverbank all through the night.[32] Gandhi wrote to Jawaharlal Nehru: 'It is nearing 10 p.m. now. The air is thick with the rumour that I shall be arrested during the night.' To the Bengali khadi worker Satis Chandra Dasgupta, he wrote in a similar vein: 'This may be my last letter—before my arrest at any rate. Tomorrow I feel they are bound to arrest me.'[33]

The police did not come to the Sabarmati Ashram that night. Gandhi awoke on 12 March a free man. He said his prayers, visited the ailing and elderly in the ashram, and gathered his walking companions around him. The group of seventy-eight included Manilal Gandhi from South Africa, and representatives from almost all parts of India. There were thirty-one marchers from Gujarat, thirteen from Maharashtra, lesser numbers from the United Provinces, Kerala, Punjab and Sindh, with Tamilnad, Andhra, Karnataka, Bengal, Bihar and Orissa sending one man apiece. The diversity was social as well as geographical, for among the chosen marchers were many students and khadi workers, several 'untouchables', a few Muslims and one Christian.[34]

Gandhi had got hundreds of requests from people wanting to join his party in the Salt March, but he chose to restrict himself to bona fide ashramites only. Women in the ashram were keen to come too, but Gandhi restricted the group to men alone.[35] This was perhaps because in the India of the 1930s, mixed groups of men and women were rare in public, and would cause consternation among the orthodox.

At exactly 6.30 a.m. on 12 March, Gandhi and his companions walked out of the ashram and turned left. Outside the ashram, the line of admirers stretched all the way to Ellis Bridge. 'Men and women, boys and girls, millionaires and mill-workers had come to see the beginnings of Gandhi's march and to be part of it for at least some distance.' The road was festooned with flags and buntings. As Gandhi walked past the line of people on either side of the road, he was showered with greetings, salutations, flowers, and even a large number of rupee notes.[36]

As the marchers left the city, the crowd behind them began to sag and thin. At ten-thirty, after three hours of walking, they reached their first stop, the village of Aslali, whose residents welcomed them with flags, flowers and the blowing of trumpets.

VI

Gandhi's first speech on the march was at Aslali. 'I can understand there being a tax on such things as the hookah, bidis and liquor,' he remarked. 'And if I were an emperor, I would levy with your permission a tax of one pie on every bidi. . . . But should one levy a tax on salt?'[37]

On the second day, the 13th, the marchers halted at the village of Baweja. When he was handed over the information he had asked for on the hamlet, Gandhi told the villagers that he 'was pained to read it. It is strange that a place so near Ahmedabad has zeroes against the columns for consumption of khadi, the number of habitual khadi-wearers and spinning-wheels at work.' In the next village, Navagam, there was but one khadi wearer and one spinning wheel at work, this in a population of close to a thousand.[38]

On the third day, Gandhi walked nine miles. He was, a reporter accompanying the party noted, 'suffering from rheumatism which became rather acute last night. He has been walking with great strain. For the major portion of this morning's tramp Mahatmaji had to lean on the shoulders of two boys.' A pony followed in case Gandhi wanted to use it; but he refused, despite repeated pleas, to ride on the animal.

The next morning, Gandhi seems to have recovered his strength, since he 'marched on without stopping for a moment'. A press car followed the marchers. The journalists were chastised by onlookers, who asked whether they were not ashamed of themselves when the sixty-one-year-old Gandhi and his colleagues were walking and thus making the ground sacred under their feet. The scribes were compelled to get out of their car and walk.

That night, Gandhi's party stopped at Dabhan, near the town of Nadiad. They had covered thirty-seven miles in the first four days of the march.[39]

As he walked towards the sea, Gandhi was attracting ever larger crowds. At Dabhan, he addressed a meeting held in the bed of a dry tank, with some 10,000 people in attendance. Among them were seven headmen, who presented their resignations to Gandhi as a mark of their own non-cooperation with the government. From Dabhan, Gandhi proceeded to Nadiad, where he addressed an even larger meeting, in the compound of a local religious sect. The crowd was estimated as being in excess of 40,000. People sat on the ground, and on ramparts of buildings and on trees.

Summing up the March so far, the *Bombay Chronicle*'s reporter observed:

> Indescribable scenes of enthusiasm marked the progress of the march of the Swaraj Army on this fourth day. . . . The rich and the poor, millionaires and mazurs [workers], 'caste' Hindus and so-called untouchables, one and all, vied with one another in honouring India's great liberator. . . . 'How can I have the "Darshan" of Bapuji' was the only anxiety of everybody. All castes, creeds, religions and

interests were merged into one irresistible wave of patriotism. All appeared a perfect Gandhi Raj. The authority of Government seemed to be almost non-existent. . . .[40]

The party reached Anand on the 16th. The next day was Monday, Gandhi's designated day of silence, and also now of rest. As he wrote to Mira on the 17th: 'Today the fatigue of the past five days made me sleep five times during the day.'[41]

From Anand, the marchers proceeded to Ras, the village where Vallabhbhai Patel had been arrested. Here, Gandhi asked all students over fifteen, and all teachers, to join the movement. As he put it: 'Wherever revolutions have taken place, that is, in Japan, China, Egypt, Italy, Ireland and in England, students and teachers have played a prominent role.'[42]

On the 19th night, the marchers crossed the river Mahi to enter Broach district. A boat had been arranged for Gandhi, but many of the others crossed on foot. The water was knee-deep, making it a 'thrilling experience to the youths accompanying' him. They slept on the other bank, and got up at dawn for prayers.

Gandhi had been on the road for a full week now. On 19 March, Jawaharlal Nehru joined the marchers. He spent the 20th morning with Gandhi, before carrying on to Baroda and Ahmedabad by car, taking with him articles written on the march by Gandhi in Gujarati and English, to be set into type at the ashram.[43]

In Gandhi's absence, the ashram was kept going by the women, supervised by Mira. They tended the vegetable garden, swept and cleansed the rooms and courtyards, and gathered water from the well. One of the few men in the ashram was Mahadev Desai, left behind to edit *Young India*, answer letters coming in from all over India and the world, and recruit students for the movement. When a reporter dropped in to see him, Mahadev was at his twice daily exercise with the charkha.[44]

Back on the march—at a village named Dehwan, Gandhi was greeted by a 105-year-old woman, who put a red tilak on his forehead and told him to return only after he had obtained swaraj. The next night the party camped in a grove of banyan and mango trees. Twelve marchers had fallen ill 'due to bad cooking arrangements'. Gandhi told them to proceed to Broach town to rest and recover, and then rejoin the march. His own stomach was clearly strong enough to withstand the village water and food.[45]

On the 23rd, the marchers reached a large village named Amod, whose roads were 'dusty', her houses 'old and dilapidated'. But now there was 'new life in the tortuous dingy lanes, new cheer on the faces of men and women who crowded in front of their houses to see Mahatmaji and his band to pass'.[46]

Two socialist activists had come down from Bombay to meet Gandhi at Amod. One, the feminist Kamaladevi Chattopadhyay, hoped to persuade him that women must be encouraged to become satyagrahis and court arrest. Gandhi answered that 'if impatient sisters will be a little patient, they will find ample scope for their zeal and sacrifice in the national struggle for freedom'.[47]

The second visitor was the trade unionist Yusuf Meherally. Meherally asked Gandhi how Muslims could be attracted to the Congress and thus 'protected from the pernicious propaganda of communalists'. Gandhi answered: 'The best way to increase Muslim interest in the Congress is for Congressmen to serve them. Convince them that the Congress is as much theirs as anybody else's. My present programme—the breaking of the salt laws—should appeal to all the communities in India, for it affects them all alike.'[48]

On the 25th, Kasturba motored down from Ahmedabad, to check on her husband and his health. He was fine, but some others were not. The number of invalids in the camp had risen to eighteen. Gandhi advised those still standing—or walking—to observe the rules of hygiene, to drink lots of hot water, and 'above all, to have firm faith in God that he might give them strength to reach Dandi safely'.[49]

Reporting on the march thus far, a journalist with the Free Press of India remarked that the popular response in the towns and villages they had passed was 'phenomenal'. All along the route, village headmen and petty officials had submitted copies of their resignation letters to Gandhi. In Ahmedabad, Kaira and Broach districts, 'almost every house [was] giving one head for [the] country's cause'. In this respect, Gandhi himself 'beats all records by allowing all adults in his family to enrol' for the satyagraha. With him on the march were his son Manilal and his grandson Kantilal. Ramdas and Devadas were expected to join soon, the latter with a group of Muslim students from Jamia Millia.[50]

On the evening of Friday, 28 March, Gandhi crossed into Surat district, using a specially constructed wooden bridge over the river Kim. He camped that night in a forest. The next morning, Gandhi marched on to a village named Esthan, where '32 men and 7 women of the untouchable class' came to him 'and took the vow to give up drink'.[51]

On Sunday, the 30th, Gandhi halted at a village named Bhatgam. The next day was a day of rest and silence. Ahead lay the city of Surat (where the East India Company had established one of its earliest factories), the town of Navsari (a stronghold of the Parsi community) and the seaside village of Dandi, where, if all went to plan, Gandhi would break the salt laws in a week's time.

It was now two and a half weeks since Gandhi had left his ashram in Ahmedabad. The police reported that while Gandhi was 'fatigued' at the end of each day's march, he continued to be 'mentally vigorous'.[52]

VII

In the first week of January 1930, Winston Churchill wrote to the viceroy, Lord Irwin, urging him to stand firm against Gandhi and the Congress. (Churchill was then out of office, having finished a long stint as chancellor of the exchequer.) With most of Ireland already gone, and the British position 'being liquidated' in Egypt, Churchill hoped that at least 'upon the supreme issue of India the British Empire will arise in its old strength'.

Irwin received very different advice from C.F. Andrews, who asked him to reach out to Gandhi, and encourage his policies of khaddar promotion so as to lessen India's dependence on foreign goods. The situation in India, commented Andrews, was 'a part of the infinitely larger question of the acknowledgement of racial equality. Until that comes, we ourselves can only expect the present friction to continue.'[53]

Irwin was not as committed a defender of British imperial supremacy as Churchill; nor as vigorous an advocate of complete racial equality as Andrews. His betwixt and between position is nicely expressed in a letter he wrote on 21 January to his friend Geoffrey Dawson, editor of *The Times* of London, and like Irwin a Fellow of All Souls College in Oxford. Here, Irwin complacently observed that 'the net result of the Lahore [Congress] proceedings has been to give a greater impetus to moderate opinion than I have seen since I have been in India. They [the Moderates] are really getting their coats off and setting to work to propaganda, and organise, and collect money, and fight the Congress at every point.'

That the Moderates were any more in a position to recover ground was wishful thinking. The radicals, led by Gandhi and the younger Nehru, had now captured the nationalist imagination. As the day of the commencement of the Dandi march drew nearer, Lord Irwin became somewhat less complacent. On 6 March, he wrote to another Fellow of All Souls that 'our affairs are not going too badly if only Gandhi would leave them alone. But he is doing his utmost to make them impossible. What an enigma the man is!'[54]

Six days later, Gandhi began his march to the sea. This created great excitement in different parts of India, duly captured in the fortnightly reports of the provincial governments. Madras told Delhi that in their bailiwick, 'the opening of Gandhi's civil disobedience campaign has completely overshadowed all other issues'. Bombay told Delhi that the march had 'created great excitement both in Gujarat and elsewhere. In Ahmedabad particularly the interest is very keen and persons from that city continue to attend Gandhi on his march and at his meetings.'[55]

The officials on the spot were agitated by the impact of the march on the public consciousness. Irwin, ensconced in his palace in New Delhi, was less worried. In the third week of the march, he wrote to his spiritual preceptor, Cosmo Gordon Lang, the Archbishop of Canterbury: 'Gandhi is continuing his theatrical march to the coast, but so far is arousing a good deal less excitement than he had anticipated. And I am quite certain that we have been right not to arrest him so far.'

Irwin had just met the Moderate politician V.S. Srinivasa Sastri, who thought that Gandhi wished above all to be a martyr. Irwin had also heard from others that Gandhi 'has sought to model his life and thought on Our Lord; and in his present march he had a pony led behind in case he wanted to ride, which some say was also with the idea of reproducing New Testament history [where Jesus, in his Second Coming, was to be accompanied by the angels of heaven riding white horses], but this strikes me as far-fetched'.[56]

For the viceroy, then, Gandhi was an object of curiosity, a subject for study, but not—or at least not yet—a political threat. The same day that he wrote to the Archbishop of Canterbury, Irwin wrote to the secretary of state for India that the government's refusal to arrest Gandhi so far 'has been an embarrassment to his plans'.[57]

VIII

One reason the viceroy was sceptical of the march's effects may have been the newspapers he was reading. The two major British-owned newspapers in India were the *Statesman* of Calcutta and the *Times of India* of Bombay. The first called the march 'a childishly futile business'; the second, speaking likewise of the 'futility of Mr. Gandhi's campaign', claimed the salt tax protected the poor from rapacious middlemen, which is why even free countries, such as Japan, had a state monopoly on the production and sale of salt.[58]

Also disparaging about Gandhi's march were visiting British reporters. A correspondent for the *Daily Telegraph* claimed that 'no one would be more disappointed than Mr. Gandhi if his expectations of his arrest before he has travelled quarter of the distance to be covered, are not fulfilled'. Gandhi was apparently travelling through a part of India 'which is unsafe for Europeans to traverse but doubts are expressed if the arrest of Mr. Gandhi would really cause more than a few hours excitement, and momentary tumultuous cheers'.[59]

The American newsmagazine *Time* shared this low estimation of Gandhi and his march. It spoke with disdain of Gandhi's 'spindly frame' and his 'spidery loins'. The magazine was even less impressed by his wife Kasturba, 'a shriveled, little middle-aged Hindu'. The crowd that sent off Gandhi from the ashram was described by *Time* as 'swirling [and] jabbering', the incoherence of the event captured in a volunteer band that 'raised their horns and blared a few bars of

"God Save the King" before they realized their mistake and subsided in brassy confusion'.

On the first day of the march, claimed *Time*, 'Mr. Gandhi's head and legs began to ache' as, 'haggard and drooping', he reached that night's destination. The next morning, as the walk continued, apparently 'not a single cheer resounded' in the villages they passed. Yet, 'Saint Gandhi called his lovely procession to a halt, gazed up and down the silent, empty street, addressed the blank windows of slumbering houses'. At the end of the second day's walking, Gandhi 'sank to the ground'. At this stage, the magazine did not believe that 'the emaciated saint would be physically able to go much further'.[60]

The view of the nationalist press was very different. The *Pratap* of Kanpur, the *Amrita Bazar Patrika* of Calcutta and the *Bombay Chronicle* all saw the march in epic and mythic terms. So did some individual patriots. An anonymous versifier in the United Provinces compared Gandhi to Lord Krishna, drinking the milk of goats rather than cows, stealing salt rather than butter, plying the charkha rather than playing the flute.[61] The entrepreneur Prafulla Chandra Ray likened the salt march to the exodus of the Israelites under Moses, while Motilal Nehru compared it to the march of Lord Ram to Lanka.[62]

IX

On 1 April, Gandhi walked into the ancient trading town of Surat, where he was met by a delegation of mill owners (who naturally warmed to his boycott of foreign cloth). That evening, he addressed a 'mammoth meeting' on the river sands, attended by more than 1,00,000 people. At this meeting, 170 village headmen presented copies of their letters of resignation to Gandhi.[63]

On the 3rd morning, the marchers left British territory for the first time to enter the native state of Baroda. 'A new feature in the meetings held in villages from Surat onwards', ran one report, was 'that a good many Mahomedans . . . attend the meeting daily'. At Dhaman village, 'a Maulvi addressing the meeting ensured Gandhiji that the Muslims would not lag behind their Hindu brethren in fighting for Swaraj'.

Gandhi, in response, spoke of the solid support extended to him by Muslim satyagrahis in South Africa.[64]

Gandhi and party spent the night of the 3rd in Navsari. The town was crowded 'with sightseers and bands of volunteers from distant parts. Mr. Gandhi and his party were received amidst tumultuous scenes of enthusiasm. Indeed it seems as if this little town in the Gaekwar's territory is vowed to outshine the British subjects in its reception to the pilgrims.'[65]

The march had now entered its last day. An eyewitness left behind this vivid description of Gandhi on the road to his final destination, Dandi:

> When I saw him on the morning of the 4th [of April] he was coming briskly up the straight road towards Vijalpur. . . . The red sun had just risen over the roof of the railway station, and his bare face and body was golden and transfigured, in the light of morning. A large crowd was behind him and the eighty and odd volunteers were lost in it. It was a quick pace, between running and walking . . . It did not seem to me he was using his staff to any purpose. He was not particularly leaning upon it. He seemed strong, lean like a lathe and fleet of foot. The municipality had watered the road very efficiently. The country road was cool and frank and beautiful. It struck me there were many ways of walking and that any other but this would have looked ridiculous. Supposing he had led the procession at slower pace, like a gipsy pedlar or a mandarin, how incongruous it would be. I realised what a consummate artist-realist the old man must be. The breathless walk made you see how urgent and downright and final was his call and his message. He did not tarry for the road-side honours from devotees. He passed on after a lady had placed a kum-kum on his forehead and a man had showered rose-water.[66]

On the 5th, Gandhi reached the village where he planned to break the salt laws. A correspondent of the *Bombay Chronicle*, accompanying the marchers, wrote that 'the simple and tiny village of Dandi now looks like a city. The route between Navsari and this village is full of visitors, many of whom have come from long distances. Drinking water is being carried to Dandi from neighbouring villages in bullock carts. A number of shops selling eatables have been opened for the convenience of the visitors.'

On 5 April, after reaching Dandi, Gandhi gave a statement to the Associated Press. He first complimented the government 'for the policy of complete non-interference adopted by them throughout the march'. He said he would commence civil disobedience at 6.30 a.m. the next morning. Explaining the significance of the date, he remarked that '6th April has been to us, since its culmination in [the] Jallianwala [Bagh] massacre, a day for penance and purification'. The reference was to the first hartal against the Rowlatt Act, held on 6 April 1919, an event which first brought Gandhi to countrywide attention.[67]

X

Dandi lay eleven miles from Navsari, the birthplace of Gandhi's early mentor Dadabhai Naoroji. In normal times, the village had a population of about two hundred souls, mostly fishermen. Its excellent climate and sea breeze had attracted a few rich people who built bungalows, including Gandhi's host, Nizamuddin Vasi, a prosperous cutlery merchant in Bombay.

This little village had now 'become a place of pilgrimage', with an 'unending stream of visitors' flowing into it because it was the first battlefield of Gandhi's campaign around salt. Dandi had only two wells, so plenty of water was bussed in from outside for Gandhi, his party, and the now very large body of sympathizers who had come here directly.

A hundred government officials, among them excise inspectors and policemen, had reached Dandi to keep watch on Gandhi. The villagers had refused to give them accommodation, so they camped outside in tents. A reporter talked to the policemen, 'and the surprise of it was that these agents of Government have not yet got a clear idea themselves about their task. They are waiting for eleventh-hour instructions from their headquarters.'[68]

Also in Dandi was the poet Sarojini Naidu. Back in February, she had (privately) mocked the idea of a struggle around salt. But as the march gained attention and acclaim, she decided she must be at hand to watch its climax.

On the night of the 5th, Gandhi had an oil massage and slept soundly (as usual). The next morning he awoke at 4.30, and after prayers, led a group of marchers towards the sea. Entering the water to sounds of 'Mahatma Gandhi ki jai', he proceeded to pick up lumps of natural salt lying in a small pit. The others followed him, even as Sarojini Naidu, addressing Gandhi, shouted: 'Hail, law breaker!'[69]

Mrs Naidu's words were to be flashed around the world by the reporters covering the event. They are still widely quoted. Less well known are her private thoughts, expressed in a letter to her daughter shortly after her famous public salutation. Here Mrs Naidu remarked:

> The little law breaker is sitting in a state of 'Maun' [silence] writing his article of triumph for Young India and I am stretched on a hard bench at the open window of a huge room that has 6 windows open to the sea breeze. As far as the eye can see there is a little Army— thousands of pilgrims who have been pouring in since yesterday to this otherwise deserted and exceedingly primitive village of fishermen.

Mrs Naidu continued:

> I wish you were here though you could not even have reached here alive. The road from Navsari is dreadful and here one cannot walk a yard without sinking in wet salt-bogs! And the food! Yesterday a mess worse than dogs' food was served up but from today there is nothing but volunteer rations: Channa and some Gur! However, I have a huge bedroom and a cleanish bathroom—God be praised![70]

The (mostly) young and (mostly) male journalists who came to Dandi were less fussy than Mrs Naidu, more willing to camp in the open, and use the fields to relieve themselves. Their focus was on getting the news of Gandhi's defiance out into the world. After the Mahatma broke the salt laws, no fewer than 700 telegrams were sent out from the post office nearest to Dandi, at Jalalpur. This extraordinarily heavy traffic had been facilitated by the postmaster general of the

Bombay Presidency, who had sent several signalmen to supplement the skeletal staff at Jalalpur.

On 7 April—a day after Gandhi broke the law—an angry letter was dispatched to Bombay by the Government of India. Was it not a mistake, it asked, to 'facilitate the advertisement that Mr. Gandhi and his followers no doubt desire'? The government had taken the precaution of banning the films made in the early stages of Gandhi's march; now that act had been nullified by the Raj's postal department's allowing 'correspondents to broadcast highly coloured and frequently inaccurate accounts of the success of the march'.

The postmaster general (an Indian named Bewoor) was unrepentant. His department, he told Simla, 'could not refuse press traffic when offered by authorised correspondents. We obtain payment for this and it is our duty to dispatch the messages.' Had Bewoor not sent additional signalmen, 'there would have been serious complaints and I would probably have been called upon to explain why I did not take proper steps to deal with the anticipated traffic'. He tellingly added that the journalists who accompanied Gandhi 'belong to all kinds of newspapers including the English Press'.

One pro-Raj paper, the *Daily Gazette* of Karachi, was outraged that facilities 'which a benign Government has created for the convenience and advancement of the general public', should have been used by Gandhi 'to project his poison through the length and breadth of this great country'. It bitterly noted that Gandhi had himself once dismissed railways and the telegraph as artefacts of modernity India could do without. And now a government he opposed had allowed him to use technologies he despised 'in furtherance of his destructive campaigns'.[71]

XI

As Gandhi broke the salt law in Dandi, similar breaches were taking place in other parts of India. In Bengal, volunteers led by Satis Chandra Dasgupta walked from the Sodepur Ashram to the village of Mahisbathan, seven miles from Calcutta, to make salt. In Bombay a batch led by K.F. Nariman marched to Haji Ali Point and prepared salt in the park nearby. In Tamil Nadu, C. Rajagopalachari led the campaign in Vedaranyam. Breaches of salt laws also occurred in the interior. Ganesh Shankar Vidyarthi, the president of the United Provinces Congress Committee, led the making of salt in Kanpur's Shraddhananda Park.[72]

Writing to Jawaharlal Nehru on 7 April, Mahadev Desai described the mood in Gujarat. Mahadev, holding the fort at Sabarmati while his master was on the coast, was 'addressing meetings the like of which I have never addressed in my life. They are all models of orderliness and silence. Ten to fifteen thousand people meeting every day at 6.30 and dispersing before dark just to hear one speech and that from me who has no pretensions to being called a speaker.'

With his letter, Mahadev enclosed a pinch of salt manufactured by Gandhi at Dandi on 6 April (which had been rushed back to Sabarmati by car). This was to 'be kept either as a memento or sold by auction, the upset price to be not less than a thousand rupees'. Mahadev himself had just sold a packet made by Gandhi for 501 rupees; he expected Jawaharlal, with his greater charisma and appeal, to sell his for at least twice the amount.[73]

The news of the upsurge in Gujarat and around the country was conveyed to Gandhi. But there was one fly in the ointment; the non-participation, indeed the active hostility, of his leading comrades from the days of non-cooperation and Khilafat, the Ali Brothers. The day after Gandhi broke the law in Dandi, Shaukat Ali wrote to him that he had started his movement 'without consulting Muslims', and now wanted 'to gain so much strength as to be "irresistible" and force us to be willy-nilly your camp-followers'.[74]

Gandhi found the letter 'astonishing'. He replied to Shaukat that 'I had no knowledge of the extent to which I had fallen in your estimation'. Could not his former friend see 'that, although I may act independently of you, it might not amount to desertion? My conscience is clear. I have deserted neither you nor the Mussalmans. Where is the desertion in fighting against the salt laws and other inequities and fighting for independence.'[75]

Some days later, in a speech in Bombay, Shaukat's brother Mohammad Ali declared: 'The non-co-operation movement which was inaugurated by Gandhi ten years ago was a genuine movement to get swaraj but . . . the present civil disobedience movement [was] aimed at establishing Hindu Raj in India.' Gandhi, claimed his former brother in arms, 'had now come entirely under the influence of the Hindu Mahasabha and was not prepared for any honourable settlement with the Muslims'. Mohammad Ali urged his followers to stay away from Gandhi's movement, adding that he himself planned to attend the Round Table Conference to place Muslim demands before the British Parliament.[76]

In the criticisms of the Ali Brothers there was perhaps more than a hint of jealousy. Back in 1920 and 1921, they had formed a trinity with Gandhi. Now, a decade later, they were denied any leadership role whatsoever. That said, it was clear that, outside of Gandhi's native Gujarat, Muslims had not participated in the Salt Satyagraha in large numbers. The reasons were several. The absence of a mobilizing motif such as the Khilafat was one. The emphasis on wearing handmade clothes was another. Thus, as one ordinary Muslim in Bombay wrote to Gandhi, 'Mahatmaji, your insistence on khaddar is noble, but under the present critical circumstances you must relax your conditions a little and allow all and sundry to join your movement for freedom.' Many people in Bombay who 'are dying to participate in the national struggle' were too poor to afford the price at which khaddar was being sold in the cities.[77]

XII

Gandhi had now decided to go from village to village, persuading people to break the salt laws and court arrest. Meanwhile, through the columns of his newspaper, he asked women not to take part in the movement against the salt laws, where 'they will be lost among the men'. Rather, for them to 'leave a stamp . . . on the history of India', they should 'find an exclusive field for themselves'. This was in promoting prohibition, whereby women could picket liquor booths and thus bring about a 'change of heart' in those addicted to drink.[78]

Some women did not heed the advice. They included Kamaladevi Chattopadhyay and Perin Captain (Dadabhai Naoroji's granddaughter), who led a satyagraha in the Dholera salt bed in

Gujarat. Gandhi congratulated Perin and Kamaladevi for their 'courage and calmness' but added that 'they would have done better to remain outside the venue of the men's fight'. He reminded the women that 'in all humility', he had 'suggested to them an exclusive field [prohibition] in which they are at liberty and are expected to show their best qualities'.[79]

Kamaladevi was undeterred. On Saturday, 12 April, she arrived at the Bombay Stock Exchange to sell the contraband salt made by her over the past week. 'She was immediately conveyed to the Trading Ring where she was cheered with cries of "Mahatmaji-ki-jai". The brokers and their clerks flocked around her to purchase the Satyagrahi salt with the result that the salt packets had to be sold by auction.' The auction lasted half an hour, realizing some Rs 4000 in all. The next day, the *Bombay Chronicle* carried a large photo of Kamaladevi Chattopadhyay, described as 'the leading lady law-breaker'.[80]

Gandhi's son Ramdas was arrested in the first week of April, as were many other satyagrahis in Gujarat. In the second week of April, Jamnalal Bajaj, Jawaharlal Nehru and Devadas Gandhi were also arrested. In response to these arrests, Vithalbhai Patel resigned from his post as president of the Legislative Assembly. Vithalbhai wrote to the viceroy on 20 April that he had always made it clear that 'Congress and Gandhi alone were in a position to deliver goods to any appreciable extent, and a Round Table Conference in which Congress leaders could not be persuaded to participate was not worth much, if anything at all'.[81]

On the same day, M.A. Jinnah also wrote to the viceroy, urging him to make a public statement on constitutional advance. At present, noted Jinnah, 'the country had got before it only one side of the question [i.e. the Congress side], which has received the greatest publicity and *ex parte* propaganda, and has gone on so long that at present it has reached fever heat, but the Government alone can put the alternative before the people and sooner it is done the better'. Irwin had asked Jinnah to make a public statement against Gandhi's movement. Jinnah said his disapproval of civil disobedience was well known, but any statement he would now make would be effective only if 'there is a definite and clear alternative' to the Congress credo.

'I have great faith in you,' wrote Jinnah to the viceroy, adding, 'but you must move faster than you are doing at present.'[82]

Gandhi was in Navsari when news reached him of a daring raid on an armoury in the Bengali port town of Chittagong. This distressed him, for, as he told the Associated Press, this showed 'that there is a large or small body of men in Bengal who do not believe in non-violence whether as a policy or as a creed. That there were such people all over India I knew but I had hoped that they would give non-violence a chance.'[83]

On 26 April, Gandhi told a meeting that what he had done in Dandi was merely to pick 'a seer or two of salt from here and there'. The time had come to go beyond this 'childish game', and raid the major government salt-making works in Dharasana. When that satyagraha commenced, he would invite the residents of Dharasana 'to join the fun'; he hoped they would join, even if it meant braving police beatings.[84]

In the third week of April, Mahadev Desai and his ashram colleague Swami Anand were arrested. So were hundreds of other Congressmen in other parts of the country. Gandhi, however, was still left free to move about.

XIII

Why had the Raj waited so long to arrest Gandhi? The day after Gandhi broke the law in Dandi, Lord Irwin wrote privately to the editor of *The Times* insisting that his policy of non-interference had been justified. He claimed that Gandhi himself hoped to be arrested early in his march, for two reasons: it would have (a) led to 'the shedding of a great lustre about his name and cause'; and (b) spared 'an elderly man the disagreeable duty of walking twelve miles a day for three weeks through dust in order to get to a hot sea-side in the end'.[85]

The view from the ground was very different. In the districts that Gandhi passed through, and in Bombay city itself, there was very clearly a 'wave of anti-Government feeling', which 'Gandhi's march is doing so much to stimulate'. Thus remarked the governor of

Bombay Presidency in a letter to the viceroy ten days after the march commenced. A week later, meeting the viceroy in Delhi, the governor again pressed the importance of acting early.[86]

Meanwhile, Gandhi broke the law in Dandi, spurring similar actions across the Presidency and in other parts of India. On 15 April, the Bombay governor told the viceroy that 'there is no doubt that Gandhi has a great emotional hold as evidenced by the numerical support of his demonstrations and the popular enthusiasm, largely among the younger generation, and, increasingly, amongst women and girls, which has been more than expected'. He added that 'Gandhi has scored a certain degree of success in attaining his objective—viz. to teach the masses . . . that the law can be defied if sufficient concerted action is brought'.[87]

The importance of punitive action finally began to dawn on Irwin. To the Bombay governor he somewhat ponderously wrote that 'my own mind is moving rather steadily in the direction of feeling that we incur graver dangers than we avoid by continuing our reluctance to arrest Gandhi'.[88] To the India Office, Irwin defensively remarked that while they 'were right to let him [Gandhi] reach the sea', they would have to arrest him soon, since the 'effect has been definitely bad in Gujerat, and I suspect in Bombay and in Calcutta. . . . I think we are reaching the time when the legend of the irresistibility of Gandhi is assuming dangerous proportions.'[89]

Knowing the viceroy's tendency to prevaricate, the Bombay government pressed him to sanction arrest. On 26 April, they wired him that 'Gandhi's exemption from arrest is having an important effect in strengthening the civil disobedience movement. His arrest would tend to check it by removing [the] brain which guides it.' Delhi answered back that Bombay should not, must not, arrest Gandhi without explicit orders from them, the central government.[90]

Gandhi had announced that he would now march towards the Dharasana Salt Works, some fifty miles south of Surat. On 30 April, Bombay wired Delhi that these works were open and not protected by fencing. The salt workers in Dharasana might either resist Gandhi's party, in which case violence would occur, and the police have to be called in. On the other hand, if the salt workers were persuaded or intimidated to join the protesters, and 'Gandhi enters into peaceable possession of large salt', then the 'news will spread like wildfire', and 'the belief already prevalent that Gandhi has beaten Government and that Government dare not arrest him will receive corroboration which no man can doubt'.

This assessment, at once alarmist and realistic, finally persuaded Irwin to act. Delhi now instructed Bombay to go ahead and detain Gandhi. However, in one last show of prevarication, they were asked to wait until 4 May so that there was enough notice to alert other provincial governments.[91]

XIV

On the evening of 4 May, Gandhi drafted a letter to the viceroy announcing that he would lead a party to raid the Dharasana Salt Works. Before the letter could be sent, he was arrested, at forty-five minutes past midnight on the morning of the 5th. He was then asleep at his camp in the village of Karadi, in Surat district. When the magistrate sent to arrest him woke Gandhi, he asked for half an hour to wash and clean his teeth. His companions said their prayers while the policemen watched. Then he was taken away, transported by train and car to the same jail in Yerwada, near Poona, where he had been incarcerated between March 1922 and January 1924.

Curiously, Gandhi was not arrested under the Salt Act, under which an offender could be sent to jail for illegal possession of salt, but under an ordinance of the Bombay government first drafted in 1827, which permitted the authorities to detain anyone deemed to be 'a menace to public order'.[92]

Once sceptical of Gandhi's challenge, Irwin now recognized the force of popular sentiment that had consolidated and crystallized. A week after Gandhi's arrest, he wrote to the former (and future) Conservative prime minister, Stanley Baldwin, that 'there is no question that the movement has caught on among the Hindus, largely out of a mistaken veneration for Gandhi and largely as the expression of a sub-conscious nationalist and self-determination movement of thought'.[93]

Irwin was not the only one to change his mind about the significance of Gandhi and his march. So did the American magazine,

Time. As the march progressed, *Time* saluted Gandhi as a 'Saint' and 'Statesman', who was using 'Christian acts as a weapon against men with Christian beliefs'. Later issues spoke of the 'spreading ripples of St. Gandhi's movement for independence', with 'unrest seething hotter and hotter all over India'. *Time*'s report on Gandhi's arrest in early May praised the dignity and composure with which he received the news, merely asking the police officer for a few minutes in which he could brush his teeth (with contraband salt).[94]

Gandhi was arrested a full eight weeks after he first set out from the Sabarmati Ashram. In these days and weeks, the details of his march, whom he met and what he said, how he was perceived and praised (and occasionally criticized), were intensively covered in the Indian press (in both English and the vernacular) and in the foreign press as well. The image of an elderly, emaciated man walking with a staff on a hot and dusty road, day after day, in a single (and singular) challenge to the greatest empire on earth, captivated the national and global imagination.

Eighty-eight years later, the Dandi March remains the best-known event of a remarkably eventful life. Yet, it could so easily have been otherwise. In a private letter written while Gandhi was on the road, the governor of the United Provinces, Malcolm Hailey, deplored the fact that Irwin was not a strong viceroy, who had shown his weakness by not arresting Gandhi before he set out on his Salt March. Drawing on three decades of life and work in India, Hailey observed that 'the East has far more respect for a ruler who misuses his powers than for one who allows his authority to be flouted'.[95]

Had the viceroy sanctioned the arrest of Gandhi before he left the Sabarmati Ashram, or shortly after the march commenced, Dandi would have remained an obscure village on the Gujarat coast, unloved by any but its few hundred inhabitants.

CHAPTER SEVENTEEN

The Prison and the World

I

Gandhi's cell in Yerwada was quite large compared to the one he had used in 1922–24—two rooms with a yard to which he had access. It had furniture and electricity as well. Shortly after he was incarcerated, Gandhi was visited by the inspector general of prisons. They discussed what newspapers he could get, and how many visitors he could receive (two family members a week was what the government suggested). Gandhi asked that he be allowed to see all prisoners in Yerwada serving sentences in connection with the civil disobedience movement. The inspector general said this would not be possible, but if Gandhi wanted a companion in the same yard that could be arranged.

The inspector general then suggested to his superiors that D.B. (Kaka) Kalelkar be transferred from Ahmedabad jail to be with Gandhi. Kalelkar was a veteran of the Sabarmati Ashram, a scholar and writer who (when not in prison) taught at the Gujarat Vidyapith. The Bombay government was happy for him to be the Mahatma's jail companion, since, as they put it, Kalelkar was 'already as "good" or as "bad" as Gandhi can make him', and sending him to Yerwada would 'prevent Gandhi getting hold of a new recruit' to his cause.[1]

Gandhi spent his first weeks in jail spinning and reading the Gita. He was, as he wrote to Mira, 'resting after many days of fatigue' brought on by his march to the sea. He took two naps during the day, one at 8 a.m. and the other at noon.

Gandhi also occupied himself by translating the *Ashram Bhajnavali*, the collection of devotional songs sung during the morning and evening prayers in Sabarmati. There were more than two hundred hymns in all, these composed in Hindi, Gujarati, Bengali, Marathi and Sanskrit. Gandhi began rendering them into English, a task initially begun for Mira's benefit, but soon acquiring a rationale of its own.[2]

The government had allowed Gandhi to see his 'blood relations' twice a week, and others only by special permission. This was relatively lenient compared to his last term in prison, when he was allowed visitors only once in three months. Yet, the prisoner rejected these terms, writing to the jail superintendent that he had 'in the Ashram and outside many widows, girls, boys and men, who are perhaps more to me than many a blood relative. If they may not see me on the same terms as relatives, to be just to the former, I must not see the latter.'

In the ashram, as well as in the wider community of Congress nationalists, Gandhi was known as 'Bapu', Father. Now, in jail, he provided the jail authorities a list of some 160 people who, he said, 'are like blood relations to me'. He wanted them to come meet him, in groups, on the same terms as he was allowed to see Kasturba and their sons. The government rejected this appeal, so Gandhi chose to have no visitors at all.[3]

Denied access to his family, both spiritual and biological, Gandhi kept in close and almost continuous contact with them through the post. In some weeks the number of letters he wrote exceeded seventy or even eighty. The letters were scrupulously non-political, offering advice or answering queries about diet, health, prayer, reading and general conduct. This was not merely because the prison authorities would have censored letters dealing with politics. For Gandhi, the moral and spiritual health of his ashram was always as important as the social or political condition of his nation.

A representative letter was written to his adopted English daughter eight weeks into his jail term. This began by expressing relief that Mira's mother's operation in London was successful. 'The West,'

Gandhi remarked, 'has always commanded my admiration [for] its surgical inventions and all-round progress in that direction.'

Gandhi came next to the vital question of diet. 'You do not tell me,' he wrote to Mira, 'how much ghee you are taking and whether you are taking oranges or not.' He then moved on to the even more vital question of spinning. 'I find the doing of 375 rounds somewhat of a strain nowadays,' he told Mira. 'I am trying to prove the cause.'[4]

Gandhi liked to refer to himself, only partly in jest, as a 'quack doctor'. He had a lifelong interest—not to say fascination—in home remedies. Queries from ashramites about health were answered with zest. A letter to Valji Desai read: 'If it is only your gums which bleed, you should gargle with salt water three or four times a day and in the morning massage them with a finger using pure, finely-powdered salt, taking care not to spit out the saliva meanwhile. You may use cocoanut oil instead of salt. You should also gargle with some potassium permanganate solution. If the bleeding does not stop with this, you should consult a dentist. Sometimes such bleeding is brought about even by indigestion. You should eat daily a little quantity of uncooked green vegetables.'[5]

In jail, Gandhi wrote many letters to individuals in the ashram, as well as a weekly collective letter to them. From July, this collective letter ended with a discourse on a specific subject—first Truth, then Ahimsa, next Brahmacharya. Other topics dealt with included fearlessness, non-possession, the removal of untouchability, and the importance of vows as regards celibacy, non-possession, truth-telling, and the like.

The letter on vows elicited a strong reaction from J.C. Kumarappa, a Columbia-educated economist who had left a flourishing career to join Gandhi. Kumarappa thought the taking of vows a tacit acknowledgement of moral weakness. 'The strong man needs no such help,' he wrote to Gandhi in October 1930. 'His ideals, determination and will-power will see him through any situation.' On the other hand, a person compelled to take vows 'ceases sooner or later—and often sooner than later—to appeal to his ideals every time a situation arises; and he acts in a particular way, not because his ideals dictate that course, but because he has taken a vow to act so'.

Gandhi answered that he was not thinking of 'vows publicly administered to audiences', but 'of a promise made to oneself'. Every human had within him Ram and Ravan, God and Satan, and vows helped in heeding the former rather than the latter. To Kumarappa, a Christian, Gandhi wrote that 'Jesus was preeminently a man of unshakeable resolution, i.e. vows. His yea was yea for ever.'[6]

Perhaps the most remarkable of all the letters that Gandhi wrote during his second term in an Indian prison was to a complete stranger. This was Pyare Lal Govil, a sub-judge in the United Provinces town of Muzaffarnagar, who had lost his only child, a daughter, to complications following pregnancy.

Govil's parents were long dead, and his only sister had also died prematurely. His daughter's death shook him deeply. He concluded that it was due to his own 'culpable mistakes'. What had he done wrong, he now asked Gandhi. Should he have taken the sick girl to another doctor? Now that she was dead, how could he atone (*prayaschitta*) for his sins? How could he 'in any way help her soul to get rest and stay in Heaven'?

Gandhi replied to Govil that he was 'quite right' in trusting the doctor he went to; Gandhi did not believe 'in constant change of doctors and hakims. No *prayaschitta* was required because 'there was no carelessness on your part'. Other doctors may not have been able to save her; indeed, 'in spite of the ablest expert help kings have to die'. No one could give rest to another soul; Govil's daughter's 'rest will come from herself'. Finally, the best way for survivors to 'help their departed dear ones' was 'by weaving into our own lives all that was good in them'.

To his own sons Gandhi could be harsh, even cruel. And yet, he could be extraordinarily compassionate to strangers. In its nobility and generosity, this letter to a grief-stricken father was very special indeed.[7]

II

In the days following Gandhi's arrest, the Bombay government received a series of unusual requests. A Parsi schoolteacher from

Khandwa in the Central Provinces asked for permission to spend his summer vacation 'as companion reader' to Gandhi in jail. He wished to read to him 'Persian and Urdu literature which contains many philosophical principles which if followed by the people, administration and statesmen will change the world for the better'. A Muslim artist from Bombay wanted the government 'to find out from Gandhiji if he would be willing to give me a few sittings'. He would come up to Poona at times convenient to Gandhi, and 'not impose on him any particular pose or cause him any worry'. Neither request was forwarded by the government.

However, some religious books posted or hand-delivered by admirers were passed on to the prisoner. So was a basket of fruits sent from Ahmedabad by the wife of Ambalal Sarabhai.[8]

In late July 1930, the *Bombay Chronicle* reported that while on occasion Gandhi had used the Singer sewing machine, he had not yet 'mastered its technicalities'. This prompted the company which made these machines to write to the jail authorities, asking for permission to send one of their experts to teach Gandhi 'the thorough and efficient use of the Sewing Machine'. Some Congress activists in Bombay had campaigned against the Singer machine on the grounds that it was British-made. By persuading Gandhi to like it even more than he did presently, Singer hoped to counteract this propaganda.

Singer assured the British government of their loyalty. Any employee 'effecting an anti-Government feeling or joining the Political Extremist Party', the company wrote, 'will be immediately dropped from service'. However, they added, since 'Mr. Gandhi does not have any prejudice against the Singer Sewing Machine, and that he uses one, or attempts to, for his personal use and pastime, we thought that if we might be allowed to extend to Mr. Gandhi the same courtesies that we do, in fact, extend to any other person desirous of learning the art of sewing this would help us materially in holding our large Organization contented and satisfied, to keep out of political activity'.[9]

The request was cleverly crafted, but the government turned it down. Perhaps they were short-sighted in not recognizing the propaganda value of a rebel against the Raj, a proponent of swadeshi, perfecting the use of a (non-violent and economically productive) British-made machine.

III

In July 1930, the novelist Arthur Conan Doyle died. Even if Gandhi read about it in the papers, it is unlikely he took much notice. However, an admirer of the creator of Sherlock Holmes now wrote to Gandhi from Banaras, saying that since Conan Doyle had spent time in South Africa during the Anglo-Boer War, 'you must have had some acquaintance, if not intimate friendship, with him. Thus I feel impelled to crave your indulgence to write a short article on the life and work of this great man and forward the same on to me so that I may have it published in [the] papers. I hope you have sufficient time these days to devote a few minutes to this all important piece of business. I trust I voice the feelings of untold novel-reading millions in both the hemispheres.'

Gandhi was not really a novel-reader, and even if he did occasionally read fiction, it was not murder mysteries. And there is no record of his having met Conan Doyle. So, it is unlikely that he would have complied with the request. But he surely would have written another article asked for by a correspondent, had that request been forwarded to him. This came from an admirer of Narayana Guru, living in the town of Alleppey. The correspondent was, he told Gandhi, aware that 'it is the duty of every Indian to give you complete rest now', but still, 'the exigency of the matter' compelled him to make this request, which was that Gandhi write and 'send a short appreciation of Swamiji' for inclusion in a planned pictorial book on Narayana Guru (who had died in 1928). Sadly, the request was withheld, thus depriving posterity of a printed assessment by one remarkable social reformer of another.[10]

The American novelist Upton Sinclair wrote to the jail superintendent in Yerwada, enclosing copies of his books *Mammonart* and *Mental Radio*. The first he described as 'a study of literature from the point of view of economics', and the second as narrating 'experiments conducted by my wife and myself in telepathy, or mind reading'. Sinclair hoped the authorities would pass on these novels to Gandhi, since 'neither book contains any reference to India or Indian affairs'.[11]

They did, and Gandhi read them almost at once, writing back to Sinclair that 'I read your Mammonart with absorbing interest and

Mental Radio with curiosity. The former has given me much to think, the latter did not interest me. Nobody in India would, I think, doubt the possibility of telepathy but most would doubt the wisdom of its material use.'[12]

Another letter came from a certain M. Pels, the railway stationmaster of Pretoria in South Africa. He reminded Gandhi that they had been introduced to each other by Henry Polak back in 1907 or 1908, and had subsequently met several times at stations where Pels was posted. The stationmaster had recently read in the *Rand Daily Mail* that Gandhi had been 'cured of an old remedy of yours, Viz. "Blood Pressure"'. The South African had been suffering from the same malady for years; even going on a vegetarian diet had not cured it. Would Gandhi, from his prison cell now perhaps 'feel disposed to favour' him with advice, for which he would 'be extremely grateful'?[13]

The letter was not forwarded to Gandhi by the jail authorities. Also kept from him was a letter by a Maharashtrian from Bombay named Jayaram Jadhav. This presented Muslims and Christians as enemies of Hindus. 'Who can say,' he told Gandhi, 'that you are not aware that the dispute between the Hindus and the Musalmans is growing day by day? Besides, owing to the encouragement of the present rulers the number of Indian Christians has been increasing among us Hindus and the number of Hindus has been dwindling down. These are the two powerful communities which are snatching morsels of flesh among the Hindu community and you also know that their powers of digestion is sufficiently intensive to assimilate the snatched morsels of flesh.'

The patriot from Bombay told Gandhi that 'the English are sure to go sooner or later. Granting that they go from here or we drive them away, shall we be able to carry on the administration of India? I think internal dissensions will increase here and a civil war will commence. Hindus and Mussalmans will first fight for supremacy and if the Hindus are successful they will again fight amongst themselves and there will be terrible bloodshed. . . . There is only one remedy if this is to be avoided and that is . . . to cause the Hindus to venerate one God, one Ved and one caste, that is to say they must merge together. There should be no reservation of powers or places, they should freely interdine and intermarry. Even their language and dress should be common.'

The letter writer told Gandhi that 'if you desire to do permanent good to India, you had better follow the path indicated by me but if you simply wish that your name should be applauded by the people, then the tall talk about independence is sufficiently good'.[14]

How might Gandhi have responded to this letter had he received it? He would have endorsed the opposition to caste discrimination, though perhaps not the wholesale uniformity in dress, language, and the like, that the correspondent advocated. And he would have disagreed with the demonization of Indians who were not Hindus. For Gandhi, Muslims and Christians were as much part of the nation-in-the-making as Hindus. Seeing them as foreigners, or as susceptible to foreign influences, was, so to say, 'foreign' to his way of thinking.

IV

Despite the leader's arrest, the civil disobedience movement continued. Gandhi had designated the respected former judge Abbas Tyabji his successor as 'dictator' of the Salt Satyagraha. Tyabji was arrested in turn, whereupon the leadership passed on to Sarojini Naidu.

Gandhi had hoped to raid the major salt works run by the government in Dharasana. With him behind bars, Mrs Naidu went there instead. 'The sudden and spectacular attack on the Dharasana Salt Works on the 21st of May,' observed a police report, 'was made by some 3,000 volunteers comprising satyagrahis from all parts of Gujarat and from Bombay encouraged by several thousand sight-seers.' The satyagrahis were met at the venue by a large contingent of police—the two sides battling for several hours. In the evening, another large body of volunteers arrived and a fresh attempt was made to rush the salt works. Several hundred satyagrahis were injured, with even the police admitting that there was 'universal condemnation of all Government measures in the press'.[15]

And not just the Indian press. Among the journalists at Dharasana was Webb Miller of the United Press International. Miller arrived too late to see or meet the Mahatma, but he was able to witness the stoic determination of his followers. The report he cabled back was partly censored by the British authorities. But even this expurgated account conveyed the intensity of the protests and the savagery of the repression. As the satyagrahis proceeded towards the salt pans, wrote Miller: 'The police kicked and prodded the non-violent raiders who swarmed the depot. . . . The spectacle of them beating the unresisting volunteers was so painful [that] I was frequently forced to turn away from the crowd.'[16]

Webb Miller's reports brought other American journalists to India. Arriving in Bombay in June, Negley Farson of the *Chicago Daily News* witnessed a police attack on a demonstration whose leader and many participants were Sikh. 'It was terrible,' cabled Farson. 'I stood within five feet of the Sikh leader as he took the *lathi* blows. He was a short heavily muscled man, like one of the old Greek gods.'

'The blows came,' continued Farson, but the Sikh

> stood straight. His turban was knocked off. The long black hair was bared with the round top-knot. He closed his eyes as the blows fell—until at last he swayed and fell to the ground.
>
> No other Sikhs had tried to shield him, but now, showing their defiance, and their determination to die rather than move, they wiped away the blood streaming from his mouth. Hysterical Hindus rushed to him bearing cakes of ice to rub the contusions over his eyes. The Sikh gave me a bloody smile—and stood up for more.
>
> For two long hours these unbelievable scenes went on. Then, at last, came the blessed rain, the monsoon like a healing balm.[17]

The accounts by Miller and Farson of how Gandhi's men and women bore beatings and courted arrest were printed around the world, garnering wide attention to, and sympathy for, the civil disobedience movement.

V

The movement was perhaps most successful in Gandhi's native Gujarat. One indication was the widespread resignation of government-appointed officials, inspired or challenged by their fellows to sunder ties with the Raj. In Surat district, 334 out of 760 village headmen resigned. The figures for Broach were 160 out of 545; in Kaira, 222 out of 665. In Bardoli taluk of Surat district, 57 per cent of land revenue remained uncollected, the figure rising to 67 per cent in Kaira's Mehmedabad taluk. In Bardoli, a police report grimly noted: 'The hostile attitude of all the inhabitants is such that, even in cases of serious crimes such as murder, all assistance and information is refused to the authorities.'[18]

Indians in other provinces were also active. A report from Madras in July noted that 'certain Tamil districts still show signs of restlessness'. In Malabar and South Kanara, there was much picketing of liquor stalls. In Guntur, district officials resigned in large numbers, while peasants refused to pay forest-grazing fees.

Other reports spoke of regular meetings, bandhs and hartals in Bombay, Karachi and Ahmedabad, with 'bands of people who go round in small processions singing songs to encourage the movement'. In the Deccan, there was an 'extensive outbreak' of violations of the forest law, and the hoisting of the Congress flag on schools and offices.

On 5 July, some four hundred people marched towards Yerwada jail to pay their respects to Gandhi on the completion of his second month in prison. The marchers were stopped by the police at the Bund Bridge, a mile away from the jail. They refused to turn back, squatting on the road in protest. Word of the impasse spread, with many more people gathering in support. When the crowd swelled, to what the police considered alarming proportions (estimates varied from two to ten thousand), they were dispersed with lathis.[19]

In 1920–22, the people of the princely states had stayed out of the non-cooperation movement. This time, as a government report noted in alarm, 'there are signs of sympathy with the agitation in British India spreading amongst the people in the larger States, and a great deal of seditious literature is finding its way into them'. In Rajkot's King Alfred High School, where Gandhi had once studied, the students 'continue[d] to give a lot of trouble', observing 'hartals on every possible occasion' and urging students of other schools in the town to likewise boycott classes.[20]

In 1920–22, women had also stayed out of the struggle. This time, they participated in large numbers. Throughout India, college girls made and sold contraband salt, picketed liquor stores, and organized processions known as *prabhat pheries* where patriotic songs were sung. Housewives and women professionals also joined them. Hundreds of women were arrested during the various breaches of the Salt Act, some signing the jail register simply as 'Miss Satyagrahi'. An intelligence bureau officer reported on 10 July that 'the awakening among women is something that I am told has taken Congressmen themselves by surprise'.[21]

VI

In the middle of July 1930, the Moderate politicians Tej Bahadur Sapru and M.R. Jayakar wrote to the viceroy asking for permission to see Gandhi in prison. The Labour government now in power was convening a round table conference in London to discuss India's constitutional future. Sapru and Jayakar were to attend; they hoped to persuade Irwin to release Gandhi so that he could come too.

The viceroy had seen how he had grievously underestimated Gandhi's popularity among his fellow Indians. The publicity garnered by Gandhi in America had also found its way back to the Viceregal Palace. So, Irwin now granted Sapru and Jayakar permission to visit Yerwada prison. They did, in the last week of July, and had long conversations with Gandhi, who said he would agree to attend the Round Table Conference only if the viceroy accepted full self-government as a goal, removed the penal application of the salt tax, and freed all political prisoners.

On 14 and 15 August, a further discussion took place in Yerwada, with Sapru and Jayakar on one side and Gandhi, the Nehrus, Vallabhbhai Patel and several other senior Congressmen (all transported by the government from their respective prisons) on the other. Afterwards, the Congress leaders wrote to Sapru and Jayakar saying that 'the time is not yet ripe for securing a settlement honourable for our country'. They took issue with the viceroy's description of the Salt Satyagraha as 'ill-timed' and 'unconstitutional', for it had been

Gandhi and Kasturba, shortly after their return from South Africa in 1915. The person standing, wearing a white turban, is the Madras publisher G.A. Natesan.

Gandhi's home, Hriday Kunj, in the Sabarmati Ashram, where he lived (when not in jail or on the road) between 1917 and 1930.

Bal Gangadhar Tilak, the great militant nationalist, whose death in 1920 allowed Gandhi to emerge as the unchallenged leader of the freedom movement.

Saraladevi Chaudhrani, with whom Gandhi once contemplated a 'spiritual marriage', photographed with her sister (*seated*).

The poet Rabindranath Tagore, a close friend and colleague, with whom Gandhi had several constructive (and instructive) arguments.

Gandhi's companion and political lieutenant, Vallabhbhai Patel, photographed at the time of the Bardoli Satyagraha in 1928, proudly bearing a peasant's moustache (which he later discarded).

Motilal Nehru, the lawyer-constitutionalist with whom Gandhi worked closely in the 1920s; here seen unusually without a moustache.

Gandhi with Jamnalal Bajaj, the businessman-turned-freedom fighter whom he thought of as his fifth son.

Maulana Azad, the leading Muslim Congressman and a member of Gandhi's inner circle for three decades.

C.F. (Charlie) Andrews, Gandhi's closest English friend, a bridge-builder between the nationalists and the Raj, known as 'Deenbandhu', friend of the poor and lowly in India and everywhere else.

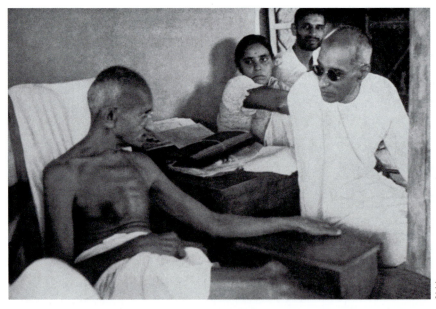

Gandhi with Chakravarti Rajagopalachari (Rajaji), his Southern Commander, a scholar-patriot whom he once referred to as 'the keeper of my conscience'.

Gandhi with the pre-eminent female Congress leader, the poet (and wit) Sarojini Naidu.

EAST & WEST.

An Indian artist's representation of Gandhi's meeting with King George V, London, 1931.

महात्मा गान्धी और सम्राट पंचम जार्ज की भेंट ।   J.P.C.S. 204.

Gandhi with the Nobel Prize–winning novelist Romain Rolland, who wrote an adulatory book about him.

Gandhi with millworkers in Lancashire, 1931. The lady in a shawl and with her hair covered is Madeleine Slade (Mirabehn), his adopted English daughter.

Everybody But Gandhi!

The Mahatma chooses to spin his own.. such as it is..
and that's *his* business! *He* needn't read this ad. But
all the rest of you gentlemen prefer to wear suits..
good suits.. and that's *our* business. So between here
and the next station, cast your eye carefully over the
most satisfying news in today's paper..7 straight facts
about the SAKSTON.. created and sold exclusively by
Saks · 34 · Street.

SAKSTON is celanese-lined and hand-tailored throughout; it has the set and feel of a suit put together by
tailors who know their job.

SAKSTON fabrics have all passed, with honors, strict
laboratory tests for quality and wearing power.

SAKSTON offers one of the largest selections of patterns and shades in the country.

SAKSTON includes two pairs of trousers with each suit.

SAKSTON comes in *every size*.. it fits the generous
type who can give two women a seat in the subway, and
those who are strictly in West Point shape.. and everybody between.

SAKSTON is 100% *right!* We're so certain of that,
that we promise to refund your money.. if you're not
satisfied, bring the suit right back.

Seventh and not least.. SAKSTON is correctly priced!
Low enough to fit the prevailing budget-trouble.. high
enough to assure you famous Saks quality.

SAKS
34 STREET
AT BROADWAY

MEN'S CLOTHING .. SIXTH FLOOR

37.50

NMML

An advertisement in the *New York Times*, circa 1931, referring knowledgeably
(and humorously) to Gandhi's scanty attire.

(By arrangement with the "Evening Standard.")

A cartoon by Low, circa late 1932, from a British newspaper, perhaps the *Evening Standard*.

The hut in the Sevagram Ashram where Gandhi lived (when not in jail or on the road) from 1936 to 1946.

entirely peaceful. 'The wonderful mass response to the movement', insisted Gandhi and his colleagues, was 'its sufficient justification'.

In early September, Sapru and Jayakar travelled again to Poona, where they had three days of conversations with Gandhi. The discussions went nowhere, for, as Gandhi put it, there was 'no meeting ground between the Government and the Indian National Congress'.[22]

Other Indian leaders were keen to attend the Round Table Conference. Among them was M.A. Jinnah, who, before leaving for London, called on the viceroy. Irwin wrote later to Stanley Baldwin that he had 'met very few Indians with a more acute intellect or a more independent outlook—not of course that he always sees eye to eye with Government! But he is not lacking in moral courage, has been outspoken against civil disobedience and is genuinely anxious to find the way to settlement.'[23]

The Round Table Conference began in London on 12 November 1930. In attendance were leaders of the Liberals, the Muslim League, the Hindu Mahasabha, the Depressed Classes and the princes. Among the subjects discussed were the rights of minorities, the creation of a federation in which British India would be partnered by princely India, and the question of whether India was ready for adult suffrage.[24]

The conference was a flop. One reason was the absence of any representative from the Congress, the most important political party in India. A second was the reactionary attitude of some British politicians, who seemed to rely 'for their policy towards India on the knowledge of that country possessed by Rudyard Kipling'.[25] A third was the failure to find any common ground between India's two major religious communities. As the undersecretary of state for India wrote to the viceroy: 'Both Hindus and Muslims at present appear to regard their differences as irreconcilable.'[26]

Among the influential Muslims at the conference was the nawab of Bhopal. Writing to the viceroy on 19 December, he blamed the failure to reach a Hindu–Muslim settlement on 'the extremists among the Hindus, who, saturated as they are by the Congress mentality of destruction and chaos, would not have a solution except on their own terms'. Despite this failure, added the nawab, 'it is a matter of great satisfaction that the Muslim solidly stands as a great Imperial asset, a powerful force for peace and order'. His own 'anxiety' was that 'nothing should happen at this stage which would drive the Muslims in a body, or even a portion of them, into the arms of the Congress . . .'[27]

This was a letter striking in its candour. The nawab did not want the British rule to end, did not want Muslims and Hindus to find a common cause, did not, in fact, want devolution of power from the British to Indians or from the princes to their subjects.

In the last week of December 1930, the annual conference of the Muslim League was held in Allahabad. With many of the League's leaders away in the United Kingdom, Muhammad Iqbal was asked to be president. An acclaimed poet in Persian and Urdu, Iqbal had taken a doctorate in philosophy from the University of Munich. Influenced by European philosophers such as Nietzsche in his youth, he became increasingly interested in the history and philosophy of Islam as he grew older.

In addressing the Muslim League, Iqbal had chosen to speak in English, his preferred language of scholarly discourse. He began by deploring the 'mistaken separation' of the spiritual and temporal realms in modern Europe, which had 'resulted practically in the total exclusion of Christianity from the life of European states'. Iqbal believed that 'religion is a power of the utmost importance in the life of individuals as well as states'.

Iqbal argued that the 'principle of European democracy cannot be applied to India without recognising the fact of communal groups'. As a major group in British India, the Muslims deserved and should demand their own political unit, whose geographical boundaries he went on to sketch. 'I would like,' said the poet, 'to see the Punjab, North-West Frontier Province, Sind and Baluchistan amalgamated into a single state. Self-Government within the British Empire, or without the British Empire, the formation of a consolidated North-West Indian Muslim state appears to be the final destiny of the Muslims at least of North-west India.'[28]

A large crowd had gathered to hear Iqbal speak in Allahabad. But they had come to listen to his poetry, not his political prescriptions. The speech went over their heads, not least because it was in English.

After he had finished, the audience shouted in Urdu for Iqbal to recite poetry. At first he declined, but as the clamour grew louder, he recited a few short verses 'in a subdued voice and without any interest', and sat down again.[29]

In jail, Gandhi had been permitted to receive newspapers. It is likely that they printed at least an abbreviated account of Iqbal's presidential address, and that he read this. Since he wasn't allowed to comment on political matters, there is no reference to it in his letters from prison. If he did indeed read it (albeit in a condensed version), it is likely that he was struck, perhaps even shaken, by it. For more than two decades now, the leaders of the Muslim League had been asking for a greater share of political power. However, their demands had been couched in terms of a greater reservation of seats in legislatures, more jobs in government, the protection of Urdu and of personal laws. Never before had they gone so far as to demand a separate state or nation. Although little noticed at the time, Muhammad Iqbal's Allahabad address marked a major turning point in the history of Hindu–Muslim relations in British India.

VII

While Gandhi was in jail, his autobiography finally appeared in the West. The Indian edition had been abridged by its editor, C.F. Andrews. He left out, among other things, the chapters on brahmacharya and fasting from *My Experiments with Truth*, while adding some material from Gandhi's South African memoir and his essays in *Young India*. This amended, reworked, autobiography was published in September 1930 under the title *Mahatma Gandhi: His Own Story*, by George Allen and Unwin in the United Kingdom (priced at 12s 6d), and by Macmillan in the United States (priced at $2.50).

In his introduction to the volume, Andrews remarked: 'One may search the pages of history in vain to find any man in any age— religious teacher, military conqueror, political statesman—who has held at one time so vast a power over so many human beings during his own lifetime. The man who sees no power in Gandhi is the man who knows no power save that of the ballot box and the battlefield.'[30]

An early, and critical, review of the book was by the Oxford scholar Quintin Hogg. Hogg's main charge was that Gandhi was

> unable to rest in a moderate opinion in any subject in which he is interested. He becomes a violent partisan of meat-eating, and again an extreme vegetarian . . . He seems to see no alternative between treating a wife 'as the object of her husband's lust' and vowing a vow of permanent abstinence. . . . Either he must regard the British Empire as so beneficent as to render it his duty to oppose even righteous rebellion (his attitude towards the Zulu revolt) or else British Government is entirely satanic. There is no alternative between active assistance and 'non-cooperation'.[31]

Somewhat more sympathetic to the book (and the author) was another Oxford scholar, Edward Thompson, who had spent some years as a college teacher in Bengal. Thompson remarked that Gandhi was 'devastatingly frank about his home, his father's courage, integrity and moral weakness; he is no less frank about his own faults and slips'. He presciently added that 'the subject himself has set on record all the materials for the inevitable "debunking" process which time will bring'.

Thompson thought Gandhi's economic ideas out of date and his political programme inconsistent. Nonetheless, 'his thinking matters because it has an elemental quality; he has so identified himself with his poorer fellow-countrymen that it is communal, not personal. In him centuries of oppression and weakness have found their voice. The reason for his overwhelming influence—so much greater than that of other Indian politicians with superior qualities of intellect or expository skill—emerges from his own story. There has hardly been a man who trusted his own intellect so absolutely, unless it was Socrates. This has simplified his life as nothing else could have done, and enabled him to sweep aside the opinions of subtler men and make them act upon his own.'[32]

The anonymous reviewer of the London *Times* likewise found Gandhi's account of his life 'exceptionally frank, even after the torrent of self-revelation by Great War veterans, actresses, and politicians'. The reader, he added, 'will experience many sensations—

astonishment, sympathy, disgust, admiration—but the last will survive when he remembers how few writers of autobiography would have made no attempt to gloss over their own baser episodes . . .'[33]

The candidness of Gandhi's exposition was also admired on the other side of the Atlantic. A New York reviewer remarked that the book was 'an almost incredible autobiography, so remote is it from our competitive world in its philosophy, so overwhelming in its simplicity, so discerning in its confession of blunders . . .'[34] A Methodist journal was impressed by 'Mr. Gandhi's ability to make and to hold friends of all sorts and conditions, Hindus, Christians, Moslems, and irrespective of race'.[35]

One last American appreciation must be noticed. This was not of Gandhi's autobiography but of his political career as a whole. It was printed in the newsmagazine Time, which, in the early months of 1930, had been so witheringly contemptuous of Gandhi and his march to the sea.

In December 1930, Time's editors sat down to choose their Man of the Year. The contenders included the golfer Bobby Jones, who had won all four major championships; Sinclair Lewis, who in the year just ended had become the first American to win the Nobel Prize in literature; Joseph Stalin, who by purging his politburo of all rivals was now 'absolute master of some 150,000,000 people'; and the 'world's most potent criminal', Al Capone, who had in 1930 been freed from prison.

While acknowledging the achievements (admirable or despicable) of Jones and Lewis, Stalin and Capone, Time concluded that 'curiously, it was in a jail that the year's end found the little half naked brown man whose 1930 mark on world history will undoubtedly loom largest of all'. The magazine recalled the Congress's declaration of independence in January 1930, the Salt March two months later, and Gandhi's arrest in May. As Time's first issue for 1931 went to press, Gandhi was still in jail, 'and some 30,000 members of his Independence movement were caged elsewhere. The British Empire was still wondering fearfully what to do with them all, the Empire's most staggering problem.' Outside the prisons, 'for Mr. Gandhi, for the Mahatma, for St. Gandhi, for Jailbird Gandhi not thousands but millions of Indians are taking individual beatings which they could escape by paying what His Majesty's Government calls, quite accurately, "normal taxes"'.[36]

And so Mohandas K. Gandhi was chosen *Time*'s Man of the Year for 1930. Himself in jail at the time, Gandhi did not read this mea culpa, but perhaps his foremost American admirer did, and felt suitably vindicated. Back in May, when Gandhi was arrested, John Haynes Holmes had written to Romain Rolland, his co-chairman as it were of the Global Gandhi Fan Club: 'I know that you are feeling as I do about the Indian situation. I can think of little else, and wish that I were more free of all my routine responsibilities that I might give all my thought and work to the support of Gandhi's cause. The Mahatma looms today a more sublime figure than ever, and justifies anew our firm conviction that he is the "greatest man in the world".'[37]

CHAPTER EIGHTEEN

Parleys with Proconsuls

I

The year 1931 began with Gandhi still in prison. In the months he had been in jail, he had spun a good amount of yarn, which he wanted to send to Ahmedabad to be woven into saris for his wife. The government, somewhat pettily, declined to do so.[1]

On 25 January, Kasturba addressed a meeting of women in Borsad, who had gathered to protest police excesses. She also visited some villages. Afterwards, she issued a press statement, in whose drafting perhaps her son Devadas had a hand. The statement read:

> Wherever I went, I saw marks of lathi blows on chest, back, head, waist, and leg . . . I was doubly grieved on hearing that police caned children, pulled women by the hair, dealt fist blows on breasts of women, and uttered indecent abuses to women. The fact that there are such policemen in India, points out the black spot of our society.
>
> This is the first occasion in my life, when I have seen such inhuman treatment meted out to ladies in Gujarat. Nowhere in India have I seen such brutalities perpetrated on women by the police.[2]

The day after Kasturba issued this statement, her husband was released. After the failure of the Round Table Conference, Ramsay

MacDonald had urged Irwin to begin talks with Gandhi. The release order was issued from Delhi; and at 11 a.m. on 26 January, Gandhi came out of Yerwada a free man.[3]

Speaking to the Associated Press, Gandhi said he had 'come out of jail with an absolutely open mind, unfettered by enmity, unbiased in argument and prepared to study the whole situation from every point of view . . .' He added, however, that all prisoners connected with the civil disobedience movement 'should be liberated immediately'.[4]

Gandhi took the train from Poona to Bombay. On his arrival in India's *urbs prima*, he was met by a large crowd, who took him in a procession to Dhobitalao. Gandhi then went on to Mani Bhavan (the home of his friend Revashankar Jagjivan), where he usually stayed when in the city. Here, too, 'large crowds besieged the building throughout the day to receive his "darshan"'.[5]

After a day in Bombay, Gandhi left for Allahabad, to attend a meeting of the CWC. On 1 February, he wrote to the viceroy saying that he 'was simply waiting for a sign in order to enable me to respond to your appeal' (for talks). But the signs he currently saw were 'highly ominous'. He gave several examples from around India of unprovoked police attacks on 'wholly defenceless and innocent women'. (The viceroy's secretary, replying on his behalf, said he saw 'no profit in the general exploration of charges and counter-charges'.)[6]

While her husband was closeted with his colleagues in Allahabad, Kasturba arrived in Bombay, to participate in a public meeting to protest the police brutalities in Gujarat. The meeting was held on 4 February. In attendance were wives of three men knighted by the British—one Muslim, one Hindu, one Parsi—as well as 'women of all classes and communities'. The report in the *Bombay Chronicle* said that 'Shrimati Kasturba Gandhi presided but owing to some trouble in the throat she could not speak'. This sounds like it must have been an alibi—always an unwilling and indifferent public speaker, Kasturba might have been intimidated by the presence of the bejewelled women around her.

Kasturba's speech was read out for her by one Kusumben Desai. It said their struggle was based on truth and non-violence, and thanked the women of Bombay for so spontaneously sympathizing with 'their village sisters' by raising a 'united protest against the atrocities of [the] police in a distant place like Borsad'.[7]

During the Rowlatt satyagraha and the non-cooperation movement, Kasturba Gandhi had stayed out of the public eye. So had women in general, with exceptions such as the emancipated and very westernized Sarojini Naidu. But in this new round of civil disobedience, women had energetically come forward to participate. Seeing college girls shout slogans and court arrest, Kasturba had decided she must play her part too.

II

Gandhi, meanwhile, was still in Allahabad, where Motilal Nehru had fallen seriously ill. On 4 February, the family decided to take Motilal to Lucknow, a city with more advanced medical facilities. Gandhi accompanied them. The journey by road, however, had been too much for the patient to take. On the morning of the 6th, Motilal died, his son and his wife at his side. He was sixty-nine.[8]

Motilal's death affected Gandhi deeply. In the next few days he spoke at several memorial meetings in Allahabad, and spent time with the bereaved family. On the 14th—a week after Motilal's death— he wrote to the viceroy asking for an interview. 'I am aware of the responsibility resting on my shoulders,' remarked Gandhi. 'It is heightened by the death of Pandit Motilal Nehru. I feel that without personal contact and heart to heart talk with you, the advice I give my co-workers may not be right.'

In the course of his life, Motilal Nehru had moved from working in assemblies and committees to courting arrest under Gandhi's direction; his death prompted his friend in turn to learn lessons from him. Now that Motilal was gone, Gandhi found it prudent to eschew struggle and return to the path of dialogue and reconciliation.[9]

Gandhi's decision to sue for peace may also have been influenced by a letter from Henry Polak. Shortly after Gandhi's release from prison, Polak wrote to him that 'you have no conception of the enormous change that has occurred in public opinion here since the

Round Table Conference opened'. An optimistic Polak believed that 'the imperialists and reactionaries are thoroughly discredited'. He thought there would soon be a consensus on the creation of 'Indian legislatures to which Indian Cabinets will be responsible'. As he wrote to Gandhi: 'If what you wanted when you set out upon your recent programme was a change of heart on the part of the British people, there can, in my opinion, be no doubt that you have got it.'[10]

When Gandhi wired the viceroy saying he would like to meet, Irwin wired back asking him to come the following week. So on 27 February—just short of a year since he began his march to the sea—Gandhi visited the Viceregal Palace, where, for three consecutive days, he spoke for several hours with Lord Irwin. The discussion ranged widely. Among the topics covered were the suspension of civil disobedience, the release of satyagrahis, the status of princely states, and the next Round Table Conference, due to be held towards the end of 1931, and at which the viceroy hoped the Congress would send a large delegation, led by Gandhi himself.

Gandhi told Mahadev Desai that 'the Viceroy desires peace because he has been touched by the struggle'. For his part, he told the viceroy: 'How can I sever my connection with you? I have so many English friends. Take for instance Mirabehn. I don't know her family and her father and yet she has completely lost herself in me. Andrews keeps sending me cables from Cape Town asking me to arrive at a settlement. How can I give up this Andrews?'

On their next meeting, Gandhi said any settlement would depend on the release of satyagrahis, the repeal or relaxation of the salt laws, and the government's recognition that peaceful picketing of shops stocking liquor and foreign goods would continue. When Gandhi assured the viceroy that picketing would be peaceful, Irwin answered that 'people were in too excitable a temper for so simple and speedy a transition as he contemplated from one sort of picketing to another to be possible'.

On salt, Irwin noted that Gandhi 'attached far greater importance to it than I had expected, and I imagine that it is mostly vanity'. The viceroy said the government could not publicly condone the breaking of the salt law, but might extend certain privileges. He asked Gandhi to suggest means whereby this compromise could be effected. Later, the viceroy noted: 'I think it may be necessary to do something to meet him on Salt.'

Gandhi also raised the question of Bhagat Singh, the revolutionary sentenced to death for his participation in acts of violence. Bhagat Singh's writings were then widely in circulation; they showed him to be a young man of uncommon intelligence and patriotism. Public sympathy for him was very high. Gandhi told the viceroy that if he postponed or retracted the execution, 'it would have an influence for peace'. Irwin was impressed that 'the apostle of non-violence should so earnestly be pleading the cause of a creed so fundamentally opposite to his own'.[11]

In this second meeting, Gandhi found the viceroy 'more cautious'. He thought 'the Viceroy was convinced of the justice of all our demands, but he talked of administrative difficulties'. One exchange recounted by Gandhi was particularly revealing. The viceroy anxiously asked: 'Now tell me whether I did not do well in arresting you in your Ashram?' Gandhi answered that the night before the march began he expected to be arrested on the morrow, but as an experienced jailbird he 'peacefully went to sleep'. Thereupon the viceroy said: 'You planned a fine strategy round the issue of salt.'

In their final interview, Irwin asked Gandhi to stay on in Delhi for some time, while he conferred with members of his executive council, spoke with provincial governors, and reported back to London on their discussions. He also asked Gandhi to consult with the CWC.[12]

In the first week of March, various drafts of an agreement between Gandhi and Irwin passed between the Government of India and the CWC. On 5 March, the *Gazette of India* published the terms of what became known as the 'Gandhi–Irwin Pact'. This stated, to begin with, that civil disobedience had been suspended, with the Congress to participate in the next Round Table Conference to discuss India's constitutional future.

The settlement made no promise about 'Dominion Status', still less 'Purna Swaraj'. This represented a climbdown from the stated position of the Congress. On the other hand, the government would allow picketing of liquor stalls and shops selling foreign goods, on the condition that it was 'unaggressive' and did not involve 'coercion, intimidation, restraint, hostile demonstration, [or] obstruction to the public'. Convicted satyagrahis would be released, and pending prosecutions withdrawn. Finally, while the government could not 'in the present financial conditions of the country, make substantial modifications in the Salt Act', it would permit villagers to collect salt for domestic consumption.

In a statement released the day the settlement was made public, Gandhi called it one which had left both parties victorious. He thanked the viceroy for his 'inexhaustible patience and equally inexhaustible industry and unfailing courtesy'. He then reiterated the Congress's and India's commitment to swaraj, deploring the fact that 'throughout the settlement one misses that enchanting word. The clause which carefully hides that word is capable, and intentionally capable, of a double meaning.'

Gandhi's statement ended with three appeals, to three sets of people. He asked the police and civil service to act as servants, not masters, of the citizens they were supposed to serve but often tended to lord over. He appealed to those who sought India's liberty through armed struggle to desist from violence, 'if not yet out of conviction, then out of expedience'. And he appealed 'to the people of the great American Republic and the other nations of the earth. I know that this struggle based as it is on truth and non-violence from which, alas, we the votaries have on occasion undoubtedly strayed, has fired their imagination and excited their curiosity. From curiosity they, and specially America, has progressed to tangible help in the way of sympathy.'

Gandhi hoped that in the days to come, the Congress would retain this sympathy. If 'India reaches her destiny through truth and non-violence', he remarked, 'she will have made no small contribution to the world peace for which all the nations of the earth are thirsting and she would also have, in that case, made some slight return for the help that those nations have been freely giving to her'.[13]

III

Following his settlement with Irwin, Gandhi received a spate of congratulatory messages from across India. A Hindu priest in

Thiruttani said he was praying 'for your long life as you are Kaliyug Rama'. S.A. Brelvi, editor of the *Bombay Chronicle*, told Gandhi that this was 'your greatest triumph'. Long-time colleagues like A.V. Thakkar and Asaf Ali also sent congratulatory messages. And then there was one from his closest English friend, sent from Cape Town, reading, simply, 'Thank God. Charlie'.[14]

There was praise unqualified, and there was advice on how to proceed further. A wire from Madras told Gandhi that the Depressed Classes 'expects much from you for its amelioration requests you to advocate separate electorates special privileges at Round Table Conference'. It added: 'Please stay in Depressed Classes Quarters when you visit Madras to know about them.'[15]

Muslim scholars wrote to Gandhi urging that the rights of minorities be protected in any future constitution for a free India. A maulana in Delhi wanted assurances that (1) Muslim places of worship and religious practice would be absolutely free of government interference; (2) the Government would not interfere with Muslim Personal Law which should, as before, be based on the principles of the Sharia; (3) the government should appoint Muslim judges in civil courts, to preside over cases involving Muslims or where Islamic law had a bearing.[16]

Some Muslims asked Gandhi not to encourage minority separatism. The rising Bombay lawyer M.C. Chagla urged him to 'remain strong on the question of joint electorates'. The national interest was not being served by separate electorates; in fact, said Chagla, these were 'harmful to Muslims themselves'.[17]

Gandhi received many messages urging him to persuade the viceroy not to execute Bhagat Singh. He was asked by Hindus, Sikhs, and even the odd Muslim to help save the revolutionary's life. Some letters from admirers of Bhagat Singh were humanitarian in nature; others, strongly ideological. A letter signed 'A Revolutionary' charged Gandhi with having betrayed the masses by his settlement with the viceroy. The radical set out his group's differences with the Congress:

> Hollow high sounding Government privileges do not make us dance
> with ecstasy. We are common human beings. We are not Christs or

Chaitanyas. And we know that murder only of oppressors can give
our Motherland a bit of relief, which no amount of boycott threats
or civil disobedience can do. Disobedience to law . . . can never
unnerve our enemy . . . Hence indiscriminate murder of Europeans
is the only panacea for the malady which is eating away the very
vitality of our nation everyday.

The most poignant mail, however, was this one:
   'Just received viceroy's order relations mercy appeal rejected last
interview bhagat singh twenty third'. It was signed: 'Kishan Singh,
Father of Bhagat Singh'.[18]

IV

Gandhi's march, arrest and release had attracted wide attention in the
United States. In the first months of 1931 he received dozens of letters
conveying the admiration of Americans for his struggle. A man from
Montana wrote saying 'your leadership in a movement which frowns
on bloodshed, is to me one of the finest projects in the annals of a race
of people striving for liberty'. The Young Men's Christian Association
of Springfield invited Gandhi to speak in their town, assuring him of
the presence of 'the leaders of a score of the principal Universities
of New England'. Chicago's Fellowship of Faith hoped that Gandhi
would come, if not now, at least in 1933, to take part with 'other
Spiritual Leaders of the world' in a Parliament of Religions planned
for that year.[19]
   A particularly moving letter came from a resident of Chicago
named Arthur Sewell. The 'Negroes of America', it said, were 'keenly
and sympathetically' following Gandhi's movement against white
racism. The blacks 'sympathize and suffer' with India and Indians,
'for here, in America, they [the white racists] not only rob us of our
possessions and hurdle us into the prisons unjustly, but they mob,
lynch and burn us up with fire . . .' But this oppression would not
last forever; for, just as the Liberty Bell in Philadelphia rang out for
American whites colonized by England, so 'will the "Liberty Bell"
toll sooner or later somewhere in notification of the independence of

all the dark peoples of the world'. 'May God Bless you,' this African American said to Gandhi, 'and enable you to carry on the great battle for righteous adjustment until you win a glorious victory for the common cause of the lowly; that is the prayer of fourteen millions of Negroes of America.'[20]

Among the more curious letters Gandhi received, one came from a certain James B. Pond of New York's Pond Bureau, a self-professed 'Managers of American Tours for World Celebrities'. Writing to Gandhi on 8 April, Pond offered as his testimonials the fact that he had previously organized one tour for Annie Besant and two tours for Rabindranath Tagore. Thus, he had 'some understanding of Indian affairs and a tremendous sympathy [for] Indian aspirations'.

'When you visit this country,' said Pond to Gandhi, 'you will receive a welcome such as no man has ever had and it is going to require the utmost knowledge, the utmost sympathy, and utmost tact on the part of a manager to meet the situation.' He offered himself as one who was 'sympathetic as well as skilled', experienced in the business of hiring halls, distributing tickets and organizing a travel itinerary. Pond understood that the idea of a commercial lecture tour might be 'repugnant' to Gandhi. But, he pointed out, 'in this country people do not value what they get free'. Pond said he was willing to travel to India to discuss with Gandhi the details of an American tour.[21]

With his own letter, Pond attached one from S.N. Ghose, the president of the American branch of the Indian National Congress. 'If and when you come', said Ghose to Gandhi, his programme should be in the hands of 'one who is a technical expert in the management of big tours'. He recommended James Pond, whom he described as 'the most reliable, the most experienced and the most sympathetic lecture manager of the country'. Ghose said Pond was soon to leave for a vacation in the Mediterranean—could Gandhi cable as to whether he should carry on to India to meet him?[22]

Pond's letter was followed a week later by one from the New York pastor John Haynes Holmes, strongly advising Gandhi against coming to America. Holmes told Gandhi that if he did come, he should take two precautions: 'First, you should place yourself absolutely in the hands of some people who can control your movements on the highest level of dignity and honor—the Quakers, for example. Secondly, there should be no preliminary trumpeting of your coming, no announcements and long preparations, but rather you should come suddenly, so to speak, and with the utmost quiet and reserve.'[23]

On receiving this letter, Gandhi cabled Holmes that he had decided not to come to America before or after London.[24] Gandhi wrote to S.N. Ghose, the eager diasporic promoter of the tour manager James B. Pond that 'as for my rumoured visit, there is nothing in it and therefore we need not discuss it any further. I must not visit America till the experiment here has become a proved success.'[25] In what was a rare departure from his usual practice, Gandhi chose not to reply to the pushy Pond himself.

V

The reactions to Gandhi in Britain were more ambivalent than in the United States. The viceroy's settlement with Gandhi had enraged some British Conservatives. Leading the charge was Winston Churchill, seeking to revive what then seemed to be a rapidly fading political career.

Back in October 1929, when Lord Irwin had suggested Dominion Status for India, Churchill called the idea 'criminally mischievous'. He thought it necessary to marshal 'the sober and resolute forces of the British Empire' against the granting of self-government to India.[26]

Over the next two years, Churchill delivered dozens of speeches where he worked up, in most unsober form, forces hostile to the Indian independence movement. Thus, speaking to an audience at the city of London in December 1930, Churchill claimed that if the British left the subcontinent, then 'an army of white janissaries, officered if necessary from Germany, will be hired to secure the armed ascendancy of the Hindu'.

In the last week of January 1931, Churchill made two major speeches demanding the Raj stand firm against the nationalists. First, in the House of Commons, he expressed his confidence that even if British politicians conceded ground, 'I do not believe our people will consent to be edged, pushed, talked and cozened out of India'. Then, at Manchester's Free Trade Hall, he urged his fellow Tory, Viceroy Lord Irwin, to resist the pressures of the Labour government and see that British rule in India 'shall not be interrupted or destroyed'.

Irwin's release of, and settlement with, Gandhi enraged Churchill, for whom it seemed to signal a prelude to a larger retreat of Britain from its imperial possessions. Speaking at the Albert Hall on 18 March, he claimed that 'to abandon India to the rule of the Brahmins [who in his view dominated the Congress party] would be an act of cruel and wicked negligence'. If the British left, said Churchill, 'India will fall back quite rapidly through the centuries into the barbarism and privations of the Middle Ages'.

Churchill targeted Gandhi personally. 'I am against these conversations and agreements between Lord Irwin and Mr. Gandhi,' he thundered. 'Gandhi stands for the expulsion of Britain from India. Gandhi stands for the permanent exclusion of British trade from India. Gandhi stands for the substitution of Brahmin domination for British rule in India. You will never be able to come to terms with Gandhi.'[27]

Churchill's most famous remarks about Gandhi, however, were made a month later, to the West Essex Conservative Association. Here, he spoke with disgust of how it was 'alarming and also nauseating to see Mr. Gandhi, a seditious Middle Temple Lawyer, now posing as a fakir of a type well-known in the East, striding half-naked up the steps of the Viceregal palace . . . to parley on equal terms with the representative of the King-Emperor'. In words as telling (if less quoted) he described his revulsion at the prospect of 'heart-to-heart discussions . . . between this malignant subversive fanatic and the Viceroy of India'.[28]

Churchill and Gandhi had met once, in November 1906. The Englishman was then undersecretary of state for the colonies; the Indian, a spokesman for the rights of his countrymen in South Africa.[29] Back then, Gandhi wore a suit and tie, as befitting a lawyer trained in London. It is not clear whether Churchill remembered their meeting, but he certainly understood the symbolism behind his adversary's new mode of dress. A week before he met the Essex Tories, Churchill told London's Constitutional Club that 'Gandhi, with deep knowledge of the Indian peoples, by the dress he wore—or did not wear, by the way in which his food was brought to him at the Viceregal Palace, deliberately insulted, in a manner which he knew everyone in India would appreciate, the majesty of the King's representative. These are not trifles in the East.'[30]

The views of Churchill, the arch-reactionary in Britain, make for an intriguing comparison with the views of arch-revolutionaries in India. Here, the fledgling Communist Party termed the Gandhi–Irwin Pact 'a stab in the back of the toiling masses'. A pamphlet issued by it spoke of the popular upsurge that the civil disobedience movement had sparked—the boycott of foreign goods, non-payment of taxes in the countryside, strikes in factories. And yet, 'at the moment when British Rule in India had already begun to crack under the pressure of the masses, the National Congress definitely disarms the movement and surrenders it to the British exploiters'. By settling with the viceroy, claimed the communists, Gandhi had 'betrayed to the British imperialists thousands of workers, peasants, and revolutionary youth'.

The Churchillian and communist views of the Gandhi–Irwin Pact were a mirror image of one another. Churchill claimed Irwin had 'surrendered' to Gandhi; the communists insisted that Gandhi had 'surrendered' to Irwin.[31]

VI

After his talks with Irwin in early March, Gandhi returned to Gujarat. Two weeks later, he was back in Delhi. He met the viceroy, who told him that local governments were 'playing the game very fairly', and had released some 14,000 prisoners in a week. The viceroy then complained about the tone of Jawaharlal Nehru's speeches, which had 'no spirit of peace' and treated the settlement merely as 'an uneasy truce'.

For his part, Gandhi once more raised the question of Bhagat Singh's execution. Could not the sentence be commuted or postponed? The execution had been fixed for 24 March, the day the Karachi Congress would begin. If it was carried out as planned, said Gandhi, 'there would be much popular excitement'. Irwin answered that he had 'considered the case with most anxious care', and concluded that he could neither commute nor postpone the sentence.

On the night of the 23rd, Gandhi was scheduled to leave for Karachi to attend the annual meeting of the Congress. Before he boarded the train, he wrote to Irwin once more urging him to stay Bhagat Singh's execution. 'Popular opinion,' he remarked, 'rightly or wrongly demands commutation. When there is no principle at stake, it is often a duty to respect it.' Gandhi had been assured by the 'revolutionary party' that if the lives of Singh and his colleagues were spared, it would stay its hand. Execution was 'an irretrievable act', Gandhi told the viceroy. Therefore, if he thought there was 'the slightest chance of error of judgment', he should 'suspend for further review an act that is beyond recall'.[32]

While Gandhi was on the train, Bhagat Singh and his comrades were hanged in Lahore. They went to the gallows shouting 'Inquilab Zindabad', Long Live Revolution. Earlier, Bhagat Singh had written to the Punjab governor asking that, since the court said they had waged war against the State, they should be treated as war prisoners, and consequently shot dead rather than hanged. They asked the governor to 'kindly order the Military Department or send a detachment or shooting party to perform our executions'.[33]

On 24 March, there was a complete hartal in Lahore, Amritsar, Sialkot, Lyallpur, Ferozepur and other towns in the Punjab to protest the executions. In Lahore's Minto Park, some 40,000 men, women and children gathered to offer prayers for the souls of the martyred men. Many of the women were dressed in black saris. Shops and schools shut down in distant Bombay too. And in towns in the United Provinces and Bengal as well.[34]

Gandhi was travelling to Karachi with the Congress's president-elect, Vallabhbhai Patel. The local reception committee had originally planned to give them a 'royal welcome', ferrying them from Karachi station to the Congress venue in a procession of twenty-four horse-drawn carriages. But the anger and resentment at Bhagat Singh's execution forced a change of plan.

On the 25th morning Gandhi and Patel got down at Malir, a station thirteen miles short of Karachi. Getting wind of the plan, a group of protesters came there, and, as the Congress leaders emerged

from the train, shouted, 'Go back, down with truce'. As one of
Gandhi's companions recalled, the militants 'broke the window panes
and entered his compartment, and began to harass and bully him.
Bapu suffered their anger with great patience.'[35]

A reporter at Malir station saw that a protester had 'offered
a black flower to Gandhiji. He accepted it with a sad smile.' The
journalist then continued: 'Little did these young men know what
efforts Mahatmaji had made to save Bhagat Singh and his comrades.
He had personally spoken to the Viceroy; he had sent influential
personages to the Viceregal Lodge to plead with His Excellency. And
even on that fateful day March 23, he had made a last desperate
effort. But he had failed.'[36]

The leading nationalist paper of the Punjab thought the anger
against Gandhi expressed by Bhagat Singh's supporters had 'not the
slightest foundation. The Mahatma did all that any human being
could have done to secure the commutation of the sentences of the
three prisoners. He went to the farthest limit of his power short of
tearing up the settlement [between the Congress and the government],
which no man with a judging head or an understanding heart could
possibly have expected him to do. . . . But while the anger against the
Mahatma and his colleagues is both unreasoning and in the highest
degree unreasonable, the dissatisfaction and resentment caused by the
sad event itself is only too well founded.'[37]

The Karachi Congress was clouded over by two things: the
execution of Bhagat Singh and his comrades; and bloody Hindu–
Muslim riots in Kanpur, in which the prominent Congressman Ganesh
Shankar Vidyarthi was killed when he sought to stop the violence.

This Congress was the first to be held in March instead of
December. It saw the (belated) election of Vallabhbhai Patel as
president. The Congress passed a major resolution on 'fundamental
rights' committing a free India to (among other things) freedom of
association and combination, freedom of the press, 'equal rights
and obligations of all citizens, without any bar on account of sex',
elections based on universal adult franchise, religious neutrality on
the part of the State, 'protection of the culture, language and scripts
of the minorities', control by the State over key industries, and the
abrogation of duty on salt manufactured in India.

At a working committee meeting held in Karachi, the Congress appointed Gandhi to represent it at the next Round Table Conference in London. In an editorial in *Young India*, Gandhi explained why he was going as the 'sole delegate. The idea was to present one, unified, Congress view. Moreover, the best Congress workers had to stay on in India.' For, 'whether at the end of the Conference it was to be peace or war, every available hand was needed in the country'.[38]

The Congress also passed a resolution on the Bhagat Singh affair. While 'disassociating itself from and disapproving of political violence in any shape or form', it placed on record 'its admiration of the bravery and sacrifice of the late Bhagat Singh and his comrades Syts. Sukdhev and Rajguru, and mourns with the bereaved families the loss of these lives'. The party described their execution as 'an act of wanton vengeance', a 'deliberate flouting of the unanimous demand of the nation for commutation'.[39]

Gandhi also weighed in with a signed article of his own. This saluted Bhagat Singh's bravery, noting that he 'did not wish to live. He refused to apologize; declined to file an appeal.' By hanging him and his colleagues, argued Gandhi, 'the Government has demonstrated its own brute nature, it has provided fresh proof of its arrogance resulting from its power by ignoring public opinion'.

While the Congress was negotiating with the government, observed Gandhi, 'Bhagat Singh's hanging was weighing upon us. We had hoped that the Government would be cautious enough to pardon Bhagat Singh and his associates to the extent of remitting the sentence of hanging.' But just because they declined to do so, the Congress could not go back on the terms of the Gandhi–Irwin Pact. 'Our dharma,' said Gandhi, 'is to swallow our anger, abide by the settlement and carry out our duty.'[40]

Before they were hanged, Bhagat Singh's colleague Sukhdev wrote an 'open letter' to Gandhi, which was smuggled out of jail and published in the press. If Gandhi really wanted the radicals to change their mind, said Sukhdev, he should have directly approached 'some of the prominent revolutionaries to talk over the whole thing with them. You ought to have tried to convince them to call off their movement.'

Sukhdev wrote to Gandhi that history was on the side of the proponents of violence. 'The hegemony of the revolutionary party in the future political struggle,' he claimed, 'is assured. Masses are rallying around them and the day is not far off when they will be leading the masses under their banner towards their noble and lofty ideal—the Socialist Republic.'

Gandhi printed Sukhdev's letter in *Young India*, and determinedly set out to refute it. He had, he remarked, presented the revolutionaries not with 'sentimental appeals' but 'hard facts'. Murder and assassination had not brought swaraj any closer; on the contrary, it had added to the country's military expenditure and brought down savage reprisals on the people. Nor was there any evidence of the revolutionaries having contributed to any 'mass awakening'. Rather, their activities had added to the woes of the masses, since it was they who 'had to bear the burden ultimately of additional expense and the indirect effect of Government wrath'.

Having defended the philosophy and practice of non-violence, Gandhi added that he did not endorse the execution of the revolutionaries. He had himself made 'every effort to secure their release'. So had the Congress. But, he pointedly observed, those radicals still at large 'must help by preventing revolutionary murder. We may not have the cake and also eat it.'[41]

VII

The execution of Bhagat Singh and his comrades was the last major act of Irwin as viceroy. In April he left India, to be replaced by Lord Willingdon. Most recently governor general of Canada, Willingdon had previously served as governor of Bombay and of Madras. In both capacities, he had dealt with Gandhi the agitator, dealings which left him with a lasting hostility to the man.

Ten days after being sworn in as viceroy, Willingdon wrote to his sister complaining about his predecessor's settlement with Gandhi. 'Was it necessary?' he asked. 'Was it wise? Didn't it place Gandhi in quite a wrong position as a plenipotentiary discussing terms of peace, instead of leaving him as he was, the leader of a very inconvenient political party? Have not our friends, the Princes, the Mohammedans, the Europeans and the Depressed Classes become very depressed as a consequence?'[42]

In the second week of May, Gandhi travelled to Simla to meet with government officials about violations of the settlement by revenue officials in Gujarat. He briefly met Willingdon, who wrote to his sister that 'Gandhi is still an enigma. I think he will go to London but he refuses to give me any definite promise. He is a weird little man, attractive in a way but as cunning as can be, and always trying to get an advantage.'[43]

Gandhi's arrival in Simla was the subject of a sensation-creating report in that often sensationalist newspaper, the *Daily Mail* of London. Entitled 'Gandhi's Effrontery: "State Entry" into Simla', the report began: 'Indians are highly elated at the "state" entry into Simla made yesterday by Gandhi, the fanatical Congress leader. It was a spectacle hitherto seen only in the case of a Viceroy, and one denied even to ruling Princes and members of the Executive Council.'

Owing to the narrowness of the Mall—the road leading to the Viceregal Palace—no cars were allowed on it, except those of the viceroy, the governor of the Punjab, and the commander-in-chief of the Indian Army. The *Daily Mail* claimed that Gandhi refused to use a rickshaw, 'so his motor-car was permitted to enter the forbidden territory, followed by three other cars containing his "suite"'.

This report led to a certain amount of alarm among the establishment in London. A question was asked in Parliament, and letters sent to the viceroy to explain what was being referred to in the press and official correspondence as 'Gandhi's motor-car incident'. Willingdon sent a long explanatory telegram, saying that it was 'entirely untrue' that Gandhi motored to the Viceregal Lodge to visit him. He had instead walked there and back, a distance of seven miles all told. However, on the day Gandhi arrived in Simla, since he had driven fifty miles from the plains, his car was allowed to proceed 'along the Lower Indian Bazar one mile beyond the ordinary barrier, and then 100 yards on the Upper Mall Road to the house where he was staying. After that Mr. Gandhi never used a car in Simla.' Willingdon added that in other cases too, the municipality had given special permission for Indians to use cars on parts of the Mall; most recently, the raja of Bilaspur was allowed to use four cars for his marriage procession. The viceroy thus hastened to assure His

Majesty's Government that, since Gandhi's car had ridden on but a small portion of the Mall, British prestige and honour were entirely intact.[44]

Gandhi's conversations in Simla were chiefly with the home secretary, H.W. Emerson. They were long but inconclusive. Emerson urged Gandhi to attend the Round Table Conference, suggesting that he go there not as his party's sole spokesman but take along other senior leaders who could serve on the conference's subcommittees. A larger delegation would be helpful, said Emerson, 'since even a Mahatma could not be in three places at once'.[45]

Emerson and Gandhi got along well. Afterwards, the home secretary wrote to a colleague that Gandhi 'has a keen sense of humour, and I found it useful, when we got on to a sticky patch, to have a comparatively frivolous diversion. He is very fair in seeing the other side of the case and is ready quietly to argue any point at issue. He is very sensitive to the personal touch, but does not mind and, in fact, rather welcomes plain speaking.'[46]

Meanwhile, Charlie Andrews wrote to Gandhi, hoping that he was coming to London for the Round Table Conference. Like the Government of India's home secretary, Andrews felt Gandhi should have, at his side, 'a small group of advisors or assessors' to help him at the conference. He suggested he bring Madan Mohan Malaviya, Jawaharlal Nehru and M.A. Ansari to make the delegation more effective. As he put it: 'All three are tried and trusted Congress representatives each differing from the other.'[47] Others thought he should take Sarojini Naidu, whose charm and speaking skills would help win over the British public, which had lately come around to the view that women could vote and become MPs too.[48] However, Gandhi was insistent that he alone would represent the Congress.

VIII

As always, politics could not be Gandhi's sole preoccupation. In between meetings with proconsuls in Delhi and Simla, he wrote essays on two subjects that had long concerned him: the position of women, and the future of caste.

The first essay was written in response to press reports of a woman committing sati after her husband's death. Gandhi, appalled at the act (which may have been coerced rather than voluntary), insisted that whatever its sanction in scripture or tradition, 'self-immolation at the death of the husband is not a sign of enlightenment but of gross ignorance'. If she was truly devoted to her husband, a wife would not commit sati but instead dedicate her life to the fulfilment of her husband's ideals 'for his family and country'.

Gandhi thought the practice of sati reflected a fundamental asymmetry between husband and wife. As he pointed out: 'If the wife has to prove her loyalty and undivided devotion to her husband so has the husband to prove his allegiance and devotion to his wife. . . . Yet we have never heard of a husband mounting the funeral pyre of his deceased wife.'[49]

The second essay was in response to a letter from a student on how to overcome caste and communal distinctions. 'I do not believe in caste in the modern sense,' remarked Gandhi. 'It is an excrescence and a handicap on progress. Nor do I believe in inequalities between human beings. . . . Assumption of superiority by any person over any other is a sin against God and man. Thus caste, in so far it connotes distinctions in status, is an evil.'

That said, Gandhi continued to believe in varna insofar as it defined and marked 'four universal occupations—imparting knowledge, defending the defenceless, carrying on agriculture and commerce and performing service through physical labour. These occupations are common to all mankind, but Hinduism, having recognized them as the law of our being, has made use of it in regulating social relations and conduct.'

This system, believed Gandhi, had been corrupted over the years, resulting in 'unnecessary and harmful restrictions' on inter-dining and intermarriage. But as Gandhi understood it, the 'law of varna has nothing to do with these restrictions. People of different varnas may intermarry and interdine. . . . [A] Brahmin who marries a Sudra girl or *vice versa* commits no offence against the law of varna.'

This was Gandhi's first statement of support for inter-caste marriages, a considerable advance on his earlier position. However, he wasn't prepared to go so far as to prescribe marriage between a

Hindu and a Muslim. He saw 'no moral objection to such unions'; yet, in the present atmosphere, he did not believe that 'these unions can bring peace. They may follow peace. I see nothing but disaster following any attempt to advocate Hindu–Muslim unions so long as the relations between the two remain strained. That such unions may be happy in exceptional circumstances can be no reason for their general advocacy.'[50]

Gandhi's adoption of a progressively radical position against caste distinctions was a consequence of his growing hold over his own community. In the decade and a half since he returned to India, he had steadily established himself as the most admired, the most influential, and the most respected Hindu. Across the country, many Brahmins, Kshatriyas, Vaishyas and Sudras now tended to follow his lead rather than that of priests or Sankaracharyas. On the other hand, the early promise of the Khilafat movement had been belied by later events. Gandhi was now confident of preaching the rules of righteous conduct to his fellow Hindus, but not, any more, to his compatriots who were Muslims.

IX

Writing in *Young India* in June 1931, Gandhi said that he was 'eager for the sake of the good name of the Congress to proceed to London and deliver its message to the R.T.C. and the British statesmen, not excluding even Mr. Churchill'. However, a week later, in a private letter to a disciple, he wrote: 'It is not at all certain whether I shall be going to England.'[51]

In early July, the maharaja of Bikaner offered to book Gandhi a first-class cabin on the ship he was himself travelling to London on, the *S.S. Mooltan*. The nawab of Bhopal had also been booked on the same ship.[52] Gandhi declined the offer, in part because he knew the princes wished to flatter him before the conference, in part because he still wasn't sure he was going. He had been receiving complaints from Congressmen in the United Provinces, the Punjab and Bengal, about how the government was not fulfilling its side of the pact. It was still arresting Congress workers, still harassing the peasantry.

In the third week of July, Gandhi went up to Simla again, where he met the home secretary, the home member and the viceroy. The discussions were about the settlement and its tardy implementation. Afterwards, when journalists asked whether he was going to attend the Round Table Conference, Gandhi answered that 'there would be no certainty until he was on board the steamer'.[53]

For his part, Willingdon continued to harbour deep suspicions about Gandhi. Once more, he blamed his predecessor. For, by negotiating with Gandhi, Irwin had made 'all future dealings extraordinarily difficult'. 'My job,' remarked Willingdon to his sister, 'has therefore been to get Gandhi back into his proper position as an ordinary and troublesome citizen under my administration. He on the other hand considers himself to be in an equal and parallel position with me . . .'[54]

On his return to Gujarat, Gandhi found the 'state of things unbearable'. The villagers were 'terror-struck' by a coercive administration. He wired Emerson to press the viceroy to intervene, or else Gandhi would 'regard [the] settlement and faith [as] broken freeing me for such action as may be necessary for [the] protection [of the] people'.[55]

On 29 July, Gandhi wrote to a Gujarati friend: 'The chances of my going [to London] are 1 against 99.'[56] Ten days later, he received a stiff letter from the Bombay government, refuting the charges of any breaches of the settlement in Gujarat. The next day, Gandhi wired the viceroy that their unyielding attitude made it 'impossible' for him to proceed to London. How, he asked, could the Bombay government presume to be 'both prosecutor and judge' in a dispute where they were themselves one of the parties?

On 13 August, the CWC met in Bombay. Afterwards, Gandhi told the press he was 'very unhappy' at being forced to call off this trip to London. 'I know what effect this will have on Lord Irwin,' he remarked, adding: 'And I also know how disappointed my numerous friends in England will be.' He had 'been hoping against hope and expected to the last moment that justice would be done' (by the government, to the terms of the settlement).[57]

On 14 August, Gandhi met B.R. Ambedkar in Bombay. This was the first meeting between the two men, one for more than a decade the most important political leader in India, the other, younger by twenty-two years, and seeking to represent his own, desperately disadvantaged community of so-called 'untouchables'. Both men knew of each other, of course; Ambedkar had been inspired by Gandhian ideas during his 'Mahad Satyagraha' of 1927, which Gandhi had praised in the columns of *Young India*.

Remarkably, Gandhi did not know that Ambedkar was born in an 'untouchable' home. In Maharashtra, people of all castes took surnames after their village of origin, so 'Ambedkar' could merely mean 'from the village of Ambed'. (Indeed, this was not Ambedkar's original surname; he had been given it by a Brahmin teacher in his school.) Gandhi seems to have thought that—like Gokhale and Tilak before him—B.R. Ambedkar was an upper-caste reformer who took an interest in the uplift of the 'untouchables'. Having worked for decades for the same cause, Gandhi was patronizing towards someone he saw as a fresh convert, a johnny-come-lately, whereas Ambedkar was in fact an 'untouchable' who had experienced acute discrimination himself. Gandhi's tone offended Ambedkar, souring the relationship at the start.[58]

The day after Ambedkar met with Gandhi, he was interviewed by the *Times of India*. 'To place the interests of Bardoli above those of India and refuse on that account to go to England to take part in the deliberations of the Round Table Conference,' he told the newspaper, 'seems to me to be the height of folly. To bother about the petty tyrannies of village officers and to be unmindful of the bigger problem, the settlement of which will enable us to exercise control on those very officers, is a thing which I cannot understand.'

Ambedkar thought Gandhi should attend the Round Table Conference. And he seemed 'somewhat sore' about one aspect of their conversation. Himself in favour of separate electorates for the Depressed Classes, he was upset that Gandhi 'refused to uphold the view and said that if he went to the Round Table Conference he would tell them that the Conference might do what they liked, but in his opinion the suggestion was absolutely suicidal so far as the depressed classes were concerned'.[59]

The day before Gandhi met Ambedkar, he had told the press he was not going to London. But a week later he had changed his mind. He sent the viceroy a telegram, saying that he was 'most anxious to avoid a breach on side issues or misunderstandings and am therefore prepared even to proceed to Simla if you think discussion necessary'.

Lord Willingdon asked Gandhi to come to Simla. Reaching the imperial summer capital on 26 August, he had a three-hour chat with Willingdon which, he told the press later, 'was fairly satisfactory'. They met again the following day. On the evening of the 27th, Gandhi took the narrow gauge mountain railway down the hills, and the next morning caught the Frontier Mail bound for Bombay.

Gandhi's *Collected Works* gives no clue as to the details of the conversations in Simla. All we have is a bland statement issued on 28 August by the viceroy's office, to the effect that as a result of their discussions, 'the Congress will now be represented by Mr. Gandhi at the Round Table Conference'. How did the viceroy persuade him to change his mind and attend the Round Table Conference? Did Willingdon promise to lean harder on the Bombay government to render justice to the peasants of Gujarat? Did he remind Gandhi of the chance the conference afforded him of putting his point of view before the British public?[60]

Apart from whatever Willingdon could have told Gandhi in Simla, his meeting with B.R. Ambedkar in Bombay may also have persuaded Gandhi that he must attend the Round Table Conference. Ambedkar was surely right in arguing that if a just constitutional settlement was reached, officials would find it harder to harass peasants in Bardoli (or anywhere else in India). Ambedkar's advocacy of separate electorates for 'untouchables' would have unnerved Gandhi; could he afford to let this go uncontested in London?

Gandhi was perhaps also influenced by a letter he received in August from an Indian whose judgement he greatly valued. This was Sir Mirza Ismail, the reform-minded diwan of Mysore. 'I do hope you are going to London for the R.T.C.,' wrote Sir Mirza, adding: 'A prophecy—you will endear yourself to the people of England, and you will do honour to them—next only to your own countrymen. It is a grand opportunity for bringing about peace and harmony and goodwill between the two countries—and to put an example to the rest of the world. And it is you and you alone that can do it.'[61]

Sir Mirza's prophecy would surely have moved Gandhi. For all his opposition to British imperialism, he had an enormous fondness for the British people. And London was a city he was deeply attached to. He had spent two years there as a law student, and two summers there lobbying for Indians in South Africa. He had also spent several months in the city en route to returning home in 1915. Now, the idea that he, and he alone, could bring India and England together drew him to London once more.

CHAPTER NINETEEN

At Home in London

I

Accompanying Gandhi on the boat to London were his secretaries Mahadev Desai and Pyarelal, his son Devadas, and his English disciple Mira. After the intense political activity of the last few months—and with more of the same awaiting him in London—Gandhi welcomed the respite the few weeks on the ship afforded him. 'Bapu is thoroughly enjoying himself,' wrote Mahadev Desai to Jawaharlal Nehru, 'if I may use the word "enjoy" about anything that he does. He sleeps on the floor on the deck without scandalising any one . . .'[1]

The ship halted en route at Aden and at Marseille, where the local post office agent was 'snowed under with demands from journalists, wire pullers and such for exclusive interviews with the Mahatma and seats on the P&O Special. The Fox Movietone had mobilised two cars of cinema equipment, one from Barcelona, to do justice to the occasion . . .'[2]

The *S.S. Rajputana* arrived in Marseille at 7 a.m. on 11 September. The crowd waiting on the quay recognized the ship's famous passenger, and a few shouted 'Vive Gandhi!' Journalists were allowed on board, one asking whether Gandhi intended to see the king of England, and if so, what dress he would wear. Gandhi answered that if invited, he would certainly go meet the king, his dress depending on the climate.[3]

II

In London, Gandhi was to stay at Kingsley Hall, a Quaker settlement in the East End run by Muriel Lester, who had visited him in Sabarmati in 1926. Born and raised in a middle-class family, Miss Lester had moved to one of London's poorest boroughs at the age of nineteen, 'bringing hope and aid to those who lived in the squalor and poverty of the East End'. In 1915, she and her sister Doris opened Kingsley Hall, which was named after their brother, who had been killed in the War. The sisters liked to refer to the settlement as a 'teetotal pub'. It served as a community centre for adults and as a school for children, open to all regardless of religious denomination or racial background.[4]

Some of Gandhi's friends were opposed to the idea of his staying with English Quakers. The industrialists Walchand Hirachand and G.D. Birla were keen that he live 'under Indian surroundings' in London. The place they had in mind was Arya Bhuvan, a vegetarian guest house run by and for Indians in Belsize Park.[5] Gandhi, however, did not share in this xenophobia, and chose to accept Miss Lester's offer to host him in the East End. 'We can arrange everything for you and your friends,' she told him: 'special food bathing prayer times flat room telephone.'[6]

As she awaited her guest, Muriel Lester read with amusement what the penny papers were saying about him. One report authoritatively stated that, along with Gandhi and his party, the *S.S. Rajputana* was carrying a pile of Ganges mud from which Hindu idols were to be made and worshipped in London. Another reported that a full flock of goats would be tethered on the roof of Kingsley Hall, to provide a regular supply of milk for the visitor. The Communist Party of Great Britain was distributing leaflets claiming that by staying in the East End, Gandhi was 'attempting to throw dust in the eyes of the British workers'. The communists believed that Gandhi's 'whole life has been a mass of deceit'; and that he was coming to London merely 'to enter into a closer alliance with the British imperialists and to secure further rights for the Indian capitalists'.[7]

Gandhi arrived in London at 4 p.m. on Saturday, 12 September, travelling by car from Folkestone. It was raining when he reached the city of his youth. He drove to Friends House in Euston, where he spoke to a mixed audience of Indians and English people.

Later that evening, Gandhi was taken to Kingsley Hall. Here, he briefly met the press, telling them: 'I am going to write to Mr. Winston Churchill and Lord Rothermere [proprietor of the *Daily Mail*], asking if they will kindly give me an interview. That is not a joke. I have always to see those who have opposed me, so that I could explain my position.'

The room Gandhi was staying in was seven feet by eight feet, had a stone floor and bare walls, a table and a chair, and a wooden plank which served as a bed. That first night, Gandhi went to slept late but woke up early. After a breakfast of cereal and goat's milk, he went to the building's roof garden. Here, in the warm morning sunshine, Gandhi began to spin.[8]

On this, his first full day in London, Gandhi spoke to an American radio audience over the Columbia Broadcasting Service. The talk was unscripted. Gandhi argued that whereas the national myths and anthems of other countries 'contain imprecations upon the so-called enemy', Indian nationalism had 'reversed the process'. It was not opposed to other nations, not even to the English. Nor would it adopt violent means. 'I, personally,' insisted Gandhi, 'would wait, if need be, for ages rather than seek the freedom of my country through bloody means.'

Gandhi alerted Americans to the struggle against untouchability, and the participation of women in the freedom movement. He ended with an 'appeal to the conscience of the world to come to the rescue of a people dying for regaining its liberty'. The last sentence of his first-ever radio broadcast delivered, Gandhi said, 'Well, that's over.' These words were also heard by the millions of listeners across the Atlantic.[9]

Three days after Gandhi reached London, Mahadev Desai wrote to Jawaharlal Nehru that 'Bapu has had an amazingly good reception, and the idea of staying with Miss Lester at [the] East End was almost inspired, I should say. Thousands crowd the entrance of the Hall at all probable hours of his entrance or exit and there is a friendliness all around for which I was not at all prepared.'[10]

Scotland Yard had assigned a police party to guard Gandhi. Two constables were on all-night duty outside the room where he slept, while four others lurked in the street. Gandhi thought their presence unnecessary. 'They are making a real prisoner of me,' he told a visitor.[11]

The policemen had been deputed to ensure 'no untoward events' happened during Gandhi's stay. Scotland Yard feared actions 'such as students dressing up in loin cloths and leading a goat', which, 'although innocuous in this country, would be bitterly resented by a vast number of his [Gandhi's] compatriots in India'. The constables loyally stuck to their man through all his peregrinations. As their superintendent exasperatedly remarked (in a note to *his* superiors): 'It is difficult to gauge what he [Gandhi] will do from one hour to another and little if any reliance can be placed on any of his suggested arrangements.'[12]

III

Gandhi's lodgings were bare, and his daily schedule punishing. He woke up at 4 a.m., and after an hour of prayers, walked through the streets, passing milkmen, newspaper boys and the odd stray dog. He then had breakfast with Mahadev and Devadas, and gave a few interviews. On most weekdays, he was at the Round Table Conference from 10 a.m. to 6 p.m. Then he came back to Kingsley Hall, to more interviews and an evening prayer meeting.

The Round Table Conference was so named because there were many parties to it. They included the Congress and the Muslim League, of course, but also representatives of the Sikhs, the Depressed Classes, and the European community in India. There were also several delegates representing the princely states.

The Quaker settlement where Gandhi was staying was some six miles away from the conference venue. His friends therefore rented a house in Knightsbridge, which served as his office, and where he would repair to between sessions, to meet with colleagues and draft statements. (However, he always returned to Kingsley Hall for the night.) Manning this town office were C.F. Andrews, Henry Polak's sister Mrs Cheesman, and a Sinhalese follower of Gandhi named Bernard Aluwihare. The first two were earnest and industrious, while the last-named added to these characteristics a wicked sense of humour. Asked to spell out Gandhi's name on the phone, when sending telegrams on his behalf, he would answer: 'G. for God, A. for Ass, N. for No one, D. for Donkey, H. for Hell, I. for Idiot.'[13]

At the Karachi Congress in March, Gandhi had been nominated the party's sole representative to the conference. Even while he was in India, however, Gandhi began having second thoughts about this. To now ask for more representatives would be to lose face, and also perhaps to play favourites—if the government agreed, who among Nehru, Patel, Rajagopalachari, Kripalani and Rajendra Prasad would he take along, and who leave behind? Instead, he asked both Willingdon and Irwin to nominate Dr M.A. Ansari as a delegate from the Nationalist Muslim Party. They declined, the viceroy writing that 'I'm afraid I can do nothing about Dr Ansari but if the S[ecretary] of S[tate] chooses to nominate him of course I should raise no objection'.[14]

Shortly after reaching London, Gandhi told a representative of the Bombay Chronicle that 'whoever committed the blunder of preventing Dr. Ansari from being selected as a delegate was responsible for committing a fatal blunder'.[15] In truth, he had contributed to the blunder himself. For, Dr Ansari was a member of the Congress. Once that organization had decided to have only Gandhi as its representative, it was hard for Ansari to be invited.

On 15 September, Gandhi spoke at the Federal Structure Committee, this his first formal presentation to the Round Table Conference. He said that his party, the Indian National Congress, 'is what it means—national'. Gandhi spoke of how the Congress had originally been conceived by an Englishman, had Muslim, Parsi and women presidents, and 'taken up the cause of the so-called untouchables'. Once a city-based forum, the Congress had since extended deep into the villages, and was now 'essentially a peasant organization'.[16]

The Congress, said Gandhi, 'claims to represent all interests and classes'. This claim had (as Gandhi well knew) long been contested by the Muslim League. Now came along a fresh challenge to the Congress conceit that it represented all of India. This was articulated by B.R. Ambedkar. As a delegate to the first Round Table Conference, Ambedkar had urged that proper attention be paid to the Depressed Classes, the so-called 'untouchables', whom he (correctly) argued were the most disadvantaged section of Indian society. To assist them in their emancipation, he thought that reservation of a percentage of seats for the Depressed Classes in any future provincial or national legislature was necessary.[17]

Ambedkar repeated this argument at the second Round Table Conference, where (unlike the first time) Gandhi as the leader of the Congress was present. The Congress had reconciled itself to separate electorates for Muslims and Sikhs. Ambedkar wanted this extended to 'untouchables', but Gandhi was not convinced. 'So far as the untouchables are concerned,' he remarked, 'I have not yet quite grasped what Dr. Ambedkar has to say; but, of course, the Congress will share the honour with Dr. Ambedkar of representing the interests of the untouchables. They are as dear to the Congress as the interests of any other body . . . throughout the length and breadth of India.'[18]

IV

The conference worked Monday to Friday only. Gandhi chose to spend most weekends outside London. The first trip outside the metropolis was to the textile-mill districts of Lancashire, where there was widespread unemployment. C.F. Andrews had urged Gandhi to visit the mill region, and offer a compromise—with boycott of lower counts to continue (to be replaced by khaddar), but that of higher counts, used by rich townspeople in India, to be withdrawn.

Andrews made Gandhi's path smoother by publishing a laudatory profile in the region's leading newspaper, the *Manchester Guardian*. He called Gandhi a 'man of his word', with a 'trained lawyer's mind' that made him 'very precise' in his public utterances. Once a prosperous advocate, he had given up his profession and embraced a life of such simplicity that he had become 'entirely one with the villagers of every part of India'. In sum, remarked Andrews rather unpersuasively, Gandhi's 'character is not unlike, in many ways, the North-country type of Englishman'.[19]

On the evening of Friday, 25 September, Gandhi took a train to Lancashire from Euston station. Andrews, Mira and Mahadev were with him. The party travelled third class. A crowd of about a hundred had gathered at Manchester's Victoria station; when the train stopped, they 'clustered round Mr. Gandhi's coach, and he came to the window in the corridor to smile at them'.

Just before midnight, Gandhi arrived at Darwen, where a large crowd greeted him at the station. On alighting, he 'entered a saloon car which was illuminated so that people could see him wave his hand in return of their welcome'.[20]

Gandhi stayed at Spring Vale, a garden village near Darwen built by the Davies family for their millworkers. He went for long walks, his loincloth and sandals attracting excited comment (especially among the children). He had several meetings with workers and their representatives. The Lancashire constabulary was out in full force, lining, at fifty-yard intervals, the roads he drove or walked on. They feared a hostile demonstration by unemployed workers. In fact, the people of Lancashire, rich and poor, were disarmed by Gandhi's gesture of coming into their midst. Wherever he went, 'the crowds behaved with the greatest good humour, and even the local Conservative Associations, in all the circumstances, with admirable restraint'.[21]

Gandhi told the weavers that 'he grieved at Lancashire's distress, but could only promise this: that if India got self-government he would agree to the prohibition of all imports of cloth other than Lancashire in so far as imports were necessary'.[22] In an interview to the *Textile Mercury*, Gandhi likewise said that if there was 'a full-hearted' political settlement between India and Britain, and supposing India had to buy foreign cloth to supplement indigenous production, whether homespun or mill-spun, 'preference would be given to Lancashire over all other foreign cloth'.[23]

Gandhi spent a weekend in October in Chichester, staying with the local bishop. 'A large crowd assembled to cheer the Mahatma when his car arrived, and he drove into the Cathedral precincts bowing and smiling broadly to the crowd.'[24] On the Sunday he drove to the nearby town of Bognor Regis, where he had lunch with the editor of the *Manchester Guardian*, C.P. Scott, whose columns had been so hospitable to reports of Gandhi's movement and to the effusive essays of C.F. Andrews in particular. Mahadev Desai, who was present, recalls Gandhi telling Scott that 'for years your paper has been an oasis in a desert of misunderstanding and misrepresentation and I thought I must see you if only to express my gratefulness'.[25]

Gandhi also spent a weekend in each of Britain's two great university towns. In Oxford, he was a house guest of the Master of Balliol, A.D. Lindsay, a distinguished scholar as well as an active member of the Labour Party. (Balliol had contributed a disproportionate share of ICS officers, both Indian and British.) Gandhi attended several gatherings, where, without making formal speeches, he readily answered questions put to him by the students. 'Mr. Gandhi,' noted a reporter accompanying him, 'evidently found himself very much at home with his undergraduate audiences, and gave the impression that he greatly enjoyed his visit.'[26]

The master's daughter later recalled some highlights of the visit. 'The routine of Gandhi's party,' she wrote, 'started early with baths at about 3 a.m. followed by prayers and morning walks which had also to be shadowed by the detective.' Through the weekend, Mira 'glided about in silent dignity looking after Gandhi's needs as best as she could in these new surroundings', while the old Yorkshire nurse who was living with the Lindsays 'protested indignantly when she found Gandhi's dhoti hanging to dry in front of her gas fire'.[27]

Gandhi also visited Cambridge, the alma mater of his friend Charlie Andrews and his disciple Jawaharlal Nehru. Andrews accompanied him. The day they arrived, their talks with dons and students carried on into the late evening. At length Andrews told the callers they must leave, as it was the Mahatma's bedtime. Then he added: 'You know, Mr. Gandhi can go to sleep within three minutes any time he wants to.' A lady who was one of the group asked gushingly, 'Can you really?', to which the Mahatma replied, quick as a flash, 'Yes. Would you like a demonstration now?'[28]

On some weekdays Gandhi made shorter excursions, within London or to its suburbs. One evening, he visited the Houses of

Parliament to address Labour MPs. The meeting carried on too late for Gandhi and his party to return to Bow in time for their customary prayer meeting at 7 p.m. So, after the MPs had dispersed and Gandhi had signed a few autographs, his party decided to say their prayers in the Parliament itself. They chanted verses from the Gita and the Bible, against the background of a large picture on the wall of 'The English Fleet pursuing the Spanish Fleet'. A Labour MP stayed behind, as per the rules of the House, which specified that all meetings in the building must have at least one MP present.[29]

Another weekday, when the conference was not in session, Gandhi visited a dairy show in Islington, posing for a photograph with the animals. Later, the animal who won first prize in the 'goats' category was (re)named 'Mahatma Gandhi'.[30]

Gandhi also reached out to the British people through the press. On 28 September the *Daily Herald* published an article by Gandhi specially written for it. The paper gave the piece the title 'Myself, My Spinning-Wheel, and Women'. Here, Gandhi said that the spinning wheel was 'the symbol of salvation' for the starving millions in India. The charkha, said Gandhi to the English, 'would teach you a great deal more than I can—patience, industry, simplicity'.

Gandhi came next to his mode of dress, which many in England found exotic and even offensive. His attire, he explained, was customary and common in India, and far better suited to the tropical climate than European clothing. Were Gandhi to come to England to work or seek citizenship rights, he would dress as the English did. But he was here 'on a great and special mission, and my loin-cloth, if you choose so to describe it, is the dress of my principals, the people of India'.

The newspaper had asked him to clarify his views on women. He answered that he believed 'in complete equality for women and, in the India I seek to build, they would have it'. He wished to see 'the opening of all offices, professions and employments to women; otherwise there can be no real equality'. Then he added a significant caveat: 'But I must sincerely hope that women will retain and exercise her ancient prerogative as queen of the household.' In Gandhi's view of the world, 'generally, it is the father who should be the bread-winner', while 'family life is the first and greatest thing. Its sanctity must remain.'[31]

On 2 October, Gandhi's birthday, the *Jewish Chronicle* printed an interview with him. He spoke of his many close Jewish friends and colleagues in South Africa. He praised the 'wonderful spirit of cohesion' displayed by Jews, and termed anti-Semitism 'a remnant of barbarism'. While sympathetic to Jews, he was less enamoured of the Zionist project per se. He understood 'the longing of a Jew to return to Palestine', but asked them to go not under the protection of British bayonets, but 'peacefully and in perfect friendliness with the Arabs'.

For Gandhi, one's faith was not necessarily tied to a specific shrine, city or territory. So, he now told his Jewish interlocutor, 'Zion lies in one's heart. . . . The real Jerusalem is the spiritual Jerusalem. Thus he can realize his Zionism in any part of the world.'[32]

V

The weekends were pleasurable, which was perhaps just as well, for the weekdays were not going smoothly for Gandhi. In the conference, the debate over separate electorates for the Depressed Classes had intensified. Ambedkar would not be budged from his conviction that these were necessary. Asked about this by a reporter, Gandhi answered; 'I do not mind Dr. Ambedkar. He has a right even to spit on me, as every untouchable has . . . But I may inform you that Dr. Ambedkar speaks for that particular part of the country where he comes from. He cannot speak for the rest of India . . .'

Gandhi said he had received 'numerous telegrams from the so-called "untouchables" in various parts of India assuring me that they have the fullest faith in the Congress and disowning Dr. Ambedkar'. In any case, the special and separate electorate that Ambedkar was demanding would do 'immense harm' to the interests of the 'untouchables' themselves. 'It would divide the Hindu community into armed camps and provoke needless opposition.'

The questioner was not entirely satisfied. He accepted that Gandhi cared for the plight of the 'untouchables', and had worked hard to protect their interests. But disadvantaged communities the world over insisted on being represented by their own people. The 'devoted Liberals' in England felt for the working class but were not workers themselves, which is why the Labour Party was born and thrived in working-class districts. Likewise, in the Indian context, 'the great stubborn fact' against Gandhi was that he was not an 'untouchable' himself.[33]

The question of separate electorates also came up in an interview with the editor of the *Spectator*. Here, Gandhi accepted that 'Dr. Ambedkar is undoubtedly clever and enthusiastic'. He added, however, that 'I have spent the best part of my life in championing their cause, I have mixed with them east, west, north and south in India, I have many of them in my own Ashram . . .'[34]

Gandhi had told the Indian students at Oxford that he had 'the highest regard for Dr. Ambedkar. He has every right to be bitter. That he does not break our heads is an act of self-restraint on his part.' Then he continued: 'He is today so very much saturated with suspicion that he cannot see anything else. He sees in every Hindu a determined opponent of the untouchables, and it is quite natural.'

For all his admiration for Dr Ambedkar, Gandhi insisted that 'the separate electorates that he seeks will not give him social reform. He may himself mount to power and position, but nothing good will accrue to the untouchables.'[35]

In a speech to the conference on 13 November, Gandhi said that 'with all my regard for Dr. Ambedkar, and for his own desire to see the untouchables uplifted, with all my regard for his ability, I must say in all humility that here the great wrong under which he has laboured and perhaps the bitter experience that he has undergone have for the moment warped his judgment'. Gandhi himself was clear that separate electorates would make the problem worse rather than better; it would further the divisions in each village and lead to endemic conflict. Therefore, he told the conference 'with all the emphasis that I can command that, if I was the only person to resist this thing, I would resist it with my life'.[36]

VI

On the defensive as regards the Depressed Classes, Gandhi was also at odds with the Muslim leaders at the conference. At a minorities committee meeting, he announced 'with deep sorrow and deeper humiliation' the 'utter failure' on his part 'to secure an agreed solution of the communal question'. He blamed this on the composition of the conference, where, except for him, all delegates had been nominated by the Imperial Government. He thought religious divisions had 'hardened' under British rule; but he hoped that, as he put it, 'the iceberg of communal differences will melt under the warmth of the sun of freedom'.[37]

On the sidelines of the conference, Gandhi had several private meetings with Muslim leaders. These were unproductive. As Mahadev wrote to Nehru, their mutual master 'had two most disappointing interviews with Shaukat Ali and the Aga Khan'. While 'Jinnah was better', he wondered why Gandhi was 'adamant' that any agreement on Muslims had to have the approval of Dr Ansari.[38] For his part, Gandhi could not understand why 'we have here today Mussalmans talking as ultra-loyalists who only a little while ago were intolerant even of British connection under any terms'.[39]

The Hindu–Muslim question also came up at a meeting with Labour MPs. One Labour leader asked Gandhi whether there was a risk of sectarian strife if the British left India. He answered that this was indeed possible, but pointedly reminded them of their own history. 'Did not the British people themselves run the maddest risks imaginable in order to retain their liberty?' he asked. 'Did they not have the terrible Wars of the Roses? Did they not fight, the English and the Scots?'[40]

When he was in Oxford, a student had asked Gandhi: 'How far is the British attitude towards the communal question an obstacle in your path?' Gandhi answered: 'Largely, or I should say half and half.' The British had followed a policy of divide and rule in India, he said, wryly adding that 'of course, if I were a British official, I would probably do the same and take advantage of dissensions to consolidate the rule. Our share of responsibility lies in the fact that we fall easy victims to the game.'[41]

VII

By coming to London as the sole representative of the Congress, Gandhi was offering to the British people the syllogism:

INDIVIDUAL=PARTY=NATION. Gandhi was the Congress which was India. This presentation was flatly rejected by the other Indian participants at the Round Table Conference. And it was denied by the British government too.

On the political front the trip to London was a failure. On the personal front it was a resounding success. The British public were charmed by Gandhi. He was warmly received in the mill districts of the north, and in the ancient universities in the south. In London itself, he was besieged by a series of visitors, famous as well as unknown. On many evenings, the children of the East End would come to see him at Kingsley Hall. Gandhi sat on the floor with kids around him, asking questions. One child asked about the language Gandhi spoke, to be told that the word *pita* in Hindi was allied to the word father in English, demonstrating that Indians and British people belonged to the same human family.[42]

Among the visitors to Kingsley Hall was the sculptor Clare Sheridan, a cousin of Winston Churchill's from his mother's side. She asked Gandhi for a couple of sittings for a bust she wished to make. Gandhi told her to be at ease despite her connections, joking that she could tell Churchill that he was 'not really so bad'. As she made her drawings, she noted the stream of callers on the great man: an Indian disciple, an Englishman who claimed to have known Gandhi in South Africa, a London doctor, a French woman lawyer, the editor of the *New Statesman*, and the wife of the actor and singer Paul Robeson (who wished to know Gandhi's opinion on the Negro question in the United States).[43]

Also among Gandhi's visitors was his old admirer, the New York clergyman John Haynes Holmes. Holmes was in Berlin when he heard Gandhi was coming to London. He rushed there to meet him. Having long venerated Gandhi from afar, Holmes now had his first glimpse of him in person. 'Where do people get the idea that Gandhi is ugly?' he later wrote. Why had some westerners described him as a 'dwarf' and as a 'little monkey of a man'? Holmes acknowledged that Gandhi's limbs and body looked emaciated, for 'his ascetic life produces no surplus flesh'. It was also true that his individual features were not especially appealing. Gandhi, wrote Holmes, 'has a shaven head, protruding ears, thick lips, and a mouth that is minus many of its teeth'. That said, 'his dark complexion is richly beautiful against the white background of his shawl, his eyes shine like candles in the night, and overall is the radiance of a smile like sunshine on a morning landscape'.[44]

The most famous individual Gandhi met in London was Charlie Chaplin. Remarkably, Gandhi had never heard of the actor. Chaplin knew something about Gandhi's fetish for the spinning wheel. He was in sympathy with India's demand for freedom, but 'somewhat confused' about Gandhi's own attitude towards machinery. The Indian answered that he was not opposed to machinery per se, but only to machines that rendered people jobless. He added that 'in cloth and food every nation should be self-contained. We were [once] self-contained and want to be that again.'[45]

The meeting (held at the home of an Indian doctor in Canning Town) was the subject of a newspaper editorial entitled 'Mahatma and Clown'. This observed that Gandhi and Chaplin had 'both established contact with larger numbers of their fellow human beings than, probably, anyone else in the history of the world'. Asking, 'What is the common quality in Mahatma and clown?', the newspaper answered: 'Perhaps, more than anything, a capacity to sympathise and to understand mass emotions. Some people make us laugh and some people make us follow them; clowns and Mahatmas.'[46]

While in London, Gandhi also heard from the great scientist Albert Einstein, who expressed admiration for his work, and hoped he might pass through Berlin on his way back. Gandhi—who certainly knew of Einstein—answered that he likewise hoped 'that we could meet face to face and that too in India at my Ashram'.[47]

A meeting that gave Gandhi great pleasure was with the animal rights activist Henry Salt. Back in 1888–89, as a young law student in London, Gandhi had read Salt's works, and joined his Vegetarian Society, and contributed essays on Indian food to its journal.[48] Now, forty-odd years later, the world-famous Mahatma addressed the society, with the octogenarian reformer in attendance. He remarked that while he had been brought up to eschew animal flesh, that was because of the caste and culture he was born into. It was only Henry Salt 'who showed me why it was a moral duty incumbent on vegetarians not to live upon fellow-animals'.[49]

A last luminary Gandhi encountered was another fellow vegetarian, George Bernard Shaw. They met at Kingsley Hall, with Mahadev Desai taking notes as Shaw interrogated Gandhi 'on a bewildering variety of topics—ethnographical, religious, social, political, economic—and his talk was illumined by his sparkling wit and sardonic humour'. Gandhi was sardonic too at times; when Shaw asked whether the Round Table Conference was trying his patience, he answered: 'It requires more than the patience of Job. The whole thing is a huge camouflage and the harangues that we are treated to are meant only to mark time.'[50]

As Shaw came out of Kingsley Hall, a reporter asked him what he thought of Gandhi. He replied in character: 'The second greatest man in the world.' This was not said entirely in jest, for it seems that he had told Gandhi that he felt in him something of 'a kindred spirit', adding: 'We belong to a very small community on earth.'[51] When he got into his car, a fellow passenger asked Shaw what he felt about the visit to Gandhi. 'He is a phenomenon and I have hardly recovered from the shock of it,' said Shaw.[52]

Gandhi met many English people, but many more wished to meet him, besieging him with letters and requests for interviews. On a drive through London with his young Quaker friend Horace Alexander, Gandhi saw a hoarding which read: 'Come and meet Gandhi at Madame Tussaud's'. Alexander thought that being immortalized in wax among all those other famous and notorious people would please Gandhi. Instead, he heard the Mahatma wryly commenting: 'I wish they would send all the letters there.'[53]

VIII

The most powerful person Gandhi met in London was the British monarch, King George the Fifth, one of whose titles was Emperor of India. On 5 November, the king hosted a reception for the delegates to the Round Table Conference. The invitation specified that those attending should wear 'Morning Dress'; finally, after much to-ing and fro-ing between the palace officials and Mahadev Desai, they decided to make an exception for Gandhi.

Two stories have long circulated about that meeting, both attributed to journalists who are said to have met Gandhi immediately afterwards. One has the reporter asking Gandhi whether he did not feel cold in his dhoti and sandals. Gandhi apparently answered: 'The King had on enough for the two of us.' The second story has the same question but a different answer, with Gandhi saying: 'The King wears plus-fours; I wear minus-fours.'

I have not been able to find a contemporary source for the first story. The second remark was not entirely made up; except that Gandhi uttered it not to the king, but to a journalist in Marseille who asked whether he would continue to wear the loincloth in England (with Gandhi's precise words being: 'In your country you put on plus-fours; I prefer minus-fours').[54]

And how did the king himself respond to Gandhi and his mode of attire? As it turns out, we do have an eyewitness account. At the palace reception, the guests lined up, and the king and queen shook hands with them, one by one. 'When Gandhi's turn came neither of Their Majesties showed any distinction or batted an eyelid but shook hands with the incongruously garbed leader just as with any one else.' Later, as the king chatted informally with the guests, our eyewitness (the British businessman E.C. Benthall) saw him 'wagging his finger at Gandhi and obviously expressing displeasure'. Gandhi 'smilingly but awkwardly answered back', and 'eventually the conversation appeared to go amicably'. A member of the royal family told Benthall that the king had asked Gandhi: 'What have I done that you should be so hostile to me nowadays? There was a time when you led an ambulance in South Africa in support of the British troops.'[55]

Put on the spot, Gandhi deftly answered: 'I must not be drawn into a political argument in Your Majesty's Palace after receiving Your Majesty's hospitality.' Overhearing the conversation was Samuel Hoare, the King's secretary of state for India. Hoare was greatly impressed by Gandhi's quickness of mind, later writing: 'What exquisite worldly manners the unworldly possess!'[56]

IX

In early October, Gandhi got a long letter from Jawaharlal Nehru, alerting him to the situation in India. 'There is a great deal of repression going on here,' wrote Nehru, 'and large numbers of young men are being proceeded against. Some are being charged under Sec 302 (the murder section) for a speech, which is extraordinary.'

Another letter from Nehru followed a week later. This spoke of how, in the United Provinces, 'the tenantry have lost hope to a large extent of any real relief being given to them'. The remissions promised them due to the failure of the rains had been withheld. Meanwhile, 'stray reports of beatings of kisans [peasants] continue to come'. [57]

On 16 October, Gandhi received a further update from Nehru about the forcible collection of rents in the United Provinces. Lands and cattle were being confiscated. The kisans were facing 'continual harassment', the situation was 'critical'. Should the local Congress start a satyagraha, asked Nehru? Or should it wait for the Round Table Conference to end?

Gandhi had been in London for a full month. The conference was going nowhere. The Hindu–Muslim question and the debate on special electorates for Depressed Classes were unresolved. The Labour Party had split in August, and Ramsay MacDonald was now being propped up by the Conservatives, who were far less sympathetic to self-government for Indians, as well as more inclined to set the Muslim League against the Congress. So, Gandhi told Nehru to 'unhesitatingly' take such steps as the situation in the countryside warranted. 'Expect nothing here,' he added. [58]

Gandhi continued to attend meetings of the conference, but without much hope that they would achieve anything. At a conference session in the last week of November, the Liberal politician Sir Hubert Carr offered this consolation: 'Without their work Mahatma Gandhi might have remained for many people in this country a more or less mythical figure, making salt in forbidden places or weaving all kinds of yarns.' Gandhi at once interjected: 'You mean spinning all kinds of yarns.' [59]

Three days later, Gandhi spoke for nearly an hour at the conference's plenary session. Once more, he argued that whereas the other parties at this meeting represented one section or another, the 'Congress alone claims to represent the whole of India, all interests'. He wished he 'could convince all the British public men, the British Ministers, that the Congress is capable of delivering the goods. The

Congress is the only all-India wide national organization, bereft of
any communal bias . . .'

With the conference having failed to arrive at a satisfactory
agreement among its parties, Gandhi contemplated having to start
civil disobedience when he returned home. The thought gave him 'no
joy and comfort', but if it had to be done, it would be, with Indians
having the 'satisfaction of knowing that it was not at least taking
lives, it was giving lives; it was not making the British people directly
suffer, it was suffering'.

Gandhi ended by saying that he would return 'carrying with me
thousands upon thousands of English friendships. I do not know
them, but I read that affection in their eyes as early in the morning
I walk through your streets. All this hospitality, all this kindness
will never be effaced from my memory no matter what befalls my
unhappy land.'[60]

For his part, Gandhi had made a considerable impression on the
British people. As he prepared to leave, the *Manchester Guardian*
organized a competition asking for submissions, in verse or prose,
bidding farewell to Gandhi, with a prize of two guineas for the best
entry.

Submissions poured in from across the country. Some were
outright hostile, as in the entry from a lady from Winchester, which
began: 'We extend to you an iron hand in a velvet glove. Shake it,
but remember; for we shall meet again in your own country,' and
continued: 'It is a pity the temperate climate of this hated land has
had no calming effect upon your fevered brain, but a distorted
imagination to a sick body. A diet of British beef would have cured
both ills.'

The *Manchester Guardian* very reasonably concluded that this
lady was 'an admirer of Mr. Churchill'. Other submissions, however,
were more sympathetic to Gandhi, as in this verse from a K.V. Bailey
from Nottingham:

Another runner passes through the night,
    Bearing a light
Tireless the hastening feet; held high the flame
    But in whose name

And on what mission has he touched our shore
 Lo! Evermore
The age-old voice replies, 'For Truth I run'
 God speed him on!

This entry won the second prize, of one guinea. The first prize went to a Reverend J.A. Wurtleburg from Harrogate, whose entry started thus:

Farewell, Mr. Gandhi! Farewell to your figure, familiar at least in the Illustrated Papers! How they will miss your loin-cloth, blanket, goggles, and the inscrutable smile! You are going back to your native land, but what you are going to do there only that ovular head knows, and perhaps even it is a little vague. We are none of us quite sure whether you are a fanatical seer with no real constructive policy, or whether you will prove a statesman who can well and truly lay the foundations of a building which might startle the ages.[61]

As befitting a prize-winning entry, this was suitably even-handed, as well as open-minded; unsure whether Gandhi was saint or charlatan, statesman or fanatic, it left it to the future to decide.

X

Gandhi left London on Saturday, 5 December, exactly twelve weeks after he arrived. Among those seeing him off at Victoria station were his Quaker hosts from Bow, the Labour leader George Lansbury (bearing a bouquet of chrysanthemums), and many students, English as well as Indian. Gandhi was placed in a second-class carriage, 'and seemed much amused to find that it was a smoker'. As the train pulled out of the station, the Eastern sage was bid Godspeed by his admirers on the platform singing, 'Auld Lang Syne' and 'He's a Jolly Good Fellow'.[62]

The Salt March had made Gandhi extremely well known in Europe. Through 1930 and 1931, he received a stream of correspondence from admirers in Russia, Poland, Czechoslovakia, Germany, Holland, Norway, Sweden, Denmark and other countries. While he was in London, invitations poured in from these places to visit them, and speak on such topics as Indian independence, non-violence and vegetarianism.[63]

In quieter times, Gandhi may have taken up some of these offers. But he had to get back soon to India, where the conflict with the government was once more intensifying. Even so, he could not leave Europe without at least seeing his friend and biographer, Romain Rolland. To get to the latter's home in the Swiss town of Villeneuve he had to go via France. To get from there to catch a ship to India, he had to pass through Italy. So he did at least manage to visit three countries in Europe.

Gandhi's first stop in Europe was Paris. He was already moderately well known in the French capital. A Paris restaurant was now using salt cellars made in the image of Gandhi, bare-chested, and with glasses.[64]

On the evening of 5 December, Gandhi spoke in a dance hall on Paris's Left Bank. The audience, some two thousand-strong, were ushered into their seats by women dressed in bright-red skirts and wearing leather boots. Gandhi spoke to them on peace and non-violence. The man and the message did not entirely resonate with the venue; for, as a journalist present observed: 'The atmosphere, part circus, part dancing hall, the overheated room, the massive columns of red marble, the flashes of magnesium from here and there, and the floodlights ready to be lit into action were not on the same level as this leader of men.'[65]

After a day in Paris, Gandhi travelled to Villeneuve to meet Romain Rolland. They had corresponded for many years; and several times in the past Gandhi had been tempted to accept invitations to visit Europe merely to see Rolland. Gandhi spent five days in Villeneuve, staying in a villa close to the writer's house, and walking there every morning and evening for a chat.

The first day of Gandhi's visit was his day of silence. Rolland spoke or lectured about the ghastly national rivalries of Europe, which had led to one World War and now threatened another. On the second day, they discussed the situation in Italy, with Rolland warning Gandhi against being taken in by the apparent order and stability of the fascist regime. If, when he visited Italy, the Indian appeared sympathetic to Mussolini, warned the writer, people would wonder why 'the great saint is with the oppressors against the oppressed'. 'Your voice must break the cordon for the people of Italy,' said Rolland to Gandhi.

On the third day of their conversations, Gandhi did most of the talking. He told Rolland about the evils of British rule in India, of the exactions of the tax collector, of the harshness of the police, and of how the colonial civil service was 'like a snake holding the whole nation in its coils'. The next day, they spoke largely of spiritual matters, of the competing claims of truth and love.

On the morning of Friday, 11 December, Gandhi came for one last time to Rolland's villa, to say goodbye. They had their last conversation, as 'rich, affectionate and varied' as the others. At one stage, Rolland's sister told Gandhi of her love for the city and university of Oxford. Gandhi conceded that the students were 'fine young men', adding, however, that for him the beauty of Oxford's buildings and grounds (and cellars) was marred 'by thoughts of the world-wide exploitation which caused these riches to flourish'.[66]

In a letter to an American friend, Rolland penned an indelible portrait of his visitor, this 'little man, bespectacled and toothless, wrapped in his white burnoose, his legs, thin as a heron's stilts, bare'. Rolland found their conversations both absorbing and exhausting. 'This little man, so frail in appearance, is tireless, and fatigue is a word which does not exist in his vocabulary.'

Rolland was less impressed with 'the hurricane of intruders, loiterers and half-wits' which Gandhi's visit brought to his house. The 'telephone never ceased ringing, photographers in ambuscades let fly their fusillades from behind every bush'. Letters were received from Italians beseeching the Mahatma to tell them the lucky numbers for the next national lottery.

On their last evening together, Gandhi asked Rolland to play him some Beethoven on the gramophone. The composer (or his work) had brought Mira to Rolland, then Mira to Gandhi, and, finally, Gandhi to Rolland. The writer played for his visitor the Andante of the Fifth Symphony.[67]

From Villeneuve Gandhi proceeded to Geneva, and from there to Rome via Milan. At several stations on the way, crowds gathered to see him. Gandhi spent two days in Rome, 12 and 13 December. On the first day he called on the educationist Maria Montessori, and also visited the Vatican museum.

While planning the trip, Mahadev Desai had written to the Italian consul general in Bombay, suggesting that Gandhi speak to the students of the University of Rome 'on the spiritual message of non-violence'. This was deemed too controversial; and the Italians instead arranged a meeting with their own resident prophet of violence, Benito Mussolini.[68]

On the evening of 13 December, Gandhi visited Mussolini in the Palazzo Venezia. Let the Rome correspondent of the *Manchester Guardian* take up the story:

> It was a strange picture when the Indian leader, wearing only his self-woven toga of white wool, below which his thin child's legs were to be seen, and with coarse sandals on his feet, stopped in front of the monumental porch of the Palazzo Venezia, where the two Blackshirts on guard presented arms. He went up the ceremonial staircase to the Duce's official apartments, which in taste and magnificence resemble the dwelling of a Renaissance condottiere, and at length appeared before the uncrowned king of Italy, the semi-naked Oriental ascetic face to face with the prophet of the new Imperium Romanum. The conversation, in English, lasted twenty minutes: the only witness was General Moris, Mr. Gandhi's host. It was significant that on coming away the general, who knew no English, had understood nothing but the frequently repeated word 'India'.

The next day, the *Guardian* correspondent asked Gandhi about what had transpired in his conversation with the Duce. In the reporter's paraphrase, Gandhi answered 'that it would not be correct for him to speak about it; then, like a new St. Francis from the East, he added: "But why not talk about Italy's domestic animals, or her vegetables, or her radiant sunlight?"'[69]

Gandhi had also wished to see the Pope, Pius XI, but the pontiff did not grant him an audience. The reason officially stated was 'other pressing engagements', but in truth it was 'the Indian leader's scant raiment' that put him off. The king of England had relented in this matter, but the Bishop of Rome would not.[70]

XI

On 14 December, Gandhi and his party boarded the *S.S. Pilsna* at Brindisi, bound for Bombay. In a letter to Rolland, he wrote down his impressions of the Italy he so briefly saw. 'Mussolini is a riddle to me. Many of his reforms attract me. He seems to have done much for the peasant class. I admit an iron hand is there. But as violence is the basis of Western society, Mussolini's reforms deserve an impartial study. His care of the poor, his opposition to super-urbanization, his efforts to bring about co-ordination between capital and labour, seem to me to demand special attention. I would like you to enlighten me on these matters. My own fundamental objection is that these reforms are compulsory.'

Gandhi thought he detected in Mussolini's speeches a 'passionate love for his people', while, on the other side, it seemed to him that 'the majority of Italian people love the iron government of Mussolini'. He wanted to know Rolland's opinions on all this, as one 'who knows infinitely more than I do about the subject'.[71]

To rush to conclusions after a fleeting visit was precisely what Rolland had warned Gandhi against. The novelist knew that the apparent order and stability of Mussolini's Italy rested on coercion. And he worried, too, about the personality cult built around Mussolini. This must have been the burden of Rolland's reply to Gandhi's letter, which, sadly, is lost.

On board *S.S. Pilsna*, Gandhi caught up on his sleep, and his correspondence. He also resumed writing for *Young India* and *Navajivan*, providing their readers with impressions of his London visit. Of his experiences at the Round Table Conference itself, Gandhi remarked that while the British politicians were 'honest', they laboured under 'a heavy handicap'; namely, their being 'spoon-fed on one-sided and often hopelessly false statements and anti-nationalist opinions received by them from their agents in India ever since the commencement of the British Raj'. The British establishment thought Indians were 'incapable of handling our own Defence and Finance, they believe that the presence of British troops and British civilians is necessary for the well-being of India'. Indeed, 'perhaps, there is no nation on earth equal to the British in the capacity for self-deception'.[72]

PART III

REFORM AND RENEWAL (1931–1937)

CHAPTER TWENTY

Arguments with Ambedkar

I

The ship carrying Gandhi back to India reached Bombay on 28 December 1931. At a press conference the same day, he was asked if he agreed with a recent statement of M.R. Jayakar that he should have taken a larger Congress delegation to the Round Table Conference. (The viceroy's home secretary had suggested that he take fourteen colleagues, since even a Mahatma could not be in several places at once.) Gandhi answered that 'it would have been a first-class tragedy, if 14 or 15 good servants of the nation had been sent out instead of keeping them here. . . . When the mandate was absolutely clear, there was no occasion for sending more than one agent unless, of course, the Congress had distrusted its agent.'[1]

One notes in this reply a tone of defensiveness, if not self-deception. The truth is that Gandhi did miss having other senior Congress leaders at hand in London. In fact, back in late August, the day before he sailed from Bombay for the conference, Gandhi had written to C. Rajagopalachari that 'there are two men whom I would like by my side in London, you and Jawaharlal. But I feel that even if both of you were available I must not have you by me. . . . Only your presence with me will have lightened my burden. But I must bear the Cross alone and to the fullest extent.'[2]

Having decided to go alone to London, Gandhi was having some regrets. He would have done well to take Jawaharlal Nehru, who had studied in England and had many friends in London, or Rajagopalachari, who had a superb legal mind, and could have aided in the negotiations with the other parties.

In not taking anyone with him, Gandhi might have been influenced by his talks with Irwin, where the two men merely had their secretaries by their side. But this was an altogether different occasion. The ability to persuade and charm an opponent face-to-face was of little use in a 'round table' conference with many parties present, representing many different interest groups.

In the event, by going alone, Gandhi found there was too much for him to do: participate in the sessions of the conference; discuss contentious issues with other delegates in private; make an impression on the British public; convey his views through the British press. Even if the younger Nehru and Rajagopalachari had to remain in India, there were other Congressmen who could have accompanied him. If Gandhi had taken Dr Ansari along, his case for the Congress's religious pluralism would have been more credible. If he had taken along a colleague from the Depressed Classes, he could have met Ambedkar's challenge more effectively. If he had taken Sarojini Naidu, he would have impressed upon British liberals that, unlike the Muslims and the princes, the Congress placed a high priority on women's rights too.

The failure of the Round Table Conference greatly pleased the new viceroy, Lord Willingdon. Lord Irwin had believed that 'whether or not democracy is a good plan for India', it is 'inevitable that they must try it'. As he put it: 'We encouraged them to have Western education, to send their students to England and all the rest of it; we can hardly wonder they caught the democratic infection that they found there raging.'[3] His successor, however, was clear that India was not fit for democracy or self-government. Lord Willingdon thought Indians were incapable of looking after their own interests. He now decided to come down hard on the nationalists. While Gandhi was on the seas, several Congress leaders were arrested, among them Jawaharlal Nehru and Khan Abdul Ghaffar Khan, for mobilizing peasants against exactions by officials. Gandhi sardonically remarked that 'I take these as Christmas presents to me from Lord Willingdon'.

These arrests presaged further conflict, perhaps a fresh round of mass civil disobedience. But, Gandhi added: 'If there is any possibility of avoiding satyagraha, I shall do my utmost to prevent it . . .'[4]

The day after he landed in Bombay, Gandhi wired the viceroy, deploring the arrest of his 'valued comrades'. He asked Willingdon to clarify whether 'friendly relations between us are closed or whether you expect me still to see you and receive guidance . . .' The viceroy sent back a stiff reply, saying that by starting a no-rent campaign in the United Provinces, the Congress had violated the terms of the Gandhi–Irwin Pact, compelling the government 'to take measures to prevent a general state of disorder'.

Gandhi answered that he could not 'repudiate' his 'valued comrades' for seeking, non-violently, to assist a depressed and defeated peasantry. He thought 'any government jealous of the welfare of the masses would welcome voluntary co-operation of a body like the Congress which admittedly exercises great influence over the masses . . .'

Gandhi now convened a meeting of the CWC, which said the arrests of their comrades 'betray no intention on the part of the bureaucracy to hand power to the people and are calculated to demoralize the nation'. The Congress called upon the government to 'institute a public and impartial enquiry' into the matters under dispute, failing which a fresh round of civil disobedience would commence.[5]

The Congress had its quarrels with the government. And, as the failure of the Round Table Conference revealed, it also had its quarrels with other Indian organizations. Gandhi's arguments with Ambedkar in particular made him realize that perhaps he (and the Congress) did not even represent all Hindus.

Now back in India, Gandhi sought to reach out to Ambedkar, albeit indirectly. On the evening of 2 January 1932, the spiritual leader Meher Baba came to see him in Mani Bhavan. The baba had followers among Parsis, Hindus, Muslims and even Christians. On hearing that Meher Baba was on his way to Nasik, a town that Ambedkar often visited, Gandhi asked that the two of them meet. The secretaries' record of the meeting has Gandhi telling Meher Baba: 'I know you can influence the Depressed Classes as you have been working for their uplift. Dr. Ambedkar personally is very considerate and reasonable, and if a personality like you can persuade him to view the question of Depressed Classes from a broader outlook of national unity and the consequent moral and spiritual strength accruing the reform, I am sure he would accept the joint electorates, and save seventy millions of our brethren from drifting away from the religious fold for paltry political gain at the cost of national disintegration. I am sure he [Ambedkar] will listen to you.'

'I will do my best,' answered Meher Baba. He too 'want[ed] this stigma of untouchability not to remain attached to Depressed Classes'. But whether he met Ambedkar and presented Gandhi's point of view to him the records do not say.[6]

II

In 1930, Lord Irwin had waited before arresting Gandhi. It was unlikely that his successor would repeat that mistake. Knowing this, on 3 January 1932, Gandhi issued instructions through the press as to what the public should do when he was taken into custody. They should wear khadi, boycott foreign goods, manufacture their own salt and picket liquor shops, in all of these actions 'discard[ing] every trace of violence'.[7]

In Bombay, Gandhi was staying as usual at Mani Bhavan. It was his custom to sleep on the terrace, the open sky above him, his disciples on the floor around him. Early in the morning of 4 January, he was woken up by the city's commissioner of police, who had come to arrest him. It was Gandhi's day of silence. Asking for a pencil and piece of paper, he wrote; 'I shall be ready to come with you in half an hour.'

Gandhi brushed his teeth, washed his face, and came back to the terrace, where his followers were waiting. They sang his favourite hymn, 'Vaishnava Jana To'. As he walked down the stairs, Kasturba followed him, saying: 'Can't I come with you?' The police gently moved her aside, although they took Mahadev, for whom too they had an arrest warrant. Later that day, they picked up Vallabhbhai Patel from another part of the city.[8]

From Bombay, Gandhi was conveyed by car and train to Yerwada prison, where he had spent two long spells already. He quickly settled into his jail routine: prayer, walk, breakfast, spinning, reading, lunch, nap, another walk, more spinning and reading, prayer, dinner, bed. This time, Gandhi was sharing a cell with Vallabhbhai Patel. Patel followed the same routine as Gandhi, except that he walked more (being younger) and (not being a food faddist) ate other things besides fruits, nuts and vegetables.

In the first month of this prison term, Gandhi read books on finance, Islam, the cow, Egypt and khadi. Later, he turned to fiction and drama, reading plays by Tagore, stories by Maithilisharan Gupt, and more novels by Upton Sinclair. He also brushed up on his Urdu, writing in that language to Raihana Tyabji, who offered corrections by return of post.

There were no restrictions on Gandhi writing or receiving letters so long as they were on non-political subjects. As before, he wrote often to his disciples in the ashram, offering advice or answering queries on diet, health, prayer. He was also allowed to receive and read a wide range of newspapers and periodicals.

III

Having burnt his bridges with the viceroy, from the jail Gandhi chose to write to Willingdon's boss, Samuel Hoare, the secretary of state for India. He assured him that he had come back from London 'with every intention of co-operating with the Government'. But, he added, 'the events he saw in India did startle me'. He had sought an interview with the viceroy but was denied one.[9]

Gandhi next wrote to the man placed immediately below the viceroy, namely, the governor of Bombay, Frederick Sykes. Recalling their 'cordial conversations' in 1931 (when a settlement was arrived at with the government), Gandhi told Sykes that the crackdown on the Congress was 'a tragic blunder'. As a 'friend wishing well to the English', he still hoped that the fight could 'be conducted honourably on either side so that at the end of it either party may say of the other that there was no malice behind its actions'.[10]

While Gandhi was confined to his cell in Yerwada, his ideas were being discussed across the world. In April 1932, a quite extraordinary advertisement appeared in the New York Times, placed by Saks, a clothing company located at the corner of 34th Street and Broadway, and covering almost a whole page of the newspaper. The ad featured an illustration of a row of four men in suits on a bench on a railway platform, all reading a newspaper.

Below this line drawing was the slogan 'EVERYBODY BUT GANDHI'. Then followed the ad copy, which ran: 'The Mahatma chooses to spin his own . . . such as it is . . . and that's *his* business! He needn't read this ad. But all the rest of you gentlemen prefer to wear good suits . . . and that's *our* business. So between here and the next station, cast your eye carefully over the most satisfying news in today's paper . . . 7 straight facts about the SAKSTON . . . created and sold exclusively by Saks. 34. Street.'

Then followed seven sober sentences listing the attributes of the suits made by Saks, as in the quality of the fabric and the tailoring, the range of colours and sizes, and their affordability.[11]

It turns out Gandhi did not have to visit the United States to be known there. This ad in the *New York Times* suggests that the well-dressed man in America knew precisely what Gandhi was wearing— or *not* wearing.

IV

While Gandhi was in jail, he heard from his wife that his eldest son, Harilal, was drinking heavily. His behaviour was often abusive. His children were with his late wife's sister; Harilal wished to take possession of them, but the children were scared to be with their father.

Gandhi now wrote to Harilal's daughter to 'tell him plainly that, as long as he does not give up drinking, he will have to assume that you do not exist. If all of us adopt such a course, Harilal might take heed. Often a drunkard gives up his evil habit when he is greatly shocked.'[12]

Denied access to his children, Harilal wrote to his father blaming him for the estrangement. Gandhi wrote back that he was preserving the letter 'so that, when you have awakened, you may see the insolence of your letter and weep over it and laugh at your folly'.[13]

Harilal wrote his father another angry letter. This time Gandhi did not reply, for (as he told his nephew Narandas) 'either he has written it in great excitement, or he was drunk when he wrote it. The language is all excitement and insolence. No attention is paid to ordinary syntax, words are left incomplete and even the signature is not completed. I think we shall completely forget him now.'[14]

In August 1932, Pranjivan Mehta passed away in Rangoon. Gandhi and Mehta first met in London in 1888, and stayed continuously in touch ever since. Mehta had funded Gandhi's work in South Africa; had underwritten his journal *Indian Opinion*; and even funded the first laudatory biography of Gandhi, written by the Non-Conformist priest Joseph Doke in 1908–09.

It was also Mehta who, before anyone else, recognized his friend's ability to move, inspire and lead people. It was Mehta who first called Gandhi a 'Mahatma'; Mehta who had long urged that Gandhi leave South Africa to work on the bigger stage that was India; Mehta who had helped fund the Satyagraha Ashram on the banks of the Sabarmati in Ahmedabad.

Writing to Henry Polak, who had known Mehta well, Gandhi called him 'a lifelong faithful friend', whose death made him 'treasure his many virtues now more than ever'. To Mehta's nephew he wrote: 'I had no greater friend than Doctor in this whole world, and for me he is still alive. But I am unable to do anything from here to keep his nest whole, and that makes me unhappy.'

In a tribute written in jail, but published many years later, Gandhi recalled both the depth of his friendship with Mehta and the doctor's own virtues. 'He had helped and supported a number of people,' he wrote. 'There was no ostentation in his help. He never boasted about it. It knew no limits of caste or community or province.' The barrister, doctor and jewellery merchant 'scrupulously followed truth both in his business and his legal practice. I know he had great hatred of falsehood and hypocrisy. His ahimsa was visible on his face and in his eyes . . .'[15]

V

In March 1932, Gandhi had read in the newspapers that the government's proposal to create separate electorates for Depressed

Classes would be announced soon. He wrote at once to the secretary
of state for India, Samuel Hoare, reminding him that at the time of
the Round Table Conference, he had said that he would resist this
'with my life'. This, insisted Gandhi now, 'was not said in the heat of
the moment, nor by way of rhetoric'.

Gandhi told Hoare that 'so far as Hinduism is concerned separate
electorates would simply vivisect and disrupt it'. Moreover, separate
electorates were 'neither penance [for the caste Hindus for their past
and present sins] nor any remedy [for the Depressed Classes] for the
crushing degradation they have groaned under'.

Gandhi informed Hoare 'respectfully' that if the government
went ahead with their announcement, he would fast unto death. This
was 'a call of conscience which I dare not disobey, even though it may
cost whatever reputation for sanity I may possess'. He added that
discharging him from jail 'would not make the duty of fasting any the
less imperative'.

Hoare answered that the matter would not be decided for at least
some weeks. He added that 'we intend to give any decision that may
be necessary solely and only upon the merits of the case', and after
taking into account 'the views that have been expressed on both sides
of the controversy'.[16]

There it rested for some months. Then on 17 August, the British
prime minister, Ramsay MacDonald, formally announced that,
apart from Muslims and Sikhs, Depressed Classes would be treated
as a 'minority community' entitled to a separate electorate. Gandhi
immediately wrote to MacDonald, reminding him of his letter to
Samuel Hoare back in March. Now that the decision had been made,
he would undergo 'a perpetual fast unto death from food of any kind
save water'. He would begin the fast on 20 September, but would call
it off if 'the British Government, of its own motion or under pressure
of public opinion, revise their decision'.[17]

Before he sent the letter, Gandhi asked his friend and fellow
prisoner, Vallabhbhai Patel, to read it. The Sardar remarked that
he had made no reference to the other parts of the prime minister's
award; did that mean that he approved of them? Gandhi answered
that it did not. The Muslims might combine with the British; but
Gandhi felt that combination could be dealt with. When freedom

came, and 'the outsider who foments quarrels is gone, we can tackle our [Hindu–Muslim] problems with success'. On the other hand, separate electorates for the Depressed Classes would 'create division among Hindus so much that it would lead [immediately] to bloodshed'. Hence, it had to be resisted, and at once.[18]

Replying to Gandhi, MacDonald said he had read the letter with 'surprise' and 'regret'. He claimed the creation of separate electorates would place the representatives of the Depressed Classes 'in a position to speak for themselves', whereas in the case of joint electorates the members could not 'genuinely represent' the Depressed Classes, since 'in practically all cases such members would be elected by a majority consisting of higher caste Hindus'. At the same time, argued MacDonald, since the Depressed Classes would also have a vote in the general Hindu constituencies, this would unite rather than separate them from the Hindus, which Gandhi had said he wanted. The British prime minister found himself 'quite unable to understand the reason' for Gandhi's decision to fast.[19]

As the correspondence between Gandhi, Hoare and MacDonald was made public, there was a rash of commentary in the press. The Depressed Classes leader from South India, M.C. Rajah, saw separate electorates as 'dangerous and suicidal', throwing lower castes into conflict with their fellow Hindus.[20] The pro-Indian British journalist, B.G. Horniman, said MacDonald's 'Communal Award' was 'designed to inspire the minds of untouchables with a spirit of antagonism and hostility to their brethren of the Hindu community and petrify the sense of separation with which they now be obsessed into a perpetual phenomenon in India's future polity'.[21]

The person most obsessed (to use Horniman's phrase) with separate electorates was B.R. Ambedkar. He had made the case for them in both the Round Table Conferences; it was largely his arguments that persuaded the British to grant them. Ambedkar was convinced that upper-caste reformers such as Gandhi could not truly understand or represent the Depressed Classes. They needed their own leaders, their own representatives in legislative assemblies across India.

Madan Mohan Malaviya now called a meeting of Hindu and Depressed Classes leaders in Delhi. The hope was that a settlement would be agreed upon, allowing Gandhi to call off his fast. Ambedkar declined to attend this meeting, telling a journalist he'd rather wait for a concrete proposal from Gandhi himself. In Ambedkar's view, 'there was no need' for Gandhi to 'impose on himself the vow of fasting. 'As soon as Mr. Gandhi's proposals are known,' said Ambedkar, 'I will give my answer in fifteen minutes.' Ambedkar added that, unlike Gandhi, 'I am not a man who allows my conscience to dominate practicality.' He said his 'supreme consideration is the interests of the Depressed Classes I represent and nothing else comes in the way'.[22]

Ambedkar followed this interview with a long, signed article expressing how 'astounded' he was by Gandhi's decision to fast. He defended separate electorates as the best way for 'untouchables' to escape 'the tyranny of the majority'. All across India the Depressed Classes were 'mercilessly' put down and exploited; therefore, 'for a community so handicapped to succeed in the struggle for life against organised tyranny, some share of political power in order that it may protect itself was a paramount necessity'.

Ambedkar continued:

> I should have thought that a well-wisher of the Depressed Classes would have fought tooth and nail for securing for them as much political power as might be possible in the new Constitution. But the Mahatma's ways of thinking are strange and certainly beyond my comprehension. He not only does not endeavour to augment the scanty political power which the Depressed Classes have got under the Communal Award, but on the contrary has staked his very life in order to deprive them of the little they have got.

Gandhi, claimed Ambedkar, had orally promised him that the Congress would encourage candidates from the Depressed Classes who contested in general seats, but in the absence of constitutional safeguards such promises meant nothing. Ambedkar thus wrote that he could not

> accept the assurances of the Mahatma that he and his Congress will do the needful. I cannot leave so important a question as the protection of my people to conventions and misunderstandings. The Mahatma is not an immortal person . . . There have been many Mahatmas in

India whose sole object was to remove untouchability and to elevate and absorb the Depressed Classes but every one of them have failed in their mission. Mahatmas have come and Mahatmas have gone. But untouchables have remained as untouchables.

Ambedkar remarked that he would have understood if the Mahatma was to fast unto death 'for stopping riots between Hindus and Mahomedans' or for 'any other national cause', but to do so to oppose the Communal Award would 'result in nothing but terrorism by his followers against the Depressed Classes all over the country'.

The last sentences of Ambedkar's powerful and poignant statement ran: 'I, however, trust the Mahatma will not drive me to the necessity of making a choice between his life and the rights of my people. For, I can never consent to deliver my people bound hand and foot to the caste Hindus for generations to come.'[23]

VI

On 16 September, Gandhi drafted a press release explaining the purposes of the fast. This urged reformers to work harder for 'the fullest freedom for the "depressed classes" inside the Hindu fold', asking them to 'count their lives of no cost to achieve the liberation of these classes and therefore [rid] Hinduism of this age-old superstition'. The same day, he also wrote letters to some friends informing them of this 'momentous step in my life'; this select group included the British Quaker Agatha Harrison, Romain Rolland, Anasuya Sarabhai, and, significantly, Saraladevi Chaudhurani.[24]

On 19 September, the *Times of India* printed a report on Gandhi's preparation for the fast, filed by its Poona correspondent. Based on leaks from the prison staff, the paper had come to know that Gandhi 'has been refraining from his usual exercise, cutting it slowly down so that to-day he is taking little or none, and thus will not feel the need of it to the same extent when he starts his fast and is compelled to conserve his energy to keep his grip on life. He still turns once a day to spinning, but more as a matter of form than to complete a daily task and maintain a regular output as his contribution to the Swadeshi movement. . . . He is even reading less than hitherto but is always bright and cheerful.'[25]

In the early hours of the 20th, Gandhi drafted a letter to Rabindranath Tagore, asking for his blessings if he approved of the fast; if not, he would 'yet prize your criticism, if your heart condemns my action'. Before he could post the letter, he was handed a telegram by the prison staff; it was from Tagore, saying he would 'follow your sublime penance with reverence and love'. Gandhi now added a postscript, saying the poet's 'loving and magnificent wire' would 'sustain me in the midst of the storm I am about to enter'.[26]

Gandhi had fasted many times in the past. However, all his previous fasts had been for a duration specified by him in advance. This was his first *indefinite* fast.

Gandhi's fast unto death to keep the Depressed Classes in the Hindu fold was to begin at 12 noon on 20 September 1932. That day, he had a meal of fruits and vegetables at 7 a.m., and a glass of honey and hot water at 11.30 a.m. Then his disciple Raihana Tyabji sang a few hymns, beginning with one of her own compositions in Hindi, whose first line (in translation) read, 'O traveller, get up, leave your bed, because it is daybreak.' When the clock struck twelve, Gandhi commenced his fast, saying he had never felt fitter in his life.[27]

Later that evening, a group of journalists were allowed to meet him. They found him in the prison courtyard, lying on a cot placed under the shade of a mango tree. Around him were Mahadev, Vallabhbhai and Kasturba, who had come down from Ahmedabad to be with her husband.

As his followers fanned away the flies, Gandhi told the visiting newsmen of his experiences seeing and speaking to 'untouchables' in different parts of India, from which he had drawn the conclusion 'that, if they are ever to rise, it will not be by reservation of seats but will be by the strenuous work of Hindu reformers in their midst, and it is because I feel that this separation [by electorates] would have killed all prospect of reform that my whole soul has rebelled against it . . .'

Gandhi said that he lived for, and was willing to die for, 'the eradication of untouchability root and branch'. He wanted 'a living pact whose life-giving effect would be felt . . . by an all-India demonstration of "touchables" and "untouchables" meeting together, not by way of a theatrical show, but in real brotherly embrace'. If untouchability was 'really rooted out', argued Gandhi, it would 'not merely purge Hinduism of a terrible blot but its repercussions will be world-wide. My fight against untouchability is a fight against the impure in humanity . . .'

In this struggle, said Gandhi, his own life was 'of no consequence. One hundred lives given for this noble cause would, in my opinion, be poor penance done by Hindus for the atrocious wrongs they have heaped upon helpless men and women of their faith.'[28]

Of Gandhi's long-standing commitment to ending untouchability, there could be no question. Even so, this moving account of how he had arrived at his decision was marred by the use of that unfortunate adjective, 'helpless'. It sounded patronizing, robbing 'untouchables' of agency, of being able to articulate their own demands and grievances. This was precisely the kind of attitude that Ambedkar was protesting against.[29]

As Gandhi fasted in Poona, a conference began in Bombay seeking ways to save his life. Attending this meeting were Malaviya, Sapru, Jayakar, Rajagopalachari and Rajendra Prasad. Ambedkar was also finally persuaded to take part. Late in the evening, Rajagopalachari and G.D. Birla went to Poona to meet Gandhi, carrying a proposal for joint electorates drafted by the former.

Meanwhile, reports were coming in from across the country of upper castes offering a concrete demonstration of repentance in response to Gandhi's call. Temples were being thrown open to 'untouchables' in, among other places, Ayodhya, Banaras, Calcutta, Allahabad, Bombay and Sirsi. The *Bombay Chronicle* carried the news under this headline: 'Orthodoxy Yields: More Temples Opened to "Untouchables": Country's Grim Effort to Save Mahatma'.[30]

On the evening of 21 September, Ambedkar left for Poona to meet with Gandhi. Before boarding the train, he gave an interview to the *Times of India*. He had heard that Gandhi wished to meet him as well as the veteran leader of the Depressed Classes in South India, M.C. Rajah. Ambedkar made it clear that he 'will have nothing to do by way of negotiation with Mr. Rajah and his party, and if Mr. Gandhi wishes to talk with them, he should do so separately. My reason for saying this is that the dispute is really between me and my party on the one hand and Mr. Gandhi on the other.'[31]

The self-confidence was striking. More than twenty years younger than Gandhi, far less known than him in India or abroad, Ambedkar saw himself as a political equal. It was an argument between his party and Gandhi's. They were the two leaders who mattered; the rest were peripheral or inconsequential.

On the 22nd, Ambedkar visited Gandhi at Yerwada jail. They talked for three hours, mostly about the compromise formula in which there would be joint electorates, but with greater representation for the Depressed Classes than in the Communal Award. One exchange, of which notes were taken down by Mahadev Desai, was telling. Ambedkar said that 'I want political power for my community. That is indispensable for our survival.' Gandhi, in reply, said that 'you are born an untouchable but I am an untouchable by adoption. And as a new convert I feel more for the welfare of the community than those who are already there.'[32]

On this day, the 22nd, Gandhi met separately with other Depressed Classes leaders, among them M.C. Rajah and Palwankar Baloo, a famous cricketer who had been an early hero of Ambedkar's. He also had discussions with Tej Bahadur Sapru and M.R. Jayakar, who, once again, were emerging as important mediators. Both were top-flight lawyers, and both had close connections with the Imperial Government.[33]

During the first two nights of his fast, Gandhi slept in the open, under the sky. During the day he spun yarn and held prayer meetings in the morning and evening. Now, however, he had been three days without food and was passing through what one newspaper described as 'the worst stage in the fast—the time when the pangs of hunger are beginning to fade and the faster is about to enter what Mr. Gandhi described as "The brooding period" where he becomes one with the subject for which he is fasting. His face is becoming more drawn and his eyes somewhat sunken. Nevertheless, he has been able to receive many visitors.'

On 24 September, the *Bombay Chronicle*'s front page carried this headline: 'SUDDEN TURN IN MAHATMA'S HEALTH CAUSES ANXIETY'. Gandhi, said the newspaper, was feeling the strain of the fast and the effect of prolonged conversations in this state. He was having bouts of nausea. His voice had grown feeble. He had difficulty keeping his eyes open. And he had lost several pounds in weight.

On the same day, the *Chronicle* carried an essay by B.G. Horniman, which argued that, beyond questions of separate versus joint electorates,

> for those who work in the field of social and religious reform there is still a stupendous task to be attacked and completed, in the emancipation of the untouchables from their outcaste status from birth to death—their right to take water from the wells, to enter the temples of their faith, for their children to sit in the schools with those of other castes and communities, and the right to live and move and have their being on equal terms with their fellow-men. All this will not be the work of a day or a year. The battle against orthodoxy will still be a hard one, and it will be prolonged.[34]

VII

From very early in his career B.R. Ambedkar had no difficulty in being alone or exceptional. At a young age, he had chosen to strike out on his own, to form his own political organization rather than join one that already existed. In an already crowded political field this was a courageous choice. Between 1913 and 1926, he was in and out of India, the years spent overseas used to acquire doctorates from Columbia University and the London School of Economics, and to qualify as a barrister at the London Bar.

Ambedkar had been politically active even as a young college student in Bombay. But it was only from the mid-1920s that politics and social reform became a full-time concern. Within a few years, he had made a considerable impact through his scholarship, his eloquence and his commitment. Recognized as the main leader of the Depressed Classes in his native Maharashtra, he had also made a powerful impression on the British rulers. They invited him as a delegate to the two Round Table Conferences, in each of which he made the case for separate electorates for his people.

A journalist who knew him well in the 1930s wrote that 'Ambedkar was undoubtedly a tall man, who appeared far taller among the pigmies surrounding him. But he had a pretty good conceit of himself. Why not? He was a self-made man and risen by his own talents. He had proved that in this secularly oppressed class there probably was an untapped reservoir of talent.'[35]

Had Ambedkar been less independent-minded, he would have either joined the Congress or taken a secure, well-paying job in the colonial administration. But in the former case, he knew he would have to play second fiddle to Gandhi, while in the latter he would not be free to express his views. In charting his own path, Ambedkar had come into conflict with the country's major political party and even with senior leaders of his own Depressed Classes. This isolation he did not mind; indeed, he was probably prepared for it. But Gandhi's fast unto death had placed him in a situation far more uncomfortable than any he had faced before. With other leaders of the Depressed Classes allying with the Congress, with the opening of temples signalling an (admittedly very belated and partial) opening of the Hindu mind, he felt far more isolated than ever before. And perhaps he felt coerced as well. Every day that Gandhi went without food added to the pressure on Ambedkar to reach an agreement. For, if the most influential Indian of the age was to succumb to his fast, how could Ambedkar continue to live with the burden of Gandhi's death on his head and on his conscience?

VIII

On 23 September, a day-long meeting was held in Poona to discuss the terms of a possible compromise. On one side were the caste Hindus, represented by Sapru, Jayakar, Rajagopalachari and the social worker A.V. Thakkar, among others. On the other side were leaders of the Depressed Classes, led by Ambedkar. One who was there recalled that 'Dr. Ambedkar and his group acted in concert and showed the greatest discipline. They proved themselves to be hard bargainers. It was the Doctor himself who did most of the speaking on behalf of the group.'[36]

The discussion centred around the key question of representation. If there were to be joint electorates, how many seats should the Depressed Classes have in the legislature? In the Communal Award with separate electorates, they were granted seventy-one seats all told in the provincial legislatures. The caste Hindus were happy to increase this number if their demand for a joint electorate was agreed upon. But by how much?

Ambedkar began by asking for a total of 197 seats. The other side thought this excessively high. It was agreed that the tally should be based on the proportion of the Depressed Classes in the total population, province by province. Census figures were presented and analysed. 'The redoubtable Doctor, strongly supported by his colleagues, fought every inch of the ground.'[37] After many hours of discussion, a figure of 148 seats was agreed upon by both parties. This was a little more than twice the number granted to the Depressed Classes by the Communal Award. The Depressed Classes were to be allocated thirty seats in both the Punjab and Bengal, twenty apiece in the Central and the United Provinces, and fifteen in Bombay. It was also agreed that 19 per cent of the general seats in the central legislature would be reserved for the Depressed Classes.

Ambedkar had asked that any agreement arrived at should be put to a referendum of the Depressed Classes after a few years. The Congress leaders were not prepared to concede this. Eventually, the matter was taken to Gandhi. It was now past nine at night. Ambedkar and Gandhi talked by the latter's bed under the mango tree. The Doctor asked for a referendum; Gandhi said he would not object to one. As the conversation continued, Gandhi's voice became noticeably weaker. Now the doctors stepped in; they would not further endanger the fasting man's health any more. He must get some rest after what for him (and everybody else) had been an exhausting, nerve-racking day.

The next day the discussions continued. Malaviya and company continued to be adamantly opposed to a referendum. Ambedkar asked for a referendum after ten years. Gandhi answered that if he distrusted the caste Hindus, it was better that he tested their conscience after five years itself. Ambedkar was not sure whether this was enough time to judge whether joint electorates were better than separate ones. Gandhi insisted that if he was unsure it was better he tested them sooner rather than later. According to one eyewitness, he even said: 'There you are. Five years or my life.'[38]

On 24 September, the doctors told Gandhi that if he did not terminate the fast, his health would rapidly deteriorate, and he would not be able to 'continue negotiations for much longer'. His 'vitality was decidedly lower', while his other parameters (urine, blood pressure, etc.) portended 'entry into the danger zone'. So that it would not be blamed in case he died, the government was considering moving Gandhi to a private residence in Poona.[39]

In their conversations, Ambedkar had seen for himself how tired and weary Gandhi was. Could he afford to have the matter unresolved much longer? After meeting Gandhi on the 24th afternoon, Ambedkar went into a huddle with his colleagues. They were still unsure as to whether it would be prudent to have a referendum before ten years had elapsed. Eventually, acting on a suggestion by Rajagopalachari, it was decided to drop the question of the referendum altogether.

At 5 p.m. on the 24th, what became known as the 'Poona Pact' was formally signed in the presence of Gandhi. This ratified the number of reserved seats, province by province, with further clauses committing its signatories to providing educational facilities to the Depressed Classes and a fairer representation in the public services. The twenty-two people (all men) who signed the pact in the first instance included Ambedkar, Malaviya, Sapru, Jayakar, G.D. Birla, Rajah, Baloo and Rajagopalachari. Notably, Gandhi himself did not sign the agreement on his own behalf, though his son Devadas did.[40]

The signatories proceeded to Bombay where, on the afternoon of Sunday, 25 September, a meeting was held in the hall of the Indian Merchants' Chambers. Speeches were made by the key actors—Malaviya, Sapru, Rajagopalachari, M.C. Rajah and, most notably, B.R. Ambedkar. Here is part of what Ambedkar said:

> I believe it is no exaggeration for me to say that no man a few days ago was placed in a greater dilemma than I was. There was placed before me a difficult situation in which I had to make a choice between two difficult alternatives.

There was the life of the greatest man in India to be saved. There was also before me the problem to try and safeguard the interests of the community which in my humble way I was trying to do . . . I am happy to be able to say that it has become [possible] through the co-operation of all of us to find a solution so as to save the life of the Mahatma and at the same time consistent with such protection as is necessary for the interests of the Depressed Classes in the future. I think in all these negotiations a large part of the credit must be attributed to Mahatma Gandhi himself. I must confess that I was surprised, immensely surprised, when I met him that there was so much in common between him and me. (Cheers).

In those intense, agonizing days in Poona, several disputes arose between Ambedkar and the caste Hindu negotiators. The Doctor said that when these disputes were carried to Gandhi, 'I was astounded to see that the man who held such divergent views from mine at the R[ound] T[able] C[onference] came immediately to my rescue and not to the rescue of the other side. I am very grateful to the Mahatma for having extricated me from what might have been [a] very difficult situation.'

Later in his speech, Ambedkar warned the audience that joint electorates should not be seen as a perfect or total solution for the problems faced by the Depressed Communities. 'Beyond this political arrangement', ways had to be found to allow the Depressed Classes to 'occupy a[n] honourable position, a position of equality of status within the community'.[41]

IX

On the day that Gandhi's fast began, 20 September, Rabindranath Tagore addressed the students and staff of Santiniketan. He told them that 'the penance the Mahatmaji has taken upon himself is not a ritual, but a message to India and to the world'. Gandhi was willing to lay down his life to dismantle a system whereby Indians had 'banished a considerable number of our own people into a narrow enclosure of insult branding them with the sign of permanent degradation'.[42]

On the 24th, Tagore left for Poona, by train. The journey was arduous at his age; he was past seventy, and he was travelling through the hottest and most humid parts of India. Two full days later, he arrived in Poona to be with Gandhi. An attendant around the prisoner's bedside wrote of how, on the afternoon of the 26th, the poet, 'bent with age and covered with a long flowing cloak proceeded step by step very slowly to greet Gandhiji who was lying in bed. Bapuji raised himself up a little bit, and affectionately embraced Tagore, and then began to comb his white beard with his shaking fingers, like a child. Soon afterwards he was exhausted, and went to sleep'.[43]

As it turned out, shortly after they met in the prison courtyard, the news came that Ramsay Macdonald's government had accepted the Poona Pact and would implement it. To celebrate, Tagore sang a verse from his Nobel Prize–winning poem, *Gitanjali*. Kasturba then offered her husband some orange juice, after which Gandhi served food to some 'untouchable' prisoners.[44]

After the celebrations had died out, Gandhi dictated a statement to the press, thanking Ambedkar, Rajah and their colleagues. The Depressed Classes leaders, he said, could 'have taken up an uncompromising and defiant attitude by way of punishment to the so-called caste Hindus for the sins of generations'. Instead, 'they chose a nobler path and have thus shown that they have followed the precept of forgiveness enjoined by all religions'.[45]

Perhaps the most interesting foreign comment on Gandhi's ordeal appeared in the *New Statesman*, which printed a poem that began:

> So, thanks to the Mahatma's fast,
> 'untouchables' and men of caste
> Have sensibly achieved, at last
>   A reconciliation.
> Does this suggest a new technique
> For bringing faction, State and clique
> In more progressive lands, to seek
>   Peace and co-operation?

Later verses urged the adoption of Gandhi's technique to Britain's leaders to stop Germany rearming, to Ireland's patriots to press

Britain into giving further concessions, to the cricketer Herbert Sutcliffe to make the game's notoriously parsimonious administrators pay professional sportsmen like him a fair wage.[46]

X

As a response to Gandhi's fast, some Hindus resolved to start an 'Anti-Untouchability League'. The industrialist G.D. Birla would serve as president, and the veteran social worker A.V. Thakkar as secretary. The league would have its headquarters in Delhi. Its objects included the opening, through non-violent means, of all public wells, roads, schools, temples and burning ghats to members of the Depressed Classes.

When he heard of the formation of this Anti-Untouchability League, B.R. Ambedkar wrote Thakkar a fascinating letter outlining two routes for the emancipation of the 'untouchables'. One was to foster 'personal virtue' in the Depressed Classes by making them stop drinking, attend schools, and read in libraries. The other was to confront the social disabilities they faced. Ambedkar strongly urged that the league adopt the latter approach, and launch a 'campaign of civic rights' to provide the Depressed Classes access to village wells, village schools, public employment, etc. Aware that this frontal attack might lead to conflict and even bloodshed, Ambedkar believed that 'such a programme if carried into the villages will bring about the necessary social revolution in the Hindu Society without which it will never be possible for the Depressed Classes to get equal social status'. The 'salvation of the Depressed Classes', insisted Ambedkar, 'will come only when the Caste Hindu is made to think and is forced to feel that he must alter his ways. For that you must create a crisis by direct action against his customary code of conduct.'

Ambedkar also wanted the league to open up the weaving departments of cotton mills to the Depressed Classes. At the time, only the lowest-paid jobs such as scavenging or manual labour were available to them. With regard to the prejudice of Indian factory owners towards the Depressed Classes, Ambedkar pointed out that 'like the Negro in America he is the last to be employed in days of prosperity and the first to be fired in days of adversity'.

Finally, Ambedkar advocated the promotion of greater social intercourse between the Depressed Classes and caste Hindus. He suggested that the latter employ them in their houses as servants or welcome them as guests. 'The live contact thus established will familiarize both to a common and associated life and will pave the way to that unity which we are all striving after.' Ambedkar pressed this method of 'fraternising with the untouchables', even if it offended orthodoxy or led to the employers being ostracized by their caste men. Once more, Ambedkar drew an analogy, and this time a more powerful one, with race relations in America. The Depressed Classes, he insisted, 'will never be satisfied of the bona fides of these caste Hindu sympathisers until it is proved that they are prepared to go to the same length of fighting against their own kith and kin in actual warfare if it came to that for the sake of the Depressed Classes as the Whites of the North did against their own kith and kin namely the Whites of the South for the sake of the emancipation of the Negro'.[47]

The formation of this new Anti-Untouchability League was one response to the Poona Pact. A second response was to restart the process of Hindu–Muslim reconciliation. The prime mover was one of the few major Muslim leaders still left in the Congress, Maulana Abul Kalam Azad. Azad met with Madan Mohan Malaviya, and then the two in turn met their long-estranged comrade Maulana Shaukat Ali. Shaukat Ali now wired the viceroy asking him to release Gandhi from prison so that he could help them reach 'an amicable and lasting settlement'. Willingdon said that would not be possible, since the prisoner had not 'definitely disassociate[d] himself from civil disobedience'.[48]

XI

After the September fast, the government modified the terms of Gandhi's detention. Attempts at Hindu–Muslim reconciliation remained verboten. But Gandhi was now permitted visitors who came to discuss the anti-untouchability campaign. Another change was to allow Kasturba to stay on in the prison; she spent the days with her husband but slept elsewhere in the jail.

After the Poona Pact, Gandhi had begun referring to the 'untouchables' as 'Harijans', a term meaning 'Children of God'. He thought it less pejorative than 'untouchable' or its equivalent in Indian languages, less patronizing than the colonial coinage, 'Depressed Classes', and more indigenous-sounding than his own earlier alternative, 'suppressed classes'.

The term 'Harijan' had first been used by the medieval poet-saint Narasinha Mehta, whom Gandhi had long admired. 'Not that the change of name brings about any change of status,' he remarked, 'but one may at least be spared the use of a term which is itself one of reproach.'[49]

On 17 October—three weeks after his last visit—B.R. Ambedkar came to see Gandhi in Yerwada. He began by asking the prisoner to formally abandon civil disobedience and attend the third Round Table Conference, to be held in London in November. Ambedkar said, 'The point is that if you do not come, we shall get nothing in England and everything will be upset. People like Iqbal who are enemies of the country will come to the forefront. We have to work any sort of constitution. Hence though I am a small man, I request you to come.'

These words are quoted from Mahadev Desai's notes of the meeting. Gandhi asked Ambedkar to elaborate this argument and write about it in the newspapers. If he made the plea public, Gandhi would 'think over it'. Ambedkar replied: 'It is not a thing that can be put down in writing. In it I have to say a lot that will hurt the Muslims and I cannot say that publicly.'

The bulk of the discussions focused on the best way to end untouchability. In a statement issued several weeks after their meeting, Gandhi recalled Ambedkar telling him: 'Let there be no repetition of the old method when the reformer claimed to know more of the requirements of his victims than the victims themselves.' Ambedkar advised Gandhi to 'tell your workers to ascertain from the representatives of the [Depressed Classes] what their first need is and how they would like it to be satisfied'. Ambedkar added that specially organized mixed dinners had 'a flavour of patronage about them. I would not like to attend them by myself. The more dignified procedure would be to invite us to ordinary social functions without any fuss.' Finally, Ambedkar told Gandhi that 'even temple-entry, good and necessary as it is, may wait. The crying need is the raising of the economic status and decent behaviour in the daily contact.'

Having quoted (from memory) these cautionary remarks by Ambedkar, Gandhi added: 'I must not repeat here some of the harrowing details given by him from his own bitter experiences. I felt the force of his remarks. I hope every one of my readers will do likewise.'[50]

The conversation pointed to the fundamental philosophical differences that—their recent pact notwithstanding—still existed between the two men. Ambedkar placed more faith in constitutional processes, in changes in the law—hence his plea to Gandhi to attend the London meeting. Gandhi saw more hope in social change, in the self-directed renewal of individuals and communities. Ambedkar emphasized the creation of jobs for 'untouchables'; Gandhi the creation of a sense of spiritual equality between Hindus of all castes. As an upper-caste reformer, Gandhi was motivated by a sense of guilt, the desire to make reparation for past sins, whereas as one born in an 'untouchable' home, Ambedkar was animated by the drive to achieve a position of social equality and human dignity for his fellows.

Two weeks after this meeting, Gandhi told a group of journalists that 'I do not take the same light view that Dr. Ambedkar does of the temple-entry question. . . . Nothing in my opinion will strike the imagination of the Hindu mass mind including Harijans as throwing [open] all public temples to them precisely on the same terms as caste Hindus. . . . After all Hindu temples play a most important part in the life of the masses . . .'

Gandhi added that he did not at all belittle the other disabilities that Ambedkar had pointed to (such as lack of access to education and dignified employment). However, he felt 'the evil is so deep-rooted that one must not make the choice between different disabilities, but must tackle them all at once'.[51]

XII

After the Poona Pact was signed, Gandhi got a truckload of correspondence from orthodox Hindus appalled at his concessions to the Depressed Classes. Many pandits and shastris visited him to make the case that temple entry was against the scriptures. One visitor from Madras asked Gandhi to accept a compromise whereby 'untouchables' could enter the flagposts of temples (normally inside the boundary walls but outside the shrine itself), but not enter the sanctum sanctorum where the deity was placed. Gandhi answered that 'there was no half-way house in the house of God. There is no such thing as temple-entry step by step. It should be unconditional and unqualified. The ["untouchables"] should be given the same equality of status as the other caste Hindus in the matter of public worship.'[52]

The orthodox backlash against Gandhi also took the form of conferences and demonstrations. In the second week of October, a meeting of the 'All Andhradesa Brahmana Mahasabha' was held in Vijayawada, attended by 500 pandits from all over the province. Temple entry for 'untouchables' was condemned as being against the Shastras. One speaker said only trustees of temples could decide who could enter them, adding that the Sarda Act (passed in 1930 to raise the age at which Hindu girls could be married) was an even greater evil than temple entry. The meeting ended with a unanimous resolution condemning both temple entry and the Sarda Act.[53]

On 17 December, Gandhi wrote to a friend: 'Those who claim to be sanatanists have put themselves in a state of rage as if I was about to violate all that is good in Hinduism . . . I can safely say that no two letters among the mass of letters I am receiving from sanatanists have agreed about the definition of untouchability. They either swear at me or enter into argument that has no bearing on the subject. . . . The correspondence I am having is a painful sign of decadence of Hinduism.'

A week later, he wrote to another friend: 'I am being visited by a great number of Shastris these days. Their plight is pitiful. It has become difficult to learn anything from them. They lack the capacity even to impart what they possess. And so I see them full of prejudices and hatreds.'

A week later still, he wrote to a third friend that 'I am having a glorious time with the *Shastris*. My knowledge of the letter of the Shastras is better but of true religion they are able to give me but little.'[54]

XIII

Two months after the Poona Pact was signed, Gandhi met with a deputation of 'untouchables'. They asked Gandhi to take concrete economic measures to aid them, such as having them admitted in the weaving department of mills (where they were currently not allowed). Then they sharply asked Gandhi: 'To what extent can we consider you as our man?' Gandhi answered: 'Since before Ambedkar was born, I have been your man. You will find all the things that he advocates in my old articles. Nobody has opposed untouchability in such strong language as I.'[55]

This was something of an exaggeration. When Ambedkar was born in 1891, Gandhi was a law student in London. Two years later he went to South Africa, where he began slowly shedding the social prejudices he had been raised with. But it was only after his return to India in 1915 that he began thinking more seriously about the iniquities of caste. Even so, his approach was gradualist and incremental. To begin with, he attacked only the practice of untouchability, seeking to keep the rest of the structure of caste intact. Then, prodded by the Ezhava reformers of Kerala, he began to advocate the practice of intermixing as well, most notably through the entry of 'untouchables' into the precincts of temples that had been barred to them. The next step was to allow, or even encourage, the eating together of people of different castes (including 'untouchables'), this striking a major blow against Hindu custom and tradition, which expressly forbade upper castes from eating in the same place or from the same vessels as those ranked below them in the caste hierarchy.

In the Hindu tradition, there was only one sin greater than eating with people of a different caste. This was to contract a marriage alliance with them. Even this last barrier Gandhi had begun to consider breaching. Thus, two months after the Poona Pact, Gandhi heard from a young Brahmin from Calcutta. This man had promised to marry a Shudra girl he knew, but was nervous to go ahead since his parents were against it. 'I am in a fix,' he told Gandhi. 'I dare not offend my parents who are my makers and to whom I still owe my existence. On the other hand I cannot disown the girl . . . I see no way to bridge the difficulty in which I am placed, viz., to marry the girl and at the same time to earn the blessings of my parents.' He beseeched the Mahatma 'to hold out to me the torch so that I may see a path in the darkness which has enveloped me and is threatening to wipe out the existence of two poor souls'.

Gandhi answered that he was 'quite clear' in his mind that 'having given your word and heart to the girl, whether she is called a Shudra or what not, and as she is deeply attached to you, you cannot get out of this sacred pledge, whatever befalls you'. Then he added: 'If the girl and you are really virtuous and would become householders, your parents will forgive the difference in caste and give you both their blessings.'[56]

Back before Ambedkar was born, Gandhi would never have advocated the marriage of a Brahmin boy to a Shudra girl. He would not have seen its merits when he returned to India in 1915, or even a decade later. The transformations in Gandhi's view of caste, his increasing willingness to challenge its prejudices and proscriptions, were a direct consequence of his encounters with reformers more radical than himself—namely, Narayana Guru and his followers, and more recently, Ambedkar. The birth and subsequent career of B.R. Ambedkar had a far greater impact on Gandhi than he was sometimes willing to acknowledge.

CHAPTER TWENTY-ONE

Shaming the Hindus

I

In the autumn of 1932, while Ambedkar and Gandhi played out their differences in Poona, the most powerful man in India was perched high on a hilltop in the Himalaya. Every summer, the viceroy and his establishment moved to Simla, along with senior officials of the government. Here, they watched what was going on in the plains below with a mixture of dismay and disgust.

In late August, when Gandhi announced he would fast if the Communal Award was not withdrawn, Lord Willingdon wrote to his sister from the Viceregal Lodge: 'I should like to let the little man kill himself, but suppose we can't do that.' Then, shortly before the fast began, he wrote that with Gandhi's life on edge, 'these neurotic and emotional folk will kick up an awful hullaballoo over this, but we must sit down, and see it through. What a life!'[1]

Five days into Gandhi's fast, Willingdon wrote to his sister again: 'What extraordinary people these are, and has anything like the present situation ever arisen in history in any country. The one person who takes all these things in her stride is B. [his wife]. Such matters as Gandhi and Constitutional Reforms don't really worry her too much. What she excels in are her entertainments which are wonderful and which keep everybody in the best of tempers.'[2]

The next letter, written three weeks after the Poona Pact was signed, began with the viceroy in a better mood: 'We are both very well,' he wrote to his sister, 'and the climate here just now is gorgeous. Quite cold at night but lovely in the day time in these marvellous Himalayas with a chain of snow mountains all round.'[3]

In the middle of October, the government moved to Delhi for the winter months. Lord Willingdon now immediately dashed to Poona and back, 1800 miles by air, not to meet the Raj's most famous prisoner, but to see a horse he owned perform in the Poona races. The horse won, which helped, as did reports from his officials that the debate about the Depressed Classes was dying down. 'Gandhi's starvation stunt is getting forgotten,' wrote Willingdon to his sister, predicting that 'its results won't be very considerable'.[4]

Poona was much closer to Delhi than to Simla. The news travelled more quickly, and it wasn't always what the viceroy wanted to hear. In December, he learnt that, upset by the laggard reaction of caste Hindus to the anti-untouchability movement, Gandhi was contemplating a fresh fast. Willingdon's last letter for 1932 was more angry and despairing than any that preceded it:

> Gandhi is still troubling us with his threats of starvation. He really is a curious little beast. At the bottom of every move that he makes which he always says is inspired by God, one discovers the political manoeuvre. . . . I wonder what Britain or America would do if Ramsay Mac or Hoover for some reason decided to starve to death. They'd tell them not to be d_d fools![5]

II

The year 1933 began with Gandhi in jail, and still obsessed with the abolition of untouchability. On 3 January, he issued a statement containing the opinion of some learned Sanskrit scholars, based on their examination of the relevant texts, that 'no class of persons today bears the brand of permanent untouchability'; therefore, the Depressed Classes should have the same rights to temples, schools, wells and roads as members of the four varnas.[6]

In early February, Ambedkar came to see Gandhi in Yerwada. The conversation, as recorded by Mahadev Desai, suggested that the Poona Pact had not entirely reconciled the two men. 'We want our social status raised in the eyes of the *savarna* Hindus,' Ambedkar told Gandhi. 'If it cannot be I should say goodbye to Hinduism. . . . I am not going to be satisfied with measures which would merely bring some relief. . . . I don't want to be crushed by your charity.'

'In accepting the Poona Pact you accept the position that you are Hindus,' responded Gandhi. 'I have accepted only the political aspect of it,' answered Ambedkar. 'The Hindu mind does not work in a rational way,' he continued. 'They have no objection to the untouchables touching them on the railway and other public places. Why do they object to it in the case of temples?'

Gandhi answered that this was precisely why he had taken 'up the question of temple-entry first of all because these people want to cling to untouchability in the temples. . . . I ask them to grant the ["untouchables"] equal status before God. It will raise their status.'[7]

III

After Gandhi's arrest in January 1932, the publication of *Young India* had been discontinued. In February 1933, Gandhi announced the publication of a new weekly to replace it. It would be called *Harijan*, and be edited by an associate of A.V. Thakkar's named R.V. Shastri. The first print run was of 10,000 copies. It would carry no advertisements. Gandhi also planned to bring out two companion journals, *Harijan Sewak*, in Hindi, and *Harijanbandhu*, in Gujarati.

The inaugural issue of *Harijan* was dated 11 February 1933. Gandhi wrote as many as seven pieces, on various aspects of the problem of untouchability. One related to the growing divergence between him and Dr B.R. Ambedkar. When they met on 4 February, Gandhi had asked him for a message for the first issue of *Harijan*. Ambedkar complied, but in characteristically blunt terms. This was his message: 'The outcaste is a bye-product of the caste system. There will be outcastes so long as there are castes. Nothing can emancipate the outcaste except the destruction of the caste system. Nothing can help to save Hinduism . . . except the purging of the Hindu faith of this odious and vicious dogma.'

Gandhi was unnerved by the message. For, it struck at the root of his own idealized conception of varnashramadharma, the division of labour according to caste. He wanted untouchability to go, he wanted all occupations to have the same value—for a Bhangi to have the same status as a Brahmin—but he wasn't yet prepared to let go of the idea of varna altogether.

Gandhi printed Ambedkar's message, with an explanation and response of his own, ten times the length. He accepted that the caste system 'has its limitations and its defects, but there is nothing sinful about it, as there is about untouchability, and, if it is a bye-product of the caste system it is only in the same sense as an ugly growth is of a body, or weeds of the crop. . . . It is an excess to be removed, if the whole system is not to perish. Untouchability is the product, therefore, not of the caste system, but of the distinction of high and low that has crept into Hinduism and is corroding it.'

Gandhi ended by asking for all reformers to come together on a common platform. Whether they believed in varnashrama (as he did) or rejected caste altogether (as Ambedkar did),

> the opposition to untouchability is common to both. Therefore, the present joint fight is restricted to the removal of untouchability, and I would invite Dr. Ambedkar and those who think with him to throw themselves, heart and soul, into the campaign against the monster of untouchability. It is highly likely at the end of it we shall find that there is nothing to fight against in varnashrama. If, however, varnashrama even then looks like an ugly thing, the whole of Hindu society will fight it.[8]

Each issue of *Harijan* was eight pages long, these printed in two columns on foolscap paper. A single copy was priced at one anna, while an annual subscription cost four rupees. Some issues started with a list of temples and wells thrown open to, and schools started for, Harijans in the previous week. Other issues began with poems on the theme of social or caste equality; yet others with a statement issued by Gandhi reminding caste Hindus of the resolutions passed after the Poona Pact, committing them to open wells, schools, roads and temples to those of any caste or none.

Gandhi asked the authorities for permission for his new weekly to be distributed to the prisoners in Yerwada jail. The government refused, on the grounds that if Gandhi and his followers were 'permitted to supply prisoners with free literature on the untouchability question, a similar privilege cannot be refused to the Sanatanists who hold different views with equal strength of feeling'.[9]

Gandhi had renamed his weekly *Harijan* because he believed that the campaign to abolish untouchability was as vital as winning political freedom. India, young and old, present and future, had to commit itself to this sacred cause. The name quickly gained currency; among the Hindu middle classes, and the nationalist press, the 'untouchables' were now regularly referred to as Harijans. However, the euphemism was rejected by B.R. Ambedkar, who never used the appellation to describe his people.

Meanwhile, the Anti-Untouchability League formed in the wake of Gandhi's fast had been renamed the Harijan Sewak Sangh, or the Service of the Untouchables Society. This was in part because Gandhi wanted to make the term 'Harijan' popular; in part because the Poona reformer V.R. Shinde already ran an Anti-Untouchability League. Someone who was unhappy with the new name was C. Rajagopalachari. He felt 'it means a continued recognition of untouchables as such'. He would rather have had 'Untouchability Abolition League', since what they were striving for was 'really abolition of a slave status and the phrase "Abolition" would be suggestive and emphatic . . . *Service* to a group of men is not really the object and aim, if we think about it. It is really the doing away with the evil.'[10]

Rajagopalachari wrote likewise to G.D. Birla and A.V. Thakkar, president and secretary of the Harijan Sewak Sangh respectively. Thakkar was a long-time member of the Servants of India Society, and had earlier founded a Bhil Seva Sangh. Rajagopalachari thought both those names logical, since India was a nation and Bhils a tribe, and both would remain whether one served them or not. But here the purpose was to *abolish* the practice of untouchability. Hence he wished the new body to be called '"Untouchability Abolition League" or Society, the word abolition being the most prominent part of the name'.[11]

Gandhi was agnostic about Rajagopalachari's idea. 'The Sangh will not succeed or fail,' he wrote, 'because of the name. It will be judged by its work.'[12] However, since it came from a colleague he enormously respected, he asked Birla and Thakkar to consider Rajaji's suggestion. They rejected it, on the grounds that the name of the society had only very recently been changed from 'Anti-Untouchability League' to 'Servants of the Untouchables Society'. The change of name, wrote Thakkar to Rajagopalachari, was approved by the board, and announced in the press, while stationery had also been printed incorporating the new name. Now, just as 'all have got used to the changed name', wrote Thakkar, came the suggestion 'that it should be changed a second time'. Thakkar admitted that there was 'much logic' in the argument that the aim was not to keep 'untouchables' as untouchables forever. However, he continued, 'if we now suggest this second change to the Board, every one will ridicule us, and may not agree to this second change. Not only the members of the Board, but the public at large and the Press will justifiably ridicule the proposal, if it is put into effect.' Therefore, the board was 'averse to the change, though it is reasonable, merely because it is not expedient to do so'.[13]

It was a typically Indian scenario. Bureaucratic inertia had triumphed over logic and reason. Worry about adverse commentary in the press, and irritation at the thought of printing stationery afresh, meant that the status quo prevailed. So the name 'Harijan Sewak Sangh' remained, although the alternative would have been less patronizing, more direct.

IV

Inspired by Gandhi's campaign, Congress members of the central legislature had introduced a Temple Entry Bill to throw open all shrines to the Depressed Classes. This provoked the head priest of one of India's most famous shrines, the Jagannatha Temple in Puri, to write an open letter to the viceroy. The Puri Shankaracharya claimed that 'these Bills, if and when passed, will really mean the sounding of the Death-knell of all possibilities for Sanatanists to lead quiet and peaceful lives of Spirituality according to the dictates of their Religion and their Conscience'. He reminded the viceroy of Queen Victoria's Proclamation of 1858 promising non-interference in religious matters. The Puri priest also targeted '"Truth-Adorers" like Mr. Gandhi', advising them to 'seek methods of peaceful intellectual persuasion and not of coercive legislation'.[14]

Another 'open letter' was penned by the head priest of the Sankeshswar-Karavir Peeth, a widely visited and well-endowed temple in southern India. This noted that the movement to abolish untouchability had 'come to a head under the evil influence of Mr. Gandhi who is guided by political motives'. It complained that 'not a single Sanatanist was consulted' on the Poona Pact, and 'still it has become binding on the Sanatanists'.

'If one closely studies Mr. Gandhi's writings,' commented this Hindu priest, 'it is clear that his religion consists of the dictates of his own heart. In fact, he and his followers do not want the authority of any religion as such, and are, in fact enemies of all the existing religions in the world.' The priest was convinced that 'it is Mr. Gandhi's ambition to force his personality on the whole world as the coming prophet of his new order of things akin to Bolshevism by destroying the hold of all other old religions and of their respective Heads. The Temple-entry movement is only the thin end of the wedge. The real motive is far deeper. They want to ultimately get a hand in the administration of temples and to divert the temple funds towards the Congress objective.'

In attacking Gandhi, this Hindu seer underscored his own loyalty to the British Empire. Observing that most servants of Europeans in India were from the lowest castes, he claimed that 'Mr. Gandhi hopes that by raising the social and religious status of the untouchables by his anti-untouchability work, this menial staff could be persuaded to leave off at a moment's notice the services of their European Employers, whose lot could then be made a hundred times more miserable than in the worst days of the Non-co-operation movement . . .'[15]

In his struggle to abolish untouchability, Gandhi was caught between radicals and reactionaries. For some, like Ambedkar, he was going too slow. For others, like the priestly orthodoxy, he was going too fast. There was a third group unhappy with Gandhi's social reform work. This comprised many of his own partymen. As the chief secretary of the United Provinces reported: 'The younger members of the Congress party are definitely opposed to Mr. Gandhi on the Harijan question and regard the movement as reactionary and a waste of time and money.'[16] One young Congressman complained to Stanley Reid, the editor of the *Times of India*, that 'Gandhi is wrapped up in the Harijan movement. He does not care a jot whether we live or die; whether we are bound or free.'[17]

In January 1933—four months after Gandhi's fast in prison—a Congressman wrote a long letter to him from Nasik. The correspondent told Gandhi he had 'a high regard for the moral and spiritual grandeur of your selfless character'. But he could not 'see eye to eye' with Gandhi 'as regards the Untouchability question'.

The Nasik Congressman criticized Gandhi's programme on four counts.

First, '90 per cent of caste Hindus are against temple-entry and you have waged a war on the major portion of Hindus in which you will fail';

Second, Gandhi was 'wounding the susceptibilities of caste Hindus and thus alienating their sympathies which you could have better utilised for the political and economic regeneration of India';

Third, that Gandhi had involved non-Hindus in a matter concerning Hindus. 'To invoke help from foreigners and ask them to make laws teasing Hindus is no phase of patriotism!';

Finally, by focusing on anti-untouchability work, Gandhi was 'killing Congress which is the only politically representative body in the Nation. Ranade, Gokhale and Tilak, though they were social reformers, kept social and religious questions apart from politics and therefore they could do something to rouse the nation.'[18]

In February 1933, a recent prisoner in the civil disobedience campaign wrote to Gandhi saying he 'cannot understand this curious haste for the uplift of the Harijans'. The young patriot accused Gandhi of betraying those who courted arrest for the sake of swaraj. The leader of the struggle against foreign rule was 'today acting faithlessly to[wards] these prisoners. Instead of carrying on the very satyagraha for which these prisoners are rotting in jail, you are today occupying your followers with the Harijans.'

This correspondent was 'surprised' to see a report of a recent speech by Rajaji arguing that 'today the work for the Harijans is more important than the acquiring of Swarajya'. 'Do you believe this?' the critic asked Gandhi. 'If you do believe it, why do you not say so publicly, so that the prisoners now rotting in jail may obtain their freedom?'[19]

Gandhi had in fact been saying such things publicly. Before and after the Nagpur Congress of 1920, he insisted that the abolition of untouchability was as important as the achievement of political freedom. The young critic did not perhaps recall those events of a decade earlier; what moved him instead were more recent events such as the opposition to the Simon Commission, the Lahore Congress and its Purna Swaraj declaration, and above all, the Salt March. Hence the charge of betrayal. The truth was that Ambedkar's challenge had compelled Gandhi to reverse his priorities. Politics had now to recede, while social reform came to the fore once more.

Facing criticism from all sides, Gandhi found cheer in the support of the friends he most valued. Jawaharlal Nehru, then in jail in Dehra Dun, was reading the first issues of *Harijan*, where, as he wrote to Gandhi, he was 'delighted to see the old rapier-touch of over-much kindness and inexhaustible patience which extinguishes, or as you say neutralises, the opponent. I pity the poor Sanatanists. With their anger and abuses and frantic cursing, they are no match for this kind of subtle attack.'[20]

From London, his even older friend Henry Polak provided a ringing endorsement of Gandhi's drive to abolish untouchability. Polak knew 'that there will be all kinds of people to tell you that the political movement is entitled to your direct leadership and guidance'. 'I do not feel that way myself', said this British Jew, since 'from all I can see and know of this great social stain (please remember that if I were in Germany I, too, would belong to an untouchable community) it is of such proportions and so vital in its nature and its demands to require the full one-hundred per cent of your capacity for public work'. Polak told Gandhi that 'it would seem that you are self-dedicated and given by God to the great task of the removal of untouchability'.[21]

V

While Gandhi was in jail in Poona, his wife Kasturba was in jail in Ahmedabad, serving a sentence for illegal picketing. In March–April 1933 she wrote him several letters, which exist, not in their original Gujarati, but in the English translations of the censor. There are all too few letters from Kasturba to Gandhi that have survived, so we must be grateful for these that do.

These letters are datelined 'Sabarmati Mandir', a reference to Gandhi himself writing and speaking of his place of incarceration as 'Yeravda [sic] Mandir'. To the satyagrahi a prison was indeed a sacred shrine, a mandir. In her letters Kasturba told Gandhi of her visitors, who included Henry Polak, with whom they had once shared a home in Johannesburg, and their relatively new companion Mira, whom she praised as 'a simple lady'.

Matters of health and diet—his and hers—naturally figured in these letters. Kasturba said she was fine, except that she suffered from constipation. On the advice of the prison doctor, she was taking liquid paraffin for her digestion. Mira, meanwhile, was making *bhakri* bread for her.

Kasturba knew that her husband would be interested in her continuing education. So she told him that she read the Gujarati edition of his magazine *Harijan*, and read Hindi books with Mira. According to the translation, she also (mysteriously or mischievously) wrote: 'I read Gujarati and Hindi and can write also but forget it also.' Kasturba updated Gandhi on their ashram, which was adjacent to her prison in Ahmedabad. Some sons and daughters of veteran ashramites were planning to leave; conveying the news, Kasturba urged her husband to put this rebellion in perspective. 'It is common knowledge that boys want everything when they grow up,' she wrote, adding: 'We had enjoyed [ourselves] also [when young]. The people do not like the habits and manners of the Ashram.'[22]

VI

In prison, Gandhi had developed a new hobby: looking at the stars. A rich admirer in Poona, Lady Premlila Thackersey (widow of the textile magnate Vithaldas Thackersey), had lent him two large telescopes. When night fell in Yerwada, Gandhi would place the telescopes in the courtyard and look through them at the sky above. As he told a visiting journalist, astronomy 'has become a passion with me. Every free minute I get I devote myself to it. It is a wonderful subject, and more than anything else impresses upon me the mystery of God and the majesty of the universe.'[23]

On 23 April, Ambedkar came again to see Gandhi in jail. He wanted an amendment in the Poona Pact, whereby the Depressed Classes candidates for the legislatures would need a minimum percentage of the 'untouchable' vote to be elected. Gandhi said he would think over the matter. He did—writing in the next issue of *Harijan*, he discussed the proposal and why he opposed it. 'Dr. Ambedkar's alternative,' he wrote, 'may well deprive the caste Hindus of any say whatsoever in the election of Harijan candidates and thus create an effectual bar between caste Hindus and Harijan Hindus.'[24]

Both Ambedkar and Gandhi were justified, from their respective points of view. Ambedkar worried that if this clause was not introduced, only candidates beholden to the upper castes would be elected. Gandhi, on the other hand, was concerned about furthering the cleavages between Harijans and caste Hindus.

In late April, disappointed by the waning of the anti-untouchability campaign, and the reports he was receiving of lack of enthusiasm among Congress workers, Gandhi decided to go on a fresh fast. This would be of a specified duration, namely three weeks, and commence on 8 May. In a statement issued on 30 April, Gandhi remarked: 'Let there be no misunderstanding about the impending fast. I have no desire to die. I want to live for the cause, though I am equally prepared to die for it. But I need for me and my fellow-workers greater purity, greater application and dedication.'[25]

On 2 May, Gandhi wired Tagore asking for his approval of the fast. Tagore wrote back in distinctly ambiguous terms. While the poet had endorsed the fast against Ramsay Macdonald's 'Communal Award', he worried that in this fresh self-purificatory exercise there was 'a grave risk of its fatal termination'. He beseeched Gandhi 'not to offer such an ultimation of mortification to God'.

Gandhi's wife Kasturba was also upset. She sent her husband a three-page letter expressing her sadness and anguish. She reminded him of how frail and weak he had felt after other (and shorter) fasts. Besides, 'penance [for past mistreatment of Harijans] is taking place under Rajagopalacharyaji at several places. He convinces people. It will have an impact . . .'

Kasturba also got Mira to send Gandhi a telegram which read: 'Ba wishes me [to] say greatly shocked feels decision [to fast] very wrong but you have not listened to any others so will not hear her she sends her heartfelt prayers.'

Gandhi replied: 'Tell Ba her father imposed on her a companion whose weight would have killed any other woman. I treasure her love. She must remain courageous to end.'

The most moving letter, however, came from Gandhi's estranged son Harilal. 'I am ready to fast on your behalf,' he wrote to his father. 'And I am ready to offer whatever this body can to you. My offer is unconditional. If we can find a way to prevent your fast, I will be very happy.' Gandhi answered that while the letter had 'touched' him, 'if this fast means your return to pure life it would be doubly blessed'. He asked Harilal to come visit him. 'I shall try [and] guide you,' wrote the father, ending, 'God Bless You.'[26]

Gandhi claimed he had been asked to fast by what he called his 'Inner Voice'. The night the idea came to him, he had 'a terrible inner struggle'. He was restless, and 'could see no way'. The 'burden of responsibility was crushing' him. Then, 'suddenly the Voice came upon me. I listened, made certain that it was the Voice, and the struggle ceased. I was calm. The determination was made accordingly, the date and the hour of the fast were fixed. Joy came over me.'[27]

Gandhi began his fast as planned on 8 May. He had a meal of papaya and lime juice at 11 a.m., with the fast commencing an hour later. Mahadev and Devadas were at his side. At noon, Gandhi shut his eyes for a few minutes of personal prayer, after which visitors were allowed in. Watching his father, Devadas was, as he wrote to a friend, struck by an 'intense mental agony. . . . I am really angry, and what's more very angry with Bapu' (for starting a fresh fast).[28]

At a quarter to seven the same evening, the government released Gandhi from jail, since they did not want to risk having his death on their hands. Gandhi now shifted to the Poona residence of Lady Thackersey, whose mansion, 'Parnakuti', was on a hill overlooking the Yerwada prison.

Before he went to bed in Delhi that night, the viceroy wrote to his sister that 'we have released that intolerable man Gandhi', whose new fast was aimed not at the government but at 'the impurities he finds all around him'. Willingdon thought 'his purpose in doing this is to restore his waning influence by doing something spectacular. His vanity is quite his worst quality and he can't bear being out of the picture.'

The viceroy ended his letter by plaintively asking: 'But why Providence has troubled the British Empire with two people like Gandhi and de Valera I can't think.'[29]

VII

After moving out of jail, Gandhi issued a statement announcing the temporary suspension of the civil disobedience movement for the duration of the fast. He wanted to make it clear that the yajna he was undertaking was wholly non-political. He did not want embarrassment to the government or himself from activists breaking laws in different parts of the country.

Three days after beginning his fast, Gandhi received what their son Devadas called 'a heart rending telegram' from Kasturba, asking to come to his side. Gandhi told her 'not to weaken or yield to nervousness'.[30]

Despite the fears of friends and family, Gandhi bore the fast well. He spent the days on Lady Thackersey's spacious veranda, looking at the countryside beyond, and often taking short naps. The fast was broken at noon on 29 May, with Gandhi accepting a glass of orange juice from Lady Thackersey. A garland was also offered to Gandhi by a Harijan boy, its sequence coupling young and old, rich and poor, high caste and low caste, male and female. Dr Ansari read from the Koran, Mahadev Desai sang a Christian hymn ('When I Survey the

Wondrous Cross'), and all present sang Narasinha Mehta's hymn 'Vaishnava Jana To'. Gandhi then thanked the doctors and friends who had attended on him during the fast.[31]

On 16 June 1933, Gandhi's youngest son, Devadas, got married to C. Rajagopalachari's daughter Lakshmi in Poona. Back in 1928, the two had been asked not to speak or write to one another by their respective fathers. Five years had now passed; the young couple had satisfied their parents of the depth and durability of their love.

Speaking at the ceremony, Gandhi told Devadas that he had 'today robbed Rajagopalachari of a cherished gem. May you be worthy of it! May you treasure it!' As for Lakshmi, Gandhi knew her to have 'justified' her name, that of the goddess of the good and beautiful. He hoped the marriage would further strengthen 'the bond of affection that has ever been growing between Rajagopalachari and me'.

Notably, Gandhi prefaced his remarks to the bridal couple by saying: 'I do not think that in celebrating this marriage anything has been done against the practice of dharma.' This was a veiled reference to the fact that this was an inter-caste marriage, specifically a union between a boy of a lower caste with a girl of a higher caste, a union frowned upon by most Shastras and Shastris. Gandhi had for some time past come around to accepting inter-caste marriages; now, indeed, to blessing one within his own family. In so doing, he explicitly set his word and reputation against that of the orthodoxy.[32]

The orthodoxy was indeed appalled by this inter-caste marriage within Gandhi's family. At a meeting of Sanatanists held in Poona's Tulsi Baug temple, one speaker said that by sanctioning this union, 'Gandhi had come out in his true colours, and asked the audience whether Gandhi could really be called a religious man'. A second speaker argued that inter-caste unions were 'the outcome of the struggle of the two civilizations, Eastern and Western, and such marriages would result in demolishing the whole fabric of the ancient Hindu civilization'. A third speaker said that 'Gandhi had deluded them thus far, because he promised to lead us to Swaraj. . . . People submitted to many of his whimsicalities, because he became a political leader. . . . But now they found that Gandhi had really betrayed their trust and he had now begun to crush their religion.' A fourth 'condemned Gandhi as a Christian in disguise, who wants to spread the gospel of Christianity and [whose] plea for his devout faith in [the Hindu] religion was false'. Gandhi, added this speaker, was not a 'Mahatma' but a 'Duratma' (wicked soul).[33]

In the third week of July, a conference of Congress leaders was held in Poona. This authorized Gandhi to resume negotiations with the government. Gandhi accordingly wired the viceroy to 'grant [an] interview with a view to exploring possibilities of peace'. Lord Willingdon stiffly replied that since the Congress had not formally and unequivocally withdrawn civil disobedience, he saw no point in talks. Gandhi now told the press that since the 'door was banged' in his face, he would not withdraw the suspension of civil disobedience. However, there would be no mass protests; rather, individuals would on their own offer satyagraha.[34]

The viceroy's refusal to meet Gandhi was vigorously debated in the House of Commons. The secretary of state for India, Samuel Hoare, claimed public opinion was behind the viceroy. George Lansbury, the leader of the Opposition, disagreed. He praised Gandhi for reaching out to Willingdon, and criticized the latter for stifling dissent. 'Mr. Gandhi's telegram is unconditional and he sincerely wants peace,' said Lansbury. 'Why not grant the interview?' To his own question the Labour leader provided this answer: 'Prestige demands that he [Gandhi] should come in a white sheet' (signifying surrender).[35]

On 26 July, Gandhi wrote to the Government of Bombay saying he was disbanding the Sabarmati Ashram and wished to hand it over to the government. The stand-off between state and subject, wrote Gandhi, demanded 'the greatest measure of sacrifice' from him, 'the author of the movement'. So he was offering his most precious possession, the ashram he had built over eighteen years, where 'every head of cattle and every tree has its history and sacred association'.

Receiving no reply, Gandhi then announced that he would leave the ashram anyway, and march to Ras, a village that he had visited en route to Dandi in 1930. His intention, he wired the government, was 'to view [with] tender sympathy [the] villages most hit' by forcible collections of land revenue.

Gandhi's new march was to begin on 1 August. This time the government arrested him the morning he proposed to set off, and transported him to Yerwada jail. 'We have had to jug that little wretch Gandhi once more,' wrote Willingdon to his sister. 'Really, he is impossible . . .'[36]

This fresh arrest of Gandhi prompted a searing critique by H.N. Brailsford, a British journalist deeply committed to Indian independence. Having just toured India and met many leaders and ordinary folk, Brailsford took apart Samuel Hoare's boast in the House of Commons that 'passive resistance' had failed. The success of the Raj in vanquishing Gandhi and his movement, he said, had

> been won partly by beating; partly by the imprisonment in overcrowded gaols under harsh conditions of tens of thousands of men and women who had committed no actual offence; partly by the suppression of the chief party of the Opposition and the confiscation of its funds.
>
> These methods are as effective in India as in Germany. The efficacy of a stout stick with a brass tip to it, as a political argument has long been understood in India. Hitler may have improved upon it by using a rubber truncheon; there is no other important difference in method. He is perhaps a little prompter over his arrests. Socialists, Communists, and Pacifists are rounded up; the door bangs upon them, and that is all.
>
> In India, there is more red tape.

The viceroy, Lord Willingdon, had said he would not meet Gandhi since the Indian leader believed in 'unconstitutional methods'. To this Brailsford sarcastically responded:

> Lord Willingdon is doubtless right on the point of fact.
>
> Mr. Gandhi's methods must be unconstitutional since they in no way resemble the model of constitutional behaviour, which the Indian Government has set.
>
> They make no use of force. One cannot expect a Viceroy to shake hands with—pacifism.

Compared with how Willingdon and the Raj had treated Gandhi and the Congress, wrote Brailsford, 'Hitler's way with Socialists is prompter and less expensive. Above all, it is less hypocritical.'[37]

In these weeks, while Gandhi disbanded the Sabarmati Ashram and courted arrest afresh, his trusted aide Mahadev Desai was not at his side. The government had separated them, by shifting Mahadev to a jail in the southern town of Belgaum, from where he followed his master's movements as best he could. The 'renunciation of the Ashram', now wrote Mahadev to Mira, 'has a poignancy which crushes me'.

Mahadev had himself given the best years of his life to the Sabarmati Ashram. He would not hide his sadness at its possible closure. But he would not lose hope, telling Mira that 'I look forward to a greater future for this resurrected Ashram' (wherever Gandhi might shift it). Nor would he lose his sense of humour. He had recently read, with delight, a poem in a British-owned newspaper satirizing Gandhi and his movements, which he copied out by hand and sent to Mira, to be shared with others in Ahmedabad and beyond. The (untitled and anonymous) poem went:

> The Press, in spite of vast 'Improvements'
> Cannot keep pace with Gandhi's movements.
> At least I always have my doubts
> As to the martyr's whereabouts.
> One day I am told he is in jail.
> The next that he is out on bail.
> And when I hear he is free at last
> He's back again and fasting fast.
> Then when I hear he is nearly dead
> He's out and eating grapes instead.
>
> But long before these are digested
> The illusive man is rearrested,
> And ten to one—poor wandering soul—
> He will be released upon parole.
> But whether he is free today
> Or not, I simply cannot say.
> I wish one of the morning Papers
> Would feature the Mahatma's capers
> An 'inset' called the 'Daily Gandhi'
> Would be, I am sure, extremely handy.[38]

VIII

On 14 August 1933—a mere ten days into his new sentence—Gandhi wrote to the government asking that, as in his last term, he be allowed to have visitors and write articles connected with the anti-untouchability movement. 'Life ceases to interest me,' he remarked, 'if I may not do Harijan service without let or hindrance.'

The government declined to grant the request. So, on the 16th, Gandhi began a fresh fast. So many fasts in such a short period of time took their toll, and within a few days the prisoner's condition had rapidly deteriorated. On the 21st he was removed to the Sassoon Hospital. He was suffering from acute nausea, and for the first time in all his experiments with fasting felt close to death, so much so that he began distributing his personal articles to the hospital staff attending on him.[39]

Seeing the prisoner's precarious condition, the government capitulated. 'Gandhi is starving again,' wrote the viceroy to his sister, 'and last night I heard that he had collapsed in prison, and we have had to release him and send him to hospital. He may insist on continuing to starve there in which case his blood will be on his own head. . . . Really he is quite abnormal now and has a megalomania for power and notoriety.'[40]

On the morning of 23 August, Gandhi was released unconditionally. He broke his fast with the usual glass of orange juice, and removed himself to Lady Thackersey's villa to recover. Meeting the press on the 25th, he said he would 'again use this unexpected freedom from imprisonment for the sake of exploring avenues of peace'.

Gandhi spent three weeks at Parnakuti, recovering his strength. On 14 September, he told the press that since his aborted prison sentence had been due to last until 3 August 1934, till that date he would not take the path of confrontation but devote himself exclusively to Harijan service.[41]

Following Gandhi's movements from afar was his American disciple Richard Gregg. Gregg had spent several years in India; he was deeply interested in khadi, agriculture and nature cure. He had been a frequent visitor to the Sabarmati Ashram, where Gandhi had given him the Indian name 'Govind'. Now, back in his homeland, he read about his master's to-and-fro journeys from prison to Parnakuti, and back again. Writing that Gandhi's address 'changes so often these days', Gregg said he was reminded of the story of the Irish boss of a tramway repair gang, called on to fix a tram that had gone off the rails three times in quick succession. The Irishman's report to his boss ran: 'Off again, on again, away again—Finnigan.'[42]

IX

Some Congressmen were impatient to launch a fresh campaign against the Raj. Their leader had other ideas. In the face of Ambedkar's challenge, social reform had to take precedence over politics. Gandhi now decided to go on an all-India tour to campaign against untouchability. He would begin at Wardha, and then move northwards to the Punjab, Sindh, Rajputana and the United Provinces. However, he was persuaded by Rajagopalachari to start in South India instead, and cover Andhra, Tamil Nadu, Mysore and Kerala in the cold weather, before returning north to complete the tour.

Gandhi's 'Harijan tour' formally began on 7 November, when, at a village near Wardha named Selu, he opened a temple to 'untouchables'. It was, he remarked, 'good fortune for me that my tour begins at Wardha, which is the geographical centre of India. I want it also to be the centre of the movement.' Jamnalal Bajaj was based in Wardha; he had already opened his family temple to Harijans. Another long-standing disciple of Gandhi's, Vinoba Bhave, had made Wardha the base for his own social work. Gandhi hoped that the commitment of Bajaj and Bhave to ending untouchability would 'prove infectious and spread through the whole of the country'.

Gandhi was heartened by the early response to his Harijan tour. As he wrote to an English friend, in the first week 'no less than 1,50,000 people must have taken part in the numerous meetings and demonstrations. If they did not want to endorse the movement, one would think that they could not possibly [have] attended in such large numbers.'[43]

Gandhi used his tour both to spread the message and to collect money for the cause. After each talk, he would ask for voluntary donations to the Harijan Sewak Sangh. Men would offer cash; women, jewellery. Next, Gandhi would pull out signed photographs of himself, and have them auctioned. 'Do rupiya ek bar', he would say, the floor price is two rupees. One member would bid higher, another still higher. Ultimately, each photo would go for ten rupees or more.

Next, photographs of Jawaharlal Nehru would be sold, in case the young men present admired him more than the Mahatma. In some places, photos of the Muslim nationalist M.A. Ansari were sold.

Apart from photographs, gifts received by Gandhi were also auctioned. At many places, he was offered a written address on embossed paper, handsomely framed. This would be put under the hammer, the selling price often exceeding 100 rupees. In one place, an oil painting of Gandhi was offered to him; this was then auctioned for 600 rupees. Occasionally, the shaving stick used by Gandhi that morning would also be bid for. By these varied means, Gandhi gathered an ever-increasing sum for his work.[44]

Gandhi's meetings were attracting critics as well as supporters. A group of orthodox Hindus from Banaras, led by one Swami Lalnath, had come south to try and stop his tour. They followed Gandhi from village to village, lying down in front of the car that conveyed him. Lifted up and taken out of the way by Congress volunteers, they then turned up at the meetings, heckling the speaker and showing black flags. Sometimes they went so far as to burn Gandhi's effigy.[45]

As was his wont, Gandhi sought out the critics. He sent for Swami Lalnath, and tried to talk him out of his opposition. The swami told Gandhi that he was paying him back in his own coin, offering satyagraha to the originator of satyagraha. As he frankly admitted: 'We want to be hurt by the police or by your volunteers. When this happens I know you would give up the tour.'

To seek 'to provoke the public to violence', said Gandhi to the swami, was the very antithesis of satyagraha. Whatever happened, he would not call the police, and had instructed his colleagues to eschew violence. He told the swami to 'go back to Benares and ask the Lord of the Universe to wean me from my error' (in opposing untouchability). Or the swami should fast to uphold his beliefs, as Gandhi had himself done. Swami Lalnath, put on the spot, shamefacedly answered: 'That we have not the ability to do.'[46]

Despite Gandhi's attempt to reach out to them, the swami and his men continued their counter-campaign. Everywhere Gandhi went, he was met by black flag demonstrations by the Sanatanists. Reporting these protests, the *Bombay Chronicle* commented that while 'the mere sight of Mahatma Gandhi being greeted with black flags anywhere in India must scandalise the vast majority of the public', the opposition could be construed as 'a healthy sign that even the most orthodox have at last been stirred out of their comfortable lethargy into action by the war that Gandhiji has declared upon an abominable ancient custom. It is a tribute to the efficacy of his campaign.'[47]

In the town of Akola, some of Ambedkar's followers came to meet Gandhi. The questions and criticisms they put to him, and the answers and explanations he gave, were noted down by a journalist:

Ambedkarites: You posed at the Round Table Conference as a Harijan leader and denied the leadership of Dr. Ambedkar.

Gandhi: No, I said there that I was the representative of millions of people of India. I said I shared along with Dr. Ambedkar the responsibility of looking after the Harijans' interests.

Ambedkarites: Dr. Ambedkar opposed you at the Round Table Conference. By doing so did he do justice or injustice to the country?

Gandhi: He thought he did justice, but I was of [the] opinion that he did injustice.

Ambedkarites: People have pictures of Lokmanya Tilak with four hands. They worship it. Do you have any objection if we had a picture of Ambedkar with four hands and worshipped it? We believe he has done us good.

Gandhi: You have a right to do that. Whenever the conversation between me and Vallabhbhai in the Yerwada Jail turned upon the Poona Pact, I used to picture in my mind's eye Dr. Bhimrao

Ambedkar, whom I wanted to please. I regularly read the *Janata*, the weekly of his party. I admire him. I may differ from his views, but admit he is a brave man. Brave men also err. I consider myself a brave man and I confess I have committed many mistakes.

The disputants parted amicably, with the Akola Ambedkarites offering Gandhi a garland, which he gratefully accepted.[48]

The government did not believe that Gandhi's anti-untouchability tour would focus on social reform alone. They worried that he might launch a fresh campaign of civil disobedience. So, they had spies clad in civilian clothes follow him everywhere, taking notes of what he did and did not say. The Raj was worried that since Gandhi had 'not yet abandoned his creed of hostility to Government', there was 'no guarantee that subscriptions given to the Harijan movement will not be used for subversive purposes'.

Based on this (mis)reading of Gandhi's intentions, a series of instructions were issued to officials in the districts the tour would pass through. First, that government property and buildings could not be used for the anti-untouchability movement. Second, that government servants were forbidden from contributing to Gandhi's Harijan fund. Third, that government servants must not be part of any reception committee for Gandhi. Fourth, that while it would be better for government servants not to attend Gandhi's meetings at all, if they did go they must make it clear that they were doing so in their private capacity.[49]

X

Gandhi had given his word that until August 1934 he would stay away from politics. But his wife had made no such commitment. On 25 November 1933, Kasturba Gandhi wrote to the home secretary of the Government of Bombay a remarkable letter which read:

Dear Sir,
When in August last my husband (M. K. Gandhi) went on a fast in prison, I was serving my own term of imprisonment as a civil

resister; and in order to enable me to attend upon and nurse him, the Government, as is their wont on such occasions, did me the courtesy to discharge me from prison.

My husband having now fairly recouped his health, and having resumed Harijan work in pursuance of his vow, I feel that I do not require to attend upon him further and that as a civil resister I may not stay away from duty any longer. I propose, therefore, to resume my work, and, to begin with, I intend to proceed to the village of Ras in the district of Kaira in order to associate myself with the civil resister sufferers in their woes and share their privations to the best of my abilities.

I hope to leave Ahmedabad for Ras on 28th November 1933.

Yours faithfully
Kasturba Gandhi

The letter was in English, but Kasturba had signed her name in Devanagari, in a not very steady hand. She knew little English and only a little more Hindi. Who drafted the letter? Perhaps it was Mahadev Desai, perhaps her son Devadas, perhaps Gandhi himself.

Kasturba left Ahmedabad for Ras on 28 November, accompanied by Vallabhbhai Patel's daughter Manibehn. They intended to preach individual civil disobedience. They were detained at Nadiad, and presented before the district magistrate, an Indian named M.S. Jayakar.

In court, Kasturba answered questions in her native Gujarati. The archival record has the English translations, these made by the magistrate for his superiors in Bombay. Kasturba gave her caste as 'Bania', her occupation as '*Deshseva*', this accurately rendered in English as 'in the service of the nation' (no doubt to the embarrassment, or anger, of the British officials who were to read it). She wanted, she said, to go to Ras to study at first-hand the condition of the agriculturists there, whom she had heard were being 'greatly harassed' by officials.

Asked whether she intended to preach civil disobedience in Ras, Kasturba answered that the breaking of unjust laws was her dharma. As her husband had recovered his health, she wished, she told the magistrate, 'to undergo the remaining period of my former sentence which had remained unexpired'.

Back in August, Kasturba had been sentenced to six months in prison. She was, however, released two weeks later to attend on her husband. The government now cancelled the order suspending the earlier sentence, and removed her to the Sabarmati prison, where she would serve the remaining five and a half months of her sentence.[50]

XI

Gandhi's 'Harijan tour' continued. After five gruelling weeks in the Central Provinces, he travelled to Delhi to attend a meeting of the Harijan Sewak Sangh. With him was Mira, who, writing to Devadas Gandhi, described the past month with her master on the road:

> I have been continually packing, unpacking and packing up again—preparing quarters only to vacate them again in a few hours—rushing 100 or even 150 miles in the day in a car, and sometimes finishing up heavy days with nights or half nights in the train. How Bapu has stood it has been marvellous. Anyone else would have broken down—but God gives him a special strength. But that does not mean we should abuse that strength. If Bapu is to fulfil the 9 months Tour it will be impossible for him to go on at this pace.[51]

Aside from meeting colleagues, Gandhi also made speeches and collected money on this visit to Delhi. The list of collections, as printed in *Harijan*, makes for interesting reading. The workers and managers of Birla Mills contributed a handsome Rs 2000. A general collection among the citizens of Delhi yielded almost three times as much. The staff and students of St Stephen's College where C.F. Andrews had taught donated Rs 152. The staff and students of the rival institution, Hindu College, gave as much as Rs 400, inspired perhaps by the fact that their long-serving principal, N.V. Thadani, was a great admirer of Gandhi.[52]

From Delhi, Gandhi and his party took a train to Madras, to commence the next stage of their Harijan tour. A Tamil Brahmin critic had claimed that 95 per cent of Harijans did not want 'the Gandhian creed'. When a journalist quoted these words to Gandhi, he answered in exasperation: 'There is no such thing as "Gandhian creed" so far as I know. I know only this. I am engaged in giving Harijans clean water. I am engaged in giving them facilities for education. I am engaged in finding accommodation for them . . . I am engaged in weaning them from drink and carrion. Do they not like all these?'[53]

Gandhi now entered the Andhra country. At the city of Vijayawada, a play was staged for him, featuring a Pariah hero. The devotion of the townsmen to the visiting saint disgusted the district magistrate, who commented that the speeches welcoming Gandhi 'were in fulsome terms which might by some people be considered nauseating, even according to the standards of what in this country is considered to be suitable flattery for an address'.[54]

Gandhi now retraced his steps southwards. In Malabar, he was once more met by black flag demonstrators. Later, at a public meeting, he remarked: 'What if those who had black flags had smeared himself as Brahmins do? . . . Brahminhood is not known by external marks. . . . He is a Brahmin who is a living treasure of scriptures, but not he who makes a demonstration of untruth by carrying a black flag.'

In the village of Badagara, a sixteen-year-old girl named Kaumudi was so moved by Gandhi's speech that she took off all her jewellery and offered it to the Harijan cause. Bangles on her hands, earrings, anklets, a gold necklace—all came off one by one and were handed over to Gandhi. He too was moved; later writing an article on how 'Kaumudi's Renunciation' had been one of the 'most touching and soul-stirring scenes' of his long and busy life.[55]

Gandhi's Quaker friend Muriel Lester (his host in London in 1931) was in India, and spent some time with Gandhi on his Harijan tour through the Madras Presidency. Miss Lester provided Charlie Andrews with a description of two days with their hero on the road:

> Well, my niece Dorothy Hogg calls Bapu 'the Speed King of Asia'.
> He has the secret of perpetual motion. We rarely eat 2 meals in
> the same place—we arrive at some Dharmshalla or Ashram at 9

pm—sleep, prayers at 4.20 (B[apu] gets up and writes at 3) we pack, have breakfast, and set off at 6.30, have perhaps 10 meetings in the day. The first day I was w[ith] him he had 50,000 people at the meetings and not counting the crowds who line the streets 16 deep—or swarm on the railway station. R[upees] 20,000 were given in . . . 2 days . . .

I've never seen him look so well—he seems radiant—tireless—jokey and all the things that endear him to people.[56]

Later in her tour, Muriel Lester was in Delhi, where she met Lord Willingdon, an old family friend. She found him 'quite hardened up . . . in the crust of his own self-righteousness'. She tried but failed to convince him of Gandhi's sincerity. The viceroy complained that Gandhi had 'given him a lot of trouble'. He accused him of 'raising a hornet's nest by asking for Temple Entry', claiming that 'the Sanatanists would do more harm now that [Gandhi] had attacked them than they would have done if left alone'.

Miss Lester told Gandhi that Willingdon had 'a grudge against you for the trouble you have given him in the past [over his fasts in jail in 1932 and 1933, among other things]. He thinks you are utterly conceited—and as that is his own weakness—he naturally dislikes it wherever he thinks he sees it in others.'[57]

Willingdon's dislike of Gandhi was intense. In late 1933, he visited the princely state of Mysore, whose diwan, Mirza Ismail, had much sympathy for Gandhi. In a recent address to the Mysore Assembly, Ismail had praised the Mahatma as 'an ardent patriot' and 'a far-seeing, sagacious statesman', who was 'qualified far better than anyone else to reconcile the conflicting elements in the country and to induce them all to march together a further stage along the road that leads to self-government'. The speech came to the attention of the viceroy, who would not countenance any talk of self-government, or indeed praise of Gandhi. 'Look here Mirza, what have you been doing?' said Willingdon to Ismail when they met, adding, 'Don't do it again.'

On his return to Delhi, the viceroy wrote to Mirza Ismail urging him to 'give up the idea of Gandhi as a leader of political thought in this country for, believe me, he is temperamentally a bad politician . . .'[58]

XII

While Gandhi toured South India, Kasturba was in jail, serving out the sentence from her involvement in the civil disobedience movement. On New Year's Day, 1934, Gandhi wrote his wife a long letter from Cuddapah. 'Can you use your dentures?' he asked. 'Do you gargle with potassium permanganate water?' For him to be free, and her to be in jail, was an unusual reversal of roles. Sensing that his wife would worry about him, he wrote: 'As Mirabehn looks after the smallest detail, I don't feel the discomfort of travelling at all.'

From personal matters, Gandhi then turned to ethical ones. He asked Kasturba to follow the 'dharma of service' both towards the prison officials and her fellow prisoners. 'Behaving towards the officials in the spirit of service means never wishing them ill, showing them due respect and not deceiving them.' Gandhi further advised Kasturba that 'women undergoing imprisonment for criminal offences should be treated as if they were your blood-sisters'.

Three weeks later, Gandhi wrote Kasturba another letter, this time from Kanyakumari. 'This is the farthest end of India,' he informed her. 'The Himalayas represent her head. We may, therefore, call this place Mother India's feet, which are daily washed by the sea. Since nobody lives here, perfect silence reigns.'

From geographical information Gandhi turned to spiritual instruction. He reminded Kasturba, lonely in prison, that the Bhagavad Gita urges the cultivation of solitude. 'We came into the world alone and shall leave it alone,' he told her, adding: 'Why, then, should we yearn for anybody's companionship during the uncertain interval between birth and death?' We should not shun the company of those we love, said Gandhi, but we should not desperately desire it either. Friends, parents, children, spouses were all fine in their time and place. But God was the 'only true friend', as well (as in the Gita) our most trusted charioteer. Thus, 'one who cultivates solitude will never be unhappy anywhere, for he sees only Vishnu in all places'.

Gandhi and Kasturba had been married for fifty years. They had often been apart—in different cities, countries and continents. When they were not in the same place, he wrote to her regularly. Sadly, not many of Gandhi's letters to Kasturba have survived; and virtually none of hers to him. To be sure, theirs was an unequal relationship. He was the teacher and she the pupil. Even so, these letters of 1934 bear testimony to the strength and depth of their marital bond.[59]

XIII

In the third week of January, a massive earthquake hit Bihar. When the news reached Gandhi, he was in the town of Tirunelveli. Speaking at a public meeting, he saw 'a vital connection between the Bihar calamity and the untouchability campaign. The Bihar calamity is a sudden and accidental reminder of what we are and what God is; but untouchability is a calamity handed down to us from century to century. It is a curse brought upon ourselves by our own neglect of a portion of Hindu humanity.'

Here, Gandhi merely coupled the natural calamity of the earthquake and the social calamity of untouchability. In his next speech, in Tuticorin, he made the latter responsible for the former, asking his audience 'to be "superstitious" enough with me to believe that the earthquake is a divine chastisement for the great sin we have committed and are still committing against those we describe as untouchables . . .'

Gandhi's remarks reached his friend and critic, the poet Rabindranath Tagore. Tagore at once issued a public statement deploring the linkage of 'ethical principles with cosmic phenomena'. Indians were, he said, 'immensely grateful' to Gandhi for having made them free 'from fear and feebleness' through his social and political campaigns. Yet, Tagore was 'profoundly hurt when any words from his [Gandhi's] mouth may emphasize the elements of unreason', especially when 'this kind of unscientific view of things is too readily accepted by a large section of our countrymen'.[60]

Tagore's chastisement of Gandhi is reasonably well known. Indeed, it was invoked again during the Nepal (and Bihar) earthquake of April 2015.[61] It is impossible to justify Gandhi's statement, but the biographer must set it in context. It stemmed from his frustration at the deep-rooted prejudices of his fellow Hindus, that he had been trying so long and heroically to combat.

In 1915, Gandhi had travelled across India in an attempt to get to know his country better. Now, this second all-India tour, conducted almost two decades after the first, sought to rouse the conscience of his compatriots against the pernicious practice of untouchability. In Gandhi's own eyes, his Harijan tour was every bit as important as the Salt March of 1930. For, he had long believed that India would be fit for freedom only when it stopped treating a section of its own population as unfree, less than human. Yet, whereas the Salt March received widespread acclaim from his countrymen, the Harijan tour evoked indifference and even hostility from many Indians. For all his preaching, Gandhi's compatriots warmed to the idea of political independence far more than to the ideal of social equality. This left him hurt, bitter, angry, confused—thus his superficially silly remarks about the earthquake in Bihar.

His irrational explanation of the Bihar earthquake did not stop Gandhi from working hard to bring succour to its victims. In every subsequent speech during his Harijan tour, he raised money for the reconstruction of homes and families in Bihar. He collected more than a million rupees, then a colossal sum, which was duly passed on to his old associate Rajendra Prasad, who was coordinating the relief efforts in his home state.[62]

Bihar was Gandhi's *karma bhumi*, the first place in India where he had worked for any length of time. The towns and villages he had travelled through in 1917 had been devastated by the earthquake. The homes of friends and colleagues in Muzaffarpur, Champaran, Motihari and Bettiah were reduced to rubble. In the last week of January, he wrote Rajendra Prasad an anguished letter. 'What do you advise me about my tour in Bihar?' he asked. 'Would it be proper for me to come there in connection with untouchability? Should I come there in connection with the alleviation of suffering? Will my not coming there be preferable?'[63]

XIV

In the end, Gandhi decided to complete his tour in South India before going to Bihar. In the third week of January, he was in the

Tamil town of Devakottai, where there had recently been clashes between Harijans and Nattar landowners. Gandhi met the Nattars, his conversation with them, snatches of which are reproduced below, making for an interesting comparison with his exchange with the Ambedkarites of Akola:

> Gandhi: I hear some Nattars, or many of you, object to Harijans wearing the clothes they wish to. You object to their making uses of the very temple to the building of which they have contributed. You insist on Harijans doing certain things for you. If any Harijan transgresses the limits, he comes in for bodily injury. Now I suggest to you it is wrong to injure any person bodily or otherwise when he does not do as you would have him to. . . . But I want to go a step further. Just now I am touring from one end of India to the other to tell the Hindus that it is a sin to consider a single human being as an untouchable, that it is sinful to consider any single human being as lower than ourselves, that Harijans have the same rights as you and I and other Hindus have.
>
> Nattar Representative: With regard to the dress, they [the Harijans] must not wear new modes of dress, when they come to our homes, and on festive and public occasions. . . . We have fixed the mode of dress to many castes according to their vocations or customs. Customs must not be transgressed. . . . I say that for Harijans not to observe customs is bad.
>
> Gandhi: Things were done in many parts of India according to custom. But when people found they were wrong, they gave it up. No man—this is the law of the land—shall determine what is good for another man or what another should or should not do.[64]

Gandhi's next stop was the Nilgiri hills, where he spent a week, mixing long walks through *shola* forests and tea estates with Harijan work. In one hamlet, he asked estate labourers from the Depressed Classes to hold him 'hostage for the due fulfilment of the [Poona] Pact'.[65]

After a week in the hills, Gandhi moved on, to the great temple towns of southern Tamil Nadu. At Srirangam, Gandhi was dismayed that the town's hallowed Vaishnavite shrine was 'not open to Harijans precisely in the same manner that it is open to caste Hindus'. A few days later, Gandhi was in Tanjore, home to the even older Brihadeeswara temple, a Saivite shrine this time, and one of the glories of Hindu architecture. On his morning walk, he had passed by the temple, which, as was customary in these parts of South India, rigorously excluded all except upper-caste Hindus. But then, 'within probably a few seconds or a few minutes of passing by the temple', Gandhi

> saw the sun rising above the horizon. I asked myself whether he rose only for caste Hindus or whether he rose for Harijans as well. I discovered at once that he was absolutely impartial and had probably to rise more for the Harijans than for the caste Hindus, who had plenty of wealth and who had shut themselves up in their palaces, shutting out light even beyond the rise of the sun. . . . If that temple designed by God opens out to the whole world, shall a man-built temple open less for Harijans?[66]

Gandhi was speaking at five or more meetings a day, each time ending with an appeal for funds. One colonial official, while obviously at odds with Gandhi's politics, was nonetheless impressed by his 'amazing toughness. Although obviously tired and exhausted . . . he did succeed in carrying through a programme which would have killed any weakling.'[67]

By now, a large amount of money—more than Rs 4,00,000—had been collected on the tour. *Harijan*'s issue for 2 March 1934 printed a list of draft rules for how it should be used. After the tour ended and the accounts were tabulated, the money would be distributed to the provinces and districts. Gandhi wanted that at least 75 per cent of the money collected in each town, district and province be spent for 'the execution of schemes for Harijan welfare work' within those territories themselves.[68]

In the next issue of *Harijan*, Gandhi printed a memorandum which had been submitted at Coonoor on behalf of the Harijans of the Tamil districts. This listed eighteen different kinds of disabilities they suffered at the hands of caste Hindus. These included lack of access to restaurants, hotels, shaving saloons, wells, tanks, post offices and of course, temples; prohibitions on burying or cremating their dead in villages where they lived; prohibitions on the kinds of clothes they could buy or wear; being shut out of public latrines and schools built by the State with public funds; harassment or even violence if their men rode bicycles; prohibitions on their commissioning musicians to perform at their weddings.

Having printed this 'formidable catalogue' of grievances, Gandhi commented that 'the shame of caste Hindus will continue so long as these disabilities are practised in the name of religion, no matter to how little or great an extent'. He called upon Sanatanists to join hands with reformers such as himself 'in protecting Harijans from humiliations heaped upon them in the name of religious custom'. He added: 'There will be no rest for me nor society, so long as untouchability persists.'[69]

In the third week of March, Gandhi finally arrived in Bihar. He spent almost a month in the province, meeting relief workers and speaking to those rendered homeless. The 'fair land' he had witnessed in 1917 was now 'a land of desolation'. In an interview with *The Hindu*, he painted a moving and meticulously detailed picture of what he had seen:

> The rich fields covered with sand, rows upon rows of houses in towns and villages utterly destroyed, water and sand shooting up through stone or cement floors, walls and pillars waist-deep, palaces a heap of bricks, solitary walls or pillars standing as a mournful reminder of the glory that was, improvised huts every moment in danger of catching fire, old sites not capable of being built upon for fear of a subsidence during rains, cattle starving for want of fodder and some dying for want of water, add to this the very real danger of floods reaching areas hitherto untouched by rains.

In his speeches in Bihar, Gandhi urged all Congressmen and social workers to cooperate with the government in the work of reconstruction, for, in the face of this calamity, it was necessary to 'forget the distinction between Hindus and Mussalmans as well as between Indians and Englishmen'.[70]

For this Bihar tour, the Quaker Agatha Harrison joined Gandhi and his party. 'I thought I knew something of crowds,' wrote Agatha Harrison to Charlie Andrews. 'But I have never seen anything like the surge of people at these meetings. Often on the edge of the crowds there would be a fringe of elephants bearing, to my mind, a far too heavy burden of people—so great was the anxiety to see this apostle of non-violence.'[71]

From Bihar, Gandhi moved further east, to the province of Assam. In one speech, at Sibsagar, Gandhi said 'he could not understand why the sweepers and workers in leather should be placed in the lowest strata of Hindu society. At some time or other, mothers performed the work of a sweeper. Doctors also did so.'[72]

XV

With civil disobedience effectively at an end, some Congress leaders were keen to revive the Swaraj Party and fight elections. It was the 1920s all over again; satyagraha, jail, and then, when out of jail, seeking once more to work the constitutional route to political progress. This time, however, Gandhi was more ready to welcome the compromise, less keen on seeing it as a capitulation. He would, he told Dr Ansari, welcome 'a party of Congressmen pursuing that programme [of council entry] rather than [they] be made sullen, discontented and utterly inactive'.

On 1 May 1934, a group of Congress leaders came to Bihar to confer with Gandhi. They included Asaf Ali, Rajagopalachari, Ansari, Rajendra Prasad, K.F. Nariman and Sarojini Naidu. They urged him to suspend civil disobedience altogether, and throw his weight behind council entry. Gandhi was unwilling to go so far. He still wanted to retain the option of individual satyagraha. He would therefore restrict 'civil disobedience to himself, provided that when and if he has the proposal for the extension of the programme of civil disobedience, the A.I.C.C. reserves the right of accepting it or not'. He also cautioned the constitutionalists that 'your parliamentary programme will be nugatory, if Hindu–Muslim unity is not achieved'.[73]

The lineage of the Swarajists went back to the 1920s, and perhaps even earlier, if we plausibly see them as ideological descendants of the Moderates of the first decade of the century. On the other side of the political spectrum, a new caucus had been formed in the Congress. This called itself the Congress Socialist Party. Its members included M.R. (Minoo) Masani and Yusuf Meherally of Bombay, Kamaladevi Chattopadhyay of Karnataka, Jayaprakash Narayan of Bihar, and Narendra Dev of the United Provinces. The informal leader or mentor of the Congress socialists was Jawaharlal Nehru.

In the last week of May, Minoo Masani called on Gandhi, then in rural Bihar. Masani, born into a westernized Parsi family, declined to get up for the prayers, but vigorously debated with Gandhi at other times of the day. Gandhi told him that 'your socialistic system is based on coercion'. Masani answered that coercion was not an end for them, but used 'for the good of the many'. Gandhi was unconvinced. 'Violence is impatience,' he pointed out, adding: 'and non-violence is patience. Great reforms cannot be introduced without great patience. In violence lies the germ of future failure.' If the socialists eschewed violence, Gandhi said to Masani, they would find 'that there is not much difference between you and me. Both of us desire the welfare of the starving millions.'

Before he departed, Masani left a copy of the socialists' programme with Gandhi. He read it carefully, before concluding that it seemed 'to ignore Indian conditions'. The socialists assumed that workers and capitalists were locked in endemic conflict. Gandhi, on the other hand, believed the two sides could work for their mutual good, so long as 'labourers and workers should know their rights and should also know how to assert them'.

The socialists' manifesto called for 'the progressive nationalization of all the instruments of production, distribution and exchange'. Gandhi thought this 'too sweeping', commenting archly that 'Rabindranath Tagore is an instrument of marvellous production. I do not know that he will submit to being nationalized.'[74]

Gandhi's view of the increasingly influential (and increasingly vocal) left wing in his party was decidedly mixed. 'Among the Socialists,' he wrote to a woman disciple, 'there are many good people, and some have the spirit of self-sacrifice in them; there are some who possess a powerful intellect and some who are rogues. Almost all of them have westernized minds. None of them knows the real conditions in Indian villages or perhaps even cares to know them.'[75]

XVI

These meetings with left-wing and right-wing Congressmen only briefly distracted Gandhi. The next stop on his Harijan tour was Orissa, home to as many fabulous ancient temples as Tamil Nadu. He had decided that he would tour the villages on foot, rather than being conveyed by motorcar. He was now almost sixty-five. He had undergone several long fasts in recent years. And May in Orissa was boiling. Yet, he comfortably walked eight to ten miles a day, and enjoyed it. As he wrote to Kasturba: 'One cannot propagate dharma by travelling in trains or cars, nor in bullock-carts. That can be done only on foot.'[76]

Gandhi now moved westwards, across the subcontinent, to Bombay. Here, he had a meeting with Ambedkar, who told him that instead of providing education or health facilities—properly the domain of the government—Gandhian social workers should 'concentrate on the primary object of securing full civic rights for Harijans, such as the right to draw water from public wells and to send children to public schools, without any discrimination being exercised against them'.

Gandhi asked Ambedkar to send him cases of continuing discrimination that came to his notice. He then said that on his tours, he had noticed a 'change for the better', but 'progress in that direction would be accelerated if he had the Doctor's valued co-operation'.[77]

In the third week of June, Gandhi arrived in Poona, a great, historic city, once home to the Peshwa kings, still home to some of the most learned scholars in the Hindu tradition. Prior to Gandhi's arrival, a procession of several hundred Sanatanists, led by a man dressed in black and riding a black horse, marched through the streets, bearing placards saying, 'Oppose the Temple Entry Bill', 'Victory Follows Tradition', and 'Do Not Give Reception to Gandhi the Destroyer of the Hindu Religion'.[78]

The anger against Gandhi in Poona soon took a more extreme form. On the evening of the 25th, he was being driven to a public meeting at Poona's municipal hall. Kasturba, who had recently completed her prison term, was with him. At 7.25 p.m. a car drove up to the hall, and the boy scouts band, thinking it was Gandhi's, began playing a tune of welcome. As the music began, a bomb was thrown from the upper storey of a house. It missed the car and exploded on the street, injuring five people, including a policeman. The bomb was aimed at Gandhi, but as it happened, the car the assailants had targeted was not his. He arrived a little later than expected; his vehicle had been held up at a railway crossing, and reached the venue three minutes after the explosion.[79]

In its editorial published the next day, the *Bombay Chronicle* offered thanks that Gandhi's life was saved. While Gandhi was unharmed, said the newspaper, 'every Indian will hang his head down in shame today because evidently it was the hand of an Indian which threw the bomb and the kind of an Indian that conceived the Satanic idea of taking away a life that has been dedicated to the service of fellow-beings in a purer and more devoted manner than that of any living human being . . .'[80]

In his own statement to the press, Gandhi said: 'The sorrowful incident has undoubtedly advanced the Harijan cause.' He continued: 'I am not acting for martyrdom, but if it comes in my way . . . I shall have well earned it, and it will be possible for the historian of the future to say that the vow I had taken before Harijans that I would, if need be, die in the attempt to remove untouchability was literally fulfilled.'

Gandhi asked his followers to exercise restraint. 'Let the reformers not to be incensed against the bomb-throwers or those who may be behind them.' He would like them instead 'to redouble their efforts to rid the country of the deadly evil of untouchability'.[81]

Those behind this unsuccessful attempt on Gandhi's life were not identified or caught. But they were almost certainly right-wing Hindus, angered by his campaign against untouchability.

XVII

Gandhi's Harijan tour had now gone on for a full eight months. With him on his journeys across India were members of his staff and a few intrepid reporters. An Andhra journalist who covered the tour wrote of how it had consolidated Gandhi's place in the affections of the ordinary Indian, who 'ran after him in crowds on foot out of the cities and sought just to touch the hem of his garments. Whether it was in the forest regions of Betul in biting winter, or on the parched dreary waste of Bellary in the hottest part of the day, whether it was in the populous cities on the plains, or in the quiet hamlets hanging on the heights of the Western Ghats—unbounded was the enthusiasm of men, women and children to catch a glimpse of him who had sworn to fast unto death to uplift the seventy million people who are depressed and made lowly and humble by age-old oppression.'[82]

In the last week of July, Gandhi arrived in Banaras, chosen as the last stop on the Harijan tour for its religious significance. On 29 July, speaking to the central board of the Harijan Sewak Sangh, he complained about the quality of the social workers who had joined his anti-untouchability campaign. 'They have not given their whole time to their work,' he said, adding: 'They do it in a leisurely fashion.' What he wanted, and the country needed, were individuals 'whose sole ambition is to devote themselves body, mind and soul to the Harijan cause. If we had ten thousand such workers—I make bold to say even if we had a thousand, we should have startling results.'

The next day, he addressed a public meeting in which the conservative element was significant, if not preponderant. A locally respected priest, one Pandit Devanayakcharya, speaking before Gandhi, had insisted that untouchability was sanctioned by the Shastras and thus part and parcel of the Hindu dharma. According to a police informer in attendance, the pandit 'spoke clearly and forcibly and held the attention of the audience until he spoilt any effect he might have had by undue verbosity and was eventually shouted down'.[83]

Gandhi spoke after the pandit. Describing the practice of untouchability as 'a blot on Hinduism', he noted that in Banaras and elsewhere in India, 'a dog can drink from a reservoir, but a thirsty

Harijan boy may not. If he goes, he cannot escape being beaten. Untouchability as practised today considers man worse than a dog.'

Gandhi dealt with the problem of untouchability on several other occasions during this visit to Banaras. In one speech, he chastised the municipality for making Harijans live in the dirtiest and most disease-prone parts of the city, 'in a place unfit even for cattle'. In another, he deplored the restrictions on inter-dining and intermingling so prevalent in Hindu society. He categorically stated that 'birth and observance of form cannot determine one's superiority or inferiority. Character is the only determining factor.' He went on: 'God did not create men with the badge of superiority or inferiority, and no scripture which labels a human being as inferior or untouchable because of his birth can command our allegiance . . .'[84]

Let's consider these sentences again. Birth *cannot* determine one's superiority or inferiority. Character is the *only* determining factor. Gandhi had clearly considerably moved on from his previously timid, hesitant attempts to question untouchability while keeping the structure of varna intact.

Back in 1916, Gandhi had chosen Banaras to make his first major political speech since his return to India. Now, almost two decades later, this ancient city of the Hindus was the place where Gandhi concluded his year-long campaign against the scripturally sanctified practice of untouchability.

CHAPTER TWENTY-TWO

A Second Sabbatical

I

Ever since his return from Europe, Gandhi had concerned himself almost exclusively with social matters. Through 1932 and 1933, and the first half of 1934 as well, he had focused on the abolition of untouchability. Stung by Ambedkar's challenge, he had sought to awaken the sometimes dormant, more often absent, conscience of his fellow Hindus against this pernicious practice.

In these years, Gandhi had, willy-nilly, shut out the world. But the world would not stop taking notice of him. In February 1932, a professor of sociology at the Yale Divinity School named Jerome Davis wrote to the social worker Jane Addams, asking her to nominate Gandhi for the Nobel Peace Prize. Addams had won the prize herself the previous year. She certainly knew about Gandhi; keen to meet him when she toured India in 1923, she was denied the chance by his being in jail.

Jerome Davis was a left-wing internationalist, who was born in Tokyo, had worked in Russia, and been a labour organizer. 'It seems to me', wrote Davis to Addams, that 'there is no one in the world today who has worked more sincerely and consistently than he [Gandhi] has for soul force and peace as over against the vise of militarism and arms'. Then he added: 'Perhaps it is too much to hope that the [Nobel] Committee would have enough impartiality to choose him, but surely those of us who do recognize the world wide character of his influence, and the heroic achievement of his efforts for peace and justice, can do no more than suggest his name to the Committee.'

In her reply, Jane Addams declined to take the request forward. In 1932 no Nobel Peace Prize was awarded. The following year, it went to the British pacifist Norman Angell. In March 1934, Davis wrote to Jane Addams again. He had prevailed upon the Chicago magazine *Christian Century* to nominate Gandhi for the Nobel Peace Prize, and wanted her to second their endorsement. Once more, Davis told Addams that 'there is no one in the world today who is more entitled to the prize than Gandhi'. He added, with a touch of exasperation: 'Would it not be a very gracious thing for you to write to the committee making this nomination?'

Addams wrote back, saying she'd rather recommend the Danish educationist Peter Manniche instead. Davis, not to be put off, said in that case he would renew his campaign in 1935. 'I am counting on you to write next fall nominating Gandhi,' he wrote to her.[1]

Gandhi did not know of this correspondence. But the recommendation of the *Christian Century* was brought to his attention by the Quaker Agatha Harrison. In its issue of 14 March 1934, the journal had asked: 'Why not award the Nobel Peace Prize to Gandhi?' Then it went on: 'It would be no personal favour to him and he probably does not want it. The honour would not greatly impress him and he would not know what to do with the money except to give it away.' 'These are all high qualifications for the prize,' commented the *Christian Century*. Noting further that the prize's original intention was 'to encourage bold dreamers and prophetic spirits whose ideas are too far ahead of their time to win attention without some adventitious aid', the journal believed Gandhi was a more worthy candidate than some 'practical politicians who merely negotiated another mile of treaty or took another mile of trench in the long campaign of humanity against bloodshed'. If Gandhi was 'not the most logical candidate for the Nobel Peace Prize', insisted the *Christian Century*, then 'the popular idea of the function and purpose of that prize needs to be revised'.

Agatha Harrison was a regular reader of the *Christian Century*; and, as it turned out, she was with Gandhi in India in the summer of 1934 when this particular issue reached her, redirected from London. Harrison read the article on a Monday, the Mahatma's day of silence. She marked the passages praising and promoting Gandhi, and handed it over to him. He read it through, twice, asked for a pencil and piece of paper, on which he wrote: 'Do you know of a Dreamer who won attention by "Adventitious Aid"?' Asked by Agatha Harrison if he wished to comment further, he shook his head, with (as she recalled) 'an amused smile'.[2]

II

Another curious manifestation of the Western interest in Gandhi in these years concerns the German priest Dietrich Bonhoeffer. Bonhoeffer, executed in 1945 for his opposition to Hitler and the Nazis, has since become a hero for religiously minded people (not just Christians) fighting political tyranny. His connection with Gandhi remains little known.

Bonhoeffer first heard of Gandhi as a teenager, from his grandmother, herself a pioneer in the fight for greater rights for women. This was in 1924, when he was seventeen. As he grew older, he read more about Gandhi, and was attracted both to his religious pluralism and his practice of non-violent resistance. In 1931—shortly before he was ordained as a priest—Bonhoeffer wrote to his twin sister Sabine that he wanted to travel to India to meet with Gandhi.[3] As he told a friend, he believed that Germans had much to learn from other cultures, and it was from the East in particular that the 'great solution would come'.[4]

In 1931, Bonhoeffer's trip to India was aborted due to lack of funds. But the idea would not go away. In May 1934, he told his grandmother he was determined to meet Gandhi, whose 'heathenism has more of the Christian spirit than our State Church'.[5] Fellow Christians put him in touch with C.F. Andrews, who wrote to Gandhi saying that 'If Pastor Bonhoeffer comes to India to enquire about what is being done for World Peace through Ahimsa or Satyagraha, I do hope you will be able to see him. I met him in Switzerland and was greatly impressed by his convictions.'[6]

Bonhoeffer also shared his India plans with the American theologian Reinhold Niebuhr. Given the complicity of the churches with Nazism, he thought Gandhi could aid German Christianity in rediscovering the message of the Sermon on the Mount. 'I plan to go to India very soon,' he told Niebuhr, 'to see what Gandhi knows about these things and to see what is to be learned there.'[7]

In October 1934, Bonhoeffer wrote Gandhi a remarkable letter from London, where he was then temporarily based. This letter has not (so far as I can tell) been seen by the two men's previous biographers. Addressing Gandhi as 'Revered Mahatmaji', Bonhoeffer told him that 'Europe and Germany are suffering from a dangerous fever and are losing both self-control and the consciousness of what they are doing'. As a pastor, Bonhoeffer felt that 'only Christianity can help our western peoples to a new and spiritually sound life'. Then he added: 'But Christianity must be something very different from what it has become in these days.'

Bonhoeffer was convinced that 'everything seems to work for war in the near future, and the next war will certainly bring the spiritual death of Europe'. What was needed therefore, was 'a truly spiritual living Christian peace movement. Western Christianity must be reborn as the Sermon on the Mount.' Having studied Gandhi and his movement, Bonhoeffer thought that 'we Western Christians should try to learn from you what realisation of faith means, what life devoted to political and racial peace means'. The German knew that the Indian was not a Christian himself, yet, as he pointed out, 'the people whose faith Jesus praised mostly did not belong to the official Church at that time either'.

Bonhoeffer told Gandhi of his 'great admiration' for 'your personal work among the poorest of your fellowmen, for your educational ideals, for your stand for peace and non-violence, for truth and its force, which has convinced me that I should definitely come to India next winter . . .' He hoped to come with a friend, a physicist. Having contemplated the journey for many years now, he did not, he told Gandhi, 'want to accuse myself of having missed the one great occasion in my life to learn the meaning of Christian life, of real community life, of truth and love in reality'.[8]

Gandhi wrote back, inviting the duo to come 'whenever you like' to 'share my daily life'. They could stay in the ashram, contributing Rs 100 per month each to its expenses (apart from paying for their own travel). Gandhi added two warnings: that the food would be vegetarian; and that he himself might have to go to prison, in which case Bonhoeffer would 'have to be satisfied with remaining in or near one of the institutions that are being conducted under my supervision'.[9]

As it turned out, Bonhoeffer could not accept Gandhi's invitation. Whether it was due to lack of funds or worry that Gandhi would be in prison, the sources do not say. But it remains an intriguing thought— what if Bonhoeffer had spent several months with Gandhi in 1934– 35, and, on his return, had conducted or led a non-violent campaign against the Nazis? At this stage, Hitler's regime was not completely in control. The attacks on Jews had commenced, but the Nuremberg Laws were not yet enacted. And the invasion of Austria lay several years in the future. The Nazis were far more ruthless than the British colonialists in India, and would have acted early to suppress any mass protest. Even so, had a movement of satyagraha, led by a charismatic Christian pastor, taken place in Germany in 1935, it could perhaps have awakened sensitive men and women in the West to the horrors that lay ahead if they did not intervene.

III

On 5 August 1934, his Harijan tour concluded, Gandhi returned to Wardha in the Central Provinces, which he had now chosen to be his home base, replacing Ahmedabad. His friend and disciple Jamnalal Bajaj lived there. Wardha's great advantage—apart from Bajaj's presence—was that it was close to the geographical centre of India.

In early September, Gandhi wrote Vallabhbhai Patel a long letter expressing his disquiet at 'the vital difference of outlook between many Congressmen and myself'. He told Patel that 'the best interests of the Congress and the nation will be served by my completely severing all official or physical connection with the Congress'.

Gandhi then turned to the 'growing group of socialists' in the Congress. He praised Jawaharlal Nehru, 'their undisputed leader', as 'courage personified'. Other members of the group were 'respected and self-sacrificing co-workers'. That said, Gandhi had 'fundamental differences' with the socialists on economic and political issues. How could they be resolved?

Gandhi understood perfectly well that by reason of 'the moral pressure' at his command, he could suppress or contain the socialists. Yet, he told Patel that 'for me to dominate the Congress in spite of these fundamental differences is almost a species of violence which I must refrain from'.[10] Patel's reply is unavailable, but he seems to have requested Gandhi to postpone his decision till the next session of the Congress, due in Bombay in October.

Word of this exchange leaked out to the press, so, in a statement of 17 September, Gandhi confirmed that 'the rumour that I had contemplated severing all physical relations with the Congress was true'. He spoke of his differences with the socialists, and of his own continuing commitment to Hindu–Muslim harmony, the abolition of untouchability, the promotion of khadi, and the revival of village industries. He added that in pursuit of this programme, 'personally I would like to bury myself in a Frontier village'. In the NWFP, his admirer Khan Abdul Ghaffar Khan had persuaded his fellow Pathans to abandon their taste for battle in favour of non-violent resistance. Gandhi felt that Ghaffar Khan's *Khudai Khidmatgars* (Servants of God) could potentially 'contribute the largest share to the promotion of [a] non-violent spirit and of Hindu–Muslim unity'.[11]

Gandhi's decision to retire from the Congress delighted the viceroy. When he heard that his bête noire was 'likely to be out of action for some time', Willingdon wrote to his sister: 'I can't help feeling grateful to Providence for giving me this relief!'[12]

At the same time, Gandhi's decision dismayed his closest political allies. 'Your retirement from the Congress will be a suicidal step,' wrote Rajagopalachari. 'That will complete the triumph of the Government over the Congress, and that of the Viceroy over you. An intense and irrevocable feeling of defeatism will spread over the whole nation, and kill political hope and enterprise . . .'[13]

These responses were in character. Far more interesting was the reaction of Henry Polak, who had known Gandhi longer than anyone living in India, whether Indian or British. In a letter to Srinivasa Sastri, Polak remarked that Gandhi had

> a temperament of restless energy, and it seems to me that he has alternations between the political mood and the social and economic reform mood. Sometimes they almost merge and blur each other. I should not at all be surprised if in the not very distant future he will feel a call to jump back into the Congress leadership once he has put his village organisation upon a proper footing.[14]

The Congress session began on 20 October in Bombay. The previous week, from Wardha, Gandhi clarified that his retirement 'was neither a threat nor an ultimatum' to his partymen to follow his diktats. Rather, he wished to focus on village work, and proposed to start an All India Village Industries Association.

Gandhi attended the Congress in Bombay, speaking at several committee meetings on Harijan work and swadeshi. The AICC passed a unanimous resolution expressing 'the country's confidence' in his leadership, and urging him not to retire. Gandhi asked them to withdraw the resolution, noting that as and when it became necessary to come back to the Congress, he would do so.[15]

After the Congress had ended, Gandhi publicly refuted the rumours that he had left the party 'in disgust'. He retained the 'highest regard for the Congress', and had 'retired not to weaken the national organization, but to strengthen it'. When India achieved its goal of swaraj, he added, 'as we will and must, the Congress will be found to have contributed the largest share in the attainment'.[16]

IV

On his return to Wardha, Gandhi wrote to the viceroy, saying he wished to visit the NWFP, to study at first-hand 'how far the teaching of non-violence by Khan Saheb Abdul Ghaffar Khan has permeated his followers'. Although 'there is no legal bar against my entering the

Frontier Province', he remarked, 'I have no desire to do anything that may bring me in conflict with the Government'.

The viceroy wrote back, saying he had consulted with his council, who were 'unanimously of [the] opinion that it was not desirable for you to pay a visit to the Frontier Province at the present time'.[17]

After his Harijan tour, Gandhi had begun to take a keen interest in the revival of the village economy. Travelling in different parts of the countryside, he noticed the widespread poverty, and the large-scale underemployment too. He thought that promoting crafts and small production units would make the rural economy self-sufficient and vigorous. Beginning in November 1934, he published a series of articles on the invigoration of the agrarian economy. Industries such as spinning and weaving, milling and grinding, could be profitably utilized to augment rural incomes, and renew social and cooperative life.

In December 1934, the All India Village Industries Association (AIVIA) formally came into being. Its president was a nationalist lawyer named Shrikrishnadas Jajooji; its secretary and chief organizer the economist J.C. Kumarappa. The AIVIA's board of advisers included Rabindranath Tagore, the chemist P.C. Ray and the Nobel Prize–winning physicist C.V. Raman.

The AIVIA's aim was defined as 'the revival, encouragement and improvement of village industries, and the moral and physical advancement of the villages of India'. Wardha had been chosen as its headquarters, 'because of being centrally situated, being a junction station and being rather a glorified village than a city'.

Meanwhile, Gandhi's series on the renewal of rural life continued. One essay focused on village sanitation, 'perhaps the most difficult task' confronting the AIVIA. Gandhi asked for the periodic cleaning and desilting of wells and tanks, and especially, for the recycling of human waste as manure (a practice not followed in India, unlike in China, where it helped to cheaply and effectively restore soil fertility).[18]

V

In January 1935, Gandhi's daughter-disciple Mira told him of her wish to start a 'real Village Ashram'. She asked whether he would join her. He told her he would, once she had created such a place. So, she began surveying the villages near Wardha for a suitable site to move to. She told Devadas Gandhi that there was, all around the town, 'fine air, good water, hills, woods, little villages—but it is difficult to get just the right place'.[19]

In mid-May, Gandhi briefly left Wardha for Bombay. The city had been an epicentre of the Rowlatt satyagraha, the non-cooperation movement and the Salt March. Congress volunteers were itching for some more direct action. Speaking to them, Gandhi said he had been told that 'there is despair and depression everywhere, that there is disappointment all around as the gateway to jail is closed'. He wondered why, when there was 'the whole of the constructive programme of work to do'.

Gandhi told the Congress radicals that while swaraj was their 'birthright', it did not depend only on jail-going. He asked the impatient activists to 'go to the villages, identify yourselves with villagers, befriend the untouchables, make Hindu–Muslim unity a concrete fact'.[20]

One Congresswoman keen to identify with village life was a princess from North India. Born in 1889 (the same year as Jawaharlal Nehru), Rajkumari Amrit Kaur was from the royal family of Kapurthala. While her ancestors were Sikh, she had herself been raised a Christian. Educated in England, a great beauty as well as a superb tennis player in her youth, she lived in Simla, and was a fixture at its games and parties.

As she entered her thirties, Amrit Kaur became dissatisfied with a life of leisure and luxury, while becoming increasingly attracted to Gandhi and the national movement. She turned her back on the court, as well as the Court, engaging instead with the All-India Women's Conference, among whose leading lights were Sarojini Naidu and Kamaladevi Chattopadhyay.[21]

In the summer of 1935, Kasturba Gandhi went to Simla to escape the searing summer of Wardha. She stayed as the guest of Amrit Kaur, in the spacious family bungalow, suitably named 'Manorville'. Kasturba returned to Wardha once the monsoon had set in. She was followed by a series of letters from Amrit Kaur to Gandhi, accompanied by a box of apples from the family orchard. The rajkumari was desperately keen to abandon her aristocratic lifestyle to come closer to the Mahatma. She expressed her desire for disciplehood in perfervid prose. 'My loyalty to your ideals,' wrote Amrit Kaur, 'and a real desire to serve the lowliest and the down-trodden with such poor capacity as is mine you will, I pray, always have—God helping me, with my shortcomings you will, I know, always exercise the utmost forbearance.'[22]

VI

In October 1935, a village in Gujarat named Kavitha became the centre of a nationwide controversy. The 'untouchables' had asked for their children to be admitted to the village school. The caste Hindus, enraged, asked for a complete boycott of the Harijans. When A.V. Thakkar brought this incident to the attention of Gandhi, he suggested that the Harijans leave the village in protest. 'If people migrate in search of employment,' he remarked, 'how much more should they do so in search of self-respect?'

When Ambedkar heard of the Kavitha incident, he said that they were treated like this because 'we have the misfortune to call ourselves Hindu'. He added: 'If we were members of another faith none dare treat us so. . . . Choose any religion which gives you equality of status and treatment.' Ambedkar urged the 'untouchables' to leave Hinduism and embrace any other religion that gave them equal status with its other members.

When Ambedkar's statement was brought to Gandhi's attention, he said he could 'understand the anger of a high-souled and highly educated person' over what had happened at Kavitha. But, he went on: 'Religion is not like a house or a cloak that can be changed at will. It is more an integral part of one's self than of one's body.' The lives of the Harijans, continued Gandhi, were, for good and for ill, intertwined with caste Hindus. Thus, reform of Hinduism rather than its rejection was the way forward.[23]

Gandhi argued that the outcry over the Kavitha incident in fact showed that the battle against untouchability was showing results. As he pointed out: 'Only a few years ago the Kavitha incident would have attracted no notice. There were very few reformers then.' Now, as it turned out, 'it was *savarna* reformers [like A.V. Thakkar] who advertised the Kavitha incident and gave it an all-India importance'. 'Let not Dr. Ambedkar's just wrath deject the reformer,' remarked Gandhi, 'let it spur him to greater effort.'[24]

In November, Gandhi published an article with the telling title 'Caste Has to Go'. This reiterated his acceptance of inter-dining and intermarriage. He argued that 'the most effective, quickest, and the most unobtrusive way to destroy caste is for reformers to begin the practice with themselves and where necessary take the consequences of social boycott'.[25]

Meanwhile, a deputation of progressive Hindus called on Ambedkar. They asked him to reconsider his decision to leave his ancestral faith. In reply, Ambedkar distinguished between the metaphysical basis of Hinduism and its social practice. As he put it: 'Though Hinduism is based on the conception of Absolute Brahma, the practices of the Hindu community as a whole are founded on the doctrines of inequality as pronounced in "Manusmriti".'

On his wish to convert to another religion, Ambedkar remarked: 'It is not a personal question and I desire to carry with me the whole untouchable community—at all events the majority of that community. I do not want it to be split up by some joining one religion or sect and others another.'

On his own political agenda, Ambedkar said: 'Being born in the untouchable community, I deem it my first duty to strive for its interests and my duty to India as a whole is secondary.'

The most striking part of the conversation was Ambedkar's hope or wish for a strong leader for India. He is reported to have said:

> Democracy is not suitable for India and popular government will not do for her. India wants a dictator, a Kemal Pasha or a Mussolini. I had hoped that Mr. Gandhi would attain the position of a dictator, but I am disappointed. My complaint is not that Mr. Gandhi is a dictator but that he is not. I feel the greatest respect for Kemal Pasha. It is he who has made Turkey into a powerful nation. If there are any people with whose religious sentiments and practice it is extremely risky to interfere, it is the Muslims. But Kemal Pasha has done it with success.[26]

This statement, even if true, should be taken as a mark of Ambedkar's desperate desire for real, rapid change in the status of 'untouchables', and not as a statement in favour of dictatorship per se.

The differences between Ambedkar and Gandhi, temporarily papered over by the Poona Pact, were once more coming to the fore. Commenting on the debate, a letter writer to the *Times of India* argued that had it not been for Gandhi's 'strenuous efforts', the 'problem of untouchability would not have attained its present importance'. Gandhi had 'set people thinking seriously', pointing them 'to the right conclusion—that untouchability is a terrible disease eating into the vitals of Hindu society'. The correspondent argued that Dr Ambedkar's decision to change his religion was inspired 'by a spirit of despondency and desperation'—it 'lacks the farsightedness of the politician that he is'. What if the Sikhs or Christians accepted Ambedkar and his followers but did not mete out equal treatment? Would he change his religion once more? 'If he has no objection to doing so,' remarked the letter writer, 'his conception of religion must necessarily be poor or inadequate for a man of his learning.'[27]

This writer was right about the limits of conversion as a means of conquering oppression. For, Sikhs and Christians in India themselves discriminated against low-caste converts. On the other hand, he was perhaps optimistic about Gandhi's campaign. For, in 1935—a full twenty years after Gandhi returned to India—untouchability was still rigorously defended by the majority of Hindu priests and scholars, and extensively practised by the Hindu laity.

VII

In 1934 and 1935, as he sought to bridge the gap between himself and his most unyielding political opponent, B.R. Ambedkar, Gandhi also sought to heal the breach with his eldest and long-estranged son, Harilal. In September 1934, Harilal wrote to Gandhi saying he had stopped drinking and wandering. He wanted to settle down, marry once more, and perhaps start a store in their native Porbandar.

Gandhi was not keen on the idea of a store. His son had failed in several business ventures before. He suggested that Harilal join the khadi or Harijan programmes instead, where he could work under the direction of Narandas Gandhi. But, he wrote to his son, 'I understand about marrying. If what you want is a companion and that must be a wife, I would not regard it as in the least blameworthy provided you find a suitable widow.'[28]

Before giving the go-ahead, however, Gandhi wanted 'independent proof' that Harilal had reformed himself. He asked his son a series of sharp questions. Was he still drinking or smoking, and did he still indulge 'in sexual pleasure through mind, speech or body'?[29]

Harilal answered that he now abstained from alcohol and sex, but hadn't yet given up smoking. Gandhi said that it 'was not in the least difficult to give up smoking' provided he adopted a prescribed diet. Meanwhile, he wrote to Devadas: 'I receive letters from Harilal. At present I am meeting his expenses. He is holding out great hopes and I too am hoping.'[30]

In the third week of February 1935, Harilal arrived in Wardha to spend some time with his father. The visit did not go well. The son still 'crave[d] for sex pleasure'. Gandhi chastised him: 'How can I, who have always advocated renunciation of sex, encourage you to gratify it.'[31]

Harilal returned to Kathiawar, then came back to Wardha to try again. He stayed a fortnight; after he returned to Rajkot, Gandhi wrote to his nephew Narandas: 'I liked his staying here. He did whatever work he could and was friendly with everybody. He says his passion for drinks has completely died out. And I understand that he has no carnal passion left, apart from the desire to marry.'

Gandhi told Narandas that if Harilal found a 'suitable wife', he would marry. 'This is Harilal's story,' remarked Gandhi philosophically. 'Let us see how fate shapes his life now. I will be content even if the treasure I have got back is not lost again, and thank God for His mercy.'[32]

Once more, the reconciliation between father and son was short-lived. 'It seems Harilal is off the rails again,' wrote Gandhi to Narandas. 'You have promised to give him some work, but if he is in the habit of telling downright lies then are you sure you have done well? How will he prove useful to you? Of late, his letters do not satisfy me at all.'[33]

Things now went swiftly downhill. On 11 July 1935, Gandhi wrote to Narandas: 'For the present Harilal may be considered as lost to us.' And, again four days later: 'Forget Harilal completely now. I have almost forgotten him.'[34]

Harilal's letters to his father now turned more truculent. Independent inquiries into what he was doing in Rajkot confirmed that the regression was complete. 'Harilal spends the whole day immersed in a tub of liquor,' wrote Gandhi to his second son Manilal in August, adding: 'All our hopes about his having been reformed are falsified. He is now worse than he was. But one keeps on hoping as long as one breathes. Accordingly, let us hope that, if he lives, some day he will reform himself.'

Six weeks later, giving his son in South Africa news of the family, he provided this single sarcastic sentence about the elder brother: 'Harilal is sanctifying his anatomy in the holy Ganga of liquor.'[35]

Reading these letters, it is impossible not to feel sympathy for Harilal. He was now in his mid-forties. He had tried several professions and failed in all. He was cut off from his children, and still missed his long-dead wife. Lonely and confused, he was desperate for companionship and for social and financial stability. Yet, the only person he could turn to for advice was his father, who, as always, wanted still to mould this now middle-aged man in his own image.

VIII

In August 1935, the British Parliament had passed an Act devolving further powers to Indians. Based on the round table conferences, and influenced by the groundswell of the national movement, in most respects this went further than the preceding Act of 1919. The franchise had been greatly expanded. The number of European representatives in provincial assemblies had been substantially reduced. In each province, the government would be formed on the basis of an elected majority; which would then choose ministers to run the various departments of home, education, health, finance, public works, etc. The ICS officers would report to these Indian ministers.

The Act went some distance in meeting Indian aspirations, but not quite far enough. For one thing, the governors would still be British, and they retained substantial reserve powers to overrule decisions taken by ministers, and to dismiss an elected government in case of a perceived threat to law and order. For another, there was no provision for a popular government at the Centre. There would be a central legislative assembly with elected members, but the real administrative powers would still be exercised by the viceroy and an executive council whose members were nominated by him.

The Congress was disappointed that the Act did not specifically promise a further evolution to Dominion Status. In the House of Commons, both Liberal and Labour MPs fought hard for an explicit commitment to this effect so that India would one day soon be placed on par with Canada and Australia, self-governing dominions with a far greater degree of autonomy than this 1935 Act would provide. However, there was a Conservative government in Britain, and many Tory MPs were unhappy even with the limited powers that the Act had devolved to Indians. So no such promise was given.[36]

Under the provisions of the Act, elections to the provincial assemblies were to be held in early 1937. How would the Congress react? Would it fight and seek to win these elections, to show that it still held the popular mood? Or would it boycott them, since the promised result fell short of Dominion Status, let alone Purna Swaraj? There were varying opinions in the party. The older Swarajists, always wedded to constitutional, incremental means, favoured the first option. The younger socialists, congenitally sceptical of representative government, favoured the second. There was also a third school of thought within the party, which wanted the election to be fought and won, but with the Congress then refusing to take charge of the provincial ministries.

Gandhi, in Wardha, was keeping in touch with the world of politics despite his professed retirement from it. He knew, and admired, leaders of all three schools in the Congress. Who could best synthesize or reconcile them? Gandhi thought it must be Jawaharlal Nehru. Nehru had been almost continuously in prison since the Salt March began. However, in September 1935, he was released on compassionate grounds. His wife Kamala was seriously ill, and he wished to accompany her to Europe to consult doctors there. Gandhi sent Mahadev Desai to meet Nehru at Allahabad. When Mahadev arrived at the family home, Anand Bhavan, he found Nehru had already left for Bombay to book berths on a ship bound for Europe.

Mahadev now dispatched Nehru a letter with the messages their mutual master had wanted him to convey. These were: (i) that Nehru should once more assume the Congress presidency, since that 'was the only way' in which 'the bitter controversies of today could be avoided and your policy and your programme could be given a fair and unobstructed trial'; (ii) that in Europe he should make no speeches or statements. Gandhi told Nehru that 'it would enhance your prestige and India's to impose upon yourself a vow of silence . . . until your return here'.[37]

Nehru agreed to be Congress president in 1936, the crucial year leading up to the elections mandated by the new Act. But he was clear in his own mind that the real leader of his party, and his country-in-the-making, was Gandhi. As he wrote to an English friend: 'The only person who represents India, more than anyone has done or can do, is Gandhi. I may differ from him in a multitude of things but that is a matter between him and me and our colleagues. So far as I am concerned he is India in a peculiar measure and he is the undoubted leader of my country. If anybody wants to know what India wants, let him go to Gandhi.'[38]

IX

In October 1935, after twenty years at the centre of public life in India, Gandhi issued a public appeal to his correspondents in the pages of *Harijan*. He was being overwhelmed by the number of letters he received. 'My capacity to overtake this ever-increasing correspondence,' he ruefully remarked, 'decreases in the same ratio as the increase in the volume of my correspondence.'

So, 'if a breakdown is not to take place', he had to 'cut off as much private correspondence as possible'. He asked for cooperation in this regard of those who wrote, and still would write, to him. He had 'prized their confidence' in the past. It had given him 'an insight

into human nature and its ultimate nobility'. And he understood
that 'nothing can be a substitute for personal contact'. But he now
had to 'urge correspondents to deny themselves the temptation of
referring to me on all kinds of problems. Let them take the trouble
of solving them themselves with such help as writings on ethics and
eternal verities can give. They will find that they will do better in the
end than if they would make of me a dictionary of reference on every
occasion.'[39]

The exasperation was justified. The openness of Gandhi's life,
the range of his activities, his willingness to engage in debate, had all
encouraged letter writers in India (and abroad) to seek his counsel on
a million myriad matters, or else dispute his utterances on a hundred
topics offered on a thousand different occasions. Back in the 1920s,
the faithful (and superbly competent) Mahadev had handled this
correspondence on behalf of Gandhi. After the volume and intensity of
the letter writers increased, Pyarelal and Amrit Kaur were also asked to
serve as additional secretaries. Now even they found it difficult to cope.

Some letters, however, would be read, answered and attended
to at once. Thus, Tagore had written to Gandhi asking for help for
funds to save Santiniketan. The poet, in his seventies, was himself
touring with a ballet troupe to raise money for his university. Gandhi
answered that he could depend 'upon my straining every nerve to
find the necessary money. . . . The necessary funds must come to you
without your having to stir out of Santiniketan.'

Some months later, Gandhi wrote to the poet again. Attaching a
draft of Rs 60,000, he said: 'God has blessed my poor effort. And here
is the money. Now you will relieve the public mind by announcing
the cancellation of the rest of the programme. May God keep you for
many a year to come.'[40]

Gandhi kept the donor's name to himself. It was the industrialist
G.D. Birla.

X

Gandhi was now living in Wardha, in a house with a large plot of
land, gifted by Jamnalal Bajaj. Here, sheds for spinning and other

crafts had sprung up. The headquarters of the All India Village Industries Association were also housed here. The settlement was named Maganwadi, in memory of Gandhi's nephew Maganlal, who had helped run the ashrams at Phoenix and Sabarmati.

Since early 1935, Mira had been living in a village called Varoda, a mile and a half from Wardha. She had been tasked with locating a village home suitable for Gandhi. She settled on a hamlet named Segaon, since it had a large population of 'untouchables', and the land in the village was owned in part by Jamnalal Bajaj.

In March 1936, Gandhi began actively planning a move to Segaon. He would live there alone or with Kasturba if she chose to join him. He told Bajaj he wanted 'as little expense as possible' to be incurred in building a hut for him, setting Rs 100 as the outer limit for the cost of labour and building materials. Another hut could be constructed for Mahadev. Gandhi would 'pay visits to Maganwadi as often as necessary'.[41]

In the third week of April, Gandhi visited Segaon and met with the villagers. He told them that they 'must have heard from Mirabehn that I have cast out all untouchability from myself, that I hold all classes of people—Brahmin, Kshatriya, Vaishya and Shudra, Rajput, Mahar, Chamar—all alike, and I regard these distinctions based on birth as immoral. We have suffered because of these distinctions, and this sense of high and low has vitiated our lives.'[42]

On 30 April, Gandhi spent his first night in Segaon. He walked the several miles from the town, and was sorrowfully seen off by the disciples who remained at Maganwadi. Mahadev Desai summed up their feelings in an article in *Harijan*: 'An unexpressed but deep-seated pang was in the heart of everyone. Some of them had been with him for the best part of their lives. Had the time come for them to be dropped out, as it had happened to the companions of Yudhisthira when he started on his march for the Kingdom of Heaven?'

One ashramite (whom Mahadev unfortunately does not name) had the boldness to tell Gandhi that instead of 'burying himself in this village', he should undertake an all-India tour to promote rural reconstruction, just as he had done for the abolition of untouchability. Gandhi answered that the comparison was invalid. 'I have been talking theory all these days,' remarked Gandhi, 'talking and giving advice on village work, without having personally come to grips with the difficulties of village work. If I undertook the tour say after passing three seasons in a village . . . I would be able to talk with knowledge and experience which I have not got today.'[43]

An early visitor in Segaon was Dr B.R. Ambedkar. He came with the industrialist Walchand Hirachand. Sadly, we do not have the details of their talks (or arguments), although we do know that, with Gandhi's hut not entirely ready, the conversation took place under a tree.

On his way to Segaon and back, Ambedkar spoke with Mahadev Desai about the personal humiliations he had suffered on account of his caste. He recalled how, as a young boy, he was not allowed to enter the village school; how he and his siblings would not be attended to by the village barber (his sister shaved them all); how, even after studying at Columbia University, he could not get a place to rent while working in Baroda; how, only the previous month, a taxi driver in Bombay refused to ferry him because of his caste.

'We are deeply ashamed,' said Mahadev on hearing this, adding: 'but do not you think the situation has changed? Do not you find numerous people to suffer with you today?' 'I see no change,' responded Ambedkar. 'And what's the good of telling me you are ready to suffer with us? If you have to suffer, it means we will have to continue to suffer still more.' Mahadev persisted, pointing to the 'healthy change' he had noticed among many upper-caste Hindus in their attitude to caste discrimination. But Ambedkar would not be convinced, saying (in Mahadev's recollection), 'One swallow does not make a summer. You are highly optimistic. But you know the definition of an optimist? An optimist is one who takes the brightest view of other people's sufferings.'[44]

On 2 May, the day after he met Gandhi in Segaon, Dr Ambedkar was felicitated by the Nagpur municipality. In his address, Ambedkar said he was 'a much maligned man' because of his arguments on behalf of separate electorates at the Round Table Conference. Ambedkar clarified that 'he never stood in the way of Dominion Status. All he wanted was protection for the minorities [among whom he included the Depressed Classes] to which they were entitled. . . . [H]e declared that if any disaster befell the country the responsibility would be on the caste Hindus and it would be judged through how they used power against the minorities.'[45]

Ambedkar had just told Mahadev Desai that he had seen 'no change' in the attitude of the caste Hindus. His statement in Nagpur suggests that he was now having second thoughts about the Poona Pact and its ability to even protect, still less enhance the rights of, the Depressed Classes.

XI

Gandhi spent a mere week in his new home, before travelling south, to the hill station of Nandi, where he had spent six weeks back in 1927. This time the cool air was not so much for him as for Vallabhbhai Patel, who had been unwell.

Gandhi and Patel walked up to Nandi from the nearest roadhead, the trek taking them two and a half hours. 'The air is beautiful,' he wrote to a disciple, 'the calmness is divine. No cars or carts or even rickshaws. . . . I do not know a more secluded, cleaner, quieter hill. Sardar is in raptures over the stillness.'[46]

One day, the physicist Sir C.V. Raman came up from Bangalore to see Gandhi. Raman's conceit was legendary. In the summer of 1930, he booked a passage for his wife and himself on a boat leaving for Europe in October, so confident was he of winning the Nobel Prize for physics that year (which he did). Now, meeting an Indian even more celebrated than himself, Raman told him: 'Mahatmaji, religions cannot unite. Science offers the best opportunity for a complete fellowship. All men of science are brothers.' 'What about the converse?' responded Gandhi. 'All who are not men of science are not brothers?' Raman had the last word, noting that 'all can become men of science'.

Raman had come with a Swiss biologist who wished to have a darshan of the Indian leader. Introducing his colleague, Raman said he had discovered an insect that could live without food and water for as long as twelve years. 'When you discover the secret at the back of it,' joked Gandhi to the Swiss scientist, 'please pass it on to me.'

Some days later, Raman came again, this time with his wife, a social worker. Gandhi was impressed with the Tamil lady's Hindi, telling her husband that it 'was as good as your science'. Raman answered that in his view English should be the link language of India. Gandhi disagreed, saying that it would be far easier for Hindi to assume that role. He asked how the scientist did not speak the language when his wife did. Raman admitted the deficiency, adding by way of justification: 'It is that conceit, you know, that I am full of as much as you.'[47]

Gandhi was in Nandi when he heard of the death of Dr M.A. Ansari. He was badly shaken by the news. As he told *The Hindu* newspaper, the Delhi doctor was 'my infallible guide in Hindu–Muslim relations'. Ansari was only fifty-five when he died. Many years younger than Gandhi, he was a close personal friend, a valued medical adviser, and a brave critic if necessary. That he was a respected Muslim leader made the loss even more acute. In anguish, and perhaps even in desperation, Gandhi wrote to the educationist Zakir Husain, vice chancellor of the Jamia Millia Islamia. 'Will you be to me what the Doctor was on the Hindu–Muslim question?' he asked. 'What distracts me is not the warmth of a gentleman-friend, of a God-believing and God-fearing doctor. It is the absence of an unfailing guide in the matter of Hindu–Muslim unity.'[48]

It was also while in Nandi that Gandhi heard that his eldest son, Harilal, had converted to Islam, taking the name 'Abdullah'. The conversion had taken place on 29 May 'in the midst of a large congregation' at Bombay's Jumma Masjid. On hearing the news, Gandhi wrote to his third son, Ramdas, that 'there could be no harm in his [Harilal] being converted to Islam with understanding and selfless motives. But he suffers from greed for wealth and sensual pleasures.'

It was overwhelmingly likely that Harilal had been offered a material inducement, with a view to embarrassing his famous father. Perhaps, given his own complicated—not to say tortured—relations with Gandhi, Harilal was also in a vengeful mood, seeing conversion as a way to finally settle accounts with an overbearing patriarch.

On 2 June 1936, Gandhi issued a press statement on Harilal's conversion. If his son's conversion was 'from the heart and free of any worldly considerations', he said, 'I should have no quarrel. For I believe Islam to be as true a religion as my own.'

Yet, Gandhi had 'the gravest doubt' that Harilal's acceptance of a new faith was 'free from selfish considerations'. He noted that Harilal's addiction 'to the drink evil' was well known, so also his 'habit of visiting houses of ill-fame'. Through his lifestyle Harilal had accumulated many debts, and until recently 'was in dread of his life from his Pathan creditors in Bombay. Now he is the hero of the hour in that city.'

Gandhi knew that 'God can work wonders. He has been known to have changed the stoniest hearts and turned sinners into saints.' Yet, the reports of Harilal's conversion 'give no such evidence. He still delights in sensation and in good living'.

Gandhi asked his Muslim friends to examine whether Harilal's conversion was done with 'a clean heart'. If it was not, they should 'tell him so plainly'. Gandhi did 'not mind whether he is known as Abdulla or Harilal if, by adopting one name for the other, he becomes a true devotee of God which both the names mean'.[49]

When the news of Harilal's conversion came, Gandhi was in Nandi, and Kasturba in Delhi, staying with her youngest son, Devadas. She was deeply upset, and poured out her feelings to Devadas, who at once wrote them out in English. Later, he had his handwritten notes typed, and published in the press under Kasturba's name, with the title, 'An Open Letter from a Mother to Her Son'.

In this extraordinary public chastisement of her firstborn, Kasturba charged Harilal with 'criticising and ridiculing your great father'. She pointed out that when (as had happened several times already) he had been hauled up before a magistrate for drunken and abusive behaviour, he was let off lightly because of whose son he was. 'Your father,' wrote Kasturba to Harilal, 'daily gets letters from people complaining about your conduct. He has to suffer all this disgrace. But you have left no place for me anywhere. For sheer shame, I am unable to move among friends and strangers. Your father always pardons you, but God will not tolerate your conduct.'

'Every morning,' said Kasturba to Harilal, 'I rise with a shudder to think what fresh news of disgrace the newspapers will bring.' Now they had brought news of his conversion to Islam. Kasturba had, she told Harilal, 'felt secretly glad even about your conversion hoping that you would now start leading a sober life'. But she had heard from friends that in fact he was 'in a condition much worse than before'. The letter ended by telling Harilal that 'your daughters and son-in-law also bear with increasing difficulty the burden of sorrow your conduct has imposed upon them'.

Kasturba also had Devadas write a shorter note, again under her own name, addressed to Harilal's 'Muslim friends'. She told them that 'a large number of thinking Mussalmans and all our life-long Muslim friends condemn the whole of his episode'. Those Muslims who had aided Harilal in his conversion were 'not doing the right thing in the eyes of God'. 'I do not understand,' said Kasturba to these new Muslim friends of her son, 'what pleasures you find in sometimes lionizing him. What you are doing is not at all in his interest. If your desire is mainly to hold us up to ridicule, I have nothing to say to you. You may do your worst.'[50]

Five months after his conversion, Harilal made a public statement that he was now thinking of returning to the Hindu fold. On hearing this, Gandhi dryly commented: 'It seems he is not getting any money from there [the Muslims] either. Maybe, too, he is tired of the whole thing.'[51] There may have been a third reason: the very public scolding by his mother. Harilal was more deeply attached to Kasturba than to Gandhi, and much more likely to seek to please her than him, or, in this case, seek not to wound her than him.

CHAPTER TWENTY-THREE

From Rebels to Rulers

I

In April 1936, Lord Willingdon was succeeded by Lord Linlithgow. The new viceroy was from a family of Scottish landowners. His father, the first marquess, was a former governor general of Australia. The son had served in World War I, then became active in the Conservative Party. He had been chairman of the royal commission of agriculture in India in 1926, and also chaired the joint parliamentary committee on the 1935 Government of India Act.[1]

These connections to India helped, as did Linlithgow's friendship with the new prime minister, Stanley Baldwin. Although not as arrogant as Willingdon, like him the new viceroy did not reach out to the Congress leadership. The journalist B. Shiva Rao, then India correspondent of the *Manchester Guardian*, met Linlithgow and urged him to invite Gandhi for a meeting. He gave the same advice to the viceroy's senior officials. Shiva Rao was told that Gandhi would have to apply for an interview, and also consent to have his name and request appear in the court circular. These conditions were naturally considered humiliating by Gandhi.[2]

After Shiva Rao tried and failed, the industrialist G.D. Birla went to ask Linlithgow to meet Gandhi. The viceroy answered: 'If I try to be overfriendly with the Congress, then I would be putting the other

509

parties at a disadvantage.' His officials had advised him that, if he invited Gandhi, the Muslims would be offended, while the prestige of the Congress would go up, helping it get more seats in the elections scheduled for next year.³ So, the most powerful man in India carefully kept his distance from the most influential Indian.

II

In the third week of June, Gandhi returned to Segaon from South India. The village, he wrote to an English friend, had 'no post office, no store for foodstuffs of quality, no medical comforts and [was] difficult of access in the rainy season'.

This was said with some pride, and satisfaction. For, Gandhi was quite excited about his new abode. He asked his (relatively) new disciple, Rajkumari Amrit Kaur, to leave her manorial home in Simla and come stay with him in Segaon. He would have a hut built for her. His own hut, he told Amrit Kaur, 'has thick mud walls, twice the breadth of [an] ordinary brick-wall. The mud is rain-proof. I think you will fall in love with the hut and the surroundings.'

Gandhi's hut had but one room, but this was quite large, twenty-nine feet by seventeen feet. Besides himself, it housed his wife Kasturba, a sadhu singer of bhajans, and a young co-worker. Amrit Kaur came as asked. The non-violent Pathan, Khan Abdul Ghaffar Khan, also arrived in Segaon to share Gandhi's hut. Mahadev Desai, however, stayed for the moment in Wardha, making the daily commute to the village, taking down letters and articles he would later have typed up in the town.⁴

Gandhi liked the idea of living in an isolated hamlet in the very centre of India. True, the railway passed not far from the village, but it took days and days to get to India's major cities. Bombay was 450 miles away to the west. Delhi lay nearly 800 miles to the north, Calcutta 800 to the east. Madras was more than 600 miles to the south.⁵

While Segaon was in the middle of nowhere, no sooner had Gandhi shifted there, it became the centre of everything. For, as Mira remarked, 'although Bapu had left the Congress officially, yet the

Congress had not left him. They wanted to go their own way, but whenever they got into difficulties they wanted Bapu to help them.'[6] Kripalani, Patel, Rajagopalachari, Nehru, Maulana Azad, Sarojini Naidu and Rajendra Prasad—if these leaders wished to consult Gandhi, they had to make the obligatory trek to Segaon, taking the train to Wardha and then a bullock cart to their leader's doorstep.

To aid his Congress colleagues, Jamnalal Bajaj had improvised a vehicle, which he called the 'Oxford', since it consisted of an old Ford car pulled by a pair of oxen. When Nehru, Patel and company went to Segaon to see Gandhi, they used this means of transport; except in the monsoon, when a standard bullock cart had to do, since the Oxford's tyres got stuck in the mud.[7]

In July 1936, a crisis broke out in the upper echelons of the Congress. Several members of the party's prestigious working committee, including Prasad, Patel and Rajagopalachari, resigned on the grounds that the president, Jawaharlal Nehru, was imposing his socialist views on the party, asking for land reforms and for greater rights for workers. The 'preaching and emphasising of socialism', they told Nehru, was 'prejudicial to the best interests of the country and to the success of the national struggle for freedom'. These leaders, who had been with the Congress longer than Nehru had, resented being treated 'as persons whose time is over, who represent and stand for ideas that are worn out and that have no present value . . .'[8]

The dispute reached Gandhi. He persuaded the stalwarts to withdraw their resignation, later writing to Nehru that if his critics were (as he had charged) 'guilty of intolerance, you have more than your share of it. The country should not be made to suffer for your mutual intolerance.'

In an article for *Harijan*, Gandhi acknowledged that Nehru and he had differences. But on the key issue of non-violence, they were as one. 'I cannot think of myself as a rival to Jawaharlal or him to me,' he remarked. If, in their common goal of achieving swaraj, they 'seem to be taking different routes', Gandhi hoped that the 'world will find that we had lost sight of each other only for the moment and only to meet again with greater mutual attraction and affection'.[9]

III

There was a crisis in Gandhi's party, and another crisis brewing outside. In May 1936, B.R. Ambedkar published a searing critique of the Hindu social order. Entitled *The Annihilation of Caste*, this was originally an address to be delivered at the invitation of a reformist group in the Punjab. When his hosts received the text of Ambedkar's speech, they withdrew the invitation, objecting to his argument that if Hindus did not abolish caste, the Depressed Classes should convert to another religion. Ambedkar went ahead and published the text at his own expense.

Ambedkar had long been interested in the sociology of caste. He had written a seminar paper on the subject when studying at Columbia, although his doctoral dissertations there and at the London School of Economics were on economic subjects. However, since his return to India he had become increasingly interested, indeed preoccupied, with the pernicious effects of the caste system, and with how to end them.

The text of *The Annihilation of Caste* ran to a mere sixty pages in print. In between a pamphlet and a book, it had the polemical zeal of the one and the scholarly rigour of the other. Ambedkar provided a magisterial overview of the history and sociology of the caste system, and of its theological justifications in the Hindu scriptures. He offered several illustrations of the cruelty and inhumanity of caste in practice. He characterized it as 'a social system which embodies the arrogance and selfishness of a perverse section of the Hindus who were superior enough in social status to set it in fashion and who had authority to force it on their inferiors'. Caste had, he added, 'completely disorganized and demoralized the Hindus', and prevented them 'from becoming a society with unified life and a consciousness of its own being'.

Ambedkar then considered and disposed of the nationalist argument that political freedom must precede social emancipation. As he put it (in what was undoubtedly a tacit comparison between Gandhi and himself), 'political tyranny is nothing compared to social tyranny and a reformer, who defies society, is a much more courageous man than a politician, who defies Government'. He also rejected the socialist argument that economic progress would on its own dissolve and destroy caste.

Ambedkar turned next to the work of well-meaning social reformers such as the people who had originally invited him. He approved of inter-dining and even more of intermarriage, yet saw them as partial, incomplete reforms. 'You must have [the] courage to tell the Hindus,' wrote Ambedkar, 'that what is wrong with them is their religion—the religion which has produced in them this notion of the sacredness of Caste.' The enemy whom reformers 'must grapple with, is not the people who observe Caste, but the Shastras which teach them this religion of Caste'.

Ambedkar asked reformers to be more bold, to seek both the annihilation of caste and the delegitimization of the holy texts that justified it. For, 'what is called Religion by the Hindus is nothing but a multitude of commands and prohibitions. Religion, in the sense of spiritual principles, truly universal, applicable to all races, to all countries, to all times, is not to be found in them . . .' Ambedkar offered as the ideals to strive for the French Revolution's trinity of Liberty, Equality and Fraternity. But, for Hindus to achieve this, they had to abolish caste altogether, and, with it, to both 'discard' and 'destroy' the 'authority of the *Shastras*'.[10]

The first edition of *The Annihilation of Caste* carries the date 16 May 1936. In the last week of the month, a conference of the Depressed Classes was held in Bombay. The meeting resolved that 'change of religion was the only remedy for the community to attain equality and freedom'. Hindu festivals would no longer be observed, nor Hindu deities worshipped, nor pilgrimages to Hindu shrines undertaken.

About 10,000 delegates attended the conference, including many women. Ambedkar gave the concluding speech, in Marathi, his two-hour-long peroration punctuated with cries of 'Dr Ambedkar ki jai'.

The *Bombay Chronicle* carried a two-column report on Ambedkar's speech under the provocative headline: 'Ambedkar's Tirade Against Mahatma'. Ambedkar, according to this report, had outlined how Hinduism had failed the 'untouchables' both socially and spiritually. The Doctor 'had also no belief in the reformers. Gandhiji, the author of the non-co-operation movement, was afraid, in his opinion, to wound the feelings of the caste-Hindus and had not offered Satyagraha in the interests of the Depressed Classes and for their emancipation.'[11]

IV

Gandhi read *The Annihilation of Caste* soon after it was published. Meeting a deputation of the Depressed Classes in Bangalore on 10 June, he remarked that 'when Dr. Ambedkar abuses us, I say it serves us right'. Gandhi claimed that 'Hinduism is a dying cult if it will not purge itself of untouchability and will perish, Ambedkar or no Ambedkar'.

Later the same day, addressing a conference of Harijan workers, Gandhi praised Ambedkar as 'intellectually . . . superior to thousands of intelligent and educated caste Hindus'. And yet, the 'orthodox Brahmin will be defiled by the touch of Dr. Ambedkar and that because of his unpardonable sin that he was born a Mahar'.[12]

Gandhi is only glancingly mentioned in *The Annihilation of Caste*. But he saw the text as a challenge to his own understanding of caste and Hinduism. So, after those first, impromptu reactions in Bangalore, he wrote a critique for publication in *Harijan*. Gandhi began by saying that 'no Hindu who prizes his faith above life itself can afford to underrate the importance of his indictment'. For, 'Dr. Ambedkar is not alone in his disgust. He is the most uncompromising exponent and one of the ablest among them. He is certainly the most irreconcilable among them.'

Acknowledging the force of Ambedkar's criticisms, Gandhi said the upper castes had, in response, got 'to correct their belief and their conduct'. He himself was clear that 'nothing can be accepted as the word of God, which cannot be treated by reason . . .'

At the same time, Gandhi believed that Ambedkar had 'over-proved his case' by picking upon 'texts of doubtful authenticity' and the current 'degraded' practice of Hindus. Naming a whole array of reformers down the ages—from Thiruvalluvar and Chaitanya down to Rammohan Roy and Vivekananda—Gandhi asked whether Hinduism was indeed as 'utterly devoid of merit as is made out in

Dr. Ambedkar's indictment'. Gandhi himself believed that 'a religion has to be judged not by its worst specimens but by the best it might have produced. For that and that alone can be used as the standard to aspire to, if not to improve upon.'[13]

Ambedkar replied to Gandhi immediately. He took up Gandhi's claim that a religion must be judged by its best practitioners. Ambedkar agreed with this statement, but, he noted, 'the question still remains— why the best number so few and the worst so many?' His own answer was that 'the religious ideal [of Hinduism] is a wholly wrong ideal which has given a wrong moral twist to the lives of the many and that the best have become best in spite of the wrong ideal'.

In this rebuttal, Ambedkar, for the first time, adopted a personal, polemical tone in challenging Gandhi. In one place, he wrote that 'the Mahatma appears not to believe in thinking'. In another, he complained of 'the double role which the Mahatma wants to play—of a Mahatma and a Politician'. Others had made the same point before, while suggesting that Gandhi stick to religious matters. Ambedkar was less charitable. 'As a Mahatma,' he remarked, Gandhi 'may be trying to spiritualize Politics. Whether he has succeeded in it or not Politics have certainly commercialized him. A politician must know that Society cannot bear the whole truth and that he must not speak the whole truth; if he is speaking the whole truth it is bad for his politics. The reason why the Mahatma is always supporting Caste and Varna is because he is afraid that if he opposed them he will lose his place in politics.'[14]

Even as he was debating with Gandhi, Ambedkar had begun a parallel conversation with B.S. Moonje of the Hindu Mahasabha. In the middle of June, the two met in Bombay. Moonje proposed to Ambedkar that he take the 'untouchables' wholesale into the Sikh faith, whereupon the Mahasabha would urge the acceptance of these 'neo-Sikhs' into the list of castes eligible for representation in the legislatures and in government bodies. Moonje was motivated by the fear that otherwise Ambedkar would convert to Christianity or Islam, faiths far more foreign to Hinduism.

After the meeting, Ambedkar issued a long and most intriguing statement. This noted that conversion to either Islam or Christianity was a feasible option for the Depressed Classes, since both religions had immense financial resources. However, conversion to either faith would 'denationalize the Depressed Classes'. If 'they go to Islam', he continued, 'the number of Muslims [in India] will be doubled and the danger of Muslim domination also becomes real'. And if they became Christians, it would 'help to strengthen the hold of the British on this country'.

If the Depressed Classes became Muslims or Christians, argued Ambedkar, they 'not only go out of the Hindu religion, but they also go out of the Hindu culture'. On the other hand, if they became Sikhs, they would 'remain within the Hindu culture'. However, as a small community, the Sikhs lacked the financial resources to compete with Muslims and Christians. This was where upper-caste Hindus came in, for, as Ambedkar put it, they could 'help the Sikhs to remove the political and financial difficulties', by contributing money, and by modifying the Poona Pact to allow Depressed Class converts to Sikhism to remain eligible to vote for and contest reserved seats.[15]

When Gandhi heard of this proposal, he deplored this 'bargaining between Dr. Ambedkar and *savarna* Hindus for the transfer to another form of several million dumb Harijans as if they were chattels'. While Dr Ambedkar and his followers were perfectly free to change their faith, it was quite another matter for political parties 'to assume such change for the mass of Harijans'. As he pointedly asked: 'And who are we, the self-constituted leaders, to barter away the religious freedom of Harijans? Has not every Harijan, however dull or stupid he may be, the right to make his own choice?'[16]

Interestingly, Christian and Muslim priests also reached out to Ambedkar. They hoped to get Ambedkar and his followers to join *their* faith instead.[17]

In June 1936, an Italian Buddhist came to see Ambedkar in Bombay, clad in the robes of a priest, carrying a bowl and an umbrella. He had adopted the name Lokananda after conversion, and now lived in Ceylon. He told a reporter that he met Ambedkar 'with the object of persuading him to become a Buddhist'. The Italian convert apparently believed 'that he has succeeded in a fair measure in convincing Dr. Ambedkar that if Harijans agreed to their conversion to the Buddhist faith they would raise themselves morally, spiritually and socially and attain a higher status in society'.

'I have reason to believe,' the Buddhist missionary added, 'that Dr. Ambedkar will come round to my view. My ambition is to convert all Harijans to Buddhism.'[18]

Ambedkar stayed his hand, however. He met and spoke to representatives of several faiths without committing himself to any. Meanwhile, he launched a fresh broadside against Gandhi for opposing his talks with B.S. Moonje. 'When Mr. Gandhi says this cannot be a matter for barter,' he remarked, 'my reply is that this argument cannot now lie in his mouth. At the time of the Poona Pact he treated the thing as one of barter. It is too late in the day now to ask people who are hungering for bread and for their elementary rights to live on spirituality.'

Ambedkar continued: 'Mr. Gandhi says that the removal of untouchability is a matter which must depend upon the voluntary effort of Savarna Hindus in the spirit of repentance. If I understand his meaning, his view is that in the removal of untouchability the untouchables should do nothing. They should wait and pray for Savarna Hindus to develop a conscience, to repent and change their ways. In my opinion, this view is as sensible as the view of a person who says to folks living in plague-stricken areas not to leave the area, but to wait and mind the disease till the municipal members repent of their neglect of duties and come forward to take measures to fight the disease.'[19]

V

Apart from brief trips to Banaras and Ahmedabad, and a week in hospital in Wardha (after he came down with malaria), Gandhi spent the second half of 1936 in Segaon. He was entirely comfortable in his new home. Charlie Andrews visited him in November, afterwards writing to a mutual friend that Gandhi 'really has never looked so fit as he does now for many years past. His recovery is marvellous and he has really found himself again in this village and he is content from here to pray for the whole world and to use not his own power but God's for the healing of the nations.'[20]

In the third week of December, Gandhi travelled to Faizpur, a Marathi-speaking hamlet in the Bombay Presidency where that year's

Congress was being held. The idea to hold the annual jamboree in a village was Gandhi's. The Congress township had been designed by a well-known (and also khadi-wearing) Bombay architect named B.K. Mhatre; the buildings and gateways embellished by drawings and sculptures provided by the Santiniketan artist Nandalal Bose.

Gandhi was delighted that the architect–artist duo had 'depended entirely on local material and local labour to bring all the structures here into being'. Inaugurating a khadi and village industries exhibition, he spoke of how he had forsaken political action for village renewal. 'I am now care-free,' he remarked, 'having cast all my cares on the broad shoulders of Jawaharlal and Sardar.' This was the first indication that Gandhi had in mind a succession plan, whereby the pre-eminent political role he had played for so long, would be passed on to a younger generation. It is notable that he singled out Nehru and Patel, and notable also that their names appeared in that particular order.[21]

On the sidelights of the Congress session, a reporter asked Gandhi what swaraj meant to him. He answered that in his conception of free India, 'there would be no difference between a Bhangi and a Maharaja, or between a Bhangi and a Brahmin'. 'No wonder the Maharajas prefer the British Raj,' wrote the journalist, adding that Gandhi's views were 'enough to make any honest Sanatanist turn an anti-Congressman'.[22]

On Gandhi's return to Segaon, a letter was waiting for him, from a villager in Birbhum in Bengal, which asked: 'What is an ideal Indian village in your esteemed opinion?' As always, when receiving an interesting query, he made his answer public through his newspaper. Thus Gandhi wrote:

An ideal Indian village will be so constructed as to lead itself to perfect sanitation. It will have cottages with sufficient light and ventilation, built of a material obtainable within a radius of five miles of it. The cottages will have courtyards enabling householders to plant vegetables for domestic use and to house their cattle. The village lanes and streets will be free of all avoidable dust. It will have wells according to its needs and accessible to all. It will have houses of worship for all, also a common meeting place, a village common for grazing its cattle, a co–operative dairy, primary and secondary schools in which industrial [i.e. vocational] education will be the central fact, and it will have Panchayats for settling disputes. It will produce its own grains, vegetables and fruit, and its own Khadi. This is roughly my idea of a model village . . .[23]

This description drew on two decades of travels through Indian villages, and six months as the resident of one. Note its salient features: homes with air and light, built of locally available materials; schools, shrines and meeting places to consolidate social solidarity; streets swept clean of dirt and dust; the collective management and use of those gifts of nature so necessary for rural life, water and pasture.

VI

In the second week of November 1936, the princely state of Travancore announced that all temples in their territory were henceforth to be open to all Hindus regardless of caste. This was the final fruit of the Vaikom satyagraha begun a decade previously by the followers of Narayana Guru, and supported by Gandhi himself. Gandhi made a public announcement congratulating the rulers of Travancore, for allowing Harijans in the state to 'feel the glow of freedom and real oneness with their caste brethren'. He further hoped that 'all other Hindu Princes will follow the noble example set by this far-off ancient Hindu State', thus 'hastening the day of the total removal of untouchability from Hinduism'.

In early December, Gandhi received a telegram from a Harijan social worker in Trivandrum about the changes the royal proclamation had set afoot. The corridors and courtyards of Travancore's temples were now 'as freely used by newly admitted devotees as caste Hindus'. Of even greater significance was 'that waters in sacred tanks attached to temples are also freely used now by Ezhavas and Harijans'. And the 'sense of horror at [the] approach of Harijans seems completely overcome'.

Reproducing the telegram in his newspaper, Gandhi said that 'the enthusiasm of the Harijans, the absence of all opposition to their entrance . . . and the willing, nay, the hearty, co-operation of the officiating priests, show the utter genuineness of the great and sweeping reform'. Only a few years previously, remarked Gandhi, 'the caste Hindus had threatened violence if Harijans crossed even certain roads leading to the Vaikom temple'. But now 'that very temple has been opened to Harijans on absolutely the same terms as to any caste Hindu'.[24]

Gandhi decided to visit Travancore to see these changes for himself. He spent the second half of January 1937 in the state, speaking at twenty-five different venues. He praised the ruler and congratulated the reformers, but urged them not to be complacent. The hosts for his first meeting called themselves the 'Ezhava Temple-entry Proclamation Celebration'. The name pointedly excluded the Pulayas and Pariahs, castes even more suppressed than the Ezhavas. Gandhi recalled how, on his first visit to Kerala, he had seen an old Pulaya man 'shaking with fear' at having transgressed the boundaries of caste by inadvertently coming close to him, a high-caste visitor. He told the Ezhavas gathered to welcome him that 'if this vast assembly does not represent these Pulayas, then I am certain that there is no place in your midst for me'.[25]

Writing in *Harijan* (which he was now editing), Mahadev Desai described a visit made by Gandhi to a hostel for Harijan boys in Trivandrum. He first asked whether the (upper-caste) superintendent ate with the boys or privately with his family. The superintendent assured him that he had all his meals with his wards. Gandhi then asked whether the buttermilk they served was more water than butter or milk. This time the answer was less cheering; yes, indeed, the proportion of water to milk was somewhat on the higher side. But, said the superintendent by way of explanation, good milk was scarce everywhere in the city. Could Gandhiji send some good cows from Gujarat?

Gandhi offered a better alternative. The priests of the great Padmanabha temple in Trivandrum were known to pour milk into gold pots for the benefit of the local Brahmins. Why not ask them, said Gandhi, to serve buttermilk to the Harijan boys, now that they had abolished untouchability?[26]

Although as a boy Gandhi had often accompanied his mother to temples and shrines, he had stopped visiting them in adult life.

This was in part because he followed Tolstoy in believing that the 'Kingdom of God is Within You', and in part because of the bar on Harijans entering temples. However, since in Travancore at any rate the bar had been lifted, on this visit Gandhi entered several temples, including Vaikom, where the struggle had first begun.

Vaikom was very close to the border between Travancore and Cochin. While in one princely state restrictions on temple entry had been lifted, in the other they were still in place. Cochin's many Hindu shrines, among them the famous Guruvayur temple, remained closed to 'untouchables'. Looking across the waters to the other state, Gandhi said in Vaikom that he was 'impatient to see that the Cochin Maharaja follows in the footsteps of the Maharaja of Travancore'.[27]

This time, among the letters waiting for Gandhi on his return from his travels was one from a Muslim friend. This man, a liberal and sceptic, wondered why, when referring to the Prophet Muhammad or the Koran, Gandhi never analysed them critically. 'I am at a loss to understand how a person like you,' this correspondent told Gandhi, 'with all your passion for truth and justice, who has never failed to gloss over a single fault in Hinduism or to repudiate as unauthentic the numerous corruptions that masquerade under it, can . . . accept all that is in the Koran. I am not aware of your ever having called into question or denounced any iniquitous injunction of Islam. Against some of these I learned to revolt when I was scarcely 18 or 20 years old and time has since only strengthened that first feeling.'

Reproducing and then answering this letter in *Harijan*, Gandhi remarked that 'I have nowhere said that I believe literally in every word of the Koran, or for that matter of any scripture in the world. But it is no business of mine to criticize the scriptures of other faiths or to point out their defects. It should be, however, my privilege to proclaim and practise the truths that there may be in them.'

Gandhi held the view that only adherents of a particular faith had the right to criticize its precepts or sanctions. By that token, it was both his 'right and duty to point out the defects in Hinduism in order to purify it and to keep it pure. But when non-Hindu critics set about criticizing Hinduism and cataloguing its faults they can only blazon their own ignorance of Hinduism and their incapacity to regard it from the Hindu viewpoint. . . . Thus my own experience of the non-Hindu critics of Hinduism brings home to me my limitations and teaches me to be wary of launching on a criticism of Islam or Christianity and their founders.'

Critics from within had the capacity and empathy to reform and redeem their faith; critics from without the tendency to mock and caricature the other's faith. Gandhi thus concluded that it was 'only through a reverential approach to faiths other than mine that I can realize the principle of equality of all religions'.[28]

Gandhi's theological pluralism was also on display in a conversation he had soon afterwards, with an American clergyman named Dr Crane. The visitor asked if Gandhi accepted that 'Jesus was the most divine' of all the religious teachers in history. 'No,' answered Gandhi, 'for the simple reason that we have no data. Historically we have more data about Mahomed than anyone else because he was more recent in time. For Jesus there are less data and still less for Buddha, Rama and Krishna; and when we know so little about them, is it not preposterous to say that one of them was more divine than another?'[29]

VII

Meanwhile, the Congress had decided to participate in the elections to provincial assemblies, notwithstanding its reservations about the limited degree of self-rule the Government of India Act had given Indians. The elections were held in February 1937, on a wider franchise than ever before. Some thirty-five million people were eligible to vote, six times as many as before. They included about four million women.

Eleven provinces in British India went to the polls. There were 1505 seats to be contested for; of which 808 fell into the 'general' category, open to all, with the rest reserved for Muslims, Sikhs, Europeans and Anglo-Indians. While a party to the decision to contest the elections, Gandhi himself did not canvass for votes. Jawaharlal Nehru led the Congress campaign, travelling 50,000 miles by train, plane, car, cart and boat, addressing over ten million people.[30]

While Nehru sought to garner the votes, the selection of candidates and the raising of funds was the responsibility of Vallabhbhai Patel. He liaised with the provincial Congress chiefs, matching candidates to constituencies and their likely opponents. He tapped merchants and industrialists for contributions to the Congress's election fund. But other leaders made their own arrangements. Thus, C. Rajagopalachari asked Devadas Gandhi to pass on an 'urgent personal call' to his employer, the Mahatma's loyal acolyte, Ghanshyam Das Birla, to send a 'very liberal cheque' to the Madras Congress. Rajaji remarked that 'Vallabhbhai [Patel] I know has fleeced everyone and he says it is too late for Central Collections to the province'.[31]

Among the main parties opposed to the Congress was the Muslim League. It was led by Muhammad Ali Jinnah, Gandhi's fellow Kathiawari and one-time friend. After leaving the Congress in protest against the non-cooperation movement, Jinnah had concentrated on his law practice. Meanwhile, his marriage ran into difficulties; he and his wife became estranged, with Ruttie Jinnah dying in 1929 of cancer, aged twenty-nine.

In the early 1930s, Jinnah attended the round table conferences, then turned his back on politics altogether, settling down in London, where his legal skills were as much in demand as in Bombay, and commanded a higher premium. In 1934, Jinnah was persuaded to come back to India and take over a languishing Muslim League. Within a year of his return, he had invigorated its provincial units, and attracted a wide array of Muslim businessmen and professionals to its flag.

Other parties which claimed a national presence were the Hindu Mahasabha and the Liberals. Although both had formidable leaders, neither had a mass base. Some parties were strong in particular provinces. The Justice Party, based on opposition to Brahmin dominance, was powerful in Madras. The charismatic A.K. Fazlul Huq's Krishak Praja Party commanded great support among the peasantry of Bengal. The Unionist Party, influential in the Punjab, was a cross-religious alliance of Hindu, Sikh and Muslim landlords. In Bombay, B.R. Ambedkar's Independent Labour Party had strong support among the working class.

When the results of the 1937 elections came in, the Congress was the major winner. It won 74 per cent of the seats in Madras, 65 per cent in Bihar, 62.5 per cent in the Central Provinces, 60 per cent in Orissa, 59 per cent in the United Provinces and 49 per cent in Bombay. The Unionists won a comfortable majority in the Punjab. Other provinces witnessed more fragmented verdicts, with no party in a position to stake a claim to form a government on its own. Taking British India as a whole, the Congress won 707 seats; with the Muslim League in a distant second place, winning 106 seats. The League performed below expectations even in constituencies reserved for Muslims. In Bengal, for example, it won just one reserved seat more (thirty-seven to thirty-six) than Fazlul Haq's Krishak Praja Party, while in the Punjab it won a solitary seat, with the cross-religious Unionist Party led by Sikandar Hyat Khan winning most constituencies reserved for Muslims.[32]

Gandhi had not campaigned at all in these elections, yet the impressive showing by the Congress owed a great deal to him, to the reputation and standing he had built up over the years. The governor of the Central Provinces spoke for several other governors when he wrote (in private, of course) that 'the name of Gandhi is unquestionably one to conjure with among the masses in this Province—not for any particular political reason—but simply because he is Gandhi—and reports from several districts indicate that the one Congress slogan which has been universally successful is—"Put your papers in the white box and vote for Gandhi"'.[33]

In the third week of March, the AICC met in Delhi to discuss the election results. Gandhi travelled from Segaon to take part. The meeting passed a resolution permitting the Congress to accept office and run the government in the provinces where it had won a majority.

At this meeting, Jawaharlal Nehru spoke out against office acceptance. The Congress had proved its popularity at the polls; but forming ministries would mean succumbing to the less-than-satisfactory provisions of the Government of India Act. Nehru was supported by, among others, the socialist Jayaprakash Narayan and the peasant leader Swami Sahajanand, for whom accepting the perks and privileges of power meant a radical departure from the high ideals the Congress had so long professed.

On the other side, C. Rajagopalachari was extremely keen on accepting office. Responding to the debate in the AICC, Rajaji said: 'Let us not distrust each other. Do not think we are hankering after jobs. . . . When they went to the Governor they had to tell him what they proposed to do and ask him if he would use his special powers. . . . [I]f he said he would not use them, they would take his words at their face value. If later he broke those words, they could come out [i.e. resign].'[34]

Gandhi had stayed away from the elections themselves. But now that the results were in, he re-entered the sphere of politics— as his friend Henry Polak had predicted. Following the AICC meeting in Delhi, Gandhi made a statement urging 'a gentlemanly understanding between the Governors and their Congress Ministers that they would not exercise their special powers of interference so long as the Ministers acted within the Constitution'. Since the British government claimed that the 1935 Act mandated provincial autonomy, the governors should recognize that it was not they but elected ministers who were now 'responsible for the wise administration of their Provinces'.

Gandhi told reporters that, in the event of the Congress taking office, rather than interfere with day-to-day administration, the British governors should simply dismiss the ministries in case of serious differences. In agreeing to accept office albeit with safeguards, said Gandhi, 'the Congress had gone as far as it could, consistent with self-esteem and with its avowed object [of swaraj]. The next move must come from the Government, if they really want the Congress to take office.'[35]

The secretary of state for India, Lord Zetland, took a tough position. He argued that close oversight by governors was necessary for social peace; that giving in to the Congress demand would be 'a grave breach of faith with the minorities and others in India'.[36] Zetland was here suggesting that the Congress was not as representative of the national mood as it claimed to be; in particular, that it did not represent the minorities. As they had done for several decades now, British politicians claimed that only British officials had the necessary impartiality to adjudicate, and hold the balance between, competing interests in India.

VIII

On 7 July 1937, the CWC permitted the party to run the ministries in provinces in which they commanded a majority. Gandhi now wrote a long piece on what the Congress ministries should do. He first explained the Congress about-turn in these terms: 'The Government of India Act is universally regarded as wholly unsatisfactory for achieving India's freedom. But it is possible to construe it as an attempt, however limited and feeble, to replace the rule of the sword by the rule of the majority.'

Gandhi then pressed three tasks on the Congress ministries. The first was to 'enforce immediate prohibition by making education self-supporting instead of paying for it from the liquor revenue'. The second was for ministers to live simply, and not be a drain on the public exchequer. The English rulers in India enjoyed an extravagant standard of living; so, if Congress ministers would 'simply refrain from copying the Governors and the secured Civil Service, they will have shown the marked contrast that exists between the Congress mentality and theirs'.

The third and most important piece of advice Gandhi offered the new ministers was to bridge the communal divide. The pro-British papers had strenuously striven to paint the Congress-majority provinces as 'Hindu', and the others as 'Muslims'. Gandhi's own 'great hope' was that 'the Ministers in the six [Congress-ruled] Provinces will so manage them as to disarm all suspicion. They will show their Muslim colleagues that they know no distinction between Hindu, Muslim, Christian or Sikh or Parsi. Nor will they know any distinction between high-caste and low-caste Hindus.'[37]

This laudable ideal immediately came under threat in two important provinces. In the United Provinces, the Congress had won 134 out of 228 seats, but none from the specifically Muslim constituencies, where the Muslim League had won as many as twenty-nine seats. The leader of the League in the United Provinces was Chaudhry Khaliquzzaman, a one-time Congressman and friend of Jawaharlal Nehru. Khaliquzzaman went to Allahabad to meet Nehru to suggest a Congress–League coalition ministry. He said that they could work out a common programme, and thus defy British attempts at divide and rule. Nehru, however, was not open to the idea. In Khaliquzzaman's recollection, Nehru believed that 'the Hindu–Muslim question in India was confined to a few Muslim landlords and capitalists who were cooking up a problem which did not in fact exist in the minds of the masses'.[38]

Meanwhile, in the Bombay Presidency, where too the Congress formed a ministry, a bitter controversy arose around the choice of who would head it. The prominent Bombay Congressman K.F. Nariman thought he had the best credentials. However, while Nariman was extremely popular in the city, he was less well known in the Marathi-speaking hinterland. In the end, B.G. Kher, also a long-standing Congressman, and a Marathi speaker, was chosen as prime minister. This was done through a secret ballot where all Congressmen elected to the assembly voted.

Nariman now accused Vallabhbhai Patel of exerting pressure on the legislators to elect Kher. His supporters, meanwhile, insinuated that Nariman's being a Parsi went against him. Patel denied this, stating 'with a full sense of responsibility that I have never, directly or indirectly, influenced this election'. He said that 'the suggestion that Nariman was not elected because he belonged to a minority community is false and malicious'.[39]

Patel may not have been prejudiced against Nariman on religious grounds. But that he had long distrusted the Bombay lawyer was a matter of record. He thought Nariman had campaigned against some Congress candidates in an earlier election, when one of Patel's closest associates, K.M. Munshi, had unexpectedly lost. He was thus more inclined to support B.G. Kher over Nariman for the prime ministership of the Bombay Presidency. Although the voting by legislators was technically done in secret, 'the proceedings', writes one historian, 'were subtly regulated and controlled by Patel'.[40]

The Congress ministries took office, without a partnership with the Muslim League in the United Provinces and with someone other than K.F. Nariman as prime minister in the Bombay Presidency. The party may have had legitimate grounds for both choices. Since they won a majority on their own in the United Provinces, they saw no reason to ally with the League. And while Nariman's past political record was impressive, it did seem a majority of the elected legislators wanted Kher as prime minister. But in both cases, seeds of suspicion were sown, damaging the Congress's credentials to represent all of India in a non-partisan fashion.

IX

As the Congress ministries took office, there was speculation as to what this portended for the future. How would a party of prison-goers convert themselves into rulers and administrators? Accustomed to breaking government laws, how would they now frame and enforce government policies? And would they be corrupted by the trappings of power? Used to austere lifestyles, how would they cope with large offices, spacious ministerial bungalows, and a bevy of peons and clerks bowing around them?

Gandhi was sceptical, on the last count especially. A fortnight after the ministries took office, he wrote to Nehru that 'the Rs. 500 salary with big house and car allowances [for the Ministers] is being severely criticized. The more I think of it, the more I dislike this extravagant beginning.'[41]

For his part, Henry Polak wondered how this new partnership between the Raj and the Congress would work, since 'each has been so accustomed to regard the other as the enemy that it is almost an obsession'. The government would not, he thought, easily come to terms with the fact that 'a political party which is not of its own liking' would henceforth issue orders to its officers. On the other side, the Congress had become 'so much accustomed to regard themselves as the disgruntled opposition that they cannot get into the habit of mind of regarding themselves as a responsible administration'.[42]

Other long-time observers of Indian politics were more hopeful. When the Congress ministers moved into the secretariat in July, G.D. Birla was in London. He met businessmen, politicians and members of the two houses of Parliament. 'Bapu is the most popular person here,' wrote Birla to Mahadev Desai. 'They talk of his commonsense, judgment and all other virtues, and his stocks have gone up very high. But what pleases me most is that they say that if the Congress could manage the provinces for five years in good order, independence will come within one-tenth of the time that we have estimated. A friend said, "By God, if you Fellows ran your administration properly, the next Viceroy will have to go with Dominion Status in his pocket".'

'When I read out to Bapu one sentence in your letter, namely that Bapu's stocks had gone up he had a very hearty but incredulous laugh,' wrote Mahadev to Birla, adding: 'Stocks in the political market as well as in the money market go up and down very suddenly, and it is only a speculator who builds much on them. I wish I could share your belief that the whole thing [collaboration with the Raj] will last very long. As Bapu said to a Minister recently, "If this thing lasts beyond a year I shall either infer that the Britishers have become angels or that our Ministers are completely kow-towing to them".'[43]

Gandhi's scepticism notwithstanding, the installation of Congress ministries in six large provinces of British India was a major milestone in the constitutional history of the subcontinent. Much more power had devolved on to the shoulder of Indians than at any previous time in the history of the Raj. Indeed, since precolonial regimes were themselves devoid of democratic representation, and were run by unelected kings who nominated their ministers, this was the furthest that Indians had thus far got in the direction of self-rule, swaraj. Surely it was now only a matter of years before the Congress, and India, achieved the next step, of Dominion Status, thus to place themselves on par with Canada, Australia and South Africa.

A sign of how much of a departure from colonial practice these elections were is underlined in a humble office order issued by the Central Provinces government after their own Congress ministry was installed. It was signed by an Indian ICS officer, C.M. Trivedi, then serving as the secretary to the general administration department. The order was sent to all commissioners and deputy commissioners, the chief conservator of forests, the inspector general of police, all secretaries to government, and a host of other senior officials (including the military secretary and the governor), almost all of whom were, of course, British. The text of the order was short and simple, albeit, in the eyes of its recipients, not altogether sweet. It read: 'In future Mr. Gandhi should be referred to in all correspondence as "Mahatma Gandhi".'[44]

PART IV

WAR AND REBELLION (1937–1944)

CHAPTER TWENTY-FOUR

The World Within, and Without

I

After the Congress ministries took office in July 1937, Gandhi did not closely monitor their performance, thinking it would be unfair on their prime ministers (among them the senior Congressmen C. Rajagopalachari in Madras, B.G. Kher in Bombay and Govind Ballabh Pant in the United Provinces). The one topic he took up was the sale of alcohol. Some of the prime ministers argued that if prohibition was imposed, it would deal a heavy blow to their province's finances, and to the key sector of education in particular. The excise tax, more or less, covered the education budget. If it went, how would they run and staff government schools?

Gandhi remained unconvinced. Prohibition had to be pushed through. The ministries must find money to run their schools regardless. When told that prohibition had failed in the United States, Gandhi answered that in that country 'drinking is not looked upon [as] a vice'—there, 'millions usually drink'. In India, on the other hand, 'drink is held reprehensible by all religions, and it is not the millions who drink but individuals who drink'.

Gandhi understood that prohibition would work only if public opinion was in its favour. He asked teachers and students in colleges to set apart a couple of hours a day to spread the word. 'They should go to the areas frequented by the drinkers, associate with them, speak to them and reason with them and do peaceful picketing of an educative character.' He recalled the picketing by women of liquor stills during the non-cooperation movement, asking them 'to revive the work under better auspices now'.[1]

In August 1937, fifteen months after he arrived in India, Lord Linlithgow finally met Gandhi. They spoke for an hour and a half, to begin with about the NWFP and Gandhi's follower in the Frontier, Khan Abdul Ghaffar Khan, who had been externed from his homeland. Gandhi urged the viceroy to lift the ban, telling him that the 'essential quality' of Ghaffar Khan 'was his sincerity, that he was truth itself, a good Moslem . . . that he . . . was destined . . . to play a great part in the future of India'. Linlithgow answered that he had heard that 'on platforms his tongue was inclined to run away with him'.

Later, the conversation turned to Jawaharlal Nehru, whom the viceroy had not yet met. Gandhi 'sang his praises at some length. He was, he said, reserved and spartan, his name Jawaharlal meant jewel, and that exactly described what Nehru was.' Gandhi told the viceroy that while his own 'mental furniture was wholly Indian', Nehru 'had English mental furniture', adding that while Nehru 'was fond of England, and got on with Englishmen well, he had been returned [as Congress president] in opposition to Imperialism', and thus might be inclined to 'regard the Viceroy as the leading instrument of Imperialism in India'. Nonetheless, Gandhi urged Linlithgow to reach out to Nehru and set up a meeting.

The viceroy's sixteen-paragraph note on the meeting ended with some reflections on Gandhi himself. He was impressed by the man, less so by his politics. Gandhi 'appeared to be in good health', wrote Linlithgow, 'his voice was firm, his mind was extremely quick and alert, his sense of humour very keen'. Then he added: 'The strong impression upon my mind was that of a man implacably hostile to British Rule in India, and who would in no circumstances hesitate (while at all times, behaving with perfect manners) to take advantage of any person or circumstance in order to advance the process, to which every fibre of his mind is entirely devoted, of reducing British power, influence and prestige in the sub-continent' (whereas every fibre of Linlithgow's own mind was devoted to maintaining or preferably enhancing British power, influence and prestige in the subcontinent).[2]

II

In the second week of October 1937, the Muslim League held a meeting in Lucknow. As one attendee recalled, 'Mohammad Ali Jinnah's position at this junction was of great responsibility and the League's fate was hanging in the balance. Muslims were earnestly looking towards him as most of their other leaders had completely betrayed their cause.'[3]

After the League's indifferent performance in the recent elections, Jinnah was working to bring it back to centre stage. He had acquired a group of devoted admirers: professionals, businessmen and students. Now, in Lucknow, itself a great centre of Islamic learning and culture, the president of the Muslim League accused 'the present leadership of the Congress' of 'alienating the Mussalmans of India more and more by pursuing a policy which is exclusively Hindu'. Jinnah claimed that in the six provinces where the Congress was in power, Gandhi's party had 'by their words, deeds and programmes shown that the Mussalmans cannot expect any justice or fair play at their hands'.

When a report of this speech reached Gandhi in Segaon, he was moved to protest. The 'whole of your speech', he wrote to Jinnah, 'is a declaration of war'. He added: 'Only it takes two to make a quarrel. You won't find me one, even if I cannot become a peace-maker.'[4]

Jinnah had, among other things, criticized the singing in government schools of the patriotic hymn 'Vande Mataram'. Composed by the great Bengali writer Bankim Chandra Chatterjee, the poem invoked Hindu temples, praised the Hindu goddess Durga, and spoke of seventy million Indians, each carrying a sword, ready to defend their motherland against invaders, who could be interpreted as being the British, or Muslims, or both.

'Vande Mataram' first became popular during the swadeshi movement of 1905–07. The revolutionary Aurobindo Ghose named his political journal after it. Rabindranath Tagore was among the first to set it to music. His version was sung by his niece Saraladevi Chaudhurani at the Banaras Congress of 1905. The same year, the Tamil poet Subramania Bharati rendered it into his language. In Bengali and Tamil, Kannada and Telugu, Hindi and Gujarati, the song had long been sung at nationalist meetings and processions.[5]

After the Congress governments took power in 1937, the song was sometimes sung at official functions. The Muslim League objected vigorously. One of its legislators called it 'anti-Muslim', another, 'an insult to Islam'. Jinnah himself claimed the song was 'not only idolatrous but in its origins and substance [was] a hymn to spread hatred for the Musalmans'.[6]

Nationalists in Bengal were adamant that the song was not aimed at Muslims. The prominent Calcutta Congressman Subhas Chandra Bose wrote to Gandhi that 'the province (or at least the Hindu portion of it) is greatly perturbed over the controversy raised in certain Muslim circles over the song "Bande Mataram". As far as I can judge, all shades of Hindu opinion are unanimous in opposing any attempts to ban the song in Congress meetings and conferences.' Bose himself thought that 'we should think a hundred times before we take any steps in the direction of banning the song'.

The social worker Satis Dasgupta told Gandhi that *Vande Mataram* was 'out and out a patriotic song—a song in which all the children of the mother[land] can participate, be they Hindu or Mussalman'. It did use Hindu images, but such imagery was common in Bengal, where even Muslim poets like Nazrul Islam often referred to Hindu gods and legends. *Vande Mataram*, argued Dasgupta, was 'never a provincial cry and never surely a communal cry'.[7]

Faced with Jinnah's complaints on the one side and this defence by Bengali patriots on the other, Gandhi suggested a compromise: that Congress governments should have only the first two verses sung. These evoked the motherland without specifying any religious identity. But this concession made many Bengalis 'sore at heart'; they wanted the whole song sung. On the other side, Muslims were not satisfied either; for, the ascription of a mother-like status to India was dangerously close to idol worship.[8]

Through the winter of 1937–38, the exchanges between Gandhi and Jinnah continued, with no quarter being given on either side.

Reading reports of his speeches, Gandhi wrote to Jinnah in the first week of February: 'I miss the old nationalist. When in 1915 I returned from the self-imposed exile in South Africa, everybody spoke of you as one of the staunchest of nationalists and the hope of both Hindus and Mussalmans.' 'Are you still the same Jinnah?' asked Gandhi. 'If you say you are, in spite of your speeches I shall accept your word.'

Jinnah, in reply, said his speeches on the Hindu–Muslim question, far from being a 'declaration of war', were in fact made in 'self-defence'. Gandhi was 'evidently' not acquainted, said Jinnah, 'with what is going on in the Congress Press—the amount of vilification, misrepresentation and falsehood that is daily spread about me— otherwise, I am sure, you would not blame me'.

Jinnah thought Gandhi's question as to whether he was the same man he had been in 1915 an unfair one. 'I would not like to say,' he remarked, 'what people spoke of you in 1915 and what they speak and think of you today. Nationalism is not the monopoly of any single individual; and in these days it is very difficult to define it . . .'

Gandhi asked Jinnah to come down to Segaon on a date suitable to both. Jinnah was open to a meeting, noting, however, that 'we have reached a stage when no doubt should be left that you recognize the All-India Muslim League as the one authoritative and representative organization of the Mussalmans of India and on the other hand you represent the Congress and other Hindus throughout the country. It is only on that basis that we can proceed further . . .'[9]

Jinnah was here proposing a threefold equivalence: personal, political and communal. On the one side, the Muslims, represented by the League, represented in turn by their major leader, Jinnah; on the other side, the Hindus, represented by the Congress, represented in turn by their major leader, Gandhi.

Jinnah was making a large, even extravagant, claim, a claim Gandhi was unlikely to accept, not least because the League had performed so indifferently in the 1937 elections. Besides, while Jinnah was the president and sole spokesman of his party, Gandhi was not at this time particularly active in Congress affairs. In his own letters to Jinnah, he had indicated that he would like other Congressmen to be involved in the discussions. He named three in particular: Jawaharlal Nehru, Subhas Bose (the party's main voice in the important province of Bengal) and Abul Kalam Azad (after M.A. Ansari's death the pre-eminent Muslim leader of the Congress).

Gandhi had always seen the Congress as representing all the castes, communities, linguistic groups and provinces of India. The Congress's fine showing in the 1937 elections seemed to confirm this wider representativeness of his party. Now Jinnah had come along to challenge this deeply cherished and long-held claim. There were two major parties in India, argued Jinnah, not just one. He led one party, representing the Muslims; Gandhi led the other party, representing the Hindus. Any long-term settlement of the communal question would have to be based on this premise.

In 1918, Sarojini Naidu had edited a collection of Jinnah's speeches, which she gave the title, 'Ambassador of Hindu–Muslim Unity'. That was then; now, twenty years later, Jinnah had become the leading advocate of Muslim separatism. The move was in part prompted by a sense of personal affront (the cold-shouldering by Gandhi and the Congress at the time of the non-cooperation movement); in part, a product of a genuine change of mind. Jinnah had come increasingly to believe that in a Hindu-majority India, Muslims would need substantial safeguards to protect their interests.

In moving from unity to separation, Jinnah was also influenced by the poet Muhammad Iqbal, who urged him to seriously consider the creation of distinct Muslim provinces or states. In letters written shortly after the 1937 elections, Iqbal told Jinnah that 'the new constitution with its idea of a single Indian federation is completely hopeless. A separate federation of Muslim provinces . . . is the only course by which we can secure a peaceful India and save Muslims from the domination of non-Muslims. Why would not we Muslims of North-West India and Bengal be considered as nations entitled to self-determination just as other nations in India and outside India are?'

Back in 1930, Iqbal had proposed a separate Muslim state in his presidential address to the Muslim League. But that was a single state, in the north-west. Now he had added a Muslim state in Bengal as well. His views made a powerful impression on Jinnah, not least because Iqbal was to him what Tagore was to Gandhi—a poet-philosopher whom this politician deeply and genuinely admired. As with Tagore and Gandhi, the admiration was mutual, with Iqbal writing to Jinnah in June 1937 that 'you are the only Muslim in India today to whom the community has the right to look up for sage guidance through the storm which is coming . . .'[10]

Jinnah's political career was once more on the rise. Opposition to the (real or perceived) 'anti-Muslim' actions of the Congress governments had provided a powerful focus for his activities. His flock of supporters and admirers grew every day. One example must stand out for what was now a much wider trend. In June 1938, Jinnah addressed a meeting of the Memon Merchants Association, Bombay. The hosts welcomed him with an address and also presented him with a purse of Rs 2154. Jinnah was exultant, remarking that while he had been 'serving the public' of Bombay for the last forty years, this was 'the first opportunity when a business community has honoured me with an address of welcome or encouraged me by eulogising my services'.[11]

Back in the days of the non-cooperation movement, Bombay's merchants, both Hindu and Muslim, saw Gandhi as their saviour, for his inherent charisma and for his programme of swadeshi. Back in 1921, the Memons of Bombay had handsomely funded Gandhi's activities. But now, with the Congress in power in the Presidency, they were anxious that a party dominated by Hindus would perhaps favour traders who were Hindus. Thus the approach to Jinnah and the League.

III

In February 1938, Gandhi attended the Congress session, held that year in Haripura, a village close to Bardoli. He had wanted the veteran Andhra leader Pattabhi Sitaramayya to be president. The mood among the delegates however decidedly favoured Subhas Bose, who appealed to the youth and the left wing, and of course to Congressmen from his own influential and populous province. It had been several years since Bengal had a president. Gandhi, who had previously told Vallabhbhai Patel that 'Subhas is not at all dependable', bowed to the wind, and endorsed Bose.[12]

On the sidelines of the Congress, ordinary folks from all over India paid their respects to Gandhi. An old man from the Punjab had come to Haripura just to have his darshan. When Mahadev Desai took him to the great man, he handed over a postal envelope with 100 rupees in it. The Punjabi had heard there were many pickpockets at the Congress, and the first thing he wanted to do was 'to relieve myself of the burden before my pocket was picked!' Then a peasant from Rajasthan came to Gandhi's hut with a huge sack of the fruit he had grown on his land. Gandhi asked how much he had spent on his train fare. Seven rupees was the answer, a not insubstantial sum, but, said the peasant: 'That was nothing, he was thankful that God had enabled him to offer fruit from his garden to Gandhiji.' A third devotee, meanwhile, had come to Haripura with his offering, this a big bundle of yarn he had spun himself, an impressive 1,25,000 yards in all.[13]

In the last week of March, Gandhi travelled to Orissa. He began his tour by opening a village industries exhibition in Delang. In his speech, he spoke sorrowfully of how the priests of the province's greatest temple, the Jagannatha shrine in Puri, did not admit low-caste Hindus. 'So long as the doors of the Jagannatha temple are closed to the Harijans,' insisted Gandhi, 'they are closed to me as well.'[14]

With Gandhi on this tour was Mahadev Desai, as well as their wives. Earlier in the year, a Western journalist had visited the ashram in Segaon, spending a week with Gandhi and his entourage. The visitor was greatly impressed by Mahadev, who was 'too arresting a figure to be missed, though he is a most self-effacing and modest man'. Yet, the ashram evidently revolved around him. Gandhi's secretary, noted the visitor, 'edits the "Harijan", [the] Mahatma's weekly paper. He does all the secretarial work and every other kind of work including cleaning, dish-washing etc. To be able to do only his intellectual job amid the perpetual va-et-vient of all India, of Europe and even of America and the Far East, all of them hammering Mahatma Gandhi with questions, is more difficult than can be realised by those not given to intellectual occupations. It means a greater self-discipline than is easily imagined.'[15]

At this time, Gandhi and Mahadev Desai had been together for twenty-one years. They had had their occasional disagreement, the odd argument even. But on this Orissa trip, their relationship met its first serious test, to pass which Mahadev required greater self-discipline than he had himself ever imagined. One day, while the men were in a meeting with social workers, Kasturba Gandhi and Durga Desai chose to make a sightseeing trip to Puri, which was a mere fifteen miles away from their camp. When they came to the gates of the Jagannatha shrine, the ladies hesitated, then stepped inside. The temple was one of the four great *dham*s set up by the legendary Hindu missionary Adi Shankara in the eighth century—Badrinath in the north, Dwarka in the west, Sringeri in the south, and Puri in the east.

Kasturba and Durga were both devout Hindus. And the Jagannatha temple was one of the holiest temples of their faith. We can, and perhaps should, sympathize with the women for wishing to see the deity from close-up. But one who didn't see it this way was Mahadev's twelve-year-old son, Narayan, who was with the ladies that day. The precocious Narayan had heard Gandhi speak disparagingly about the shrine in several speeches. Now he urged his mother and (adoptive) aunt not to go inside. Bapu would be cross with them, he said. The temple was not holy, because it refused to admit Harijans.

Kasturba and Durga disregarded the boy. He stayed outside, while they paid their respects to Lord Jagannatha. After they came out, and went back to the men and their camp, the twelve-year-old Narayan told Gandhi about what had happened.[16]

Gandhi was, according to one account, 'almost prostrate with grief over the carelessness of his wife and Mahadev Desai's wife'.[17] His grief—perhaps we should say 'anger'—was compounded when he learnt that Mahadev had known the women were going to Puri, but had not alerted them as to what they could, and could not, do there. His mental agitation aggravated his blood pressure, which rose to an alarmingly high level.

Gandhi said that the women who entered the Puri temple were not to blame, but Mahadev and he were. Clearly, his own teaching had not been sound enough. How could Kasturba, he asked, 'at all go there after having lived with me for fifty years'? And 'Mahadev was more to blame in that he did not tell them what their dharma was and how any breach would shake me'.

Mahadev had been chastised by his master before, but never on an issue at once so sensitive and substantial. He began a fast of atonement, and also told Gandhi he could relieve him of his services. Gandhi answered that while fasting was 'no remedy for thoughtlessness or wrong-thinking', there was 'no question of your leaving'. The advice he gave Mahadev was 'to read less, but think more'.[18]

Mahadev Desai wrote about the controversy in *Harijan*, recounting his wife's transgression and his own indirect aiding of it. This mea culpa was drafted by Mahadev, and it appeared under his name in *Harijan*. But as the original manuscript held in the archives of the Sabarmati Ashram shows, it had been heavily edited by Gandhi. Several lines had been rewritten, several words changed (thus Mahadev referred to the pandas of the Puri temple as 'potbellied', which Gandhi changed to 'unscrupulous'). Also changed was the title of the article itself—with Mahadev's 'A Blunder—and an Expiation', becoming, under Gandhi's direction, 'A Tragedy'.

Gandhi also excised an entire paragraph from Mahadev's original draft. This read:

> I narrate these facts in order that the bare narration may serve somewhat to expiate me for my wrongs. Better expiation it is not in my power to do at the present moment. I am not a hot crusader to the extent of believing that service of the Harijans in the shape of befriending them, having them in your homes, feeding them and clothing them, counts as naught before service of them in the shape of boycotting temples not open to them. I wish I was guilty of the blind love of my wife. She does not credit me with it. She is an obstinate person, but she has more purity than I can ever attain. Ba, inspite of her intellectual limitations, is perhaps the purest specimen of womanhood that one can hope to come across. Both Ba and my wife do their humble best for the service of Harijans, and to think that their having gone to the Puri temple was something in the nature of adharma seems to me to carry the emphasis on creed rather than on works too far.

Here, Mahadev was noticeably sympathetic to the women concerned, pointing to the dignity and decency in their general conduct. Striking, too, was the refusal to make a fetish of temple entry; befriending Harijans and treating them as equals in everyday life, was in his eyes, as important as permitting them to worship idols they had previously not been allowed to see. Treating Harijans as equals was what Kasturba and Durga did every day in the ashram; to so severely scold them now for entering the Puri temple was surely, as Mahadev put it, 'to carry the emphasis on creed rather than on works too far'.

This telling paragraph did not pass *Harijan*'s in-house censor. Fortunately, Gandhi did not cut, from the printed version, a quatrain that captured Mahadev's feelings, a quatrain that was perhaps imperfect in grammar yet remains immortal in essence:

> To live with the saints in heaven
> Is a bliss and a glory
> But to live with a saint on earth
> Is a different story.[19]

IV

After his Orissa trip, Gandhi stopped in Calcutta, where he met the governor of Bengal, Lord Brabourne. The governor reported Gandhi as saying that the aim of the Congress was 'bringing the British people to realise that the present Act must, fairly soon, be replaced by a much more liberal one . . . that if we did this voluntarily and graciously the Congress would also act graciously but that if we did not he could see nothing for it but, sooner or later, a mass civil disobedience movement.'

The governor's notes of the meeting continued:

> I asked him what his real aim was—was it to sever the connection with the British as quickly as possible? His reply was emphatic—he wishes to see a complete break of all ties with the Empire but that the break should come, not as a result of a revolt or mass movement in India but as a gesture from us. His view is that were we to make such a gesture India would, eventually, be only too ready to cooperate with us as partners, though not as members of the British Empire.[20]

A week later, Gandhi met the viceroy himself. With Congress ministries in power, a sort of truce was in existence. Gandhi did most of the talking, and began by asking for the release of all political prisoners. He then said that in several cases, governors were refusing to be guided by the advice of their ministers even in matters 'entirely domestic to the province' concerned. Next, speaking about the prospects for an all-India federation, he urged the viceroy to lean on the princes to send representatives who represented the popular will of their subjects rather than being nominees of the rulers themselves. Finally, Gandhi touched on the still unfinished task of restoring lands to peasants in Gujarat seized during the satyagrahas of the early 1930s.[21]

On returning from his travels, Gandhi set about finding a mutually convenient time to meet Jinnah. Harmonizing their extremely busy calendars was not the only problem. Gandhi asked if Maulana Azad could accompany him to the meeting; Jinnah wired back that he 'would prefer to see you alone'. Both leaders were acutely aware of the symbolism at stake; Gandhi wanted to take along a Muslim Congressman, Jinnah determined to convey that he alone represented Muslims while the Congress and Gandhi represented Hindus alone.

Jinnah had recently had an acrimonious correspondence with Jawaharlal Nehru. Jinnah charged the Congress press with printing canards and falsehoods about him and the League; Nehru answered that there was no such thing as the 'Congress Press', and in any case the Urdu press printed 'astounding falsehoods' about the Congress and its leaders. The two men also debated specific matters, such as cow slaughter, the protection of Islamic culture, Urdu versus Hindi, Muslim representation in administration, etc., with Nehru striving hard but unavailingly to convince Jinnah that the Congress had and would behave responsibly on all these questions.

Nehru's reading of the Indian problem emphasized the importance of economics. He invited Jinnah and the Muslim League to join the Congress in 'our anti-imperialism . . . our attempt to remove the exploitation of the masses, agrarian and labour protests, and the like'. Jinnah saw the problem more in cultural terms; the key question, he told Nehru, 'is of safeguarding the rights and the interests of the

Mussalmans with regard to their religion, culture, language, personal laws and political rights in the national life, the government and the administration of the country'.

The crucial, and irreconcilable, difference, however, remained the question of representativeness. Writing to Jinnah on 6 April 1938, Nehru somewhat loftily remarked: 'I do not understand what is meant by our [the Congress] recognition of the Muslim League as the one and only organization of Indian Muslims. Obviously the Muslim League is an important communal organisation and we deal with it as such. But we have to deal with all organisations and individuals that come within our ken. We do not determine the measure or importance or distinction they possess.' Nehru went on to note that the Congress itself had 1,00,000 Muslim members.

In his reply, dated 12 April, Jinnah stated:

Your tone and language again display the same arrogance and militant spirit, as if the Congress is the sovereign power and, as an indication you extend your patronage by saying that 'obviously the Muslim League is an important communal organisation and we deal with it as such, as we have to deal with all organisations and individuals that come within our ken . . .' Here I may add that in my opinion, as I have publicly stated so often, that unless the Congress recognises the Muslim League on a footing of complete equality and is prepared as such to negotiate for a Hindu–Muslim settlement, we shall have to wait and depend upon our inherent strength which will 'determine the measure of importance and distinction it possesses'.[22]

Seeking to heal the breach, Gandhi had now reached out to Jinnah himself. A meeting was fixed for 28 April 1938. It would be held in Bombay. A week prior, Gandhi issued a press statement saying that he would 'not leave a single stone unturned to achieve Hindu–Muslim unity'. He asked 'all lovers of communal peace' to pray that Jinnah and he could find the right means to achieve that ever more elusive end.

This public plea for communal peace was prefaced by a strange, intriguing admission of personal frailty. Thus Gandhi wrote: 'I seem to have detected a flaw in me which is unworthy of a votary of truth and ahimsa. I am going through a process of self-introspection, the results of which I cannot foresee. I find myself for the first time during the past 50 years in a Slough of Despond.'[23]

One wonders what readers of the press statement made of this decidedly odd interpolation. To them, the cause, manifestation and the precise nature of this flaw was left unelaborated. Gandhi's close disciples knew the details; and the labours of the editors of his *Collected Works* have since made them public for us to examine it.

Here is what happened. On 14 April 1938, Gandhi awoke with an erection; and despite efforts to contain his excitement, had a masturbatory experience. He was sleeping alone, and it was decades since he had been aroused in such a way.

The details of the incident were kept from his 'political' followers such as Jawaharlal Nehru, but discussed with the spiritual followers who had stayed with him in Sabarmati and Ségaon. To one Gujarati ashramite he wrote that 'I was in such a wretched and pitiable condition that in spite of my utmost efforts I could not stop the discharge though I was fully awake. . . . After the event, restlessness has become acute beyond words. Where am I, where is my place, and how can a person subject to passion represent non-violence and truth?'

To Mira, Gandhi wrote in a language even more vivid in its self-abasement: 'That dirty, degrading, torturing experience of 14th April shook me to bits and made me feel as if I was hurled by God from an imaginary paradise where I had no right to be in my uncleanliness.'

To his other close woman disciple, Amrit Kaur, Gandhi spoke of 'an unaccountable dissatisfaction with myself'. But he had not lost faith, and was resolved to overcome the memory of his failure. 'The sexual sense is the hardest to overcome in my case,' he remarked. 'It has been an incessant struggle. It is for me a miracle how I have survived it. The one I am engaged in may be, ought to be, the final struggle.'[24]

Gandhi had taken a vow of brahmacharya, as far back as 1906. He thought sex was necessary only for procreation, and rejected the idea that sex might be pleasurable in and of itself. In his writings and speeches, he had often spoken of the importance of the preservation and husbanding of sperm, which he termed 'the vital fluid'. As he told the readers of *Harijan*: 'All power comes from the preservation and sublimation of the vitality that is responsible for creation of life. If the vitality is husbanded instead of being dissipated, it is transmuted into creative energy of the highest order.'[25]

After this (to him) shocking experience, how could Gandhi best control his passions, best preserve and husband that vital fluid? Several ashramites (Amrit Kaur among them) thought he should avoid close physical contact with women, especially younger women. He should abandon ashram girls as supports while walking (he rested his hands on their shoulders to propel his frail frame along), and discontinue the practice of having his nails cut or his body massaged by women disciples. Gandhi was not convinced of the sagacity of this advice. He had, he reminded one disciple, not 'advocated total avoidance of innocent contact between the two sexes and I have had a certain measure of success in this'. To Amrit Kaur, he insisted that 'it is not the woman who is to blame. I am the culprit. I must attain the required purity.'[26]

Gandhi had wanted to write about the experience of 14 April in *Harijan*, baring to the world his failure and lack of self-control. He discussed this with Rajagopalachari, who was then in Segaon. Rajaji dissuaded him from making his experience public. Afterwards, Rajaji wrote to his son-in-law Devadas, who was also Gandhi's son. The Mahatma, he said, was deeply worried 'that he was still unable to overcome the reflex action of his flesh. He discovered, it seems, one day and he was so shocked and felt so unworthy that he was deceiving people and he wrote an article about it for publication in Harijan, which, thank God, I have stopped, after a very quarrelsome hour.'[27]

Gandhi had once called Rajagopalachari 'the keeper of my conscience'. Back in 1921, Rajaji had saved Gandhi from public embarrassment, and possibly political humiliation too, when he prevailed upon him to not go ahead with his 'spiritual marriage' to Saraladevi Chaudhurani. Now, seventeen years later, he had sensibly urged Gandhi to keep his private obsessions private.

V

On 28 April, Jinnah and Gandhi had their long-delayed meeting in Bombay. After it ended, Gandhi issued a terse public statement, saying merely that they had 'three hours friendly conversation over the Hindu–Muslim question'. The same night, Gandhi caught the Frontier Mail to Peshawar, in the NWFP, to which his follower Khan Abdul Ghaffar Khan had recently been allowed to return, and to which he had himself finally been granted permission to visit.[28]

Gandhi was close to Ghaffar Khan; but his visit was as much political as personal. The 1930s had seen a steady movement of the Muslims away from the Congress. There were some outstanding Muslim scholars in the party, such as Maulana Azad and Dr Zakir Husain, but few mass leaders. Ghaffar Khan was an exception; by identifying with him and his movement, Gandhi hoped to show afresh that the Congress was more than a 'Hindu' party.

An Urdu newspaper claimed Gandhi had come to emasculate the mighty and warlike Pathans; in fact, he had come to see at first-hand the work of the Khudai Khidmatgars, which had demonstrated that 'true non-violence is mightier than the mightiest violence'.

Not all Pathans were convinced. One, an educated and learned professor, asked Gandhi if pacifism had its limits. Could Mussolini's invading army have been effectively resisted through non-violence by the Abyssinians? Gandhi thought it not inconceivable. If the Italians had been met with 'quiet, dignified and non-violent defiance', they would have had to retreat. To the objection that 'human nature has not been known to rise to such heights', Gandhi replied: 'But if we have made unexpected progress in physical sciences, why may we do less in the science of the soul?'

From the Frontier, Gandhi returned to Bombay, where he once more met Jinnah. Their talks, he told Rajagopalachari later, were 'cordial but not hopeful, yet not without hope'.[29] To Amrit Kaur, he was more gloomy. Describing Jinnah as 'a very tough customer', he observed that 'if the other members of the League are of the same type a settlement is an impossibility'.[30]

The other members of the Muslim League did indeed seem to be 'of the same type'. In late March 1938, less than a year after the provincial elections, the League had appointed a committee to report on the 'hardship, ill-treatment and injustice that is meted out to the Muslims in various Congress Governments and particularly to those whose are workers and members of the Muslim League'. The six-member committee submitted its report in November 1938. It listed a number of grievances of Muslims in the Congress-ruled provinces, among them:

(1) Forcing children in schools to sing '*Vande Mataram*' despite it being 'positively anti-Islamic and idolatrous in inspiration';
(2) Hoisting at school and office functions the Congress flag which was 'purely a party flag and nothing more';
(3) Exclusion of Muslims from local bodies;
(4) Demanding a ban on cow slaughter and intimidating Muslims to give up eating beef, and attacking Muslim butchers—this, claimed the report, was inspired by Gandhi, 'whose fundamental motives are religious', and whose religion was 'based on the fundamental Hindu scripture, the Bhagavad Gita';
(5) Discrimination against the Urdu language, by promoting Hindi in the Nāgarī script and foisting languages such as Marathi and Oriya on Urdu-speaking Muslims.[31]

All over the world democratically elected governments have been accused of betraying their mandate within a year or two of coming to power. Here, in the India of the late 1930s, the Muslim League adroitly seized on this mood of anti-incumbency against the Congress. Some of their grievances were real; for, unlike Gandhi, Nehru or Bose, many lesser Congressmen saw themselves as Hindus first, and in the arrogance that followed their electoral triumph sought to encode their ideas (and prejudices) in policy and in practice. On the other hand, the Muslim League was not above embellishing or exaggerating reports of alleged 'discrimination'.

Who or what was responsible for this growing atmosphere of distrust is still a matter of keen historical debate.[32] But that the distrust intensified in this period no one disputes. Before the elections of 1937, the Congress and the Muslim League were rivals; now, they were adversaries.

VI

The one part of India where the Muslims had stood solidly behind the Congress was the NWFP. In October 1938, Gandhi set off for a second, and longer, trip to the Frontier. This time he spent a full five weeks there, being escorted by Ghaffar Khan to towns and villages, through hilltops and valleys. He enjoyed the air, the scenery and the fresh fruit, writing to a disciple that 'the climate is excellent. The peace is beyond description. One will not get such peace anywhere else.'[33]

Ghaffar Khan told Gandhi that 'violence has been the real bane of us Pathans'. The 'entire strength of the Pathan', he added, 'is today spent in thinking how to cut the throat of his brother'. This cult of violence and revenge split brother from brother, village from village, clan from clan. If his and Gandhi's campaign to wean the Pathan away from the gun and sword succeeded, said Ghaffar Khan, 'this land, so rich in fruit and grain, might well [become] a smiling little Eden . . .'[34]

While Gandhi and Ghaffar Khan discussed the redemptive potential of non-violence, in distant Europe war clouds were gathering. Touring the Continent in the autumn of 1938, Jawaharlal Nehru sent regular reports about what he saw and heard. In late August, Nehru wrote to Gandhi from Budapest that there was a 'fever of anxiety' across Europe. 'It is extraordinary how much today depends,' he remarked, 'on the will of one man and that man a semi-neurotic like Hitler.' If war came, said Nehru to Gandhi, 'very vital decisions will have to be taken by us. I earnestly trust that we shall act wisely . . .'

Two weeks later, Nehru wrote to Gandhi from Geneva. He was 'feeling very unhappy at the way Chamberlain and Co. are preparing to abandon Czechoslovakia'. A month later still, now in London, Nehru wrote in dismay of Britain's betrayal of the Czechs through the pact between the British prime minister, Neville Chamberlain, and the German chancellor, Adolf Hitler. 'Whatever happens to the world or to Europe,' he predicted, 'the British Empire is doomed.'[35]

Reading the press reports alongside Nehru's letters, Gandhi decided to make his first major statement on world affairs. It took the form of a long essay called 'If I Were a Czech'. At Munich, Chamberlain had effectively told Hitler that he could invade Czechoslovakia at a time of his choosing. Gandhi thought this was because 'democracy [only] threatens to spill blood', whereas 'the philosophy for which the two dictators [Hitler and Mussolini] stand calls it cowardice to shrink from carnage. They exhaust the resources of poetic art to glorify organized murder.'

Gandhi advised the hapless Czechs to offer satyagraha to Hitler's army when they came. 'If I were a Czech,' he wrote, 'I would not be a vassal to any nation or body. I must have absolute independence or perish. To seek to win in a clash of arms would be pure bravado. Not so, if in defying the might of one who would deprive me of my independence I refuse to obey his will and perish unarmed in the attempt. In doing so, though I lose the body, I save my soul, i.e., my honour.'

Gandhi had been told by a colleague (unnamed, but probably Jawaharlal Nehru) that since 'Hitler knows no pity', his philosophy of satyagraha 'will avail nothing before him'. Gandhi answered that 'my honour is the only thing worth preserving. That is independent of his pity.' Thus, his advocacy of satyagraha to the Czechs, 'a weapon not of the weak but of the brave. There is no bravery greater than a resolute refusal to bend the knee to an earthly power, no matter how great, and that without bitterness of spirit and in the fulness of faith that the spirit alone lives, nothing else does.'[36]

Another (and also unnamed) friend told Gandhi that satyagraha might work with the British because they were lovers of liberty, whose democratic instinct 'restrains them from lengths to which autocrats will go'. Gandhi refused to accept that his doctrine was limited in scope. 'If we can succeed with the English,' he argued, 'surely it is an extension of faith to believe that we are likely to succeed with less cultured or less liberally-minded nations.'[37]

The article on the Czechs written and dispatched, Gandhi's tour of the Frontier continued. It was the holy month of Ramzan, with many Pathans observing the dawn-to-dusk fast it mandated. As an expert in fasting himself, Gandhi was troubled to see Pathan men 'losing temper over trifles or indulging in abuse during the sacred month of Ramzan. If there is the slightest delay in serving the repast at the time of the breaking of the fast, the poor wife is hauled over live

coals.' This was both a travesty of faith and of their political credo. 'If
you really want to cultivate non-violence,' Gandhi told the Pathans,
'you should take a pledge that come what may, you will not give way
to anger or order about members of your household or lord it over
them.'[38]

VII

Gandhi had chastised the Pathans for being harsh and cruel to their
wives. He had by now reached a comfortable modus vivendi with
his own wife. While he was unquestionably the dominant partner,
no longer did he order Kasturba about. In their letters and one
presumes in their conversations, there were moments of deep love
and companionship. Yet, in his wider dealings with Indian women,
Gandhi could be condescending and patronizing.

Consider thus an article he wrote in *Harijan* in December 1938,
entitled 'Students' Shame'. This excerpted a letter from a college
girl in the Punjab, complaining about the teasing and harassment
she and her companion experienced at the hands of prowling young
men. 'First of all,' this young lady asked Gandhi, 'tell me how, in
the circumstances mentioned above, can girls apply the principle of
ahimsa and save themselves. Secondly, what is the remedy for curing
youth of the abominable habit of insulting womenfolk?'

Replying in *Harijan*, Gandhi recognized that such molestation by
men was a 'growing evil' in India. He recommended that 'all such
cases should be published in the newspapers. Names of the offenders
should be published when they are traced.' For, 'there is nothing
like public opinion for castigating public misconduct'. Indeed, he
argued, 'crime and vice generally require darkness for prowling. They
disappear when light plays upon them.'

Gandhi urged well-behaved young men to chastise the deviants
among them. They should, 'as a class, be jealous of their reputation
and deal with every case of impropriety occurring among their mates'.
Gandhi also accepted the need for young women themselves to 'learn
the art of ordinary self-defence and protect themselves from indecent
behaviour of unchivalrous youth'.

Gandhi spoilt his case by launching an unprovoked attack on the modern woman. For all the evil that males did and do, he wrote, 'I have a fear that the modern girl loves to be Juliet to half a dozen Romeos. She loves adventure. My correspondent seems to represent the unusual type. The modern girl dresses not to protect herself from wind, rain and sun but to attract attention. She improves upon nature by painting herself and looking extraordinary. The non-violent way is not for such girls.'[39]

Gandhi's article was read by a group of young women in Calcutta. They sent in a spirited response, addressed to their 'Most revered Mahatmaji', which began by observing that Gandhi's remarks were 'not very inspiring', since they seem to 'put the whole slur upon the injured female who suffers most due to the malevolent social custom'.

The letter continued: 'Some may find modern girls' dresses and deportments a bit different than they wish them to be but to brand them as exhibitionistic generally is a positive insult to her sex as a whole. Strength of character and chaste behaviour are necessary not only for modern girls but for men as well. There may be a few girls playing Juliets to a dozen Romeos. But such cases presuppose the existence of half a dozen Romeos, moving around the streets in quest of a Juliet, thereby pointing out where the proper correction lies.'

Since the root of the problem was the deportment of men, not women, Gandhi's remarks in *Harijan* were unfortunate, wrote these young Bengalis. For, 'a statement like this once again holds brief for that worn-out and un-becoming saying—"woman is the gate of Hell". And naturally clouds of doubt gather over the much-vaunted progress that man has made since the birth of that saying.' These women told Gandhi that 'a Gokhale, a Tilak, a Deshbandhu [C.R. Das] would have surely hesitated to come out with such an ungenerous statement as you have done. Woman has been called a boa-constrictor, but that is in a different land and by a different man. What befits a Bernard Shaw with his hands touching the ground and legs kicking the air does not befit a Mahatma.'

This passionate, intensely felt letter ended with this moving passage:

Lastly, from the foregoing remarks, it should never be concluded that modern girls have no respect for you. They hold you in as much respect as every mother's son does. To be hated or pitied is what they resent most. They are ready to amend their ways if they are really guilty. Their guilt, if any, must be conclusively proved before they are anathematized. In this respect they would neither desire to take shelter under the covering of 'ladies, please' nor they would silently stand and allow the judge to condemn them in his own way. Truth must be faced, the modern girl or Juliet as you have called her, has courage enough to face it.[40]

Gandhi printed large chunks of the letter in *Harijan*, leaving out, however, the references to Gokhale, Bernard Shaw et al., as well as the (even more telling) sentence pointing out that to dress differently was not necessarily to be exhibitionist. Then, as was his wont, he set out to respond. His tone was notably defensive. 'My correspondents do not perhaps know,' he remarked, 'that I began service of India's women in South Africa more than forty years ago when perhaps none of them were born.' He continued: 'I hold myself to be incapable of writing anything derogatory to womanhood.' His original article, he explained, 'was written to expose students' shame, not to advertise the frailties of girls. But in giving the diagnosis of the disease, I was bound, if I was to prescribe the right remedy, to mention all the factors which induced the disease.'

In conclusion, Gandhi invited his correspondents 'to initiate a crusade against the rude behavior of students. God helps only those who help themselves. The girls must learn the art of protecting themselves against the ruffianly behaviour of man.'[41]

VIII

In Europe, many Jews had begun to join the exodus to Palestine, where, from the late nineteenth century, Zionists had hoped to create a state that would save Jews from the savage persecution they faced in the nations, large and small, of Europe.

Gandhi received several letters asking him to comment on the Arab–Zionist question in Palestine and the situation of the Jews in Germany. In November 1938, he answered his correspondents collectively via an article in *Harijan*. This began by saying that his 'sympathies are all with the Jews'. They were 'the untouchables of Christianity. . . . Religious sanction has been invoked in both cases for the justification of the inhuman treatment meted out to them.'

This sympathy did not blind Gandhi to the requirements of justice for the Palestinians. If the Jews needed a national home, why should the Arabs pay for it? He was not supportive of the rising wave of migration from Eastern Europe to the Holy Land, promoted by energetic Zionists. He was distressed that Jews from Europe had sought to enter Palestine 'under the shadow of the British gun'. A 'religious act', he insisted, 'cannot be performed with the aid of the bayonet or the bomb'. If the Jews wanted to settle in Palestine, they should do so 'only by the goodwill of the Arabs'. As things stood, however, the Jews had become 'co-sharers with the British in despoiling a people who have done no wrong to them'.

Gandhi acknowledged that 'the German persecution of the Jews seems to have no parallel in history. The tyrants of old never went so mad as Hitler seems to have done.' He also accepted that 'if there ever could be a justifiable war in the name of and for humanity, a war against Germany, to prevent the wanton persecution of a whole race, would be completely justified'.

Gandhi still hoped that Hitler could be resisted by other than violent means. He asked the Jews in Germany to themselves 'resist this organized and shameless persecution'. He invoked to them, as he had done to the Czechs, the example of the non-violent movements he had led against the racist regime in South Africa. Gandhi claimed that 'the Jews of Germany can offer satyagraha under infinitely better auspices than the Indians of South Africa'. They were a 'compact, homogeneous community'; they were 'far more gifted than the Indians of South Africa'; they had 'organized world opinion behind them'. Gandhi was 'convinced that if someone with courage and vision can arise among them to lead them in non-violent action, the winter of their despair can in the twinkling of an eye be turned into the summer of hope'. Such a movement, thought Gandhi, would be 'a truly religious resistance offered against the godless fury of dehumanized man. The German Jews will score a lasting victory over the German gentiles in the sense that they will have converted the latter to an appreciation of human dignity.'[42]

So far as one can tell, Gandhi's essay on the Czechs elicited no major reactions. However, his essay on the Jews was followed by a torrent of responses. First off the mark was a writer from Berlin, who claimed that no non-German had the right to criticize his country or its actions. Gandhi thought this a false doctrine, for 'in this age, when distances have been obliterated, no nation can afford to imitate the frog in the well. Sometimes it is refreshing to see ourselves as others see us.'[43]

The complaints from Germans, betraying hurt national pride, were followed by anguished reactions from Jewish writers, who thought Gandhi had not understood the depth of their suffering. Two of the foremost Jewish intellectuals of the day, Martin Buber and J.L. Magnes, each wrote a long reply, these printed together in a pamphlet.

Martin Buber had for long admired Gandhi and closely studied his writings. In 1930, when Gandhi commenced the Salt March, Buber wrote an essay on his attempts to spiritualize politics. He praised Gandhi as a 'clear-sighted' and 'truthful' thinker, whose moral courage and capacity for self-criticism were 'worthy of the purest admiration'.[44]

Now, eight years later, Buber addressed Gandhi directly, in the form of a personal letter, which he took weeks to compose, anguishing over, drafting and redrafting its sentences and paragraphs. The letter as finally sent argued that Gandhi's idea of satyagraha, while 'praiseworthy' in conception, was totally inapplicable to Jews in Germany. Buber pointed out that the comparison with Indians in South Africa was inapt; for, while the latter were discriminated against, they were not 'persecuted, robbed, maltreated, tortured, [and] murdered' as the Jews in Germany were. Moreover, when Gandhi conducted his struggle against that racist regime, he could always look for assistance, moral and financial, from his motherland. The 1,50,000 Indians in South Africa had drawn immense sustenance from the support of the 200 million Indians at home.

The Jews were treated infinitely worse in Europe; and the Jews had (as yet) no homeland. But they must have one, argued Buber, to protect them in the present and the future. Invoking the ancient settlements of Jews in Palestine, and the sacrality of that land as enunciated in their holy books, Buber said the 'question of our Jewish destiny is indissolubly bound up with the possibility of in-gathering, and this in Palestine'.

Unlike some other Zionists, Buber believed in a binational state, to be peopled by Jews and by Arabs. Like Gandhi, he respected the rights of the Arabs, except that he suggested that these were acquired by conquest. And he was less than impressed by what he called the 'primitive state of fellah agriculture'. He claimed the Arabs were clinging to unproductive forms of cultivation; and that the Jews were necessary to modernize them and their ways. As he put it, 'Ask the soil what the Arabs have done for her in thirteen hundred years and what we have done for her in fifty! Would her answer not be weighty testimony in a just discussion as to whom this land "belongs"?'

Buber told Gandhi he had taken so long to draft the letter as he wanted to make sure he did not fall 'into the grievous error of collective egotism'. In the end, he did fall into that error; not against Gandhi, nor against the Indians, but against the Arabs. He saw them—in an economic and technological sense—as a distinctly inferior race. Thus he remarked:

> This land recognizes us, for it is fruitful through us, and through its fruit-bearing for us it recognizes us. . . . The Jewish peasants have begun to teach their brothers, the Arab peasants, to cultivate the land more intensively. We desire to teach them further . . .[45]

J.L. Magnes's letter to Gandhi was equally long, but less combative. He too had followed the Indian leader's career closely and read many of his writings. Gandhi's statement on the Jews, wrote Magnes, was 'a challenge, particularly to those who have imagined ourselves your disciples'.

Like Buber, Magnes drew attention to the brutal authoritarianism of Hitler's regime. If a political prisoner went on a hunger strike in England or America, it might rouse public opinion. But in Germany, it would 'make not even a ripple'. And while Indians had the great Gandhi, said Magnes, 'we have no one comparable to you as [a] religious and political leader'. How could one even begin to conceive of satyagraha in such a situation?

Magnes had long thought of himself as a pacifist. But as far as Hitler was concerned, his pacifism had been placed in 'a pitiless crisis'. The world was now confronted with 'a choice of evils—a choice between the capitalisms, the imperialisms, the militarisms of the western democracies and between the Hitler religion'. It was thus that he concluded that war was necessary against the Nazis, a war 'against the greater evil'. 'Or do you know of any other choice?' he asked Gandhi.[46]

The Buber–Magnes pamphlet was posted to Gandhi in India. Yet there is no sign that he ever received it. Did it get mislaid on its way across the seas? Did it get mislaid in India, while being redirected from Segaon to wherever he was? Did one of his secretaries (surely not Mahadev) not show the pamphlet to Gandhi because the criticisms were so direct? We shall never know. Had Gandhi seen the letters, he would almost certainly have replied to them. But he very likely didn't, and we were thus denied the chance of reading an exchange between Gandhi and Buber, two of the greatest moralists of the twentieth century.[47]

Gandhi did, however, get to see a critique by another (if less well-known) Jewish thinker. This was Hayim Greenberg, a widely travelled activist, born and raised in Eastern Europe, who eventually made a home in America. Like Buber and Magnes, Greenberg had for long admired Gandhi (since 1914, in his recollection). In 1937, he wrote asking Gandhi why, in his varied and voluminous writings, he had not yet drawn attention to the sufferings of the Jews.

When Gandhi spoke on the subject a year later, what he said dismayed Greenberg. Gandhi, he remarked, demanded heroism from his fellow Indians but, from the Jews, 'a measure of super-heroism unexampled in history'. He had suggested that the Jews offer non-violent resistance to Hitler; but, as Greenberg observed, 'a Jewish Gandhi, should one arise, could function for about five minutes and would be promptly taken to the guillotine'.

Like Buber and Magnes, Greenberg was also disappointed that Gandhi did not endorse a Jewish National Home in Palestine. Why was this? 'With all my respect for the Mahatma (I doubt if there is another man living who evokes within me such a moral awareness of his loftiness),' wrote Greenberg, 'I cannot avoid the suspicion that so far as the Palestine problem is concerned, Gandhi allowed himself to be influenced by the anti-Zionist propaganda being conducted among fanatic pan-Islamists' (in India).[48]

When Greenberg's article was brought to his notice, Gandhi replied to it in *Harijan*, arguing that while non-violence would surely be harder against dictators, it must still be tried. 'Its real quality is only tested in such cases,' he observed. 'Sufferers need not see the result during their lifetime. They must have faith that if their cult survives, the result is a certainty. The method of violence gives no greater guarantee than that of non-violence.'[49]

In his reflections on the Jews, Gandhi was surely guilty of naïveté. He had referred to the Jews as the 'untouchables' of Christianity (a formulation first suggested to him by his friend Henry Polak). But he was hopelessly out of touch with the rapidly developing situation in Europe. Once merely segregated and discriminated against, Jews were now being butchered and murdered. Pogroms in Eastern Europe were followed by organized state violence against them in Germany. Hitler had already announced his desire to eliminate the Jews completely. Even as Gandhi was composing his article for *Harijan*, the Nazis were planning the attacks on Jewish shops and homes since known to history as Kristallnacht.

Gandhi was wrong to see the Jewish situation in Germany as akin to the Indian situation in South Africa. It was far, far worse. A Jewish Gandhi in Germany was an impossibility. But could there have been a Christian Gandhi in Germany in 1934? That was the year when Dietrich Bonhoeffer wrote asking whether he could come to Segaon and stay with, and learn from, Gandhi. Gandhi invited him to the ashram, but in the end, Bonhoeffer did not come. What if he had? Could Bonhoeffer then have returned to Germany and mobilized his fellow Christians in a non-violent resistance movement against the Nazis?

In 1934, when Bonhoeffer contacted Gandhi, Hitler had not fully consolidated his regime. Had a brave, charismatic Christian priest opposed the authoritarian ruler of a Christian country, he may not—in 1934—have been shot at sight. Could a popular movement have crystallized around the figure of a Gandhi-inspired Bonhoeffer, awakening the conscience not merely of his fellow Germans but of democrats around the world, forcing the other European powers and America to intervene much before they did, forestalling the horrific loss of life in the Second World War?

Had Gandhi replied to Buber in 1939, it would have enriched intellectual and moral discourse. On the other hand, had Bonhoeffer apprenticed with Gandhi in 1934, it might—just—have influenced social and political history as well.[50]

CHAPTER TWENTY-FIVE

(Re)capturing the Congress

I

Through 1938, Gandhi became increasingly engaged with the politics of the 500-odd princely states. These covered roughly one-third the territory of the subcontinent, and were indirectly rather than directly ruled by the British. The partial self-government mandated by the Government of India Act, and the coming to power of the Congress in many provinces of British India, had in turn inspired the residents of the states to demand greater rights for themselves. Popular movements against autocratic rule, demanding elected assemblies and ministries on the British Indian pattern, arose across the subcontinent; in the princely states of Travancore and Mysore in the south, in Hyderabad in the Deccan, in Jaipur in the north, in Dhenkanal in the east, and in Rajkot in the west.

Gandhi had initially advocated a policy of non-interference on the part of the Congress as regards the states. As someone who had grown up in princely India, he retained a residual affection for it. He thought it premature to organize satyagrahas to put pressure on the princes, hoping that they would on their own devolve power to their subjects. But the movements carried on regardless. In Travancore and

Mysore, democrats, inspired by the ideals of the Congress, organized a series of street protests, provoking repression from the rulers. Some protesters were killed in police firing; others were arrested and put in jails, more accurately described as dungeons and even torture chambers.

The escalating cycle of protest and repression moved Gandhi to speak out. In September 1938 he wrote:

> If the States persist in their obstinacy and hug their ignorance of the awakening that has taken place throughout India, they are courting certain destruction. I claim to be a friend of the States. Their service has been an heirloom in my family for the past three generations, if not longer. I am no blind worshipper of antiquity. But I am not ashamed of the heirloom. All the States may not live. The biggest ones can live only if they will recognize their limitations, become servants of their people, trustees of their welfare and depend on their existence not on arms, whether their own or British, but solely on the goodwill of the people.[1]

Gandhi called the popular movements in the states 'a very significant event in the national struggle for independence'. He hoped the princes and their advisers would recognize this awakening 'and meet the legitimate aspirations of the people'. Will 'they not read the handwriting on the wall'? he asked.[2]

They would not, at least not yet. In January 1939, the Chamber of Princes met in Bombay. Opening the conference, the maharaja of Bikaner suggested the creation of a common police force to more effectively deal with popular movements for democratic rights. More focused repression, argued the maharaja, should be combined with inducements to the leading agitators, by giving them State jobs and thus shutting their mouths. Bikaner termed the policy he was advocating 'kicks and kisses'.

Quoting this speech, Gandhi thought there was 'a nefarious plot to crush the movement for liberty which at long last has commenced in some of the States'. But, he hoped, 'if the people have shed fear and learnt the art of self-sacrifice, they need no favours. Kicks can never cow them.'[3]

II

In December 1938, the popular American magazine *Reader's Digest* carried a long essay on Gandhi. This chronicled Gandhi's life and work, his dietary experiments and political struggles, interspersing the narrative with quotes from the man himself.

Written by the widely travelled journalist John Gunther, the essay was appreciative, even cloying. It called Gandhi 'an incredible combination of Jesus Christ, Tammany Hall and your father', the 'greatest Indian since Buddha', who, like the Buddha, 'will be worshipped as a god when he dies'. Speaking on the one side of his 'colossal spiritual integrity', and on the other of his 'very considerable charm', the profile continued: 'Despite his 40 years of celibacy, he adores the company of women, and he likes to flirt. He is a saint, but a laughing one.' It then passed on the (unverified) story that, as secretary of state for India, Samuel Hoare instructed the new viceroy, Lord Willingdon, not to meet Gandhi 'in order to prevent him [from] succumbing to his formidable charm'.[4]

The essay in the *Reader's Digest* was a further sign of the growing interest in, and admiration for, Gandhi in America. In his own homeland, however, Gandhi was not without his critics and adversaries. Indeed, even as Gunther was crafting his laudatory profile, its subject was seeking to retain control over his own party. Subhas Bose wanted to continue as Congress president. A second term was very rare; it had been given only twice before, once in the exceptional circumstances of the Salt March when all the major leaders were in jail. Gandhi was not in favour of Bose's re-election. He looked around for a suitable successor. He first tried Azad, then Nehru. Both refused. So he settled on the Andhra Congressman Pattabhi Sitaramayya, who had been in the running in 1938 as well.[5]

Although he had been Congress president only once (in 1924), Gandhi was in effect, a super-president. Even at times when he was focusing on constructive work, even when he was officially on sabbatical from the Congress, the party looked to him for guidance. His advice was always sought on the choice of president. When major disputes broke out between party factions, the matter was always brought to him for arbitration.

Subhas Bose had the support of his provincial committee, and of many younger Congressmen, disenchanted with what they saw as maladministration and corruption in governments run by their party. These critics claimed that, in its year and a half in office, the Congress had steadily lost its lustre and credibility. Its long legacy of sacrifice and struggle was put at risk by its embrace of opportunists motivated solely by greed of office.[6]

Subhas Bose found support from the young and the left wing in the party, as well as from the one Indian whom Gandhi considered his moral and spiritual equal, namely, Rabindranath Tagore. In late November 1938, Tagore wrote to Gandhi about the question of the Congress presidency. He began by apologizing for the suggestion he was making despite his 'utter lack of training in politics'. Then he continued: 'The prospect of a prolonged agony of humiliation for my Province compels me at last to appeal to you with an earnest request that you may use your influence to offer Subhas [Bose] another chance of Presidentship for the next Congress.'

Tagore knew that Bose was regarded, and not by Gandhi alone, as somewhat hot-headed and temperamental. But he thought (or hoped) that 'lately he has been thinking and working hard to make himself ready for any great task of responsibility that his country may claim from him and I assure you that I myself will try my best to help him from my own vantage ground if he desires it'.[7]

There is no reply to this letter in the *Collected Works*. It may be that Gandhi was too embarrassed to reply, or that he talked with Tagore about the matter in person (over the telephone, since he was in Segaon at the time). Tagore was the least parochial of men, who had once urged Gandhi to shed his xenophobia and embrace the world. Now, twenty years on, he was urging the claims of his province. It is often the case that as men grow older, the attachment to their roots, their native language and their ancestral culture, grows. Even so, the letter is uncharacteristic. The poet had never before interfered in Congress politics. Was he put up to this by Subhas Bose or his supporters?

In the second week of December, Subhas Bose himself came to Segaon. Gandhi and he had long discussions, with Mahadev and Jawaharlal Nehru in attendance. Bose refused to be shaken from his decision to seek a second term.

It had been many years since the Congress had a presidential election. Since Gandhi's emergence as the party's pre-eminent leader, the president had always been chosen by consensus. But now, with neither side backing down, an election was organized by the AICC. This was held in the last week of January 1939. Bose won comfortably, getting the support of 1580 AICC members, some 200 more than Sitaramayya did.

Bose was a superb orator who had the ability, as Nirad Chaudhuri once remarked, to 'say a thousand times the same thing in different forms, and to get animated without end in the face of the same objects'. By contrast, his opponent, Sitaramayya, was a sober, stolid Congressman, without any charisma, and without the credibility of other Gandhians such as Abul Kalam Azad or Rajendra Prasad either. Had Prasad or Azad stood instead of him, they would have given Bose a much tougher fight, and perhaps even defeated him.[8]

Gandhi did not attend the AICC session. He was at Bardoli when he heard the news of Bose's re-election. He issued a statement which began:

> Shri Subhas Bose has achieved a decisive victory over his opponent, Dr. Pattabhi Sitaramayya. I must confess that from the very beginning I was decidedly against his re-election for reasons which I need not go into. I do not subscribe to the facts or the arguments in his manifestos. I think that his references to his colleagues were unjustified and unworthy. Nevertheless, I am glad of his victory. And since I was instrumental in inducing Dr. Pattabhi not to withdraw his name as a candidate when Maulana Saheb withdrew, the defeat is more mine than his.

Subhas Bose responded with a statement of his own. He was grieved that Gandhi saw it as 'a personal defeat', since the voters in the Congress presidential election were not called upon to vote for or against him.

Bose acknowledged that the result of the election had been interpreted as a victory of the Left within the Congress. Even so, he thought this would not or should not presage a split within the party, as many feared. He himself assured Congressmen that 'there will be no violent break with the past in the parliamentary or in the extra-parliamentary sphere'.

Bose ended with a profession of regard for Gandhi himself. Though they differed on some 'public questions', he would 'yield to none in my respect for his personality'. Bose insisted that 'it will always be my aim and object to try and win his confidence for the simple reason that it will be a tragic thing for me if I succeed in winning the confidence of other people but fail to win the confidence of India's greatest man'.[9]

Bose's statement was generous, as well as conciliatory. But even if Gandhi had been open to a compromise, the Gandhians were not. In response to Bose's re-election, most members of the CWC resigned. They included Patel, Kripalani, Bajaj and Rajendra Prasad, all Gandhi loyalists. The resignation of these working committee members left 'the Congress with a president marked for the helm, but without a crew to run the ship'.[10]

III

From the affairs of his party, Gandhi now turned back to the problems of princely states—or, to be more precise, the problems of his own princely state. This was Rajkot, where he had lived between 1874 and 1888, as a schoolboy and married man, and again in 1892–93, as a lawyer. His father had been diwan of the state. Many of his family members still lived there.

For forty years, from 1890 to 1930, Rajkot had an exceptionally broad-minded ruler, named Lakhajiraj. The Thakore Saheb (as the ruler was known) had inaugurated a representative assembly of the state's citizens, its members drawn from all major groups: traders, farmers, labourers, artisans and professionals. This council was free to make recommendations on policy, although the final decisions on whether or how to implement them rested with the ruler and his advisers.

After Lakhajiraj's death, his son and successor, Dharmendrasinhji, disbanded the people's council. While the new ruler busied himself with the pleasures of the flesh, the state was run by his autocratic diwan, Darbar Virawala. Popular discontent grew. In 1936, the workers in Rajkot's cotton mills went on strike for better wages. The Thakore Saheb was forced to agree to the formation of a labour union. Now other sections of society began to organize themselves. Peasants protested against the harsh rates of land assessment. Lawyers and intellectuals demanded greater rights of representation in the councils of the state.

These movements for democracy were encouraged by Vallabhbhai Patel, who kept in close touch with activists in Rajkot. In September 1938, Patel met a senior adviser of the Thakore Saheb, and put forward a charter of demands. In November, the ruler agreed to appoint a ten-member inquiry committee, whose three members were to be state officials and the remaining seven nominated by Patel. This committee was charged with, among other things, fixing a limit on the ruler's expenses, and recommending reforms so as to 'give the widest possible powers to [the] people consistent with [the ruler's] obligations to the paramount power and with [his] prerogatives as an adviser'.

However, the Thakore Saheb resiled from this agreement. Of the names sent by Patel, several were claimed not to be residents of Rajkot. Then the ruler and his advisers insisted that there should be representatives of Muslims, the Depressed Classes and the nobility (known as Bhaiyats). The State clearly wanted to ensure that their representatives would have a majority in the committee.

After the ruler reneged on his promise, a satyagraha was organized, in which Patel's daughter Manibehn was arrested. Kasturba was close to Manibehn, whom she saw as akin to a daughter, and of course, through her husband she had her own strong ties to Rajkot. She was keen to join the struggle in the state, and after some hesitation, Gandhi agreed to let her go. Soon after she entered the state, Kasturba was placed under detention, prompting her husband to go to Rajkot himself.[11]

Gandhi arrived in Rajkot on 27 February 1939. In his first week there, he spoke to a wide cross section of the population. He paid special attention to the groups that had stayed away from the struggle: Hindu landlords with large holdings, Muslims and the Depressed Classes. He also met the British Resident and members of the Durbar.

Gandhi had hoped that as a result of his intervention, the Thakore Saheb of Rajkot would honour his promise to Vallabhbhai Patel, by ensuring peasant leaders majority representation in the arbitration committee. When he did not, Gandhi went on a fast (his first for almost five years), which began on 3 March. Kasturba was allowed to spend the days with him, going back in the evenings to her detention camp. On the 6th, she was released, so as to be with him day and night.

The fast ran for four days. It was called off on the 7th after the viceroy personally intervened in the dispute. Linlithgow prevailed upon the Thakore Saheb to agree to the appointment of the Chief Justice of India, Sir Maurice Gwyer, as an arbitrator between the State and the protesters. It was agreed that Gwyer's decision on who would staff the arbitration committee would be final.

During Gandhi's fast, the viceroy in Delhi, and the secretary of state in London, were besieged with telegrams asking them to intervene and save Gandhi's life. These pleas came from, among others, the Marwari Chamber of Commerce, the Indian Cotton Association and the Bombay Assembly Congress Association. G.D. Birla sent a personal telegram to the secretary of state saying that if Gandhi were to die, it would 'be disaster [of the] first magnitude both to India and Empire'.[12]

The British press covered Gandhi's fast extensively, its comments ranging from the sceptical and sneering to the pejorative and hostile. The *Daily Telegraph* claimed Gandhi was attempting 'to substitute suicide for discussion'. The *Birmingham Post* remarked that 'nowadays Mr. Gandhi seems less than ever to need provocation to martyrdom'. The *Glasgow Herald* observed that the fast proves yet again 'how difficult saints are to deal with in the days of their flesh— especially when they choose to exercise their saintliness in the sphere of politics'.

Amidst this general tone of suspicion, an editorial in the *News Chronicle* stood out. Entitled 'BEYOND THE SWORD', it ran:

> Mr. Gandhi's fast, undertaken to secure democratic reforms from the ruler of Rajkot State, has ended in a settlement which is not merely a great personal triumph but a remarkable victory for the method of passive resistance.

Unlike violence, personal sacrifice tends to have a disarming effect on those to whom it is directed and breeds conciliation. The Viceroy would never have intervened in so conciliatory a way if Mr. Gandhi had led an armed attack on Rajkot State.

It is not a method which can be applied at the moment in Western Europe, but we cannot afford to forget that in the long run it is the human spirit that triumphs, not the sword.[13]

This was a brilliant summation of the philosophy behind Gandhian satyagraha. By suffering oneself, and drawing attention to that suffering, a protester could open up a channel of communication with his or her adversaries. To be sure, satyagraha could not be used against Hitler in Germany. But in normal times, normal places and against normal rulers, as a means of protest it was always more moral, and often more effective, than violence.

IV

From Rajkot, Gandhi went to Delhi, where he met with the viceroy. They discussed the stand-off in Rajkot, and the broader question of what role the princes could play in a future All-India Federation. Linlithgow told Gandhi that the Congress 'must carefully avoid frightening the Princes or driving them into a panic. They were a very stiff proposition.' The viceroy's notes of the meeting continue: 'I took the opportunity to remark to Mr. Gandhi that he had criticised me a great deal over the appointment of British Dewans. I must frankly tell him that I found it quite impossible to find Indians of the requisite quality. He said he was quite unable to agree with that . . .'

Gandhi had criticized British diwans for their distance, linguistic and cultural, from the subjects of the states, and for their partiality to the Raj. In defending them so determinedly, while disparaging Indians in the same position, did Linlithgow know that Gandhi himself was the son and grandson of diwans? If he did, it was an extraordinarily insensitive thing to say.

Linlithgow and Gandhi also discussed the idea of 'Pakistan', now being talked about in the Muslim League circles. Coined in 1933 by a

Cambridge student called Choudhry Rahmat Ali, the term expanded on the idea suggested by Muhammad Iqbal in his Muslim League presidential address of 1930, in recommending a sovereign Muslim state in the north-west of British India. 'P' stood for Punjab, 'A' for the 'Afghan Province' of British India (i.e., the NWFP), 'K' for Kashmir, and 'S' for Sindh, with the last four letters denoting both 'state' in Urdu as well as the fifth province to be included in this future nation, Baluchistan. Moreover, 'Pakistan' also meant 'Land of the Pure' in both Urdu and Persian.

Linlithgow later noted that 'before we concluded I thought it well to mention the Pakistan project to him [Gandhi] and to ask him whether he thought it had any life in it. He said he understood not; but that that might come. I replied that I had in mind to give the idea an airing very soon in my own way and get it out of the way. Mr. Gandhi said he was sure that it was the right course; that he doubted if it would stand any detailed examination though it no doubt had wide possibilities. I asked whether by that he meant that it might represent an upsurge running back into the depths of the Muslim world. He said that that might indeed be the case, in certain circumstances, but that even if Pakistan admitted of realisation it could never settle the communal question in India or represent more than a sharp division which might in due course give rise to a major calamity.'[14]

V

Because of his preoccupations in Rajkot, Gandhi had missed the annual session of the Congress, held that year in Tripuri, in the Central Provinces. The session reflected the growing split within the party. The so-called 'Old Guard', led by the United Provinces prime minister, Govind Ballabh Pant, were determined to push Subhas Bose towards resigning as president. At Tripuri, Pant introduced a resolution whose operative sentence was as follows: 'In view of the critical situation that may develop during the coming year and in view of the fact that Mahatma Gandhi alone can lead the Congress and the country during such crisis, the [All India Congress] Committee regards it as imperative that the Congress executive should command his implicit confidence and requests the President to nominate the Working Committee in accordance with the wishes of Gandhiji.'

Bose was, in effect, being asked to renominate members who had resigned in February. But how could a president function with a working committee with whose members he had such sharp differences of opinion?

Bose's elder brother, Sarat Chandra Bose, wrote a hurt letter to Gandhi. Meanwhile, Subhas Bose had fallen ill. Writing to Subhas on 24 March, Gandhi denied he had anything to do with Pant's resolution. Then he added these decidedly ambiguous lines: 'The initiative lies with you. I do not know how far you are fit to attend to national work. If you are not, I think you should adopt the only constitutional course open to you.'

Bose replied that the initiative for uniting the party lay with Gandhi, not with him. He told Gandhi that 'the main problem appears to me as to whether both parties can forget the past and work together. That depends entirely on you. If you can command the confidence of both parties by taking up a truly non-partisan attitude, then you can save the Congress and restore national unity.'

Bose also rejected the suggestion that he step down because of poor health. He had 'not the slightest desire to stick to office', yet did not 'see any reason for resigning because I am ill. No President resigned when he was in prison . . .'

Two days later, Bose wrote to Gandhi again. Once more, he said that while there was a wide gulf between the two factions, Gandhi alone could bridge it. 'It is in your hands to save the Congress and the country,' he wrote. 'People who are bitterly opposed for various reasons to Sardar Patel and his group, still have confidence in you and believe that you can take a dispassionate and non-partisan view of things. To them you are a national figure—above parties and groups—and you can, therefore, restore unity between the warring elements. If for any reason that confidence is shaken—which God forbid—and you are regarded as a partisan, then God help us and the Congress.'[15]

Bose was correct in identifying Vallabhbhai Patel as his main opponent within the party. The two had an old rivalry, at once personal and political. Their relationship rapidly deteriorated after the death of Vallabhbhai's elder brother Vithalbhai in 1933. Bose had nursed Vithalbhai during his last illness. In his will, the elder Patel left three-fourths of his estate to Bose, to be used 'preferably for publicity work on behalf of India's cause in other countries'. Vallabhbhai now cast aspersions on the authenticity of the will. A long legal battle ensued, which ended in a triumph for Vallabhbhai, with Vithalbhai's next of kin getting the money instead of Subhas.

This familial history apart, Patel was also opposed to Bose's militant socialism. When, in 1938, Gandhi decided to propose Bose's name for the presidency of the Congress, Patel opposed it. Gandhi overruled his objection. In 1939, when Bose sought a second term, Patel opposed him again, unsuccessfully. 'I never dreamt,' wrote Patel to Rajendra Prasad, 'that he [Subhas] will stoop to such dirty mean tactics for re-election.' In another letter, he told Prasad that 'it is impossible for us to work with Subhas'. The resignation of the working committee members in February, and Pant's resolution at Tripuri in March, were both approved of—if not instigated by—Patel.[16]

In his letters to Gandhi in the last week of March, Subhas Bose urged him to take a more adversarial stance towards the Raj. The international crisis had convinced Bose that 'the time has come to force the issue of *purna swaraj*'. But Gandhi, he complained, was 'obsessed with the idea of corruption within the Congress. Moreover, the bogey of violence alarms you.' Bose wanted the Congress to issue an ultimatum to the British; and if (as expected) it was not met, to resign from their ministries and launch a full-fledged agitation for freedom. He told Gandhi that he was 'so confident, and so optimistic on this point, that I feel that if we take courage in both hands and go ahead, we shall have swaraj inside of 18 months at the most'.

Replying to Bose, Gandhi said that he should form his own working committee, formulate its programme and place this before the AICC. If the AICC accepted his programme, then Bose could 'prosecute it unhampered by the minority'. If it was rejected, however, Bose should resign and make way for a new president.

In his letter, Gandhi made clear his disagreement with Bose on the political route he had proposed. He himself saw 'no atmosphere for non-violent mass action'. Gandhi told Bose that 'I smell violence in the air I breathe. But the violence has put on a subtle form. Our mutual distrust is a bad form of violence. The widening gulf points to the same thing.'[17]

Subhas Bose's own commitment to non-violence was less than certain. In his book *The Indian Struggle* (first published in 1935), he had criticized Gandhi for encouraging India's 'inordinate belief in fate and the supernatural—her indifference to modern scientific development—her backwardness in the science of modern warfare, the peaceful contentment engendered by her latter-day philosophy and adherence to Ahimsa carried to the most absurd length'. While praising Gandhi's purity of character and the struggles he had led, Bose was clear that he had to be superseded. As he wrote: 'Mahatma Gandhi has rendered and will continue to render phenomenal service to his country. But India's salvation will not be achieved under his leadership.'[18]

His fair-minded biographer, Leonard Gordon, writes that 'Bose felt that in her struggle against the British, India needed a strong, vigorous, military-type leader—perhaps even himself—not a hesitating, confused, reformist guru'.[19] By no means an instinctive democrat, Subhas Bose thought that 'the next phase of world-history will produce a synthesis between Communism and Fascism'.[20]

Behind the ideological differences, there was also a provincial rivalry at play. A letter signed by seventy-five men from Bengal was addressed to 'Mr Gandhi', since the angry Bengalis 'cannot but betray our conscience to address you as the "Mahatma" considering the inconceivable meanness and the vindictive sordidness shown by you and your followers' (in seeking to unseat Bose). Gandhi and Patel were accused of 'shameless hankering after power and underhand plotting', and of a long-held prejudice against Bengal as when Gandhi 'vehemently opposed Deshbandhu [C.R.] Das' in 1923, and opposed Bose's resolution for complete independence in 1928.[21]

The greatest Bengali of his age also chose (once more) to bat for Subhas Bose. Thus, Rabindranath Tagore telegraphed Gandhi: 'At the last Congress session some rude hands have deeply hurt Bengal with ungracious persistence. Please apply without delay balm to the wound with your own kind hands and prevent it from festering.'

Gandhi wrote back saying that 'the problem [was] difficult', and he had made some suggestions to Bose to find a way out of the impasse.[22]

In early April, Bose wrote to Gandhi again, this time proposing a 'composite' working committee including members of both factions. But behind the offer of compromise a deep sense of hurt remained. 'There is a world of difference,' wrote Bose to Gandhi, 'between yourself and your lieutenants, even your chosen lieutenants.' He claimed that at the Tripuri Congress, which Gandhi had to miss, 'the Old Guard cleverly dropped out of the picture and more cleverly pitted me against you'. Gandhi answered that Bose's suspicions about the 'Old Guard' were unjustified. 'Nobody put me up against you,' he remarked. 'You are wrong if you think that you have a single personal enemy among the Old Guard.'[23]

Apart from Subhas Bose and Gandhi, the person who read their correspondence most attentively was Mahadev Desai. He opened Bose's letters before passing them on to Gandhi, and helped Gandhi in drafting his replies. In mid-April, after a month of these increasingly contentious exchanges, Mahadev wrote to a friend that 'his [Bose's] behaviour and his endless letters in which he contradicts himself are enough to try the patience of a Job'.[24] One suspects that, on the other side, Subhas Bose's own closest confidant, his elder brother Sarat, saw it quite differently. Gandhi's stubbornness could be very trying too.

Since he came out of jail in August 1933, Gandhi's principal concern had been with the abolition of untouchability. He paid some attention to rural renewal, some (as always) to Hindu–Muslim harmony, but from the day-to-day affairs of the Congress Party he was now somewhat removed. These were largely in the hands of his two trusted lieutenants, Nehru and Patel.

Subhas Bose's bid for re-election brought Gandhi back into active involvement—perhaps we should say interference—in Congress politics. While Gandhi had personal affection for the Bengali leader, he was not nearly as close to him as to Patel or Nehru. Patel he could absolutely depend upon in all circumstances. Nehru and he often disagreed on political questions, but their personal ties were so close that these, in the end, overrode ideological differences. At the crunch, the younger man generally deferred to Gandhi's judgement.

Like Nehru, Subhas Bose was on the Left in a political and economic sense. Like Nehru again, his personality and ideas greatly appealed to the young. However, while Bose admired Gandhi, he was not deferential towards him. Both Nehru and Patel would have been incapable of the direct, personal challenge that Bose had now mounted against Gandhi.

VI

On 9 April, Gandhi returned to Rajkot, spending two weeks seeking a solution to what was now a prolonged dispute. He met leaders of the Muslims and the Depressed Classes, groups somewhat distant from the Congress.

While Gandhi was in Rajkot, B.R. Ambedkar arrived in the town. He met the Thakore Saheb, representatives of the Depressed Classes, and then Gandhi himself. On coming out of their meeting, Ambedkar told a reporter that 'Mahatma Gandhi still persists in using arguments which I am accustomed to hear from him from before the Poona Pact, namely that he or the Congress represented all'.[25]

A rumour was abroad that Jinnah too would soon come to Rajkot, and conduct a rival fast on behalf of the state's Muslims. The Bombay correspondent of the *Manchester Guardian* even claimed that 'a number of rich Bombay Indians have booked [hotel] rooms at Rajkot in the hope of seeing Mr. Gandhi and Mr. Jinnah, who are bitter political rivals, fasting on adjacent beds'.[26]

The story was without foundation. Jinnah was not a man to miss his morning or evening meal in any case. Interviewed in Sholapur, Jinnah said 'a large body of Hindus, untutored and unsophisticated are being exploited by the Congress by giving them the impression that they are fighting for a Hindu raj'. Jinnah deplored 'the wrongheaded policy pursued by the Congress in the last eighteen months in and outside legislatures', a policy which, in his view, had 'led to a complete estrangement between the two communities and created intense bitterness'. For the Muslims, said Jinnah, 'the moral is obvious. We have to organize and when we begin to count ourselves in crores instead of lakhs the Paramount Power would be awakened to their sense of responsibilities towards the Muslims.'[27]

Gandhi's own trip to Rajkot had not been a success. His conversations with Muslims and Bhaiyats were unfruitful. The former viewed the Congress with suspicion; the latter were bound to the Thakore Saheb by ties of caste and kin. Their reservations came out into the open during one of his prayer meetings, where both Muslims and Bhaiyats waved black flags at Gandhi while shouting slogans in praise of the ruler. Gandhi walked up to the demonstrators and tried to reason with them. The shouting did not stop. After the meeting ended, Gandhi silently but stoically walked back to a waiting car, abuse ringing in his ears.[28]

From Rajkot, Gandhi travelled across the country to Calcutta. In the last week of April, he had long conversations with Subhas Bose, with Jawaharlal Nehru sitting in. But these three days of intense discussion failed to resolve the deadlock. On 29 April, Bose announced that he was resigning from the Congress presidency. In a statement to the press, he described the various attempts at finding a meeting ground with Gandhi. These having failed, he felt his 'presence as President may be a sort of obstacle or handicap in the path' of the Congress as it sought to reconcile its two wings. The statement was uncharacteristically restrained, attracting a letter of praise from Tagore, who wrote to Bose that 'the dignity and forbearance which you have shown in the midst of an aggravating situation has won my admiration and confidence in your leadership. The same perfect decorum has still to be maintained by Bengal for the sake of her own self-respect and thereby to help to turn your apparent defeat into a permanent victory.'[29]

On Subhas Bose's resignation, the old Gandhi loyalist, Rajendra Prasad, was appointed interim president. Bose, writes one biographer, 'was comprehensively outwitted and outmaneuvred by Gandhi in Congress politics during the spring of 1939'.[30] The party had returned to the control of the man who had taken it over in Nagpur two decades ago.

The Congress recaptured, Gandhi went back to the town where he had grown up, graduated from high school, and first lived as a married man. On 17 May, he issued a press statement apologizing for the fast he had undertaken back in March. That had put unfair pressure on the ruler of Rajkot, by bringing the viceroy into the picture. His fast, he said, had been tinged with *himsa*, coercive violence. It had also 'become a potent cause of angering the Muslims and Bhaiyats against me'.

Gandhi now voluntarily renounced the award reached in March, by which the Chief Justice of India was to be the arbiter. He wished the dispute to be settled within the parameters of the state itself. He appealed to the Thakore Saheb and his advisers 'to appease the people of Rajkot by fulfilling their expectations and dispelling their misgivings'.[31]

Why did Gandhi withdraw from the fray in Rajkot? The demonstration against him by Muslims and Bhaiyats had certainly unnerved him. Rajkot was his own state; did he want to push the confrontation further, embarrassing a House his own father had worked for?

Gandhi may have been perfectly sincere when he said that his fast in March had been coercive. He acknowledged a moral lapse. But this may also have been a tactical retreat. Did he want to stake his reputation on a dispute in what, after all, was a small princely state? Would it not adversely affect the larger struggle for self-government in British India? He had just come through an arduous battle of wits with Subhas Bose, which had dented his image among many Bengalis, and many younger Congressmen as well. It seemed unwise to risk further damage to his reputation in Rajkot.

CHAPTER TWENTY-SIX

One Nation, or Two?

I

In March 1939, the Nazis overran what remained of Czechoslovakia. In May, they signed a pact with Italy. In between, the Spanish Civil War had come to an end, with the victory of the authoritarians in uniform.

Gandhi was following these events from afar. On 23 July, he sat down to write a letter to the man who had seeded the war clouds gathering over Europe. 'Friends have been urging me,' said Gandhi to Hitler, 'to write to you for the sake of humanity.' (The friends were unnamed, but they most likely were British pacifists.) So, he made his 'appeal for what it is worth', which was: 'It is quite clear that you are today the one person in the world who can prevent a war which may reduce humanity to the savage state. Must you pay that price for an object however worthy it may appear to you to be? Will you listen to the appeal of one who has deliberately shunned the method of war not without considerable success?'[1]

The letter was withheld by the Government of India. So Hitler did not see it. Whether he would have at all taken it seriously is extremely doubtful. On 1 September, Germany invaded Poland. Two days later, Britain and France finally declared war on Germany. Immediately, the viceroy, Lord Linlithgow, committed the people and resources of India to the Allied war effort.

Gandhi was now asked by the viceroy to meet him in Simla. Afterwards, Gandhi issued a statement to the press. He began by saying that he had met the viceroy as an ordinary Indian, and only the Congress could arrive at an understanding with the government as to what to do next. Gandhi added that, on his part, 'I told His Excellency that my own sympathies were with England and France from the purely humanitarian standpoint. I told him that I could not contemplate without being stirred to the very depth the destruction of London which has hitherto been regarded as impregnable. And as I was picturing before him the Houses of Parliament and the Westminster Abbey and their possible destruction, I broke down.'[2]

For all his opposition to British imperialism, Gandhi was deeply attached to London. He had lived in the city for long stretches— between 1888 and 1891, in 1906, 1909, 1914, and (most recently) 1931. He had walked through most of its boroughs. He had many friends in the city, and quite a few admirers. The grief he expressed in public, about the prospect of London being bombed, was manifestly sincere. As Linlithgow's personal secretary later recalled: 'Mr. Gandhi came to see the Viceroy in Simla at the outbreak of war and I remember vividly how he told me of his grief at what had happened, and his sorrow at the thought of the destruction that might come to so many landmarks familiar to him . . .'[3]

Gandhi's sympathy for the English people was not matched, at least on the viceroy's part, with a corresponding sympathy for Indian hopes and aspirations. After their meeting, Linlithgow assured London that he had told Gandhi that 'there was not any commitment of any sort [on Indian self-government] that I could enter into as regards the future'. Meanwhile, Linlithgow was 'anxious to shepherd all the Muslims into the same fold so far as the prosecution of the War is concerned', adding that 'the Princely response has been as good as one would have expected it to be'. Clearly, the viceroy was shoring up support from quarters other than the Congress, seeking to marginalize the main party of Indian politics.[4]

In the second week of September, the CWC met in Wardha to consider the European war and its fallout. Its resolution, drafted by Jawaharlal Nehru, began by pointing out, first, that the viceroy and the colonial government had committed India and Indians to the war without their consent, and had also used their emergency powers to impose substantial curbs on the elected provincial governments; and, second, that the Congress had for its part 'repeatedly declared its entire disapproval of the ideology and practice of Fascism and Nazism and their glorification of war and violence and the suppression of the human spirit'.

The resolution drafted by Nehru continued: 'If the war is to defend the status quo—imperialist possessions, colonies, vested interests and privileges—then India can have nothing to do with it. If, however, the issue is democracy and a world order based on democracy, then India is intensely interested in it.' If Great Britain genuinely wished to promote and protect democracy, the Congress argued, then it must end imperialism in her own possessions, and facilitate a Constituent Assembly where Indians would design their own constitution, paving the way for the establishment of full democracy in India and other colonies.

The CWC asked the British government for a clear declaration of what their war aims were. If it declared that these aims included the 'elimination of imperialism and the treatment of India as a free nation', then the Congress was 'prepared to give their co-operation'.

Jawaharlal Nehru was a long-standing critic of both fascism and Nazism. In 1933, he had written that after Mussolini came to power in Italy, 'an extraordinary orgy of violence and terrorism took place'. There was 'repression and arrests on a large scale'. Fascism, wrote Nehru, had 'the unique distinction of having no fixed principles, no ideology, no philosophy behind it'; what it had instead was 'a definite technique of violence and terrorism'.

In the same year, 1933, Nehru had observed that 'you will find all the elements of fascism in Hitlerism', such as 'a savage attack on all liberal elements and especially workers'. Behind the 'intensely nationalistic' programme of Nazism, he continued, 'lay an extraordinary philosophy of violence'. What was 'unique' about the Nazi terror, noted Nehru, was that it was 'not an outcome of passion and fear, but a deliberate, cold-blooded, and incredibly brutal suppression of all who did not fall in line with the Nazis'. So there had been 'savage beatings and tortures and shooting and murder on a vast scale, both men and women being victims. . . . Enormous numbers of people have been put in gaols and concentration camps . . .'[5]

In the same year, 1933, that Nehru excoriated fascism and Nazism, Winston Churchill described Mussolini as 'the Roman genius . . . the greatest lawgiver among living men'. The two men had met several times, and considered each other friends. Churchill was convinced the Duce had restored order to an anarchic country, and brought hope to its poor and divided people.[6]

Churchill was, of course, less sympathetically disposed towards Hitler. Yet, many other British politicians admired Hitler for having united the Germans and given them a sense of national purpose. The former Liberal Prime Minister David Lloyd George called Hitler 'a great man'. The former Labour Foreign Secretary Arthur Henderson thought Hitler was 'sincerely pacific'. And there was a long list of Conservative Party grandees who not only praised Hitler but rushed to Berlin to meet him after he took power. They saw him both as a friend of Britain, and as a bulwark against communism.[7]

On the other side, Nehru's own views were widely shared by Congressmen. The head of the party's foreign affairs cell, Ram Manohar Lohia, was a political scientist trained in Berlin, where he had seen the rise of the Nazis at first-hand. As a left-wing radical, he had to flee the country after Hitler took power. Other leading Congress socialists, such as Jayaprakash Narayan, were implacably opposed to both Hitler and Mussolini. So was Mahadev Desai, who kept himself up to date with international affairs.

The leaders of the Congress were, from the first, struck by the hypocrisy of the British claim that by going to war with Hitler, they were defending democracy and freedom. When the British (and the French) had denied freedom and democracy to their colonial subjects in Asia and Africa, how could they claim to be consistently in favour of these values? If they wanted credibility for their war against Hitler, said the Congress, then the British should at once commit themselves to granting full freedom to the colonies they controlled.

In a statement to the press on the working committee resolution, Gandhi pointed out that its author, Nehru, was, notwithstanding his 'implacable opposition to imperialism in any shape or form', a 'friend of the English people'. He was an 'ardent nationalist' whose 'nationalism is enriched by his fine internationalism'. Endorsing the resolution wholeheartedly, Gandhi hoped for 'a mental revolution on the part of British statesmen'. Will Great Britain, he asked, 'have an unwilling India dragged into the war or a willing ally co-operating with her in the prosecution of a defence of true democracy? The Congress support will mean the greatest moral asset in favour of England and France.'[8]

By offering moral and material support to Britain in its war with Germany, the Congress was abandoning its doctrinal commitment to non-violence. While Gandhi might still wish to preach ahimsa, his party (under Nehru's urgings) had decided that the dangers of a Nazi triumph were too great for them to go along with his views in this regard. This was a significant change of perspective, a climbdown even; but the viceroy, unfortunately, did not see it this way. He rejected the Congress's offer of cooperation since it came with the condition that independence be granted to India once the war was won.

The industrialist G.D. Birla, who kept in close touch with both the viceroy and Gandhi's party, thought the former bore principal responsibility for the breach between the government and the Congress. 'Lord Linlithgow's tragic failure to consult the Legislature before forcing India into the War immediately on its outbreak,' he wrote, 'was too strong a dose for the [Congress] Ministers to swallow. . . . Had the Viceroy the wisdom to consult India I doubt not that she would have supported Britain.' He added: 'The blunder made by Lord Linlithgow in not even going through the motions of appearing to consult the Legislature, or Indian public opinion, before declaring India a belligerent seemed irretrievable.'[9]

II

Gandhi's seventieth birthday by the Christian calendar fell on 2 October 1939. Some months previously, the philosopher Sarvepalli Radhakrishnan had set in motion the preparation of a collection of essays in his honour. Radhakrishnan was an admired teacher at Mysore, Calcutta, Andhra and Oxford Universities, as well as the author of many books published in India and the West. He canvassed widely for contributions to this Gandhi Festschrift he was editing. Some famous people refused; such as J.M. Keynes and H.G. Wells, the latter saying: 'I will not write a line to boost up that old publicity bore.'[10]

Other famous people sent in tributes. They included the Nobel laureates Albert Einstein, Pearl S. Buck and Romain Rolland. In his contribution, the Spanish writer-diplomat Salvador de Madariaga termed Gandhi 'the most symbolic man of our day', while the Japanese poet Yone Noguchi remarked that 'Gandhi cannot find any higher way of worshipping God than by serving the poor and identifying with them'. The scholar Ananda Coomaraswamy submitted a learned disquisition on the many meanings of the term 'Mahatma'. In his article, the Labour politician George Lansbury said Gandhi 'has demonstrated in his own life and the lives of his many millions of friends and supporters in India and elsewhere the mighty strength of Passive, Non-violent Resistance against every form of evil and wrong-doing'.

Quakers and Theosophists were well represented among the contributors. Gandhi's close friends Charlie Andrews, Henry Polak and Rabindranath Tagore also sent tributes. The sole Muslim contributor was the diwan of Mysore, Sir Mirza Ismail, who called the Mahatma 'a force for moderation, for reason, for practicality in politics', adding that his message of peace and reconciliation should be heeded by warring communities within India, as well as warring countries elsewhere. In his own introduction to the volume, Radhakrishnan said that despite his public profile as a politician and reformer, Gandhi was 'an essentially religious person endowed with the highest and most human qualities and made more lovable by the consciousness of his own limitations and by an unfailing sense of humour'.

Among the longer and more perceptive pieces was one from the Liberal politician Herbert Samuel. Samuel admitted to being often exasperated by Gandhi, who had a habit of saying things that seemed 'unreasonable and perverse'. But, since the British were 'a self-respecting people' who 'respect self-respect in others', he had to acknowledge that, notwithstanding his strange language and stranger methods, Gandhi had 'taught the Indian to straighten his back, to raise his eyes, to face circumstance with steady gaze'. Moreover, 'in this fuller dignity, in this stronger striving, he showed it to be vital that the women of India should also share'. As well as the so-called 'untouchables', for, as Samuel remarked, Gandhi had done a 'great service . . . to take up, with vigour and power, the cause of the depressed classes; to bring it into the forefront of Indian politics; and to set it well on the road to success'.

Some contributions came in from South Africa, among them a pungent piece by Jan Christian Smuts. Between 1906 and 1913, General Smuts had, as a senior minister in the Transvaal and Union governments, several times ordered the arrest of the Indian leader. Now, a quarter of a century later, Smuts recalled how Gandhi's early satyagrahas, raising 'a most troublesome issue', were 'very trying to me', creating 'a wild and disconcerting commotion', to control which 'large numbers of Indians had to be imprisoned for lawless behaviour and Gandhi himself received—what no doubt he desired—a short period of rest and quiet in gaol'.

At first sight 'remote from the ways of democracy and indeed of Western civilisation', Gandhi's technique, argued Smuts, carried echoes of 'the Great Sufferer on the Cross', reminding Christians of their own first martyrs and protesters. Gandhi's 'distinctive contribution to political method', said his old adversary, was to make 'himself a sufferer in order to move the sympathy and gain the support of others for the cause he has at heart. Where ordinary political methods of reasoning and persuasion fail, he falls back on this new technique, based on the ancient practices of India and the East.'[11]

Radhakrishnan had hoped to present this volume to Gandhi on 2 October 1939. But shortly before that date, war had broken out in Europe. The book was published anyway, at a time when its honorand's distinctive contribution to political method seemed increasingly irrelevant to global affairs.

III

On 17 October—six weeks after taking India into the war—the viceroy finally made a statement of his government's political agenda and intentions. This was long, rambling and—from the Congress point of view—unpromising. Linlithgow praised the 1935 Act as a model of constitutional progress, and hoped that it could be built upon so that 'India may attain its due place among the Dominions'. The viceroy had been authorized by His Majesty's Government 'to say at the end of the war they will be very willing to enter into consultations with representatives of the several communities, parties and interests, in India, and with the Indian Princes, with a view to securing their aid and co-operation in the framing of such modifications [of the 1935 Act] as may seem desirable'.

Linlithgow was temperamentally disinclined to granting more political rights to India in any case. Moreover, the Congress notwithstanding, many Indians were signing up to enlist to fight on the side of Britain. The Punjab and the Frontier Province, which had provided close to 4,00,000 soldiers for the First World War, provided fertile recruiting ground this time too. Other volunteers came from the south and the west of India. Even the traditionally 'non-martial' Bengalis were sending soldiers to the front. Notably, Muslims were more likely to volunteer than Hindus, and lower-caste Hindus more likely than upper-caste Hindus.[12]

The viceroy, alerted to this flow of recruits, was further encouraged to withhold the assurance of freedom the Congress had asked for. The party's working committee, meeting in Wardha, said Linlithgow's statement was 'wholly unsatisfactory and calculated to rouse resentment among all those who are anxious to gain, and are intent on gaining, India's independence'. They asked the Congress ministries to tender their resignations in protest.

Later, speaking to the *Times of India*, Gandhi underlined that 'what the Congress wants is the clearest possible acceptance of the fact that India is to be treated as an independent nation. For India to become enthusiastic about participation in this war it is necessary to speak to her in the language of precision, admitting of no other meaning.' He was also dismayed at 'how the minorities are being played against the Congress'. The Congress stood for a representative Constituent Assembly, in which 'the Muslims, the Scheduled Classes and every other class will be fully represented . . . and they will have to decide their own special rights.'

On 23 October—a week after the viceroy's declaration—Gandhi cabled a statement for the world's press, which was carried in the *New York Times*, the *Daily Herald*, *Paris-Soir* and other papers across Europe and in Soviet Russia and Japan too. This clarified that the 'Congress had demanded no constitutional change during [the] war'. Rather, it had asked for a 'declaration that Britain's war aims necessarily include India's independence according to the charter framed by her elected representatives after [the] war'.

The growing estrangement between the government and the Congress was not helped by Lord Zetland, the secretary of state for India, claiming in the House of Lords that the Congress was merely a 'Hindu organization'. Gandhi was moved to protest, telling the *Manchester Guardian* that Zetland's 'misdescription of the Congress is untimely, disturbing and calculated to increase irritation and bitterness' (as it did). There could not, he said, be a 'grosser libel' than calling the Congress a communal organization. The party had been founded by an Englishman, and since had Muslim, Christian and Parsi presidents. Even now, it had several important Muslim leaders; indeed, 'today the Working Committee does not move without Maulana Abul Kalam Azad's co-operation and wise guidance'.

Gandhi insisted that 'the Congress embodies the hope and aspirations of India. . . . Its traditions unfit it to represent Hindus as against Muslims or vice versa.'[13]

IV

On 27 October 1939, the Congress ministries resigned. The next day, the outgoing prime minister of Madras, C. Rajagopalachari, wrote Mahadev Desai a long letter unburdening himself of a growing difference between himself and their common mentor. This concerned relations between Hindus and Muslims. Rajaji was not as sanguine as Gandhi on the subject. He believed that the Congress had in fact lost a large measure of Muslim support. As he wrote to Mahadev:

> Whatever may be the motives and the deft exploitation by the British
> people of the Hindu–Muslim cleft, the fact must be recognised

that today the ablest and most disinterested leaders of the Muslim community have led their entire people to feel that they stand apart and must continue to stand apart from the Hindu population. It is not flatterers and office seekers, but a man like Jinnah that have made up the Muslim mind in this direction and we cannot afford to deceive ourselves by proceeding on the assumption that the Muslim leaders are tools of the British. The British may use them, but the decision is their own, and cannot be brushed aside as a corollary of British wickedness.

How should the Congress respond to this growing Muslim consolidation? Rajaji sensed that Gandhi was considering a fresh campaign of civil disobedience against the British, a move he was decidedly against. Such a campaign, he argued, would 'only widen the cleft. We may secure . . . success in the programme against the British, but it cannot solve the problem as against the Muslim leaders and their social following, unless indeed we envisage complete anarchy and civil war . . .'

Rajaji hoped that Gandhi, and the Congress, would think instead of a programme that could evoke appreciation and trust instead of jealousy and fear among the Muslims.[14]

Of the major leaders of the Congress, Rajaji was on this question the most alert, pragmatic and unsentimental. For Patel, Kripalani and Rajendra Prasad, Hindu–Muslim relations had never been a principal concern. Nehru's socialism made him assume that economic interests would override communal ties, so poor Muslims would have more in common with poor Hindus than with their affluent co-religionists. Gandhi himself looked nostalgically back to the Khilafat movement and to the struggles he led in South Africa, where he had succeeded in bringing Hindus and Muslims on a common platform. True, they had since become somewhat estranged; but could they not, if he worked hard enough, come together again?

It is not clear whether Mahadev showed Gandhi Rajaji's letter (there is no reference to it in the *Collected Works*). Since it was addressed to him and not to Gandhi, perhaps he did not. Nor is it clear either, whether Gandhi saw all of the angry letters from Muslims themselves, addressed directly to him, that were pouring into Segaon.

Back in the 1920s, Gandhi had read and replied to almost every letter he got; now, however, as his incoming correspondence grew ever larger, he was much more selective. He had even issued an appeal through the pages of *Harijan*, asking Indians not to burden him with too much correspondence. He had neither 'the time nor the energy' to cope with it.[15]

In the circumstances, it was left to Mahadev and Pyarelal to sift through the correspondence and decide which letters to place before Gandhi. They were assisted by Amrit Kaur, and by Sushila Nayar, a medical doctor (and sister of Pyarelal's) who had become an integral part of Gandhi's entourage.

Many Muslims wrote to Gandhi in these years, expressing discontent with the Congress and sometimes with him personally. The president of the Muslim League in the southern town of Bezwada wrote complaining about the installation by the local Congress of a Gandhi statue in a park in a predominantly Muslim locality, this when 'statues [and] idols offend [the] Muslim religion'. Five of his colleagues wrote a separate letter, complaining that portraits of Gandhi had been put up in town schools, offending the 'religious sentiments' of Muslims whose children studied there. 'It would amount to nothing short of religious tyranny,' wrote the protesters, 'if the majority community, being in possession of power, forces the Muslims to show respect and reverence to Mr. Gandhi and adopt his preachings which are opposed to Islamic religion and are injurious to the young and impressionable minds of the Muslim pupils.'[16]

Even Gandhi's attempts to positively invoke the Koran in his writings and prayer meetings invited protest. 'Can't you realise,' wrote a research scholar in Aligarh to Gandhi, 'that nothing can offend the religious susceptibilities of a Mussalman more than to see a non-Muslim citing the scriptures for his own purpose? Well, the Mussalmans have had thirteen centuries to know what the Koran teaches and to practice what it means. The Muslims, of course, do not need a Mahatma to interpret their own holy book.'[17]

Muslims in Gandhi's own party were worried about the deepening alienation of their co-religionists from the Congress. A Congressman in Lahore complained that too few Muslims were nominated to the boards of the All India Spinners Association and the Harijan Sewak

Sangh. Although such representation would help in 'politicizing the Muslim masses and bringing them into the Congress fold', in practice, 'the Hindu Nationalists who are managing and governing these institutions have scrupulously tried their utmost to prevent the inclusion of Muslim nationalists . . .' Meanwhile, a Muslim legislator from the Central Provinces told Gandhi that in his area, the Congress was hand in glove with the Arya Samaj and the Hindu Mahasabha in taunting and provoking Muslims, by playing music before mosques, etc. 'It is time Gandhiji that you cry a halt,' he urged. 'If you don't patch up the Hindu Muslim differences I would think that your whole life of noble ideas and constructive genius was a gruesome failure.'[18]

These letters were, it seems, not shown to Gandhi by his secretaries. But some others were. A League legislator sent Gandhi a news clipping about a recent firing by the United Provinces police on a meeting of a Muslim militant group known as the Khaksars. The writer bitterly complained that while 'Hindu and Muslims fought shoulder to shoulder in the old days of freedom', now 'Muslims can only serve as targets for rifle practice'. Comparing the United Provinces government to the Nazis, likewise an example of 'militant aggrandizement in action', he asked: 'How long is this reign of terror for Muslims to last in U. P.; is there to be any deliverance; is U. P. to remain an inferno for the Muslims, you and you alone can answer.'[19]

Gandhi sent a brief reply. 'Your letter is bad, unbalanced and full of anger,' he began. Then, in a more conciliatory tone, he added: 'I quite agree with you that resort to firing is not non-violent action.' He asked the correspondent to write to the United Provinces government 'to find out the true position'.[20]

Among the many letters from Muslims that Gandhi received in this period, perhaps the most telling was from Dr Zakir Husain, the vice chancellor of the nationalist Muslim university, the Jamia Millia, and a man for whom the Mahatma had enormous respect. In November 1939, on returning from a long trip to Europe, Zakir Husain found that in his absence relations between Hindus and Muslims had rapidly deteriorated. Meanwhile, the stock of the Muslim League had steadily appreciated. Dr Husain urged Gandhi to recognize and deal with this changed scenario. 'Many a lover of India,' he wrote, is looking up to you for a solution of the Hindu Muslim problem which has become the central problem of our political life. . . . If I were you, Bapuji (what an idea!) I would unhesitatingly deal with the Muslim League as the representative of Muslim interests in India and give them what they want. I could never give them too much, and there would be nothing to lose and everything to gain. All the aberrations born of mutual suspicion and deep-rooted prejudice will be brushed aside at a stroke and the whole atmosphere in the country would lose its present suffocating weight—we would all breathe more freely and be able, perhaps, to plan something really good even if not very great.

To this anguished plea, Gandhi replied, 'I am trying my best,' adding: 'But you should come and help me. It is worthwhile your coming here [to Segaon] for that one purpose!'[21]

Zakir Husain did not accept the invitation. He was a scholar, not an activist. He had diagnosed the problem as he saw it; and now looked to Gandhi to solve it.

V

Individual Muslims complained to Gandhi in private; Muslim leaders and Muslim newspapers attacked Gandhi in public. Representative was an editorial carried in a pro-League newspaper published from Calcutta, two weeks after the Congress ministries had resigned from office. This recalled Muhammad Iqbal's speech of 1930, which had argued that the problem in India was not national but international. Any solution must therefore 'accord the fullest political accommodation to the Muslim Community'. However, remarked the newspaper: 'The Totalitarian Junta of Wardha is still far from seeing this light. They have not descended from the starry heavens of sickly metaphysics.'[22]

Gandhi's old adversary B.R. Ambedkar had also entered the debate. In an interview with the Associated Press, Ambedkar claimed that 'the Minorities' problem will never be solved unless Mr Gandhi and the Congress give up their egoistic and insolent attitude towards persons and parties outside the Congress. Patriotism is not a monopoly of the Congressmen . . .' Ambedkar hoped that 'wisdom and statesmanship will dawn on the Congress in time to prevent India being divided into two parts and Scheduled Classes merging themselves with a powerful and influential Minority'. This was a veiled (or perhaps not so veiled) threat that if his criticisms were not heeded, Ambedkar would enter into a compact with the Muslim League.[23]

The Muslim League had charged the Congress with oppressing the Muslims in the provinces where they had ruled. Their grievances, real or imaginary, accurate or embellished, had been articulated in a report they had commissioned. Now, in a brilliant tactical move, Jinnah decided to celebrate the resignation of the Congress ministries as a 'Deliverance Day' for Muslims. The terminology was intriguing; for, after the Congress demitted office, the powers reverted entirely to the British governor and his senior officials, almost all also British. In Jinnah's mind, the Muslims of India were far better off being governed by the British than by the Congress.

Jinnah chose to mark 22 December 1939 as 'Deliverance Day'. It was a Friday, the day Muslims went to pray at the mosque, the day of the week when they would be most likely to come out and support their community.

On 21 December, the viceroy wrote a long letter to the secretary of state. Linlithgow suggested that in the dispute between the Congress and the Muslim League, the government should side with the League. He meaningfully noted that Muslims 'have made the largest actual and are capable of making one of the largest additional contributions to the war'. The Punjab in particular had provided tens of thousands of Muslim soldiers. Furthermore, after the resignation of their ministries, the prestige and the morale of the Congress was low. Conceding their demand for a Constituent Assembly would, said the viceroy, now 'immeasurably strengthen' the Congress, while Muslims would think the British were 'undependable allies'.

Linlithgow also feared a Constituent Assembly because it might, under the influence of Nehru and even Gandhi, ask for independence rather than Dominion Status. As the viceroy wrote to his superior in London: 'After all, we framed the constitution as it stands in the Act of 1935 because we thought that was the best way—given the political situation in both countries—of maintaining British influence in India. It is no part of our policy, I take it, to expedite in India constitutional changes for their own sake, or gratuitously to hurry the handing over of controls to Indian hands at any pace faster than that which we regard as best calculated, on a long view, to hold India to the Empire.'[24]

Linlithgow was clearly delighted that the influence of the Congress seemed to be on the wane. He was an old-fashioned imperialist, determined to concede as little as possible, and this as slowly as possible, to the rising tide of nationalist opinion. Whatever the public proclamations made by British politicians in London, their man in New Delhi was determined to retain the imperial position in India.

The day after the viceroy's letter was posted to London, the Muslim League celebrated its 'deliverance' from Congress rule in the provinces. With the Ali Brothers no longer alive (Mohammad Ali having died in 1931 and Shaukat Ali in 1938), Jinnah was now the unchallenged leader of the Muslim League, and, in his view, of all Muslims in India. Through this countrywide mobilization of Muslims against Congress (mis)rule, Jinnah sought to demonstrate that his claim had substantial foundation.

On 'Deliverance Day', Jinnah himself was the lead speaker at a great gathering of Muslims in Bombay's Mohammed Ali Road. On the podium with Jinnah were his father-in-law the Parsi magnate Sir Dinshaw Petit, and B.R. Ambedkar, whose presence was a coup for the League and its leader. In his speech, Jinnah boasted that for the first time in the history of the Muslim League, all the minorities had gathered on the same platform.

Similar meetings were held in Delhi, Lahore, Lucknow, Shillong, Sylhet, Madras, Hyderabad, Bangalore, Jabalpur, Peshawar and Rangoon—some in mosques, others in parks and gardens. One of the largest gatherings was in Calcutta, where after *jumma* prayers in mosques a massive crowd gathered in front of the Ochterlony Monument, to hear speeches condemning Congress governments for their 'tyranny', 'oppression' and 'failure to safeguard the rights and interests of Moslems and other minorities'.[25]

Jinnah's propaganda had a substantial effect. The size of the meetings held on 22 December and their geographical range was impressive—and unprecedented. This, from Gandhi's point of view, was worrying enough. And there were further complications; as the observance of 'Deliverance Day' showed, the League preferred the British rulers to the Congress; and as Linlithgow's letter to London demonstrated, the British had chosen to side with the League against the Congress.

Watching the developments closely was the Liberal leader V.S. Srinivasa Sastri. Once a great believer in British justice, who had long thought that Dominion Status was preferable to full independence since it would keep the British connection intact, Sastri was now deeply disenchanted with the rulers. He wrote to a British friend that the viceroy and his government were cold-bloodedly aiding 'the intransigence of the Muslims'. 'Britain must now placate the Muslims,' he remarked. 'The Muslims must therefore put forward impossible claims in order to get some of them recognised and to get the maximum out of the others.'[26]

VI

Gandhi spent the first weeks of 1940 in Segaon. He read in the papers that Jinnah had met Ambedkar again, had begun talks with the non-Brahmin Justice Party of South India, and might even be meeting V.D. Savarkar, the president of the Hindu Mahasabha. Writing in *Harijan*, he said he regarded these developments

> as thoroughly healthy. Nothing can be better than we should have in the country mainly two parties—Congress or anti-Congress, if the latter expression is preferred. Jinnah Saheb is giving the word 'minority' a new and good content. The Congress majority is made up of a combination of caste Hindus, non-caste Hindus, Muslims, Christians, Parsis and Jews. Therefore it is a majority drawn from all classes, representing a particular body of opinion; and the proposed combination becomes a minority representing another body of opinion. This may any day become a majority by commending itself to the electorate. Such an alignment of parties is a consummation devoutly to be wished. If the Quaid-e Azam can bring about the

combination, not only I but the whole of India will shout with one acclamation: 'Long Live Quaid-e-Azam Jinnah'. For he will have brought about permanent and living unity for which I am sure the whole nation is thirsting.

Gandhi sent an advance copy of his piece to Jinnah, addressing him (for the first time) as 'Dear Quaid-e-Azam' (the Great Leader), since he had heard that he was 'always called' that 'in League circles'. He praised Jinnah's 'plan to amalgamate all the parties opposed to the Congress [which] at once gives your movement a national character'. If he succeeded, Gandhi told Jinnah, 'you will free the country from [the] communal incubus and, in my humble opinion, give a lead to the Muslims and others for which you will deserve the gratitude not only of the Muslims but of all the other communities. I hope that my interpretation is correct. If I am mistaken, you will please correct me.'[27]

Gandhi was urging Jinnah to focus on the politics of numbers rather than the politics of community. He had in mind Western models of democratic politics, where two national parties competed for office. Labour and Conservative in Britain, or Democratic and Republican in the United States, were parties based on policies and ideologies, not on religion or caste.

Gandhi saw the Congress as being a non-denominational party too. It had, as he was never tired of proclaiming, Muslim and Christian members as well as Hindu ones; Muslim and Parsi presidents as well as Hindu ones. Congressmen who were themselves Hindus came from different castes. From varied social backgrounds, the members of the Congress were bound together by their party's manifesto. In Gandhi's famous formulation of the 1920s, the Congress was a sturdy bed with four legs: those of inter-religious harmony, inter-caste equality, economic self-reliance and non-violence.

Gandhi welcomed the move to build a broad coalition of forces opposed to the Congress. If Jinnah did that, he could construct a non- or trans-denominational alliance, that, at the national level, could challenge (and one day defeat) the non- or trans-denominational Congress, thus bringing India closer to the standard norm of democratic politics in other parts of the world.

Gandhi's suggestion was well meant. But Jinnah rejected it outright. Replying to Gandhi, he said his talks with Parsis, Scheduled Castes leaders and non-Congress Hindus were 'partly a case of "adversity bringing strange bedfellows together"', and partly because a common interest may lead Muslims and [other] minorities to combine'. Jinnah stuck to the position that 'India is not a nation, nor a country. It is a sub-continent composed of nationalities, Hindus and Muslims being the two major nations.'

Gandhi was keen to see Jinnah as more than a Muslim leader. Jinnah, on the other hand, was determined to see Gandhi as a Hindu leader alone. 'More than any one else,' he wrote, 'you happen to be the man today who commands the confidence of Hindu India and are in a position to deliver the goods on their behalf. Is it too much to hope and expect that you might play your legitimate role and abandon your chase after a mirage?' Gandhi, in Jinnah's eyes, was the leader exclusively of the Hindus; in which capacity he could, if he so wished, meet and negotiate with Jinnah himself, the leader of the Muslims.[28]

Jinnah released his letter to the press. Gandhi did likewise with his reply, where he said that the response of the League's leader 'dashes to the ground all hope of unity if he represents the Muslim mind'. Jinnah's 'picture of India as a continent containing nations according to their religions', remarked Gandhi, 'if it is realized, would undo the effort the Congress has been making for over half a century'. Muslims in India, he pointed out, were largely converts from Hinduism or descendants of converts. Just as Englishmen who converted to Islam did not lose their nationality, 'Muslims of the different provinces [of India] can never cut themselves away from their Hindu or Christian brethren'.[29]

VII

In the first week of February 1940, Gandhi travelled to Delhi to meet the viceroy. The talks were cordial, but the British were in no mood to make any commitment to Indian independence during or after the Second World War. There was vague talk of granting Dominion Status at some unspecified time, but, as Gandhi pointed out afterwards, the existing dominions such as Australia, New Zealand, Canada and South Africa were part of an imperial system that privileged one race over others. He thus insisted that 'India cannot be one of the many Dominions, i.e., partner in the exploitation of the non-European races of the earth. . . . If India is not to be co-sharer in the exploitation of the Africans and the degradation of our own countrymen in the Dominions, she must have her own independent status.'[30]

From Delhi, Gandhi took a train to Calcutta. His close friend Charlie Andrews was ailing, and the man who brought them together, Rabindranath Tagore, was getting on in years too. From the station, he went straight to the hospital where Andrews was lying, and after a few hours of intense, emotional conversation, carried on to Santiniketan. Approaching his eightieth birthday, Tagore was acutely aware of his own mortality, and Gandhi (who was eight years younger) also sensed that this might be their last meeting.

Gandhi returned to his ashram on 3 March. The name of the village where he had made his home had now changed. It would henceforth be called Sevagram, not Segaon. This was because there was another village named Shegaon, some 130 miles west of Wardha, and the post office wanted to avoid confusion. The new name pleased Gandhi, for it meant the 'Village of Service'.

On 13 March, at a meeting of the East India Association in London, a Punjabi youth named Udham Singh shot dead Sir Michael O'Dwyer, who had been lieutenant governor of the Punjab during the troubles of 1919. Several other Englishmen were injured, among them Lord Zetland, the secretary of state for India. Hearing the news, Gandhi called it 'an act of insanity'. Noting that such acts of violence 'have been proved to be injurious to the causes for which they are committed', he hoped the murder of O'Dwyer would 'not be allowed to affect political judgment', by which he meant the attitude of Britons to India and of India to Britons.[31]

Gandhi heard of Udham Singh's murder of O'Dwyer in Ramgarh, in Bihar, where that year's Congress was being held. In a meeting of the working committee, he said the Constituent Assembly the Congress had asked for would be elected on the widest possible franchise. If this assembly was constituted, 'we will lay down no conditions for the British Government. The army will remain and so will their administrative machinery.'[32] This was a concession to his party, the majority of whose members were not as dogmatically committed to non-violence as he was. What the Congress wanted was concrete steps towards self-government, while recognizing that self-government itself would come only after the war had ended.

Since the early 1930s, after the mass arrests during the Salt March, the Congress session was held in spring rather than in December. This year, 1940, Maulana Abul Kalam Azad had been elected Congress president, in recognition of his services to the party over the decades, but perhaps also as a tactical move to quell the charge—made most consistently by Jinnah—that the Congress was in essence a Hindu party. It had rained heavily the night before the Congress began, and the open-air venue was dense with slush. Volunteers worked hard to restore a semblance of order and cleanliness.

Azad began his presidential address by referring to the weather. The fight for freedom, he said, must continue 'through rain, flood and storm'. He then referred to the world crisis. 'India cannot endure the prospect of Nazism and Fascism,' said Azad, 'but she is even more tired of British imperialism.'

Britain had refused to recognize India's claims for independence and justice. Worse, Britain had chosen a cynical policy of divide and rule, seeking to exploit and further Hindu–Muslim differences. Himself a considerable scholar of Islamic texts and theories, Azad saw no contradiction between being both Indian and Muslim at the same time. As he said in Ramgarh:

> It was India's historic destiny that many human races and cultures and religions should flow to her, finding a home in her hospitable soil, and that many a caravan should find rest here. . . . One of the last of these caravans, following the footsteps of its predecessors, was that of the followers of Islam. This came here and settled here for good.
>
> . . . Full eleven centuries have passed by since then. Islam has now as great a claim on the soil of India as Hinduism. . . . Just as a Hindu can say with pride that he is an Indian and follows Hinduism, so also we can say with equal pride that we are Indians and follow Islam. I shall enlarge this orbit still further. The Indian

Christian is equally entitled to say with pride that he is an Indian and is following a religion of India, namely Christianity.

Eleven hundred years of common history have enriched India with our common achievement. Our languages, our poetry, our literature, our culture, our art, our dress, our manners and customs, the innumerable happenings of our daily life, everything bears the stamp of our joint endeavour. . . .

This joint wealth is the heritage of our common nationality, and we do not want to leave it and go back to the times when this joint life had not begun. If there are any Hindus amongst us who desire to bring back the Hindu life of a thousand years ago and more, they dream, and such dreams are vain fantasies. So also if there are any Muslims who wish to revive their past civilization and culture, which they brought a thousand years ago from Iran and Central Asia, they dream also, and the sooner they wake up the better.[33]

Here was stated, in stirring prose, the thesis of a composite culture, the theory, or belief, that by living together for so long and in such proximity, Hindus and Muslims in the Indian subcontinent had forged bonds so close that manipulative politicians (on either side) could not entirely tear them apart.

Azad's view of Hindu–Muslim relations was broadly Gandhi's too. This was a compelling thesis, here outlined in lyrical language. But it would not go unchallenged.

VIII

In the second decade of the twentieth century, the Congress and the Muslim League had met in back-to-back sessions at the same venue. At that time, League members often were Congressmen too. By 1940, however, the two organizations had drifted wide apart. They now usually met in the same month, but in different towns.

In recent years, the Muslim League had steadily grown in strength. Once dominated by nobles and large landlords, under Jinnah's leadership it had attracted many doctors, lawyers, teachers and traders into its fold. In 1931, when the League held its annual session in Delhi, this was described as 'a languid and attenuated House of scarcely 120 people in all'. But by the end of the decade, these sessions were attracting tens of thousands of eager and enthusiastic participants.[34]

The Congress session in Ramgarh ended on 20 March 1940. Two days later, the Muslim League started its annual session in Lahore, the capital of the Punjab. The two sessions were separated marginally by time, more substantially by space—Lahore is some seven hundred miles north-west of Ramgarh—and, most radically, by political agenda.

The permanent president of the Muslim League was M.A. Jinnah. This year, the session began with a poem in praise of Jinnah, which, recalled an adoring eyewitness, 'sent the audience into rapturous ecstasies'. Then the leader himself rose to speak. He was dressed in 'an immaculate white achkan and churidar pyjama', a dress more suited to the crowd and occasion than the European clothes he normally wore. He began in Urdu, but then quickly changed to a language he was more comfortable in, telling the audience that 'the world is watching us, so let me have your permission to have my say in English'.[35] In his address, Jinnah noted with satisfaction that, when war broke out in Europe, the viceroy called *both* Gandhi and him for talks. This, claimed Jinnah, 'was the worst shock that the Congress High Command received, because it challenged their sole authority to speak on behalf of India. And it is quite clear from the attitude of Mr. Gandhi and the High Command that they have not yet recovered from the shock.'

Jinnah urged that this symbolic victory be consolidated by hard organization on the ground. He then explained that the idea of a Constituent Assembly, promoted by the Congress was not suitable because in this body Muslims would be outnumbered three to one.

What then was the solution? Jinnah argued that 'the problem in India is not of an inter-communal character, but manifestly of an international one . . . So long as this basic and fundamental truth is not realised, any constitution that may be built will result in disaster . . .' The British government, urged Jinnah, must realize that 'the only course open to us all is to allow the major nations separate homelands by dividing India into "autonomous national states"'.

Why were two nations needed, why were they necessary? This was because, in Jinnah's view, Hindus and Muslims could not live together peaceably in a single state. His understanding of how the two communities had related to one another down the centuries was radically opposed to Maulana Azad's. Islam and Hinduism, argued Jinnah,

> are not religions in the strict sense of the word, but are, in fact, different and distinct social orders; and it is a dream that the Hindus and Muslims can ever evolve a common nationality; and this misconception of one Indian nation has gone far beyond the limits and is the cause of more of our troubles and will lead India to destruction if we fail to revise our notions in time. The Hindus and Muslims belong to two different religious philosophies, social customs, and literature[s]. They neither intermarry nor interdine together, and indeed they belong to two different civilisations which are based mainly on conflicting ideas and conceptions. Their aspects on life, and of life, are different. It is quite clear that Hindus and Mussalmans derive their inspiration from different sources of history. They have different epics, their heroes are different . . . Very often the hero of one is a foe of the other, and likewise their victories and defeats overlap. To yoke together two such nations under a single state, one as a numerical minority and the other as a majority, must lead to growing discontent, and final destruction of any fabric that may be so built up for the government of such a state.[36]

The next day, the 23rd, the League met in open session, with Jinnah presiding. In the afternoon, the prime minister of Bengal, A.K. Fazlul Haq, arrived to resounding cheers of 'Sher-e-Bangla Zindabad'. This Tiger of Bengal had a complicated relationship with the Muslim League. Fazlul Haq had once been a member of the Muslim League, then left to start his own Krishak Praja Party, which in March 1940 was in a coalition government with Jinnah's party in Bengal.

Fazlul Haq was not formally a member of the Muslim League. But his party was in partnership with the League in an important, heavily populated province where he was the most powerful leader. Now, in another brilliant tactical move, Jinnah got Fazlul Haq to propose the main resolution of the day. This asked that 'geographically contiguous units are demarcated into regions which should be constituted with such territorial readjustments as may be necessary that the areas in which the Muslims are numerically in a majority, as in the North-western and eastern zones of India should be grouped to constitute "independent states" in which the constituent units shall be autonomous and sovereign'.

In his own speech, Fazlul Haq said that if a unitary constitution was proposed, the Muslims must make it 'absolutely unworkable'. He dismissed Maulana Azad's Congress speech advocating a single nation as 'unIslamic'. And he appealed to Muslims across India 'to remain united and . . . remember that we have to stand on our own feet and cannot rely on anybody'.[37]

The resolution proposed by Fazlul Haq at Jinnah's instance was passed by a show of hands. It soon became known as the 'Pakistan Resolution', although in fact that term had not actually been used in the discussion. A significant feature of the resolution was that it spoke of Muslim *states*, in the plural, one in the north-west, the other in the east. What relation these states would have towards one another was not specified. Fazlul Haq himself may have believed that they would be separate and distinct, and that he might, in time, become the first prime minister of an independent, sovereign, Muslim-majority nation of Bengal.[38]

Though Jinnah had asked Fazlul Haq to move the key resolution, the Lahore meeting of the Muslim League was from first to last his own show. Before and after the League met, Jinnah addressed other public meetings in Lahore, where his words visibly moved and impressed the Muslims of Punjab's premier city. As an activist visiting from Bombay later recalled: 'This was the time when Jinnah, perhaps, gauged his strength for the first time. This was the time when he realised how much devotion he had earned from his followers by sheer service. This was the time when he felt how much confidence Musalmans of India had already reposed in him.'[39]

Back in 1929, Lahore had been the venue for the Congress session which proposed 'Purna Swaraj', Complete or Full Independence (that is, not mere 'Dominion Status'). That resolution envisaged the creation of a single, free, united Republic of India, for which a flag had already been prepared. Gandhi had led his Salt March hoping to bring that republic into being. From 1930, every 26 January had been celebrated by Congressmen as 'Independence Day', with the 'national' flag hoisted, khadi spun and patriotic songs sung.

Now, eleven years later, it was Lahore, again, which saw the anticipatory announcement by a political party of a free India; this, however, to be not one indivisible unit, but two or perhaps three separate, sovereign nations, each defined by religion.[40]

IX

Observing the Lahore session of the Muslim League with keen interest was Penderel Moon, a scholar of All Souls College, Oxford, a senior member of the Punjab cadre of the Indian Civil Service, and one of the most astute British observers of Indian politics. In March 1940, Moon was serving as private secretary to the governor of Punjab. He prepared a note for his boss, this passed on in turn to the viceroy.

For Penderel Moon, the three main lessons of the recently concluded Muslim session in Lahore were: '(a) The importance of the League as the real representative Muslim organisation has been immensely enhanced; (b) Jinnah's own personal prestige has greatly risen. His position as the one all-India Muslim leader is now unchallenged; (c) Muslim opinion is now, outwardly at least, unanimous in favour of the partition of India. Only a very courageous Muslim leader would now come forward openly to oppose or even criticise it.'

Moon thought that the League's Partition resolution 'has completely torpedoed the Congress' claim to speak for India as a whole'. That said, 'was it also meant as a serious solution of India's difficulties'? Moon wrote that the 'unthinking rank and file [Muslim] may so regard it. But I find difficulty in believing that the responsible Muslim leaders regard it—at present at any rate—as a constructive proposal.' The scholar-civil servant concluded that, as things stood, in 1940, 'Muslims will accept something less than partition, but the longer time that elapses, without any concrete alternative being put forward, the more the support and favour partition proposals are likely to gain.'[41]

What did Jinnah's main political rival think of the Muslim League meeting and its Pakistan resolution? Writing in *Harijan*, Gandhi admitted that the developments in Lahore had created 'a baffling situation'. But he himself did not believe 'that Muslims, when it comes to a matter of actual decision, will ever want vivisection. Their good sense will prevent them.' For Gandhi the two-nation theory was an 'untruth', neglecting as it did the shared culture of Hindus and Muslims, as well as more recent examples of political partnership. Was Islam 'such an exclusive religion' as Jinnah claimed? Was there, asked Gandhi, 'nothing in common between Islam and Hinduism or any other religion? Or is Islam merely an enemy of Hinduism?'[42]

Gandhi's response to the Muslim League's proclamation of the two-nation theory was intense and heartfelt. Meanwhile, Mahadev Desai had penned a more detached analysis of why things had come to such a pass. In Mahadev's view: 'the principal authors of the two nations theory were the Empire builders of Britain.' He quoted various British politicians and officials such as Lord Dufferin, John Morley and Malcolm Hailey, who had emphasized the divisions between Hindus and Muslims and worked to cast them in stone. Thus, remarked Mahadev: 'We cannot fix the guilt either of the monstrosity or the originality of the suggestion of Jinnah Saheb. It was conceived and defined by the "rulers".'[43]

X

On 5 April 1940, Charlie Andrews died in Calcutta. He was buried not in the grand European cemetery in Park Street, where generals and civil servants were laid to rest, but across the street in the more modest Lower Circular Road cemetery, amidst Indian members of his faith, the workers, artisans and middle-class professionals of Calcutta who had converted to Christianity. In death, as in life, he had chosen to identify with the humble and the lowly.

In a brief statement issued the next day, Gandhi called Andrews 'one of the greatest and best of Englishmen'. Later, in a quite wonderful tribute in *Harijan*, Gandhi wrote of how, at their last meeting in a

Calcutta hospital, Andrews had told him, 'Mohan, swaraj is coming.' He could have shared other such memories from their twenty-five years of intimate friendship, but Gandhi chose instead to reflect on what Andrews's life and legacy meant for Indians and Englishmen. 'At the present moment,' wrote Gandhi,

> I do not wish to think of English misdeeds [in India]. They will be forgotten, but not one of the heroic deeds of Andrews will be forgotten as long as England and India live. If we really love Andrews' memory, we may not have hate in us for Englishmen, of whom Andrews was among the best and noblest. It is possible, quite possible, for the best Englishmen and the best Indians to meet together and never to separate till they have evolved a formula acceptable to both.[44]

In the last week of April, a British friend of Charlie Andrews named R.O. Hicks came to see Gandhi in Sevagram. He spent a couple of weeks in the ashram, observing how its founder lived and worked. Gandhi's room was tiny, with just enough space for his cot and for a few people to sit on the floor. Above the cot was a punkah, pulled by a rope. Gandhi himself sometimes looped the rope around his big toe and pulled the fan. There was a single shelf, with some books and a pen. Papers needing attention were kept on the floor, with stones acting as paperweights. On the wall was a motto, which said: 'If you are in the right you can afford to keep your temper; if you are in the wrong you cannot afford to lose it.'

Since Andrews had just died, Hicks asked Gandhi 'what a lot of little Charlies could do in his place'. Gandhi answered that they must have 'the very broad love he had for India, born out of his love for humanity'. He added: 'And on that account, Charlie's love for England burned all the brighter instead of growing dim.'

Gandhi also reported to the visiting Englishman his several, invariably dispiriting talks with Lord Linlithgow. In one meeting the viceroy had told him: 'In spite of everything we may say, we shall be in India a long time, a very long time.' Gandhi's impression of the most powerful person in India was that he was hostage to 'an invincible stupidity'.[45]

XI

As Gandhi and Jinnah, the Congress and the Muslim League, jostled for space in India, the war further intensified in Europe. In April 1940, the Nazis invaded Norway and Denmark. In early May, they invaded France, Belgium, Luxembourg and the Netherlands.

These dramatic advances left the British as the only major country in the fight against the Nazis. Drastic measures were called for, and they were taken. On 14 May, Winston Churchill replaced Neville Chamberlain as prime minister. Despite his rather wayward political career, Churchill had a reputation as a fighter. He had once been a soldier himself, and had written many works of military history. He was much admired in the United States (a country thus far neutral in the war) on account of his writings and his familial connections (his mother was American).

Within Britain itself, Churchill's appointment led immediately to a rise in morale. Meanwhile, the main opposition party, Labour, decided to join the Cabinet. So did some independent MPs, making this a truly national government.

Three days after Churchill took over as prime minister, Lord Linlithgow wrote a note entitled 'The Congress position on 13/5/40', reproduced below in toto:

> It is important to note that the position of Congress is weakening very rapidly, and the risk of c[ivil] d[isobedience] receding at the same pace.
>
> Since Friday [10 May], Congress is the weaker—
>
> (a) By the immense sympathy now felt for the Allied cause by the whole population in North America.
> (b) By the virtual cancellation of the nuisance value of German propaganda about India. No American will now listen to German chatter about India, and no newspaper will print such.
> (c) By the inclusion of Liberals and Labour in the Cabinet, and by the focusing of all public opinion in Great Britain upon the war. The press will be equally bored with India, the more so as they are cut off their newsprint.

(d) By the tremendous (and vocal) movement of sympathy for the Allied cause, and the fear of a new and very different master, enabled by the war crisis.

So Congress has in fact lost the whole of what remained of the 'claque', during the past 3 days. [The Quaker] Agatha Harrison and her friends, [the writer] Edward Thompson and a few besides are what is left of the old man [Gandhi]'s fans in three continents.
We can do what we wish.

L. 13/5/40.[46]

Always suspicious of the Congress, the viceroy now saw an opportunity to marginalize it altogether. The note of triumphalism was marked, and unfortunate. That the main representative of the British Empire in India had such hatred for the main political party in India sat oddly with the claim that this war against Hitler was being fought to preserve democracy and freedom. Gandhi's characterization seemed right; Linlithgow was not particularly quick-witted; and he thought his Raj was immortal and invincible.

CHAPTER TWENTY-SEVEN

Pilgrimages to Gandhi

I

The preceding chapters have inevitably been intensely political, since these were the years when the Congress formed ministries for the first time; when it was bitterly opposed by a resurgent Muslim League; when the Nazis rose in Germany to the alarm and consternation of other nations in Europe; when the Second World War broke out; when the Congress and Gandhi tried unavailingly to come to an agreement with the Raj that would allow them to aid the war effort on terms they considered honourable.

This chapter is more personal in character. It recounts visits made by curious travellers to Gandhi's home in central India, and the conversations, often illuminating and sometimes eccentric, they had with him.

In December 1935, the American feminist Margaret Sanger came to Wardha to meet Gandhi. She was on an extended trip to India, travelling 10,000 miles and visiting eighteen cities, speaking with doctors and social activists on birth control and the emancipation of women.

Mrs Sanger arrived at the ashram on 3 December, a tonga sent by Gandhi meeting her at the railway station. It was her host's day of silence, so the visitor was taken by Mahadev Desai to see the village industries coming up in Wardha—the oil presses, the handmade paper machines, the spinning wheels.[1]

The next morning Mrs Sanger accompanied Gandhi on his morning walk, and also spent the afternoon with him.

They had long conversations, the details noted down by Mahadev Desai, as well as by the visitor's secretary. Mahadev remarked that 'both seemed to be agreed that woman should be emancipated, that woman should be the arbiter of her destiny'. But whereas Mrs Sanger believed that contraceptives were the safest route to emancipation, Gandhi argued that women should resist their husbands, while men for their part should seek to curb 'animal passion'.

Gandhi had always opposed artificial methods of birth control. Back in December 1934, a women's rights activist from Kerala had asked him: 'May not birth-control through contraceptives be resorted to, as the next best thing to self-control, which is too high an ideal for the ordinary man or woman?'

Gandhi answered: 'Do you think that the freedom of the body is obtained by resorting to contraceptives? Women should learn to resist their husbands. If contraceptives are resorted to as in the West, frightful results will follow. Men and women will be living for sex alone. They will become soft-brained, unhinged, in fact mental and moral wrecks . . .' Gandhi, however, added that 'though I am against the use of contraceptives in the case of women, I do not mind voluntary sterilisation in the case of man, since he is the aggressor'.[2]

Speaking to Margaret Sanger, Gandhi likewise spoke disparagingly of 'carnal passion'. Mrs Sanger distinguished between 'sex lust', as manifest in men who went to prostitutes, and 'sex love', this based on a deep and enduring relation between one man and one woman, as between husband and wife. Mrs Sanger believed that the latter form of 'sex expression is a spiritual need'. As she pointed out: 'Women have feelings as deep and as amorous as men. There are times when wives desire physical union as much as their husbands.' Did Gandhi, she asked, 'think it possible for two people who are in love, who are happy together, to regulate their sex act only once in two years, so that relationship would only take place when they wanted a child'? This is where contraceptives were useful, necessary, even vital, in enhancing the control of women over their bodies.

Gandhi, on the other hand, regarded all sex as lust, or, to use a phrase he himself used often, 'animal passion'. Like most Indian men, Gandhi denied the possibility of women themselves desiring sex. In answer to Mrs Sanger's question, he did believe it possible to have sex only when husband and wife wanted children. Procreation was the sole legitimate purpose of sexual union. Speaking of his own marriage, he claimed that 'the moment I bade good-bye to a life of carnal pleasure our whole relationship became spiritual. Lust died and love reigned instead . . .' When Mrs Sanger persisted in arguing that sex was necessary and pleasurable, and contraceptives were the only way to prevent unwanted pregnancies, Gandhi made a small concession—instead of encouraging contraceptives, he would urge that sex be confined to the 'safe period' of the menstrual cycle. Mrs Sanger was unconvinced, writing later of Gandhi's 'appalling fear of licentiousness and over-indulgence'.

To Mrs Sanger, as to other advocates of birth control, Gandhi argued that the best way was for women to resist their husbands. The American, in reply, asked him to 'consider the turmoil, the unhappiness it means for the woman if she resists her husband! What if he puts her out of the house? In some states in the United States, a wife has no rights if she resists her husband.' Surely, the use of contraceptives was a better way of assuring marital concord.[3]

Mrs Sanger had hoped to win Gandhi over to the cause of contraception. On a visit to Bombay's tenements, she had met young women who had five or six children, but were still 'haunted by the fear of more and more and still more pregnancies'.[4] How much could their lives be enhanced if they could use contraception? She left Wardha with warm feelings towards Gandhi himself; as she wrote to him after her return to America, 'I shall always look upon my visit at Wardha and the delightful walks and talks with you as one of the great privileges bestowed upon me.'[5] Yet, she also carried back a deep sense of disappointment at his failure to approve of her campaign. Later, reading Gandhi's autobiography, and juxtaposing its contents with their conversations, she was 'convinced that his personal experiences at the time of his father's death was so shocking and self-blamed that he can never accept sex as anything good, clean or wholesome'.[6]

There was a later experience of Gandhi's which was also critical in shaping his views on the subject. Indeed, he referred to that experience in his conversation with Mrs Sanger. He spoke here of 'a woman with a broad cultural education', a 'woman with whom I almost fell. It is so personal that I did not put it in my autobiography.' The reference, of course, was to Saraladevi Chaudhurani. When he met and 'fell' for this woman, said Gandhi to Mrs Sanger, he asked himself: 'Could we not develop a close contact?' He continued: 'This was a plausible argument, and I nearly slipped. But I was saved, I awoke from my trance. . . . I was saved by youngsters [i.e. Rajagopalachari and Mahadev] who warned me.'[7]

As much as the experience of having sex with his wife when his father was dying, it was the near miss in not falling for Saraladevi that lay behind Gandhi's rejection of contraception. For him, all sex was lust; sex was necessary only for procreation. Modern methods of birth control legitimized lust. Far better that women resist men, and men control and tame their animal passions.

II

Shortly after Mrs Sanger left Wardha, Gandhi was diagnosed as having high blood pressure. He was advised bed rest, and told to stop writing altogether. But he was allowed to read, so he went through the draft manuscript of Jawaharlal Nehru's autobiography, which he liked on the whole. He had one reservation: that Nehru's 'attack on the Liberals seems to have been overdone', and marred 'the grace and beauty of the narrative'. Gandhi reminded his younger, left-wing compatriot that Liberals such as Gokhale, Sapru and Sastri had 'served the country in their time according to their lights, and while we may have our serious differences with them we do not exactly serve the cause of the country by publicly pillorying them'.[8]

After two months of rest, Gandhi's health improved, and he was free to meet visitors once more. In February 1936, the black intellectual Howard Thurman came to Wardha with his wife. Thurman had grown up reading about Gandhi in the African-American press. In the 1920s, black newspapers marvelled at Gandhi's fight against British imperialism; by the 1930s, they increasingly presented him to their readers 'as one of the foremost sages and seers of human history'. And they asked the question: when, and how, could we have our own Gandhi?[9]

With Mrs Sanger, Gandhi had discussed the problem of gender; with Dr Thurman, the equally urgent problem of race. Gandhi asked the visitors whether prejudice on the basis of colour was growing or dying out. They answered that it had declined in some places but was solidly intact in others.

Dr Thurman and Gandhi discussed the technique of satyagraha. The American asked how they could 'train individuals or communities in this difficult art'. 'There is no royal road,' replied Gandhi, 'except through living the creed in your life which must be a living sermon.'

Mrs Thurman then urged Gandhi to visit the United States. 'We want you not for white America,' she remarked, 'but for the Negroes; we have many a problem that cries for solution, and we need you badly.' 'How I wish I could,' answered Gandhi, 'but I would have nothing to give you unless I had given an oracular demonstration here of all that I have been saying. I must make good the message here, before I bring it to you.'

Dr Thurman discussed with Gandhi the centrality of Christianity to black politics and spiritual life. His wife then sang, to Gandhi's delight, two songs illustrating this: 'Were You There When They Crucified My Lord' and 'We Are Climbing Jacob's Ladder'.

As the Thurmans prepared to leave, Gandhi offered them this hopeful prediction: 'It may be through the Negroes that the unadulterated message of non-violence will be delivered to the world.'[10]

Years later, Thurman remembered how he had been subject to an intense examination by Gandhi: 'persistent, pragmatic, questions about American Negroes, about the course of slavery, and how we had survived it'. Gandhi was puzzled that in order to escape or defy oppression, the slaves had not converted to Islam, since, as he put it, 'the Moslem religion is the only religion in the world in which no lines are drawn from within the religious fellowship. Once you are in, you are all the way in.'

Thurman was impressed both by Gandhi's curiosity and his range of interests. Gandhi, he recalled, 'wanted to know about voting rights, lynching, discrimination, public school education, the churches and how they functioned. His questions covered the entire sweep of our experience in American society.'

As a parting gift, Gandhi handed over to Mrs Thurman a basket of fruit. Thurman boldly asked for something for himself as well. The American said he would love to have a sample of cloth woven from the yarn Gandhi had spun that day. Some months later, a piece of cloth arrived at the Thurmans' house through the post.[11]

III

After Gandhi moved to his new home in Sevagram, a steady flow of foreigners found their way there. Journalists, missionaries, educationists, all came to interrogate him or seek his counsel. In December 1936, a Polish professor of philosophy descended on the village. Like so many of his compatriots, he was a devout Catholic. His conversation with Gandhi was mostly on religious matters. At one stage, the Polish scholar remarked: 'If you became a Catholic you would be as great as St. Francis.' Gandhi answered with a mixture of humour and exasperation: 'But not otherwise? A Hindu cannot be a St. Francis? Poor Hindu!'

The Polish professor was followed by an American clergyman of African extraction. He asked Gandhi for a word of advice to his 'Negro brethren'. The Indian answered: 'With right which is on their side and the choice of non-violence as their only weapon, if they will make it such, a bright future is assured.'[12] Travelling around the country, the visitor had noticed how Gandhi's movement had 'given the Indian masses a new conception of courage'. Perhaps his techniques, when practised by African Americans, could embolden and empower them too.[13]

Shortly afterwards, a visitor from Germany arrived who was not merely a bird of passage. As a young man in Nazi Germany, Herbert Fischer had read about Gandhi in a magazine called *Tao*, published from Switzerland by Werner Zimmermann. Zimmermann was an admirer of Tagore and generally of things Indian, and his journal carried news of the national movement. Fischer was already oriented towards vegetarianism and organic farming, and from what he read in *Tao*, the Mahatma seemed to combine the simple life with anti-authoritarian politics. In 1935, he wrote a letter addressed to 'Mahatma Gandhi, India', asking to be allowed to work with him. A reply came back, explaining the harsh ashram regimen, and adding that he was welcome if he could abide by it.

When Fischer finally arrived in Sevagram, late in 1936, Gandhi was not at home. He had left with his entourage for the annual Congress meeting being held at Faizpur, in the Khandesh region of Maharashtra. The German found his own way to Faizpur, to be greeted by Gandhi with the words: 'So you have come.' He did not speak more, but told Fischer to report to J.C. Kumarappa, the general secretary of the AIVIA. This was the first Congress ever held in a village, to mark which the Gandhians had set up a khadi and village industries exhibition. Fischer worked here by day, and stayed in the dormitories by night. At some point, his jacket was stolen, his passport and papers along with it. The German consulate in Bombay said they would give him a new passport on the condition he returned to his country and joined the military. He refused, returning to Wardha instead.

For the next year and a half, Fischer worked with the AIVIA. From the beginning, he was treated not as a visitor but a co-worker. Certainly, the colonial police saw him as such, for in a report on Fischer, they noted that 'he is a regular wearer of khadi'. He often cycled the seven miles from Maganwadi, the AIVIA's headquarters, to the ashram in Sevagram. There, Gandhi and he had friendly arguments. Gandhi, ever the attentive host, ordered that Fischer be served an egg a day, which he believed necessary for the European body. The visitor demurred, arguing that even cold-blooded Germans could remain vegetarian. A more weighty disagreement was political. Gandhi thought that Fischer should return home and commence a satyagraha campaign against the Nazis. The German answered that Hitler 'was not Judge Broomfield' (the English judge who had called Gandhi a saint while being forced to sentence him).[14]

After England declared war on Germany in September 1939, Herbert Fischer was declared an enemy alien and imprisoned. When the war ended, he was released and returned to his now de-Nazified homeland. Years later, he wrote a remembrance of his days with Gandhi, which gives a vivid feel of the annual Congress session as held in that party's pomp: the 'huts erected from light bamboo mats on bare fields', the 'discussions [which] took place in the open on a raised platform' such that 'everyone could hear what the leaders said', and, looming above it all, the presence and personality of the Mahatma:

> After the sessions, during the meals and at other functions, there was always a great rush. A path for Gandhi could be found with difficulty. Everyone wanted to see him from near, or touch him. A man threw himself on the floor to touch his feet, even though he was in danger of being trampled upon by the crowd. Such worship of a living man I had not so far seen. I had to think back to the New Testament for a similar instance.

On Sunday, their day of rest, the workers at Maganwadi would walk or cycle over to Sevagram, where Fischer studied Gandhi with attention and fascination. He writes that after early morning prayers and the obligatory walk, Gandhi

> withdrew to a corner of his room, the only one in the house which was surrounded on all sides by a two metre wide verandah. The long sides each had two doors, the others one apiece. All six doors were always open and there was continuous coming and going. The other corners were also used. When I once came in, I saw a young man reading aloud from Nehru's autobiography, which had just been published. In another corner a beginner was playing a musical instrument. Gandhi's wife came in from time to time to fetch a lid or cooking vessel. All this did not distract him . . . [H]e sat on the floor on a grass mat covered with a khadi sheet, with a white cushion at the back. On his thigh he held a board which served as writing support. Next to him was a desk barely half-a-metre high, in which he kept paper and writing material. If his secretary or a visitor came, they sat before him. To save time he shaved while talking—naturally without a mirror—or he did his spinning. Only during very important conversations did he content himself with just listening and speaking.

Gandhi, recalled Fischer, was addicted to argument. 'For him, a requirement was debate with those of different opinion. This helped him to check his own train of thought.' Fischer likened him to a chess player. 'As a chess player considers in advance the opponent's next move and his own, so it appears to me that Gandhi made his move with reference to the expected answer. He did not play chess or other games for passing time, for time was too precious for him and life itself offered an interesting pastime!'

Gandhi's thought, commented Herbert Fischer, was constantly evolving and adapting. In taking a decision to have a poisonous snake in the ashram killed, 'he did not bind himself in literal interpretations [in this case, of ahimsa], but decided each situation on humanitarian grounds'. Gandhi was often reproached for being inconsistent but, as Fischer noted, 'there was consistency in his inconsistency, as his words and actions were determined by the prevailing conditions'. He changed his mind as the facts themselves changed.[15]

IV

Herbert Fischer was a new German disciple of Gandhi, and a gentile. In 1937 a very old friend of Gandhi, also German-speaking but a Jew, came on a visit. This was the architect Hermann Kallenbach. Gandhi and Kallenbach had once shared the latter's spacious home in the upmarket Johannesburg locality of Orchard; now they shared Gandhi's single-room hut in the village of Sevagram. Kallenbach, wrote Gandhi to Amrit Kaur, 'has no desire to see anything in India. He has come just to be with me as long as he can.' Gandhi was pleased that, despite running a successful practice with branches in four cities, and thirty-five architects working under him, Kallenbach was 'in his personal life just as simple as when I left him in 1914'.[16]

Like other Indians in Gandhi's circle, Mahadev Desai had heard many stories about Kallenbach. Writing about his visit in *Harijan*, Mahadev described Kallenbach as 'a princely giver', who 'believed in earning in order to give'. The visitor was 'proud to call himself a Jew, but would prefer not to be known as a German'.

Reading this description in print, Kallenbach clarified that he was once happy to call himself a German too. But Hitler had compelled him to disavow that affiliation. After the 'persecution of the Jews', said Kallenbach to Mahadev, 'I was ashamed to call myself a German'. His own firm had stopped importing German goods in protest. He was dismayed that so many articles in use in India were made in Germany: knives, paper products, lanterns, among others. 'Whoever takes German goods helps to consolidate the power of Hitler,' remarked Kallenbach.[17]

In the first week of July, a Nazi journalist and SS officer named Captain Strunk came to Sevagram. The visitor first asked Gandhi what he meant by independence for India. Gandhi replied: 'What we mean by independence is that we will not live on the sufferance of any people on earth and that there is a big party in India which will die in vindicating this position. But we will not die killing, though we might be killed. It is a novel experiment, I know. Herr Hitler, I know, does not accept the position of human dignity being maintained without the use of force. Many of us feel that it is possible to achieve independence by non-violent means. It would be a bad day for the whole world if we had to wade through blood.'

The Nazi journalist then asked why Gandhi was against Western medicine. He answered that he did 'not despise all medical treatment. I know we can learn a lot from the West about safe maternity and the care of infants. Our children are born anyhow and most of our women are ignorant of the science of bringing up children. Here we can learn a great deal from the West.'

At the same time, Gandhi continued: 'The West attaches an exaggerated importance to prolonging man's earthly existence. Until the man's last moment on earth you go on drugging him even by injecting.' The odd thing, remarked Gandhi, was that this desperate desire to prolong life was 'inconsistent with the recklessness with which they [the West] will shed their lives in war'.

As Captain Strunk prepared to leave, Gandhi introduced him to Hermann Kallenbach, with these words: 'Here is a live Jew and a German Jew, if you please. He was a hot pro-German during the War [of 1914–18].' Gandhi then asked the Nazi: 'I should like to understand from you why the Jews are being persecuted in Germany.'

Put on the spot, Captain Strunk tried to explain why his party and government were opposed to Jews. He accepted that they fought for their country during the conflict of 1914–18, but (he claimed) it was 'the Jews who overran Germany after the War, who ousted Germans from their jobs, and who "guided" the fight against Hitler who were not being tolerated'.

'I personally think we have just overdone it,' continued Gandhi's Nazi visitor. 'That's the mistake revolutions always do,' he added. 'Oh, there is such a lot of hate in Europe,' said Captain Strunk. 'And it has reached its climax in Spain. It is cruel, heartless, stupid, inhuman—this Spanish War. It can't be compared with any other war.'[18]

V

Many of the visitors to Sevagram were, of course, ordinary Indians rather than exotic foreigners, come to have a darshan of their most famous countryman. In the winter of 1938 a young Punjabi named Bhisham Sahni arrived at Wardha station. He was a writer-in-the-making, whose elder brother Balraj (an aspiring actor) had based himself in Sevagram, and wished to introduce Bhisham to the ashram and what it meant. They accompanied Gandhi on his morning walk, where Bhisham marvelled at the number of people who clustered around the leader, peppering him with questions. 'Anyone can join in,' said Balraj to his brother, adding: 'There is a dark-skinned fellow, an "Ashramite", who accompanies Gandhiji everyday. He smells awfully. Whenever he finds anyone sticking too long to Gandhiji, he quietly starts walking by his side and the fellow falls back within seconds. That is Gandhiji's non-violent method of regulating interviews.'

'Doesn't Gandhiji feel his smell?' asked Bhisham. 'Gandhiji has no sense of smell,' answered Balraj. Recounting this incident many years later, Bhisham said he still didn't know whether his brother was pulling his leg or not.[19]

In the first week of December 1938, a Japanese member of Parliament came to Sevagram to meet Gandhi. He asked how Japan and India could develop friendly relations. Gandhi answered that 'it can be possible if Japan ceases to throw its greedy eyes on India'. He complained that the Japanese 'flood India with your goods which are often flimsy'. Nor was he much enthused about Japan's call for Asian solidarity under its leadership. 'I do not subscribe,' remarked Gandhi, 'to the doctrine of Asia for the Asiatics, if it is meant as an anti-European combination.'[20]

A month later, the participants in an economists' conference in Nagpur visited Gandhi. When they asked if he was against large-scale production, he said not always, only where the goods in question could be made in villages. Asked whether cottage and big industries could be nationalized, Gandhi answered: 'Yes, if they are planned so as to help the villages. Key industries, industries which the nation needs, may be centralized.' But in Gandhi's scheme, 'nothing will be allowed to be produced by cities which can equally well be produced by the villagers'.[21]

In February 1939, a certain *S.S. Tema* came calling. A Johannesburg pastor and a member of the African National Congress (ANC), Tema had come to India to attend a World Missionary Conference in Tambaram. The first question he asked Gandhi was what the ANC could learn from the Indian National Congress. Gandhi thought that the leaders of the ANC were excessively Europeanized, wearing Western dress and professing the Christian faith, in both respects standing apart from the majority of Africans. 'You must become Africans once more,' he told the visitor.

Tema then asked Gandhi about his opinion on a future Indo-African front in South Africa. Gandhi thought it would be a mistake, as the two groups faced very different problems. 'The Indians are a microscopic minority,' he told the African. 'You, on the other hand, are the sons of the soil who are being robbed of your inheritance. . . . Yours is a far bigger issue.' That said, keeping the movements separate did not 'preclude the establishment of the friendliest relations between the two races'.

Gandhi believed that the best way Indians could help the Africans was 'by always acting on the square towards you. They may not put themselves in opposition to your legitimate aspirations, or run you down as "savages" while exalting themselves as "cultured" people in order to secure concessions for themselves at your expense.'

Finally, the visitor asked if Christianity could bring 'salvation to Africa'. Gandhi's answer is worth quoting in full:

> Christianity, as it is known and practised today, cannot bring salvation to your people. It is my conviction that those who today call themselves Christian do not know the true message of Jesus. I witnessed some of the horrors that were perpetrated on the Zulus during the Zulu rebellion. Because one man, Bambatta, their chief, had refused to pay his tax, the whole race was made to suffer. I was in charge of an ambulance corps. I shall never forget the lacerated backs of Zulus who had received stripes and were brought to us for nursing because no white nurse was prepared to look after them. And yet those who perpetrated all those cruelties called themselves Christians. They were 'educated', better dressed than the Zulus, but not their moral superiors.[22]

These remarks were a decisive advance on, and in some respects, a clear repudiation of, Gandhi's older views on Africans. When, in the 1890s, he had first gone to South Africa, he was quite strongly prejudiced against Africans. In petitions to the colonial authorities, he had asked for Indians to be better treated than (what in his opinion were) the less civilized natives. However, over the two decades he lived in South Africa, Gandhi steadily shed these racist views. His journal, *Indian Opinion*, regularly carried reports about discrimination against Africans.[23]

Now, two decades after he had left Africa, Gandhi had deepened his understanding of Africans and their predicament. He no longer believed in a hierarchy of civilizations where Christians and Hindus were at the top and animists at the bottom. He had long since rejected his once benign view of imperialism; Europeans were not morally superior to Zulus; in pursuit of wealth and power, professedly 'Christian' nations could be entirely barbaric.

The most interesting aspect of Gandhi's remarks was the clear recognition that, in South Africa, Indians were less exploited than Africans. Theirs was a 'far bigger issue'. He knew Indians had a reputation for being collaborators, for cosying up to the whites in order to extract concessions for themselves. Indeed, his own early efforts in the 1890s had been of this nature. But over time, he came to reject such self-serving behaviour. He now argued that Indians should not seek to extract concessions from the rulers at the expense of Africans.

That Gandhi now wanted the 'friendliest relations' between Indians and Africans was a refreshing departure from his own practice. In his time in South Africa, the two communities had tended to stay apart. Within the Indian community, Gandhi himself had friends who were Tamil and Gujarati, Hindu, Muslim and Parsi, workers, hawkers and prosperous merchants. He had many Europeans friends, these Christian, Jewish and Theosophist. But he had not a single African friend. However, since his return, and especially after the Salt March, people of colour had come to seek him out. At his ashram in Sevagram, he had entertained several African Americans, and now this black pastor from Johannesburg. In what he said to them, and how he received them, he demonstrated that he had comprehensively transcended the prejudices of his youth.

CHAPTER TWENTY-EIGHT

Somewhere between Conflict and Cooperation

I

In the summer of 1940, the Hindu–Muslim question was much on Gandhi's mind. From the letters he was receiving, and the press cuttings he was reading, Gandhi had reached the melancholy conclusion 'that I am believed to be the arch enemy of Islam and Indian Muslims'. He insisted that 'in nothing that I am doing, saying or thinking, I am their enemy. They are blood-brothers and will remain so, though they may disown me for ever.'[1]

Pursuing the path of reconciliation, Maulana Azad had, as Congress president, written to Jinnah saying that his party was in favour of a national, multiparty government for the duration of the Second World War. He asked whether Jinnah would be open to the idea, or whether the Muslim League's participation was conditional on the acceptance of their two-nation theory. Instead of clarifying the point, Jinnah wrote a vicious and hurtful reply which he then released to the press. 'I refuse to discuss with you,' said Jinnah to Azad,

> by correspondence or otherwise, as you have completely forfeited the confidence of Muslim India. Can't you realise you are made a 'Muslim showboy' Congress President to give it colour that it is national and [thus] deceive foreign countries. You represent neither

Muslims nor Hindus. The Congress is a Hindu body. If you have
self-respect resign at once. You have done your worst against the
League so far. You know you have hopelessly failed. Give it up.[2]

Jinnah was accusing Maulana Azad of being a traitor to his community,
of siding with the rival community for his own personal gain. Such
an accusation was damaging in normal circumstances; and its power
was heightened further during this World War, when Pétain, in
France, and Quisling, in Norway, had (so to say) abandoned their
countrymen by making peace with the enemy.

Jinnah's astonishing arrogance was noted by Srinivasa Sastri.
'Nobody can gauge the precise extent of Jinnah's influence,' wrote
Sastri to Gandhi. 'As a man [and] as a politician, he has developed
unexpectedly. It is no violence to truth to describe him today as a
monster of personal arrogance and political charlatanry. Nevertheless
Congress is unable to ignore or neglect him; how can the British
Government do so?'

Sastri saw clearly that, for the British, 'Muslim displeasure
is [now] a greater minus than Congress adhesion is a plus'. So, he
told Gandhi that 'it profits little now to blame the Hindu–Muslim
tension on Britain. . . . We can't abolish Jinnah, any more, than we
can abolish Britons.'[3]

Although they had long since gone their separate ways, Sastri,
Gandhi and Jinnah had all at one stage been groomed and mentored
by Gopal Krishna Gokhale. Now, one Gokhale disciple, Sastri, was
suggesting to a second, Gandhi, how to deal with a third, Jinnah. The
Congress, he was saying, should seek a compromise with the Raj as
well as with the Muslim League, instead of fighting both.

II

In the spring and summer of 1940, the Nazis swept through northern
and western Europe. In the last week of May, Gandhi wrote to the
viceroy suggesting that it might be prudent for the Allies to 'sue for
peace for the sake of humanity' so that this 'mad slaughter' could
stop. 'I do not believe,' remarked Gandhi, 'Herr Hitler to be as bad

as he is portrayed.' If the idea appealed to the British government, he continued, 'I am prepared to go to Germany or anywhere required to plead for peace not for this interest or that but for the good of mankind.'

The viceroy answered that the British government had 'done their best in the past' to avoid war. But now they could not 'place any reliance in the light of events on any understanding or any promise that Herr Hitler might give to them. There is nothing for it . . . but to go on until victory is won.'

Once the British refused his offer to act as peacemaker, Gandhi wrote a piece in *Harijan* entitled 'How to Combat Hitlerism'. The Germans 'had robbed the small nations [of Europe] of their liberty', but, asked Gandhi, 'what will Hitler do with his victory? Can he digest so much power? Personally he will go as empty-handed as his not very remote predecessor Alexander. For the Germans he will have left not the pleasure of owning a mighty empire but the burden of sustaining its crushing weight. For they will not be able to hold all the conquered nations in perpetual subjection. And I doubt if the Germans of future generations will entertain unadulterated pride in the deeds for which Hitlerism will be deemed responsible.'

Having predicted the (eventual) fall of Hitler and Hitlerism, Gandhi yet wished that the Czechs, the Poles, the Norwegians, the French and the English had chosen to resist the Nazis not by arms but through non-violence. 'I dare say,' he wrote, 'in that case Europe would have added several inches to its moral stature.'

In the last week of June, Gandhi travelled to Delhi to meet with the viceroy. The viceroy said he would ask London to announce that India would become a self-governing dominion (on the model of Australia and Canada) within a year of the war's termination, subject to an agreed understanding on the status of the princes, on British commercial interests, and on the rights of minorities. Gandhi answered that this was too little too late, and asked that the British instead offer an unequivocal declaration of independence for India after the war.

The viceroy then said he hoped to expand his executive council, by inviting more Indians to join. Gandhi answered that no Congressman would serve on the council unless the commitment to full independence was made.

From Indian politics, the discussion turned to the global situation. Gandhi repeated his advice, earlier conveyed by letter, that Britain and Germany should begin peace negotiations to stop the senseless slaughter of innocents. With reports coming in of attacks on British towns by the Luftwaffe, the viceroy must have had a hard time containing his exasperation at hearing Gandhi's 'appeal to the British people to accept the non-violent method at this supreme juncture in their life as also the life of mankind'.[4]

Having failed with the viceroy, Gandhi now went public, with an article addressed to 'every Briton', urging them to fight Nazism not by the force of arms but through non-violence. He asked them 'to invite Herr Hitler and Signor Mussolini to take . . . possession of your beautiful island, with your many beautiful buildings. You will give all these, but neither your souls, nor your minds. If these gentlemen [sic] choose to occupy your homes, you will vacate them. If they do not give you free passage out, you will allow yourself, man, woman and child, to be slaughtered, but you will refuse to owe allegiance to them.'[5]

Gandhi claimed he was writing as 'a lifelong and wholly disinterested friend of the British people'. But his public appeal was poorly timed. In the summer of 1940, the war had entered its most savage phase yet. The British were fighting desperately for survival. Russia and America, those two great and coming powers of the age, were in July 1940 still neutral. Stalin had signed a non-aggression pact with Hitler. Across the Atlantic, the Americans were waiting and watching, the pro-British elements among their political class countered by an equally influential group of isolationists. At this stage, for Gandhi to offer the advice he did was spectacularly ill-judged.

Gandhi sent a copy of his appeal to the viceroy, asking him to convey it to 'the proper quarters'. Linlithgow did, later conveying to Gandhi the response of the British government that 'with every appreciation of your motives they do not feel that the policy which you advocate is one which it is possible for them to consider, since in common with the whole Empire they are firmly resolved to prosecute the war to a victorious conclusion'.[6]

The argument between Gandhi and Linlithgow, or between the Congress and the Raj more generally, was an argument of right versus right. The war was professedly being fought for the defence of freedom and democracy. How then could the British deny freedom to India and Indians? The argument was compelling, except that, in the summer of 1940, Britain was battling heroically for its own survival. Its national honour was at stake in Europe just as much as India's (putative) national honour was at stake in Asia.

It was this clash of national identities, indeed of national egos, that made the situation so painful, and a meeting ground so difficult to find. And Gandhi's stubborn insistence that non-violence had an important place in international (as distinct from intra-national) affairs, with his unsolicited advice to Britons not to resist Hitler with arms, made it much more difficult still. Besides, virtually all British officials in India, from the viceroy downwards, had close family members on the battlefront in Europe. Some of these relatives had been killed, others captured, still others were missing in action.

Linlithgow and his advisers were temperamentally disinclined to abandon the British hold over India. In peacetime, they were happy to consider proposals for the (incrementally) greater involvement of Indians in government. But now, in the depths of this most bloody war, to be asked to promise India full independence was something they could never countenance.

On the Indian side, the war in Europe was unpopular not only because its aims were seen as hypocritical, but also because it bore down heavily on the population. In 1940 and 1941, Gandhi received dozens of letters from correspondents across India, complaining of forcible collections for the War Fund. In some districts, peasants were made to buy war lottery tickets and students 'V for Victory' tickets. Motorcar owners were levied a war tax. Cows were seized and slaughtered to feed British troops. As large quantities of food and other commodities were transported to the theatres of war, their prices rose within India itself.[7]

III

On 10 May 1940, the Germans had begun their invasion of France. The government in Paris finally collapsed in the last week of June—

the fall of France being by far the Nazis' greatest triumph to date. In early July, the CWC met in Delhi, and 'in the light of the latest developments in world affairs', once more offered a compromise to the Government. If they committed themselves to complete independence for India after the end of the war, and meanwhile formed a provisional national government at the Centre, the Congress would 'throw in its full weight in the efforts for the effective organization of the defence of the country'.

The resolution was drafted by C. Rajagopalachari, who had, from the outset of the war, warned against an attitude of confrontation with the government. It was supported by Jawaharlal Nehru, whose own hatred of the Nazis was of long standing, based on his own extended visits to Germany and other parts of Europe in the mid-1930s.

The resolution was also supported by Vallabhbhai Patel. Nehru, Patel and Rajaji were sometimes known as Gandhi's 'heart, hand, and head' respectively. They were indisputably his closest political colleagues. But through this resolution, they were making it clear that they, as well as the Congress as a whole, did not share Gandhi's absolute and fundamental commitment to non-violence.

Gandhi was present at the working committee meeting, which was held in Delhi. Writing afterwards in *Harijan*, he explained how, and why, he and his most trusted followers of the past twenty years 'were drifting away from each other in our outlook upon the political problems that face us'. He could not carry the Congress, which meant, as he told his readers, that 'Rajaji's resolution represents the considered policy of the Congress'. As 'a disinterested but staunch friend' of the British, he now advised them that they 'should not reject the hand of friendship offered by the Congress'.

A month after the CWC's (albeit awkwardly worded) hand of friendship, the viceroy made a statement rejecting any idea of a national government. He suggested, as he had done before, that the authority of the Congress to speak for India was 'directly denied by large and powerful elements in India's national life'. All he would, or could, offer was an expanded executive council. Those fighting in Europe for freedom had, once again, declined to commit themselves to freedom in and for India.

The Congress replied 'in deep pain and indignation'. To the 'friendly offer' they had held out, said the working committee, the viceroy had in effect responded that 'the present autocratic and irresponsible system of Government must continue so long as any group of people or the Princes . . . or perhaps even foreign vested interests raise objections'.

The Congress made its statement public; meanwhile, Gandhi wrote a private note to Linlithgow, more in sorrow than in anger. He had read the viceroy's statement, and 'it made me sad. Its implications frighten me. I cannot help feeling that a profound mistake has been made' (in spurning the Congress offer).

Gandhi also sent a cable to the British press, saying the viceroy's statement had 'widen[ed] the gulf between India, as represented by the Congress, and England. Thinking India outside the Congress, too has not welcomed the pronouncement.' He then asked once more the question that he, and others like him, had asked a hundred times since the beginning of the war. How could Britain 'claim to stand for justice, if she fails to be just to India'?[8]

IV

In the second week of September 1940, Gandhi travelled to Bombay for a working committee meeting. Back in July, the mood was all in favour of a settlement; now that the government had spurned their offer, the mood had swung back towards opposition. Gandhi played a leading part in the meeting, advocating a programme of graded and guided satyagraha, to be offered by individuals in the first instance.

Even in the midst of his political preoccupations, Gandhi still found time to offer advice on health to his friends. Saraladevi Chaudhurani had come down to Sevagram. After their aborted 'spiritual marriage' now twenty years in the past, they had settled down to an amicable (if mostly distant) friendship, with Kasturba not standing in the way.

Saraladevi had not been well. While in Bombay for the Congress meeting, Gandhi consulted the Poona-based naturopath Dinshaw Mehta, who thought Sarala might wish to try his methods of cure. Gandhi passed on the advice to the patient, via a letter to Amrit Kaur.

Dr Mehta, he said, 'was ready to take charge of her [Sarala] whenever she can go to Poona. If she will not go, he is of opinion that she will not be cured except by quinine taken under observation. The spleen must be reduced. She ought not to trifle with her body.'[9]

In the last week of September, Gandhi travelled to Delhi, to meet the viceroy in a last bid to avoid confrontation. Gandhi had been receiving more letters on the exactions levied by British officials, who were—often against the popular will—collecting money and materials for the war. India had been dragged into the war against its wish; now, if the Congress wanted to preach against these forcible exactions, why should it not be allowed to do so?

Linlithgow said the restrictions on press freedom would not be removed; nor could the Congress be allowed to peacefully preach against the war. For his part, Gandhi made it plain that 'the Congress is as much opposed to Nazism as any Britisher can be'; at the same time, the people of India made 'no distinction between Nazism and the double autocracy [of the British and the Princes] that rules India'. He was disappointed that they were not even able 'to arrive at an agreement on the single issue of freedom of speech'.[10]

Later, in a press statement, Gandhi spoke in despair of 'a certain cold reserve about the British official world which gives them their strength and isolation from surroundings and facts'. This remark was based on forty years of talking with British officials—in South Africa, in India and in Britain itself. Of all the representatives of the ruling race Gandhi had dealt with, Linlithgow was in many ways the most unsympathetic. When India needed a viceroy who could understand how Indians felt, it had been given one who could think only of his own country and his own countrymen.

Three weeks after his failed meeting with the viceroy, Gandhi announced that the Congress would commence a programme of restricted civil disobedience. One by one, individuals nominated by Gandhi would peacefully preach against the war and the war effort, and thus court arrest.

Gandhi wanted to put pressure on the British, but not to embarrass them unduly. Hence the decision to launch a movement of individuals, and not a popular mass upsurge like those he had led in 1920–21 or in 1930. He wrote to the viceroy that he was 'taking extraordinary precautions to ensure non-violence', to which end he was 'restricting the movement to the fewest possible typical individuals'. He, and the Congress, hoped that, by protesting in this restrained and controlled fashion, they might be able to bring the government back to the path of dialogue and negotiation.

Since he was now seventy-one, Gandhi believed that 'this will perhaps be the last civil disobedience struggle which I shall have conducted. Naturally I would want it to be as flawless as it can be.' The individual chosen to start the campaign was Vinoba Bhave, the austere scholar who had joined Gandhi as far back as 1916, a man who, in his abolition of 'every trace of untouchability from his heart', his readiness to take part 'in every menial activity of the Ashram from scavenging to cooking', was the model ashramite, more so since, as Gandhi added, 'for perfect spinning probably he has no rival in all India'.[11]

Writing to Gandhi's son Devadas, Mahadev Desai said Vinoba was selected as the first satyagrahi because he understood his master's principles so thoroughly. 'The uppermost consideration in Bapu's mind, throughout these anxious days,' wrote Mahadev, 'has been that of non-violence, and though he seems to have now lost caste with Government, no one thinks of Government's interests more than he.'[12]

From 17 October, Vinoba Bhave began going from hamlet to hamlet, preaching against the war. Speaking in Hindi and Marathi, he said, 'The soldiers of the British are full of vices. It is not seen what character a recruit in the Army possesses. It is considered enough if he has a chest measuring 36 inches. For them it is always considered a qualification if they are devoid of human considerations.'[13]

On 18 October, *Harijan* received a letter from the government forbidding it from reporting speeches made by Vinoba. On the 21st he was arrested. Three days later, Gandhi announced that in view of the press censorship he was suspending publication of *Harijan* and its Gujarati and Hindi counterparts. At the same time, he exhorted every patriot to 'become his own walking newspaper and carry the good news [of the ongoing satyagraha] from mouth to mouth. . . . This no Government can overtake or suppress. It is the cheapest newspaper yet devised and it defies the wit of Government, however clever it may be.'

The second satyagrahi nominated by Gandhi was Jawaharlal Nehru, a man he had described to the viceroy as 'one who will be the future leader of all India'. Nehru was detained on the last day of October, before he could begin making speeches on the ground.

Gandhi now contemplated going on a fast himself. But the working committee dissuaded him from doing so; instead, it advised that the programme of individual satyagraha be extended. Since his letters were read by the censor, Gandhi sent Mahadev Desai on a tour of the provinces, asking Congress leaders to prepare their own lists of which individuals would offer satyagraha, and in what order.

Mahadev carried with him a charter of instructions prepared by Gandhi. Each protester had to inform the district magistrate of where, when and how he would offer satyagraha. The method followed was to shout, in the appropriate regional language, this message: 'It is wrong to help the British war effort with men or money. The only worthy effort is to resist all war with non-violent resistance.' The satyagrahis should say 'they sympathize with the British in their effort to live, but they want also to live themselves as members of a fully free nation'.

Slowly, the satyagraha spread. One by one, designated Congressmen in different provinces began to court arrest, among them Patel, Rajaji, Azad and other stalwarts. Once the movement had gathered momentum, Gandhi also allowed women, likewise carefully chosen for their credibility, to become satyagrahis.[14]

Through the second half of 1940, the individual satyagraha campaign gathered pace. A table compiled by the government was involuntary proof of its success. This showed that a large proportion of Congress members of provincial legislative assemblies had courted arrest; fifty out of ninety-nine in Bihar, fifty-six out of ninety-seven in Bombay, 109 out of 164 in Madras, eighty-six out of 151 in the United Provinces.[15]

The government now deliberated as to whether to arrest Gandhi himself. Higher officials in Delhi and Bombay were keen that he be detained. Those closer to the ground advised caution. 'As regards Mr. Gandhi's arrest,' wrote the deputy commissioner of Wardha,

'I am strongly against this being done at the present time. . . . So far, he has guided the movement so as to cause the least amount of embarrassment and there are no signs that he proposes to do otherwise. Such being the case, it would be a great mistake to arrest him.' His colleague in the neighbouring district, Nagpur, concurred, saying that if they did go ahead and detain Gandhi, 'the moment he is arrested and the controlling hand is removed, there will be indiscriminate satyagraha. . . . [L]eftists are looking forward to his arrest, so that they may get an opportunity to lead the movement.'[16]

V

Gandhi had chosen the method of individual satyagraha to avoid a total confrontation with the British. He still hoped that they would be amenable to a compromise. In November, he sent Mahadev Desai to Delhi, to meet the viceroy's private secretary, Gilbert Laithwaite. Mahadev told Laithwaite that Gandhi's desire was to convert all mankind to non-violence; but this did not mean that he was in any way anti-British. In fact, the Congress was anti-fascist as well as anti-Nazi. If Hitler came to India, said Mahadev, Gandhi would launch a non-violent struggle against him. He added that if India was granted independence now, the Congress would most likely help the British in the war, even if Gandhi himself would step aside and continue to preach ahimsa.

In Delhi, Mahadev held a press conference, where he said that Gandhi himself 'thinks all the twenty-four hours of the British people and the British rulers and how best to help them, and yet knows that these regard him as their enemy'.[17] Before returning to Sevagram, Mahadev left with Laithwaite a draft of a statement he hoped the viceroy would issue, to the effect that since Gandhi had made it clear that he did not intend 'to paralyse [the] war effort', but merely 'to prevent people from being dragged into helping the war against their will', the government was now 'pleased to announce that those who are opposed to the prosecution of war on conscientious grounds, whether of a political or ethical character, are free to express their views, provided they do not prevent those who are inclined to help the war and provided they do not in doing so transgress the bounds of restraint or non-violence'.

Mahadev was heroically trying to find a face-saving formula, that is to say, to save the face of the Imperial Government and his master at the same time. Laithwaite noted of their talks that 'Mr. Desai's good temper and good will were obvious'. However, the statement proposed by Mahadev could not be issued by the government since 'we could not and would not have any anti-war propaganda, and that our determination not to do anything which might impede or reduce [the] war effort was complete and unalterable'.[18]

The secretaries to Gandhi and Linlithgow got along far better than their bosses did. After Mahadev returned to Sevagram, Laithwaite wrote thanking him for coming all the way to Delhi to see him. However, the envelope in which the letter was posted was under-stamped. Mahadev wrote back enclosing the envelope, saying that 'although we are "at war", we might have fun occasionally'. Surely, he asked, the private secretary to the viceroy was 'supposed to know and obey the law better than the ignorant public'? Mahadev had to pay eight annas to the postman 'for the ignorance of "Government"!'

Laithwaite, in reply, guiltily enclosed one rupee. Mahadev now joked: 'To wreak "vengeance" on you I was half inclined to send the amount on to the Civil Disobedience Fund! But lest you should take it as vengeance, I am sending it on to a Red Cross Fund in your name (using your initials). I hope you will not mind that.'[19]

The regard that Laithwaite had for Mahadev was atypical. For, most British officials in India distrusted Gandhi and the Congress. The war had intensified their dislike; and now, the individual satyagraha campaign had turned distrust and dislike into something akin to hatred. Representative here was a pamphlet issued in October 1940 by an ICS official in the Central Provinces named E.S. Hyde entitled 'Why We Should Support India's War Effort'. Addressed to Indians, this stated that 'what Mr. Gandhi and the Congress leaders of all grades, none of whom have had the courage or the patriotism to join the fighting forces, are asking you is to stab in the back your own countrymen, the cream of India's manhood, who with their comrades in arms of Britain, the Dominions and the Colonies are all that stand between you and the predatory totalitarian powers'.

Hyde's immediate superior was an Indian, C.M. Trivedi. He thought the pamphlet and its wording improper. In any case, said Trivedi to Hyde, 'it is not the business of District Officers to become propagandists in attacking Mahatma Gandhi and the Congress'. Hyde was unrepentant. The Congress, he insisted, 'must be shown up for what it is; a treacherous organisation stabbing in the back its own countrymen who are fighting India's enemies; an ally of Hitler and Mussolini'.[20]

The war had, it seems, opened up a racial divide even within the ranks of the Indian Civil Service. Note that Trivedi used the honorific 'Mahatma' in referring to Gandhi, whereas Hyde preferred the plain 'Mr'. The average Indian ICS officer must surely have had some sympathy with the aspirations for freedom of his compatriots; the average British ICS officer, none at all.

VI

Gandhi's campaign had angered the British in India, and it had also alienated one of his closest friends in England. This was Henry Polak. Through the 1920s and 1930s, Polak had moved closer to the position of liberals like V.S. Srinivasa Sastri, which was that self-government should be won step by step, by constitutional means, not sought to be seized by mass protest. Polak and Gandhi remained friends, but, over the decades, their correspondence grew more erratic.

Polak was Jewish, and also British. These twin claims, of community and nation, made him intensely hate Hitler and the Nazis, whose prime ambitions, of course, were to subjugate Britain and exterminate the Jews. When, in October 1940, Gandhi asked Congressmen to court arrest, one by one, Polak was dismayed. He wrote to an Indian friend that 'the resort to civil disobedience in certain quarters and the circumstances in which it has been undertaken, have been regarded as entirely without justification in this country, and disastrous if they were to have any serious consequences'. The 'kind of stuff' that Vinoba Bhave and Jawaharlal Nehru had been saying, remarked Polak, 'could not be allowed for a moment in this country, nor could even strict pacifists here justify it'.

Polak was living, as he had long done, with his family on the outskirts of London. The bombs were falling all around them. 'We are still getting daily attacks on London,' wrote Polak to his friend, 'but, notwithstanding the mischief and inconvenience, it is astonishing how little damage has been done upon the whole. Even the loss of life and injuries, painful as they are to note, are regarded with comparative equanimity. The spirit of the public is amazingly firm, courageous and determined. There will certainly be no collapse of morale here, whatever may happen elsewhere. Indeed, I seem to detect a growing uplift and an increased sense of ultimate triumph in the cause for which we are fighting. The personal risks are not even being considered.'[21]

The letter was heartfelt, and accurate. The British had, through all the raids and bombs, sustained their morale. They were determined to defend their island, their nation, to the end. Yet, the irony was that the traits that Polak ascribed to his people were also displayed by nationalists in India. The spirit of Gandhi, Nehru et al. was likewise 'firm, courageous, and determined'. Despite the hostility of the British, despite the decades of struggle, their morale remained high, as did the 'sense of ultimate triumph' in the cause for which they were fighting.

The incommensurability of viewpoints was striking, even tragic. Locked in their respective fights for freedom, neither Indian nor Briton could properly recognize or empathize with the other. This was true even of the most intimate friends. That Polak could not understand why Gandhi, in the evening of his life, would wish to launch a final struggle for freedom, or Gandhi appreciate why his campaign would cause such hurt and anguish to Polak, was symptomatic of a much wider and much deeper misrecognition.

VII

Gandhi's attitude towards the war had also alienated some Indian politicians. One was Sir Sikandar Hyat Khan, prime minister of the Punjab. Sikandar Hyat was a leader of the Unionist Party, a cross-religious alliance of landlords, Hindu, Sikh and Muslim, all utterly loyal to the British. Sikandar Hyat and the Unionists had enthusiastically supported the war effort, and tens of thousands of soldiers from the Punjab had enlisted to serve in Europe and the Middle East.

In early October, Sikandar Hyat made a speech in Gurgaon, attacking Gandhi for opposing the recruitment of Indian soldiers. Claiming that 99 per cent of the Punjab was for the war, he charged Gandhi with 'stabbing the British in the back' and with 'a betrayal of the best interests of India and the Islamic world'. A report of the speech reached Gandhi, who responded in *Harijan*, by saying that the Punjab had always been 'one of the best recruiting grounds for the British rulers'. Soldiering was a profession like any other, he said, and 'these professionals will lend their services to whomsoever will pay them good wages and enough practice for their professions'.

Gandhi was suggesting that by enlisting for the war, the Punjabi soldier was merely doing a job, for which he was paid. Service in uniform did not in any way imply an endorsement of imperialism. As Gandhi put it: 'The Punjabi soldier is as much interested in the issue [of British rule] as the black soldiers trained by General Franco were interested in his politics or in his ambition.'[22]

Sikandar Hyat was furious with Gandhi's suggestion that the Punjabis had enlisted not for ideals but for money. In a speech at Lahore's Badshahi mosque on 1 November, he said Gandhi had insulted all Punjabis—Hindus, Sikhs and Muslims—by calling them mercenaries. If India was threatened by invasion, it would be the people of the Punjab and the Frontier who would have to resist them, while Gandhi would be safe in his ashram in Sevagram. 'If Mahatma Gandhi wants to pursue the policy [of ahimsa] which is beyond the comprehension of ordinary beings,' remarked Khan, 'it would be better for him to go to [the Himalayan holy places of] Amarnath or Rishikesh where he can have a full play of his Mahatmaship.'[23]

Meanwhile, another prominent Punjabi Muslim, a religious leader this time, had taken issue with the individual satyagraha movement. 'A large majority of Muslims are standing out as a body from your present programme,' wrote this divine to Gandhi, adding: 'At the same time the present antipathy between the two communities is bound to increase and the idea of a Hindu–Muslim unity will become a still fading dream.'

Gandhi wrote back defending his campaign. 'If independence is obtained as a result of this struggle', he remarked, it would be 'obtained by all and not for Congressmen merely. And why should antipathy between the two [communities] increase because both get extended freedom soon if it be as a result of action taken by only one? Do I not deserve special credit from you if without putting you to any trouble, I secure you a mango as well as one for myself? The utmost you can do is reject the gift but surely not get angry with me.'[24]

The language showed stress; the mango metaphor was strained. It seems that Gandhi, estranged from the British, and now from the Muslims too, was exasperated by the impediments to the freedom he had so long striven for, yet hoped nonetheless to inspire a fresh movement of sacrifice and struggle to achieve that ever elusive goal.

VIII

By December 1940, several thousand satyagrahis were in prison, arrested one by one, as each shouted slogans against the war and thereby breached the law. Now, as a gesture of goodwill, Gandhi announced that there would be no courting of arrest between 24 December 1940 and 4 January 1941, so as to allow the officials to celebrate Christmas and New Year with their families.

On Christmas Eve, Gandhi sat down to write a letter to Adolf Hitler. Having previously urged the British to sue for peace, he now asked the German leader to do so. Hitler believed the Germans had perfected the 'science of destruction'; but couldn't he see that other nations might exceed them in this regard? 'If not the British,' said Gandhi to Hitler, 'some other power will certainly improve upon your method and beat you with your own weapon.'

Gandhi continued: 'You are leaving no legacy to your people of which they should feel proud. They cannot take part in [a] recital of cruel deed, however skilfully planned. I, therefore, appeal to you in the name of humanity to stop the war. You will lose nothing by referring all the matters of dispute between you and Great Britain to an international tribunal of your joint choice.'

Gandhi also offered a primer on Indian politics to Hitler. 'Ours is a unique position,' he remarked. 'We resist British Imperialism no less than Nazism.' Indians had long fought, non-violently, for their freedom. 'We know what the British heel means for us and the non-European races of the world,' said Gandhi to Hitler. 'But we would never wish to end the British rule with German aid.'[25]

This letter was better judged, and better timed, than Gandhi's appeal to Britons. The Raj, however, decided to suppress the letter altogether, principally because Gandhi had referred to the subjugation of India by British imperialism.

The archives have a moderately fat file on Gandhi's 'Open Letter to Hitler', where various officials give free rein to their views—and prejudices. The first to comment was an arch-imperialist in the home department, who claimed this was 'not a genuine message to Hitler, but a message to the people of India', which 'notwithstanding its skilful manipulation of the peace motive, the Christmas spirit and so on', had as its 'main object' to 'bring [the British] Government [in India] into hatred and contempt'.

On 28 December, the chief press adviser to the government, an Englishman named Desmond Young, called in some Indian editors to discuss the letter. Among them was Gandhi's son, Devadas, editor of the *Hindustan Times*. Devadas said he had not seen the letter, though he had been aware that his father was composing it. When shown the full text, Devadas told the chief press adviser that on balance the letter was anti-Hitler and gained in credibility by stating the case against British imperialism. He said that 'even if the letter did not move Herr Hitler, it would help the British Government in the U. S. A. and elsewhere and damp down German propaganda about India'. Devadas suggested that Gandhi be invited by All India Radio to broadcast the appeal in full, with the broadcast relayed to the United States and Great Britain.

Desmond Young was a former editor himself. He was convinced that there was 'a genuine and sincere desire on the part of the great majority of Indian newspaper editors for the defeat of the Axis Powers'. Young knew that many of these editors 'were opponents of Nazism and Fascism long before the outbreak of war and I see no reason to suppose that their views have changed'.

Then Young added: 'On the other hand, there is an equally genuine and sincere reluctance, not altogether discreditable, to oppose what professes to be a movement for India's freedom, led by a man whom Indians respect and admire, perhaps beyond reason. These views may be mutually contradictory in the present circumstances but that does not prevent them being honestly held.'[26]

This nuanced understanding of the predicament of intelligent and patriotic Indians was rare. It was not of course shared by most British officials in India, nor by ordinary Britons in Britain, not even by Gandhi's old comrade Henry Polak.

IX

In January 1941, the viceroy expanded his executive council to include some half a dozen Indians. Among the new councillors were two former Congressmen, M.S. Aney and N.R. Sarkar, as well as several Muslim notables. Meanwhile, Subhas Chandra Bose disappeared from his house in Calcutta. After leaving the Congress he had formed a new party, the Forward Bloc, which, however, did not gain much traction. Now Bose had left India for an unknown destination. The colonial police believed his destination was Japan, from where he would smuggle arms back to India.[27] (In fact, he had gone overland to Afghanistan, and from there to Germany.)

Gandhi did not comment in public either on the expanded executive council or on Subhas Bose's disappearance. His main concern was the deteriorating communal situation. In the first months of 1941, Hindu–Muslim riots broke out in Dacca, Ahmedabad and several other cities. Gandhi was distressed by the violence, and more particularly by the fact that, as he put it, 'individual cases apart, the Congress produced little or no influence over either the Muslims or the Hindus in the affected areas'.[28]

In the second week of June 1941, the senior Congress leader Rajendra Prasad came to Sevagram to discuss the communal situation with Gandhi. Prasad told Gandhi that:

(a) I am losing my hold over Bihar.
(b) The Muslims are frankly aggressive.
(c) The Hindus are equally aggressive, and are organizing themselves.
(d) The Hindu Mahasabha is gaining ground.[29]

The emergence of communal blocs was disturbing. Clearly, the Pakistan resolution had consolidated a sense of communal pride among young, militant Muslims, giving them a concrete ideal to fight for—that of a Muslim homeland. On the other side, the Hindu Mahasabha was also increasing its influence. The Mahasabha's leader, V.D. Savarkar, was a bitter critic of Gandhi, whom he claimed had 'loaded the Moslems with favoured treatment'. Now, he was encouraging young, militant Hindus to pick up the sword to settle their disputes with Muslims.[30]

X

On 22 June 1941, Germany invaded Russia, breaking the non-aggression pact the two countries had signed two years previously. Russia had now joined the Allies. In India, communists who had previously disparaged the 'Imperialists War' began supporting the British, since this had become a 'Peoples War'. To better understand what all this meant, Gandhi sent Mahadev to the sub-Himalayan town of Dehradun, where Jawaharlal Nehru was incarcerated.

In late June, Gandhi received an anguished letter from Jayaprakash Narayan, a prominent young socialist in the Congress. Narayan was in a detention camp in Deoli, after being arrested for offering individual satyagraha. From here he wrote to Gandhi in Hindi, urging a more widespread struggle against the Raj. A translation follows:

> One feels like weeping at the slow pace of the struggle. And you used to say that the fight will now be carried on more intensively. The state and the lack of purpose of the Congress have together made us helpless. In future we must endeavour to rid ourselves of this helplessness.[31]

Gandhi's reply is unavailable. Some part of him certainly wanted to intensify the struggle. But another part urged caution. The war had entered its critical phase. In India itself, Hindus and Muslims were becoming ever more estranged.

Not long after Narayan wrote asking him to take on the British more directly, Gandhi received a letter from a Muslim friend, Shwaib

Qureshi, an associate from the Khilafat days and the son of one of his South African comrades. Qureshi, who was now working for the nawab of Bhopal, wrote beseechingly to Gandhi to take the lead in reducing Hindu–Muslim tensions, growing across India. If 'the present dangerous drift in communal relations is allowed to continue much longer', he warned, 'anything might happen. It may be that Fates have decreed otherwise and that renewed efforts are doomed to failure but he will be taking too great a responsibility in history who would take the deluge for granted and resigning himself to it in a pathetic, almost tragic, spirit of fatalism refuses to make any effort. If an effort is to be made there is only one man who can make it. I need not tell you who. Will you?'

Gandhi, in reply, said it was unfair to put 'the whole burden' on him. He reminded his Muslim friend that 'I have gone down on my knees to Quaid-e-Azam as I had to your knowledge to the Aga Khan and Co. in London' (during the Round Table Conference). He would, he said, 'gladly give my life for settling the question'. But he needed help. 'If you simply throw the burden on me,' said Gandhi to Qureshi, 'you will break me. If you shoulder it with me even if it means leaving Bhopal for a time, it can be done, God willing.'[32]

XI

Rabindranath Tagore died on 7 August 1941. He had been ailing for some time. Since *Harijan* was no longer being published, Gandhi issued a short statement calling Tagore 'the greatest poet of the age', an 'ardent nationalist who was also a humanitarian'. There 'was hardly any public activity on which he has not left the impress of his powerful personality', he remarked.[33]

The man who had brought Gandhi to Tagore was Charlie Andrews. Andrews had died in April 1940; now Tagore had passed away, a year and a few months later. These twin losses must surely have hurt Gandhi greatly. Andrews was by some distance his closest friend. And, after Gokhale (who died in 1915), Tagore was by some distance the Indian whom Gandhi most admired. Now both had gone.

Gandhi had been in Sevagram from the beginning of the year. Through the first half of 1941, he monitored the progress of the individual satyagraha programme. He had deliberately kept Mahadev out of the campaign, for he needed him to travel between provinces, carrying messages and bringing back reports. By late 1941, some 2500 Congressmen had been arrested.

Mahadev also kept Gandhi up to date with the progress of the World War. It was through him, and the clippings he brought to his notice, that Gandhi learnt of the fierce fighting between the Germans and the British in North Africa, of the German conquest of Greece and Yugoslavia, of the freezing of German and Italian assets in the United States, and, most momentously, of the German invasion of Russia.

Except for one brief trip to Allahabad, Gandhi had stayed put in Wardha since October 1940. A year later, in October 1941, he wrote a long and most interesting letter to his Quaker friend Agatha Harrison on how he saw the world, from his own particular vantage point. Within India, he noted, 'distrust of the Rulers is growing and spreading. The distance is increasing. We here perceive no difference between Hitlerism and British Imperialism. Hitlerism is a superfine copy of Imperialism and Imperialism is trying to overtake Hitlerism as fast as it can. Democracy is nowhere.'

Gandhi saw the war as an 'unholy duel' between two immoral antagonists. The British, naturally, saw it very differently. If many Indians distrusted their white rulers, they, in turn, were increasingly exasperated with the inability of Gandhi and the Congress to recognize the fight for life and death the British were engaged in. Henry Polak had told Agatha Harrison that if their friend Gandhi was (like them) living in London, his non-violence would not survive the stress of bombs falling near his feet and his loved ones being crushed to death. When Harrison passed on this criticism, Gandhi replied in a somewhat defensive tone. 'I rehearse such situations,' he remarked. 'I pray that the faith might not break under such strain.' He reminded his Quaker friend that 'I did shed a silent tear when I read about the damage done to the Houses of Parliament, the Westminster Abbey and St. Paul's'.[34]

CHAPTER TWENTY-NINE

Towards 'Quit India'

I

On 7 December 1941, Japan bombed Pearl Harbour, and the United States finally entered the war on the side of Britain and Russia. Asked to comment, Gandhi said he did 'not know whether America could have avoided the entry'. He himself wished it had stayed neutral, thus to play 'its natural part' as an 'arbitrator and mediator between the warring nations'.

Gandhi believed that by her 'territorial vastness, amazing energy, unrivalled financial status and owing to the composite character of her people', America was 'the one country which could have saved the world from the unthinkable butchery that is going on'. Now, with her entry into the war, 'there is no great Power left which can mediate and bring about peace for which I have no doubt the peoples of all lands are thirsting'.[1]

In the last week of December 1941, the CWC met in Bardoli, Gandhi making the overnight trip from Wardha to attend. The other CWC members who had been arrested the previous year were now out of jail, having completed their sentences. With the Soviet Union and the United States entering the war, this had become a truly global conflict; meanwhile, Japan was advancing on British possessions in South East Asia, bringing the war closer to India itself. The gravity

642

of the situation was grasped by the working committee's more internationalist members such as Nehru and Rajagopalachari. They thus decided to make a fresh move for compromise.

In a resolution passed at Bardoli, the working committee chose to offer cooperation with the war effort in exchange for a clear commitment to independence for India once the conflict had ended. In Gandhi's words, the Congress had 'made a small opening for violence just with a view to shaking hands with Britain'.[2] Following the Bardoli resolution, Gandhi formally suspended the individual civil disobedience movement, and wrote to the viceroy of his decision. He also decided to restart his three weeklies to give public expression to his views.

In January 1942, Gandhi travelled to Banaras to deliver the Silver Jubilee Convocation address at the Banaras Hindu University. He had come at the invitation of the vice chancellor, Sarvepalli Radhakrishnan, the philosopher who, some years previously, had edited a festschrift of tributes to Gandhi.

Gandhi's address was given extempore. A previous speaker had boasted that the university's new engineering faculties were its pride and joy. Gandhi, characteristically, said that this did not, and would not, distinguish BHU from universities in the West. But the BHU could make a special contribution if it actively fostered harmonious relations between India's two major communities. A good way to begin would be to pursue closer ties with a university that carried 'Muslim' rather than 'Hindu' in its name. And so, Gandhi asked his audience:

> Have you been able to attract to your University youths from Aligarh? Have you been able to identify with them? That, I think, should be your special work, the special contribution of your University. Money has come in, and more will come in if God keeps Malaviya ji in our midst for a few more years. But no amount of money will achieve the miracle I want—I mean a heart-unity between Hindus and Muslims.[3]

This holy city of the Hindus had previously been witness to other speeches where Gandhi had asked his audience to grow beyond their prejudices. In 1916, then relatively unknown, Gandhi had spoken in Banaras of the importance of middle-class Indians identifying with the poor. In 1934, then famous and celebrated, he had spoken in Banaras of the importance of ending untouchability. Now, even more famous and respected, he spoke in Banaras of the importance of Hindu–Muslim unity.

II

On 11 February, Jamnalal Bajaj died of a cerebral haemorrhage. He was only fifty-two. The death affected Gandhi deeply. 'Bapu is in greatest need of consolation,' wrote Mahadev Desai to Rajagopalachari. 'I think his grief is as deep and profound as it was on Maganlal Gandhi's death.'

Bajaj was, in effect, a fifth son to Gandhi. He had put his wealth at the service of the freedom struggle, his personality at the service of his leader. Other industrialists such as Ambalal Sarabhai and G.D. Birla had given Gandhi moral and material support. But they had not gone to jail on his behalf. Bajaj had, several times. He had also acted as the treasurer of the Congress, and was instrumental in Gandhi's move to central India. Indeed, the ashram in Sevagram was built on what was once Bajaj's ancestral property.

In a fine tribute, Mahadev wrote of Bajaj that this 'treasurer of the nation's wealth was also the treasurer of the nation's honour. He was among the very few capitalists who recklessly threw themselves in the fray for the nation's freedom and bore the rigours of imprisonment every time the call had been made'. Bajaj had, by opening his family temple to 'untouchables', 'risked the wrath of his hide-bound community'. He was equally committed to Hindu–Muslim unity, 'for which he cheerfully bore heavy blows in the course of a riot . . .'[4]

Soon after Bajaj died, Gandhi had a meeting with his family. He told the elder son, Kamalnayan, to take over and run his father's businesses; and the younger son, Ramkrishna, to 'dedicate your whole life to service and completing whatever work Jamnalal has left incomplete'.[5]

In between these memorial meetings for Bajaj, Gandhi made a quick trip to Calcutta. The Chinese leader Chiang Kai-shek was visiting India to canvass support for resistance to the Japanese. He had hoped to come to Sevagram to see Gandhi. In the event, this proved unfeasible, so Gandhi travelled to Calcutta to meet him.

Chiang and his wife were staying at Government House. Gandhi was staying at the residence of the industrialist G.D. Birla, which is where the meeting took place, on 18 February 1942, with the Indian spinning away at his wheel while they talked. Madame Chiang had been educated in America, so Gandhi asked why she didn't interpret instead of the official translator the Generalissimo had brought along. 'Surely he did not marry an interpreter,' responded Madame Chiang, 'he married a woman.'

Chiang told Gandhi that while non-violence might work against the British, it would never work against the Japanese. As Mahadev Desai (who was present) reported: 'He was naturally full of indignation at what Japan had done and was doing in China, and he had grave fears of India having to go through China's terrible fate if the Japanese overran India.'

Writing to Vallabhbhai Patel, Gandhi summarized the gist of Chiang's argument in these words: 'Help the British anyhow. They are better than the others and will improve further hereafter.'[6] Meanwhile, Chiang wrote in his diary that 'after meeting Gandhi yesterday, I'm disappointed. My expectations were too great, but perhaps the pain of being ruled by the British has hardened his heart.'[7]

As soon as Gandhi returned to Sevagram, Mahadev Desai fell ill. Mahadev had just completed twenty-five years in the service of Gandhi—and India. He was his master's amanuensis and shadow, his secretary, nurse and cook, his translator and his interpreter.

Mahadev had always worked ferociously hard. But in the past two years he had, if anything, worked even harder. He had been continuously on the road, travelling often to Delhi to negotiate with government officials and across the country to monitor the individual satyagraha movement. He was now utterly exhausted. His blood pressure had risen alarmingly. Gandhi advised him 'to take prolonged rest'.[8]

III

Just before the meeting between Gandhi and Chiang Kai-Shek, Singapore fell to the Japanese. This was a serious blow to the British; weeks later, in a blow to the Dutch, the Japanese overran the island of Java.

In the first week of March, a Lahore Congressman named Jagannath wrote identical letters to Nehru and Rajagopalachari saying that the freedom of India was paramount, and everything else was secondary. Hence a struggle against the British had to be launched immediately. Nehru wanted his country to be independent too, but, as he now told the Lahore patriot: 'We cannot isolate India from the rest of the world and I do think that it is important that we give our moral sympathy completely to China and Russia. Their defeat will be a tragedy from the larger point of view and from the point of view of the future of Indian freedom.' Nehru thought that 'we have become too obsessed with our hatred of British imperialism not to see this larger picture. Britain is already a second class power and the British Empire cannot survive. It will be dangerous for us to allow things to happen which lead to other empires being formed.'

Rajaji likewise warned the Lahore Congressman that a struggle against the British now would only help the Axis powers. 'I do not hope to get Indian independence,' he wrote, 'through the intervention of the Japanese at this juncture. We must get it if at all now by playing a[n] honourable part on the side of the British. If unfortunately the British lose and the Japanese take possession of India, we will have to be prepared for a new kind of dominion for a good long time to come.'[9]

Gandhi did not recognize the Japanese threat as fully as Nehru and Rajaji. Besides, he still contemplated a mass non-violent struggle against the British. However, for the moment he went along with the Bardoli resolution of the working committee, which had sought to make one last effort for compromise with the British.

As the Congress, led by Nehru and Rajaji, made fresh overtures towards the British, from the other side the Labour members of the British Cabinet also pushed for a rapprochement. The prime minister, Winston Churchill, was a diehard imperialist, who—as the secretary of state for India, Leo Amery, noted in April 1941—'just dislikes the idea of anything being done in India at all . . . and just hopes that we can sit back and do nothing indefinitely'.[10] However, Amery himself was less hostile to Indian aspirations, while his Cabinet colleagues from the Labour Party, such as Clement Attlee and Stafford Cripps, had long been committed to the independence of India. Attlee warned Churchill not to 'accept and act on the crude imperialism of the Viceroy, not only because I think it is wrong, but because it is fatally short-sighted and suicidal'.[11] Cripps, who shared Attlee's views in this regard, was in addition a friend of Nehru's and Gandhi's; shortly after war broke out in September 1939, he had come to India to meet them both.

Meanwhile, left-wing anti-colonialists in Britain were urging an immediate pact with Indian nationalists. Writing in the *Observer* in February 1942, George Orwell said the Indian people could be won over only by 'some concrete unmistakable act of generosity, by giving something away that cannot afterwards be taken back'. Orwell himself offered a three-part proposal: 'First, let India be given immediate Dominion status, with the right to secede after the war, if she so desires. Secondly, let the leaders of the principal political parties be invited at once to form a National Government, to remain in office for the duration of the war. Thirdly, let India enter into formal military alliance with Britain and the countries allied to Britain.'[12]

In March, the British Cabinet finally decided to send Stafford Cripps to India to seek a provisional settlement. The brief he was given promised Dominion Status after the war had ended—rather than immediately, as both the Congress and Orwell had urged. When the war had been won, a constitution would be designed by an elected body of Indians, albeit with each province having the right to accept or reject it. Meanwhile, the British-controlled Government of India would 'bear the responsibility' for 'organizing to the full the military, moral and material resources of India' in prosecuting the war, albeit 'with the co-operation of the peoples of India'.[13]

IV

Stafford Cripps arrived in New Delhi on 23 March. Four days later he met Gandhi, who had travelled to the capital. The conversation was civil, but there remained a fundamental disagreement. Gandhi thought that the clause allowing provinces to reject the Constitution 'was an invitation to the Moslems to create a Pakistan'.[14]

Cripps spent three weeks in India. He met with leaders of the Sikhs, the Muslims, the princes and the Depressed Classes. And he spoke extensively to leaders of the Congress. Though he met both Gandhi and Nehru, Cripps spent more time with Maulana Azad, then Congress president. Azad, for his part, consulted regularly with Nehru (and to a lesser extent with Gandhi) on his talks with Cripps.

Both Cripps and Azad brought an open mind to the discussions. Both wished for a compromise, both acted in good faith. Cripps, like Attlee and other senior Labour leaders, believed that the Allied cause would be given more legitimacy if the Congress, the leading voice for freedom in Britain's largest colony, was brought on board. Azad, like Nehru, Rajaji and Gandhi, empathized with the British predicament; like Nehru and Rajaji (but unlike Gandhi), he had no doctrinal commitment to absolute non-violence, and so was willing, if offered honourable terms, to participate in the war.

Cripps and Azad spoke for many hours and wrote many letters to one another. The Congress, said its president, had three major disagreements with the British Cabinet. First, whatever Linlithgow and Churchill might claim, the Congress spoke for far more than caste Hindus. Second, while the Congress was happy to form a national government with the Muslim League and other parties, it hoped for a clear devolution of power to Indian hands, with the viceroy being to the government what the king was to the British Cabinet. Third, the Congress believed that if it had to join the war effort, an Indian member of the viceroy's executive council should bear ultimate responsibility for the defence of the country.

The third point proved to be the stickiest. For, the British would not trust anyone but an Englishman with the defence of India. Cripps suggested that the existing commander-in-chief of the Indian Army be made war member in the executive council, with an Indian member taking on other responsibilities such as 'public relations', 'all canteen organizations', 'stationery, printing, and forms for the Army', etc. Azad (and the Congress) found this condescending, and even humiliating. The C-in-C could remain in charge of military matters, but the defence member had to be Indian. For, as Azad pointed out, 'the chief functions of a National Government must necessarily be to organize defence, both intensively and on the widest popular basis, and to create [a] mass psychology of resistance to an invader'.[15]

Liberals like Sapru and Jayakar, placed between the Congress and the Raj, told the viceroy that 'the adoption of an Indian Defence Member will have a great effect on Indian psychology. It will inspire the people with confidence . . . We think that the presence of such a Member will, far from weakening the military position in India, strengthen it, and the political effects of this step will be very wholesome.'[16]

However, an Indian as defence member was not acceptable to Linlithgow. The viceroy wrote to the secretary of state for India that 'morale in [the] sense of willingness to suffer for a national cause is a non-existent quality in India and could not be evoked by any political concessions. Among Indians and especially Hindus who preponderate in threatened areas the ruling instinct is self-preservation and the preservation of family and property.'

This was an extraordinary comment to make, especially at a time when Indians (many of them Hindus) were winning battles for the British in North Africa.[17] Yet, it was entirely in character. Linlithgow had no sympathy with the Cripps Mission, no desire at all to build bridges with the Congress. While Cripps wished desperately to bring the Congress on board, Linlithgow resisted every attempt to make the government more representative of Indian interests.

On 12 April, when it was clear that the Cripps Mission had failed, Jawaharlal Nehru addressed a press conference in Delhi. Nehru said the Congress made it clear to Cripps that on the battlefield per se the (British) commander-in-chief would and should have full autonomy. But having an Indian as defence member or minister would 'make it a popular war', would 'make every man and woman do something for the war'. Only then would 'India feel that she was fighting her own war for her freedom'.

The request was refused; meanwhile, Cripps, who had begun these discussions talking of the formation of an interim 'National Government' composed of Indians, soon reverted to speaking of an expanded viceroy's 'Executive Council'. Nehru said he was 'amazed' at this change of nomenclature. Had, he asked, Sir Stafford 'been pulled up by his senior partner in England or someone here'? It was a pertinent question. The Labourite in Cripps was committed to Indian independence, but his prime minister did not envisage the British leaving India any time soon (if at all), and nor, of course, did the incumbent viceroy himself.[18]

When Churchill heard that Cripps's talks with the Congress leaders had finally collapsed, he danced with glee around the Cabinet room. 'No tea with treason,' he declared: 'No truck with American or British Labour sentimentality, but back to the solemn—and exciting— business of war.'[19]

The most acute contemporary assessment of the Cripps Mission was offered by the radical British journalist H.N. Brailsford. Cripps went to India with good intentions, wrote Brailsford, but 'when he asked the Indians for an act of faith, the sour memories of all that has been amiss from Clive's day to Churchill's surged up, to wreck our hopes and their ambitions'.

Brailsford pointed out that 'liberal Indians, who follow international affairs closely, were as hostile to the Axis as we are ourselves, but we had wounded them by making India a belligerent without her consent'. Cripps's offer had promised the substance of 'independence' but had refrained from using that 'magic word', had outlined the elements of a 'National Government' but without using 'that inspiring term'.[20]

V

In April 1942, soon after Stafford Cripps returned home empty-handed, the Japanese bombed ports on the east coast, including Vizagapatnam and Kakinada. The war was coming closer to India. American troops were arriving to assist the beleaguered British. Writing in *Harijan*, Gandhi said the 'introduction of foreign soldiers' into India was 'a positive danger thoroughly to be deplored and distrusted'. He thought it would be better 'for Britain to offer battle in the West and leave the East to adjust her own position'. If the Japanese or the Nazis then chose to invade India, claimed Gandhi, 'they will find that they have to hold more than they can in their iron hoop. They will find it much more difficult than Britain has. Their very rigidity will strangle them.'[21]

In the last week of April, the AICC met in Allahabad, to consider their future course of action. Gandhi did not attend, but sent a draft resolution which asked the British to withdraw and leave India to Indians. Nehru dissented, saying the proposal, if accepted by the Congress, would 'inevitably make the world think that we are passively lining up with the Axis powers'. Nehru felt that 'the whole thought and action of the draft is one of favouring Japan. It may not be conscious . . . It is Gandhiji's feeling that Japan and Germany will win. This feeling unconsciously governs his decision. The approach in the draft is different from mine.'

Nehru was here being slightly unfair to Gandhi. It was not so much that he felt the Japanese would win, but that he thought his own time on earth was running out. The deaths of Andrews, Tagore and, most recently, Jamnalal Bajaj, had brought home to him his own mortality. For some time, Gandhi had been planning another mass struggle against colonialism. He had kept that on hold so long as there was any hope of compromise with the British. Now that hope had disappeared, with the failure of the Cripps Mission. Hence his demand that the British leave India to the Indians.

At the Allahabad meeting, the socialist Achyut Patwardhan vigorously disagreed with Nehru. 'Jawaharlalji's attitude,' he claimed, 'will lead to abject and unconditional co-operation with British machinery.' Noting the growing presence of American troops on Indian soil, Patwardhan said, 'I doubt America is a progressive force.' Rajendra Prasad, speaking as a long-term Gandhi loyalist, added that 'we have to strengthen Bapu's hands'. The Assam leader Gopinath Bordoloi and the Oriya Congressman Biswanath Das also felt that it was right and proper to ask the British to withdraw.

The younger socialists favoured Gandhi's draft because they hated Britain (and America). The older conservatives favoured it because to them Bapu's word was God. But one long-term Gandhian held out. This was Rajagopalachari, who said 'our reaction to [the] evils of Britain should not make us lose our sense of perspective' and 'run into the arms of the Japanese'.[22] Later, writing to Gandhi on his return to

Madras, Rajaji told him that 'your as—yet—uncrystallised ideas of concentrating on moral opposition to Britain are most unfortunate. I have worked with you so long and have I been an altogether bad counsellor? Do not do it for God's sake. . . . Your appeal [for the British to withdraw from India] will not be responded to. . . . The only effect will be national weakening of any opposition such as there is to Japan and great moral assistance to the enemy at a most critical moment. Do not take the Congress that way at the end of all these years.'[23]

VI

On 11 May 1942, Gandhi issued an appeal through the pages of *Harijan* 'to every Briton'. He recalled here that at the start of his 'public career', he had written 'An Open Letter to Every Briton in South Africa' about the disabilities faced by Indians in that land. Now, more than forty years later, he asked 'every Briton to support me in my appeal to the British at this very hour to retire from every Asiatic and African possession and at least from India'.[24]

The reference to his early petition in South Africa was a reminder, not least to himself, of how long Gandhi had been in public life. From 1893 to 1914, he had fought steadily for greater rights for Indians in South Africa. From 1915 to 1942, he had campaigned for Hindu–Muslim harmony, for the emancipation of low castes and women, and for the freedom of India from British rule. This last was the campaign that had attracted him the most followers within India, and the most attention outside India. Yet, it remained unfulfilled. Hence this desperate appeal to the British to quit.

Three days after he drafted this appeal, a representative of the *News Chronicle* interviewed Gandhi in Bombay. He asked how the administration would function if the British did as he had asked, and simply withdrew. The British, replied Gandhi, 'have to leave India in God's hands, but in modern parlance to anarchy, and that anarchy may lead to internecine warfare for a time or to unrestrained dacoities. From these a true India will rise in the place of the false one we see.'[25]

Gandhi made this startling statement on 14 May; six days later, Burma fell to the Japanese. The war was coming closer and closer. The several hundred thousand Indians who lived in Singapore, Malaya and Burma had now witnessed it at first-hand. They had experienced the brutality of the Japanese, but also the amorality of the British, most notably in Burma, where the whites were evacuated on ships, leaving Indians to find their own way back to their homeland by trekking across hill and forest, many perishing in the process.[26]

Many of the Indians in South East Asia were Tamils. News of their plight reached their fellow Tamil, C. Rajagopalachari. The Japanese advance made Rajaji even more determined to find a way to cooperate with the British. He sought and obtained Gandhi's permission to go see Jinnah in Bombay. Jinnah told Rajaji that he wanted 'separate sovereignty' for areas in which Muslims were in a majority, to be ratified or rejected by a referendum after the war. If the Congress conceded this, Jinnah's Muslim League would form a coalition government with them, so long as the British then agreed to leave India once the war was won. When this proposal was put to Gandhi, he was lukewarm, since it might pave the way for the partition of India on religious lines.[27]

On 28 May, a representative of *The Hindu* asked Gandhi about the report that he had 'matured plans for some big offensive'. He replied: 'There are certainly many plans floating in my brain. But just now I merely allow them to float in my brain.' Noting that he had 'never believed in secrecy', he said that, as in the past, 'British authority will have a full knowledge of anything I wish to do before I enforce it'.[28]

VII

In the first week of June 1942, Louis Fischer came to Sevagram. Fischer was a famous (and controversial) American journalist, who had lived for many years in Soviet Russia and admired Stalin before the truth about that brutal dictator belatedly dawned on him. In the 1940s, on the rebound, he visited India, and found his way to the village home of the subcontinent's most famous (and most controversial) man.

Before coming to see Gandhi, Louis Fischer had called on the viceroy. Linlithgow told the visiting American that had Gandhi 'remained the saint that he was in South Africa he would have done a lot of good to humanity. But unfortunately politics absorbed him here and have made him vain and egoistical.'[29]

Fischer spent a week in Sevagram, where he had long discussions with Gandhi, recording his words as he spoke, later writing them up as a short book. The first question, however, was posed by Gandhi himself. It was: 'You have lived in Russia for fourteen years. What is your opinion of Stalin?' Fischer answered: 'Very able and very ruthless.' When Gandhi asked whether Stalin was 'as ruthless as Hitler', the American replied: 'At least.'

The conversation then turned to the Cripps Mission and why it had failed. Gandhi explained the sources of disagreement; stressing, as Azad and Nehru had done to Cripps himself, that 'there must be civilian control of the military'. He gave this striking example: 'If the British in Burma wish to destroy the golden [Shwedagon] pagoda because it is a beacon to Japanese airplanes, then I say you cannot destroy it, because when you destroy it you destroy something in the Burmese soul.'

The next day, Gandhi told Fischer that while the Congress had asked for the constitution of a provisional national government of all parties, British and American troops could remain in India for the course of the war. 'I do not wish Japan to win the war,' he said, emphatically. 'I do not want the Axis to win.' He added that 'Britain is morally indefensible while she rules India'.

Fischer interpreted this (correctly) as a major climbdown from Gandhi's earlier position on the subject. From 'The British Must Go', he was now saying, 'The British army can stay and conduct the war from India'. Gandhi was now 'ready to tolerate the war effort and, under certain circumstances, support it'.

Asked by Fischer about Hindu–Muslim relations, Gandhi said that in recent years, 'thanks to the British government, the divergence between the two communities has been widened'. Gandhi himself believed that 'in actual life it is impossible to separate us into two nations'. Across India, Hindus and Muslims lived in the same villages; they ate the same food; spoke the same language. He acknowledged the existence of conflict, such as over cow protection and music before mosques, pointing out, however, that 'it is our superstitions that create the trouble and not our separate nationalities'.

The next stop on Louis Fischer's Indian journey was the princely state of Hyderabad. On the long train ride through the Deccan, he reflected on his conversations with Gandhi. 'Part of the pleasure of intimate intellectual contact with Gandhi,' thought Fischer, 'is that he really opens his mind and allows the interviewer to see how the machine really works.' Other politicians chose their words carefully, so as to 'bring their ideas out in final perfect form so that they are least exposed to attack'. Gandhi, on the other hand, 'gives immediate expression to each step in his thinking'. It was as though a writer was to publish the first draft of his story, then the second, then a third, changing his mind and refining his arguments for all to see.

Fischer had also met Jinnah several times. He admired his intellect, and knew him to be personally incorruptible. Yet, whereas Gandhi spoke spontaneously, Jinnah, wrote Fischer,

> talked at me. He was trying to convince me. When I put a question to him I felt as though I had turned on a phonograph record. I had heard it all before or could have read it in the literature he gave me. But when I asked Gandhi something I felt that I had started a creative process. I could see and hear his mind work. With Jinnah I could only hear the needle scratch the phonograph record. But I could follow Gandhi as he moved to a conclusion. He is, therefore, much more exciting [for an interviewer] than Jinnah. If you strike right with Gandhi you open a new pocket of thought. An interview with him is a voyage of discovery, and he himself is sometimes surprised at the things he says.[30]

VIII

In the second week of June, Jawaharlal Nehru visited Sevagram. He and Gandhi spent the better part of three days closeted together. Their talks remained private, but it appears that Gandhi finally persuaded

Nehru that the time had come for one last struggle against the British. However, Nehru exacted a price: he got Gandhi to write a letter to Chiang Kai-shek, explaining that while India wanted freedom, it would never choose the Japanese over the British.

In his letter to Chiang, Gandhi offered sympathy and admiration for the heroic resistance of the Chinese against the Japanese, now in its sixth year. 'My appeal to the British power to withdraw from India,' said Gandhi, 'is not meant in any shape or form to weaken India's defence against the Japanese or embarrass you in your struggle.'

Nehru had persuaded his mentor to abandon, for this specific purpose and aim, his commitment to non-violence. So Gandhi told Chiang that if India gained its independence immediately, 'I would personally agree that the Allied Powers might, under treaty with us, keep their armed forces in India and use the country as a base for operations against the threatened Japanese attack'.

Chiang, in reply, sent a brief telegram indicating that he desired the status quo to continue. The war, he said, 'appears to be at [a] critical stage', and so 'nothing should take place in India to harm prosecution of the war and which would also harm India in those countries sympathetic to her'.[31]

Meanwhile, Gandhi offered the same proposal in a wired interview to Reuters, as well as in an article in *Harijan*. Prompted by Nehru, he said that an independent India would sign a treaty with the Allies, aimed specifically at repulsing the Japanese. 'India must not,' he remarked, 'by any act of hers short of national suicide let China down or put the Allied powers in jeopardy.' He wished 'British opinion could realize that [the] Independence of India changes [the] character of [the] Allied cause and ensures [its] speedier victory'.[32]

Gandhi stood firm on his demand for immediate independence. But, in deference to Nehru, he had not allowed his own pacifism to get in the way of a coordinated response to the Japanese. As he told a group of British Quakers visiting Sevagram in late June, he 'was confident that a free India will wish to keep the British and even the American soldiers in the country in order to resist a Japanese invasion, as there is no prospect that a free India will accept his [Gandhi's] pacifist convictions'.[33]

IX

While Gandhi, in Sevagram, was planning his next move, a correspondent of the BBC was in Bombay, speaking to his chief political rivals. In a single week in June 1942, the BBC reporter met Ambedkar, Jinnah and the Hindu Mahasabha leader V.D. Savarkar. Ambedkar was angry with the BBC and its Indian arm, All India Radio, 'for not giving him a platform'. He demanded that the AIR give Gandhi, Jinnah and himself the opportunity to each deliver one talk a month. Ambedkar told the visiting journalist: 'We scrap and revile each other in print, why not on the air? Public meetings do no harm, why are you afraid of air combat? At present India is all in sects, and each sect listens to its titular deity. I am the titular deity of the Depressed Classes. I also want to talk to the Hindus. For 2,000 years the Brahmins have been carrying out propaganda: I want to have my propaganda against them, which Hindus will listen to. They may not the first time, or the second, but one time they will listen. And I know I can persuade them.'

Ambedkar was arguing that he was as important a player in Indian politics as Gandhi and Jinnah, and that like them, he commanded the loyalty of tens of millions. The claim was tenuous— at any rate in 1943. At this time, Ambedkar commanded the support of his own Mahar community in western India, and of sections of the Depressed Classes elsewhere. He was by no means an all-India leader in the sense that Gandhi had been since 1920, and Jinnah since 1937.

While undoubtedly as personally courageous as Gandhi, and as intellectually alert as Jinnah, Ambedkar was not—in 1943—as politically consequential as they. Yet, his belief in himself was so strong that he demanded parity with the two most influential leaders of the time. He thus represented the political landscape in India as a three-cornered contest, between the Hindus, the Muslims and the Depressed Classes, with Gandhi, Jinnah and himself being the titular deities of these three sects respectively.

The next day, the BBC reporter met Savarkar, who 'was very anxious for me to put the Hindu Mahasabha case in England'. Savarkar claimed that while the 'English thought of Muslims and

Congress', the contest now was between 'Muslims and Hindu Mahasabha. Congress is nothing any longer.'

Later the same day, the reporter called on Jinnah. The Muslim League leader argued that a united India would mean a Hindu Raj, and that was something Muslims could not accept. Jinnah charged the Congress with wanting 'Hindu caste rule', adding that Ambedkar and the 'untouchables' 'are much more bitter about the Hindus than I am'. Jinnah said he had been in public life for three decades, and 'after years of patiently working it out' had 'decided for Pakistan'.[34]

Jinnah's commitment to the idea of Pakistan was manifest in many public statements made by him since the resolution demanding a separate homeland was passed by the Muslim League in Lahore in March 1940. In November of that year, he said in New Delhi that 'Pakistan is our sheet anchor'. The Congress, he insisted, 'must give up their dream of a Hindu *raj* and agree to divide India into [a] Hindu homeland and [a] Muslim homeland'. The next month he told an audience in Karachi that 'Pakistan is the only solution of Hindu–Muslim tension'. Speaking in Madras in April 1941, he claimed that not since the fall of the Mughal Empire had Muslims in India been 'so well organised and so alive and so politically conscious' as they now were. In February 1942, he wrote to a British MP that 'the partition of India demand, the Muslim idea, is not only a political reality, it is our creed and our article of faith'. In April, he rejected the Cripps Mission since in its proposals 'Pakistan was not conceded unequivocally and the right of Muslim self-determination was denied'.

To the Congress and the British, Jinnah insisted that the partition of India into what he called Hindu and Muslim homelands was the only solution the League would accept. Meanwhile, he told his followers that they must be prepared to fight to realize that ideal. Speaking to a group of Muslim students, he remarked: 'Muslims must assert themselves in this country and outside and although our enemies . . . are carrying on false propaganda against us yet, I am sure, no power on earth can resist the onward rush of 80 millions [of Muslims] who are determined to materialize their ideal of Pakistan and to stand united on a soil which they can call and claim as their homeland.'[35]

X

As Jinnah grew more uncompromising on the question of Pakistan, Gandhi, prodded by Nehru, was making a last-ditch attempt at finding a meeting ground with the British. Hence his abandonment of non-violence, if only in return for a clear declaration of Indian independence. Having written in this vein to Chiang Kai-shek, he now wrote to the one man who did have some influence on the British and their recalcitrant prime minister—namely, the American President, Franklin Roosevelt. Gandhi knew that if he posted the letter, the British censor would read it, and perhaps (as had happened previously with his letter to Hitler) not allow it to reach its recipient. Even if the censor passed the letter on, the staff at the White House might not show it to Roosevelt. So, to make absolutely sure the American President saw it, Gandhi sent the letter by personal courier, through Louis Fischer, who was now going back to his homeland.

Gandhi's letter to FDR began by noting that many of his compatriots had been educated in America, while he himself had 'profited greatly by the writings of Thoreau and Emerson'. Gandhi then added that despite his 'intense dislike of British rule', he had 'numerous personal friends in England whom I love as dearly as my own people'. Besides, he had been educated there. Therefore, said Gandhi to Roosevelt, he had 'nothing but good wishes for your country and Great Britain'.

Gandhi told Roosevelt that 'the Allied declaration that the Allies are fighting to make the world safe for freedom of the individual and for democracy sounds hollow so long as India and, for that matter, Africa are exploited by Great Britain and America has the Negro problem in her own home'. He proposed to Roosevelt that if India was made independent, then the Allies could keep their troops in the country, 'not for keeping internal order but for preventing Japanese aggression and defending China'. Gandhi said while he personally abhorred war and violence, he recognized that not everyone had 'a living faith in non-violence'. Therefore, he was willing, provided India was offered freedom, to countenance armed resistance to the Japanese to be conducted from Indian soil.[36]

Gandhi's letter to Roosevelt was dated 1 July 1942. In the same week, the members of the CWC descended on Sevagram. They had nine days of intense discussions, following which they passed a resolution on 14 July, asking for the withdrawal of British power from India. The working committee noted that ever since the war began, the Congress had 'steadily followed a policy of non-embarrassment'. Yet, the British had responded by seeking to strengthen their hold over India. The Congress, having patiently waited three years, now made a final offer, namely, that the British should grant immediate independence, whereupon, in exchange, any 'provisional Government' of free India would allow Allied troops to continue to use Indian soil to fight the Japanese.

The working committee hoped the British would accept this 'very reasonable and just proposal', made 'not only in the interest of India but also that of Britain and the cause of freedom, to which the United Nations proclaim their adherence'. However, if the appeal was rejected, then the Congress would 'be reluctantly compelled to utilize all the non-violent strength it might have gathered . . . for the vindication of the political rights and liberty'. This struggle, said the resolution, would 'inevitably be under the leadership of Mahatma Gandhi', and the final decision as to how it was to be conducted was to be taken at a meeting of the AICC, scheduled in Bombay on 7 August.[37]

Present in Sevagram was a large group of journalists, both Indian and foreign. Immediately after the working committee meeting ended, they crowded around Gandhi, peppering him with questions. The interrogation began on the evening of 14 July, continuing well into the next day. Gandhi was asked what methods of struggle he had planned. All, he answered, so long as they were non-violent. He also said that he might, if arrested, resort to fasting, adding: 'Though I would try to avoid such an extreme step so far as possible.'

A British journalist (whom Mahadev Desai observed was 'full of the doubts and fears of the average Englishman') asked Gandhi whether, if the viceroy asked him to come to Delhi, he would go to meet him. 'Oh yes,' he replied. 'Would the campaign collapse if [the] Government sent you and thousands of followers to jail?' now asked the anxious Englishman. Gandhi replied: 'I hope not, on the contrary it should gain strength if it has any vitality.'

A journalist from the *Chicago Daily News* asked Gandhi whether he was apprehensive that the Congress's decision would 'antagonize American opinion'. Perhaps it might, he answered, but why, he asked in turn, should the American or even the British people 'fight shy of a just demand for absolute freedom'? As for the provisional government that he envisaged, Gandhi said he hoped the Muslim League would also participate in its formation; at any rate, 'no one party would take the lead'.[38]

XI

A conspicuous absentee from the working committee meeting in Sevagram was C. Rajagopalachari, Gandhi's 'Southern Commander', who was now at odds with his master and his party.

Rajaji had been opposed to a fresh round of civil disobedience. Now, reading the reports of the working committee meeting, he wrote to Gandhi that the resolution demanding the British leave India was fraught with danger, for it asked for 'the withdrawal of the government without a simultaneous replacement by another'. If put into effect, the proposal would lead to 'anarchy' and 'wide-spread self-inflicted suffering'. Rather than demand the British quit, said Rajaji, the Congress and the Muslim League should come together, and press for an interim national government 'which can take over power and preserve the continuity of the state'.[39]

Rajaji's critique was worded soberly, as was his wont. More anguished was a letter written by a Polish woman who had converted to Hinduism and joined Ramana Maharshi's ashram in Tiruvannamalai. She charged Gandhi with betraying freedom and humanity by planning to launch his Quit India movement. Anything that hindered the Allied war effort, she argued, 'prolongs the sufferings of 250 million people under the Nazis' rule of whose moral and physical agonies you have not even the slightest idea; comparing [*sic*] with them Indians are till now in a heaven of peace and freedom . . .'

The lady in Tiruvannamalai had received reports from her native Poland of the brutality of its Nazi occupiers. A satyagraha at this juncture, she insisted, would be akin to stabbing the British in the back. 'If an ordinary politician, a worldly, narrow nationalist—like Subhas Bose—would push towards such [a] movement,' she remarked, 'it would at least be logical from the worldly political point of view—justified; as crude nationalism cares little for Humanity, and for the repercussions of its own exploits on other nations. But one who claims to be a spiritual man, to care for the religious spirit, for Truth . . . It is impossible to understand.'[40]

While long-time admirers expressed their disappointment directly, Gandhi's long-term adversaries, the officials of the British Raj, were quietly planning their own response. In a meeting held in the home department on 25 July, it was decided that action would be taken when the AICC met in Bombay in August. As soon as this larger body ratified the resolution asking the British to quit India, the government would detain Gandhi, Nehru and other 'dangerous members of the Working Committee'. These arrests, it was decided, 'should not be made at the meeting, but as quietly as possible afterward, preferably during the night', perhaps at the railway station if some members were leaving Bombay by train.

The officials planned to confine the working committee leaders in one place, but Gandhi in another. Back in May 1941, the government had, in anticipation of such an eventuality, leased a large double-storeyed house in Poona owned by the Aga Khan. Some officials thought Gandhi should be sent, as so often before, to the Yerwada prison. Others argued that the 'Aga Khan Palace' (as it was called) would be a better choice, not least because the Americans would be less cross if they knew Gandhi was, as it were, in a palace. To further sugar the pill, Gandhi's close companions in the ashram, such as Mahadev, Mira, Pyarelal and Sushila Nayar, would be allowed to live with him.[41]

Such were the opinions of the officials; meanwhile, their boss, the viceroy, had some interesting ideas of his own. Linlithgow thought that 'if a break is forced upon us by the Congress', the government should put Gandhi in the Aga Khan Palace, old and ailing members of the working committee elsewhere in India, and dispatch the rest to a British colony in Africa (perhaps Uganda or Nyasaland) for the duration of the war. The viceroy believed that 'a dramatic move of this nature might well produce a deep impression on followers of the Congress and create a degree of confidence which would be of value among other individuals who, from fear that there would be an early settlement with [the] Congress, may be disposed to give us more lukewarm assistance than might otherwise be the case'.[42]

The British commander-in-chief of the army in India warmed to Linlithgow's proposal. He proposed to send Nehru, Patel and company in flying boats, promising that the Royal Air Force (RAF) 'would arrange European style food for the whole party. If Indian food is required I don't quite know what we would do, but that must be thought about.' A senior RAF man he consulted 'rather pooh-poohs the idea of any of the gentlemen going on hunger-strike in the flying-boat; he says travelling at 12,000 feet will soon put a stop to that'.[43]

Also enthusiastic was the governor of Nyasaland. He had identified a good hotel at Dedza, 120 miles north of Zomba 'in high healthy climate' which could be made ready in a week to house the deportees. The hotel was owned and managed by Europeans, had electricity and hot water, and was well-furnished. The governor would provide an African guard under a European officer.[44]

However, the governors of India's major provinces came out strongly against the viceroy's scheme. The governor of Bihar said sending Nehru and Patel to Africa would 'be regarded as unduly harsh', leading to 'a serious revulsion of even moderate feeling in Bihar'. The governor of Bombay likewise remarked that deportation would 'shock moderate opinion in India and alienate support from us'. Only the governor of the Punjab (where the Congress had the least influence) was in favour.[45]

Linlithgow now reluctantly dropped his proposal. The working committee members would be sent instead to the Ahmednagar Fort, in the Deccan, which was surrounded by a moat and approached by a drawbridge, so that (even though they were in India and not Africa) the prisoners would still be 'completely cut off from the outside world'.[46]

XII

In the third week of July 1942, Gandhi published a letter addressed to the Asian nation whose army was pressing upon India. Published in several Japanese papers, and also in English (the language in which it was originally written), this began by Gandhi squarely stating: 'I intensely dislike your attack upon China. From your lofty height you have descended to imperial ambition.'

Gandhi told the Japanese that their wish 'to take equal rank with the great powers of the world' was a 'worthy ambition'. Yet, their 'unprovoked attack against China', their 'merciless devastation of that great and ancient land', was 'surely an unwarranted excess of the ambition'. Noting the reports of a planned attack on India, Gandhi asked the Japanese 'to make no mistake about the fact that you will be sadly disillusioned if you believe that you will receive a willing welcome from India'.[47]

The open letter to the Japanese had followed upon a public appeal to the British, and private letters written to Chiang and FDR. Gandhi wanted to launch what he knew to be his last struggle with clean hands. A week after his appeal to the Japanese, Gandhi printed an appeal to the Muslims of India. Jinnah had recently said that 'Pakistan is an article of faith with Muslim India and we depend upon nobody but ourselves for the achievement of our goal'. Quoting this remark, Gandhi observed that 'today there is neither Pakistan nor Hindustan. So I say to all India, let us first convert into the original Hindustan and then adjust all rival claims.'

Gandhi then made a direct appeal to Jinnah. 'If the Quaid-e-Azam really wants a settlement,' he wrote, 'I am more than willing and so is the Congress.' He urged Jinnah to 'accept the Congress President's offer that Congress and League representatives should put their heads together and never part till they have reached a settlement'.[48]

Jinnah did not reply to Gandhi directly. But, in a public statement issued on 31 July, he said the Congress's ultimatum to the Raj was 'the culminating point of the policy and programme of the Hindu Congress of blackmailing the British and coercing them' to transfer power to the Congress, thereby 'throwing the Muslims and other minorities at the mercy' of 'a Hindu Raj'.[49]

Meanwhile, Gandhi's other great rival, B.R. Ambedkar, had been recently elevated to the viceroy's executive council. In a speech in Bombay on 22 July, he said it was the 'patriotic duty' of all Indians to resist the Congress, for the struggle they wished to launch would create 'anarchy and chaos' at a time when 'aggressive Japan [is] standing right at the gates of India'. Ambedkar was in 'no doubt that to start [a] civil disobedience movement at such a juncture would be directly playing the game of the enemy. It is a game we will not allow the Congress or anybody else to play. It is a game of treachery to India.' He continued: 'I yield to none in my desire for the freedom of this country, but I do not want to drive out the British to help [the] establishment of Japanese rule over this country.'[50]

Gandhi was perhaps not entirely surprised by what Jinnah and Ambedkar had said. What may have worried him more was the fact that President Roosevelt had not yet replied to him. And the British had turned their backs on Gandhi altogether. The Labour Party, once so sympathetic to the Congress and to Indian independence, now called the working committee resolution 'proof of political irresponsibility'. The British papers, conservative, liberal and socialist, all united in attacking Gandhi and the Congress.[51] Their own national existence was at peril; at this time, the British had no thought for people of other nations still struggling to be born.

Gandhi now made one last appeal, to the people of the United States, a country he had never visited, but where he knew he had many admirers. This was written on 3 August, on the train to Bombay, where he was going to attend the meeting of the AICC. He told the Americans of his admiration for Thoreau, Ruskin and Tolstoy, three writers from the three nations now battling Hitler and the Nazis. 'After having imbibed and assimilated the message of [Ruskin's] *Unto This Last*', he wrote, 'I could not be guilty of approving of Fascism or Nazism, whose cult is suppression of the individual and his liberty.'

Gandhi warned Americans against the 'interested propaganda' that painted him 'as a hypocrite and enemy of Britain under disguise'. He also reminded them that, by making common cause with Britain in the war, 'you cannot therefore disown responsibility for anything that her representatives do in India'. He therefore urged America, and Americans, 'to look upon the immediate recognition of India's independence as a war measure of first class magnitude'. [52]

XIII

That Gandhi, and the Congress, now planned a major countryside struggle against colonial rule was a matter of public record. That some, perhaps many, Indians opposed the idea was also known. That the British would act swiftly and punitively was also understood. What remained private at the time, and largely unknown since, was this— that, in July 1942, Gandhi was actively contemplating a hunger fast.

Gandhi had fasted many times, on occasion to atone for a lapse of one or more of his disciples, on other occasions to compel Indians to change their ways, so as to promote Hindu–Muslim harmony (as in Delhi in 1924), or to stop the practice of untouchability (as in Yerwada in 1932). But he had never, so far, actually fasted in opposition to British rule per se. His campaigns against colonialism had always taken the form of the breaking of what he considered unjust laws. And these breaches had always been collective, involving many other satyagrahis apart from himself.

It was now almost three years since the war had broken out. In that time, Gandhi and the Congress had made repeated overtures to the government. Gandhi had even resiled from his commitment to non-violence to permit Indian soil being used for military purposes— so long as an assurance of political independence was given. Yet, all these attempts were in vain. The colonial government in India, and His Majesty's Government in Great Britain, refused to trust the Congress. Linlithgow, Churchill and company could not bring themselves to see the fundamental contradiction between their claim to be fighting the Nazis on behalf of democracy and freedom and their denial of democracy and freedom to the people of India. Tired of trying, and increasingly aware of his own mortality, Gandhi now thought of dramatic measures to force the British into the concessions they were so far reluctant to make.

Gandhi's own writings give no hint that he was planning to fast against the British in July 1942. But the letters of his disciples do.

On 23 July, Mahadev Desai, at Gandhi's side in Sevagram, wrote to Amrit Kaur, then at her family home in Simla:

> Bapu is well but the Fast idea, he says, is getting more and more [active]. It would be a tremendous blunder, I am afraid, for these folks will spare no effort to mis-represent him to the World and we have so [far] declined to make people listen to us. There is such amount of misunderstanding and equal amount of wilful distortion and mischievous propaganda that there could not be [a] more inauspicious moment for a step like that. But I am hoping and praying that God will guide him. . . . I want to have a good argument with him one of these days. The W[orking] C[ommittee] people did not discuss it at all—They all sat mum—and Bapu took the silence to mean consent.[53]

Mahadev himself had been unwell for months, a product entirely of the hard work he had put in on his master's behalf the past quarter of a century. Earlier that year he had had a mild heart attack. Rest was prescribed, but Mahadev would not take it, for who else could then work for and with Gandhi? And, if the occasion demanded, chastise him too?

On hearing of Gandhi's proposed fast, Amrit Kaur wrote back to Mahadev:

> How tragic B[apu]'s fast would be. You must prevent it at all costs. I do not see how such acts can affect people who are already enraged and who have no eyes to see or hearts to understand. That is why I have been pleading for delaying action until the tide of war has definitely turned in their favour or, at any rate, is not so dead against them as it is today. . . . Personally I feel that if a last appeal with a reasonable time limit is given there will be a response from those quarters which are antagonised today. Fasting against people who are in the throes of a life and death struggle is surely wrong.[54]

Mahadev was determined to have that 'good argument' with Gandhi—although, unusually for him and their relationship, it was initiated by means of a written communication. On 27 July, Mahadev wrote Gandhi an anguished letter urging him not to fast. 'You are,' he told him, 'mistaken in your belief that the Working Committee approves of this step. Its silence was not consent but sullenness.' Mahadev warned Gandhi that 'there is bound to be a very big class of people who honestly do not understand about [such] a fast; and we would lose the sympathy of those few in England who understand you'. And if Gandhi died as a result of a fast, he 'would be leaving behind a legacy of hatred for the English for ever till the existence of [the] sun and [the] moon'. In sum, said Mahadev bluntly to Gandhi, the 'entire idea [of a fast] is delusionary'.[55]

Gandhi decided in the end to drop the idea of putting pressure on the British by offering his own life as a sacrifice, and instead stay with the well-tried, and less morally coercive, route of non-violent mass protest. Mahadev Desai had done Gandhi many favours since he joined him in 1917; persuading him not to fast in July 1942 was one of the most substantial.

XIV

Of Gandhi's oldest and most valued colleagues, C. Rajagopalachari was most bitterly opposed to the launching of a mass movement against the British. Jawaharlal Nehru was ambivalent, but eventually reconciled himself to the idea. Vallabhbhai Patel, on the other hand, was enthusiastic from the start. This man of peasant stock, one of whose forefathers had taken part in the great rebellion of 1857, was now itching for a fresh round of struggle.

On 26 July 1942, Patel addressed a public meeting in Ahmedabad. More than one hundred thousand people heard him say that 'every Indian should act as a free man as soon as the struggle is launched'. Two days later, addressing students in the same city, Patel said, 'Mahatma Gandhi's last struggle will be short and swift, and will be finished within a week.' The key word here was, of course, 'last'.[56] Having served as Gandhi's chief lieutenant in Kheda in 1918, and in Bardoli in 1928, and in several other campaigns besides, Patel was extremely keen to play a key part in what he sensed would be the final struggle of his master.

Patel now proceeded to Bombay, where the CWC and the AICC were due to meet. On Sunday, 2 August, he addressed a massive crowd at the Chowpatty beach, the audience standing or squatting on the sands. Patel rehearsed how India 'was dragged into the war against her consent'. The Congress had been prepared to help the British in their war efforts if a national government was formed. Patel spoke of how through its indifference to Gandhi's pleas, 'the British Government had lost the support of one whose love towards them had been true and sincere'. Now Gandhi was seventy-two years old, and 'felt that Britain should withdraw her rule from India'. The Mahatma, said Patel, believed that 'the continuation of British imperialism would act as a temptation for another imperialist power [Japan] to covet this land. In this vortex of imperialist ambitions, wars would extend and continue.'[57]

It was in Bombay that Gandhi had his most long-standing and steadfast political supporters. The city had rallied to the Rowlatt Satyagraha, the non-cooperation movement, the Salt March. With Gandhi old and ailing, Patel was acting as His Master's Voice, rousing the masses before the crucial Congress meetings in their city.

Impressed by the response to Patel's speech was that other long-time loyalist of Gandhi, the *Bombay Chronicle* newspaper. 'The mammoth meeting held on the Chowpatty sands on Sunday evening,' it noted, 'is a phenomenon which it will be unwise for [the] Government to ignore. It symbolically demonstrates for the thousandth time the deep loyalty of crores of Indians to Congress and Gandhiji. It will be dangerous for [the] Government to flout the Congress by banking on the differences within it, and between it and other political bodies.'

The *Chronicle* reminded the British that Gandhi had reached out to them 'by permitting the continuance of Allied troops in India to resist Japanese aggression'. Since the political aims of the Congress and Gandhi were 'in substance similar' to those made by other parties, the paper warned that if these demands 'are not substantially conceded at once, the inevitable result will be wide and acute discontent, whatever shapes it may take'.[58]

Gandhi himself arrived in Bombay on Monday, 3 August, with Mahadev and Kasturba in tow. They were met at Dadar station by

Patel and prominent Bombay Congressmen, including B.G. Kher and Yusuf Meherally. 'An eager and enthusiastic crowd filled the platform and cheered the Mahatma as he walked to the waiting car.'[59]

The CWC met on the 4th and 5th, with Gandhi present throughout. In the evenings he held his customary prayer meetings. He was also examined by two Bombay doctors closely associated with the Congress, M.D. Gilder and Jivraj Mehta. They 'found him better and stronger. He has put on weight. But they were of [the] opinion that his period of rest should not be encroached upon.'[60]

On 6 August, speaking to the press in Bombay, Gandhi said he 'definitely contemplated an interval between the passing of the Congress resolution [which would ask the British to "Quit India"] and the starting of the struggle'. He planned to write a letter to the viceroy, 'not as an ultimatum but as an earnest pleading for avoidance of a conflict'. He continued: 'If there is a favourable response, then my letter can be the basis for negotiation.'[61]

The much-awaited meeting of the AICC began at 2 p.m. on 7 August, at the Gowalia Tank Maidan in central Bombay. On his arrival, 'Mahatma Gandhi and the other leaders had to pass through serried ranks of cheering humanity along the road to the pandal and in the pandal itself.'[62]

In his speech to the gathering, Gandhi urged Congressmen to under no circumstances show sympathy for the Japanese. 'At a time when I am about to launch the biggest fight in my life,' he remarked, 'there can be no hatred for the British in my heart.' 'The coming in of Japan,' he warned, 'will mean the end of China and perhaps of Russia, too.' Gandhi also urged Congressmen to 'not resort to violence and put non-violence to shame'.

The next day, speaking to the AICC again, Gandhi focused on the deepening divide between Hindus and Muslims. He recalled the days of the Khilafat movement, 'when every Mussalman claimed the whole of India as his motherland', and 'Muslims throughout the country accepted me as their true friend'. But now Muslim newspapers demonized him, and were even more savage in their treatment of Maulana Azad, who was 'being made a target for the filthiest abuse'. He asked why Jinnah allowed the vilification of Muslims who were still with the Congress.

Gandhi deplored the separatism of the Muslim League, but he did not approve of Hindu majoritarianism either. As he put it: 'Those Hindus who, like Dr. Moonje and Shri Savarkar, believe in the doctrine of the sword may seek to keep the Mussalmans under Hindu domination. I do not represent that section.'

Gandhi told the audience that the struggle that the Congress was contemplating would not start immediately. 'I will now wait upon the Viceroy and plead with him for the acceptance of the Congress demand. That process is likely to take two or three weeks.' In the meantime, he advised members of the Congress to promote spinning and other elements of the constructive programme, and to 'consider yourself a free man or woman, and act as if you are free and are no longer under the heel of this imperialism'.[63]

On 8 August, the AICC passed a resolution asking for the immediate end of British rule in India. Once India became independent, it would become an ally of the Allies, 'sharing with them in the trials and tribulations of the joint struggle for freedom'. The resolution envisaged a provisional government, this not dominated by the Congress but 'a composite government, representative of all important sections of the people of India'.

The AICC held that 'the freedom of India must be the symbol of and prelude to the freedom of all other Asiatic nations under foreign domination'. The French, the Dutch and the British should withdraw from their colonies, and 'it must be clearly understood that such of those countries as are under Japanese control now must not subsequently be placed under the rule or control of any other colonial power'.

The AICC hoped that Britain and the Allies would heed this plea for freedom for India. But if they did not, then the Congress could not 'hold the nation back from endeavouring to assert its will against an imperialist and authoritarian government'. Therefore, 'for the vindication of India's inalienable right to freedom and independence', the AICC was sanctioning the 'starting of a mass struggle on non-violent lines on the widest possible scale', which would 'inevitably be under the leadership of Gandhiji'.[64]

The resolution was moved by Nehru, and seconded by Patel, once more establishing these two as Gandhi's most trusted, loyal lieutenants as well as his designated political successors. Their speeches, and of course Gandhi's too, were listened to with 'rapt attention' by the 'enthusiastic mass of humanity' that had occupied 'every inch of the 35000 square feet of the pandal'.[65]

After his long speech to the AICC on the 8th, Gandhi told Mahadev and Vallabhbhai that when he got up to speak he did not know what he would say. 'Now I know why I was not able to sleep last night,' he said in Gujarati. 'There was so much on my mind; I did not know whether I would be able to express it all or not. . . . I have said practically all I wanted to say to the country.'[66] That a man who normally slept so easily was so restless is an indication that Gandhi sensed that, approaching his seventy-third birthday, this was indeed the last major political battle of his life.

The motion passed by the Congress on 8 August 1942 is customarily known as the 'Quit India' resolution. Remarkably, that redolent, now celebrated, phrase does not occur in the resolution as worded and passed. There is an intriguing parallel, for the likewise famous 'Pakistan Resolution' passed by the Muslim League in Lahore in March 1940 had not actually used the word 'Pakistan' either.

XV

In December 1920, at a well-attended Congress meeting in Nagpur, Gandhi had launched his non-cooperation movement. It took more than a year for the British to arrest him. A decade later, he launched the Salt March; once more, rather than detain him at once, the British allowed him to undertake his slow, majestic march to the sea, to break the law and attract worldwide attention before they eventually acted.

Gandhi may have thought that this time too, the British would behave in a fashion customary to them, tardily from one point of view, if gentlemanly from another. On the night of the 8th, he told Mahadev that he did not believe that the British would arrest him after his speeches to the AICC, which had displayed respect, even affection, for the British.[67]

But the rulers were now less indulgent. Linlithgow was less charitably disposed to Gandhi than either Reading or Irwin. The

Second World War had greatly clouded relations between Indian nationalists and the Raj. Fighting their own desperate battle for survival, the British were not disposed to look at all kindly on the needs and aspirations of other peoples.

The Quit India resolution was passed on the evening of 8 August. Early the next morning, at around 5 a.m., Gandhi was served a notice of arrest at the Bombay residence of the industrialist G.D. Birla, where he was staying. Gandhi was given half an hour to gather his effects. He used the time to have his customary breakfast of goat's milk and fruit juice. A Muslim member of the Sevagram Ashram, who was present, then recited verses from the Koran, which was followed by a collective rendition of '*Vaishnava Jana To*'. Gandhi packed his bag for prison with, among other things, the Bhagavad Gita, the Koran, an Urdu primer and 'his inevitable "Charkha"'.[68]

Gandhi—along with Mahadev Desai, Sarojini Naidu and Mira, all also staying in Birla House, all also now placed under arrest— was taken in a police convoy to the station and put in a special train to Poona. The group was made to get off at Chinchwad station (ten miles short of Poona) and conveyed in a police car to the Aga Khan Palace. An eyewitness who saw them drive off reported that 'Mahatma Gandhi was seen cracking jokes with Sarojini Naidu' in the car.

Meanwhile, the other major Congress leaders, Nehru, Patel, Azad and company, were also detained and taken to 'an unknown destination'. The government declared the Congress and its affiliated organizations 'unlawful' under Section 16 of the Indian Criminal Law Amendment Act, 1908, on the grounds that they constituted 'a danger to the public peace'. Congress offices all over India were sealed.[69]

Justifying its pre-emptive attack, the government issued a communiqué saying that the AICC resolution was in effect an invitation to the Axis powers to attack India. 'The Congress Party is not India's mouthpiece,' said the viceroy and his government. It charged the Congress with 'pursuing a totalitarian policy' of imposing its view on all Indians.[70] The use of the term, 'totalitarian', normally reserved for absolutist regimes such as those run by Hitler and Stalin, was of course outrageous hyperbole when applied to a party with no power and no arms. It reflected the bitter, indeed extreme, hostility which Linlithgow and his officials had developed for Gandhi and his party.

The day after Gandhi was arrested, the War Cabinet met in London. Churchill was in a jovial mood, for, as he told his assembled colleagues, 'We have clapped Gandhi into prison.' General Smuts introduced a note of seriousness, telling Churchill that Gandhi 'is a man of God. You and I are mundane people. Gandhi has appealed to religious motives. You never have. That is where you have failed.' Churchill, with a grin, replied: 'I have made more bishops than anyone since St. Augustine.' But Smuts was not amused; as an eyewitness reported, 'his face was very grave'.[71]

CHAPTER THIRTY

A Bereavement and a Fast

I

The Aga Khan Palace, where Gandhi and his companions were incarcerated, was built in the 1890s. It was five miles outside Poona city, on a small hill, commanding a fine view of the countryside. Two storeys high, it was enclosed by a wide and shady veranda running along the house. There were nine large bedrooms, while the drawing room had chandeliers hanging from the ceiling, and portraits of previous Aga Khans on the wall.

Seventy acres of grounds came with the main building, with twelve gardeners to tend them. There was a deer park on the premises, as well as several greenhouses. In the salubrious climate of Poona, both trees and plants grew abundantly. From the terrace, one saw a profusion of colours all around.

The Aga Khan Palace had been acquired in 1941, just in case Gandhi had to be arrested. The Bombay government sent a long note to the viceroy on its size and character, along with photographs, noting that this description 'will make as much impression as is necessary on the American public!' The rent paid to the Aga Khan was Rs 12,000 a year, the money remitted to him in Geneva, with the arrangement kept secret from the public.

After the Aga Khan Palace was acquired, certain alterations were made to the premises by the public works department. The cost of these alterations was some 9000 rupees; the Government of Bombay, mindful of its pennies, successfully got this reimbursed from the Government of India, since it was they who had got Gandhi interned. The amount was debited under the heading: 'Miscellaneous Expenditure connected with the War: Payments to Provincial Governments'. Delhi also accepted liability for the salaries of the jailers and soldiers keeping a watch on Gandhi, of a doctor kept on duty in the palace, of the malis tending the garden, and (among other things) for the installation of a telephone.

A recurring sum of Rs 450 per month was also sanctioned to take care of the food and other items supplied to Gandhi and his party (this was later increased to Rs 550, and in time to Rs 700, to keep pace with wartime inflation).[1]

Early in 1942, as the confrontation between the Congress and the government sharpened, the authorities began building a barbed wire fence around the property. Fourteen new sentry boxes were also constructed. They decided that, as and when Gandhi was arrested, they would post a certain A.E. Kately in charge of the palace prison. Kately was a Gujarati-speaking Parsi, who had been a jailer in Yerwada when Gandhi was confined there in 1932–33, and so knew him well. He was in place, with seventy-six constables to assist him, when Gandhi was taken to Poona from Bombay in the second week of August 1942.[2]

Gandhi had never lived in such luxurious surroundings before— whether as a convicted satyagrahi or as a free man. The government had sent Kasturba and Pyarelal to be with him; with Mahadev, Mira and Sushila Nayar also at hand, he had family and close disciples around him. But he was not happy at being incarcerated. He had met previous prison sentences quite willingly; this time, however, he felt the government had acted in haste.

Gandhi arrived at the Aga Khan Palace on 9 August. Two days later, he began drafting a letter to the viceroy. On the 14th, he finally sent it. The letter began: 'The Government of India were wrong in precipitating the crisis. The Government resolution justifying this step is full of distortions and misrepresentations.' The resolution charged the Congress with preparing to launch 'violent activities', although, as Gandhi pointed out, 'violence was never contemplated at any stage'. In any case, why could the government not have waited till mass action was launched?

Gandhi's letter, perhaps unconsciously, brought to the fore the intense debates within the Congress that preceded the Quit India resolution. Thus he wrote to the viceroy: 'The Government of India think that the freedom of India is not necessary for winning the cause. I think exactly the opposite. I have taken Jawaharlal Nehru as my measuring rod. His personal contacts make him feel much more the misery of the impending ruin of China and Russia than I can—and may I say than even you can. In that misery he tried to forget his old quarrel with imperialism. He dreads more than I do the success of Fascism and Nazism. I have argued with him for days together. He fought against my position with a passion which I have no words to describe. But the logic of facts overwhelmed him. He yielded when he saw clearly that without the freedom of India that of the other two was in jeopardy.'

Given Nehru's views, well known and widely publicized, Gandhi told the viceroy that 'surely you are wrong in having imprisoned such a powerful friend and ally. If notwithstanding the common cause [the defeat of Nazism and fascism], the Government's answer to the Congress demand is hasty repression, they will not wonder if I draw the inference that it was not so much the Allied cause that weighed with the British Government, as the unexpressed determination to cling to the possession of India as an indispensable part of the imperial policy.'[3]

II

Ever since they had been arrested, Mahadev Desai had been worried that Gandhi might embark on a fast unto death. On the night of the 14th, he unburdened his worries to Sarojini Naidu. The next morning, Mahadev got up early, prepared Gandhi's musambi juice and his breakfast, and then went back to the book he had been reading the previous night, *The Art of Living* by André Maurois. Later, he joined

Gandhi for a stroll in the garden. As ever, he had many ideas buzzing in his mind. He told Gandhi that he wished, when they were released, to bring out an anthology of instances of non-violence in literature.

As they walked around the garden, Gandhi and Mahadev also indulged in nostalgic remembrance. Gandhi asked his secretary what Vallabhbhai Patel was like before he met him in 1917. Mahadev told him that the Sardar was a fastidious dresser, who had his suits made by the best tailors. He was also inordinately fond of bridge. He made enough money in a week's work in the court to spend the rest of the month on the card table at the Gujarat Club.

After their walk, Gandhi went for his daily massage, given by Sushila Nayar. Shortly afterwards, Kasturba rushed in to call Sushila. Mahadev, she said, was having a fit. He complained of feeling giddy, and then fell down. When Sushila reached where Mahadev was, she found his pulse had stopped beating, and there was no sound in his heart either. The prison authorities were called in; they declared him dead.

Sarojini Naidu was convinced that it was the worry about Gandhi fasting that killed his secretary. 'If ever a man laid down his life for another it was Mahadev,' she told the others in the palace prison.[4]

Mahadev had turned fifty earlier in the year. He was relatively young, ate simple ashram food, and exercised regularly. However, he had not been keeping well for some time. Twenty-five years of continuous work and travel had weakened him. The months and years since the war broke out had been filled with tension, indecision, an agonizing back and forth between reaching out to the Raj and confronting it. As the prime messenger and mediator between Linlithgow and Gandhi, Bose and Gandhi, Nehru and Gandhi, Rajaji and Gandhi, the various provincial Congress leaders and Gandhi, the troublesome/possessive ashram disciples and Gandhi, Mahadev had borne it all. Although the official cause of death was cardiac arrest, Mahadev had in fact died of overwork. He had given his life in the service of his master and their yet-to-be-free country.

When Mahadev collapsed on the morning of 15 August, Gandhi cried out, in Gujarati, 'Mahadev, arise! Arise!' Mahadev had (mostly) listened to Gandhi ever since he joined him, but this was one order he could not follow. When it became clear that he was dead, his clothes were taken off. He was, as always, wearing a dhoti and shirt made of khadi. In a side pocket of the shirt was an edition of the Gita; in the front pocket, a pen. Both were symbolic, of a life devoted to work and to sacrifice.

Gandhi himself washed Mahadev's body. Sushila Nayar, who was in the room, recalled that Gandhi's 'hand was shaking and he could hardly carry the mugful of water. I was afraid that he might slip and fall. I, therefore, went in and quietly started helping him. He needed the help and accepted it. I poured the water and Bapu rubbed the body with the wash cloth. Mahadevbhai often used to walk barefoot. So the feet needed thorough cleaning. Bapu insisted that his feet must be absolutely clean. He then asked me to turn his body over so that he could wash his back.'[5]

The towel Gandhi used to dry the body was handed over to Sushila Nayar, with the instruction that it should eventually be passed on to Narayan, Mahadev's teenage son. Mira decked the body with flowers gathered from the garden. Sushila applied some sandalwood paste on the forehead. As they did so, Gandhi sat next to Mahadev's body, reciting verses from the Gita.

During the day, a space was cleared in the grounds for the cremation. A bier was made from tree branches, and carried by Pyarelal, Mira, Sushila and some of the prison staff, with Gandhi leading the way, holding an earthen pot with a flame inside. The body was placed on the ground. Hymns were sung, while Gandhi lit the fire that consigned the body to the flames. Kasturba, herself ailing, sat on a chair alongside.[6]

The next day, the suitcase Mahadev had brought with him to the prison was opened by Gandhi. Apart from his clothes, it contained a copy of the Bible (presented to him by Agatha Harrison), some newspaper clippings and several books, among them a copy of Tagore's play *Muktadhara* and a book called *Battle for Asia*. Gandhi took the last two with him, knowing that Mahadev had kept them to read and digest their findings on his behalf.

Thereafter, every morning, Gandhi would go to the spot Mahadev had been cremated and recite Chapter 12 of the Gita, on the path of bhakti, or devotion. Some of Mahadev's ashes were kept in a box; on the morning of 18 August, noted Sushila, 'Bapu again put a little bit of Mahadevbhai's ashes on his forehead which Ba did not like.'[7] By this act, Gandhi wished perhaps to symbolically imbibe some of Mahadev's learning, to the evident displeasure (or at least puzzlement) of his wife.

III

The news of Mahadev Desai's passing took time to seep out of the jail. But, as it did, a wave of condolences came in from across the country. A file in the archives has more than 300 letters/telegrams of condolences on Mahadev's death, addressed to his wife Durga, their son Narayan, or to Gandhi. These were written in Gujarati, Hindi, English and Marathi, with a couple even in Tamil. They came from, among other places, the Gujarati Mitra Mandali, Secunderabad; the district boards or municipalities of Madura, Nellore, Chidambaram, Jalgaon, Thana and Andheri; the staff and students of the Bombay University School of Sociology and Economics (calling Mahadev 'one of the most devoted workers in the country's cause'); the cooperative banks of Dhulia and Bulsar; the Ahmedabad Bar Association (noting that Mahadev was a former member); the Sahitya Sabha of Surat (for, Mahadev was an accomplished and widely published littérateur as well); the Poona Journalists Association (which noted that apart from his services to Gandhi and the nation, 'as a journalist Shri Desai distinguished himself as an outstanding champion of the freedom of the Press'); and the Society of Intelligentsia, Ghatkopar (saying that in Mahadev's death, 'the Nation has lost a great philosopher, an erudite, a free journalist and a beloved friend of the youths of India').

There were also plenty of letters from individuals. The Lahore Congressman Mian Iftikharuddin wrote to Mrs Desai saying 'your loss is nation's loss'; a man from Murshidabad said Mahadev was Gandhi's 'true friend' and also 'a sympathetic friend to the public'; an advocate from Abbottabad said Mahadev 'was the right hand man to him [Gandhi] and could hardly be spared at this critical juncture'. The propaganda secretary of the Punjab Students' Federation (a communist front, in theory opposed to the Congress) wrote to Narayan Desai that 'your father's loss is an irreparable loss to the nation. India is today intellectually poorer than it was four days back' (and so it was). An old Congressman from the Andhra country wrote to Durga Desai that the last time he met Mahadev in Wardha, 'he was teaching your son and also writing some Guzerathi short stories in prose'. The American missionary Dick Keithan and his wife, long-time supporters of the freedom struggle, based in Madurai in deepest South India, wrote to Durga offering thanks for 'such a life giving itself for us all even to the last moment', and thanking her for 'sharing Mahadev with us all and with Mother India'.

In his travels and tours, and through his writing and speaking, Mahadev Desai touched or moved, influenced or shaped, countless Indians across the land. But his wife Durga, staying at home, may not have realized the extent of her husband's influence until these letters and telegrams came pouring in after his death.

The most poignant of all the letters came from the wife of a Congressman in Delhi in whose house Mahadev had often stayed. The hostess remembered the affection and intelligence of a man she had come to regard as a brother. 'Hum kya saara Bharat unké liyé rotaa hai,' she said. (Why only me, the whole of India weeps for him today.) And added: 'Jab tak Hindusthan aur Mahatma ji ka nam rahega tab tak Mahadev bhai bhi jinda hain.' (Till such time as India and the name of Mahatma Gandhi are known, the name and memory of Mahadev will be alive too.) Sadly, it has turned out otherwise. Seventy-five years on, India is independent and democratic, Gandhi is much memorialized (and much criticized), but the role of Mahadev Desai in the making of the Mahatma and the nation the Mahatma helped father is mostly forgotten.[8]

Gandhi once remarked that Mahadev's 'greatest characteristic' was his 'ability to reduce himself to zero, whenever occasion demanded it'.[9] These occasions occurred regularly and even ubiquitously in the twenty-five years he spent in his master's cause. Gandhi himself recognized how deep was Mahadev's sacrifice, how rich the range of his contributions. The Quaker Muriel Lester wrote of how 'one day Gandhiji began to describe to me what sort of salary [Mahadev] might have had, the sort of position normally due to such a brilliant intellect and character of such integrity'. Lester continued: 'But Mahadev, sitting on the mud floor wide-minded, objective, interested in everything, never so absorbed in serious affairs to banish his fleeting humorous smile, owning only his pen, and his spectacles and his ever living spirit, obviously chose the better part.'[10]

There was a nice tribute to Mahadev Desai in the *Manchester Guardian*, which focused on his love of books and of friendship. The (anonymous) obituarist had worked with Mahadev during the Round Table Conference in 1931, when his 'selfless service impressed me deeply, as did his intelligence and reliability—to say nothing of his sense of humour, without which we could not have survived those strenuous days'. Mahadev, recalled this English friend, 'liked going into English homes and seeing how people lived. No sooner was he inside them that he would gravitate to the bookshelves. It could be seen how much he loved books by the way he handled them. And one could be quite sure of finding him in some bookshop if he had a few minutes to spare.'[11]

The appreciation I myself like best came from the anthropologist-activist Verrier Elwin. In the late 1920s, Elwin had been a regular visitor to the Sabarmati Ashram. Gandhi adopted him as his English son, even as Mira/Madeleine was his English daughter. Elwin then went to work with the tribes of Central India, whose culture and lifestyle made him sceptical of the Gandhian credo of abstinence from sex and alcohol. He drew away from the Mahatma, but remained in contact with Mahadev.

Elwin was in his village home in the Gond country when he heard the news of Mahadev's death on the radio. This brought forth a score of memories: 'I remembered him on the battle-field among his beloved peasants at Bardoli; I recalled how he had taught me to read Tolstoy at Sabarmati; I remembered going to see him in prison and how the mean and gloomy little office where we had our interview seemed transformed by the vitality and beauty of this man whom no chains could bind.'

Mahadev was officially merely Gandhi's secretary, but, as Elwin pointed out, 'he was much more than that. He was in fact Home and Foreign Secretary combined. He managed everything. He made all the arrangements. He was equally at home in the office, the guest-house and the kitchen. He looked after many guests and must have saved ten years of Gandhi's life by diverting from him unwanted visitors.

He had a wonderful way with elderly ladies. . . . When he went to England, he so charmed my own mother that she, of very orthodox [Evangelical] stock, was completely converted to his politics and half-converted to his religion in an afternoon.'

Elwin praised Mahadev's literary abilities, these too undertaken exclusively in his master's cause. Through his 'clear, clean, idiomatic English style', Mahadev had made Gandhi 'perhaps the best known man in the world, certainly the best loved. The punctual, vivid, intimate stories that appeared week by week in *Young India* and *Harijan* displayed to readers all over the world a personality so lovable that love was inevitably aroused in response.'

Elwin wrote of Mahadev's wit, his generosity, his goodness, his extraordinarily self-effacing character. For more than two decades, he was the most important person in the life of the most important Indian. And yet, 'never was a man less pompous. Never was a man less conscious of his own great powers. His heart was filled with pity, gentleness and love; his mind was dominated by a great and holy cause. There was no room for selfishness and egotism. He was too busy to be mean.'[12]

Had Gandhi been free, he would have written a remembrance of Mahadev in English for *Harijan*, and doubtless another one in Gujarati too. But since he was in jail, we do not have an extended tribute from Gandhi after Mahadev's death. To sense what his secretary meant to him, we must make do with some words of chastisement offered in September 1938, when Mahadev had come close to a breakdown because of overwork and his refusal to take a holiday. 'Shall we say you have a mania for work?' wrote Gandhi to Mahadev. 'Don't you know if you were to be disabled, I would be a bird without wings? If you became bed-ridden, I would have to wind up three-fourths of my activities.'[13]

IV

In the country at large, the 'Quit India' movement was gathering momentum. The pre-emptive strikes against the Congress leaders had generated widespread anger and resentment. In Bombay itself, where the famous/notorious meeting of the AICC was held, trouble erupted on a wide scale the day after the arrest of Gandhi. 'Crowds in which students were the most prominent got into local trains, broke glass windows, destroyed cushions of compartments and pulled alarm chains.' Telephone wires were cut and post offices broken into. 'Municipal property—street lamps, lamp-posts, refuse carts, hydrants etc.—was destroyed or damaged.' Markets and bazaars 'in Hindu localities' were closed, as were most schools and colleges.

There were similar protests, albeit on a slightly less intense scale, in other towns of the Bombay Presidency, such as Poona, Ahmedabad, Surat and Ahmednagar.

When, on 15 August, the news of Mahadev Desai's death reached Ahmedabad, there was a citywide hartal. Efforts were made to hold a condolence meeting but the authorities prevented it. Broach, Surat and the Panchmahal also observed hartals in Mahadev's memory.

On 3 September an 'illegal Congress radio' came on air in Bombay. 'Subversive literature was widely distributed and a large quantity of it was seized.' 'Gandhi Week' was celebrated from 2 to 8 October. On the opening and closing days of this week, flag salutation ceremonies were held in different parts of the city, these dispersed by the police. Many mills and shops were closed on these days. Meanwhile, in Ahmedabad, Broach and Kheda, there were processions on 2 October, Gandhi's birthday.[14]

Across the country, in Bengal, the protests were, if anything, even more intense. Between the middle of August and the end of November, hundreds of incidents were reported of the cutting of telegraph wires, the burning of mailbags and letter boxes, the pasting on walls of leaflets saluting 'Azadi ki Larai' (The Fight for Freedom), threats to village headmen and petty officials that if they didn't resign, their houses would be looted. Congress radicals moved around the countryside calling for a no-tax, no-rent campaign. There were strikes in high schools and colleges (including some where there were only girl students). Young men hoisted the tricolour on college buildings. Law courts were picketed. Judges were made to take off their official robes and shout '*Vande Mataram*'.[15]

The 'present position in Bengal', wrote the Hindu Mahasabha leader N.C. Chatterjee to a colleague in Nagpur, is that the entire Hindu population is with Gandhiji and his movement and if anybody wants to oppose it, he will be absolutely finished and hounded out of public life. The unfortunate statement issued by Veer Savarkar [opposing Quit India] made our position rather difficult in Bengal. It is rather amusing to find that Mr. Jinnah wants the Mussalmans not to join the Congress movement and Mr. Savarkar wants the Hindus not to join the same. Even when the Congress movement has made a great stir and it shows that it has got thousands of adherents.[16]

Meanwhile, a Bengali newspaper printed behind the censor's back commented: 'In their pride and arrogance the English have kicked at Gandhi who is the symbol incarnate of Indians and their inner soul. But the day has arrived when the legs of those who kicked, will break off themselves and become unworkable . . .'[17]

In Assam, the province that bordered Bengal on the east, the main Congress leaders were arrested soon after the AICC resolution. Undaunted, students and other activists hoisted flags, raised slogans and, in more remote parts, destroyed bridges, cut telegraph wires and attacked government offices. In response, the government enacted Section 144 throughout the province, rounding up hundreds of activists (including quite a few women) and putting them in jail.[18]

In Orissa, the province immediately to the south of Bengal, Congress leaders were taken into protective custody in the days following the Quit India resolution. But, as elsewhere, protests erupted, often led by students. In the countryside, telegraph wires were cut. Post offices were ransacked and police stations attacked. In remote Koraput, noted a police report, the speed with which some completely irresponsible Congress adherents managed to pass word round in distant hill-tribe villages that the British Raj was no more, was rather surprising.'[19] Acting on this report—or rumour—tribals stormed courts and police stations, shouting slogans in praise of Gandhi and freedom, asking their fellows to stop paying taxes to a government that, in their eloquently expressive and completely unGandhian words, was (as the English translation had it) 'not worth a single pubic hair'.[20]

Moving further south, in the Andhra country, 'telephone wires were cut; rails were removed in several parts of the province. In Guntur District some stations, goods sheds and Railway Carriages were burnt. Trains were de-railed in Bellary and Karnool, Guntur, Kistna, Godavary and Vizag Districts. In Nellur District [a] police station was burnt. In Cuddapah district postal bags were looted in two places. Students abstained from attending schools and colleges en masse.' The government responded sharply: 'Heavy firing took place in Tenali, Guntur and Bhimavaram, and there were nearly 30 people dead. The district Congress leaders were detained. Collective fines were imposed on villages and towns where Government property was destroyed.'[21]

Andhra bordered Karnataka, where the 'most phenomenal feature' of the movement was the response of the student community, which organized boycotts and hartals in Belgaum, Dharwad, Gadag, Bangalore, Mysore, Mangalore, Bijapur, Bellari, Sirsi and other places. In Dharwad, on the 23 October, two students, a Miss Shenolikar and a Miss Gulawadi, entered the district court, hoisted the national flag, told the district judge (who was present) that he was dismissed from his office, distributed leaflets, and disappeared.[22]

Hindi-speaking North Indians were as energetic in their protests as their compatriots who spoke Marathi, Gujarati, Oriya, Bengali, Telugu, Kannada or Tamil. In the holy city of Banaras, a large crowd, acting 'in the name of Congress, marched to the Collectorate and Government buildings in order to destroy and burn papers and files in those offices and to hoist the Congress flag'. In neighbouring Ballia, a crowd of over a lakh marched to the collector's house and then to the SP's home too. The officials caved in, whereupon the crowd then entered their offices, and proceeded to burn the files inside. The United Provinces government sent in the military, while even bombs and machine guns were used in suppressing the rebellion.

The incidents were witnessed by a prosperous zamindar with holdings in both Ballia and Banaras. He noted the scale of the protests but was dismayed rather than impressed by it. For, in the United Provinces, there was now an 'iron rule' of the government, and 'Hindus have had to pay dearly for all this. Muslims are laughing up their sleeves. They have been benefitted by a thousand and one ways. War-contracts, jobs and key-positions, all are being given to Muslims.'

After witnessing the protests first-hand, the zamindar went to the provincial capital, Lucknow. When he complained to a senior British official that the repression was excessive, the official replied that 'Mr. Gandhi had succeeded admirably in bringing about an awakening and as long as it was a case of criticising us from outside the ring, it was alright'. He said that the British were sensitive to world opinion, and were thus willing to recognize the force of Gandhi's criticisms of imperial rule. The official continued: 'Had Mr. Gandhi not put on gloves, and entered the boxing ring, meaning the August Resolution, we were going to yield much more than you Indians had ever thought or expected. The moment Mr. Gandhi got into the ring, it was a case of he knocking us out, or us knocking him out.'[23]

The imperial capital, New Delhi, was not left untouched by the protests. The city's main Congress leaders were quickly arrested, yet younger radicals at large persuaded students not to attend classes. They also distributed handbills and newsletters critical of the government. A cyclostyled sheet printed on 2 October said: 'Today is Gandhi Jayanti Day. The people of India are called upon to fast today and offer prayers in mosques, churches and temples for the life of our leader and for the success of our struggle. All shops should observe complete hartal. Prabhat pheris, processions . . . should be carried out.'[24]

V

Hundreds of thousands of Indians had come out in support of Gandhi's call for the British to withdraw. They had expressed this support in many ways, not all of which would have been approved by the leader. This was no armed revolt; no protester carried a gun or used it. On the other hand, the storming of government offices, the cutting of telegraph wires, the defacement of railway stations—these were not acts of non-violence either. Gandhi, if he was a free man, would not have countenanced them.

It is striking that the targets of these attacks were so often identified with the colonial state. District offices and police stations, railway tracks and telegraph wires—these were all crucial to the maintenance of British power in India. By attacking them, the protesters were calling into legitimacy a state ruled by non-Indians.

Gandhi's Quit India movement brought to the fore the manifest patriotism of large numbers of Indians. On the other side, there were the hundreds of thousands of Indians enlisted to serve in the British Army. Even if they were not mercenaries (as Gandhi charged), these Indian soldiers in Europe, Africa and Asia were certainly apolitical. They did not side with Gandhi or with the Congress.

And there were also some Indians who actively and publicly opposed the Quit India movement and its leaders. Four weeks after Gandhi was arrested, B.R. Ambedkar, now a member of the viceroy's executive council, gave a long interview to a British newspaper. He began by calling the Congress a Hindu party, which had no right to speak for the Depressed Classes. The 'freedom' that Gandhi spoke of and wanted, claimed Ambedkar, was 'the freedom of traditional India, and that means India dominated by Brahmins who believe we pollute them by our presence'. He added that 'Gandhi certainly created a solid Hindu-India, but in America after the Civil War a solid South came into being and its real object was to keep down Negroes'.

Ambedkar continued: 'We [the Depressed Classes] are in the same position as those Negroes, so what comfort can we draw from the prospect of a free and solid Hindu India?'

Ambedkar clarified that he was not 'in favour of domination by the British. But I do not want to escape subjection by the British only to fall victim to complete domination by Hindus.'[25]

Recall that, back in 1939, Ambedkar and Jinnah had briefly contemplated an alliance. That had proved infructuous. Now, some years later, he was bitterly opposed to both Gandhi and Jinnah. In a talk in Poona in January 1943, Ambedkar observed:

> It would be difficult to find two personalities who rival Mr. Gandhi and Mr. Jinnah in their colossal egotism, to whom personal ascendancy is everything, and the country's cause a mere counter on the table. They have made Indian politics into matters of personal

feud, and the consequences hold no terrors for them. Between them Indian politics would become frozen, and no political action would be possible. Their feeling of supremacy and infallibility is strengthened by the Indian press. Indian journalism today is written by drummer boys to glorify their heroes. Never has the interest of a country been sacrificed so senselessly for the propaganda of hero worship.[26]

While Ambedkar attacked Gandhi, in India, others were attacking him abroad. On 9 September, a month after Gandhi's arrest, Winston Churchill told Leo Amery: 'I hate Indians. They are a beastly people with a beastly religion.'[27] A few days later, Churchill launched a blistering attack on Gandhi and the Congress in the House of Commons. The Congress, claimed Churchill, 'did not represent the majority of the people of India'; it 'did not even represent the Hindu masses'. Churchill characterized Gandhi's party as 'a political organisation built around a party machine and sustained by certain manufacturing and financial interests (cheers and laughter)'.

Gandhi might claim to advocate non-violence; but, said Churchill, his party had now 'come out in the open as a revolutionary movement designed to paralyse communications by rail and telegraph and generally to promote disorder . . .' Churchill charged the Congress with being 'committed to hostile and criminal courses', and worse, of being aided 'by Japanese fifth columnists'.

Churchill's speech led to a long debate, spilling over into several sessions of the house. The Labour leader Arthur Greenwood said the prime minister's harsh language would further embitter Anglo-Indian relations. He reminded his fellow MPs that 'there are nations who do not look kindly on our attitude towards subject people'. The Independent Labour Party (ILP) MP James Maxton went further; noting that, in the 1937 elections, the Congress Party had got an 'overwhelming majority and that mandate was as good as Mr. Churchill's or the Conservative party here'. His ILP colleague Campbell Stephen went further still, urging that, since they commanded an 'overwhelming majority' of Indian opinion, the government should 'let the Congress leaders out of jail at once', and 'appoint Mr. Gandhi as Viceroy'.

Seeking to calm the waters, the secretary of state for India, Leo Amery, said that Britain did not have a claim to 'permanent domination' of India, and would, when conditions permitted, restart the process of constitutional reform, so that India could 'go forward with our goodwill to build her future with her own leadership'. The Indophile Labour MP Sydney Silverman interjected: 'Is that the Prime Minister's view?' Knowing that it was not, Amery ducked the question, instead saying that British policy towards India was 'to go forward not to fly apart, to build, not to break up', adding that any settlement must take account of the 'great Moslem community' and of the Depressed Classes.

The debate was closed by Clement Attlee, now deputy prime minister in the War Cabinet. His Labour Party was committed to freedom for India, but this had to be balanced against the demands of the war now being fought. Attlee rode the tightrope delicately and diplomatically. His own interest in India was stoked by his having been a member of the Simon Commission in 1928; fourteen years later, he realized 'how little I know and how great are the difficulties'. He complained about the Congress Party, but in tones gentler than Churchill's. He had thought the Congress would accept the Cripps offer, but they 'departed altogether from methods of democracy and tried the method of coercion'. Attlee nonetheless believed that India might, once the War was won, 'set a lead in Asia for democracy'. He was still hopeful that the Congress would change its mind, and 'join in our effort to defeat tyranny and thereby hasten the time when the Indian peoples may themselves decide on their own free Government for the future'.[28]

Meanwhile, Attlee's colleague in party and government, Stafford Cripps, chose to present the British case to the American people. Writing in the *New York Times*, Cripps deplored that 'at a critical time' in the course of the war, Gandhi should have persuaded the Congress party to carry out 'a campaign of civil disobedience which can do nothing except give comfort and encouragement to the enemy'. Cripps charged that Gandhi's campaign would 'embitter different sections of Indian opinion and so make agreement upon a new Constitution more difficult'. As proof of Britain's good faith, Cripps spoke of the Indianization of the civil services, and the elections of

1937, adding that once the war had ended, steps would be taken to ensure that 'India should have self-government as free as that of Canada or the United States'.

Cripps then explained to the American reader the political configuration in India, with parties other than the Congress representing the Muslims, the Sikhs, the Depressed Classes and the princely states. Cripps claimed that 'these Indians, who are considerably more than half the population, do not want Great Britain to walk out of India while the war is on, do not want the chaos Mr. Gandhi had suggested (quite rightly) that his plan would bring, but they do want to help the United Nations defend India against Japan'.[29]

Cripps's piece was almost certainly written on the advice of his Cabinet. A left-wing Labour leader, one moreover who knew Gandhi and Nehru and had quite recently attempted to arrive at a compromise with the Congress, was more likely to sway American public opinion than one of his Tory counterparts. Even so, his arguments were somewhat disingenuous. That 'India should have self-government as free as that of Canada or the United States', was as he well knew, surely not consistent with his own prime minister's views. Churchill and Linlithgow were loath to cede power to the Indians—a factor that had contributed to the decision by Gandhi and the Congress to launch a fresh mass struggle for freedom.

That Ambedkar and Cripps should take on Gandhi at this time was not surprising. More remarkable, perhaps, was the decision of Henry Polak, a friend of forty years standing, to enlist in the ranks of those opposing Gandhi. As we have seen, ever since the war broke out, Polak, as a British Jew, had strongly felt that the need to defeat Hitler was paramount. His disenchantment with the Congress's refusal to unambiguously support the war effort was at first expressed in private to Indian friends. When his criticisms had no effect, he decided to make them public.

In July 1940, Polak had written to the India Office, saying he would like to go on a government-sponsored lecture tour of the United States, to 'help to place Indo-British relations and Indian cultural values and national aspirations in a fair perspective and to create a sympathetic understanding of each country's difficulties and endeavours'. The India Office was taken with the idea; since 'America has had an abundant share of Congress propagandists over the last two or three years', they were 'anxious to get one or two people of independent views to put a more balanced picture before the American public'.[30]

Polak himself wanted freedom for India, but in slow, steady steps, with the British connection kept intact. He was in this respect closer to Srinivasa Sastri than Gandhi. Had Polak gone on a lecture tour of neutral America in 1940, he would have tried to be even-handed between Britain and India, Linlithgow and Gandhi. As it turned out, Polak was finally sent to America by the India Office only in the second half of 1942. By this time, after the failure of the Cripps Mission and the Quit India movement, Polak had—in a political sense—become extremely hostile to his housemate and intimate friend of his Johannesburg days. That America itself had now entered the war made him even more determined to speak out against Gandhi and the Congress.

Polak's tour of the United States was arranged and paid for by the British Information Services. He spoke in many cities, and also gave several radio interviews. On 15 October 1942, for example, he took part in a public debate in Philadelphia on the question 'What Should Be Done About India'. The other participants were J.J. Singh, president of the India League of America; and Frederick L. Schuman, professor of government at Williams College. Polak himself was described in the programme as a lawyer and journalist, an adviser to the British Labour Party, and 'a former law associate of Gandhi'.

The first speaker in the debate was J.J. Singh, here representing the Congress point of view. Singh said that if a coalition government was formed in Delhi 'by the popular leaders of India', then India as a whole would 'fight shoulder to shoulder with the United Nations against the Axis', thus 'to fight and to die for freedom and democracy'. An unambiguous declaration, without any 'ifs' and 'buts', to the effect that India would be granted independence at the end of the War, would enable Indians to wholeheartedly join the Allies. What stood in the way, said Singh, were the 'reactionary British Tories who are still indulging in the pipe dream of their old glory and cannot bear to see the end of their imperialism'.

Polak, speaking next, accused Singh of painting 'too beautiful a picture' for it to be credible. The Cripps Mission promised independence after the war, but the Congress wanted a declaration of 'immediate independence', and when that was not granted, launched a movement of disobedience and sabotage. Polak went on to speak scathingly of how

> within the Congress Party itself there is a strong pacifist and defeatist element, led by my old friend, Gandhi, who is convinced that the United Nations cannot win the war and who, in any case, would defend India against the enemy only by non-violent means. But Gandhi, would, in fact, if his advice was accepted, urge his countrymen to disband the Indian army (he said so) and make peace with the Japanese, who, he believes, would not invade India if the British and American forces were withdrawn (he said that too).

A sharp argument now began between Gandhi's relatively new follower and his old but now estranged comrade. Singh refuted the claim that Gandhi was an appeaser wanting to make terms with the Japanese. Singh quoted Gandhi as saying: 'I'm more interested than the British in keeping the Japanese out. If Japan wins, then we are losers of everything. I would rather die than cooperate with the Japanese.'

Polak answered by referring to Gandhi's letters offering to negotiate with the Japanese, and even with Hitler. At this stage, the moderator remarked: 'I'm afraid that we can't get anywhere if we disagree over the facts.'

It was time now for the third panellist, the American professor, to speak. Britain's leaders did not trust the Indian nationalists, he said, and the Indian nationalists did not trust Britain's leaders. There was no trust before the Cripps Mission, no trust during it, and certainly no trust after, now that 'too much blood has flowed, too many hearts have been broken, too much bitterness has been bred by the tragic conflict which is still going on in India'.

Professor Schuman suggested that a United Nations commission be constituted, headed by an American, to work out a provisional war government of representative Indians. To this end, the British should release the Congress leaders, and the Congress should call off the civil disobedience movement.[31]

The professor's proposal was well meant, yet with no chance of being heard. The British, led by Churchill, were in no mood to recognize their own fallibilities or imperfections. Imperial arrogance would never permit an impartial arbiter between Britain and India, even if it be America.

VI

These arguments conducted in his name were (at the time) unknown to Gandhi. He was in jail, cut off from his country, his countrymen and the world. Unlike in previous jail terms, he was not allowed to write even non-political letters to his friends and disciples. Few visitors were allowed. He was, however, permitted to subscribe to newspapers.

What we know of Gandhi's daily regimen in prison, c. 1942–43, comes from the colonial archives. It appears that he got up at 6.30 a.m. (somewhat later than at Sevagram), and after ablutions and breakfast, read books or newspapers. From 8.15 to 9 a.m. he walked in the garden with Pyarelal, Sushila Nayar, Mira and his grand-niece Manu. This was followed by a massage by the doctor in his party (Sushila), and a bath.

From eleven to noon, Gandhi ate lunch, slowly, while Mira talked to or read to him. A short rest followed, after which he spent about an hour discussing the newspapers with Pyarelal, who, after Mahadev's death, was now serving as his master's secretary.

As the afternoon progressed, Gandhi taught his grand-niece Manu (precisely what the sources do not say), before supervising the indexing of newspaper cuttings by Pyarelal and Sushila. As sunset approached, Mira read to Gandhi once more. He then took a long walk in the garden, followed by an hour or more at the spinning wheel.

A prayer meeting, then a light evening meal, an hour of conversation with family and friends took up the rest of the day. Gandhi usually went to bed at 10 p.m.[32]

Other glimpses of Gandhi's life in prison come from a memoir written by one of his companions, Sushila Nayar. She reports that on 5 November 1942, the newspapers reported the death in combat of the son of the former viceroy, Lord Irwin (now known as Lord Halifax). Gandhi wrote a message of condolence for the government to pass on. He then told his colleagues in the palace prison that 'you will not find a single nobleman in England whose son has not gone to war. They set an example for the common people and generate a spirit of self-sacrifice and stiff resistance in the whole nation.'[33]

Due to the restrictions on his correspondence, and the fact that Gandhi could not write his weekly columns for his own newspapers, the *Collected Works* are unusually sparse for this period. The only letters that are preserved are those that he wrote to officials. We thus know that he was distressed by reading, in the newspapers, summaries of government resolutions and statements vilifying him and the Congress, accusing them of being complicit with the Axis powers and of practising 'totalitarian' politics. The government had also claimed that Gandhi himself was responsible for the violence that the protests after his arrest had sometimes led to.

In February 1943, the government published an eighty-six-page booklet consolidating these claims. It bore the accusatory title, *Congress Responsibility for the Disturbances, 1942–3*. Its author, a senior home department official named R. Tottenham who detested Gandhi, had so arranged a series of carefully chosen quotes as to seek to show that: (a) Gandhi did not ever intend the movement to be non-violent; and (b) Gandhi preferred the Japanese to the British. The 'entire phraseology of Mr. Gandhi's writings in connection with the movement', this report claimed, 'is of a type associated in the ordinary man's mind with violence'. Indeed, 'Mr. Gandhi knew that any mass movement started in India would be a violent movement. . . . In spite of this knowledge, he was prepared [to] take the risk of outbreaks of rioting and disorder.' Gandhi's stated willingness to allow Allied troops to remain in India, the report further claimed, was insincere; apparently 'he had no intention of allowing them to operate effectively in resisting Japan'.[34]

It is not clear whether the printed report reached Gandhi in the Aga Khan Palace. But the excerpts reproduced in the newspapers certainly did. These charges angered Gandhi, and he wrote directly to the viceroy to refute them. Gandhi reminded Linlithgow that he had always stood out against violence. 'Was not,' he asked, 'the drastic and unwarranted action of the Government responsible for the reported violence?' He also insisted that the Congress was 'definitely against Fascism in every shape and form'.

Hurt and angered by what he considered false and malicious allegations, Gandhi told the viceroy that he planned a twenty-one-day fast, beginning on 9 February 1943.[35]

The viceroy, in reply, stood by his claim that the Congress and Gandhi personally were responsible 'for the lamentable disorders of last autumn'. As for what Gandhi planned to do by way of protest, Linlithgow cleverly used his adversary's language against him, saying that 'I regard the use of a fast for political purposes as a form of political blackmail (*himsa*) for which there can be no moral justification . . .'[36]

There was one doctor with Gandhi in prison—his disciple Sushila Nayar. Sushila was concerned about Gandhi's health, and asked the government to allow three experienced medical men—B.C. Roy, Jivraj Mehta and M.D. Gilder, to be present at the Aga Khan Palace during the fast. Her suggestion was endorsed by the inspector general of prisons, who was 'worried about Mr. Gandhi bearing in mind the sudden collapse of Mahadeo Desai'. He regarded it as 'of very great importance to have a really good medical adviser on the spot'.

One of the men asked for, Jivraj Mehta, was a prominent Congressman, currently imprisoned in Yerwada. The government did not want him near Gandhi. However, B.C. Roy was given permission to come from Calcutta, and M.D. Gilder to come from Bombay. The knowledge that these respected doctors would attend on Gandhi would, the Bombay government hoped, 'have a calming effect on public opinion outside'.[37]

VII

Gandhi had originally planned to begin his fast on 9 February. In the event, it started a day later, on the 10th. On the first day of the fast, the Valmiki Ramayana was read out to Gandhi. On the second day, he read some religious literature himself. By the third day, he was experiencing bouts of nausea. On the fifth day, 'he seem[ed] very weak and exhausted . . . and did not want the usual Gita recitation'.[38]

Some Indian members of the viceroy's executive council pressed for the release of Gandhi. Linlithgow was unmoved. On 17 February, as the fast entered its second week, M.S. Aney, H.P. Mody and N.R. Sarkar resigned from the executive council in protest.[39]

The government would not release Gandhi, but it did now permit him visitors. His old, albeit recently estranged, comrade C. Rajagopalachari came from Madras to see him. His sons Ramdas and Devadas came from Delhi and Nagpur respectively. Saraladevi Chaudhurani got permission to see him too, arriving by train from Lahore.

Of these visitors, one of the few to leave a (brief) record was the editor of the *Bombay Chronicle*, S.A. Brelvi. He found Gandhi 'passing through unprecedented mental agony'. It 'distressed him beyond words' that the government had falsely charged him, one who had dedicated his whole life to non-violence, with inciting violence. It 'hurt him deeply' that the government had given him no opportunity to refute the grave charges against him.[40]

Those who could not personally visit Gandhi sent messages. Hundreds of telegrams were sent to him during the fast, these not forwarded to him at the time. Some were messages of support, others prayers for the fast's success, yet others were pleas to him to abandon it. These messages came from, among others, the Indian Merchants Association of Gibraltar, the Transvaal Indians, the Agra University Students Union, the medical students of Chittagong, the cigar workers of Trichnopoly, the Indian Tea Planters Association of Jalpaiguri, the Bombay Musical Instruments Merchants Association, and the District Harijan Association of Bijapur. The odd wire expressed dissent; one, from the 'Frontier Muslims' of Kohat, read: 'Disapprove practice of fasting as instrument to achieve political ends.'

There were many messages from individuals as well, some formulaic, others more idiosyncratic. A Larry Page of Tasmania wired: 'Play Beethoven's Moonlight Sonata using Indian instruments daily.' A naturopath from Mysore named Sharma advised Gandhi to 'pray use pure water instead citric acid light enema alternate day'.[41]

VIII

At Gandhi's bedside, his disciple and doctor, Sushila Nayar, was maintaining a diary, which minutely recorded, hour by hour and sometimes minute by minute, his sleep, his mood, his pains, his bowel and kidney motions, his baths and massages, his pulse rate, his blood samples and what they revealed, and the coming and going of visitors.

The entry for 19 February began: 'Yesterday (8th day) Gandhiji had a bad day. Severe headache persisted throughout the day. He felt as if the head "would burst". There was disinclination to talk, answer questions or to see or hear anything.'

The next morning, Sushila Nayar noted in her diary that 'yesterday Gandhiji was a little more interested in his surroundings till midday, but after that headache, earache and restlessness returned. He did not like to be disturbed for anything and lay listless with closed eyes. The voice sank to a whisper. He can not now turn in bed by himself and does not like the bed to be tilted up for drinking water.'

On the 21st morning Dr Nayar wrote: 'Yesterday (11th day), G had a bad day. Exhaustion was pronounced, headache, general uneasiness and salivation persisted. Most of the time he lay apathetic in bed and at times appeared drowsy. He finds it difficult to turn in bed or to stretch his legs by himself.'[42]

The fast was now halfway through its course. Visiting him on the 20th, the surgeon general of the Bombay Presidency thought 'a fatal result was at hand'.[43] The Bombay government had sent a message to Delhi that Gandhi's condition was serious. This prompted some discussion on what the government might do if Gandhi died as a consequence of his fast. Should, asked one senior official in the home department, they close government offices for a brief period 'as a mark of respect for an individual who is held in such universal respect, in spite of the fact that he is our political opponent and also, in his own words, an open rebel'?

The viceroy did not think it should. Writing to the governors of the provinces on 18 February, Linlithgow said that considering 'Gandhi's position as our prisoner and a declared rebel, there can be no question of half-masting flags or sending official messages of condolence to his widow'. He thought that, if Gandhi did die in prison, 'any message on the part of Government must contain no unction, no excuse for or explanation of Government's part in Gandhi's end; no word of recrimination against the man himself, while on the other hand any eulogy would equally jar. My own view therefore favours something to the effect that "The Government of India regret to announce that Mr. Gandhi died while in detention at Poona at . . . on . . . from collapse/heart failure following a self-imposed fast".'[44]

While some British officials, with their ear close to the ground and their long Indian experience, knew how widely Gandhi was admired and even venerated, the dour Linlithgow only saw him as 'a declared rebel'.

The news of Gandhi's deteriorating health reached and alarmed the Indian politicians outside prison. On 21 February, a meeting of prominent public figures was held in Delhi, cutting across party lines (the Muslim League only excluded). The gathering appealed to the viceroy to release Gandhi, whose life was in danger because of his fast. They said: 'We firmly believe that if the Mahatma's life is spared a way will be opened to the promotion of peace and goodwill as surely his death as a British prisoner will intensify public embitterment.' They added that 'wise and liberal statesmanship will solve the Indo-British problem more speedily and effectively than stern repression'. This resolution was wired to the British prime minister, Winston Churchill. He sent back a terse reply, saying that Gandhi and other Congress leaders had been jailed 'for reasons which have been fully explained and well understood'. The responsibility for the situation, said Churchill, 'rests entirely with Mr. Gandhi himself'. Churchill added that 'the first duty of the Government of India and of His Majesty's Government is to defend the soil of India from invasion by which it is still menaced, and to enable India to play her part in the general cause of the United Nations'.[45]

IX

In the prison palace, the fast continued. On the afternoon of 23 February, Gandhi's Quaker admirer Horace Alexander arrived for a visit. Gandhi told the Quaker that his principal reason for fasting was to clear his name. He was distressed that he, who had striven for non-violence for almost fifty years, should be accused of 'deliberately instigating the violence that has been and still is happening in the country today'. Gandhi said that if he were free, he would do all he could to rid India of violence, and also work to relieve the distress of those suffering from scarcity of food.[46]

Gandhi was clearly under enormous mental stress. His physical condition was poor too. Sushila Nayar's diary for 23 February noted that 'Gandhiji had a very bad day. He was extremely exhausted, and suffered from restlessness, headache, nausea and salivation.' The 'nausea became so severe that he could not even look at water'. The 'pulse became thready, almost imperceptible and he nearly fainted'.

The next day, Gandhi continued to look 'tired and weak', but the following twenty-four hours were slightly less worrisome to him and his minders. Despite a slight headache, he had 'a comfortable day on the whole'. He also slept well, and so, as Sushila wrote with relief, 'this morning he feels better & the voice is stronger & he looks more rested and cheerful'.[47] The Bombay government wired their bosses in Delhi that 'medical circles in Bombay were now optimistic about Mr. Gandhi's ability to survive his fast . . .'[48]

On the 24th, Gandhi had 'a fairly comfortable day. There were many visitors and he was tired at the end of the day.' On the 25th too, 'Gandhiji had a comfortable day on the whole, except that he felt weaker'. His doctor said 'he looks rested and cheerful'. His fast was now into its third and final week. On the 26th, he complained of a 'slight headache and a flattened out feeling', but he slept well that night, and was 'refreshed and cheerful' when he awoke. The next day, the eighteenth of his self-imposed ordeal, he 'felt weak, but otherwise very well'. He even read a book (we do not know which one) for about forty-five minutes. At 4.15 p.m., C. Rajagopalachari came for a visit. After a few minutes of chit-chat, 'G started talking on the subject of non violence. He was deeply moved, became exhausted and pulse became very feeble. The interview had to be terminated immediately at 4.55. After that he had a drink of water, quietened down and went off to sleep. He slept for 45 minutes and felt better for the sleep.'

There were now a mere three days to go. On the 28th, Dr Sushila Nayar was pleased to record sixty-three ounces of fluid intake, including nine of sweet lime juice. The urine output was likewise satisfactory. The penultimate day, 1 March, saw Gandhi feeling tired and weak, perhaps because there had been a rush of visitors to see him as it became clearer that he (and they) had come successfully through his (and their) ordeal.[49]

Meanwhile, six American correspondents, temporarily stationed in India, had asked the government for permission to be present in the Aga Khan Palace when Gandhi broke his fast. They said they would not question or interview him, but take photographs and write background stories for their newspapers.

The Bombay government said it did not want a 'tamasha' (their phrase), so the request was refused. A note on file by a senior officer reveals how, despite being on the same side in the war and despite sharing strong ties of language, culture and religion, the British upper class still harboured disdain for their trans-Atlantic cousins. Of this request to meet Gandhi, the officer remarked: 'Truly American! These correspondents . . . practically burst into tears at the thought of Gandhi's dying; but they flock like vultures to Poona in the hope of a funeral; and when cheated of that exciting privilege they clamour to invade his sick room and snap cameras at him, regardless of the fact that (in their own estimation) he is still at death's door . . .'[50]

X

Gandhi broke his fast on 3 March 1943. Two days later, the doctors attending on him said 'his progress was satisfactory', and no further bulletins would be issued unless necessary. Meanwhile, the nature cure expert, Dinshaw Mehta, had come to Aga Khan Palace to help Gandhi recover faster from the after-effects of his ordeal. On his advice, Gandhi was taking diluted goat's milk, fruit juice and fruit pulp. (Mehta had also attended on Gandhi after his fasts in Yerwada in 1932 and 1933.)

On 10 March, a week after the fast had ended, the home member of the viceroy's executive council told the Bombay government that

'Dr Ambedkar has asked me whether we have received reports of Gandhi's weight from day to day during his fast'. If this information was available, Ambedkar wanted to see it.

Why did Ambedkar want this information? Why did he wish to know how his great political opponent had fared during his fast? The possibilities are intriguing. But we must resist speculation, and stick here to the facts. Ambedkar's request resulted in the following table, compiled by the Bombay government: [51]

Weight at commencement of fast	109 lbs
On 17/2	105 lbs
On 19/2	97 lbs
On 24/2	90 lbs
On 2/3	91 lbs

Always spindly and spare, Gandhi had become utterly emaciated during his ordeal. He had lost close to 20 per cent of his body weight in the three weeks he went without food. For a man now well into his seventies, to undertake such a long fast was an act of bravado; to see it through safely must be reckoned some kind of medical marvel.

XI

In September 1942, a month after Gandhi was jailed, Winston Churchill wrote to the secretary of state for India, Leo Amery: 'Please let me have a note on Mr. Gandhi's intrigues with Japan and the documents the Government of India published, or any other they possessed before on this topic.' Three days later, Amery sent Churchill the note he asked for, which began: 'The India Office has no evidence to show, or suggest, that Gandhi has intrigued with Japan.' The 'only evidence of Japanese contacts [with Gandhi] during the war', the note continued, 'relates to the presence in Wardha of two Japanese Buddhist priests who lived for part of 1940 in Gandhi's Ashram'.[52]

Before the Quit India movement had even begun, Churchill had convinced himself that Gandhi was intriguing with the Japanese. In February 1943, when Gandhi went on a fast in jail, Churchill convinced himself that Gandhi was secretly using energy supplements. On 13 February, Churchill wired Linlithgow: 'I have heard that Gandhi usually has glucose in his water when doing his various fasting antics. Would it be possible to verify this.'

Two days later, the viceroy wired back: 'This may be the case but those who have been in attendance on him doubt it, and present Surgeon-General Bombay (a European) says that on a previous fast G. was particularly careful to guard against possibility of glucose being used. I am told that his present medical attendants tried to persuade him to take glucose yesterday and again today, and that he refused absolutely.'

On 25 February, as the fast entered its third week, Churchill wired the viceroy: 'Cannot help feeling very suspicious of *bona fides* of Gandhi's fast. We were told fourth day would be the crisis and then well staged climax was set for eleventh day onwards. Now at fifteenth day bulletins look as if he might get through. Would be most valuable [if] fraud could be exposed. Surely with all those Congress Hindu doctors round him it is quite easy to slip glucose or other nourishment into his food.'

By this time, the viceroy was himself increasingly exasperated with Gandhi. But there was no evidence that the fasting man had actually taken any glucose. So, he now replied to Churchill in a manner that stoked both men's prejudices. 'I have long known Gandhi as the world's most successful humbug,' fumed Linlithgow, 'and have not the least doubt that his physical condition and the bulletins reporting it from day to day have been deliberately cooked so as to produce the maximum effect on public opinion.' Then, going against his own previous statement, the viceroy claimed that 'there would be no difficulty in his entourage administering glucose or any other food without the knowledge of the Government doctors' (this when the same government doctors had told him exactly the reverse). 'If I can discover any firm of evidence of fraud I will let you hear,' said Linlithgow to Churchill, adding, somewhat sadly, 'but I am not hopeful of this.'

This prompted an equally disappointed reply from Churchill: 'It now seems certain that the old rascal will emerge all the better from his so-called fast.'[53]

XII

An interesting sideways perspective on Gandhi's fast was provided by the American diplomat William Phillips, who had served as his country's ambassador to Belgium and Italy, as well as assistant and undersecretary of state. Phillips had come out to India in January 1943 as President Roosevelt's personal representative, seeking to lean on the British to reach out to the Congress.

Gandhi, we may recall, had written to President Roosevelt on 1 July 1942, arguing that the Allied claim to be fighting for freedom would be credible only if India was made free. Roosevelt sent a brief reply a month later, choosing his words very carefully. He said that the United States had 'consistently striven for and supported policies of fair dealing', and that, with other nations, they were now 'making a supreme effort to defeat those who would deny forever all hope of freedom throughout the world'. Roosevelt told Gandhi that he hoped 'our common interest in democracy and righteousness will enable your countrymen and mine to make common cause against a common enemy'.[54]

Gandhi didn't get to read Roosevelt's letter, for by the time it reached India he was in jail, where all his correspondence was censored. The Quit India movement, meanwhile, had further soured relations between the nationalists and the Raj. Roosevelt now decided to send William Phillips out to India as his personal envoy. Phillips stayed for almost four months, touring the country and meeting Indian politicians of all stripes, many senior British officials (from the viceroy downwards) and several princes too.

Phillips was extremely keen to visit Gandhi in prison. But, as he told President Roosevelt two weeks after he arrived, he wanted to wait a while before requesting permission to see him. For, 'just now, my call upon him would raise speculation to fever heat without any compensating advantage'.[55]

A month after Phillips arrived in India, Gandhi began his fast. The American observed that there was 'widespread sympathy for Gandhi' among Indians, even those who didn't normally support the Congress. 'The general feeling seems to be that "the grand old man" is being persecuted by our oppressors and therefore he has our entire sympathy and support.'

When Gandhi was halfway through his fast, Phillips went to a large dinner given at the Imperial Hotel by Sir J.P. Srivastava, civil defence member of the viceroy's executive council. The dinner was held in honour of the visiting British governor of the United Provinces. About one hundred people were present. Phillips was told that more than fifty guests had backed out because of the government's intransigence towards the fasting Gandhi. However, noted Phillips, 'Doctor Ambedkar, the Depressed Classes Member, ridiculed the whole excitement and insisted that there was nothing to it, that the Government could not possibly have taken any other course. He hates Gandhi because of the refusal to permit the Depressed Classes to have an electorate independent from the Hindus.'

At the same time, continued Phillips, 'my host [Sir J.P. Srivastava], however, took a different attitude. He said neither his wife nor his two daughters would come to the dinner because of their intense feeling against the Government, of which he was a member. He said that many families were thus divided and that the situation was terribly complicated. If Gandhi dies, he saw infinite trouble.'[56]

Later, in a letter to President Roosevelt, his envoy to India wrote:

It is difficult for Anglo-Saxons to understand the deep-seated feelings which have been aroused by this performance of an old man of 73 years. . . . That such a being is willing to sacrifice himself for the cause that every Indian has at heart, namely, the independence of India, has touched the people as a whole. While, of course, Gandhi's methods in the past are not approved, probably by the majority, nevertheless his honesty of purpose is respected and Indians who have been violently against him have now joined the chorus of appeals on his behalf.

The viceroy, wrote Phillips to Roosevelt, 'has remained adamant' in the face of many appeals to release Gandhi and restart negotiations with Indian leaders. Phillips thought Linlithgow 'does not feel, I fear, the pathos in the appeal of these millions for freedom for their own country. . . . Perhaps he is a "chip off the old block" that Americans knew something about in 1772.'

In his next letter, sent ten days later, Phillips said that the 'only result' of Gandhi's fast, now successfully completed, 'has been increasing bitterness against the British from large sections of the public. The Government has handled the case from the legalist point of view. Gandhi is the "enemy" and at all cost British prestige must be maintained.'

But, continued Phillips, 'Indians look at it from a different angle. Gandhi followers regard him as semi-divine and worship him. Millions who are not his followers look upon him as the foremost Indian of the day and that since he has never had an opportunity to defend himself it is a case of persecution of an old man who has suffered much for the cause which every Indian has at heart—freedom for India. And so presumably Gandhi comes out of the struggle with an enhanced reputation as a moral force.'

After spending two months speaking to a cross section of people, Phillips could clearly see that most Indians were now 'caught in the new idea which is sweeping over the world, of freedom of oppressed peoples'. Yet, Churchill and Linlithgow were determined not to transfer any power to Indians. Phillips thought his fellow Americans should seek to break the deadlock. He proposed that a conference of all major Indian political parties and their representatives be convened under the blessings of the king-emperor, the U.S. President, and the President of the Soviet Union. The conference could be held in any city in India other than Delhi, and be 'presided over by an American who could exercise influence in harmonizing the endless divisions of caste, religion, race and political views'. The British, for their part, should free Gandhi and other leaders to attend this conference.

Phillips believed his proposal offered 'a way out of the impasse, which if allowed to continue, may affect our conduct of the war in this part of the world and our future relations with colored races. It may not be successful, but, at least, America will have taken a step in furthering the ideals of the Atlantic Charter.'[57]

Roosevelt himself had never visited India. While more sympathetic than Churchill to the rights of coloured people, for him too the demands of the war were more pressing than any other. Meanwhile, Phillips continued his travels around India. He met Ambedkar several times, noting: 'He is always interesting but far from constructive.' He also had long conversations with Jinnah, writing later: 'Undoubtedly he has a brilliant mind. He is tall and slender and well dressed, and he looks far more like an Englishman than an Indian.'

Jinnah, observed Phillips, 'hates and distrusts Gandhi and firmly believes that the latter has no intention of helping to create a Coalition Government with Hindus and Muslims. . . . He warned that the more support which was given to the Congress Party from abroad the more obstinate Gandhi would be in his demands.' Jinnah spoke to the American diplomat 'about his *right* to Pakistan, and said that the new Muslim State which, he insisted, would be a continuous block in the North representing forty million Muslims, would be able to take care of itself economically and financially'.[58]

Phillips also went for a tiger shoot with the viceroy in the sal forests of Dehradun. He had tried several times to get permission to see Gandhi; now, amidst the campfires, he tried once more, and failed again. In a farewell press conference held in Delhi in the last week of April, Phillips remarked that in his extended tour of India, he had travelled extensively and met hundreds of people 'from all walks of life and representing all types of opinion, occupation, and profession'. There remained, however, one significant omission. As he delicately put it: 'I should have liked to meet and talk with Mr Gandhi. I requested the appropriate authorities for permission to do so and was informed that they were unable to grant the necessary facilities.'[59]

William Phillips' reservations about the viceroy were shared by some Englishmen too. The novelist and historian Edward Thompson wrote to a friend in April 1943 that 'there is no hope whatever [of a resolution in India] until you get a new Viceroy. The present man is a humiliating combination of high-mindedness and arrogance.'[60]

CHAPTER THIRTY-ONE

The Death of Kasturba

I

As he recovered from the after-effects of the fast, Gandhi resumed his daily routine, walking, writing, reading and spinning. He had been subscribing to the Muslim League's newspaper, *Dawn*. He saw there that in a League meeting in Delhi, Jinnah had asked Gandhi to write directly to him if he was interested in a settlement.

Early in May 1943, taking up the offer, Gandhi wrote to Jinnah to come meet him in prison. 'Why should not,' asked Gandhi, 'both you and I approach the great question of communal unity as men determined on finding a common solution, and work together to make our solution acceptable to all who are concerned with it or are interested in it?'[1]

The government did not forward the letter to Jinnah. As the viceroy wrote to the secretary of state for India, the 'Congress at the moment are beaten and disheartened', and thus 'it would suit us best to preserve the status quo here until the war with Japan is won . . .'

Word of the suppressed letter got around, forcing the government to issue a formal communiqué, saying they could not permit 'political correspondence or contact to a person detained for promoting an illegal mass movement which he has not disavowed, and thus gravely embarrassing India's war effort at a critical time'.[2]

Jinnah himself called Gandhi's invitation 'meaningless'. He had hoped Gandhi would come to an agreement with the Muslim League on the basis of Pakistan, in which case 'we were willing to bury the past and forget it'. He added: 'This letter of Mr. Gandhi can only be construed as a move on his part to embroil the Muslim League to come into clash with the British Government solely for the purpose of helping his release so that he would be free to do what he pleases thereafter.'[3]

Never short of self-confidence, Jinnah had even more reason to be pleased with himself at this time. The Congress's absence from the political field had allowed the Muslim League free play. Their membership had continued to grow steadily, with many new recruits among college students and professionals. The League was now part of ruling governments in Punjab, Sindh, Assam and Bengal. The membership of the party, once in the mere thousands, was now close to two million.

The appeal of the League rested in part on the image of its leader. Jinnah was seen by his followers as upright and incorruptible, and of a high intellectual calibre, so high that (unlike other Muslim leaders in the past, such as the Ali Brothers), he could not be taken for a ride by the crafty Congress bosses. The idea of a sovereign Muslim state was also greatly appealing to them. Thus, as one historian of this period observes, 'the demand for Pakistan reminded Muslims of their past glory and opened before them vast and fascinating vistas of future greatness. It was this stimulant which put life and vigour into the Muslim League.'[4]

Jinnah himself often placed this image of a future Muslim state before his followers. On 23 March 1943, he issued a statement reminding everyone, not just the Muslims, that on this day three years previously 'was declared, at Lahore, for the first time authoritatively from the platform of the All-India Muslim League, the final goal of Muslim India, which later on came to be known as the "Pakistan scheme"'.

The 'progress that Mussalmans, as a nation, have made, during these three years,' said Jinnah with noticeable (but also well-merited) satisfaction,

is a remarkable fact. Never before in the history of the world has a nation rallied round a common platform and a common ideal in such

a short time as the Muslims have done in this vast sub-continent.
Never before has a nation, miscalled a minority, asserted itself so
quickly, and so effectively. Never before has the mental outlook of
a nation been unified so suddenly. Never before has the solidarity
of millions of population been established and demonstrated in so
limited a time and under such peculiar circumstances as are prevalent
in India. Three years ago Pakistan was a resolution. To-day it is an
article of faith, a matter of life and death with Muslim India.[5]

II

In the summer of 1943, Gandhi asked for and received a copy of
the government report entitled *Congress Responsibilities for the
Disturbances, 1942–43*. He spent several weeks poring over its
contents, and then drafted a reply rebutting its contents. Replete
with long quotations from his own writings (sourced by Pyarelal),
this rebuttal runs to some ninety pages of Gandhi's *Collected Works*.
Contrary to the government's claims and charges, Gandhi insisted that:

1. He never had and never would countenance violence in any
   popular movement against colonial rule;
2. He had consistently opposed Nazism and fascism;
3. He was by no means pro-Japanese, and had condemned their
   attacks on China;
4. He was not at all anti-British, had many British friends and felt
   deep sympathy for the British people;
5. He had always sought a compromise before deciding to launch a
   mass struggle.[6]

This extraordinary letter showed the depths to which Gandhi had been
wounded by the calumnies to his reputation. In fifty years in politics,
he had often been abused and vilified, but usually by individuals, not
by governments. That a British viceroy questioned his motives and his
character so harshly was something he would not leave unchallenged.

Gandhi's hurt, extended response to the government's charges
also reveals the stress he was under. Physically, he had not yet

recovered fully from his fast earlier in the year; emotionally, he had not yet recovered from the loss of Mahadev in August 1942. Age, ill health and mental weariness had made him far more prickly about criticism than he had perhaps ever been before.

In September, Lord Linlithgow's term as viceroy finally ended. He had served in the post longer than anyone else, not because of his inherent qualities or his suitability for the job, but because once the war broke out, continuity at the top was deemed important. In a farewell letter, Gandhi told him: 'Of all the high functionaries I have had the honour of knowing, none has been the cause of such deep sorrow to me as you have been. . . . I hope and pray that God will some day put it into your heart to realize that you, a representative of a great nation, had been led into a grievous error.'[7]

III

While Gandhi was in prison in Poona, on the other side of the subcontinent famine was looming. In their bid to stop a Japanese invasion, the British had destroyed thousands of country boats in Bengal. They did not want the enemy to get hold of them. However, these boats were traditionally used by the villagers of Bengal to buy and sell goods crucial for subsistence. Food and other essential commodities now became scarce. The government did not react, and people began to starve to death. Still there was no response. Rice was sequestered for the city of Calcutta (where large numbers of British and American troops were based) while the districts of the province were left without supplies. The famine got worse, and worse. Perhaps more than a million died in 1943 alone.[8]

Meanwhile, the most prominent living Bengali, Subhas Bose, had joined the Japanese side in the war. After he was forced to resign from the Congress presidency in 1939, Bose formed a group called the Forward Bloc, which he saw as a left-wing vanguard of the Congress. Addressing a meeting in Madras in January 1940, Bose remarked that 'to say that we must spin our way to *swaraj* or that spinning is the acid test of our fitness for *swaraj* is something too big to swallow'.[9]

Bose hoped he would be able to rejoin the Congress Party, and tame the conservatives. This proved impossible. After a series of combative speeches excoriating the British, he was put under house arrest. In January 1941, he escaped, and made his way across Afghanistan to Germany. He made contact with Indian exiles, and sought an audience with Hitler. He had decided that, on the principle of 'the enemy's enemy is my friend', he would seek the support of the Axis powers to deliver India from British rule.[10]

Bose was in Germany through much of 1941 and 1942. But Hitler did not much care for India or Indian independence. His officials suspected that Bose had pro-Soviet sympathies. Disappointed, in February 1943, Bose left by sea for the East, hoping now to solicit the help of the Japanese for his cause.[11]

Bose got a more sympathetic reception here. An Indian Independence League had been set up by the Japanese; this was converted into an Indian National Army, with Subhas Bose placed in charge. This Azad Hind Fauj (to give it its Hindustani name) was largely composed of former soldiers of the British Indian Army, who had surrendered to the Japanese in Singapore and Malaya, and now hoped to free their country under Bose's leadership.[12]

There is a vast (and ever proliferating) literature on Subhas Chandra Bose and the Indian National Army (INA). I flag here only an important point obscured in the stirring tales of Bose's disappearance from India, his controversial appeal to Hitler, his final concord with the Japanese, the battles his army fought—namely, that this rebel retained a deep attachment to the party in which he had cut his political teeth. Of the four brigades of the INA, three were named after Gandhi, Jawaharlal Nehru and Maulana Azad (the fourth was named, after he yielded to his sycophants, after Bose himself). These were all Bose's old Congress comrades; besides, he knew of the enormous appeal their names carried within India. Like Gandhi and Nehru, Bose also remained a vigorous proponent of Hindu–Muslim harmony, and of equality for women. He even started a women's regiment, this named after the nineteenth-century warrior-queen, the Rani of Jhansi. But on the question of non-violence he differed with Gandhi, and on the question of who were more evil, the Allies or the Axis, he differed with Nehru.[13]

On 2 October 1943, Subhas Bose spoke over the radio from Bangkok. This, he reminded his Indian listeners, was the birthday 'of their greatest leader, Mahatma Gandhi'. His address rehearsed Gandhi's contributions; how, when he started his non-cooperation movement in 1920, 'it appeared as if he had been sent by Providence to show the path to liberty. Immediately and spontaneously the whole nation rallied round his banner.'

In the twenty-odd years since Gandhi emerged as the nation's leader, continued Bose, Indians had 'learnt national self-respect and self-confidence'. They had also 'now got a country-wide organisation representing the whole nation'. The 'service which Mahatma Gandhi has rendered to India and to the cause of India's freedom', said Bose, 'is so unique and unparalleled that his name will be written in letters of gold in our National History—for all time'.

Subhas Bose ended his radio address with these words: 'Mahatma Gandhi has firmly planted our feet on the straight road to liberty. He and other leaders are now rotting behind the prison bars. The task that Mahatma Gandhi began has, therefore, to be accompanied by his countrymen—at home and abroad.'[14]

Bose did not overstate Gandhi's role in stoking Indian political consciousness. Yet, coming from him, the tribute was uncommonly generous. For, just four years previously, Gandhi had forced Bose out of the Congress presidency and out of the party itself. Now Bose had, in the larger interest of India's freedom, set aside those old quarrels, and handsomely praised Gandhi for consolidating a diverse and divided population into a nation-in-the-making.

In his speeches on Azad Hind Radio, Subhas Bose referred to Gandhi as the 'Father of the Nation'. This seems to be the first time Gandhi was called this. The usage soon became ubiquitous.

IV

Towards the end of 1943, Kasturba Gandhi's health began to deteriorate. In December, she had two mild heart attacks. She had difficulty breathing, and was now, more or less, confined to bed.

Devadas Gandhi rushed to Poona from Delhi to visit his mother. Afterwards he wrote to his father-in-law (Rajaji) that Kasturba was 'bedridden with breathlessness and a heart which has little vitality left now. . . . Bapu takes a serious and fatalistic view of Ba's condition and she herself is in great despair . . . But I was glad to see Bapu in fairly good health. His smack of my back had more than the usual punch.'[15]

In early January, Gandhi wrote to the jail superintendent that his wife 'has got into very low spirits. She despairs of life, and is looking forward to death to deliver her. If she rallies on one day, more often than not she is worse on the next.' He asked that she be allowed to see her relatives more often, as this 'may give her some peace'. In particular, he asked that their nephew Kanu Gandhi, both an expert nurse and an accomplished singer, be allowed to stay with them in prison. If that was not possible, he hoped that Kanu could at least visit daily and sing some bhajans for his aunt.[16]

The government allowed Kanu Gandhi to visit every day, and also permitted Kasturba's sons to come from time to time. While Devadas and Ramdas came often, Harilal's visits were rationed by the government. The government thought Harilal was 'an irresponsible man', and would leak out the security details of the palace. When Gandhi heard this, he laughed and said: 'Perhaps [the Government thinks] I may take advantage of Harilal's weakness and ask him to do something [illegal] for me.'[17]

Later in January, the patient asked for Kanu Gandhi to attend on her day and night. The permission was refused on the grounds that while 'the request for Kanu Gandhi might be perfectly genuine, Mr. Gandhi regards it as merely a thin end of the wedge, and proposes to ask for more favours'.[18]

The high officials of the Raj intensely disliked Gandhi. With Kasturba on her deathbed, they struggled to balance elementary humanity with their hatred for her husband. With the war against the Japanese entering its climatic phase, they were more prone than ever to regard him as a mortal enemy.

Passed on the correspondence, the home member of the viceroy's executive Council, R.M. Maxwell, said that, if more help was needed, the Bombay government should provide professional nurses. 'I do not know,' commented Maxwell angrily, 'why it is assumed that anyone connected with the Gandhi family is so sacred that they can only be nursed by Congressites.'[19] However, after Kasturba had another heart attack in the last week of January, Kanu was allowed to move into the palace prison.

A series of articles appeared in the Indian press urging the government to release Kasturba. One newspaper wrote sarcastically that, while in London, the authorities had released the fascist Oswald Mosley, 'Britain's Enemy Number 1', they would not release this old lady, perhaps believing that doing so 'would bring a catastrophe to the rule of "law and order" in India'. Another newspaper likewise remarked that while 'frail, weak, old Kasturba loved by millions of Indian people is good where she is' (in jail), 'the fat, strong Oswald Mosley hated by all people, suffering from slight indisposition was not good in detention and had to be released'.[20]

On 5 February, Devadas Gandhi met the senior home department official R. Tottenham in Delhi, and asked him to have Kasturba released from prison, and allow her to move to Sevagram or Delhi, since 'the change of air or scene might be good for her'. Devadas's proposal was endorsed by H.V.R. Iyengar of the Bombay government, who thought it possible that 'freedom will give her [Kasturba] happier psychological environments and make her last days easier'. The Indian ICS man made a 'radical' proposal, which was to release Kasturba, let Gandhi out on parole, and allow both to stay in Lady Thackersey's bungalow in Poona, on the condition that Gandhi did not leave its premises, stayed away from political discussions, and gave no interviews.

Tottenham rejected Iyengar's proposal, since it would, from the government's point of view, 'give rise to far too many complications. Mrs Gandhi might live for many months yet; parole [for Gandhi] might have to be indefinitely extended; Lady Thackersey's bungalow might become a centre of attraction to an extent to which even she might object; and even if Mr. Gandhi did not agree to talk politics, it is difficult to give that word a precise definition and anyhow he would be continually in the public eye.'[21]

As Kasturba's condition further deteriorated, her three sons in India—Devadas, Ramdas and Harilal—came to see her every day.

(Manilal was in South Africa.) Kanu Gandhi gave massages and sang bhajans for her. In the first week of February, the Bombay government, as advised by the prison authorities, ordered three oxygen cylinders and sent them to Poona for Kasturba's use.[22]

The physician in charge of Kasturba was Dr M.D. Gilder, an old Congressman jailed for supporting the Quit India movement. An Ayurvedic physician from Lahore had come to Poona as well. He stayed at the Thackersey mansion, Parnakuti, and visited the Aga Khan Palace during the day. Gandhi's old and trusted naturopath, Dinshaw Mehta, was also attending on Kasturba twice daily, giving enemas and massages to help her sleep better.

These treatments gave some relief but then, in the third week of March, Kasturba came down with pneumonia. Gandhi now agreed to go back to allopathic treatment. Dr Gilder asked whether the government could procure the new wonder drug, penicillin, for Kasturba. The Bombay government made inquiries, and were told that only the military had stocks. The British Army had exhausted their supplies, so a request was made to the American Army's headquarters in India. The Americans located some stocks in Calcutta and agreed to fly them to Poona.[23]

V

As Kasturba's health began to fade perceptibly, Sushila Nayar began maintaining a daily, hourly diary on her health, as she had done during Gandhi's 1943 fast. This diary was in Hindi, not English—in keeping both with the linguistic preferences of the doctor and the special relationship she had with her patient. Sushila's entries record the physical suffering and the emotional restlessness of this elderly woman prisoner. At 5.10 a.m. on 18 February, Sushila wrote of Kasturba: 'Chathi mein dard honé laga. Bhitar jalan si honé lagi.' (The chest pained; the insides burnt.) Five hours later she noted: 'Bechaini rahi' (the restlessness remained). Kasturba dozed off briefly in the afternoon, but at 3.20 p.m. her devoted doctor-attendant noted: 'Khansi aane sé neend tooti' (a coughing fit woke her up). For the rest of the night, her sleep was interrupted at regular intervals.

Through the 19th, Kasturba was restless. She slept fitfully through the day, alternately mumbling to herself and dozing. To still her coughing, she was given doses of the bronchodilators, deriphyllin and ephedrine. Her last hours were approaching, and Gandhi had been reconciled to making them as painless as possible, even if this meant departing from the natural methods he had so often advocated and practised.

The next morning, Kasturba was calmed by the singing of her husband's favourite *Ramdhun*. She was taken into the veranda and into the garden, which pleased and further calmed her. But in the evening the sense of agitation (*bechaini*) returned.

That night, at 10.45, Sushila administered her *'neend ka dawa'*, a sleeping pill, though the diaries do not record which one, and whether it was made from synthesized Western chemicals or organic native herbs. A chest massage was also administered. For two hours, she fell into *'gehri neend'* (deep sleep). But in the early hours of the morning, once more the restlessness returned. A great weakness (*bahut kamzori*) manifested itself. She complained of a burning stomach (*pet mé jalan*) and of pain in the liver. Sushila pressed a wet cloth gently on the aching parts. But an hour later, it was reported that *'bechaini kaafi rahi'* (the restlessness remained). The head also ached. Now a handkerchief soaked in cologne water was placed on her head. Gandhi came and sat next to her, and she calmed down again.

On the 21st, Kasturba coughed badly during the day. At 1.30 in the afternoon, she was put on an oxygen cylinder. Two hours later, asthmatic pills were also administered. Gandhi stayed close to her throughout. The entry for 4.30 to 5 p.m. is bilingual: *'Bechaini.* Excitement over Harilal Bhai. [Her eldest, long-estranged son, who had come to see her, apparently in a drunken state.]'

At 7.45 p.m., Sushila gave Kasturba a cup of hot Horlicks, followed by an injection of deriphyllin. She slept, and wetted her bed. Sushila changed her clothes and the sheets without her waking up. At 1.30 in the morning of the 22nd, Kasturba woke up, complaining of *'sirr mé chakkar'* (a whirling head). Then she dozed off again. At 3.45 a.m., M.D. Gilder checked Kasturba's pulse. At 6.30 a.m. her husband came to see her. That calmed Kasturba, and for three hours she had a spell of peaceful rest. By noon, she was once more overcome by a great weakness. By now, she was too far gone to be revived, whether by pills or the presence of her husband and sons. The last page of Sushila Nayar's diaries has this entry for the afternoon of 22 February 1944: '*Swashtya jaada bigad gaya tha*'—her health had deteriorated massively.[24]

Devadas Gandhi had reached Poona on the 21st evening to find his mother in a 'semi-conscious' state. She seemed 'greatly comforted' when her husband came and attended on her for an hour. The next morning she refused her medicines, but opened her mouth for a drop of Ganga water. At 3 p.m., she called for Devadas and told him, 'I must go some day, why not today?' She then joined her hands in prayer, her words translated from the Gujarati by her youngest son as 'God, my refuge, thy mercy I crave.'

At about 5 p.m. on the 22nd, word came that the penicillin had finally arrived. Was it now too late or too dangerous to inject her with the drug? Devadas was in favour of the injections, but Gandhi was not. 'You can't cure your mother whatever wonder-drugs you may muster,' he told his youngest son, 'I will yield to you if you insist. . . . [But] remember you are seeking to cause physical pain by an injection every four or six hours to a dying mother.'

Gandhi then turned to Sushila. 'Are you and Dr. Gilder sure that it should be given?' he asked. 'Are you sure it will help her?' Sushila later recalled how she felt at being asked the question directly: 'I could not say yes. Ba's condition was so grave that we could not be very sure that it would help her. . . . I was sorry that we could not try penicillin, which might have helped her. I was also somewhat relieved, as the prospect of giving her repeated injections had not been very pleasant.'

So the injections were not given. Later that evening, Kasturba called for Gandhi. He leaned her against his shoulder and sought to comfort her. Shortly afterwards, she passed away.[25]

VI

The day after Kasturba died, all shops and businesses closed as a mark of respect for her memory in Bombay, Ahmedabad, Surat, Broach,

Miraj, Nasik, Jabalpur and other towns. Condolence meetings were held in many parts of India, organized by schools, colleges, merchants' associations, and a range of political parties, from the Communist Party of India on the left to the Hindu Mahasabha on the right. There were also meetings in her memory in Durban and in Johannesburg, where 5000 pounds was raised on the spot, to commemorate her life and spirit in the form of a girls' school in the Phoenix Settlement.[26]

On 24 February, Kasturba's body was cremated in the grounds of the palace. The next day, Devadas collected her ashes to immerse in the Ganga in Allahabad, for, as Gandhi told him, 'what crores of Hindus do as a sacrament is what would please your mother'.

Devadas ended his essay on his mother's last days by describing what they had meant to his father:

> He was looking obviously fagged. He grieves over this tragic gap which has come into his life, for she in large measure is responsible for what he is to-day. But he maintains a philosophic calm . . . The atmosphere around him was one of sadness without gloom and when my brothers and I parted company with the camp on Friday [the 25th], he cracked his customary jokes as a substitute for tears.[27]

Gandhi and Kasturba had been married for sixty years. They had made homes together in Rajkot, Durban, Johannesburg, Bombay, Ahmedabad and Wardha. They had raised four children together. Their own relationship had passed through many phases, from Gandhi seeing her as an object of his lust, to demanding that she follow him blindly in his activist and personal choices, to a maturing accommodation where they came to respect and love one another—this companionship briefly interrupted by the Saraladevi episode, now well in the past.

As with Mahadev, with Kasturba too hundreds of messages of sympathy came pouring in for Gandhi—though it is not clear whether he was shown them at the time. These condolences came from, among others, many district Congress committees; the staff and students of numerous schools and colleges across India; merchants' bodies; trade unions; youth associations. The Harijans of Vizag district condoled the 'model *mahila*'s expiration'; the Pan Cigarettes Shopkeepers Union of Lahore expressed 'great sorrow of death of Mata Kasturba' (which was generous, since her husband so strongly disapproved of the goods they sold); the Cloth Merchants Association of Chakwal hoped that 'mother's tragic death may terminate the period of slavery'; the Kathiawar Political Conference, Wadhawan, called Kasturba the 'embodiment of self-effacement [and] pure service', adding that 'she met nobler death as prisoner of war'; the All India Momin Conference (representing millions of lower-caste Muslims) said Kasturba's death was a 'stunning blow' to their community as well as to the 'entire humanity'.

As with Mahadev, the grief felt was spontaneous and widespread, coming from different castes and communities, and all over the subcontinent. This was an indirect tribute to Gandhi, to his cross-class and pan-Indian appeal, so that in his loss his compatriots could, burying past and present differences, unite to console him.

There were also messages from outside India. The Muslim and Tamil communities of Galle (who had seen Kasturba on her visit to Ceylon with Gandhi in 1928) sent a wire, as did the Cape Indian Congress; the Transvaal Indian Congress; the Indian communities of dozens of towns in South Africa, and some in East Africa and New Zealand too.

An astonishing number of associations in Ahmedabad—home to Kasturba between 1915 and 1934—wrote letters, reflecting the social diversity of the city, here united in tribute: the staff and students of the H.L. Commerce College and the S.L.D. Arts College; the Chawl Owners Association; the Ahmedabad Share and Stock Brokers Association; the Mahagujarat Dalit Harijan Samaj (saying that 'Harijans mourning this irreparable loss as if they have lost their own mother'); the Gujarat Committee of the Communist Party of India; and many more.

The individuals who wrote in included the veteran social worker Hridyanath Kunzru, for whom Kasturba 'typified in herself the highest ideals of Indian womanhood'; a Bombay palmist and astrologer named M.S. Rao, for whom Kasturba's 'death has caused a shadow of sorrow in every Indian Home and coming as it does so soon after Mahadeva Desai's death, the blow is too great for words to describe'; the photographer Umrao Singh Sher-Gil, who had lost his own gifted painter-daughter, Amrita Sher-Gil, some years previously, and now hoped that Gandhi, with his 'real spiritual outlook', would 'be able to bear it with greater equanimity than people like us can bear our sorrows'. A letter from the Poona writer and nationalist S.L. Karandikar acutely observed that while Gandhi himself was 'the support of millions', Mahadev and Kasturba 'were supports to you. Cruel death has snatched away both these supports! The highest degree of courage and patience would be required to struggle with the sense of bereavement. I earnestly pray to God that He should give you both on this occasion as He has done on many an occasion before.'[28]

Condolence messages also came from the former British Prime Minister David Lloyd George; the former Viceroy Lord Irwin (now Lord Halifax); the Archbishop of Canterbury—showing that (select) sections of the British establishment still retained the common courtesies despite the deep rift between Gandhi and themselves.

So far as one can tell, there were no messages of condolence from Linlithgow, Ambedkar, Savarkar or Jinnah. However, the Muslim League's newspaper published an affecting tribute to Kasturba, praising her 'silent, uncomplaining heroism' in keeping faith with Gandhi's radical personal and political choices, with the cults that surrounded him and his own 'inner voice', with the 'extraordinary courses of action' he would periodically embark upon. 'For any woman,' wrote *Dawn*, 'to watch by the side of a husband undertaking prolonged fasts, sometimes according to capacity, sometimes unto death, must be a harrowing ordeal, but she endured all . . .'[29]

Perhaps the two messages that would have meant the most to Gandhi (had he seen them) came from old, intimate friends with whom he had had political disagreements. The first was C. Rajagopalachari. Rajaji was one of Gandhi's oldest political colleagues, and also his *sambandi* with whom he had shared grandchildren. It was he who rescued the Gandhi–Kasturba marriage when Gandhi's infatuation with Saraladevi threatened to disrupt it. But Rajaji was also, more recently, a disputant and renegade, who was at liberty while his long-time comrades were in prison.

Rajaji's letter, posted three days after Kasturba's death, said that 'Ba has found final release. If there be any truth in the Hindu Dharma she has lived up to it and fulfilled her earthly trial.' There was, he continued, 'no life-story in our generation where woman has stood her trial so much in the manner of our Hindu . . . traditions as Ba has triumphantly done'.[30]

The second tribute one hopes Gandhi saw came from Henry Polak. When Kasturba died, Polak (her former housemate) was in Orkney, lecturing to the troops on education. On hearing the news, Polak sent a short telegram to the India Office to forward to Gandhi, reading: 'Deepest loving sympathy wish you all God's blessings Henry [and] Millie Polak.'

Polak also composed a longer wire, sent as a statement to the press. This read:

> death Mrs Gandhi — ba (mother) as she was generally known — not unexpected advanced age stop devoted wife mother in many ways independent personality stop but she was real martyr husbands causes learning uselessness beyond certain point resisting his firmly held principles austere practices stop Gandhi declared learnt first lessons passive resistance from her stop her first imprisonment occurred south african indian struggle 1913 thereafter several times later interned India during Gandhis civil disobedience movement stop death may have been expedited by anxiety for husbands many self imposed fasts during one of which she had saved his life by inducing him modify oath against use milk by taking goats milk stop her many friends grieving her death will rejoice her release.[31]

The contrast between the two telegrams sent by Polak is striking. A short private message of love to Gandhi, and a much longer statement to the press that was strongly pro-Kasturba, presenting her (not untruthfully) as a martyr to his many (and often mysterious) causes. Polak knew the marriage better (and longer) than any Indian associate of Gandhi, and therefore wished that the extent of Kasturba's sacrifice be made known to the British public. It seems the wire was intended as an obituary in the press—it is not clear, however, if it was ever published.

VII

In October 1943, Lord Wavell had replaced Linlithgow as viceroy. A former commander-in-chief of the British Indian Army, Wavell knew the country well. His appointment was seen by some as a demotion. Churchill did not warm to Wavell, and wanted to shift him out of active military service. So, he sent him to oversee the administration of Indian civilians, about whose welfare the British prime minister had never greatly cared about. As Wavell wrote in his journal: 'He [Churchill] has a curious complex about India and is always loth to hear good of it and apt to believe the worst.' Leo Amery, the secretary of state for India, was even more blunt; as he put it (again, in private), Churchill knew 'as much of the Indian problem as George III did of the American colonies'.[32]

The first argument that Wavell and Churchill had was about food aid to Bengal. When the viceroy asked for more supplies to be sent to the famine-stricken districts of eastern India, the prime minister 'spoke scathingly of India's economic efficiency' and said the available stocks were better used within Europe. Wavell concluded that Churchill thought it 'more important to save the Greeks and liberated countries from starvation than the Indians . . .' The prime minister was hostile to Indians in general and to one Indian in particular, telling the viceroy 'that only over his dead body would any approach to Gandhi take place'. Churchill joked to Wavell that he had 'one great advantage over the last few Viceroys'. They 'had to decide whether and when to lock up Gandhi', whereas Wavell 'should find him already locked up'.

When Wavell went to call on Linlithgow, he found his predecessor as sceptical of Indian aspirations as the prime minister. Linlithgow told Wavell that 'he did not believe that any real progress is possible while G[andhi] lives', adding that 'we [the British] shall have to continue responsibility for India for at least another 30 years'.[33]

Gandhi, perhaps nursing bad memories of Wavell's predecessor, did not write to the new viceroy for some time. Finally, on 17 February, he wrote to Wavell saying that though in some quarters he was considered the greatest enemy of the British, in fact he saw himself as their friend. That said, 'the spirit of India demands complete freedom from all foreign dominance and would, therefore, resist [the] Japanese yoke equally with [the] British or any other'.[34]

Shortly after Kasturba's death, Wavell sent a message of condolence. Gandhi, in reply, told the viceroy of what Kasturba meant to him. After his vow of celibacy in 1906, he wrote, 'we ceased to be two different entities. Without my wishing it, she chose to lose herself in me. The result was that she became truly my *better* half.'

Gandhi had read reports of Wavell's air travels across India, among them a visit to the victims of the terrible famine in Bengal, which had claimed more than a million lives. 'May I,' wrote Gandhi to the viceroy, 'suggest an interruption in your scheduled flights and a descent upon Ahmednagar and the Aga Khan's Palace in order to probe the hearts of your captives? We are all friends of the British, however much we may criticize the British Government and system in India.' If Wavell met the Congress leaders, said Gandhi, 'if you can but trust, you will find us to be the greatest helpers in the fight against Nazism, Fascism, Japanism and the like'.

Wavell wrote a long reply, polite but firm. He said he was committed to self-government for India, and only sought 'the best means to implement it without delivering India to confusion and turmoil'. He did not accuse Gandhi or the Congress 'of any wish deliberately to aid the Japanese'. He continued: 'But you are much too intelligent a man, Mr. Gandhi, not to have realized that the effect of your [Quit India] resolution must be to hamper the prosecution of the war . . .' Calling himself a 'sincere friend' of India, the new viceroy said he hoped to get 'very considerable co-operation from the majority of Indians'.

Gandhi appreciated the desire for cooperation, yet told Wavell that this required 'equality between the parties and mutual trust. But equality is absent and Government distrust of Congress can be seen at every turn'. As 'I visualize India today', remarked Gandhi, 'it is one vast prison containing four hundred million souls. You are its sole custodian.'[35]

While neither side yielded much ground, at least the correspondence was courteous. Wavell was encouraged now to release Gandhi from jail. In mid-April, Gandhi had a bout of high fever, which persisted for almost a week. Medical reports showed that his blood pressure was high, his kidneys malfunctioning. The onset of coronary thrombosis was a worry. 'Deterioration in Gandhi's health,' wrote Wavell to London on 4 May, 'appears such that his further participation in active politics is improbable and I have no doubt that death in custody would intensify feeling against Government . . .'

Wavell issued orders for the prisoner's discharge, and Gandhi left the Aga Khan Palace on the morning of 6 May. His first stop, as so often in the past, was the Thackerseys' grand home on the hill, Parnakuti. On the way, he thought of his wife Kasturba and his secretary Mahadev: 'She had been so eager to get out of prison, yet I know she could not have had a better death. . . . Both she and Mahadev . . . have become immortal.'[36]

PART V

THE LAST YEARS (1944–1948)

CHAPTER THIRTY-TWO

Picking Up the Pieces (Again)

I

Gandhi was released on 5 May 1944. The next day, the *New York Times* wrote in an editorial that 'Mr. Gandhi passes from his prison and will pass into history as a man of many contradictions'. The accompanying news report was even less complimentary. It began: 'Seventy-four-year-old Mohandas K. Gandhi, whose followers in 1942 proposed to yield India to the Japanese without a fight, will be released tomorrow from his luxury prison in the Aga Khan's $100,000 palace of Poona.' The report went on to compare Gandhi's release with that of the British fascist Oswald Mosley. Both events, said America's paper of record, were 'a happy sign of change in the fortunes of war'.[1]

From the early 1920s till the late 1930s, the *New York Times* had adopted a broadly sympathetic attitude towards the Indian national movement and its leader. However, the onset of the war, and Germany's pounding by air of Britain, introduced a certain ambivalence. After Pearl Harbor and the entry into the war of the United States, the balance began to shift further. Once the Quit India movement was launched, mainstream American opinion decidedly took the side of Churchill against the Congress. Now, the *New York Times* was going so far as to suggest that Gandhi's career had ended, that he had 'passed into history'.

Gandhi is unlikely to have read this premature political obituary. After his discharge from jail, he spent a week in Poona before moving to Bombay, where—as in 1924—on his doctors' advice he based himself in a seaside cottage in Juhu, recovering his strength and his health. Characteristically, he would also be his own doctor, his self-medication on this occasion being a voluntary vow of silence, for a full fifteen days, from 14 to 29 May. 'Just now,' he wrote to Rajaji, 'I am passing the time reading some literature I have not read and the correspondence which Pyarelal chooses to show me.'[2]

From early June, Gandhi began writing some (short) letters himself, and also holding his daily prayer meetings. One evening, the rush of the crowd seeking to see and touch him was so frenzied that he was compelled to chastise them. 'You have gate-crashed and broken in,' he remarked, 'if that is so, I do not wish to have your *darshan*, neither do I wish to give you my *darshan*.' Gandhi retreated into the cottage, but not before asking the unruly crowd to contribute to the Harijan Fund to redeem themselves.

On 17 June, Gandhi wrote to Lord Wavell, asking for permission to see the CWC members in jail. He wished to call on the viceroy himself once his doctors gave him permission to travel. Wavell, in reply, declined both requests, saying: 'If, after your convalescence and after further reflection, you have a definite and constructive policy to propose for the furtherance of India's welfare, I shall be glad to consider it . . .'[3]

Meanwhile, the government posted Gandhi some eighty books that had been sent to him in jail but withheld by the authorities. They included works in Hindi, Urdu, Gujarati and English; on Christ, the Gita, the Gujarati poet Narmad, Theosophy, and Mahadev Desai (in Marathi); also a pamphlet called 'Gandhi against Fascism'; and another entitled 'A Dirty Little Rebel—That's What You Are Little Man'.[4]

After Gandhi was released from prison he received thousands of letters from admirers from all parts of India, and from some public figures too, these written in English, Hindi and Gujarati, seeking advice, offering suggestions, recounting what happened to the Quit India movement in their district or state after Gandhi was jailed, offering prayers for his long life and good health, etc.

These letters lie buried in the archives. But one at least deserves to be exhumed. It came from Saraladevi Chaudhurani. Sarala had written to Gandhi soon after he was released but got no reply. Worried that her letter might have been lost, she wrote again, this time from her late uncle Tagore's home, 'Uttarayan' in Santiniketan. 'I had mentioned,' said Sarala to Gandhi, 'that I was free for a fortnight . . . to visit you at any place suitable to you for placing before you certain ideas.'⁵

What could have been these 'certain ideas' she wished to discuss? Political or personal? There is, alas, no reply to this letter in the *Collected Works*. It may be that Pyarelal did not show it to Gandhi. Back in 1919–20, when the Gandhi–Saraladevi relationship was at its most intense, Pyarelal had not joined Gandhi's entourage. He must surely have heard later about the relationship, and how and why it was aborted. Despite his devotion, Pyarelal was by no means as close to, or as trusted by, Gandhi as his great predecessor Mahadev Desai. He was also more obsessively protective of his master's reputation, whereas, for Mahadev, the interests of Truth generally predominated. Mahadev would have shown Saraladevi's letter to Gandhi. But perhaps Pyarelal did not.

There is, of course, another possibility. This is that Gandhi saw this letter, and replied to it, but did not share his reply with Pyarelal (whereas he would certainly have done so with Mahadev), which is why there is no record of it in the *Collected Works*.

II

After a month by the sea in Juhu, Gandhi travelled to Poona, for two weeks of further recuperation at the clinic of his naturopath, Dinshaw Mehta. On 29 June, a group of local Congressmen came to see him. His doctors allowed him half an hour to meet them, which he spent on a speech underlining his core beliefs. He had heard of incidents of arson and sabotage during the Quit India movement, which distressed him deeply. He also made clear once more his opposition to Japan. 'I do not want a change of masters,' remarked Gandhi. 'I want to be free of all foreign control.'⁶

From Poona, Gandhi proceeded up the Western Ghats to Panchgani, where he could escape the fierceness of the Indian summer. As his health recovered, he slowly began engaging once more in the political process. On 17 July, he wrote to M.A. Jinnah. The letter began somewhat patronizingly: 'There was a time when I was able to persuade you to speak in our mother tongue [Gujarati]. Today I venture to write in the same.' As he had done while he was in jail, Gandhi asked Jinnah for a meeting, at a time and place of his convenience. 'Please do not regard me as an enemy of Islam and the Muslims here,' he remarked. 'I have always been a friend and servant of yours and of the whole world. Do not dismiss me.'

Knowing that Jinnah did not read Gujarati easily, Gandhi enclosed a translation in Urdu. In his reply (in English, of course), the Muslim League leader said he would be glad to receive him in his Bombay home any time after mid-August. Jinnah added: 'I am very pleased to read in the Press that you are making very good progress, and I hope you will soon be all right.'[7]

A week later, Gandhi wrote to the viceroy, offering to withdraw that still active resolution of the Congress advocating civil disobedience. He proposed that 'full co-operation in the war-effort should be given by the Congress, if a declaration of immediate Indian independence is made and a national government responsible to the Central Assembly be formed subject to the proviso that, during the pendency of the war, the military operations should continue at present but without involving any financial burden on India'.

This was at least half an olive branch, but the viceroy did not see it that way. In a stiff reply, Wavell characterized Gandhi's proposal as 'quite unacceptable'. So long as the war continued, a 'national government' of Indians was inconceivable. Wavell made it 'quite clear that until the war is over, responsibility for defence and military operations cannot be divided from the other responsibilities of Government, and . . . His Majesty's Government and the Governor-General must retain their responsibility over the field'.[8]

The viceroy's coldness might have been amplified by his advisers, who had not forgiven Gandhi, or the Congress, for organizing the Quit India movement when the British had their backs to the wall fighting Hitler. On the last day of July 1944, Wavell's private secretary wrote

to his predecessor on Linlithgow's staff: 'Lots of political doings
here since old Mr. G. came out of [the] jug *in articulo mortis*. The
latest, as you know, is that Mr G. writes to Jinnah in Gujerati—copy
in Urdu enclosed—calling him "brother" & suggesting a meeting.
Jinnah replies agreeing to "receive" G. at his house. Aren't they
an astounding pair of humbugs? And what a disaster it is that they
should have so much influence here just now.'[9]

On 3 August, with the doctors satisfied with his progress and
the rains having set in, Gandhi returned to his ashram in Sevagram,
almost exactly two years after he had left it for the momentous AICC
meeting in Bombay. He found a letter from B.R. Ambedkar waiting
for him. Ambedkar was then, as he had been since 1942, a member of
the viceroy's executive council. He now reminded Gandhi that, apart
from the Hindu–Muslim question, there was 'a communal problem
between the Hindus and the untouchables, which is also awaiting
solution'. If Gandhi was as 'anxious to solve the Hindu–untouchable
problem as you are to solve the Hindu–Muslim problem', Ambedkar
would be 'glad to formulate points on which a settlement is necessary'.

Gandhi's reply combined anxiety with hope, expectation with
exasperation. He noted, as he had to, his own long struggle to end
untouchability. 'But I know to my cost,' added Gandhi wistfully, 'that
you and I hold different views on this very important question. . . . I
know your great ability and I would love to own you as a colleague
and co-worker. But I must admit my failure to come nearer to you. If
you can show me a way to a common meeting ground between us I
would like to see it. Meanwhile, I must reconcile myself to the present
unfortunate difference.'[10]

IV

Gandhi and Jinnah had planned to meet in mid-August. Writing to a
Gujarati friend, Gandhi admitted that the Muslim League leader 'has
hated me since the day [in 1915] I asked him in a meeting to give up
English and speak Gujarati'. But he still hoped to reach out to, if not
convert, him. For, 'nobody has ever told me that I have done anything
in bad faith. Thus it was that I won over Motilal [Nehru], C.R. Das

and others' (in 1920, on the question of non-cooperation). Now he wished 'to conquer even Jinnah with trust and love. I have no other weapons at all.'[11]

Gandhi had met Jinnah many times before, yet they had drifted further and further apart. How he hoped now to convert him with 'trust and love' was not clear. A lawyer who had worked closely with Jinnah for many years wrote that he had 'never come across any man who has less humanity in his character than Jinnah. He was cold and unemotional, and apart from law and politics he had no other interests.' The lawyer further added that 'Jinnah's dominant characteristic was tenacity. Once he made up his mind, nothing in the world could divert him from his chosen objective.'[12]

In the event, the meeting had to be postponed, since Jinnah fell ill. This disappointed Gandhi, for, as he wrote to the Muslim League leader, 'the whole world was looking forward to our meeting'. He now hoped that 'God will soon restore you to health, hasten the meeting . . . and that the meeting will lead to the welfare of India'.[13]

The meeting was now rescheduled for September. On the 8th of that month, Gandhi took the overnight train from Wardha to Bombay. The next morning he met Jinnah, spending three hours with him, the first of numerous conversations they would have over the next twenty days.

In September 1944, Gandhi and Jinnah had known of each other for almost fifty years. Both had Gujarati as their mother tongue (though Jinnah spoke it indifferently), both were lawyers educated in London (though Jinnah succeeded at the Bombay Bar whereas Gandhi failed), both once considered themselves protégés of Gopal Krishna Gokhale. They differed substantively in their politics— Jinnah having left the Congress in 1920, and more recently leading the Muslim League in opposition to Gandhi's Congress—and even more spectacularly, in their lifestyle. Gandhi lived in a mud hut in the middle of nowhere; Jinnah in a stately mansion on Malabar Hill, Bombay's most exclusive locality. Gandhi wore more or less nothing, whereas Jinnah took great care over his attire.[14]

Gandhi had taken, as the basis for their discussion, a proposal made by C. Rajagopalachari. This had first been discussed sixteen months ago, when Rajaji came to meet Gandhi in prison. The proposal had six clauses: first, that the Muslim League and the Congress would cooperate in the formation of a provisional government at the Centre; second, after the war ended, a commission would demarcate contiguous Muslim-majority districts in the north-west and east of India, where a plebiscite would be held (ideally, with all adults participating) on whether these regions wanted to be part of a free and united India or not; third, that all parties could freely propagate their views before the plebiscite; fourth, if the Muslim areas voted for separation, an agreement for cooperation on defence, commerce and communications would be worked out; fifth, that any transfer of population would be voluntary; and, finally, that all this was naturally contingent on the British transferring power to Indian hands.[15]

Gandhi took the Rajaji proposal to Jinnah off his own bat, so to speak. He did not consult his closest lieutenants, Nehru and Patel. Or perhaps we should say 'could not', since those two men were still in prison, along with other members of the CWC. This was probably just as well, for it is overwhelmingly likely that Nehru and Patel would have opposed these parleys with Jinnah. Nehru distrusted Jinnah; Patel distrusted both Jinnah and Rajaji. He would not forgive Rajaji for (as he saw it) letting down the party in 1942.

Back in January 1915, at a reception hosted by the Gujaratis of Bombay, Jinnah had urged Gandhi to help 'bring about unanimity and co-operation between the two communities so that the demands of India may be made absolutely unanimously'. Gandhi had tried to do this ever since, albeit with mixed success. In seeking to further that cooperation he had corresponded with Jinnah and met with him on occasion too. This meeting was a last chance to heal a rift that had become as much personal as communal.

The Gandhi–Jinnah talks began on 9 September 1944. They were held at Jinnah's bungalow on Malabar Hill. As the car carrying Gandhi arrived there, shortly before four in the afternoon, the visitor 'was warmly received by Mr. Jinnah at the portico. The beautiful lawn in front of Mr. Jinnah's house was alive with a battalion of Press representatives, foreign war correspondents and camera-men who had assembled there long before.'[16]

The two men went inside, and spoke for three hours. Afterwards, Gandhi prepared a long report for Rajaji to read.

> It was a test of my patience . . . I am amazed at my own patience. However, it was a friendly talk.
>
> In the middle of the talk he came back to the old ghost: 'I thought you had come here as a Hindu, as a representative of the Hindu Congress'. I said, 'No, I have come here neither as a Hindu nor as a representative of the Congress. I have come here as an individual'.
>
> . . . We came back to the [Rajaji] Formula. He wants Pakistan now, not after independence. . . . He said, 'The Muslims want Pakistan. The League represents the Muslims and it wants separation.' I said, 'I agree the League is the most powerful Muslim organization. I might even concede that you as its President represent the Muslims of India, but that does not mean that all Muslims want Pakistan. Put it to the vote of all the inhabitants of the area and see.' He said, 'Why should you ask non-Muslims?' I said, 'You cannot possibly deprive a section of the population of its vote. You must carry them with you, and if you are in the majority why should you be afraid?'[17]

Gandhi and Jinnah met again the next day, and the next. No record was kept of their conversations, and with Mahadev Desai dead, there was no one to press Gandhi to record his impressions as soon as he came out of Jinnah's bungalow on Malabar Hill. But we do have the letters that the two leaders wrote one another in the intervals between their talks. Writing on 10 September, Jinnah worried that, with Gandhi claiming to speak as an individual, the talks lacked a representative character. If Gandhi agreed to speak as the leader of the (Hindu) Congress, then it would be easier to come to an agreement. He was also concerned about the commission for demarcation proposed by Rajaji; how would it be set up, who would be its members, and what would be its mandate? Gandhi, in reply, assured Jinnah that he was 'pledged to use all the influence I may have with the Congress to ratify my agreement with you'. As for the commission, this would be set up by the proposed provisional government, its membership and terms of reference based on the widest possible consultation.[18]

As the talks proceeded, Gandhi and Jinnah refused to give any updates to the pressmen outside. But the journalists were hungry for details, sometimes seeing them in visual signs. One reporter kept a day-long watch on the window of the first-floor lounge where the talks were taking place. From his vigil he concluded 'that Mr. Jinnah did most of the talking today. Framed in this window was Mr. Jinnah's sharp profile, and one could see him raising his delicate index finger to make a point, or lurch forward to emphasise another. At least on one occasion, he was seen bringing his right fist heavily down into his left palm and straighten himself up in his seat.'[19]

After this, the fourth day of the talks, Gandhi told Rajaji that Jinnah 'drew a very alluring picture of the Government of Pakistan. It would be a perfect democracy. . . . Sikhs would have Gurmukhi if they wanted and the Pakistan Government would give them financial aid.' 'On my part,' added Gandhi, 'I am not going to be in a hurry. But he can't expect me to endorse an undefined Pakistan.'[20]

On the 13th, the two men were closeted together for the best part of the day. After the morning session, as they emerged into the garden, a reporter asked, 'Anything for us?' 'No,' replied Gandhi, adding, 'yesterday you read something in our faces. Here we are both. I would like you not to read anything in our faces except hope and nothing but hope.' Gandhi then turned to Jinnah and asked, 'Am I right?' Jinnah answered dryly, 'Why bother?' (with what the press wrote, that is).[21]

On the 15th, after their talks for almost a week, Gandhi wrote Jinnah a letter outlining the situation as he saw it. 'The only real, though awful, test of our nationhood,' he wrote here, 'arises out of our common political subjection. If you and I throw off this subjection by our combined effort, we shall be born a politically free nation out of our travail.' But if Jinnah's idea of two separate and distinct nations was implemented, Gandhi saw 'nothing but ruin for the whole of India'.

Gandhi ended his letter by repudiating Jinnah's long-standing charge that he was merely a 'Hindu' leader. 'Though I represent nobody but myself,' he remarked, 'I aspire to represent all the inhabitants of India, for I realize in my own person their misery and degradation, which is their common lot, irrespective of class, caste or creed.' Then, however, he appended a significant concession. 'I know that you have acquired a unique hold on the Muslim masses,' he told Jinnah. 'I want you to use this influence for their total welfare, which must include the rest.'[22]

That Jinnah was a genuine mass leader Gandhi would not have stated or believed as recently as 1937. The emphatic victory of the Congress in the elections held that year had, it seemed, proved that the party of Gandhi and Nehru represented a majority of Indians, among them many Muslims too. But, after the Congress ministries took office, Jinnah's claim that they practised anti-Muslim policies acquired increasing salience. When the Congress ministries resigned in 1939, the success of the League's 'Deliverance Day' celebrations confirmed that it was now the major party of the Muslims of the subcontinent.

When the leading Congressmen were in jail, Jinnah travelled through the towns of north and east India. Once aloof and distant, cerebral and somewhat snobbish, he now worked hard to make connections with the ordinary Muslim. And he succeeded, as this account of a meeting in Allahabad in 1942 demonstrates:

> The procession [conveying Jinnah from the railway station] passed under 110 arches, each named for a person important in Indian Islamic history, beginning with the first Muslim sultan to land on India's shores and ending triumphantly with Muhammed Ali Jinnah. He addressed the Momins, the poor of the Muslim community, descending from the truck to do so and speaking of mutual loyalty between them and the League. Honorific speeches were presented to him, including one which brought his name in the line of Prophet and the Asar saints (companions and successors of Mohammed). Oratory, lights, pageantry and general excitement reign at the League meetings. The Pakistan flag is flown, money is collected, and Mr. Jinnah's speech—a short part in unaccustomed Urdu and a long part in English—produces a near frenzy in the audience.[23]

Now, in September 1944, even Gandhi was speaking of Jinnah's 'unique hold on the Muslim masses'.

The concession, or flattery if you will, did not move Jinnah. Replying to Gandhi, he doggedly defended his two-nation theory. 'We [Muslims in India] are a nation of [a] hundred million,' he said, 'and what is more, we are a nation with our own distinctive culture and civilization, language and literature, art and architecture, names and nomenclature, sense of value and proportion, legal laws and moral codes, customs and calendar, history and traditions, aptitudes and ambitions; in short, we have our own distinctive outlook on life and of life. By all canons of international law we are a nation.'

Like Gandhi, Jinnah also claimed that his proposal was for the good of all, Hindus and Muslims alike. And he offered some flattery of his own. 'You are a great man and you exercise enormous influence over the Hindus, particularly the masses,' wrote Jinnah to Gandhi, 'and by accepting the road I am pointing out to you, you are not prejudicing or harming the interests of the Hindus or of the minorities. On the contrary, Hindus will be the greater gainers. I am convinced that true welfare not only of Muslims but of the rest of India lies in the division of India . . .'[24]

Gandhi told Jinnah that unity was in the best interest of Muslims. Jinnah answered that separation was in the best interest of Hindus. Could there be any meeting ground? Gandhi thought that there could. 'Can we not,' he now wrote to Jinnah, 'agree to differ on the question of "two nations" and yet solve the problem on the basis of self-determination?' If the regions with Muslim majorities wanted to become a separate nation, he said, then 'the grave step of separation should be specifically placed before and approved by the people in that area'.

Jinnah was, however, not willing to put his theory to the test of popular opinion. Muslims in India, he argued, 'claim the right of self-determination as a nation and not as a territorial unit, and . . . we are entitled to exercise our inherent right as a Muslim nation, which is our birth-right'. Gandhi answered that 'mere assertion is no proof', adding that 'all the people inhabiting the area ought to express their opinion specifically on this single issue of division'.[25]

On 21 September, with the Gandhi–Jinnah talks well into their second week, the *Bombay Chronicle* ran a thoughtful editorial on the question of untouchability. It noted that the central executive of B.R. Ambedkar's Scheduled Caste Federation was soon to meet in Madras, where its leader would surely speak of the implications of the Gandhi–Jinnah talks for the position of the Depressed Classes. Ambedkar had often said that though he was born a Hindu, he would not die a Hindu. However, commented the newspaper, although 'large sections of his community wish to repudiate Hinduism he found little response even from his known followers'. Conversion was a matter of individual choice and conscience, not of one person compelling others to follow him into a new faith.

The newspaper agreed with Ambedkar that 'Harijans ought to have a fair share of political power in almost every representative body and state service'. Then the editorial continued:

> Above all, the system of untouchability, the root cause of disharmony, must be destroyed root and branch without any avoidable delay. Unfortunately, however, very few persons are concentrating their efforts on this specific task. Many Harijan leaders neglect this because they fear that once their grievance is gone their prominence in championship goes with it. And many caste Hindu leaders, though they abominate untouchability, think that their main, if not sole duty is to be kind and generous to Harijans. They spend lakhs over this service to Harijans but sadly neglect the root cause of the trouble, namely, their own belief in untouchability caused by superstition or social selfishness or sheer custom. It is time Gandhi and other leaders who want to destroy untouchability consider the Harijan problem afresh in all its bearings, with a view in particular to the speedy eradication of untouchability itself.[26]

As the *Chronicle* had predicted, Ambedkar spoke out against the Gandhi–Jinnah talks at the meeting of his followers in Madras. 'The Hindu–Moslem problem,' he remarked here, 'was not the only one confronting the country. Christians, Scheduled Castes and other minorities were involved . . .' He warned Gandhi not to 'give more to Jinnah' at the expense of the Scheduled Castes. He then launched a furious broadside against Gandhi, calling him 'a man who has no vision, who has no knowledge, and who has no judgment, a man who has been a failure all his life . . .' This prompted a puzzled editorial in a local newspaper. 'Dr Ambedkar's is undoubtedly one of the best causes in the world today,' remarked the *Indian Express*. 'Why is he then so keen on spoiling it by intemperate attacks on others, who have at least as much claim as he has to their own viewpoints?'[27]

As it turned out, the parleys in Bombay that Ambedkar so objected to were going nowhere. Two weeks after their first meeting, Gandhi told Jinnah that 'our talks and our correspondence seem to run in parallel lines and never touch each other'. He now suggested they call in 'outside assistance' to help them (he probably had Rajaji in mind). Gandhi also asked Jinnah to allow him to address the council of the Muslim League. Jinnah rejected both proposals; the second of which he characterized as 'a most extraordinary and unprecedented suggestion'.[28]

Since these talks had been on for close to three weeks now, and there was no word on how they were progressing, there was much tension among those who were following them. On the 26th, as Gandhi walked into Jinnah's bungalow, journalists crowded around him. 'Is there any hope?' asked one. Gandhi answered: 'Patience, patience, patience.'[29]

As it turned out, this was the last day the two men met. Afterwards, Gandhi wrote to Jinnah that 'you keep on saying that I should accept certain theses, while I have been contending that the best way for us, who differ in our approach to the problem, is to give body to the demand as it stands in the [Lahore] Resolution and work it out to our mutual satisfaction'.

The exasperation was palpable. It was answered by exasperation and anger. Thus Jinnah wrote to Gandhi: 'If one does not agree with you or differs from you, you are always right and the other party is always wrong, and the next thing is that many are waiting prepared, in your circle, to pillory me when the word goes, but I must face all threats and consequences, and I can only act according to my judgment and conscience.'[30]

On 29 September, the *Bombay Chronicle* ran a two-column editorial on the failure of the Gandhi–Jinnah talks. It was almost certainly written by the editor, S.A. Brelvi, a Muslim, yet a staunch

Congressman who had been jailed several times in the nationalist cause. The *Chronicle* observed that the talks had raised 'great and pleasant hopes', and that their failure 'will cause an unprecedented shock of pain and disappointment to every Indian who truly loves his country, yearns for heart-unity between Hindus and Muslims and desires national freedom'.

The editorial argued that Jinnah was to blame for the failure of the talks, and for two reasons. First, Jinnah had suggested that Gandhi was meeting him in an individual capacity and not as a representative of the Congress, and hence he did not know how far any agreement would have validity. The *Chronicle* asked how Jinnah could ever have questioned, 'in a petty, legalistic spirit, the representative capacity of Mahatma Gandhi'? Surely, Jinnah knew that if Gandhi said he could convince Congress of any agreement, his party, whose leader he had been for the past twenty-five years, would go along with him?

The second reason the *Chronicle* blamed Jinnah was because of his refusal to allow a plebiscite. As the newspaper pointed out, the Lahore Resolution had spoken of Muslim-majority 'regions' and 'areas', not provinces. And in both Bengal and Punjab, there were large non-Muslim minorities, and even districts where non-Muslims were in a majority. Hence Gandhi had suggested a vote on separation in which all residents of these provinces would participate. But Jinnah demanded the separation of Bengal and of the Punjab and of Sindh, the NWFP and Baluchistan without any consultation with the non-Muslim inhabitants of these provinces. Jinnah's 'refusal to agree to a joint plebiscite of all inhabitants of these provinces', wrote Brelvi, 'is repugnant to any conception of democracy and fairplay and is, therefore, certainly un-Islamic'.[31]

On the same day, the Muslim League newspaper, *Dawn*, also carried a long editorial on the subject. This was most likely written by its editor, Pothan Joseph, a Christian by birth and upbringing. *Dawn*'s interpretation was radically opposed to the *Chronicle*'s. It put the blame for the failure of the talks squarely on Gandhi. In his letters to Jinnah, said the newspaper, Gandhi had raised 'a series of conundrums' about 'the qualifications entitling a people to regard themselves as a nation'. The 'tortuous procedure' adopted by the Congress leader, remarked *Dawn*, suggested that 'compliance with the Muslim claim [for Pakistan] lies on Mr. Gandhi's lips and does not come from the heart'.

Dawn saw the demand for Pakistan as a priori and non-negotiable, and even non-testable. The creation of Pakistan, it argued, was 'essential for the survival of the Muslims in India and vital to the civilised purpose of preventing a Central hegemony dominated by the Caste Hindus of this sub-continent'. 'No one,' it continued, 'can deprive the Indian Mussalman of that intense feeling [for Pakistan] which is supported by the material conditions of his struggle for existence.'[32]

V

Gandhi and Jinnah had known of each other since 1897, and known each other since 1915. Over the years, they had met and often corresponded with one another. But this was the first time the two men had such extended contact and conversations. At the end, when the talks had clearly and finally failed, Gandhi issued a press statement expressing 'deep regret' that no agreement was reached. But he hadn't completely given up hope, saying that now each party was free to offer its views to the public, and 'if we do so dispassionately and if the public co-operate, we may reach a solution of the seemingly insoluble at an early date'. The 'chief thing', he added, 'is for the Press and the public to avoid partisanship and bitterness'.

As Gandhi later explained to the veteran Moderate politician Tej Bahadur Sapru, the talks had broken down on two key issues. First, Jinnah would not accept the suggestion of a plebiscite, insisting 'that the other communities should have no voice as to Pakistan which was [the] Muslims' exclusive right wherever they were in a majority'. Second, while Gandhi, in a significant concession, 'accepted the concrete suggestion of division of India as between members of the same family' who might still forge a 'partnership [in] things of common interest' (such as defence and communications), Jinnah 'would have nothing short of the two-nation theory and therefore complete dissolution amounting to full sovereignty in the first instance'.[33]

A week after their final meeting, Jinnah told a British journalist that Gandhi's suggestion of a plebiscite was 'an insult to intelligence'. The interim national government asked to conduct it would be 'a Hindu majority Government', which would, he claimed, so demarcate boundaries and organize the plebiscites as to favour Hindus at the expense of Muslims. 'The fact is,' said Jinnah to this reporter, 'the Hindus want some kind of agreement which will still give them some form of control over Muslims. They will not reconcile themselves to our complete independence.'[34]

No sooner had the talks ended than the correspondence between the two men was leaked to the press. It was thought this occurred as a result of a lapse by Gandhi's staff. As a senior journalist commented: 'Things have been very different around and about Mr Gandhi since his precious Secretary, Mahadev Desai's, death. The Mahatma's present entourage has caused many a chuckle among all sane-minded people visiting him.'[35]

Among those who read the leaked correspondence was the viceroy. He thought the letters 'a deplorable exposure of Indian leadership', since if Gandhi and Jinnah had worked out the elements of a solution, or at least been more civil and courteous to one another, that would have been 'the best way' to embarrass the rulers. As it turned out, wrote Wavell in his journal, 'the two great mountains have met and not even a ridiculous mouse has emerged'.[36]

VI

Since his release from jail, Gandhi had been active in the functioning of the Kasturba Gandhi Memorial Trust, formed by some friends shortly after his wife's death. He helped raised money for the trust, and also laid down guidelines for its functioning. By early September 1944, some Rs 5.7 million had already been collected, with a further Rs 10.7 million promised. (Among the cheques received was one for ten pounds sterling from Henry and Millie Polak, a small contribution of huge symbolic value.) By mid-1945, provincial units had been set up to disburse money and oversee programmes. Numerous letters and applications for support were coming in from social work organizations across India.

The trust deed listed four aims: (i) the 'conduct and promotion of such charitable activities as would conduce to the general welfare of the condition of poor and needy women and children in the rural areas of India'; (ii) the establishment of hospitals for women and children, maternity homes, widows' homes and orphanages; (iii) the promotion of primary education and training in handicrafts and cottage industries for women and children in rural areas; (iv) the assisting of other institutions carrying out the objects mentioned in (i) to (iii) above.[37]

Addressing a meeting of the Kasturba Memorial Trust in Sevagram, Gandhi said the money collected thus far should be spent in villages and not cities, and preferably for the education of women and children. To foster local participation, he asked that 75 per cent of the money collected in a particular district or region be spent there itself, the rest going into a central fund.[38]

Meanwhile, in a display of churlishness, the Bombay government passed an order making it illegal for government servants to contribute to the trust set up in Kasturba Gandhi's name. A lady doctor, who worked in a government hospital in Bombay, was barred from serving on the medical advisory council of the trust.[39]

Even more spiteful than the Bombay government was V.D. Savarkar, who issued a statement carried by the press under this headline: 'THE HINDU SANGHATANISTS SHOULD NOT CONTRIBUTE A SINGLE PIE TO THE CONGRESSITE KASTURBA FUND'. In this angry and impassioned, bitter and resentful statement, Savarkar attacked Gandhi and the fund from two fronts. First, as a former revolutionary himself, he said Gandhi had never shed a tear for the martyred men and women hung or shot by the British in pursuit of their armed attempts to overthrow British rule. For Savarkar, Kasturba's sacrifice was 'relatively insignificant' compared to the sufferings of those women whose husbands and brothers were tortured, killed or transported for life for opposing colonial rule.

Rather than praising their sacrifices, Gandhi, in Savarkar's words, saw these revolutionaries as 'a blot on the "Indian" culture and the Ahimsa/Charkha politics'. In a sharp comment on Gandhi's loyalist beginnings, he asked: 'Has the Congress spent a single word in commemoration of the heroic Madam Cama who championed the cause of Independence publicly, when the Congress could not dare even to claim Home Rule and Gandhiji was dancing to the tune of the British Imperial Anthem and prided himself on his hearty loyalty to the Chains that bound Mother-India!'

Second, Savarkar claimed that the money collected in Kasturba's name would be used to promote the Congress credo of Hindu–Muslim unity to which he and his party, the Hindu Mahasabha, were so totally opposed. He invoked the memory of a previous fund with which Gandhi was associated, the Tilak Swaraj fund, a large part of which, according to Savarkar, was spent 'to enrich the Moslem purse' and in 'exterminating the Tilakite principles'. He now claimed that from the money collected in memory of Kasturba, the Congress would once more 'contribute huge sums to the Moslems as soon as they are demanded'.[40]

Savarkar's statement reeked of jealousy and decades-long animosity. More interesting was a letter from another (if less embittered) Hindu Sanghatanist, the Poona writer S.L. Karandikar. He approved of a memorial to Kasturba, but thought it should take a form different from that Gandhi had outlined for it. Why, he asked, open schools for women, when Kasturba was not herself a pioneer in female education? Any memorial should reflect or represent what she stood for. And, in Karandikar's view, Kasturba was 'a typical Hindu lady, whose sole joy is to be a part of the life of her husband. Kasturba's life and death is this beyond anything else.' By her death, wrote this correspondent, 'Kasturba has enriched the tradition of Hindu Womanhood who, during the last fifty years, have suffered silently when either the husband, the son, the father, or the brother suffered in response to the call of the country.'

Therefore, argued this Poona Hindu, the best memorial to Kasturba would be a picture gallery of women saint-martyrs, this either in a central location in Delhi or the Aga Khan Palace where she died. Here would be featured pictures of Tilak's wife, who died when he was in Mandalay prison; of the wife of Ganpatrao Savarkar, who died when her husband and brother-in-law were in the Cellular jail in the Andamans, and of other such women who died when their male relatives were incarcerated, and 'whose silent suffering and sacrifice is the foundation of our achievements, in all spheres of life'. This memorial would allow 'the rising youth of the country [to] have a Darshan of these women martyrs of modern India'.

The letter was not without a grain of truth. For, Kasturba was merely Gandhi's long-suffering wife, her life dictated by his. In that sense she embodied the orthodox, ancient and irredeemably patriarchal Hindu ideal of a wife's devotion to her husband. But while Gandhi had treated Kasturba as an extension of himself, he now wanted her memory to inspire women to educate themselves and make their own, unfettered choices about the lives they would like to lead.

VII

While he was in jail, Gandhi followed the course of the war through the newspapers that he was permitted to read. But, due to the severe censorship imposed by the Raj, news of the Bengal famine was scarce. Now that he was out, he began receiving reports of its scale, intensity and long-term impacts. This so distressed him that in November 1944, he thought of fasting to compel the government to more actively bring succour to the citizens of rural Bengal. His doctors (and disciples) dissuaded him; given his age and his recent illnesses, it seemed not to be worth the risk.[41]

In December, Gandhi's health took a turn for the worse. He was 'feeling fatigued. Even after the noonday siesta, the brain seemed tired. There was a complete disinclination to speak or write.' Rajaji came to Sevagram, and seeing the state he was in, told Gandhi 'to stop all this ceaseless mental activity if you want to avoid a disaster'. Gandhi therefore decided to be silent, not for one day in a week as was his wont, but for a full four weeks at a stretch. From 4 to 31 December, he would 'discontinue all public activities, all interviews for public or private purposes and all correspondence of any nature whatsoever'. He wouldn't even read newspapers.[42]

Gandhi was lonely as well as ill. 'Rajaji is leaving today,' wrote Pyarelal to G.D. Birla on 6 December. 'I wish there was someone like him to take his place by Bapu's side. In spite of all the detachment that Bapu has cultivated he is very human and the presence of someone from among his Old Guard cannot be over-estimated.'

But Rajaji had work and family in Madras. Without any companion he could truly trust, Gandhi was desperately lonely. Bajaj, Tagore, Andrews, Mahadev and Kasturba were all dead. Nehru and Patel were absent in jail. 'There is something frightening in his utter spiritual isolation,' wrote Pyarelal to Birla. 'In a measure it is inseparable from greatness. But surely something could be done to mitigate it'.[43]

A month's rest helped, and, as the year 1945 dawned, Gandhi expressed afresh a desire to visit Bengal. His doctors, however, forbade him from criss-crossing the country. He was now seventy-five, and weak, and still recovering from his prison ordeal. 'Bapu is very low,' wrote his disciple Mridula Sarabhai to a friend in the second week of January. 'Everybody tries to give him as much rest as possible.'[44]

On 26 January, Gandhi was in Sevagram. He had a quiet day; elsewhere, enthusiastic young patriots were celebrating the first 'Independence Day' since their leader's release from prison. In Bombay, many meetings, processions and flag hoistings were held. The city's cotton, bullion and share markets remained shut on the day.

Independence Day was also celebrated in Lahore, Calcutta, Poona and other cities. However, in the provinces of Bihar, Sindh and Madras, the British authorities had issued orders prohibiting the celebrations. Quite a few people defied the bans, hoisting or carrying the tricolour, and were duly arrested.[45]

In the last week of March, Gandhi travelled to Bombay for a month of meetings with friends, sympathizers and social workers. He was in Bombay when he heard that his former housemate and fellow Tolstoyan, Hermann Kallenbach, had died in Johannesburg. This was one more loss to add to the others, of close associates who had died in recent years. Gandhi had known Kallenbach longer than Andrews or Tagore, Bajaj or Mahadev. When Kasturba and he had sailed for India in 1914, Kallenbach was with them. Had war not broken out when they were en route to England, and had Kallenbach not been technically a German citizen and hence an 'enemy alien', he would have come with the Gandhis to India, sharing their life and labours in

Gandhi's remarkable secretary, Mahadev Desai, at his side as always, and as so often, explaining a word or phrase to him.

Jawaharlal Nehru, Gandhi's designated political successor, at Sevagram.

Gandhi on his morning walk, in or near the Sevagram Ashram. To his left is the Pathan proponent of non-violence, Khan Abdul Ghaffar Khan; to Khan's left is Mahadev Desai.

A meeting of white-clad Congress nationalists in the North-West Frontier Province, 1938. Gandhi and Ghaffar Khan are on the podium.

Subhas Chandra Bose at the Haripura Congress of 1938 where he was first elected party president (Maulana Azad is behind him, and Jawaharlal Nehru behind Azad).

A crowd greeting Gandhi at a wayside railway station, late 1930s.

No. 2039-2458-II

GOVERNMENT OF THE CENTRAL PROVINCES AND BERAR
GENERAL ADMINISTRATION DEPARTMENT.

MEMORANDUM

To

The Registrar, High Court of Judicature, Nagpur.

All Commissioners of Divisions.

The Commissioner of Settlements and Director of Land Records.

The Chief Engineer, Public Works Department.

The Legal Remembrancer to Government.

The Chief Conservator of Forests.

The Inspector-General of Civil Hospitals.

The Director of Public Instruction.

The Inspector-General of Police.

The Inspector-General of Prisons.

The Director of Veterinary Services.

All Deputy Commissioners.

All Superintending Engineers.

All Conservators of Forests.

The Director of Public Health.

The Director of Industries.

The Registrar, Co-operative Societies.

The Commissioner of Excise, etc.

The Superintendent, Government Printing.

All Secretaries to Government.

The Secretary to His Excellency the Governor.

The Military Secretary to His Excellency the Governor.

The Registrar, Civil Secretariat.

All Departments of the Secretariat.

The Publicity Officer.

Nagpur, the 2nd September 1938.

In future Mr. Gandhi should be referred to in all correspondence as " Mahatma Gandhi ".

Secy. to Govt., C. P. & Berar,
General Administration Department.

An office order of the Congress government in the Central Provinces in 1938, instructing all (and especially British) officials, to henceforth refer to Gandhi as 'Mahatma'.

Gandhi with General and Mrs Chiang
Kai-shek, Calcutta, 1942.

Muhammad Ali Jinnah, leader of the Muslim
League, founder of the state of Pakistan, with
whom Gandhi argued often through the 1930s
and 1940s.

After Jinnah, B.R. Ambedkar was Gandhi's most formidable political opponent; one argued that the Congress did not represent Muslims, the other that Gandhi could not represent the Depressed Classes. Here is Ambedkar, photographed with the American journalist Louis Fischer in a Bombay tenement, circa 1942.

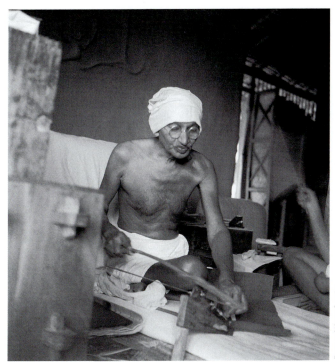

Gandhi at work in the ashram, early 1940s.

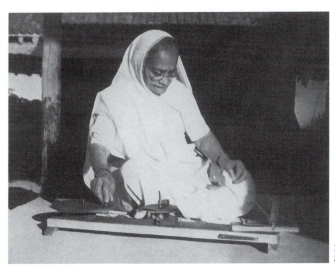

Kasturba at work in the ashram, early 1940s.

Gandhi, sombre.   Gandhi, smiling.

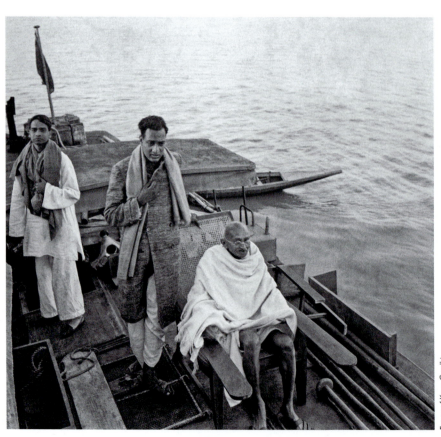

Gandhi on a river ferry in rural Bengal, 1945.

Sabarmati and Sevagram, and many other places besides. In a short but moving tribute, Gandhi called Kallenbach 'a very dear and near friend', who 'used to say often that when I was deserted by the whole world, I would find him to be a true friend going with me, if need be, to the ends of the earth in search of Truth'.[46]

In late April, Gandhi went to the Western Ghats, where he spent two months in Mahableshwar and Panchgani, rebuilding his health away from the torrid heat of the plains.

VIII

At a meeting of the All India Spinners Association in Sevagram in late March 1945, some members complained of B.R. Ambedkar's harsh, and continuing, criticisms of the Congress. Gandhi told them that 'if the followers of Ambedkar oppose us we should not let ourselves be provoked or give up our work because of it. We should reach their hearts and understand their feelings. If we had gone through the experiences that the Harijans have gone through, there is no telling how embittered we might not have become and how little our ahimsa would have endured. Therefore on such occasions we should look inwards and if there is the slightest vestige of untouchability left we should purge ourselves of it.'[47]

This was one of several statements Gandhi made at this time, re-emphasizing his commitment to ending untouchability. He no longer had time even for the caste system itself. In Bombay, in answer to a question about whether caste was 'consistent with democracy and democratic organizations', Gandhi replied: 'I do not need to refer to my past writings to say what I believe today, because only what I believe today counts. I wish to say that the caste system as it exists to-day in Hinduism is an anachronism. It is one of those ugly things which will certainly hinder the growth of true religion. It must go if both Hinduism and India are to live and grow . . . The way to do [this] is for all Hindus to become their own scavengers, and treat the so-called hereditary Bhangis as their own brothers.'[48]

Two weeks later, when Gandhi was in Mahableshwar, a Congressman from Tamil Nadu, come to visit him, and asked why he had not visited a famous shrine on a nearby hilltop. Gandhi answered that it was because it practised caste discrimination. 'As long as the doors of the temples are not open to the Harijans,' he said, 'I shall never enter them.'[49]

In mid-April, Gandhi's old friend and supporter Ambalal Sarabhai wrote him a remarkable letter from Ahmedabad. Sarabhai, we may recall, had saved Gandhi's ashram in 1915 when he admitted an 'untouchable' family and other patrons backed out. Now, thirty years later, he sent Gandhi a thoughtful update on the battles yet to be won. In the years since Gandhi's famous fast at Yerwada, much progress had been made in admitting 'untouchables' in schools, trains, buses, etc., yet 'very little success had been attained in the treatment of Harijans on equal footing of touchable Hindus, in private life and social intercourse'.

Sarabhai had started an experiment in his own mill, Calico, with Harijans encouraged to use the same restaurant as the other workers. Those Hindus and Muslims who objected to being served with Harijans were told that they would be served outside, much as the Harijans had been previously. This bold experiment however had not succeeded, since some Harijans who ate inside the restaurant were later set upon by Hindu and Muslim weavers, who also smashed some of the crockery in the restaurant. Sarabhai thought that those who opposed the experiment were perhaps 20 per cent of all workers, but sadly the majority had been silenced by the reactionary militants. Meanwhile, it was very hard for Harijans to find employment as weavers (who were better paid than unskilled labourers) since the thread had to be 'kissed' (sucked) from the shuttle, and both Hindus and Muslims objected to the kissing of a shuttle used by Harijans.

Sarabhai had asked the labour union, whose leaders were sympathetic to his scheme, to convene a meeting of workers, and tell them that the union and management both desired to end this discrimination against the Harijans. If a majority favoured non-discrimination, they should see that the small minority 'do not molest the Harijans or take other retaliatory action'. He hoped to open the restaurant again when this agreement was reached, with the objectors served their refreshments outside.

Sarabhai was keen that Gandhi himself wrote on this matter. If he did, 'it would be very effective and carry great weight. It would also help the Labour Union to bring about speedily a reform for which they are striving. . . . I am sorry to trouble you at a time when you are not well and have pressure of work. But you have always stood out for what you believe to be right. A person thinking only of an objective to be reached, would not like you have brought to the fore-front the issue such as Untouchability before Swaraj had been attained. You had the rare courage to do so, in spite of the knowledge that it might partially weaken the caste Hindu support, which you had formerly.'[50]

Gandhi wrote a brief reply, saying he would write on the subject when he had the time.[51] Perhaps he did send a statement to be circulated among the workers in Ahmedabad. Unfortunately there is no trace of it in his papers. But we do know that in these months, Gandhi thought often about the subject of caste, and, as he did, adopted positions far more radical than he had once adopted. In May 1945, some Gujarati colleagues decided to reprint an old pamphlet of Gandhi's on the caste system. They asked him for a fresh foreword, which he disarmingly began by saying: 'I do not have the time to read this book again. I do not even wish to.' He then outlined his *current* thinking on caste. While the Hindu scriptures spoke of four varnas, in his view 'there prevails only one varna today, that of Shudras', or, you may call it, Ati-Shudras', or Harijans' or untouchables. . . . Just as it is not dharma but *adharma* to believe in the distinctions of high and low, so also colour prejudice is *adharma*. If a scripture is found to sanction distinctions of high and low, or distinctions of colour, it does not deserve the name of scripture.' Given how far he had moved on in this regard, Gandhi requested the reader 'to discard anything in this [older] book which may appear to him incompatible with my views given above'.[52]

IX

On 14 June 1945, the viceroy announced the release of the members of the CWC. In a broadcast the same day, Wavell said he was inviting representative leaders of Indian opinion for a conference in Simla to arrive at 'a settlement of the communal issue, which is the main stumbling block'. He hoped this would lead, in the short run, to a new, expanded executive council, an 'entirely Indian Council, except for the Viceroy and the Commander-in-Chief, who would retain his position as War Member'. For the first time, Indians would hold the crucial finance and home portfolios. This new council was, Wavell emphasized, a first step towards a 'final constitutional settlement'.[53]

Wavell had, in fact, wanted to release the Congress leaders much earlier. In October 1944, he wrote to Churchill suggesting that he, as viceroy, invite the main leaders of the Congress and the Muslim League for talks. He saw this gesture of reconciliation as crucial to Britain's long-term interests in Asia. 'Our prestige and prospects in Burma, Malaya, China and the Far East generally,' the viceroy told his prime minister, 'are entirely subject to what happens in India. If we can secure India as a friendly partner in the British Commonwealth our predominant influence in these countries will, I think, be assured; with a lost and hostile India, we are likely to be reduced to the east to the position of commercial beggars.'

Wavell was working towards the best possible British position in a post-imperial world. Churchill, on the other hand, did not think the Empire should end at all. He delayed for months in responding to the viceroy's proposal. Meanwhile, the term of his government was coming to an end. More thoughtful Conservatives warned Churchill that if he was too obdurate towards Wavell (and India), the viceroy might resign, which would be used against their party in the forthcoming elections. So, in June 1945, the prime minister finally consented to setting free the Congress leaders who had been detained since the Quit India movement.[54]

On being released from prison, the members of the CWC headed straight to see Gandhi in Panchgani. As he arrived at that hill town, Vallabhbhai Patel was besieged by journalists asking for comments on the political situation. He said he had been shut away in jail for three years, and in any case would need to consult with his colleagues first. 'There is one sentence, however, in the Viceregal declarations on which I must speak,' said Patel, 'not as a member of the Working Committee but as a Congressman. It is that the parity between caste

Hindus and Mussalmans must be preserved. If this condition subsists the Congress can have no place at the Conference. The Congress is not a sectional organisation. It represents Indians belonging to all creeds and races. It can be and has been represented by Muslim, Hindu, Christian and Parsi Presidents. I hope no nationalist will be party to any arrangement which has as its basis a religious division. I express these sentiments not only on my behalf but all those Congressmen who are with Gandhiji at this moment.'[55]

Wavell had mentioned Gandhi by name as one of the invitees to the Simla conference. Gandhi said he would come, but in an individual capacity, not as a, still less *the*, representative of the Congress Party. Only the president and working committee members could serve that function.[56]

Gandhi reached Simla on 24 June. The same day he met the viceroy, this their first meeting. They spoke for over an hour, Wavell noting that Gandhi 'was rather vague and discursive, but on the whole gave his blessings to the proposals'. The viceroy was puzzled by Gandhi's frequent digressions, such as 'a most graphic digression of the death of his Private Secretary, and the relation of his carrying down the wounded General Woodgate from Spion Kop in 1899'. We should be less puzzled, since Mahadev Desai meant more—far more—to Gandhi than any private secretary had to any viceroy, while by his recounting of his aid during the Boer war, Gandhi was indicating that he bore no ill will towards the British.

Immediately after he met Gandhi, Wavell had an equally long meeting with Jinnah, who was 'much more direct than Gandhi, but whose manners are far worse'.[57]

Apart from the participating politicians and their hangers-on, a horde of journalists had also descended on the imperial summer capital to cover the conference. In a conversation on the sidelines, Gandhi told one of these reporters that 'Jawaharlal Nehru is my heir. He has got ability, knowledge and close touch with the public here and can interpret India's mind.'[58]

While Gandhi was in Simla, he received numerous telegrams urging the claims of different communities. Religious minorities like Christians and Sikhs, vulnerable economic groups like fisherfolk and pastoralists, all asked him not to neglect their interests in any future settlement. Muslim associations in Allahabad, Gulbarga and other places told Gandhi that only Jinnah and the League represented them. Some correspondents asked Gandhi to tell Maulana Azad to 'avoid helping Kafirs and side with Muslims', since he would have to show his 'face to God on the day of resurrection'. On the other hand, the Sialkot Pathans assured Gandhi they had 'full confidence in you in Simla Conference', while the association of 'Bhisti Mussalmans' (water-carriers by profession) said they recognized not Jinnah but Azad as their 'true representative'.

One of the more curious wires received by Gandhi in Simla came from a certain Babasaheb from Bombay, representing the 'Universal Astrological and Statistical Bureau'. Dated Thursday, 12 July, it read: 'Stars position changes strongly favourable from next Monday resulting Viceroy's plan success to empower Congress in spite of present unfavourable position eleventh hour change for better Jinnah's collapse or surrender.'[59]

The astrologer's prediction did not come to pass. The Simla conference failed, mostly on the question of Muslim representation. The Congress wanted the right to nominate its members to an expanded executive council regardless of religion, but the Muslim League insisted that only it could nominate Muslims. Even the Congress president, Maulana Azad, was effectively barred by the League's veto.[60]

On 14 July 1945, the day the conference ended, Jinnah issued an angry statement blaming the viceroy for not granting the Muslim League complete parity in the proposed executive council. He insisted that the Muslims his party represented were 'not a minority but a nation'. The Muslim League had, he said, 'repeatedly made it clear to the British Government several times since 1940, that we cannot consider or enter into any provisional interim Government unless declaration is made by the British Government guaranteeing the right of self-determination of Muslims and pledging that after the war, as soon as it may be possible, the British Government would establish Pakistan . . .'

Wavell's own statement, issued on the same day, was more restrained. If the conference had succeeded, he remarked: 'Its success would have been attributed to me, and I cannot place the blame for its failure upon any of the parties. I ask the party leaders to accept this view, and to do all they can to ensure there are no recriminations.'[61]

The Congress president, Maulana Azad, put aside his personal disappointment and wrote Wavell a warm letter, saying that the failure in Simla notwithstanding, they must continue to explore 'future possibilities of finding a way out, honourable to all concerned, and leading to the objective of Indian freedom'. Towards that end, he asked the government to nurture a cooperative atmosphere, by releasing all political prisoners, lifting the ban on the Congress and its allied organizations, and restoring full freedom of the press.

The war in Europe had been won, but the war in the East was still being fought. So, Azad reminded Wavell 'on behalf of the Congress that whatever the result of your promised effort [to try and break the deadlock] the Congress is and has always been against the Japanese. Therefore, there will always be on the part of the Congress a desire for the defeat of Japan in her designs upon China or any other aggression on her part.' However, 'the effort now being made on Indian soil [against Japanese aggression] will continue to be looked upon as a British and Allied effort, so long as there is not at the Centre a popular government assisted by provincial popular governments'.[62]

Gandhi wrote to Wavell on the same day as Azad (15 July), but in more anguished tones. 'It grieves me,' he remarked, 'to think that the conference which began so happily and so hopefully should have ended in apparent failure—due exactly, as it would seem, to the same cause as before. This time you have taken the blame on your own shoulders. But the world will think otherwise. India certainly does.'

'I must not hide from you,' Gandhi continued, 'the suspicion that the deeper cause is perhaps the reluctance of the official world to part with power, which the passing of the virtual control into the hands of their erstwhile prisoners would have meant.'[63]

Wavell himself thought that it was not so much British obduracy as the inability of Indians to forge a united front that impeded the transition to self-government. In a long letter to the British monarch about the Simla conference, Wavell remarked that 'the root cause of the failure was Jinnah's intransigence and obstinacy. But it represents a real fear on the part of the Muslims, including those who do not support Jinnah, of Congress domination, which they regard as equivalent to a Hindu Raj. . . . It shows more openly than ever before the great rift between Hindus and Muslims, which the events of the last few years have accentuated.'[64]

CHAPTER THIRTY-THREE

Prelude to Partition

I

In the last week of July 1945, the Labour Party won a landslide victory in the UK General Elections, securing 393 out of 641 seats in the House of Commons. The Conservatives, who had as many as 386 MPs in the outgoing house, won a mere 197. The result was entirely unexpected. Most observers thought that the war hero, Winston Churchill, would be rewarded with another term as prime minister. But the British electorate thought otherwise. Seeking to rebuild their lives and their economy, they put their trust in Labour and its understated, uncharismatic leader, Clement Attlee.

The Labour Party had long been committed to ending British rule in India. When, on 15 August, Japan surrendered and the war was finally over, Attlee's government restarted the democratic process in Britain's largest colony. On 21 August, the Government of India announced that fresh elections would take place to the provincial and central legislatures. A month later, the viceroy said the elections would be followed by the establishment of a body to design a constitution for a free India.

The elections for the central legislature were to be held in December 1945; those for the provincial assemblies, in January 1946. The Congress preparations for the polls were, as they had been back in 1937, principally in the hands of two men: Vallabhbhai Patel, who took charge of candidate selection and campaign finance; and Jawaharlal Nehru, who was the chief speaker at the party rallies. Gandhi himself took little interest in choosing candidates, election propaganda, and the like.

The veteran socialist-feminist Frederick Pethick-Lawrence (he had added his wife's surname to his own) was appointed secretary of state for India in Attlee's Cabinet. Gandhi had first met Pethick-Lawrence in 1906, in England, when he was lobbying for the rights of Indians in South Africa. That summer the suffragettes had been particularly active on the streets of London, defying the police by holding large marches and making stirring speeches. Gandhi followed their activities with admiration. He met some of their leaders, among them Emmeline Pethick, as well as her socialist husband. Forty years later, Gandhi wrote Pethick-Lawrence a warm letter of congratulation, saying: 'If the India Office is to receive a decent burial and a nobler monument is to rise from its ashes, who can be a fitter person than you for the work?'[1]

II

In July 1945, B.R. Ambedkar published a book called *What Congress and Gandhi Have Done to the Untouchables*. This argued that Gandhi's campaign to lift the Depressed Classes had failed, and for three reasons. First, 'Gandhi's sermons on Untouchability have completely failed to move the Hindus', who 'hear his after-prayer sermons for few minutes and then go to the comic opera'. Second, that while Gandhi claimed to be against untouchability, he had himself never launched a concerted political (as distinct from social) campaign for its abolition. Third, that (as Ambedkar saw it) 'Gandhi does not want the Untouchables to organize and be strong. For he fears that they might thereby become independent of the Hindus and weaken the ranks of Hindus.'

Ambedkar argued that 'it is to kill this spirit of independence among the Untouchables that Mr. Gandhi started the Harijan Sevak Sangh'. He claimed that 'the whole object of the sangh is to create a slave mentality among the untouchables towards their Hindu masters. Examine the Sangh from any angle one may like and the creation of slave mentality will appear to be its dominant purpose.'

When asked why there were no Harijans in the governing body of the Harijan Sewak Sangh, Gandhi had answered that it was an institution that asked caste Hindus to make reparations for the sins of the past. The exploiters had to make amends themselves. Ambedkar saw this as a cunning ploy to keep the 'untouchables' forever subservient. He claimed that 'if the Sangh was handed over to the Untouchables Mr. Gandhi and the Congress will have no means of control over the Untouchables. The Untouchables will cease to be dependent on the Hindus. . . . [T]he Untouchables having become independent will cease to be grateful to the Hindus.'[2]

Ambedkar had often criticized Gandhi in the past, but this was the first time he had devoted a full book to the subject. In August, shortly after *What Congress and Gandhi Have Done to the Untouchables* was published, a Congress social worker, himself from a low-caste background, came to see Gandhi. The conversation turned to B.R. Ambedkar, and his recently published attack. The social worker asked whether Ambedkar had 'proved himself to be more than a match to Gandhi'. To this Gandhi responded:

> My answer is 'Yes' and 'No'. Dr. Ambedkar is a fierce and fearless man. He does not scruple to beat the Hindu dog with any stick he can get. He wants to destroy Hinduism. It is open to him to do it. . . . I want Harijans to be as able and earnest as Dr. Ambedkar but in a different way. I want you to do even better. I want you to produce sterling men who will reshape the whole of our society.[3]

In truth, although Gandhi was by now quite accustomed to Ambedkar's attacks, this latest assault had shaken him. He worried that it might erode the credibility of the Congress, already undermined by the growth of the Muslim League. So, he asked C. Rajagopalachari to write a pamphlet rebutting the arguments of *What Congress and the Gandhi Have Done to the Untouchables*. 'There is no other person,' he told his long-time friend and comrade, 'as well-informed and able as you to answer Dr. Ambedkar's indictment of the Congress on the question.'[4]

Of all of Gandhi's associates, Rajaji had been most solidly behind him in the campaign to abolish untouchability. Where Nehru and Patel saw it as a distraction from the freedom struggle, Rajaji understood both its social and political significance. After he had abandoned his flourishing legal career because of non-cooperation, the sole appearance he made in court was to defend an 'untouchable' who entered a temple to which caste Hindus had denied him access. In December 1931, while Gandhi was returning to India after the Round Table Conference, Rajaji was active in a campaign to have 'untouchables' enter the famous (and famously orthodox) Guruvayur temple. As he told an audience assembled there: 'It would certainly help us in the fight for Swaraj if we open the doors of this temple. One of the many causes that keeps Swaraj away from us is that we are divided among ourselves. Mahatmaji received many wounds in London. But Dr. Ambedkar's darts were the worst. Mahatmaji did not quake before the Churchills of England. But he had to plead guilty to Dr. Ambedkar's charges. Mahatmaji pleaded that the removal of untouchability was an accepted national programme in India and that he himself was the greatest exponent of it. If therefore we postpone this quarrel, Swaraj would be more distant than ever.'[5]

In December 1945, Rajaji's little book *Ambedkarism Refuted* was published. Ambedkar, said Rajaji, 'heaps ridicule on the slow pace of the progress achieved' by the Congress in emancipating the 'untouchables'. Surely, this was because of colonial rule? Once India was independent, the pace of reform would accelerate. In any case, argued Rajaji, 'the progress of conditions regarding the Scheduled Castes in India does not compare ill with what has been done in America for Negroes, or in the South African republic for the natives of Africa, or for the Jews in civilized Europe'.

Where Ambedkar had savaged Gandhi, Rajaji felt 'that any fair-minded person must appreciate the service rendered by Gandhiji to the cause of social reform in India and admire him for having brought about a revolutionary upheaval of conscience about the so-called untouchables'. He continued: 'Carping criticism of the pace of results in a Herculean task benefits no one'; no one, that is to say, except the rulers, the 'British imperialist caste', who used criticisms such as Ambedkar's 'as an answer to world-opinion in regard to their obstinacy towards Indian political aspirations'.

Rajaji demonstrated that Ambedkar had been extremely selective, even tendentious, in his quotations from Gandhi's writings. But he spoilt an otherwise good case by casting personal aspersions on his master's fiercest critic. Gandhi and the Congress, he said, wished to remove the disabilities of *all* erstwhile 'untouchables', which would hurt educated members of this community most, since they could no longer claim special status. This, claimed Rajaji, 'is the material explanation for the violent dislike of Gandhiji exhibited by Dr. Ambedkar who looks upon this great and inspired reformer as the worst enemy of the "untouchables", meaning thereby of the educated and ambitious among them who find that the depressed status furnishes a short cut to positions'.[6]

While his old adversary Ambedkar attacked him on one side, on the other side, Gandhi was carrying on an argument with one of his closest disciples. This was Jawaharlal Nehru. Nehru was a vigorous votary of rapid industrial development. He saw India's failure to adopt the scientific method as the main cause of its subjugation at European hands. Now, after both Gandhi and he were out of jail and the negotiations for the transfer of power had begun, Nehru made it clear that when India became independent, it would adopt a model of economic development based on the factory and the city rather than the farm and the village.

Gandhi had several times stated that Nehru was his political heir. This implied that Nehru, rather than Patel, Rajaji, Azad or Prasad, would be the prime minister of a Congress-led government when freedom finally came. Nehru and he were on the same side when it came to Hindu–Muslim harmony, the rights of women, and the like. But Gandhi worried about this fundamental difference on the economic question. His worry deepened when, in the third week of September, the CWC met in Poona, and Nehru and he had a long argument on the best way to achieve all-round economic and social progress in an independent India.

The details of the conversations in Poona are not available. But we do have a letter that Gandhi wrote Nehru shortly afterwards, where he explained why he believed that the village must be placed at the centre of India's economic renewal. 'If India, and through India the world, is to achieve real freedom,' wrote Gandhi, 'then sooner or later we shall have to go and live in the villages—in huts, not palaces.' It 'does not frighten me at all', he continued, 'that the world seems to be going in the opposite direction. For the matter of that, when the moth approaches its doom it whirls faster and faster till it burns up. It is possible that India will not be able to escape this moth-like circling. It is my duty to try, till my last breath, to save India and through it the world from such a fate.'

Gandhi hoped that Nehru and he could meet soon to discuss these differences. He knew that their bond was so deep that it 'can never be broken'. The bond was personal, and it was political—'we both live for India's freedom', he remarked, 'and will be happy to die too for that freedom'. But while Gandhi was 'an old man', Nehru was 'comparatively young'. That was why, observed Gandhi, 'I have said that you are my heir. It is only proper that I should at least understand my heir and my heir in turn should understand me. I shall then be at peace.'[7]

Nehru's reply was equally long, and equally considered. He thought Gandhi idealized the Indian village, which, far from being an embodiment of truth and non-violence, was 'backward intellectually and culturally'. The needs of the masses for food, clothing, housing, education, etc. would be better served by modern factories, modern science and technology, and modern means of transport. Nehru, however, agreed that industrial development need not be concentrated; with the availability of electric power, light and medium industries could be dispersed across India.

Industrialization, argued Nehru, was necessary not only to meet basic human needs, but also to protect the nation's sovereignty. In a world of competitive nation states, technical modernization was mandatory to ward off military aggression. To be sure, Nehru deplored the 'tremendous acquisitive tendency both in individuals and groups and nations, which leads to conflicts and wars'. He hoped, within and outside India, to work to replace competition with cooperation.[8]

IV

Since his release from jail, Gandhi had been keen to visit Bengal, to study the destitution that the great famine of 1943 had left in its wake. His slow recovery from his jail illness, and the fluctuating and unstable political environment, had forced him to postpone his trip several times. For, travel through Bengal was even more arduous than in other parts of India. The trains were irregular and the roads bad (or non-existent), while in the deltaic districts, canoes where passengers rocked from side to side were the only viable means of transport.

Gandhi had a long and very complicated relationship with Bengal. He had first visited the province in 1896, and been back often. He had intense arguments with the bomb-throwing revolutionaries of Bengal, and less polemical, but arguably more productive, debates with its greatest poet, Tagore. Although the Congress was very strong in Bengal, its leaders there, from C.R. Das to Subhas Bose, were never as subservient to Gandhi as were Congressmen from other provinces.

Gandhi's connection with Bengal was political and it was personal. His sole romantic attachment after marriage was with that gifted and independent-minded bhadramahila, Saraladevi Chaudhurani. In August 1945, Gandhi met Saraladevi's son, Dipak, who said that his mother was ill and depressed. On 19 August, Gandhi wrote to her: 'Dipak gives me a sorrowful account of you. Disease like birth and death is part of us. May you have the strength to suffer what comes as your lot.' Saraladevi had in fact died the previous day, the news not having reached Gandhi when he wrote to her.[9]

Gandhi was finally permitted by his doctors to go to Bengal in December 1945. He travelled to some districts in the interior, but was otherwise based at the Sodepur Ashram, run by his long-time disciple Satis Chandra Dasgupta, and an hour away from Calcutta by road. Here, he met citizens who came to see him. He occasionally ventured out into the city, and had several meetings with the governor of Bengal, a bluff, engaging Australian named Richard Casey.

After two weeks in and around Calcutta, Gandhi left for Santiniketan. This was his first trip there since the death of Tagore. He spoke to students, urging them to become messengers of international fellowship and peace, laid the foundation stone of a hospital carrying the name of C.F. Andrews, and walked around the place, reviving old memories. Asked by a professor whether Santiniketan should 'allow itself to be drawn into political work', Gandhi answered that its goals were different. While supporting the cause of India's independence, while serving the poor and needy, the students and staff of Santiniketan should 'keep out of the present-day political turmoil', fulfilling instead its founder's intellectual, cultural and moral ideals.

In the last week of December, Gandhi visited the district of Midnapore, which had been extremely active during the Quit India movement of 1942, so much so that activists had even at one stage set up a parallel government. Gandhi did not approve of the means the rebels had used. They had, among other things, blown up railway tracks, burnt a court and seized a police station. Gandhi chastised local Congress workers for 'committing the mistake of thinking that all that did not involve killing was non-violence'. He warned Bengali admirers of Lenin that 'our tradition is wholly different from Russia's'. A non-violent revolution, he pointed out, aimed not at the 'seizure of power', but rather at 'a transformation of relationships ending in a peaceful transfer of power'.[10]

Shortly after reaching Calcutta, Gandhi met with the governor, Richard Casey. The two men got along well, so at regular intervals Gandhi went back to Government House. Their first conversation turned to the question of food and famine. Later, Gandhi heard the governor speak on the radio, proposing an ambitious dam-building scheme to capture the waters of Bengal before they went into the sea. Gandhi wrote to the governor that 'your gigantic project will come to nothing until the whole mass of the people of Bengal is interested in the Government of the province'. As important as utilizing 'waste water', he pointed out, was utilizing 'waste labour'. The millions of peasants in Bengal must be encouraged to take up weaving and other artisanal crafts to make every hour of their day productive. If the governor thought the idea 'practical and capable of immediate application', Gandhi was happy to send him 'a detailed scheme' to be implemented with the aid of the Spinners and Village Associations that he had founded.[11]

Casey wrote a long and fascinating reply, setting out his differences with Gandhi as regards rural uplift. 'While I am at one with you in looking forward to the regeneration of village life through the provision of healthy village occupations,' he wrote,

> I still believe that I am correct, at least in the circumstances of Bengal, in laying all the stress that I can on the control of physical environment as fundamental to prosperity. I believe that the fundamental curse of Bengal (I don't claim to know about the rest of India) is poverty, which brings in its train illiteracy and disease. So long as the people are under-nourished and impoverished so long will it be impossible (to my way of thinking) for them to be happy or, in any complete sense, free. You know the saying: 'Things are in the saddle and ride mankind'—which in Bengal are land and water—so that mankind may ride free.
>
> It seems to me that we both have the same goal but we proceed to it in different ways. The goal is human happiness—that is, freedom in the complete sense. I wish to create the physical circumstances which, in my belief, are a prerequisite to happiness. Your bolder vision, if my interpretation is correct, sees its attainment without the control of these physical circumstances.

Casey told Gandhi that he did have 'regard for home spinning and weaving', and would 'be glad to see the renaissance of village craft'. Yet, he could not see 'that this would be a real cure in itself for the ills of Bengal. These ills are shortage of food, under-nourishment and poverty. They derive from the insufficient productivity of the land, and, in my belief, they could be largely cured by the integration and development of the land and water of the province.'

'Maybe, mine is not a panacea,' remarked Casey. 'I remember reading somewhere that "human nature is the greatest puzzle that God has set for man in this world, and when we have solved it we shall have solved everything". I do not look, as perhaps I should, to solve the problem of human nature, but I do look to the creation of circumstances in which human nature can best fulfil itself.'[12]

Gandhi also wrote to Casey asking him to release all political prisoners. Many of those detained in Bengal's jails had been put away on the basis of police testimonies that the accused had not seen or had any chance of contesting. Gandhi had it on good authority that 'there is no terrorism to be feared'. He added: 'The prisoners are all likely to be public-spirited. But that can be no reason for keeping them behind prison bars.' Urging Casey to discharge these political detainees 'without the slightest ado', Gandhi asked for 'a little grace before, as you and I hope, the transference of powers [to Indian hands] comes'.[13]

Casey passed on a record of his talks with Gandhi to Lord Wavell. Apart from spinning, agriculture, political prisoners, and the like, they had spoken about the value of massages and masseurs, and even about Gandhi's renegade son, Harilal, about whom the father said (in the governor's recollection) that he 'had not put any impediment in the way of his becoming a Muslim. He'd said to him that if his becoming a Muslim resulted in his giving up drink, he would be glad. But it didn't.'

Gandhi had told Casey that 'the I.C.S. were responsible for a great deal of India's troubles and difficulties. They were loyal to the British, but not to India. He said that this all started with Warren Hastings and Lord Clive, who might be heroes to [the British], but they certainly were not to Indians.'

Casey then asked Gandhi what the British should now do in India. The notes continue:

> He said that he supposed we looked at the Congress and at the Muslim League—and said to ourselves, 'Which shall we choose between'—on the one hand, there is the Congress who represented a very great proportion of the people of India, but who had been rebellious and difficult for a number of years—and, on the other hand, the Muslim League, who had co-operated with us for a long time, but who represented only a relatively small proportion of India—and who now took the point of view that India must be divided up, which we (the British) must realise was wrong. Were we going to support the majority (the Congress) who, in spite of the difficulties that they might have created for us in the past, now wanted the right and proper thing (a united India)—or those who had been our friends in the past and who wanted the wrong thing—a divided India? If we decided for the Muslims—for Pakistan, the

Congress would never accept such a decision, and we would be doing India a final and very great disservice.[14]

On the larger political question of which side the British should support in the Congress–League battle, Casey had no say. It would be the viceroy, the secretary of state and the Labour government in London who would plan out India's constitutional future. But on matters within his domain, the governor was more than ready to help. He released political prisoners in batches, forty or fifty at a time, till the jails of Bengal only had criminals qua criminals. He provided sales tax exemptions for dhotis, lungis and saris, so as to reduce the burden on the poor. Finally, he instructed his officers to allow salt to be used for home consumption without being taxed. Thus, as he told Gandhi, in this respect at least 'the Gandhi–Irwin Pact is being administered in a fair—and even generous—way in this part of the world'.[15]

In his diary, Casey jotted down some observations he had kept out of his letter to Wavell. He recalled Gandhi saying 'that Jinnah had told him that he (Gandhi) had ruined politics in India, by dragging up a lot of unwholesome elements in public life and giving them political prominence . . .' Casey himself thought that Gandhi 'clearly has a certain rather feminine streak in him'. The Australian was also impressed by how the ordinary Indian saw Gandhi; as he noted: 'Each night he came to see me, his departure was remarkable in that probably 150 of our servants (Muslim and Hindu) lined the passages and the entrance to the house, to see him—all salaaming profoundly.'

Later that month, Casey also met Nehru, Patel and Azad. In his diary entry for 10 December 1945, he noted:

I can well believe that a good deal of our trouble and difficulty in India has been our own fault, particularly in the last 20 years or so. We (or at any rate a good many amongst us) have not sought company or the friendship of Indians for their own sake. . . . We make them feel ill-at-ease and inferior. In its train comes the natural reaction—bitterness and dislike. We have, to an appreciable extent, dug our own grave in India by our high-hattedness—although the metaphor is not a very happy one.

Casey then continued:

> There is a lack of warmth and generosity in our dealings with
> Indians, both Hindus and Muslims. It may be said—why should
> we show warmth and generosity to rebels? Well, we've got to make
> up our minds about it—whether they are to be regarded as rebels
> against constituted British authority or the people to whom we're
> about to hand over the control of India. They're the same people.[16]

Reading these noticeably empathetic lines, one is tempted to say: if
only Casey rather than Linlithgow had been viceroy of India in 1939!
History, and historians, have rightly paid much attention to Gandhi's
interactions with General Smuts in South Africa and with Lord Irwin
in India, encounters that had a direct bearing on politics and public
policy. However, of all the imperial proconsuls Gandhi dealt with
in three continents, the one he perhaps most enjoyed speaking (and
arguing) with was the Australian, R.G. Casey.

On Gandhi's last day in Calcutta, he gave an interview to the
United Press of India, the conversation focusing on the great, and
recently deceased, hero of Bengal, Subhas Chandra Bose. (Bose had
died in an air crash in August, after Japan's surrender to the Allies—
he was apparently en route to Russia.) Gandhi was generous to a man
with whom he had had major political and philosophical differences.
He warmly endorsed the adoption of the Indian National Army's
slogan *Jai Hind* (glory to India), noting that just because it had been
used in war, it need not 'be eschewed in non-violent action'. As for
Bose himself, Gandhi remarked that he 'always knew of his capacity
for sacrifice. But a full knowledge of his resourcefulness, soldiership
and organizing ability came to me only after his escape from India.'
He added: 'The difference of outlook between him and me as to the
means is too well known for comment.'[17]

V

After seven weeks in eastern India, Gandhi moved down the
Coromandel Coast to Madras. He spent ten days in the city,

meeting social workers, speaking to them of the importance of taking Hindustani, the putative link language of free India, to Tamil and Telugu speakers. In Madras, Gandhi also visited the ailing Liberal leader Srinivasa Sastri several times. The two had a long, if occasionally contentious, relationship. Both disciples of Gokhale, one had moved into mass politics while the other remained in the realm of constitutional discussion. Sastri deplored satyagraha, his opposition largely principled, but also inflected by a measure of personal jealousy at Gandhi's ever-growing popularity.

In the late 1930s, Gandhi's devoted secretary, Mahadev Desai, had asked Sastri to help him edit the second, revised English edition of *The Story of My Experiments with Truth*. As draft chapters were conveyed between Sevagram and Madras and back, Sastri and Desai debated in a friendly manner about a man the former had reservations about and whom the latter unreservedly admired. While ready to improve the Gujarati's English, the Madras scholar was loth to make his part public. Sending the last set of chapters with his corrections, Sastri instructed Desai to ensure that 'my name shall never be disclosed in the preface or introduction or press notices'. He agreed that Gandhi himself could be told; otherwise, 'the fewer the people that are let into the secret the better'.[18] When the second edition of Gandhi's autobiography appeared, in 1940, Mahadev's preface explained that this fresh translation had 'the benefit of careful revision by a revered friend, who, among many other things, has the reputation of being an eminent English scholar. Before undertaking the task, he made it a condition that his name should on no account be given out. I accept the condition. It is needless to say that it heightens my gratitude to him.'[19]

Now Mahadev himself was dead. The Quit India movement had come and gone. Sastri was sick and seemingly on his deathbed. Gandhi gamely forgot their differences and went to chat and console him. Seeing his visitor come into the hospital room, Sastri, overcome with emotion, struggled to rise from his bed and hug him. Sastri was an acknowledged authority on the Ramayana; now, he told Gandhi, the 'living Rama' had come to meet him. When Gandhi protested against such extravagantly hyperbolic comparisons, Sastri answered, 'Ha! don't I know Gandhi, though you have come to me as my friend that you are the greatest fellow living in the world today?'[20]

In early February, Gandhi left for the inland town of Madurai, whose famous Meenakshi temple had finally, reluctantly, opened its gates to those stigmatized as 'untouchables'. In a speech the day he left Madras, he explained that for him the maidan 'was really the best temple of God. They had the fine blue sky for their roof, under which there was no difference between the rich and the poor, the master and the servant, the millionaire and the worker, or the Hindu, the Muslim, the Christian and the Parsi.'

Gandhi's own prayer meetings were always held in the open. He did not feel the need to go to temples to pray. While 'no idol worshipper' himself, he yet knew the 'great place idol-worship has among Hindus'. At railway stations on the way to Madurai, he told those who had come to hear him that he was travelling to the temple town as a pilgrim, to see and experience for himself the mixing of savarnas and Harijans which was now, for the first time ever, being practised there.

Before entering the Meenakshi temple, Gandhi addressed a public meeting in Madurai town. The gathering was mammoth—in excess of five lakh. Gandhi thanked the crowd for showing their love and affection, but urged them not to follow him into the temple itself. He wanted to go there in solitude; he was, as he put it, on this occasion 'himself a Harijan who wanted to worship there'.[21]

In the first week of February 1946, Gandhi returned to Sevagram, after nine weeks on the road. 'It's been a marvellous tour,' wrote Amrit Kaur to a friend, 'but of course a tremendous strain on all & most of all on Bapu. It is only his iron will & power of the spirit that sustains him. I am amazed at the physical strength he gains thereby. The people's love is unrestrained but one can't blame them. I've never seen women in such crowds.'[22]

Gandhi was now seventy-five years old. This tour in Bengal and Madras had been physically arduous but emotionally satisfying, the groundswell of love and goodwill renewing his spirit, wounded by the loss in recent years of his wife, his secretary, and his closest friends.

Meanwhile, Gandhi's English weekly *Harijan*—shut since the Quit India movement of 1942—had been revived, and, with its

Gujarati counterpart *Harijan Bandhu*, became once more the chief vehicle for his speeches, talks and articles. These spoke, as always, of Hindu–Muslim harmony, of the emancipation of the so-called 'untouchables', and the promotion of khadi.

After their long absence, the potential readership of Gandhi's weeklies had massively increased. The Quit India movement had brought many young patriots into the Congress fold; they all wanted to read, in English, Hindi or Gujarati, what their hero was saying or writing. When the first three issues quickly sold out, the print run was revised radically upwards. In February 1946, the Navajivan Press was printing 60,000 copies of *Harijan*, 40,000 of *Harijan Bandhu*, and 25,000 of *Harijan-Sevak*, or 1,25,000 in all. This required some 3,90,000 pounds of newsprint, which the government was finally persuaded to provide.[23]

For some readers, *Harijan* without Mahadev Desai was not what it used to be. One patriot in the town of Unnao wrote to Pyarelal that while he was thankful that *Harijan* had resumed publication, Mahadev was 'sorely missed'. For, 'he was such a fine and loveable personality, so simple and yet so acute—a true interpreter of Gandhiji, his philosophy and all that he stands for. His pen pictures were simply beautiful.'[24]

VI

While Gandhi was travelling in eastern and southern India, elections were being held for the central legislature and the provincial assemblies. With the franchise restricted by education and property, some forty-one million Indians were eligible to vote, of whom about six million were women.

The Muslim League campaigned principally on the plank of Pakistan. It warned Muslims that a vote for the Congress would lead to the construction of a 'Hindu Raj'. On the other side, the Congress promised economic development and social progress, while reminding voters of its sacrifices during the Quit India movement.

Between 1937 and 1946, the League's reach had enormously expanded. Once a party of large landholders, it had now attracted to its fold many professionals and many students too. Muslim doctors, lawyers, professors and businessmen were increasingly nervous of their prospects in a free but undivided India, where they would have to compete with their more numerous, and often better-educated, Hindu counterparts.

By early February 1946, the votes had been counted. The results revealed a divided electorate, itself mirroring a divided land. Across India, the League took a majority of seats reserved for the Muslims. It won seventy-five out of eighty-six in the Punjab, 114 out of 119 in Bengal, and twenty-eight out of thirty-four in Sindh. These were all provinces that would form part of any future Pakistan. Yet, even in provinces that would never be part of a Muslim homeland, the League did extremely well. For example, it won all thirty Muslim seats in Bombay, and all twenty-nine in Madras. It was only in the NWFP, where Khan Abdul Ghaffar Khan and his Khudai Khidmatgars were strong, that the Congress could count on Muslim support. Here, the seats reserved for Muslims were divided almost equally between the League and the Congress.

The steady growth of the Muslim League through the war years had been confirmed at the polls. Jinnah's party, once confined to large landlords and aristocrats, had now drawn millions of other people into its fold. They were fired with the idea of creating an Islamic nation in the subcontinent, seeking to join the growing ranks of Muslim states across Asia. Turkey, Iran, Syria, Iraq, Saudi Arabia and Egypt already existed as independent countries with a Muslim majority; the hope, and expectation, was that Pakistan would soon join this list.[25]

Since Muslim seats were often a small percentage of the total, the Congress still did well overall in these elections. In Madras and Bombay, despite losing all Muslim seats, it won a majority and formed the government. The Congress also formed governments in Orissa, Bihar, the United Provinces and the Central Provinces.[26]

The elections of 1946 dealt a decisive blow to the Congress's claims to represent Muslims. However, it could take some consolation in its performance in that other important category of reserved seats, that of Scheduled Castes. Out of 151 seats reserved for the erstwhile 'untouchables' across India, the Congress won 142, while Ambedkar's

Scheduled Caste Federation (SCF) won only two. The SCF was wiped out in Bombay, where it had won twelve seats in 1937. Congress was able to capitalize on the Quit India movement and the sacrifice of its leaders in prison, at a time when Ambedkar himself sat on the viceroy's executive council.[27]

The 1946 elections were a body blow to one of Gandhi's great rivals, B.R. Ambedkar. But they were a cause of enormous satisfaction to his other, and older, rival, M.A. Jinnah. Across India, Muslim voters had vindicated Jinnah's claim that the League, and more or less the League alone, represented their interests. If the elections were to be seen as a referendum on the two-nation theory, then the result was an emphatic vindication of Jinnah and his party. This would make the task of the Congress, and of Gandhi himself, far harder in any future negotiations with the British.

VII

On 18 February 1946, Gandhi left Sevagram for a stint in a nature-cure clinic in the village of Uruli Kanchan, on the outskirts of Poona. No sooner had he reached there than news came of a naval mutiny having broken out in Bombay. Protesting against bad food, inadequate housing and inhuman working conditions, Hindu, Muslim and Sikh ratings stopped work, took down the flag of the Royal Navy and raised nationalist slogans.

The mutiny in Bombay found its echoes in Karachi and Calcutta, where Indians on British ships likewise struck work. The leaders of the strike were placed under arrest, intensifying the protests. Many millhands came out in support of the striking seamen. American flags were burnt, a British soldier in uniform beaten up. The Raj's reaction was swift, and punitive. Fighter planes flew menacingly overhead, while a British battalion fired on the protesters, killing six ratings and wounding several others.[28]

Gandhi was one of the heroes of the rebellious navy men. Their leaders had invoked both the Salt March and the Quit India movement. 'Mahatma Gandhi ki jai' was one of the slogans the protesters shouted. ('*Hindu–Muslim Ek Ho*' was another.) But

Gandhi, of course, could not approve of their methods. From Poona, he issued a statement deploring the use of violence by the rebellious ratings. The methods they had used were 'not the way to swaraj as defined by the Congress. Burning of tram-cars and other property, insulting and injuring Europeans is not non-violence of the Congress type, much less mine.' Left-wing commentators had praised the rebels for disregarding religious differences. For Gandhi, however, 'a combination between Hindus and Muslims and others for the purpose of violent action is unholy and will lead to and probably is a preparation for mutual violence—bad for India and the world'.

Vallabhbhai Patel, who was in Bombay at the time, was more ambivalent in his response. He agreed that 'the destruction of property was wantonly thoughtless'; yet, he recognized the deep 'resentment of distinction between Europeans and Indians' that sparked the uprising. Patel persuaded the ratings to surrender unconditionally, promising them the Congress would ensure that 'full justice would be done and that there would be no victimization'.[29]

In the second week of March, Gandhi came to Bombay for a meeting of the CWC. On the sidelines, he met some returned former soldiers of Subhas Bose's Indian National Army. 'The real test of the I. N. A.,' he told them, 'was to come only now. In the fighting line there was the romance and excitement, not so in civil life. The country today was faced with the spectre of famine. Would they help the people to fight it with the same courage, cohesion, doggedness and resourcefulness which they had shown on the battle-field?' Gandhi praised the INA soldiers for their 'physical stamina, discipline, and . . . a feeling of solidarity and oneness, untainted by narrow communalism'. These attributes now put them 'in a singular position of vantage for introducing non-violent discipline and organization among the masses'.[30]

VIII

In late March, a three-man 'Cabinet Mission' arrived from England to seek to formalize the transfer of power from British to Indian hands. Announcing this initiative in the British Parliament, Clement

Attlee noted that 'the idea of nationalism is running very fast in India and indeed all over Asia. . . . It is no good applying the formula of the past to the present position. The temperature of 1946 is not the temperature of 1920, 1930 or even 1942.' Attlee pointed out that in the two World Wars, thousands of Indians had sacrificed their lives for the freedom of others. Now it was time that India 'should herself have freedom to decide her destiny'. He himself hoped and felt 'that political India might be the light of Asia'.[31]

It was the kind of speech Attlee's predecessor could never have made. We don't know whether Churchill was in the house when the prime minister spoke. He would surely have been dismayed by what Attlee said and how he said it. In India, the speech was received very warmly. The Cabinet Mission's members included Frederick Pethick-Lawrence and Stafford Cripps, both of whom Gandhi knew and liked (the third member was also a senior Labour politician, A.V. Alexander). Indeed, on arriving in India, Pethick-Lawrence had written Gandhi a warm letter, saying he was 'greatly looking forward to seeing you again and renewing the acquaintanceship & friendship which began some 40 years ago when you came to lunch with us in Clements Inn'.[32] So, Gandhi now chose to re-engage with politics, travelling to Delhi to be at hand while the mission talked with Congress leaders and with other political interests.

Gandhi's patron and disciple, G.D. Birla, invited him to stay at his capacious house in New Delhi. Gandhi chose to stay in the Bhangi (sweepers') colony instead. Birla now hastened to install electricity and provide fresh water to the humble home which his master had chosen to grace. Gandhi sent a note to Birla, via Pyarelal, hoping that these 'arrangements will be permanent. If the wires are removed the moment he goes out of the Bhangi Niwas, the whole thing will become a farce.'

Gandhi arrived in Delhi on 1 April. The same evening, at a prayer meeting, he called 'Untouchability the blackest spot in Hinduism'. The 'least expiation' caste Hindus could do was 'to share with the Harijans their disabilities and to deny ourselves the privilege[s] which the latter cannot share'.

On 2 April, Gandhi wrote to Pethick-Lawrence that he should lean on the viceroy for 'the immediate release of *political* prisoners irrespective of the charge of violence or non-violence'. This would be welcomed by all parties, not just the Congress, and create a conducive atmosphere for talks. He also hoped that the salt tax would finally be abolished.

On the 3rd, Gandhi had his first meeting with the Cabinet Mission. He told them that he was not an authorized representative of the Congress; any formal proposals they had should be conveyed to the party president, Maulana Azad. But he would say, in his personal capacity, that the Muslim League's two-nation theory was 'dangerous'; for, the Muslims in India were themselves sons of the soil.

In his prayer meeting on 6 April, Gandhi recalled the same day twenty-seven years previously. That was when the Rowlatt Satyagraha began, when 'for the first time the entire masses of India from one end to the other rose like one man'. In that, his first major national campaign, 'Hindus and Muslims for the time forgot all their differences'. In the city in which he now spoke, a 'monster gathering' of Hindus and Muslims had come together in the great Jama Masjid, to be addressed by Swami Shraddhananda. That, recalled Gandhi wistfully, 'was a glorious day in India's history, the memory of which we shall always treasure'. But, he added sadly, 'the situation has changed today. We have gone wrong somewhere. The hearts of Hindus and Muslims are sundered. The air is poisoned with communal bitterness and rancour. A section of the Muslims have begun to claim that they are a separate nation.'

In the years following the Rowlatt Satyagraha, 6 to 13 April had been observed as 'National Week'. Gandhi now asked the citizens of Delhi to recall those events and those associations, to work anew for communal harmony and for the fulfilment of the constructive programme for 'the attainment of non-violent swaraj'. Back in 1919, 'every home in the Punjab hummed with the music of the spinning-wheel'. Could Indians now not recreate that mood and that magic, by undertaking 'sacrificial spinning' and 'by purging our hearts of any trait of communal hatred'?[33]

Not many young Muslims were listening, however. A student leader in Bareilly, a passionate supporter of the Pakistan movement, wrote to Gandhi that 'like the Hindus, Muslims want complete independence, which you have yourself nurtured in them. Rightly or wrongly they have decided to have Pakistan. How are you going

to crush the spirit fostered by you? By force? That will result in
bloodshed. You alone can avoid it.'

Gandhi replied wearily, and in Hindi: '*Mere paas talwar nahin
hai na mein chahta hoon. Jis ko mein samjha sakta hoon woh talwar
kabhi istamaal nahin kar sakte.*

*Rahi baat Pakistan ke chahne valon ki. Ve kahte hain "ham lad
kar lenge". Agar aisa hai to ve hi talwar khichenge.*'[34]

(I do not have a sword, nor do I want one. Those whom I can
persuade will never use a sword either.

There remain the people who ask for Pakistan. They say they will
fight for it. If that is so they will be the ones who draw the sword.)

IX

In early May, the Cabinet Mission shifted its base to Simla. Stafford
Cripps asked Gandhi also to come up from the plains to continue
their discussions. He did, and on his first prayer meeting in the hills
expressed the hope 'that this time the Cabinet Mission will do the
right thing by India and that the British power would finally and
completely be withdrawn'.[35]

The Cabinet Mission had prepared a draft for discussion, which
proposed a Union government in control of foreign affairs, defence
and communications, with all remaining powers to be vested in
the provinces. They further proposed parity between five 'Muslim-
majority' provinces (Punjab, Bengal, Assam, Sindh, the NWFP
and Balochistan) and six 'Hindu-majority' ones (Madras, Bengal,
Bombay, the United Provinces, Bihar, Assam and Orissa), with the
two groups being represented equally in the discussions on a future
constitution and in any future federal parliament. The position of
the princely states was left ambiguous; they could remain part of the
federation, and join a province with which they shared a boundary.
But the possibility of some larger states striking out on their own for
an independent status was not explicitly ruled out.

Shown the proposal, Gandhi found his enthusiasm for the
Mission rapidly evaporate. The designated 'Muslim' provinces had
a combined population of some ninety million; the so-called 'Hindu'

provinces, more than twice as many. To place them at par seemed grossly biased.[36]

In the second week of May 1946, with the talks deadlocked, Nehru suggested to Jinnah that an 'Umpire' who was not Muslim, Hindu, Sikh or English be appointed to arbitrate on differences between the parties.

This was a fascinating suggestion. For, the idea of an umpire was quintessentially British, coming in fact from that most English of games, cricket. Nehru wanted an umpire who would be from some other Asian country or perhaps an American. Jinnah, however, only trusted the British to see or take his side. And so, he rejected the proposal.[37]

In Simla, as in Delhi, the Cabinet Mission failed to bring the Congress and the League anywhere close to an agreement. Gandhi himself thought his presence in Simla unnecessary, and returned to the plains. On his last day in the imperial summer capital, he told a prayer meeting that while the Mission appeared to have failed, 'it would not necessarily mean that all was over. After all, Hindus and Muslims are brothers. Some day they are certainly going to unite.'[38]

On 16 May, the Cabinet Mission issued a long statement focusing on the Hindu–Muslim question. The Muslim League had demanded a 'separate and fully sovereign State of Pakistan', which would include all of Bengal, the Punjab, NWFP, Sindh and Balochistan, and possibly chunks of Assam too. The mission found it unjustified to include in any such state those districts of Bengal and Punjab which were predominantly non-Muslim. A second alternative would be to partition these two large and crucial provinces; but this too would render asunder populations with a 'common language and long history and tradition'. The mission thus concluded that 'neither a larger nor a smaller sovereign State of Pakistan would provide an acceptable solution for the communal problem'.

The immediate creation of Pakistan ruled out, the Mission went back to its original proposal of a loose federation, with the Centre controlling a few areas, the rest left to the provinces, these combined into groups. Any province could, after ten years, opt out of its assigned group and, at a pinch, out of the Union itself. This scheme, said Pethick-Lawrence and Co., would not 'completely satisfy all parties', but perhaps 'at this supreme moment in Indian history statesmanship demands mutual accommodation'.[39]

Sent this document, Gandhi wrote to Pethick-Lawrence to protest the grouping scheme, since some provinces (such as Assam and NWFP) might not wish to join the group assigned to them. He further noted the lack of any assurances to the people of the princely states, these 'groaning under a double yoke', that of their rulers and of the British Raj. Gandhi was disappointed that the Mission had not called for the immediate formation of a national government, and dismayed that it had not made clear that British troops would have to leave India for good when the Raj ended.

The secretary of state wrote back in stiff, formal terms, saying that he 'quite definitely' disagreed with Gandhi on the questions of a national government and troop withdrawal. Gandhi archly replied that this letter was 'in the best imperialistic style which I had thought had gone for ever'.[40]

The degeneration in tone was unpropitious. By the middle of May, it was clear that the Cabinet Mission plan was going nowhere. It pleased neither the Muslim League, since it did not explicitly concede Pakistan; and it alienated the Congress, since it seemed to leave behind a weak Centre with little control over potentially secessionist provinces and always autocratic princes. The negotiations dragged on till the middle of June, before finally being proclaimed a failure.

Meanwhile, the viceroy, Lord Wavell, was seeking to form a provisional government at the Centre, composed (unlike the executive councils of the past) wholly of Indians. There would even be an Indian war member, or defence minister.

Which parties or individuals would be represented in this interim government? In his correspondence with Wavell, Jinnah had demanded parity between the Congress and the Muslim League. He suggested that these parties nominate five ministers each, with Sikhs and Christians, themselves small but distinct minorities, nominating one minister apiece. Jinnah further told Wavell that he would not allow Maulana Azad to represent the Congress in talks regarding Cabinet formation, even though Azad was—as he had been since 1940—the party's president. The opposition was personal, but also strategic—by denying Azad a place at the negotiating table, Jinnah would further solidify the League's claim to represent the interests of all Indian Muslims.

Gandhi met Wavell in Delhi on 11 June. When the viceroy put Jinnah's conditions to him, Gandhi gently expressed his own reservations about parity. He was more forceful in condemning Jinnah's bid to keep Azad out of the talks. The Congress, he told Wavell, 'could not be expected to sacrifice its faithful servant of twenty-five years standing whose self-sacrifice and devotion to the national cause had never been in question'.[41]

A week later, the CWC met in Delhi. Gandhi told them that if asked to nominate members for this interim government, they must choose at least 'one nationalist Muslim and one woman'. He stressed that the 'Congress will lose its prestige if it ceases to have a national character'.[42]

The Congress's negotiating position was weakened by Jinnah's obduracy, and by the unrelenting hostility towards them of many British members of the Indian Civil Service, who had not forgotten the uprising of 1942. The governor of the United Provinces told Wavell that 'we must stop Congress getting a dominating position, with Gandhi as de facto dictator behind the scenes. This can only be done if HE [Wavell] accepts Jinnah's nominees [for the interim government], even if it crashes the conference.'[43]

This was advice the viceroy was prepared to heed. To be sure, Wavell was more sympathetic to Indian aspirations than his predecessor. Unlike Linlithgow, he knew the British must, for their own sake as much as for their subjects, leave soon. Yet, he retained deep reservations about India's pre-eminent political party. He could not forgive the Congress for launching the Quit India movement at a time when the fate of the World War hung in the balance; when, as the commander-in-chief of the Indian Army, he was himself organizing the defence of the subcontinent against the Japanese. He thought that Gandhi's party was adroit at raising 'mob passion and mob support', writing somewhat hyperbolically that the Congress 'do not hesitate to use the worst and most violent elements in the population for their purposes'. He was enraged that Gandhi, Nehru and company had—as he saw it—'chosen to exalt and glorify the few thousands of traitors of the INA, who were mostly the cowards and softlings; and to neglect the magnificent men who really fought for them'. Such were the sentiments that led Wavell, when the Cabinet Mission was in India, to confide to his journal that 'I sympathise with the Muslims rather than with Congress . . .' He sympathized least of all with the Congress's long-time leader, telling his journal that 'I have always regarded G[andhi] as our most inveterate, malignant and rather hypocritical enemy'.[44]

X

In the last week of June 1946, the Cabinet Mission departed for England, having failed to bring about a resolution of the dispute between the Congress and the League. Another way, and some other interlocutors, would have to be found to take the transfer of power from British to Indian hands forward.[45]

Meanwhile, the Indian National Congress had to choose a new president. The war, Quit India and the incarceration of their main leaders had disrupted the normal process of having fresh elections every year. Maulana Azad had, willy-nilly, served as Congress president from 1940 to 1946. Now it was time to choose a suitable successor.

J.B. Kripalani, the Congressmen who had known Gandhi longest, wanted to throw his hat in the ring. Twelve of the fifteen secretaries of the provincial Congress committees nominated Vallabhbhai Patel, in acknowledgement of his role in building and rebuilding the party. But Gandhi himself wanted Jawaharlal Nehru. In the event, his will prevailed, and the working committee nominated and selected Nehru.[46]

Why did Gandhi choose Jawaharlal Nehru over Vallabhbhai Patel? The question was debated somewhat at the time, and has in fact been debated far more intensely in recent years, when—in part due to the misdeeds of his descendants—the popular mood in India has turned fiercely against Nehru and his legacy.[47] First, Gandhi knew that, with independence imminent, the person who became Congress president in 1946 would most likely become the prime minister of a free India. Second, for at least a decade now, Gandhi had regarded

Nehru as his political heir. In statements both private and public, he had made this choice clear. This was something Patel himself was quite aware of, which is why he did not press his candidacy but withdrew in favour of Nehru. Patel also knew that while the provincial secretaries may have backed him, he would not have won a vote against Nehru in the wider AICC, still less among the party membership as a whole.

Gandhi chose Nehru as his political heir because he most reliably reflected the pluralist, inclusive idea of India that the Mahatma stood for. The two other alternatives—Patel and Rajagopalachari—had, by contrast, somewhat sectional interests and affiliations. Patel was seen as a Gujarati Hindu; Rajaji as a South Indian Brahmin. But Nehru was a Hindu who was trusted by Muslims, a North Indian who was respected in the south, and a man committed to equal rights for women.

Like Gandhi, but like no one else in the Congress, Nehru was a genuinely all-India leader. His popularity among the public at large had been amply demonstrated through the leading role he played in the election campaigns of 1937 and 1946. He had two further attributes: he was the most internationalist among the Indian nationalists, and he was much younger than the other contenders, and thus likely to have a longer tenure.[48] That is why, and despite their differences on economic policy, Gandhi had from at least the mid-1930s clearly and consistently identified Nehru as his political heir.

CHAPTER THIRTY-FOUR

Marching for Peace

I

Gandhi had rarely spoken about what a free India would look like. In July 1946, a correspondent asked him for a 'broad and comprehensive picture of the Independent India of your conception'. Gandhi obliged with an article in *Harijan* which argued, first, that independence should mean the independence of the whole of India, including the princely states and the areas under French and Portuguese control; second, that it 'must begin at the bottom' so that 'every village will be a republic or *panchayat* having full powers'; third, that 'in this structure composed of innumerable villages, there will be ever-widening, never-ascending circles. Life will not be a pyramid with the apex sustained by the bottom. But it will be an oceanic circle whose centre will be the individual always ready to perish for the village, the latter ready to perish for the circle of villages, till at last the whole becomes one life composed of individuals, never aggressive in their arrogance but ever humble, sharing the majesty of the oceanic circle of which they are integral units.'

Gandhi said that in the India of his conception, every religion would have 'its full and equal place'. As for the economy, 'there would be 'no room for machines that would displace human labour and that would concentrate power in a few hands'. To be sure, 'every machine that helps every individual has a place'.[1]

This was Gandhi's idea of India, a nation built from the bottom up, village loyalties blending into regional loyalties and so on upwards.

II

In three decades of fighting for freedom, Gandhi had two main challengers: two individuals who stood for ideas and interests that did not harmonize with Gandhi's own. One was M.A. Jinnah, whose Muslim League had, by 1946, radically undermined the Congress's claim to represent all of India. Through its growth during the Second World War, and its performance in the elections held after the war had ended, the League compelled the Raj to concede them parity with the Congress, as demonstrated in the Simla conference of 1945 and the Cabinet Mission discussions of 1946.

While Jinnah and the League grew in strength and visibility, Gandhi's other great rival, B.R. Ambedkar, had seen his once rapidly advancing political career receive a series of setbacks. This former member of the viceroy's executive council had seen his Scheduled Caste Federation fare miserably in the elections of 1945–46. When the Cabinet Mission came to India, it met with representatives of the 'Nationalist Scheduled Castes' such as Jagjivan Ram, making it clear that (even in British eyes) Ambedkar was not the sole or even the main leader of the community.

Ambedkar now sought to reach out to the Congress. In July 1946, Ambedkar met Patel through an intermediary (the trade unionist N.M. Joshi), and they discussed a possible alliance between the Congress and his Scheduled Caste Federation. During and after the war, leaders of the Muslim League had sought to make common cause with followers of Ambedkar, based on their mutual dislike of Gandhi and the Congress. Patel knew of (and deplored) these attempts;[2] now, with Ambedkar himself seeking to make peace with the Congress, Patel sensed an opportunity to neutralize one former adversary, while making the Congress's case against the adversary that remained, the Muslim League, more robust.

When Patel wrote to Gandhi about his meeting with the Scheduled Caste leader, he wrote back that 'it was a good thing that you met

Bhimarao Ambedkar'.[3] However, as the discussions progressed, Ambedkar set a condition for an alliance—20 per cent of all seats should be reserved for his party. When Patel wrote to Gandhi about this new development, Gandhi replied that he saw 'a risk' in forging such an alliance, since Ambedkar

> follows one single principle, viz., to adopt any means which will serve his purpose. One has to be very careful indeed when dealing with a man who would become a Christian, Muslim or Sikh and then be reconverted according to his convenience. There is much more I could write in the same strain. To my mind it is all a snare. It is a 'catch'. Besides, it is not necessary for him at present to insist on 20 p[er cent]. If India becomes independent in the real sense— the provinces to some extent are—and if the caste Hindus are true to themselves, all will be well. But if the number of fair-minded persons is small and if power passes into the hands of fanatics, there is bound to be injustice, no matter what agreements you make today. You may come to any understanding you like today—but who are the people who beat up Harijans, murder them, prevent them from using public wells, drive them out of schools and refuse them entry into their homes? They are Congressmen. Aren't they? It is very necessary to have a clear picture of this. I therefore feel that at present we should not insist on an agreement such as you suggest. However, we should stress the capacity of the Congress to do justice. Mine may be a voice in the wilderness. Even so I prefer it that way. Therefore, if we negotiate with Ambedkar out of fear of the League we are likely to lose on both the fronts.[4]

Gandhi did not entirely trust Ambedkar. He had seen him accept the Poona Pact, then reject it; seek to convert his followers to Sikhism, then abandon the idea; strongly ally with the British during the war but now, with independence imminent, seek to come closer to the Congress. Beyond these disagreements on tactics lay a more fundamental divergence of views. Gandhi did not believe in mass conversion, particularly if (as Ambedkar had once proposed) it arose not through any genuine spiritual desire but for purely instrumental purposes. At the same time, while Ambedkar put great faith in state action, Gandhi thought that real change would come only if upper-caste Hindus themselves repented of their past behaviour towards the 'untouchables'.

Patel wrote back, once more making the case for an alliance with Ambedkar. Gandhi replied: 'I have your letter. If you see no risk in it, what is there for me to say? Do by all means settle with [Ambedkar].'[5]

Ambedkar now sent Patel a detailed memorandum, proposing reservation for Scheduled Castes in the public services (as well as in the legislature), state support for them in high school and university, and state funding for the foreign education of their best students. Ambedkar also urged the renewal of the system of separate electorates, since the recent 1946 elections had, in his view, 'proved how the Scheduled Castes can be completely disenfranchised under the existing system'. In his covering letter to Patel, Ambedkar said that 'if you have an open mind I hope to convince you that they [separate electorates] are not so bad as it is generally made out'.

Patel, in reply, said that he had read Ambedkar's memorandum and given 'the most anxious consideration to your proposals'. But, he noted, their 'approach to the whole question' differed, with the Congress aiming at 'the assimilation of the Scheduled Castes into the general Hindu community' while Ambedkar intended 'to provide safeguards which would perpetuate the separation of the Scheduled Castes from the general Hindu community'.

Patel then continued:

Of course, I am always willing to meet you and be convinced of any error of judgment the Congress may have made. No human institution can claim infallibility for itself. I can, however, give you this assurance that the Congress has never wished wilfully to damage the interests of the Scheduled Castes but I must not conceal from you the suspicion with which I and other Congressmen have viewed your activities. Your language has often been highly provocative and inflammatory and you have been reckless in your statements against the Congress and its great leader, Mahatma Gandhi. So far as I am aware, hardly any of the charges hurled by you against the Congress would bear impartial scrutiny.

Patel was here unburdening himself of years of suspicion and anger. That Ambedkar had opposed and vilified the Congress; that Ambedkar served in the viceroy's executive council during the Quit India movement; that Ambedkar had often spoken disparagingly about his Mahatma, Gandhi—all this weighed on Patel's mind. He did, however, end his letter on a conciliatory note: 'If therefore, you can convince me to the contrary, please do come. I am willing to listen and discuss. Naturally the Congress would be glad to enlist your great ability for the promotion of what must be and is common cause between you and the Congress.'

Ambedkar did not reply to Patel for more than a month, doing so only when he was just about to leave for the United Kingdom. His letter started by complaining that the Congress press had represented his approach to Patel 'as an act of surrender'. Then he came to the main point of disagreement, evidently personal rather than political, namely, Patel's veneration of the Mahatma which Ambedkar could not and did not share. So, Ambedkar now wrote:

Your reference to my quarrel with Mr. Gandhi is, to say the least, in my judgment, quite out of place. This is not the first time that you have known that I 'abuse' Mr. Gandhi. Whether you agree or not, I have reasons to be angry with him. I have written a whole book giving my reasons why I am opposed to Mr. Gandhi on the issue of the Scheduled Castes. . . . Many agents have been engaged to refute the allegations contained in my book. Unfortunately for Mr. Gandhi, they have all failed ignominiously. You seem to think that I am the only one who 'abuses' Mr. Gandhi. I know hundreds who do the same. . . . The only difference between them and me is that they 'abuse' Mr. Gandhi privately and praise him publicly. My misfortune is that I have not learnt the art of double-dealing, say one thing in public and quite opposite of it in private. Since you have taken my attack on Mr. Gandhi to heart in a manner which shows that but for the 'abuse' there would have been a settlement, I must say that you think Mr. Gandhi is greater than the country. My view is different. I think the country is greater than the greatest man. You think to be Congressmen and to be nationalists are synonymous. I think a man can be a nationalist without being a

Congressman. If you will forgive me, I will cite my own case. I am
a greater nationalist than any Congressman and if on occasions I
have not been able to present the full front of a nationalist, it is
because men like Mr. Gandhi have been stabbing me in the back
by their opposition to the demand of the Untouchables for political
safeguards.

Ambedkar ended by saying that though Patel had ended his letter by
offering to meet, he was sure 'it can serve no purpose'.[6]

Ambedkar's dislike for Gandhi was intense. In 1946, his Bombay
publishers, Thackers and Co. brought out a book by the Gandhi-
worshipping journalist Krishnalal Shridharani, entitled *The Mahatma
and the World*. Climbing the stairs to his publisher's office, Ambedkar
was outraged to see a poster advertising this book. 'The number of
books that people write on this old man takes my breath away,' he
grumbled, pointing at the display board. Not long afterwards, he met
the journalist Vincent Sheen, and told him that if Americans loved
Gandhi so much, they should import him to the United States so that
Indians would at last be rid of him.[7]

III

Meanwhile, Gandhi's other long-standing rival, M.A. Jinnah, was
making his most daring move yet. After the Cabinet Mission failed,
Jinnah decided to take the case for Pakistan to the streets. A meeting of
the League's leaders on 29 July resolved that 'the Muslims of India will
not rest content with anything less than the immediate establishment
of an independent and full sovereign state of Pakistan'. The 'time has
come for the Muslim nation', it added, 'to resort to direct action in
order to achieve Pakistan and assert their just rights and to vindicate
their honour and to get rid of the present slavery under the British and
contemplated future of Caste Hindu domination'.

The Muslim League, said Jinnah, had never done 'anything
except by constitutional methods and by constitutionalism. But now
we are obliged and forced into this position. This day we bid good-
bye to constitutional methods.' The League had, he said, to change

its methods to combat the 'authority and arms' of the British Raj and the 'mass struggle and non-co-operation of the Congress'. As Jinnah bluntly put it: 'To-day, we have also forged a pistol and are in a position to use it.'[8]

Sixteenth August was designated Direct Action Day. On this day, Muslims were asked to organize processions all over India, shut down shops and schools, and in other ways press the case for Pakistan.

Jinnah had a lifelong faith in constitutional methods. Indeed, he had broken with Gandhi and the Congress in 1920 on precisely this question. He had wanted a continuing dialogue with the British, not a programme of 'non-co-operation' with them. Long comfortable only in the law court and the assembly chamber, he had in recent years become more of a mass leader. Still, the call for 'direct action' was utterly inconsistent with his temperament, and his public career so far.

In abandoning constitutional methods, Jinnah may have been acting in part out of frustration (at the Congress's rejection of the Cabinet Mission's grouping plan). But he was also responding to the signals from his own rank and file. This was the view of Penderel Moon, the ICS man who arguably knew India better than any of his colleagues. In the first week of August 1946, Moon wrote to an English friend that 'extremist Muslims are as crazy, irrational and fanatical as their leaders. The more moderate elements are in a "nobody loves me" mood of self-pity. Fear of being eaten up by the Hindus is becoming a quite widespread obsession.' In a second letter, he added that 'the Muslims are deeply, however irrationally, stirred. . . . They are likely to act desperately and impulsively.'[9]

On 16 August, followers and cadres of the Muslim League took to the streets. Their largest show of strength was in Calcutta, where, with their own party in power, winking at their violations of the law, they had, for a full twenty-four hours, the run of the place.

A large meeting of Muslims had been called in the Calcutta Maidan. On their way to the maidan, Muslim League activists forced shopkeepers to close their shops, and threw burning rags into houses en route. On their way back, drunk with the power that comes from hearing heady speeches, they attacked more homes and shops. The riot spread across the city, with stabbings and murders in localities across north Calcutta, the weapons used including knives, iron rods and fire bombs.

The next day, the Hindus retaliated, led by their own communal organization, the Hindu Mahasabha. 'As people came back home from different parts of the town they brought back tales of maimed women, burnt houses, looted shops and so on. Some of these were later on found to be wrong; but people had become panicky and were eager to believe every atrocity story.' Through the 17th and 18th, the riots intensified and spread, as 'people lost their senses from fright and reacted violently in the hope of self-defence. The police were nowhere, and the only chance of living, they thought, must be through extermination of Muslims—as if that were possible or desirable.'

On the 19th, detachments of the British Indian Army were called in, and slowly the city became calm. A teacher in Calcutta University, walking around the city, saw 'dozens of corpses lying about. They swelled in a day or two, the air became foul, and vultures for a whole week littered the roofs of Calcutta, and feasted on the corpses until they could do no more.' Soon 'relief works sprang up everywhere and have been doing a splendid amount of work. Money, services, clothes, vegetables started coming in profusely, but the sting has remained. There is hardly any centre where you find both Hindu and Muslim refugees. There is a clear-cut division.' As the teacher talked to people, 'numerous cases of Hindus sheltering Muslims and Muslims sheltering Hindus have come to light; but, taken as a whole, the fear and distrust on both sides is intense. People are shifting from one quarter to another; but God knows if that is any solution.'[10]

As details of the violence in Calcutta and elsewhere reached him in Sevagram, Gandhi issued an anguished appeal for peace. In a statement dated 19 August, he noted that Muslim League leaders were 'preaching violence in naked language'. The road to 'Pakistan of whatever hue', he remarked, 'does not lie through senseless violence'. Rather 'what senseless violence does is to prolong the lease of the life of British or foreign rule'.

'Would that,' Gandhi hoped, 'the violence of Calcutta were sterilized and did not become a signal for its spread all over.' He added that 'this depends on the leaders of the Muslim League of course, but the rest will not be free from responsibility. They can retaliate or refrain. Refraining is easy and simple, if there is the will.'[11]

In the last week of August, Gandhi travelled to Delhi, for discussions with the viceroy on the formation of an interim government. Nehru and Gandhi met Wavell on the 28th, with the viceroy asking them to accept the Cabinet Mission's 'grouping' scheme so as to smooth the path for a Congress–League coalition at the Centre.

On 2 September 1946, the members of an interim government were sworn in. Jawaharlal Nehru headed it, with the (interim) designation of vice president. Patel was home minister, Rajaji minister for education, Rajendra Prasad minister for food and agriculture, the Delhi Congressman Asaf Ali railway minister. The Sikhs had sent a representative, Baldev Singh, as defence minister, but the Muslim League had kept away. Gandhi advised the new ministers to 'ever seek to attain communal harmony', and 'resolve never to use British troops'.[12]

With the Muslim League refusing to join the government, and with its leaders (including Jinnah) making incendiary speeches, the subject of religious harmony figured often in Gandhi's prayer meetings. On 7 September, he said: 'I am not a Muslim but I venture to say that Islam does not preach enmity towards anyone. I think I am as much a Christian, a Sikh and a Jain as I am a Hindu. Religion does not teach one to kill one's brother however different his belief.'[13]

In the last week of September, Gandhi met the viceroy at the latter's request. Wavell told him: 'The League must be brought in somehow' (into the interim government). Gandhi answered that the Congress was happy to facilitate this—why not Jinnah meet Nehru and discuss the matter? The viceroy then said that the 'stumbling block' was the inclusion by Congress of Asaf Ali, a Muslim, as a minister, since Jinnah and the League claimed the exclusive right to represent Muslims. Gandhi replied that while he was all for a Congress–League collaboration, the Congress could not disown non-League Muslims who had stayed loyal to them for so long.[14]

In a fresh attempt at a Congress–League compromise, the nawab of Bhopal met Gandhi in Delhi in the first week of October. They then jointly signed a statement, the first part of which represented a significant climbdown on the part of the Congress. This read: 'The

Congress does not challenge and accepts that the Muslim League now is the authoritative representative of an overwhelming majority of the Muslims of India. As such and in accordance with democratic principles they alone have today an unquestionable right to represent the Muslims of India.' Then came a caveat: 'But the Congress cannot agree that any restriction or limitation should be put upon the Congress to choose such representatives as they think proper from amongst the members of the Congress as their representatives.'[15]

This agreement paved the way for the Muslim League to join the interim government. In this new coalition, Congress had six ministers, the League five, with three posts for other parties. Gandhi's party retained Asaf Ali in the Cabinet. On the other side, Jinnah retaliated by nominating a non-Muslim as minister. This was the Scheduled Caste leader from Bengal, Jogendra Nath Mandal.

Since Nehru was now heading the interim government, he gave up the Congress presidency. The veteran nationalist J.B. Kripalani, Gandhi's friend from the days of the Champaran struggle, was chosen to replace Nehru as head of the party.

IV

On 2 October 1946, Gandhi turned seventy-seven. As ever, he received many letters from friends and well-wishers. The Vietnamese nationalist Ho Chi Minh conveyed his 'warmest compliments on your seventy eighth [*sic*] birthday and wish you live twice seventy eight years'. The Burmese nationalist Aung San sent a telegram addressed to 'Mahatma Gandhi Care Pandit Jawaharlal Nehru New Delhi', reading: 'On the occasion of your eightieth [*sic*] birthday I send you on behalf of our people respectful felicitations. May you live long to usher in and enjoy full freedom of India.'

The British Labour leader Stafford Cripps wrote a letter in red ink, wishing Gandhi on his 'double-seven' birthday on behalf of his wife Isobel and himself. Since Gandhi had 'devoted so many years' to the freedom of his people, remarked Cripps, he must be happy that 'at last Jawaharlal, Vallabh[bh]ai, and others are where they ought to be, at the head of Indian Government. A few short steps and the final act will have been completed and then we can all rejoice together in the accomplishment of Indian Freedom.'

The file in the Gandhi Papers containing these letters from the Great Men of History also has a lovely letter from an unknown American, who wrote:

Today at lunch I got the urge to tell you that small towns, like Forty Fort [in Pennsylvania] where I live, all over the world have been made better because of your life.

Perhaps it is not so strange after all that you, Hindu leader, should remind the world and Palestine to adopt the methods of Jesus, our Christ. Jesus lives today and perhaps he speaks through you.

To me it is one of my great blessings that I have lived in the same generation with you.

You feel and know, I am sure, that the world is getting better; and, that we are drawing closer to the people of India and China.

Gandhi's secretary, Pyarelal, surely showed him the telegrams from Ho and Aung San, and the letter from Cripps. One hopes he showed Gandhi the letter from Forty Fort too.[16]

V

While Gandhi was in Delhi, the situation in Bengal was rapidly deteriorating. In Calcutta, the Direct Action Day had started with a show of strength by the Muslim League. But as the rioting spread in what was a Hindu-majority city, Muslims themselves became victims of the mayhem their leaders had unleashed. When the violence finally subsided, hundreds of Hindus had lost their lives, but a greater number of Muslims had perished in the conflagration.

As news of the violence spread through rural Bengal, calls for revenge were heard. These were loudest in Noakhali, a district where Muslims were more than 80 per cent of the population, and which housed many Islamic seminaries, which trained preachers who went on to lead congregations in all parts of Bengal. Hindus were a small minority in Noakhali, but they owned large tracts of land, as well as shops, making them obvious and visible targets.

On 29 August, thousands of Muslims gathered in Noakhali town, calling for 'a revenge of Calcutta'. A local League leader named Ghulam Surwar led a mob through the Hindu localities of the town, looting and torching shops and homes. The violence then spread out into the countryside. Hindu men were made to shout 'Pakistan Zindabad'; Hindu girls were taken away and married to Muslim boys. Many Hindus were forcibly converted to Islam. Those who protested or resisted were killed.[17]

The Muslims of Noakhali were mostly poor peasants and artisans, whose already fragile economic condition had been worsened by the war and the famine. Now, wrote one contemporary observer: 'Their bitterness was skilfully exploited by the propagandists of the Muslim League. The Hindus, specially the zamindars and the merchants, became the target of their virulent attacks. The starving Muslim peasants were asked to kill rich Hindus and loot their property. They were told that they would enjoy untold blessings in Pakistan, but Pakistan could not be established before the extermination of Hindus.'[18]

The news of the bloodbath in East Bengal reached Gandhi in Delhi. In a prayer meeting on 15 October, he wondered aloud 'where his duty lay'. Should he rush to Noakhali, or stay on in the capital? 'God would show him the way.' Meanwhile, he insisted 'that it was the duty of every Hindu not to harbour any thoughts of revenge on Muslims in spite of what they did in Noakhali'. Two days later, he spoke about how, more than the killings, what hurt him 'was the fact that women were being carried away, abducted and converted to Islam'. But there was still 'no inner call' to go to Noakhali. 'When it comes,' he told his co-workers, 'nothing will hold me back.'[19]

Amidst the deepening gloom, there was some good news from Bombay, where the new Congress government had passed a comprehensive law removing social disabilities for the 'untouchables'. They would now have access to all wells, temples, schools, shops, playgrounds, cremation grounds, etc., where caste Hindus had previously denied them entry. Those who prevented them from

exercising these rights would be sentenced to a term in prison or made
to pay a heavy fine.

Gandhi welcomed the new Act, but warned his readers not 'to be
over-sanguine about it. Unfortunately for us, we know that we pass
resolutions by acclamation and allow them to become [a] dead letter.
The greatest vigilance will have to be exercised by the Government
and the reformers in the strict enforcement of the law.'[20]

VI

In Delhi, Gandhi was receiving regular updates from Bengal,
these sent by the Quaker Horace Alexander, then working on a
relief mission among the victims of the Bengal famine. Alexander
had several meetings with the chief minister of the province, H.S.
Suhrawardy of the Muslim League, who was thought to have played
an extremely partisan role during Direct Action Day. The Quaker,
on the other hand, found Suhrawardy, (as he wrote to Gandhi) a
'curiously mixed personality. He can be the most fire-eating and
rabid of communalists, and also the best of peace-makers. I believe he
would welcome a coalition [with the Congress], with a radical policy
of social and economic reform.'[21]

This was written in early September. A month later, after the
reports from Noakhali became more dire, Alexander met Suhrawardy
again. This time he took along his senior Quaker colleague Muriel
Lester, in whose Kingsley Hall settlement Gandhi had stayed in
London back in 1931. They had a long talk with Suhrawardy, and
found him now more amenable to talk of peace. 'My own belief,'
wrote Alexander to Gandhi, 'is that he has sufficient sense now
to realise that the present troubles can do only infinite harm to
Bengal until the leaders of the two communities can get together. I
know enough of Suhrawardy's black record, including even things
he has done within the past few weeks, to realise something of the
feeling of those who are asked to walk into his parlour again. But
he may be in a different mood now. For in the end continuance of
the present horrors can do nothing but harm to the man who is
chief minister.'

Alexander continued:

> The situation in Bengal is so desperate that it can only be cured by
> a heroic remedy. That does not mean ruthless repression. It may
> mean heroic efforts to turn the enemy into a friend. 'Walk cheerfully
> over the world, answering that of God in every man' was the brave
> word of the first Quaker, George Fox. By every man, I take it he
> meant literally every man, for in every man, however he may try to
> hide it, something of God remains. I have seen it very plainly visible
> in Suhrawardy. I hope you and your colleagues will find it there
> too. So I hope you will encourage them boldly to join the peace
> committee. Nothing can be lost by so doing. Much may be gained.
> Is it worth while to try? Surely it is.[22]

This letter is in Gandhi's papers. Although there is no reply in the
Collected Works, the fact that he left Delhi for Bengal soon afterwards
strongly suggests that these British Quakers spurred him to take on
the challenge of bringing peace to Noakhali, and beyond.

Gandhi reached Calcutta on 29 October; the next day, he called
on the governor (no longer R.G. Casey, but an unimaginative trade
unionist named Frederick Burrows with no previous experience
outside England), and the chief minister, H.S. Suhrawardy. Gandhi
hoped to push on to Noakhali, but Suhrawardy asked him to wait till
the situation stabilized. Meanwhile, Gandhi had also developed a bad
cough, and the prominent Calcutta physician and Congressman, Dr
B.C. Roy, advised him not to travel till the cough had cleared up. To
aid his recovery, he was drinking fresh coconut juice, mixed with hot
water and honey.[23]

In Calcutta, Gandhi was shocked by the physical residues of the
communal violence the city had lately witnessed. Thus, 'as one drove
through the deserted streets with garbage heaps, at places banked up
nearly two feet high against the pavements, and entire rows of gutted
shops and burnt-out houses in the side-streets and by-lanes as far as
the eye could reach, one felt overcome with a sinking feeling at the
mass madness that can turn man into less than a brute'.[24]

While he was in Calcutta, Gandhi got news of riots that had
lately broken out in Bihar, where, to avenge the killings of their

co-religionists in Noakhali, Hindus had gone on the rampage against Muslims. This was the Bengal situation in reverse—Hindus killing Muslims with a Congress (or majority Hindu) government in power, as against Muslims killing Hindus with the League in power. 'If half of what I hear is true,' wrote Gandhi to Nehru, 'it means that Bihar has lost all humanity.' He asked Nehru to pass on the letter to the Bihar government so that they could take remedial action.[25]

Gandhi left for eastern Bengal on 6 November. Shortly before he left, he issued a public appeal to the people of Bihar. 'A bad act of one party,' he told the Biharis, 'is no justification for a similar act by the opposing party, more especially when it is rightly proud of its longest and largest political record. . . . And is counter-communalism any answer to the communalism of which Congressmen have accused the Muslim League? Is it Nationalism to seek barbarously to crush the fourteen per cent of the Muslims in Bihar?'

Gandhi said 'though Bihar calls me, I must not interrupt my programme for Noakhali'. He told the Hindus of Bihar that they were 'honour bound to regard the minority Muslims as their brethren requiring protection, equal with the vast majority of Hindus. Let not Bihar, which has done so much to raise the prestige of the Congress, be the first to dig its grave.' If the 'erring Biharis' did not turn over a 'new leaf', he might even consider going on a fast unto death.[26]

Gandhi's first speech in eastern Bengal was in Chandpur, where refugees had demanded that the government post Hindu officers and policemen in the riot-torn districts. Gandhi reminded them that 'Hindu officers, Hindu police and Hindu military have in the past done all these things—looting, arson, abduction, rape'. In another speech, he spoke wistfully of his trip through eastern Bengal with the Ali Brothers, twenty-five years previously, when Hindus and Muslims lived and laboured together, and fought together, non-violently, under the banner of Khilafat and non-cooperation. He himself remained 'a servant of both the Hindus and the Mussalmans'.[27]

While holding out a message of hope, Gandhi was disturbed by what he saw: temples and schools razed to the ground, Hindu homes charred or abandoned, Hindu women missing or abducted, those still with their families too scared to wear the bindi on the forehead or the sindoor in their hair that signified their faith.

Gandhi addressed a meeting every evening. A heartening sign was the large number of Muslims who turned up to hear him speak. A reporter on the spot estimated that 80 per cent of the crowd was from that community. When the time came for namaz, Gandhi cut short his speech so that the faithful could go to the mosque to pray.[28]

Gandhi had come with several colleagues, among them Pyarelal, Sushila Nayar, Satis Chandra Dasgupta and a spirited Punjabi Muslim follower named Bibi Amtus Salam.

These Gandhians were joined by a band of Sikhs, led by Niranjan Singh Gill and Jiwan Singh, both former officers of the Indian National Army. The sturdy Sikhs helped move luggage from village to village, erected temporary shelters, and repaired and drove motor vehicles. The work of social succour, of consoling the victims and helping them rebuild their lives, was in the hands of the Bengali Gandhians and their 'Noakhali Rescue, Relief and Rehabilitation Committee'.[29]

After the first few villages, the attendance at Gandhi's meetings began to decline. Muslims who had previously come in large numbers now chose to stay away. Perhaps the novelty had worn off, or perhaps his message of peace and reconciliation did not resonate. One Muslim woman told Gandhi that the menfolk would attend his meetings only if the Muslim League leaders instructed them to. Gandhi asked the few Muslims who had come to hear him to take his message to the others.[30]

After a week touring the countryside, Gandhi decided that rather than be together as a party, each social worker would be based in a different village, and hold herself or himself hostage for the safety and security of the Hindu minority there. These sevaks would observe non-violence, live on a frugal diet, refrain from bathing in tanks used by villagers for drinking water, etc. Satis Chandra Dasgupta defined their work as follows:

> Ideal: The ideal should be to bring together the two communities
> on the basis of fearlessness. The members of both the communities
> should learn to shed fear of each other and also of the Government.
> They should learn to respect each others' religious sentiments. . . .
> The attainment of freedom in this one matter of religion, may be
> symbolic of the other freedoms.

Work: The Sevak should regard himself as the lowliest servant of the village. He [or she] will rejoice in cleaning night soil, in cleaning tanks, in repairing roads, in keeping public places of worship or education etc in a fit condition. He should strive to attend the sick and be a nurse wherever possible.

He [or she] should be helpful in rehabilitating the villagers and of setting them up in life.[31]

Gandhi himself decided to settle in a village named Srirampur, which, despite its name, had a Muslim majority. In fact, at this time, only one Hindu family remained, the rest having fled or been killed. Gandhi moved into the house of one of the Hindu families that had fled, this sited in the middle of a courtyard, with a coconut grove and a large tank in the compound.

In Srirampur, Gandhi had two companions. One was the anthropologist Nirmal Kumar Bose, who had taken leave of absence from his university in Calcutta to serve as Gandhi's interpreter. Bose also helped Gandhi with his Bengali lessons, reading aloud poems (by Tagore, among others), translating as he went along. Gandhi also practised handwriting; soon he was able to 'write some Bengali words'.[32] The second person with Gandhi in Srirampur was a stenographer from South India named R.P. Parasuram, proficient in typing and in taking dictation.

Gandhi's separation from them upset the possessive ashramites who had come with him to Noakhali, such as Pyarelal and Sushila Nayar. 'Bapu, you are going alone,' a journalist reported them as saying. 'When will we meet you again?'[33]

On 20 November, his first day in the village, Gandhi issued a press statement, where he said: 'I do not propose to leave East Bengal till I am satisfied that mutual trust has been established between the two communities and the two have resumed the even tenor of their life in their villages. Without this there is neither Pakistan nor Hindustan—only slavery awaits India, torn asunder by mutual strife and engrossed in barbarity.'

On the same day, he also wrote a short letter to the inmates of the Sevagram Ashram, saying: 'I am afraid you must give up all hope of my returning early or returning at all to the Ashram.'

Gandhi had not lived without a core of devoted disciples fussing around him for many years now. In Srirampur, he had to shave and massage himself, peel his own oranges and bananas. After his morning bath, he went around the village, speaking to the local Muslims. In the afternoon, he completed his (self-inflicted) quota of spinning, and then addressed a prayer meeting, on occasion amidst the ruins of a charred house. Some days he ventured out into the countryside, meeting people in other hamlets.

Shortly after moving to Srirampur, Gandhi came down with a stomach upset, probably caused by a bitter local vegetable that he had eaten the previous night. On the 23rd, his tour of neighbouring villages was repeatedly interrupted by visits to paddy fields to relieve himself. He felt exhausted, and Nirmal Bose urged him to return to Srirampur. Gandhi refused, since, as he put it, a meeting had been scheduled in the next village, and 'a promise should never be broken'.[34]

Asked how Gandhi was faring without his trusted core of helpers, the stenographer Parasuram said he was managing fine, 'doing his household duties such as arranging his own bed, books, food and even cleaning his things and utensils'. The one problem was 'the noise of jackals, who roamed near about Gandhi's cottage'.[35] Parasuram was probably speaking for himself. Neither howling animals nor rattling trains (nor indeed, closed and stuffy prison cells) had ever interfered with Gandhi's capacity to sleep at night.

Soon the entourage in Srirampur had a new member: Gandhi's grand-niece Manu. Manu had lost her mother early, and was brought up by Kasturba and Gandhi. After Kasturba died, Gandhi became both father and mother to her. Manu was with them in the Aga Khan Palace, and continued to live with and travel with Gandhi after his release. Now she had joined him in Noakhali. Her exact date of birth is unknown, but at this time, February 1947, Manu was probably in her early twenties. In Srirampur, she helped Gandhi with his bath, and prepared his meals, tasks she was accustomed to doing.[36]

From Srirampur, Gandhi made short trips to nearby hamlets, returning to home base in the evening. 'It is my intention,' he wrote to G.D. Birla on 26 November, 'to stay on here so long as the Hindus and Muslims do not start living together as sincere friends. . . . At the moment I have forgotten Delhi, Sevagram, Uruli and Panchgani.'

For many years now, Gandhi had observed his weekly day of silence on Monday. This was now changed to Sunday, as that was the day the weekly bazaar was held in this part of eastern Bengal. Gandhi adjusted his schedule to the local rhythms, staying silent on the day when the villagers had to buy or sell their wares, while holding prayer meetings on Monday and through the rest of the week.

While Gandhi was in Srirampur, newspapermen came from time to time to see and speak with him. When, on 2 December, one journalist asked whether, in a future division of India, he would approve of a migration of peoples to create consolidated Hindu and Muslim provinces, Gandhi called the proposal 'unthinkable and impracticable'. Even here, in Noakhali, his aim was 'to go on foot, where possible and necessary, from village to village and induce the evacuees to return'. In the village and the country of his conception, 'everyone is an Indian, be he a Hindu, a Muslim, or of any other faith'.

To get refugees to return was an arduous task. As Gandhi wrote to Suhrawardy on 3 December: 'In spite of all my efforts exodus continues and very few persons have returned to their villages. They say the guilty parties are still at large . . . that sporadic cases of murder and arson still continue, that abducted women have not all been returned, that forcibly converted persons have not all returned, that burnt houses are not being rebuilt and generally the atmosphere of goodwill is lacking.'

Suhrawardy, stung by these (implicit, and mostly valid) criticisms of his government, wrote back, suggesting that Gandhi's place was not in Bengal but in Bihar, where it was the Muslims who were being hounded and persecuted.[37]

Other Muslim leaders in Bengal were also unhappy with Gandhi's pilgrimage of peace in Noakhali. In the third week of December, a member of Suhrawardy's government named Maulvi Hamiduddin Ahmed launched a savage attack on Gandhi. 'Everyone is aware,' he remarked, 'why Gandhiji has become a "Bengali" and an "inhabitant of Noakhali".' This League leader claimed that while Hindu propagandists had issued 'strange and exaggerated reports', only about a hundred people were killed in Noakhali, and that there was no forcible conversion. On the other hand, in Bihar, 'the manner in which thousands upon thousands of men and women of a particular community were inhumanly done to death, is without a parallel in the history of the world'. And yet, said this leader sneeringly, 'Mr. Gandhi does not wish to remain in Bihar.'

'It was known to everyone,' continued this critic of Gandhi's peace mission, 'that the oppressed community in Noakhali was Hindu and that in Bihar it was Musalman. Would it be wrong for anyone to feel that by riveting the attention of the whole world to Noakhali, Mr Gandhi's purpose is to draw attention away from Bihar?'[38]

Gandhi had ignored attacks as fierce (and as unfair) as this, published in *Dawn* and other League newspapers. But this time, since the accuser was a senior minister in the Bengal government, Gandhi was moved to reply. He had come to Noakhali, he said, merely to 'make my humble contribution to a lasting and heart peace between the two communities'. He had not come to indict the League or its conduct, but to ask it to 'shed its complacency and do good solid work for the sake of itself and India'. He then asked his critic to work with him, cooperatively. 'For I believe that if you and I can produce in Bengal the right atmosphere, the whole of India will follow.'[39]

Gandhi had now been more than a month in Noakhali. His work had begun bearing modest fruit; a news report in mid-December spoke of how 'panicky people have picked up courage and many [Hindu] refugees have returned to their homes today in villages of Srirampur and Kamardiya'.[40]

VII

Having embraced many causes, multiple campaigns, it was Gandhi's fate to be called away by one cause while seeking to focus his attention on another. This had happened to him all through his time in India. The last months of 1946 were no exception. As he was engaged in bringing Hindus and Muslims together in Bengal, he got an urgent request from a friend in London, asking him to bring Dr B.R. Ambedkar and the Congress together.

After his talks with Vallabhbhai Patel in the autumn of 1946 had failed, Ambedkar turned against the Congress once more. He organized a satyagraha movement against upper-caste oppression, but this fizzled out, as the national mood was now entirely focused on independence. In October 1946, Dr Ambedkar visited London, where he met many politicians and public men, but failed to find support for his views. British MPs knew that the Congress would soon be in power in India, and they didn't want to unduly encourage a lifelong opponent of that party.

Among the people Ambedkar met in London was Carl Heath, a prominent member of the 'India Conciliation Group' of British Quakers. Heath was an admirer of Gandhi who, in 1944, had published a short but entirely sympathetic portrait of him, to combat the 'widespread misrepresentation and defamation of a noble and prophetic personality' in the hyper-nationalist British press.[41] Now, two years later, he met Ambedkar, whom he found to be 'very bitter', this bitterness largely directed at Gandhi and the Congress. Speaking 'as a personal friend and in a human sense', Heath asked Gandhi to reach out to Ambedkar. Thus he wrote:

You have done so much for and are always continuing the . . . struggle over the Harijans. That I know is central and essential to you, and a deeply religious matter. But these people can scarcely be expected to wait quietly for political redress until all those who oppress them are converted. In an awakened India men like Ambedkar brought into the Central Government of India call for certain action now, when all the rest are endeavouring to meet each others' claims. It should be possible to accomplish a political justice in this matter without breaking the moral and spiritual ties of the community [to] Hinduism.

I am not presuming to urge what the action needed is. But when Dr Ambedkar returns very shortly to India will you not invite him to come and see you? He will not seek such a meeting himself I know; but I have good reason to believe that he would respond to your call.

The letter was redirected to Gandhi in Srirampur. In his reply (which is not in the *Collected Works*), Gandhi told Heath that Ambedkar

represents a good cause but he is a bad advocate for the simple reason that his passion had made him bitter and made him depart from the straight and narrow path. As I know to my cost, he is a believer in questionable means so long as the end is considered to be good. With him and men like him the end justifies the means. Have you read his book [*What Congress and Gandhi Have Done to the Untouchables*]? It is packed with untruths almost from beginning to end. I am sorry to have to say this of a countryman who has himself been obliged to put up with insults which have embittered men mightier than Dr. Ambedkar. You need not take all I say as gospel truth. I have written this to you in order to give you my [view] that if I do not go out of my way to seek contact with Dr. Ambedkar it is not for want of will or want of regard for you and friends like you but because I know that such seeking will, in my view, harm the cause [rather] than help it. I can say that the question of prestige has never interfered with my doing that I believed was a duty. I have laboured to show that in this case duty points the other way.[42]

Through the 1930s, Gandhi had shown an indulgent, generous attitude towards Ambedkar's criticisms of his work. That generosity had waned in recent years, in part because of Ambedkar's joining the viceroy's executive council when Gandhi and his comrades were in jail, in part because Ambedkar's latest book had dismissed, in what many considered a cavalier fashion, the twenty years (and more) of hard, patient work for the abolition of untouchability that had earned Gandhi much hostility and abuse from orthodox circles, this manifest not only in words but also in physical attacks, as in the failed assassination attempt in Poona in June 1934.

Gandhi would not take the initiative in effecting a reconciliation with Ambedkar—at least not yet. His letter to Carl Heath on this subject showed an unyielding attitude missing in (for example) his correspondence with Muslim League critics such as Maulvi Hamiduddin Ahmed.

VIII

Gandhi's walks, talks and prayers in Noakhali continued. In a meeting in Srirampur on 10 December, he said no religion was 'without its blemishes'. Islam had forgotten its ideals and taken to violence, Christians very often forgot that their master asked them to love their enemies, while, as the status of 'untouchables' showed, 'in Hinduism, too, diabolical wrong has been perpetrated in the name of religion'.[43]

On Christmas Day, Gandhi chose for his prayer meeting an excerpt from the New Testament, which in English read: 'Love is patient, love is kind. It does not envy, it does not boast, it is not proud. It does not dishonour others, it is not self-seeking, it is not easily angered, it keeps no record of wrongs. Love does not delight in evil but rejoices with the truth. It always protects, always trusts, always hopes, always perseveres.' Nirmal Bose translated the passage into Bengali for the audience.

Later the same week, Jawaharlal Nehru and J.B. Kripalani came to see Gandhi in Srirampur. They discussed the Hindu–Muslim question not only in Bengal but also in other parts of India. Gandhi was keen that, in the Congress-ruled state of Bihar, an impartial inquiry committee be set up to report on the cause of the riots there. Nehru then tried, unsuccessfully, to get Gandhi to leave Noakhali and return to Delhi to help with the crucial negotiations on the transfer of power that lay ahead.[44]

On 2 January 1947, Gandhi left Srirampur. He had spent forty-three consecutive nights in the hamlet, the longest period in any place in India apart from his ashrams in Ahmedabad and Sevagram (and the jails in Poona). He now resumed his walking tour, going from one village to another. As he left the village, 'one Muslim elderman of Srirampur stopped him and presented him four oranges and requested [him to] come again in their midst'.[45]

At his first stop, Chandpur, Gandhi spoke about how, rather than pit one religion against another, the people of Bengal should work on ridding their homes of dirt and disease, on increasing the productivity of their lands, and thus 'convert their villages into cleaner abodes of peace and prosperity'. In another village, Karpara, he reminded Hindus and Muslims that both 'are nourished by the same corn and live under the same sky, quench their thirst by the same water, in [natural] calamities that overtake the country are afflicted in the same way, irrespective of their religious beliefs'.[46]

GANDHI

Gandhi spent the night wherever possible in a Muslim home. One meeting had 'a large gathering of Muslims'; in another, 'he got a grand ovation by a large number of Muslims'. Both Hindus and Muslims had begun to warm to him. As one enthusiastic reporter wrote, the villagers of Noakhali 'have begun to wonder as to the fire Gandhiji's life is made of. . . . [M]en, women and children, Muslims and Hindus, come out of their huts and look at him. An old man of 76 with a bamboo stick marches in brisk pace and in his way whoever comes [he] greets always [with] an immediate smiling response.'[47]

In the village of Bhatialpara, a Hindu family who had fled during the riots asked Gandhi to reinstall their family deity in the home they had returned to. Gandhi agreed, thus performing the duties of a priest for the first time in his life. As he came out of the shrine, 'three influential Muslims greeted him and said: "Now that you have installed the image of the family deity here, we will stand surely for its protection." Mr. Gandhi replied that it was just what was expected of them.'[48]

On 20 January, Gandhi reached the village of Sirandi. His disciple Amtus Salam was based here. In the last week of December, after three ceremonial swords used in Hindu prayers were stolen, Amtus Salam went on a fast. She said she would not eat until the swords were returned.

Two weeks into her fast, Amtus Salam was struck by a high fever. She had a bad cough, bringing up large quantities of sputum. She was now extremely weak.[49]

A local police inspector was called in to persuade the Gandhian to break her fast. He convened a joint meeting of Hindus and Muslims, which was followed by the recovery of two of the stolen swords, given back by two young Muslims. Amtus Salam said she would break her fast only when the third sword too was recovered, 'whereupon she was reported to have been abused in filthy language by one Muslim'. The search recommenced. The suspicion fell on a man called Kasem, who had, however, absconded from the area and could not be traced.[50]

When Gandhi reached the village of Shirandi, Amtus Salam had been fasting for twenty-five days. Her fever and cough remained, and she found it hard even to drink water. But, as the doctor at her side (Sushila Nayar) noted, she was 'at peace and cheerful', had 'completely resigned herself to God', and insisted on the 'Koran and Gita being read to her daily'.[51]

Gandhi sought to succeed where the policeman had failed. He called a meeting of the residents of four villages in the neighbourhood (Shanktola, Shirandi, Rajarampur and Madhyapara), and drafted a pledge which, once it was translated into Bengali, he got them all to sign.

The pledge ran as follows:

> With God as witness, we solemnly declare that we bear no antagonism towards the Hindus or members of any other community. To each one, to whatever faith he might belong, his religion is as dear as Islam is to us. There can, therefore, be no question of interference by anybody in the observance of the religious practices of others. We understand that Bibi Amtussalaam's object is the establishment of Hindu–Muslim unity. The object is gained by the signing of this pledge. We wish, therefore, that she should give up her fast.

Gandhi took the signed pledge to Amtus Salam, and persuaded her to break her fast, which she did, by accepting a glass of orange juice from him.[52]

Gandhi's colleagues in the Congress were again urging him to come out of Noakhali. The ministers in the interim government wished to consult him; and they could scarcely make regular trips to the deepest corners of East Bengal. In early February, Abul Kalam Azad wrote beseechingly to Gandhi, asking him to at least move his base to Calcutta 'so that we may have the privilege of coming and seeing you and seeking your valuable advice on important questions. We have for years become accustomed to act on your advice that it has now become difficult for us to take any decision without your guidance. Jawahar[lal] is also feeling the same thing every moment. He also is anxious that there may be some way to be near you as early as possible. I hope you will give your sympathetic consideration to my appeal.'[53]

Gandhi heard the appeal, but rejected it. The ministers would have to fend for themselves. Noakhali needed him more than they did. In early February, he was joined by Phillips Talbot, an American journalist based in India. Talbot's friends in Delhi, both Indian and British, saw 'the aging leader's absence from today's political arena as a demonstration of weakness and caprice'. One official told him Gandhi was 'dotty' not to be in Delhi when the crucial transfer of power talks were taking place. Meanwhile, the Muslim League newspaper, *Dawn*, was demanding that their chief minister in Bengal, Suhrawardy, expel Gandhi from the province.

Talbot went to Noakhali in early February 1947. He followed the Mahatma around from village to village, writing that 'the Gandhi march is an astonishing sight'. It began just before dawn, with Gandhi setting off on the road, accompanied by a party of about a dozen aides, among them a 'Sikh attendant who fawns as much as Gandhi permits'. Then, as the sun began to climb, peasants from hamlets on the way came along, 'swelling the crowds as the snows swell India's rivers in spring'. They joined in the singing of hymns of prayer and of peace. The peasants pressed in on Gandhi, men and women, young and old, and many children too. 'Here, if I ever saw one,' wrote the American journalist, 'is a pilgrimage. Here is the Indian and the world's—idea of sainthood: a little old man who has renounced personal possessions, walking with bare feet on the cold earth in search of a great human ideal.'[54]

CHAPTER THIRTY-FIVE

The Strangest Experiment

I

When Gandhi went to Noakhali, he was closer to eighty than to seventy. The terrain in deltaic East Bengal was not exactly conducive to a walking tour; badly maintained village roads intersected by rivulets that one crossed over on a string of bamboo poles masquerading as a bridge. Sometimes, Gandhi walked from place to place; at other times, he took a country boat, which ferried him through canals green with water hyacinth. The huts in the villages were more modest than even in Sevagram; and there were many more flies and mosquitoes, some carrying malaria. To walk through these parts so recently soaked in blood was an act of heroism, or, as the visiting American journalist had it, of saintliness.

But recall Mahadev Desai: 'To live with a saint in heaven is bliss and glory / To live with a saint on earth is a different story.' In the midst of this heroic, saintly pilgrimage for peace, Gandhi was conducting the strangest of his experiments with (as he had it) 'truth'. The goal of the experiment was his old, continuing, obsession with brahmacharya—the instrument, his grand-niece Manu.

Sometime in late December 1946, Gandhi asked Manu to join him in the bed he slept in. He was seeking to test, or perhaps further test, his conquest of sexual desire. Somehow, the idea had entered his mind that the rise of religious violence was connected to his own failure to become a perfect brahmachari. The connection was a leap of faith, an abdication of reason, and perhaps also an expression of egotism. He had come round to the view that the violence around him was in part a product or consequence of the imperfections within him.

When Gandhi commenced his experiments with Manu, his Bengali interpreter Nirmal Kumar Bose objected. Bose was a man (and scholar) of conspicuous independence of mind. Although he admired Gandhi and had compiled an important anthology of his writings, he found this latest experiment both puzzling and indefensible. He urged Gandhi to abandon it, but without success.[1]

The other person in the entourage, the stenographer Parasuram, was also unhappy with the experiment. He expressed his anguish in a long letter, where he asked why Gandhi could not practise celibacy without having to prove it in such a public manner. Thus Parasuram remarked:

> Apart from the question of any effect on you what about the effect on girls. They might imagine that instead of an old man there is a young and handsome man lying nearby. You know how in India girls marry themselves to stone images of Krishna and are content by visualising that Krishna is their real husband.
>
> Leave this also. Let there be no effect on the other party or on you. Even then the whole thing is considered wrong by the world. I do not like it. Nirmal Babu does not. Sucheta ben [Sucheta Kripalani, one of Gandhi's educated women disciples] does not like it and said 'However great he may be, he cannot do such things. What is this?' You must admit that there is something in our objection. You cannot waive it aside.

Parasuram continued:

> As far as Manu is concerned I must say she is a good girl. She won't become neurotic. But I must say the thing is bad. Why should you do it. Your brahmacharya should be like of [the legendary *sanyasi*] Suka. He did not experiment. He did not boast of it. Yet he was

a perfect brahmachari. The Apsaras bathing in the water without clothes did not feel shame when he passed by. Yet they felt shame and put their clothes on when Vyasa his father passed by in search of his son. Your brahmacharya should be like that of Suka. It should be felt by other people without your effort.

Parasuram had joined Gandhi hoping to serve him until the end of his life. He knew, as he told Gandhi, that 'the good things you have done are so innumerable. You have taken us so far along the path of freedom and independence. You have shaken the Hindu's concept of untouchability etc. which even slavery under 1000 years of Muslim rule did not do.' But now, unless Gandhi discontinued the practice of sharing a bed with Manu, he would have to leave. Gandhi refused to abandon the experiment, so Parasuram left Srirampur and made his way back to South India.[2]

Some of Gandhi's oldest disciples were also opposed to his sharing a bed with Manu. These dissenters included Narhari Parikh, who had joined Gandhi as far back as 1917. The criticisms of those close to him prompted a remarkable letter written by Gandhi to Satish Chandra Mukerji, a patriot who was one of the pioneers of the national education movement in Bengal. Mukerji was several years older than Gandhi; and, perhaps more significantly, had renounced worldly pursuits to become a sanyasi, taking renunciation so far as to discard his clothes altogether (earning him the affectionate appellation, 'Nanga Baba', or naked saint). Gandhi and he recently had an exchange on the meaning and purpose of *Ramanama*, the repeated uttering of the name of Rama, a practice favoured by both men. Now, writing to Mukerji on 1 February, Gandhi said:

I put before you a poser. A young girl (19) who is in the place of granddaughter to me by relation shares the same bed with me, not for any animal satisfaction but for (to me) valid moral reasons. She claims to be free from the passion that a girl of her age generally has and I claim to be a practised brahmachari. Do you see anything bad or unjustifiable in this juxtaposition? I ask the question because some of my intimate associates hold it to be wholly unjustifiable and even a breach of brahmacharya. I hold a totally opposite view. As you are an experienced man and as I have regard for your opinion, I put the question. You may take your own time to answer the question. You are in no way bound to answer it if you don't wish to.[3]

It is not known whether Mukerji answered this 'poser'. But we do know that, following the criticisms of Bose, Parikh, Sucheta Kripalani and Parasuram, Gandhi himself was conflicted about his experiment. The day he wrote to Mukerji, he was reported in a speech as having 'referred to "small-talks, whispers and innuendos" going round of which he had become aware. He was already in the midst of so much suspicion and distrust, he told the gathering, that he did not want his most innocent acts to be misunderstood and misrepresented. He had his granddaughter with him. She shared the same bed with him. The Prophet [Muhammad] had discounted eunuchs who became such by an operation. But he welcomed eunuchs made such through prayer by God. His was that aspiration. It was in the spirit of God's eunuch that he had approached what he considered was his duty. It was an integral part of the yajna he was performing and he invited them to bless the effort. He knew that his action had excited criticism even among his friends. But a duty could not be shirked even for the sake of the most intimate friends.'[4]

A week later, Gandhi wrote to his long-time disciple Vinoba Bhave, a man he valued highly for his scriptural learning, and for being a more thoroughgoing ascetic than himself. Bhave had never married, never had a relationship with a woman. Even in matters of diet, clothing and transport, he was far more abstemious than his master. Gandhi now told Bhave that 'the friends in our circle have been very much upset because of Manu's sleeping with me'. These friends included Narhari Parikh, who had been with Gandhi as long as Bhave, and K.G. Mashruwala and Swami Anand, who had also been in the ashram for decades. But these criticisms notwithstanding, Gandhi said 'my own mind, however, is becoming firmer than ever, for it has been my belief for a long time that that alone is true *brahmacharya* which requires no hedges'.

Should his grand-niece Manu, Gandhi asked Bhave, stop sleeping in his bed 'out of deference to custom or to please co-workers'? If she did stop, would Gandhi 'not be a hypocrite of the type described in chapter III [of the *Gita*]? If I do not appear to people exactly as I am within, wouldn't that be a blot on my non-violence?' Gandhi asked Bhave, as a man more learned than him in these spiritual matters, to let him have his view on them.

Bhave replied two weeks later. 'For the sake of achieving brahmacharya,' he remarked, the experiment conducted by Gandhi was irrelevant. 'Even if we do this for the sake of consolation,' he continued, 'sleeping naked is unnecessary. A father never does it with his daughter even innocently.'

In Vinoba's view, to be self-conscious about the difference between man and woman was contrary to brahmacharya. As he put it: 'If I don't think of sleeping with a man, what is the purpose of sleeping with a woman?' If Gandhi had indeed become a proper or true brahmachari, if he had indeed achieved that 'passionless state', he wouldn't need to sleep with a woman to confirm or prove it.[5]

J.B. Kripalani was also not approving of Gandhi's latest experiments. And Vallabhbhai Patel was 'very angry' with him.[6] Patel's anger was political rather than personal. He worried that word of these experiments would get out, and Jinnah and the Muslim League, not to speak of the viceroy and the British, would use it to diminish or demean Gandhi's reputation.

But Gandhi stubbornly persisted. Why? The answer may lie in a conversation he had with A.V. Thakkar in the last week of February. Thakkar was the same age as Gandhi, and had a long record as a social worker. Known as 'Bapa' (Father), he was a greatly respected if also occasionally forbidding figure in nationalist circles. Now, when Thakkar came to see him in Noakhali, Gandhi told him the spread of violence in India had called into question his own lifelong practice of, and faith in, ahimsa. 'Ever since my coming to Noakhali,' said Gandhi to his visitor, 'I have been asking myself the question, "What is it that is choking the action of my ahimsa? Why does not the spell work? May it not be because I have temporized in the question of *brahmacharya*?"'

Thakkar reassured him that his ahimsa had not failed. 'Just think,' he remarked, 'what would have been the fate of Noakhali if you had not come.' Then he added: 'The world does not think of *brahmacharya* as you do.'

Gandhi was unpersuaded. Even if his experiments led to his being 'debunked' by 'millions', he would carry on. For, as he put it, 'on the lonely way to God on which I have set out, I need no earthly companion'.[7]

To understand this, the strangest of Gandhi's 'experiments with truth', one needs to look beyond rationalist or instrumental explanations of why men behave as they do. For some forty years now, Gandhi had been obsessed by brahmacharya. Both his early mentors, the Jain thinker Raychandbhai and the Russian sage Tolstoy, considered conquest of sexual desire a crucial step towards living a more spiritually fulfilled, and socially worthy, life. Now, at the end of his own life, with his dream of a united and peaceable India in ruins, Gandhi was attributing the imperfections of society to the imperfections of this society's most influential leader, namely, himself.

But there may have been another reason for Gandhi's strange, bizarre, perhaps ultimately inexplicable, experiments. This is alluded to in a letter not available in the *Collected Works*, and so far as I know not seen by previous scholars or biographers of Gandhi.

While the Indian press had stayed scrupulously silent on Gandhi's latest experiments, a Reuters report had alluded indirectly to them. This was read by Agatha Harrison in London, who wrote to Horace Alexander, then in Bengal, for an explanation. Alexander provided this in one very long paragraph, reproduced below:

> When I was with him in East Bengal, during one of our talks, he said: 'If that is all on the subject (I forget which item on my agenda it was) then there is something I want to talk to you about on which I would like to have your opinion'. He then proceeded to tell me about the girl who was with him, how she had come to Sevagram, and how, after some time, there had been talk of her being in love with Pyarelal; how she had gone away, but had protested that she was totally innocent of any sexual feeling in connection with anyone; how she had felt it necessary to test her sincerity, and had asked her if she was prepared to undergo the severest test, with him. She had said 'Yes' and that her feelings towards him were as to her Mother (note the sex). He felt that it was necessary both for him and for her

to undergo this test, but if for one moment he felt himself failing in it, he would stop it at once and admit his failure. He went on to tell me of certain cases he had known of where under acute difficulties of accommodation a woman of undoubted purity had been forced to share a bed with a man. And he added that he thought it would be a great thing for mankind to have it demonstrated that men and women could so purify themselves in mind and spirit that they could share a bed without either being put to shame. Then we had to go to prayer-time, and I was left to think about it during the night. Next morning I told him that in principle I saw nothing wrong in what he was doing, but I could not see the absolute necessity of it: that one of my mottoes was 'Moderation in all things' and that the character of [the fifth-century Syrian ascetic] St. Simeon Stylites had never appealed to me. He said he agreed about 'Moderation in all things' and about St. Simon (of whose private character he had evidently read more than I had). But he thought I missed the point. The necessity of it all arose from the need to test the girl, and her claim to be pure from all sexual feeling. It was true that I had thought he was justifying it as a step he had to take, and I had said I thought it was a pity for him to undertake this 'experiment with truth', which was bound to cause misunderstanding, just when he was asking everyone to give undivided thought to the communal problem. He now made it quite clear that the benefits for the world would be secondary, and that it was for her sake that he was thus impelled to 'sanctify himself'. This, to my mind, put a very different complexion onto the whole affair. Of the paramount necessity of such a ruthless testing of her I still could not judge. But, as I had already said, I saw nothing inherently wrong in what he was doing, provided the circumstances made it necessary. In this case, clearly the circumstances were subjective, not objective. The girl was present, doing chores, most of the time we were talking, and she knew he was discussing it with me. Her English is not good, but she would understand most of what we said. Two other points. One reason why he opened up on it was that Patel had written strongly protesting at his action (whether on principle, or in relation to the need for concentrating his energies on other issues, I do not know). Also, MKG pointed out that all the pressmen and others with him knew that only one bed was made up each night, and he regarded it as a remarkable token of their loyalty that none had written it up for the press or made any protest or raised the issue with him. Well, I hope that covers it. Perhaps it is just as well that there has been occasion to put this on record, as it might lead to all sorts of foolish argument in the future. You will realise that I felt acutely that he was treating me as if I were a ghost of CFA[ndrews], and I also realised that my reply, if I was to be true to him and to the memory of CFA, must be my reply, not what I surmised CFA's might have been.[8]

This letter of Alexander provides an altogether new perspective. We do know, from other sources, that Pyarelal was indeed deeply attracted to Manu Gandhi, and may even have proposed marriage to her. This was not reciprocated; besides, as an ashramite from a very early age, Manu herself had been schooled (dare we say, indoctrinated?) in the virtue and necessity of conquering sexual desire. While they were in Srirampur, Nirmal Bose reported to Gandhi that Manu had told him that 'she had been steadily losing respect for P[yarelal] because the latter had been pursuing her in spite of clear rejection, and how he had even talked of suicide to her on a former occasion. It was also a surprise to me to learn how his sister [Sushila Nayar] had been pleading and pressing her to accept the love of her brother even after she knew her mind.'[9]

So, contrary to what has become the received wisdom on this subject, there may have been, as it were, two sides to the story. Both Gandhi and Manu may have wanted to go through this experiment, or ordeal. To be sure, there was a certain amount of imposition—from his side. It was Gandhi who felt it was necessary 'both for him and for her to undergo this test', Gandhi who wanted to 'have it demonstrated that men and women could so purify themselves in mind and spirit that they could share a bed without either being put to shame'.

II

Gandhi saw his experiments as untainted because of his special relationship with the young girl with whom he shared his bed. Manu had lost her mother early, and Kasturba and Gandhi had come to be her foster parents. After Ba's death (Manu was at her side then), Gandhi became both father and mother to her.

While Manu was with Gandhi in eastern Bengal, she maintained a daily diary, in Gujarati. This was published many years later in English translation, and possibly with some redactions. Notwithstanding the editing and excision it may have gone through, it remains the sole account of the experiment as seen from the perspective of its lesser-known participant. The published diary has many references to Gandhi's obsession with brahmacharya, along with a few remarks that may (or may not) be construed as coded references to the experiments they were to do together, albeit on his instructions.[10]

When asked by Gandhi to join her in Noakhali, Manu was in Udaipur. She reached Srirampur on 19 December 1946, accompanied by her father. Gandhi told him: 'She will be put to a very severe test by the situation. I consider this Hindu–Muslim unity problem an altar for sacrifice. Not a trace of impurity can pass muster here. If there is even a speck of it in Manu, she will fail and go to pieces. Let's all be clear on this point. She can return now. Better to do so now than with shame and dishonour afterwards.'

From this it does appear that Gandhi was asking the father for permission for his daughter to take part in this strange (if to his eyes, necessary) experiment. Before he could reply, Manu did. 'I will,' she said to Gandhi, 'willingly suffer to the last all my trials and troubles. I have the fullest faith and trust in you. And now, the more terrible and darker the picture you draw of Noakhali, the more is my mind steeled to stay on here.' To this Manu's father added: 'Now that she has decided to stay here, you may keep her with you as long as you like. Why should I worry over her when she is with you?'

Shortly after joining Gandhi, Manu asked him to give her informal lessons on the Gita, which she had studied when at the Aga Khan Palace but stopped thereafter. Gandhi commenced doing so on 22 December, the monthly anniversary of Kasturba's death, to whom Manu had been devoted. The next day, Gandhi told Manu: 'You know this is a holy sacrifice; and our old Puranic sacrifices demand perfect purity on the part of the performers. Satanic urges in man such as lust, anger, infatuation, etc. have to be totally overcome.'

Apart from sharing a bed in this experiment to prove each other's conquest of lust, Manu's duties included preparing Gandhi's meals, accompanying him on walks and boat rides through the ravaged countryside, and massaging his tired legs at day's end. He also dictated letters to her.

One morning, some three weeks after Manu joined him, Gandhi launched into a reverie about how while 'nowadays marriage panders mainly to lust', it was meant to be about companionship and mutual understanding. He told Manu that Kasturba and he had learnt to practise a brahmacharya that was 'entirely passionless'. He praised his late wife for her participation in that experiment, and for her other services to him, saying that 'it is Ba who really deserves the credit for the title of Mahatma which the people have chosen to confer upon me'.

As recorded in Manu's diary, Gandhi regularly returned to the importance of brahmacharya in his conversations with her. There were some men, he told his grand-niece, who did not touch women for fear it would arouse them. That was a brahmacharya born out of fear, not courage. For, how could a man's 'passion be aroused by a woman's touch when he considers all women as his mothers, sisters, or daughters!' The true brahmachari, claimed Gandhi, would 'remain passionless' even when faced with 'the most beautiful damsel on earth'.

The conversations reported by Manu show Gandhi to have a distinct aversion to women seeking to make themselves attractive to men. He deplored modern hairstyles, and modern clothes even more. 'What a pity,' he told Manu, 'that the modern girl attaches greater importance to following the code of fashion than to the protection of her health and strength!'

When it came to women's clothing, Gandhi was opposed to modern fashion, but also to archaic custom. When a Muslim at a prayer meeting asked whether the 'moral beauty' of women would 'be better preserved if the custom of the veil for them is strictly enforced', Gandhi answered that a 'woman who throws a veil about her face for mere show and at the same time looks at another person with lustful eyes from behind the purdah, is simply shaming chastity'. Gandhi opposed the veil because 'it harms women's health; they can't get sufficient air and light and they remain disease-ridden'. In any case, he argued, if 'the original object behind the purdah system was self-restraint', then 'that woman alone observes it in the right spirit, who keeps the invisible purdah of self-control'.

Manu was a grand-niece who was also a devotee, and an especially starry-eyed one at that. When Gandhi cut his soles walking and she had to clean his wounds, she burst into tears. 'I filled the cuts with ghee,' she wrote later in her diary: 'There is a specially deep cut at the joint below the great toe. What a difficult ordeal Bapuji has chosen to go through at this age! How very sad must the plight of Indian people be, if they cannot understand this great man! Or could it be that such is the fate destined by God for exceptionally noble men? It was only because Ramachandraji voluntarily suffered for 14 long years the torments of a secluded and dangerous life in fearful jungles, that he is worshipped as a god today.'

The diary of Manu Gandhi's Noakhali travels is entitled *The Lonely Pilgrim*. Another short book that she wrote about Gandhi is called *Bapu, My Mother*. Odd though it may seem in light of the experiment they performed together, Gandhi did see himself as stepping into his late wife's shoes as the adoptive mother of a girl who had lost her own mother when very young. After one of his long talks with—or long lectures to—her, Gandhi told Manu: 'I am simply discharging my duty as your mother. I am feeding you with what my mind is filled with.'

A few days later, after Gandhi expressed concern at her having to carry a large bucket of water, Manu herself noted in her diary: 'Bapu's conversation was filled with affection greater than any mother could feel. What a deep loving insight into my needs! And that in the midst of all his worries! . . . Which male shows motherly care and love as he does?' Then she added: 'And oh, joy! I am actually having that experience! It is I who am that beloved child of Mother Bapu! I am immensely happy at my rare good fortune.'

The ashramites and other close disciples called Gandhi 'Bapu', Father. 'Mother Bapu' in the original Gujarati must have been 'Ma Bapu', or, put in plain English, 'Mother Father'. This curious, indeed unique, appellation shows that at least in the eyes of Manu, Gandhi had transcended not just sexual desire but also the boundaries of gender. The Father of the Nation was also, and at the same time, the Mother of this young woman.

III

In the last week of January 1947, the INA officer working with Gandhi, Niranjan Singh Gill, met H.S. Suhrawardy in Calcutta. When he sought to brief him on the situation in East Bengal, the chief minister said he 'would doubt his bona fides until he [Gandhi] with his men worked in Bihar just as assiduously as in Noakhali'. When Gill reported this to Gandhi, Gandhi took the chastisement to heart, and sent the Sikh to Bihar for a tour of inspection and analysis. He asked Gill to meet leaders of all parties in Bihar, study the condition of the (mostly Muslim) refugees, and 'prepare a fairly exhaustive report'.

Niranjan Singh Gill toured Bihar, and on his return, 'strongly recommended' that Gandhi go there, since the situation was far graver than he had previously thought it to be. Gandhi wrote to Nehru, asking him to pass on Gill's report to the Bihar government, run by the Congress, on whom it reflected rather badly. He thought he might indeed now have to go to Bihar himself.[11]

Just as the rioters in Noakhali had sought to avenge Calcutta, the rioters in Bihar sought to avenge Noakhali. In the last week of October 1946, Patna was plastered with handbills asking Hindus not to light lamps that year at Diwali, to mourn the attacks on their co-religionists in East Bengal. This was followed by hartals and processions, which culminated in attacks on Muslims in Patna and in the surrounding countryside.[12]

Patna was followed by Gaya and Bhagalpur, where too, large meetings of Hindus were held to protest against the killings in Noakhali, these sparking further attacks on Muslims. As one report had it: 'The Police appear to have been flabbergasted by the extent of the trouble at most places . . .' They remained flabbergasted—and flat-footed—for weeks on end, unable or unwilling to save the minorities from the mobs. Close to four thousand Muslims were killed in the riots, while some 1,20,000 Muslims lost their homes. About half of them fled to Bengal, where they felt more secure.[13]

In early March 1947, Gandhi decided he must study the situation in Bihar at first-hand. There was 'consternation among the Hindus' in Noakhali when they heard he was to leave them. He had brought some kind of peace; now, in his absence, they feared a fresh round of attacks. Gandhi told Suhrawardy that he hoped 'the fear will prove groundless and that you will do all you can to allay the fear'.[14]

The last village where Gandhi stayed in Noakhali was named Haimchar. Before he left the hamlet, and the district, he was visited by the popular and charismatic Bengali politician, A.K. Fazlul Huq. Back in the 1920s, Fazlul Huq had been a Congressman, as well as a member of the Muslim League, a dual affiliation not uncommon at the time. Later, he formed his own Krishak Praja Party, becoming prime minister of Bengal between 1937 and 1943. For much of this period, he was in alliance with the Muslim League; he had even been chosen by Jinnah to move the 'Pakistan Resolution' in Lahore in March 1940.

Huq later broke with the Muslim League (and with Jinnah). Huq thought Jinnah did not adequately recognize the place and importance of Bengali Muslims, seeking only to consolidate his position among the Muslims of North and West India.[15] The elections of 1946 brought a League government to power in Bengal, and Huq's rival, Suhrawardy, became chief minister. Out of power, Huq continued to command a large following in Bengal.

Fazlul Huq came to meet Gandhi in Haimchar on 2 March. Huq's next stop was the town of Mymensingh, where he spoke to the local bar association. After characterizing Gandhi's work in East Bengal as 'really praiseworthy', Huq 'announced his intention to spend the rest of his life in preaching goodwill among Hindus and Muslims just as Mr. Gandhi was doing'. This, he added, 'would make Bengal really happy and prosperous'.[16]

That the mover of the Pakistan Resolution was now speaking of how Hindus and Muslims could and must live together represented a major change of heart. Or perhaps of tactics, for one does not know how much Huq was moved by Gandhi's mission, how much by his own political compulsions. Even so, that Fazlul Huq now spoke as he did counted as a moral triumph for Gandhi.

IV

Gandhi reached Bihar's capital, Patna, on 5 March. He met government ministers, and also Muslim refugees. In a speech the same day, he said, 'Bihar has sullied the fair name of India.' He felt embarrassed, or even ashamed, of his party as well as his country, for 'any sin committed by India comes to the door of the Congress'. This assertion was at once problematic and admirable; an increasing number of Indians no longer felt that the Congress represented them, yet for Gandhi the emotional equation, Congress=India, still held, so in his eyes, crimes committed by one set of Indians on another had still to be redeemed by his party alone.

Gandhi spent three weeks in Bihar. Some days, he stayed in Patna as a stream of Muslim refugees came to him and narrated their woes; on other days, he travelled through the countryside to see the devastation the riots had left in their wake. He saw Muslim homes burnt, mosques vandalized, the looms of Muslim weavers destroyed. His speeches at prayer meetings mixed sorrow with anger. When he had first heard of the loot and murder, he remarked, 'I thought the version was greatly exaggerated. I did not believe that man could be so depraved or that Biharis could stoop so low. But today I witnessed it with my own eyes. When Muslims fled you either looted their property or destroyed it. They had not harmed you in any way.'

Gandhi conceded 'that the Muslims behaved very viciously in Calcutta and Noakhali. But how can that be avenged in Bihar?' Amidst the carnage, he took solace in the residents of a village named Bir, who had formed a peace committee and ensured that 'Hindus and Muslims lived like brothers despite the prevailing lawlessness'. Gandhi asked Hindus in Bihar to rebuild Muslim homes, clean up village streets and sink new wells, for then, and then only, would the Muslims trust them enough to return from the camps.[17]

Gandhi had hesitated for a long time in coming to Bihar, thinking he was needed more in Noakhali. But, he now told Satis Chandra Dasgupta, 'I see how vitally necessary it was for me to come.'[18] He had to rebuke the Hindus here as he had rebuked the Muslims there, to seek security for the Muslims here as he had done for the Hindus there. For, as he told a meeting in the town of Jehanabad, 'to me the sins of the Noakhali Muslims and the Bihar Hindus are of the same magnitude and equally condemnable'.[19]

V

Gandhi's grand-niece, Manu, was also with him in Bihar. But his experiments in the practice of brahmacharya had ceased. As he wrote to Vinoba Bhave: 'Nowadays Manu does not sleep in my bed. It is her own wish and is due to a pathetic letter from [Thakkar] Bapa.'[20]

The experiment had been stalled, but Gandhi was not sure it was misplaced in the first place. Writing to his disciple Amrit Kaur, he said that despite the criticisms of some of his closest co-workers,

> you will have no difficulty in accepting at its face value my statement that not one of our company knows the full value and implications of brahmacharya, and that among these ignoramuses I am the least ignorant and the most experienced. With one solitary exception I have never looked upon a woman with a lustful eye. I have touched perhaps thousands upon thousands. But my touch has never carried the meaning of lustfulness. I have lain with some naked, never with the intention of having any lustful satisfaction. My touch has been for our mutual uplift. I would like those who have felt otherwise, if there are any, truly to testify against me. Even the one solitary instance referred to by me was never with the intention of despoiling her. Nevertheless my confession stands that in that case my touch had lustfulness about it. I was carried away in spite of myself and but for God's intervention I might have become a wreck.

The 'solitary exception', of course, was Saraladevi Chaudhurani, with whom Gandhi's relations were, for a brief, intense period, shot through with (in the end unconsummated) passion.

Gandhi's letter to Amrit Kaur continued:

> My meaning of brahmacharya is this:
> One who never has any lustful intention, who by constant attendance upon God has become proof against conscious or

unconscious emissions, who is capable of lying naked with naked women, however beautiful they may be, without being in any manner whatsoever sexually excited. Such a person should be incapable of lying, incapable of intending or doing harm to a single man or woman in the whole world, is free from anger and malice and detached in the sense of the Bhagavadgita. Such a person is a full brahmachari. Brahmachari literally means a person who is making daily and steady progress towards God and whose every act is done in pursuance of that end and no other.[21]

Let us give the last word to the anthropologist Nirmal Kumar Bose, an admirer (not disciple), a scholar (not ideologue), who was with the great man when he conducted the strangest of all his experiments. Of Gandhi's obsession with brahmacharya, Bose wrote to a friend that 'from a serious study of Gandhiji's writings I had formed the opinion, which was not perhaps unjustified, that he represented a hard, puritanic[al] form of self-discipline, something which we usually associate with medieval Christian ascetics or Jain recluses'.

Bose also knew that many of Gandhi's disciples had 'a kind of emotional unbalance'; some even 'regarded Gandhiji as their private possession'. When Bose first heard of Gandhi's most recent *prayog*, or experiment, he was 'genuinely surprised'. It seemed an extreme (Bose did not, but could have said, 'unbalanced') form of self-trial; and a blind devotion on the part of those who participated in it. 'Personally, I would never tempt myself like that,' remarked Bose, adding: 'Nor would my respect for women's personality permit me to treat her as an instrument of an experiment only for my own sake.'

'Whatever may be the value of the *prayog* in Gandhiji's own case,' wrote Bose, '*it does leave a mark of injury on the personality of others* who are not of the same moral stature as he himself is, and for whom sharing in Gandhiji's experiment is no spiritual necessity.'[22]

When he wrote this, Bose may not have known that (if we are to believe Gandhi) the experiment was at least in part a product of Manu's own need to be seen as sexually pure. Even if that were so, the asymmetry in age, familial relationship, and social power, meant that it was to some extent forced on the young girl for whom, as Bose put it, the experiment was 'no spiritual necessity'.

Had Kasturba been around, she would have taken care of Manu in the ashram while Gandhi was on the road. Had Mahadev Desai been around, he would have been with Gandhi, and quite conceivably argued him out of it. That Mahadev's friend Narhari Parikh was disapproving adds to the weight of this speculation. Like Vallabhbhai Patel, Mahadev would have been keenly aware of the political fallout of a possible sensationalization of the experiments. But he might have seen them as spiritually unnecessary too.

Had he been with Gandhi in Bengal, C. Rajagopalachari would have also surely advised against the experiment. Rajaji had been instrumental in subverting Gandhi's 'spiritual marriage' to Saraladevi, convincing him that it would hurt the nationalist cause. He might have made the same objection again, perhaps adding that such tests were unnecessary to prove one's spiritual sincerity.

One can't see Charlie Andrews endorsing the experiment either. In his confusion, Gandhi saw Horace Alexander as a proxy CFA, but Alexander was too young and too deferential towards Gandhi to challenge or question him. Facing his ideal of a united, harmonious India crumbling around him, and without Kasturba, Andrews and Mahadev to console or assist him, Gandhi sought to tame the (stark, manifest) violence without by taming the (probably non-existent) passions within.

CHAPTER THIRTY-SIX

Independence and Division

I

Gandhi had wanted to stay longer in Bihar, and even undertake (as in Noakhali) a walking tour through the villages. But a new viceroy had now taken over in Delhi, and it was important for them to meet. Lord Mountbatten was as flamboyant as his predecessor was dour, as loquacious as Wavell was taciturn. A career naval officer, Mountbatten had been the supreme commander of the Allied Forces in South East Asia. He was also related to the British royal family, being the uncle of Prince Philip, who would shortly be engaged to be married to Princess—later Queen—Elizabeth.[1]

Mountbatten's appointment as viceroy was preceded by a major declaration by the British prime minister, Clement Attlee. Speaking to the House of Commons on 20 February 1947, Attlee announced that the British would leave India not later than June 1948. They would put in place arrangements to hand over power to Indians so that they could—at last—realize their long-cherished dreams of self-government. Although Attlee did not spell out the details of how and to whom power would be transferred, the fixing of a definite deadline for the end of British rule was noteworthy.[2]

Mountbatten arrived in Delhi on 22 March. The same day, he wrote to Gandhi that he hoped 'we shall be able to meet soon'. He understood that 'it may be difficult for you to come to Delhi at once in view of your preoccupations in Bihar', but asked that Gandhi come when he felt able to.[3]

Gandhi reached Delhi on 31 March, staying at the sweepers' colony. The next day, he made the trek to the Viceregal Palace. Mountbatten asked Gandhi some questions about his early life, his education in London and his struggles in South Africa. The conversation then turned to the present. Gandhi made a startling suggestion—that the viceroy invite Jinnah to form a government at the Centre, to which the Congress would give full support. It is not clear when Gandhi thought up this idea—perhaps even as recently as on the train from Patna to Delhi. But it was clearly inspired (if that is the word) by the horrific communal violence he had witnessed in Bengal and Bihar. If the price of Hindu–Muslim harmony was a Muslim League government in Delhi headed by Muhammad Ali Jinnah, Gandhi was willing to pay it. But would the Congress agree? It appears that, at this stage, they had not even been consulted. This was Gandhi's idea, and Gandhi's alone.

Mountbatten asked Gandhi to put his proposal in writing. Gandhi drafted a one-page note, which suggested that Jinnah be asked to form a Cabinet, and appoint the ministers of his choosing. Despite having a majority in the Central Assembly, the Congress would cooperate with this ministry 'freely and sincerely', so long as its proposals and actions were 'in the interests of the Indian people as a whole', with—in case of a dispute—the 'sole referee' of what constituted the interests of India being Lord Mountbatten. As prime minister, Jinnah would be free to present for acceptance his scheme for Pakistan even before the formal transfer of power, provided he did so by appealing 'to reason and not to the force of arms which he abjures for all time for this purpose'. Finally, Gandhi's proposal asked that 'if Mr. Jinnah rejects this offer, the same offer be made *mutatis mutandis* to Congress'.

Gandhi now took the proposal to the CWC. Nehru and Patel rejected it, as did all other members, except Ghaffar Khan, the Pathan whose commitment to non-violence and religious harmony was exceptional and exemplary. Gandhi conveyed the news back to Mountbatten.[4]

It is not clear whether the proposal was ever formally put to, or even informally discussed with, Jinnah himself. If it was, any attraction he may have felt for reasons of personal vanity would have vanished on considering the larger political implications. Could he trust Gandhi, and more importantly, the Congress Party? Would they not use their majority in the assembly to block or thwart him? By now, relations between the Congress and the League had broken down completely. The mutual hatred and animosity of recent years would have been hard, if not impossible, to put behind.

Gandhi's proposal was a grand but futile gesture, admirable in theory but hopelessly unworkable in practice. On 6 April, Jinnah and his sister Fatima had come to dine at the Viceregal Palace. Afterwards, Lady Mountbatten wrote in her diary: 'Two very clever and queer people . . . I rather liked them but found them fanatical on their Pakistan and quite impracticable.'[5]

II

In Delhi, Gandhi held daily prayer meetings as was his wont. These did not always go smoothly. One day, a young man objected to the reading of passages from the Koran. He came closer to Gandhi, shouting his dissent. Finally, he was removed from the premises, without Gandhi's consent. He would have wished to listen to and answered his criticisms.

Communal violence had broken out in the Punjab, where a coalition ministry, of which the Congress was a part, had just collapsed. A partisan governor had hastily sworn in a Muslim League-minority government. This enraged the Congress, as well as the Sikhs and their militant leader, Master Tara Singh. On 4 March, while the assembly met, a large Muslim crowd gathered outside shouting pro-Pakistan slogans. Hindus and Sikhs led by Master Tara Singh shouted counter slogans. The police intervened to calm the situation.

The following week saw many demonstrations in the streets of Lahore, some for Pakistan, others against. Soon there were clashes between Hindus and Muslims, followed by police firing and curfews.

The violence quickly spread into the countryside. The caretaker government resigned, the governor took charge of the administration—but the flames lit on the 2nd could not now be doused. The violence spread into the countryside, Hindus and Sikhs on the one side pitted against Muslims on the other. Both Punjabi Muslims and Punjabi Sikhs had fought in large numbers in the recent World War; often, the mobs were directed in the use of arms and arson by these ex-soldiers.[6]

Friends in the Punjab wrote asking Gandhi to come and calm tempers. Meanwhile, he continued to receive 'doleful wires' from Noakhali, suggesting 'increasing lawlessness' there.[7] Eventually, Gandhi chose to return to Bihar. This may have been because while in Noakhali Muslims were the aggressors, and in the Punjab it was a three-way fight between Hindus, Muslims and Sikhs, in Bihar the majority of riot victims were Muslims, the majority of perpetrators, Hindu. And Gandhi thought that if he could tame and contain the violent elements in his own faith, he could make his mission more credible in the eyes of Muslims. As he put it in a speech in Patna on 15 April, 'whatever may be the deterioration in the situation in the Punjab, Bengal and Sind, Hinduism will be saved if Bihar at any rate follows the right path. Even if the Muslims in the Punjab, Bengal and Sind harm the Hindus there, and if Bihar shows true courage in protecting and comforting Muslims and their children, Bihar will have raised India in the estimation of the world.'

Gandhi spent the second half of April in Bihar, meeting ministers and refugees, and addressing public meetings. There was an occasional note of despair, as when he told an audience that 'if you can carry my voice to Bihar Sharif [a town that had witnessed much violence], tell the Hindus there that they should not go on troubling an old man like me'.[8]

While he was in Patna, Gandhi received a long 'Open Letter' from a Hindu lawyer in Calcutta, accusing him of working for Muslim interests. Gandhi, he claimed, had advised Hindus to face death and Hindu women to take poison when attacked, but he daren't advise Muslims similarly. 'Is it your idea,' asked the critic, 'that all Hindus in Bengal will die, so that the flag of independence can be safely unfurled in Pakistan?'

The angry Hindu continued: 'What have you done in Noakhali and Calcutta? You succeeded in winning the hearts of Hindu miscreants

in Behar but did you win a single Muslim heart in Noakhali? . . . You
are the cause of death and ruin of so many Hindus, who went back
to their houses according to your advice. But you need not fast, as the
Muslims will never repent for their misdeeds.'

Gandhi replied to the Bengali in hurt tones. He was 'surprised'
that an educated solicitor could write such a letter. Had he studied
the facts beforehand, he would have been 'unable to prove me guilty
under any of your many counts'. For, 'whatever I am saying here to
the Hindus, I said unequivocally to the Muslims of Noakhali'.[9]

Before he came to Bihar himself, Gandhi had sent a former major
general of the Indian National Army, Shah Nawaz Khan. Shah Nawaz
and six other INA men worked with Muslim refugees, rebuilding their
homes and villages. Shah Nawaz 'had been told by Mahatmaji that the
success of our work in Bihar would have a good effect on the whole
of India and might even be a cure against the poison of communalism
which is destroying the country'. Some officials obstructed their
work, but this stopped when Gandhi arrived. 'Mahatmaji's presence
and speeches in Bihar,' observed Shah Nawaz, 'have had a good effect
on the masses of Bihar. Their attitude with me was very cooperative.
They were prepared to listen to Mahatmaji and make his work a real
success.'[10]

With Gandhi in Bihar was Mridula Sarabhai, daughter of
Ambalal Sarabhai, who had saved the ashram in Ahmedabad from
going under in 1915. Mridula had known Gandhi all her life, but this
was the first time she had seen at such close quarters his method of
working. She was impressed by how, through his prayer meetings,
Gandhi spread the message of religious toleration. These began with
a Buddhist prayer taught to him by a Japanese monk who had lived
in Sevagram, and continued via verses from the Koran, the Gita, the
Bible and the Zend-Avesta to Gandhi's favourite Ramdhun, whose
last verse he had tweaked to *Ishwar Allah téré naam, sabh ko sanmati
dé Bhagwan* (God is called both Ishwar and Allah, and may He give
good sense and wisdom to all).

Mridula observed that 'it was Gandhiji's practice to investigate
every complaint himself. His insistence on satisfying himself in every
matter, big or small, compels everybody working with him to be
continually vigilant.' Visiting a village where many Muslims were

reported to have been killed, he was told by the local magistrate and police officers that the reports were false. But Gandhi saw some wells had been filled up; he had them excavated, to find many decaying corpses within.[11]

III

While urging ordinary Hindus to repent and make amends, Gandhi continued to have reservations about the Muslim leadership. 'If you are true representatives of the League,' he told Muslim League functionaries in Bihar, 'you should frankly tell Jinnah Saheb or Liaquat Ali Saheb that they are going in the wrong direction; only then you would be serving the League faithfully. Noakhali, Bengal and the Punjab are still witnessing massacres by Muslims. I do not deny that Hindus too are perpetrating such crimes, but both Jawaharlal and I have been strongly condemning their misdeeds and publicly appealing to them to desist. Has any representative of the League made any such appeal to Muslims?'[12] The criticism, or complaint, was not without foundation: Jinnah and his second in command, Liaquat Ali Khan, were by no means as forthright in speaking out against Muslim communalism as were Gandhi and Nehru with regard to Hindu communalism.

Negotiations regarding the transfer of power were reaching a crucial stage. Nehru and Patel thus wanted Gandhi back in Delhi. He returned to the capital for a week, consulting with leading Congressmen, and also meeting Mountbatten and Jinnah. It now looked more and more likely that, when the British left, they would leave behind not one nation but two. Jinnah's campaign for Pakistan was on the verge of success. Gandhi still hoped it would not come about; arguing that 'the Congress should in no circumstance be party to partition'.[13]

Gandhi met Jinnah in Delhi on 6 May; afterwards, the League leader issued a statement saying that Gandhi 'thinks division is not inevitable, whereas in my opinion, not only is Pakistan inevitable but this is the only practical solution of India's political problem'.[14] But Gandhi yet hoped to stall the inevitable; writing to the viceroy that 'it would be a blunder of the first magnitude for the British to be a party in any way whatsoever to the division of India'.[15]

In truth, the increasing polarization was manifest at Gandhi's own prayer meetings, with many Hindus objecting to the recital of verses from the Koran. One correspondent wrote saying the Koran's philosophy 'is an anti-thesis of all the Gita teaches'. Gandhi's reading of these verses, charged the critic, was an 'expression' of his 'appeasement policy'. Another writer sarcastically commented that 'in order to support the Congress, the Hindu need not become an ardent admirer of the "Quran" or allow it to be sung [sic] at his place of worship'. If this practice continued, he warned, 'the Congress will cease to exist as the Hindus are no longer in a mood to be treated in the way they have been'.[16]

From Delhi, Gandhi proceeded to Calcutta, where a movement had arisen for a 'united Bengal', for a state that would not join Pakistan but unite Bengali speakers regardless of religious affiliation. Among its chief advocates were Subhas Bose's younger brother Sarat Chandra Bose and H.S. Suhrawardy. On the other hand, it was opposed by the Hindu Mahasabha leader Syama Prasad Mookerjee, who claimed it was promoted largely by British commercial interests. The scheme was also rejected by the Muslim League, for whom Bengal was as big a prize for Pakistan as the Punjab. Gandhi met both proponents and opponents of the idea. While he did not commit himself to either side, the idea of unity on the basis of 'a common culture and a common mother tongue' appealed to him. But, as he told Sarat Bose, the proposal had to be put to the democratic test of the citizens of Bengal. However, Nehru and Patel also came out against the United Bengal scheme, so, as Gandhi wrote to Bose, he would now have to persuade *both* the Congress and the League, an impossible task.[17]

Gandhi moved on to Patna again, talking to citizens and volunteers, pursuing his campaign for communal harmony. He was disappointed by the lack of commitment of Congressmen to 'establishing good relations among the Hindus and the Muslims'. He struck a note of despair, saying, 'a rot has set in in the Congress. It means that Congressmen are no longer honest. If those who are selfish capture the Congress it cannot function well.'[18]

In the last week of May, Gandhi returned to Delhi. His prayer meetings were now regularly obstructed by protesters. These were often Hindu refugees from West Punjab, thrown out of their homes and villages as the violence in the province grew progressively more intense. Gandhi was also receiving many abusive letters. As was his wont, he read out excerpts from these letters in these meetings. He did not contest their facts, while pointing out that no one could cast the first stone, since 'the Hindus in Bihar have not lagged behind in committing atrocities. Not only were the atrocities of Noakhali avenged, but much more was done.' On the other side, 'we shall have to tell the Muslims that [violence] is not the way to achieve Pakistan'.[19]

Partition had now become inevitable. On 3 June, Mountbatten announced that the British government had recommended that British India be divided into two successor states, India and Pakistan, both remaining in the British Commonwealth, but retaining the right to secede from it. The 15th of August was set as the date of formal transfer of power. British India was to be partitioned; so too would be two of its largest provinces, Bengal and the Punjab. Cyril Radcliffe, a British judge with no previous experience of India and Indians, was tasked with drawing the line that divided India from Pakistan in the east and in the west.

Once Pakistan came into being, said Gandhi at a prayer meeting on 7 June, then 'it becomes the duty of the Congress to . . . make its best efforts in the portion that remains with it. Let the people in Pakistan go ahead of the Congress in their efforts to bring progress to their land.' Five days later, he remarked that 'geographically we may have been divided. But so long as hearts too have not been divided, we must not weep.' Four days later still, he insisted that even if Pakistan and India became two different countries, 'if I have to go to the Punjab, I am not going to ask for a passport. And I shall go to Sind also without a passport and I shall go on walking. Nobody can stop me.'

Gandhi urged his audiences to ensure that those Muslims who stayed back in India were treated as full citizens. Their safety and security must be assured. At the same time, there was no question of separate electorates for Muslims. Those electorates 'were a poisonous weed planted by the British but we shall be just to them. Their children will have as much opportunity of education as other children.'[20]

IV

Through the second quarter of 1947, the situation in the Punjab continued to deteriorate. The province was 'submerged under suspicion and hatred', wrote one Punjabi: 'Passions are running high. Killings, loot, arson, abductions and forcible conversions have hardened the people. All classes of men are feverishly arming themselves.'[21] The governor of the Punjab threw up his hands, writing to a colleague in late May, as houses and localities were being set ablaze in Lahore, that 'we haven't the water or the fire-engines to exercise more than a very elementary control. No answer that HMG [His Majesty's Government] can devise will really meet the Punjab situation . . .'[22]

Gandhi was reading the newspapers, and getting reports from Congressmen in the province. 'Is Pakistan,' he asked, 'to be raised over the ashes of Lahore and Amritsar?' He found himself in a dilemma. Punjab called, but so did Bihar, and so also Noakhali, where his 'work was just started and [had] given much comfort to the Hindus'.

In a prayer meeting on 10 July, Gandhi said: 'There are still thirty-five days to August 15. Let us cease to be beasts and become men. We have all been put to the test and that includes the British.' He had heard that, in Noakhali, Hindu refugees worried that once Pakistan came into being, they would not be resettled or compensated. Gandhi insisted that 'the Pakistanis must demonstrate that the Hindus living in Pakistan will not be harmed in any way. Then we shall have reason to celebrate 15th of August as Independence Day. But if this does not happen, this independence is not for me nor, I am sure will it be for you. A lot can happen in these thirty-five days.'

In another prayer meeting two weeks later, Gandhi said that after Partition, 'the Congress can never become an organization of the Hindus. Those who seek to make it such will be doing great harm to India and Hinduism.' Muslims, Christians, Sikhs, Parsis who lived in India would have equal rights. For, 'people professing different religions have mingled to form the Indian nation and they are all citizens of India and no section has the right to oppress another section'.[23]

The creation of Pakistan was a great personal triumph for Muhammad Ali Jinnah. His idea of a separate nation for Indian Muslims had been widely scoffed at and mocked. As recently as 1942, Jawaharlal Nehru had written:

> Hindu and Muslim 'cultures' and the 'Muslim nation'—how these words open out fascinating vistas of past history and present and future speculation! The Muslim nation in India—a nation within a nation, and not even compact, but vague, spread out, indeterminate. Politically the idea is absurd, economically it is fantastic; it is hardly worth considering.[24]

Within five years of this magisterial dismissal, this absurd and fantastic idea had been fulfilled, albeit at a horrific human cost. Did Jinnah think it worth the price? We do not know, since his feelings on the division of India were, unlike Gandhi's, not shared with the public. Meanwhile, Penderel Moon cynically wrote to a friend: 'One man with two stenographers having created two kingdoms—J's [Jinnah's] own description of his achievement. He is apparently quite satisfied and doesn't much mind if they both go to blazes . . .'[25]

V

On the last day of July, Gandhi left Delhi for Kashmir. This was at the request of Jawaharlal Nehru. The situation in that princely state was rapidly reaching boiling point. Once Independence came, on 15 August, all princely states would have the option of joining India or joining Pakistan, depending on which new nation its borders abutted. Of these five hundred-odd principalities, some the size of Jersey or Guernsey, some the size of Great Britain, the state of Jammu and Kashmir was one of the very few which had the choice of joining either India or Pakistan, since its borders touched both.

The viceroy, Lord Mountbatten, urged the princes to join either state before 15 August. Several dithered, among them the maharaja of

Kashmir and the nizam of Hyderabad, both of whom fancied staying independent. In Kashmir, a vigorous popular movement had arisen for democratic rule, led by the charismatic Sheikh Abdullah. The maharaja had responded with repression, throwing Abdullah and many of his colleagues in jail.

The ruling family of Jammu and Kashmir was Hindu. The bulk of the population, however, was Muslim. While Sheikh Abdullah was a Muslim, he was also a close friend of Jawaharlal Nehru, sharing his socialist views. In terms of the religious composition of its population, the princely state was aligned more to Pakistan, but by the character and ideology of its major mass leader, drawn more to India. The Congress naturally wanted to focus on the latter, so as to facilitate Jammu and Kashmir's accession to New Delhi.

In June 1947, Nehru told Mountbatten that 'he thought he would soon have to go to Kashmir to take up the cudgels on behalf of his friend [Sheikh Abdullah] and for the freedom of the people'. The viceroy dissuaded him from going, since he was needed in Delhi, and since Nehru had been arrested by the maharaja the last time he went to Kashmir (in 1946), and Mountbatten didn't want the trouble to escalate. Nehru said in that case the viceroy must permit Gandhi to go instead.[26]

Shortly before he left Delhi for Srinagar, Gandhi said: 'The people of Kashmir should be asked whether they want to join India or Pakistan. Let them do as they want.'[27] He took a train to Rawalpindi, from where he was to proceed by road to Kashmir. The train stopped at Amritsar, where angry Hindus waved black flags and asked him to go back. His disciple Brij Krishna Chandiwala, who was with him, thought immediately back to 1919, when Gandhi was a folk hero in Punjab, his arrest leading to mass protests culminating in the massacre at Jallianwala Bagh. 'The same Gandhi was now the target of abuse by the people of that very province who 28 years ago, respected him so much.'[28]

However, when Gandhi reached Kashmir he received a terrific reception. He drove from Rawalpindi to Srinagar, and on his entry into the town was met by thousands of people on either side of the road, shouting 'Mahatma Gandhi ki jai'. Since the bridge across the river Jhelum had been taken over by the crowd, Gandhi took a boat to the other side, where he addressed a public meeting of some twenty-five thousand women, convened by Sheikh Abdullah's wife.

In Kashmir, Gandhi spent three days in the Valley and two days in Jammu. He met the maharaja, Hari Singh, as well as his controversial prime minister, Ram Chandra Kak. He also met the Sheikh's political deputy, Bakshi Ghulam Mohammad, who 'was most sanguine that the result of the free vote of the people, whether on the adult franchise or on the existing register, would be in favour of Kashmir joining the [Indian] Union provided of course that Sheikh Abdullah and his co-prisoners were released . . .'[29]

VI

Gandhi had asked Sushila Nayar to stay back in Rawalpindi, to help with refugee relief. She was herself originally from West Punjab, and Gandhi trusted her to provide him reliable reports of what was, and what was not, happening. He had, meanwhile, proceeded by train to Calcutta, from where he hoped to push on to Noakhali. But when he reached Bengal's capital on 9 August, he found it convulsed by a fresh round of rioting.

On the 11th, Gandhi went on a two-hour tour of the riot-affected areas of Calcutta by car. He was accompanied by, among others, Satis Chandra Dasgupta. A police contingent followed. In his tour, Gandhi 'saw some burnt-out and devastated bustees and passed through roads lined with abandoned and shattered houses, the occupants having been evacuated'. At various places, his car was halted by crowds, where men and women narrated their experiences. 'Mr. Gandhi, who was observing his day of silence, listened quietly to the tales of woe, occasionally jotting down notes.'[30]

Gandhi now decided to stay on and 'see if he could contribute his share in the return of sanity in the premier city of India'. He met H.S. Suhrawardy, now about to be jobless, since with the division of Bengal, there would be new chief ministers in its Indian and Pakistani sections. Gandhi persuaded Suhrawardy that they should stay together in a riot-torn part of the city to instil confidence simultaneously in Hindus and Muslims.

On 13 August, Gandhi and Suhrawardy moved into the Hydari Manzil, a once grand but now derelict home of a Muslim merchant in the east Calcutta locality of Beliaghata. Manu Gandhi records that this was a 'very shabby house', with 'only one latrine used by hundreds of people, including a number of volunteers, policemen and visitors'. Besides, 'every inch of the place was covered with dust. In addition, rain had made the passages muddy.'[31]

On their first day in this dismal place, an angry mob of Hindus came and shouted slogans against Gandhi. He invited in their leaders, who asked why he was staying in a Muslim locality rather than a Hindu one. Did he not know or remember what the Muslims had done on Direct Action Day in August 1946?

Gandhi acknowledged that 'what the Muslims did was utterly wrong. But what is the use of avenging the year 1946 in 1947?' He had come there 'to serve not only Muslims but Hindus, Muslims and all alike'.[32]

During the 14th, many visitors and deputations came to see the two leaders. 'The local Hindus were reassured, the Muslims received fresh hopes.' A large crowd had gathered for the evening prayers at 6 p.m. Suhrawardy was too nervous to come out; he lay inside the house, 'his eyes shut'. Gandhi's speech was heard in silence at first, but then some young men began to shout for Suhrawardy.

Gandhi went back in, and then, a little later, as the shouting continued, came to the window of the house, and

> began to talk in a quiet voice to the youths just outside. Quickly the noise grew less, till there was absolute quiet. After ten minutes Suhrawardy joined Gandhi at the window, and began to speak. At first there were shouts of disapproval but soon the crowd listened and in spite of occasional taunts about his own responsibility for the past killings they gave him close attention; in response to an interruption he confessed to shame for the horrors of a year ago; and the crowd applauded his solemn assurances that he would go on working with Gandhi for peace in any part of Calcutta or East Bengal or wherever it might be needed.

Later in the evening, an army officer brought news of a big procession elsewhere in the city of Hindus and Muslims celebrating together. This was communicated to the crowd outside, who then 'left in peace'.[33]

The 15th of August was Independence Day. In cities across India, ran one report, 'lusty crowds have burst the bottled-up frustrations of many years in an emotional mass jag. Mob sprees have rolled from mill districts to gold coasts and back again. Despite doubts about the truncated, diluted form of freedom descending on India, the happy, infectious celebrations blossomed in forgetfulness of the decades of sullen resentment against all that was symbolized by a sahib's sun-topi.'[34]

One man who was not entirely pleased with Independence Day was Lord Mountbatten. He had hoped to continue as governor general of both the newly independent dominions, India and Pakistan. But while Nehru and Patel were happy to have Mountbatten stay on, Jinnah was determined that he would himself be head of state. Mountbatten now wrote bitterly to Stafford Cripps:

> My private information is that Mr. Jinnah's immediate followers are horrified at the line he has taken; and it seems almost incredible that a man's megalomania should be so chronic as to cause him to throw away such material advantages to his own future Dominion for the sake of becoming 'His Excellency' some eight months earlier than he would in any case have assumed that title.
>
> Jawaharlal Nehru is convinced of this view, but Vallabhbhai Patel ascribes more sinister motives to Mr. Jinnah and thinks that he wishes to set up a form of Fascist dictatorship with ultimate designs against the Dominion of India.[35]

In truth, this was a clash of two egomaniacs, Jinnah *and* Mountbatten. The latter felt cheated that, after 15 August, he would be governor general of merely one of the Raj's successor states, not both. Someone who had more (substantial) reason not to see this day as one of joy or triumph was, of course, Gandhi. He was devastated that the freedom for which he had so long struggled had resulted in two nations, not one, these formed against a backdrop of bloody violence. On 10 August, when the new chief minister of West Bengal, Dr P.C. Ghosh, asked him how the 15th should be celebrated, Gandhi answered that it should be spent praying, fasting, and at the spinning wheel. 'What else could they do,' he remarked, 'when all around the country was burning, when people were dying from lack of food and clothing?'[36]

But when the day came, Gandhi was slightly less depressed. For, in Calcutta on 15 August, the violence miraculously stopped. Muslims and Hindus together flew the tricolour, together shouted patriotic slogans. Gandhi was, inevitably, reminded of Khilafat days.

At hand, to see and record the violence slowly ebb away and finally end, was Horace Alexander. In Calcutta on the 15th, he wrote: 'The fears and enmities of yesterday seemed to have vanished like a black cloud or a hideous nightmare. The dawn of freedom was also the dawn of goodwill. Freedom and peace had kissed each other. Hindus and Muslims crowded into lorries together, waved the new tricolour flags and shouted "Jai Hind" all over the city. In "Bustees", where for months people had not dared to cross a road separating one community from the other, and where the women had kept indoors, men and women were fraternising.'

What explained this transformation? As Alexander saw it,

the change from fear and dread to joy and peace was so sudden as to seem spontaneous. Probably the truth is that the common people were all longing for peace and reconciliation. But someone had to touch the hidden spring. Only a great soul could do that. The Mahatma's decision to take Suhrawardy into close and affectionate partnership was the symbolic act that touched the spring. But he knows better than any man that the work of reconciliation is only just begun. The partners must strive day by day to consolidate the ground they have won.[37]

The new governor of West Bengal, C. Rajagopalachari, told the city's Rotary Club that 'Mahatma Gandhi has achieved many things in his lifetime, but I do not think he has achieved anything so great, so grand, as he has achieved in Calcutta'.[38]

VII

As Hindus and Muslims were fraternizing in Calcutta, a reconciliation of a different kind was being effected in New Delhi. When, on 15 August, Jawaharlal Nehru handed over the list of Cabinet ministers in his new government to the viceroy, it included the name of B.R. Ambedkar, as law minister. This bitter, long-standing opponent of the Congress had been inducted into a Congress-led government. How did this happen?

After his party's rout in the 1946 elections, Ambedkar had sought to mend fences with the Congress. He had long talks with Vallabhbhai Patel in July/August, but these finally broke down. Then, while in London in November 1946, he had indicated to mutual friends that he would like to be reconciled with the Congress, asking, however, that the first approach be made by Gandhi.

Through the winter of 1946–47, Ambedkar saw himself increasingly isolated from the political process. Independence was imminent; the British were soon to depart India for ever. What then would be his political future? In the second week of February 1947, the writer Kanji Dwarkadas met Ambedkar in Bombay. He found him 'for a very strong centre', and also 'very anti-Jinnah [and the] Muslim League stand'. Ambedkar told Dwarkadas that 'in spite of all the differences with the Congress, he was a nationalist first and would not behave as Jinnah is behaving. I found that he was willing to come to terms with the [Congress] high command and I think very soon the Congress and Dr Ambedkar and his party will make common cause.'[39]

In the Constituent Assembly, Ambedkar met and spoke with many Congress members. One of them was Rajkumari Amrit Kaur. In the middle of April, Amrit Kaur wrote to Gandhi that she has 'seen a good deal of Dr. Ambedkar during the fortnight[ly] sittings of the Fundamental Rights Committee. He has been very reasonable in these sittings.'

On 15 April, Ambedkar sent a message through the economist K.T. Shah, saying he wanted to talk privately with Amrit Kaur. They had a long meeting, the gist of which she now passed on to Gandhi. Ambedkar told her that he 'would like to come to an agreement with Congress'. He said his party's minimum demand was for separate electorates, with the present reservation of seats in the legislatures. Amrit Kaur then 'pleaded with him for joint electorates with no reservations now that untouchability is going to be abolished by law. In the second instance, as second best, I pleaded for joint electorates with reservation of seats. His plea is that the recent elections have proved that the Hindu vote overwhelms the Sch[eduled] Caste vote & the true representatives of the latter don't come to the top.'

Amrit Kaur conveyed her conversations with Ambedkar to Nehru, Rajaji and Kripalani. Patel was out of town. She now asked Gandhi: 'What is your reaction? Please let me know as I am on the Minorities Committee. What would be the maximum you would concede to him? He wants the concession for 20–25 years at the most. If he doesn't get his way he says he will have to walk out.'[40]

Gandhi replied to Amrit Kaur's letter that he was 'quite clear that Dr. Ambedkar's demands cannot be conceded'. Gandhi held to his position that joint electorates with reservation of seats was the best solution. 'Such evil as there is in joint electorate[s],' he told Amrit Kaur, 'can be obviated only by right type of education and enlightenment. If Dr. Ambedkar's objections were upheld for any length of time, be it ever so little, it would undermine [a] solution.'[41]

The next reference in the archives to this subject is dated 11 July, when Nehru wrote to C. Rajagopalachari that he had spoken to Ambedkar, who had agreed to join the Cabinet. He asked Rajaji to persuade another veteran critic of the Congress, R.K. Shanmukham Chetty of Madras's Justice Party, to come aboard too, as finance minister.[42]

What happened between April and July to make Gandhi change his mind and give the go-ahead to Ambedkar's reconciliation with the Congress? We do know that, on his side, Ambedkar dropped his demand for separate electorates, agreeing instead to joint electorates with reservation of seats, which is what finally found its way into the Indian Constitution. But it appears that the advice of his close disciple, Amrit Kaur, made Gandhi more amenable to mending fences with his long-time opponent. The Congress Harijan leader Jagjivan Ram also seems to have played a role in effecting this reconciliation. He met Ambedkar several times, writing to Gandhi that if their old adversary would join hands with them, this might ensure that 'the problem of the Scheduled Castes is solved before it takes a serious turn and goes adrift like the Muslim question'.[43]

To allow Ambedkar to serve in the Cabinet, however, he had first to be made a member of the Constituent Assembly. When that assembly was first convened, in December 1946, Ambedkar was elected a member from the then undivided province of Bengal, whose eastern wing had a strong Scheduled Caste presence. But with Partition, Ambedkar lost his seat. Vallabhbhai Patel prevailed upon the chief minister of the Bombay Presidency, B.G. Kher, to 'make arrangements for Dr. Ambedkar's election' from that province. Kher did the needful, by making a Congress member vacate his seat and getting Ambedkar elected in his place.[44] Ambedkar was now appointed law minister in the first Cabinet of free India, as well as chairman of the drafting committee of the Constitution.

The credit for effecting this reconciliation with Ambedkar lies largely with Amrit Kaur, through her discussions with him on the sidelines of the Constituent Assembly. She was a Christian of Sikh background, and a woman too. Ambedkar would surely have perceived Amrit Kaur in less antagonistic terms than he had those powerful upper-caste Hindu males: Gandhi, Nehru and Patel.

VIII

It is now seventy years since Independence and Partition, yet a fierce historiographical (as well as popular) debate still rages on the subject. Which was most responsible for Partition, this debate asks, Hindu intransigence or Muslim separatism? Who contributed most to this process of estrangement: Gandhi, Jinnah or Nehru? Should the blame be put rather on the British Raj, for whom divide and rule was a strategic imperative? Was the real villain of the piece the policy of separate electorates, which made religious identity so central to democratic politics?

One reason this debate is so intense is the sheer scale of the violence. More than a million people died in the Partition riots, and more than ten million were rendered homeless, with Hindus and Sikhs fleeing from Pakistan into India and Muslims fleeing from India into Pakistan. Five provinces of British India: the Punjab, Bengal, Bihar, United Provinces and the NWFP, were absolutely ravaged by the violence. Sindh and the Bombay Presidency also witnessed much suffering, and there was episodic rioting in the Central Provinces as well. Among the major provinces of British India, only the Madras Presidency escaped relatively unscathed.

A second reason the debate has carried on for so long is the enduring enmity between India and Pakistan. The two countries have fought four wars since Independence and Partition; even in times of 'peace', soldiers of both sides are regularly killed in cross-border firing, and hostile propaganda (again, on both sides) continues unabated. Meanwhile, the communal question has scarcely been solved by Partition; with Muslims being victimized within India, and Hindus and Christians being persecuted within Pakistan.

This persistence of national rivalry and sectarian conflict means that the question of who (or what) caused Partition has never gone away. And it has promoted this follow-up question: could Partition have been avoided? Had the Congress been generous enough to form a coalition government with the Muslim League in the crucial state of the United Provinces in 1937, would this have arrested the growth of separatist sentiment? Had the Congress (or Gandhi specifically) not launched the Quit India movement in 1942, and supported the war effort instead, would this have encouraged the British to hand over power to a single national government (headed by the Congress) after the war had ended?

The idea, or thought, or hope, that Partition could have been avoided raises a further set of questions still. What would have happened to Indian unity if the Cabinet Mission Plan of 1946 had been accepted? Would not that have left the large areas occupied by princely states quasi-independent? Would this not have made travel across India difficult, impeded the growth of a national market and hence economic development, and also fragmented the idea of nationhood itself? Would Hindus and Muslims have lived peaceably ever after, or would they have had further conflicts, even a civil war? Would they ever have agreed on a common national language?

The idea that India could have been constituted and run as a single country was vigorously disputed by Jinnah and the Muslim League; and, long before them, by many British officials as well. In Chapter 8, I quoted a home secretary as saying that Gandhi, in seeking to build a compact between Hindus and Muslims in the 1920s, had ignored 'the essential differences which divide the two great religions—differences due to conflicting ethical standards as much as to political jealousy'. These differences had been given formal legal sanction by the creation of a separate electorate for Muslims in 1909. Is that year the point of no return then, after which Hindus and Muslims were fated to become distinct and opposed political entities, resulting in the creation in 1947 of the distinct and opposed nations of India and Pakistan?

I have my own answers to these (admittedly) important questions, but this is not the place to offer them. The biographer's task is to document what happened at the time, not to pose counterfactuals. Earlier chapters have outlined the process by which the Congress and the Muslim League, Hindus and Muslims, Jinnah and Gandhi, diverged in their perceptions and priorities so that in the end Partition became inevitable. Once it happened, however, Gandhi was determined to stem the flow of blood that it caused. He had, it seems, succeeded in Calcutta; he had now to take himself and his mission to other parts of the subcontinent.

CHAPTER THIRTY-SEVEN

The Greatest Fasts

I

Through July and August 1947, Congressmen in the Punjab were sending Gandhi gory details of the massacres and the looming refugee crisis.[1] From Delhi, Amrit Kaur, herself a Punjabi, wrote saying 'your "miracle" in Calcutta is a bright spot in an otherwise gloomy picture. The Punjab situation is bad beyond measure. A Sikh said to me that "Pindi has been avenged fourfold". . . . The tragedy is that most of us inwardly rejoice when our community gets its own back on the other. . . . I am filled with fear as to where we are drifting.'[2]

'When do you think', wrote Gandhi to Nehru on 24 August, 'I should go to the Punjab if at all?' Nehru replied that he 'should go [to the Punjab] but not just yet'.[3] So, Gandhi went back to his original plan, which was to return to Noakhali. He planned to leave on 2 September, but then, on the last day of August, a fresh round of rioting broke out in Calcutta. A series of stabbings were reported. As night fell, the violence reached the Hydari Manzil itself. A crowd surrounded the house, and began throwing stones at the windows. A few panes cracked and broke. Then there was an attempt to cut off the electricity supply. Gandhi went outside and spoke to the demonstrators, in Hindustani, a language which few of them understood. Two policemen arrived, and the mob finally dispersed.

As Gandhi wrote later to Vallabhbhai Patel, 'every one suspects the Hindu Mahasabha' was behind the attack.

The same evening, Gandhi commenced an indefinite fast. In a press statement, he said that 'if India is to retain her dearly won independence all men and women must completely forget lynch law'. His fast would 'end only if and when sanity returns to Calcutta'.

The new governor of West Bengal, C. Rajagopalachari, tried hard to persuade Gandhi not to go on a fast. If he died, said Rajaji, 'the conflagration would be worse'. Gandhi calmly answered: 'At least I won't be there to witness it. I shall have done my bit. More is not given a man to do.'[4]

Rajaji then appealed to the people of Calcutta. They must, as soon as possible, restore communal peace and goodwill in the city, as 'Mahatma Gandhi had hard work before him in the Punjab, for which he must be spared'. Indians, he added, could 'throw the blame on no outsider or foreign Government if [Gandhi's] precious life ebbs away in Calcutta. This time it is not aliens, but we . . . that have it in their power to save his life or let him die.'[5]

The leading English newspaper in the city, the British-owned *Statesman*, had long been hostile to Gandhi. But after his work in Noakhali and Bihar, it began to soften its stance. It had once referred to him only as 'Mr Gandhi'; after 15 August, it began to adopt the name most Indians used for him, 'Mahatma'.[6] Now, on the day that Gandhi began his fast, the *Statesman* issued a further mea culpa:

On the ethics of fasting as a political instrument we have over many years failed to concur with India's most renowned practitioner of it, expressing our views frankly. But never in a long career has Mahatma Gandhi, in our eyes, fasted in a simpler, worthier cause than this, nor one more calculated for immediate effective appeal to the public conscience. We cordially wish him unqualified success, and trust that happy termination of the ordeal may be speedy.[7]

From the morning of 2 September, Gandhi received a steady stream of callers asking him to end his fast. The chief minister of West Bengal came and assured him the government was taking 'stringent measures' to maintain public order. The Hindu Mahasabha leader,

S.P. Mookerjee, came and said 'the general feeling here now is in favour of peace'. A brother of Subhas Chandra Bose came and promised Gandhi that 'there would be no more incidents'.[8]

On 3 September, Gandhi woke up as usual at 3.30 a.m. He participated in the morning prayers, but then—in a departure from past practice—refused to have a shave, saying he would only have one after the fast ended. His last fast had been in the Aga Khan Palace back in 1943. He had, he told his assembled disciples, wanted to survive that fast, 'which was directed against the despotism of Linlithgow'. But now he did not care whether he lived or died. Of course, he hoped that peace would come to Calcutta, but, he said, 'this fast will not go beyond ten days. There shall either be peace within that period or else I shall die.' He was not without hope; for, he knew 'from personal experience of a number of instances where ruffians had been converted to peaceful ways'.[9] Perhaps Gandhi had in mind here a 'personal experience' from 1908, where a group of ruffians tried to kill him in Johannesburg but later repented, asked for forgiveness, and joined his non-violent campaign for greater rights for Indians in South Africa.[10]

As the day progressed, there was a noticeable improvement in the communal situation. There were fewer incidents, with less than five deaths reported. A number of peace processions passed through the city shouting unity slogans. Some 5000 students marched through different localities, 'urging the people to stand against goondaism to save the life of Mahatma Gandhi'.[11]

At 8 a.m. on 4 September, the entire police force of Calcutta, 'including Europeans and Anglo-Indians' started a fast in sympathy with Gandhi.[12] Later in the morning, a bunch of hooligans came to Beliaghata, begged for forgiveness, and placed their weapons at Gandhi's feet. These rowdies included the Hindu leaders of the attack on the Hydari Manzil on the night of 31 August/1 September. They would, they now told Gandhi, 'submit to whatever penalty you may impose'. He asked them 'to go immediately among the Muslims and assure them full protection. The moment I am convinced that real change of heart has taken place, I will give up my fast.'

The ruffians who had repented included Muslims as well as Hindus. One Muslim leader, weeping, urged Gandhi: 'Please give up your fast.

We were with you in the Khilafat fight. I take the responsibility of seeing that no Muslim in this locality creates any disturbance.'

These hooligans-turned-peacemakers then visited all parts of the city, coming back in the evening to tell Gandhi that 'there was quiet everywhere'. They promised to ensure that there would be no more rioting anywhere in Calcutta. An undertaking was signed by five leaders—two Bengali Hindus, one Bengali Muslim, one Punjabi Hindu and one Punjabi Sikh—and given to Gandhi. This pledged that 'now peace and quiet have been restored in Calcutta once again, we shall never again allow communal strife in the city, and shall strive unto death to prevent it'.

After some reflection, Gandhi decided to break his fast. He was doing so, he said, 'so that I might be able to do something for the Punjab'. He hoped and expected 'that the Hindus and Muslims here will not force me to undertake a fast again'. A few prayers were recited and hymns sung, and then, at 9.15 in the evening of the 4th, Gandhi drank a glass of lemon juice offered by Suhrawardy.[13]

The return of peace to Calcutta prompted Mountbatten to write to Gandhi that 'in the Punjab we have 55 thousand soldiers and large scale rioting on our hands. In Bengal our force consists of one man, and there is no rioting.'[14] This tribute has been widely quoted. Less well known, but perhaps more moving and insightful, are two contemporary assessments by Gandhi's fellow Indians, both, as it happens, Muslims. When Gandhi broke his fast in Calcutta, in Patna a member of the Bihar government remarked: 'We are ashamed of ourselves for creating conditions in which the ordeal had to be undertaken, but we are supremely happy that the penance was only short-lived and that its reaction on Calcutta was literally miraculous.' The minister continued: 'Gandhiji is not a man of a particular place or community. He belongs to the world and his efforts for the restoration of mutual concord and harmony in Bengal or Bihar symbolise his services to humanity at large.'

Gandhi's fast, said the minister, prompted the question: 'Why is it that while we are engaged in petty things and indulging in violence and slaughter, retaliation and reprisal, an old man of 80 is moving about on his tottering legs from one end of the country to the other asking people to give up madness and return to sanity?'

The Bihar minister thought the continuing riots proved that the division of the country, 'which was supposed to be the panacea of all the evils of the Indian Muslims, has been nothing but an undiluted curse for all'. He chastised the Muslim League for having given 'a consistently wrong lead to the Indian Muslims'. Indians of all religions should now follow 'the lead of Mahatma Gandhi which alone can ensure peace and security in India'.[15]

This was a public statement, which Gandhi may or may not have seen. Meanwhile, he received a letter from Bangalore, written by Mirza Ismail, the widely admired former diwan of Mysore. Ismail told Gandhi that 'you are rendering the greatest possible service to India in her most trying time. Your moral influence on all communities— Hindu, Muslim, Christian, Sikh, alike, and on all races, whether in or outside India, is at its highest to-day. May the Almighty spare you for the benefit, everlasting benefit, of India for very many years to come, for without your physical presence in our midst, India is lost. She will lose both her soul and her independence.'[16]

To these Muslim appreciations let me add a Hindu one, that of R.P. Parasuram, the typist who had left Gandhi in early 1947 objecting to his experiment with Manu. He had since found a new job, in the office of the Socialist Party in Bombay. After reading about Gandhi's fast on the other side of the subcontinent, Parasuram wrote to Nirmal Bose that 'I was glad to find that you were with him once again'. Then he ruefully added: 'I was one of those who thought that Bapu had perhaps outlived himself. He ought to have died. Then the creed of non-violence would have had greater success as one would not be faced with the spectacle of the author of non-violence himself frustrated in his attempt at stopping violence. But recent events have shown that Bapu is more needed than ever. In the present turmoil he is the only man to whom both the minorities can look up to with hope in their hearts.'[17]

Meanwhile, a Tamil journalist wrote that after his deeds in 1947, surely Gandhi would be awarded the Nobel Peace Prize. His name had been mentioned off and on in this connection for twenty years. This year too his name had come up; the Tamil hoped the speculation 'was well-founded', for the other names being mentioned, such as the Czech politician Edvard Beneš and the British biologist John Boyd

Orr, 'though worthy enough persons and entitled to recognition on other meritorious grounds, are not in the same light'.[18]

Alas, the Nobel Committee thought otherwise. The prize went in 1947 to the Quaker relief organization, the Friends Service Committee.

II

On 8 September, Gandhi left Calcutta for Delhi. He was met at Shahdara station by Vallabhbhai Patel and Amrit Kaur, who told him of the continuing violence in the capital. They took him to the large house of G.D. Birla, where they said he would be safer than in his preferred location, in the sweepers' colony.[19]

Birla House was located in the heart of New Delhi, close to the Claridges Hotel. It was a spacious two-storey house, with a large lawn adjoining it. Birla's family moved to the upper storey, allowing Gandhi and his party the exclusive use of the ground floor. Knowing that there would be daily prayer meetings, to which uninvited guests and admirers would come, Birla had erected a platform on the lawn for Gandhi to speak from, equipped with microphones and loudspeakers. He had also placed one of his cars at the service of the Mahatma, to take him around the city or to run errands for his staff.[20]

Gandhi had wished to go further north, to the Punjab. His disciple Amrit Kaur had recently been there, and come back with a 'horrific tale of woe'. Hindus had fled West Punjab while Muslims had fled East Punjab, in each case experiencing 'loss of all property and goods, brutal atrocities, no news of relatives—black despair'. There was, noted Amrit Kaur grimly, a 'complete lack of confidence on the part of the minorities in the police administration both in West and East Punjab'.[21]

Gandhi was being called to the Punjab, but he was detained in Delhi by the continuing violence in the capital. In a statement to the press, he said, 'I must do my little bit to calm the heated atmosphere. I must apply the old formula "Do or Die" to the capital of India. . . . I am prepared to understand the anger of the refugees whom fate has driven from West Punjab. But anger . . . can only make matters worse in every way. Retaliation is no remedy. It makes the original disease much worse. I, therefore, ask all those who are engaged in the senseless murders, arson and loot to stay their hands.'[22]

In Delhi, the main sufferers were the Muslims, who were, at Partition, some 33 per cent of the city's population. The happenings in West Punjab, as carried by Hindu and Muslim refugees, inflamed local passions. Muslims were driven out of their homes in the Old City. Shops owned by them and mosques where they prayed were vandalized. In many cases, Hindu refugees from West Punjab had moved into Muslim-owned properties.

Homeless Muslims had taken refuge in the capital's ancient monuments. Tens of thousands huddled together in the Purana Qila and in the tombs of the Mughal emperor Humayun and the Sufi saint Nizamuddin Auliya. Others were accommodated on the grounds of the Jamia Millia Islamia.

Camps had also come up to house Hindu and Sikh refugees from the Punjab. These were on the grounds of temples and schools, and in parks. Towns close to Delhi, such as Kurukshetra, had witnessed a vast influx of Hindus and Sikhs from across the new international border.

Gandhi visited both those displaced by the violence in Delhi and by the violence in West Punjab. While he did, as he stressed, understand the anger of the refugees from Pakistan, he did not wish it to be visited on the innocent Muslims of Delhi. 'I would like to request you,' he told the audience at his prayer meeting on 12 September, 'not to regard the Muslims as your enemies. . . . Just because the country has been divided into India and Pakistan, it does not befit us to slaughter the Muslims who have stayed behind.' Would, he pertinently asked, attacks on Muslims in Delhi 'mitigate the sorrows of the Hindus and Sikhs of the Punjab in any way'?

At the same time, Gandhi appealed to the Muslims who had stayed behind to 'open-heartedly declare that they belong to India and are loyal to the Union'. He also wanted 'the Muslims here to tell the Muslims of Pakistan who have become enemies of the Hindus, not to go mad'.

Gandhi was himself now reconciled to the fact and existence of Pakistan. But the violence on either side had put into question future relations between the two countries. He hoped that both governments would 'come to a mutual agreement that they have to protect the minorities in their respective countries'.[23]

Gandhi was in Delhi, but the Punjab continued to call. A civil servant wrote to him from Lahore that the situation in West Punjab was still very bad, with attacks by armed gangs on trains and refugee convoys. 'The stock excuse given by everybody here, high and low, for this undesirable state of affairs,' wrote the official, 'is that the East Punjab Govt. is permitting worse things to happen on their side . . . *This is a vicious cycle that only you can break.*'[24]

The Punjab called Gandhi, but while the capital of India was not at peace with itself, how could he go there just yet?

III

It was not merely its status as the new nation's capital that compelled Gandhi to stay on in Delhi. He had an old and intimate connection with the city. He first visited it in 1915, to speak at St Stephen's College in Kashmiri Gate, where his friend C.F. Andrews had once taught. He came back often during the days of Khilafat and the non-cooperation movement. He knew and admired two great Delhi doctors: Ajmal Khan, trained in the Unani style, and M.A. Ansari, trained in modern medicine. Both were also patriots; both had been presidents of the Congress. Gandhi was particularly close to Ansari, and was devastated by his death in 1936.

Gandhi knew, from personal experience, how Muslims had defined the city of Delhi, its architecture, its literature, its musical and its medical traditions. In a speech on 13 September, he remembered that when he first came here, in 1915, he 'was told that Delhi was ruled not by the British but Hakim [Ajmal Khan] Saheb. . . . He was a Unani Hakim but had made considerable study of the Ayurvedic system. Thousands of Muslims and thousands of poor Hindus used to come to him for treatment.'

The Muslim character of Delhi had been diluted when the British moved their capital here in 1911. The lovely old mosques and forts of Delhi had to share visual and social space with the grand new imperial structures built by Lutyens and Baker. Now, a mere three and a half decades later, the threat to Delhi's Muslims was not merely aesthetic and symbolic, but physical and existential. Hindu and Sikh refugees were seeking revenge against the Muslims of Delhi for the suffering they had experienced at the hands of the Muslims of West Punjab. They demanded that these Muslims go away to Pakistan, vacating their homes, shops and schools for them to occupy.

Gandhi had praised his late friend Hakim Ajmal Khan for healing his Muslim and Hindu patients. He too had now come to Delhi as a healer, albeit of souls, seeking to reconcile Hindus and Muslims and help them rebuild their lives and their country. And not just in India, but in Pakistan too. As he told H.S. Suhrawardy, who came to see him on 18 September, 'both Governments should make a clean breast of their mistakes and failures'. Suhrawardy was on his way to Karachi; Gandhi told him to tell Jinnah 'to face up to his own declaration respecting the minorities which were being honoured more in the breach than the observance'.

The same day, addressing a gathering of Hindus and Sikhs in Delhi, he urged them to ensure that Muslims lived, not as slaves, but as full and equal citizens of India. He hoped to soon leave for Pakistan, where, as he put it, 'I shall not spare them. I shall die for the Hindus and the Sikhs there. I shall be really glad to die there.'

That trip to Pakistan would be contingent on the establishment of peace in India. There were millions of Muslims in the country; scattered across its villages, districts and states. There were even some in his own village, who were so 'loyal to Sevagram, they would lay down their lives for it'. And yet, some Hindus questioned the loyalty of *all* Muslims who had chosen to stay behind.

In one speech, Gandhi asked his audience: 'Are you going to annihilate all the three-and-a-half or four crore Muslims? Or would you like to convert them to Hinduism? But even that would be a kind of annihilation. Supposing you were so pressurized, would you agree to become Muslims? . . . It is senseless to ask Muslims to accept Hinduism like this. . . . Am I going to save Hinduism with the help of such Hindus?'[25]

On 27 September, Winston Churchill, speaking in the British Parliament, argued that the communal violence in the subcontinent was a vindication of imperial rule. Churchill claimed that India had known a 'general peace' under 'the broad, tolerant and impartial rule of the British Crown and Parliament'. The departure of the white rulers, claimed Churchill, was leading to 'a retrogression of civilization throughout these enormous regions, constituting one of the most melancholy tragedies which Asia has ever known'.

In his prayer meeting the next day, Gandhi referred to this speech. He praised Churchill's role during the war, the saving of his nation from the Nazis, but thought that by this speech, 'Mr. Churchill has harmed his country which he has greatly served'. For, the British themselves bore much responsibility for the communal violence. 'The vivisection of India,' commented Gandhi, 'unwittingly invited the two parts of the country to fight each other.' That said, Gandhi accepted that Indians had contributed to the troubles by their own partisan acts. 'Many of you,' said Gandhi to his audience in Delhi, 'have given ground to Mr. Churchill for making such remarks. You still have sufficient time to reform your ways and prove Mr. Churchill's prediction wrong.'[26]

IV

On 2 October 1947, Gandhi turned seventy-eight. From the morning a stream of visitors came to wish him. They included his close lieutenants Nehru and Patel, now prime minister and home minister respectively in the Government of India. His devoted English disciple, Mira, had decorated the chair he customarily sat in with a cross and the words Hé Ram, made of flowers.

Gandhi was not displeased to see his old friends and comrades. But his overall frame of mind was bleak. 'What sin have I committed,' he told Patel in Gujarati, 'that He should have kept me alive to witness all these horrors?' As he told the audience at that evening's prayer meeting: 'I am surprised and also ashamed that I am still alive. I am the same person whose word was honoured by the millions of the country. But today nobody listens to me. You want only the Hindus to remain in India and say that none else should be left behind. You may kill the Muslims today; but what will you do tomorrow? What will happen to the Parsis and the Christians and then to the British? After all, they are also Christians.'

Ever since his release from jail in 1944, Gandhi had spoken often of wanting to live for 125 years. Now, in the face of the barbarism around him, he had given up that ambition. 'In such a situation,' he asked, 'what place do I have in India and what is the point of my being alive?' Gandhi told the crowd who had gathered to wish him at Birla House that 'if you really want to celebrate my birthday, it is your duty not to let anyone be possessed by madness and if there is any anger in your hearts you must remove it'.[27]

Delhi had not yet completely dispossessed itself of its madness. But Calcutta had. C. Rajagopalachari sent Gandhi editorials published in two Muslim newspapers in that city, which, while wishing him a long life, nicely outlined what he stood for and why he was still needed. The *Star of India* remarked that the 'baser passions to which many in the country have given a free rein threaten to make a messy thing of freedom—something entirely different from the Swaraj of Gandhiji's conception. There is a crying need to rehabilitate men's minds and there is also a unanimous feeling that no one is better qualified to do it than Gandhiji.'

The *Morning News*, meanwhile, described Gandhi as 'a symbol of the soul of India', who had 'held aloft the blazing torch of liberty', who had 'won freedom by his own sacrifices for ¼ of the world's people'. The newspaper continued:

Calcutta will never forget the superhuman effort Gandhiji made to make sanity return to the city when it seemed to have taken temporary leave of some of its citizens. . . . He showed his real greatness in the miraculous way he was able to bring about a change of heart even among Calcutta's criminals. . . . Some of Gandhiji's own co-religionists have undoubtedly betrayed him, made his message of non-violence a mockery. The prophet, as is proverbial, is never honoured in his own country. But Gandhiji, as he steps into his 79th year, crowned with the laurels, must have the supreme satisfaction of having used a technique with superb success against the mightiest military machine in the world. He has the rare distinction of having lived to see the fruits of his own labours. May he live long to see India tread the primrose path of its newly-won freedom.[28]

V

On 9 October 1947, H.S. Suhrawardy came to see Gandhi. Suhrawardy had just returned from Karachi, where he had tried, but failed, to get Jinnah to sign 'a declaration of cooperation and mutual assistance between the two dominions', committing both to protecting their minorities and to not making provocative statements against one another. Gandhi had already signed the statement, which may have made Jinnah even more averse to joining in. Jinnah received Suhrawardy coldly, accusing him of being 'taken in' by Gandhi. When the Bengali reported this to him, Gandhi commented that 'there cannot be a worse libel . . . You should know that I am incapable of deceiving anybody or wishing anybody ill.' He urged Suhrawardy not to give up on his peace mission, saying: 'If only you could get Jinnah to do the right thing, peace between the two Dominions might return.'[29]

In late October, a force of Afridis and Pathans, encouraged, funded and advised by the Pakistan government, entered Kashmir to seek to forcibly incorporate it into their country. Commenting on this invasion, Gandhi said 'it is not possible to take anything from anyone by force'. He added: 'If the people of the Indian Union are going there to force the Kashmiris, they should be stopped too, and they should stop by themselves.'

This was said on 26 October. The next day, the first batch of Indian troops was flown to Srinagar. The maharaja had asked for them in the wake of the invasion. Nehru came to Gandhi and apprised him of why the troops were sent. Gandhi accepted that the action was necessary for protecting the Valley from the raiders. But after the soldiers had saved Srinagar and Kashmir, what would happen next? Gandhi answered the question thus: 'All that would happen would be that Kashmir would belong to the Kashmiris.' To the Kashmiris, not to the maharaja.

Gandhi was happy that the popular leader Sheikh Abdullah had been released in time to help repulse the invaders. 'If anyone can save Kashmir, it is the Muslims, the Kashmiri Pandits, the Rajputs and the Sikhs who can do so. Sheikh Abdullah has affectionate and friendly relations with all of them.'[30]

On 28 October, Gandhi met the governor general. When the conversation turned to the conflict in Kashmir, Gandhi said that if 'Sheikh Abdullah and his men stood side by side with them [the Indian troops] in defence of their hearth and homes and womenfolk it would have a wonderful effect throughout India, whatever the outcome of the battle. The fact that Moslems and Sikhs and Hindus had fought together in a common cause would be a turning point in history.'[31]

In between visits to refugee camps and his own daily evening prayer meeting, Gandhi had many visitors at Birla House. Nehru and Patel came often to see him, usually separately. This was not only because he had intimate relations with both, but also because the two had recently begun drifting apart. They had different views on the communal question. Patel was still sore with the Muslims of the south and the west voting for the League in 1946 even when their districts would never be part of Pakistan. He wanted the Muslims who stayed behind in India to prove their loyalty to the Union. Nehru, on the other hand, argued that by staying back, they had already demonstrated their loyalty. He further insisted that whatever Pakistan did to its minorities, India must ensure that Muslims (and Christians) would have equal rights in the republic.[32]

Nehru and Patel also disagreed on the functioning of the Cabinet system. Patel thought the prime minister was merely the first among equals. He was cross that Nehru had deputed his secretary to inquire into a riot in Ajmer, when law and order came under his home ministry. Nehru answered that as the head of the government, he could send an official wherever he wished.

Nehru and Patel took their disagreements to Gandhi, independently. Both threatened to resign. To the mountain of worries confronting Gandhi, here was a new, unexpected and unwelcome one: a fight between the two men he had thought would, working together, unite the nation after he was gone. He worried too that he had lost his authority over the two men, and that Patel in particular thought his ideas had no relevance any more. As Gandhi told Kripalani (whom he had known longer than he had known either Nehru or Patel), 'Jawaharlal at least tries to understand me, though he may not follow my advice, but Sardar thinks that I am now no good [and that] I am living in the clouds and have lost touch with the reality of the situation.'[33] Speaking to his grand-niece Manu about the conflict between Nehru and Patel, Gandhi remarked: 'Today we miss Mahadev as never before. Had he been alive, he would never have allowed things to come to such a pass.'[34]

VI

In the middle of November, the AICC met in New Delhi. Addressing the delegates, Gandhi told them: 'You represent the vast ocean of Indian humanity. You will not allow it to be said that the Congress consists of a handful of people who rule the country. At least I will not allow it.'

Gandhi's talk at the AICC focused on religious harmony. 'India does not belong to Hindus alone,' he insisted, 'nor does Pakistan to Muslims.' Congressmen may 'blame the Muslim League for what has happened and say that the two-nation theory is at the root of all this evil and that it was the Muslim League that sowed the seed of this poison; nevertheless I say that we would be betraying the Hindu religion if we did evil because others had done it.' Gandhi reminded the delegates that 'it is the basic creed of the Congress that India is the home of Muslims no less than of Hindus'.[35]

That India did not belong to Hindus alone was also a recurrent theme in his prayer meetings. On 19 November, he spoke of how, in the old, historic locality of Chandni Chowk, shop owners who were Muslim were being forcibly driven out. Two days later, he reported that some 130 mosques in and around Delhi had been damaged or destroyed; such acts, he commented, 'can only destroy [the Hindu] religion'.[36]

Gandhi also spoke of the abduction of women by rioters. In West Punjab, Hindu and Sikh girls had been captured and often forcibly converted to Islam. On the Indian side of the border, Hindus and Sikhs had acted likewise with Muslim women.

Some of Gandhi's disciples, such as Mridula Sarabhai and Rameshwari Nehru, were working on restoring these girls and women to their families.[37] They estimated that the number of abducted women was close to forty thousand in all, a large, perhaps we should say alarming, figure. 'We have become barbarous in our behaviour,' remarked Gandhi mournfully. 'It is true of East Punjab as well as of West Punjab. It is meaningless to ask which of them is more barbaric. Barbarism has no degrees.'[38]

In the second week of December, there was a meeting of social workers in Delhi. To his colleagues working on khadi, village uplift, and Harijan work, Gandhi unburdened himself of his worries at the rather quick corrosion of values among those Congressmen who had entered the legislature or had become ministers. 'Anybody who goes into politics gets contaminated,' he said. 'Let us keep out of it altogether. Our influence will grow thereby. The greater our inner purity, the greater shall be our hold on the people, without any effort on our part.'

Gandhi added that 'the Congressmen are not sufficiently interested in constructive work. If they were, it should not have been necessary for us to meet here.' He urged constructive workers to strive to 'resuscitate the village, make it prosperous and give it more education and more power'. When told that the government sometimes obstructed their efforts, Gandhi replied: 'If the people are with you, the Government are bound to respond. If they do not, they will be set aside and another installed in their place.'[39]

The conflict in Kashmir had escalated. The maharaja had acceded to India, enraging Pakistan, who now threw regular troops into the battlefield, to supplement the raiders they had previously promoted. In the first week of January, the Government of India decided to take the matter to the United Nations. Gandhi felt that it might have been better to keep this a bilateral affair. He thought it not too late to invite Pakistan's representatives to Delhi, and 'with God as witness find a settlement'.[40]

VII

Four weeks after Partition and Independence, Lord Mountbatten had written to Prime Minister Attlee that 'we are now under a far greater pressure than at any time since we came out here . . . Nevertheless I honestly feel that we are all beginning to get a grip on a wellnigh desperate situation, and I feel we shall pull through all right if none of my vital ministers are bumped off—a factor which is not impossible of fulfilment with the fear-crazed, half-mad crowds of people roaming the streets of Delhi.'[41]

The fear was real, the madness partly provoked. The riots of 1946–47 had brought radicals on both sides to the fore. On the Muslim side, it was the Muslim National Guards and the Khaksars; on the Hindu side, the Hindu Mahasabha and the Rashtriya Swayamsevak Sangh (RSS). Founded in 1925, the RSS was now led by M.S. Golwalkar, an intense man of extreme views, determined to purge India of all non-Hindu influences. RSS cadres had played an active part in the violence in the Punjab. Now, in Delhi, they sought to crystallize and take advantage of the swarm of Hindu and Sikh refugees that had come into the city.[42]

On 8 March 1947, a rally of RSS workers of the Delhi province was held. Some 1,00,000 volunteers participated. The chief guest was M.S. Golwalkar, who told the gathering that it 'was the duty of every Hindu to defend his religion'.

Two days later, a meeting of RSS leaders was held in the home of one Sham Behari Lal in Daryaganj. The attendees seemed to be mostly Hindu merchants. The fragile Hindu–Muslim situation in Punjab was discussed. One Lala Hari Chand presented a purse of Rs 1,00,000 to M.S. Golwalkar on behalf of the Delhi branch. Golwalkar, in his speech, said that if the Hindus perished, the Sangh would perish. Golwalkar added that 'the disunity among Hindus in the Punjab was the cause of the present calamity. The Sangh should unite the Hindus and the capitalists should help by funds.'[43]

In the last week of September 1947, Gandhi spoke to a group of RSS workers in the Harijan Colony. He praised their discipline and the absence of untouchability within their ranks, but told them that 'in order to be truly useful, self-sacrifice had to be combined with purity of motive and true knowledge'. Many allegations that the Sangh was against Muslims had been brought to Gandhi's notice. He reminded the Sangh workers that Hinduism was not an exclusive religion, and that Hindus 'could have no quarrel with Islam'. The strength of the Sangh, said Gandhi, 'could be used in the interests of India or against it'.[44]

Gandhi was ambivalent about the RSS; the Sangh, for their part, actively distrusted him. An article in their magazine, *Organiser*, savagely attacked Gandhi's attempts at forging communal peace in Bengal. 'Nero fiddled when Rome burnt,' it remarked. 'History is repeating itself before our very eyes. From Calcutta Mahatma Gandhi is praising Islam and crying Allah-o-Akbar and enjoining Hindus to do the same, while in the Punjab and elsewhere most heinous and shameless barbarities and brutalities are being perpetrated in the name of Islam and under the cry of Allah-o-Akbar.'

Gandhi had reached out to the Muslims; but the RSS believed that 'Muslims do not attach any importance to Gandhiji and his words unless it suits them. His policy towards the Muslims has utterly failed to the chagrin and detriment of Hindus. He is, however, still held in great reverence and esteem by the Hindus, although they are in no mood to appreciate his subtleties and much less his Islamic preaching and appeasement.'

This article in the *Organiser* urged Gandhi to put his acknowledged leadership of the Hindus to other ends. The Mahatma, it said, 'has unprecedented opportunity of organising and consolidating Hindus and making them and Hindusthan great and strong within and without to be reckoned with by any aggressive nation of the world'.[45]

This was at once a critique and a lament. If only Gandhi would use his status and position to actively and militantly lead the Hindus, thus to show Muslims their place while simultaneously forcing Hindus themselves into the councils of the world! From the point of view of the RSS, Gandhi was a leader gone awry. Their own endeavour, as a policeman assigned to their beat reported, was 'for building the Hindus physically strong and for establishing Hindu rule in India'. The RSS believed 'that the present government was not cent per cent a Hindu Government but still they were not opposed to it as with the help of this government they would be able to establish purely a Hindu State'.

The police report continued:

According to the Sangh volunteers, the Muslims would quit India only when another movement for their total extermination similar to the one which was started in Delhi sometime back would take place. . . . They were waiting for the departure of Mahatma Gandhi from Delhi as they believed that so long as the Mahatma was in Delhi, they would not be able to precipitate their designs into action. They were further of the opinion that at the time of the forthcoming Id-ul-Zuha festival, if the Muslims would slaughter any kine [cows] of which the Sangh people would get a scent, then there was every possibility of communal disturbances in Delhi.[46]

In November 1947, M.S. Golwalkar returned to Delhi. He collected money from supporters, met RSS cadres and assessed the progress of the Sangh in Delhi. Several thousand new members had been enrolled. An intelligence bureau report dated 15 November noted that 'the workers of the Rashtriya Swayamsevak Sangh, especially those coming from West Punjab as refugees, intend starting communal trouble in Delhi after the Diwali festival. They say they could not tolerate the sight of Muslims moving about in Delhi and collecting large amounts from business while the Hindu and Sikh refugees, who were made destitute for no fault of theirs but only because they opposed the Muslim League and establishment of Pakistan, were dying of starvation and would have to freeze dead with chill in the coming winter. . . . It is reported that some [RSS] workers have gone out to fetch arms and ammunition for the purpose.'[47]

The annual function of the Delhi RSS was celebrated at Ramlila Ground on 7 December. The main speech was by Golwalkar, who spoke for an hour and a half. He began on a visible note of self-congratulation: 'The RSS had so many branches throughout the length and breadth of India that it would take twenty to twenty-five years to visit all of them. Despite continuous touring he had succeeded in seeing only a few of them. People were surprised to see the progress of this organisation, which was not heard of a few years back, and regarding which they had seen nothing in the press . . .'

Golwalkar then turned to the aims and ideals of the Sangh. After eulogizing the medieval warrior-kings Shivaji and Rana Pratap, he spoke of the importance of Hindu unity and self-respect. 'We should not be ashamed to call ourselves Hindus,' he remarked. 'The Sangh had taken a vow to keep up our ancient culture . . .'

The following evening, a smaller and more focused meeting was held in the Sangh's camp on Rohtak Road. Some two thousand RSS full-timers were present. Addressing this group of activists, Golwalkar said, 'We should be prepared for guerrilla warfare on the lines of the tactics of Shivaji. The Sangh will not rest content until it had finished Pakistan. If anyone stood in our way we will have to fight him too, whether it was Nehru Government or any other Government. The Sangh could not be won over.'

Also in the meeting was a policeman in plain clothes. His report noted that 'referring to Muslims', M.S. Golwalkar

> said that no power on Earth could keep them in Hindustan. They would have to quit the country. Mahatma Gandhi wanted to keep the Muslims in India so that the Congress may profit by their votes at the time of election. But, by that time, not a single Muslim will be left in India. . . . Mahatma Gandhi could not mislead them any longer. We have the means whereby such men can be immediately silenced, but it is our tradition not to be inimical to Hindus. If we are compelled, we will have to resort to that course too.[48]

The mood in Delhi during the second half of 1947 was very ugly. Angered by the violence in the Punjab, inflamed by the stories carried by Sikh and Hindu refugees, RSS militants in India's capital wished to purge this ancient city of its Islamic influences, of its large and well-established Muslim population. M.S. Golwalkar and the RSS were even thinking of having men like Gandhi and Nehru—who stood in the way of making India a Hindu theocratic state—'immediately silenced'.

VIII

In Birla House, a new member had joined Gandhi's entourage, a young English Quaker named Richard Symonds. He first met Gandhi with Horace Alexander in June 1942, and then caught up with him again in late 1945. In September 1947, Symonds returned to India to work among Partition refugees. In December, he fell seriously ill with typhoid, and was admitted into a hospital, from where Gandhi had him removed to Birla House, where he spent several weeks recovering.

Every day, Gandhi would drop in to see the patient, and have a chat. When Symonds, agitated, spoke of Partition and its consequences, Gandhi instead turned the conversation to when he was studying law in London, the 'only time he said, he was popular with the British', because at dinner his fellow students could have his share of the wine allotted to their table. On Christmas Day, Gandhi had Symonds's room decorated with streamers, and when he saw that Alexander had brought some celebratory sherry, remarked: 'I see you are having high jinks. Well, what would not be right for me may be right for you.'

Decades later, reflecting on Gandhi's kindness towards him, Symonds marvelled at how 'this great man at a time of acute anxiety, pressure and sadness, had found it possible every day to nurse and chat and joke with a man of no importance'. In truth, Gandhi probably found the experience nourishing too; despite his hostility to British imperialism, he was enormously fond of the British, and in this time of tension and stress, conversations with a sensitive young Englishman would have been a relaxation.[49]

Another young white man in Delhi in the winter of 1947–48 was Alan Moorehead, a tough and hard-nosed war correspondent originally from Australia. In the first years of the World War, Moorehead had met Gandhi several times, and had several arguments with him about the respective merits of violence and non-violence. Now, back to cover Partition and Independence, Moorehead found Gandhi, in essence and in spirit, unchanged: 'He was still getting up at four in the morning to exercise, he was still the nimblest (and I think the gayest) good brain in India, and he was still talking in parables on precisely the same theme' (of combating violence with non-violence). When the Australian went to hear him address his daily prayer meeting at Birla House, he thought Gandhi 'looked like some great gaunt bird with long, bare legs, and his little dark bird-like head poking out of his white cotton dhoti. His voice was tired, but he spoke with the mind of a mental athlete.'[50]

On the first day of 1948, one Gandhi disciple in Delhi wrote to another in Calcutta: 'Bapu is extraordinarily well and I feel that his influence is permeating slowly but surely.'[51]

At his prayer meetings in Delhi, Gandhi now wore a straw hat. Asked about this, he answered that he valued the hat for three reasons: that it was presented to him by a Muslim peasant in Noakhali; that it doubled up as an umbrella; and that it was made of local materials.[52]

Not all questions were so harmless. During the prayer meeting on 10 January, a sadhu clad in saffron got up and said he wanted to read a note he had written criticizing Gandhi. When Gandhi said he could hand the note over, to be read later, the sadhu insisted on reading it out aloud to the gathering. After some argument with the crowd, he finally agreed to sit down.[53]

The public mood in Delhi remained angry, and soon rioting broke out once more in the city. Gandhi further postponed his plans to visit Punjab. This was just as well, for the trouble escalated. In Mehrauli, a village on the outskirts of Delhi, there was a celebrated Sufi shrine, visited by tens of thousands of people, including Hindus and Muslims. Now the Muslims whose families had tended the shrine for hundreds of years were hounded out by a Hindu mob.[54]

On 12 January, Gandhi informed his prayer meeting that he was commencing a fast the next day. The recent riots had been contained by police and military action, but there was yet a 'storm within the breast. It may burst forth any day.' So, he had decided to go on a fast, which would end when he was 'satisfied that there is a reunion of hearts of all communities brought about without any outside pressure, but from an awakened sense of duty'.[55]

The *Hindustan Times*, edited by Gandhi's son Devadas, reported that the decision to fast had come 'as a complete surprise to his colleagues and the members of the Government'. Gandhi's close associates 'cannot conceal their anxiety' at his decision, said the paper, as his health was still frail, after the fast in Calcutta. But Gandhi disregarded them, for 'he had been very much affected by the all-round misery and chaos, thousands of refugees streaming to him with tragic tales'.

Meanwhile, in a private letter to his father, Devadas Gandhi wrote: 'By your strenuous efforts [for communal harmony] lacs of lives were saved and lacs more would have been saved. But all of a sudden you lost patience. What you can achieve while living, you cannot achieve by dying.'[56]

Gandhi would not be moved. On the morning of the 12th, he went to the Viceregal Palace to inform Mountbatten of his fast. Later, Nehru came to Birla House and sat with Gandhi for two hours. Although the stated reason for the fast was the deteriorating communal situation, it seems Gandhi was also upset with the government's decision to withhold from Pakistan its share of the sterling balances owed by Britain to (undivided) India after the Second World War. Because of Pakistan's invasion of Kashmir, the Indian government had delayed the payment. But in Gandhi's view of the world, financial debts to another person or entity, whether friend, enemy, or neither, had to be discharged immediately.[57]

On the 13th, Gandhi had his usual morning meal of goat's milk, boiled vegetables and fruit juice. Then he had a long conversation with Vallabhbhai Patel. The fast formally began at 11.15 a.m., after which some prayers were said.

On the 13th itself, Rajendra Prasad, now president of the Congress, issued a statement urging citizens to restore communal peace and thus save Gandhi's life. The Congress president appealed to citizens to desist from violence, since to let Gandhi die as a result of his fast would be 'an eternal blot on the name of Delhi'. The prime ministers and assemblies of Bengal and Madras urged the re-establishment of peace so that Gandhi could call off his fast.

Another report noted that 'the most pleasant surprise caused in the capital today apropos Mahatma Gandhi's fast was the news of reactions in Pakistan'. One Pakistani politician, Ghazanfar Ali Khan, said Gandhi's decision to fast should make the leaders of the two countries come together and sort out their differences. Another, Mumtaz Daultana, said Gandhi had 'rendered noble services in the cause of Hindu–Muslim unity'. A third, Feroz Khan Noon, remarked— during a session of the West Punjab assembly ostensibly devoted to discussing the budget—that 'Mahatma Gandhi's services in restoring peace in Calcutta during the recent past are only a small example of his great achievement towards restoration of sanity and peace'.[58]

On the evening of the first day of his fast, Gandhi attended the daily prayer meeting and gave his address as usual. He spoke of, among other things, the perception that Indian Muslims trusted both him and Nehru, but not Patel. Gandhi thought this slightly unfair.

'The Sardar is blunt of speech,' he remarked. 'What he says sometimes sounds bitter. The fault is in his tongue.' He asked his Muslim friends to 'bring to the Sardar's notice any mistakes which in their opinion he commits'.[59]

On the 14th, the second day of his fast, Gandhi met members of the Indian Cabinet, a deputation of refugees from the NWFP, and a large number of other visitors, including the maharaja of Patiala and G.D. Birla. Elsewhere in the city, the violence continued. Hindu and Sikh refugees attacked Muslims in the Ajmeri Gate area, whereupon a group of Congress volunteers came and took the victims to the safety of a nearby mosque. In another incident, a group of Muslims, returning to their temporary camp in Humayun's Tomb after a train they hoped to take to Pakistan had no place for them, were stopped and beaten up.

On the evening of 14 January, a batch of angry men arrived on bicycles at Birla House and raised what were described as 'communal and anti-Gandhi slogans'. Inside the house, speaking with Gandhi, were Patel, Azad and Nehru. When the trio came out and heard the demonstrators say, 'Let Gandhi Die', Nehru shouted: 'How dare you say that. Come and kill me first.' At this, the demonstrators dispersed, but no sooner had Nehru's car sped away, than they reassembled. One of Gandhi's doctors, Jivraj Mehta, tried to reason with them. They told him that the slogans were on behalf of the refugees who needed food, homes, clothes and jobs.[60]

At the prayer meeting that day, Gandhi spoke of reports of attacks on Sikhs and Hindus in Pakistan; if these ceased, they would have a beneficial effect on India. He then turned to his present ordeal. 'They tell me I am mad,' he said, 'and have a habit of going on fast on the slightest pretext. But I am made that way.' When he was a boy growing up in Kathiawar, he had a dream 'that if the Hindus, Sikhs, Parsis, Christians and Muslims could live in amity not only in Rajkot but in the whole of India, they would all have a very happy life. If the dream could be realized even now when I am an old man on the verge of death, my heart would dance.'[61]

On the 15th, the third day of Gandhi's fast, an American writer visiting India went to see him at Birla House. He saw him lying on a cot in the porch. Gandhi, reported this writer to his wife in New York, was asleep, lying on his side in an embryo position. He was completely covered in a khaddar cloth, including his head, and framing his face. . . . An old man's face and not attractive. In his sleep, he seemed to have lost control and it showed what he perhaps was feeling—suffering, intense suffering . . . Somehow we never think of a Gandhi fast as a terrible physical experience. We think of it as a political manoeuvre, a strike, a gesture. But here it was in human terms, a process. Here was a 79 year old man deliberately killing himself in the most difficult and excruciating way.[62]

Elsewhere in the city, a young student from Gorakhpur, walking through Connaught Circus, came across a group of men in khaki shorts, white shirts and black caps, exercising while vigorously waving sticks. They were volunteers of the RSS. As they walked and jumped, these RSS men shouted at the top of their voices, 'Boodhé ko marné do' (Let the old man die).[63]

At evening prayers on the 15th, Gandhi was visibly weak. From his bed, with a microphone next to him, he spoke in a barely audible voice for a minute. The rest of his speech, read out for him by Pyarelal, explained that his fast was on behalf of the minorities *both* in Pakistan and India. Conducted in the first instance 'on behalf of the Muslim minority in the [Indian] Union', it was 'necessarily against the Hindus and Sikhs of the Union and [against] the Muslims of Pakistan'.[64]

After the meeting, the crowd filed past him, one by one, bowing with folded hands, first the children, then the women, finally the men.

Meanwhile, news reached Birla House that the government had agreed to pay the sterling balances owed to Pakistan, as their contribution 'to the non-violent and noble effort made by Gandhiji, in accordance with the glorious traditions of this great country, for peace and goodwill'. The Government of India had bowed to Gandhi's will; when would the city of Delhi do likewise?[65]

IX

On 16 January, Prime Minister Nehru spoke to a crowd of over a lakh in Delhi, urging them to maintain peace and save their leader's life. 'We must not allow Gandhiji to suffer for our sins,' he said. The post office in Delhi was now marking all letters they received or sent with the words 'Communal harmony will save Gandhiji' written in English, Urdu and Hindi.

Political parties and civil society organizations made appeals of their own. A statement by the Sikh political party, the Akali Dal, said: 'No Sikh should at any cost, in a state of excitement or under stress of provocation, do anything which may endanger the peace of the country or Hindu–Sikh–Muslim unity.' Syed Muttalabi, secretary of the Mewati Conference, wired Jinnah that Indian Muslims were 'determined' to save Gandhiji's life, since his life was 'a bedrock against inhuman barbarities committed in both the Dominions'. The Meos had suffered greatly during the riots, but had decided to stay back in India because of 'Gandhiji's untiring efforts' on their behalf. The Meo leader appealed to Jinnah and the people of Pakistan 'to stop the killing of the minority community and create conditions for the return and resettlement of Hindus and Sikhs in Pakistan'.[66]

Following these developments from Calcutta was C. Rajagopalachari, the governor of West Bengal. He wrote anxiously to Devadas Gandhi: 'I hope Jawaharlalji will do something and get Bapu to give up his fast. No one else can do this now.'[67]

On Saturday the 17th, Gandhi entered the fifth day of his fast. His doctors issued a bulletin saying he was 'definitely weaker and has begun to feel heavy in the head'. Besides, 'the kidneys are not functioning well'.

Meeting Maulana Azad in the morning, Gandhi laid down seven conditions for breaking his fast. These were: 1. The annual fair (the Urs) at the Khwaja Bakhtiyar shrine at Mehrauli, due in nine days' time, should take place peacefully; 2. The hundred-odd mosques in Delhi converted into homes and temples should be restored to their original uses; 3. Muslims should be allowed to move freely around Old Delhi; 4. Non-Muslims should not object to Delhi Muslims returning to their homes from Pakistan; 5. Muslims should be allowed to travel without danger in trains; 6. There should be no economic boycott of Muslims; 7. Accommodation of Hindu refugees in Muslim areas should be done with the consent of those already in these localities.

Gandhi's influence was finally permeating across the city of Delhi, 'slowly but surely'. Two lakh people signed a peace pledge, which read: 'We the Hindu, Sikh, Christian and other citizens of Delhi declare solemnly our conviction that Muslim citizens of the Indian Union should be as free as the rest of us to live in Delhi in peace and security and with self-respect and to work for the good and well-being of the Indian Union.'

In Subzi Mandi, Paharganj and Karol Bagh, residents said they were willing to welcome Muslims back in their midst. Muslim villagers of Mehrauli sent their representatives to Birla House to tell Gandhi that conditions for peacefully holding their Urs now existed.[68]

On the 17th evening, Gandhi somehow summoned the strength to speak at his prayer meeting. He thanked all those who had written or wired their good wishes (many from Pakistan). But he insisted that his fast was not 'a political move in any sense of the term. It is in obedience to the peremptory call of conscience and duty.'[69]

On the morning of 18 January, Hindu, Muslim and Sikh leaders met at Rajendra Prasad's house. Here they signed a pledge assuring Gandhi that the seven conditions he had stipulated would be fully met. The Urs would be held at Mehrauli as usual, Muslims would be able to move freely all across Delhi, the mosques taken away from Muslims would be returned to them, and so on. They all then trooped over to Birla House to present the undertaking to Gandhi. Reassured and convinced, shortly after noon, Gandhi accepted a glass of lime juice.

When Gandhi broke his fast, the room he was in was

> filled with Ministers of the Cabinet, leaders of the various communities, inmates of Gandhiji's camp, Pressmen and photographers.
>
> Reclining on the pillow, Gandhiji chuckled aloud when Maulana Azad handed him a glass of lemon juice sweetened with glucose. The room rang with shouts of 'Gandhiji-ki-jai'. A smile appeared on the face of Pandit Jawaharlal Nehru who had worn an anxious look all these days.

Outside, the city of 'Delhi was jubilant: its efforts to convince Gandhiji that the era of communal madness in the capital was over had succeeded'. The news that the fast had been broken brought thousands of people to Birla House, despite it being a rainy day.[70]

Over the past thirty-five years, Gandhi had gone on fast every other year. The provocations had been various: sexual transgressions in the ashram; violence committed in the name of nationalism; the oppression of 'untouchables'; and, of course, the need for communal harmony.[71] On 16 January 1948, he wrote to a disciple now living in the Himalaya, who had been at his side in several previous fasts, that this latest yajna in Delhi was his 'greatest fast'.[72] It was, with the possible exception only of the fast that immediately preceded it, undertaken in Calcutta in September 1947.

CHAPTER THIRTY-EIGHT

Martyrdom

I

When he broke his fast on 18 January, Gandhi told those who had signed the pledge presented to him that while it bound them to keep the peace in Delhi, this did not mean that 'whatever happens outside Delhi will be no concern of yours'. The atmosphere that prevailed in the capital must prevail in the nation too.[1]

That same evening, Jawaharlal Nehru addressed a large public meeting at Subzi Mandi, where he remarked that 'there is only one frail old man in our country who has all along stuck to the right path. We had all, some time or the other, strayed away from his path. In order to make us realize our mistakes he undertook this great ordeal.' Congratulating the people of Delhi for taking the pledge to restore communal harmony, Nehru said the next step was to ensure peace 'not merely in Delhi but in the whole of India'.

Later that evening, a group of Muslims returned to Subzi Mandi, where they 'were given a hearty welcome in the vegetable market where they [had] felt somewhat insecure'.[2]

Monday the 19th was a day of silence for Gandhi. He spent it attending to his correspondence and writing articles for *Harijan*. In their daily report, the doctors attending on him said: 'There is considerable weakness still. There are signs of improvement in his kidneys. The diet is being slowly worked up. He is still on liquids.'

Also on the 19th, the general secretary of the Hindu Mahasabha issued a statement saying that while they were relieved that Gandhi was out of danger, the Mahasabha had not signed the peace pledge, since 'the response to his fast has been wholly one-sided, the Pakistan Government still persisting in its attitude of truculence . . . The net result of the fast has been the weakening of the Hindu front and strengthening of the Pakistan Government.' The statement went on: 'What we oppose is the basic policy of Mahatma Gandhi and the followers of his way of thinking that whatever might be done to the Hindus of Pakistan, Muslim minorities in India must be treated equally with other minorities. This is a policy that the Hindu Mahasabha can never accept . . .'[3]

At his prayer meeting on the 20th, Gandhi said he hoped to go to Pakistan, but only if the government there had no objection to his coming, and only when he had regained his strength. As he was speaking, there was a loud explosion. This scared Manu Gandhi, sitting next to him, as well as members of the audience. Gandhi, however, was unruffled. After the noise died down, he continued his speech.[4]

The explosion was the sound of a bomb going off behind the servants quarters of Birla House, some 200 feet from the prayer meeting. Inquiries revealed that a group of men had come earlier in the evening in a green car and 'moved around in a suspicious manner'. After the explosion, watchmen arrived on the scene, and apprehended a young man who had a hand grenade. His accomplices had meanwhile fled. The man, named Madan Lal Pahwa—who was 'well dressed, of fair complexion and of medium height'—said he was opposed to Gandhi's peace campaign since he 'had lost everything he had in West Punjab'. A refugee from Montgomery district, he was living in a mosque in Paharganj from where he had just been evicted (as it had been restored to the Muslims).

On hearing of the incident, Nehru came to Birla House, met Gandhi and also discussed the matter with the police.[5]

II

The doctors had told Gandhi to wait a fortnight after his fast ended before travelling out of Delhi. While he wished to go to the Punjab, he hadn't been in his ashram in Sevagram since August 1946. His devoted (and always possessive) disciples called him there. He now planned to leave for Wardha on 2 February, stay two weeks in the ashram, and then come back north and carry on to the Punjab and Pakistan.

On 26 January, the Urs, or annual festival of homage, began in the shrine of the thirteenth-century saint Qutubuddin Bakhtiyar at Mehrauli. The holding of the Urs was a crucial part of the peace pledge presented to Gandhi. On the 27th, he went to Mehrauli himself. Gandhi had never felt the need to pray in, or even visit, formally sanctified structures. He had made an exception in the case of the Meenakshi temple in Madurai when it finally admitted Harijans. He would make another exception now for this tomb outside Delhi.

When Gandhi reached Mehrauli, a large crowd, estimated at close to 10,000, had assembled to welcome him. Gandhi was escorted around the site and told the life story of the saint. He expressed distress at the damage to the marble trellis. A custodian of the tomb thanked Gandhi for creating the conditions in which the Urs was celebrated. A representative of Ajmer Sharif (the tomb of the even greater Sufi saint Hazrat Moinuddin Chishti) told Gandhi that many Muslims had fled Ajmer, and asked him to come 'to allay the panic of the Muslims who were still there'.[6]

Later, in a brief speech, Gandhi requested 'the Hindus, Sikhs and Muslims who have come here with cleansed hearts to take a vow at this holy place that you will never allow strife to raise its head, but will live in amity, united as friends and brothers'.[7]

Gandhi visited the shrine in Mehrauli, but Muslims in the city continued to feel insecure. That evening, at the prayer meeting in Birla House, Gandhi asked how many Muslims were present. One, was the answer. 'Sirf ek?' (only one?), he said, sadly, before urging those present to bring their Muslim friends along the next day.[8]

III

Through 1947, as he was seeking to douse fires in Bengal, Bihar and Delhi, Gandhi had been peppered with a series of letters from a friend with whom he had long been out of touch. His name was John Cordes. A Christian priest of German extraction, based in Rhodesia, in 1907 Cordes had left the ministry and joined Gandhi's rural settlement in Natal. Here, he lived with contentment for some years, before discovering theosophy, and travelling to India to meet Annie Besant. He soon returned, disenchanted, and spent his time shuttling between different parts of South Africa. In between, he had rejoined the Church, and then left it again.[9]

In May 1947, Cordes wrote to Gandhi out of the blue. He was looking 'around for fields anew', and thought of coming over to India to join his old friend. He had, he told Gandhi, 'devised a remarkably interesting way of teaching History, Geography, Art & International bridging of nationalities and Races'. He could also translate articles from German for Gandhi's papers. His letter continued:

> All this if approved by you. I bow to your services, as of yore. You are the man on the spot. Then as now I should have to be approved by the Settlers themselves. For you I have a remarkable study (Gnostic-Chinese-Chaldean-Indian etc) on Longevity. It may make you 127 or 157, just a generation longer. Then as now I can be of modest financial assistance again. I should prefer to come via Calcutta to see Sri Paramah Ramakrishna Kali Temples & possibly Sri Sri Anandamayiji & possibly Budha Gaya and Benares. Then as now, I do not proselytize for Adyar, Theosophy nor for Christ, but if allowed I like to join in appeals for womenfolk & children . . .[10]

Gandhi wrote back asking Cordes to come to Sevagram. He did, but first undertook a leisurely trip through India itself. In late November, he finally made his way, via Madras, Calcutta and Rajasthan, to Sevagram, accompanied by fifteen trunks of luggage, which included some four hundred books. Gandhi was himself in Delhi, so his nephew Chhaganlal helped him settle into the ashram, and began teaching him Hindustani.

From Sevagram, Cordes wrote a series of frenzied mails to the ashram's absent founder. In a letter of December 1947, he told Gandhi that he 'attended the Prayer meeting at 7.30 pm, & listened (in bed) to the 4.30 puja. It is too cold then to sit in the dark & wind on the cold ground, but when warmth and light return I shall be of the party.' In another, he told of being asked to recite a Christian prayer, whereupon, as he wrote, 'I chose the following as in your Spirit (adapted from Liberal Catholic Liturgy): Almighty God, unto whom all hearts be open, all desires be known & from whom no secrets are hid; cleanse the thoughts of our hearts by the inspiration of Thy Holy Spirit that we may perfectly love Thee, & worthily magnify Thy Holy Name; Teach us, O Lord, to see Thy life in all men and in all the peoples of Thine earth & so guide the nations into the understanding of Thy laws that peace and goodwill may reign upon earth. Amen.'[11]

In the midst of his walks and fasts for communal harmony, Gandhi must have welcomed the diversion provided by Cordes's letters. They reminded him of his formative years in South Africa, of the friendships he forged there, and the comparatively less strenuous struggles he had waged in that country. Cordes, for his part, was impressed by his friend's commitment and resolve. Thus, one letter thanks Gandhi for his 'charming note of the 4th Dec. Fancy finding the time in this turmoil of hectic days & incessant audiences to write to me!' In another letter he wrote: 'How on earth your dear letter of the 19th 5.45 am could have reached me at 10 o'clock today I have not fathomed yet. You still chase yourself to death, up at 4 am, & to bed a little bit before that! Miraculous and superhumanlike!'[12]

IV

On 29 January, the postman brought, as always, many letters addressed to Gandhi. Among the letters was one from Henry Polak. With Kasturba and Pranjivan Mehta dead, perhaps no person alive knew Gandhi better and longer than Polak. Yet, their relationship had recently undergone some strain. His former housemate in Johannesburg, his second in command in his years in South Africa, had taken against Gandhi during the World War, going so far as to visit the United States to preach against him.

After Kasturba died, Polak had sent a letter of consolation and also written a warm tribute for publication. There had been messages sent and received from mutual friends. The process of reconciliation had begun. Scars remained, on Gandhi's side especially. Polak knew that, and was seeking to remove them. In this latest letter, posted from Folkestone on 23 January and arriving in Delhi on the 29th, he asked Gandhi whether he had 'got our two anxious telegrams'. He and his wife Millie were, he said, 'greatly relieved' at the conclusion of his recent fast. 'We deeply hope, with you,' wrote Polak to Gandhi, 'that the peace will be real and lasting, and that you may not have to resort again to a fast—at least, on this account. It is tragic to think that this fast should have become necessary for the restoration of communal peace, when I recall that some 24 years ago you had to resort to a fast to ensure communal unity. To-day's news is that your strength is beginning to return and that you hope soon to have got back to normal. We, too, most earnestly hope so.'

Polak seems to have realized afresh what had been obscured during the anguished choices and partisan politics of the Second World War; that the friend he had once called 'Bada Bhai', elder brother, was one of the great figures of the age. So, in this letter of reaching out and reconciliation, Polak underlined his own intimate ties to Gandhi. Thus he wrote:

> I am now a member of the Executive Committee of the London Vegetarian Society, of which you were an early member . . . I have often shown at vegetarian gatherings your membership badge, which you gave me years ago in Johannesburg. I still have—and frequently refer to—your signed copy of the Song Celestial that we used to read together. I have read nearly 40 English renderings of the Bhagavad Gita, but like you I prefer Arnold's rendering to the rest, and quote from it when I have occasion to refer to the B.G. in my lectures.

The letter then turned to family matters, speaking of Millie, who had dislocated her shoulder; of their son, Leon, who 'is a great standby in the professional work' [of law]; of their grandchildren. Polak said he often mentioned in legal circles that he had been professionally articled to Gandhi, who was thus, in a matter of speaking, his 'father-in-law'. Further underlining the once very close, now somewhat distant, personal connections, he mentioned meeting the Indian journalist Krishnalal Shridharani, and telling him that 'our relations had been those of Bhai and Chhotabhai. He at once insisted on addressing me as Kakaji!' (father's younger brother).

The letter's last line read: 'Hoping to continue to get good news of you and of India and communal relations, and with our love.' Polak had started by addressing Gandhi as 'My dear Bhai', and signed off as 'Henry (C)', the 'C' standing for 'Chotabhai'.[13]

Although one can't be absolutely certain, Pyarelal must have brought this letter to Gandhi's attention. He would have read it with pleasure, affection, and perhaps, a certain sense of relief.

V

It was now five months since Independence, and Gandhi was increasingly disenchanted with the behaviour of the Congressmen who had taken office. On 29 January, he drafted a short note arguing that the Congress itself should be disbanded, since it had 'outlived its use' as 'a propaganda vehicle and parliamentary machine'. It must keep itself 'out of unhealthy competition with political parties and communal bodies'.

Other parties could contest elections and run governments, but the Congress, argued Gandhi, should now become a Lok Sevak Sangh (Society for the Service of the People). The workers of this new organization (habitual khadi wearers of course) should focus on rural reconstruction, on making India's villages 'self-contained and self-supporting through their agriculture and handicrafts'. They should 'educate the village folk in sanitation and hygiene' and enrol them for voting in local, state and national elections.[14]

This document was prompted by reports of the arrogance and misconduct of Congress legislators and ministers. Gandhi hoped to circulate it among party members across India. He had not yet shown it to Nehru and Patel, who would most likely have dismissed it as idealistic. If the Congress suddenly left office, who would run the government? Rather than leave the running of the State to untested or malevolent men, surely it was wiser to have people of quality and credibility at the helm of power?

Gandhi had been upset by the bickering between Nehru and Patel. Despite their differences, however, the two men had been working independently to create a united and peaceable India. On 29 January, the day that Gandhi wrote his note asking for the disbanding of the Congress, Patel held a press conference in Delhi, where he briefed reporters on the princely states that had already joined the Union. As regards the recalcitrant nizam of Hyderabad, Patel insisted that the 'accession of Hyderabad was inevitable'. The same day, Nehru addressed a meeting in Amritsar, where, 'trembling with anger and emotion', he spoke of an incident where some people (most likely angry Hindu refugees) had trampled upon the national flag on 26 January. Nehru insisted: 'Whoever insults the National Flag— be he a Pakistani, a Britisher, a Hindu [Maha]Sabhaite or an R.S.S. man—will be considered a traitor and will be treated as such.'[15]

These activities of Gandhi's key political lieutenants were captured on the front page of the *Hindustan Times* of 30 January 1948. The top story on the left of the page carried the headline, 'BLOODLESS REVOLUTION IN STATES'; the lead story on the right carried the headline, 'NEHRU DARES COMMUNALISTS TO COME OUT IN OPEN'.

VI

On 30 January 1948, Gandhi woke up as usual at 3.30 a.m. After his toilet, he attended morning prayers, had a glass of water mixed with honey and lime juice, and then a short nap. His first appointment was at 7 p.m., with a social worker on her way to America. After a massage, he read the morning papers, revised his note on the future of the Congress, had his daily Bengali lesson, and then ate his breakfast, which consisted of boiled vegetables, goat's milk, raw radish, tomatoes and orange juice.

After his morning meal, Gandhi had another nap. His first appointments on waking up were with the leaders of Delhi's Muslims, the maulanas Hifzur Rahman and Ahmed Said. A conference of constructive workers had been called in Sevagram on 2 February. Gandhi was keen to attend; moreover, he had not been back to his ashram for more than a year. But he would leave Delhi only if he was certain that the Muslims in the city felt secure. Maulana Hifzur Rahman told him that now he had made their city peaceful and their community safe, he was free to travel to Sevagram. Gandhi then asked his associate Brij Krishna Chandiwala to book the train tickets to Wardha.

At about 1 p.m. on 30 of January, the Gujarati philanthropist Shantikumar Morarjee came to see Gandhi. They discussed the writing of a biography of Mahadev Desai, and the editing of his diaries, with Morarjee willing to foot the bill. Gandhi suggested that since Mahadev's old friend Narhari Parikh was not well, another long-time ashramite, Chandrashankar Shukla, be asked to do the job.[16]

Through the afternoon, Gandhi met with visitors. They included refugees, Harijans, Congress leaders and social workers. A diplomat from Ceylon also called with his daughter. The historian Radha Kumud Mukherjee also came.[17]

The most important visitor of the day arrived at 4.30 in the afternoon. This was Vallabhbhai Patel. They discussed the growing rift between him and Nehru, which Gandhi thought was 'disastrous'. Perhaps one of them should leave the Cabinet to leave the field clear for the other person. The discussion was intense and prolonged; so much so that Gandhi was late for the prayer meeting. Nehru himself had planned to come and talk to Gandhi after the prayers were over.[18]

At about quarter past five on the evening of 30 January, Gandhi stepped out of Birla House, and began walking towards the garden, where the prayer meeting was to be held. He had, as was now customary, his hands around the shoulders of his grand-nieces Manu and Abha. As he climbed the steps to the platform from where he would speak, a man in a khaki tunic advanced towards Gandhi, as if to touch his feet. Since they were late, Abha tried to stop him. The man roughly pushed her aside; she stumbled backwards, Gandhi's notebook, spittoon and rosary falling from her hands. The interloper then 'suddenly stepped out in front of him and whipping out a pistol, fired three shots at him at point-blank range. One bullet hit Gandhiji in the chest and two in the abdomen.' He collapsed and fell to the ground, muttering 'Hé Ram', an invocation to his favourite mythological figure and lifelong icon, the god-king Ram.

On hearing the shots being fired, 'a terrible cry rose from the crowd, who closed in on the assailant'. He was overpowered, and handed over to the police. Gandhi was carried into Birla House. Nothing could be done to revive him. He had been killed almost instantaneously.[19]

As news of the assassination spread, the first to arrive at Birla House were Devadas Gandhi and Maulana Azad. They were followed by Nehru, Patel, the Mountbattens, other ministers and senior officials (including the army chief, General Roy Bucher). As one report went, 'Pandit Nehru and Sardar Patel sat for long beside the body and gazed hard baffled by the sudden catastrophe. Maulana Azad after a while retreated to a secluded corner to mourn in silence. The Governor-General, Lord Mountbatten, hearing someone say that it would be a day of mourning for the whole country, remarked that it would be a day of mourning for the entire world.'[20]

As the dignitaries crowded into Birla House, an enterprising reporter went out of the premises, and walked over to the nearest police station, at the intersection of Aurangzeb and Tughlak Roads. There, in a dark, unlit room, was Gandhi's assassin. When the reporter set eyes on him, 'blood was pouring from his forehead and had practically covered the whole left side of his face. This I was told was due to the blows which the spectators had heaped upon him. The police told me that contrary to the original report the assassin had not tried to shoot himself but some nearby spectators who saw him shooting at Gandhiji had pounced upon him and mauled him.'

The assassin, who was handcuffed, got up when the reporter entered the room. He said his name was Nathuram, and that he was from Poona. He gave his age as twenty-five, but the journalist thought 'he looked considerably older'.

When asked whether he had anything to say, Gandhi's murderer 'smiled blandly' and remarked: 'For the present I only want to say that I am not at all sorry for what I have done. The rest I will explain in court.'

At this stage the police intervened, and disallowed further questions. On his way out, the reporter asked a policeman what Nathuram was carrying apart from his gun (a Beretta automatic). Four hundred rupees, was the answer.[21]

Back in Birla House, Gandhi's body was draped in a white khadi cloth, put on a plain bier, and carried to the terrace. Floodlights were put on to make the body visible to the crowds below. 'Shouts of "Mahatma Gandhi ki jai" rent the air. People wept and sobbed.'[22]

At 2 a.m., after the crowds had dispersed, Gandhi's associates brought the body inside to give it a bath. A tub was filled with cold water. The task of bathing the dead Mahatma was handed over to Brij Krishna Chandiwala, who was from an old Delhi family, and had associated himself with Gandhi from the time he heard him speak at his college, St Stephen's, in 1919. Brij Krishna now took off Gandhi's blood-splattered loincloth and gave it to Devadas. The woollen shawl, displaying the three holes through which the bullets had entered, was also handed over to Gandhi's youngest son. Because of the blood they contained, the clothes stuck to the body; as he wrenched them off, Brij Krishna burst out sobbing.

Writing some years later of how he felt at the time, Brij Krishna remarked:

> Bapu's body now lay on the plank. I filled a tumbler with cold water from the tub and stretched out my hand to pour it on Bapu's body, but almost automatically my hand was arrested. Bapu never took a cold bath. It was 2 a.m. At this late hour, in the month of January,—a terribly cold January too—how could I pour this icy water on his body? . . . A cry burst forth from my despairing heart, and I could not control it.

Brij Krishna composed himself once more, and bathed Gandhi with the cold water he had never used when alive. He dried the body, and then dressed it in a loincloth he had spun himself for Gandhi on his last birthday, 2 October 1947. Around Gandhi's neck, Brij Krishna placed a garland, once more of yarn spun by himself, as well as the rosary that Gandhi used when chanting the name of Ram. A vermilion tilak was placed on the forehead, and rose petals around the hands, chest and feet. Now the body, bathed, dressed and decorated, could proceed on its final journey.[23]

Gandhi had written several times in the past that he expected to die a violent death. And so, albeit in private, had his old comrade Henry Polak. On hearing in April 1934 that Gandhi was planning a fresh fast, Polak had written to a friend: 'He [Gandhi] has a chronic tendency to offer himself up as a public sacrifice, and I can never feel any sense of certainty that he will in the normal course of events pass away in any but the most dramatic circumstances.'[24]

VII

On 30 January, Sushila Nayar was in Multan, in West Pakistan, carrying on her work for refugee rehabilitation. At 4 p.m. that day she met the deputy commissioner of Multan. His wife asked, 'When is Gandhiji coming to us?' For Sushila, 'it was gratifying to see the erstwhile "Enemy No.1 of Islam", looked upon as the friend of the Muslims both in India and Pakistan. In my mind I rehearsed, how pleased Bapu would be when he heard my report.'

Two hours later, the deputy commissioner's wife rushed in with the news that Gandhi had been killed. Sushila motored through the night to Lahore, from where she took a morning flight to Delhi. Also on the plane was Mian Iftikharuddin, a lifelong Congressman who, shortly before Partition, had opportunistically joined the Muslim League. On seeing Dr Nayar, Iftikharuddin said, with tears in his eyes, 'Every one of us is responsible for Gandhiji's death.'

Sushila Nayar reached Birla House at 11.30, just in time to join the procession carrying Gandhi's body for the cremation. She climbed into the open car in which the body lay, a Dodge belonging to the Eighth Company of the army's electrical and mechanical engineers, and driven by one Ram Chand. In the vehicle she saw 'the Sardar sitting near the feet of his dead master, sad and serene. . . . Pandit Nehru stood near the head with his grief-stricken face.' Also in the car

were two other long-time devotees of the Mahatma, Rajkumari Amrit
Kaur and J.B. Kripalani.[25]

The Dodge began its journey at 11.45 a.m. Its destination lay
four miles to the north-east, by the banks of the river Jamuna. On a
normal day, the drive would have taken fifteen to twenty minutes. On
this day, however, the car had to crawl through the streets, through
the great crowds that milled in and around them.

From Birla House, the car turned left and then right, towards the
War Memorial at India Gate. The entire 'central vista was one mass
of seething humanity. Wherever there were trees, the branches hung
with the burden of people. People were seen perched on the top of the
150-foot War Memorial and on lamp-posts along the route.'

There were some people watching from even higher up.
Mountbatten's staff had climbed up to the great dome of the Durbar
Hall, from where they saw the procession carrying Gandhi's body go
down Kingsway, the massively broad avenue that ran from India Gate to
the Viceregal Palace. Now, remarked Mountbatten's private secretary,

> the man who more than anyone else had helped to supersede the Raj
> was receiving in death homage beyond the dreams of any Viceroy.
> Gandhi died one evening and is taken for cremation the following
> morning. Here is no long-heralded State funeral; all the same, the
> people have flocked within the hour and by the hundred thousand to
> have one last glimpse of him. Who, in the face of the overwhelming
> tribute, can honestly assert now that Gandhi had no genuine mass
> following?[26]

From Kingsway, the Dodge turned left, making its way northwards
towards the Jamuna. As the procession proceeded, it was met with
a continuous shower of flowers and shouts of 'Mahatma Gandhi
Amar Rahe'. When it approached Delhi Gate, three Dakotas flying
overhead dipped in salute.

The cortège was now coming closer to its destination. At Delhi
Gate, it turned right and approached the river. 'The banks of the
sacred Jumna were packed with multitudes as far as the eye could see.
People who had been silent so far were shouting "Mahatma Gandhi
Zindabad".'

Reporters on the spot, faced with these 'unbelievably colossal crowds', found it 'impossible to form even the roughest estimate of the number'. The general in charge of managing the arrangements later provided an estimate. The funeral procession was more than two miles long, with an estimated 1.5 million mourners.[27]

Starting out before noon, the procession finally reached its destination at 4.20 p.m. The body was placed on an elevated wooden platform built overnight by the public works department. For the cremation itself, some fifteen maunds of sandalwood, four maunds of ghee and one maund of coconut had been procured. With Gandhi's eldest son estranged and his second son in South Africa, the pyre was lit by his third son, Ramdas Gandhi. Afterwards, as the body was being consumed by the flames, 'the great mass of people gathered on the Jumna bank rose en masse and observed a minute's silence and garlands and flowers poured in all the while'. As 'the red flames rose against the evening sun, the multitude with one voice raised the cry, "The Mahatma has become eternal"'.[28]

VIII

Speaking on All India Radio on the evening of the 30th, Jawaharlal Nehru said 'the light has gone out of our lives', and then immediately corrected himself, saying, 'No, the light shines and will continue to shine thousands of years hence.'

Another prompt tribute was offered by Muhammad Ali Jinnah, who said: 'I was shocked to learn of the most dastardly attack on the life of Mr. Gandhi resulting in his death. There can be no controversy in the face of death.'

Jinnah went on to create a controversy nonetheless. 'Whatever our political differences,' he remarked, Gandhi 'was one of the greatest men produced by the Hindu community and a leader who commanded their universal confidence and respect'. Jinnah continued: 'I wish to express my deep sorrow and sincerely sympathize with the great Hindu community and his family in their bereavement at this momentous, historical and critical juncture so soon after the birth of freedom for Hindustan and Pakistan.'[29]

For all its apparent generosity, this appreciation was damaged by its one moment of churlishness. Even in death, even after his last, heroic fasts for inter-religious harmony, Gandhi would be seen by Jinnah as merely a 'Hindu' leader.

Other Pakistani politicians rose to the occasion. Jinnah's second in command, Liaquat Ali Khan, called Gandhi 'the great figure of our times', whose 'recent efforts for communal harmony will be remembered by all lovers of peace'. Gandhi's 'removal from the stage of Indian politics at this juncture', remarked Khan, 'is an irreparable loss'.

Another leading Muslim League politician, Muhammad Saadulla, a former prime minister of Assam, said that 'the fact that Mahatma Gandhi in his prayer meetings used to have recitations from the Koran, clearly demonstrated the breadth of his outlook and his sincere endeavour to bring into one whole different religious-minded people of the sub-continent—India'.

The Muslim League's newspaper, *Dawn*, published out of Karachi, said 'all Muslims in Pakistan are bowed with grief at the ghastly ending of so great a life', adding: 'Should the Mahatma's supreme self-sacrifice in the cause of peace and amity lead to a genuine stirring of the conscience of Hindus of India, the Muslims on this side of the frontier will not fail to respond with all sincerity.' This was somewhat grudging, although *Dawn* did (so far as I know for the first time) call Gandhi a 'Mahatma'.[30]

A more generous assessment of Gandhi's life and legacy came from the *Pakistan Times*, published in Lahore. This said that in Gandhi's death, 'the world has been deprived of the sight and sound of his frail body and aged voice—a body and voice that in the last few months have almost lost for a large section of mankind their personal and ephemeral character and become tireless symbols of compassionate love and fearless rectitude'. The newspaper hoped that Gandhi's sacrifice would 'yet save the lives of millions for which this life was given. Once Hindus and Muslims of undivided India mingled their blood to fight for freedom under Gandhiji's banner during the Khilafat days: let us hope that they will now mingle their tears on his glorious dust to retain their peaceful freedom under the independent flags of India and Pakistan.'[31]

The *Pakistan Times* called Gandhi (in a direct refutation of Jinnah's claim) 'the best-loved and most venerated political leader' of the subcontinent. 'There have been great heroes in history,' it remarked, 'who lived and fought and died to preserve their own people from dangers that threatened and from enemies lying in wait. It would be hard to name any who has fallen fighting his own people to preserve the honour of a people not his own. No greater sacrifice could be rendered by a member of one people to another and no greater tribute could be paid to the supremacy of fundamental human values as opposed to passing factional squabbles.'

Published as an unsigned editorial, this piece was written by the newspaper's owner, Mian Iftikharuddin, who had spent more time in the Congress than in the Muslim League, and was now struck by remorse at abandoning an inclusive form of nationalism for a sectarian one. Meanwhile, a less emotional, but nonetheless handsome, tribute was penned by the newspaper's editor, the poet Faiz Ahmad Faiz. This emphasized that 'the passing of Gandhiji is as grievous a blow to Pakistan as it is to India. We have observed distressed looks, seen moistened eyes and heard faltering voices in this vast sprawling city of Lahore to a degree to be seen to be believed. We have also seen spontaneous manifestations of grief on the part of our fellow citizens in the shape of observance of a holiday and a hartal.'[32]

Gandhi's death evoked much grief in East Pakistan too, especially in the district of Noakhali, where he had started his peace mission in the last months of 1946. Young activists of the Pakistan movement, who had opposed him at the time, were consumed by guilt for not heeding his message of Hindu–Muslim harmony while he was alive. 'I will suffer and my conscience will bite me for the rest of my life,' confided one activist to his diary. On 2 February, Dacca observed a complete hartal in the Mahatma's memory. Shops, offices, schools and colleges were all closed. In the afternoon, 'a mile long procession of the Hindus and the Muslims with a life-size portrait of Gandhi' walked silently through the city, ending with a prayer meeting where verses from the Bible, the Koran and the Gita were read.[33]

There were tributes from Britain, the country where Gandhi had lived and studied, and against whose policies he had long fought, while befriending many of its people. The British prime minister

Clement Attlee, while praising in glowing terms Gandhi's idealism and courage, then added: 'He represented, it is true, the opposition of the Indians to being ruled by another race but also expressed the revulsion of the east against the west. He himself was in revolt against western materialism and sought for a return to a simpler state of society.'

Later, at a memorial service in Westminster Abbey, Stafford Cripps said Gandhi 'stood out head and shoulders above all his contemporaries as one who believed and who fearlessly put his beliefs into practice'. Cripps praised Gandhi's 'supreme effort' for religious harmony, and continued: 'His attitude to the British as individuals was always one of friendliness and even so far as that somewhat impersonal entity the British people he had no wishes except for their happiness. Many people will remember his visit to Lancashire at a time when there was bitter feeling against the Indians over the affairs of the cotton industry. He walked as was his custom among the workers and by his personality and sympathy met with their almost universal acclaim.'[34]

The reactions of a viceroy who had dealt with Gandhi were more ambivalent. Writing in his journal, Wavell remarked that while Gandhi did not have 'much of the saint in his composition', he was nonetheless 'an extremely astute politician', who 'certainly hastened the departure of the British, which was his life's aim'. Then he added: 'I always thought he had more of malevolence than benevolence in him, but who I am to judge, and how can an Englishman estimate a Hindu? Our standards are poles apart; and by Hindu standards Gandhi may have been a saint; by any standards he was a very remarkable man' (this last a verdict he would not have offered while dealing with him as viceroy).[35]

There were, of course, plenty of tributes in the popular press, a particularly fine one appearing in the *News Chronicle*. 'The hand that killed the Mahatma,' said this newspaper, 'is the same hand that nailed the Cross; it is the hand that fired the faggots; it is the hand that through the ages has been growing ever more mightily in war and less sure in the pursuit of peace. It is your hand and mine.'[36]

Gandhi's first English friends were the vegetarians of London, whose meetings he had attended as a law student and in whose journal he had published his first articles on social affairs. The *Vegetarian News* now devoted a special issue to Gandhi, its lead editorial spelling out his significance to their movement and to the world at large. 'By any standard of judgment,' wrote this organ of the London vegetarians who had once been proud to claim him as a member, 'Mahatma Gandhi was one of the greatest men of modern times; by ours, the greatest.' If 'any public man in our time can be said to have outlived the vanity of personal praise', remarked the journal, 'it was Gandhi; he wanted only to carry conviction'. Beyond what he did for India and the world, for his old flesh-eschewing comrades in England, Gandhi's significance was that 'he saw, and tried to communicate, the significance of the impulse towards universal non-violence that moves all of us in our better moments, which gives meaning to the vegetarian ethic as it explains the source of the benefit that we derive from it—an integration of imaginative and physical nutrition, a gesture towards harmony in the individual personality'.[37]

The tribute by a European that most stood out came from the veteran French socialist Léon Blum. 'I never saw Gandhi,' said Blum. 'I do not know his language. I never set foot in his country, and yet I feel the same sorrow as if I had lost someone near and dear.' Unlike many others, prone to seeing Gandhi as the Sage of the East, Blum seemed to glimpse the fact that Gandhi was also a symbol of what was best in the West.

From Cape Town, Gandhi's old political sparring partner Jan Christian Smuts sent this message: 'Gandhi was one of the great men of our time and my acquaintance with him over a period of more than 30 years has only deepened my high respect for him however much we differed in our views and methods. A prince among men has passed away and we grieve with India in her irreparable loss.'[38]

Among the tributes by Americans, perhaps the most insightful came from the widely travelled journalist Edgar Snow. Snow first met Gandhi in 1931, and had several long conversations with him over the years. He saw Gandhi as both a saint and socialist, who 'against 3000 years of prejudice raised a crusade for the human rights of 50,000,000 untouchables', who 'never ceased to unite his countrymen and indeed the whole world under the homely injunctions common to all faiths;

individual perfection, tolerance, humility, love of nature (God), equality, brotherhood and co-operation'. Of his own relationship with Gandhi, Snow wrote:

> I don't pretend to have understood Gandhi or to have moved upon the stage where I could take in the metaphysics of his philosophy or his personal dialogues with God. I am an agnostic and pragmatist, an ex-Catholic turned Taoist, a Hegelian fallen among materialists, and one who chastised the Mahatma for denying the righteous battle in 1942 and for leading his open rebellion against our allies, the British. For years I had felt out of sympathy with him. Yet even in this dull clod, the avatar had finally struck a spark before he died, when in my last visit, I became conscious of my size in the mirror of him, and I saw him as a giant.[39]

On 1 February 1948, a memorial service was held for Gandhi at the Community Church of New York, with his old admirer John Haynes Holmes in the chair. Among the speakers was the Jewish thinker-activist Hayim Greenberg, who had criticized Gandhi in the late 1930s for not supporting Zionism. Now, seeing Gandhi's life in the round, he praised him for departing from the saintly tradition of withdrawal, and instead engaging actively with the world. Gandhi, he remarked, 'did not ignore Caesar. He did not seek to "bribe" him or pay him a "ransom". His passionate aim was to destroy tyranny, to unseat Caesar from his throne—but with Gandhi's own, "un-Caesarian" weapons. Instead of becoming a *sadhu*, he became a social crusader.'[40]

Meanwhile, the New York journal *Politics*, edited by the cultural critic Dwight McDonald, assembled a special issue of essays on Gandhi by some well-regarded writers, a collection all the more remarkable for the fact that none of the contributors had met the man. Comparing the Mahatma's murder to the Crucifixion, the novelist Mary McCarthy thought Gandhi was killed because 'what he stood for in his life—simplicity, good humour, steadfastness—affronted his killer's sense of human probability'. The Italian writer Nicola Chiaromonte said that compared to his mentor Tolstoy, Gandhi was far less hypocritical—indeed, 'it is difficult to think of another man in all known history, for whom Thought and Deed were so utterly inseparable as Gandhi'. The magazine's editor, in his own piece, marvelled that the Indian leader could practise 'tolerance and love to such an extent that he seems to have regarded the capitalist as well as the garbage-man as his social equal'. Gandhi, wrote Dwight McDonald,

> was the last political leader in the world who was a person, not a mask or a radio voice or an institution. The last on a human scale. The last for whom I felt neither fear nor contempt nor indifference but interest and affection. He was dear to me—I realize it now better than I did when he was alive—for all kinds of reasons. He believed in love, gentleness, persuasion, simplicity of manners, and he came closer to 'living up to' those beliefs than most people I know—let alone most Big Shots, on whom the pressure for the reverse must be very powerful. He was dear to me because he had no respect for railroads, assembly-belt production, and other knick-knacks of liberalistic Progress, and insisted on examining their human (as against their metaphysical) value. Also because he was clever, humorous, lively, hard-headed, and never made speeches about Fascism, Democracy, the Common Man, or World Government. And because he had a keen nose for the concrete, homely 'details' of living which make the real difference to people but which are usually ignored by everybody except poets. And finally because he was a good man, by which I mean not only 'good' but also 'man'.[41]

More grudging in their response to Gandhi's death were writers in the Soviet Union. Their leader, Stalin, had refused or forgotten to send a condolence message. After this was commented on in the Indian press, a Russian writer tried to make amends, while staying faithful to the Marxist catechism. So, he praised Gandhi for 'draw[ing] the great labouring masses into the movement', adding that he was however a 'decided opponent of class struggle', whose tactics of class collaboration 'undoubtedly retarded the development of the national liberation struggle'.[42]

There was no public reference to Gandhi's death by Winston Churchill. There was no public comment either by B.R. Ambedkar, despite him being a member of Nehru's Cabinet. However, a week after Gandhi's death, Ambedkar wrote a fascinating letter to his future wife Dr Sharada Kabir. Here, he called the murder a 'foul deed', adding: 'You know that I owe nothing to Mr. Gandhi and he has not contributed to my spiritual, moral and social makeup. . . . Nonetheless I felt very sad on hearing of his assassination.'

Ambedkar went to Birla House on the 31st morning, where he 'was very much moved on seeing his [Gandhi's] dead body'. He walked with the funeral procession for a short distance and returned home, but later in the afternoon went to the cremation site, where the massive crowds made him turn back again.

Writing to the friend whom he was to marry, Ambedkar remarked that 'great men are of great service to their country, but they are also at certain times a great hindrance to the progress of their country'. He further elaborated:

> Mr. Gandhi had become a positive danger to his country. He had choked all the thoughts. He was holding together the Congress which is a combination . . . agreed on no social or moral principle except the one of praising and flattering Mr. Gandhi. . . .
>
> As the Bible says that something good cometh out of evil, so also I think that good will come out of the death of Mr. Gandhi. He will release people from bondage to superman, it will make them think for themselves and it will compel them to stand on their own merits.[43]

More generous was Vasant Moon, a young Ambedkarite in Nagpur then in his teens, and in the fullness of time to become the chief editor of B.R. Ambedkar's collected works. As he and his friends heard the news of Gandhi's murder, recalled Moon, 'everyone's mind almost unconsciously sank into depression. In the sky clouds began to gather. If some great man dies nature reflects the despondency. . . . We had never felt much sympathy for Gandhi; we understood Ambedkar's opposition to him. Even so we were conscious that he was a great man.'[44]

Ideological opponents were moved by Gandhi's death, and so were former associates who had fallen out with him. One of them was R.P. Parasuram, the typist who had quarrelled with Gandhi and left

his entourage in eastern Bengal a year previously. Gandhi's Calcutta
fast had stoked feelings of guilt, these made stronger by the manner
of Gandhi's death. In early January, Parasuram had wanted to go and
see Gandhi in Delhi, but didn't have the money for a long-distance
railway ticket. So, he thought he would go and see Gandhi when
he visited Sevagram, which was closer to Bombay (where Parasuram
then worked). Now that wouldn't be possible either. 'His going away
like this, after the two successful fasts,' wrote Parasuram sorrowfully
to Nirmal Kumar Bose,

> makes me feel completely foolish and greatly guilty. To the end of
> my days I shall have to remember that I put him to great trouble and
> deserted him at a time when my attendance was necessary. Even in
> July last he had given me a hint that he would welcome me back.
> But I was too conceited and proud.
>
> It is no use crying over what one cannot undo. I know that
> [then] I thought sincerely. Whether I thought rightly, only the future
> could have shown. Yet my mind shall continue to be troubled. The
> only thing I can now do, in whatever little way I can, what all he has
> asked us to do. That way alone shall I find some peace.[45]

An interesting (and also prophetic) reaction came from the industrialist
J.R.D. Tata. While (unlike Jamnalal Bajaj and G.D. Birla) Tata had
never explicitly identified with the Congress, Gandhi was fond of
him, not least because his uncle Ratan Tata had funded his struggle
in South Africa. When Gandhi was murdered, J.R.D. Tata was in
Switzerland, from where he wrote to a colleague:

> I was horrified, as you all must have been, at the news of Gandhiji's
> assassination. It is a World tragedy but who knows whether his
> paying the ultimate price may not in the end have done more for
> the cause of peace, tolerance and communal harmony for which he
> gave his life than he would have achieved by remaining alive. It may
> have, amongst other things, brought about greater solidarity and a
> tightening of the ranks in the Cabinet and the Congress and healed,
> at least for the crucial time being, the differences and fissiparous
> tendencies which were beginning to make themselves conspicuous

in government circles. . . . I trembled to think what would happen
if Jawaharlal met the same fate. I hope however, that the grief
and anger caused by Gandhi's murder amongst the great mass of
the people of India and the realisation of the righteousness and
soundness of what he stood for, will keep . . . the extremists from
further mischief and wean away many from their fold.[46]

IX

After he was cremated on 31 January, Gandhi's ashes were collected
and placed in several dozen boxes, these distributed to different parts
of the country. On Thursday, 14 February, in a grand, coordinated
ceremony, the ashes were immersed in rivers or in the sea, in towns
and cities across India.

In Bombay, a city Gandhi knew intimately and which had
witnessed the ups and downs of his political career, some half a
million people participated in the immersion ceremony. The ashes
were placed overnight for public viewing in the town hall, and taken
the next day to Chowpatty beach in a procession of open vehicles.
'Every inch of the roads was packed and every window and vantage
point occupied. Flowers continued to be showered as the procession
passed through Churchgate Street, Bazar Gate Street, Hornby Road,
Sheikh Memon Street, Bhuleshwar, C.P. Tank, Vithalbhai Patel Road
and Sandhurst Road to Chowpatty.'

In Calcutta, a city which had recently witnessed Gandhi's epic
fast for peace, the immersion took place in the Hooghly River at
Barrackpore. It was observed by a 'vast crowd, consisting of men,
women and children of all castes and communities'. A boat was taken
into the river, and the urn with the ashes lowered into the water by
the West Bengal governor, C. Rajagopalachari, his hands shaking
with emotion.

There were similar ceremonies in Patna, capital of Bihar, the state
where Gandhi had organized his first Indian campaign; in Poona,
home to his early mentor Gopal Krishna Gokhale; and in Paunar,
near Wardha, where his disciple Vinoba Bhave had his ashram, not
far from Gandhi's own last ashram at Sevagram.[47]

With Manilal having arrived from South Africa, Gandhi's sons took one urn for immersion in Allahabad, where the Ganga and Jamuna met. At every station along the way, Indians of all castes, creeds, classes and ages thronged the train to pay respects. At the industrial city of Kanpur, an estimated four lakh people turned up to have a last darshan. Even at the small railway town of Tundla, there was a crowd a lakh strong, 'perched on roof-tops, railway wagons, railway engines, trees, lamp posts—any vantage point available . . .'[48]

X

Who was the man who murdered Gandhi? Why was he moved to act as he did? These details emerged in the course of the year 1948, as the trial of the murderer and his companions proceeded.

Nathuram Vinayak Godse was born in 1910, the son of an employee in the postal department. His was a family of Brahmins, well versed in the scriptures but also open to the currents of the modern world. In about 1930, his father was posted in Ratnagiri, where V.D. Savarkar also lived. Once a militant (and secular) revolutionary, Savarkar now propounded a philosophy he called 'Hindutva', which saw Hindus, and Hindus alone, as the true and proper inhabitants of India. Visiting his father in Ratnagiri, Nathuram met Savarkar, and soon 'became thick with Savarkar's activities and worked with him'.[49]

Through the 1930s and 1940s, Godse worked to further a militant, muscular form of Hinduism. He formed rifle clubs, and ran a newspaper. He joined the Rashtriya Swayamsevak Sangh, then left it. He also met many leaders of the Hindu Mahasabha, and retained a veneration for Savarkar himself, visiting him often in Bombay, where Savarkar now lived.

In February 1938, Nathuram Godse wrote Savarkar a long letter outlining how the Hindu Mahasabha could challenge the Congress in the political field. To strengthen the Mahasabha organization, argued Godse, it should bring in non-Brahmins and the Depressed Classes representatives into leadership positions, and make more active propaganda through newspapers and speeches.

Godse complained about an 'inferiority-complex' among Mahasabhites in Poona, who felt they couldn't achieve 'solid results' to match those of the Congress. Godse himself thought the Mahasabha could learn a lesson or two from Gandhi's party. His letter to Savarkar concluded:

> In the last two years the Congress President Jawahar Lal [Nehru] has done a great deal of real work. He went by air from place to place, made speeches in the villages round about. Therefore the succeeding president will have responsibility of heavier work than that, and it seems they will successfully carry that out too.
>
> The name of the Hindu Mahasabha President must resound as well. Maharaj, individually you do great work ceaselessly, but that work is not getting to-day the necessary publicity, and hence its importance does not become known to the public.
>
> I have gone beyond my privilege in writing [such a] letter, but it is requested that you will be generous enough to excuse [me] for the same.[50]

Between 1941 and 1944, Godse wrote many letters addressed to 'Venerable Barrister Tatyarao Savarkar', praising his attempts at promoting Hindu Sanghatanist ideology, offering to organize Savarkar's own tours through Maharashtra and to accompany him if he chose to tour Kashmir.[51] Godse later recalled that under Savarkar's 'magnetic lead', the 'Hindu Sanghatan Movement got verily electrified and vivified as never before'. The man who became Gandhi's murderer claimed that Gandhi's old rival, Savarkar, was looked upon by right-wing Hindus as 'the chosen hero, the ablest and most faithful advocate of the Hindu cause'.[52]

In 1946 and 1947, Godse was the editor and publisher of a Marathi magazine called *Agrani*. The magazine impressed Savarkar, who gave Godse and his colleague Narayan (Nana) Apte a grant of Rs 15,000, at the time a not inconsiderable sum.[53] The articles printed by *Agrani* spoke of 'Muslim goondas' and their 'terrible atrocities' which led to 'pools of [Hindu] blood and flesh' being created, compared the leaders of the Muslim League to Nader Shah and Genghis Khan, and attacked the Congress (and Nehru and

Gandhi personally) for not protecting the interests of Hindus. One article, published in March 1947, claimed that 'whether it is Punjab or Bengal the real culprits in setting ablaze the conflagration that is seen flaring up far and wide with growing speed today are Gandhi and his followers, Congressmen'. It further spoke of 'Gandhi's incessant efforts for not allowing any spirit to be created in the Hindu community anywhere', charged the British with favouring fanatical Muslims, and asked Hindus and Sikhs to take heart from (and follow the methods of) the medieval warriors Rana Pratap, Shivaji and Guru Govind.[54]

Godse's closest collaborator was Narayan Apte, like him a Poona Brahmin. Others in his circle had a shared background of caste, language and ideology. Poona had long been a centre of Hindu extremism. Anti-Muslim sentiment ran deep amongst its intelligentsia and upper castes.

Godse detested Gandhi for his philosophy of non-violence, and for his tolerance of, or love for, Muslims. There was also a partisan flavour to his aversion—many Maharashtrians had reservations about Gujaratis, and many Brahmins saw Banias as scheming. In 1944, Godse had shouted angry slogans at a meeting Gandhi addressed in Panchgani. But it was with the partition of India and the flight of Hindus and Sikhs from the Punjab that his hatred for Gandhi turned venomous. When India should be taking on Pakistan, when Hindus should be subduing Muslims, the presumed 'Father of the Nation' was preaching peace and reconciliation.

It was in early January that Godse and Apte made up their mind to murder Gandhi. They travelled to Delhi on the 17th, stayed under assumed names at the Marina Hotel in Connaught Place, and made a reconnaissance of Birla House. On the 20th, they travelled to Kanpur and then on to Bombay, perhaps to meet fellow conspirators. On the 29th, they were back in Delhi.

In his testimony to the court, Godse said:

My idea was to shoot him twice-at-point-blank range so that none else might get injured. I bowed [to] him with the pistol between my two palms. I had removed the safety-catch when I had taken out the pistol from inside my bush-coat pocket. . . . After I had fired the shot there was a lull throughout for about half a minute. I had also got excited. I then shouted 'Police-Police—come'.

The bow before releasing the trigger was apparently in acknowledgement of Gandhi's age, and his past services to the nation, *before* the recent events that had so completely turned Godse against him.

Godse told the court that he had 'never made a secret about the fact that I supported the ideology or the school which was opposed to that of Gandhiji. I firmly believed that the teachings of absolute "Ahimsa" as advocated by Gandhiji would ultimately result in the emasculation of the Hindu Community [and] thus make the community incapable of resisting the aggression or inroads of other communities especially the Muslims.'

The judges asked Godse whether he was acting under the advice or inspiration of Savarkar. He rejected what he called an 'unjust and untrue charge', which was, he said, an 'insult to my intelligence and judgment'.

Godse claimed that when he and Apte came to Delhi in early January, their plan was merely to organize a demonstration on behalf of the refugees. Then, 'while moving in the camps my thoughts took a final and definite turn. Chancely I came across a refugee who was dealing in arms and he showed me the pistol. I was tempted to have it and bought it from him. It is the same pistol that I later used in the shots I fired. On coming to the Delhi Railway Station I spent the night of the 29th thinking and re-thinking about my resolve to end the present chaos and further destruction of the Hindus.'[55]

In his article in the *Pakistan Times*, Mian Iftikharuddin had characterized Gandhi's killer as a 'poor idiot or maniac'. That the murderer was crazy was the immediate reaction of others who knew and revered the Mahatma, such as C. Rajagopalachari. However, as the trial proceeded, it became clear that this was no idiot or maniac but a focused and ideologically driven individual, committed to a form of Hinduism and of nationalism totally opposed to Gandhi's own. While Godse may have left the RSS, there was little question that, like M.S. Golwalkar and his organization, he detested the Mahatma

for seeking to make Indian Muslims safe in India. Since by his acts
Gandhi was (as Godse thought) weakening the consolidation of the
Hindus, he had to be (as it were) 'immediately silenced'.

XI

On 31 January 1948, a former Punjab civil servant named Malcolm
Darling wrote in his diary:

> Gandhi was assassinated yesterday. A talk with Arthur Lall [an
> Indian friend, then posted in London] on the telephone. He thought
> this was the end of civilization in India. Very difficult to say what will
> happen, but it is as if a ship had lost its keel. Further disintegration
> seems inevitable, and what will happen to the 40 million Muslims
> left in India, now that they have lost their chief protector? Arthur
> Lall fears Nehru will be the next victim. I wonder if sooner or later
> we will have to go back.[56]

Darling was by no means a typical ICS man. A graduate of the
famously liberal King's College in Cambridge, a protégé of E.M.
Forster, he was an urbane, cultivated cosmopolitan, who saw himself
as a friend of India and Indians.[57] Yet, even he was here thinking that
perhaps Indians wouldn't be able to run their country after Gandhi
died, and the British might have to return to take charge.

They didn't, of course. One reason was that the immediate fallout
of Gandhi's death was the reconciliation of Nehru and Patel. Two
days after the Mahatma was murdered, Nehru wrote to Patel that
'with Bapu's death, everything is changed and we have to face a
different and more difficult world. The old controversies have ceased
to have much significance and it seems to me that the urgent need of
the hour is for all of us to function as closely and co-operatively as
possible . . .' Patel, in reply, said he 'fully and heartily reciprocate[d]
the sentiments you have so feelingly expressed . . . Recent events had
made me very unhappy and I had written to Bapu . . . appealing to
him to relieve me, but his death changes everything and the crisis that
has overtaken us must awaken in us a fresh realisation of how much

we have achieved together and the need for further joint efforts in our grief-stricken country's interests.'[58]

I have written elsewhere about the 'further joint efforts' by Nehru and Patel to unite India. In the aftermath of Gandhi's death, his two lieutenants submerged their differences, and held the ship of state together. Between 1948 and 1950, Nehru and Patel, and their colleagues in government and administration, tamed a communist insurgency and brought the princely states into the Union, promulgated a Constitution assuring equal rights to minorities and women, and mandating a multiparty system based on adult franchise. While Patel died in December 1950, the first General Election, held in the first months of 1952, further consolidated the nation.[59]

While Malcolm Darling's presumption that the British would have to go back betrayed an unconscious racism, he did raise one pertinent question: what would be the fate of the millions of Muslims in India now that they had lost their 'chief protector'? That, in those first, fraught months after Partition, Gandhi spoke out most bravely for the rights of minorities was reassuring for them. When, in the winter of 1947–48, Gandhi stayed at Birla House, a diplomat whose office was across the street noted that every day 'people of all communities rich and poor came to visit him for guidance, assistance or consolation'.

Among those seeking succour and consolation from Gandhi, one community was especially evident. Thus, wrote the diplomat, 'day in and day out, too, Muslims of all classes of society, many of whom had also suffered personal bereavements in the recent disturbances, came to invoke his help. Normally too fearful even to leave their homes, they came to him because they had learned and believed that he had their interests at heart and was the only real force in the Indian Union capable of preserving them from destruction.'[60]

What would happen to the Muslims of India after Gandhi was assassinated? The fears for their safety were genuine. However, it was not the case that he was their only protector, the only politician who had 'their interests at heart'. So did Jawaharlal Nehru. No sooner had he heard the news, and confirmed the identity of the assassin, Nehru was quick-witted enough to say on the radio that it was a Hindu who had murdered Gandhi. Later, in public speeches and letters to chief ministers, he repeatedly emphasized the need to treat Muslims (and Christians) as equal citizens of the land. Meanwhile, the government quickly banned the RSS, whose cadres had actively spread hatred against Muslims before, during and after Partition.

Another associate of Gandhi who was resolute on this question was C. Rajagopalachari. In an address to the Calcutta University not long after his master's death, Rajaji said: 'May the blood that flowed from Gandhiji's wounds and the tears that flowed from the eyes of Indian women everywhere when they learnt of his death serve to lay the curse of 1947, and may the grisly tragedy of that year sleep in history and not colour present passions.'[61]

Rajaji's hope was realized. The lead came from the top, but the ordinary Hindu was himself appalled at this act of parricide. The passions unleashed during Partition were quickly tamed, from without and from within. For more than a decade after Gandhi's death, there were no serious communal riots in India.

Some thirty-nine years before the event, Gandhi himself had anticipated the manner of his death—and what purpose it might serve. Writing to his nephew Maganlal on 29 January 1909, he had remarked: 'I may have to meet death in South Africa at the hands of my countrymen. If that happens you should rejoice. It will unite the Hindus and Mussalmans. . . . The enemies of the community are constantly making efforts against such a unity. In such a great endeavour, someone will have to sacrifice his life. If I make that sacrifice, I shall regard myself, as well as you, my colleagues, fortunate.'[62]

EPILOGUE

Gandhi in Our Time

I

In September 1924, Gandhi went on a fast in Delhi in response to Hindu–Muslim riots in northern India. 'I am striving to become the best cement between the two communities,' he said. 'My longing is to be able to cement the two with my blood, if necessary. But, before I can do so, I must prove to the Mussalmans that I love them as well as I love the Hindus. My religion teaches me to love all equally.'[1]

This credo, of loving all religions as his own, Gandhi practised throughout his life, with erratic results on those around him. From 1915 to 1948, periods of relative religious peace were followed by bouts of often savage violence. But before and through his death, he did radically reduce tensions between Hindus and Muslims, allowing the new nation state to craft institutions that could hold it together, and, through the practice of multiparty democracy, give the majority of its citizens some sort of stake in its functioning.

The first major religious riots in independent India took place in 1963–64. The 1970s were punctuated by episodes of Hindu–Muslim conflict. The temperature then escalated alarmingly in the late 1980s, because of the Ram Janmabhoomi movement, which sought to demolish a Mughal mosque in the town of Ayodhya that many Hindus believed was built on the spot where Lord Ram had been born. The campaign led to a wave of rioting across northern and western India, in which tens of thousands of people perished, a majority of them Muslims.[2]

In 1990, when the Ram Janmabhoomi campaign was at its height, the veteran Gandhian Dr Sushila Nayar went on a peace mission to Ayodhya. She held a prayer meeting outside the disputed site, where—as was done in Gandhi's time—texts from different scriptures were read and hymns sung. A small crowd had gathered to witness the event. One of the songs was an old melody in praise of Lord Ram, whose lyrics Gandhi had tweaked to suit his own inclusive and ecumenical purposes. When Dr Nayar and her colleagues came to the line '*Ishwar Allah Téré Naam*' (God is named both Ishwar and Allah), there were catcalls and boos. The elderly Gandhian, confused by the reception, called the protesters to her side. We have come representing (the spirit and memory of) Gandhi, she told them (*Hum Gandhiji ki taraf sé aayé hain*). And we have come representing Godse (*aur hum Godse ki taraf sé*) was the devastating reply.[3]

There remains a small cult of Nathuram Godse active today, which seeks to perpetuate the memory of Gandhi's assassin by building statues and observing his birth and death anniversaries.[4] More worryingly, there is a wider disenchantment with Gandhi's ideas of religious pluralism. In recent years, his own Congress Party has very inconsistently followed his beliefs and his practice, and in any case the Congress's political significance has steadily declined.

The force that now dominates Indian politics is the Bharatiya Janata Party (BJP), which stands for a muscular Hindu assertiveness. The BJP's ideological arm, the Rashtriya Swayamsevak Sangh, distrusted Gandhi while he was alive, partly for his philosophy of non-violence but mostly for his belief that in independent India, Muslims and Christians must have the same rights as Hindus. Now, in the context of Gandhi's formal standing as the 'Father of the Nation', the BJP and the RSS profess respect for him in public. At the same time, they seek to diminish his stature by elevating their own heroes. In 2003, during the BJP's first spell in power at the Centre, the portrait of V.D. Savarkar was installed in the Central Hall of Parliament.[5]

Meanwhile, state governments run by the BJP have rewritten school textbooks to accord Savarkar a larger role in the Indian freedom struggle than Gandhi.[6]

Since 2014, the BJP has once more been in power in New Delhi. Its prime minister, Narendra Modi, quotes and praises Gandhi from time to time. However, on social media, Gandhi is regularly abused by individuals who simultaneously declare themselves to be admirers of Modi. Echoing Savarkar's dismissal of 'Ahimsa/Charkha politics', radical Hindu preachers deliver sermons claiming that Gandhi's role in winning independence for India was vastly exaggerated. If Gandhi's ideas retain their influence, they warn, then India will fall prey to Islamic fundamentalists and Christian missionaries. In pursuit of their virile and strong Hindu nation, they ask that the nineteenth-century Arya Samaj ideologue Dayanand Saraswati be anointed 'Father of the Nation' instead.[7]

Religious pluralism in India was, and will always be, hard won. Although the almost continuous bloodletting of the period 1989–93 has not been repeated, the country is never far away from a riot. Most often Muslims are the main sufferers, as in Gujarat in 2002, and in Kokrajhar and Muzaffarnagar in 2013. At other times it is Christians, as in Kandhamal in 2008; or Sikhs, as in New Delhi in 1984. Hindus have not escaped either, being purged from the valley of Kashmir by the Islamic radicals who now hold sway there.

With the rise of Islamic fundamentalism around the world, and in neighbouring Pakistan and Bangladesh as well, and with the political ascendancy of Hindu fundamentalist forces within the country, Gandhi's commitment to interfaith harmony is more relevant than ever before.

II

Not long after Sushila Nayar's failed peace mission to Ayodhya, I came across an interview with Kondapalli Seetharamaiah, the leader of a group of Maoist revolutionaries then active in eastern India. The Indian Maoists are known as Naxalites, after the village of Naxalbari in north Bengal, where their movement began in 1967. Two years later, in 1969, the world celebrated the centenary of Gandhi's birth. In that year, the Naxalites brought down statues of Gandhi in towns and villages across the country. Occasionally, by way of variation, they entered a government office to vandalize his portrait.

The Naxalites were suppressed and defeated by the Bengal Police in the 1970s. But they later revived, and by the early 1990s, were particularly active in the southern state of Andhra Pradesh. Their rise owed much to the work of Seetharamaiah, a former schoolteacher whose People's War Group mounted a series of daring attacks on railway stations and police camps. The police finally arrested 'KS', as he was known; but then he feigned illness, and was admitted to hospital, from where he escaped.

It took the police two years to recapture the Maoist leader. A journalist later asked KS what he had done when on the run. He replied that he went from the hospital in Hyderabad to Gandhi's birthplace in Gujarat, 600 miles away. Here the revolutionary got off the train and took a rickshaw to Gandhi's parental home, now a museum dedicated to his memory. 'I went there and spat on the *maggu*,' KS told the reporter, 'maggu' being the Telugu word for the painted decorations that are placed outside many Indian shrines. This Maoist's hatred of Gandhi was so intense that he travelled incognito across the country merely to spit on the doorstep of the home in which Gandhi was born.[8]

The movement led by KS was eventually crushed by the police. The Maoist cadres then crossed from Andhra Pradesh into Madhya Pradesh, where they dug strong roots, especially among the tribal people whose lands and forests (and the rich mineral ores that lay under them) were coveted by outsiders. Those districts now form part of the state of Chhattisgarh. Visiting the strife-torn region in 2006, I met some Maoist revolutionaries, whose dislike of Gandhi was as extreme as that of their predecessors. But I also saw that the violence unleashed by rebels had provoked savage reprisals by the state.

The Maoist hostility to Gandhi has many sources. They oppose his political method, seeing non-violence as a diversionary tactic designed to suppress the revolutionary instincts of the masses and keep the ruling classes in power. Gandhi and his Congress Party claimed to have freed the country from British rule in 1947; the Maoists, however, still see India as a 'semi-colony' in thrall to Western capitalism and Western imperialism. Gandhi may have been a theological pluralist; but the fact that he so often used a religious idiom in his speeches and writings is antithetical to these self-proclaimed 'scientific socialists'. Finally, there is also a regional tinge to the hatred: the Maoist movement began in Bengal and many of its leaders have been Bengalis, from a province where Gandhi faced the greatest opposition during his political career.

Although they name themselves after a Chinese leader, the Indian Maoists may also be seen as ideological descendants of the HSRA of the 1920s. However, their main adversary, the Indian State, has not acted as Gandhi might have. Politicians and administrators have not sought to understand the roots of tribal discontent, or to begin (as Gandhi would have) a conversation with the angry young men who direct discontent through channels of blood. Instead, the police and paramilitary have burnt villages, harassed and violated women, and further escalated the violence. In between revolution and repression stand the unhappy tribals, squeezed by both sides.[9]

III

In arguments with religious extremists and proponents of armed struggle, the imperatives of pluralism and democracy compel one to stand on Gandhi's side. More complex are the afterlives of another long-running battle that Gandhi had in his lifetime: with B.R. Ambedkar, on the question of the abolition of untouchability.

Ambedkar and Gandhi were political adversaries in the 1930s and 1940s. They were partially reconciled in 1947, when Ambedkar joined the first Cabinet of free India, as law minister, working alongside Gandhi's protégés, Nehru, Patel, Amrit Kaur and others. Between 1947 and 1951, Ambedkar played a key role in the Union government, overseeing the drafting of the Constitution, and promoting the reform of personal laws in the direction of gender equality.

In 1951, Ambedkar left the Cabinet, and restarted his party, the Scheduled Caste Federation. He fought the 1952 elections in opposition to Nehru's Congress. His party fared disastrously, and he himself lost the seat he contested. Ambedkar was now back to where he had been before, a bitter opponent of the Congress Party. In 1955, he gave an interview to the BBC where he denounced Gandhi in terms as polemical as in his writings of the 1930s and 1940s.[10]

A Bombay writer who knew him well remarked that Ambedkar 'never recognized the chapter in the life of the Mahatma exclusively devoted to the cause of the untouchables. The Doctor at no time peeped into the Mahatma's Ashram where the touchable and the untouchable lived in peace and harmony and the former smilingly performed all the menial tasks the latter did in the world of caste-ridden Brahmins. To him the name of the Mahatma was saturated with evil. It was calamity for his community to have such a benefactor! The learned Doctor set his face to obliterate the collective record of all caste Hindu social reformers and thus eclipse them all, especially Gandhi.'[11]

Others read Ambedkar's situation more sympathetically. In early 1944, Horace Alexander, then doing relief work for the victims of the Bengal famine, had lunch with Ambedkar. He found him 'a tragically lonely man'. Ambedkar seems to have recognized that sitting on the viceroy's executive council at a time the heroes of Quit India were in jail would cost him politically. But did he have any other option? 'I wonder what might have happened,' remarked Horace Alexander, 'if some of the Congress leaders had shown him warm and generous friendship when he was young. Perhaps they tried. I do not know. But today he is lonely and embittered, fighting a forlorn battle on all fronts at once, nursing an impossible political ambition.'[12]

Their personal rivalry apart, there were, of course, major philosophical differences between the two men. Ambedkar had great faith in the reformist powers of the State, which he saw as the chief instrument for ending untouchability. Gandhi was suspicious of State power, instead emphasizing moral transformation through individual and social self-correction. While Gandhi hoped to save Hinduism by ending untouchability, Ambedkar concluded that the only way for the 'untouchables' to emancipate themselves was by converting to another faith. He pondered long about which religion to join, considering and rejecting Sikhism, Islam and Christianity before becoming a Buddhist in October 1956. Tragically, he died six weeks later, at the age of sixty-four.

In recent years, the Gandhian term 'Harijan' has been replaced by the term 'Dalit' to denote the erstwhile 'untouchables'. As one activist told an anthropologist in the 1980s: 'Harijan means what we can never be allowed to become by the caste Hindu, and what we may not want to be anyway. It was a superficial way for Gandhi to resolve his guilt.'[13] Although 'Dalit', meaning 'the oppressed', was used in parts of northern India from the late nineteenth century, it only gained wider currency in the 1970s, following its adoption by a group of radical activists in Maharashtra who called themselves the Dalit Panthers. Now it is ubiquitously used across India, by Dalits and non-Dalits alike, whereas 'Harijan' has deservedly fallen out of favour.[14]

Meanwhile, since his death, the political significance of B.R. Ambedkar and his ideas have steadily grown. In his lifetime, Ambedkar had a popular following in his native Maharashtra, yet in other parts of India he was known only to educated Dalits. Now, however, he is revered by Dalits across the land. Photographs and statues of Ambedkar adorn homes, schools, factories, shops and offices; his books are read and reread; and stories about him are told and retold as well.

Dalits venerate Ambedkar for his searing critiques of the caste system; for his work in drafting the Indian Constitution; and for being an exemplar and inspiration in their own continuing struggles for dignity and self-respect. Many Dalit intellectuals who admire Ambedkar simultaneously denigrate Gandhi, whom they see as patronizing their hero, deceiving him in the negotiations during the Poona Pact, and being an apologist for the caste order himself.[15]

Gandhi and Ambedkar debated with one another while they lived; now, long after their deaths, ideologues still represent them as political adversaries. In 1997, the right-wing journalist Arun Shourie published a book dismissing Ambedkar as a 'false god'. He made two main charges against Ambedkar: first, that he sided with British colonialists rather than with Indian nationalists; and second, that he used sharp and occasionally abusive language against the Father of the Nation, Gandhi.

While he stopped short of calling him a traitor, Shourie repeatedly insinuated that Ambedkar worked against the interests of India and Indians. The first page of his book set the tone: 'There is not one instance,' claimed Shourie, 'not one single, solitary instance in which Ambedkar participated in any activity connected with the struggle to free the country. Quite the contrary—at every possible turn he opposed the campaigns of the National Movement, at every setback to the Movement he was among those cheering the failure.'[16]

The very chapter titles of Shourie's book charged Ambedkar with opportunism. One read: 'Where Was Ambedkar in 1942? How Did He Get There?' Another was 'The Loyal Minister'. The text took these accusations further. Thus, Shourie remarked that 'as Congress leaders rotted in jails [following the Quit India movement], Ambedkar was broadcasting over the radio on behalf of the British Government'.[17]

Shourie accused Ambedkar of uttering 'calumnies' about Indian culture and civilization, of 'adding some even more garish colours to the caricature that the missionaries and rulers had put out'. He further charged him with being a collaborator, of seeking to divide the national movement in the manner of Jinnah and Syed Ahmad Khan, who urged the Muslims to side with the British, with Ambedkar later asking the Depressed Classes to do likewise. Shourie wrote that 'Ambedkar and Jinnah became not just accomplices of Imperial politics, they became the best of agents, agents who had been so flattered into self-importance that they did not see that they had made the cause of the Imperial rulers their own'.[18]

In the 600 pages of Arun Shourie's book, there was not one instance, not one single, solitary instance in which Shourie documented, or even acknowledged, the horrific discrimination against the 'untouchables' that was such a marked, and disfiguring, feature of the India in which Ambedkar and Gandhi lived. He did not pause to ask why, at crucial times in his political career, Ambedkar thought it necessary to side with the British. This was because the Congress was dominated by Brahmins and other upper castes, who had oppressed Dalits in the past, and might do so again if they came to power in independent India. In an interview in

1934, Ambedkar remarked: 'I am sure there are many nationalists among the Depressed Classes and, if they have not joined the Congress, it is because they love their country more than they love the Congress.'[19] Six years later, he put it more polemically, saying: 'That the Congress is fighting for the cause of the country is humbug. The Congress is fighting to obtain the keys of power in its own hands.'[20]

This may have been slightly unfair to Congressmen like Gandhi, Nehru, Patel and Kripalani, Congresswomen such as Sarojini Naidu and Kamaladevi Chattopadhyay. They were animated by a deep patriotism. But it was certainly true of lesser Congress leaders. Moreover, other great low-caste reformers such as Jyotirao Phule in Maharashtra and Mangu Ram (the leader of the Adi-Dharm movement in the Punjab) had also thought the Raj a lesser evil when compared to the Congress.[21] For an 'untouchable' leader to take the side of the British government against the Congress was certainly a plausible and defensible political option.

Arun Shourie has now found his left-wing counterpart in the writer Arundhati Roy, who, in a book-length essay published in 2014, dismissed Gandhi as a false Mahatma. She claimed that Gandhi was a conservative defender of the caste system who changed his views 'at a glacial pace'.[22]

In seeking to paint him as a slow-moving reactionary, Arundhati Roy made much of Gandhi's idealized conception of varnashramadharma, while omitting to add that, from the time he returned to India, Gandhi sharply attacked the practice of untouchability. Let me refresh the reader's memory by quoting once more two of the many remarks he made to this effect. As early as 1915, Gandhi said it was 'no part of real Hinduism to have in its hold a mass of people whom I would call "untouchables". If it was proved to me that this is an essential part of Hinduism, I for one would declare myself an open rebel against Hinduism itself.' And in 1920, he stated:

> We cannot compare the sufferings of the untouchables with those of any other section in India. It passes my understanding how we consider it dharma to treat the depressed classes as untouchables; I shudder at the very thought of this. My conscience tells me that

untouchability can never be a part of Hinduism. I do not think it too much to dedicate my whole life to removing the thick crust of sin with which Hindu society has covered itself for so long by stupidly regarding these people as untouchables. I am only sorry that I am unable to devote myself wholly to that work.

In her critique of Gandhi, Arundhati Roy did not cite these remarks—or others like them. Instead, she presented Gandhi as a thoroughgoing apologist for caste, further arguing that this was in line with his views on race. Gandhi, she suggested, was casteist in India because he had been racist in South Africa. Roy claimed that Gandhi 'feared and despised Africans'; this he certainly did in his twenties, but just as certainly did not in his forties and fifties. Reading Roy, one would not know that Gandhi decisively outgrew the racism of his youth, a fact that people of colour themselves acknowledged, and appreciated. This book has quoted letters written to Gandhi from African Americans 'keenly and sympathetically' following what they called his 'great battle for righteous adjustment', fought in 'the common cause of the lowly'. And documented in the *Collected Works* are numerous visits by African Americans, as well as Africans, to Sevagram to seek Gandhi's counsel. Why, if Gandhi was a racist, were black intellectuals and activists so keen to meet him, befriend him, and, in their own battles against social oppression, learn from his methods?

Both Arun Shourie and Arundhati Roy see history in terms of heroes and villains. Neither seeks to place the choices made by Gandhi and Ambedkar in context, seeking only to elevate one by disparaging the other. Roy has all of Ambedkar's polemical zeal but none of his scholarship or sociological insight. Shourie, meanwhile, perhaps loves India as much as Gandhi did, but he loves it in the abstract, without empathy for those Indians who suffer discrimination at the hands of their compatriots. Both seek—by the technique of *suppressio veri, suggestio falsi* so beloved of ideologues down the ages—to prove a verdict they have arrived at beforehand: that Gandhi was the Enemy of the Dalits, for Roy; that Ambedkar was the Enemy of the Nation, for Shourie.

Gandhi's commitment to ending untouchability was evident from soon after his return to India. Meanwhile, he steadily became more direct in his critique of the caste system as a whole. At first, he attacked untouchability alone, while leaving the other rules of caste intact. Then, through his temple-entry movement, he began advocating intermingling and inter-dining as well. Finally, he insisted that the only marriage he would solemnize in his ashram was one between a so-called 'untouchable' and a member of the upper castes, thus calling into question the very basis of the caste system itself.[23]

In her essay, Arundhati Roy made the astonishing charge that Gandhi was a 'Saint of the Status Quo'. In truth, the Hindu leaders of his own time saw Gandhi as a dangerous revolutionary who sought to destroy the traditional social order. His campaign to abolish untouchability struck at the very core of Hindu orthodoxy. The Sankaracharyas were enraged that a mere Bania who knew little Sanskrit dared challenge scriptural injunctions that mandated untouchability. During Gandhi's anti-untouchability tour of 1933–34, Hindu Mahasabha activists showed him black flags, threw faeces at him, and in Pune in June 1934 even attempted to assassinate him.

Indeed, Gandhi's campaign was unpopular within his own Congress Party. Nehru, Bose, Patel and company believed that the Mahatma should have set social reform aside and focused exclusively on the winning of swaraj.

In a speech to college students in Karachi in July 1934, Gandhi succinctly outlined his own position, between the radicals and the reactionaries. Ambedkar had recently told him there was 'no Hindu family in Poona which would accept me as a colleague or friend'. 'Whose shame is this?' asked Gandhi of the Karachi students. 'How can one who has been put to such treatment be won over?' Then he added: 'At the same time, we have to touch the heart of [the] Shankaracharya. Those two are poles apart. How can they be brought together? We stand between these two.'[24]

Among those who understood the depth of Gandhi's challenge to Hindu orthodoxy was the British liberal J.A. Spender, who had travelled through India and closely studied Indian affairs. 'Gandhi is often very irritating as a politician,' he wrote in 1935, 'but the work on which he is now engaged of rousing the Indian people to cast off this bondage is beyond all praise and the little periodical "Harijan" shows the fine spirit and high courage that he is bringing to it. Only an Indian, and only a very influential Indian who is prepared to stake everything in a battle against long-rooted custom and prejudice, could even make a beginning on it. Even Gandhi is met with the cry "Religion in Danger".[25]

As Gopal Guru has argued, despite not being an 'untouchable' himself, Gandhi felt 'morally tormented' by the practice of untouchability. He saw that it had a corrosive impact both on those who practised discrimination and those who were at the receiving end of such discrimination. This set him apart from socialists such as Jawaharlal Nehru, whose reading of inequality was economistic, with caste being entirely subsumed by class. Gandhi, on the other hand, saw 'untouchability as a deeply social question'.[26]

To be sure, despite his courage and consistency in attacking untouchability, Gandhi's approach could be patronizing. During his famous fast in Yerwada prison in 1932, he argued that if the suppressed castes 'are ever to rise, it will not be by reservation of seats but will be by the strenuous work of Hindu reformers in their midst'. While putting the onus on the upper castes to reform themselves, this perspective robbed the Dalits of agency. Why couldn't the suppressed castes rise through organizing themselves for (non-violent) action against injustice and discrimination?

In retrospect, Gandhi may have made a mistake in not endorsing Rajaji's suggestion to rename the Harijan Sewak Sangh the Untouchability Abolition League. Normally so astute in understanding the importance of the right word, the most evocative symbol, he did not here perceive that 'abolition' conveyed a far more emphatic meaning than mere 'service'. Moreover, the social workers who ran the Harijan Sewak Sangh placed more emphasis on fostering personal virtue in upper- and lower-caste individuals than in removing the civic and social disabilities that the 'untouchables' suffered from.

Perhaps the most subtle scholarly assessment of the Gandhi–Ambedkar relationship is contained in the social theorist D.R. Nagaraj's book *The Flaming Feet*. Nagaraj argued that the narrative of Indian nationalism was akin to the Ramayana in that it had place for only one Great Hero, with everyone else asked to support, even revere, this central and defining character. But Ambedkar was too proud a man, too conscious of his abilities and his own historic role, to wish to play the role of Sugreeva to Gandhi's Ram. Thus, he charted his own path, autonomous of and often antagonistic to that of Gandhi and the Congress. And yet, as D.R. Nagaraj showed, their exchanges and debates changed both men, with Gandhi increasingly more willing to acknowledge the material roots of discrimination, and Ambedkar, in turn, appreciating that moral transformation might be as important as legal reform.[27]

Nagaraj writes that 'from the viewpoint of the present, there is a compelling necessity to achieve a synthesis of the two'. This is absolutely correct. Social reform takes place only when there is pressure from above and from below. Slavery would not have been abolished had not guilt-ridden whites like Abraham Lincoln responded to the critiques of the likes of Frederick Douglass. Civil rights would not have been encoded into law had Lyndon Johnson not recognized the moral power of Martin Luther King and his movement. The vote was granted to women in England only because the heroic struggles of the suffragettes were heeded by liberal male politicians, inspired by progressive thinkers such as John Stuart Mill.

Although they were rivals in their lifetime, from the vantage point of history, Gandhi and Ambedkar played complementary roles in the undermining of an obnoxious social institution. No upper-caste Hindu did as much to challenge untouchability as Gandhi. And Ambedkar was the greatest leader to emerge from within the ranks of the Dalits. Although the practice of untouchability has been abolished by law, discrimination against Dalits still continues in many parts of India. To end it fully, one must draw upon the legacy of both Ambedkar and Gandhi.

IV

There were, indeed still are, two fundamental axes of social inequality in India. Caste is one, and gender is the other. In his political career, Gandhi did not pay as much attention to the emancipation of women as he did to the abolition of untouchability. In his personal life, Gandhi often thought and acted like a Hindu patriarch. That said, over the thirty years he was in India, Gandhi did a great deal to undermine traditional gender hierarchies. He attacked the pernicious system of purdah which, at the time, was extensively practised in both Hindu and Muslim households. He energetically promoted the education of girls, in his own ashram school and in 'national' colleges as well. Within the ashram, there was no gendered division of labour; men had to cook and clean, and women to teach and spin yarn.

In the future India of Gandhi's conception, women were to be fully equal to men. Once, when meeting with Congress workers in Bengal, Gandhi noted that few women were present, and those who were, not as forthcoming as the men. 'Is Azad Hindustan' (free India), he sharply asked, 'then going to be for men only and are women for ever to be in Zenanistan?' (i.e. behind the purdah).[28]

Gandhi's greatest contribution to the emancipation of women, however, was to make them part of social and political movements. In his South Africa satyagrahas, Indian women (including his wife Kasturba) had courted arrest. When he returned to India, however, he at first kept women out of his civil disobedience campaigns. Except for a few wives of Congressmen arrested for selling khadi on the road, women were largely absent during the non-cooperation movement. However, after his release from prison, Gandhi worked actively to have Sarojini Naidu appointed president of the Congress. While Gandhi asked women to lead the picketing of liquor shops, he was initially not keen to have them participate in the Salt March; Kamaladevi Chattopadhyay persuaded him to reconsider, whereupon many women broke the salt law and courted arrest. A decade later, women participated in large numbers in the Quit India movement.

Gandhi did not use the language of modern feminism. While strongly supportive of women's education, and open to women working in offices and factories, he thought the burden of child-rearing and homemaking should be borne by women. By the standards of our time, therefore, Gandhi must be considered conservative. By the standards of his own time, however, he was undoubtedly progressive, proof of which is the involvement of women in Congress meetings, in his satyagrahas, and in his programmes of constructive work. By contrast, there were few women active in Jinnah's Muslim League, or in Ambedkar's Scheduled Caste Federation, or in the Indian Liberal Party of Sapru and Srinivasa Sastri. And if we widen the comparative frame to take in countries other than India, many more women joined the freedom struggle led by Gandhi than the movements of Lenin, Mao, Ho or Castro.[29]

Even had the Labour Party in Britain or the Democrats in America a system of choosing presidents for one-year terms in 1925, it is hard to see either having a woman head the party, as Gandhi's Congress did that year. Two decades later, when India became independent, it had a woman governor (Sarojini Naidu) and a woman Cabinet minister (Rajkumari Amrit Kaur), while the work of refugee rehabilitation was led by other remarkable women, among them Kamaladevi Chattopadhyay, Mridula Sarabhai, Subhadra Joshi and Anis Kidwai. When the M.S. University was established in Baroda in 1949, it chose a woman (Hansa Mehta) as its vice chancellor. (It was to be another three decades before top American universities began choosing women presidents.)

Women were perhaps as prominent in public life in the India of the 1940s and 1950s as in the United States of the same period. And they were far more prominent than in the other newly independent countries of Asia or Africa. To be sure, these women ministers, governors, vice chancellors, etc. came from the upper-caste elite. Even so, in a culture whose two main religions, Hinduism and Islam, are so intensely patriarchal in their scripture as well as in their social practice, the rise of these women to positions of distinction and influence must count as one of Gandhi's major (if insufficiently acknowledged) achievements.

V

After a visit to Yerwada prison in August 1932, the respected newspaper editor S.A. Brelvi called Gandhi 'the truest nation-builder since [the Mughal Emperor] Akbar's time', adding, 'of the two [he] will prove to be the greater'.[30]

In 1932, the independence of India lay many years in the future. But as a close observer of Gandhi's politics, Brelvi understood how he was nurturing the nation-in-the-making. He had seen Gandhi build bridges between Hindus and Muslims, take the nationalist message to the south and east of the country, urge that 'untouchables' be treated as equals, and steadily undermine the patriarchy which characterized India's two major religions, Hinduism and Islam.

India today is a flawed and fault-ridden democracy. Its many failures include widespread poverty, the malfunctioning of public institutions, political corruption and crony capitalism. On the other side, unlike so many ex-colonial countries, India regularly conducts free and fair elections; women have equal rights under the Constitution; it has successfully nurtured linguistic diversity; the state is not (or not yet) identified with a particular religion; and it has extensive programmes of affirmative action for those of underprivileged background. These achievements are owed to a generation of visionary nation builders, among whom Gandhi was—in all senses—pre-eminent.

Gandhi's successes in forging a sense of dignity and national purpose were in large part a product of his methods. A country so large, so staggeringly diverse and so desperately divided could never have been united by a leader (or leaders) marked by ideological rigidity or personal arrogance. Travelling through India in 1938, meeting Gandhi and studying his work, talking to his followers and his critics, the American journalist John Gunther came to the conclusion that perhaps the most striking thing about Gandhi was 'his inveterate love of compromise. . . . Surely no man has ever so quickly and easily let bygones be bygones. He has no hatreds, no resentments; once a settlement is reached, he co-operates with enemies as vigorously as he fought them.'[31]

Gandhi himself expressed it slightly differently. In November 1936, an English visitor to Sevagram asked for details of Gandhi's village programme. He answered: 'I cannot speak with either the definiteness or the confidence of a Stalin or Hitler, as I have no cut-and-dried programme I can impose on the villagers. My method, I need not say, is different. I propose to convert by patient persuasion.'[32]

Promoting an ethic of dialogue and compromise was one way in which Gandhi brought different kinds of Indians together. A second was through the Congress Party, which, under his direction, transformed itself from a body of urban middle-class professionals into a mass political organization, with branches in states and districts, its networks touching every part of India and virtually every section of Indian society. By promoting the mother tongue, Gandhi drew peasants, workers and artisans into a continuing conversation with lawyers, businessmen and intellectuals.

The social base of the Congress was far deeper than that of the Muslim League, one reason why democracy has established itself more solidly in India than in Pakistan, a point that some Pakistani scholars themselves acknowledge.[33] Another key difference between Gandhi and his great rival Muhammad Ali Jinnah was that the former assiduously nurtured leaders for the future, whereas Jinnah was verily the Great and Only Leader. There were no analogues in his party of Nehru, Patel, Rajaji, Azad and others.

That, amidst the wreckage of Partition, there were some capable men and women at hand to build a nation anew was largely the handiwork of Gandhi. I have already spoken of the partnership between Jawaharlal Nehru as prime minister and Vallabhbhai Patel as home minister. A third Gandhi associate, Maulana Azad, served as education minister; a fourth, Rajkumari Amrit Kaur, as health minister. Formally placed above them all, as the President of the Indian Republic, was Rajendra Prasad, whose potential Gandhi first saw in Champaran in 1917.

One of Gandhi's closest colleagues, J.B. Kripalani, left the Congress shortly after Independence to start his own party. A second, C. Rajagopalachari, served as the governor of West Bengal and as the last governor general while the country was still a dominion, and as home minister of India and chief minister of Madras province after the country became a republic. However, he became increasingly disenchanted with Nehru's policies, and in 1959 formed a new party, Swatantra, promoting the values of market liberalism in opposition to the centralized economic planning that the prime minister favoured. Meanwhile, as an opposition member of Parliament, J.B. Kripalani was relentlessly harrying Nehru on his appeasement of Chinese communism.

Gandhi himself had little interest in constitutional processes or the functioning of Parliament. But indirectly, he played a considerable role in stabilizing the democratic institutions of independent India. Through the 1950s and 1960s, some of the men and women he had trained ran the ship of state, while others were in the Opposition, holding the government to account. It was also followers and admirers of Gandhi, such as Kamaladevi Chattopadhyay and J.C. Kumarappa, who laid the foundations of the civil society movement in India, by working to promote cooperative housing projects, revive traditional handicrafts, and renew the rural economy.[34]

As the major leader of the freedom struggle in the largest colony of the world's greatest Empire, Gandhi also profoundly influenced anti-colonial movements elsewhere. Gandhi was admired by such (widely different) African nationalists as the Kenyans Jomo Kenyatta and Tom Mboya, the Zambian Kenneth Kaunda, the Tanzanian Julius Nyerere, and the Ghanaian Kwame Nkrumah.[35] In Botswana, when the British exiled the extremely popular king, Seretse Khama, chiefs and headmen refused to elect a new leader, and said they would not pay taxes unless Seretse returned with his honour and position intact. Their movement of civil disobedience was inspired by their knowledge of the satyagrahas led by Gandhi in India and South Africa.[36]

In South Africa itself, the struggles against apartheid were directly inspired by Gandhi. The long-time leader of the African National Congress, Albert Luthuli, counted himself a disciple of Gandhi, and so, less surprisingly, did leaders of the Indian community such as Monty Naicker and Yusuf Dadoo. The first major mass movement against apartheid, the Defiance Campaign of 1952, used methods pioneered by Gandhi, with African and Indian protesters defying racial laws by entering offices, train compartments and other public spaces designated for 'Europeans only'.[37]

In 1960 the African National Congress (ANC) abandoned non-violence. For the next thirty years it practised various forms of armed struggle. But the Gandhian element returned after the release of Nelson Mandela in 1990 and the negotiations for the transfer of power. After the ending of apartheid, and his taking office as the first President of a democratic South Africa, Mandela promoted a Gandhi-like path of reconciliation with the white race, and among the different sections of South African society. That the Constitution of democratic South Africa refused to privilege a particular race, religion, or linguistic group also owed something to the Indian, or one might even say, Gandhian, experience.

VI

As the second millennium of 'the Christian era' drew to a close, *Time* magazine decided to choose a Person of the Century, a once-in-a-hundred-years variation on its annual Person of the Year. The magazine organized an online poll, which threw up the name of the singer Elvis Presley. Fortunately, it had a backup plan, namely, nomination by a jury of experts. This ranked the scientist Albert Einstein first, and Gandhi second (jointly with Franklin Roosevelt).

Even professedly, 'global' magazines are not immune to nationalist sentiment, and doubtless *Time*'s choice of Einstein as the Person of the Century was influenced by the fact that he was an American, and a naturalized American at that, thus further feeding into the myth of the Lady of Liberty who always provides refuge to the worthy and the needy. But Einstein himself would have been embarrassed at being so anointed. For, he absolutely venerated Gandhi, as the first of the three epigraphs to this book demonstrates. An authoritative recent study of the scientist's political views states unambiguously that 'for Einstein it is clear that Gandhi was the supreme moral compass'.[38] In Einstein's Berlin study, there were portraits of Newton, Faraday and Clerk Maxwell. When he moved to Princeton in 1935, he added a portrait of Gandhi. However, a scientist friend who visited him in 1954 observed that while the portraits of the physicists had been taken down, that of Gandhi remained. When asked about this, Einstein answered that the Mahatma was 'the greatest man of our age'.[39]

Einstein had lived in Europe and America, and seen the work of Churchill, Roosevelt and Truman at close quarters. He would never speak of them in remotely the same terms as he did about Gandhi. Nor was he alone. In a memoir of his boyhood in the Italy of the 1930s, the writer Italo Calvino observed: 'When I think back to the personalities who dominated world news at the time, the one who stands out from all the others in terms of his visual image is without a doubt Gandhi. Although huge numbers of anecdotes about him circulated, and he was very often caricatured, his image managed to instill the idea that there was something serious and true in him, albeit very remote from us.'[40]

To the verdicts of Einstein and Calvino let me add that of the widely travelled British man of letters Malcolm Muggeridge. In the 1920s, Muggeridge taught in a college in Kerala. Many years later, he wrote that the 'three outstanding men of action' of his time were Gandhi, Stalin and De Gaulle. 'Of my three men,' he continued, 'Gandhi, without disposing of so much as a popgun, got us out of India, where Churchill had said we must remain for many a year to come. No one who saw, as I did, the fabulous following he had among the poorest of the poor in India could doubt the reality of his influence, unsupported, as it was, by any sort of ceremonial trappings or material resources' (trappings and resources which both Stalin and De Gaulle, as well as Roosevelt and Churchill, had in abundance).[41]

Einstein, Calvino and Muggeridge lived through the tumultuous interwar decades when Gandhi was at the height of his influence and renown. Yet, in our own time, this curiosity in, and admiration for, Gandhi, is manifest in many parts of the world, and among human beings mighty as well as powerless. Two examples must suffice. As a state senator in Illinois, Barack Obama had a photo of Gandhi in his office, alongside portraits of Nelson Mandela, Martin Luther King and Thurgood Marshall. Many years later, after he was elected President of the United States, a journalist asked Obama which person in history, dead or alive, he would most like to have dinner with. Mahatma Gandhi, answered the President, wittily adding that it would have to be a frugal meal.

Obama's interest in and admiration for Gandhi was impressive; but not, in itself, entirely surprising. One would expect an African-American graduate of Columbia and Harvard universities to know of Gandhi's influence in India and (via the civil rights movement) within the United States too. My second illustration of Gandhi's global reach may be more striking. Early in Obama's second term as President, I was visiting his country, to promote my book *Gandhi Before India*. A waiter who brought me tea in my New York hotel room saw the book lying on the table. Not knowing that I was the author, he saw the cover photo and asked: 'That's the young Mr. Gandhi, isn't it?' I answered in the affirmative. 'In my country we admire him a great deal,' said the waiter. 'And which country are you from?' I asked. The surprising answer was the Dominican Republic.

Gandhi probably did not know of the Dominican Republic. But, long after he was dead, one of its citizens knew about him and admired him; they could even identify him in a rare photo where he was clad in a suit and tie rather than his trademark loincloth.

This posthumous, worldwide praise for Gandhi would have amazed the men who jailed him in British India. Successive viceroys dismissed him as a humbug, a hypocrite, a back number. Their insolence towards him could be extreme: during the Second World War, Gandhi was reduced to corresponding with, and being reviled by, an additional secretary in the home department, who reported to the home secretary who reported to the home member who reported in turn to the viceroy. But who now remembers that arrogant civil servant, or his boss, or his boss's boss's boss, who once sat in a grand palace atop Raisina Hill in imperial New Delhi? This revenge of history is a mark of the greatness of Gandhi the man, and of the profound political changes he helped bring about: namely, the dismantling of the British Empire and the institutional and ideological edifice that once sustained it.

VII

For a man who has been dead seventy years, and who held no public office, Gandhi is extraordinarily well known across the globe. The world knows of him, but what should it know about him? In what ways does Gandhi speak to the predicaments and peoples of the twenty-first century?

Gandhi is still relevant on account of the method of social protest he pioneered. In 1931, a British journalist based in India wrote to Gandhi that 'whether or not you are to be the architect of India's new constitution, your advocacy of the doctrine of non-violence as a political weapon will remain throughout history as your greatest contribution to the world'.[42] Four years later, the *Bombay Chronicle* observed that 'the gospel of Satyagraha is the choicest gift that Gandhiji, the Congress and India have given to the world. And we are confident that ere long the world will be grateful for the gift.'[43]

These verdicts were prophetic. After Gandhi's death, his techniques of non-violent protest have been successfully used in several continents. Martin Luther King and his colleagues applied the force of truth to shame the American government into overturning racial legislation. Across Soviet-controlled Eastern Europe, Lech Walesa, Vaclav Havel and their comrades used the power of non-violence to replace communist dictatorships with democratic regimes.

Gandhi himself used satyagraha to oppose colonial rule. But even when countries are formally free, and formally democratic, non-violence can play a crucial role in challenging injustice and discrimination. Such was the case in the United States of the 1950s and 1960s, when the denial of equal rights of citizenship for African Americans was confronted, and overcome, by the civil rights movement. And such is the case in India today, where multiparty democracy and an independent judiciary exist side by side with pervasive social inequalities.

In his own country, Gandhi's methods of satyagraha have been applied in different ways and to different ends. In the 1970s, peasants in the Himalaya launched the Chipko movement, protesting the deforestation caused by logging companies by threatening to hug the trees still standing. In the 1980s, tribals in Central India launched a series of satyagrahas in protest against a massive dam that would submerge their homes, lands and shrines, and devastate large areas of forest as well. Most recently, in the summer of 2011, tens of thousands of Indians held rallies and fasts to protest against the large-scale corruption of the country's political class. These movements have all drawn inspiration from Gandhi, carrying his portrait, humming the hymns he liked, starting or ending their campaigns on the day he was born, 2 October, or the day he died, 30 January.[44]

Non-violent opposition to the arbitrary use of state power is one manifestation of the legacy of Gandhi today; social work among the poor and disadvantaged is another. Gandhi himself placed as much importance on reconstruction as on protest. Men and women inspired by him have nurtured rural cooperatives, restored ravaged habitats, and in other ways built up the social capacity of vulnerable groups. One of the more noteworthy of these Gandhian initiatives is SEWA, the Self-Employed Women's Association, headquartered in his own town of Ahmedabad, which has organized more than a million women in producer cooperatives, the provision of child and maternal health care, and even a cooperative bank.[45]

Gandhi was nominated for the Nobel Peace Prize several times. He was never chosen, in part because of Norway's extremely close relationship to Britain. That Gandhi was never awarded the prize remains a matter of deep embarrassment to the Nobel Committee in Oslo. They have since tried to make amends, by awarding prizes to (among others) Albert Luthuli, the Dalai Lama, Archbishop Desmond Tutu and Aung San Suu Kyi, all of whom were inspired by Gandhi.

VIII

The theory and practice of non-violent resistance to unjust authority has been, as those prescient journalists of the 1930s predicted, Gandhi's most enduring legacy. But there are others too. I myself think that his ideas on religious pluralism and interfaith harmony speak directly to the world we live and labour in today.

Gandhi was born in 1869, a decade after the publication of Charles Darwin's *The Origin of Species*. This was a time of widespread scepticism among the educated classes in Europe, a sentiment captured in the title of Thomas Hardy's poem, 'God's Funeral'. Outside the Continent, this was also a time of heightened missionary activity. In their new colonies in Africa and Asia, European priests sought to claim the heathen for Christianity.

Gandhi rejected both the atheism of the intellectuals as well as the arrogance of the missionaries. He did not think science had all the answers to the mysteries of the universe. Faith answered to a deep human need. Yet Gandhi did not think that there was one privileged path to God either. He encouraged inter-religious dialogue so that individuals could see their faith in the critical reflections of another.

Despite his long battles with the Hindu orthodoxy, Gandhi still called himself a Hindu. Perhaps this was out of sentimental attachment to an ancestral faith, or for tactical reasons, since positioning himself as an outsider would make it harder to persuade India's Hindu majority of his reformist and egalitarian credo. Yet, Gandhi's faith resonates closely with spiritual (or intellectual) traditions that are other than 'Hindu'. The stress on ethical conduct brings him close to Buddhism, while the avowal of non-violence and non-possession is clearly drawn from Jainism. The exaltation of service is far more Christian than Hindu. The emphasis on the dignity of the individual echoes Enlightenment ideas of human rights.

The best tribute to Gandhi's religious ecumenism that I have come across relates to a memorial meeting held after his death in the Tamil town of Tirupattur. Presiding over the meeting was the founder of a Christian ashram modelled on Sevagram. 'The most moving speech,' he reported later, 'was that of the Secretary of the local Muslim League, who said: "Mahatma Gandhi was the twentieth century Christ, and he died for us Muslims."'[46]

Gandhi's respect for other religions was intimately connected with his philosophy (and practice) of non-violence. He opposed injustice and authoritarian rule, but without arms. He reached out to people of other faiths, with understanding and respect. Where the proselytizer took his book (and sometimes his bayonet) to the heathen, Gandhi chose instead to study Islamic and Christian texts, bringing to them the same open, yet not uncritical, mind that he brought to Hindu scriptures. In a world riven by inter-religious violence and misunderstanding, Gandhi's ideas and example may yet provide a moderating influence.[47]

IX

Gandhi and his legacy also speak directly to the question of environmental sustainability. That quintessentially Gandhian question—How much should a person consume?—has never been more relevant than today, when the populous countries of Asia increasingly challenge the West's monopoly on modern lifestyles. Back in 1928, Gandhi had warned about the unsustainability, on the global scale, of Western patterns of production and consumption. 'God forbid that India should ever take to industrialization after the manner of the West,' he had said. 'The economic imperialism of a single tiny island kingdom [England] is today keeping the world in chains. If an entire nation of 300 million took to similar economic exploitation, it would strip the world bare like locusts.'[48]

The key phrase here is *after the manner of the West*. Gandhi wished to free the people of India from poverty, ill health, illiteracy and the lack of dignified employment. He was keen to enhance human productivity, and was happy to use modern science towards that end. At the same time, Gandhi had an intuitive understanding of the global limits to resource-intensive, energy-intensive industrialization. As he put it in 1926, to 'make India like England and America is to find some other races and places of the earth for exploitation'. Since the Western nations had already 'divided all the known races outside Europe for exploitation and there are no new worlds to discover', he pointedly asked: 'What can be the fate of India trying to ape the West?'[49]

The advice was disregarded. Whether under state planning in the past or under the business-friendly regime now in place, India's economic and technological policies have taken little (often no) account of the country's resource endowments or of broader questions of environmental sustainability. As a result, India is an ecological disaster zone, marked by deforestation, species loss, chemical contamination of the soil, declining soil fertility, depleting groundwater aquifers, and massively high rates of atmospheric and river pollution. One recent study estimated that the annual cost of environmental degradation in India was equivalent to 5.7 per cent of the Gross Domestic Product.[50] The costs are economic and they are social, for the burden of environmental abuse falls disproportionately on the poor. Fisherfolk are thrown out of work by polluted rivers, pastoralists by degraded grazing land, farmers by man-made droughts and tribal communities by unregulated mining, while the slum dwellers in the cities suffer much more—health-wise and work-wise—from air and water pollution than the rich who live in gated communities.

Not just India, but China too is aiming to 'ape the West', and perhaps they will together strip the world bare like locusts unless they stop, step back and forge policies that can eliminate poverty and destitution without destroying the earth that sustains us all. Notably, Gandhi himself had a keen interest in practical forms of conservation. He endorsed the ideas of Albert Howard, a pioneer of organic farming who had lived for many years in India. He set his disciple J.C. Kumarappa to work at rebuilding the village economy on sustainable lines, by promoting water conservation, community forest management and chemical agriculture.[51]

X

In his 'Reflections on Gandhi', George Orwell wrote that 'regarded simply as a politician, and compared with the other leading political figures of our time, how clean a smell he has managed to leave behind!'[52] This lack of odour around Gandhi was a product of the openness of his political (and personal) life. There were no security men posted outside Gandhi's ashram; visitors of any creed and nationality could walk in when they chose. Those who could not visit sent their questions and criticisms in the mail; these were read by Gandhi, and often answered by him as well.

Perhaps no political leader in modern times knew his land and his people as intimately as Gandhi. He travelled around India by train, car, bullock cart and on foot, traversing thousands of miles of desert, mountain, valley, plain, plateau, delta and the coast, while spending the nights in towns and hamlets and sometimes in open fields as well.

There were no bodyguards with Gandhi in these journeys. In this age of terrorism, politicians may not be able to live the public life he did. But they might yet note that Gandhi's politics was marked by an absence of dissemblance and an utter lack of reliance on 'spin' (as distinct from spinning). His campaigns of civil disobedience were always announced in advance. His social experiments were minutely dissected in the pages of his newspapers, the comments of his critics placed alongside his own.

Gandhi's heightened self-awareness and openness to self-criticism stand in striking contrast to the arrogance of those in positions of power today. Gandhi once admitted to making a 'Himalayan Blunder'; but contemporary activists, as much as contemporary politicians, are loath ever to admit to even a simple mistake.

The poet Paul Valéry once remarked that 'in general the things that people hide from each other are of an emotional or physiological nature; defects, manias, lusts, passions, and superstitions'.[53] Among all the public figures of his time (or ours), Gandhi was singular in that he exposed his defects, his manias, his lusts, his passions and his superstitions, to the whole world, through his writings in periodicals he himself edited and published. And the odd dark thought that he kept for correspondence with friends was posthumously (and unsentimentally) exposed by the editors of his *Collected Works*.

As an English Quaker who interacted with him over a period of twenty years pointed out, 'Gandhiji *had no private life*, as we Westerners understand the expression.'[54] God knows what we would think of other celebrated figures (whether in politics or business, sports, science or the arts) if we were so directly exposed to the intimacies of their lives and thoughts. Beyond satyagraha, interfaith harmony, environmental responsibility, the ending of the British Empire, and the delegitimizing of untouchability, the practice of, and the largely successful quest for, truth may in fact be Gandhi's most remarkable achievement.

Acknowledgements

This book is the product of months and years in the archives, so it must be the keepers of the records I consulted who get pride of place here. I am grateful to the staff of the National Archives of India, New Delhi; of the Maharashtra State Archives, Mumbai (as well as of its Vidarbha branch office in Nagpur); of the library of the University of Mumbai and of Mani Bhavan, also in Mumbai; of the Uttar Pradesh State Archives, Lucknow; of the British Library, the National Archives of the United Kingdom, Friends House, and the Bishopsgate Institute, all in London; of the University of Southampton: of the Cambridge South Asia Centre; of Rhodes House, Oxford; of the Library of Congress in Washington, D.C.; of the New York Public Library, New York; of the Swarthmore College Peace Collection, Swarthmore; of the Houghton Library of Harvard University; of the Watson Institute, Brown University, Providence; and of the Doe Library of the University of California, Berkeley.

Two archives and their keepers deserve special mention. These are the Sabarmati Ashram Archives in Ahmedabad, where I found hundreds of rare, and rarely seen, letters to Gandhi; and the Nehru Memorial Museum and Library (NMML) in New Delhi, where—apart from dozens of other collections—I consulted the massive hoard of Gandhi Papers that for decades had remained unclassified and closed to scholars. My guides in Sabarmati were the terrific trilingual scholar

931

Tridip Suhrud (the three languages he works in being the three that Gandhi wrote or spoke in) and the superbly skilled archivist Kinnari Bhatt.

The Sabarmati Ashram is a place I had only occasionally visited before starting research on Gandhi. On the other hand, the NMML has sustained me all my working life. For this, as for all my previous books, I have spent many joyous weeks and months in its manuscripts section, where I could count on the professionalism of Neelam Vatsa, Shazia Faridi, Jyoti Luthra, Soumya Mohanty, D.S. Rawat and Sanjeev Gautam. I owe a colossal debt to Deepa Bhatnagar, who supervised the indexing of the Gandhi Papers, and to Dr N. Balakrishnan, who took the courageous decision to open these papers, previously held in private hands, to the public. Both Deepa and Dr Bala have a thorough knowledge of the NMML's wide-ranging collections, and gave me (as they did other scholars) many tips on where I might find more, or more interesting, material on the person or themes I was exploring. Now that they have both retired, one can safely, and sadly, say that the NMML shall never know their like again.

In the research and writing of this book, I received advice and assistance from many other people, among whom I must especially mention Sekhar Bandyopadhyay, Arpita Basu, Ajit Bhide, Rudra Chaudhuri, the late Mahendra Desai, the late Narayan Desai, Swati Ganguly, Jagadev Gajare, Ira Guha, Keshava Guha, Diva Gujral, Salima Hashmi, Kamu Iyer, Rajesh Joshi, Cara Jones, Gunjan Jhunjhunwala, Sunil Khilnani, Nirmala Lakshman, Mark Lindley, Mallikarjuna G.S., J. Martinez Alier, the late Swapan Mazumdar, Nandini Mehta, Ramanuj Mukherjee, Rudrangshu Mukherjee, Archana Nathan, Anil Nauriya, Prashant Panjiar, Aakar Patel, Dina Patel, Dinyar Patel, Vijay Prashad, Vikram Raghavan, M.V. Ravishankar, M.R. Sharan, Dilip Simeon, Hemali Sodhi, Taylor Stoehr, Peter Straus, the late Govind Talwalkar, R. Ullagadi, Saumya Vaishnava, and the doyenne of historians of the Dalit movement, the late Eleanor Zelliot. I owe a special debt to Vijay Jain of Prabhu Book Service, Gurgaon, and to K.K.S. Murthy of Select Bookshop, Bengaluru, for supplying me with numerous out-of-print and rare books and pamphlets relevant to this project. And I am particularly grateful to Shanuj V. C. for his meticulous copy-editing of the manuscript, and to Christine Shuttleworth for preparing such an excellent index to the printed book.

The Hindi letters and reports cited in this book were translated by myself. However, the Gujarati letters I have drawn upon were translated by Urvish Kothari. My late father, Dr S.R.D. Guha, translated some extremely useful materials from French and German, while a key document in Spanish was translated by Aditya Balasubramanian.

The draft manuscript of this book had the benefit of close readings from two outstanding historians, David Gilmour and Srinath Raghavan; and from two great Gandhi scholars, E.S. Reddy and Gopalkrishna Gandhi. Gopal has saved me from many errors of fact and interpretation. Mr Reddy, ninety-three years young as I write, continues to inspire me with his example and nourish me with his knowledge.

My agents, Gill Coleridge in London and Melanie Jackson in New York, have provided critical support and encouragement through the long decade in which this biography of Gandhi was conceived, researched and written. Gill and Melanie placed me with a superb set of editors and publishers: Meru Gokhale and Tarini Uppal in New Delhi, Simon Winder in London, Anne Collins in Toronto, and Dan Frank and Sonny Mehta in New York, who have all provided extremely valuable comments that have helped me shape, cut, revise and reshape successive drafts of the book. I owe a special debt to Sonny Mehta for taking such a strong personal interest in the project. Over long lunches in New York and New Delhi, and through many phone conversations, Sonny has helped me seek to strike a balance between the man and his ideas, the leader and his followers, the politician and his rivals, the individual and his times.

I grieve that two of my early mentors, the sociologist Anjan Ghosh and the historian Basudev (Robi) Chatterji, are no longer alive to see this work in print. Anjan and Robi were Indian intellectuals remarkably unmarked by prejudice or dogmatism; and I was one of many scholars younger than them, who benefited from their generosity and open-mindedness. I wish they were here still; I hope the spirit of their teachings is not entirely absent from these pages.

Notes
ABBREVIATIONS USED IN THE NOTES

ABP   *Amrita Bazar Patrika* (newspaper published from Calcutta)

Autobiography   M.K. Gandhi, *An Autobiography, or the Story of My Experiments with Truth*, translated from the Gujarati by Mahadev Desai (first published in 1927; second edition: Ahmedabad, Navajivan Press, 1940—reprinted many times since). There are many print editions of Gandhi's autobiography around the world, licensed by Navajivan; and there will be many more, especially since the work is now out of copyright. The pagination of these works varies enormously. Therefore, in my references to this book, I have cited Part and Chapter rather than page numbers. However, since the book originated from a series of newspaper articles, each chapter is only a few pages long, so my citations will be relatively easy to track down.

APAC/BL   Asia, Pacific and Africa Collections, British Library, London

BC   *Bombay Chronicle* (newspaper published from Bombay)

CWMG   *Collected Works of Mahatma Gandhi* (New Delhi: Publications Division, 1958–1994)

D   *Dawn* (newspaper published from Delhi till 1947, and later from Karachi)

DTDG	Mahadev H. Desai's *Day-to-Day with Gandhi,* in six volumes, edited by Narhari D. Parikh, translated from the Gujarati by Hemantkumar G. Nilkanth (Varanasi: Sarva Seva Sangh Prakashan, 1968)
FR	Fortnightly Report
GoI	Government of India
GBI	Ramachandra Guha, *Gandhi Before India* (New York: Alfred A. Knopf, 2014)
H	*Harijan* (weekly published from Ahmedabad)
HT	*Hindustan Times* (newspaper published from Delhi)
IAR	*Indian Annual Register* (edited by H.N. Mitra, and published from Calcutta from 1919 to 1947)
IOR	India Office Records
MSA	Maharashtra State Archives, Mumbai
MG	*Manchester Guardian* (newspaper published from Manchester, predecessor of *Guardian*)
MP	Mountbatten Papers
N	*Navajivan* (weekly published from Ahmedabad)
NAI	National Archives of India, New Delhi
NAUK	National Archives of the United Kingdom, Kew
NMML	Nehru Memorial Museum and Library, New Delhi
NYPL	New York Public Library, New York
PRMGMC	*Printed Record of the Mahatma Gandhi Murder Case (in the High Court of Judicature for the Province of East Punjab at Simla),* eight volumes, in the Rare Book Collection, Law Library, Library of Congress, Washington, D.C.
PSV	Private Secretary to Viceroy
SN	Serial Number
SAAA	Sabarmati Ashram Archives, Ahmedabad
Source Material	N.R. Phatak, editor, *Source Material for a History of the Freedom Movement in India,* published in multiple volumes and parts (Bombay: Government of Maharashtra, 1965)
ToI	*Times of India*
ToP	Nicholas Mansergh, editor, *Constitutional Relations Between Britain and India: The Transfer of Power, 1942–47,* published in twelve volumes (London: His Majesty's Stationery Office, 1970–1983).
TS	*The Statesman* (newspaper published from Calcutta)
TT	*The Tribune* (newspaper published from Lahore)
UP	United Provinces

VAN   Vidarbha Archives, Nagpur

YI   *Young India* (weekly published from Ahmedabad)

Preface

1. Gandhi to C.F. Andrews, 15 June 1933, *CWMG*, LV, pp. 198–99.
2. Josiah Oldfield, quoted in 'Victor French' (pseudonym), *Lord Willingdon in India* (Bombay: Karnatak Printing Press, 1934). On Oldfield's early friendship with Gandhi, see *GBI*, pp. 44–45, 216–17, etc.
3. *CWMG*, LXXXV, p. 151.
4. The most readily accessible biographical study by an Indian is by Rajmohan Gandhi, who was born in 1935; that by a non-Indian, by Joseph Lelyveld, who was born in 1937. I was born in 1958.
5. 'Higher Education', H, 9 July 1937, *CWMG*, LXVII, p. 159.
6. Pattabhi Sitaramayya, quoted in C.D. Narasimhaiah, *The Writer's Gandhi* (Patiala: Punjabi University, 1967), pp. 54–55. To this, Narasimhaiah adds his own assessment, which was that Gandhi 'broke the cumbrous, Victorian periods which had enslaved the Indian writer like his counterpart in England . . . and made us speak like men who had something to say, and not exhort like gods or rant like demons.'
7. See V.S. Naipaul, *Letters between a Father and Son* (London: Little, Brown and Company, 1999), pp. 29–30.
8. Quoted in Ved Mehta, *Mahatma Gandhi and His Apostles* (Harmondsworth: Penguin, 1977), p. 35.

Chapter One: The Returning Hero

1. Gandhi to G.A. Natesan, c. 29 October 1909, *CWMG*, IX, pp. 506–07.
2. *CWMG*, XII, pp. 507, 521.
3. On the friendship between Gandhi and Kallenbach in South Africa, see *GBI*, pp. 187–88, 418–19, 459–60, 600–01, etc. Cf. also Shimon Lev, *Soulmates: The Story of Mahatma Gandhi and Hermann Kallenbach* (Hyderabad: Orient Blackswan, 2012).
4. *Autobiography*, Part IV, Chapter XXXVIII.
5. Sarojini Naidu to Lady Pherozeshah Mehta, undated letter reproduced in the *Indian Review*, January 1915. See also James Hunt, *Gandhi in London* (New Delhi: Promilla Books, 1993), p. 163, for a later (but equally colourful) recollection of Mrs Naidu's.
6. See *Autobiography*, Part IV, Chapter XXXVIII, 'My Part in the War'.

7. See *GBI*, pp. 135–37, 193–94.

8. *CWMG*, XII, pp. 523–25.

9. Olive Schreiner to Hermann Kallenbach, 2 October 1914, in Kallenbach Papers, NAI; Schreiner to Gandhi, 2 October 1914, letter quoted in Ruth First and Ann Scott, *Olive Schreiner: A Biography* (New York: Schocken Books, 1980), pp. 304–05, emphasis in the original. On Gandhi's friendship with Olive Schreiner and her brother, the liberal politician W.P. Schreiner, see *GBI*, pp. 328, 433–34, 494–95, 527.

10. Gandhi to Maganlal, 18 September 1914, *CWMG*, XII, pp. 531–32.

11. Gandhi to Pragji Desai, 15 November 1914, *CWMG*, XII, pp. 554–55. During the Anglo-Zulu war of 1906, Gandhi, while officially on the British side, ministered to many Zulus as well. See *GBI*, p. 194.

12. Gandhi, *Autobiography*, Part IV, Chapter XLI, and Part V, Chapter IV.

13. *CWMG*, XII, pp. 523–25.

14. Andrews to Gokhale, 27 December 1912, in File 11, G.K. Gokhale Papers, NAI, emphases added. In the time they spent together in South Africa, Andrews and Gandhi had become very close, with the Englishman acquiring an acute understanding of the Indian's mind. See *GBI*, pp. 500–09.

15. *BC*, 11 January 1915.

16. See *GBI*, pp. 342–44.

17. Narandas Gandhi to Chhaganlal Gandhi, 21 January 1915, S.N. 6114, SAAA.

18. *BC*, 13 January 1915.

19. *CWMG*, XIII, p. 7.

20. *BC*, 15 January 1915.

21. See *GBI*, pp. 129–30.

22. See Stanley Wolpert, *Jinnah of Pakistan* (Delhi: Oxford University Press, 1985), Chapters 2 and 3.

23. Jinnah's speech was reproduced in *BC*, 15 January 1915.

24. *CWMG*, XIII, pp. 9–10.

25. *BC*, 16 January 1915.

26. Narandas Gandhi to Chhaganlal Gandhi, 21 January 1915, S.N. 6114, SAAA.

27. Japaan to Chhaganlal Gandhi, 6 March 1915, S.N. 6161, SAAA.

28. *Autobiography*, Part V, Chapter III, 'With Gokhale in Poona'.

29. *CWMG*, XIII, pp. 26–28.

30. See P. Kodanda Rao, *The Right Honourable V.S. Srinivasa Sastri: A Political Biography* (Bombay: Asia Publishing House, 1963).

31. Entries for 22 and 27 February 1915, in 'Diaries for 1915–1920', V.S. Srinivasa Sastri Papers, NMML. 'Hariji' was Hriday Nath Kunzru,

later a member of the influential States Reorganization Commission of independent India.

32. *Source Material*, Volume III, Part I, p. 3.
33. See Gopalkrishna Gandhi, editor, *A Frank Friendship: Gandhi and Bengal* (Kolkata: Seagull, 2015), pp. 47–50.
34. See *GBI*, pp. 419–23, 509–10, etc.; S.R. Mehrotra, *The Mahatma and the Doctor: The Untold Story of Dr Pranjivan Mehta, Gandhi's Greatest Friend and Benefactor* (Mumbai: Vakils, Feffer & Simons Private Limited, 2014).
35. *CWMG*, XIX, p. 251. Cf. also J.T.F. Jordens, *Swami Shraddhananda: His Life and Causes* (New Delhi: Oxford University Press, 1981).
36. 'Mr. Gandhi's Visit', *St. Stephen's College Magazine*, number 32, April 1915.
37. *CWMG*, XIII, p. 47; Manian Natesan, 'Bapu and I', *Indian Review*, February 1958; A.S. Iyengar, 'Gandhiji's First Visit to Madras', *Indian Review*, May 1965.
38. *CWMG*, XIII, pp. 51–52, 58–61.
39. Letter of 4 May 1915, *CWMG*, XIII, p. 72.
40. Entry for 30 April 1915, in 'Diaries for 1915–1920', V.S. Srinivasa Sastri Papers, NMML.
41. K. Venkatappayya to Gandhi, 26 April 1915, in SAAA. For the later development of the Andhra movement, and Gandhi's own endorsement of it, see Ramachandra Guha, *India After Gandhi* (London: Macmillan, 2007), Chapter 9.
42. Bhushan Chandra Joshi to Gandhi, 24 April 1915, S.N. 6177, SAAA. Cape Comorin, now known as Kanyakumari, is the southernmost tip of India.
43. K. Natarajan to Gandhi, 26 May 1915, S.N. 6195, SAAA.
44. *GBI*, pp. 201–04, 413–18, 502–03, 510–11, etc.
45. Gandhi to Narandas Gandhi, 14 March 1915, *CWMG*, XIII, p. 36.
46. The letter is reprinted in full and in English translation in C.B. Dalal, *Harilal Gandhi: A Life*, translated from the Gujarati by Tridip Suhrud (Hyderabad: Orient Longman, 2007), Appendix 1, pp. 127–45.
47. Gandhi to Narandas Gandhi, 25 April 1915, *CWMG*, XIII, p. 62.
48. See Kenneth L. Gillion, *Ahmedabad: A Study in Indian Urban History* (Berkeley: University of California Press, 1968).
49. The family home of Mangaldas Girdhardas in Ahmedabad has now been converted into a splendid heritage hotel named 'House of *MG*'.
50. *CWMG*, XIII, pp. 84–87.
51. Achyut Yagnik and Suchitra Sheth, *Ahmedabad: From Royal City to Megacity* (New Delhi: Penguin Books, 2011), pp. 195–96.
52. 'Draft Constitution for the Ashram', *CWMG*, XIII, pp. 91–98; *Autobiography*, Part V, Chapter IX.

53. Untitled notes by Satyananda Bose, c. 1915, S.N. 6184, SAAA.
54. *GBI*, pp. 195–98, 200–01.
55. Robin Lane Fox, *Augustine: Conversions to Confessions* (London: Allen Lane, 2015), pp. 107, 111, 336, etc.
56. *GBI*, p. 195f.
57. *Autobiography*, Part V, Chapter X.
58. *CWMG*, XIII, p. 94.
59. J.M. Lazarus to Gandhi, dated Durban, 21 December 1914, S.N. 6068, SAAA.
60. *CWMG*, XIX, p. 154.
61. *CWMG*, XIII, pp. 127–28.
62. Howard Spodek, *Ahmedabad: Shock City of Twentieth Century India* (New Delhi: Orient Blackswan, 2012), pp. 33–39.
63. Gandhi, *Autobiography*, Part V, Chapter X.
64. *Source Material, Vol. III*, pp. 7–8.
65. Quoted in B.R. Nanda, *Gandhi, Pan-Islamism, Imperialism and Nationalism in India* (Bombay: Oxford University Press, 1989), p. 1.

Chapter Two: Coming out in Banaras

1. See Arthur H. Nethercot, *The Last Four Lives of Annie Besant* (London: Rupert Hart-Davis, 1963), pp. 62–63, 161–63, 242–43.
2. As reported in the *Pioneer*, 6 February 1916.
3. Lord Hardinge of Penshurst, *My Indian Years, 1910–1916* (London: John Murray, 1948), p. 137.
4. Gandhi's edited version is in *CWMG*, XIII, pp. 210–16; the unexpurgated text is available in File Number 221 of 1916, General Administrative Department, Uttar Pradesh State Archives, Lucknow (hereafter cited as File 221).
5. Macaulay's 'Minute on Education' can be accessed at http://www.columbia.edu/itc/mealac/pritchett/00generallinks/macaulay/txt_minute_education_1835.html.
6. As recounted in the statement of E.M. Nanavatty, ICS, Officiating District and Sessions Judge, Banaras, dated 9 February 1916, in File Number 221.
7. This account of how Gandhi's speech was interrupted and ended is based on documents in File 221.
8. Typescript entitled 'The Benares-Gandhi Incident', signed 'An Observer', Simla, 25 February 1916, in Reel number 4, Annie Besant Papers (on microfilm), NMML.

9.   *CWMG*, XIII, pp. 216–17.

10. *CWMG*, XIII, pp. 217–18.

11. Statements by Annie Besant in *New India*, 10 and 16 February 1916.

12. Commissioner, Banaras Division, to Chief Secretary, 7 February 1916, in File 221.

13. Chief Secretary to Lieutenant Governor, 9 February 1916, in ibid.

14. Note by J.S. Meston, Lieutenant Governor of the United Provinces, dated 17 March 1916, in ibid.

15. Hardinge, *My Indian Years*, pp. 79–81.

16. *CWMG*, XIII, pp. 244–45.

17. *CWMG*, XIII, pp. 350–51.

18. 'Railway Passengers', *CWMG*, XIII, pp. 284–86.

19. 'The Hindu Caste System', *CWMG*, XIII, pp. 301–03.

20. Gandhi to Narhar Shambhurao Bhave, 7 June 1916, *CWMG*, XIII, p. 279.

21. C. Rajagopalachar[i], 'M.K. Gandhi: His Message to India', *Indian Review*, May 1916.

22. *CWMG*, XIII, pp. 303–04.

23. Polak to Kallenbach, 18 November 1916, Kallenbach Papers, NAI.

24. H.F. Owen, 'Towards Nationwide Agitation and Organization: The Home Rule Leagues, 1915–18', in D.A. Low, editor, *Soundings in Modern South Asian History* (Berkeley: University of California Press, 1968).

25. D.V. Tahmankar, *Lokamanya Tilak: Father of Indian Unrest and Maker of Modern India* (London: John Murray, 1956), pp. 241–42.

26. See Wolpert, *Jinnah of Pakistan*, Chapter 4.

27. S.R. Mehrotra, *A History of the Indian National Congress: Volume One, 1885–1918* (Delhi: Vikas Publishing House, 1995), pp. 142–43.

28. Khwaja Razi Haider, *Ruttie Jinnah* (Karachi: Oxford University Press, 2010), pp. 17–18.

29. Ruttie Petit to Padmaja Naidu, 7 January 1917, in Padmaja Naidu Papers, NMML.

30. Entry for 24 December 1916, 'Diaries for 1915–20', V.S. Srinivasa Sastri Papers, NMML.

Chapter Three: Three Experiments in Satyagraha

1.   B.B. Misra, editor, *Select Documents on Mahatma Gandhi's Movement in Champaran, 1917–18* (Patna: Government of Bihar, 1963) (hereafter *Select Documents*), pp. 54–55.

2.   See Bhairav Lal Das, editor, *Gandhiji Ké Champaran Andolan Ké Sutradhar Raj Kumar Shukla Ki Diary* (Darbhanga: Maharajadhiraj Kameshwar Singh Kalyani Foundation, 2014).

3.   *Autobiography*, Part V, Chapter XII.

4.   Quoted in Kalikinkar Datta, *Gandhiji in Bihar* (Patna: Government of India, 1969), pp. 3–4.

5.   See Mohammad Sajjad and Afroz Alam Sahil, 'The Unsung Heroes of the Champaran Satyagraha', https://thewire.in/123622/champaran-pir-munis-raj-kumar-shukla/ (accessed on 19 April 2017).

6.   This account of the indigo economy of north Bihar is based on Jacques Pouchepadass, *Champaran and Gandhi: Planters, Peasants and Gandhian Politics* (New Delhi: Oxford University Press, 1999), especially Chapters I to III. But cf. also Girish Mishra, *Agrarian Problems of Permanent Settlement: A Case Study of Champaran* (New Delhi: People's Publishing House, 1978).

7.   Pouchepadass, *Champaran and Gandhi*, pp. 165f.

8.   As related in R.M. Lala, *Encounters with the Eminent* (Bombay: International Book House, 1981), p. 48.

9.   *Select Documents*, pp. 58–62.

10.   *CWMG*, XIII, p. 363.

11.   Rajendra Prasad, *Satyagraha in Champaran* (Madras: S. Ganeshan, 1928), pp. 137–40. Motihari was the birthplace of Eric Blair, later known as George Orwell.

12.   Gandhi to District Magistrate, Champaran, 16 April 1917, *CWMG*, p. 367.

13.   Gandhi to Private Secretary to Viceroy, 16 April 1917, *CWMG*, XIII, pp. 368–69.

14.   Letters to Polak and Kripalani, both dated 17 April 1917, *CWMG*, XIII, pp. 371–72. For more on Naidoo, Sorabji and Cachalia, see *GBI*, pp. 308–09, 323, 352–53, etc.

15.   Prasad, *Satyagraha in Champaran*, pp. 146–49.

16.   See *Select Documents*, pp. 68–78.

17.   Prasad, *Satyagraha in Champaran*, pp. 153–56.

18.   J.B. Kripalani, *My Times: An Autobiography* (New Delhi: Rupa and Co., 2004), pp. 66–68.

19.   Herbert Cox, Secretary, Bihar Planters' Association, to L.F. Morshead, Commissioner, Tirhut Division, 28 April 1918, in *Select Documents*, pp. 95–96.

20.   Quoted in Datta, *Gandhiji in Bihar*, p. 37.

21.   W.H. Lewis, Subdivisional Officer, Bettiah, to W.B. Heycock, District Magistrate, Champaran, 29 April 1917, in *Select Documents*, pp. 99–104.

22. *CWMG*, XIV, pp. 542–44.
23. *CWMG*, XIV, pp. 150–52.
24. *CWMG*, XIII, p. 479.
25. *Select Documents*, pp. 396–99.
26. Quoted in D.G. Tendulkar, *Gandhi in Champaran* (New Delhi: Government of India, 1957), pp. 97–98.
27. Untitled, undated note, c. July 1921, by H. McPherson, Member of Council, Bihar and Orissa, in File No. 65 of 1921, Home (Political), NAI.
28. David Hardiman, *Peasant Nationalists of Gujarat: Kheda District, 1917–1934* (Delhi: Oxford University Press, 1981), pp. 59, 80.
29. See Narhari D. Parikh, *Sardar Vallabhbhai Patel, Volume 1* (1953; reprint Ahmedabad: Navajivan, 1996), Chapters I to VI.
30. See Narhari D. Parikh, *Mahadev Desai's Early Life*, translated from the Gujarati by Gopalrao Kulkarni (Ahmedabad: Navajivan Publishing House, 1953), pp. 45–53 and passim.
31. *Autobiography*, Part IV, Chapter XXI.
32. Cf. http://gandhiashramsabarmati.org/en/about-gandhi-ashram-menu/history-menu.html (accessed on 24 September 2014).
33. Hardiman, *Peasant Nationalists of Gujarat*, p. 89.
34. *CWMG*, XIV, pp. 68–69.
35. 'Speech at Gujarat Political Conference', Godhra, 3 November 1917, in *CWMG*, XIV, pp. 48–66.
36. Parikh, *Sardar Vallabhbhai Patel, Volume 1*, Chapter IX.
37. Hardiman, *Peasant Nationalists of Gujarat*, Chapter 5.
38. Bombay Government, fortnightly report for second half of January 1918, in Proceedings No. 18 of May 1918, Home Department (Political-Deposit), NAI.
39. *DTDG*, Volume I, pp. 17–18, 96–97.
40. Sujata Patel, *The Making of Industrial Relations: The Ahmedabad Textile Industry, 1918–1939* (Delhi: Oxford University Press, 1987), Chapter III.
41. Mahadev Desai, *A Righteous Struggle*, translated from the Gujarati by Somnath P. Dave, edited by Bharatan Kumarappa (Ahmedabad: Navajivan, 1951), pp. 4–7.
42. See Ela Bhatt, editor, *Motaben: Anasuya Sarabhai (1885–1972)* (Ahmedabad: Shantisadan, 2012).
43. Gandhi to Ambalal Sarabhai, Motihari, 21 December 1917, *CWMG*, XIV, p. 115.
44. Erik H. Erikson, *Gandhi's Truth: On the Origins of Militant Nonviolence* (London: Faber and Faber, 1970), pp. 330–33.

45. Desai, *A Righteous Struggle*, pp. 16–17.
46. *CWMG*, XIV, pp. 224–25, 232–33, 237–39, 248–49, etc.
47. *CWMG*, XIV, pp. 229–30. The letter was, of course, originally written in Gujarati. The translation was most likely the handiwork of C.N. Patel, the Deputy Editor of the *Collected Works*.
48. Spodek, *Ahmedabad*, pp. 61–62.
49. Desai, *A Righteous Struggle*, pp. 25–26.
50. *CWMG*, XIV, pp. 258–67.
51. Desai, *A Righteous Struggle*, pp. 92–93.
52. Hardiman, *Peasant Nationalists of Gujarat*, pp. 104–07.
53. *DTDG*, I, pp. 84, 92–93.
54. *Hindusthan*, 2 April 1918, in *Report on Newspapers in the Bombay Presidency, January to December 1918*, L/R/5/174, APAC/BL.
55. *CWMG*, XIV, pp. 369–70.
56. Gandhi to PSV, 30 April 1918, *CWMG*, XIV, pp. 380–81.
57. *CWMG*, XIV, pp. 479, 493.
58. Erikson, *Gandhi's Truth*, pp. 370–71.
59. *CWMG*, XIV, pp. 414–19.
60. *CWMG*, XIV, pp. 240, 447–48.
61. Letters of 29 and 31 July 1918, both written from Nadiad, *CWMG*, XIV, pp. 515, 517.
62. Gandhi to Pranjivan Mehta, 2 July 1918, *CWMG*, XIV, p. 467.
63. *CWMG*, XV, pp. 21–23.
64. *CWMG*, XV, pp. 32, 67, 70–71.
65. H.S.L. Polak to Mahadev Desai, 20 February 1919, SN 6428, SAAA.
66. Gandhi to Harilal, 1 May 1918, *CWMG*, XIV, p. 385. For this and later letters between Gandhi and Harilal, I have sometimes supplemented the *CWMG* version with that found in Mahadev Desai's diaries.
67. *DTDG*, I, p. 165.
68. Gandhi to Manilal, 31 January 1918; Gandhi to Ada West, 31 January 1918, *CWMG*, XIV, pp. 178–79. The relations between Gandhi and his second son are explored in greater detail in Uma Dhupelia-Mesthrie, *Gandhi's Prisoner? The Life of Gandhi's Son Manilal* (Cape Town: Kwela Books, 2005).
69. Gandhi to Manilal, 31 July 1918, *CWMG*, XIV, pp. 517–18.
70. Cf. Neelima Shukla-Bhatt, *Narasinha Mehta of Gujarat: A Legacy of Bhakti in Songs and Stories* (New York: Oxford University Press, 2014).
71. *DTDG*, I, pp. 100–01.

72. Gandhi to Devadas, 2 February 1919, *CWMG*, XV, pp. 83–84.
73. C.M.C. Marsham, Superintendent of Police, Champaran, to L.F. Morshead, Commissioner, Tirhut Division, 12 September 1917, in *Select Documents*, p. 333.
74. *Select Documents*, Appendix VII, pp. 532–47.
75. *DTDG*, I, pp. 138–39, 154–55.
76. Gandhi to H.S.L. Polak, 8 March 1918, *CWMG*, XIV, p. 245.
77. Gandhi to Haribhai Desai (father of Mahadev), 8 April 1918, *CWMG*, XIV, p. 318.
78. Gandhi to Mahadev Desai, 9 May 1918, *CWMG*, XIV, pp. 393–94.
79. Letter of 5 February 1919, *CWMG*, XV, p. 84.

Chapter Four: Going National

1. S.D. Waley, *Edwin Montagu: A Memoir and an Account of His Visits to India* (London: Asia Publishing House, 1964), pp. 134–35.
2. Edwin S. Montagu, *An Indian Diary*, edited by Venetia Montagu, (London: William Heinemann, 1930), pp. 3–4, 184–85.
3. Ibid., pp. 57–58, 65–66.
4. Ibid., pp. 104, 116, 220–21.
5. Ibid., p. 193.
6. Arthur Berriedale Keith, *A Constitutional History of India, 1600–1935* (first published 1930: second, enlarged edition, Delhi: Low Price Publications, 2011), pp. 247–59.
7. Peter Heehs, *The Bomb in Bengal: The Rise of Revolutionary Terrorism in India, 1900–1910* (New Delhi: Oxford University Press, 1993).
8. Montagu, *An Indian Diary*, p. 156.
9. *Sedition Committee Report* (Calcutta: Government of India, 1918), pp. 25, 145–46, 179, 190, 201, etc.
10. Secretary of State to Viceroy, 10 October 1918; Viceroy to Secretary of State, 19 November 1918, both in Mss Eur E 264/4, APAC/BL.
11. Desai, *DTDG*, I, p. 271.
12. *CWMG*, XV, pp. 86–88.
13. Jamnadas Dwarkadas to Annie Besant, 27 February 1919, in Reel 11, Annie Besant Papers, NMML.
14. *CWMG*, XV, pp. 102–03, 125–26. Gandhi called his youngest son 'Devdas', but the son himself spelt his name 'Devadas'.
15. Jawaharlal Nehru, *An Autobiography: With Musings on Recent Events in India* (first published 1936: second edition London: The Bodley Head, 1942), pp. 41–42.

16. *Source Material, Vol. III, Part I*, p. 104.

17. IAR, 1920, Volume I, Part I, pp. 34–35.

18. H.F. Owen, 'Organizing for the Rowlatt Satyagraha of 1919', in Ravinder Kumar, editor, *Essays on Gandhian Politics: The Rowlatt Satyagraha of 1919* (Oxford: Clarendon Press, 1971).

19. Rajmohan Gandhi, *The Rajaji Story: I: A Warrior from the South* (Madras: Bharathan Publications, 1978), pp. 67–70.

20. *CWMG*, XV, pp. 128–66.

21. See D.W. Ferrell, 'The Rowlatt Satyagraha in Delhi', in Kumar, editor, *Essays in Gandhian Politics*.

22. Banerjee to Sir William Vincent, 3 April 1919, in Progs Nos 141–47, May 1919, in Home (Political-B), NAI.

23. *CWMG*, XV, pp. 183–86.

24. *Mufid-e-Rozgar*, 13 April 1919, in *Report on Newspapers in the Bombay Presidency, January to June 1919*, L/R/5/175, APAC/BL.

25. *New Times*, 8 April 1919, in ibid.

26. See Progs Nos 284–300, April 1919, Home (Political-B), NAI.

27. *CWMG*, XV, pp. 190–203.

28. Testimony to Hunter Commission by J.P. Thompson, Chief Secretary of the Punjab, in V.N. Datta, editor, *New Light on the Punjab Disturbances in 1919. Volume One* (Simla: Indian Institute of Advanced Study, 1975), pp. 36–37.

29. *Disorders Inquiry Committee, 1919–1920: Report* (Calcutta: Government of India, 1920), p. xxxiii.

30. *CWMG*, XV, pp. 207–08; Desai, *DTDG*, II, p. 25.

31. Progs Nos 514–15, May 1919, Home (Political-B), NAI.

32. K.L. Gillion, 'Gujarat in 1919', in Kumar, ed. *Essays in Gandhian Politics*, pp. 136–38.

33. Gandhi to PSV, 14 April 1919, *CWMG*, XV, pp. 218–20.

34. *CWMG*, XV, pp. 220–24.

35. *Disorders Inquiry Committee, 1919–1920: Report*, p. 19.

36. Gandhi to Tagore, 5 April 1919; Tagore to Gandhi, 12 April 1919, *CWMG*, XV, pp. 179–80, 495–96.

37. *CWMG*, XV, pp. 243–44, 265–66.

38. IAR, 1920, Volume I, Part I, pp. 42–44.

39. Nigel Collett, *The Butcher of Amritsar: General Reginald Dyer* (Delhi: Rupa and Co., 2005), especially Chapter 16; *Disorders Inquiry Committee, 1919–1920: Report*, pp. 29–40; anon., 'By a Voice from the Punjab', *YI*, 9 June 1919. Cf. also the retrospective justification of the repression in the Punjab by the province's

Lieutenant Governor at the time—Michael O'Dwyer, *India As I Knew It: 1885–1925* (London: Constable and Company, 1925), especially Chapter XVII.

40. Mss Eur F 137/13, APAC/BL.

41. Gandhi to J.L. Maffey, 16 May 1919, *CWMG*, XV, p. 311.

42. *CWMG*, XV, pp. 354–62, 445–49.

43. *DTDG*, 2, p. 40.

44. *CWMG*, XV, pp. 399–400; XV, pp. 28–29.

45. *CWMG*, XVI, pp. 3–4.

46. Gandhi to M.A. Jinnah, 28 June 1919, *CWMG*, XV, pp. 398–99.

47. Letter to Private Secretary to Governor of Bombay, 25 August 1919, *CWMG*, XVI, pp 60–62.

48. See Gail Minault, *The Khilafat Movement: Religious Symbolism and Political Mobilization in India* (first published in 1982; reprint New Delhi: Oxford University Press, 1999).

49. A copy of this petition was provided to me by the Gandhi scholar and collector E.S. Reddy.

50. Minault, *The Khilafat Movement*, pp. 32–34.

51. Abdul Bari to Gandhi, Lucknow, 27 April 1919, SN 6567, SAAA.

52. See *CWMG*, XVI, pp. 90–91.

53. *CWMG*, XVI, pp. 151–52.

54. 'Turkey', *Navajivan*, 7 September 1919, *CWMG*, XVI, pp. 104–05.

55. *CWMG*, XVI, pp. 226–27.

56. George Lloyd to Lord Halifax, 1 November 1919, in Mss Eur B 158, APAC/BL.

57. Preface to *CWMG*, XVI, p. ix, unsigned, but this assessment is most likely the work of C.N. Patel, the editor of the Gujarati section of the *Collected Works*.

58. *CWMG*, XVI, pp. 221–22.

59. *CWMG*, XVI, pp. 180–81.

60. Pravrajika Atmaprana, *Sister Nivedita of Ramakrishna-Vivekananda* (first published in 1961; reprint Calcutta: Ramakrishna Sarada Mission, 1992), p. 245.

61. Saraladevi's life and career (but not her relationship with Gandhi) are discussed in, among other works, Bharati Ray, *Early Feminists of Colonial India* (New Delhi: Oxford University Press, 2002); Chitra Deb, *Women of the Tagore Household,* translated by Smita Chowdhry and Sona Roy (New Delhi: Penguin India, 2010); Sunil Gangopadhyay, *First Light,* translated from the Bengali by Aruna Chakravarti (New Delhi: Penguin India, 2001).

62. *CWMG*, XVI, p. 316.
63. This account of Gandhi's visits to Lahore, Amritsar and other places in the Punjab is based on *CWMG*, XVI, pp. 283, 286–87, 296–97, etc.
64. *BC*, 30 October 1919.
65. Quoted in Richard Cashman, *The Myth of the Lokmanya: Tilak and Mass Politics in Maharashtra* (Berkeley: University of California Press, 1975) p. 205.
66. Minault, *The Khilafat Movement*, p. 82.
67. *CWMG*, XVI, pp. 363–67.
68. *GBI*, p. 43.

Chapter Five: The Personal and the Political

1. *CWMG*, XVI, pp. 512–13, 516.
2. Gandhi to Maganlal, c. 23 January 1920, *CWMG*, XVI, pp. 496–97.
3. *CWMG*, XVI, p. 517.
4. *CWMG*, XVII, pp. 29–33.
5. *CWMG*, XVII, p. 56f.
6. *CWMG*, XVII, pp. 53–54; *Source Material, Vol. III*, pp. 251–52.
7. *YI*, 11 February 1920.
8. 'The Message of the Punjab', *YI*, 24 March 1920.
9. Saraladevi Chaudhurani, 'What is an Ideal Gurukul', *YI*, 12 May 1920; idem, 'At the Point of the Spindle', *YI*, 2 February 1921.
10. *CWMG*, XVII, pp. 73–75.
11. *CWMG*, XVII, pp. 75, 105–07.
12. See Afzal Iqbal, editor, *Select Writings and Speeches of Maulana Mohamed Ali* (Lahore: Shaikh Muhammad Ashraf, 1944), pp. 165–73.
13. See Minault, *The Khilafat Movement*, pp. 86–90.
14. 'Pledges Broken', *YI*, 19 May 1920, *CWMG*, XVII, pp. 434–36.
15. For more details, see Ian Bryant Well, *Jinnah's Early Politics: Ambassador of Hindu–Muslim Unity* (Delhi: Permanent Black, 2005), Chapter 5.
16. C.F. Andrews to Gandhi, letters of 16 November 1919 and 8 September 1920, SN 6979 and SN 7245 respectively, SAAA (emphasis in the original).
17. Nanda, *Gandhi: Pan-Islamism, Imperialism and Nationalism in India*, pp. 211, 374.
18. 'Hindu–Muslim Unity', N, 29 February 1920, *CWMG*, XVII, pp. 58–60.
19. See *Report of the Commissioners Appointed by the Punjab Sub-Committee of the Indian National Congress* (Bombay: Karnatak Printing Press, 1920), pp. 156–60.

20. *Disorders Inquiry Committee, 1919–1920: Report*, pp. xl–xli.
21. 'How to Work Non-Co-operation', *YI*, 5 May 1920, *CWMG*, XVII, pp. 389–92.
22. *CWMG*, XVII, p. 71.
23. 'Uses of Khadi', N, 25 April 1920, *CWMG*, XVII, p. 329.
24. Bhatt, *Motabehn*, p. 40.
25. Gandhi to Saraladevi, 30 April 1920, *CWMG*, XVII, pp. 358–59.
26. Gandhi to Saraladevi, 1 May 1920, *CWMG*, XVII, pp. 365–66.
27. Gandhi to Saraladevi, 2 May 1920, *CWMG*, XVII, pp. 374–76.
28. Gandhi to Balwantrai Mehta, c. 2 September 1927, *CWMG*, XXXIV, pp. 439–40.
29. Gandhi to Kallenbach, 10 August 1920, *CWMG*, XVIII, pp. 129–31.
30. Rajagopalachari to Gandhi, 16 June 1920, in Gopalkrishna Gandhi, editor, *My Dear Bapu* (New Delhi: Penguin 2012), pp. 37–39.
31. Progs No. 19 for July 1920, Home (Political-B), NAI.
32. *CWMG*, XVII, pp. 502–04.
33. *CWMG*, XVIII, pp. 4–7, 55–57.
34. Reports in *BC*, 30 July 1920.
35. *BC*, 2 August 1920, quoted in Ravinder Kumar, *Essays in the Social History of Modern India* (Delhi: Oxford University Press, 1983), p. 248.
36. *BC*, 2 August 1920; *CWMG*, XVIII, pp. 107–09.
37. *CWMG*, XVIII, pp. 104–06.

Chapter Six: Capturing the Congress

1. 'Mr. Montagu's Threat', *YI*, 1 August 1920, *CWMG*, XVIII, pp. 100–02.
2. Chelmsford to Montagu, 4 August 1920, Mss Eur E 264/6, APAC/BL.
3. *CWMG*, XVIII, pp. 143ff.
4. Minault, *The Khilafat Movement*, pp. 123–24.
5. Gandhi to C.F. Andrews, 23 August 1920, *CWMG*, XVIII, p. 190.
6. 'Madras Tour', N, 29 August 1920, *CWMG*, XVIII, p. 210.
7. *DTDG*, II, p. 217.
8. *CWMG*, XVIII, pp. 191, 193–94.
9. On the ambivalence of Bengal and Bengali politicians towards Gandhi, c. 1920, see J.H. Broomfield, *Elite Conflict in a Plural Society: Twentieth-Century Bengal*, pp. 147–51. Cf. also Leonard A. Gordon, *Bengal: The Nationalist Movement, 1876–1940* (Delhi: Manohar, 1979), Chapter 6.

10. *ABP*, issues of 2, 3 and 4 September 1920.

11. See Gopalkrishna Gandhi, *A Frank Friendship*, p. 75.

12. *CWMG*, XVIII, pp. 230–31.

13. *CWMG*, XVIII, pp. 245–49, 260.

14. See J.H. Broomfield, 'The Non-Cooperation Decision of 1920: A Crisis in Bengal Politics', in Low, editor, *Soundings in South Asian History*.

15. See IAR, 1920, Vol. I, pp. 130–31.

16. Desai, *DTDG*, II, pp. 279–81; Mushirul Hasan, *A Nationalist Conscience: M.A. Ansari, the Congress and the Raj* (New Delhi: Manohar, 1987), p. 99.

17. IAR, 1920, pp. 131–35.

18. Mahadev Desai to Devadas Gandhi, 22 November 1920, SN 7351, SAAA.

19. Gandhi to Muhammad Iqbal, c. 27 November 1920, *CWMG*, XIX, p. 34.

20. Muhammad Iqbal to Gandhi, 29 November 1920, SN 7361, SAAA.

21. *CWMG*, XVIII, pp. 373–77.

22. Letter by H.A. Popley and G.E. Phillips, printed in *YI*, 1 December 1920.

23. *YI*, 12 January 1921.

24. Undated letter, c. November–December 1920, SN 7425, in SAAA.

25. S. O'Brien to Gandhi, Cannanore, Malabar, 1 January 1921, SN 7427, SAAA.

26. *CWMG*, XVII, p. 471.

27. *CWMG*, XIX, pp. 7–9, 73.

28. Quoted in V.B. Kulkarni, *M.R. Jayakar* (New Delhi: Publications Division, 1976), pp. 84–85.

29. 'The Caste System', *YI*, 8 December 1920, *CWMG*, XIX, pp. 83–85.

30. C.B. Dalal, *Gandhi: 1915–1948: A Detailed Chronology* (New Delhi: Gandhi Peace Foundation, 1971).

31. Cf. *History of Indian Railways* (Delhi: Government Press, 1964).

32. *DTDG*, III, p. 135.

33. See Sarvepalli Gopal, *Jawaharlal Nehru: A Biography: Volume One: 1889–1947* (Bombay: Oxford University Press, 1976), Chapter 4.

34. As stated in Chapter 5, the bulk of Sarala's letters to Gandhi was destroyed after his death by the latter's family. But we do not know—how or why—these letters of October 1920 survived the bonfire, and now rest in the archives of the Sabarmati Ashram in Ahmedabad.

35. Saraladevi to Gandhi, 10 October 1920, SN 9876, SAAA.

36. Saraladevi to Gandhi, 14 October 1920, SN 9877, SAAA.

37. Saraladevi to Gandhi, 16 October 1920, SN 9878, SAAA.
38. Saraladevi to Gandhi, 22 October 1920, SN 9889, SAAA.
39. *CWMG*, XIX, p. 93.
40. *DTDG*, III, p. 178.
41. Tagore to Andrews, 18 September 1920, in Rabindranath Tagore, *Letters from Abroad* (Madras: S. Ganesan, 1924), pp. 20–21.
42. *CWMG*, XIX, pp. 137–38.
43. Gandhi to Rajagopalachari, 24 August 1924, *CWMG*, XXV, p. 137.
44. Report in *BC*, 22 December 1920.
45. *CWMG*, XIX, pp. 147–54.
46. *CWMG*, XIX, p. 159.
47. See File 13 of 1920, AICC Papers, 1st Instalment, NMML.
48. *CWMG*, XIX, pp. 185–87.
49. IAR, 1921, Part II, p. 144.
50. B. Pattabhi Sitaramayya, *The History of the Indian National Congress (1885–1935)* (Madras: Congress Working Committee, 1936), pp. 348–49.
51. See S.S. Pirzada, editor, *The Collected Works of Quaid-e-Azam Mohammad Ali Jinnah*, Volume 1 (1906–1921) (Karachi: East and West Publishing Company, 1984), pp. 402–06.
52. Viceroy to Secretary of State, 5 January 1921, in Mss Eur E 264/6, APAC/BL.

Chapter Seven: The Rise and Fall of Non-cooperation

1. Gopal Krishna, 'The Development of the Indian National Congress as a Mass Organization, 1918–1923', *Journal of Asian Studies*, Volume 25, Number 3, May 1966.
2. Ibid., p. 425.
3. *CWMG*, XIX, pp. 288–90 (emphasis in the original).
4. Desai, *DTDG*, III, pp. 254–55.
5. *GBI*, pp. 143–44.
6. 'The National Flag', *YI*, 13 April 1921, *CWMG*, XIX, pp. 561–62. See also Arundhati Virmani, *A National Flag for India: Rituals, Nationalism and the Politics of Sentiment* (Delhi: Permanent Black, 2008).
7. Speech in Marehra, Etah district, 13 May 1921, in File 111 of 1921, Home (Political), NAI.
8. Speech in Jhansi, 20 November 1920, in ibid.
9. R.A. Graham of the Madras Government to S.P. Donnell of the Government of India, 18 April 1921, in File 241/1A of 1921, Home (Political), NAI.

10. Quoted in P.C. Bamford, *Histories of the Non-Co-operation and Khilafat Movements* (Delhi: Government of India Press, 1925), p. 54.

11. Speech in Broach, 1 June 1921, translated in File 11 of 1921, Home (Political), NAI.

12. See M. Naeem Qureshi, 'The "Ulama" of British India and the Hirat of 1920', *Modern Asian Studies*, Volume 3, Number 1, 1979.

13. See Minault, *The Khilafat Movement*, p. 131.

14. Quoted in *Trial of Gandhiji* (Ahmedabad: High Court of Gujarat, 1965), p. xiv.

15. Minault, *The Khilafat Movement*, pp. 142–45.

16. *CWMG*, XIX, pp. 277–78.

17. Gandhi to Lala Lajpat Rai, c. 30 June 1921, *CWMG*, XIX, p. 300.

18. *CWMG*, XIX, pp. 4659–771.

19. *CWMG*, XX, p. 286.

20. *Source Material, Volume III, Part I*, pp. 415–17.

21. See File No. 5, AICC Papers, First Instalment, NMML.

22. *CWMG*, XX, pp. 454–55, 472.

23. Bamford, *Histories of the Non-Co-operation and Khilafat Movements*, pp. 100–09.

24. Cf. Sumit Sarkar, *'Popular' Movements and 'Middle Class' Leadership in Late Colonial India* (Calcutta: K.P. Bagchi, 1983); Majid H. Siddiqi, *Agrarian Unrest in North India: The United Provinces, 1918–22* (New Delhi: Vikas, 1978); Ramachandra Guha, *The Unquiet Woods: Ecological Change and Peasant Resistance in the Himalaya* (Delhi: Oxford University Press, 1989).

25. 'Ethics of Destruction', *YI*, 1 September 1921, *CWMG*, XXI, pp. 41–44.

26. *Young India*, 27 April 1921, *CWMG*, XX, pp. 42–43.

27. *Letters from Abroad*, pp. 123–24.

28. 'English Learning', *YI*, 1 July 1921, *CWMG*, XX, pp. 158–59.

29. These remarks by Tagore are quoted in L.K. Elmhirst, *Poet and Plowman* (Calcutta: Visva-Bharati, 1975), pp. 20–22.

30. Tagore, 'The Call of Truth', *Modern Review*, October 1921, reprinted in R.K. Prabhu and Ravindra Kelekar, editors, *Truth Called Them Differently: Tagore–Gandhi Controversy* (Ahmedabad: Navajivan Press, 1961), p. 72f.

31. Gandhi, 'The Great Sentinel', *YI*, 13 October 1921, *CWMG*. The reader interested in a fuller account of the Tagore–Gandhi debate should read Sabyasachi Bhattacharya, editor, *The Mahatma and the Poet: Letters and Debates between Gandhi and Tagore* (New Delhi: National Book Trust, 1997).

32. 'The Inner Meaning of Mahatma Gandhi's Non-co-operation', *YI*, 22 September 1920.
33. Dwijendranath Tagore to Gandhi, 1 September 1921, marked 'Most Private and Confidential', SN 7607, SAAA.
34. P.C. Ray to Gandhi, 5 October 1921, SN 7634, SAAA.
35. See File No. 188/IV of 1922, Home (Political), NAI.
36. Shaukat Ali to Gandhi, 11 September 1921, SN 7611, SAAA.
37. See D.A. Low, 'The Government of India and the first non-co-operation movement, 1920-2', in Kumar, ed., *Essays in Gandhian Politics*, pp. 305-07.
38. 'My Loin-Cloth', published in N, 2 October 1921, and in English in *The Hindu*, 15 October 1921, CWMG, XVIII, pp. 225-26.
39. Conrad Wood, *The Moplah Rebellion and Its Genesis* (New Delhi: People's Publishing House, 1987), Chapter 5.
40. Quoted in Wood, *The Moplah Rebellion*, p. 225.
41. *CWMG*, XXI, pp. 116-18, 120-21.
42. *CWMG*, XXI, pp. 232-33.
43. Gandhi to Mahadev Desai, 31 October 1921, *CWMG*, XX, p. 375.
44. *CWMG*, XX, p. 350f.
45. *CWMG*, XXI, pp. 462-64, 481.
46. 'The Moral Issue', *YI*, 24 November 1921; 'Rights of Minorities', *YI*, 1 December 1921, *CWMG*, XXI, pp. 484, 501-02.
47. Abul Kalam Azad to Gandhi, Calcutta, 6 December 1921, SN 7692, SAAA.
48. 'One Year's Time Limit', N, 11 December 1921, *CWMG*, XXI, pp. 557-58.
49. *CWMG*, XXII, p. 15.
50. See clipping from the *Pioneer*, 15 March 1922, in File 489 of 1922, Home (Political), NAI.
51. *CWMG*, XXII, pp. 94-101, 166-68.
52. *CWMG*, XXII, pp. 191-92.
53. Governor of Bombay to Viceroy, 4 January 1922; Note by S.P. O'Donnell, 6 January 1922, both in File 489 of 1922, Home (Political), NAI.
54. *CWMG*, XXII, p. 271.
55. *CWMG*, XXII, pp. 287-98.
56. Gandhi to Viceroy, dated Bardoli, 1 February 1922, *CWMG*, XXII, pp. 302-05.
57. *CWMG*, XXII, pp. 512-14.
58. *CWMG*, XXII, pp. 344-50.

59. See Shahid Amin, *Event, Metaphor, Memory: Chauri Chaura, 1922–1992* (New Delhi: Oxford University Press, 1995), pp. 14–17.
60. *CWMG*, XXII, pp. 350–51.
61. *CWMG*, XXII, p. 377.
62. *CWMG*, XXII, pp. 377–80.
63. Gandhi to Devadas Gandhi, 12 February 1922, *CWMG*, XXII, p. 397.
64. See Gandhi to Jawaharlal Nehru, 19 February 1922, *CWMG*, XXII, p. 435.
65. See 'The Crime of Chauri Chaura', *YI*, 16 February; 'Shaking the Manes', *YI*, 23 February 1923, *CWMG*, XXII, pp. 415–17, 457–58, etc.
66. These paragraphs on the Government of India's prolonged discussion on whether to arrest Gandhi are based on the correspondence in File No. 489 of 1922, Home (Political), NAI.
67. *CWMG*, XXIII, pp. 84–85.
68. *Source Material, Volume III, Part I*, pp. 465–66.
69. This account is based on a pamphlet called *The Historic Trial of Mahatma Gandhi*, printed at the International Printing Works, Karachi, and reproduced in *Source Material, Volume III, Part I*, pp. 657–66.
70. Francis Watson, *The Trial of Mr. Gandhi* (London: Macmillan, 1969), pp. 61–62.

Chapter Eight: The Mahatma from Above and Below

1. Bamford, *Histories of the Non-Co-operation and Khilafat Movements*, p. xiii.
2. E.M. Craik, Finance Secretary, Government of Bombay, to H.D. Craik, Home Secretary, Government of India, 16 July 1921, in File No. 170 of 1921, Home (Political), NAI.
3. C.F. Andrews, 'Mahatma Gandhi at Amritsar', TT, 7 November 1919.
4. See Proceedings Nos 174–82 for September 1919, Home Department (Political-B), NAI.
5. See *GBI*, pp. 348–49.
6. Anon., *27 January 1915: A Historical Occasion celebrated 53 years ago: Title Mahatma and Address Offered to Mahatma Gandhi at Gondal* (Gondal: The Rasashala Aushadhashram, 1968).
7. *CWMG*, XIX, p. 216.
8. These lines are based on *Source Material, Vol. III, Part I*, pp. 201–04, 561–67. 'Kavi' is Gujarati (and Hindi) for poet.

9. Raihana Tyabji to Gandhi, 17 March 1922, SN 7996, SAAA.

10. Desai, *DTDG*, III, pp. 262–65

11. See Shahid Amin, 'Gandhi as Mahatma: Gorakhpur District, Eastern UP, 1921–2', in Ranajit Guha and Gayatri Chakravorty Spivak, editors, *Selected Subaltern Studies* (New York: Oxford University Press, 1988).

12. Untitled note, c. February 1921, on agrarian disturbances in Oudh, in Mss Eur 264/5, APAC/BL.

13. See Proceedings Nos 195–216A for February 1921, Home Department (Political-B), NAI.

14. See File No. 525 of 1922, Home (Political), NAI.

15. Bamford, *Histories of the Non-Co-operation and Khilafat Movements*, pp. 60–61.

16. N.E. Marjoribanks, Chief Secretary, Madras Government to S.P. Donnell, Home Secretary, Government of India, 2 September 1921, in File No. 241/1A of 1921, Home (Political), NAI.

17. See K.P.S. Menon, *C. Sankaran Nair* (New Delhi: Publications Division, 1967).

18. C. Sankaran Nair, *Gandhi and Anarchy* (Madras: Tagore and Co., 1922), pp. xii, xiv, 10, 17, 45, 47, 51, 58, 109–110, 121, etc.

19. M. Ruthnaswamy, *The Political Philosophy of Mr. Gandhi* (Madras: Tagore and Co., 1922), pp. 1–4, 46–47, 82–90, 50–51, 80, 75–76, 93, 95.

20. S.A. Dange, *Gandhi vs Lenin* (Bombay: Liberty Literature Co., 1921), especially Chapter III. Cf. also Muzaffar Ahmad, *Myself and the Communist Party of India, 1920–1929* (Calcutta: National Book Agency, 1970), pp. 108–12.

21. M.N. Roy, 'Non-Violence and Revolution', *Advance Guard*, Volume 1, No. 5, December 1922, clipping in File No. 128 of 1922, Home (Political), NAI.

Interestingly, Roy's assessment of Gandhi and his movement was not shared by Lenin himself. The Bolshevik leader, basing himself on Marx's five-stage theory of history, thought that Gandhi was leading a bourgeois-nationalist revolution that would destroy the feudal remnants in Indian society. Thus it must be supported, for it would in time lead to the next and highest stage of human evolution, namely, socialism. Roy vigorously disagreed, arguing that Gandhism was a reactionary movement which communists should reject rather than support. See, for more details, Sibnarayan Ray, *In Freedom's Quest: Life of M.N. Roy, Volume I* (Calcutta: Minerva Associates, 1998).

22. Kantilal Amratlal to Gandhi, 31 December 1920, SN 7434, SAAA.

23. Note by W.S. Marris, 2 June 1919, in Proceedings No. 705 for June 1919, Home Department (Political-B), NAI.

24. J.H. Du Boulay, Home Secretary, Government of India, note dated 23 April 1919, in Proceedings Nos 763 to 685, Part B, May 1919, in Home (Political), NAI.

25. Letter by W.S. Irwin in the *Pioneer*, 21 June 1917.

26. *Gandhi and the Anglican Bishops* (Madras: Ganesh and Co., 1922), pp. 45, 49–51, 53, 55–56.

27. See W.B. Heycock, District Magistrate, Champaran, to L.F. Morshead, Commissioner, Tirhut Division, 5 June 1917, in *Select Documents*, pp. 201–03.

28. Note by H.D. Craik, Home Secretary, Government of India, dated 25 June 1921, in File 49 of 1921, Home (Political), NAI.

29. Gilbert Murray, 'The Soul as It Is, and How to Deal with It', the *Hibbert Journal*, Volume 16, Number 2, January 1918.

30. Valentine Chirol, *Indian Unrest* (London: Macmillan and Co., 1910), pp. 41ff.

31. Valentine Chirol, *India Old and New* (London: Macmillan and Co., 1921), pp. 165, 175, etc.

32. Anthony Clyne, 'M.K. Gandhi', *Review of Reviews* (London), April 1922.

33. Sir Michael F. O'Dwyer, 'Gandhi and the Prince's Visit to India', *Fortnightly Review*, February 1922.

34. The article in the *Glasgow Herald* was reprinted in *YI*, 4 August 1921.

35. The *Tribune* report is reproduced in the *Rangoon Mail*, undated clipping in SN 7506, SAAA.

36. Clare Price, 'Gandhi and British India', the *New York Times*, 10 July 1921.

37. See John Haynes Holmes, *My Gandhi* (New York: Harper and Brothers, 1953), pp. 21, 29–31.

    Some Englishmen in India were appalled by the comparison of Gandhi to Jesus, and wrote in protest to Reverend Holmes, who, just as spiritedly, defended and expanded upon the comparison. This correspondence is reproduced in 'The Gandhi–Jesus Parallel', *Searchlight*, 26 November 1922, clipping in SN 8653, SAAA.

38. 'Gandhi as World Savior', report in *New York Times*, 13 March 1922.

39. Sudarshan Kapur, *Raising Up a Prophet: The African-American Encounter with Gandhi* (Delhi: Oxford University Press, 1993), Chapter 2 and passim.

40. Myrtle and Gordon Law, 'Gandhi in Jail', *Outlook*, 19 April 1922.

41. 'E.M.S.', 'Gandhi at First Hand', *Atlantic Monthly*, May 1922.
42. 'Her Impressions of Gandhi', *New York Times*, 23 April 1922.
43. See Harnam Singh, *The Indian National Movement and American Opinion* (New Delhi: Rama Krishna and Sons, 1962), pp. 188–89.
44. See *GBI*, pp. 120–21.
45. 'The New Light of Asia', the *Nation*, 14 September 1921.

   For an overview of Gandhi's reception in the West in the 1920s, see Sean Scalmer, *Gandhi in the West: The Mahatma and the Rise of Radical Protest* (Cambridge: Cambridge University Press, 2011), Chapter 1.
46. J. Augustin Leger, 'Mahatma Gandhi', *Revue de Paris*, Volume 29, Number 2, 1 April 1922.
47. See Keith Kyle, 'Gandhi, Harry Thuku and Early Kenyan Nationalism', *Transition*, Number 27, 1966; Ngugi Wa Thiong'o, *Dreams in a Time of War: A Childhood Memoir* (London: Harvill Secker, 2010), pp. 188–91.
48. Cf. S. Natarajan, *A History of the Press in India* (Bombay: Asia Publishing House, 1962); Milton Israel, *Communications and Power: Propaganda and Press in the Indian Nationalist Struggle, 1920–1947* (Cambridge: Cambridge University Press, 1994); N.S. Jagannathan, *Independence and the Indian Press* (New Delhi: Konark Publishers, 1999).

Chapter Nine: Prisoner Number 827

1. See *Source Material, Volume III, Part II*, p. 5.
2. C. Rajagopalachari, 'My Great Disappointment', *YI*, 6 April 1922.
3. *CWMG*, XXIII, pp. 122–28.
4. *CWMG*, XXIII, pp. 553–54, 129–36.
5. See *Source Material, Volume III, Part II*, pp. 2–3.
6. Ibid., pp. 27–29.
7. *CWMG*, XXIII, pp. 143–53.
8. 'My Jail Experiences–XI', *CWMG*, XXV, pp. 125–27.
9. 'My Jail Experiences–IX', in *CWMG*, XXIV, pp. 289–92.
10. See SN 8078, SAAA.
11. *Source Material, Volume III, Part II*, p. 191.
12. *CWMG*, XXIII, Appendix VI.
13. Jane Addams to J.H. Holmes, Delhi, 10 February 1923, copy in E.S. Reddy Papers, NMML.
14. See *CWMG*, XXIII, Appendix IV.
15. YI, 18 May 1922.

16. YI, 1 June 1922.
17. YI, 22 June 1922.
18. YI, 20 July 1922.
19. YI, 28 September 1922.
20. IAR, 1923, Volume I, pp. 812, 835, 872ff.
21. IAR, 1923, Volume II, pp. 143–44, 161–66.
22. See the correspondence in File 10 of 1922, AICC Papers, First Instalment, 1922, NMML.
23. Jordens, *Swami Shraddhananda*, p. 143.
24. Viceroy to Secretary of State for India, 18 December 1922, File No. 14 of 1922 Home (Political), NAI.
25. *CWMG*, XXIII, pp. 178–88.
26. YI, 26 July 1923.
27. *CWMG*, XXIII, pp. 161–62.
28. These paragraphs are based on documents printed in *Source Material, Volume III, Part II*, pp. 33–34, 73–74, 105–08, 137, 141, 193, 827.
29. Ibid., p. 186.
30. This section is based on material in File 606 of 1922, Home (Special), MSA.
31. *Select Writings and Speeches of Maulana Mohamed Ali*, pp. 248, 276.
32. Colonel Maddox to Home Secretary, Bombay Government, 19 January 1924, in File 355(35) M of 1924, Home (Special), MSA.
33. *BC*, 14 January 1924. The European nurse tried hard to convince Gandhi to temporarily abjure his vow and take cow's milk to regain his strength. He refused. See SN 8189, SAAA.
34. Colonel Maddox to a 'Sir Maurice', 18 January 1924, in File 355(35) M of 1924, Home (Special), MSA.
35. *BC*, 20 January 1924.
36. File note dated 15 January by Home Secretary, Bombay Government, in File 355(35) M of 1924, Home (Special), MSA.
37. *Source Material, Volume III, Part II*, pp. 216–18.
38. See Home Secretary, Bombay Government, to Home Secretary, Government of India, 1 February 1924, in File 355(35) M of 1924, Home (Special), MSA.
39. Colonel Maddox to Home Secretary, Bombay Government, 30 January 1924, in ibid.
40. See *DTDG*, IV, pp. 17–21, 48–49.
41. Devadas Gandhi to 'Dear Friend' (whom I have been unable to identify), from Sassoon Hospital, Poona, 6 February 1924, SN 8286, SAAA.

42. Gandhi to Mohammad Ali, from Sassoon Hospital, Poona, 7 February 1924, *CWMG*, XXIII, pp. 199–202.
43. Gandhi to Mohammad Ali, 5 March 1924, *CWMG*, XXIII, p. 221.

Chapter Ten: Picking Up the Pieces

1. 'Appeal to the Public', 24 March 1924, *CWMG*, XXIII, pp. 305–06.
2. Ruttie Jinnah to Gandhi, 31 March 1924, SN 8630, SAAA. We do not know whether Ruttie had shown her (handwritten) letter to her husband before sending it to Gandhi.
3. Letter dated 2 April 1924, SN 8645, SAAA.
4. Polak to Gandhi, 24 March 1924, SN 8566, SAAA.
5. *CWMG*, XXIII, pp. 238–40.
6. See Robin Jeffrey, 'The Social Origins of a Caste Association, 1875–1905: The Founding of the S.N.D.P. Yogam', *South Asia*, Volume 14, Number 1, 1975.
7. *CWMG*, XXI, pp. 185–88.
8. On the background and origins of the Vaikom Satyagraha, see T.K. Ravindran, *Eight Furlongs of Freedom* (New Delhi: Light and Life Publishers, 1980), Chapter 2; George Gheverghese Joseph, *George Joseph: The Life and Times of a Kerala Christian Nationalist* (Hyderabad: Orient Longman, 2003), Chapter 9.
9. K.P. Kesava Menon, Secretary, Kottayam District Congress Committee, to Gandhi, 12 March 1924; Gandhi to K.P. Kesava Menon, Secretary, Kottayam District Congress Committee, 19 March 1924, *CWMG*, XXIII, pp. 560–61, 272–73. Cf. also George Joseph to Devadas Gandhi, 31 March 1924, SN 10264, SAAA.
10. Mary Elizabeth King, *Gandhian Nonviolent Struggle and Untouchability in India: The 1924–25 Vykom Satyagraha and the Mechanisms of Change* (New Delhi: Oxford University Press, 2015), pp. 131–32.
11. These paragraphs are based on Ravindran, *Eight Furlongs of Freedom*, pp. 57ff.
12. See *CWMG*, XXIII, pp. 419–20.
13. Gandhi to George Joseph, 6 April 1924; 'Vaikom Satyagraha', 1 May 1924, *CWMG*, XXIII, pp. 391, 515–16. On the same principle, Gandhi also asked a group of Sikhs to close a free kitchen they had started in Vaikom. The 'Hindu reformers of Malabar', he pointed out, 'will estrange the entire Hindu sympathy if they accept or encourage non-Hindu interference or assistance beyond sympathy'. See 'Vaikom Satyagraha', *YI*, 8 May 1924, *CWMG*, XXXIV, p. 7.

14. 'Vykom Satyagraha', *YI*, 24 April 1924, *CWMG*, XXIII, pp. 476–77.
15. 'Interview to Vaikom Delegation', *CWMG*, XXIV, pp. 90–94.
16. See *GBI*, p. 473f.
17. *CWMG*, XXIII, pp. 413–14.
18. *CWMG*, XXIV, pp. 109–11, 585–88.
19. IAR, 1924, Volume II, pp. 25f.
20. M. Asaf Ali to Gandhi, 28 April 1924, SN 10378, SAAA.
21. YI, 29 May 1924, *CWMG*, XXIV, pp. 136–54.
22. See undated clipping, c. May–June 1924, SN 8948, SAAA.
23. *CWMG*, XXIV, pp. 371–73, 403–05, 434–38.
24. *CWMG*, XXIV, p. 518.
25. *CWMG*, XXIV, pp. 267–68, 307.
26. Motilal Nehru to Gandhi, 28 July 1924, *CWMG*, XXIV, pp. 595–96.
27. 'Who Shall Be President', *YI*, 17 July 1924, *CWMG*, XXIV, pp. 398–99.
28. *CWMG*, XXV, pp. 171, 174–76.
29. Reports in *BC*, 18 and 19 September 1924.
30. *CWMG*, XXV, pp. 181–83.
31. *CWMG*, XXV, pp. 199–202.
32. *Aaj*, 23 September 1924.
33. *BC*, 27 September 1924.
34. Rajagopalachari to Devadas Gandhi, 26 September 1924, Devadas Gandhi Papers, NMML.
35. See M. Mohd Shoaib to Gandhi, 21 September 1924, SN 10190, SAAA.
36. *BC* and *Aaj*, issues of 1 and 2 October 1924.
37. C.F. Andrews, 'How the Fast was Broken', *YI*, 16 October 1924.
38. *Aaj*, 13 October 1924.
39. *BC*, 29 October 1924.
40. *CWMG*, XXV, pp. 425–26.
41. *CWMG*, XXV, pp. 464–70.
42. Eugene F. Irschick, *Politics and Social Conflict in South India: The Non-Brahmin Movement and Tamil Separatism, 1916–1929* (Berkeley: University of California Press, 1969), pp. 268–69. Ramasamy was later to break with the Congress—whose approach to attacking caste he found too timid—and found the Dravida Kazhagam, the forerunner of the Dravida Munnetra Kazhagam (DMK). A sharp critic of idol-worship and of patriarchy, he remains a figure much admired by intellectuals and activists in South India.
43. 'Vykom Satyagraha', *YI*, 19 February 1925, *CWMG*, XXVI, pp. 158–59.

44. *CWMG*, XXVI, pp. 269–71.
45. Mahadev Desai, *The Epic of Travancore* (Ahmedabad: Navajivan Karyalaya, 1937), pp. 17–21. Mahadev Desai was appalled at the combination of insolence and ignorance that the Namboodiris showed; their 'haughty air', he remarked, would 'put to shame those of the Nagars [Gujarati Brahmins] in their heyday'. *DTDG*, p. 56.
46. *CWMG*, XXVI, pp. 293f.
47. M.K. Sanoo, *Narayana Guru: A Biography*, translated from the Malayalam by Madhavan Ayyappath (first published in 1978: reprint Bombay: Bharatiya Vidya Bhavan, 1998), pp. 189–90.
48. Quoted in Ravindran, *Eight Furlongs of Freedom*, p. 13.
49. *CWMG*, XXVI, pp. 303–04.
50. See M.S.A. Rao, *Social Movements and Social Transformation: A Study of Two Backward Classes Movements in India* (first published in 1979: reprint New Delhi: Manohar, 1987), p. 66.
51. The two statements appear side by side in IAR, 1925, Volume I, pp. 97–106.
52. Letter of March 1925, quoted in John Grigg, 'Myths about the Approach to Indian Independence', in Wm. Roger Louis, editor, *More Adventures with Britannia: Personalities, Politics and Culture in India* (Austin: University of Texas Press, 1998), p. 211.
53. E.A. Ross, 'The United States of India', typescript of article published in *Comrade*, 22 January 1926, copy in L/PJ/12/229, IOR, APAC/BL.
54. Clarence Marsh Case, 'Gandhi and the Indian National Mind: A Fragment and a Suggestion', in *Journal of Applied Sociology* (Los Angeles), July 1923, pp. 293–301.
55. Harry F. Ward, 'Lenin and Gandhi', in *The World Tomorrow*, April 1925.
56. See *Romain Rolland and Gandhi Correspondence* (New Delhi: Publications Division, 1976), pp. 3–10.
57. Romain Rolland, *Mahatma Gandhi: The Man Who Became One with the Universal Being* (New York and London: The Century Co., 1924), pp. 3–5.
58. Ibid., p. 227.
59. Ibid., pp. 241–42, 247–48.
60. Holmes to Romain Rolland, 15 January 1924, Box 3, John Haynes Holmes Papers, Library of Congress, Washington D.C.
61. A useful introduction to Mariátegui's life and work is contained in the chapter on him in Enrique Kreuze, *Redeemers: Ideas and Power in Latin America* (New York: HarperCollins, 2011).

62. See 'Gandhi', in José Carlos Mariátegui, *La Escena Contemporánea* (first published in Lima in 1925), available at https://www.marxists. org/espanol/mariateg/1925/escena/06.htm.

63. *CWMG*, XXVII, pp. 229, 251–52, 354–55.

64. Ibid.

65. *CWMG*, XXVII, pp. 248–49.

66. *CWMG*, XXVIII, pp. 275–76.

67. Annie Besant to David Graham Pole, 11 June 1925, Mss Eur F 264/6, APAC/BL.

68. Rajagopalachari to Devadas Gandhi, 19 July 1925, Devadas Gandhi Papers, NMML.

69. *CWMG*, XXVII, pp. 73, 259–60.

70. Madeleine Slade to Gandhi, 29 May 1925, SN 10541, SAAA; Madeleine Slade, *The Spirit's Pilgrimage* (London: Longmans, Green and Co., 1960), Chapters XV to XVII.

71. *CWMG*, XXIX, pp. 280–82.

72. IAR, 1925, Volume II, p. 320.

73. Aldous Huxley, *Jesting Pilate: The Diary of a Journey* (first published in 1926: reprint London: Chatto and Windus, 1948), pp. 98–100.

74. Mirabehn to Devadas Gandhi, 28 December 1925, Devadas Gandhi Papers, NMML.

Chapter Eleven: Spinning in Sabarmati

1. 'Indulgence or Self-Denial', *YI*, 7 January 1926, *CWMG*, XXIX, pp. 380–82.

2. 'How Should Spinning Be Done', N, 11 July 1926, *CWMG*, XXXI, pp. 119–21.

3. Cf. Lisa Trivedi, *Clothing Gandhi's Nation: Homespun and Modern India* (Bloomington: Indiana University Press, 2007), Chapter 2 and passim.

4. On the assistance given to Miss Mayo by British officials in India, see Manoranjan Jha, *Katherine Mayo and India* (New Delhi: People's Publishing House, 1971), p. 29f.

5. *CWMG*, XXX, pp. 119–24.

6. Charles I. Reid to Gandhi, 28 April 1926, SN 12470, SAAA.

7. Letter dated 21 April 1926, *CWMG*, XXX, p. 337.

8. Gandhi to Manilal Gandhi, 3 April 1926, *CWMG*, XXX, p. 229; Mesthrie, *Gandhi's Prisoner?*, pp. 175–77.

9. *CWMG*, XXXII, pp. 564–67.

10. Gandhi to G.D. Birla, 4 December 1926, *CWMG*, XXXIII, p. 387.
11. 'The Ten Greatest Living Indians', *Indian National Herald*, 21 December 1926.
12. *CWMG*, XXXII, pp. 445, 450.
13. Jordens, *Swami Shraddhananda*, pp. 166–67.
14. *CWMG*, XXXII, pp. 451–54.
15. 'Letter to Ashram Women', 27 December 1926, *CWMG*, XXXII, p. 464.
16. 'Speech at Bettiah', 23 January 1927, *CWMG*, XXXIII, p. 3
17. 'Tear Down the Purdah', *YI*, 3 February 1927, *CWMG*, XXXIII, pp. 44–45.
18. Gandhi to Manilal, 8 February 1927; Gandhi to Sushilabehn Mashruwala, 13 February 1927, *CWMG*, XXXIII, pp. 55–56, 73–75.
19. 'Silence Day note to Manilal Gandhi', 7 March 1927, *CWMG*, XXXIII, p. 148.
20. 'A Revolutionary's Defence', *YI*, 12 February 1925, *CWMG*, XXVI, pp. 136–41.
21. See Sehri Saklatvala, *The Fifth Commandment: A Biography of Shapurji Saklatvala* (Calcutta: National Book Agency, 1996).
22. See IAR, 1927, Volume I, pp. 63–68; Sehri Saklatvala, *The Fifth Commandment*, pp. 292–93.
23. *CWMG*, XXXIII, pp. 163–66. Interestingly, while criticizing Gandhi in public, in private Saklatvala appealed to him to use his influence with the Tatas to release the pension due to the communist from his days working with the firm. See Shapurji Saklatvala to Anasuya Sarabhai, 16 April 1927, SN 124941, SAAA.
24. *CWMG*, XXXIII, pp. 209–10, 489.
25. See Rajagopalachari's letter to Mahadev Desai, 17 April 1927, copy in Devadas Gandhi Papers, NMML.
26. The most informative biography of Ambedkar remains Dhananjay Keer, *Dr. Ambedkar: Life and Mission* (first published in 1954; third edition, Bombay: Popular Prakashan, 1971).
27. *CWMG*, XXXIII, pp. 267–68.
28. These letters are quoted in P.D. Tandon, *The Unforgettable Nehru* (New Delhi: National Book Trust, 2003), pp. 67–68.
29. Gandhi to Motilal Nehru, 14 May 1927, *CWMG*, XXXIII, pp. 320–21.
30. Gandhi to Jawaharlal Nehru, 25 May 1927, *CWMG*, XXXIII, pp. 364–65.
31. Jawaharlal Nehru to Gandhi, 22 April 1927, SN 12572, SAAA.
32. Gandhi to Motilal Nehru, 19 June 1927, *CWMG*, XXXIV, pp. 30–31.
33. Gandhi to M.A. Ansari, 10 August 1927, *CWMG*, XXXIV, pp. 304–05.

34. Katherine Mayo, *Mother India* (first published in 1927: thirty-third printing, New York: Blue Ribbon Books, 1931), p. 11.

35. Ibid., p. 5f.

36. Ibid., p. 16.

37. Ibid., p. 22.

38. Ibid. pp. 300, 378.

39. Mrinalini Sinha, 'Editor's Introduction', in *Selections from Mother India* (New Delhi: Kali for Women, 1998), p. 37.

40. Lajpat Rai's book first appeared as a series of articles in the *Bombay Chronicle* in October 1927. See File 715 of 1927, Home (Special), MSA.

41. *BC*, 24 October 1927.

42. Letter written to the *Manchester Guardian* by Rabindranath Tagore, reproduced in *ToI*, 7 October 1927.

43. Sinha, 'Editor's Introduction', in *Selections from Mother India*, p. 2. These rejoinders included a twelve-part series called 'The Facts about India: A Reply to Miss Mayo', by Gandhi's and Tagore's friend C.F. Andrews, published in *Young India* between May and August 1928.

44. 'Drain Inspector's Report', *YI*, 15 September 1927, *CWMG*, XXXIV, 529–37 (emphases added).

45. *CWMG*, XXXV, pp. 98–99, 112.

46. Gandhi to Prabhashankar Pattani, 8 November 1927; Gandhi to C.F. Andrews, 11 November 1927, *CWMG*, XXXV, pp. 223, 227–28.

47. Quoted in the Earl of Birkenhead, *Halifax: The Life of Lord Halifax* (London: Hamish Hamilton, 1965), pp. 246–47.

48. Handy S. Perinpanayagam to Gandhi, 28 July 1927, in Gopalkrishna Gandhi, editor, *Gandhi and Sri Lanka, 1905–1947* (Ratmalana, Sri Lanka: Vishva Lekha Publishers, 2002), pp. 25–26.

49. Mahadev Desai, *With Gandhiji in Ceylon* (Madras: S. Ganesan, 1928), pp. 3–4, 31–32.

50. Report in the *Ceylon Independent*, 28 November 1927, in Gopalkrishna Gandhi, *Gandhi and Sri Lanka*, p. 242.

51. Ibid., p. 265.

52. *CWMG*, XXXV, pp. 324–27.

53. Desai, *With Gandhiji in Ceylon*, pp. 3–4, pp. 155–59.

54. *CWMG*, XXXV, pp. 265–66.

55. Gandhi to Surendra, 28 November 1927, *CWMG*, XXXV, pp. 339–40.

56. As recalled by Devadas and Lakshmi's eldest son, Rajmohan Gandhi, in a talk in Bangalore in 2007.

57. See IAR, 1927, Volume I, pp. 90–93.
58. Shaukat Ali to Gandhi, letters of 4 March and 11 July 1927, SNs 12566 and 12604, SAAA.
59. IAR, 1927, Volume II, pp. 39ff.
60. File G-64, AICC Papers, First Instalment, NMML.
61. 'Hindu–Muslim Unity', YI, 1 December 1927, CWMG, XXXV, pp. 352–54.
62. CWMG, XXXV, pp. 420–21, 538–39.
63. See IAR, 1927, Volume 2, pp. 98–99, 384–86.
64. See Jawaharlal Nehru, *Soviet Russia: Some Random Sketches and Impressions* (Allahabad: Allahabad Law Journal Press, 1928).
65. Gandhi to Jawaharlal Nehru, 4 January 1928, CWMG, XXXV, pp. 432–33.
66. Nehru to Gandhi, 11 January 1928, CWMG, XXXV, pp. 540–44.
67. Gandhi to Nehru, 17 January 1928, CWMG, XXXV, pp. 467–68.

Chapter Twelve: The Moralist

1. See GBI, pp. 55–56, 86–87, 140–42, etc.
2. CWMG, XXXII, p. 96.
3. Ibid., pp. 115–16, 123, 146.
4. Ibid., pp. 224, 366,
5. Ibid., pp. 132–34.
6. Ibid., pp. 153–55, 164.
7. Ibid., p. 141.
8. Ibid., p. 366.
9. Mahadev Desai, *The Gospel of Selfless Action, or the Gita According to Gandhi* (Ahmedabad: Navajivan Press, 1946), pp. 18, 4.
10. 'Crime of Reading Bible', YI, 2 September 1926, CWMG, XXXI, pp. 350–51.
11. CWMG, XXXV, pp. 461–62.
12. As described by Mahadev Desai, writing in YI, 19 January 1928.
13. See Ramachandra Guha, *Savaging the Civilized: Verrier Elwin, His Tribals, and India* (Chicago: University of Chicago Press, 1999), pp. 37–38.
14. CWMG, XXXVI, pp. 136–37.
15. See CWMG, Volume XXXII, pp. 512–16, 586–88.
16. See CWMG, XXXI, pp. 486–87, 506–07, 541; XXXII, pp. 15–17.
17. 'When Killing May Be Ahimsa', YI, 4 October 1928, CWMG, XXXVII, pp. 310–12.

18. 'The Tangle of Ahimsa', *YI*, 11 October 1928; 'A Conundrum', *YI*, 18 October 1928, *CWMG*, XXXVII, pp. 338–39, 360–61 (emphasis added).
19. Gandhi to C. Rajagopalachari, 21 October 1928, *CWMG*, XXXVII, p. 386.
20. 'Speech to Students of Satyagraha Ashram, Ahmedabad', c. July 1920, *CWMG*, XVII, pp. 535–39.
21. *CWMG*, XXIX, pp. 270, 289–91.
22. See *CWMG*, XXXIV, pp. 371–74.

Chapter Thirteen: The Memoirist

1. I am grateful to Gopalkrishna Gandhi for this point.
2. On the writing and reception of *Hind Swaraj*, see *GBI*, Chapter XVI.
3. *CWMG*, XXXI, p. 491.
4. The fifty or more languages the autobiography has appeared in range from Swedish to Swahili, and from Tibetan to Turkish. Gopalkrishna Gandhi, 'Gandhi's Autobiography: The Story of Translators' Experiments with the Text', a talk at the School of Cultural Texts and Records, Jadavpur University, October 2008.
5. *Satyagraha in South Africa* (first published in 1928: reprint Ahmedabad: Navajivan Publishing House, 1972), p. 5.
6. *Satyagraha in South Africa*, p. 33.
7. Ibid., p. 94.
8. Ibid., p. 123.
9. Ibid., p. 132.
10. Ibid., p. 258.
11. Ibid., p. 168.
12. Ibid., p. 307.
13. I am here adapting terms first used by Clifford Geertz in his *Works and Lives: The Anthropologist as Author* (Stanford: Stanford University Press, 1988). Geertz distinguishes between three types of narratives: 'author-evacuated', 'author-saturated' and 'author-supersaturated'. I have added a fourth category, 'author-inflected', logically placed between the first and the second.
14. *Autobiography*, Part I, Chapter II.
15. Ibid., Part II, Chapter III.
16. Ibid., Part II, Chapter XXII.
17. Ibid., Part III, Chapter VIII.
18. Ibid., Part IV, Chapter X.
19. Ibid., Part IV, Chapter XXIII.

20. Ibid., Part V, Chapter I.
21. Ibid., Part IV, Chapters XXX and XXXI; Part V, Chapter XXIX.
22. Ibid., Part V, Chapter XXVI.
23. H.S.L. Polak to Mahadev Desai, 19 March 1928, SN 13590, SAAA; Gandhi to H.S.L. Polak, 12 October 1928, *CWMG*, XXXVIII, p. 356.
24. See Sonja Schlesin to Manilal Gandhi, 1 October 1928, SN 15047, SAAA.
25. Sonja Schlesin to Gandhi, 4 May 1928, SN 15039, SAAA (emphasis in the original).
26. Sonja Schlesin to Gandhi, 15 June 1928, SN 15041, SAAA.
27. Gandhi to Manilal Gandhi, 15 July 1928, *CWMG*, XXXVII, pp. 65–66 (emphasis in the original).
28. Gandhi to Jane Howard, 12 March 1928, *CWMG*, XXXVI, p. 101.
29. C. Rajagopalachari to Mahadev Desai, 6 February 1926, Subject File, No. 46, C. Rajagopalachari Papers, Fourth Instalment, NMML.
30. 'The Supreme Egotist', *Times of India*, 10 April 1929.
31. 'A Saint on His Case', *The China Press* (Shanghai), 16 February 1930.
32. Gandhi to Niranjan Singh, 12 May 1928, *CWMG*, XXXVI, p. 310.
33. Holmes to Gandhi, letters of 14 April and 13 May 1926, SNs 32219 and 32222, SAAA.
34. Gandhi to F.H. Brown, 25 May 1928, *CWMG*, XXXVI, p. 337.
35. *Autobiography*, last, unnumbered chapter entitled 'Farewell'.
36. *Sun* (Baltimore), 15 May 1928.
37. See SN 14305, SAAA.
38. Report in the *Manchester Guardian*, 14 January 1929.
39. See C.F. Andrews to Gandhi, 2 August 1928, SN 14369, SAAA.

Chapter Fourteen: Once More into the Fray

1. *CWMG*, XXXV, pp. 499–500
2. Gandhi to N.R. Malkani, 8 February 1928, *CWMG*, XXXVI, p. 12.
3. Edward Cadogan, *The India We Saw* (London: John Murray, 1933), pp. 10, 19–20, 25, 64–66, 75, 119, 132–33, 161–65, 192.
4. This account of the Simon Commission debate in the Legislative Assembly is based on IAR, 1928, Volume 1, pp. 186–201.
5. See reports in Home (Special) File 584-E, Part I of 1928, MSA.
6. Reports in *BC*, 10 March and 2 April 1928.
7. *BC*, 30 April 1928.
8. See reports in Home (Special) File 584-E, Part I of 1928, MSA; Mahadev Desai, *The Story of Bardoli: Being a History of the Bardoli Satyagraha*

of 1928 and Its Sequel (first published in 1929; reprint Ahmedabad: Navajivan Publishing House, 1957).

9. 'The Only Issue', *YI*, 17 May 1928; 'Bardoli on Trial', *YI*, 31 May 1928; 'The Yajna at Bardoli', *N*, 10 June 1928, *CWMG*, XXXVI, pp. 319–22, 353–54, 384–86. These methods of managing conflict and suppressing dissent are traditionally ascribed to the great political theorist of ancient India, Kautilya.

10. Mirabehn to Devadas Gandhi, 19 July 1928, Devadas Gandhi Papers, NMML.

11. N.R. Malkani, *Ramblings and Reminiscences of Gandhiji* (Ahmedabad: Navajivan Publishing House, 1972), p. 129.

12. Gandhi to L.W. Ritch, 27 February 1928, *CWMG*, XXXVI, pp. 60–61.

13. 'My Best Comrade Gone', *YI*, 26 April 1928, *CWMG*, XXXVI, pp. 261–63.

14. *CWMG*, XXXVII, p. 35.

15. Reports in Home (Special) File 584-E, Part V of 1928, MSA: *ToI*, 24 July 1938.

16. Bombay Government note dated 28 July 1928, in Home (Special) File 584-E, Part VIII of 1928, MSA.

17. Bombay Government note dated 31 July 1928, in ibid.

18. *BC*, 7 August 1928; *ToI*, 7 October 1928.

19. Police report dated 12 August 1928, in Home (Special) File 584-E, Part V of 1928, MSA.

20. Desai, *The Story of Bardoli*, p. 219.

21. Letter of 19 February 1929, in Mss Eur F 150/1, APAC/BL.

22. *All Parties Conference 1928: Report of the Committee Appointed by the Conference to Determine the Principles of the Constitution of India* (Allahabad: All India Congress Committee, 1928), pp. 71–72.

23. Ibid., p. 18.

24. Ibid., Chapters II, III, VII and VIII.

25. Gandhi to Motilal Nehru, 21 August 1928, *CWMG*, XXXVII, p. 194.

26. Gandhi to B.G. Horniman, 28 August 1928, *CWMG*, XXXVII, p. 212.

27. C.F. Andrews to Gandhi, 3 August 1928, SN 14370, SAAA.

28. These paragraphs are based on reports and posters in File 143-K-VIII of 1928, Home (Special), MSA.

29. IAR, 1928, Volume 2, pp. 94–95.

30. 'The Assault on Lalaji', *N*, 4 November 1928; 'The Inevitable', *YI*, 8 November 1928; *CWMG*, XXXVIII, pp. 16–17.

31. *CWMG*, XXXVIII, p. 65.

32. Lord Irwin (Viceroy) to Frederick Sykes (Governor of Bombay), 15 December 1928, Mss Eur F 150/1, APAC/BL.

33. Gandhi to Motilal Nehru, 15 July 1928, *CWMG*, XXXVII, p. 64.

34. Ibid., p. 69.
35. 'Crown of Thorns', *YI*, 26 July 1928, *CWMG*, XXXVII, pp. 91–92.
36. Subhas C. Bose to Gandhi, 26 July 1928, SN 13650, SAAA.
37. Saiyid Haidar Raza to Gandhi, Leonards-on-Sea, Sussex, 6 June 1928, SN 14322, SAAA.
38. See Narayani Gupta, *Delhi Between Empires, 1803–1931: Society, Government and Urban Growth* (Delhi: Oxford University Press, 1981), pp. 149–51.
39. http://hosted.law.wisc.edu/wordpress/sharafi/files/2010/07/Middle-5.01.pdf (accessed on 7 April 2015).
40. Shaukat Ali to Gandhi, 16 July 1928, SN 13465, SAAA.
41. Gandhi to Shaukat Ali, letters of 18 July and 3 August 1928, *CWMG*, XXXVII, pp. 69–71, 121.
42. Shaukat Ali to Gandhi, 25 November 1928, SN 13733, SAAA.
43. Gandhi to Shaukat Ali, 30 November 1928, *CWMG*, XXXVIII, pp. 129–32.
44. 'Curse of Assassination', *YI*, 27 December 1928, *CWMG*, XXXVIII, pp. 274–76.
45. *CWMG*, XXXVIII, p. 271.
46. See A.R. Venkatachalapathy, 'Street Smart in Chennai: The City in Popular Imagination', in C.S. Lakshmi, *The Unhurried City: Writings on Chennai* (Delhi: Penguin India, 2004).

Chapter Fifteen: Father, Son, Holy Spirit

1. Entry for 8 April 1929, Diary of Lady Haig (wife of Harry Haig, then Home Secretary, Government of India), in the Haig Papers, Centre for South Asian Studies, Cambridge.
2. http://www.shahidbhagatsingh.org/biography/c8.htm (accessed on 8 April 1929).
3. *CWMG*, XL, pp. 223, 259–61.
4. See IAR, 1929, Volume 1, pp. 78–80.
5. *CWMG*, XL, pp. 262–63, 317–18, 359–60, 380–81, 411, 432–33, etc.
6. Gandhi to Mirabehn, 6 May 1929, *CWMG*, XL, pp. 346–47.
7. 'In Andhra Desa (VII)', *YI*, 30 May 1929, *CWMG*, XL, pp. 346–47.
8. See Vijaya Lakshmi Pandit, *The Scope of Happiness: A Personal Memoir* (1979; reprint Delhi: Orient Paperbacks, 1981), pp. 57–58.
9. Jawaharlal Nehru to Gandhi, 13 July 1929, SN 15428, SAAA.
10. Cf. Michael Brecher, *Nehru: A Political Biography* (London: Oxford University Press, 1959), Chapter V and passim.

11. See Sarvepalli Gopal, *Jawaharlal Nehru: A Biography: Volume One, 1889–1947* (Bombay: Oxford University Press, 1976), pp. 126–27.
12. Qamar Ahmad to Gandhi, 3 February 1929, SN 15323, SAAA.
13. See IAR, 1929, Volume 1, pp. 362–66; Volume 2, pp. 350–52.
14. See Subject File 1, M.A. Ansari Papers, NMML.
15. Motilal Nehru to Gandhi, 14 September 1929, Personal Correspondence Files, Gandhi Papers, First and Second Instalments, NMML.
16. Gandhi to Jawaharlal Nehru, 7 August 1929, *CWMG*, XLI, p. 256.
17. 'Interview with Mr. Jinnah', *YI*, 15 August 1929, *CWMG*, XLI, p. 289.
18. *CWMG*, XLI, pp. 351–53.
19. *CWMG*, XLII, pp. 220–21.
20. See http://cinnamonteal.in/authors/salima-tyabji/ (accessed on 9 April 2015).
21. 'Position of Women', 17 October 1929, *CWMG*, XLII, pp. 4–6.
22. 'Letter to Ashram Women', 21 October 1929, *CWMG*, XLII, p. 27.
23. IAR, 1929, Volume 2, pp. 47–49.
24. Sarojini Naidu to Gandhi, 9 November 1929, SN 15567, SAAA.
25. Polak to Gandhi, 5 December 1929, Personal Correspondence Files, Gandhi Papers, 1st and 2nd Instalments, NMML.
26. Polak to Gandhi, 12 December 1929, SN 16211, SAAA.
27. News report in TT, 3 December 1929.
28. Front page report in TT, 25 December 1929.
29. 'Minutes of conversation between His Excellency the Viceroy and Mr. Gandhi, Pandit Motilal Nehru, Sir T.B. Sapru, Mr. Jinnah and Mr. Patel on 23rd December 1929', in Subject File No. 57, Gandhi Papers, First and Second Instalments, NMML.
30. Report in TT, 26 December 1929.
31. Report in TT, 27 December 1929.
32. TT, issues of 14 and 27 December 1929.
33. IAR, 1929, Volume 2, pp. 288–97.
34. *CWMG*, XLII, p. 320.
35. IAR, 1929, Volume 2, pp. 298ff.

Chapter Sixteen: The March to the Sea

1. *CWMG*, XLII, p. 313. (The translation, from the original Hindi, has been slightly modified to make it more accurate.)
2. 'The Cult of the Bomb', *YI*, 2 January 1930, *CWMG*, XLII, pp. 361–64.
3. The Hindustan Socialist Republican Association Manifesto', pamphlet printed c. January 1930, signed by Kartar Singh, President of HSRA,

Subject File No. 57, M.K. Gandhi Papers, First and Second Instalments, NMML.

For a fine historical analysis of these Indian revolutionaries and their attitude to Gandhi, see Kama Maclean, *A Revolutionary History of Interwar India: Violence, Image, Voice and Text* (London: C. Hurst and Co., 2015).

4. Manishankar Upadhyaya to Gandhi, c. January 1930, Subject File No. 57, M.K. Gandhi Papers, First and Second Instalments, NMML.

5. Satyananda Bose to Gandhi, Calcutta, 10 January 1930, Subject File No. 57, Gandhi Papers, First and Second Instalments, NMML.

6. Shaukat Ali to Gandhi, 16 February 1930, Personal Correspondence Files, Gandhi Papers, First and Second Instalments, NMML.

7. M.A. Ansari to Gandhi, 13 February 1930, reproduced in *CWMG*, XLII, pp. 518–22.

8. Hasan, *A Nationalist Conscience*, p. 209.

9. Gandhi to Ansari, 16 February 1930, *CWMG*, XLII, pp. 510–11.

10. Motilal Nehru to Ansari, 17 February 1930, in *A Bunch of Old Letters: Written Mostly to Jawaharlal Nehru, and Some Written by Him* (Bombay: Asia Publishing House, 1958), pp. 81–83.

11. *CWMG*, XLII, pp. 376–77, 382.

12. 'Independence Day', *YI*, 16 January 1930, *CWMG*, XLII, pp. 398–400.

13. See Fortnightly Reports for the second half of January 1930, File No. 18/II of 1930, Home (Political), NAI.

14. Saifuddin Kitchlew to Gandhi, 27 January 1930; Satyapal to Jawaharlal Nehru, 27 January 1930, both in Subject File No. 57, Gandhi Papers, First and Second Instalments, NMML.

15. 'Clearing the Issue', *YI*, 30 January 1930, *CWMG*, XLII, pp. 432–34.

16. 'The Salt Tax', *YI*, 27 February 1930, *CWMG*, XLII, pp. 499–501.

17. 'Answers of Rammohun Roy to Queries on the Salt Monopoly (March 19, 1832)', in Jatindra Kumar Majumdar, editor, *Raja Rammohun Roy and Progressive Movements in India: A Selection from Records (1775–1845)* (Calcutta: Art Press, 1941), pp. 467–69.

18. Quoted in J.B. Pennington, 'The Salt Tax', *Indian Review*, December 1902.

19. Malcolm Darling, *Apprentice to Power: India, 1904–1908* (London: Hogarth Press, 1966), p. 81.

20. *Indian Opinion*, 8 July 1905, *CWMG*, V, p. 9.

21. *CWMG*, XLIII, pp. 2–8.

22. *CWMG*, XLIII, p. 51.

23. Four-page note prepared by A. Tottenham, of the Criminal Investigation Department, 8 February 1930, in File No. 59 of 1930, Home (Political), NAI.

24. See *CWMG*, LXXII, p. 390.

25. Sarojini Naidu to Padmaja Naidu, Ahmedabad, 15 February 1930, Padmaja Naidu Papers, NMML.

26. Reports in *BC* (Sunday Edition), 2 March 1930.

27. *BC*, 9 March 1930.

28. *CWMG*, XLIII, pp. 27–28.

29. Thomas Weber, *On the Salt March* (New Delhi: HarperCollins India 2000), pp. 92–96.

30. For more details, see *GBI*, Chapter 20.

31. 'Satyagrahis' March', N, 9 March 1930, *CWMG*, XLIII, pp. 33–35.

32. Interview with Valji Govindji Desai, Oral History Transcript Number 221, NMML.

33. *CWMG*, XLIII, pp. 48–49.

34. *CWMG*, XLIII, pp. 454–55; Weber, *On the Salt March*, pp. 490–95.

35. See interview with Anand T. Hingorani, Oral History Transcript Number 512, NMML.

36. *Pratap*, 16 March 1930.

37. *CWMG*, XLIII, pp. 62–63.

38. *CWMG*, XLIII, pp. 66, 72.

39. *ABP*, 16 March 1930.

40. *BC*, 16 March 1930.

41. *CWMG*, XLIII, p. 89.

42. *CWMG*, XLIII, pp. 101–02.

43. *ABP*, 21 March 1930.

44. 'The Ashram Without Mahatmaji', *ABP*, 22 March 1930.

45. Reports in *ABP*, 21 and 22 March 1930.

46. *ABP*, 25 March 1930.

47. As reported in *ToI*, 25 March 1930.

48. *CWMG*, XLIII, pp. 117–18.

49. *ABP*, 26 March 1930.

50. *ABP*, 28 March 1930.

51. *BC*, 30 March 1930.

52. *Source Material, Volume III, Part III*, p. 25.

53. Winston Churchill to Irwin, c. first week of January 1930; C.F. Andrews to Irwin, 3 February 1930, both in Mss Eur C 152/19, APAC/BL.

54. Irwin to Lionel Curtis, 6 March 1930, in ibid.

55. Fortnightly reports for the second half of March 1930, in File No. 18/IV of 1930, Home (Political), NAI.

56. Lord Irwin to Archbishop of Canterbury, 31 March 1930, in Mss Eur C 152/19, APAC/BL.

57. Letter of 31 March, in File No. 18/IV of 1930, Home (Political), NAI.

58. TS, quoted in *ABP*, 13 March 1930; *ToI*, 13 March 1930.

59. Ashmead Bartlett, quoted in *ABP*, 16 March 1930.

60. Report in *Time*, 24 March 1930.

61. See Shahid Amin, 'The Pedagogy of Nationalism', *Seminar*, issue number 686, October 2016, p. 37.

62. See IAR, 1930, Volume 1, p. 76.

63. Reports in *ABP*, 2 and 3 April 1930.

64. *ABP*, 4 April 1930.

65. *ToI*, 5 April 1930.

66. K.C.B., 'The Great Trek: Personal Impressions', *BC*, 20 April 1930.

67. *CWMG*, XLIII, pp. 179–80.

68. 'All About Dandi', *ABP*, 8 April 1930.

69. *ABP*, 7 April 1930.

70. Sarojini Naidu to Padmaja Naidu, Dandi, 6 April 1930, Padmaja Naidu Papers, NMML.

71. This account is based on the letters, memos and clippings in File 223 of 1930, Home (Political), NAI.

72. Reports in *BC* and *ABP*, 7 April 1930.

73. Mahadev Desai to Jawaharlal Nehru, 7 April 1930, Jawaharlal Nehru Papers, NMML.

74. Shaukat Ali to Gandhi, 7 April 1930, Subject File 18, Gandhi Papers, First and Second Instalments, NMML.

75. Gandhi to Shaukat Ali, 17 April 1930, *CWMG*, XLIII, pp. 280–81.

76. Fortnightly Report for Bombay, second half of April 1930, in File No. 18/V of 1930, Home (Political), NAI.

77. Letter to Gandhi from 'A Muslim', Bombay, 30 April 1930, SN 16760, SAAA.

78. 'To the Women', *YI*, N, 6 April 1930, *CWMG*, XLIII, pp. 189–90.

79. See *CWMG*, XLIII, p. 269.

80. *BC*, 13 April 1930.

81. Vithalbhai Patel to Irwin, 20 April 1930, Mss Eur C 152/24, APAC/BL.

82. Jinnah to Irwin, 20 April 1930, in ibid.

83. Statement to Associated Press, Navsari, 21 April 1930, *CWMG*, XLIII, p. 301. Ironically, the men in the Chittagong raid had raised slogans

of 'Mahatma Gandhi ki jai'. See Manini Chatterjee, *Do & Die: The Chittagong Uprising, 1930–34* (1999: reprint New Delhi, Picador India, 2010).

84. Gandhi to Narandas Gandhi, 26 April 1930; 'Speech at Chharwada', 26 April 1930, *CWMG*, XLIII, pp. 325, 330–32.

85. Irwin to Geoffrey Dawson, 7 April 1930, Mss Eur F 152/19, APAC/BL.

86. Sykes to Irwin, 23 March 1930; Notes of a meeting held in New Delhi on 27 March 1930, both in ibid.

87. Governor of Bombay to Viceroy, 15 April 1930, Mss Eur Mss C 152/19, APAC/BL.

88. Irwin to Sykes, 21 April 1930, Mss Eur F 150/2, APAC/BL.

89. Lord Irwin to Sir Arthur Hitzel (Undersecretary of State for India), 21 April 1930, Mss Eur C 152/19, APAC/BL.

90. Bombay Government to Government of India, telegram dated 26 April 1930; Government of India to Bombay Government, telegram dated 29 April 1930, both in Mss Eur F 150/2, APAC/BL.

91. J.E.B. Hotson, Member of the Bombay Executive Council, to Private Secretary to Governor, Mahableshwar, 29 April 1930; Bombay Government to Government of India, telegram dated 30 April 1930; Government of India to Bombay Government, telegram dated 30 April 1930, all in ibid.

92. *CWMG*, XLIII, pp. 389, 399.

93. Irwin to Baldwin, 13 May 1930, in Mss Eur F 150/2/APAC/BL.

94. Reports in *Time*, 31 March, 28 April, 5 and 12 May 1930 respectively.

95. Hailey, quoted in Sarvepalli Gopal, 'Drinking Tea with Treason: Halifax in India', in *Imperialists, Nationalists, Democrats: The Collected Essays of Sarvepalli Gopal*, edited by Srinath Raghavan (Ranikhet: Permanent Black, 2013), p. 89.

Chapter Seventeen: The Prison and the World

1. *Source Material, Volume III, Part III*, pp. 135–37, 141–44.

2. Gandhi to Mira; Gandhi to Narandas Gandhi; both written on 12 May 1930, *CWMG*, XLIII, pp. 402–03. Gandhi's cellmate Kaka Kalelkar helped with the Marathi translations; whereas for the Bengali songs, Gandhi used versions rendered into English by Tagore.

3. Gandhi to R.V. Martin, 11 June 1930, *CWMG*, XLIII, p. 435; same to same, 8 July 1930, *CWMG*, XLIII, pp. 10–11.

4. Gandhi to Mira, 7 July 1930, *CWMG*, XLIV, p. 7.

5. Gandhi to Valji G. Desai, 2 September 1930, *CWMG*, XLIV, p. 113.

6. This exchange was reprinted as 'The Importance of Vows: A Correspondence', *Gandhi Marg*, Volume 3, Number 2, April 1959, pp. 127–31.

7. Gandhi to Pyare Lal Govil, 19 November 1930, *CWMG*, XLIV, pp. 324–25.

8. *Source Material, Volume III, Part III*, pp. 201–02, 219–20, 224.

9. Ibid., pp. 380–85.

10. P. Subba Rao to Gandhi, 9 July 1930; Tata Vasudevan to Gandhi, 4 June 1930, *Source Material, Volume III, Part III*, pp. 278–79, 504–05.

11. Upton Sinclair to Superintendent, Yerwada Jail, 9 August 1930, *Source Material, Volume III, Part III*, p. 279.

12. Gandhi to Upton Sinclair, 30 October 1930, *CWMG*, XLIV, p. 263.

13. *Source Material, Volume III, Part III*, pp. 531–32, 643.

14. Jayaram Jadhav to Gandhi, 23 May 1930, addressed to 'Dear and Revered Bapuji', in ibid., pp. 595–96.

15. FR for Bombay, combined for second half of May and first half of June, in File No. 18/VII of 1930, Home (Political), NAI.

16. Webb Miller, '630 Hurt as Police Beat Salt Raiders in 2 India Clashes', *New York Herald Tribune*, 22 May 1930. Cf. also Webb Miller, *I Found No Peace: The Journal of a Foreign Correspondent* (Harmondsworth: Penguin Books, 1940), Chapters XI and XII.

17. Farson's report was reprinted in *Time*, 7 July 1930.

18. Confidential letter from Chief Secretary, Government of Bombay, 17 June 1930, in File No. 214 of 1930, Home (Political), NAI.

19. See reports in File No. 18/VIII of 1930, Home (Political), NAI.

20. FR for western India states for first half of August 1930, in File No. 18/IX of 1930, Home (Political), NAI.

21. See Anon, 'Women Join the Struggle', *Current*, 9 November 1960.

22. This account is based on *CWMG*, XLIV, pp. 81–84, 117–21, 470–72; IAR, 1930, Volume II, pp. 83–96.

23. Irwin to Baldwin, 13 September 1930, in Mss Eur C 152/19, APAC/BL.

24. A summary of the proceedings is in IAR, 1930, Volume II, pp. 288–324.

25. Nawab of Bhopal to Irwin, London, 21 November 1930, in Mss Eur C 152/19, APAC/BL.

26. H.G. Haig to Lord Irwin, 18 December 1930, in Mss Eur C 152/19, APAC/BL.

27. Nawab of Bhopal to Irwin, 19 December 1930, APAC/BL.

28. Iqbal's Presidential Address is printed in full in Nadeem Shafiq Malik, editor, *The All India Muslim League and Allama Iqbal's Allahabad Address 1930* (Lahore, Iqbal Academy, 2013), pp. 372f.

29. Ibid., pp. 38–41.
30. Andrews, as quoted in the *Daily Boston Globe*, 1 November 1930.
31. Review in *The Saturday Review of Politics, Literature, Science and Art*, 4 October 1930.
32. Edward Thompson, 'The Voice of Gandhi', *Christian Science Monitor*, 25 October 1930.
33. Review in *The Times*, 23 September 1930.
34. Review by Lewis Gannett, in the *New York Herald Tribune*, 25 September 1930.
35. *The Methodist Review*, July 1930.
36. *Time*, 5 January 1931.
37. Holmes to Rolland, 26 May 1930, Box 3, John Haynes Holmes Papers, Library of Congress.

Chapter Eighteen: Parleys with Proconsuls

1. *Source Material, Volume III, Part III*, pp. 169–70.
2. BC, 29 January 1931.
3. *CWMG*, XLV, pp. 425–27.
4. *CWMG*, XLV, pp. 127–28, 130.
5. FR for Bombay City for second half of January 1931, in File No. 18/1931, Home (Political), NAI.
6. *CWMG*, XLV, pp. 136–38.
7. BC, 5 February 1931.
8. B.R. Nanda, *The Nehrus: Motilal and Jawaharlal* (London: George Allen and Unwin, 1962), pp. 337–39.
9. *CWMG*, XLV, pp. 175–76.
10. Polak to Gandhi, 28 January 1931, SN 16940, SAAA.
11. See Alan Campbell-Johnson, *Viscount Halifax: A Biography* (New York: Ives Washburn, Inc. 1941), pp. 313–14. Irwin's contemporary response is at odds with some recent works that claim that Gandhi did not do enough to save Bhagat Singh's life. For a fair-minded analysis of this controversy, see V.N. Datta, *Gandhi and Bhagat Singh* (New Delhi: Rupa and Co., 2008).
12. This account of the Gandhi–Irwin meetings is based on *CWMG*, XLV, pp. 185–207; and Irwin's notes of his interviews with Gandhi on 27 February and 1 March 1931, Mss Eur C 152/6, APAC/BL. Cf. also S. Gopal, *The Viceroyalty of Lord Irwin, 1926–1931* (Oxford: Clarendon Press, 1957), Chapter VI.
13. *CWMG*, XLV, pp. 432–36, 250–56.

14. See Subject File 81, Gandhi Papers, First and Second Instalments, NMML.

15. Chinniah, Secretary of the Depressed Classes Prajanika Sangam, Madras, to Gandhi, 19 March 1931, in Subject File 78, Gandhi Papers, First and Second Instalments, NMML.

16. Mohammed Kitayatullah, President, Jamiat Ulamai Hind, Delhi, to Gandhi, 22 March 1931, in Subject File No. 2, Gandhi Papers, First and Second Instalments, NMML.

17. M.C. Chagla to Gandhi, 16 March 1931, in ibid.

18. These mails are based on Subject File 78, Gandhi Papers, First and Second Instalments, NMML.

19. Raymond Chagnon to Gandhi, 30 March 1931; Chas. S. Field to Gandhi, undated, c. May 1931; Blake A. Hoover to Gandhi, 27 April 1931; Charles Frederick Waller to Gandhi, 17 April, 1931; all in Correspondence File Number 18, Gandhi Papers, First and Second Instalments, NMML.

20. Arthur Sewell to Gandhi, 26 January 1931, Correspondence File No. 19, Gandhi Papers, First and Second Instalments, NMML.

21. James D. Pond to Gandhi, 8 April 1931, in ibid.

22. Sailendra N. Ghose to Gandhi, 8 April 1931, in ibid.

23. John Haynes Holmes to Gandhi, 17 April 1931, in ibid.

24. John Haynes Holmes to Gandhi, 23 April 1931, in ibid

25. *CWMG*, XLVI, pp. 70–71.

26. See Martin Gilbert, *Winston S. Churchill: Volume V, 1922–1939* (London: Heinemann, 1976), pp. 355–57.

27. Winston S. Churchill, *India: Speeches and an Introduction* (London: Thornton Butterworth, 1931), pp. 37–38, 75, 120–28.

28. Quoted in Gilbert, *Winston S. Churchill: Volume V*, p. 390.

29. *GBI*, pp. 22–23.

30. See Churchill, *India*, pp. 138–39.

31. A four-page pamphlet issued by the Communist Party of India, Subject File 81, Gandhi Papers, First and Second Instalments, NMML.

32. *CWMG*, pp. 313–15, 319, 333.

33. TT, 25 March 1931.

34. TT, 26 March 1931.

35. Brijkrishna Chandiwala, *At the Feet of Bapu* (Ahmedabad: Navajivan Publishers, 1954), pp. 67–68.

36. See reports in TT, 27 March 1931.

37. See editorial in TT, 28 March 1931.

38. *CWMG*, XLV, pp. 370–71, 403–04.

39. *CWMG*, XLV, p. 363.

40. 'Bhagat Singh', N, 29 March 1931, *CWMG*, XLV, pp. 359–61.

41. *CWMG*, XLVI, pp. 397–99, 29–31.

42. Lord Willingdon to Florence Brooks, 29 April 1931, in Mss Eur F 237/3, APAC/BL.

43. Lord Willingdon to Florence Brooks, 21 June 1931, in Mss Eur F 237/3, APAC/BL.

44. See clippings and notes in L/PO/6/24, APAC/BL.

45. *CWMG*, XLVI, pp. 409–13.

46. H.W. Emerson, Home Secretary, Government of India, to Malcolm Hailey, Governor of the United Provinces, 16 May 1931 (copy), in IOR, R/3/1/289, APAC/BL.

47. C.F. Andrews to Gandhi, 10 June 1931, in Correspondence File No. 19, Gandhi Papers, First and Second Instalments, NMML.

48. 'I do not see how Mr. Gandhi can be in London without you,' wrote the Punjab politician Fazl-i-Husain to Mrs Naidu. Letter dated 15 July 1931, in Waheed Ahmad, editor, *Letters of Mian Fazl-i-Husain* (Lahore: Research Society of Pakistan, 1976), p. 163.

49. 'A Twentieth-Century Sati', *YI*, 21 May 1931, *CWMG*, XLVI, pp. 73–75.

50. 'Caste and Communal Question', *YI*, 4 June 1931, *CWMG*, XLVI, pp. 302–04.

51. *CWMG*, XLVI, pp. 309, 381.

52. Ganga Singh, Maharaja of Bikaner, to Gandhi, letters of 4 and 9 July 1931, Subject File 84, Gandhi Papers, First and Second Instalments, NMML.

53. *CWMG*, XLVII, pp. 146–47, 149–50, 177.

54. Lord Willingdon to Florence Brooks, 25 July 1931, in Mss Eur F 237/3, APAC/BL.

55. Gandhi to H.W. Emerson, 24 July 1931 (from Bardoli), *CWMG*, XLVII, p. 200.

56. Gandhi to Amritlal Sheth, 29 July 1931, *CWMG*, XLVII, p. 235.

57. *CWMG*, XLVII, pp. 445–46, 281, 287.

58. See Dhananjay Keer, *Dr. Ambedkar: Life and Mission* (first published in 1954; reprint of fourth edition, Mumbai: Popular Prakashan, 2015), pp. 165–68; *The Diary of Mahadev Desai: Volume I: Yeravda-Pact Eve, 1932*, translated from the Gujarati and edited by Valji Govindji Desai (Ahmedabad: Navajivan Publishing House, 1953), p. 52, which quoted Gandhi as saying, on 1 April 1932: 'Till I went to England I did not know that he [Ambedkar] was a Harijan. I thought he was some Brahman who took deep interest in Harijans and therefore talked intemperately.'

59. 'Dr. Ambedkar on Mr. Gandhi's Folly', *ToI*, 17 August 1931.
60. *CWMG*, XLVII, pp. 330–31, 357, 449–50.
61. Mirza Ismail to Gandhi, 30 July 1931, Personal Correspondence Files, M.K. Gandhi Papers, NMML (emphasis in the original).

Chapter Nineteen: At Home in London

1. Letter dated 31 August 1931, Jawaharlal Nehru Papers, NMML.
2. British Consul General to Foreign Office, 12 September 1931, in L/PO/6/73, APAC/BL.
3. *The Times*, 12 September 1931. Gandhi's arrival at Marseille is captured on film in www.youtube.com/watch?v=Se0kpkJIhH8.
4. Obituary of Muriel Lester in *The Times*, 13 February 1968. Lester's life and work are also discussed in Seth Koven, *The Match Girl and the Heiress* (Princeton: Princeton University Press, 2015).
5. Walchand Hirachand to G.D. Birla, telegram dated 11 July 1931, Subject File 84, Gandhi Papers, First and Second Instalments, NMML.
6. See Muriel Lester to Gandhi, 13 March 1931, in Subject File 81, Gandhi Papers, First and Second Instalments, NMML.
7. Muriel Lester, *Entertaining Gandhi* (London: Ivor Nicholson and Watson, 1932), pp. 34–35.
8. *The Observer*, 13 September 1931.
9. *CWMG*, XLVIII, pp. 8–10.
10. Letter of 16 September 1931, Nehru Papers, NMML.
11. Reports in *MG*, 14 September 1931, and in the *Observer*, 13 September 1931.
12. Police note dated 18 September 1931, MEPO 38/156, NAUK.
13. Agatha Harrison, '88 Knightsbridge, London', in Chandrashanker Shukla, *Gandhiji as We Know Him* (Bombay: Vora and Co. Ltd, 1945), pp. 82–88.
14. Lord Willingdon to Gandhi, 4 September, 1931, SN 17642, SAAA.
15. *CWMG*, XLVIII, p. 12.
16. *CWMG*, XLVIII, pp. 13–20.
17. See Vasant Moon, editor, *Dr. Babasaheb Ambedkar: Writings and Speeches, Vol. 2* (Bombay: Government of Maharashtra, 1982), pp. 596–99.
18. *CWMG*, XLVII, pp. 26–34.
19. C.F. Andrews, 'Mr. Gandhi: The Champion of the Very Poor', *MG*, 24 September 1931.
20. *MG*, 26 September 1931.

21. See Margarita Barns, *India: Today and Tomorrow* (London: George Allen and Unwin, 1937), p. 80.

22. *Manchester Guardian*, 28 September 1931.

23. CWMG, XLVIII, pp. 24–25.

24. *Observer*, 11 October 1931.

25. Police note dated 12 October 1931, MEPO 38/156, NAUK; C. Rajagopalachari and J.C. Kumarappa, editors, *The Nation's Voice: Being a Collection of Gandhiji's Speeches in England and Sjt. Mahadev Desai's Account of the Sojourn* (Ahmedabad: Navajivan Press, 1932), p. 243.

26. *Observer*, 1 November 1931. Among the students who heard Gandhi was an American, Dean Rusk, later to be his country's Secretary of State. 'Despite his slight frame and loincloth and his philosophy of non-violence,' recalled Rusk, 'Gandhi was far stronger than he is usually portrayed. He was a dynamic personality, vibrant and inspiring, not at all weak or feeble.' Dean Rusk (as told to Richard Rusk), *As I Saw It* (New York: Penguin Books, 1990), p. 72.

27. See Drusilla Scott, *A.D. Lindsay: A Biography* (Oxford: Basil Blackwell, 1971), pp. 214–16; idem, 'Gandhi in Oxford', *Balliol College Annual Record 1994*, pp. 58–62.

28. Untitled memoir by R.O. Hicks, in Hicks Papers, Centre for South Asian Studies, Cambridge.

29. *MG*, 17 September 1931.

30. *MG*, 24 September 1931.

31. CWMG, XLVIII, pp. 79–80.

32. CWMG, XLVIII, pp. 106–07.

33. CWMG, XLVII, pp. 160–61.

34. CWMG, XLVIII, p. 179.

35. CWMG, XLVIII, p. 223.

36. CWMG, XLVIII, pp. 297–98.

37. CWMG, XLVIII, pp. 115–16.

38. Mahadev Desai to Jawaharlal Nehru, 25 September 1931, Nehru Papers, NMML.

39. Interview with the *Daily Herald*, CWMG, XLVIII, p. 207.

40. CWMG, XLVIII, pp. 140–41.

41. CWMG, XLVIII, p. 229.

42. *MG*, 21 September 1931.

43. Clare Sheridan, *To the Four Winds* (London: Andre Deutsch, 1957), pp. 264ff.

44. John Haynes Holmes, 'I Meet Gandhi', *Unity*, 23 November 1931.

45. *CWMG*, XLVIII, pp. 47–48; Lester, *Entertaining Gandhi*, pp. 79–80.
46. *MG*, 23 September 1931.
47. Gandhi to Albert Einstein, 18 October 1931, *CWMG*, XLVIII, p. 183.
48. See *GBI*, pp. 42–44, 47–50.
49. *CWMG*, XLVII, pp. 326–27.
50. *CWMG*, XLVII, pp. 272–73.
51. Michael Holroyd, *Bernard Shaw: Volume III, 1918–1950: The Lure of Fantasy* (London: Penguin Books, 1993), p. 286.
52. Mahadev Desai to Hermann Kallenbach, 4 November 1931, Kallenbach Papers, NAI.
53. Copy of printed article by Horace Alexander, 'Mahatma Gandhi: What Manner of Man', date and source unknown, in Box 2, Benthall Papers, Centre for South Asian Studies, Cambridge.

   Alexander had visited Gandhi in Sabarmati in 1928, and kept in close touch since. See Geoffrey Carnall, *Gandhi's Interpreter: A Life of Horace Alexander* (Edinburgh: Edinburgh University Press, 2011), Chapter 3 and passim.
54. See Dalal, *Gandhi: 1915–1948*, p. 92.
55. 'Gandhi', undated 10-page typescript in Box 2, Benthall Papers, Centre for South Asian Studies, Cambridge.
56. Viscount Templewood, *Nine Troubled Years* (London: Collins, 1954), pp. 59–60.
57. Jawaharlal Nehru to Gandhi, letters of 27 September and 4 October 1931, SNs 17863 and 17973, SAAA.
58. *CWMG*, XLVII, p. 173.
59. *CWMG*, XLVIII, p. 351.
60. *CWMG*, XLVIII, pp. 356–68.
61. *MG*, 16 December 1931.
62. *MG*, 7 December 1931.
63. See, for example, the material in Correspondence File No. 18, Gandhi Papers, First and Second Instalments, NMML, as well as SNs 17993 and 18060, SAAA.
64. See photograph in Subject File 81, Gandhi Papers, First and Second Instalments, NMML.
65. See Mira Kamdar, 'When Paris Met the Mahatma', *Caravan*, December 2011.
66. See *Romain Rolland and Gandhi Correspondence*, pp. 166–234.
67. *CWMG*, XLVIII, pp. 395–98, 498–500.
68. Mahadev Desai to Dr Scarpa, 2 December 1931, copy in D.G. Tendulkar Papers, NMML.

69. Report by the Rome correspondent, *MG*, 18 December 1931.
70. 'Pope Refuses to Meet Gandhi in Scanty Garb', Associated Press, 12 December 1931, in Subject File 312, Gandhi Papers, First and Second Instalments, NMML.
71. Gandhi to Romain Rolland, 20 December 1931, *CWMG*, XLVII, pp. 429–30.
72. 'A Retrospect' *YI*, 31 December 1931, *CWMG*, XLVIII, pp. 432–36.

Chapter Twenty: Arguments with Ambedkar

1. *CWMG*, XLVIII, p. 445.
2. Gandhi to Rajagopalachari, 28 August 2016, *CWMG*, XLVII, p. 372.
3. Lord Irwin to Viscount Cecil of Chelwood, 1 October 1930, in Mss Eur C 152/19, APAC/BL.
4. *CWMG*, XLVIII, pp. 446–47.
5. *CWMG*, XLVIII, pp. 459, 500–02, 472–75, 469–72.
6. See *Source Material, Volume III, Part IV*, pp. 454–56.
7. *CWMG*, XLVIII, pp. 490–92.
8. *CWMG*, XLVIII, pp. 2, 531–32.
9. Gandhi to Samuel Hoare, 15 January 1932, *CWMG*, XLIX, pp. 10–11.
10. Gandhi to Frederick Sykes, 23 January 1932, *CWMG*, XLIX, pp. 19–20.
11. *New York Times*, 7 April 1932, clipping in Subject File 312, Gandhi Papers, First and Second Instalments, NMML.
12. Gandhi to Manu Gandhi, 4 April 1932, *CWMG*, XLIX, p. 269.
13. Gandhi to Harilal Gandhi, 27 April 1932, *CWMG*, XLIX, p. 375.
14. Gandhi to Narandas Gandhi, 26 May 1932, *CWMG*, XLIX, p. 498.
15. See *CWMG*, XL, pp. 327–31, 335–36.
16. Gandhi to Hoare, 11 March 1932; Hoare to Gandhi, 13 April 1932, *CWMG*, XL, pp. 190–91, 533–34.
17. Gandhi to Ramsay Macdonald, 18 August 1932, *CWMG*, XL, pp. 383–84.
18. *CWMG*, XL, pp. 466–69.
19. Macdonald's letter was reproduced in *BC*, 13 September 1932.
20. See *BC*, 6 September 1932.
21. B.G. Horniman, 'Tragedy Must be Averted', *BC*, 13 September 1932.
22. Interview in *BC*, 17 September 1932.
23. Ambedkar's statement was reproduced in full in *BC*, 19 September 1932.

24. *CWMG*, LI, pp. 62–63, 66–68.
25. *ToI*, 19 September 1932.
26. *CWMG*, LI, pp. 101, 109.
27. Report in *ToI*, 21 September 1932; IAR, 1932, Volume 2, p. 242.
28. *CWMG*, LI, pp. 116–20.
29. *Source Material, Volume III, Part IV*, pp. 835–36.
30. See reports in *BC*, 21 September 1932.
31. *ToI*, 22 September 1932.
32. *CWMG*, LI, pp. 458–60.
33. Reports in *BC*, 23 September 1932; *ToI*, 23 September 1932.
34. Horniman, 'Enthusiasm for Temple-Entry Must Not Be Allowed to Wane', *BC*, 24 September 1932.
35. Aloysius Soares, *Down the Corridors of Time: Recollections and Reflexions, Volume I: 1891–1948* (Bombay: published by the author, 1971), p. 327.
36. Pyarelal, *The Epic Fast* (Ahmedabad: Navajivan Press, 1932), p. 63.
37. Ibid., p. 65.
38. Ibid., p. 71.
39. *Source Material, Volume III, Part IV*, pp. 206–10, 491.
40. Pyarelal, *The Epic Fast*, pp. 153–56.
41. Reports in *BC*, 26 September 1932.
42. See Rabindranath Tagore, *Mahatmaji & the Depressed Humanity* (Calcutta: Visva-bharati Bookshop, 1932), pp. 4–5.
43. Chandiwala, *At the Feet of Bapu*, p. 74.
44. Letter dated Poona, 29 September 1932, addressed to 'My Dear Charlie', from a person signing himself 'Bond', in Mss Afr.s. 2307, Box 7, File 3, Rhodes House Library, Oxford.
45. *CWMG*, LI, pp. 143–44.
46. MacFleck, 'The Moral of the Fast', *New Statesman and Nation*, 1 October 1932.
47. B.R. Ambedkar to A.V. Thakkar, 14 November 1932 (copy), SN 18642, SAAA.
48. IAR, 1932, Volume 2, pp. 257–58, 281–82.
49. 'Why "Harijans"', *CWMG*, LIII, pp. 266–67.
50. *CWMG*, XLI, pp. 347–48, 462–63.
51. *CWMG*, LI, pp. 376–77.
52. *CWMG*, LII, p. 211.
53. News reports in Subject File No. 23, C. Rajagopalachari Papers, Fourth Instalment, NMML.

54. Gandhi to M.A. Ananta Rau, 17 December, 1932; Gandhi to Mathurudas Trikumji, 23 December 1932; Gandhi to Jawaharlal Nehru, 31 December 1932, in *CWMG*, LII, pp. 219, 269, 311–12.
55. *CWMG*, LII, pp. 435–36.
56. Kamal Kumar Banerji to Gandhi, 6 December 1932, SN 18664, SAAA; Gandhi to Kamal Kumar Banerji, 14 December 1932, *CWMG*, XLII, p. 191.

Chapter Twenty-One: Shaming the Hindus

1. Lord Willingdon to Florence Brooks, letters of 23 August and 12 September 1932, in Mss Eur F 237/4, APAC/BL (emphasis in the original).
2. Lord Willingdon to Florence Brooks, 25 September, 1932, in ibid.
3. Lord Willingdon to Florence Brooks, 10 October 1932, in ibid.
4. Lord Willingdon to Florence Brooks, 30 October 1932, in ibid.
5. Lord Willingdon to Florence Brooks, 30 December 1932, in ibid.
6. *CWMG*, LII, pp. 347–50.
7. *CWMG*, LII, pp. 498–500. The meeting took place on 4 February 1933.
8. 'Dr. Ambedkar and Caste', *Harijan* (hereafter H), 11 February 1933, *CWMG*, LIII, pp. 260–62.
9. Home Secretary to Inspector General of Police, 28 February 1933, *Source Material, Volume III, Part VI*, p. 477.
10. C. Rajagopalachari to Gandhi, 12 December 1932, *CWMG*, LII, p. 434 (emphasis in the original).
11. C. Rajagopalachari to G.D. Birla, 10 January 1933, SN 20198, SAAA.
12. Gandhi to A.V. Thakkar, 19 January 1933, *CWMG*, LIII, p. 54.
13. A.V. Thakkar to C. Rajagopalachari, 19 January 1933, SN 20057, SAAA.
14. 'An Open Letter on Temple Entry to the Viceroy & Governor-General of India and the Central Legislature of India, by His Holiness Jagadguru Shri Shankaracharya of Puri', an eight-page letter published by the All India Varnashrama Swarajya Sangh, and printed at the Delhi Printing Works, n.d., c. June 1933, SN 21582, SAAA.
15. *The Authoritative Opinion of His Holiness Shree Shankaracharya of Sankeshwar-Karavir Peeth on the Anti-Religious Bills Now Pending Before the Legislative Assembly* (Bombay: The Gomantak Press, 1934).
16. Chief Secretary, United Provinces, to Home Secretary, Government of India, 10 August 1934, in L/PJ/7/595, APAC/BL.

17. See 'Gandhi's Ambedkar', in Ramachandra Guha, *An Anthropologist Among the Marxists and Other Essays* (New Delhi: Permanent Black, 2001).

18. L.R. Pangarkar to Gandhi, 15 January 1933, SN 20047, SAAA.

19. See *Source Material, Volume III, Part V*, pp. 90–95

20. Jawaharlal Nehru to Gandhi, 7 March 1933, SN 19008, SAAA.

21. Polak to Gandhi, 1 June 1933, SAAA.

22. Kasturba to Gandhi, letters of 13 March, 9 April and c. 24 April 1933, in *Source Material, Volume III, Part VI*, pp. 127, 201–03, 242–43.

23. *CWMG*, LIV, p. 235.

24. *CWMG*, LV, pp. 16, 38.

25. *CWMG*, LV, pp. 74–75, 77.

26. These paragraphs are based on *CWMG*, LV, pp. 55, 92, 121–22, 128, 441; Kasturba to Gandhi, 5 May 1933, SN 21170, SAAA; Harilal to Gandhi, 5 May 1933, SN 21213, SAAA; Mira to Gandhi, 2 May 1933, SN 21110, SAAA.

27. The Beginning of the Yajna', *Harijanbandhu*, 7 May 1933; 'All About the Fast', H, 8 July 1933, *CWMG*, LV, pp. 135–36, 254–56.

28. Devadas Gandhi to Padmaja Naidu, 8 May 1933, Padmaja Naidu Papers, NMML.

29. Lord Willingdon to Florence Brooks, 8 May 1933, in Mss Eur F 237/5, APAC/BL.

30. Devadas Gandhi to Padmaja Naidu, 8 May 1933, Padmaja Naidu Papers, NMML.

31. *CWMG*, LV, pp. 177–78, 444–45.

32. *CWMG*, LV, pp. 200–01.

33. Police report dated 17 June 1933, in F. 800 (40) (4) AA-II, Home (Special), MSA.

34. *CWMG*, LV, pp. 265–69, 276.

35. IAR, 1933, Volume 2, p. 329.

36. Lord Willingdon to Florence Brooks, 1 August 1933, in Mss Eur F 237/5, APAC/BL.

37. H.N. Brailsford, 'Hitlerism Wins in India', originally in *Reynold News*, reprinted in *Free Press Journal*, 13 August 1933, clipping in F. 800 (40) (4) AA-II, Home (Special), MSA.

38. Mahadev Desai to Mira, 12 October 1933, in Ghanshyam Das Birla, *Bapu: A Unique Association* (in four volumes) (Bombay: Bharatiya Vidya Bhavan, 1977), Volume I, pp. 323–28.

39. *CWMG*, LV, pp. 353–54, 468–69, 393.

40. Lord Willingdon to Florence Brooks, 21 August 1933, in Mss Eur F 237/5, APAC/BL.
41. CWMG, LV, pp. 373, 425–26.
42. Richard Gregg to Gandhi, 31 August 1933, Personal Correspondence Files, Gandhi Papers, NMML.
43. Gandhi to Agatha Harrison, 16 November 1933, CWMG, LVI, pp. 232–33.
44. These methods are described in some detail in the intelligence reports contained in L/PJ/7/595, APAC/BL; as well as in S. Mahadevan, *Mahatma Gandhi's Warning and Flashes in Harijan Tour* (Madras: Journalist Publishing House, 1936), passim.
45. BC, 11 November 1933.
46. CWMG, LVI, pp. 250–53.
47. BC, 24 November 1933.
48. Mahadevan, *Mahatma Gandhi's Warning and Flashes*, pp. 8–12.
49. Letter dated 17 November 1933 from the Chief Secretary, Central Provinces, to all Commissioners and Deputy Commissioners, in File No. 9 of 1933, Political and Military Records, Nagpur Division, VAN.
50. This account is based on letters and documents in File No. 800 (40) (17) of 1933, MSA.
51. Mira to Devadas Gandhi, 12 December 1933, Devadas Gandhi Papers, NMML.
52. See H, 5 January 1934.
53. CWMG, LVI, p. 345.
54. District Magistrate, Kistna, to Chief Secretary, Madras, 22 December 1933, in L/PJ/7/595, APAC/BL.
55. CWMG, LVI, pp. 460–61, 465, 470; CWMG, LVII, pp. 18–19.
56. Muriel Lester to C.F. Andrews, 16 February 1934, Mss Afr.s. 2307, Box 7, File 3, Rhodes House Library, Oxford.
57. Muriel Lester to Gandhi, c. April 1934, Personal Correspondence Files, M.K. Gandhi Papers, First and Second Instalments, NMML.
58. Mirza Ismail, *My Public Life* (London: George Allen and Unwin Ltd, 1954), pp. 27–30.
59. See CWMG, LVI, pp. 416–17; CWMG, LVII, pp. 35–36.
60. CWMG, LVII, pp. 45–47, 503–04.
61. See http://www.thehindu.com/opinion/op-ed/taking-a-comprehensive-view-of-quakes/article7216725.ece; article/724133/suggesting-religious-reasons-for-quakes-isnt-new-mahatma-gandhi-did-that-in-1934 (accessed 22 May 2015).

62. See Gandhi to Rajendra Prasad, c. 28 January 1934, *CWMG*, LVII, p. 61.

63. Letter dated c. 31 January 1934, *CWMG*, LVII, p. 74.

64. Mahadevan, *Mahatma Gandhi's Warning and Flashes in Harijan Tour*, pp. 135–40.

65. *CWMG*, LVII, p. 112.

66. *CWMG*, LVII, p. 160.

67. Collector of North Arcot, quoted in Chief Secretary, Madras, to Home Secretary, Delhi, 1 March 1934, in L/PJ/7/595, APAC/BL.

68. 'Draft Rules for the Disbursement of Gandhi's Harijan Purse Tour Fund', H, 2 March 1934.

69. 'Our Shame', H, 9 March 1934, *CWMG*, LVII, pp. 259–62.

70. *CWMG*, LVII, pp. 288–89, 358.

71. Agatha Harrison to C.F. Andrews, Patna, 7 April 1934, in Temp Mss 883/1/12, Agatha Harrison Papers, Friends House, Euston.

72. Chief Secretary, Assam, to Home Secretary, Delhi, letters of 21 April and 4 May 1934, in L/PJ/7/595, APAC/BL.

73. *CWMG*, LVII, pp. 338, 352, 363–64, 449–54.

74. *CWMG*, LVIII, pp. 27–29, 37–38; Minoo Masani, *Bliss Was It in That Dawn: A Personal Memoir upto Independence* (New Delhi: Arnold-Heinemann, 1977), pp. 56ff.

75. Gandhi to Premabehn Kantak, 10 September 1935, *CWMG*, XLI, p. 403.

76. *CWMG*, LVII, pp. 474–75.

77. *CWMG*, LVIII, p. 82.

78. Home Secretary, Bombay, to Home Secretary, Delhi, 17 July 1934, in L/PJ/7/595, APAC/BL.

79. 'Attempt on Mr. Gandhi's Life at Poona', *ToI*, 27 June 1934; 'Poona Bomb Outrage on Mahatma', *BC*, 26 June 1934.

80. 'Congratulation', *BC*, 26 June 1934.

81. *CWMG*, LVIII, pp. 108–09.

82. Mahadevan, *Mahatma Gandhi's Warning and Flashes in Harijan Tour*, Preface.

83. See Chief Secretary, United Provinces, to Home Secretary, GoI, 10 August 1934, in L/PJ/7/595, APAC/BL.

84. *CWMG*, LVIII, pp. 259–61, 266–68, 273–74, 277–78.

Chapter Twenty-Two: A Second Sabbatical

1. This account is based on copies of the original correspondence in E.S. Reddy Papers, NMML.

2.   See Birla, *Bapu, Volume I*, pp. 358–59.

3.   Eric Metaxas, *Bonhoeffer: Pastor, Martyr, Prophet, Spy* (Nashville, Texas: Thomas Nelson, 2010), pp. 46–47, 76, 115.

4.   Larry Rasmussen, 'Gandhis Einfluss auf Bonhoeffer', Xerox of undated article in the E.S. Reddy Papers, NMML.

5.   Letter excerpted in ibid.

6.   C.F. Andrews to Gandhi, 14 May 1934, Personal Correspondence Files, Gandhi Papers, NMML.

7.   Bonhoeffer to Niebuhr, 13 July 1934, copy in the E.S. Reddy Papers, NMML.

8.   Bonhoeffer to Gandhi, 17 October 1934, Personal Correspondence Files, Gandhi Papers, First and Second Instalments, NMML.

9.   Gandhi to Bonhoeffer, 1 November 1934, *CWMG*, LIX, p. 273.

10. Gandhi to Vallabhbhai Patel, c. 5 September 1934, *CWMG*, LVIII, pp. 403–05.

11. *CWMG*, LIX, pp. 3–9.

12. Lord Willingdon to Florence Brooks, 28 September 1934, in Mss Eur F 237/5, APAC/BL.

13. C. Rajagopalachari to Gandhi, 28 September 1934, in Subject File No. 3, Rajagopalachari Papers, Fourth Instalment, NMML.

14. H.S.L. Polak to V.S. Srinivasa Sastri, 31 October 1934, Sastri Papers, NMML.

15. *CWMG*, LIX, pp. 174–80, 220f.

16. *CWMG*, LIX, p. 261.

17. *CWMG*, LIX, pp. 348–49.

18. *CWMG*, LIX, pp. 355–56, 411–12, 449–53; *CWMG*, LX, pp. 130–31, 190–92.

19. Mira to Devadas Gandhi, 13 February 1935, Devadas Gandhi Papers, NMML.

20. *CWMG*, LXI, pp. 88–89.

21. Pamela Kanwar, *Imperial Simla: The Political Culture of the Raj* (second edition: New Delhi: Oxford University Press, 2003), pp. 238–39.

22. Rajkumari Amrit Kaur to Gandhi, letters of 2 and 8 September 1935, Personal Correspondence Files, Gandhi Papers, NMML.

23. *CWMG*, LXII, pp. 11, 37.

24. 'On Its Last Legs', H, 26 October 1935, *CWMG*, LXII, pp. 64–65.

25. 'Caste Has to Go', H, 16 November 1935, *CWMG*, LXII, pp. 120–21.

26. See *ToI*, 30 November 1935.

27. Letter from D.D. Pinglay, Manmad, published in *ToI*, 5 November 1935.

28. Gandhi to Harilal Gandhi, 19 September 1934, *CWMG*, LIX, pp. 27–28; Gandhi to Narandas Gandhi, 19 September 1934, *CWMG*, LIX, p. 29.

29. Gandhi to Harilal Gandhi, 3 October 1934, *CWMG*, LIX, pp. 110–12.

30. Gandhi to Harilal Gandhi, 17 October 1934, *CWMG*, LIX, pp. 187–88; Gandhi to Devadas Gandhi, 25 November 1934, *CWMG*, LIX, pp. 399–400.

31. Gandhi to Harilal Gandhi, 12 April 1935, *CWMG*, LX, pp. 410–11.

32. Gandhi to Narandas Gandhi, 5 May 1935, *CWMG*, LXI, p. 37.

33. Gandhi to Narandas Gandhi, 25 June 1935, *CWMG*, LXI, p. 199.

34. Gandhi to Narandas Gandhi, letters of 11 and 15 July 1935, *CWMG*, LXI, pp. 246, 257.

35. Gandhi to Manilal Gandhi, letters of 15 August 1935 and 11 October 1935, *CWMG*, LXI, p. 333; *CWMG*, LXII, p. 21.

36. For more details, see Keith, *A Constitutional History of India*, Chapters IX and X.

37. Mahadev Desai to Jawaharlal Nehru, 6 September 1935, *CWMG*, XLI, pp. 474–75.

38. Jawaharlal Nehru to Agatha Harrison, 25 September 1935 (copy), Personal Correspondence Files, Gandhi Papers, NMML.

39. *CWMG*, LXII, pp. 24–26.

40. Gandhi to Tagore, letters of 13 October 1935 and 27 March 1936, *CWMG*, LXII, pp. 34, 290.

41. Gandhi to Jamnalal Bajaj, 19 March 1936, *CWMG*, LXII, p. 272.

42. *CWMG*, LXII, pp. 331–32, 345, 350, 358, 379.

43. 'Weekly Letter', H, 9 May 1936.

44. M[ahadev] D[esai], 'A Story to Make Us Think', H, 9 May 1936.

45. As reported in *BC*, 4 May 1936.

46. Gandhi to Amrit Kaur, 11 May 1936, *CWMG*, LXII, p. 392.

47. *CWMG*, LXII, pp. 388–89, 463–65; H, issues of 30 May and 6 June 1936.

48. *CWMG*, LXII, pp. 389–90, 392, 441–42.

49. *CWMG*, LXIII, pp. 5–6.

50. R.K. Prabhu, editor, *Sati Kasturba: A Life-Sketch* (Bombay: Hind Kitabs, 1944), pp. 65–67.

51. Gandhi to Dev[a]das Gandhi, 12 November 1936, *CWMG*, LXIV, p. 23.

Chapter Twenty-Three: From Rebels to Rulers

1. Dharmjit Singh, *Lord Linlithgow in India, 1936–1943* (Jalandhar: ABS Publications, 2005).
2. B. Shiva Rao, 'Gandhiji: Some Anecdotes', *Illustrated Weekly of India*, 14 May 1961.
3. G.D. Birla, *In the Shadow of the Mahatma: A Personal Memoir* (Calcutta: Orient Longman, 1953), p. 207.
4. *CWMG*, LXIII, pp. 69, 71, 140–41.
5. Rambhau Mhaskar's Hindi pamphlet *Sevagram* (published by the Sevagram Ashram, no date) provides a charming, but also fact-filled, history of how the settlement was founded and nurtured.
6. Mirabehn (Madeleine Slade), *The Spirit's Pilgrimage* (London: Longmans, Green and Co. Ltd, 1960), p. 190.
7. B.R. Nanda, *In Gandhi's Footsteps: The Life and Times of Jamnalal Bajaj* (New Delhi: Oxford University Press, 1990), pp. 220–21.
8. See Nehru, *A Bunch of Old Letters*, pp. 182ff.
9. *CWMG*, LXIII, pp. 127–28, 164–65.
10. B.R. Ambedkar, *Annihilation of Caste*, first published in 1936, reprinted in *Dr. Babasaheb Ambedkar, Writings and Speeches, Volume 1* (Bombay: Government of Maharashtra, 1979), pp. 26–80.
11. *BC*, 1 June 1936.
12. *CWMG*, LXIII, pp. 31, 33–38, 42–45.
13. *CWMG*, LXIII, pp. 134–36, 153–54.
14. See *Dr. Babasaheb Ambedkar, Writings and Speeches, Volume 1*, pp. 86–96.
15. IAR, 1936, Volume 2, pp. 276–78.
16. *CWMG*, LXIII, pp. 174–75, 233–34.
17. Cf. reports in File No. 800 (40)(4) A-IV-B-II, Home (Special), MSA.
18. Report in *ToI*, 11 June 1936.
19. Report in *BC*, 8 August 1936.
20. C.F. Andrews to Amrit Kaur, Wardha, 8 November 1936, copy in SAAA.
21. *CWMG*, LXIV, pp. 170–72.
22. Report in *Bombay Sentinel*, 22 December 1936.
23. *CWMG*, LXIV, p. 217.
24. *CWMG*, LXIV, pp. 26–27, 47–48.
25. *CWMG*, LXIV, p. 237.
26. M[ahadev] D[esai], 'Weekly Letter', H, 13 February 1937.
27. *CWMG*, LXIV, pp. 233–37, 275–78, 297.

28. 'Need for Tolerance', H, 13 March 1937, CWMG, LXIV, pp. 331–33.
29. CWMG, LXIV, pp. 399–401.
30. See Bombay Sentinel, 8 February 1937.
31. C. Rajagopalachari to Devadas Gandhi, 21 January 1937, Devadas Gandhi Papers, NMML.
32. See IAR, 1937, Volume 1, pp. 28ff.
33. Quoted in John Glendevon, The Viceroy at Bay: Lord Linlithgow in India, 1936–1943 (London: Collins, 1971), p. 49.
34. CWMG, LXV, pp. 3–4, 456–57; IAR, 1937, Volume 1, pp. 190–97.
35. CWMG, LXV, pp. 37–38, 261–62.
36. CWMG, LXV, pp. 174–75.
37. 'Congress Ministries', H, 17 July 1937, CWMG, LXV, pp. 406–08.
38. Choudhry Khaliquzzaman, Pathway to Pakistan (Lahore: Longmans, Green and Co., 1961), pp. 153–57.
39. See CWMG, LXV, p. 472.
40. Rani Dhavan Shankardass, Vallabhbhai Patel: Power and Organization in Indian Politics (Hyderabad: Orient Longman, 1988), p. 153. Cf. also Shankerprasad S. Nanavaty, Khurshed Nariman (Bombay: Bombay Chronicle Press, 1959).
41. Gandhi to Nehru, 22 July 1937, CWMG, LXV.
42. Polak to T.R. Venkatarama Sastri, 30 April 1937, in H.S.L. Polak correspondence, T.R. Venkatarama Sastri Papers, Fourth instalment, NMML.
43. G.D. Birla to Mahadev Desai, 17 July 1937; Mahadev Desai to G.D. Birla, 1 August 1937, in Gandhi Papers, First and Second Instalment, NMML.
44. See File 54C of 1938, General Administration Department, Central Provinces, in VAN.

Chapter Twenty-Four: The World Within, and Without

1. CWMG, LXVI, pp. 58–60, 78–79.
2. See P.N. Chopra, editor, Towards Freedom, 1937–1947, Volume 1, Experiment with Provincial Autonomy, 1 January–December 1937 (New Delhi: Indian Council of Historical Research, 1985), pp. 821–88.
3. Matlubul Hasan Saiyid, Mohammad Ali Jinnah: A Political Study (Lahore: Shaikh Muhamad Ashraf, 1945), p. 571.
4. CWMG, LXVI, pp. 468–69, 257, 296–97.
5. See Sabyasachi Bhattacharya, Vande Mataram: The Biography of a Song (New Delhi: Penguin Books, 2003).
6. Ibid., pp. 11–14.

7. Subhas Chandra Bose to Gandhi, 20 October 1937; Satis Chandra Dasgupta to Gandhi, 21 October 1937, both in Subject File No. 17, Gandhi Papers, First and Second Instalments, NMML.

8. *CWMG*, LXVI, pp. 296–97.

9. See Syed Sharifuddin Pirzada, editor, *Quaid-e-Azam Jinnah's Correspondence*, third revised and enlarged edition (Karachi: East and West Publishing Company, 1977), pp. 88–95.

10. Iqbal's letters are reproduced in Pirzada, editor, *Quaid-e-Azam Jinnah's Correspondence*, pp. 138–42. Cf. also Bimal Prasad, 'Congress versus the Muslim League', in Richard Sisson and Stanley Wolpert, *Congress and Indian Nationalism: The Pre-Independence Phase* (Delhi: Oxford University Press, 1988); V.N. Datta, 'Iqbal, Jinnah and India's Partition', *Economic and Political Weekly*, 14 December 2002.

11. Typed excerpt from news report in *Roznama-e-Khilafat*, 8 June 1938, in Box 4, *Harijan/Young India* Files Collection, SAAA.

12. See Gandhi to Jawaharlal Nehru, 1 October 1937; Note to Vallabhbhai Patel, 1 November 1937, *CWMG*, LXVI, pp. 183, 285.

13. M[ahadev] D[esai], 'Haripura Notes', H, 18 March 1938.

14. *CWMG*, LXVI, pp. 413–14.

15. Untitled typescript by an unnamed visitor to Gandhi, in Box 3, *Harijan/Young India* Files Collection, SAAA.

16. This account is based on conversations with Narayan Desai in Sevagram, 2006, and in Ahmedabad, 2009.

17. D.G. Tendulkar, *Mahatma: Life of Mohandas Karamchand Gandhi* (reprint New Delhi: Publications Division, 1990), volume 4, p. 238.

18. *CWMG*, LXVI, pp. 452–53, 455–56.

19. The printed version of Mahadev Desai's expiation appeared under the title 'A Tragedy', in *Harijan*, 9 April 1938, and is reprinted in *CWMG*, LXVII, pp. 445–47. The original manuscript, with Gandhi's handwritten excisions, is in Box 3, *Harijan/Young India* Files Collection, SAAA.

20. 'Notes of a conversation with Mr M.K. Gandhi, 7 April 1938', by the Governor of Bengal, R/3/2/60, APAC/BL.

21. 'Note of Interview between His Excellency the Viceroy and Mr. M.K. Gandhi, at New Delhi at 11.30 a.m., on Friday, 15th April, 1938', in L/PO/6/96, APAC/BL.

22. Copies of the letters exchanged between Jinnah and Nehru are in File No. 976 of 1939, Home (Special), MSA. See also IAR, Volume 2, pp. 362–78; and Pirzada, editor, *Quaid-e-Azam Jinnah's Correspondence*, pp. 246–69.

23. *CWMG*, LXVII, pp. 30, 36–37.

24. Gandhi to Amritlal T. Nanavati, 2 May 1938; to Mira, 3 May 1938; to Amrit Kaur, 7 May 1938; *CWMG*, LXVII, pp. 58, 60–61, 69.

25. 'How Non-Violence Works', H, 23 July 1938, *CWMG*, LXVII, pp. 195–96.

26. Gandhi to Balwantsinha, 11 June 1938; to Amrit Kaur, c. 11 June 1938; *CWMG*, LXVII, pp. 116–18.

27. C. Rajagopalachari to Devadas Gandhi, 20 May 1938, Devadas Gandhi Papers, NMML.

28. *CWMG*, LXVII, p. 50.

29. Gandhi to Rajagopalachari, 21 May 1938; to Amrit Kaur, 22 May 1938, *CWMG*, LXVII, pp. 90, 92.

30. *CWMG*, LXVII, pp. 62–68, 75–76.

31. See *Report of the Inquiry Committee Appointed by the Council of the All-India Muslim League to Inquire into Muslim Grievances in Congress Provinces* (Lucknow: Pioneer Press, 1938).

32. See, among other works, Salil Misra, *A Narrative of Communal Politics: Uttar Pradesh, 1937–39* (New Delhi: Sage Publishers, 2001); William Gould, *Hindu Nationalism and the Language of Politics in Late Colonial India* (Cambridge: Cambridge University Press, 2005); Venkat Dhulipala, *Creating a New Medina: State Power, Islam and the Quest for Pakistan in Late Colonial North India* (Cambridge: Cambridge University Press, 2014).

33. Gandhi to D.B. Kalelkar, 18 October 1938, *CWMG*, LXVIII, p. 22.

34. D.G. Tendulkar, *Abdul Ghaffar Khan: Faith Is a Battle* (Bombay: Popular Prakashan, 1967), pp. 253–54. Cf. also Pyarelal, *A Pilgrimage for Peace: Gandhi and Frontier Gandhi among N.W.F. Pathans* (Ahmedabad: Navajivan, 1950).

35. Jawaharlal Nehru to Gandhi, letters of 30 August, 16 September and 10 October 1938, Personal Correspondence Files, Gandhi Papers, First and Second Instalments, NMML.

36. 'If I Were a Czech', H, 6 October 1938, *CWMG*, LXVII, pp. 404–06.

37. 'What Are the Basic Assumptions?', H, 22 October 1938, *CWMG*, LXVII, pp. 435–37.

38. *CWMG*, LXVII, pp. 28, 43, 47.

39. *CWMG*, LXVIII, pp. 244–48.

40. Letter, c. mid-January 1939, signed by eleven young women of Calcutta, all Hindus going by their names, in Box 5, *Harijan/Young India* Files Collection, SAAA.

41. 'The Modern Girl', *CWMG*, LXVIII, pp. 348–50.

42. 'The Jews', H, 20 November 1938, *CWMG*, LXVIII, pp. 137-39.

43. *CWMG*, LXVIII, pp. 189-90.

44. Martin Buber, 'Gandhi, Politics and Us', 1930, reprinted in Buber, *Pointing the Way: Collected Essays* (New York: Harper and Brothers, 1957).

45. Buber was here reflecting the widespread prejudice of cultures based on settled agriculture against cultures based on pastoralism and shifting cultivation. The historical roots and sociological implications of this prejudice have been brilliantly explored by James C. Scott. See his works, *Seeing Like a State* and *The Art of Not Being Governed*, published by Yale University Press in 1998 and 2009 respectively.

46. *Two Letters to Gandhi from Martin Buber and J.L. Magnes* (Jerusalem: Bond, 1939). Buber's letter is also reprinted in Nahum N. Glatzer, editor, *The Letters of Martin Buber: A Life of Dialogue* (New York: Schocken Books, 1991).

47. The Buber–Magnes pamphlet was printed in Jerusalem in April 1939, and presumably posted immediately to Segaon. However, Gandhi was on the road all of April and May; he was back in Segaon between 8 and 20 June, and then out again till end-July.

48. Originally published in his magazine *Jewish Frontier*, this essay is reprinted in Hayim Greenberg, *The Inner Eye: Selected Essays* (New York: Jewish Frontier Association, Inc. 1953), pp. 230-38.

49. *CWMG*, LXIX, pp. 289-90.

50. Interestingly, in January 1944, when Bonhoeffer was in jail, he was reminded once more of Gandhi, when his fiancée Maria wrote to him: 'Ina [her sister] came in from school and said she had learnt about Gandhi in geography class, that he always did hunger strike in prison and asked whether you cannot do the same. I am not in agreement with this suggestion.' Letter dated 19 January 1944, in *Brautbriefe Zelle 92: Dietrich Bonhoeffer Maria von Wedemeyer, 1943–1945* (Munich: C.H. Beck, 1994), p. 123.

Chapter Twenty-Five: (Re)capturing the Congress

1. 'The States and Responsibility', H, 17 September 1938, *CWMG*, LXVII, p. 350.

2. 'States and their People', H, 3 December 1938, *CWMG*, LXVIII, pp. 151-53.

3. '"Kicks and Kisses"', H, 4 February 1939, *CWMG*, LXVIII, pp. 354-56.

4. 'The Incredible Mr. Gandhi', *Reader's Digest*, December 1938.

5.   See Gandhi to Jawaharlal Nehru, 21 December 1938, *CWMG*, LXVIII, p. 227.

6.   See '*Kangress ké Kharabiyan aur Unké Dur Karné ké Upay*' (The Defects in the Congress and the Means to Remove Them), Hindi pamphlet (undated, but probably published in November or December 1938) in Subject File No. 63, Gandhi Papers, First and Second Instalments, NMML.

7.   Rabindranath Tagore to Gandhi, 22 November 1938, Gandhi Papers, First and Second Instalments, NMML.

8.   James C. Wilson, 'Bose vs. Gandhi: Tripuri and After', in Jagdish P. Sharma, editor, *Individuals and Ideals in Modern India: Nine Interpretative Studies* (Calcutta: Firma KLM Private Limited, 1982), pp. 148–196 (the Chaudhuri quote is on p. 164).

9.   *CWMG*, LXVIII, pp. 359–60, 487–88; Rudrangshu Mukherjee, *Nehru and Bose: Parallel Lives* (New Delhi: Viking, 2014), Chapter 6.

10. Leonard A. Gordon, *Brothers against the Raj: A Biography of Sarat and Subhas Chandra Bose* (New Delhi: Viking, 1989), p. 375.

11. These paragraphs are based on John R. Wood, 'Rajkot: Indian Nationalism in the Princely Context: the Rajkot Satyagraha of 1938–9', in Robin Jeffery, editor, *People, Princes, and Paramount Power: Society and Politics in the Indian Princely States* (Delhi: Oxford University Press, 1980). Cf. also the correspondence printed in H, 4 February 1939.

12. See IOR, L/P&S/13/1500, APAC/BL.

13. The press clippings quoted in the preceding paragraph are contained in Mss Eur F 138/22, APAC/BL.

14. 'Note on Discussion on General Topics between H.E. the Viceroy and Mr. Gandhi on 15th March 1939', in Mss Eur F 138/22, APAC/BL.

15. *CWMG*, LXIX, pp. 80, 90, 96–97, 448–54.

16. Rajmohan Gandhi, *Patel: A Life* (Ahmedabad: Navajivan Publishing House, 1991), pp. 236–38, 264, 277–81.

17. Bose to Gandhi, letters of 29 and 31 March 1939, Gandhi to Bose, 2 April 1939, *CWMG*, LXIX, pp. 448–54, 96–97.

18. Subhas Chandra Bose, *The Indian Struggle*, as edited by Sisir K. Bose and Sugata Bose (first published in 1935; new edition Delhi: Oxford University Press, 1997), pp. 126, 326–33, etc.

19. Gordon, *Brothers against the Raj*, pp. 287–88.

20. *The Indian Struggle*, p. 351.

21. Letter to Gandhi, c. 20 March 1939, signed by members of the Bengal Provincial Youth Association, in Subject File No. 68, Gandhi Papers, First and Second Instalments, NMML.

22. *CWMG*, LXIX, p. 99.
23. Bose to Gandhi, 6 April 1939; Gandhi to Bose, 10 April 1939, *CWMG*, LXIX, pp. 455–60, 125–27.
24. Mahadev Desai to V.S. Srinivasa Sastri, 15 April 1939, Srinivasa Sastri Papers, Last Instalment, NMML.
25. Clipping from the *National Call*, 20 April 1938, in L/P&S/13/1500, APAC/BL.
26. *MG*, 9 May 1939.
27. News report in *Hindustan Times*, 5 May 1939.
28. Report in the *National Call*, 17 April 1939, in IOR, L/P&S/13/1500, APAC/BL.
29. See Sisir Kumar Bose and Sugata Bose, editor, *Netaji Collected Works, Volume 9: Congress President, Speeches, Articles and Letters, January 1938–May 1939* (Delhi: Permanent Black, 2004), pp. 107–09.
30. Sugata Bose, *His Majesty's Opponent: Subhas Chandra Bose and India's Struggle against Empire* (Cambridge, Massachusetts: Harvard University Press, 2011), pp. 163–64.
31. *CWMG*, LXIX, pp. 460–62, 269–71.

Chapter Twenty-Six: One Nation, or Two?

1. *CWMG*, LXX, pp. 20–21.
2. *CWMG*, LXX, pp. 160–61.
3. Gilbert Laithwaite, 'Gandhi', unpublished typescript, c. 1967–68, in Mss Eur F 138/172.
4. See Mushirul Hasan, editor, *Towards Freedom: Documents on the Movement for Independence in India, 1939, Part I* (New Delhi: Indian Council of Historical Research, 2008), pp. 293–94.
5. Jawaharlal Nehru, *Glimpses of World History* (first published in 1934: reprint London: Lindsay Drummond, 1949), pp. 813–20, 911–22.
6. See Richard Lamb, *Mussolini and the British* (London: John Murray, 1997), p. 3 and back flap.
7. See Ian Kershaw, *Making Friends with Hitler: Lord Londonderry and Britain's Road to War* (London: Allen Lane, 2003), whose early chapters demonstrate how, apart from the leading politicians of all parties, many British newspapers (not least *The Times*) were extremely indulgent towards Hitler until as late as 1938.
8. *CWMG*, LXX, pp. 409–13, 175–77.
9. Birla, *In the Shadow of the Mahatma*, pp. 250, 256.

10. See Sarvepalli Gopal, *Radhakrishnan: A Biography* (Delhi: Oxford University Press, 1989), pp. 156–57.

11. These paragraphs are based on the essays in S. Radhakrishnan, editor, *Mahatma Gandhi: Essays and Reflections on His Life and Work* (London: George Allen and Unwin, 1939).

12. See, for more details, Srinath Raghavan, *India's War: World War II and the Making of Modern South Asia* (New York: Basic Books, 2016), Chapter 4.

13. These paragraphs are based on CWMG, LXX, pp. 414–20, 267–68, 279–80, 290, 327, 341–42.

14. C. Rajagopalachari to Mahadev Desai, 28 October 1939, Personal Correspondence Files, Gandhi Papers, First and Second Instalments, NMML.

15. 'To Correspondents and Message-Seekers', H, 17 December 1939, *CWMG*, LXXI, p. 43.

16. President, Muslim League, Bezwada, to M.K. Gandhi, 9 May 1939; Representation, c. October 1939, addressed to M.K. Gandhi by five Muslim members of the Municipal Council, Bezwada, both in Subject File No. 15, Gandhi Papers, First and Second Instalments, NMML.

17. S.M. Yusuf to Gandhi, 29 July 1940, in Box 21, *Harijan/Young India* Files Collection, SAAA.

18. Sirajuddin Piracha to Gandhi, Lahore, 22 December 1938; Abdul Rahman Khan to Gandhi, 8 December 1939, both in Subject File No. 15, Gandhi Papers, First and Second Instalments, NMML.

19. Hussain Imam to Gandhi, Gaya, 9 October 1939, in Subject File No. 21, Gandhi Papers, First and Second Instalments, NMML.

20. Gandhi to Hossain Imam, 14 October 1939 (not in *CWMG*), in ibid.

21. Zakir Husain to Gandhi, 22 November 1939; Gandhi to Zakir Husain, 26 November 1939 (not in *CWMG*), both in ibid.

22. *Star of India*, 13 October 1939.

23. Report in *Star of India*, 11 October 1939.

24. Viceroy to Secretary of State for India (Marquess of Zetland), 21 December 1939, copy in Mss Eur F 138/22, APAC/BL.

25. See reports in TS, 23 December 1939.

26. Sastri to H.S.L. Polak, 13 March 1940., V.S. Srinivasa Sastri Papers, First and Second Instalments, NMML.

27. 'A Welcome Move', H, 20 January 1940; letter to Jinnah, 16 January 1940, *CWMG*, LXXI, pp. 109–10, 117.

28. Jinnah to Gandhi, 21 January 1940, in K.N. Panikkar, editor, *Towards Freedom: Documents on the Independence of India, 1940, Part I* (New Delhi: Oxford University Press, 2009), pp. 543–44.

29. *CWMG*, LXXI, p. 133.

30. *CWMG*, LXXI, pp. 186–91.

31. *CWMG*, LXXI, pp. 334, 346–47.

32. *CWMG*, LXXI, p. 337.

33. IAR, 1940, Volume 1, pp. 228, 290–300.

34. See Khalid B. Sayeed, *Pakistan: The Formative Phase, 1857–1948* (second edition: Lahore: Oxford University Press, 1969), Chapter 6, 'The Muslim League: Its Role and Organisation'.

35. Mian Mohammad Shafi, 'The Historic League Session', in Jamil-ud-din Ahmad, editor, *Quaid-i-Azam as Seen by His Contemporaries* (Lahore: Publishers United Ltd, 1976), p. 130.

36. Jinnah's speech is available in full at http://www.columbia.edu/itc/ mealac/pritchett/00islamlinks/txt_jinnah_lahore_1940.html. But see also IAR, 1940, Volume 2, pp. 308–11.

37. IAR, 1940, Volume 2, pp. 311–12.

38. Indeed, a year and a half later, Haq had broken with Jinnah and the Muslim League.

39. Saiyid, *Mohammad Ali Jinnah*, pp. 693–94.

40. Cf. also Muhammad Aslam Malik, *The Making of the Pakistan Resolution* (Karachi: Oxford University Press, 2001).

41. Note drafted by Penderel Moon, c. April 1940, in Mss Eur F 230/39, APAC/BL.

42. 'A Baffling Situation', H, 6 April 1940, *CWMG*, LXXI, pp. 387–90.

43. M[ahadev] D[esai], 'The Hand of the Devil?', H, 4 May 1941.

44. *CWMG*, LXXII, pp. 394–409.

45. Untitled memoir by R.O. Hicks, in Hicks Papers, Centre for South Asian Studies, Cambridge.

46. Note entitled 'The Congress position on 13/5/40', signed 'L.', i.e. Linlithgow, in Mss Eur F 138/23, APAC/BL.

Chapter Twenty-Seven: Pilgrimages to Gandhi

1. Lawrence Lader, *The Margaret Sanger Story: And the Fight for Birth Control* (New York: Doubleday, 1955), pp. 287–90.

2. Interview with a social worker of Cochin named Mrs C. Kuttan Nair in Delhi, *CWMG*, LX, pp. 67–69.

3. This account of the Gandhi–Sanger conversations is based on *CWMG*, LXII, pp. 156–60; M[ahadev] D[esai], 'Mrs Sanger and Birth Control', H, 25 January 1936; 'Gandhi and Mrs Sanger Debate Birth Control', *Asia*, November 1936.

4. 'Gandhi and Mrs Sanger Debate Birth Control', p. 700.

5. Sanger to Gandhi, 20 October 1936, in the Margaret Sanger Papers, on microfilm, Doe Library, University of California, Berkeley.

6. Lader, *The Margaret Sanger Story*, p. 290.

7. 'Gandhi and Mrs Sanger Debate Birth Control', p. 701.

8. *CWMG*, LXII, pp. 169–72.

9. Kapur, *Raising Up a Prophet*, Chapter 3, 'We Need a Gandhi'.

10. *CWMG*, LXII, pp. 198–200.

11. *With Head and Heart: The Autobiography of Howard Thurman* (San Diego: Harcourt Brace & Company, 1979), pp. 130–34.

12. *CWMG*, LXIV, pp. 71, 203–04, 229.

13. See Benjamin E. Mays, 'The Color Line Around the World', *Journal of Negro Education*, Volume 6, Number 2, 1937, p. 141 and passim.

14. These paragraphs are based on a long interview I conducted with Herbert Fischer in Berlin in April 1995.

15. Herbert Fischer, *Mahatma Gandhi, Personlich Erlebt* (Mahatma Gandhi, as Seen in Person) (Berlin: Gandhi Informations Zentrum, 1994), passim.

16. Gandhi to Amrit Kaur, 29 May 1937, *CWMG*, LXV, pp. 55–56.

17. Cf. Mahadev Desai's weekly letters in H issues of 29 May 1937, 5 and 12 June 1937.

18. *CWMG*, LXV, pp. 360–62.

19. Bhisham Sahni, *Balraj My Brother* (New Delhi: National Book Trust, 1981), p. 68.

20. *CWMG*, LXVIII, pp. 187–88.

21. 'Discussion with Economists', H, 28 January 1939, *CWMG*, LXVIII, pp. 258–59.

22. 'Interview to S.S. Tema', H, 18 February 1939, *CWMG*, LXVIII, pp. 272–74.

23. See *GBI*, pp. 396, 536, etc.

Chapter Twenty-Eight: Somewhere between Conflict and Cooperation

1. 'Hindu–Muslim', H, 8 June 1940, *CWMG*, LXXII, pp. 131–34.

2. Report in *Bombay Sentinel*, 13 July 1940.

3. Srinivasa Sastri to Gandhi, 16 July 1940, V.S. Srinivasa Sastri Papers, First and Second Instalments, NMML.

4. *CWMG*, LXXII, pp. 100–01, 187–89, 212–14.

5. 'To Every Briton', H, 6 July 1940, *CWMG*, LXXII, pp. 229–31.

6. *CWMG*, LXXII, p. 232.

7. See Subject Files 287 and 288, Gandhi Papers, First and Second Instalments, NMML.

8. These paragraphs are based on *CWMG*, LXXII, pp. 467, 254–56, 472–75, 370–71, 384.

9. Gandhi to Amrit Kaur, 15 September 1940, *CWMG*, LXXIII, p. 3.

10. *CWMG*, LXXIII, pp. 450–51, 70–71, 79.

11. 'Civil Disobedience', H, 20 October 1940, *CWMG*, LXXIII, pp. 102–07, 137–38.

12. Mahadev Desai to Devadas Gandhi, 6 November 1940, Subject File 289, Gandhi Papers, First and Second Instalments, NMML.

13. As quoted in File No. 6 of 1940–41, Political and Military, VAN.

14. *CWMG*, LXXIII, pp. 87, 124–25, 155–59, 186.

15. See R/3/5/41, APAC/BL.

16. Deputy Commissioner, Wardha, to Commissioner, Nagpur, 26 December 1940; Deputy Commissioner, Nagpur, to Commissioner, Nagpur, 30 December 1940, both in File No. 18 of 1941, Political and Military, VAN.

17. Desai, quoted in a letter to the editor by Horace G. Alexander, *MG*, 13 February 1941.

18. Notes of talks with Mahadev Desai on 13 and 14 November 1940 made by Gilbert Laithwaite, Private Secretary to Viceroy, in L/PJ/7/4171, APAC/BL.

19. Mahadev Desai to Gilbert Laithwaite, letters of 3 and 10 December 1940, in L/PJ/7/4171, APAC/BL.

20. C.M. Trivedi, Secretary, Political and Military Department, Government of the Central Provinces and Berar, to E.S. Hyde, Deputy Commissioner, Mandla, 25 October 1940; Hyde to Trivedi, 4 November 1940, Box VIII, E.S. Hyde Papers, Centre for South Asian Studies, Cambridge.

21. Polak to T.R. Venkatarama Sastri, 31 October 1940, in HSL Polak correspondence, T.R. Venkatarama Sastri Papers, Fourth Instalment, NMML.

22. See *CWMG*, LXXIII, pp. 95–96.

23. News clipping of Sikandar Hyat Khan's speech, undated; Amrit Kaur to Sikandar Hyat Khan, undated; Sikandar Hyat to Amrit Kaur, 12 November 1940, all in Subject File No. 286, Gandhi Papers, First

and Second Instalments, NMML; Gandhi to Khan, 17 November 1940 (not in *CWMG*), Subject File No. 286, Gandhi Papers, First and Second Instalments, NMML.

24. Sahibzada Abdul Wadud Sarhadi (President of Jamiat-ul-Ulma-e-Sarhad) to Gandhi, 6 December 1940; Gandhi to Sarhadi, 13 December 1940 (not in *CWMG*), both in Subject File No. 18, Gandhi Papers, First and Second Instalments, NMML.

25. *CWMG*, LXXIII, pp. 253–54.

26. Note by R. Tottenham, in the Home Department, 25 December 1940; Notes by Chief Press Adviser, 31 December 1940 and 16 January 1941, all in R/3/1/342, APAC/BL.

27. Note by G.J.B. Janvrin, Deputy Commissioner of Police, 1 February 1940, in R/3/2/21, APAC/BL.

28. *CWMG*, LXXIV, pp. 26–27.

29. *CWMG*, LXXIV, p. 404.

30. Cf. 'Two Parties: Br. Savarkar's Reply to Gandhiji', in Subject File No. 17, Gandhi Papers, First and Second Instalments, NMML.

31. Jayaprakash Narayan to Gandhi, 22 June 1941, Personal Correspondence Files, Gandhi Papers, First and Second Instalments, NMML. Cf. also Ram Manohar Lohia, '"Immediate Satyagraha"', H, 1 June 1940.

32. Shwaib Qureshi to Gandhi, 15 July 1941 (emphasis in the original); Gandhi to Qureshi, 19 July 1941 (not in *CWMG*), Subject File No. 21, Gandhi Papers, First and Second Instalments, NMML.

33. *CWMG*, LXXIV, p. 218.

34. Gandhi to Agatha Harrison, 22 October 1941, *CWMG*, LXXVI, pp. 37–38.

Chapter Twenty-Nine: Towards 'Quit India'

1. *CWMG*, LXXV, p. 180.

2. *CWMG*, LXXV, pp. 450–52, 197–98, 298.

3. *CWMG*, LXXV, pp. 241–45.

4. M[ahadev] D[esai], 'Jamnalalji', H, 22 February 1942.

5. *CWMG*, LXXV, pp. 306, 312–13, 315–16, 342–49, 454–55.

6. *CWMG*, LXXV, pp. 333–34, 359–60; M[ahadev] D[esai], 'A Historic Meeting', H, 1 March 1942.

7. Quoted in Rana Mitter, *China's War with Japan, 1937–1945: The Struggle for Survival* (London, Allen Lane, 2013), p. 248.

8. *CWMG*, LXXV, pp. 354–55.

9. Jawaharlal Nehru to Jagannath, 6 March 1942 (copy); C. Rajagopalachari to Jagannath, 17 March 1942 (copy) in Subject File No. 293, Gandhi Papers, First and Second Instalments, NMML.

10. See John Barnes and David Nicholson, editors, *The Empire at Bay: The Leo Amery Diaries, 1939–1945* (London: Hutchinson, 1988), p. 678.

11. Quoted in Peter Clarke, *The Cripps Version: The Life of Sir Stafford Cripps* (London: Allen Lane, 2002), pp. 278–79.

12. See *Orwell: The Observer Years* (London: Atlantic Books, 2003), p. 3.

13. CWMG, LXXV, pp. 356–58.

14. CWMG, LXXV, pp. 458–59.

15. Cripps to Azad, 7 April 1942; Azad to Cripps, 10 April 1942, in Mss Eur F 138/30, APAC/BL.

16. Memorandum by T.B. Sapru and M.R. Jayakar, 5 April 1942, in ToP, Volume 1, p. 643f.

17. As documented most recently in Raghavan, *India's War.*

18. IAR, 1942, Volume I, pp. 238–39.

19. See Warren F. Kimball, '"A Victorian Tory": Churchill, the Americans, and Self-Determination' in William Roger Louis, editor, *More Adventures with Britannia: Personalities, Politics and Culture in India* (Austin: University of Texas Press, 1998), pp. 225–26.

20. H.N. Brailsford, 'What Happened at Delhi', *New Statesman and Nation*, 16 May 1942.

21. 'Foreign Soldiers in India', H, 26 April 1942, CWMG, LXXVI, pp. 49–50.

22. Minutes of AICC meeting, held at Allahabad, 27 April to 1 May 1942, Subject File No. 298, Gandhi Papers, First and Second Instalments, NMML.

23. C. Rajagopalachari to Gandhi, 6 June 1942, Subject File 349, Gandhi Papers, First and Second Instalments, NMML.

24. 'To Every Briton', H, 17 May 1942 (written on 11 May), CWMG, LXXVI, pp. 98–100.

25. CWMG, LXXVI, pp. 105–06.

26. See Yasmin Khan, *The Raj at War: A People's History of India's Second World War* (London: The Bodley Head, 2015); Indivar Kamtekar, 'The Shiver of 1942', *Studies in History*, Volume 18, Number 1, 2002.

27. C. Rajagopalachari to Gandhi, 2 July 1942, Personal Correspondence Files, Gandhi Papers, First and Second Instalments, NMML.

28. CWMG, LXXVI, pp. 155, 159, 163.

29. As reported in Birla, *In the Shadow of the Mahatma*, pp. 255–56.

30. Louis Fischer, *A Week with Gandhi* (New York: Duell, Sloan and Pearce, 1942), pp. 12, 17–18, 32–33, 39, 45–46, 68–69, 116–18.

31. Gandhi to Chiang Kai-Shek, 14 June 1942, *CWMG*, LXXVI, pp. 223–26.

32. *CWMG*, LXXVI, pp. 236, 241.

33. Letter dated 10 July 1942 from a member of the Friends Ambulance Unit, Calcutta, to Paul D. Stuege, Friends House, London, copy in IOR/R/3/1/293, APAC/BL.

34. This section is based on 'Diary of Mr. L. Brander's Indian Tour, May–August 1942', in the Brander Papers, Centre for South Asian Studies, Cambridge. Cf. also John Evelyn Wrench, *Immortal Years (1937–1944): A View from Five Continents* (London: Hutchinson and Co., 1944), Part II, where the author, a long-time editor of the *Spectator*, narrates his conversations with Ambedkar, Jinnah, Savarkar, Gandhi and Nehru in 1942.

35. Waheed Ahmad, editor, *Quaid-i-Azam Mohammad Ali Jinnah: The Nation's Voice, Volume II: Annotated Speeches and Statements, April 1940–April 1942* (Karachi: Quaid-i-Azam Academy, 1996) pp. 85–87, 96, 212, 386–87, 446, 132, etc.

36. Gandhi to Franklin D. Roosevelt, 1 July 1942, *CWMG*, LXXVI, pp. 264–65.

37. *CWMG*, LXXVI, pp. 451–53.

38. *CWMG*, LXXVI, pp. 298ff; also Subject File No. 295, Gandhi Papers, First and Second Instalments, NMML.

39. C. Rajagopalachari to Gandhi, 18 July 1942, in Subject File No. 72, Gandhi Papers, First and Second Instalments, NMML.

40. Umadevi (pseudonym) to Gandhi, 18 July 1942, Subject File No. 293, Gandhi Papers, First and Second Instalments, NMML.

41. 'Proceedings of a meeting held in the Home Department on the 25th July, 1942, to discuss the mechanics of the proposed action against the Congress', in IOR/R/3/1/293, APAC/BL.

42. Viceroy to the Secretary of State for India, 19 July 1942, in IOR, R/3/1/297, APAC/BL.

43. General Hartley, acting C-in-C, Indian Army, 22 July 1942, to R. Tottenham, Home Department, in ibid.

44. Governor of Nyasaland to Viceroy, 9 August 1942, in ibid.

45. Bihar Governor to Viceroy, 26 July 1942; Bombay Governor to Viceroy, 28 July, both in ibid.

46. Viceroy to the Secretary of State for India, 1 August 1942, in ibid.

47. 'To Every Japanese', statement written on 18 July 1942, published in H, 26 July 1942, *CWMG*, LXXVI, pp. 309–12.

48. 'For Muslim Friends', H, 26 July 1942, *CWMG*, LXXVI, pp. 315–16.

49. As reported in *BC*, 1 August 1942.

50. As reported in *BC*, 23 July 1942.

51. See ToP, Volume II, p. 455 fn., etc; also *CWMG*, LXXVII, pp. 330–31.

52. 'To American Friends', H, 9 August 1942.

53. Extract of letter from Mahadev Desai to Amrit Kaur, 23 July 1942, in IOR/R/3/1/293, APAC/BL.

54. Amrit Kaur to Mahadev Desai, Simla, 31 July 1942, Subject File No. 299, Gandhi Papers, First and Second Instalments, NMML (emphases in the original).

55. Narayan Desai, *The Fire and the Rose* (Ahmedabad: Navajivan Publishing House, 1995), pp. 684–88.

56. Reports in *BC*, 28 and 30 July 1942.

57. Report in *BC*, 3 August 1942.

58. Editorial entitled, 'Why Not Now?', *BC*, 3 August 1942.

59. *BC*, 4 August 1942.

60. Reports in *BC*, 5 and 6 August 1942.

61. *CWMG*, LXXVI, p. 375.

62. *BC*, 8 August 1942.

63. *CWMG*, LXXVI, pp. 377–81, 384–91.

64. *CWMG*, LXXVI, pp. 458–61.

65. *BC*, 8 August 1942.

66. As recollected in Sushila Nayar, *Mahatma Gandhi's Last Imprisonment: The Inside Story* (New Delhi: Har-Anand Publications, 1996), pp. 32–33.

67. Nayar, *Mahatma Gandhi's Last Imprisonment*, pp. 33–34.

68. 'Mahatmaji's Arrest', H, 16 August 1942.

69. Reports in *BC*, 10 August 1942; File No. 1110(3) of 1942, Home (Special), MSA.

70. *CWMG*, LXXVI, pp. 463–64.

71. See Lord Moran, *Churchill: The Struggle for Survival, 1940–1965* (Boston: Houghton Mifflin, 1966), p. 57.

Chapter Thirty: A Bereavement and a Fast

1. See File Nos 111085, 1110(85)-D, 1110(85)-F and 1110(85)-H of 1942–43, Home (Special), MSA.

2. These details on the Aga Khan Palace draw from the notes and letters in IOR/R/3/1/290, APAC/BL.

3. Gandhi to Lord Linlithgow, 14 August 1942, *CWMG*, LXXVI, pp. 410–11.

4. These paragraphs are based on remembrances by Sushila Nayar and Sarojini Naidu in H, issues of 17 February and 18 August 1946.

5. Nayar, *Mahatma Gandhi's Last Imprisonment*, pp. 65–66.

6. This account of Mahadev Desai's cremation draws on Narayan Desai, *The Fire and the Rose*, Chapter 1.

7. Nayar, *Mahatma Gandhi's Last Imprisonment*, pp. 76, 78.

8. These paragraphs are based on Subject File No. 404, Part I, Gandhi Papers, First and Second Instalments, NMML.

9. *CWMG*, LXXXV, p. 151.

10. The untitled two-page reminiscence by Muriel Lester, c. 1942/43, Gandhi Papers, First and Second Instalments, NMML.

11. 'Mah[a]dev Desai', *MG*, 19 August 1942.

12. Verrier Elwin, 'Mahadev', in D.G. Tendulkar, M. Chalapathi Rau, Mridula Sarabhai and Vithalbhai K. Jhaveri, editors, *Gandhiji: His Life and Work* (Bombay: Keshav Bhikaji Dhawale, 1944), pp. 14–18.

13. Gandhi to Mahadev, 14 September 1938, *CWMG*, LXVII, p. 338.

14. See *Bombay: Six Months of the Congress Movement* (New Delhi: Government of India Press, 1943), printed document marked Secret, copy in IOR, R/3/2/357, APAC/BL; Jim Masselos, 'Bombay, August 1942: Re-readings in a Nationalist Text', in Masselos, *The City in Action: Bombay Struggles for Power* (New Delhi: Oxford University Press, 2007).

15. See IOR, R/3/2/33, APAC/BL.

16. N.C. Chatterjee to B.S. Moonje, 14 August 1942 (intercepted letter), in ibid.

17. Translation of a Bengali article published in *Harijan Patrika*, 16 August 1942, in ibid.

18. See the forty-eight-page transcript entitled 'A General Survey of the Political and Economic Condition of Assam since August, 1942 to June, 1944', in Volume 23, Series 5, Gandhi Papers, Twelfth and Fourteenth Instalments, NMML.

19. *Narrative Account of Congress Disturbances in the Different Districts of the Province of Orissa, August–December 1942*, thirteen-page printed document marked Secret, copy in IOR, R/3/2/367, APAC/BL.

20. See Chandi Prasad Nanda, 'Mapping the Mahatma: Literary Tracts and Rumours in Late Colonial Orissa', in Martin Brandtner and Shishir

Kumar Panda, editors, *Interrogating History: Essays for Hermann Kulke* (Delhi: Manohar, 2006).

21. See 'Memorandum of the Andhra Pradesh Youth and Students' Congresses' (handwritten), Bezwada, 4 July 1944, in Volume 7, Series 5, Gandhi Papers, Twelfth and Fourteenth Instalments, NMML.

22. *Karnatak in Revolt*, a forty-four-page pamphlet published by the Karnataka Pradesh Congress Committee in 1944, copy in ibid.

23. Vijay Anand, c/o Vizianagaram Palace, Banaras, to Gandhi, 21 June 1944, in Volume 1, Series 4, Gandhi Papers, Twelfth and Fourteenth Instalments, NMML.

24. A cyclostyled sheet, entitled 'Congress Newsletter No. 18', Delhi, 2 October, issued by Delhi PCC with the instructions: 'PLEASE PASS ON THIS NEWSLETTER AFTER READING', in IOR, R/3/1/310, APAC/BL.

    For a valuable compilation of government records on the spread of the Quit India movement after Gandhi's arrest, see Partha Sarathi Gupta, editor, *Towards Freedom: Documents on the Movement for the Independence in India, 1943–44, Part 1* (New Delhi: Indian Council of Historical Research, 1997). See also File Nos 3/16/42, 3/31/42, and 3/79/42, Home (Poll.), NAI.

25. Clipping from *Daily Herald* (London), 4 September 1942, copy in Mss Eur F 158/40, APAC/BL.

26. As reported in telegram dated 20 January 1943, from New Delhi to India Office, in ibid.

27. See *The Empire at Bay*, p. 832.

28. See IAR, 1942, Volume I, pp. 344–66.

29. Sir Stafford Cripps, 'Britain and India', *New York Times Magazine*, 23 August 1942.

30. Polak to Joyce of the India Office, 6 July 1940; Joyce to Polak, 30 July 1940, copies in E.S. Reddy Papers, NMML.

31. This account is based on a printed transcript of the discussion, in Box 50, Sydney Hertzberg Papers, NYPL.

32. 'The daily routine of Mr. Gandhi', a note in IOR, R/3/1/313, APAC/BL.

33. Nayar, *Mahatma Gandhi's Last Imprisonment*, p. 123.

34. Anon, *Congress Responsibility for the Disturbances, 1942–3* (New Delhi: Government of India Press, 1943), pp. 15, 21, 39, etc.

35. Gandhi to Linlithgow, letters of 31 December 1942 and 29 January 1943, *CWMG*, LXXVII, pp. 49–53, 54–56.

36. Linlithgow to Gandhi, 5 February 1943, *CWMG*, LXXVII, pp. 446–47.

37. Governor of Bombay to Viceroy, 10 February 1943, in IOR, R/3/1/298, APAC/BL.
38. Untitled, undated, notes by Mirabehn, in Subject File No. 300, Gandhi Papers, First and Second Instalments, NMML.
39. See Subject File No. 13, H.P. Modi Papers, NMML.
40. *CWMG*, LXXVII, p. 65.
41. See Subject File No. 406, Gandhi Papers, First and Second Instalments, NMML.
42. Notebooks/Diaries, Serial No. 1, in the Gandhi Papers, Third and Fourth Instalments, NMML.
43. 'Note of Mr. Gandhi's Fast, February 10th to March 3rd', Sd R.H. Candy, Surgeon General, Bombay Presidency, 5 March 1943, in R/3/1/298, APAC/BL.
44. Note dated 17 February 1943 by R. Tottenham, in IOR; Viceroy to Governors, 18 February 1943; Viceroy to Secretary of State for India, 19 February 1943, all in R/3/1/298, APAC/BL.
45. 'Leaders' Conference Demand Turned Down: Churchill's Reply: Endorsement of Viceroy's Attitude', *Hindustan Times*, 25 February 1943.

 The appeal that Churchill rejected was signed by, among others, the liberals T.B. Sapru, H.N. Kunzru, Bhulabhai Desai, M.R. Jayakar and N.M. Joshi, the Hindu Mahasabha leaders B.S. Moonje, S.P. Mookerjee and N.C. Chatterjee, the communist B.T. Ranadive, the industrialist J.R.D. Tata, the former Prime Minister of Sindh, Allahbuksh, C. Rajagopalachari (now an ex- or expelled Congressman), and several women social workers, among them Saraladevi Chaudhurani, described as 'President, Women's Hindu–Muslim Unity Committee'.
46. 'Report on Visit to Poona, Feb–March 1943', in Temp Mss 577/82b, Friends House, Euston.
47. Notebooks/Diaries, Serial No. 1, in Gandhi Papers, Third and Fourth Instalments, NMML.
48. Note by R. Tottenham, 24 February 1943, in R/3/1/298, APAC/BL.
49. Notebooks/Diaries, Serial No. 2, in Gandhi Papers, Third and Fourth Instalments, NMML.
50. Note by R. Tottenham, 1 March 1943, in R/3/1/298, APAC/BL.
51. This table is reproduced in R/3/1/298, APAC/BL.
52. ToP, II, pp. 961, 978–79.
53. ToP, III, pp. 659, 669, 730, 737, 744.
54. Roosevelt to Gandhi, 1 August 1942, copy in IOR, R/3/1/326, APAC/BL.
55. Phillips to Roosevelt, 22 January 1943, in Mss Am 2232 (33), William Phillips Papers, Houghton Library, Harvard University.

56. Diary entries for 17 and 22 February 1943, in Mss Am 2232 (33), William Phillips Papers, Houghton Library, Harvard University.

57. Letters dated 22 February and 3 March 1943, in ibid.

58. Diary entries for 7 and 10 April 1943, in Harvard, Mss Am 2232 (34), William Phillips Papers, Houghton Library, Harvard University (emphasis in the original).

59. Report in *The Statesman*, 26 April 1943.

60. E.J. Thompson to Norman Cliff, 2 April 1943, in Mss C 798, APAC/BL.

Chapter Thirty-One: The Death of Kasturba

1. Gandhi to M.A. Jinnah, 4 May 1943, *CWMG*, LXXVII, pp. 75–76.

2. Letter of 13 May 1943, press communiqué of 27 May 1943, both in IOR/R/3/1/300, APAC/BL.

3. As reported in *Dawn*, 29 May 1943.

4. Sayeed, *Pakistan*, p. 179.

5. See Jamil-ud-din Ahmad, editor, *Some Recent Speeches and Writings of Mr. Jinnah* (Fourth edition: Lahore: Shaikh Muhammad Ashraf, 1946), pp. 519–20.

6. Gandhi to Additional Secretary, Home Department, Government of India, 15 July 1943, *CWMG*, LXXVII, pp. 105–99.

7. Gandhi to Lord Linlithgow, 27 September 1943, *CWMG*, LXXVII, p. 201.

8. See, among other works, Amartya Sen, *Poverty and Famines: An Essay on Entitlement and Deprivation* (Oxford: Oxford University Press, 1981); Paul Greenough, *Prosperity and Misery in Rural Bengal: The Famine of 1943–1944* (New York, Oxford University Press, 1983); Madhusree Mukerjee, *Churchill's Secret War: The British Empire and the Ravaging of India During World War II* (New York: Basic Books, 2011).

9. As reported in *ToI*, 13 January 1940.

10. See R/3/2/21, APAC/BL.

11. Cf. Romain Hayes, *Bose in Nazi Germany* (Delhi: Random House India, 2011); Christopher Sykes, *Troubled Loyalty: A Biography of Adam von Trott zu Solz* (London: Collins, 1968), Chapter 14, 'The Story of Bose'.

12. Peter Ward Fay, *The Forgotten Army: India's Armed Struggle for Independence, 1942–1945* (Delhi: Rupa & Co., 1944).

13. Cf. M. Sivaram, *The Road to Delhi* (Rutland, Vermont: Charles E. Tuttle and Co., 1967), Chapter 7 and passim.

14. K.M. Tamhankar, editor, *On to Delhi: 23 Enthralling Speeches of Subhas Chandra Bose* (Bombay: Phoenix Publications, 1946), pp. 1–7.

15. Devadas Gandhi to C. Rajagopalachari, 6 December 1944, in IOR/R/3/1/313, APAC/BL.

16. Gandhi to Ardeshir Kateli, 6 January 1944, *CWMG*, LXXVII, pp. 215–16.

17. Note dated 29 January 1944, in File No. 76-I of 1943–44, Home (Special), MSA.

18. Bombay Home Department note, 22 January 1944, File No 76, 1943–44, Home (Special), MSA.

19. Note by R.M. Maxwell, 22 December 1943, in IOR/R/3/1/313, APAC/BL.

20. Clippings in File No 76-IV, 1943–44, Home (Special), MSA.

21. R. Tottenham, Additional Home Secretary, Government of India, to H.V.R. Iyengar, Home Secretary, Bombay Government, 7 February 1944; Iyengar to Tottenham, 12 February 1944; Tottenham to Iyengar, 15 February 1944, all in File No 76-IV, 1943–44, Home (Special), MSA.

22. See Files Nos 76-I and 76-II of 1944, Home (Special), MSA.

23. H.V.R. Iyengar to R. Tottenham, 7 February 1944; Notes by R. Tottenham, dated 16 and 21 February 1944, all in IOR/R/3/1/313, APAC/BL.

24. See Notebooks/Diaries, Serial Nos 4 and 5, Gandhi Papers, Third and Fourth Instalments, NMML.

25. Devadas Gandhi, 'Last Moments with Kasturba', *BC*, 29 February 1944; Nayar, *Mahatma Gandhi's Last Imprisonment*, p. 341.

26. Reports in *BC*, 25 February 1944.

27. Devadas Gandhi, 'Last Moments with Kasturba'.

28. See Subject File No. 409, Parts I to V, Gandhi Papers, First and Second Instalments, NMML, which has some 600 telegrams/letters of condolence to Gandhi on Kasturba's death.

29. 'Mr. Gandhi's Bereavement', D, 24 February 1944.

30. Letter dated 25 February 1944, in *My Dear Bapu*, p. 234.

31. Copies of these telegrams from Polak are in the so far unclassified E.S. Reddy Papers, NMML.

32. Lord Wavell, *The Viceroy's Journal*, edited by Penderel Moon (Oxford: Oxford University Press), pp. 3–4, 12.

33. Ibid., pp. 19, 23, 25, 33.

34. Gandhi to Lord Wavell, 17 February 1944, *CWMG*, LXXVII, pp. 22–23.

35. Gandhi to Lord Wavell, 9 March 1944; Wavell to Gandhi, 28 March 1944; Gandhi to Wavell, 9 April 1944, *CWMG*, LXXVII, pp. 244–50, 462–64, 257–60.

36. *CWMG*, LXXVII, pp. 262–63, 487–88.

Chapter Thirty-Two: Picking Up the Pieces (Again)

1. The *New York Times*, quoted in M.S. Venkataramani, 'The United States and the Release of Mahatma Gandhi, May 1944', in V.D. Rao, editor, *Studies in Indian History: Dr A.G. Pawar Felicitation Volume* (Kolhapur: Dr Appasaheb Pawar Satkar Samiti, 1968), p. 373.

2. Gandhi to C. Rajagopalachari, 26 May 1944, *CWMG*, LXXVII, p. 291.

3. Gandhi to Wavell, 17 June 1944, Wavell to Gandhi, 22 June 1944, *CWMG*, LXXVII, p. 317.

4. The list of books is in Volume 147, Series 4, Gandhi Papers, Twelfth and Fourteenth Instalments, NMML.

5. Saraladevi to Gandhi, 20 July 1944, in Volume 13, Series 5, Gandhi Papers, Twelfth and Fourteenth Instalments, NMML.

6. *CWMG*, LXXVII, pp. 338–41.

7. See *CWMG*, LXXVII, pp. 393–94.

8. Gandhi to Wavell, 26/27 July 1944; Wavell to Gandhi, 15 August 1944, *CWMG*, LXXVII, pp. 425–26, 480–82

9. G.E.B. Abell to Gilbert Laithwaite, 31 July 1944, in Mss Eur F 138/161, APAC/BL.

10. Gandhi to Ambedkar, 6 August 1944, *CWMG*, LXXVIII, p. 13.

11. Gandhi to Jagdish Munshi, c. 12 August 1944, *CWMG*, LXXVIII, pp. 23–24.

12. M.C. Chagla, *Roses in December: An Autobiography* (1973: reprint Bombay: Bharatiya Vidya Bhavan, 1994), pp. 55, 80.

13. Gandhi to Jinnah, 18 August 1944, *CWMG*, LXXVIII, p. 39.

14. A journalist who followed his career for many years remarked that Jinnah, 'apart from being an egotist, was also a narcissist. He spent a lot of time looking at himself in the mirror. He liked dressing up in Western clothes and with meticulous care. He wore a stiff collar, in fashion or out of fashion, in season or out of season. His trousers were creased to sabre-point sharpness. His thinning hair was pressed downwards. He wore a monocle for effect, while a pair of "spring"

glasses were held from a black band for reading . . . His well-made shoes were shined to a mirror glossiness . . .'

   J.N. Sahni, 'Pakistan's Quaid-e-Azam', *Illustrated Weekly of India*, 26 December 1976.

15. See *CWMG*, LXXVII, Appendix VIII, p. 456.
16. D, 10 September 1944.
17. *CWMG*, LXXVIII, pp. 87–90.
18. *CWMG*, LXXVIII, pp. 401–03, 92–93.
19. D, 13 September 1944.
20. *CWMG*, LXXVIII, pp. 96–97.
21. *BC*, 14 September 1944.
22. Gandhi to Jinnah, 15 September 1944, *CWMG*, LXXVIII, pp. 101–03.
23. 'Pakistan', an anonymous typescript deposited in Mss Eur C 313/18, APAC/BL, most likely written by a senior British civil servant.
24. Jinnah to Gandhi, 17 September 1944, *CWMG*, LXXVIII, pp. 406–08.
25. Gandhi to Jinnah, letters of 23 and 24 September 1944, Jinnah to Gandhi, 21 September 1944, *CWMG*, LXXVIII, pp. 116–17, 122–23, 409–10.
26. 'The Harijan Problem', *BC*, 21 September 1944.
27. *Indian Express*, 25 and 26 September 1944, clippings in File No. 3, C.B. Khairmonday Collection, University of Mumbai.
28. Gandhi to Jinnah, letters of 19 and 22 September 1944, Jinnah to Gandhi, 26 September 1944, *CWMG*, LXXVIII, pp. 124, 130–31, 415–16.
29. *BC*, 27 September 1944.
30. Gandhi to Jinnah, 26 September 1944, Jinnah to Gandhi, 26 September 1944, *CWMG*, LXXVIII, pp. 131–32, 416–17.
31. 'Not the End', *BC*, 29 September 1944.
32. 'Lessons of Failure', D, 29 September, 1944.
33. Gandhi to Sapru, 26 February 1945, *CWMG*, LXXIX, pp. 168–69.
34. 'Mr Jinnah's Interview to the Representative of the "News Chronicle", London, on 4 October 1944', in *Jinnah–Gandhi Talks (September 1944): Text of Correspondence and Other Relevant Documents, etc.* (Delhi: All India Muslim League, November 1944), pp. 75–78.
35. A.F.S. T[alyarkhan], 'Bull's Eye', *Blitz*, 30 September 1944, in Volume 27, Series 4, Gandhi Papers, Twelfth and Fourteenth Instalments, NMML.
36. Wavell, *The Viceroy's Journal*, p. 91.
37. See Volumes 21 to 25, Series 4, Gandhi Papers, Twelfth and Fourteenth Instalments, NMML.

38. *CWMG*, LXXVIII, pp. 149–51.

39. See File No. 40 of 1944, Home (Special) MSA.

40. See clipping in Volume 21, Series 4, Gandhi Papers, Twelfth and Fourteenth Instalments, NMML.

41. See correspondence in Volumes 8 and 29, Series 4, and in Volumes 125 and 135, Series 5, Gandhi Papers, Twelfth and Fourteenth Instalments, NMML.

42. 'Statement to the Press', 1 December 1944, See *CWMG*, LXXVIII, pp. 371–72.

43. Birla, *Bapu*, Volume IV, pp. 349–50.

44. Mridula Sarabhai to Indira Gandhi, 12 January 1945, in Reel No. 57, Mridula Sarabhai Papers, on microfilm, NMML.

45. See reports in File 212-III of 1945–47, Home (Special), MSA.

46. *CWMG*, LXXIX, p. 301.

47. *CWMG*, LXXIX, p. 299.

48. *CWMG*, LXXIX, pp. 383–84.

49. *CWMG*, LXXX, p. 63.

50. Ambalal Sarabhai to Gandhi, 16 April 1945, in Volume 49, Series 4, Gandhi Papers, Twelfth and Fourteenth Instalments, NMML.

51. Gandhi to Sarabhai, 21 April 1945, *CWMG*, LXXIX, p. 405.

52. *CWMG*, LXXX, pp. 222–24.

53. *CWMG*, LXXX, pp. 440–42.

54. Adrian Fort, *Archibald Wavell: The Life and Times of an Imperial Servant* (London: Jonathan Cape, 2009), pp. 382–86.

55. Statement to the press by Vallabhbhai Patel, Panchgani, 17 June 1945, in Volume 148, Series 4, Gandhi Papers, Twelfth and Fourteenth Instalments. NMML.

56. Gandhi to Wavell, 16 June 1945, LXXX, pp. 335–36.

57. Wavell, *The Viceroy's Journal*, p. 14.

58. 'Interview to Preston Grover', 29 June 1945, *CWMG*, LXXX, p. 383.

59. The telegrams quoted here are in Subject File No. 36, Gandhi Papers, First and Second Instalments, NMML.

60. Cf. note by Evans Jenkins, c. late July 1945, in R/3/1/108, APAC/BL.

61. See Bimal Prasad, editor, *Towards Freedom: Documents on the Movement for Independence in India, 1945* (New Delhi: Indian Council of Historical Research, 2008), pp. 365–68.

62. Azad to Wavell, 15 July 1945, copy in Volume 150, Series 4, Gandhi Papers, Twelfth and Fourteenth Instalments. NMML.

63. Gandhi to Wavell, 15 July 1945, *CWMG*, LXXX, p. 426.
64. Wavell to King George VI, 19 July 1945, ToP, V. p. 1279.

Chapter Thirty-Three: Prelude to Partition

1. Gandhi to Lord Pethick-Lawrence, 4 August 1945, *CWMG*, LXXX, p. 69.
2. B.R. Ambedkar, *What Congress and Gandhi Have Done to the Untouchables* (Bombay: Thacker and Co., 1945).
3. *CWMG*, LXXXI, pp. 119–20.
4. *CWMG*, LXXXI, p. 169.
5. Excerpts from speech of 20 December 1931, in Subject File No. 23, C. Rajagopalachari Papers, Fourth Instalment, NMML.
6. C. Rajagopalachari, *Ambedkarism Refuted* (Bombay: Hind Kitabs, 1945), pp. 5–6, 13, 16–17, 23–27, 32–33, etc.
7. Gandhi to Jawaharlal Nehru, 5 October 1945, *CWMG*, LXXXI, pp. 319–21.
8. Nehru to Gandhi, 9 October 1945, in Uma Iyengar and Lalitha Zackariah, *Together They Fought: Gandhi–Nehru Correspondence, 1921–1948* (New Delhi: Oxford University Press, 2011), pp. 452–56.
9. Letter of 19 August 1945, *CWMG*, LXXXI, p. 140.
10. *CWMG*, LXXXII, pp. 236–42, 277–79, 333–35,
11. Gandhi to Casey, 8 December 1945, *CWMG*, LXXXII, pp. 180–81.
12. Casey to Gandhi, 10 December 1945, in Diaries of R.G. Casey, Accession Number 3284, on microfilm, NMML.
13. Gandhi to Casey, letters of 12 and 16 December 1945, *CWMG*, LXXXII, pp. 180–81, 201–02, 215.
14. 'Extracts from the Governor of Bengal's diary notes dated 22nd December 1945', in R/3/2/57, APAC/BL.
15. Casey to Gandhi, letters of 30 January and 1 February 1946, in Volume 155, Gandhi Papers, Series 4, Twelfth and Fourteenth Instalments, NMML. Cf. also R.G. Casey, *An Australian in India* (London: Hollis and Carter, 1947), pp. 55–63.
16. Diaries of R.G. Casey, Accession Number 3284, on microfilm, NMML.

  Casey's wife was also greatly taken with their visitor. Gandhi 'had an extraordinary power over Indian people', she wrote. Whenever he 'came and went through the portals of Government House all our staff, clerks, domestics, gardeners, of whatever religion or caste—all living creatures—crowded the entrance hall on his arrival and departure, greeting him reverently after their own fashion. This happened to no one else who visited us.' Cf. Maie Casey, *Tides and Eddies* (London: Michael Joseph, 1966), pp. 155–56.

17. *CWMG*, LXXXII, p. 415.

18. Sastri to Desai, 7 July 1939, in V.S. Srinivasa Sastri Papers, Last Instalment, NMML.

19. See Translator's Preface to M.K. Gandhi, *An Autobiography, Or the Story of My Experiments with Truth*, translated from the original in Guajarati by Mahadev Desai (first published in 1927: second, revised edition Ahmedabad: Navajivan Press, 1940).

20. T.N. Jagadisan, *V.S. Srinivasa Sastri* (New Delhi: Publications Division, 1969), pp. 182–83. Sastri died on 17 April 1946. Gandhi, who was then in Delhi, issued a brief, dignified statement, noting that 'though we differed in politics, our hearts were one and I could never think that his patriotism was less than that of the tallest patriot'. See *CWMG*, LXXXIV, p. 19.

21. *CWMG*, LXXXIII, pp. 75, 78–81.

22. Amrit Kaur to N.K. Bose, 5 February 1946, Group 14, Nirmal Kumar Bose Papers, NAI.

23. Jiwanji Desai to Khan Sahib Mohammed Nasrullah, Assistant Secretary, Department of Industries and Supplies, Government of India, 25 February 1946, in Volume 136, Series 5, Gandhi Papers, Twelfth and Fourteenth Instalments, NMML.

24. Lalit Mohan Garg to Pyarelal, 17 February 1946, in ibid.

25. See Sho Kuwajima, *Muslims, Nationalism and the Partition: 1946 Provincial Elections in India* (New Delhi: Manohar, 1998); David Gilmartin, *Empire and Islam: Punjab and the Making of Pakistan* (Berkeley: University of California Press, 1988); idem, 'A Magnificent Gift: Muslim Nationalism and the Election Process in Colonial Punjab', *Comparative Studies in Society and History*, Volume 40, Number 3, July 1998.

26. See, for more details, Kuwajima, *Muslims, Nationalism and the Partition*.

27. See Sekhar Bandyopadhyay, 'Transfer of Power and the Crisis of Dalit Politics in India, 1945–7', *Modern Asian Studies*, Volume 34, Number 4, 2000.

28. This account of the 1946 naval mutiny draws on B.C. Dutt, *Mutiny of the Innocents* (Bombay: Sindhu Publications, 1971); Percy S. Gourgey, *The Indian Naval Revolt of 1946* (Hyderabad: Orient Longman, 1996). Cf. also IAR, 1946, Volume I, pp. 285ff.

29. *CWMG*, LXXXIII, pp. 171–72, 426–27.

30. *CWMG*, LXXXIII, pp. 245–46.
31. See *CWMG*, LXXXIII, Appendix XI, pp. 432–33.
32. Pethick-Lawrence to Gandhi, 28 March 1946, in Volume 157, Series 4, Gandhi Papers, Twelfth and Fourteenth Instalments, NMML.
33. *CWMG*, LXXXIII, pp. 354–55, 437–38, 376–77.
34. Z.A. Khan to Gandhi, 17 April 1946; Gandhi to Z.A. Khan, 24 April 1946 (not in *CWMG*), both in Volume 91, Series 4, Gandhi Papers, Twelfth and Fourteenth Instalments. NMML.
35. *CWMG*, LXXXIV, pp. 92–93.
36. *CWMG*, LXXXIV, pp. 462–63, 122–23.
37. See *Correspondence and Documents Connected with the Conference between the Cabinet Mission and His Excellency the Viceroy and Representatives of the Congress and the Muslim League, May 1946* (Cmd. 6829: London: HMSO, 1946).
38. *CWMG*, LXXXIV, p. 150.
39. *CWMG*, LXXXIV, pp. 467–76.
40. Gandhi to Pethick-Lawrence, letters of 19, 20 and 22 May; Pethick-Lawrence to Gandhi, 20 May, *CWMG*, LXXXIV, pp. 165, 172–74, 183, 477.
41. Gandhi to Wavell, 12 June 1946, *CWMG*, LXXXIV, p. 320.
42. *CWMG*, LXXXIV, p. 345.
43. See Maurice Hallet (Governor, United Provinces) to Francis Mudie (Home Member, Government of India), undated letter, c. late June 1946, in Mss Eur F 164/1, APAC/BL.
44. Wavell, *The Viceroy's Journal*, pp. 197, 220, 260–61, 413.
45. For a broader analysis of the Cabinet Mission and why it failed, see Clarke, *The Cripps Version*, Part V.
46. For the details of how Nehru became Congress president in 1946, see Rajmohan Gandhi, *Patel*, p. 369f.
47. Cf. my essay 'Verdicts on Nehru: The Rise and Fall of a Reputation', in Ramachandra Guha, *Patriots and Partisans* (New Delhi: Allen Lane, 2012).
48. Cf. also Rajmohan Gandhi, *The Good Boatman: A Portrait of Gandhi* (New Delhi: Viking, 1995), Chapter 10, 'Sons and Heirs'.

Chapter Thirty-Four: Marching for Peace

1. 'Independence', H, 28 July 1946, *CWMG*, LXXXV, pp. 32–34.
2. Cf. D.P. Mishra to Vallabhbhai Patel, Nagpur, 9 September 1946, in Durga Das, editor, *Sardar Patel's Correspondence, 1945–50* (in

ten volumes; Ahmedabad: Navajivan Press, 1971–74), Volume III, p. 161.

3. Gandhi to Patel, letters of 21 and 23 July 1946, CWMG, LXXXV, pp. 35, 45.
4. Gandhi to Patel, 1 August 1946, CWMG, LXXXV, p. 102.
5. Gandhi to Patel, letters of 3 August 1946, CWMG, LXXXV, p. 120.
6. Ambedkar to Patel, 12 August 1946; Patel to Ambedkar, 1 September 1946; Ambedkar to Patel, 14 October 1946, all in Volume 20, Series 4, Gandhi Papers, Twelfth and Fourteenth Instalments, NMML.
7. See Salim Yusufji, editor, Ambedkar: The Attendant Details (New Delhi, 2017), pp. 73, 84.
8. IAR, 1946, Volume II, pp. 177–78.
9. See Penderel Moon to Major J.M. Short, letters of 6 August and 2 September 1946, in Mss Eur F 189/13, APAC/BL.
10. This account of the Calcutta riots of 1946 is based on a first-hand account by the anthropologist Nirmal Kumar Bose, dated 2 September 1946, the copy in Volume 90, Series 4, Gandhi Papers, Twelfth and Fourteenth Instalments, NMML.
11. 'What can Violence Do?', H, 25 August 1946, CWMG, LXXXV, pp. 186–87.
12. CWMG, LXXXV, pp. 515–16, 215–16, 235.
13. CWMG, LXXXV, pp. 276–77.
14. CWMG, LXXXV, pp. 383–86, 521–22.
15. CWMG, LXXXV, p. 416.
16. The letters quoted in this section are all in Volume 88, Series 4, Gandhi Papers, Twelfth and Fourteen Instalments, NMML.
17. See notes and reports in Volume 132, Series 4, Gandhi Papers, Twelfth and Fourteenth Instalments, NMML.
18. Anon, Noakhali Tipperah Tragedy, a fifteen-page pamphlet in Box 1, Louis Fischer Papers, NYPL.
19. CWMG, LXXXV, pp. 464–65, 480–81.
20. CWMG, LXXXVI, pp. 30–32.
21. Alexander to Gandhi, 5 September 1946, in Volume 90, Series 4, Gandhi Papers, Twelfth and Fourteenth Instalments. NMML.
22. Alexander to Gandhi, 19 October 1946, in ibid.
23. Reports in Searchlight, 3 and 5 November 1946.
24. Speech at a prayer meeting, 31 October 1946, CWMG, LXXXVI, p. 65.
25. Gandhi to Nehru, 5 November 1946, CWMG, LXXXVI, pp. 78–79.
26. 'To Bihar', CWMG, LXXXVI, pp. 81–82.

27. *CWMG*, LXXXVI, pp. 89, 98, 106.

28. Cf. reports in *Searchlight*, 11 and 12 November 1946.

29. See, for more details, Volumes 132 and 133, Series 4, Gandhi Papers, Twelfth and Fourteenth Instalments, NMML.

30. See *Searchlight*, 20 November 1946.

31. Dasgupta, 'General Principles upon which Service to Hindu–Muslims of Noakhali is to be based on Gandhiji's Camp', note in Volume 39, Series 5, Gandhi Papers, Twelfth and Fourteenth Instalments, NMML.

32. As reported in *Searchlight*, 30 November 1946.

33. *Searchlight*, 22 November 1946.

34. Nirmal Kumar Bose, *My Days with Gandhi* (Calcutta: Nishana, 1953), pp. 64–65.

35. As reported in *Searchlight*, 24 November 1946.

36. Manubehn Gandhi, *Bapu—My Mother* (Ahmedabad: Navajivan Publishing House, 1955).

37. *CWMG*, LXXXVI, pp. 144–45, 147, 149–52, 162, 182, 185, 195.

38. 'Literal translation of Maulvi Hamiduddin Ahmed's statement published in the Azad of 14.12.46', in Volume 110, Series 5, Gandhi Papers, Twelfth and Fourteenth Instalments. NMML.

39. Gandhi to Hamiduddin Ahmed, 27 December 1946, *CWMG*, LXXXVI, pp. 273–76.

40. As reported in *Searchlight*, 12 December 1946.

41. Carl Heath, *Gandhi* (London: George Allen and Unwin, 1944).

42. Carl Heath to Gandhi, 14 November 1946; Gandhi to Heath, 2 December 1946 (not in *CWMG*), both in Volume 138, Series 4, Gandhi Papers, Twelfth and Fourteenth Instalments, NMML.

43. *CWMG*, LXXXVI, pp. 213–14.

44. *CWMG*, LXXXVI, pp. 266–67, 283, 287.

45. As reported in *Searchlight*, 4 January 1947.

46. *CWMG*, LXXXVI, pp. 313, 349.

47. Reports in *Searchlight*, 6, 9 and 10 January 1947.

48. As reported in TS, 17 January 1947.

49. Note by Sushila Nayar, dated 6 January 1947, in Volume 133, Series 4, Gandhi Papers, Twelfth and Fourteenth Instalments, NMML.

50. 'Enquiry Report about the cause of Hunger-strike by Miss Amtus Salam at Sirandi about the recovery of a Kharga (sacrificial sword)', by Raihen Ali, S[tation] I[nspector], Ramganj Police Station, 12 January 1947, copy in Volume 136, Series 4, Gandhi Papers, Twelfth and Fourteenth Instalments, NMML.

51. Note dated 20 January 1947, in ibid.
52. See *CWMG*, LXXXVI, pp. 373–76.
53. Azad to Gandhi, 2 February 1947, in Volume 33, Series 4, Gandhi Papers, Twelfth and Fourteenth Instalments, NMML.
54. Phillips Talbot to Walter S. Rogers, 16 February 1947, copy in Box 1, Louis Fischer Papers, NYPL.

Chapter Thirty-Five: The Strangest Experiment

1. Bose, *My Days with Gandhi*, pp. 130–37.
2. R.P. Parasuram to Gandhi, 1 January 1947 (copy), serial number 53 in Group 14, Nirmal Kumar Bose Papers, NAI; Gandhi to Parasuram, 2 January 1947, *CWMG*, LXXXVI, pp. 299–300.
3. *CWMG*, LXXXVI, p. 414.
4. *CWMG*, LXXXVI, pp. 419–20.
5. Gandhi to Vinoba Bhave, 10 February 1947, *CWMG*, LXXXVI, pp. 452–53; Vinoba Bhave to Gandhi, 25 February 1947, SN 32683, SAAA.
6. See *CWMG*, LXXXVII, pp. 15–16; *CWMG*, LXXXVI, p. 476.
7. 'Discussion with A.V. Thakkar', *CWMG*, LXXXVII, pp. 14–16.
8. Horace Alexander to Agatha Harrison, Calcutta, 19 March 1947, in Box 12, Horace Alexander Papers, Swarthmore College.
9. Bose to Gandhi, 4 February 1947, Group 14, Nirmal Kumar Bose Papers, NAI.
10. This section is based on Manu Gandhi, *The Lonely Pilgrim: Gandhiji's Noakhali Pilgrimage* (Ahmedabad: Navajivan Publishing House, 1964), passim. The quoted remarks are from pp. 9, 12, 31, 90–91 157, 194, 243, 83, 93, 111.
11. *CWMG*, LXXXVI, pp. 400–01, 486; *CWMG*, LXXXVII, pp. 7, 13.
12. See Volume 141, Series 4, Gandhi Papers, Twelfth and Fourteenth Instalments, NMML.
13. Note by K.B. Sahay (Home Minister, Bihar), 1 January 1947; note by T.P. Singh, ICS, early January 1947, both in Volume 139, Series 4, Gandhi Papers, Twelfth and Fourteenth Instalments, NMML.
14. Gandhi to H.S. Suhrawardy, 1 March 1947, *CWMG*, LXXXVII, p. 31.
15. Cf. Sana Aiyar, 'Fazlul Haq, Region and Religion in Bengal: The Forgotten Alternative of 1940–43', *Modern Asian Studies*, Volume 42, Number 6, 2008.
16. As reported in the *Statesman*, 4 March 1947.

17. *CWMG*, LXXXVII, pp. 42–46, 114–16, 125–26.
18. Letter of 19 or 20 March 1947, *CWMG*, LXXXVII, pp. 128–29.
19. *CWMG*, LXXXVII, p. 168.
20. Gandhi to Bhave, 10 March 1947, *CWMG*, LXXXVII, p. 63.
21. Gandhi to Amrit Kaur, 18 March 1947, *CWMG*, LXXXVII, p. 107.
22. Bose, *My Days with Gandhi*, pp. 173–74 (emphasis added).

Chapter Thirty-Six: Independence and Division

1. Philip Ziegler, *Mountbatten* (London: Collins, 1985).
2. See IAR, 1947, Volume 1, pp. 142–43.
3. Mountbatten to Gandhi, 22 March 1947, in Volume 161, Series 4, Gandhi Papers, Twelfth and Fourteenth Instalments, NMML.
4. *CWMG*, LXXXVII, pp. 179–180, 199, 254–55.
5. Quoted in Janet Morgan, *Edwina Mountbatten: A Life of Her Own* (London: HarperCollins, 1991), p. 394.
6. 'Report of the recent disturbances in the Punjab (March/April 1947)', twenty-one-page transcript sent by Rameshwari Nehru to Edwina Mountbatten (author unknown), in MB1/Q79, Mountbatten Papers, University of Southampton.
7. *CWMG*, LXXXVII, pp. 183, 221, 223.
8. *CWMG*, LXXXVII, pp. 288–89, 298.
9. B.M. Das to Gandhi, 16 April 1947; Gandhi to B.M. Das, 20 April 1947 (not in *CWMG*), both in Volume 118, Series 4, Gandhi Papers, Twelfth and Fourteenth Instalments, NMML.
10. Shahnawaz Khan, 'Report on Relief and Rehabilitation Work done by me in P.S. Masaurhi—Bihar from 24th March–5th July 1947', in Volume 121, Series 5, Gandhi Papers, Twelfth and Fourteenth Instalments, NMML.
11. See Sucheta Mahajan, editor, *Towards Freedom: Documents on the Movement for Independence in India, 1947, Part II* (New Delhi: Indian Council of Historical Research, 2015), pp. 1974–88.
12. *CWMG*, LXXXVII, p. 337.
13. 'Discussion with Aruna Asaf Ali and Ashok [*sic*] Mehta', 6 May 1947, *CWMG*, LXXXVII, p. 421.
14. *CWMG*, LXXXVII, p. 551.
15. Gandhi to Mountbatten, 8 May 1947, *CWMG*, LXXXVII, p. 435.
16. Letters by S. Banerji and G.J. Khan, 8 and 9 May 1947, respectively, in Volume 122, Series 4, Gandhi Papers, Twelfth and Fourteenth Instalments, NMML.

17. *CWMG*, LXXXVII, pp. 452, 464, 526; *CWMG*, LXXXVIII, p. 103.

18. *CWMG*, LXXXVII, p. 514.

19. *CWMG*, LXXXVIII, pp. 6–7, 42.

20. *CWMG*, LXXXVIII, pp. 99, 112, 164.

21. Sant Singh to Major J.M. Short, 9 April 1947, Mss Eur F 189/17, APAC/BL.

22. Evans Jenkins to Gilbert Laithwaite, 25 May 1947, in Mss Eur F 138/161, APAC/BL.

23. *CWMG*, LXXXVIII, pp. 209, 313–14, 452–53.

24. Nehru, *An Autobiography* (1942 edition), p. 469.

25. Moon to Major J.M. Short, 11 July 1947, in Mss Eur F 189/17, APAC/BL.
    There is a voluminous literature on the partition of India; on what caused it, on how it might have been averted. Of these (at least several hundred) books, permit me to mention just three: C.H. Philips and Mary Doreen Wainwright, editors, *The Partition of India: Policies and Perspectives* (London: George Allen and Unwin, 1970), valuable for, among other things, its diversity of viewpoints and contributors (including some who witnessed the Partition and its effects first-hand); Sucheta Mahajan, *Independence and Partition: The Erosion of Colonial Power in India* (New Delhi: Sage Publications, 2000), a sober, scholarly analysis of the complex forces at work; and Alex von Tunzelmann, *Indian Summer: The Secret History of the End of an Empire* (New York: Henry Holt, 2007), a fast-paced, vividly written account of the final few months of the British Raj and the birth of the two nations that succeeded it.

26. See R/3/1/94, APAC/BL.

27. *CWMG*, LXXXVIII, p. 461.

28. Chandiwala, *At the Feet of Bapu*, pp. 169–70.

29. *CWMG*, LXXXXIX, pp. 7–8.

30. Reports in TS, 10, 11 and 12 August 1947.

31. Quoted in Gopalkrishna Gandhi, *A Frank Friendship*, p. 483.

32. *CWMG*, LXXXXIX, pp. 27, 28, 33–34; TS, 13 and 14 August 1947.

33. Horace Alexander, 'India Achieves Freedom and Gandhi Starts on a New Adventure', four-page transcript, Calcutta, 16 August 1947, in Volume 114, Series 4, Gandhi Papers, Twelfth and Fourteenth Instalments, NMML.

34. Phillips Talbot to Walter S. Rogers, 19 August 1947, Talbot Papers, Centre for South Asian Studies, Cambridge.

35. Mountbatten to Cripps, 9 July 1947, in MB1/E5, Mountbatten Papers, University of Southampton.

36. *CWMG*, LXXXIX, p. 21.

37. Alexander, 'India Achieves Freedom and Gandhi Starts on a New Adventure'.

38. As reported in TS, 20 August 1947.

39. Kanji Dwarkadas to Lord Scarborough, 11 February 1947, Mss Eur F 253/53, APAC/BL.

40. Amrit Kaur to Gandhi, 17 April 1947, in Volume 146, Series 4, Gandhi Papers, Twelfth and Fourteenth Instalments, NMML.

41. Gandhi to Amrit Kaur, Patna, 20 April 1947, *CWMG*, LXXXVII, p. 315.

42. This (handwritten) letter by Nehru is in the C. Rajagopalachari Papers, NMML.

43. Jagjivan Ram to Gandhi, 9 November 1945, in Volume 19, Series 4, M.K. Gandhi Papers, Twelfth and Fourteenth Instalments, NMML. Cf. also Indrani Jagjivan Ram, *Milestones: A Memoir*, translated from the Hindi by Tara Joshi (New Delhi: Penguin Viking, 2010), p. 122.

44. Vallabhbhai Patel to B.G. Kher, 1 July 1947, in, Durga Das, editor, *Sardar Patel's Correspondence, 1945–50* (in ten volumes: Ahmedabad: Navajivan Press, 1971–74), Volume V, pp. 149–51.

Chapter Thirty-Seven: The Greatest Fasts

1. See, for example, Bhim Sen Sachar to Gandhi, 12 July 1947, in Volume 61, Series 5, Gandhi Papers, Twelfth and Fourteenth Instalments, NMML.

2. Amrit Kaur to Gandhi, 24 August 1947, in Volume 76, Series 5, Gandhi Papers, Twelfth and Fourteenth Instalments, NMML.

3. *CWMG*, LXXXXIX, p. 83; *Together They Fought*, p. 513.

4. *CWMG*, LXXXXIX, pp. 126–27, 130–34.

5. TS, 2 September 1947.

6. Cf. Denis Dalton, *Gandhi: Nonviolent Power in Action* (New York: Columbia University Press, 1993).

7. Editorial in TS, 2 September 1947.

8. *CWMG*, LXXXXIX, pp. 139–40, 149.

9. As reported in Manubehn Gandhi, *The Miracle of Calcutta*, translated from the Gujarati by Gopalrao Kulkarni (Ahmedabad: Navajivan Publishing House, 1959), pp. 85–86.

10. *GBI*, pp. 273–74, 328–29.

11. Reports in TS, 4 September 1947.

12. TS, 5 September 1947.

13. *CWMG*, LXXXXIX, pp. 151–154; TS, 5 and 6 September 1947; Manubehn Gandhi, *The Miracle of Calcutta*, pp. 88–92.

14. Letter of 26 August 1947, original in Volume 161, Series 4, Gandhi Papers, Twelfth and Fourteenth Instalments, NMML.

15. Statement by Abdul Qayum Ansari, President, All-India Momin Conference and a Minister in the Bihar Government, in *Searchlight* (Patna), 7 September 1947, copy in Volume 130, Series 4, Gandhi Papers, Twelfth and Fourteenth Instalments, NMML.

16. Sir Mirza Ismail to Gandhi, 16 September 1947, in Volume 32, Series 4, Gandhi Papers, Twelfth and Fourteenth Instalments, NMML.

17. R.P. Parasuram to N.K. Bose, 15 September 1947, Group 14, Nirmal Kumar Bose Papers, NAI.

18. Vigneshwara (pseudonym), 'Sotto Voce', *Swatantra*, 27 September 1947.

19. TS, 10 September 1947.

20. Medha M. Kudaisya, *The Life and Times of G.D. Birla* (New Delhi: Oxford University Press, 2003), pp. 190–91.

21. 'Notes by Rajkumari Amrit Kaur on visits to refugee camps in East and West Punjab, 26th to 28th August 1947', in MB 1/Q60, Mountbatten Papers, University of Southampton.

22. *CWMG*, LXXXIX, pp. 166–68.

23. *CWMG*, LXXXIX, pp. 173–77.

24. Brijlal Nehru to Gandhi, Lahore 18 September 1947, in Volume 63, Series 5, Gandhi Papers, Twelfth and Fourteenth Instalments, NMML (emphasis added).

25. *CWMG*, LXXXIX, pp. 179–80, 199–201, 210–11, 388.

26. *CWMG*, LXXXIX, pp. 253–54.

27. *CWMG*, LXXXIX, pp. 273, 524–25.

28. The clippings from the *Star of India* and the *Morning News*, both dated 2 October 1947, are in Volume 114, Series 4, Gandhi Papers, Twelfth and Fourteenth Instalments, NMML.

29. *CWMG*, LXXXIX, p. 307.

30. *CWMG*, LXXXIX, pp. 413, 432–33.

31. 'Note of an interview between H.E. the Governor General, Mr. Gandhi and Lord Ismay on Tuesday, 29th October, 1947', in MB1/E112, Mountbatten Papers, University of Southampton.

32. Nehru's Secretary, H.V.R. Iyengar, summarized this divergence in these words: 'Nehru in many of his public utterances, just like Gandhi, tended to start off by chastising the Hindus and Sikhs and then going on to say that the Muslims were just as bad. Patel, on the other hand, would start off by saying that the Muslims were

responsible for all the trouble and then advise the Hindus and Sikhs to hold their hands.'

Iyengar, quoted in A.C.B. Symon, UK High Commissioner, Delhi, to Commonwealth Relations Office, London, 20 January 1948, in DO/142/307, NAUK.

33. J.B. Kripalani, *My Times: An Autobiography* (New Delhi: Rupa, 2004), p. 720.

34. See Manuben Gandhi, *Last Glimpses of Bapu* (Delhi: Shiva Lal Agarwala and Co., 1962), p. 16.

35. *CWMG*, XC, pp. 37–43.

36. *CWMG*, XC, pp. 71–73, 79.

37. For a moving personal account of these attempts at succour and rehabilitation, see Anis Kidwai, *In Freedom's Shade*, edited and translated by Ayesha Kidwai (New Delhi: Penguin India, 2011).

38. *CWMG*, XC, pp. 191–94.

39. *CWMG*, XC, pp. 215–21.

40. *CWMG*, XC, pp. 356–57.

41. Mountbatten to Attlee, 12 September 1947, in MB1/E5, MP.

42. On the RSS ideology and its role in Indian politics from the 1940s, see, among other works, Jyotirmaya Sharma, *Terrifying Vision: M.S. Golwalkar, the R.S.S., and India* (New Delhi: Penguin India, 2011), Gyanendra Pandey, *Remembering Partition* (Cambridge: Cambridge University Press, 2001).

43. CID Report for 8 and 9 March, 1947, in File 137, Delhi Police Records, Fifth Instalment, NMML.

44. Report in H, 28 September 1947; *CWMG*, LXXXIX, pp. 173–75.

45. Raghu, 'Whither Mahatma Gandhi?', *Organiser*, 11 September 1947.

46. 'Source Report', 24 October 1947, signed Bhagwan Das Jain, S[tation] I[nspector], in File 138, Delhi Police Records, Fifth Instalment, NMML.

47. Reports dated 10, 15 and 17 November, in ibid.

48. Reports by Kartar Singh, Inspector, CID, 7 and 9 December 1947, in ibid.

49. Richard Symonds, 'Gandhi: Some Recollections and Reflections', talk delivered on 3 February 1998, unpublished, copy in the author's possession. Cf. also Symonds, *In the Margins of Independence: A Relief Worker in India and Pakistan, 1942–1949* (Karachi: Oxford University Press, 2001).

50. Alan Moorehead, 'Gandhi: A Last Look', *Observer*, 1 February 1948.

51. Amrit Kaur to Rajagopalachari, 1 January 1948, Subject File 57, C. Rajagopalachari Papers, Fifth Instalment, NMML.

52. HT, 3 January 1948.
53. HT, 11 January 1948.
54. *CWMG*, XC, pp. 266, 282.
55. *CWMG*, XC, pp. 408–09.
56. Manuben Gandhi, *Last Glimpses of Bapu*, pp. 133–34.
57. HT, 13 February 1948.
58. Reports in HT, 14 January 1948.
59. *CWMG*, XC, pp. 413–16.
60. Reports in HT, 15 January 1948.
61. *CWMG*, XC, pp. 423–25.
62. Letter from Sidney Hertzberg, quoted in Hazel Whitman to Louis Fischer, 5 February 1948, in Box 3, Louis Fischer Papers, NYPL.
63. Akhil Anand, 'Let the Old Man Die', *Mainstream*, 5 October 2002.
64. *CWMG*, XC, pp. 425–29.
65. Reports in HT, 16 January 1948.
66. Reports in HT, 17 January 1948.
67. Letter of 17 January 1948, in C. Rajagopalachari correspondence, Devadas Gandhi Papers, NMML.
68. HT, 18 January 1948.
69. *CWMG*, XC, pp. 438–40.
70. Reports in HT, 19 January 1948.
71. For a complete list of Gandhi's fasts, see https://www.gandhiheritageportal.org/chronology/event-chronology-listing/MTA=.
72. Gandhi to Mira, 16 January 1948, *CWMG*, XC, p. 430.

Chapter Thirty-Eight: Martyrdom

1. *CWMG*, XC, pp. 438–40.
2. HT, 19 January 1948.
3. HT, 20 January 1948.
4. *CWMG*, XC, p. 465.
5. HT, 21 January 1948.
6. HT, 28 January 1948.
7. *CWMG*, XC, pp. 501–02.
8. Vincent Sheean, *Lead, Kindly Light* (London: Cassell and Co., 1950), p. 193.
9. See *GBI*, pp. 247–50, 258.
10. Cordes to Gandhi, letters of 6 May and 2 July 1947, in Volume 106, Series 4, Gandhi Papers, Twelfth and Fourteenth Instalments, NMML.

11. Cordes to Gandhi, letters of 13 and 20 December 1947, in Volume 82, Series 5, Gandhi Papers, Twelfth and Fourteenth Instalments, NMML.

12. Cordes to Gandhi, letters of 18 and 20 December 1947, in ibid. After Gandhi's assassination in January 1948, Cordes stayed on in Sevagram, until his own death in 1960.

13. Polak to Gandhi, 23 January 1948, Volume 99, Series 5, Gandhi Papers, Twelfth and Fourteenth Instalments, NMML.

14. *CWMG*, XC, pp. 526–28.

15. HT, 30 January 1948.

16. Manubehn Gandhi, *The End of an Epoch*, translated from the Gujarati by Gopalkrishna Gandhi (Ahmedabad: Navajivan Publishing House, 1962), pp. 38–39.

17. Chandiwala, *At the Feet of Bapu*, pp. 249–54. Pyarelal, 'The Fateful Friday', H, 15 February 1948.

18. *CWMG*, XC, pp. 534–35.

19. These paragraphs draw on 'MAHATMA GANDHI KILLED BY ASSASSIN'S BULLET', front-page story in HT, 31 January 1948; Chandiwala, *At the Feet of Bapu*, pp. 255–56.

20. 'GANDHIJI'S ASSASSIN ARRESTED ON SPOT/LAST SAD MOMENTS AT BIRLA HOUSE', back-page report in HT, 31 January 1948.

21. 'THE ASSASSIN', front-page report in HT, 31 January 1948.

22. *ToI*, 31 January 1948.

23. Chandiwala, *At the Feet of Bapu*, pp. 259–60.

24. H.S.L. Polak to P. Kodanda Rao, 27 April 1934, Kodanda Rao Papers, NMML.

25. S[ushila] N[ayar], 'He Lives', H, 8 February 1948.

26. Alan Campbell-Johnson, *Mission with Mountbatten* (London: Robert Hale Limited, 1951), p. 278.

27. General Sir Roy Bucher to Louis Fischer, 1 December 1948, in Box 2, Louis Fischer Papers, NYPL.

28. This account of the procession and cremation is based on reports in the HT and the *ToI*, 1 February 1948.

29. HT, 1 February 1948.

30. These paragraphs draw on the tributes reprinted in *India News*, 5 February 1948, issued by the High Commission for India, London, copy in APAC/BL.

31. *Pakistan Times*, 31 January 1948.

32. 'Long Live Gandhiji', *Pakistan Times*, 2 February 1948.

33. See A.H. Ahmed Kamal, 'The Assassination of Gandhi and the Early Signs of Crisis of Muslim Nationalism in East Bengal', in Sekhar Bandyopadhyay, *Decolonization and the Politics of Transition in South Asia* (Hyderabad: Orient Blackswan, 2016).

34. See copy of speech in MB 1/Q60, Mountbatten Papers, University of Southampton.

35. Wavell, *Viceroy's Journal*, p. 439.

36. Reprinted in *India News*, 5 February 1948, issued by the High Commission for India, London, copy in APAC/BL.

37. *Vegetarian News*, Summer 1948.

38. The tributes by Blum and Smuts were reprinted in *India News*, 5 February 1948.

39. Edgar Snow, 'The Message of Gandhi', *Saturday Evening Post*, 27 March 1948.

40. Greenberg, *The Inner Eye*, pp. 137–41.

41. See *Politics*, Winter 1948, pp. 1–7.

42. A. Dfyakov, 'The Assassination of Gandhi', *New Times* (Moscow), 18 February 1948.

43. See M.V. Kamath, *A Reporter at Large* (Mumbai: Bharatiya Vidya Bhavan, 2002), pp. 238–39.

44. Vasant Moon, *Growing up Untouchable in India: A Dalit Autobiography*, translated from the Marathi by Gail Omvedt (Lanham, Maryland: Rowman and Littlefield, 2001), pp. 105–06.

45. R.P. Parasuram to N.K. Bose, 15 September 1947, Group 14, Nirmal Kumar Bose Papers, NAI.

46. J.R.D. Tata to Ardeshir Dalal, 6 February 1948, in Arvind Mambro, editor, *J. R. D. Tata: Letters* (New Delhi: Rupa and Co., 2004), pp. 114–15.

47. Reports in *ToI*, 14 February 1948; Bimanesh Chatterjee, *Thousand Days with Rajaji* (New Delhi: Orient Paperbacks, 1975), p. 9.

48. *The Free Press Journal*, 13 February 1948, clipping in Box 3, Louis Fischer Papers, NYPL.

49. Statement of Prabhakar Trimbak Marathe, recorded on 5 February 1948, in Subject File No. 18, D.P. Mishra Papers, First and Second Instalments, NMML. Marathe was married to Nathuram's sister.

50. *PRMGMC*, Volume V, pp. 17–20. These letters were originally written in Marathi.

51. *PRMGMC*, Volume IV, pp. 202–16.

52. See K.L. Gauba, *The Assassination of Mahatma Gandhi* (Bombay: Jaico Publishing House, 1969), p. 383.

53. See Gopal Godse, *Gandhiji's Murder and After*, translated from the Marathi by S.T. Godbole (Delhi: Surya Prakashan, 1989), p. 171.
54. *PRMGMC*, Volume IV, pp. 89–123.
55. See *PRMGMC*, Volume II, pp. 12–21.
56. Diary entry of 31 January 1948, Box 60, Malcolm Darling Papers, CSAS, Cambridge.
57. Cf. Clive Dewey's *Anglo-Indian Attitudes: The Mind of the Indian Civil Service* (London: Hambledon Press, 1993).
58. See the correspondence between Nehru and Patel in Durga Das, editor, *Sardar Patel's Correspondence*, Volume VI, pp. 8–31.
59. See Guha, *India After Gandhi*, especially Chapters 3 to 6.
60. A.C.B. Symon, UK High Commissioner, New Delhi, to Secretary of State for Commonwealth Relations, nine-page report dated 4 February 1948, in DO/142/307, NAUK.
61. C. Rajagopalachari, *University Addresses* (Bombay: Hind Kitab Ltd, 1949), p. 75. The speech was delivered on 20 March.
62. *CWMG*, IX, p. 175. To be sure, there was one (not insignificant) difference. In 1909, Gandhi faced a possible assassination attempt from Pathans opposed to his policies. In 1948, it was a Hindu, not a Muslim, who killed him. Even so, the prediction of the likely consequences of his meeting a violent death is uncanny.

Epilogue: Gandhi in Our Time

1. *CWMG*, XXV, p. 202.
2. See A.G. Noorani, *The Babri Masjid Question 1528–2003: A Matter of National Honour*, two volumes (New Delhi: Tulika Books, 2003).
3. Personal communication from Gopalkrishna Gandhi, who was told this story by Dr Nayar herself.
4. Cf. http://www.thehindu.com/news/national/hindu-mahasabha-launches-a-website-for-nathuram-godse/article7880713.ece (accessed on 24 April 2016).
5. Cf. Anil Nauriya, 'Portrait as Mirror', *The Hindu*, 3 March 2003.
6. See http://www.hindustantimes.com/india-news/in-new-rajasthan-textbooks-veer-savarkar-overshadows-gandhi-and-nehru/story-NGzReSVik2uLKCRQDAsQ5I.html (accessed on 4 July 2017).
7. See, for example, this discourse by an Arya Samaj preacher: https://www.youtube.com/watch?v=ec8JxbBq5eM (accessed on 3 July 2017).

8.   Unfortunately, I did not retain a clipping of the newspaper in which I read this interview. It was probably published in the *Times of India* or the *Indian Express*.

9.   Cf. Nandini Sundar, *The Burning Forest: A Savage War in the Heart of India* (New Delhi: Juggernaut, 2016).

10.   See https://www.youtube.com/watch?v=ZJs-BJoSzbo (accessed on 25 April 2016).

11.   Joachim Alva, *Men and Supermen of Hindustan* (Bombay: Thacker and Co., 1943), p. 20.

12.   Talk by Horace Alexander at the Royal Institute of International Affairs, 9 March 1944, Temp Mss 577/11, Friends House, Euston.

13.   See R.S. Khare, *The Untouchable as Himself: Identity, Ideology and Pragmatism among the Lucknow Chamars* (Cambridge: Cambridge University Press, 1984), pp. 119–20.

14.   Cf. Eleanor Zelliot, *From Untouchable to Dalit: Essays on the Ambedkar Movement* (Delhi: Manohar, 1992).

15.   Representative of this new Ambedkarism is the website www. roundtableindia.in (which describes itself as being 'for an informed Ambedkar age').

16.   Arun Shourie, *Worshipping False Gods* (New Delhi: ASA Publications, 1997), p. 3.

17.   Ibid., p. 102.

18.   Ibid., pp. 43, 64, 229.

19.   *ToI*, 25 October 1934.

20.   Quoted in *ToI*, 25 September 1940.

21.   Rosalind O'Hanlon, *Caste, Class and Ideology: Jotirao Phule and Low-Caste Protest in Nineteenth Century Western India* (Cambridge: Cambridge University Press, 1985); Mark Juergensmeyer, *Religion as Social Vision: The Movement Against Untouchability in Twentieth Century Punjab* (Berkeley: University of California Press, 1982).

22.   Arundhati Roy, 'The Doctor and the Saint', pp. 15–179 in S. Anand, editor, B.R. Ambedkar, *Annihilation of Caste: The Annotated Critical Edition* (New Delhi: Navayana, 2014).

23.   The growing radicalization of Gandhi's views on caste and the abolition of untouchability was first set out in Dennis Dalton, 'The Gandhian View of Caste, and Caste After Gandhi', in Philip Mason, *India and Ceylon: Unity and Diversity* (London: Oxford University Press, 1967), a superb if now little-known essay that should be required reading for all students of the subject. Cf. also Nishikant Kolge, *Gandhi Against Caste* (New Delhi: Oxford University Press, 2017).

24. *CWMG*, LVIII, pp. 166–67.

25. *The Free Press Journal*, 27 June 1935.

26. See Gopal Guru, 'Ethics in Ambedkar's Critique of Gandhi', *Economic and Political Weekly*, 15 April 2017.

27. D.R. Nagaraj, *The Flaming Feet* (first published in 1983: second edition, Ranikhet: Permanent Black, 2011).

28. *CWMG*, LXXXII, p. 362.

29. Cf. Madhu Kishwar, 'Gandhi and Women', in two parts, *Economic and Political Weekly*, 5 and 12 October 1985.

30. Notes by S.A. Brelvi, 8 August 1932, SN 19603, SAAA.

31. John Gunther, *Inside Asia* (London: Hamish Hamilton, 1939), pp. 404–05.

32. See *CWMG*, XLIV, p. 71.

33. See, among other works, Tariq Ali, *The Duel: Pakistan on the Flight Path of American Power* (New York: Simon and Schuster, 2008); Farzana Shaikh, *Making Sense of Pakistan* (London: C. Hurst and Co., 2009).

34. Of this cohort of Gandhi's direct disciples, Vallabhbhai Patel died earliest, in 1950. Jawaharlal Nehru lived on till May 1964, having been prime minister for close to seventeen years at the time of his death. Maulana Azad died in 1958, Amrit Kaur in 1964; both served in Nehru's Cabinet for more than a decade. Rajendra Prasad demitted office as President of the Republic only in 1962, dying the next year. Of those in the Opposition and in civil society, Kumarappa passed away in 1960, Rajaji in 1973, Kripalani in 1982 and Kamaladevi as late as 1988.

35. Cf. Anil Nauriya, *The African Element in Gandhi* (New Delhi: National Gandhi Museum, 2006).

36. See Susan Williams, *Colour Bar: The Triumph of Seretse Khama and His Nation* (London: Allen Lane, 2006), Chapter 11.

37. See Leo Kuper, *Passive Resistance in South Africa* (New Haven: Yale University Press, 1957).

38. Richard Crockatt, *Einstein and Twentieth-Century Politics* (Oxford: Oxford University Press, 2016), p. 19.

39. Ronald W. Clark, *Einstein: The Life and Times* (London: Hodder and Stoughton, 1973), pp. 498, 581.

In May 1953, Einstein wrote to a Brooklyn schoolteacher who asked his opinion of the McCarthyite hearings: 'Frankly, I can only see the revolutionary way of non-cooperation in the sense of Gandhi's. Every individual who is called before one of these communities ought to refuse to testify.' See Walter Isaacson, *Einstein: His Life and Universe* (New York: Simon and Schuster, 2007), p. 529.

    For a detailed analysis of Einstein's views on Gandhi, from the 1920s to the 1950s, see Bhikhu Parekh, 'Einstein on Gandhi's Non-Violence', in his *Debating India: Essays on Indian Political Discourse* (New Delhi: Oxford University Press, 2015).

40. Italo Calvino, 'Il Duce's Portraits', *New Yorker*, 6 January 2003.

41. Malcolm Muggeridge, *Tread Softly, for You Tread on My Jokes* (London: Fontana, 1968), p. 187.

42. J.R. Glorney Bolton to Gandhi, 2 August 1931, Subject File 82, Gandhi Papers, First and Second Instalments, NMML.

43. *BC*, 9 November 1935.

44. On the Chipko movement, see Guha, *The Unquiet Woods*, Chapter 7; on the Narmada movement, see Amita Baviskar, *In the Belly of the River: Tribal Conflicts over Development in the Narmada Valley* (New Delhi: Oxford University Press, 1995).

45. Rajni Bakshi, *Bapu Kuti: Journeys in Rediscovery of Gandhi* (New Delhi: Penguin India, 1998); Ela Bhatt, *We Are So Poor, But So Many: The Story of Self-Employed Women in India* (New York: Oxford University Press, 2005).

46. Savarirayan Jesudason, 'Bapu', in Chandrashanker Shukla, editor, *Reminiscences of Gandhiji* (Bombay: Vora and Co., 1951), p. 182.

47. The tragedy of the Rohingyas is further proof of the relevance of Gandhi's ideas in this regard. Notably, while Aung San Suu Kyi has been reluctant to take on the fundamentalists of her own faith, the Dalai Lama has not been lacking in courage in this regard. The Tibetan leader has thus shown himself to be a better Gandhian, as well as a better Buddhist, than his counterpart in Myanmar. It is noble and brave to lead a non-violent struggle against an oppressive state; but perhaps nobler, and braver, to display compassion towards, and express solidarity with, those oppressed by one's own community.

48. 'Discussion with a Capitalist', *YI*, 20 December 1928, *CWMG*, XXXVIII, p. 243.

49. 'The Same Old Argument', *YI*, 7 October 1926, *CWMG*, volume 31, p. 478f.

50. Muthukumara Mani, editor, *Greening India's Growth: Costs, Valuations, and Trade-Offs* (New Delhi: Routledge, 2013).

51. See Venu Madhav Govindu and Deepak Malghan, *The Web of Freedom: J.C. Kumarappa and Gandhi's Struggle for Economic Justice* (New Delhi: Oxford University Press, 2016).

52. 'Reflections on Gandhi' (first published in 1949), reprinted in George Orwell, *Essays*, selected and introduced by John Carey (New York: Alfred A. Knopf, 2002), p. 1357.

53. Quoted in Joseph Epstein, *Friendship: The Exposé* (Boston, Houghton Mifflin, 2006), p. 71.

54. Reginald Reynolds, *To Live in Mankind: A Quest for Gandhi* (London: Andre Deutsch, 1951), p. 18 (emphasis in the original).

Index